CW01656170

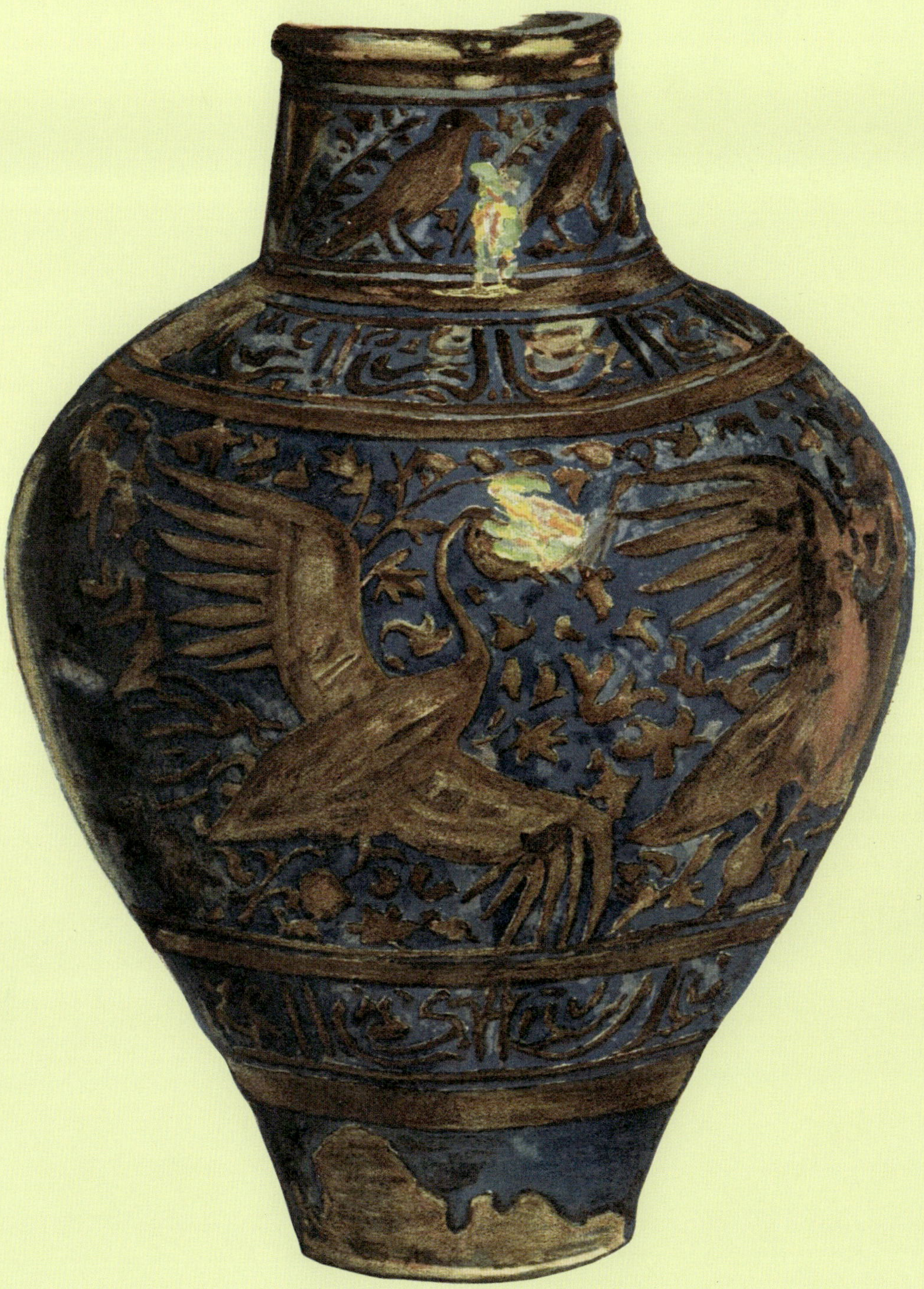

HENRY WALLIS

From Pre-Raphaelite Painter to Collector/Connoisseur

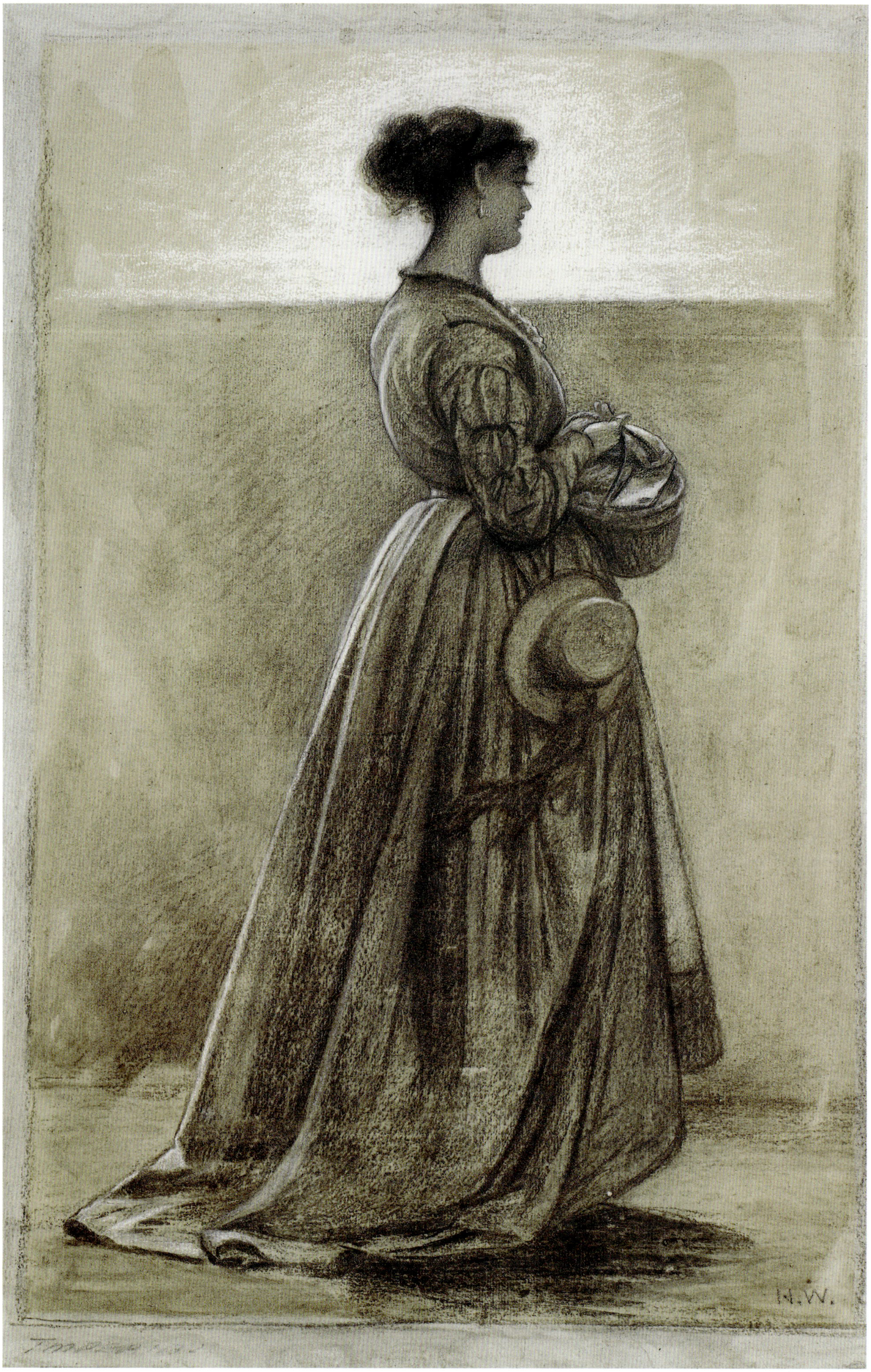

HENRY WALLIS

(1830-1916)

FROM PRE-RAPHAELITE PAINTER TO COLLECTOR/CONNOISSEUR

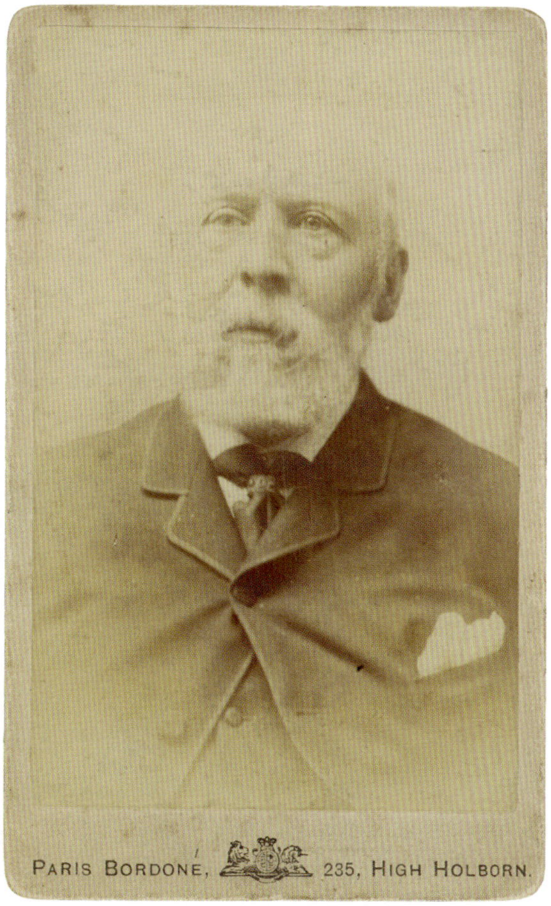

Ronald Lessens • Dennis T. Lanigan

ACC ART BOOKS

© 2019 Ronald Lessens and Dennis Lanigan
World copyright reserved

ISBN: 978-1-78884-027-9

The rights of Ronald Lessens and Dennis Lanigan to be identified as authors of this work have been asserted by them in accordance with the Copyright, Designs and Patents Act 1988

All rights reserved. No part of this publication may be reproduced, stored in a retrieval system, or transmitted in any form or by any means electronic, mechanical, photocopying, recording or otherwise, without the prior permission of the publisher

British Library Cataloguing-in-Publication Data

A catalogue record for this book is available from the British Library

The authors and publisher gratefully acknowledge the permission granted to reproduce the copyright material in this book. Every effort has been made to trace copyright holders and to obtain their permission for the use of copyright material. The publisher apologises for any errors or omissions in the text and would be grateful if notified of any corrections that should be incorporated in future reprints or editions of this book.

Cover:
The Death of Chatterton [Cat. 22]
1855-56; oil on canvas
62.2 x 93.3 cm. (24½ x 36 in.)
IMAGE BY PERMISSION OF TATE BRITAIN, LONDON

Endpapers:
Chromolithographs by W. Griggs after Wallis's original watercolours of lustre vases from *Notes on some Examples of Early Persian Lustre Ware*, published in 1889 [see: Cat. 216].

Frontispiece:
Study of a Young Woman Standing [Cat. 70]
c.late 1860s; black and white chalk with brown wash on blue-grey laid paper
51.5 x 33.5 cm. (20⁵⁄₁₆ x 13³⁄₁₆ in.)
IMAGE BY PERMISSION OF BIRMINGHAM MUSEUMS TRUST.

Title page:
Henry Wallis c.1890
Cabinet photo
IMAGE BY PERMISSION OF THE BODLEIAN LIBRARIES, UNIVERSITY OF OXFORD, MS ENG.E.3396.

FSC www.fsc.org MIX Paper from responsible sources FSC® C124385

Printed in China for ACC Art Books Ltd.,
Woodbridge, Suffolk, IP12 4SD, UK

www.accartbooks.com

ACC ART BOOKS

CONTENTS

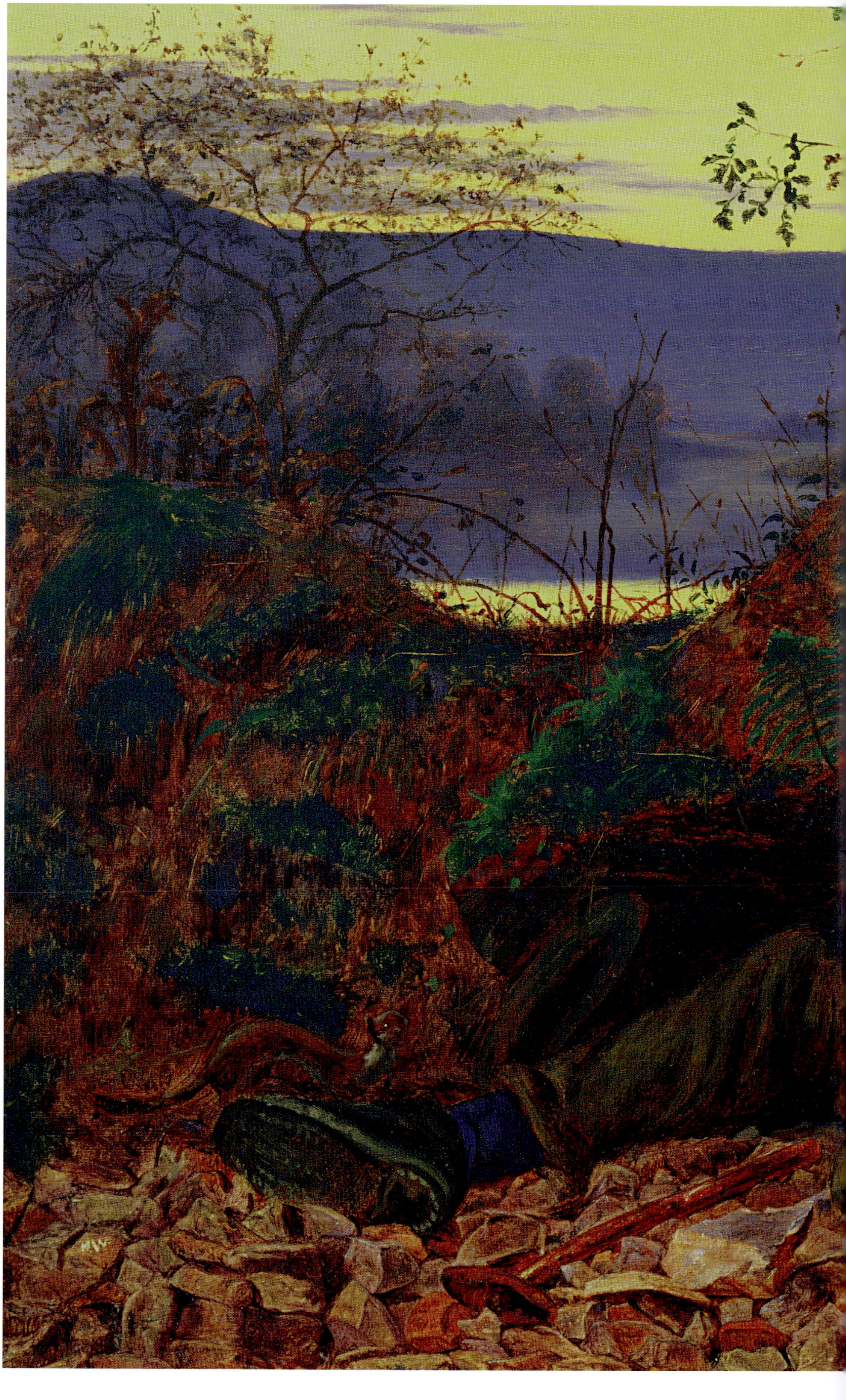

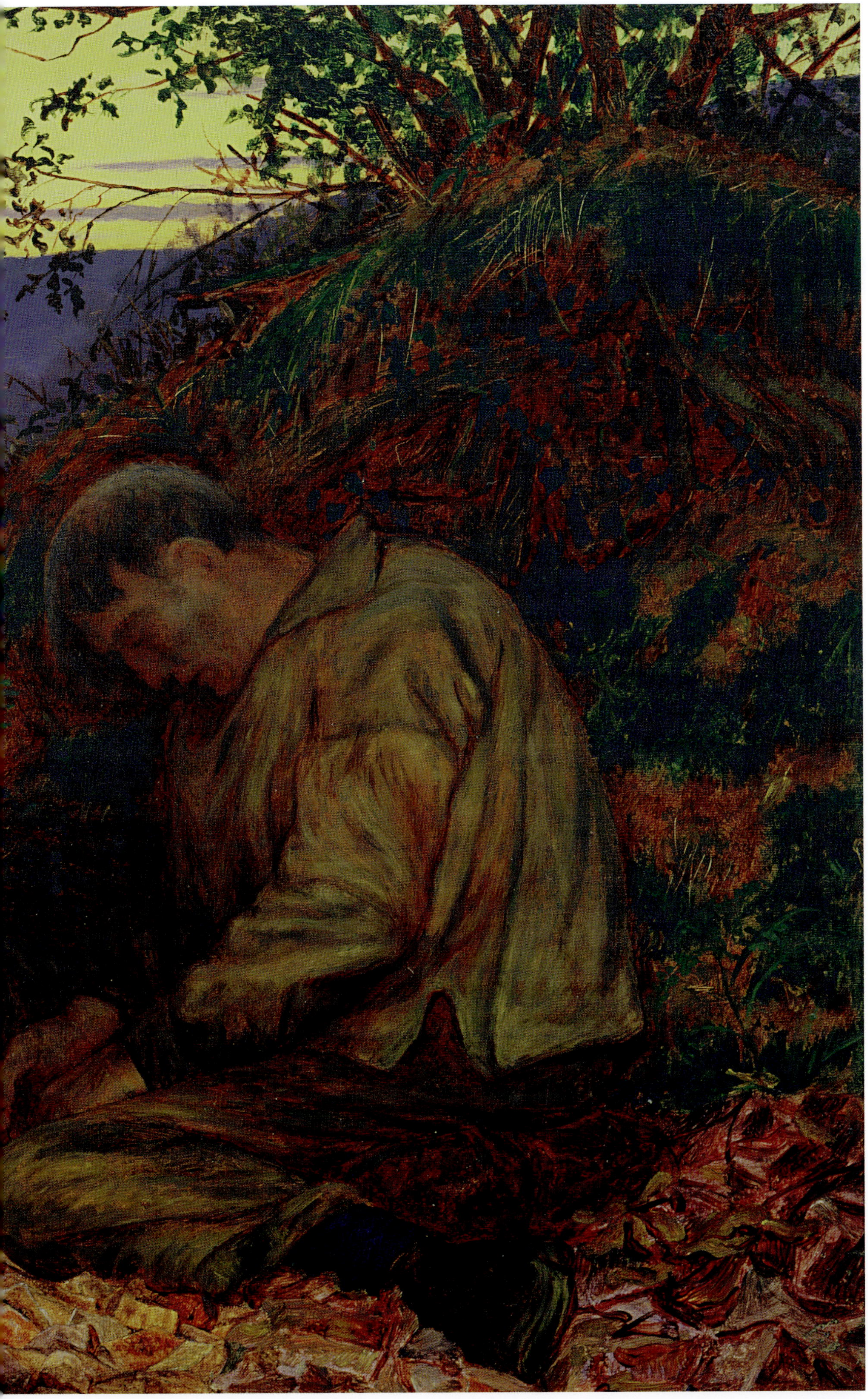

The Stonebreaker
[Cat. 28a]
c.1857; oil on canvas;
38.1 x 45.7 cm
(14½ x 18 in.)
The Makins Collection

PREFACE

"One of the pressing tasks of contemporary art history is to expand the frontiers of research heretofore limited by excessive hero worship."[1]

"We know a lesser life does not seem lesser to the person which leads one.
His life is very real to him; he is not a minor figure in it."[2]

It happened during my first visit to Tate Britain. While walking through the Pre-Raphaelite section, I was struck at the sight of *Chatterton*, painted by Henry Wallis, an artist who was scarcely known to me. I imagined I had come back to 1856, when the Royal Academy visitors showed their enthusiasm for the stupendous contrast between the chestnut-coloured hair, the purple-blue silk breeches and the red jacket, as well as the balance between the curve of the corpse and the garret's window.

I wondered why this painter was barely mentioned in histories of British art written in the early and mid-portions of the 20th century and was totally absent from early editions of the *Dictionary of National Biography* (although of course he was still alive at the time of the very first edition). After his death, hardly anyone seemed to remember him. In 1982, in fact, K. Z. Cieszkowski, a former librarian at the Tate Gallery, made the astounding statement that "Later, Wallis gave up painting altogether – there is no painting of his dating from after 1861."[3] Only in 1973 did Diane Johnson begin to do him belated justice in her biography of Mary Ellen Meredith. Fortunately, this situation has changed now. About ten years ago Nicholas Joukovsky started to present some relevant unpublished material found among Mary Ellen's letters. I had the same strange feeling as Diane Johnson when she started her inquiry into the life of "the first Mrs Meredith": "At first it seemed that nothing could be known. Meredith, or someone, had bitterly destroyed any letters or manuscripts that might have survived. No one knew anything about Henry Wallis, not even the art historians, who said they had always wondered about Henry, and about what could have happened to the many paintings he exhibited at the Royal Academy, famous paintings, during his lifetime. All parties – except Meredith – seemed to have disappeared without a trace, and that in itself is a provoking comment on time and immortality."[4]

Four decades later, Henry Wallis is no longer unknown among scholars, though few episodes of his life have been well documented. Until recently we knew only that Henry Thomas was born on 21 February 1830 in London, father unknown. In 1845 his mother, Mary Ann Thomas, married Andrew Wallis, a prosperous London property owner and Henry subsequently took his name. Henry wanted to be an artist and went to the Royal Academy Schools and then he continued his studies in Paris at Gleyre's studio. Later, he developed a passion for Italian and Eastern ceramics and became an authority on this. He exhibited at the Royal Academy from 1854 to

1877, and at the Old Water-Colour Society, of which he became an associate in 1878 and a full member in 1880. Finally, we know that he died at Croydon on 20 December 1916 during the middle of the Great War.

This is unfortunately a meagre result for an artist and connoisseur well known in his day. Books did not give us much more information, since they reduce him to the painter of two famous works: *Chatterton* and *The Stonebreaker*. Clearly no one felt the need, nor took the trouble to scroll through the archives. Despite the detailed but limited studies of Timothy Wilson on Wallis the ceramic-collector, and Nicholas Joukovsky on his affair with Mary Ellen Meredith, the first part of his long life remained obscure. The truth is that after Mary Ellen's death in 1861, her father, her daughter and her former husband did everything they could to destroy all the evidence related to the "affair".

The Bodleian Library houses a number of Wallis letters, but the majority of them were written after 1880 and deal with his passion for ceramics and his numerous journeys abroad. Seventy letters up to 1880 is not a large number, and it is necessary to look to other contemporary sources to learn more. I was lucky enough to discover a letter written by Peter Augustin Daniel (although his friends always knew him as Peter Austin Daniel), Wallis's fellow student at the R.A. Schools, just before the affair with Mary Ellen started. It shows how charming a person Wallis must have been.[5] To find anything about his youth, however, has proven to be well nigh impossible.

This lack of documentation does not prove that Wallis led an uninteresting life; on the contrary, as we hope this book will demonstrate.

Ronald Lessens

In November of 2014 I received an email from Ronald Lessens, a scholar with whom I had corresponded on a number of occasions in the past about various aspects of Henry Wallis and his career. Ronald wanted to send me a draft of his book on Wallis in its present state and, as a favour, to ask my opinion as to "what was good and what needs corrections." When the book arrived, it was obvious that Ronald had done a great deal of research and that Parts I and the Appendices were largely completed. The book needed some editing to rearrange some material and to delete redundancies and some material which, although interesting, was not essential to a book dealing with Wallis. Information specifically relating to Wallis as an artist and how he fit into the Victorian art world needed to be expanded. I also felt that Wallis's contributions as a collector/connoisseur needed more emphasis, because this was one area that made him stand out from his contemporaries and made him equally as interesting.

I have been a collector of Victorian art since the early 1970s and I know how much dedication and study it involves to move past being someone who collects art purely for its esthetic appeal to one who is a serious scholar in their chosen collecting field. Wallis made a significant impact with his writing and lectures on the ceramics he so avidly collected.

I edited the book and sent my various suggestions back to Ronald. He obviously felt my suggestions were helpful and asked if I would become a co-author on the book. To be honest I resisted the idea initially, but finally agreed to help. My major contribution to the book I think has been to expand the Catalogue section, which has proved a difficult task. Unlike major Pre-Raphaelite artists like Rossetti, Millais and Holman Hunt, most of the whereabouts of Wallis's oeuvre remains unknown and his work has seldom come on the market except for when family descendents have sold works. Although based on exhibition histories we know the titles of many of Wallis's works, we have no idea of dimensions and, in many cases, even what the medium was remains unclear. Fortunately, Wallis was a great friend of F. G. Stephens who generally reviewed Wallis's works when they were shown at the Old Water-Colour Society (Society of Painters in Water Colours) exhibitions. Contemporary reviews have allowed us to recover the original titles of some of Wallis's works that have later appeared on the art market and should allow us to identify additional works in the future. When I started this project I, like most people interested in the Pre-Raphaelites, primarily knew Wallis as the painter of two Pre-Raphaelite masterpieces, *Chatterton* and *The Stonebreaker*. After researching Wallis's life and oeuvre, however, I have come to have a much greater appreciation of Wallis as a man and as an artist. The contribution he made to art history was considerable through his writings and illustrations, particularly to a greater appreciation and understanding of Middle Eastern ceramics. Wallis's abundant correspondence gives valuable insights into the Victorian art world and to the travel conditions of his time.

Dennis T. Lanigan

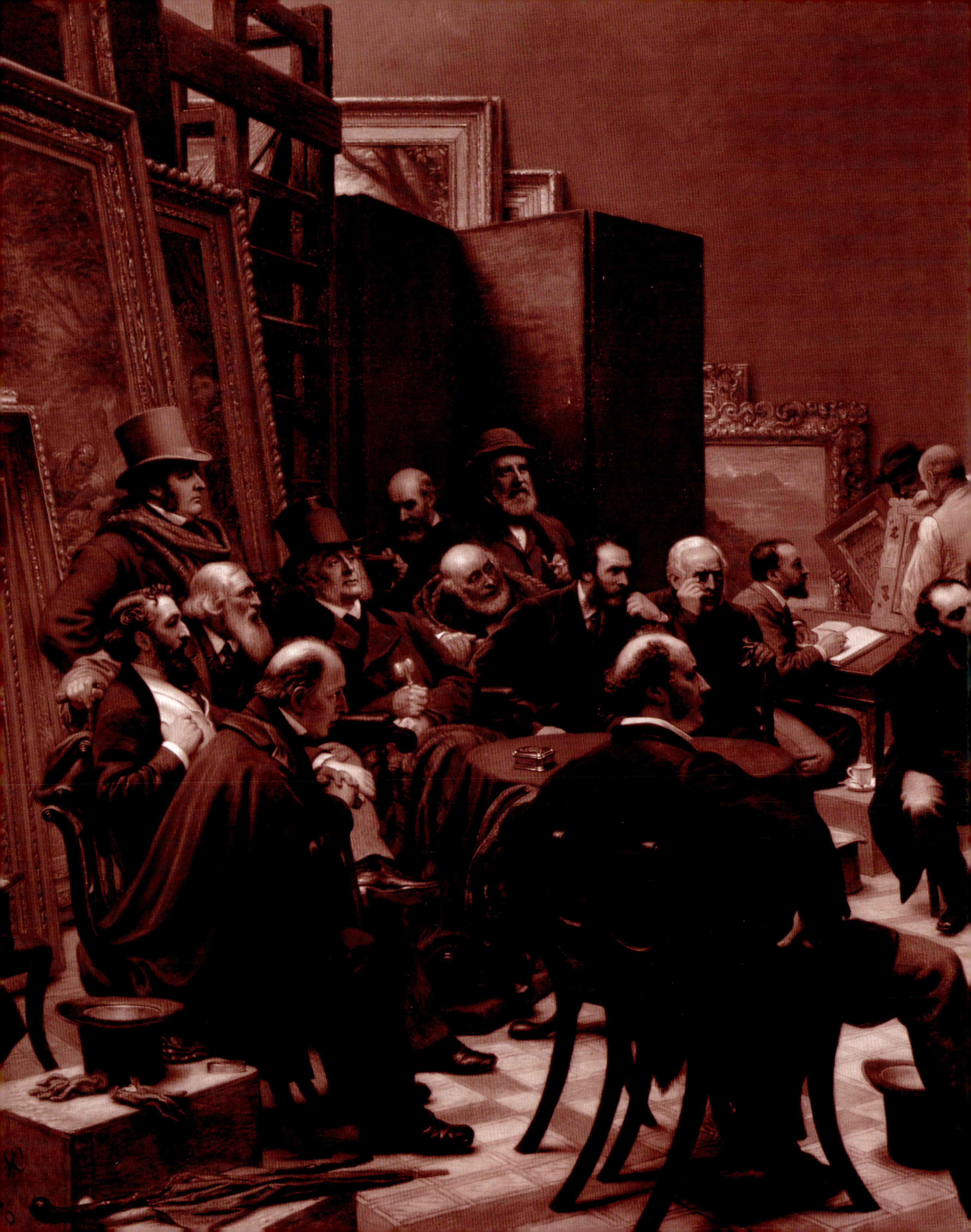

Part One
An Uncommon Life

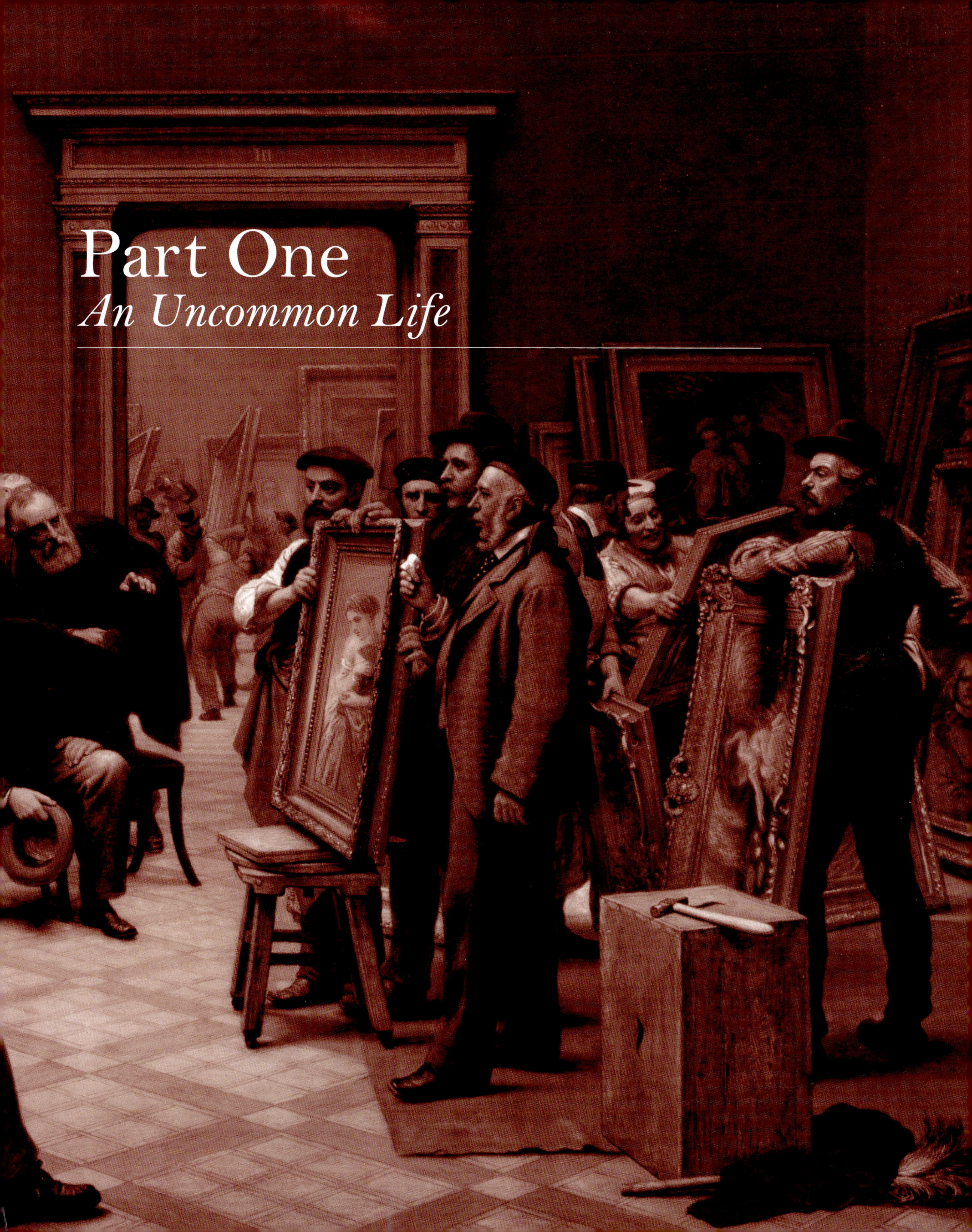

Chapter One

CHILDHOOD AND STUDIES

Henry Wallis was born on 21 February 1830 in London. His father was officially unknown, which implies that his mother Mary Ann Thomas had had a pre-marital relationship, not unusual in Victorian times. By consulting different genealogical websites and indexes, it can be gleaned that Henry's initial surname was Thomas, his mother's maiden name, and that he was christened on 27 November 1831 at St Pancras Old Church. When Henry was fifteen, his mother married Andrew Wallis, a wealthy property owner and the assumption has been that Henry simply took his family name on that occasion.[1] However, the 1841 census shows that Henry, aged 11, already lived with Andrew and was registered as Henry Wallis. According to the marriage certificate, the nuptials took place on 14 April 1845 at St James, Clerkenwell. It is interesting to learn that the bride and groom already shared the same residence at Clarence Place, Pentonville, in the district of Islington, which strongly suggests that they had known each other for quite a long time and that Andrew was likely Henry's actual father. The marriage made their relationship official, however, and gave the boy legal protection.[2]

Of Henry's youth, we know almost nothing, except from one French passport found by Diane Johnson, "for Andrew Wallis & son", stamped at Boulogne on 10 August 1845, "à reprendre à Paris", which means that Henry was accompanying his "father" to Paris. A later passport for Italy, stamped in 1852 – now in the Andrew Gordon collection, New York – tells us that he was 1m 71cm (5ft. 7in.) tall, that he had light brown hair, grey eyes and an oval face.

What we do know is that Henry Wallis had fixed upon a career as an artist by his mid-teens and that, in order to have access to the Royal Academy Schools, he initially enrolled at Sass's Academy, like so many others. The school had been established by Henry Sass (1788-1844) in 1818 and was notable for admitting female pupils from 1832. It was located in Bloomsbury near the British Museum at 6 Charlotte Street, now 10 Bloomsbury Street. Sass, born in London, was a portrait and history painter and exhibited at the Royal Academy from 1808 to 1838. But, according to William Powell Frith: "Though

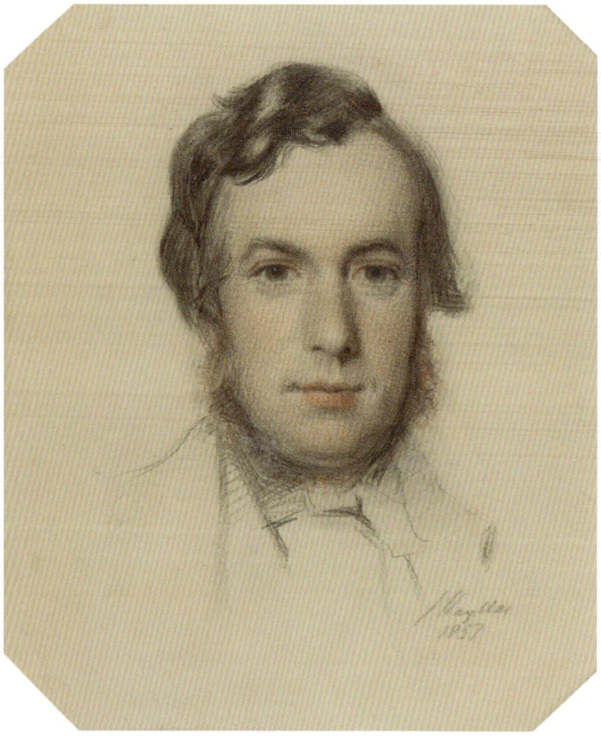

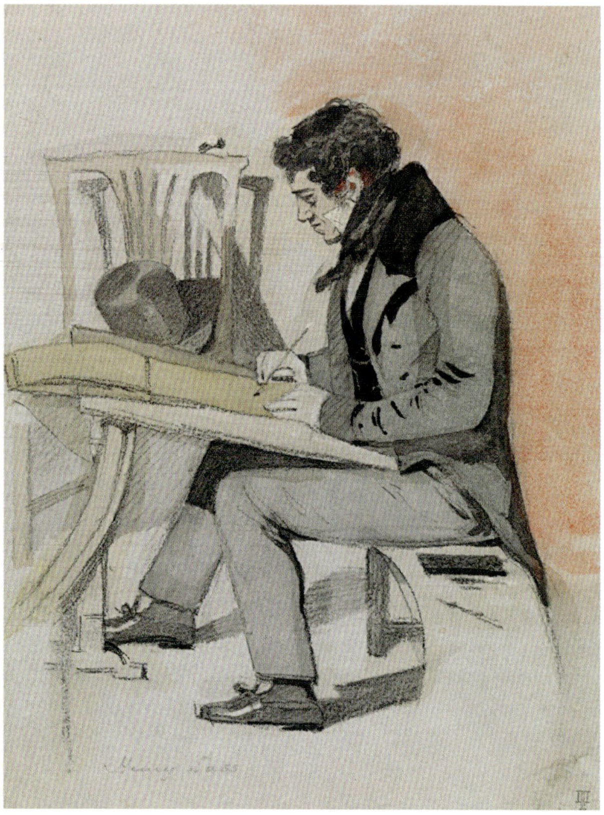

Far left:
James Hayllar, *F.S. Cary*, 1851
Image courtesy of National Portrait Gallery, London

Left:
Daniel Maclise, *Henry Sass*, c.1830
Image courtesy of the Yale Center for British Art, New Haven (Reproduced in Robinson, Michael, *The Lives and works of the Pre-Raphaelites*, Wigston, 2012, p.13)

Opposite page:
Back from Marston Moor [Cat. 39b.], 1859
Engraving by William Ridgway after H. Wallis, hand coloured
Illustration from *Contemporary Art*, 1886
Dennis Lanigan collection

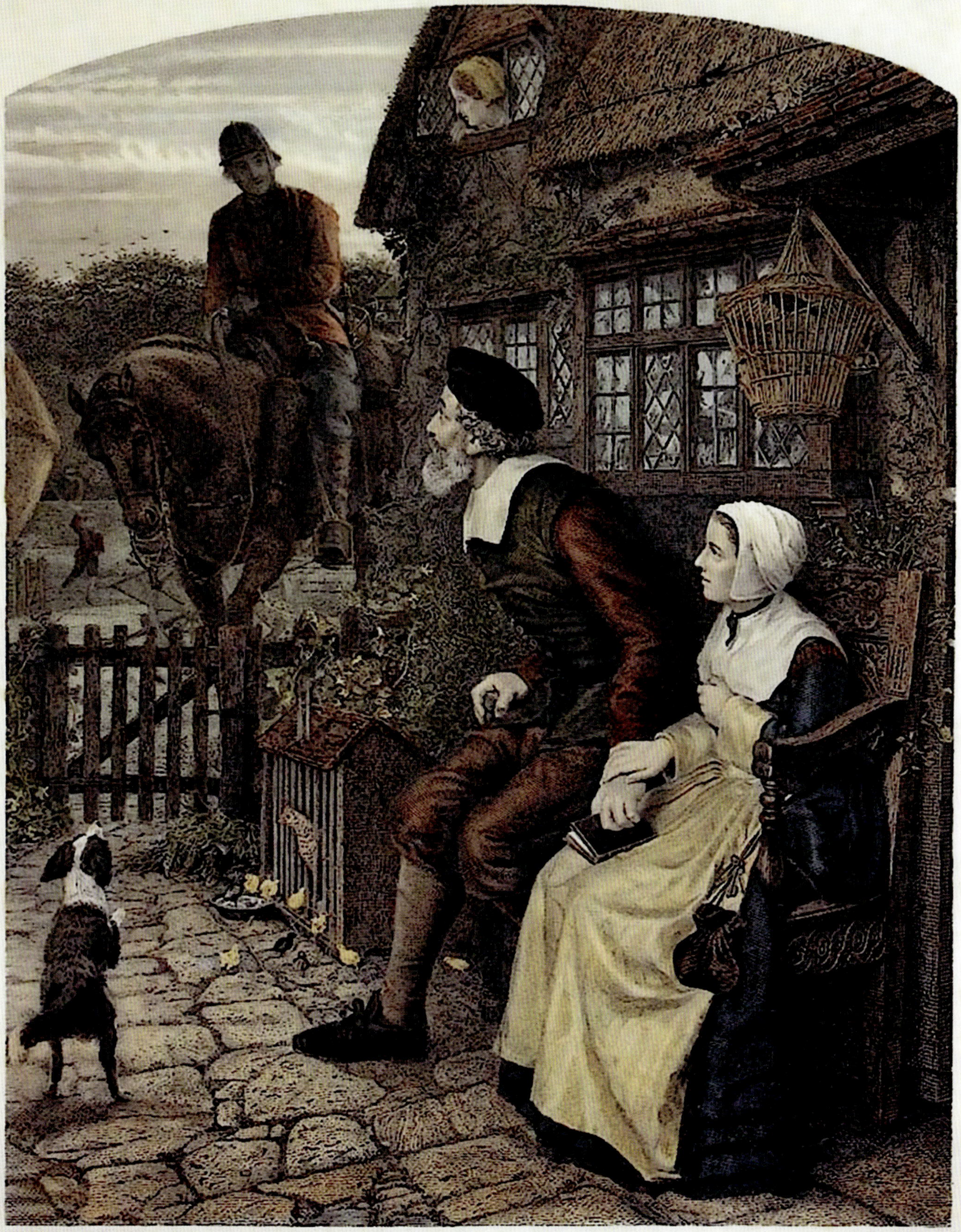

H. WALLIS PINXᵀ W. RIDGWAY SCULPᵀ

BACK FROM MARSTON MOOR.

FROM THE PICTURE IN THE POSSESSION OF THE PUBLISHERS.

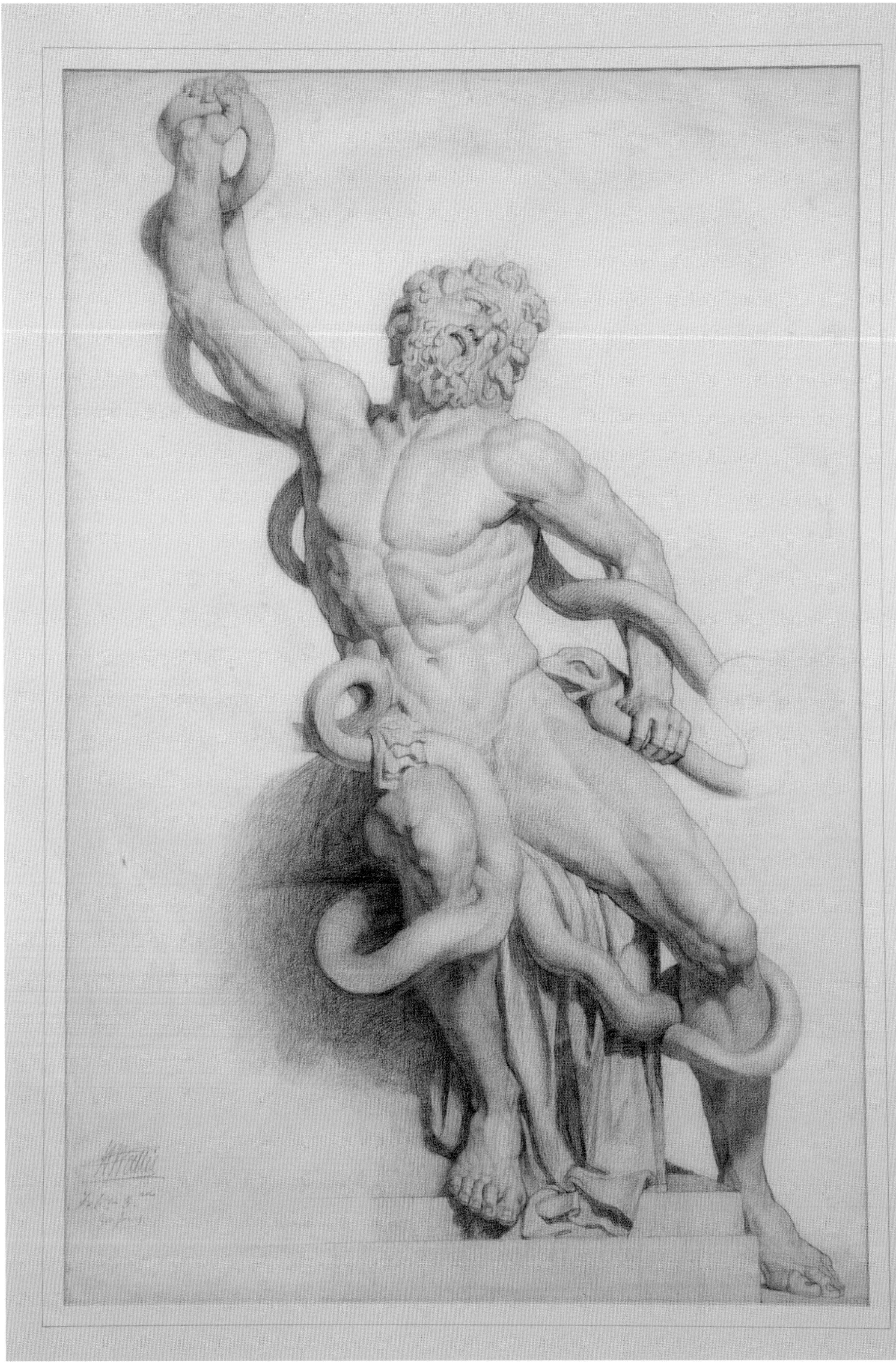

Mr. Sass thoroughly understood the principles of art, and could most efficiently inculcate them, he never succeeded in putting them satisfactorily into practice on his own account. His pictures were coldly correct, never displaying an approach to the sacred fire of genius."[3]

In 1842, due to health problems, Sass handed the direction over to one of his students, Francis Stephen Cary, the son of the Rev. Henry Francis Cary, the translator of Dante's *The Divine Comedy*. F.S. Cary renamed the institution Cary's School or Cary's Drawing Academy. Cary found inspiration in history and in Shakespeare. During the first part of his career, Wallis painted Shakespearian subjects, as well as national heroes, possibly as a result of having attended Cary's school. These subjects may also have been inspired by the competitions for the decoration of the new Palace of Westminster. It should also be remembered that "throughout the nineteenth century, one in five of all literary subject paintings shown at the Royal Academy featured a Shakespearean theme. This number rose during the middle decades of the century, when the popularity of literary subjects reached its zenith."[4]

Other pupils who attended Sass's or Cary's school included Augustus Leopold Egg, Dante Gabriel Rossetti, John Everett Millais, Walter Deverell, Simeon Solomon, Joanna Boyce and William Powell Frith. Frith gives an interesting description of how courses were given: "… A huge white plaster ball, standing on a pedestal, was the next object of attention, by the representation of which in Italian chalk and on white paper the student was to be initiated into the first principles of light, shadow and rotundity.... I spent six weeks over that awful ball (the drawing exists still, a wonder of line-work), the result being a certain amount of modeling knowledge very painfully acquired."[5] These tedious learning methods in the Antique School of the Royal Academy is likely the reason that Wallis left for Paris where he could enter the Life School of an atelier immediately.

The Royal Academy was founded in 1768, under George III, who generously financed the institution out of his own funds. Unlike those on the Continent, no academies then existed in England but only a few private institutions, which due to financial difficulties did not survive long. Forty Academicians (RAs) and twenty Associates (ARAs) were members, and a President was elected each year.

The Academicians had to supervise the drawing and the painting classes, but their main task was to prepare the annual exhibition. In order to be admitted to the Schools, students had to show their ability and produce drawings and studies from the antique. The Academician G.D.

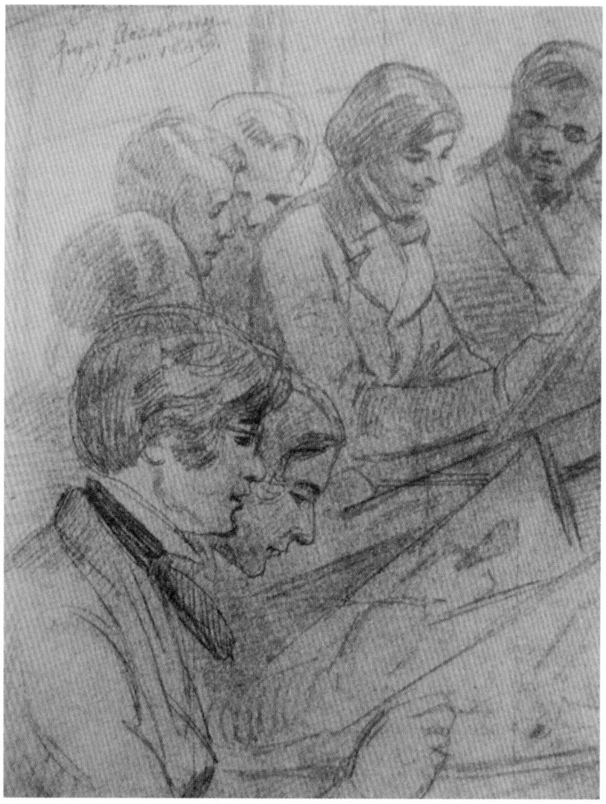

Leslie, who entered the Schools in 1852, describes the way things had to be done. A prospective student had to send a chalk drawing from the antique, an anatomical drawing and a drawing from a skeleton, the whole to be accompanied by an introductory letter certifying the student's morals. "If an applicant's drawing was approved by the Keeper, he or she was admitted as a 'Probationer', which meant he or she was given three months to prepare a set of drawings or models in the Academy, including a skeleton and an anatomical figure. It these were accepted by the Council (the ruling body of the Academy) as showing sufficient promise, the student was formally enrolled in the Antique school."[6]

Like so many others, Wallis was recommended by F.S. Cary. On 7 January 1848, shortly before his eighteenth birthday, Wallis entered on probation, and on 31 March of the same year, he was admitted to the Antique School.[7] Students were allowed to stay seven years at the Schools, though Wallis seems to have left after only two, for it is certain that he was in Paris in 1851.[8] It is possible that Wallis tired of drawing from casts and was anxious to advance to drawing from life such as he could experience from the start under the French system of training in an atelier. From what Wallis wrote to F.G. Stephens in 1881, after he had stopped exhibiting at the Academy, we can deduce that he found no stimulus in the academic system of teaching: "The schools of the Academy have always been detrimental to the advance of the best Art in this country. Of course they are useful to throw dust in the eyes of the public & for self glorification."[9]

Opposite page:
Study of the Laocoön [Cat. 1], made by Wallis at the Royal Academy Schools
Diane Johnson collection, Paris

Top right:
Until recently, the only known portraits of Wallis were the two cartes de visite photographs from the Bodleian Libraries at Oxford showing Wallis at approximately aged 60 (see title page and p.63). While studying the life and work of Arthur Hughes, Roberts and Wildman discovered Carl Haag's drawing made at the Royal Academy Schools on 17 November 1849, in which we may identify (starting from back right): Peter Austin Daniel, Arthur Hughes, unknown, Henry Wallis (sideways) then aged 19, unknown, James Hayllar and John Bagnold Burgess.
(Reproduced in Roberts, Leonard & Wildman, Steven, *Arthur Hughes: His Life and Work*, Woodbridge, 1997, p.12. Photograph from an original in Eton College, a gift of the Furnival family).

Chapter Two
PARIS: THE ATELIER GLEYRE

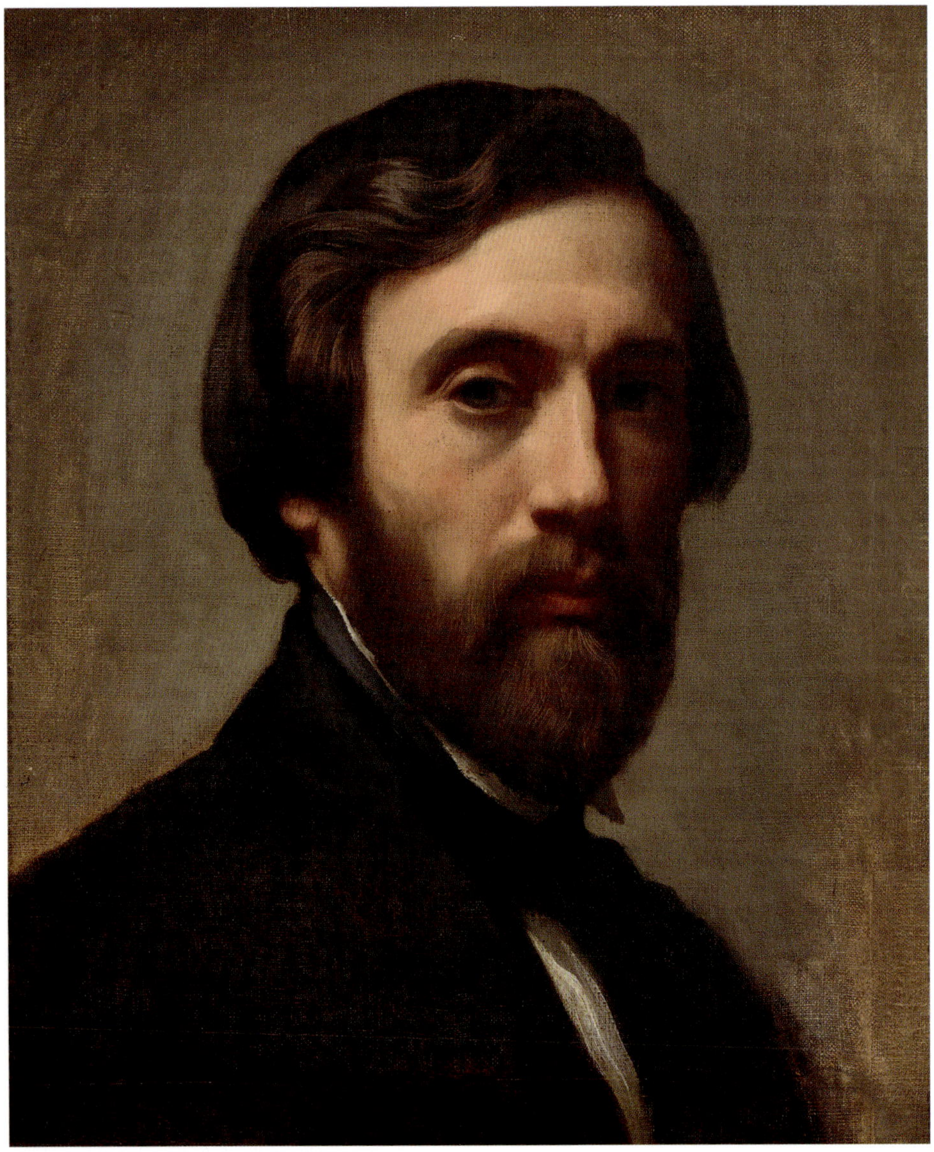

Charles Gleyre, self-portrait, Palace of Versailles
IMAGE BY PERMISSION OF CHÂTEAU DE VERSAILLES, DIST. RMN-GRAND PALAIS / CHRISTOPHE FOUIN

Medal-winners at the Royal Academy were provided with funds so that they could make a journey on the Continent.[1] In comparison with his contemporaries, Wallis seems to have been a diligent, but not a distinguished student. Despite never winning a student prize, he decided to undertake further studies in Paris; although students might have acquired technical skills at the Royal Academy, many were fascinated by the Parisian studios.

At that date, Paris was the centre of the world in matters of art. Thomas Armstrong, who, together with Thomas Lamont, George du Maurier, Edward Poynter, Val Prinsep and James Whistler, attended Gleyre's studio in the mid-1850s, vouches for the French ignorance of foreign art: "The French artists I lived among, mostly in the student stage, knew little or nothing, even by hearsay, of British art; indeed they would ask: 'Est-ce que l'on fait de la peinture en Angleterre?' Some of them had heard of Hogarth perhaps and knew Flaxman's outlines, which were much esteemed. Bonington's position was high. Turner was unknown, except from engravings, and only few of them."[2] This situation would change however, following the Exposition Universelle

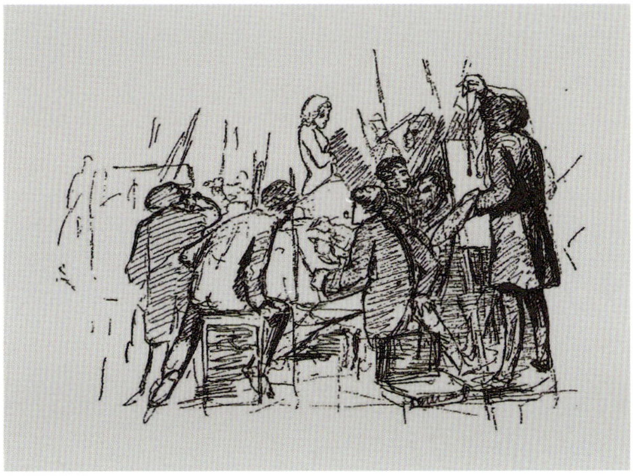

held in Paris in 1855, which allowed the French a greater exposure to contemporary British art.

Henry had previously been in Paris with his father in 1845. According to Morris and McKay,[3] he was registered at Gleyre's studio as early as 1851. Having trained in Paris in 1825 and attended Louis Hersent's studio, Gleyre spent some years travelling – first to Rome and then Sicily, Corfu, Turkey, Rhodes, Egypt and Nubia – where he produced many watercolours. On his return to Paris Gleyre was particularly successful at the 1843 *Salon* with his painting *Le Soir*.[4]

More than for his artistic achievements, Gleyre is now best remembered for having taken over Delaroche's studio, previously run by David and Gros.[5] "The ateliers [were] a survival from the medieval guild tradition, [and] the clearest indication of this heritage was the designation for the master as *patron*, an ancient term originally referring to the artisan in charge of a workshop. ... The term *patron* implied the practical rather than the theoretical training offered in the atelier."[6]

Since there were no formal programs of instruction at the École des Beaux-Arts, the skills necessary to become a successful artist were acquired haphazardly. "The private studios, formed by celebrated painters outside of their usual activities, were meant to fill in the gaps and thus provide the elementary student the essential preparation in drawing and other areas that would help him pass the examinations."[7]

Gleyre's studio (or *atelier*) became famous and was attended in the early 1860s by the future Impressionists Bazille, Monet, Sisley and Renoir. But British artists had preceded them: Wallis in around 1851, Philip Hermogenes Calderon in 1852, Felix Moscheles in 1855, Willie O'Connor, James Whistler, George du Maurier and T.R. Lamont in 1856, Edward Poynter in 1857 and Val Prinsep in 1859.

Among the students who wrote their memories, the Swiss painter Albert Anker reported that: "... he entered the studio softly, and started his round whereby he stopped at every easel. He only spoke to the student whose work needed correction, or rather he whispered so that the neighbour could hardly understand a word. He never generalized as Paul Delaroche did at the École des Beaux-Arts, who shouted so as to be understood in both study rooms. At the end of his round, he would leave just as quietly after having lighted his cigarette."[8]

In his novel, *Trilby*,[9] the satirist George du Maurier described the atmosphere within the studio[10] in the following terms: "Thirty or forty art students drew and painted from the nude model every day but Sunday from eight till twelve, and for two hours in the afternoon, except on Saturdays. One week the model was male, the next female. ... The bare walls were adorned with endless caricatures – *des charges* – in charcoal and white chalk; and also the scrapings of many palettes – a polychromous decoration not unpleasing. ...A stove, a model-throne, stools, boxes, some fifty strongly-built low chairs with backs, a couple of score easels and many drawing-boards, completed the *mobilier*."

Despite du Maurier's description in his novel, the models were not entirely naked, as a drawing by Wallis, now at the Birmingham Museum, proves. Jean Renoir, the painter Pierre-Auguste

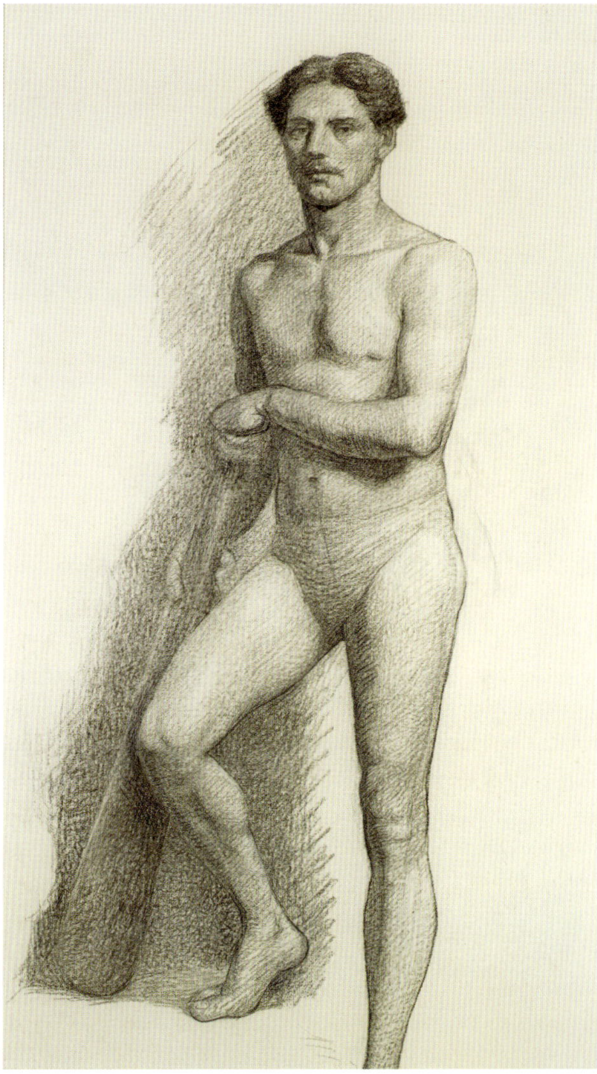

Above:
George du Maurier, *The Atelier Gleyre*, c.1857
(Felix Moscheles, *In Bohemia with du Maurier*, p.18.)

Right:
Henry Wallis, *Study of a Nude Man with Club* [Cat.3], c.1851-2
Image by permission of Birmingham Museums Trust

Renoir's son, confirms this: "His mind went back when at twenty he first entered the Atelier Gleyre and saw that big room crowded with young art students working away at their easels. A large bay window at the north side shed a grayish light on a nude male model. Old Gleyre had made the model wear a pair of short drawers so as not to offend the female students. There were three women in the class, one of them a young English girl, who was chubby and covered with freckles. Every time she came to the school she asked if the model could be allowed to take off his 'little panties'. Gleyre, a sturdy Swiss, who wore a beard and was near-sighted, refused flatly."[11]

Little evidence has been discovered of Wallis's presence in Paris and at Gleyre's studio, and it is not easy to find out much about how he lived there. Fortunately, other testimonies survive, for example, those of George du Maurier, Thomas Armstrong and Felix Moscheles, all of whom attended Gleyre's studio a few years after Henry had left, and which give us insights into a typical English art pupil's life.

Val Prinsep explained, "Normally a new student was subject to hazing as part of the rite of initiation into the studio. ... The newcomer was expected to purchase refreshment for the whole group, the traditional *bienvenue*, as a sign of his acceptance. Failure to do so, or even resistance could result in ridicule or expulsion from the group. Whistler recalled that when he was in Gleyre's studio an unpopular student was forced to leave after an open coffin was placed near his easel."[12]

Most of the students were penniless and tried to make both ends meet by doing small jobs. According to Moscheles, the penurious students' only means of support was derived from painting what is called *Les Stations de la Croix* (the Stations of the Cross). Moscheles explained, "These pictures destined to decorate the village churches in France and generally in Catholic countries, are produced in a more matter-of-fact than artistic way. The employer with an eye to the advantages of division of labour, has the subjects printed on canvas. Then a batch of Station No. 1, perhaps some six or eight canvases at a time, are given out to artist No. 1, who puts in the landscape and surroundings, from there they go to artist No. 2, who paints the draperies, and finally to No. 3, who fills in heads, hands, and feet."[13] This exercise was useful in teaching students how to draw the human body and may have been as effective as any Academy attendance. It is unknown whether Wallis had to do this kind of work, but as his (step)father was a wealthy man, it seems reasonable to think he did not. The question remains unanswered, however. Wallis is said to have done "patient, beautiful drawings of all the statues in the Louvre, to perfect his knowledge of anatomy."[14] Certainly, copying paintings and sketching from art works in the Louvre was considered an essential part of an art student's training in Paris and Wallis appears to have been no exception.

Gleyre gave his students a great deal of freedom, but he continued a strict academic tradition: only the antique ideal of beauty mattered, not reality; and a hierarchy had to be followed, with history paintings at the top. He simply perpetuated the system that others before him had used, such as Delaroche.

Renoir, Sisley and the other would-be "Impressionists", who attended Gleyre's studio at the beginning of the 1860s found his teaching principles outdated. Since he thought that nature was uninteresting and that artists should idealise their subject, Gleyre tried to "correct" their "errors". Monet remembered Gleyre saying: "Remember, young man, that when drawing a figure, you should always have the antique in mind. Nature, my friend, is all right for a study, but in itself it is uninteresting. You see, style is the only thing."[15]

As to Gleyre's influence on the British artists, Boime correctly points out that "it is not coincidental that Gleyre's English pupils, Edward Poynter and Val Prinsep, promoted their own brand of domesticated antiquity not too dissimilar in approach from that of the 'Néo-grecs'... We may also mention here the bond between Albert Moore and Whistler, whose joint obsession with Greek art in the 1860s might very well be traced to Gleyre. Thus, the antique scenes so prevalent in England from the sixties on, which evidently provided Victorians relief from the disturbing Pre-Raphaelite offshoots, stemmed in good measure from the work of Gleyre and his disciples."[16]

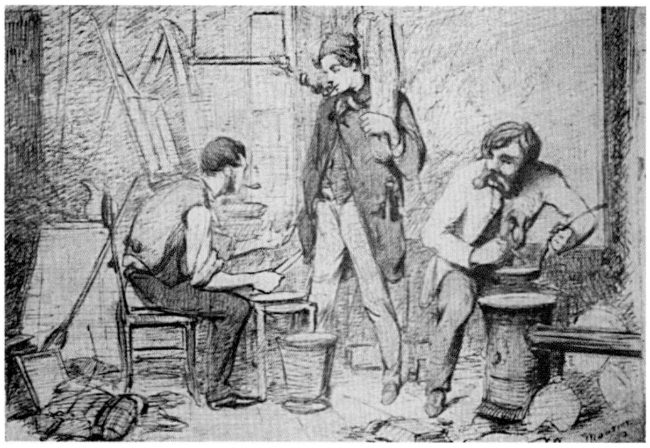

George du Maurier, *Cooking the Dinner in the Studio*, pen and ink sketch. L.M. Lamont: *Thomas Armstrong, C.B. A Memoir*, Martin Seckler, London, 1912, opposite p.138.

Despite his devotion to the ideal in art matters, Gleyre "taught personal theories that seemed revolutionary to the Academicians. He advised students to prepare their tones in advance before starting to paint. This would resolve their struggle with colours and they would be able to focus on contours and on drawing. Indeed, Gleyre

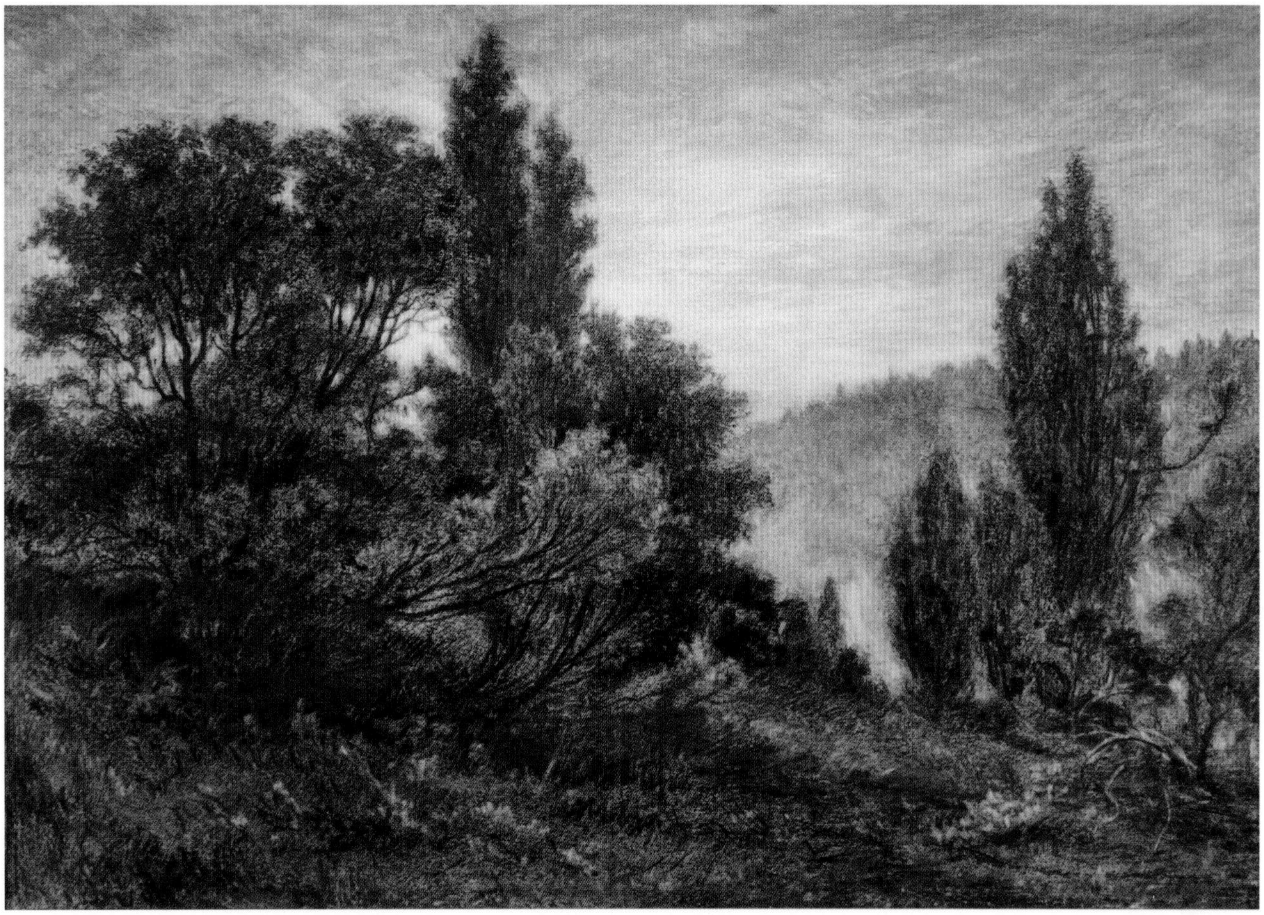

Henry Wallis,
Landscape Study with Trees [Cat. 85],
*c.*1870s
IMAGE COURTESY DIANE JOHNSON, SAN FRANCISCO, CALIFORNIA.

was always anxious that the 'damned colour' would go to the students' heads."[17]

We do not know whether Wallis, who entered the studio in 1851, was influenced by such theories. In the years of his apprenticeship he certainly painted historical topics – and Shakespeare was his hero – but never in a pompous academic manner. Rather his approach was a more intimate personal one.[18]

In August and September 1864, Gleyre closed his studio, for want of money and because of sight-related problems. Bazille wrote to his parents: "Mr Gleyre is quite ill, it seems the poor man is going to lose his sight. All the students are sad because they are very fond of him."[19] It has sometimes been assumed that the studio had closed its doors for good following this, but Hauptman has reason to believe that Gleyre continued to teach at least until 1870.[20] The French critic and historian Hippolyte Taine greatly admired the painter: "In creating a style and a grand style, few are superior to him; considering his good taste, his knowledge and his ideas, his continuous pursuit of and almost constant devotion to pure beauty and to perfection – physical and moral, Christian and pagan – he is first class."[21]

Although it is certain that Wallis was a student at Gleyre's, as the early Birmingham academic drawing and the 1852 passport seem to confirm, it is doubtful that he was admitted at the École des Beaux-Arts. Investigation of their archives leads to the inescapable conclusion that Wallis was unknown there because his name does not appear in the indexes of staff and students' files. No doubt the widely propagated claim that he had studied at the École des Beaux-Arts is no more than an initial assumption and subsequent legend. Despite this, with his combination of training at the Royal Academy Schools and Gleyre's atelier, Wallis had achieved a good solid foundation of the craft of painting. Later reviewers frequently complimented him both on his draughtsmanship and his use of colour. *The Athenaeum*, in particular, pointed out Wallis's skill as a draughtsman: "In this country Mr. Wallis's noble drawings are well known, and several examples of this mode of art have been seen at the Black and White Exhibition. The process is a highly artistic one, and possesses precious advantages for the skilled draughtsman."[22] A reviewer for *The Illustrated London News* noted: "Mr. Henry Wallis has often proved himself a colourist approaching the Venetian standard."[23] This is high praise from critics and gives a good indication as to how well Wallis had indeed mastered his craft.

Chapter Three
THE ROYAL ACADEMY AND ITS RIVALS: WALLIS AND THE VICTORIAN ART WORLD

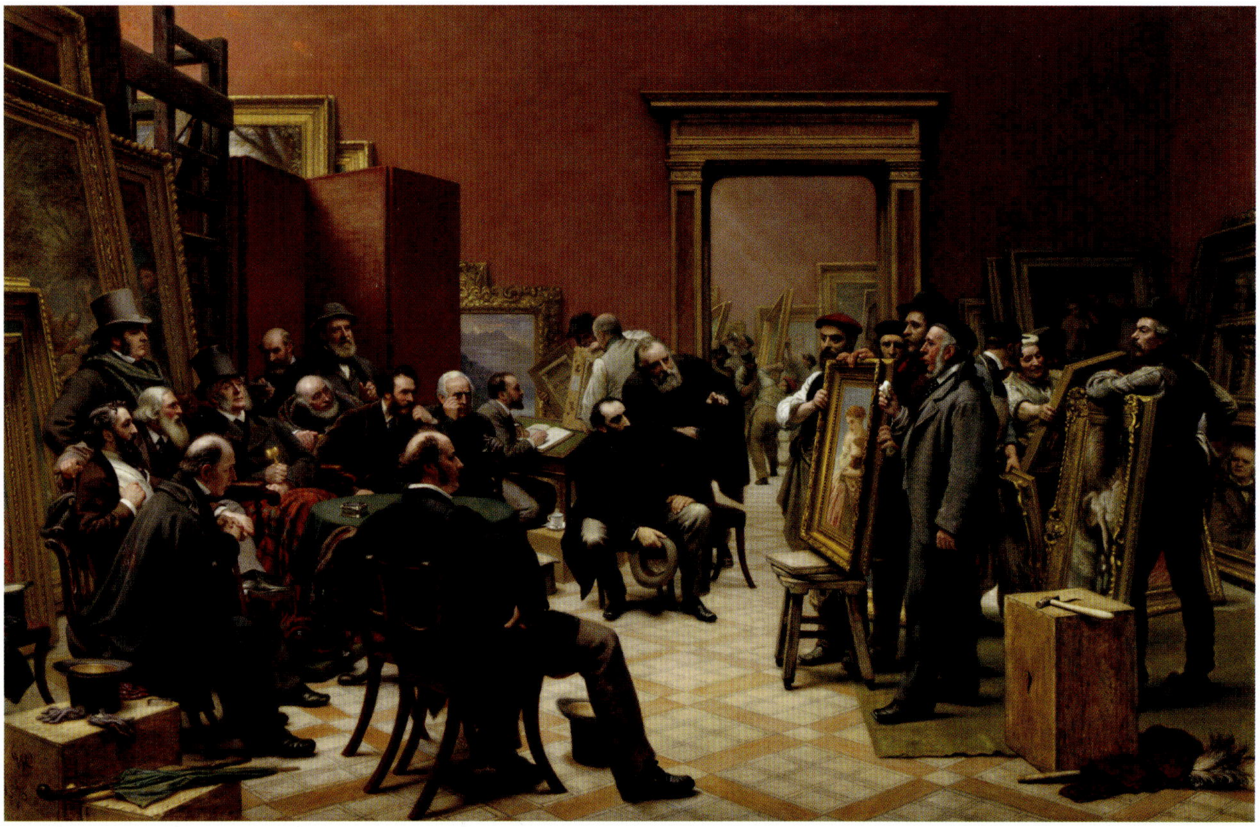

Charles West Cope RA (1811 - 1890), *The Council of the Royal Academy selecting Pictures for the Exhibition, 1875*, oil on canvas, 1876
This painting shows the Council of the R.A. selecting pictures for the Summer exhibition of 1875. Wallis had two works selected that year, *Fugitives from Constantinople* (No. 386) and *On the Ponte Della Paglia; Going to the Council* (No. 405).
© Royal Academy of Arts, London; photographer: John Hammond

Wallis, like all artists of his generation, had a wide choice of exhibiting venues to which he could submit works. Early in his career his paintings were primarily exhibited at the Royal Academy. At the time when Joshua Reynolds was President, the Academy had its premises at Somerset House (presently housing the Courtauld Institute of Art), but in 1837 the government took the building over for their own administration,[1] and from then on, the Royal Academy shared the buildings of the National Gallery on Trafalgar Square. Finally, in 1868, it found its current location in an imposing building at Burlington House, Piccadilly.

One can hardly imagine today the prestige that surrounded the R.A.s and the A.R.A.s in the Victorian era, but it was considerable, and the full members in particular were able to sell their works at a high price. At a time when the average salary was less than £100 a year, some Academicians could easily earn up to £5,000 per annum.[2]

It was not easy during the 1850s to challenge the monopoly of the Royal Academy if one wished to be considered a serious artist. It was the natural place to start one's career, and even the Pre-Raphaelites followed this path. Wallis regularly exhibited at the R.A. between 1854 and 1877. Although the 1850s were his years of greatest success, with masterpieces such as *Chatterton* and *The Stonebreaker*, even well into the 1870s he continued to draw the critics' attention with works such as *A Despatch from Trebizond* and *Fugitives from Constantinople*.

Wallis stopped exhibiting at the Royal Academy in 1877, the very year that the Grosvenor Gallery opened its doors, but in Wallis's case a link does not seem to exist between the two. Holman Hunt was never elected an A.R.A; in his letters to Wallis, he constantly criticised the Royal Academy so it is possible that Hunt's arguments eventually induced Wallis to cease exhibiting there. Hunt and Wallis were not the only ones disaffected by the policies of the Royal Academy. Thomas Armstrong stopped exhibiting there the same year as Wallis. In 1877 William Bell Scott also launched his own attack on the Academy. According to W.E. Fredeman, Scott's avowed purpose was "to expose the total inability of the Academy to represent in any adequate sense the artists of England in the seventh decade of the 19th century. Its restrictive membership (40 R.A.'s and 20 Associates) limits arbitrarily and invidiously the recognition that competent British artists have every right to expect, and he accuses the Academy of being no more than a 'trade monopoly', committed to the perpetuation of 'modest mediocrity'."[3]

Attacking the Royal Academy was not a new phenomenon, opposition to the institution had started early in the nineteenth century: "The main substance of the complaints was that Academies in general were of no use and that the Royal Academy in particular was unfair to artists who were not numbered in its membership."[4] At the time of Wallis's studentship, Sir Martin Archer Shee (1769-1850) was the President, but his successor Sir Charles Eastlake (1793-1865) achieved some significant improvements, such as opening its doors to engravers and women artists. As early as 1859, violent opposition came from anonymous writers who called themselves "the Council of Four" and who stated in their *Royal Academy Review*[5] that "the Royal Academy has survived – a self-elected, self-governing, self-serving conclave, appropriating to itself a large revenue derived through others excluded from its management or enjoyment" and that "the Institution has done little or nothing for art. As a school it is not successful. The most excellent painters are those who either were not distinguished students, or those who have emancipated themselves from the Academical instruction."[6] A criticism that dominated the whole century was that "the rule which constitute the Royal Academicians – who are themselves exhibitors – to be the arbiters and judges of the whole of the pictures sent for selection, – which enables them to exhibit eight pictures, no matter what their size or merit, and which afford to them the very best positions on the walls or right, are every one of them bad and unjust."[7]

In 1863, a Commission was set up to inquire into the position of the Royal Academy which met for the first time on 13 January 1863 under the chairmanship of Lord Elcho.[8] Among the witnesses were artists, including Mulready, Landseer, Holman Hunt and Millais, art critics, such as Ruskin, and three Members of Parliament. The final report was very much in the Academy's favour. Nevertheless, several recommendations were made, including: that more architects and sculptors should be elected to bring the total number of Academicians to 50; that the number of Associates should also be increased to 50; and that they should have equal rights with Academicians in running the Academy's affairs.[9] Most of these suggestions for reform were ignored, however.

During the 1870s, Hunt's and Wallis's opposition to the Academy expanded and Hunt said that his remedies "would be to limit membership to ten years, no past member being eligible for re-election; that the duties should be to analyse artists' materials and guard against adulteration, and to manage the schools, appointing a supervisor in the full vigour of his faculties; that elections should be made not by the body itself but by every exhibitor of three years' standing; and that the title should signify simply that the person was an important and respected member of his profession."[10]

In 1878, Frederic Leighton became President and, during his tenure, he improved the teaching and a new life-school was set up. These measures seemed insufficient to the opponents, which is why artists, among them Holman Hunt and Walter Crane, sought the aid of the press and published their first article concerning reforms in the *Pall Mall Gazette* in June 1885. Marion H. Spielman summarized the points on which reform was demanded as follows:

1. An alteration in (a) the test-examination for admission to the schools, and (b) the teaching after admission is obtained;

2. The recognition of (a) water-colour painting, (b) original engraving, and (c) the minor decorative arts, and the qualification of their professors for membership;

3. A modification of (a) the present mode of election into the Academy, and (b) the constitution of the Selection and Hanging Committees; and chiefly,

4. The limitation of the number of works that any one artist may send in for admission to the Annual Exhibition.[11]

Finally, in 1887, a Committee was appointed to consider the proposals, but, as Spielman pointed out, the results were disappointing: "Two recommendations have been made to the Council, and await confirmation by the General Assembly: (1) No student is eligible for probationship after he or she has passed the age of twenty-two; and (2) No more than four works of any exhibitor, either Member or Outsider, may be hung on the line. ... What has been done to hint that the professors of watercolour painting, and original etching, and drawing in black-and-white merit a place as 'artists' in the Royal Academy? Nothing."[12]

The influence of the Royal Academy was for obvious reasons regularly questioned by rival societies, such as the Old and the New Water-Colour Societies. The Royal Academy did not

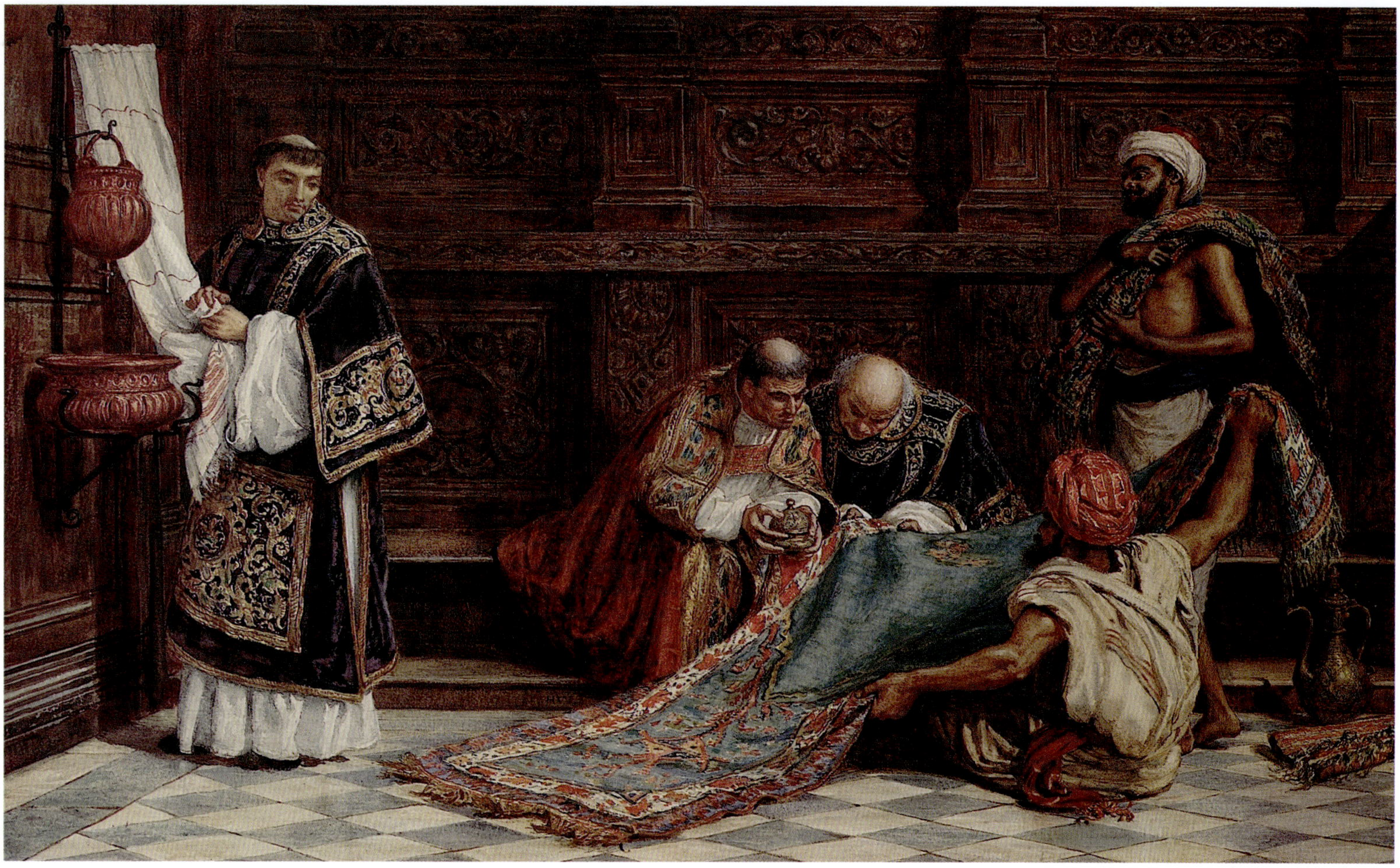

favour watercolours in its exhibitions, considering them not to be an appropriate medium for serious artistic expression. It only admitted oil painters, sculptors and architects to membership.[13] The Society of Painters in Water Colours (the Old Water-Colour Society), created in 1804, was the first of its kind.[14] Among its members were such diverse artists as Turner and Burne-Jones. Wallis became an associate member in 1878 and a full member two years later. He exhibited numerous watercolours that he had made on his travels, or later worked up in his studio from studies, that received favourable reviews in the periodicals of the time. At the time of Wallis's election, John Gilbert was the Society's President and would hold office until his death in 1897.[15] The Old Water-Colour Society should not be confused with the New Society of Painters in Water Colours, originally founded in 1807, which in 1863 became known as the Institute of Painters in Water Colours and in 1883 the Royal Institute of Painters in Water Colours. It had been set up in protest because of the "fogeyism" and exclusivity that continued to mark the Old Water-Colour Society. In April 1881, the Institute had suggested to its rival that they should amalgamate, but this proposition was ultimately rejected.[16] Wallis had been a negotiator on behalf of the Old Water-Colour Society.

The British Institution (1806-1867)

Located in Pall Mall, The British Institution "was founded by a number of noblemen and gentlemen to encourage art, and it was not in any way intended to be a rival to the Royal Academy, members of which body continued to exhibit their works there in large numbers until the expiration of the lease in 1867."[17] Unlike the Royal Academy, the British Institution actively bought works with a view towards a permanent collection. The largest portion of these works ultimately became part of the collection of the National Gallery, which had been created in 1824. The exhibition room at the British Institution was small and guarded by an armed grenadier. Malicious gossip coming from people like William Bell Scott maintained that the manager was an autocrat and that a condition to have one's paintings hung in a prominent position was to have them framed by the latter's own son.[18] Wallis did not exhibit here frequently, but did show *The Parlour of Anne Hathaway's Cottage* in 1854.

The New British Institution

In 1870 the New British Institution was opened at 39 Old Bond Street, where a Spring exhibition of oil paintings and a Winter exhibition of watercolour drawings was held. Unlike the Royal

Above:
Henry Wallis, *In a Sacristy, the Carpet Merchant* [Cat. 120], exhibited at the O.W.S. 1878
IMAGE COURTESY OF BONHAMS, LONDON

Opposite page:
Henry Wallis, *The Parlour in Anne Hathaway's Cottage* [Cat 16], which was shown at the British Institution in 1854.
IMAGE COURTESY CHRISTIE'S, LONDON.

Academy, contributors elected the Committee for selecting and hanging works, and it was not requisite that a successful candidate be a member of the General Committee of the Institution. There was to be no favour shown to members of the Committee, or any other persons, as to exhibition, and no artist was to be allowed to exhibit more than two works.[19] Wallis exhibited several works at this venue, including *Blue Bells* [Cat. 75] and *Ser Pandolfo* [Cat. 80] in 1870 and *Assunta* [Cat. 87] in 1871, before it closed in 1876.

Society of British Artists

Another competitor to the Royal Academy was the Society of British Artists founded in 1823, which was supposed to promote the career of British artists. Located in Suffolk Street, it was the particular haven of landscape painters and its shows were intended to rival the Royal Academy's Summer Exhibition. Despite only having a loose affiliation with the Society, Wallis exhibited at least five works there, including *A Night Study* [Cat. 17] in 1854, *A Study at Fontainebleau* [Cat. 20] and *The Present [Cat. 21]* in 1855 and *Arranging for the Marriage – An Idyll of the Sacristy* [Cat. 109] in 1876-77.

Despite their opposition to the Royal Academy, not many of these societies actually had a more "progressive" exhibition policy. Only members of the Old Water-Colour Society, for instance, were allowed to exhibit, and their display rules were identical to those of the Royal Academy.[20] Both the New British Institution and the New Society of Painters in Water Colours, however, allowed nonmembers to exhibit alongside members. The opening of two new exhibiting venues was therefore welcomed by artists, particularly the Dudley Gallery with its liberal exhibition policies. The Dudley Gallery opened its doors at the Egyptian Hall in 1865 and initially just displayed watercolour paintings. It was primarily run by young artists with liberal views and quickly became a favourite venue for the Pre-Raphaelites and many of the young painters associated with the nascent Aesthetic Movement.[21] Oil paintings were also exhibited after 1867. Although Wallis preferred to exhibit his watercolours at the Old Water-Colour Society, he did exhibit oil paintings and drawings at the Dudley Gallery.

The Grosvenor Gallery and The New Gallery

In 1877, the art world experienced a major innovation with the opening of the Grosvenor Gallery in New Bond Street by Sir Coutts Lindsay. Firstly, Lindsay "admitted artists by invitation, rather than through the juried systems that discouraged young talent at other venues."[22] Secondly, the Gallery had an original way of displaying works. At the Royal Academy, a lucky few had their works hung "on the line", with most of the paintings hung in a floor-to-ceiling arrangement, the so-called "Salon style". The Grosvenor hung all paintings on the line, and, more importantly, grouped them by artist, which was not the case at the Royal Academy. This was a major advantage for artists exhibiting at the Grosvenor Gallery. At other venues like the Royal Academy an artist could have his painting rejected, accepted but not hung, or hung in a position that was unfavourable to view the work,

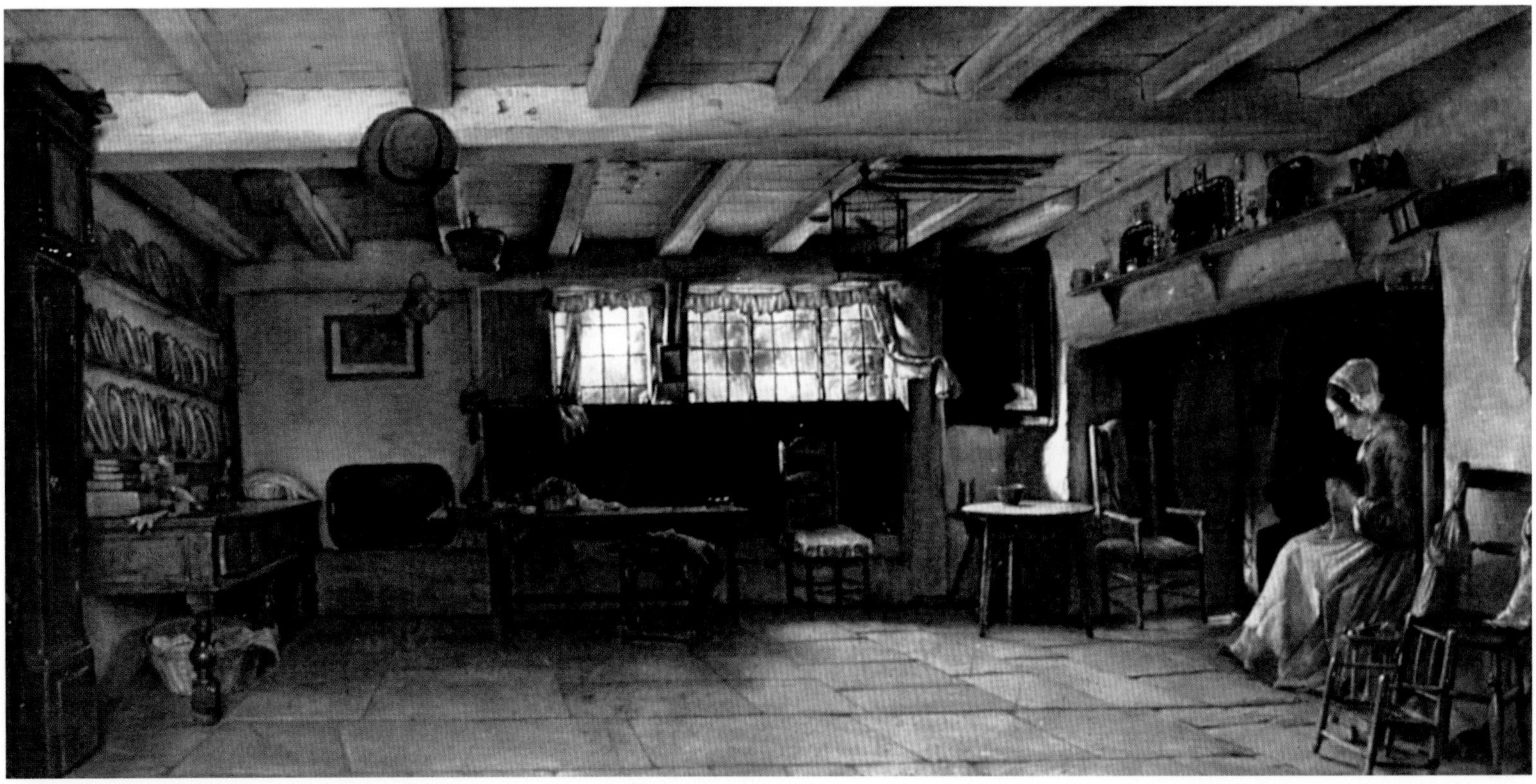

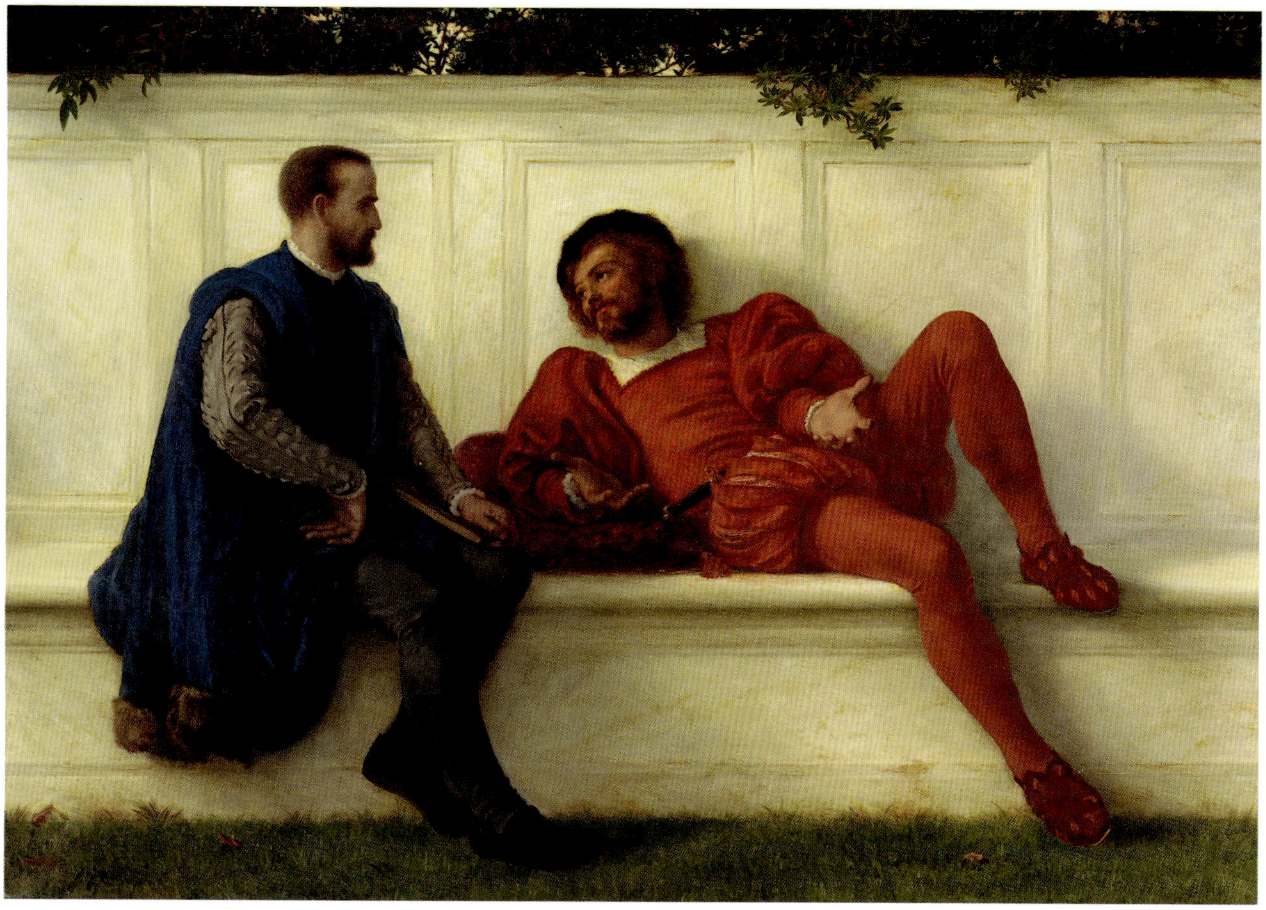

either from a height standpoint, or because it was hung in between works that were not compatible with it.[23] Although the Grosvenor Gallery was short-lived, having stopped its activities in 1890,[24] it proved to be of great assistance to progressive artists, especially those associated with the Aesthetic Movement. It made famous such names as Edward Burne-Jones, John Roddam Spencer Stanhope, George Frederic Watts, Albert Moore, and James Whistler, as well as many women artists such as Princess Louise (Queen Victoria's daughter), Evelyn De Morgan and Marie Spartali Stillman.[25] Though Wallis did not exhibit at the Grosvenor Gallery itself, he did show *Pot of Honey from Mount Hymettus* [Cat. 191] at its successor, The New Gallery. The New Gallery, at 121 Regent Street, was founded in 1888 by J. Comyns Carr (1849-1916) and Charles Hallé (1846-1914), who had previously been co-directors of the Grosvenor Gallery. Many of the artists who had previously exhibited at the Grosvenor transferred their allegiance to the New Gallery, including Burne-Jones, Alma-Tadema, Watts, Hunt and Leighton.[26]

By the second half of the nineteenth century, the art market had dramatically changed. Middle-class buyers of recent fortunes, such as financiers, manufacturers, cotton traders and industrialists, were progressively replacing the earlier aristocratic patrons of art.[27] Certainly, it was this middle-class group of buyers who primarily patronised Wallis, as can be seen from the catalogue raisonné section of this book. Independent dealers appeared and, with them, new exhibiting galleries not affiliated with any Society. Artists could try the French Gallery in Pall Mall, founded in 1854 by Ernest Gambart, the famous Belgian art dealer,[28] which held two annual events, the Winter Exhibition of British Art and the spring French Exhibition or the Society of French Artists at 168, New Bond Street, opened in 1870 by Paul Durand-Ruel, and run by Charles Deschamps. Wallis exhibited at both the galleries, including *The Golden Scarf* [Cat. 58] and *After Supper at Capri* [Cat. 59] at the French Gallery in Winter 1866 and Dartmoor Oaks [Cat. 103] in 1875 and *A Morning Call, Ladies of Smyrna* [Cat. 143] in 1889 at The Society of French Artists.

Above:
Henry Wallis, *His Highness and His Excellency the Ambassador of the Florentine Republic (Cesare Borgia and Machiavelli)* [Cat. 79], which was exhibited at the Dudley Gallery in 1871.
Image courtesy of private collection c/o Martin Beisly Fine Art

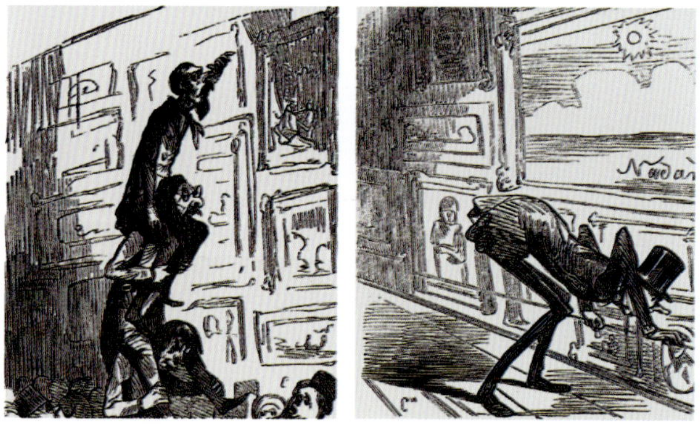

Left:
The hanging policy at the Academy and the Salon: two sketches by the famous French photographer Nadar, first published in the journal *Le petit journal pour rire,* (1848-1855) and reprinted in *Les petits albums pour rire: On nous écrit de Paris.*

Chapter Four
THE PRE-RAPHAELITE CIRCLE

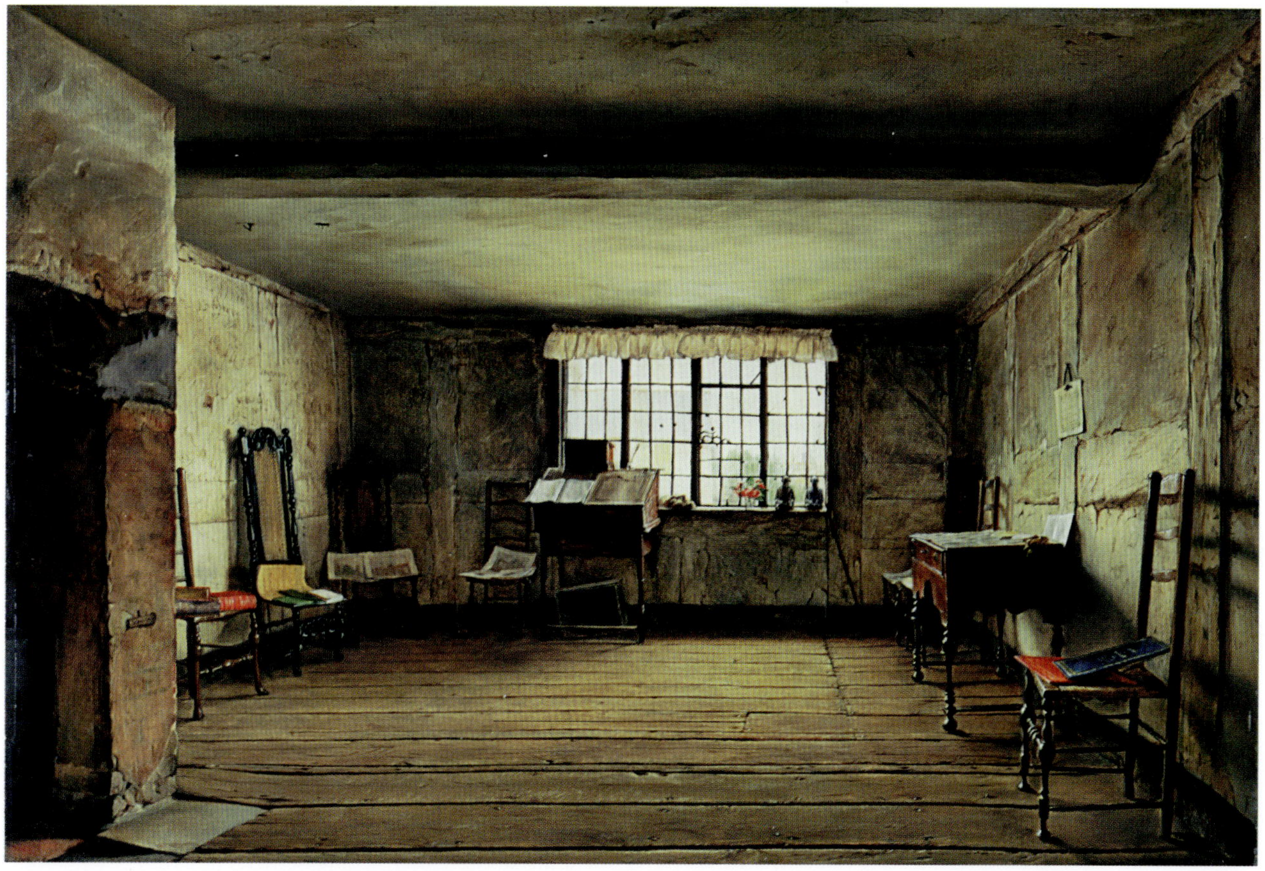

Henry Wallis,
The Room in which Shakespeare was Born
[Cat. 8], 1853
Wallis has painted the room in remarkable detail; a true early Pre-Raphaelite picture.
IMAGE BY PERMISSION OF TATE, LONDON, 2016

The freedom that Wallis and other students experienced at Gleyre's studio was unknown at the Royal Academy Schools, where emphasis was placed on a hierarchy of artistic subjects, on drawing, on painting indoors in the studio as opposed to *en plein air*, on a smooth and invisible brush stroke, and last, but not least, on a reference to Classical Antiquity and to the High Renaissance. In Britain, this constant reference to the High Renaissance provoked a reaction among certain young artists who refused to limit themselves to the so-called perfect conventional pose and idealised beauty, as found in the work of Raphael and his followers. This led to the birth of the Pre-Raphaelite Brotherhood (PRB), founded in 1848 by John Everett Millais, William Holman Hunt, William Michael and Dante Gabriel Rossetti, Thomas Woolner, Frederic George Stephens and James Collinson.

Though he never played a formal part in the movement, Wallis is famous for his paintings, *The Death of Chatterton* and *The Stonebreaker*, both considered masterpieces within the Pre-Raphaelite oeuvre. Wallis also had considerable contact with important members of both the first and second phases of Pre-Raphaelitism – Arthur Hughes, William Holman Hunt and Frederic George Stephens were among his closest friends. He was also on good terms with Robert Braithwaite Martineau, G.P. Boyce, W.B. Scott, Edward Burne-Jones, William Morris, the Rossetti brothers, Algernon Swinburne, Charles Fairfax Murray and George Howard. Being a member of the Hogarth Club, Wallis would have known all the young progressive artists and architects of the time.[1]

Arthur Hughes

Wallis and Arthur Hughes had struck up a friendship as students at the Royal Academy Schools. Arthur Hughes had entered the Royal Academy Schools on 17 December 1847, three months before Wallis,[2] and both were obviously still there on 17 November 1849 when Carl Haag made his drawing. Wallis and Hughes often met during the 1850s and both were present at a meeting of the Hogarth Club on 4 May 1858.[3] That year, Hughes moved to Maidstone in Kent

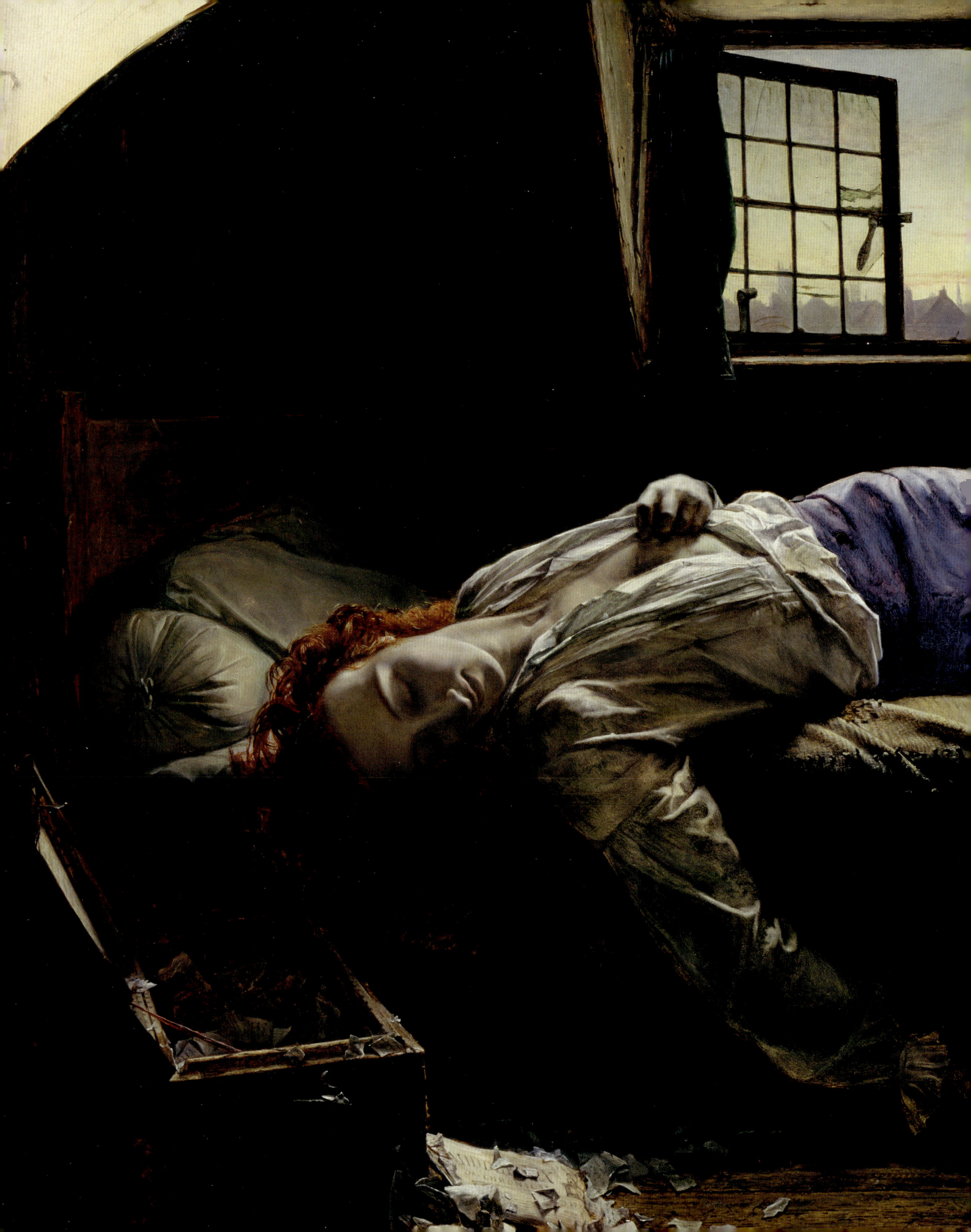

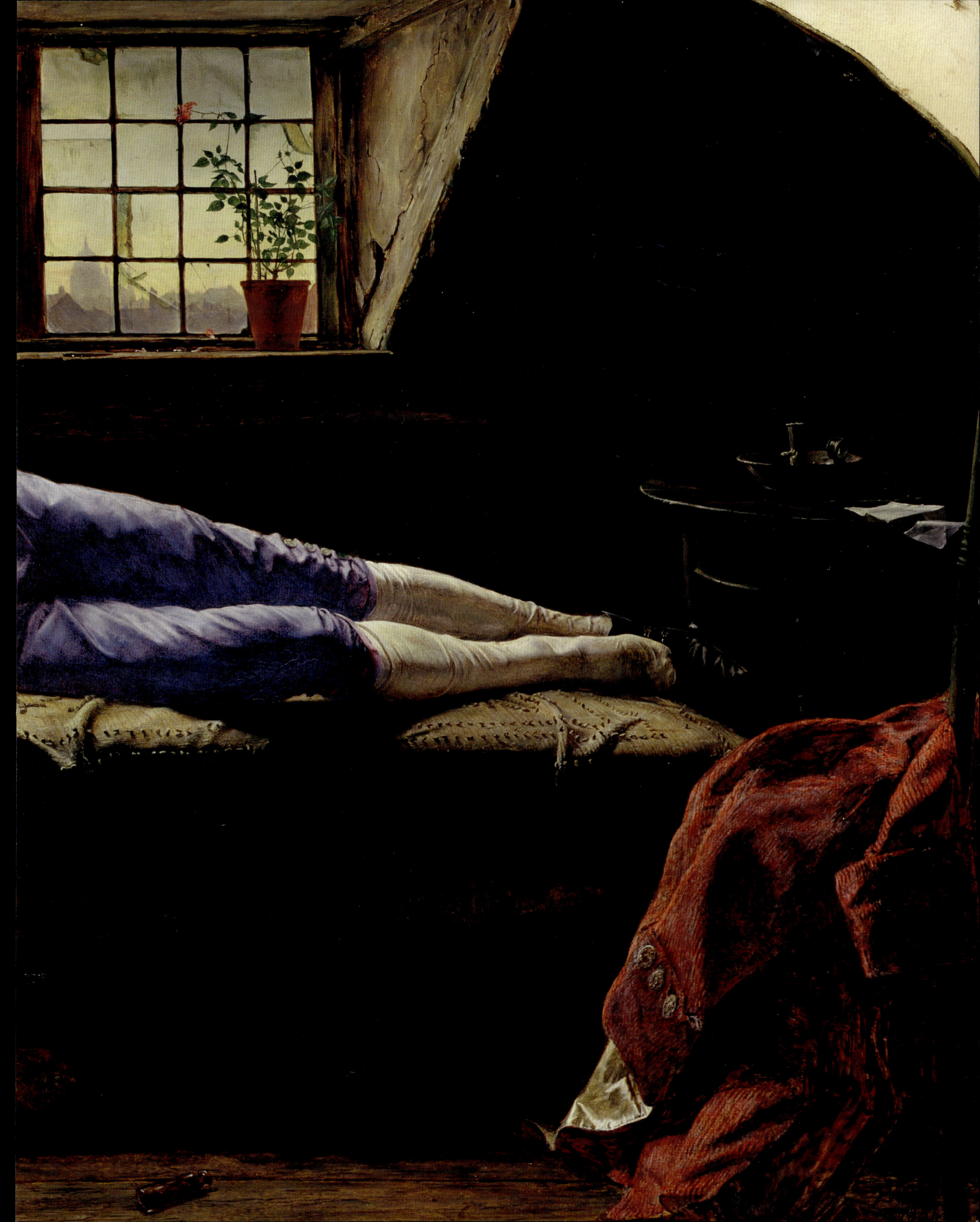

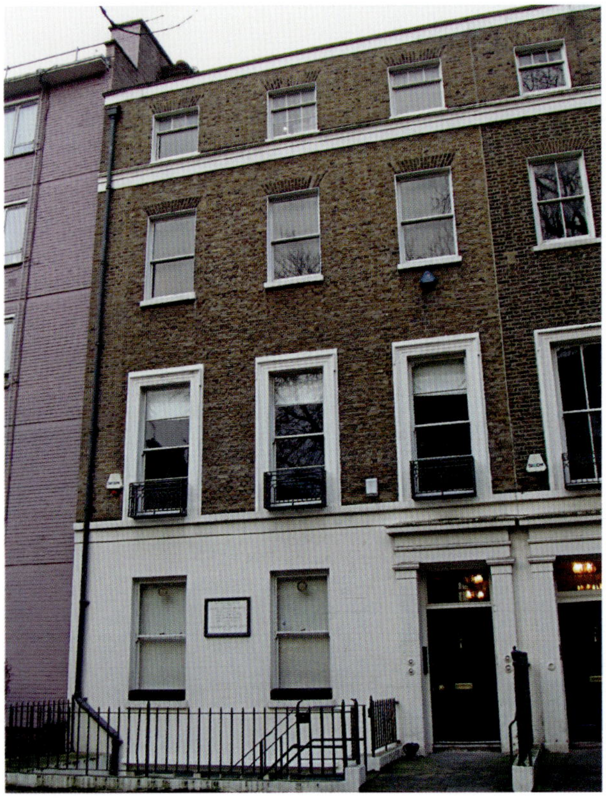

No. 17, Red Lion Square. Rossetti, Burne-Jones and Morris lived here during the 1850s. In 1873, Wallis lived at no. 9, a house similar to this one, but that has since been demolished.
PHOTOGRAPH BY RONALD LESSENS

while Wallis, who had started his affair with Mary Ellen Meredith, spent the winter with her at Capri. It is likely that they were in touch less after this time, although they did remain friends during the following decades.

The month before his death on 22 December 1915, Hughes asked Wallis for financial help.[4]

To Wallis, 4 November 1915:

"My dear Wallis. I am laid up on my last illness and so despairing at leaving my dear people, in dire want and trouble (all from my want of care and dutifulness) that I try to think that among the old pictures I have, there might be one that you remember with favour, such as Botticelli "Calumny" old copy – or the St Jerome I lent the Burlington Club – reproduced in Burlington Magazine. Do you think at a modest price you could add such to your collection? Affectionately yours."[5]

Wallis was a wealthy man and always helped a friend when he could. He did not fail to do so on this occasion, as we learn from Hughes's next letters, written on 8 and 9 November:

"My dear Wallis. Alas – Yes it was this Hughes who wrote the dismal letter. How to thank you, I hardly know, for the kind thought. I am awfully sorrowful. And I am very sorrowful too by the evidently diminished sight as shown by your writing, but you have done supreme work with those eyes – and I hope there are loving other eyes to read to you about you at hand. This is only to thank and acknowledge this mornings letter. Affectionately yours."[6]
"My dear Wallis. Thanks many for your letter by this mornings post – about pricing the two pictures. I have been offered some time ago £80 for Botticelli Calumny and St Jerome has been valued in several hundreds. But in these times I wonder if I may ask you

	£
Calumny	*50*
St Jerome	*150*

I am very truly o(b)liged to you for this last letter. Ever sincerely yours."[7]

Though there is no further correspondence as evidence, it seems highly likely that Wallis bought the paintings as he always liked to help his friends. Hughes died on December 22, 1915 and was buried at Richmond cemetery. Whether Wallis was present at the funeral is unknown, though it is unlikely as he was in poor health himself at the time.

Introduction to the PRB

Wallis was closest to the Pre-Raphaelites and their extended circle during the 1850s and 1860s. In the spring of 1851, the sculptor Alexander Munro had introduced Hughes to Dante Rossetti and Ford Madox Brown[8] and it is likely that Hughes would have introduced Wallis to his Pre-Raphaelite friends. Wallis's name appears only occasionally in the diaries and in the correspondence of the Pre-Raphaelites, but he seems to have been liked by them. He is mentioned for the first time in George Price Boyce's diary with an entry on 8 February 1854: "Wallis said he liked my drawings and asked the price of the Westminster Abbey – 15 gns."[9] Wallis is mentioned again in a letter dated 14 May 1854, from Dante Gabriel Rossetti to the collector Francis MacCracken:[10] "I have once seen a small picture by the H. Wallis you ask about, and should venture to say that any work of his must have some degree of value if not a *very* high one, at any rate something preferable to any "Mill" by any "Brandard", to any "vacant" thing whatever by "John Bridges" or even to anything I could suppose likely to fall under Redgrave"s notice while "returning from Church". … Hughes could tell you more than I could about Wallis and his works, as he knows him well I believe. I see by notices of the R.A. that he has a picture there from the life of Dr. Johnson, which seems to attract some attention."[11]

This letter shows that by early 1854 Wallis was not yet acquainted with D.G. Rossetti. Wallis must have stayed in Paris at least until the end of 1852, and possibly even into 1853. We do know that he had returned to London at least by early February 1854, as he exhibited four paintings at

Previous spread:
The Death of Chatterton
[Cat. 22]
1855-56; oil on canvas
62.2 x 93.3 cm. (24½ x 36 in.)
IMAGE BY PERMISSION OF TATE BRITAIN, LONDON

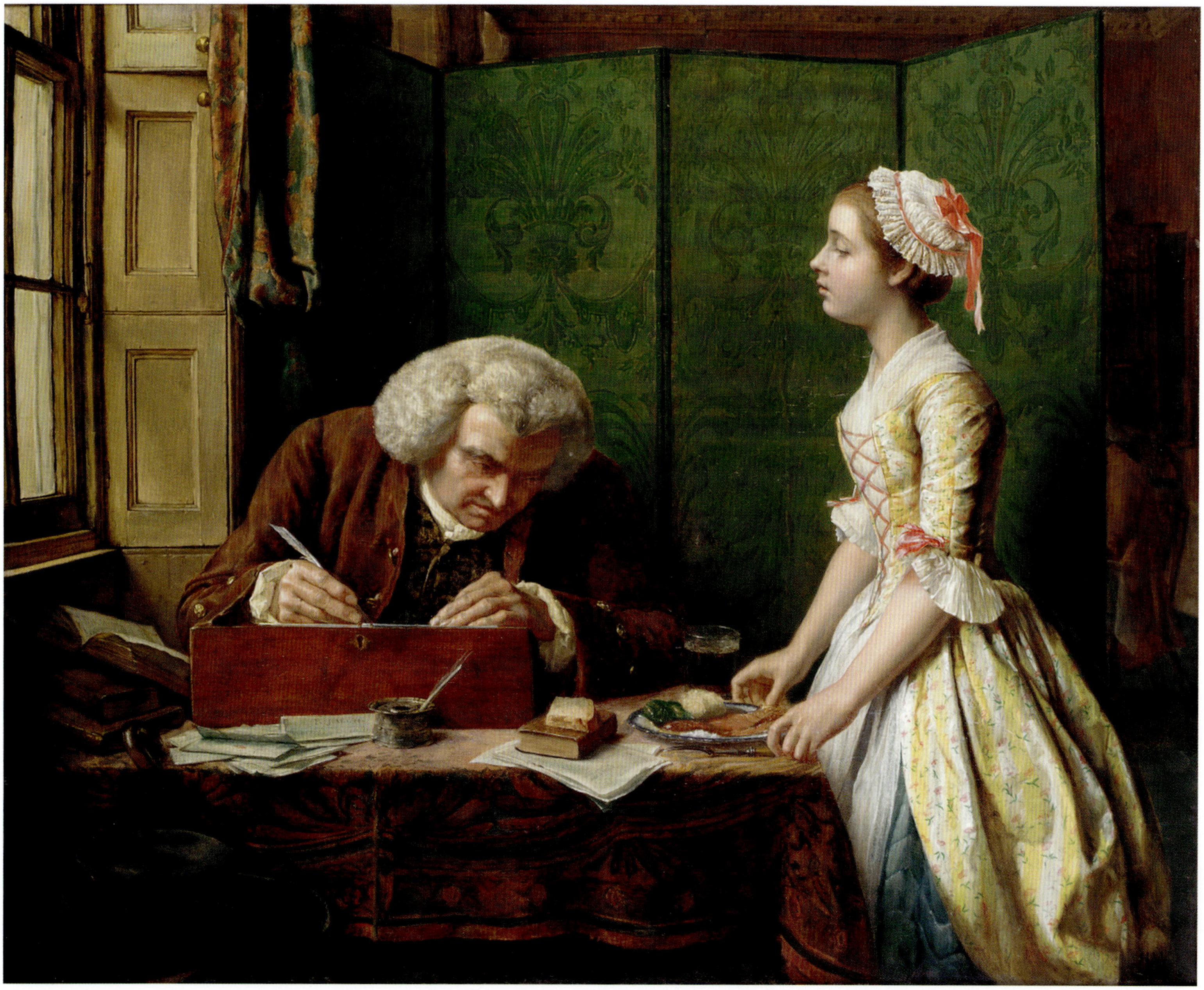

the annual Royal Academy summer exhibition that year. It is likely that Wallis was introduced to the Pre-Raphaelite circle then.

The Pre-Raphaelites extolled the virtues of the artists who had been active before the period of the High Renaissance, hence their name. Ruskin's *Modern Painters* had also deeply influenced them, particularly his suggestion that artists should go "to nature in all singleness of heart… rejecting nothing, selecting nothing, and scorning nothing…rejoicing always in the truth."[12] This return to authenticity resulted in studies in which human emotions played a more central part, and historical figures were represented as if closer to daily life, rather than idealised. In his *Christ in the House of His Parents*, Millais had dared transform the Virgin Mary, Joseph and Jesus into a proletarian family. This realistic perception caused outrage and was firmly condemned by conservative critics, even by writers such as Charles Dickens. Then, as now, artists who wanted to take a novel approach were often criticised. The advocates of good taste might allow their feelings to be challenged, but not profoundly upset!

Opposition to the Pre-Raphaelites came more from the art critics, rather than from the Royal Academy itself. It would be a mistake to think that this venerable institution deliberately crushed these young artists at the beginning of their careers. The Academician George Dunlop Leslie has explained "…there is a prevalent idea that the Pre-Raphaelite Brotherhood movement was treated by the Academy with hostility, but this is entirely erroneous. Millais's and Holman Hunt's early works were invariably well hung – at a time, too, when they were being condemned with the utmost virulence by the generality of the critics in the press, and even before the powerful voice of Ruskin had been heard in their favour."[13]

Quite remarkably, the Liverpool Academy actively supported the Pre-Raphaelites and systematically awarded non-member prizes to

Henry Wallis, *Dr Johnson at Cave's, the Publisher* [Cat. 10], 1854
PRIVATE COLLECTION. IMAGE COURTESY OF SOTHEBY'S, LONDON

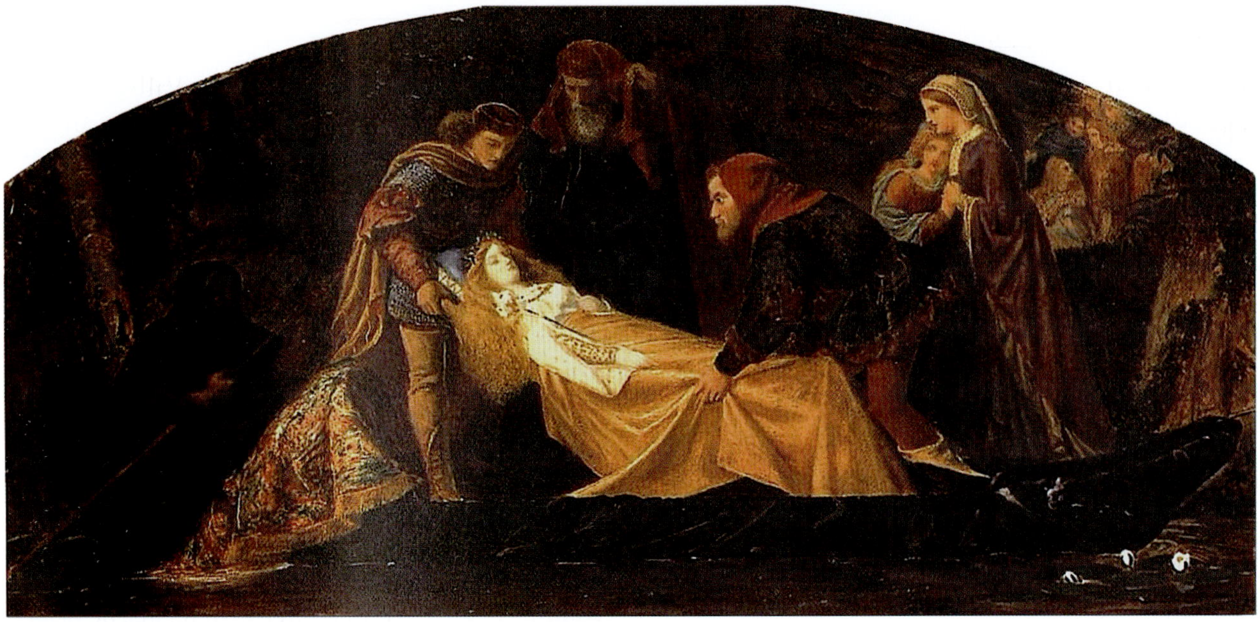

Hunt, Millais and Madox Brown between the years 1851 and 1856.[14] Pre-Raphaelite art also attracted the attention of Liverpool collectors such as John Miller (1796-1876), a tobacco merchant and ship owner.[15] This favouritism generated an opposition within certain members of the Liverpool Academy itself, which the *Art Journal* quickly relayed to its readers: "The Academy has procured itself somewhat unenviable notoriety…this act of the Academy has already thrown dissension among its members…there cannot be a doubt that many of its friends will be alienated from the institution by the perpetration of such folly on the part of a few only of the Liverpool academicians."[16]

Indeed, in 1857, some members of the Academy founded a rival Society of Arts. The threat prompted the Pre-Raphaelite artists to lend assistance to the Liverpool Academy. Although Wallis numbered among them, he does not seem to have been overly enthusiastic in his support. In his diary entry for 10 June 1858, George Price Boyce writes: "To Hunt's. At 7.30 we came to dinner and found in the room Wallis, Halliday, Martineau, Barwell, and Miss Hunt.... After dinner came Prinsep, Jones, Brett, Egg, F.G. Stephens and Stanhope... After some time, Hunt mooted the subject that was the cause of the gathering, viz. the importance of supporting the old Liverpool Academy. All adhered, Wallis alone rather throwing cold water on the project."[17]

While serious recognition of the PRB had come initially only after Ruskin's intervention, opposition in London was still a fact. Aristocrats had ceased to be the sole patrons of the arts. After Waterloo and with the economic boom, a new middle-class had arisen, which had understood that collecting works of art was a way of achieving respectability, though some patrons like Frederick Leyland, William Graham and George Rae also happened to be men of taste and true art lovers.[18]

Art collectors from the industrial Midlands and North were amongst the first to acquire Pre-Raphaelite paintings, which explains why Pre-Raphaelite works are so well represented in the public collections of these regions to this day. The main collectors included Thomas Plint and John Sheepshanks (Leeds), John Miller and Frederick Leyland (Liverpool), Thomas Fairbairn, Samuel Mendel and Joseph Arden (Manchester), Thomas Miller (Preston), Francis MacCracken (Belfast), James Leatheart (Newcastle), John Gibbons (Birmingham) and George Rae (Birkenhead). Thomas Plint, who made a great deal of money on the stock market, seems to have been Wallis's chief initial patron. According to William Michael Rossetti, Plint started collecting in 1856,[19] not only works by the founders of the PRB, but also young and unknown disciples, such as Wallis, Hughes and Burne-Jones. Plint died in 1861, aged only 38; his collection, which had cost him around £25,000, was sold at Christie's on 7 and 8 March 1862. Four of Wallis's works appear in the catalogue: *Elaine* (which sold for 475 guineas), *Return from Marston Moor* (135 guineas), *Marten in Chepstow Castle* (221 guineas), and *Gondomar watching Raleigh's Execution* (190 guineas), as well as the sketch of *Elaine*, which sold for 110 guineas.[20]

Wallis, like many of his Pre-Raphaelite friends, was enthusiastic about music. G.P. Boyce testified in his diary: "1870. November 14. Wallis dined with me here, and we went to St. James's Hall for Beethoven Concert. Glorious music."[21] Wallis was a frequent guest at Arthur Lewis's famous musical entertainments, first in Jermyn Street and later at Moray Lodge after Lewis's marriage to Kate Terry in 1867. Other constant guests at these gatherings were G.P. Boyce, P.H. Calderon, G.A. Storey, G. du Maurier, Stacey Marks and Fred Walker.[22] Thomas Armstrong has described these parties: "After Mr. Lewis removed from his rooms in

Henry Wallis, *Elaine* [Cat 44a], *c.*1861
Both the painting and this preliminary sketch were in the Plint collection
Image courtesy of Sotheby's

Jermyn Street to the more spacious and sumptuous quarters at Moray Lodge these gatherings became less frequent, taking place only four times a year, but with a very numerous attendance. They had a great vogue, and people of all ranks sought for invitations, and no wonder, for the entertainment was of the most agreeable kind. Fred Walker designed the cards of invitation.[23] First came a set programme of glees and part-songs performed by the Moray Minstrels, and when that was over a good supper was served, in which oysters were an important feature. After supper volunteers were invited to amuse the company. Marks used to sing his comic songs and preach his American sermon, while du Maurier was always called on for some of his songs, by that time well known."[24]

There was obviously a large circle of artists who knew each other very well and often gathered, as can be deduced from their diaries and correspondence. From Boyce's diary, 10 February 1865: "Dined at Arts Club. Full table. Had a lot of friends to tea (afterwards) at my studio (Chatham Place). The two Rossettis, Clayton, Wells, Walter Field, F. Burton, Henry Wallis and Val Prinsep."[25]

Holman Hunt

Since the 1850s, Wallis had been very close to Holman Hunt. He shared Hunt's concerns about the Royal Academy hanging policy and about the lack of copyright law that would protect artists. As George Price Boyce's diary and Dante Rossetti's letters show, Hunt and Wallis met frequently. They shared a passion for pottery of all kinds.[26] Their surviving correspondence, however, mainly dates from the mid-1880s, when Wallis explored Egypt. While Hunt was a welcome guest in Pre-Raphaelite circles, and was appreciated for his energy, for his wit, and for his knowledge, some found him difficult as a person and not everyone considered him a likeable man. Besides their mutual concern about Royal Academy reform, the correspondence between Hunt and Wallis sometimes dealt with Hunt's faith and Wallis's alleged atheism. Hunt was a Christian, but as Nicholas Tromans has pointed out: "He regarded all organized religion with suspicion. He was baptized into the established Anglican Church, and later stated that the Church of England was his chosen denomination. But this was a relationship conducted entirely on Hunt's own terms: he prided himself on retaining his independence of thought and never saw a necessity to conform to the details of the Church's teachings."[27]

In a long letter that he wrote to Wallis from Jerusalem on 9 March 1892, Hunt stated that: "One difference between you and me is, I still think, that you don't believe in an overruling Providence, while I do. It may be very foolish, but I have really taken a good deal of pains to cure myself. I have read Voltaire, Volney, Gibbon, Bolingbroke, Hume, Payne, and a man you once recommended strongly to me as good medicine for the malady. I mean Renan.[28] ... And so I still believe that in some mysterious manner the ruler of the world has dimly

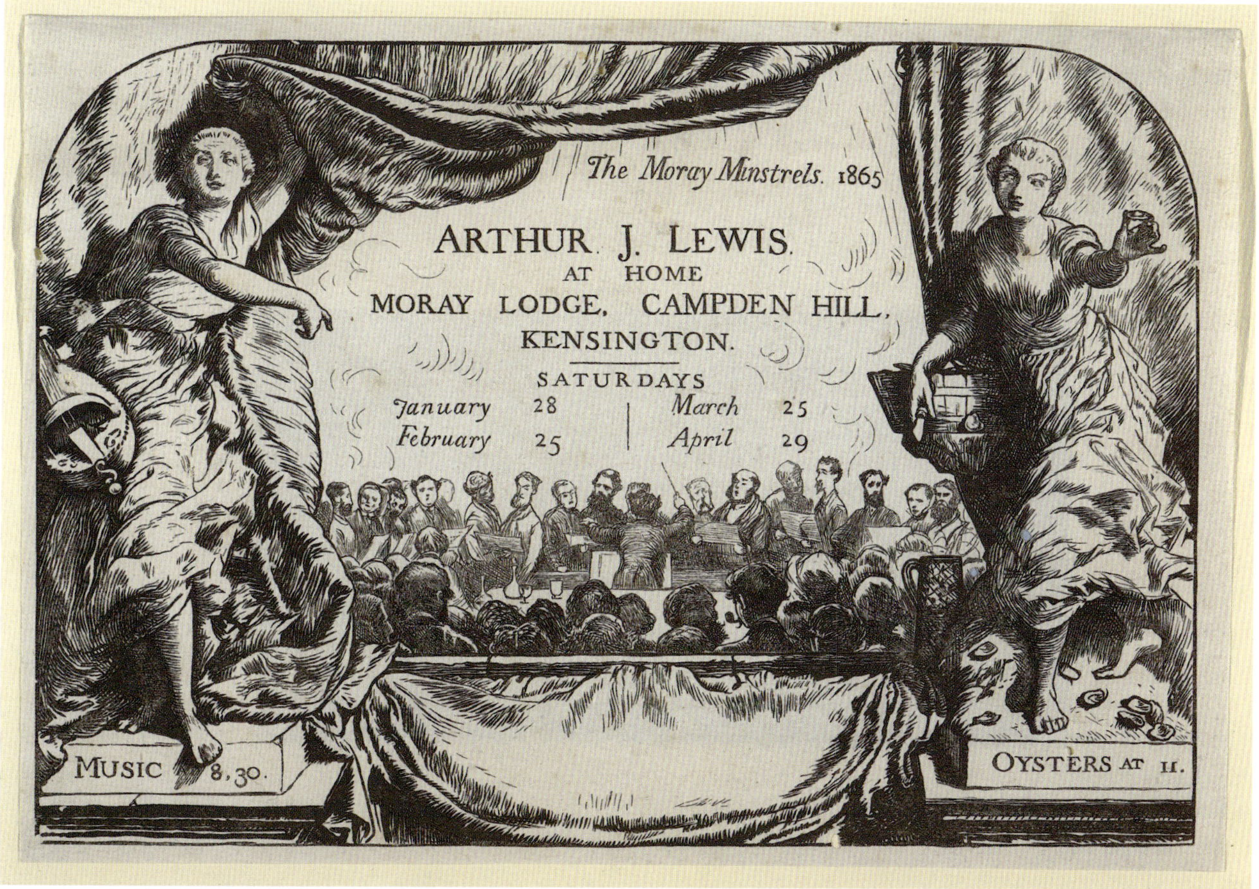

W.H. Hooper after Fred Walker, *Moray Minstrels' Invitation Card*, 1865
It is uncertain whether Wallis is illustrated here, but it is possible to pick out certain artists such as Charles Keene, for example, who can be seen in the back row, mid-right of centre.
Image courtesy of the Metropolitan Museum of Art, New York

made known his programme of events by the pens of men of old belonging to the Jewish race. And it can be doubted that the idea they expressed was that in the far future war should cease. All the people now working to encourage this idea are not believers in revelation. I know of some who would call themselves atheists, and many more who are professed agnostics. Their idea of the superiority of insight of these predecessors of theirs of three thousand years back is, and could not but be, extraordinary. They don't now act with any thought of fulfilling prophecy. They judge of the value of the proposal without allowing prejudice to turn them from the work of hastening its accomplishment. I believe my dear fellow that you too on further thought will agree that they are right."[29]

Another influence of Hunt on Wallis may have been to encourage him to make his numerous journeys abroad to Europe and the Middle East. The effect of these travels on Wallis's art was primarily to change him from working in oils to watercolours, which would have been far more convenient. The fact that Wallis was a wealthy man after the death of his stepfather may also have influenced his desire to travel and the shift from oils to watercolours, because now Wallis did not really need to earn a livelihood from his painting. This change to painting in watercolour may obviously have influenced Wallis's decision to stop exhibiting at the Royal Academy as well.

In his *Reminiscences*, William Michael Rossetti, the historian of the Pre-Raphaelite movement, recalls Wallis briefly: "With Henry Wallis, the painter of the very admirable picture of the *Death of Chatterton* (now likewise in the National British Gallery and clearly one of the best products of the Præraphaelite movement), I was acquainted somewhat later than with most of the preceding. I say the less of him, in that he is still alive.[30] I have found him a very agreeable companion, of solid character and open mind. He was also of some special interest to me as having known Thomas Love Peacock, the friend of Shelley; he once gave me two hairs from Shelley's head, which, to my shame, seem to have disappeared. On one occasion I sat to him for a head in one of his pictures – I forget which. Needless to say that Mr. Wallis has for many years past been a leading authority on oriental and other ceramics."[31]

William Bell Scott

Another good friend was the painter and poet William Bell Scott (1811-1890), who was associated with the Pre-Raphaelite movement through his friendship with the Rossetti brothers. He produced oils and watercolours of Biblical and historical scenes and also landscape paintings in the Pre-Raphaelite style.[32] Being constantly in touch with the Pre-Raphaelite circle, Wallis must have seen Scott regularly. A drawing has recently resurfaced at auction showing that their close friendship dated back to at least 1862. The drawing, entitled *Shadows on the Wall*, and executed on 20 December 1862 at Ellison Place, Newcastle shows the profiles of William Bell Scott, Alice Boyd, Dante Gabriel Rossetti, Algernon Swinburne and Henry Wallis.[33] We know that in September 1873 he spent several weeks at Penkill Castle, where Scott lived with his mistress Alice Boyd and where Scott made Wallis's portrait.[34] The few letters between them that remain all date from 1885-6, at a time when Scott had developed a serious heart condition and after Wallis had enquired after his health.[35]

The correspondence starts on 20 June 1885, with Scott giving some details about his disease: "I found your card left yesterday with peculiar gratification, in returning from our drive. This illness I have undergone has been the most serious I have ever had,[36] and lying so long in bed from week to week I have had time to think of every thing and had determined to write to you, inviting you to call. Feebleness and the disposition to do nothing not even write a note have prevented me doing so till now, when we are about to leave for Penkill.[37] For some time we have taken a daily drive but still I am weak as water, and the doctors won't let me mount a stair or do any action needing the slightest gestion, and tell me I should be off for change of air. However I am getting on by slow degrees and when I get back to town again at the end of autumn I shall hope to see you."[38]

On 17 August of the same year, besides other details about his disease, he enquires about Wallis's forthcoming journey to Egypt: "... I hope you will go to Egypt as you speak of [39] and bring home some material for new works. There must be plenty surely between the most ancient and the most modern oriental life. I shall be vegetating here long time. If you do go let me hear from you on your return. Miss Boyd, my best of friends

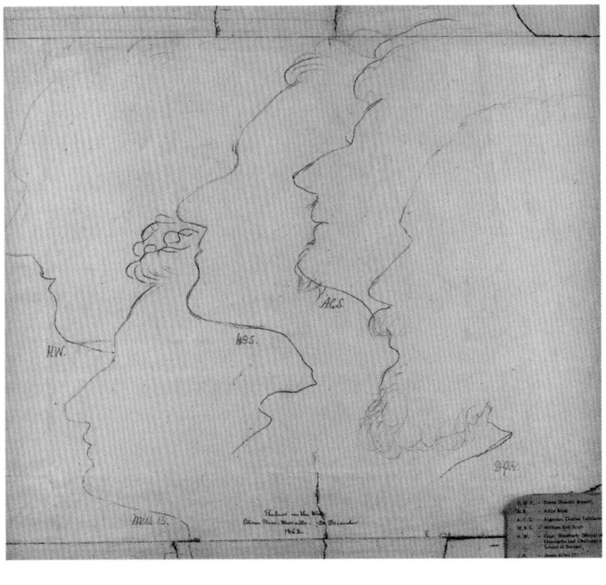

Circle of William Bell Scott, *Shadows on the Wall.*
Pencil silhouettes of "H.W." (Henry Wallis), "Miss B" (Alice Boyd), "W.B.S." (William Bell Scott), "A.C.S." (Algernon Charles Swinburne) and "D.G.R." (Dante Gabriel Rossetti). This drawing was made on 20 December 1862 at Scott's residence Ellison Place in Newcastle upon Tyne.
Image courtesy of Abbott and Holder, London.

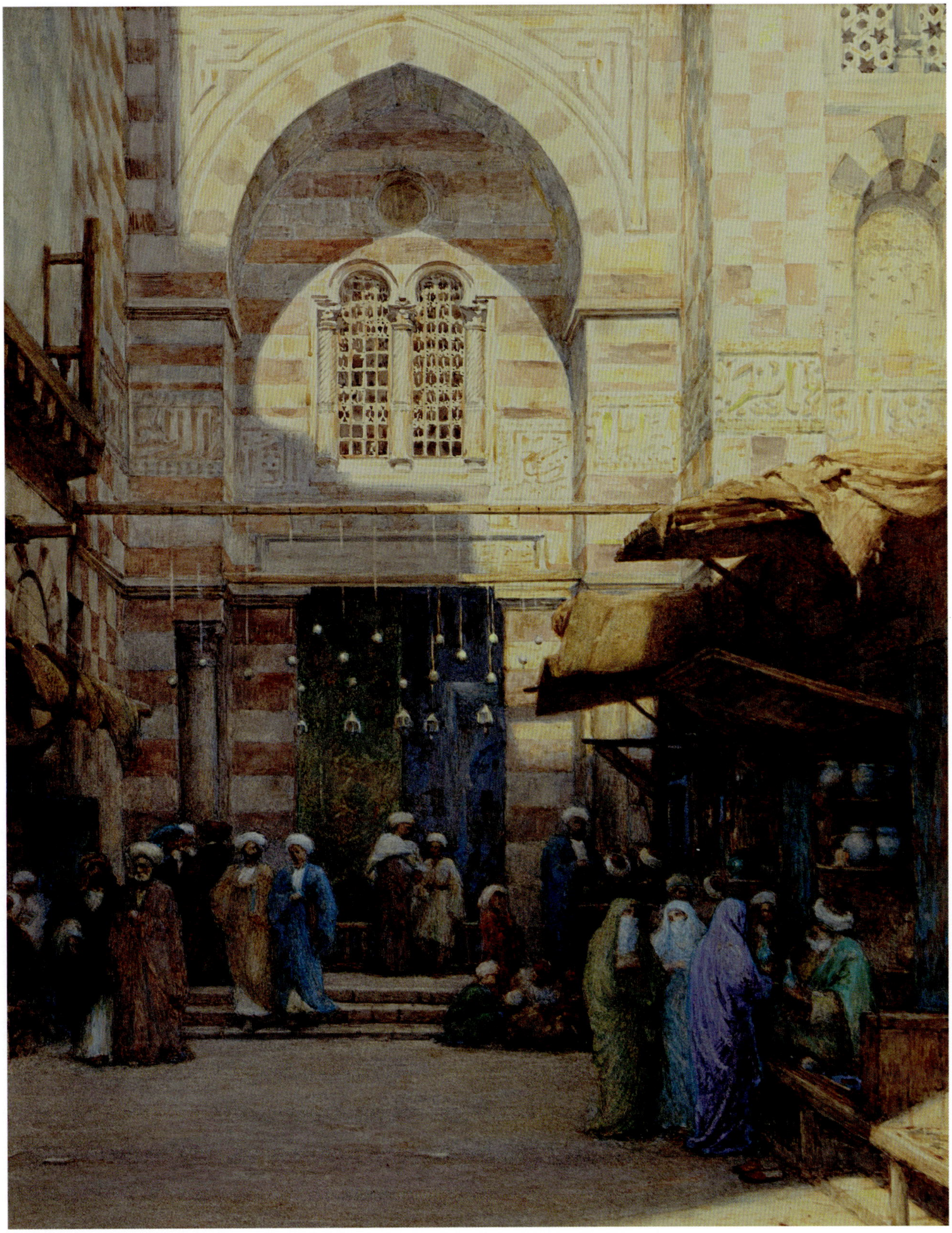

Henry Wallis, *The Principal Entrance to the Mosque of Sultan Kalaun* [Cat. 223], 1895
DIANE JOHNSON COLLECTION, SAN FRANCISCO, CALIFORNIA

and nurses, who has preserved my life certainly, send[s] you kindest remembrances. She is disappointed you do not mention Felix.[40] We hope he is all right."[41]

In his next letter, dated 18 February 1886, he gave Wallis advice about keeping a sketchbook: "I hope you are keeping a sketchbook and using it daily. My experience of artistic life is entirely in favor [*sic*] of so doing. The slightest scribble when named and dated becomes invaluable in two ways: firstly it recalls the whole scene in wch you make it, and the period when it was done, and secondly it entails a habit of rapid exactitude in designing and a truthfulness of expressing nature even when we have it not before us. Our friend D.G.R[ossetti]. never had a sketchbook in his hand, and up to the end of his life, made the wall of a house about the thickness of cardboard, and drew a human arm in this way [sketch of an arm]."[42] Wallis must either have already been in the habit of keeping a sketchbook, or he took Scott's words to heart. To date, 31 sketchbooks are still known to exist.[43]

Chapter Five
THE MEREDITH AFFAIR

Until recently a whole episode of Wallis's life remained largely unexplored: his relationship with Mary Ellen Peacock, George Meredith's first wife. Biographers have shown curiosity, but Mary Ellen's family appear to have destroyed nearly every document that could have shed some light on it. Her father Thomas Love Peacock, her daughter Edith, and her husband George Meredith attempted to leave no trace of what was indeed a notorious scandal in those days.

Lionel Stevenson, Meredith's biographer, seems to have had access to documents shedding full light on Mary Ellen's liaison with Henry Wallis. These documents were gathered by Sir Walter Peacock[1] and communicated to his cousin H.E. Wallis. Neither this cousin, nor Stevenson, were allowed to reveal details, as the latter explained to Diane Johnson: "When I was working on the Meredith book in England I was put in touch with a person who had inherited from a cousin a mass of notes on the Meredith marriage. The notes had been compiled by a retired solicitor [Sir Walter Peacock], who was planning a history of the Peacock family, and he had spent much time in consulting records, only to become so distressed by the evidence of Mrs. Meredith's misconduct that he abandoned the project. He placed his cousin [H.E. Wallis] on oath not to reveal details that might be embarrassing or painful to the surviving descendants of the Wallis liaison, and the cousin in turn required me to take a similar vow before I was allowed to see the material. It was fully documented, and confirmed hints that I had picked up."[2] Unfortunately, Stevenson gave no more details and Diane Johnson, when writing her biography of Mary Ellen, was denied access as well. She was, however, the first to spotlight this remarkable lady. Thanks to Nicholas Joukovsky's efforts, some of her letters, as well as those of her circle, have been found and subsequently published. This allows us a more objective and calmer look at the events that transpired.

Born in July 1821,[3] Mary Ellen was the daughter of Thomas Love Peacock, the poet and novelist, popular in his time, who was the executor of Shelley's will after the poet died in 1822. She seems to have spent a happy youth with a father who did not share common Victorian prejudices. Diane Johnson explains as follows: "As the Chinese bound the feet of their women, Englishmen bound their minds."[4] Peacock had decided that Mary Ellen would be educated, liberating her from the restrictions typically imposed on Victorian women.

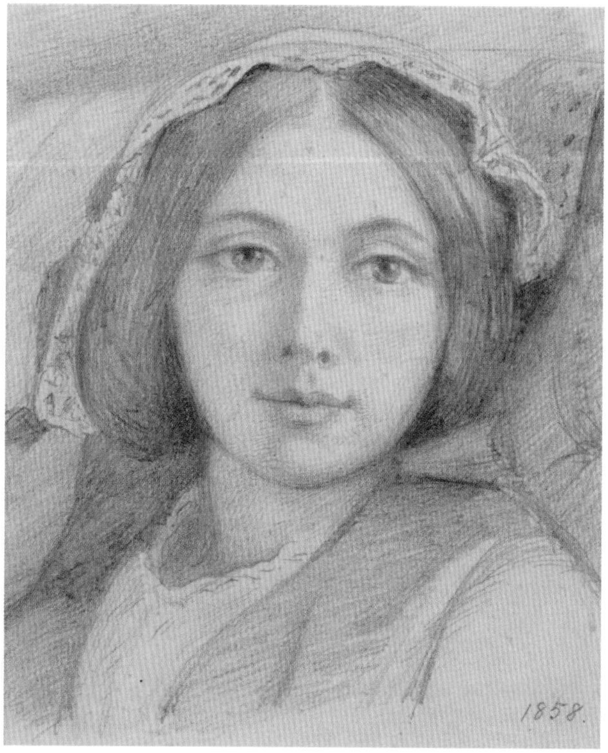

Henry Wallis, *Portrait of Mary Ellen Meredith* [Cat. 32], 1858 Oxford, Ashmolean Museum
IMAGE COURTESY OF BONHAMS, LONDON

In 1843, aged 21, she met Edward Nicolls, the first love of her life. Their marriage was celebrated in January the following year. On 11 March 1844, Edward, a naval officer in command of the HMS *Dwarf*, drowned in the Shannon estuary while rescuing people in distress. Joukovsky points out that it seems "clear not only that Mary Ellen was with Edward aboard the *Dwarf*, as has long been known, but that she actually encouraged him to undertake the rescue attempt in which he lost his life – a circumstance that suggests her grief may have been compounded by a sense that she herself had been at least partly responsible for the tragedy."[5] According to her friend Mrs. Bennett, Mary Ellen never really got over this tragedy. She had been pregnant at the time of her husband's death and moved back to her father's house with her baby daughter, Edith.

In 1846, George Meredith had started to work as a clerk with Richard Charnock, a solicitor and Fellow of the Society of Antiquaries. Charnock

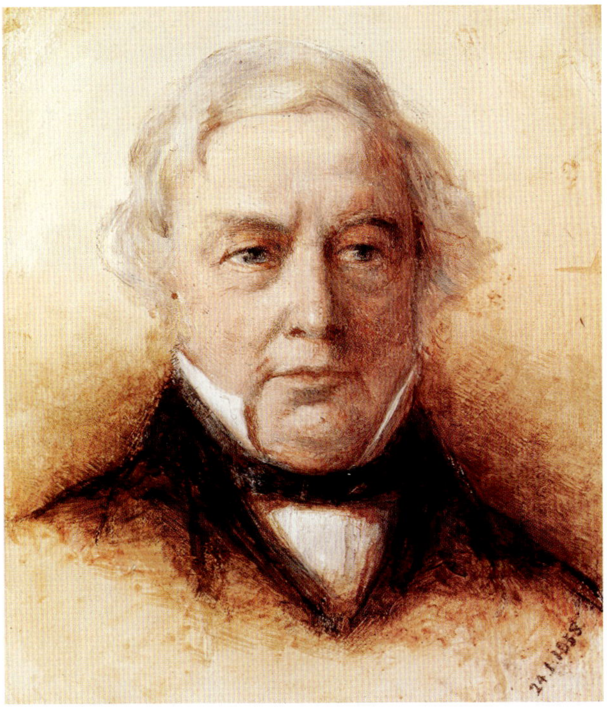

introduced Meredith to his set of intimates, mainly writers and artists, including Mary Ellen and her brother Edward, as well as Wallis's fellow student at the Royal Academy schools, Peter Austin Daniel.[6] The literary achievements of this group were published in *The Monthly Observer*. Mary Ellen was too young to retreat into a widow's loneliness, and being a sensual young woman, who enjoyed the company of the witty young men in her literary circle, she captured the heart of the aspirant novelist George Meredith. This does not mean that she immediately accepted a shared life with him because she had come to enjoy the freedom that widowhood allowed her. In fact, she rejected his proposals six times before agreeing to marry him.[7]

In addition, in 1848 Meredith was only aged twenty while she was twenty-seven. She had already tried her hand at poetry and was a good cook, being convinced that "the stomach, not the heart, as poets write, is the great centre of existence and feeling."[8]

When it comes to describe their natures and their relationship, there are two schools of thought: the feminist – D. Johnson – and the masculinist – R. Sencourt.[9] Johnson claims that Peacock did not like Meredith and, in fact, none of those gentlemen who took his daughters away. On the contrary, Sencourt says that Meredith was accepted at once by Peacock and that he was fond of Edith, Mary Ellen's daughter by her first husband. Her marriage to Meredith eventually took place on 9 August 1849 at St. George's, Hanover Square, in the presence of the bride's father. Their honeymoon was to the Rhine Valley where George had been to school. Meredith's youth had not been a happy one, as he recognised himself: "When I was young, had there been given me a little sunshine of encouragement what an impetus to better work would have been mine."[10] When he was thirteen, his widowed father married his housekeeper and George was sent to a boarding school at Neuwied, a small town on the Rhine.

Mary Ellen suffered several miscarriages before she gave birth to a son, Arthur, in 1853. However, it appears that the Merediths had already been quarrelling since 1850 and by that date were already no longer close.[11] In fact, according to Banerjee, theirs was "a marriage that was in trouble almost from the start."[12] It is sad to read in Mary Ellen's *Commonplace book of extracts*: "Terrible moment when we first dare to view with feelings of repugnance the being that our soul has long idolized."[13] This single statement sheds a great deal of light about her dissatisfaction with the marriage.

Joukovsky has discovered and published notes based on writings by Anne Ramsden Bennett, who had known Mary Ellen well and was devoted to her.[14] Mrs. Bennett seems to have met Mary Ellen in June or July 1860, when the latter was living at Weybridge, and sympathy quickly turned into friendship. Mrs. Bennett emphasizes Mary Ellen's striking physical appearance as well as her impressive intellectual qualities, and also that "as long as she was silent her face wore a very serious almost stern expression but the moment she smiled she seemed almost transfigured into an ideal of gaiety & sociality. Her conversation was charming, full of original ideas and brimming over with wit – everything indeed which might

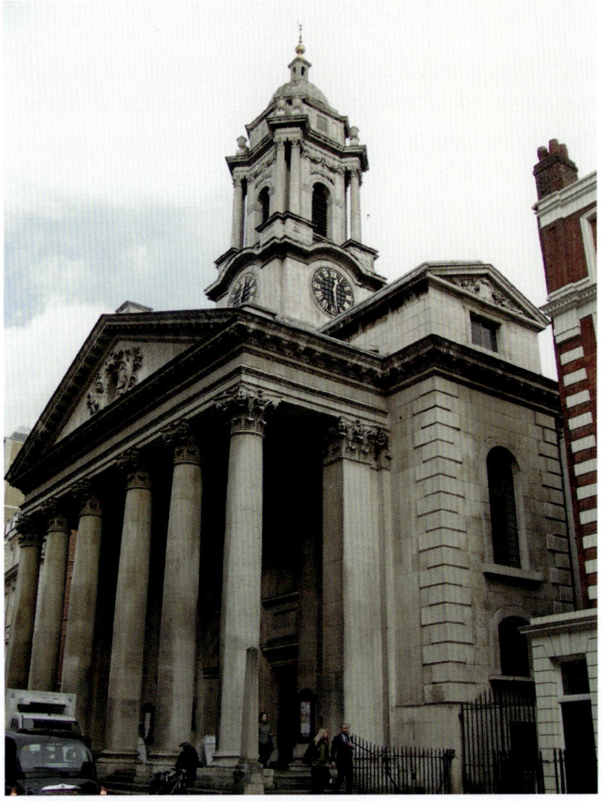

Above:
Henry Wallis, *Thomas Love Peacock* [Cat. 34], 1858
London, National Portrait Gallery
Image courtesy of De Agostini Picture Library/Bridgeman Images

Right:
St. George's, Hanover Square, where the Meredith marriage took place
Photograph by Ronald Lessens

be looked for from Mr. Thos Love Peacock's daughter."[15] She assisted Mary Ellen until the end of her life and, seeing that Mary Ellen was thrown into panic at the idea of her children's future, Mrs. Bennett promised to look after Harold, her son by Wallis.

Mrs. Bennett does not mention any kind of mental instability, the reason that George Meredith would later give to explain their separation.[16] On the contrary, Bennett found her "wonderfully pleasant and reviving."[17] On the other hand, Bennett's notes are interesting, because she is the only one to give a plausible motive for the couple's dissension. Before their marriage, George seems to have told his wife that he originated from an ancient Welsh family, among whom even princes could be traced. The truth was that his father, Augustus Meredith, was a tailor who had emigrated to South Africa in 1849. Having learned of the lie later, Mary Ellen was bitterly disappointed, and her love and esteem for her husband vanished.

Their long-lasting poverty may also help to explain their difficulties. The Merediths were in financial need, though this had nothing to do with George's refusal to accept a "down-to-earth" job, as it has sometimes been suggested. The Joukovsky documents prove that Peacock and the Merediths – especially Mary Ellen – did their utmost to procure George a decent position.[18] In a letter she wrote to Wallis before their affair started, Mary Ellen explained that "George did not obtain the place we were trying for & I am racking my brains to see what I can do. Whether all the intelligence I ever possessed is quite swallowed up by my long illness, or whether the attempt to begin work in this tremendous heat is the cause of failure I have not yet made up my mind, but I am much discouraged that it is ten days since I began to hunt for an idea & that I have not found one."[19] Peacock himself had been poor – had even been in debtor's prison for a short time[20] – before he had been appointed to the East India House, and now he tried to introduce his son-in-law to a position there as well. Such a job was not onerous and would not have prevented George from continuing his literary activities, for, as Peacock explained, a day at the India House took place as follows:

From ten to eleven, ate a breakfast for seven;
From eleven to noon, to begin 'twas too soon;
From twelve to one, asked, "What's to be done?"
From one to two, found nothing to do;
From two to three began to foresee
That from three to four would be a damned bore.[21]

However, Peacock did not manage to help George and retired during that period. The Merediths subsequently tried to secure a position for George as under-secretary to the Society of Arts, which was less lucrative than the other post, but at least could provide them with some security. Mary Ellen wrote in this regard to their friend Henry Cole, who would later run the South Kensington Museum; but this hope, too, vanished.

Whatever the reasons for the breakdown of their marriage, it seems obvious, according to Mrs. Bennett,[22] that George did not really love Mary Ellen for what she was – an independent and resolute woman, who had freed herself from the surrounding prejudices, even if she was a victim of them. His feelings for her may have been genuine, but, if so, he often had an unpleasant Victorian way of showing them. The Merediths quarrelled frequently during their marriage. Catherine Horne, in a letter dated 18 November 1852 to her husband Richard Hengist Horne, described one of the most violent of these quarrels. "I presently heard the two above disputing; and after about half an hour of this, one evidently accusing the other, there came a series of dreadful screams. I rushed upstairs and met Mr. M. at the door, very pale – he begged me to go in, and went down stairs. Mrs. M. was sitting in a chair, with her hair all down, crying and screaming and calling out 'Take him away, take him away!' As soon as he shut the door she rushed to it and bolted it and then ran to open the window, which you know is directly over the river. I never saw anyone in such a devilish passion before thought she was actually mad and wanted to throw herself in the river, so I prevented her opening it and made her sit down. Presently G. came up again and tried to speak to her and take her hand (fool) but she said 'no George, never again, you've gone too far this time, I'll never speak to you again.' I left the room rejoicing at the 'never again' and hoping she really meant it." Mrs. Horne, does not appear to have been the most impartial of witnesses and was heavily prejudiced in Meredith's favour; it is possible that she was in love with him herself.[23]

Marital dissatisfaction led Mary Ellen to having an affair with the chemist Charles Blachford Mansfield,[24] who died from burns after an accident in his laboratory. Although Meredith was probably aware of this affair, he continued to have a high opinion of Mansfield and was devastated by his death. In a letter of March 1855 to Mary Ellen's half-sister, Susan Mary Abbott, Meredith writes: "You have heard of our dear Charles Mansfield's death. That has given us a great shock. I say, you have heard, for I doubt not one of your correspondents has stated to you the sad accident which befell that noble fellow, one of the noblest & best of the men of this earth... But few will pass away regretted like Charles Mansfield."[25]

The Merediths subsequently met the painter

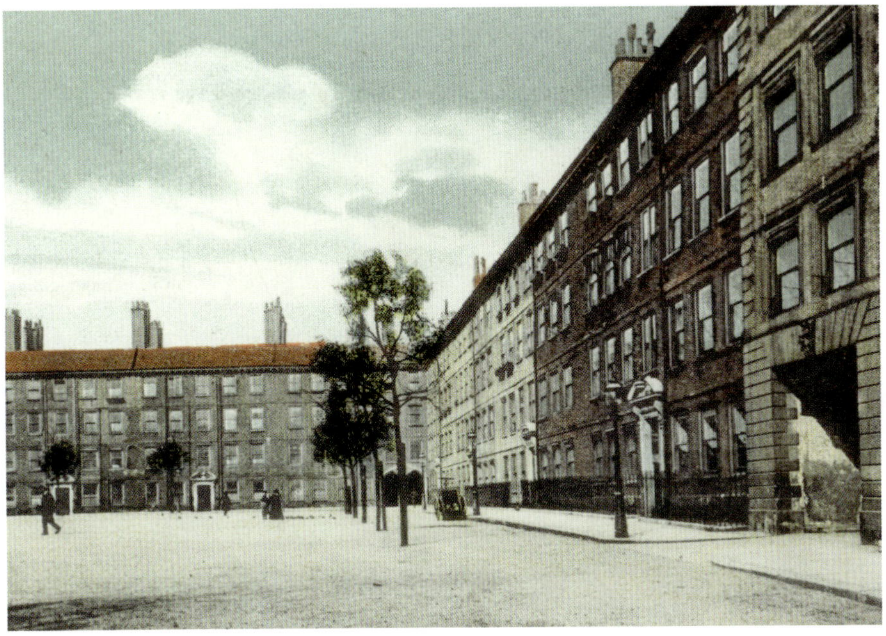

Gray's Inn Square, c.1910
© Chronicle/Alamy Stock Photo

Between 1855 and 1858, Wallis shared rooms with Peter Austin Daniel at no. 8. After having lived at no. 62 Great Russell Street, Wallis came back and rented an apartment at no. 6 from 1862 to 1865. His friend Daniel came over in 1864 and stayed at least until 1870.

Henry Wallis, probably through Peter Austin Daniel, although Mervyn Jones states that it was through Mary Ellen's brother Edward. Wallis used George as a model for his *Chatterton.* Joukovsky points out that the real Chatterton had been in a similar position to Meredith, as had Mary Ellen's father, Thomas Love Peacock; all had been poor and neglected poets. As well as using George as a model, Mary Ellen sat for his painting *Fireside Reverie* (now untraced). In the beginning, Mary Ellen was not especially attracted to him. During his trips to France and to Spain, however, he wrote to her and, slowly but surely, she became fond of him and invited him to meet her in her husband's absence.

Nothing was known about the period preceding August 1856, until a letter was discovered at the Bodleian Library to Wallis from his friend P.A. Daniel, dated 24 June 1856, that suggests that the affair was imminent.[26] "Meredith stayed with us till Friday afternoon when he and I went down to Seaford by the six o'clock train from London Bridge. And there I stayed till Monday morning the 23ᵈ June having passed a couple of days pleasantly enough considering the state of the weather... But talking of attractiveness what the deuce did you do to your grim old mug[27] to make all women at Seaford mad after you. There was Mʳˢ M. who talked about nothing but 'her Wallis' and even venerated me as having the supreme honor [*sic*] of his friendship. The pink, the pattern and perfection of men to whom in all seriousness she sends her 'love & duty'. Even Mʳˢ Ockenden talked of the 'poor dear man', for whom she had heated gruel and other slops potent against chilly humours of the nasal organs. On the whole a rabid Wallisomania gnawing at the heart of Seaford."

Their intimate relationship had not really started at this time, however, because in a letter dated 4 August 1856, she still addresses him as "Dear Mʳ Wallis", but one feels there was something more than sympathy, even if she only wanted to fill in the emotional gap that her unhappy marriage had created: "Your letter was a most agreeable surprise, I had hardly ventured to expect one during your travels: and though I am afraid you wrote under the impression that you ought to reply to me … I cannot help rejoicing to have it, a description written on the spot & impressions noted as they occur are so much more graphic than any after recollection of either can be. … If you come back by way of Dieppe of course we shall see you. And whether returning that way or not if you like to come & stay here on your return, I need not say how glad we shall be."[28]

Joukovsky speculates that their affair likely began in September or October 1856.[29] George Meredith's biographer S.M. Ellis states: "He [Wallis] found her alone at Seaford, in difficulties and debt and distress of heart. He helped her – and she yielded."[30] Certainly by 6 July 1857 the tone of her letter is more intimate and she begins the letter without a salutation, which was a conventional sign of intimacy between correspondents during the 19th century. Mary Ellen says she has kept some "tonic medicine" [wine] which she will be happy to share with him: "When are you coming? I have laid in *nine gallons* of *Tonic medicine* for you, but such is my good nature that I will help you through with it."[31]

Their love affair was by now quite obviously a fact. In the summer of 1857, Mary Ellen left the matrimonial home; a scandalous act in Victorian times. Despite what has frequently been claimed, she did not immediately elope with Wallis. She initially went to live in Seaford with her two children. Wallis subsequently asked her to accompany him through Wales and, as Mary Ellen knew very well that her marriage had disintegrated, she agreed. She left Arthur with Mrs. Chapman, the publisher's wife, but during her absence George Meredith came and reclaimed his son, as the law permitted him to do. In Wales, the lovers visited Maentwrog, Mary Ellen's birthplace, and the waterfalls at Cain, Mawddach and Dolymelynllyn.[32]

After she came back in September, now pregnant, she went to live at Home View House, Clevedon, a resort overlooking the Bristol Channel. From there, she wrote Henry a letter on 29 September 1857, which confirms that the Merediths were already separated and that Meredith had the intention of dealing with the domestic crisis legally, even though he never did so. Mary Ellen writes: "If we have to stay in England let us be at Clifton. I have no answer from George. I imagine he wants to see Darvall before writing. If he gives no reply in a week I shall take his silence for freedom and go abroad without another word, if you will like it, and where you will... I am always dreading to lose you because I feel I have no right to you, and I love you so really, so far beyond anything I have known of love, that there are ways in which I believe I could bear to lose you. God knows how hard it would be; but I believe I could bear it. Not by Death or weariness or anger. By Death I could not lose you

The love where Death has set his seal
Nor age can chill, nor rival steal
Nor falsehood disavow-,[33]

But I do not fear your Death, because I feel how much you owe to Life, how much Life has for you, and surely I shall in no shape lead you Delilah-like to Death, since it is my one aim to add to your strength, my one prayer 'God grant that I may do this man no harm'. And for weariness or anger, if we begin to thread either of those paths we will part before they possess us."[34]

On 5 October 1857, Wallis left Tintern, where he had been working on his painting *Henry Marten in Chepstow Tower*, and took the train to Clifton to be with Mary Ellen. Wallis appears to have divided his time between London and visiting Mary Ellen at Elm Cottage, Redland, near Clifton where she spent most of the last six months of her pregnancy.

Baby Harold, born on 18 April 1858, became known as 'Felix', meaning "son of their happiness."[35] On 4 May 1858, a few weeks after Harold's birth, she wrote to Henry: "I am not suffering from anything, & am getting on well but I am very weak, as I have never been before, dragging pains in my limbs, & swelled ankles, but I have no doubt caution & rest will remove these."[36]

In the autumn of that year, Henry took Mary Ellen to Capri, the climate of which was supposed to strengthen her. "It is not clear whether little Harold went with them, but probably he did."[37] Although biographers have repeatedly stated that the lovers went there in 1858, the validity of this assumption has to be questioned to some extent because there is no specific documentary evidence to prove it. Diane Johnson and others relied on what S.M. Ellis stated in his biography of Meredith, but Joukovsky in his articles has proven how unreliable Ellis was. If Wallis took Mary Ellen someplace to recuperate, it is likely he would have taken her some place warm and the area around Sorrento in Italy would have been a logical choice. Capri was definitely a favourite place for Wallis in the early 1860s because we know for certain that he spent several winters there with his son after Mary Ellen's death. Hickox points out that Capri might have been a logical place for the lovers to go because it seems to have been a place where no questions were asked with respect to relationships, which may explain why John Brett and his mistress Madame Loeser went there in 1865. Wallis was not the only English artist to favour Capri's favourable climate. His friend Frederic Leighton, for instance, spent five weeks on the island in the early summer of 1859.[38]

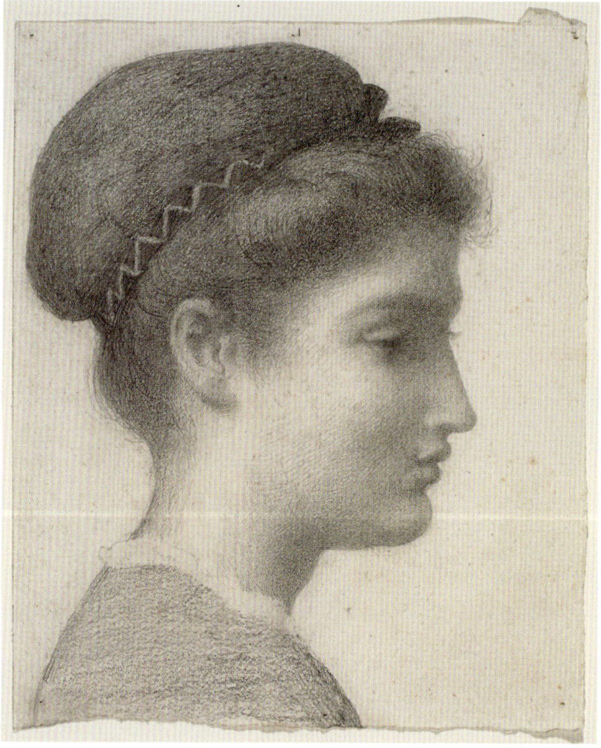

Henry Wallis, (Alleged) *Portrait of Mary Ellen Meredith* [Cat. 33], c.1857
Dr Dennis Lanigan, Saskatoon, Canada
IMAGE COURTESY OF THE NATIONAL GALLERY OF CANADA, OTTAWA.

Mary Ellen apparently returned from Capri on her own[39] by early February 1859 and some biographers claim that Wallis had deserted her.[40] However, Johnson thinks it more likely that "they went underground, to provide for an undisturbed and scandal-free future."[41] After Henry returned, it seems that they intended to live together; in the Wallis papers, Diane Johnson found answers to an advertisement Wallis placed in *The Times* in January 1859 looking for apartments for "a gentleman and a lady."[42] However, we do not know why this did not happen and, therefore, no firm conclusions can be reached. A recent biographer speculated that Wallis "may well have been the sort of man who preferred to live without a woman, a preference that in his time was not considered extraordinary."[43] It is also possible that Mary Ellen was unfaithful to Henry, or Henry to her, or that the two over time simply found themselves to be incompatible. Capri is known to have been a meeting place for the gay community during the nineteenth century and it has been suggested that Henry may have been homosexual, though there is little supporting evidence for this (see Chapter Twelve).[44]

Mike Hickox feels there is a more logical reason why Wallis and Mary Ellen separated after Capri. The short periods during which they cohabited, were in Wales and Capri, out of the public eye. To live together openly in London would have been a totally different matter. The ensuing scandal could have had a deleterious effect on Wallis's rising career, just as he was achieving success following his recent triumphs at the Royal Academy exhibitions. P.A. Daniel's journal for 25 June 1857 records: "A lucky dog is Wallis – he made a great hit last year with his 'Death of Chatterton' and now people seek him out and beg him to paint pictures for them at his own price and he is very successful."[45] A public scandal may very well have dashed Wallis's hopes for future commissions and favourable reviews at exhibitions. The scandal would also have been a public humiliation for George Meredith, who may then have exercised his legal right to remove Harold from his wife's custody, just as he had his own son. Meredith had been listed as the baby's father on Harold's birth certificate. By keeping a low profile, this did not occur and Wallis was able to claim his son following Mary Ellen's untimely death. Although the scenario of Meredith claiming Harold seems highly unlikely, even the possible threat of it might have been sufficient to keep the couple living apart.[46]

It is known that Wallis remained in cordial contact with Thomas Love Peacock and with Mary Ellen's daughter Edith Nicolls for the rest of his life. This fact alone certainly argues against the traditional view of Wallis as a callous deserter. It is, therefore, possible that Henry and Mary Ellen continued an inconspicuous relationship. Joukovsky thinks the houses where Mary Ellen lived after Harold's birth, at 4 Crown Crescent, Twickenham, in 1859, and at 2 Sussex Villas, Cambrian Road, Richmond Hill, in 1860, would likely have been leased in her name but paid for mainly by Wallis.

It is interesting to note that Wallis never married and that in the 1881 England and Wales Census, Henry Wallis's marital status is listed as "widower". He may have done this to cover up Felix's illegitimacy, or he may have considered himself a widower despite never having been formally married to Mary Ellen. We know that Wallis retained mementos of Mary Ellen for the rest of his life and which were subsequently inherited by the family.

What we do know for certain is that after they apparently separated, Wallis rented an apartment, facing the British Museum, at no.62 Great Russell Street – an apartment that would later be taken over by Edward and Georgiana Burne-Jones.[47]

Mary Ellen went to live at no. 4 Crown Crescent, Twickenham. She tried to re-establish a more cordial relationship with her husband, but he refused, and he forbade her to see their son. Only when she was dying, did Meredith allow contact between Arthur and his mother. According to Johnson, Wallis was never mentioned in Victorian art studies, because Meredith felt resentful about the "traitor" who "stole" his wife from him.[48] This seems highly unlikely, however.

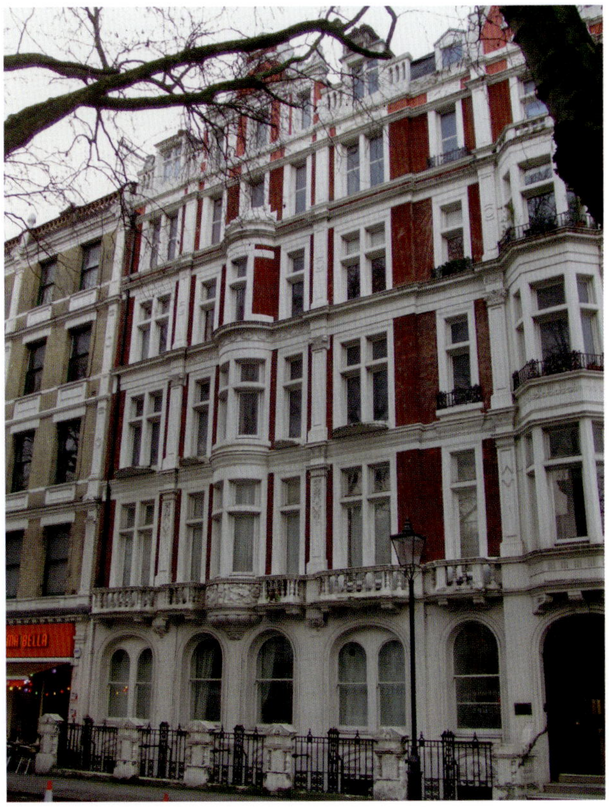

After his affair with Mary Ellen had come to an end, Wallis settled for two years at no. 62 Great Russell Street, opposite the British Museum. George du Maurier and his wife Emma were neighbours, as well as George Price Boyce who had moved into the 1st Floor at no. 60 in 1852. In 1862, Wallis let the apartment to the Burne-Joneses, who would later let it to Edward Poynter. In 1868, Whistler lived here for a while
PHOTOGRAPH BY RONALD LESSENS.

Mary Ellen's health had never been good and she suffered from a kidney disease that would ultimately prove fatal. Even as early as March 1855, Meredith writes in a letter to Mary Ellen's half-sister, Susan Abbott: "Mary has been very unwell again".[49] In addition to her medical problems, her correspondence proves that she was confronted with financial difficulties, which seems odd since Wallis had become a wealthy man after his stepfather's death.[50] It is uncertain why he did not help his former lover. Joukovsky suggests several possibilities: Firstly, that Wallis did not receive his inheritance immediately after his stepfather's death; Secondly, that Mary Ellen was too proud to accept assistance from him; or, indeed, that he did help her, but she still ran out of money.

It is only fair to mention that Mary Ellen did get some monetary assistance from John William Parker Jr., the editor of *Frazer's Magazine*, whom she had known since 1851.[51] Early in 1860, Parker gave her two sums of money to help her in this difficult time but, that summer, relations between them came abruptly to an end: "During the summer, she took a house at Richmond and let it to Parker for his sister who was ill. After a few weeks, Mary accused Miss Parker's servants of damaging her furniture. The charge was denied by Parker and relations between them terminated in considerable bitterness."[52]

During the last period of her life, Mary Ellen lived at Grotto Cottage in Oatlands Park, Weybridge, close to her father's house. This allowed the latter to pay her almost daily visits during her last illness, as we learn from letters he wrote to his friend Lord Broughton: "Day after day, I have tried to write to you, but always in vain. It seemed as if I could not trace the letters for what I had to say. At the same time with your last kind letter, I received a message from my eldest, and only surviving daughter, that she was extremely ill, and earnestly wished to see me…I have never seen such a fearful change in so short a time. I have been with her every day. She seems to grow rapidly worse. But while there is life, there is hope."[53] During her illness, "Mary Ellen sent a lock of her hair, a long, shining, light-brown tress, to Harold's nurse [Mrs. Bennett], for Harold to keep as he grew up. It is the hair of a young woman, with no trace of gray."[54] This lock, which Johnson saw among the Wallis estate, was inserted in an envelope dated 9 August 1861 with a note in Mary Ellen's writing: "His mother's hair for dear Harold: care of Mrs. Bennett"; this has subsequently been purchased by a New York collector.

Mary Ellen was only aged 40 when she died on 22 October 1861. A letter from George Meredith to his friend Bonaparte Wyse, 1 December 1861, states: "My wife is dead – All is much the same here. Arthur flourishes."[55] He could not have been more laconic and unsympathetic.

S.M. Ellis claimed that Mrs. Meredith died virtually alone, and her only mourners were a Mr. Howse, a Miss Bennett, and her former maid Jane Wells. Joukovsky disputes this, however, noting that Ellis was writing sixty years after the event and Mary Ellen had friends who were living in Weybridge who likely would have attended.

That Mary Ellen and Wallis must have remained on good terms is shown by the fact that she allowed Wallis to take Felix travelling with him to Europe during her last illness.[56] There has been speculation as to why Wallis did not attend her funeral, but the simple fact of the matter is that he was out of the country at the time. It is unlikely that it had anything to do with Wallis not wanting to taint her memory with scandal or that, being an atheist, he did not want to attend a religious ceremony.

A major question remains, however, why Henry would choose to go abroad at that time when she was obviously very ill. Possibly he did not expect her to die so quickly, or at this point was he simply indifferent to her fate? In the absence of documentary evidence, it is not possible to give a plausible answer and it remains a baffling mystery.

No tombstone has ever been placed over her unmarked grave, despite her father initially planning to do so.[57] The lines that she hoped might have been inscribed over her grave were these:

"Come not, when I am dead,
To drop thy foolish tears upon my grave,
To trample round my fallen head,
And vex the unhappy dust thou wouldst not save.
There let the wind sweep and the plover cry;
But thou, go by.
…
I am sick of Time,
And I desire to rest."[58]

It is a sad thing to say, but perhaps Mary Ellen could not cope with the kind of freedom she dreamt of. Even as early as in 1844, Claire Clairmont, in a letter to Mary Shelley, wrote: "Poor Mary Peacock – who can deny Fate who knows her history – Nothing she does ever succeeds."[59]

Peacock was devastated by the death of his daughter, as he explained in a letter to his friend Lord Broughton on 21 November 1861: "I have struggled in vain against the double weight of mental depression and physical fatigue. A few quiet days with you and your daughters present, not merely the greatest, but the only attraction the external world can offer me: but I am totally unable to avail myself of your kindness. I have been too long, perhaps, in bringing myself to the conclusion, but you will pardon me in consideration of my extreme reluctance to admit it."[60] The absence of Peacock at his daughter's funeral is difficult to explain. It may partly be the result of his anti-religious sentiments but it is far more likely that illness prevented him from attending. Her death was an emotional blow from which he never totally recovered.

The Survivors

George Meredith

George Meredith never forgave Mary Ellen for having "eloped" with Wallis. As Diane Johnson explains, "he had had to endure that most humiliating experience, especially humiliating to a Victorian, of being left by his wife, more or less with the approval of people connected with her, and of knowing that everyone (the World as he was to call it in his fiction) knew it, and that they knew she had taken up with Wallis, and that, eventually, they knew about the baby."[61] In a letter to William Hardman dated 3 June 1864, Meredith wrote of Harold: "There is, or was a child – not mine, who was taken by the father, and of whom I hear and shall hear nothing." [62]

The failure of his first marriage left a wound that never fully healed. A sense of guilt obliged him to think about his past errors, and his letters leave no doubt that he became more considerate and tolerant as he got older. He wrote about his unrest in one of his greatest works, *Modern Love*, a sequence of sonnets about the disintegration of a marriage. In it he refers to his own case and the opening lines are revealing:

Like sculptured effigies they might be seen
Upon their marriage-tomb, the sword between.

"The sword which separates them is emblematic of the endemic violence of their relationship."[63] He began to think about women's rights, which had no legal basis, although in reality, many women "wore the trousers". In Victorian times, marriage was a dreadfully serious matter and the "negotiations" between Meredith and his second father-in-law are a good example of it. He had to fill in a detailed questionnaire about his past life and marriage and to present a list of persons who could guarantee his honourability.[64] A few years after Mary Ellen's death, he fell desperately in love with Marie Vulliamy, who would become his loving and docile wife – quite the contrast to that Peacock lady who had always gone her own way! Unfortunately, Marie Vulliamy died from cancer aged 45, after two painful operations that had left her unable either to speak or move.[65]

Such difficult moments in his personal life could not but help induce Meredith to become more humane, even a "feminist" *avant la lettre*. It may seem paradoxical that he later stood up for women's rights more actively than many women did at the time. In fact, his thoughts on the rights of women ultimately evolved so as to be able to write to his publisher the following: "Since I began to reflect I have been oppressed by the injustice done to women, the constraint put upon their natural aptitudes and their faculties, generally much to the degradation of the race. I have not studied them more closely than I have men, but with more affection, a deeper interest in their enfranchisement and development, being assured that women of the independent mind are needed for any sensible degree of progress. They will so educate their daughters, that these will not be instructed at the start to think themselves naturally inferior to men, because less muscular, and need not have recourse to particular arts, feline chiefly, to make their way in the world."[66]

Harold 'Felix' Wallis

Harold Wallis was born in Bristol on 18 April 1858. When his mother died, he was aged 3. He spent most of the time with Mrs. Bennett until he was old enough to go to school. But Henry would sometimes leave Harold in the charge of his mother and would write to enquire about his health, referring to him affectionately by his nickname: "My dear Mother, I was sorry to hear Felix is no better. If it is measles, I suppose you had better let the doctor see him. I do not think it is necessary to give medicine for measles or only something very simple. Write and let me know how he comes on. Give him my love & kisses & tell him I hope to hear that he is patient I shall come & see him the first opportunity." [67] A letter from Mrs. Bennett to Henry, gives us a small insight into Harold's childhood: "...I am going to ask you if you would be so kind as to see if you can get for me a good collection of the old fashioned English nursery stories, not put into modern dress. I do not wish to have any German mixture, but simply such tales as Jack the Giant Killer, Tom Thumb ... Jack & The Beanstalk which is Harold's favorite - so far as I can tell it to him, but unfortunately I always stick fast in the middle for want of memory. I do not want expensive binding or illustrations."[68]

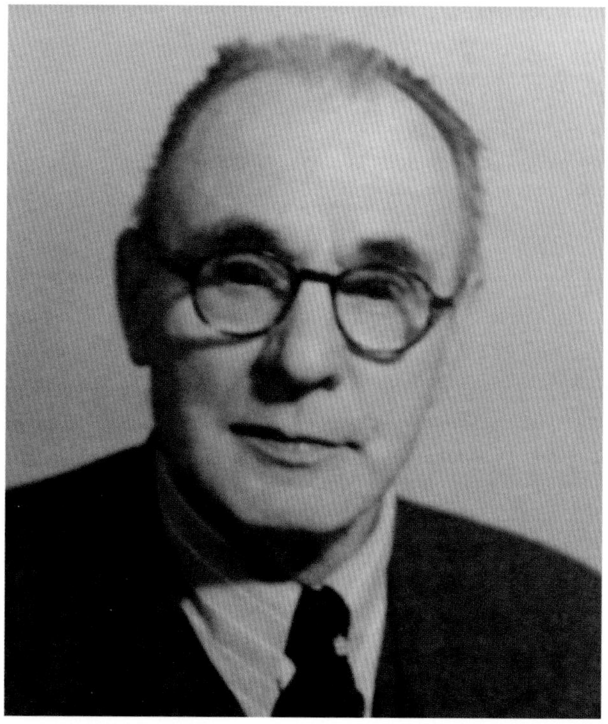

Cabinet photo, (presumably) Harold Wallis

This photograph was found alongside those of Henry. In a letter to Diane Johnson, dated 29 January 1968, Marshall, Liddle & Downey, solicitors at Croydon and executors of Harold's will, wrote: "You ask what Mr. Harold Wallis was like – he was a tall thin man who always appeared to wear a long black cloak."

IMAGE BY PERMISSION OF BODLEIAN LIBRARIES, OXFORD, MS PHOTOGR.150, FOL.38.

Henry early on often spent the winters around the Mediterranean. One of Wallis's passports, now at the Bodleian Library, was stamped at Boulogne on 15 December 1860: "Request...to allow Mr. Henry Wallis, British subject going to Paris, and his son"[69] and was possibly used for their journey to Italy, since the passport was stamped again at Paris for Rome on 6 June 1861. Georgiana Burne-Jones in her *Memorials*, states that "before the birth of our first child [Philip, born on 1 Oct 1861] we removed into a larger set or rooms just left by Mr. Wallis."[70] This implies that Henry and his son must have started their journey to Capri sometime in August or September 1861, which meant that he could not attend Mary Ellen's funeral in October.

The contemporary testimony of a British traveller who visited Capri in 1860 describes the arduous journey: first crossing the English Channel by boat to Boulogne, then by train to Paris; from here by rail to St-Jean-de-Maurienne in the French Alps, before transferring to a stagecoach to Turin, via Mont Cenis; on to Genoa, and then a steamer to Naples.[71] Once in Naples, one could go by rail to Sorrento and then on to Capri by boat. It was only shortly after 1860 that a steamboat service linked up Naples, Sorrento and Capri, but then still only irregularly. Travelling abroad was thus serious business and it is astonishing to imagine that Wallis took his very young son with him that distance and on such a difficult journey. In the winters of 1861 and 1862 they went to Capri, and from 1863 to 1865 to Rome.[72] In a letter to his mother, from Rome, dated 27 December 1863, Wallis wrote: "Harold is very fond of acquiring languages. I think I shall let him begin German. He has been trying his hand on Greek lately - the joke against him is that he begins a fresh language every day."[73]

When Harold was seven or eight years old his father sent him to a boarding school in Chester, managed by the Rev. Charles Wicksteed and his wife, where Harold stayed several years.[74] Henry also considered sending his son to a German or a Swiss school, as we learn from his correspondence. In a letter dated 15 June 1868, Mathilda Lufton, one of Mr Wicksteed's teachers, wrote: "I feel very glad that you should have decided on Germany in preference to France, but do you really think that English boys or indeed any boys are benefited by a foreign education commenced so early. I mean before 16 or 17? My impression was the contrary. I know I have heard that the greatest scapegraces in the German schools are the English boys, and I, perhaps somewhat luckily [?] took it for an axiom that boys were better for the control that the public opinion of their own country exercises on them. I have fancied that I perceived in children brought up abroad a sort of homeless [?] feeling. They do not regard the feelings nor opinions of those among whom they live, and they are too far from their own country to feel it a [burned] home [?] and when they return, often seem more aliens than many foreigners."[75] Perhaps on this advice, Henry gave up the idea of sending Harold abroad for schooling. It seems that Harold lived with his grandmother at least until he was twelve, as the 1871 census has shown.

Harold was educated at University College School and matriculated at the University of London in 1875. He was initially employed as a clerk at the Magdeburg Insurance Company but on 22 March 1877, aged 18, he entered the Bank of England where he stayed 42 years until his retirement.[76]

He married Alice Julyan Roberts,[77] who gave him two children: Edwin Harold and Violet Grace.[78] Harold died on 4 February 1933, aged 74, at the house of his daughter Violet Grace at Purley. The cause of death was listed as hypostatic pneumonia, chronic interstitial myocarditis and arteriosclerosis.[79]

Henry's letters to his son were quite affectionate, always starting with "My dear Felix" and ending with "Your loving father". Harold sometimes paid a visit to his father when the latter was abroad. In a letter dated 6 August 1879 to Frederic George Stephens, Henry mentioned that "Felix came to see me at the Hague for a few days, he enjoyed the trip immensely."[80]

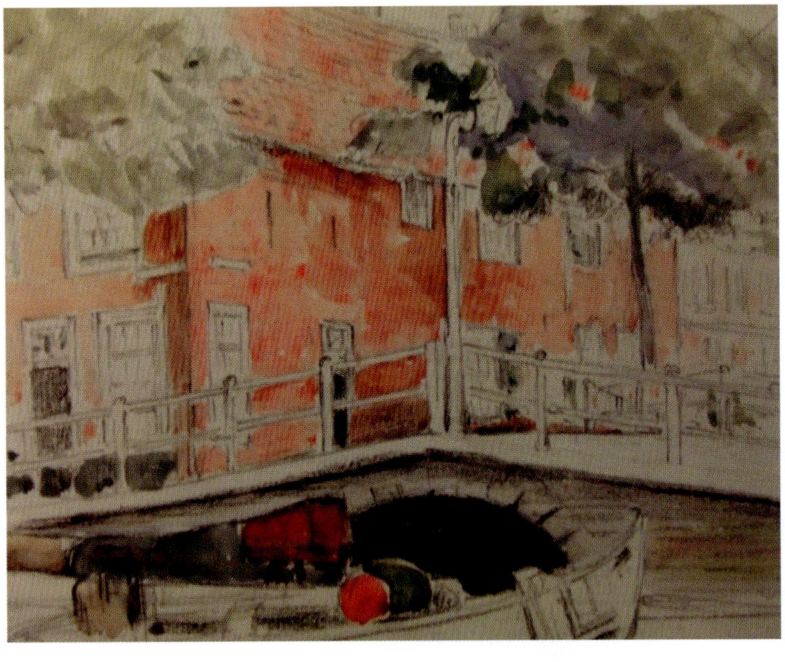

Delft (the Netherlands). From Wallis's sketchbooks [Cat. 312]
IMAGE BY PERMISSION OF THE BODLEIAN LIBRARIES, UNIVERSITY OF OXFORD (MS. ENG. D. 3553, FOL. 11R)

Chapter Six
THE "WIDOWER"

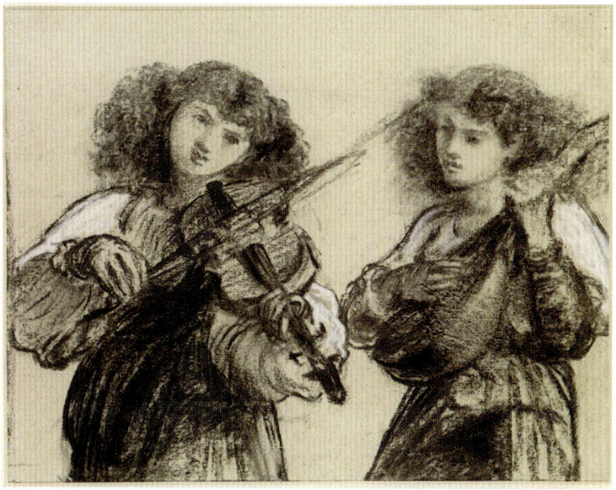

Wallis continued exhibiting at the Royal Academy until 1877. During the 1860s he mainly produced historical scenes, such as *Gondomar witnessing the execution of Sir Walter Raleigh* (1861, whereabouts unknown), *Shakespeare and Spenser* (1864, private collection) and *Luther and Melancthon* (1867, private collection). In the 1870s, however, he became increasingly fond of Italy and Renaissance art. "Venetian" subjects, and Italian landscapes became predominant, such as *A Despatch from Trebizond* (1873, private collection), *Found at Naxos* (1875, private collection) and *On the Ponte della Paglia, going to the Council* (1875, whereabouts unknown).

At the end of the 1870s, he was constantly on the move, mostly painting high-quality watercolours, which he sent to be exhibited at the Old Water-Colour Society (Society of Painters in Water-Colour) of which he had become a member. While only indirect evidence documents his movements in the 1860s to early 1870s, from this point onwards his correspondence allows us to trace him almost week by week.

Some scholars have wondered how Wallis managed to finance his lifestyle with his numerous journeys abroad. It should not be forgotten, however, that the cost of living was much cheaper in those days and even cheaper abroad. When George Frederic Watts won a £300 prize in the 1840s for his design for the decoration of the new Houses of Parliament, it allowed him to spend several years in Italy. Even in the early

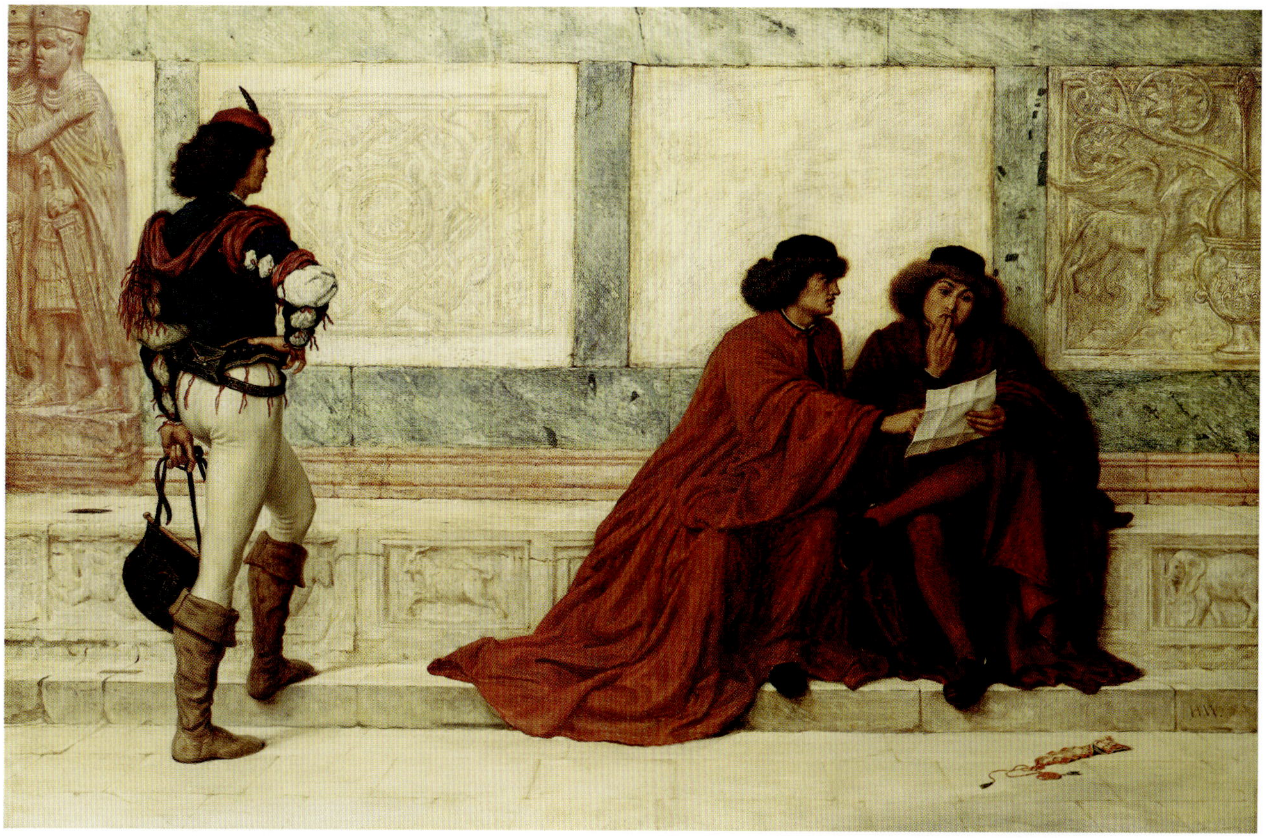

Above:
Henry Wallis, *Study of Two Italian Girls Playing Violin and Lute* [Cat. 134], 1870s?
Image courtesy of Birmingham Museums Trust

Right:
Henry Wallis, *A Despatch from Trebizond* [Cat. 95], 1873
Image by permission of Christie's Images/Bridgeman Images

1850s, Wallis must have had an allowance from his parents in order to settle in Paris and study at Gleyre's studio. It has been said that Wallis was a wealthy man following the inheritance he received from his stepfather after his death in 1859. The latter's estate was under £6,000, which, though not a vast fortune was still a considerable sum. (The purchasing power of £6,000 in 1859 would be equivalent to greater than £550,000 today.)[1]

From 1855 on he sold his pictures, not only at the Royal Academy, but also at other venues and even privately. John Forster, for example, never managed to purchase one of Henry's important pictures (see Appendix II Letters, L2). In the 1860s and 1870s his pictures sold from between £150 and £950, which were very good prices. An average middle-class family could live comfortably for a year on £300 in the 1860s. After 1878, when he began to exhibit at the Old Water-Colour Society, he regularly sold works at prices that varied between £40 and £200.

As we learn from his correspondence, part of his money was invested in stocks and shares.[2] In his own will, Henry Wallis mentions "my freehold land and houses at Finchley and at Whitfield". He never mentioned these properties in his letters and it is likely he inherited them from his father, or from his mother after she died in 1873. These would have provided a steady and not inconsiderable income.

In the 1870s, or possibly earlier, Wallis started to deal in ceramics and other decorative objects; and this activity became more important in the 1880s. He not only collected pieces for himself, but also sold many examples to museums, which would have helped to finance his journeys. For example, in 1886 he sold 300 textiles to the South Kensington Museum for £300. In 1896 the museum offered him £200 for three maiolica plates. His biggest sale came in 1907, when he sold 56 pieces of Spanish lustreware to the same museum for £3,000.

As Isabelle Gadoin points out, the Hogarth Club, of which he had been a member since its foundation in 1858, was perhaps the meeting place that convinced Wallis to become a collector in addition to his activities as a professional painter.[3] Membership of the Hogarth Club was eclectic and, in addition to professional painters and architects, members also included prominent collectors and critics. Ford Madox Brown, Dante Gabriel Rossetti and John Roddam Spencer Stanhope were the driving forces behind the Hogarth Club. It was "a meeting-place for artists and amateurs in sympathy with us", where they could "use the walls for exhibiting [our] sketches and pictures to members and friendly visitors."[4] In 1857, the year before the foundation of the club, some of their works had been refused or badly hung at the Royal Academy. They, therefore, decided to look for a permanent exhibition facility where their works could be hung in good conditions. Thirty members would have been financially sufficient to establish such a club, and on 10 April 1858 the inaugural meeting was held. Wallis was involved from the very start in this undertaking.[5] The Hogarth Club opened at no. 178 Piccadilly, before moving to no. 6 Waterloo Place. The shows were strictly private and allowed members, art lovers, and collectors by invitation to view pictures before they were exhibited elsewhere. On occasion artists would hang pictures that had already been displayed in other venues. For example, at the inaugural exhibition held in 1859, Wallis hung his *Stonebreaker*, which had been a great success at the Royal Academy the previous year. He was not the only one to do similarily. Hunt followed his example because displaying a painting in more than one place meant increased coverage, not to mention increased prestige. Because the Hogarth Club was a private venue, works exhibited here could later be exhibited at public galleries, such as the Royal Academy, which otherwise would have disallowed works that had been exhibited previously.

However, from 1859, some members began to disagree about the displaying policy. The hanging committee had refused Madox Brown's furniture design, which led to his resignation, and Rossetti threatened to do the same in sympathy with Brown. Members also quarrelled about the social activities of the Club. Burne-Jones, for instance, considered it a place meant for social contact, but others wanted it to concentrate solely on artistic matters. John Ruskin resigned because a billiard room had been installed. In 1861, Madox Brown was reinstated as chairman but membership decreased and, to improve the financial situation, "Brown gave his casting vote to a resolution introducing paying exhibitions."[6] This decision met with massive refusal from the membership as a whole and the Club was eventually dissolved in December of the same year.[7]

Whatever influence the Hogarth Club may have had on Wallis's future career, it is a fact that membership brought him into contact with collectors of European and Oriental works of art. In the 1850s and 1860s Wallis had made trips to France and to Spain and had been fascinated by what is called Spanish-Moresque ware. By the 1870s W.M. Rossetti remarked that Wallis was the owner of a substantial collection of this kind of art: "*Friday 7 February* [1873]. Spent the evening by invitation at Wallis's at Red Lion Square.... Wallis has a very fine show of Spanish-moresque lustreware."[8] Until the mid-1880s, Wallis also travelled through Italy and became an experienced and passionate lover of *maiolica* (faience) and of Renaissance art. His travels may have influenced his work towards being less sentimental in comparison to his previous 'Pre-

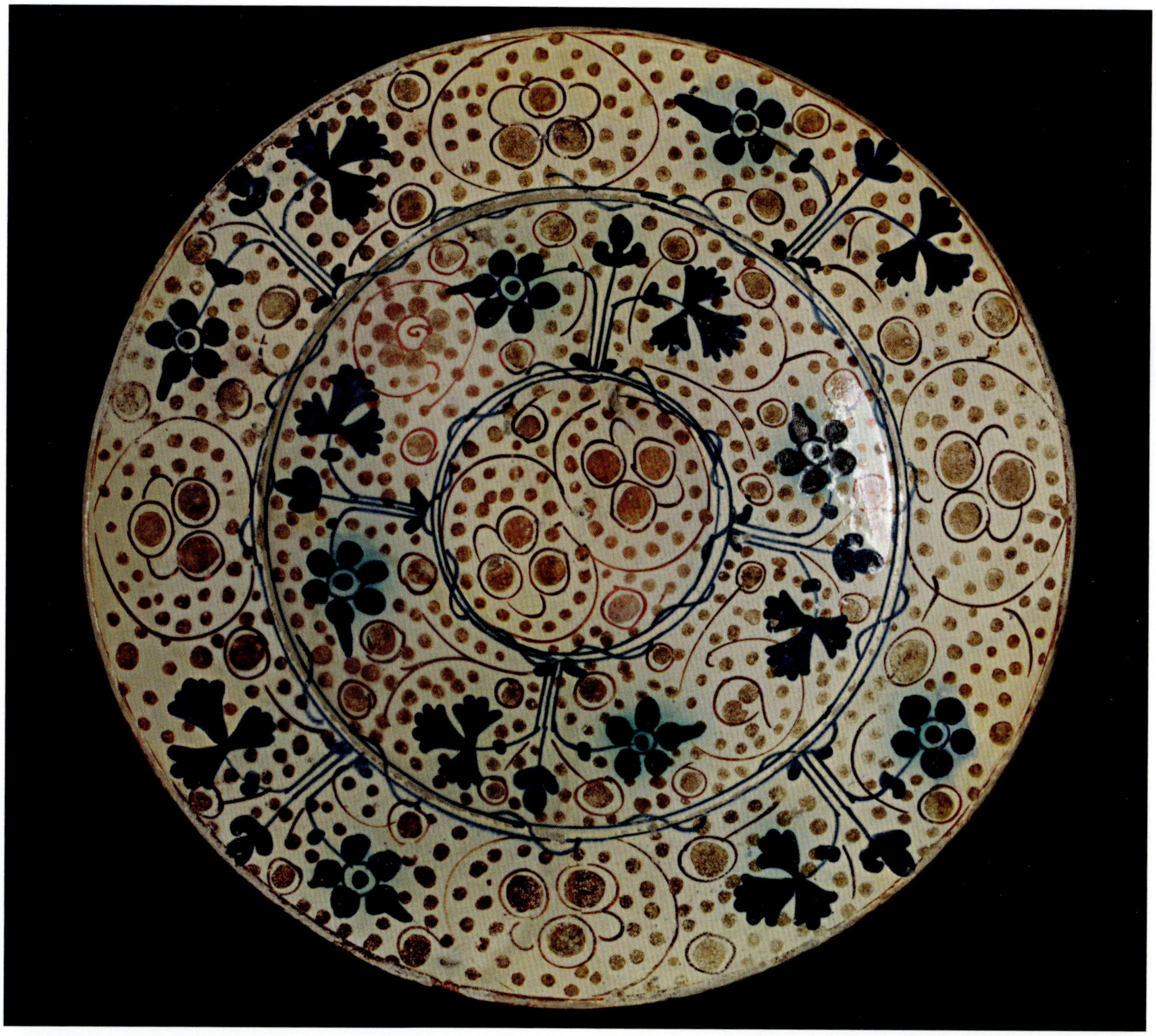

Hispano-Moresque plate, formerly in the Henry Wallis collection
Image courtesy of the Victorian & Albert Museum, London

Raphaelite' works as well as his move away from oil paints to watercolours.

Another more prosaic reason to explain his journeys to Italy and later to Egypt, even though his passion for the art of these regions was obviously genuine, was that he suffered from rheumatism and the climate in these warmer places favoured his medical condition. He explained to F.G. Stephens in a letter dated 28 October 1879 (he was then aged 49): "I am at present diverting myself with an attack of rheumatism, it is a pastime which has its inconveniences out of which is you can neither sit, stand or lie down…"[9] Years later, on 22 March 1892, he sent a similar complaint to Harold, from Taormina in Sicily: "Since I have been here the weather has changed to cold & wet, wch has given me a sharp attack of rheumatism – or rather I believe lumbago. It is not an agreeable exercise, since you cannot get down, rise, go to bed, get up, dress or perform any of the ordinary functions of life wthout suffering violent pain in the muscles of the small of the back."[10]

Later in life, Wallis was a member of the Burlington Fine Arts Club (BFAC) –in Savile Row – where exhibitions were held twice a year and where one could meet likeminded people connected to the arts such as Whistler, Ruskin, the Rossettis and the architect Edwin Lutyens. The Club[11] was founded when connoisseurs like Felix Slade and Wollaston Franks merged with the Fine Arts Club which, since 1857, had been a meeting place for collectors to compare and discuss their acquisitions. This resulted in the BFAC, which initially took its premises in December 1866 at no. 177 Piccadilly, but which later moved to a more suitable location in Savile Row. Candidates were supported by full members and elected by a committee. Once elected they had to pay £5 5s, which was also the annual membership fee. One or two exhibitions were held every year. As early as 1868, Oriental art began to be admired by club members. Wallis's interest in Persian and Hispano-Moresque pottery developed during the 1870s and it is, therefore, not impossible to imagine that he was the driving force behind some of the Club exhibitions. His specialized knowledge of Oriental art was recognized when a decision was made to show important pieces of Egyptian art and Wallis was asked to write the introduction to the catalogue, *The art of ancient Egypt: a series of photographic plates representing objects from the exhibition of the art of ancient Egypt*, London, 1895. He remained a Club member for the rest of his life.[12]

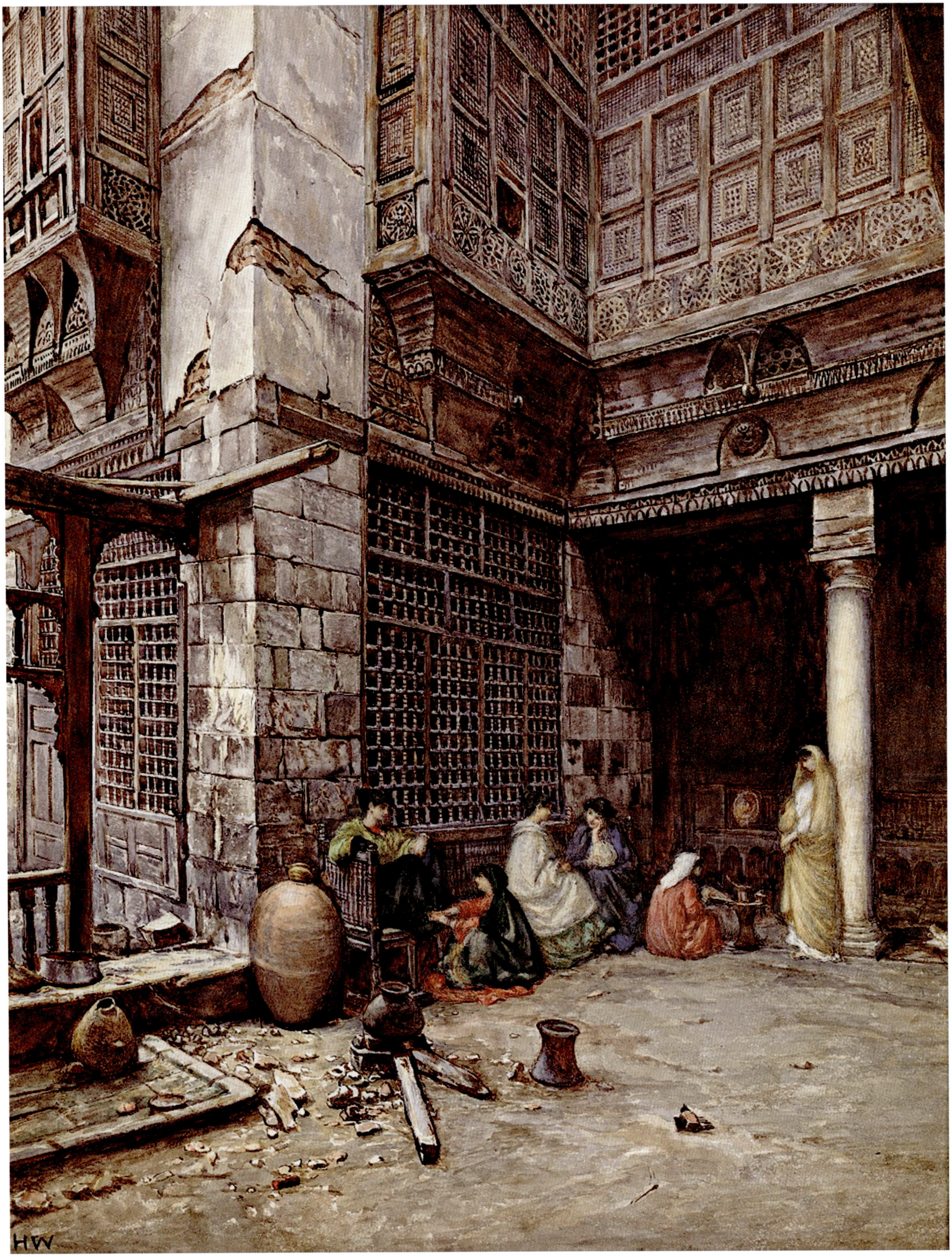
HW

Chapter Seven
THE JOURNEY TO EGYPT

In the 1880s and 1890s Egypt became a favourite destination for Wallis. He might initially have been inspired to visit there because his teacher, Gleyre, had made the journey to Egypt in the mid-1830s, and his friend Holman Hunt had toured in the Orient as early as in 1854 with Thomas Seddon. From 1885 to 1901 Wallis spent most of his winters in Egypt, which he explored from top to bottom; this was an Egypt that tourism had already 'invaded' by the standards of the time. After Thomas Cook set up package tours in 1869 and opened an office at Cairo, the number of tourists to Egypt had increased, requiring an infrastructure which extended from special trains to local dragomen. To have an idea of how people travelled, it is only necessary to consult a travel guide of the time.[1] The many possibilities offered for travel to the Middle East proves that it had become "big business". Between 1869 and 1891 Thomas Cook's Eastern tours led 12,000 visitors to the region, primarily British and Americans.[2] Besides tourists, one could meet businessmen and diplomats, as well as soldiers serving in the far corners of a British Empire at the peak of its glory.

To reach Cairo, there were various sea routes and overland routes available to the intrepid Victorian traveller. In the first case, it was possible to start from London, Southampton, Liverpool or Manchester. From London, there were weekly P.&O. services and fortnightly services of the Orient-Pacific liners, arriving at Marseille almost a week later, and at Port Said in another 4 days. In addition, the British India Company, the Prince Line, or the Japanese Mail Line provided further alternatives and dispatched a fortnightly steamer, but the voyage was slower and offered less comfort. Starting from Southampton, the Norddeutscher Lloyd Company was in favour with English travellers and Wallis used it at least once, as shown in one of his letters written aboard the *Prinz Heinrich*, in the winter of 1900.[3] After arrival at Port Said, passengers could reach Cairo by train in 4-and-a-half hours.

Henry Wallis, *Interior Courtyard of a Jew's House at Cairo – Preparing Coffee* [Cat. 184], 1886
Image courtesy of Bonhams, London

Alternatively, having crossed the Channel, travelers could take a luxury train to one of the ports of embarkation: Marseille, Brindisi, Venice, Naples, Genoa or Trieste. The port of Marseille had become a favourite boarding place with English travellers to Egypt, since the railway journey lasted 22 hours rather than the 45 hours to Brindisi. From Brindisi tourists took a mail steamer to which passengers were also admitted. The mail steamer was scheduled on Sunday evening and arrived at Port Said early on Wednesday morning. However, travel guides did not recommend it because of the less comfortable accommodation it offered.

Another option was the Austrian-Lloyd steamer, which connected Trieste and Alexandria in four days; Wallis took this on at least one occasion in 1893. In 1895-96, he took a steamer of the *Navigazione Generale Italiana* line, leaving Naples for Alexandria.

To go up the Nile from Cairo, Messrs. Cook & Son offered the possibility of taking an express steamer – leaving on Friday and reaching Luxor the following Thursday and Assouan on Saturday – or a more leisurely tourist steamer for a twenty-day trip. Tourist guides declared Egypt suited for a winter residence, but advised that Cairo was to be avoided because of its poor standard of hygiene and high risk of epidemics. It was, therefore, recommended to go up the Nile and come back to Cairo in February. Wallis followed this advice. In 1892-3, for instance, he arrived at Cairo on 4 December, left for Assouan at the end of the month, then came back via Philae, Medinet Habu, Luxor and Karnak, and reached Cairo on 20 February.[4]

With regards to Cairo's unhealthy conditions, and sometimes unfavourable weather, we have reports not only from Wallis, but also from Holman Hunt. On 4 April 1892, Hunt wrote to Wallis, from Jerusalem: "Happily after having written the above, my wife got better and as it was evident that Cairo was pestilential, we came away at once."[5] From Cairo, on 17 November 1895, Wallis wrote to Frederic George Stephens: "Cairo has not even surface drains for the streets & when such a catastrophe as has occurred the last few days – in torrential rains – the streets are canals & lakes of mud & water. Villages in the suburbs have been swept away by the torrents from the hills. And the popular notion is that it never rains in Egypt! Lately, even when not raining one has to take a carriage to go a hundred yards."[6]

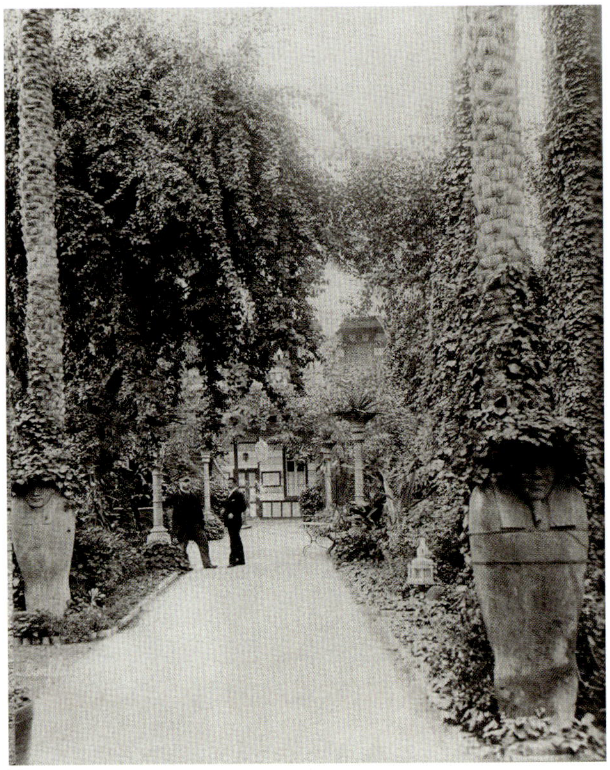

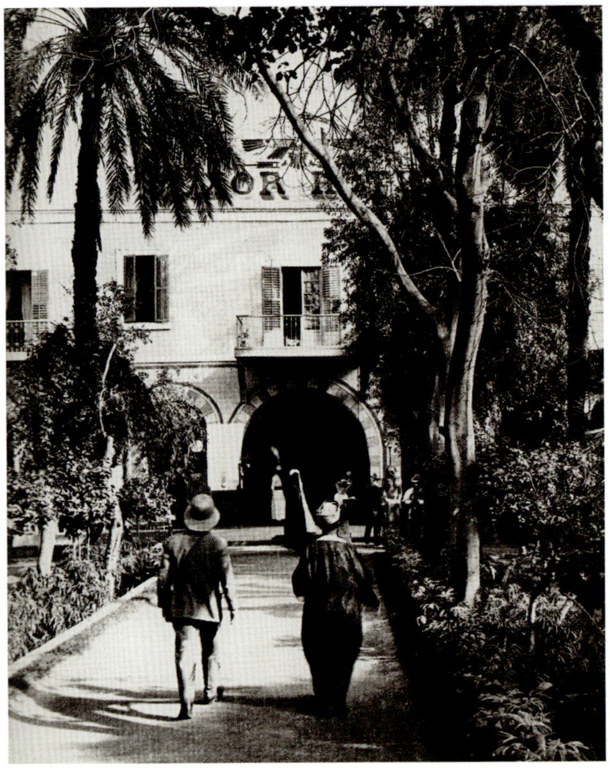

When he was in Egypt, Wallis would nearly always choose good quality hotels, but rarely the luxurious palaces aimed at tourists wanting social recognition. In Cairo, for example, instead of staying at the fabulous Shepheard's[7] or at the Savoy, he contented himself with the Grand Hôtel Royal in 1892-3 and the Hôtel du Nil in 1885-86, 1895-96 and 1897-98. The famous archaeologist Flinders Petrie also chose the latter hotel for his stays in Cairo, perhaps on Wallis's recommendation.[8] At Luxor, Wallis was fond of the Hôtel Luxor (1901-2), the Hôtel Karnak (1901) and particularly of the Grand Hôtel Thewfikieh, which many visitors preferred because of its affordable prices, its quiet atmosphere and its large garden.

In Wallis's time the journey to Egypt had become hugely popular, and a pioneering role had been played by the artists who had earlier gone "to the Orient" to forget civilization. As Holman Hunt explained: "Suddenly, I discovered how to escape the pretences of Civilisation."[9] Other artists, like John Frederick Lewis and Edward Lear, were looking for fresh inspiration, new energy, and exotic scenes to paint. As William Makepeace Thackeray (writing as M.A. Titmarsh) stated: "There is a fortune to be made for painters in Cairo, and material for a whole Academy of them. I never saw such a variety of architecture, of life, of picturesqueness, of brilliant colour, and light and shade. There is a picture in every street, and at every bazaar stall."[10]

In Wallis's case, it is extremely unlikely he wanted to escape civilization. His motive is more likely to have been his increasing interest in pottery and historical research. Wallis also painted a great many watercolours here, most of which are now, unfortunately, untraceable. He painted the local scenery, but unlike many Orientalists, he rendered what he saw, without interpreting it through Western eyes.

Wallis first travelled to Egypt in 1885 and wrote weekly to his son. His first impressions were mixed. He was enthusiastic about the beauty of the scenery seen from the Nile, but unhappy with the filth and dirt of Cairo. On 22 November 1885, shortly after his arrival at Cairo, he wrote: "Glad to hear you have a servant that promises to do, hope she will continue satisfactory. Is she equal to lighting an occasional fire in the studio & keeping it up for a few days? It seems curious talking of fires here, where the weather is like our August. Cloudless skies, since I have been here & too hot to be pleasant in this terribly dusty country. Flies, fleas & mosquitoes are a regular plague. People say the season is rather warmer than usual. Certainly the sun at midday is broiling. This day I went to Sakkarah, it was roasting. Cook[11] gave

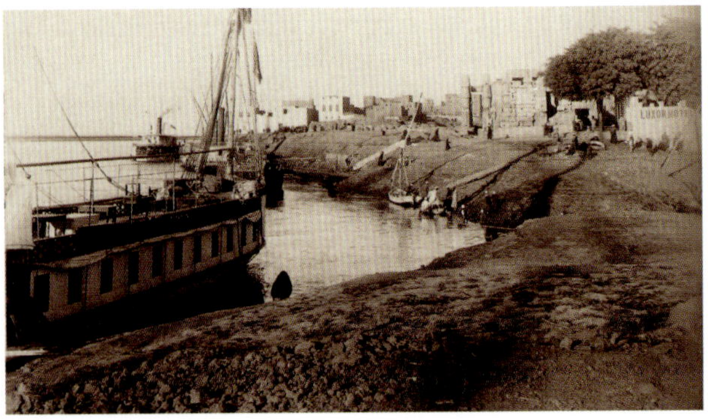

Top left:
Cairo, Hôtel du Nil, c.1875
Reproduced from Robert Solé, *Voyage en Égypte*, du Chêne, Paris 2003, by kind permission of the publisher; © collection Walter

Top right:
Luxor, Luxor Hotel, c.1930
Reproduced from Robert Solé, *Voyage en Égypte*, du Chêne, Paris 2003, by kind permission of the publisher; © collection Walter

Left:
The mail steamer leaving the Luxor Hotel, c.1880.
Reproduced from Robert Solé, *Voyage en Égypte*, du Chêne, Paris 2003, by kind permission of the publisher; © collection Walter

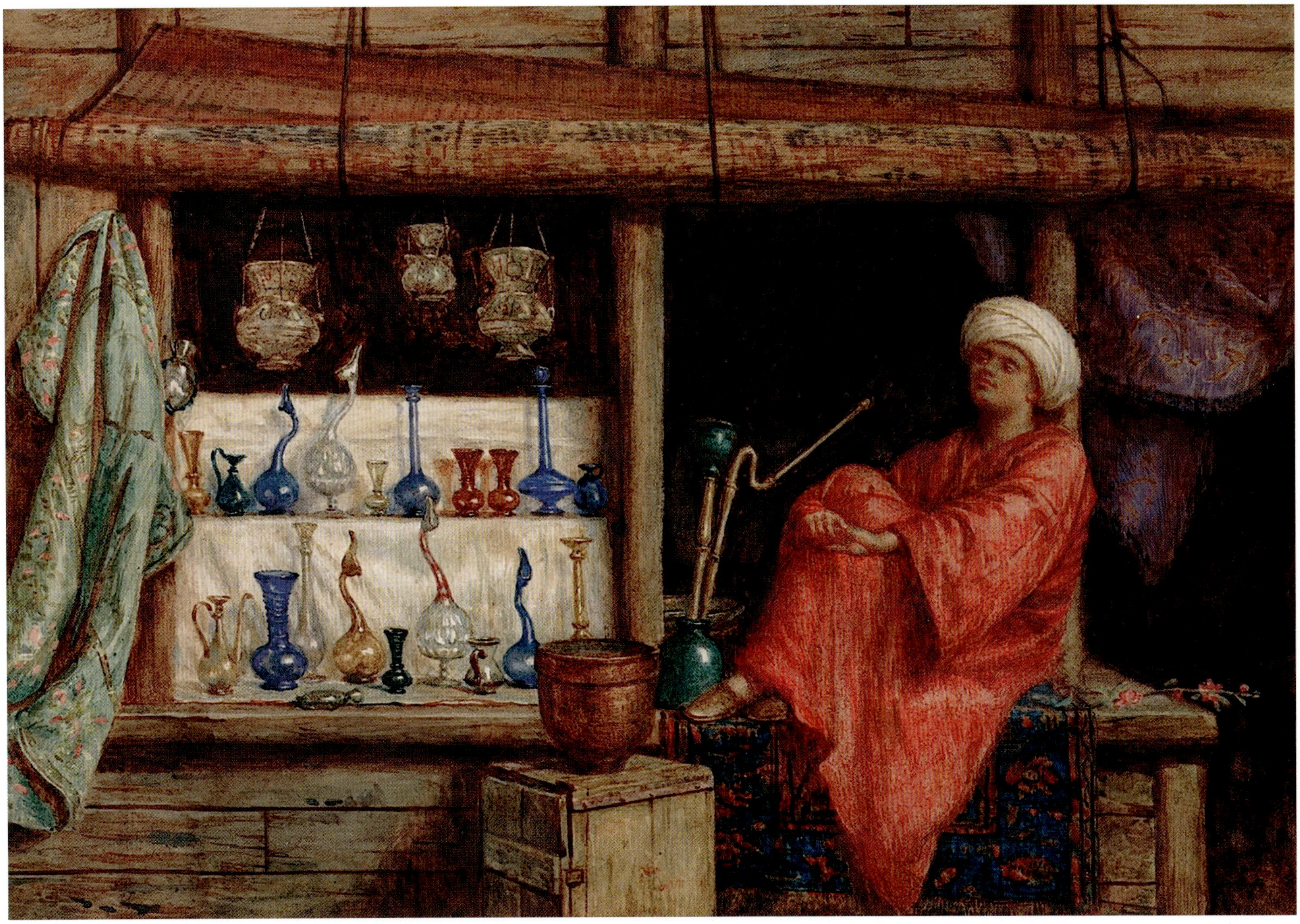

Henry Wallis, *An Oriental Glass Merchant* [Cat. 177], 1885
Private collection
IMAGE COURTESY OF BONHAMS, LONDON

half a dozen of us a pleasant excursion. We found the carriages waiting at Shepheard's at 7.45, drove to the Rlwy [railway], in an hour we arrive at Bedreshayn[12] & then mounted the donkeys that had been brought by train. Then we started across the strip of cultivated land, through palm groves to the desert, saw the tombs, pyramids &c, lunched (No.1) & then to Memphis.[13] Then to the banks of the Nile where a launch took us an hour up stream (lunch No.2). The steam back to Cairo was very delightful from the beauty & variety of the scenery. Altogether it was not so bad being personally conducted in this way. Cook was very pleasant & homely, & finished up his hospitality by giving us a dinner."[14]

A few weeks later, on 12 December, in a letter to Frederic George Stephens, Wallis mentioned the situation in Upper Egypt: "The unsettled state of the country in Upper Egypt has, I suppose, scared away tourists.[15] There seem to be more this year. I sh^ld^ like if [I] can manage it to see something of the country up the Nile, at present. I hear the military authorities refuse permission to go further than Luxor;[16] but that I think must be a canard. In any case, it will not be very agreeable travelling. The more sanguine natives expect the Soudanese will be down here before a couple of months."[17]

The British position in Egypt being threatened by the French, Wallis's anti-French feelings became dominant. To his son, on 13 January 1891, he wrote: "The French display an incapacity wch is simply incredible - unless it is intentional. Their paper, the Bosphore - the organ of the French Consul General is more rabid & abusive than ever. I suppose it is on a par wth the Irish home rule papers. I occasionally see Paris papers, & they are equally virulent in their anti-English feeling, now they are furious at the fiasco of the Irish, showing that their rooted feeling is a malignant hatred of England...It seems that there will be nothing for it but to effectually draw their teeth, & I think it is a pity Germany did not do so 20 years ago."[18]

Wallis was certainly well known in Egyptian archaeological circles, as confirmed by more than one witness. E.A. Wallis Budge,[19] who made several journeys through Egypt and Mesopotamia on behalf of the British Museum, repeatedly recalled Wallis's presence and Wallis was renowned both as

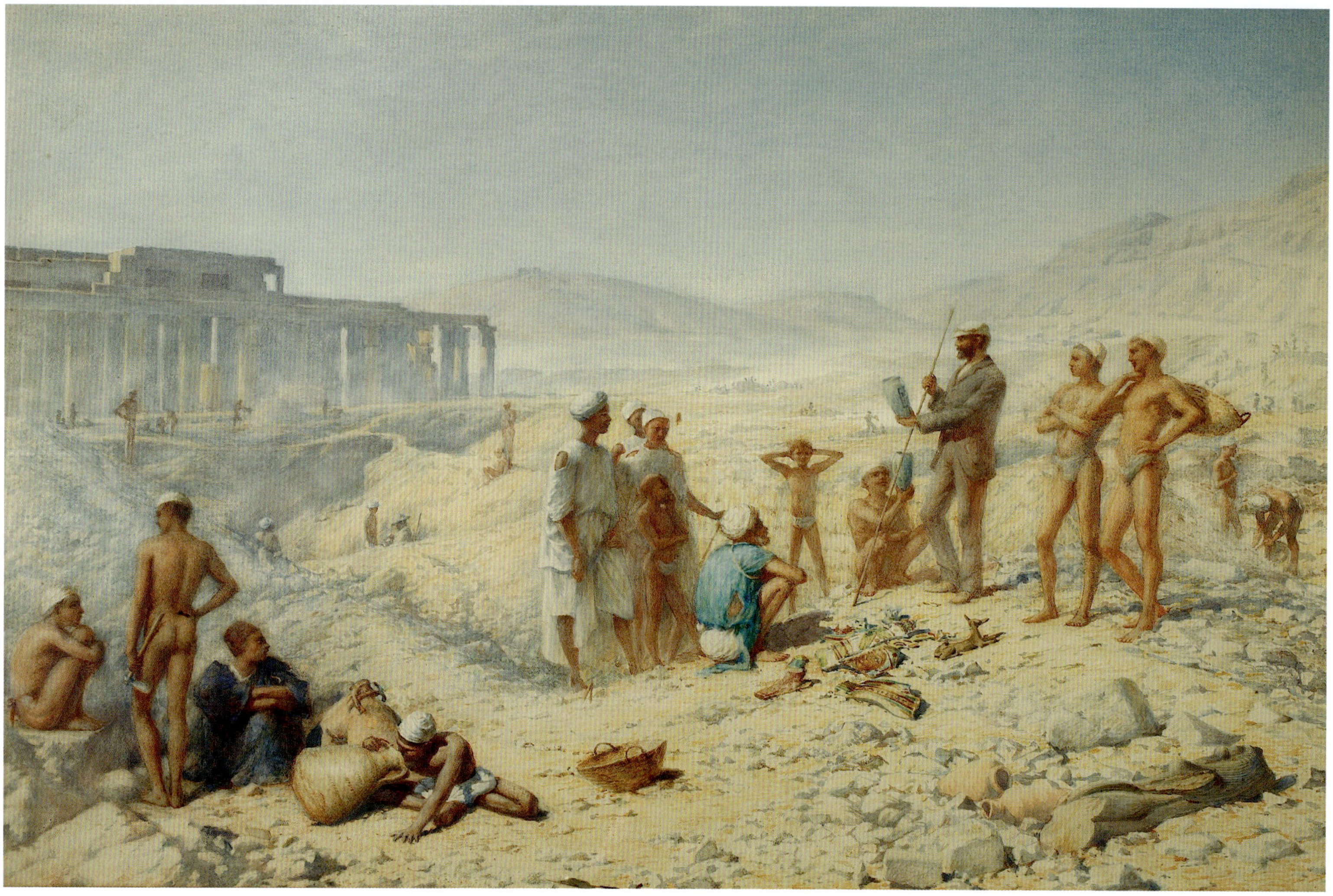

an artist and as a ceramic-collector. Furthermore, according to Budge, Wallis seems to have been instrumental in welcoming the famous Heinrich Schliemann at Assouan in January 1887: "In January Dr. H. Schliemann, the distinguished archaeologist and excavator, visited Aswan in one of the old dhahabiyahs, which were so roomy and comfortable. As soon as he arrived his secretary, or companion, landed and sent some of the crew to announce to the native officials that his great master had arrived, but with what object he did this no one understood. The British military authorities had not been instructed from Cairo to give Dr. Schliemann a public reception, and they did nothing. Mr. Henry Wallis, the artist, who very kindly made for me many drawings of the Aswan tombs, was very anxious that some one should show civility to Dr. Schliemann, and offered to act as guide for him over the tombs. Therefore he, Major Plunkett, and I were rowed over to the dhahabiyah, and announced ourselves. The butler received us civilly, and led us into the large reception room in the stern of the vessel, and after the usual salutations and coffee and cigarettes, Major Plunkett acted as spokesman, and said that we had called to offer him our boat and crew if he wished to go over to the tombs, and that we were ready to accompany him at any time, and show him what we had done. Dr. Schliemann replied very stiffly, 'It is very kind of you to be so amiable. I should like to place my archaeological science at your disposal by showing and explaining to you the tombs, but I have not the time as I am going up to Halfah.' He then reached out one hand, and lifted up a paper-bound copy of the Greek text of Homer's 'Iliad', in the Teubner Series, which he was holding in his hand when we entered (it was then lying face downwards on the cushion), and went on with his reading. Major Plunkett, lighting another cigarette, asked in a sweetly soft voice if we had his permission to withdraw, and we did so with as much dignity as was possible under the circumstances."[20]

During the winter of that year, both men met again and Wallis Budge remembered: "Henry Wallis the artist, who had made some excellent coloured drawings of the Aswan tombs."[21] They travelled together up the Nile, as Henry explained to his son: "I started early on Tuesday morning wth Budge on the dirtiest bit of railway travelling in the world, the line to Asyout, & we had 10 hours of it arriving at 6.30. We came on board the

Henry Wallis, *Flinders Petrie admiring a find, the Ramesseum, Western Thebes* [Cat. 224], 1895
During the 1895 excavations, Petrie stayed near Luxor and was cataloguing the Theban tombs. Petrie, Milne and others camped beside the Ramesseum. In that period, Wallis came over for a couple of days and made the present watercolour, which must have been executed between 18 December 1895 and 26 January 1896.
Image by permission of University College Museum, London

steamer at once & started the next morning at a little after six, just as the day was dawning, a time that I never like to miss on the Nile."[22]

Still in 1887, Wallis met George Howard, the future ninth Earl of Carlisle and a distinguished amateur artist, who spent the winter in Egypt with his wife Rosalind and their children, in an attempt to save their marriage. From Luxor, 29 December 1887, Wallis wrote to Harold: "I don't think I shall stop & work here, I had a notion of doing something on the other side – Thebes – but there w^ld^ be a difficulty about getting accommodation there & the getting across & ride over the plain every morning w^ld^ be a long & fatiguing affair if one had to work after it.

I spent Xmas day on that side, went over wth George Howard[23] & his family who I found staying here, we had a long day, climbing over the mountain to the valley of Kings & visiting the tomb of Seti I[24] – whose alabaster sarcophagus is in the Soane museum.[25] Last night I went to see the temple of Karnac by moonlight, a time when the gigantic ruins look the most impressive, & when, if there are no other tourists, one is not pestered by the swarm of bawling natives that are such a nuisance in the day. At night – full moon – one sees all the general masses, just the right amount of detail w^th^out the fissures & defacements that mar the effect by day. There, as at Thebes & indeed every where up the Nile, the neglect of the monuments is very saddening, the wilful destruction is great, for the want of efficient guarding & an insignificant expense in cement, monuments wch might be preserved for eyes will be wrecked in the course of a few years."[26]

Wallis was also well acquainted with Flinders Petrie,[27] the famous archaeologist who revolutionized excavation methods by dating even the tiniest fragments unearthed. Before him, scholars were interested only in whole pieces and contemptuously rejected the numerous fragments that were to be found in the mounds around Cairo. In his letters from Egypt, Wallis often mentioned Petrie and was lucky enough to accompany him to Naucratis, a site that Petrie had previously excavated. In a letter to Harold on 17 November 1890, Wallis writes: "We had a very pleasant voyage to Alexandria, arriving there on Thursday morning, the wind was favourable & we had no bad weather though it was not exactly smooth. It was very cold on starting & fairly warm on arriving. We stayed the day at Alexandria & then on Friday left by an early train for the nearest station to Naucratis,[28] a five miles [*sic*] walk in a brilliant sun. Petrie was glad to visit the scene of his former labours. We passed most of the day in walking about the site of the ancient city & among the myriads of fragments of pottery found some interesting pieces. Then we took the evening train arriving at Cairo at night."[29]

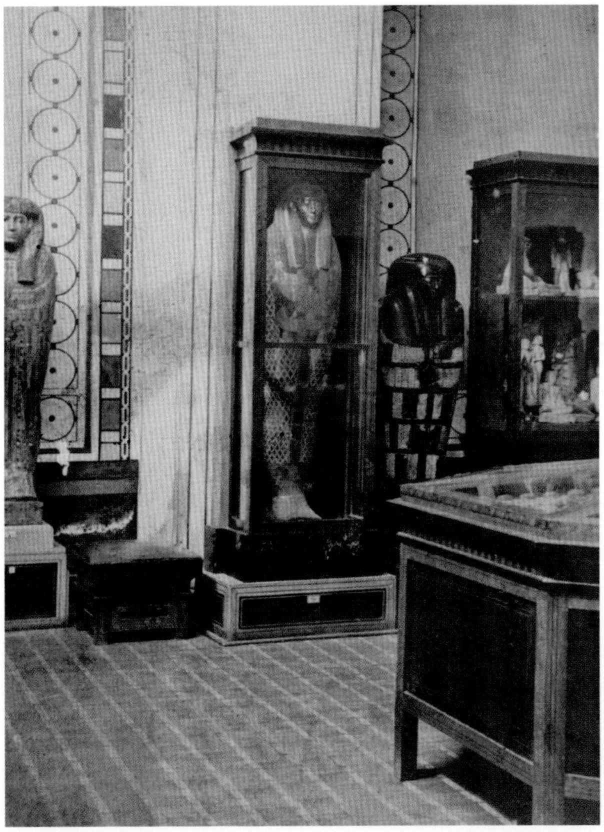

The Bulaq Museum in the 1860s. The museum was founded by Auguste Mariette in 1863. Due to dampness and to an increasing number of items, the collection was first moved to Giza, and then to the present museum in 1902 (Photograph from Ben Mahmoud, Feriel, *Le voyage en Orient, 1850-1930*, 2008, p.94).

Wallis may also have been in touch with the young Howard Carter, who worked as Petrie's assistant for a few years. Between 1893 and 1899, Carter had been appointed as principal artist to Swiss Egyptologist Édouard Naville at Deir-el-Bahri, and we know that Wallis visited the site during the winter of 1895-1896. No written trace seems to have survived about a meeting with the famous discoverer of King Tutankhamun's tomb, however.

Chapter Eight
THE ARCHAEOLOGIST-COLLECTOR/CONNOISSEUR

The best general discussion of Wallis's activities as an Archaeologist-Collector/Connoisseur is found in Isabelle Gadoin's chapter, written in French, on "Henry Wallis, the Pre-Raphaelite painter specialist in Islamic ceramics."[1] Although his major passion was for ceramics, Wallis had wide collecting interests that also encompassed fabrics, including Oriental rugs, manuscripts, metal work, glassware, antiquities, and fine art.[2] Gadoin suggested that it was Wallis's work as an artist that led him to become successful as a ceramic specialist: "c'est l'art, et l'œil affûté de l'artiste, qui menèrent à l'expertise". [It is art, and the sharp eye of the artist, that led to expertise.]

As Wallis often travelled through Italy, one might think that his first publications would be

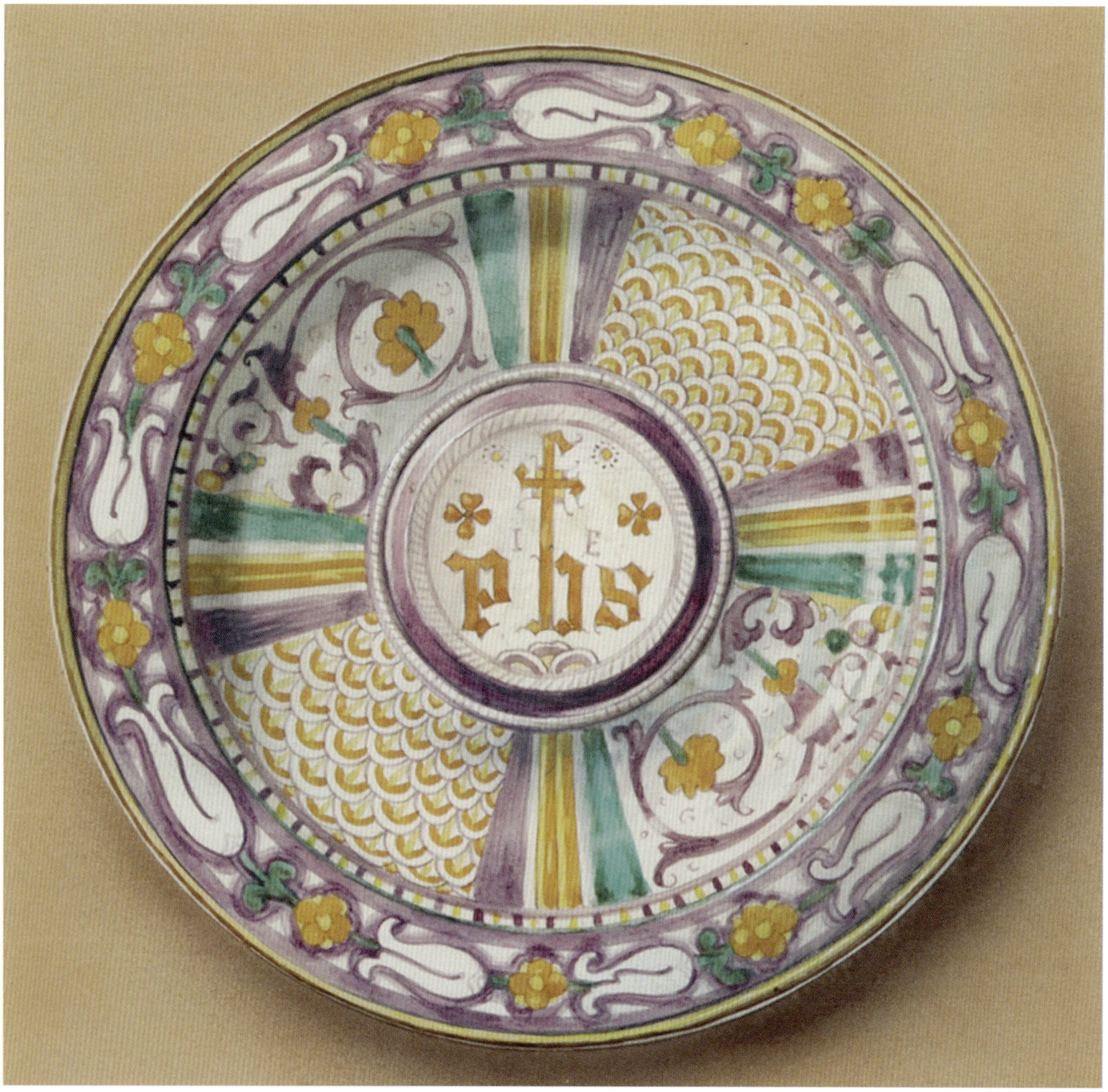

Henry Wallis, *Watercolour of a Renaissance Plate* [Cat 231]
Image courtesy Diane Johnson, Paris

devoted to Italian art. However, his love for Persian and Arab art dates as far back as the late 1850s, when he had travelled to southern Spain and where he first had fallen under the spell of Moorish art. By the 1870s, Wallis had formed a fine collection of Hispano-Moresque pottery. This initial passion then led him to the Italian Renaissance ceramics and finally to Egyptian pottery. His research focused primarily on their reciprocal links and influences. As Timothy Wilson has pointed out, "by the 1890s his enthusiasm was increasingly for fourteenth- and fifteenth-century, so-called 'primitive' Italian pottery."[3] In Wallis's obituary,[4] his friend Albert Van de Put, though not crediting him with any new discoveries, recognised his knowledge: "Excavation, documentary and other research, he for the most part left to others concerned, either by bent or professionally. ... Mr. Wallis's real knowledge of ceramics in certain departments would have equipped two or three professed archeologists to treat thereof with greater appearance of learning, but with the dryness still supposed in certain quarters, proper to the exposition of all manifestations whatsoever of art or science."[5] He also wrote: "Everywhere peeps out the wisdom begotten of pilgrimages to little-known museums, in quiet old cities; of the quest-ceramic pursued between Berlin and Bitonto, and from Sevres to Fostat, sketch-book in hand; of discussions with *conservatori*; and of arguments with all and sundry."[6]

However, posterity has given him proper recognition: "Wallis must particularly be credited with having been among the first to recognize the influence of the Fatimid art upon later Islamic productions. It was his belief that any scholarly study on ceramics must be based upon the Egyptian ceramic art...; throughout the centuries, its influence can be found in the Byzantine and Persian art, then in the art of medieval Egypt and Syria, as well as in the Italian *maiolica* ... Later studies on Islamic art have proved this influence, in particular on lustre faience."[7]

With regards to Italian *maiolica*, Wallis was "one of the first students to realize the importance of excavated fragments, and particularly of wasters."[8] He also succeeded in dating pottery by analyzing their representation in paintings. The role he played in the study of the *istoriato* (*maiolica* based on Renaissance designs) was far from negligible: he discovered "that the scenes on the maiolica plates by Nicola da Urbino in the Museo Correr in Venice are derived from woodcuts in the *Ovidio Metamorphoseos vulgare* and the *Hypnerotomachia Poliphili*, published in Venice in 1497 and 1499 resp."[9] He also wrote about "oak-leaf jars", the ware decorated in relief blue and made in the mid-fifteenth-century in Florence, which he had probably come to know through the artist-dealer-connoisseur Charles Fairfax Murray."[10] Timothy Wilson points out that "the term seems to have been coined by Wallis in 1903."[11] Charles Fairfax Murray, an artist who later on specialised in dealing in Pre-Raphaelite and Italian Renaissance art, was both a friend and a correspondent of Wallis's. One major difference between them as collector/connoisseurs is that Murray only trusted his own knowledge and instinctively mistrusted academics, whom he considered as being out of touch with reality. Unlike Murray, Wallis always seemed to need the approval and confirmation of other scholars. This might be taken as a symptom of a lack of self-confidence but could also be interpreted as a need by Wallis to take part in scholarly debate with his peers.

To contradict Van de Put's statements about Wallis not being involved with "excavation, documentary and other research", Wallis *did* in fact perform fieldwork and visited many principal excavation sites, as his correspondence and sketchbooks eloquently prove. This is one of the reasons why he was able "to thoroughly discuss about the dating of ceramic items and greatly contribute to refine the classifications previously established by experts such as Augustus Wollaston Franks and Charles Drury Fortnum."[12] The hundreds of letters he sent to his son and friends bear witness to his many connections with art dealers and museum directors, as well as to his bargaining skills, although diplomacy was not one of his major virtues!

Wallis was in close contact with the British Museum and the South Kensington Museum (now the V&A). He was not only a go-between in negotiating the purchase of interesting items that he had found on the market, but he also lent parts of his own collection to exhibitions in both museums. Occasionally, he also sold them pieces. Given that it was easier in those days to take antiquities out of a country, and considering the number of items in his possession, it is clear that he was involved in the export of many antiquities.

During his first journey to Egypt (1885) he collected many textiles, as reported by Arthur Hughes in a letter dated 26 April 1886 to their mutual friend William Bell Scott: "I saw Wallis yesterday, lately back from Wady Halfa or about the edge of the Soudan and whose common talk of Thebes & Philoe and early Coptic, and whose tables are spread with remnants of Gorgeous ~~emboss~~ pattern woven dresses that travel with their wearers before Pharaoh / trifles they hardly allowed him to bring away again from Vienna & Paris, and such as he graciously allows the British Museum to take of him at the price he paid. I hope we shan't get too proud, but <u>now</u> we are far in advance in these matters of Paris & Vienna."[13]

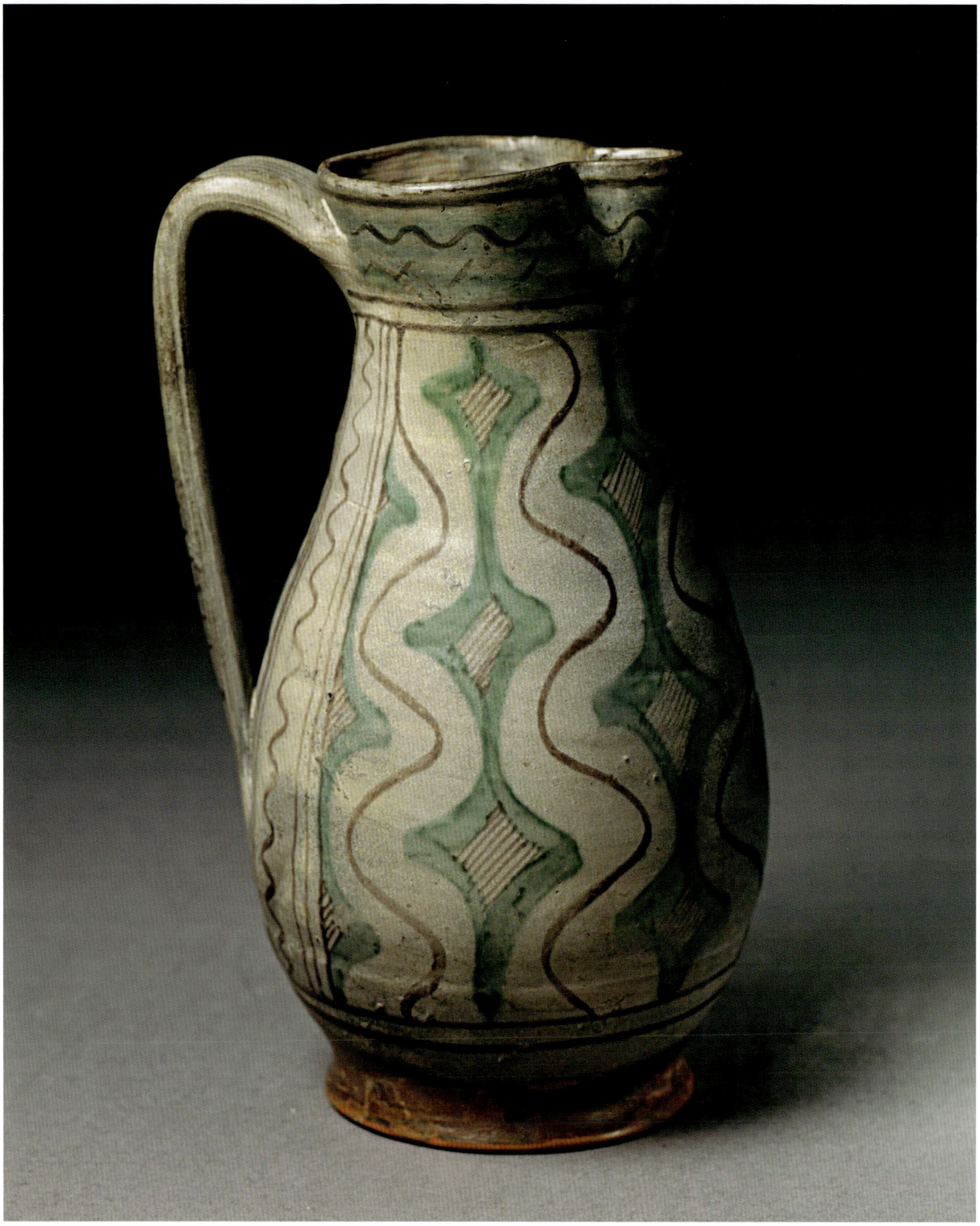

Tin-glazed earthenware jug painted in copper and manganese, late 14th or early 15th century, probably Tuscany

Height: 24.6 cm; diameter: 14.3 cm.

V&A Museum number: 1148-1904. In 1903, Wallis lent this jug, and others, to the museum for inspection. They were shown at the Museum Meeting on 7 July 1903 and were recommended for acceptance on loan.
Image courtesy of the V&A, London

In fact, Wallis sold his textiles to the South Kensington Museum – and not to the British Museum – as Timothy Wilson explains: "In 1886, Wallis offered for sale a collection of early textiles from Egypt. Thomas Armstrong, Director for Art, reported that the textiles were 'of the greatest interest as much from the decorative as from the archaeological point of view.' ... In accordance with South Kensington practice, a member of the Museum's team of art referees, the artist Lawrence Alma-Tadema, was asked for a second opinion. He reported that the textiles were from the Roman period, some Ptolemaic or Byzantine, and recommended the price as reasonable; whereupon the collection was bought for £300, forming the foundation of the Museum's extensive collection of these textiles."[14]

Two years later, Wallis gave the South Kensington Museum "6 illuminations in Coptic MSS and 4 Ancient Book cover", and in 1891 he offered to lend them a collection of Egyptian pottery.[15] In 1896, the museum offered him £200 for three Maiolica plates, which he accepted. In 1898, he proposed lending the museum his collection of early Italian pottery (vases, drug jars, etc.), which as Arthur Banks Skinner,[16] the Director of the V&A from 1905 to 1908, noted: "are of a very considerable interest as illustrations of the early wares – for the most part 15th century of Italy."

Wallis's biggest sale came in 1907, when he sold about fifty-six choice pieces of Spanish lustreware to the same museum for the huge sum of £3,000 (paid in two instalments).[17] A French dealer had asked Wallis to sell him his Spanish lustreware on behalf of Mr. Hillingdon, a Chicago collector. In his report to the Board of Education at South Kensington, the Chairman F.G. Ogilvie mentioned that "he [Wallis] had received the letter, but was quite agreeable to giving us the opportunity of acquiring the collection for £3,000."[18] It is worth mentioning that the transaction was finalized thanks to the favourable reports of Walter Crane, William Blake Richmond and Frederick DuCane Godman.[19]

Wallis's collection of decorative arts had become so valuable and important that he would lend pieces to major exhibitions. For the 1885 show of Arab and Persian art held at the Burlington Fine Arts Club "Wallis lent twenty-five pieces, covering the whole range of items exhibited: ceramic tiles and other specimens, specially classified lustreware, as well as metal work, ivory and carved wood, a rug and a manuscript page."[20] This was his first involvement in organising an exhibition for which he also wrote the catalogue. From this date onwards, he wrote extensively about Persian art, which had been his first area of research. The more he explored Egypt, however, the more his interest in Egyptian art became predominant. Because of Wallis's contacts with eminent scholars and archaeologists, he helped the Burlington Fine Arts Club, of which he was a member,[21] to organise an important exhibition, 'The Art of Ancient Egypt'. Professors Adolf Erman, Gaston Maspero and Flinders Petrie, the Rev. William MacGregor, the banker F.G. Hilton Price, and Henry Wallis made up the exhibition committee; all lent pieces from their own collections. This was a typical Victorian exhibition with encyclopedic ambitions. More than 1,900 pieces were on display – the majority of them obviously very small – of which Henry Wallis contributed more than 400, including vases and bowls, heads of statues, finger rings, *ushabtis*,[22] pectorals and more than fifty pottery specimens.

Wallis wrote the general introduction to the catalogue, pointing out that "in their forms

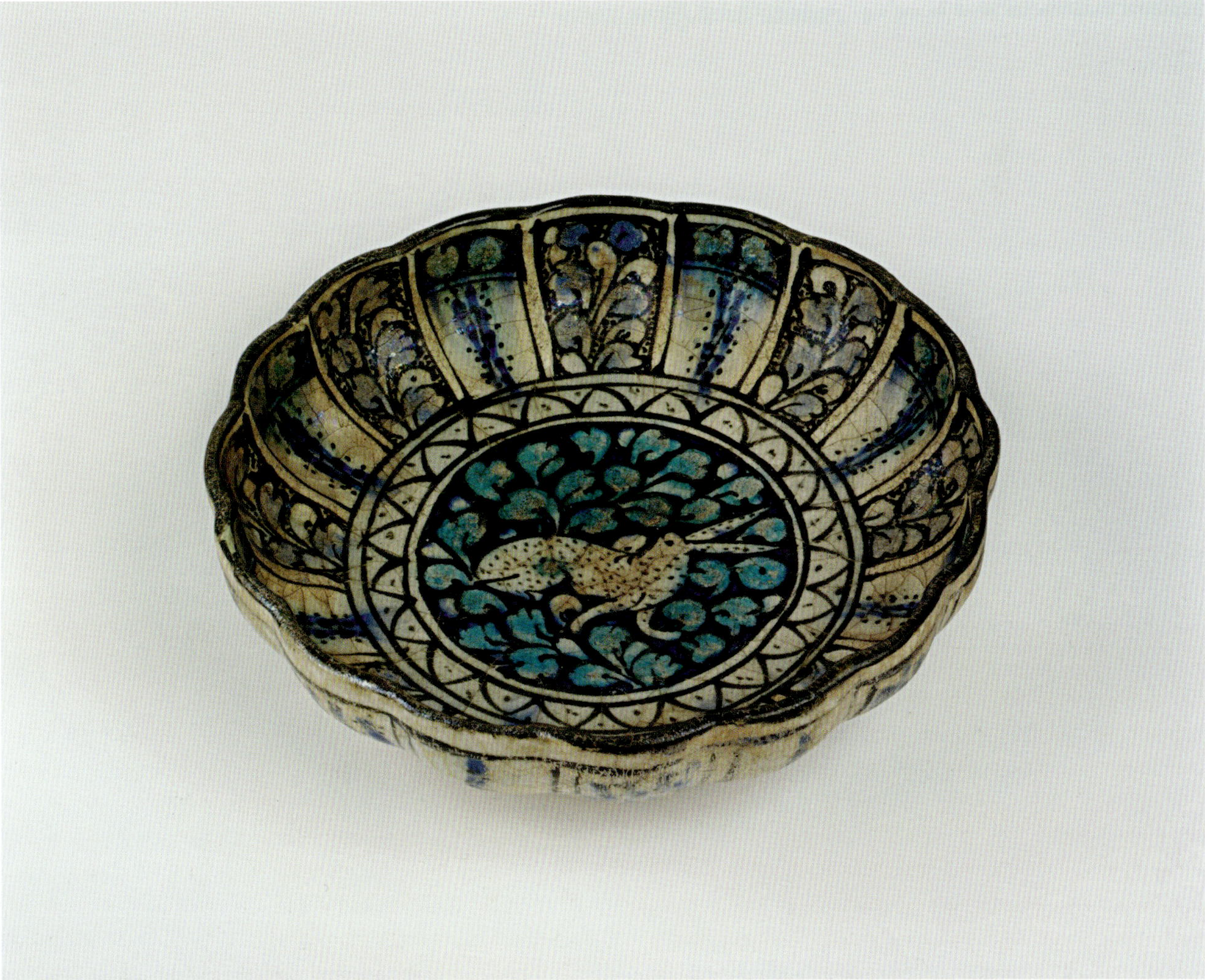

Fritware bowl of shallow form with lobed walls, on small foot with underglaze painting in black, blue and turquoise on a white slip, 1260-1350, Iran

Height: 5.4 cm; diameter: 17.7 cm.

V&A Museum number: c.414-1918. Formerly the property of Henry Wallis, father of the vendor [Harold Wallis], exhibited as a loan at the Museum in 1908-1911 and 1917 until the date of purchase in 1918
IMAGE COURTESY OF THE V&A, LONDON

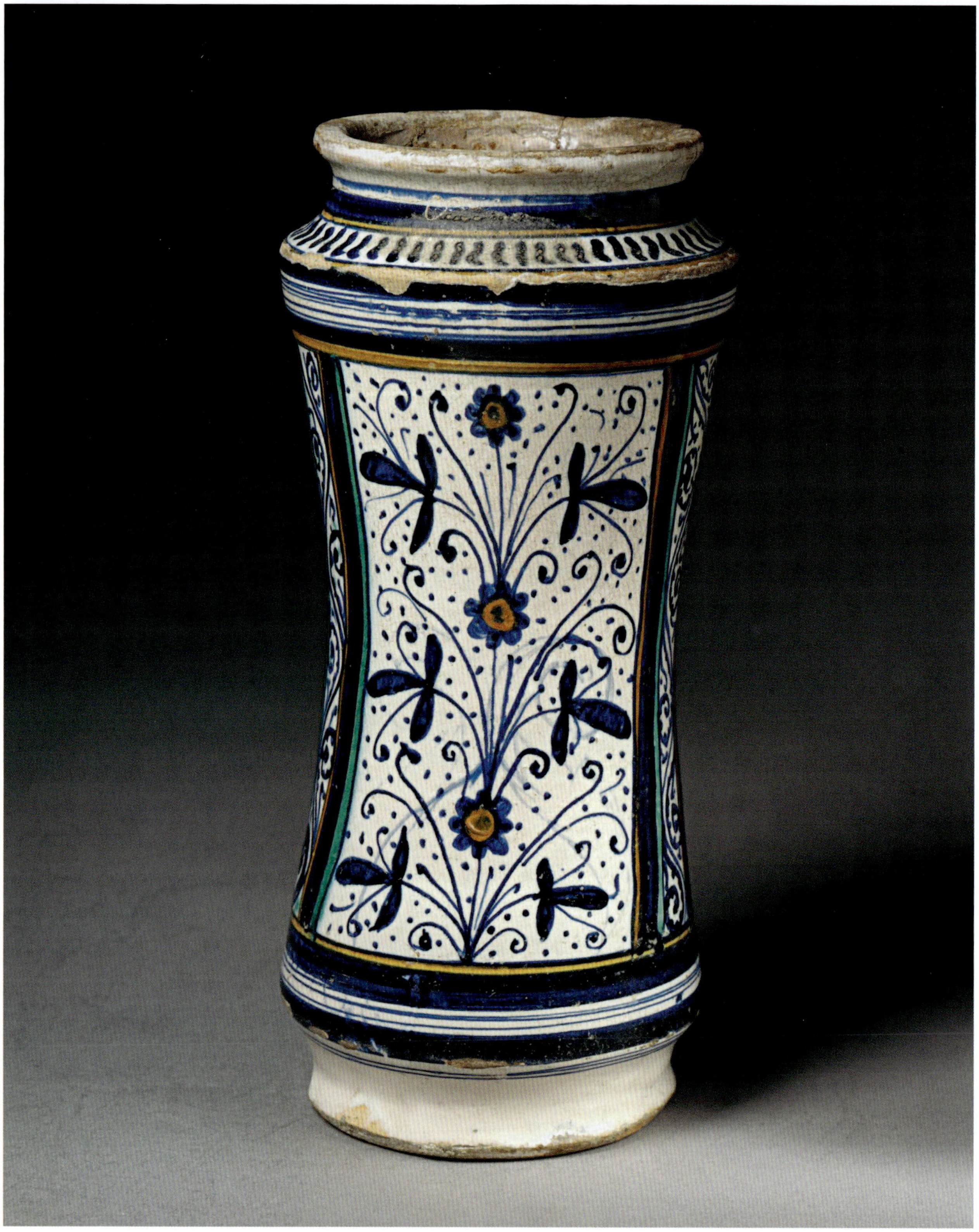

the artists aimed at elegance. Above all, their art was very human. They faithfully portray the husbandman at his labours, the artisan in his workshop, the scenes of the market place and the Nile navigation, banquets and funerals. Nothing was too high or too low for delineation by the dexterous and industrious chisels and pencils of the Egyptian sculptors and painters."[23]

With regards to the art of the Saitic period,[24] which was considered a kind of "Renaissance" in antiquity, Wallis stated that "admiration of the ancient art prompted the artists to attempt the imitation of its forms and style; the revival of its spirit was a more arduous undertaking – indeed, an impossible one. The eye as readily detects the difference between a *cinque cento* gem or bronze and a veritable antique, or a picture by Overbeck[25] and one by Perugino, as it does between a work of the time of Psametik and its prototype of the earlier dynasties."[26] As to reciprocal influences, Wallis's

Tin-glazed earthenware drug-jar (albarello), *c.*1480, Pesaro, Italy

Height: 30 cm; diameter: 13.5 cm.

V&A Museum number: 1126-1904. From Henry Wallis's collection, 1904
Image courtesy of the V&A, London

idea was that "Egypt has been the donor, not the recipient" and that "the influence of Egyptian art on that of the other great civilizations of antiquity can be traced in all directions".[27]

At first glance Wallis, unlike many of his artistic contemporaries, does not appear to have shown a great deal of interest in Chinese or Japanese earthenware, although several items had found a place in his collection. At one time Wallis had considered leaving his friend P.A. Daniel a bequest of two pieces of Chinese porcelain in his will. At a Bonhams sale on 5 March 2002 (lot 70), thirteen items of Oriental ceramics from Wallis's collection were sold, including Qianlong pieces with four- and six-character marks, as well as a pale-celadon water pot. How and when these items had been purchased is unknown, but it must have been through the numerous dealers with whom he was in contact.

There is no doubt, however, that Wallis's most lasting contribution to art is not just his own oeuvre – the paintings, watercolours and sketches – but the many books he wrote and lectures he gave on ancient ceramics, on which his contemporaries recognised him as an expert. *The Academy* called Wallis "the eminent connoisseur of lustre-ware". Thomas Kirby, in his catalogue of the Henry Marquand Collection, stated: "Mr. Henry Wallis, was probably the best living authority on Persian tiles."[28] The reviewer for *The Athenaeum*, in his review of Wallis's book on *Persian Ceramic Art belonging to Mr. F. D. Godman*, stated: "Mr. Wallis is so much in love with his subject, and he treats it with such artistic fervour, that we cannot do better than let him state his own case… 'It is the seeing eye that profits by seeing,' while the dull eye sees nothing at all. Mr. Wallis's criticisms on the more strictly technical charms of the curves and colouration which appeal to the aesthetic sense of artists like himself are such as every connoisseur

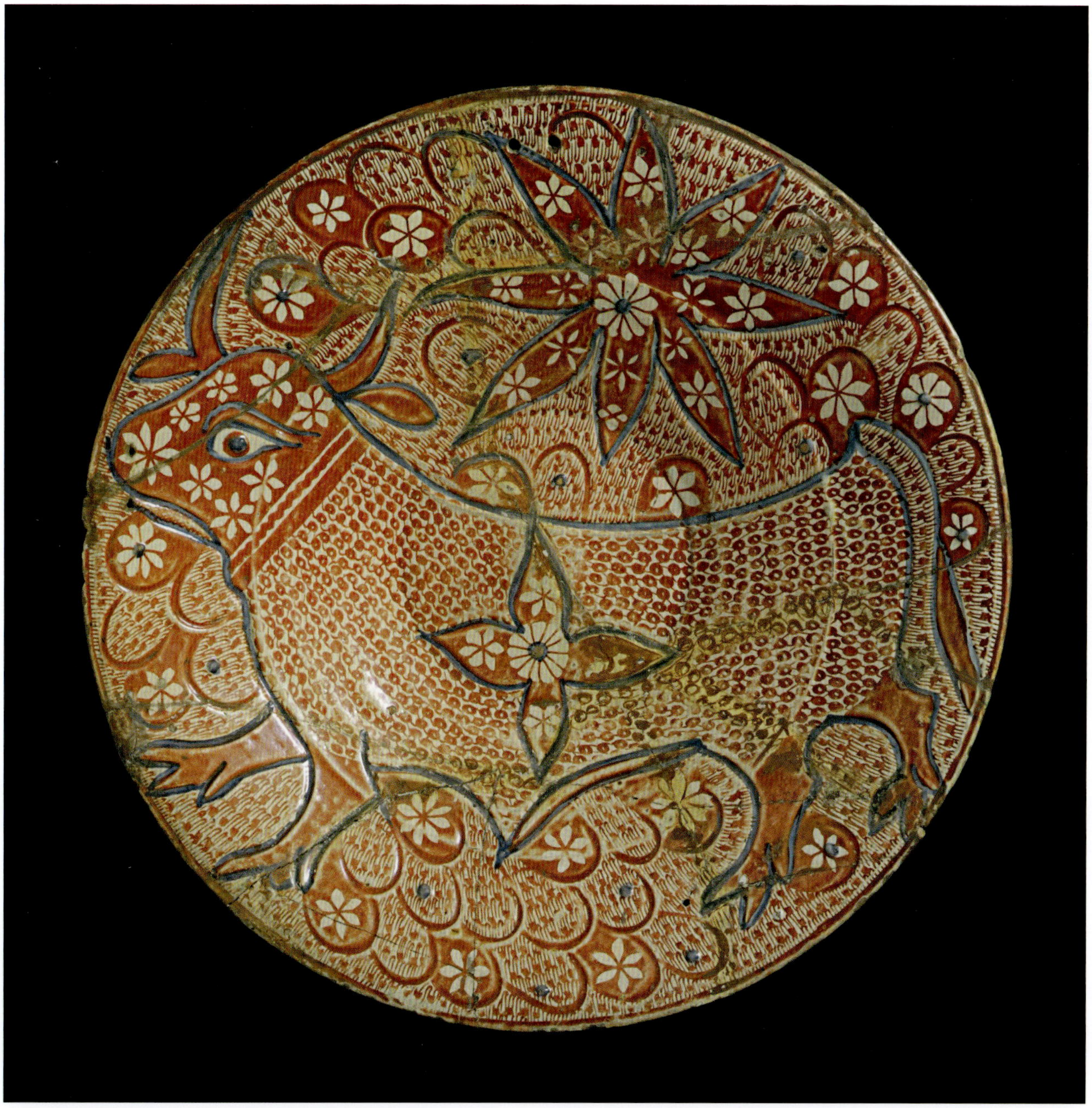

Tin-glazed earthenware dish with lustre decoration, *c.*1500, Manises, Spain

Height: 6.8 cm; diameter: 47.4 cm.

V&A Museum number: 16-1907. Purchased from Henry Wallis in 1907
IMAGE COURTESY OF THE V&A, LONDON

is sure to sympathize with and appreciate. His pages come to us as a revelation of a lost art, redolent of the romance and peculiar beauty of the East."[29] *The Times* when reviewing Wallis's book on Persian Ceramic Art noted: "In dealing with this branch of art the authority of Mr. Wallis is beyond dispute."[30] A number of artists within the Pre-Raphaelite circle collected ceramics, such as D.G. Rossetti and J.M. Whistler, with their collections of blue and white Japanese and Chinese porcelain. Frederic Leighton collected Islamic pottery from Iran, Turkey and Syria, and lined the famous Arab Hall in his house in Holland Park with rare tiles from the late 15th and early 16th cenuries, primarily from Damascus. Lawrence Alma-Tadema, William Holman Hunt,[31] and William Bell Scott[32] also collected ceramics. None, however, reached the same status of collector/ connoisseur when compared to Wallis.

After Wallis's death, the major part of his collection was split between the British Museum and the Victoria and Albert Museum, not without some quarrel, as Timothy Wilson has explained: "A final episode brought to the surface a long-submerged rivalry between the V&A and the British Museum. Among the items that had been on loan to the V&A and withdrawn in 1911 was a fifteenth-century Syrian vase which had long been coveted by Sir Hercules Read, Keeper of British and Mediaeval Antiquities at the British Museum. Read, who had known Wallis for nearly forty years, was by this time immensely grand - a knight and past President of the Society of Antiquaries - and claimed the right to buy it from Harold Wallis for the British Museum. Rackham [from the V&A] stuck to his guns, and Read withdrew, with an ill grace."[33] However, part of the collection remained in the family and in 1963 and 1964, Mary Elizabeth Aymes, Harold's daughter-in-law, donated a collection of antiquities to British Museum and Victoria and Albert Museum in memory of her husband Edwin Harold Wallis.

Wallis was an astute businessman and knew the exact value of the items of his collection. He also had become a shrewd and tough negotiator. In a letter to Charles Hercules Read, dated 2 December 1908, he wrote: "Before buying I sh^{ld} make a careful examination, but then it is always best wth the Italians to buy at once, not giving them an opportunity to consult other people or to communicate wth other w^{ld} be buyers."[34] Even his friend Wilhelm von Bode would be asked to pay for the items that were sent to the Berlin Museum: "Respecting the Persian plate, I sh^{ld} always be delighted to give you anything I c^{ld} for your collection, but when the object has to go to a public museum I am afraid one must look at it from a business point of view."[35] Wallis preferred to negotiate with the staff of museums, because he did not trust amateurs and self-proclaimed experts. It has to be said in his favour that he never tried to enrich himself in the process: "he rather wanted the objects themselves to be secured for the coming ages."[36]

With regard to Wallis's contacts with the London museums, it has already been pointed out that a large part of their collections of maiolica, textiles and Islamic pottery is due to him. He could not put up with endless negotiations, however. In 1910, for example, he offered to sell to the Victoria and Albert Museum two crates of eastern pottery and Italian majolica for £5,000, but the museum dragged on and he abruptly withdrew his offer. Confronted with the carelessness and the shambles at the South Kensington Museum (later the V&A), he could only agree with what William Morris had written to him on 11 March 1882: "I have just this moment come from the S.K.M. which I have found in its usual state of muddle: that museum is overburdened with articles & don't know where to put them, it is true that about one third of the articles are useless & ought to be destroyed, but even if that were done there would still not be room for a proper arrangement of what is left."[37]

Gadoin has summarised the importance of Wallis as a collector/connoisseur of Middle Eastern ceramics: "It is due to these vast perspectives opened by Victorian collectors that the history of Islamic art continues to gain interest. Wallis occupies pride of place in these discoveries. He played on several strings: he possessed not only the eye but also the expert hand of the artist. Not content to excel in the game of attribution, classification and dating, as that of 'connoisseur' in the noblest sense of the term, he also possessed rare qualities of images broadcaster, by his virtuosity as an illustrator. Finally, through his close contacts with the merchants, along with his lighthearted diplomacy, evident from reading his letters, he was an emissary in museums choices and that of major collectors. His career irrefutably shows that between dream and knowledge, there is no antithesis. We use the knowledge of what we first loved, fantasized, and in this progressive knowledge acquired, together with respectful investigation and the imperialistic posession seems to slowly disappear. But the love of art, united with the collector's passion of the acquisition, develops the knowledge that the West may have of the East – a necessarily subjective knowledge (in charge of the affect of the amateur) and at the same time objective (probing the objects)."[38]

Lustred vase after Henry Wallis, c. 1889, chromolithograph on paper, plate taken from *Notes on some Examples of Early Persian Lustre Ware*, published by W. Griggs, London, in 1889. (William Griggs (1832-1911) was the inventor of photo-chromo-lithography.) This vase was later reproduced in black and white as fig. 3, p. 1, in *Persian Ceramic Art in the Collection of Mr. F. DuCane Godman, F.R.S. The Thirteenth Century Lustred Vases*, 1891.
IMAGE COURTESY OF THE DENNIS LANIGAN COLLECTION

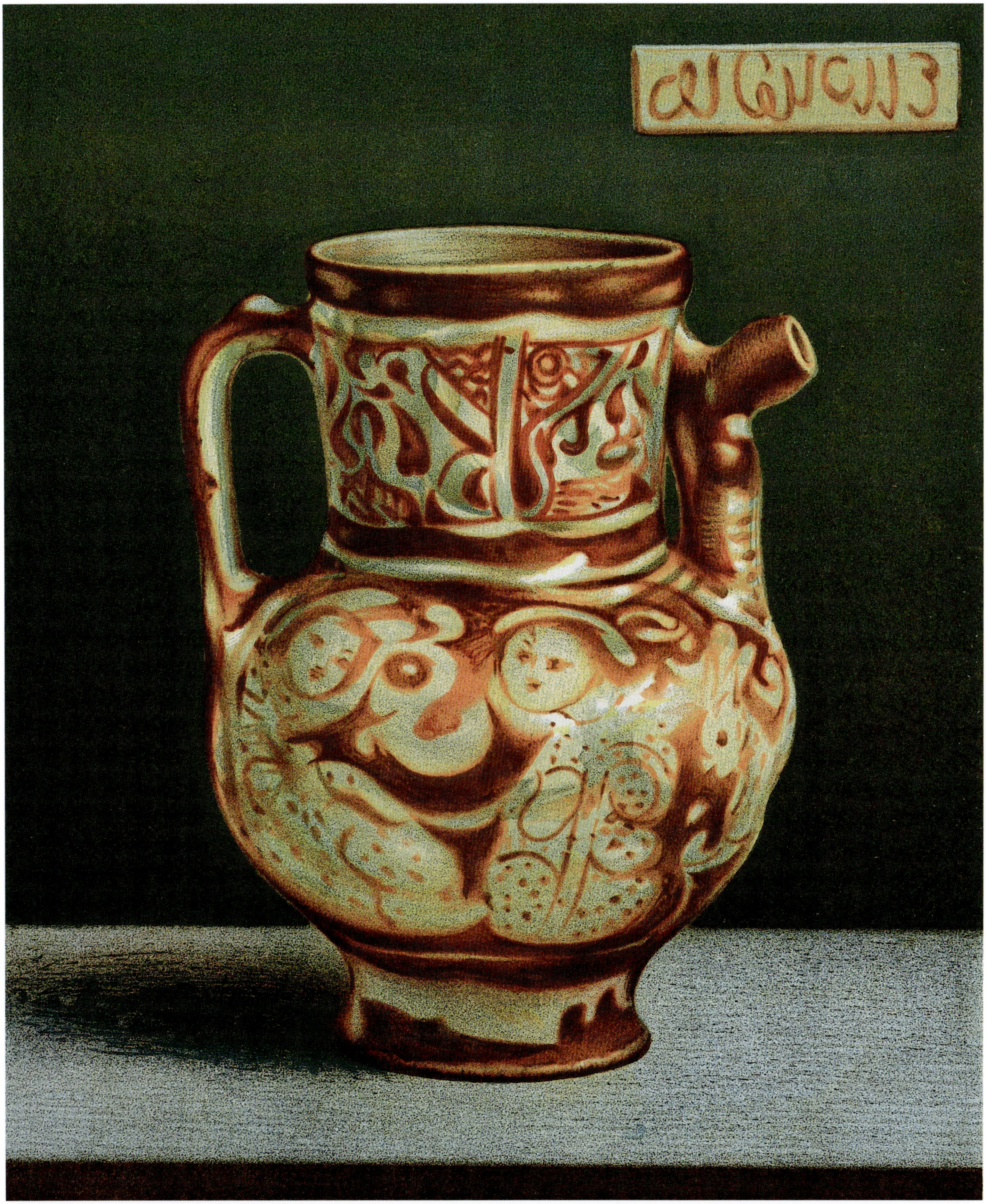

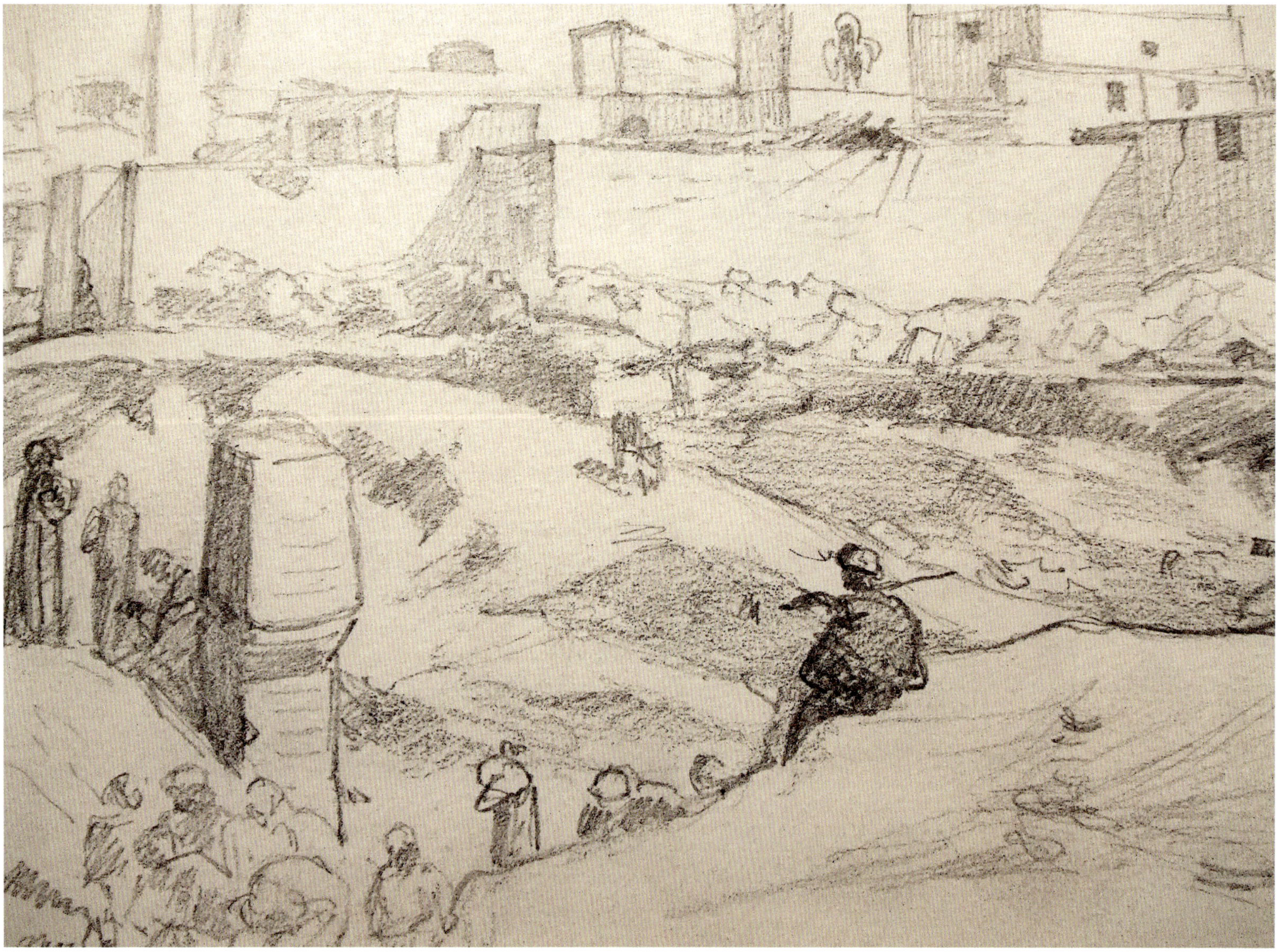

Chapter Nine
PROTECTION OF ANCIENT BUILDINGS

From 1879 onward, Wallis joined William Morris in his defense of ancient buildings. Morris was a leading figure within the Society for the Protection of Ancient Buildings (SPAB) founded two years earlier, whose original role was to preserve the buildings important to British heritage. One of Morris's early campaigns, however, concerned what he considered a disastrous restoration of St Mark's, Venice. Convinced as he was of British superiority in the care of ancient buildings and of the carelessness of the Italian authorities, Morris had formed an International Committee for the Preservation of the Basilica of St Mark.[1] Wallis as Honorary Secretary of the committee wrote a spirited letter about the "scandalous" restoration of St. Mark's to the editor of *The Times*, published on 8 November 1879. Morris then sent memoranda to the Italian Ministry of Public Works, although the work on St Mark's was actually supervised by the Ministry of Public Instruction.[2] He even asked

Excavating in Egypt [Cat. 316], February 1886, from Wallis's sketchbooks
Image by permission of the Bodleian Libraries, University of Oxford (MS. Eng. e. 3418, fol. 14r)

British Members of Parliament to intervene. As Fiona MacCarthy has pointed out: "In pursuing his campaigns Morris shows perhaps surprising purist narrowness, attacking individual work and naming names, castigating the restoring architects with a zealousness that verges on the cruel."[3]

The Italians, shocked at this humiliating attack, reacted agressively but, nevertheless, postponed the work. This unforeseen but natural reaction forced Morris to show more diplomacy in his official requests, although in private he and Wallis were less guarded in their comments.[4] Other problems that Wallis brought to the attention of Italian authorities were the state of the Baptistery of Ravenna, particularly the interior mosaic decorations, and the proposed restoration of the chapel painted by Melozzo da Forlì in the church of San Girolamo at Forlì.[5]

Wallis was also involved in the protection of the Egyptian monuments. On 8 August 1888, a meeting was held at Edward Poynter's house. In attendance were the painters Lawrence Alma-Tadema, Frank Dillon, and Henry Wallis, Sir Frederick Burton, the Head of the National Gallery, Wallis Budge, Keeper at the British Museum, as well as Flinders Petrie. They decided to create a Society for the Preservation of the Monuments of Ancient Egypt[6] and to give effective support to the Egyptian authorities by suggesting the appointment of appropriate guardians and custodians. Poynter and Wallis were to act as secretaries. Among the early members of the society were Lord Wharncliffe, Frederic Leighton, Thomas Armstrong, Sidney Colvin, William Holman Hunt, Edward Burne-Jones, George Frederic Watts and Sir Henry Layard (excavator of Nimrud). The members repeatedly criticised the Egyptian authorities for their shortcomings and, leaving aside the paternalistic mentality of those times, such criticism seems justified. One only needs to look at ancient photographs to realize that nothing was being done to protect, let alone to restore, Egypt's ancient buildings. As Flinders Petrie pointed out: "It is sickening to see the rate at which everything is being destroyed, and the little regard paid to its preservation – Nothing seems to be done with any uniform and regular plan; work is begun and left unfinished."[7] At a meeting of the Society held on 14 March 1890 the following resolution, proposed by Henry Wallis and with an amendment by General Brackenbury, was passed: "That this meeting has heard with feelings of profound grief and dismay the account of the recent wanton mutilation of the ancient monuments at Beni Hassan, Tel-el-Amarna, and El-Bersheh, in Upper Egypt – a disaster, as Prof. Sayce truly observes, exceeding all that has befallen the remains of Egyptian art during the past half-century; and that this meeting earnestly hopes that the Egyptian Government will take steps for the appointment of an efficient staff for the custody and inspection of important monuments, to prevent acts of this nature being again committed."[8]

Wallis had crossed Egypt several times since 1885 and, as a scholar and a collector, he could offer an expert opinion on this matter. In the 1890 issue of *The Nineteenth Century*, he published an article on the 'Destruction of Egyptian Monuments', in which he set out the reasons for the dilapidated state of the monuments. He stated that the usual scapegoat was the tourist, which he considered unrealistic. In his opinion, the tourists may sometimes have scattered the leftovers of their luncheon, but as to carving names and graffiti, some of the ones remaining dated back to Napoleon's expedition of 1798-1801 and were still clearly visible as far as Philae.

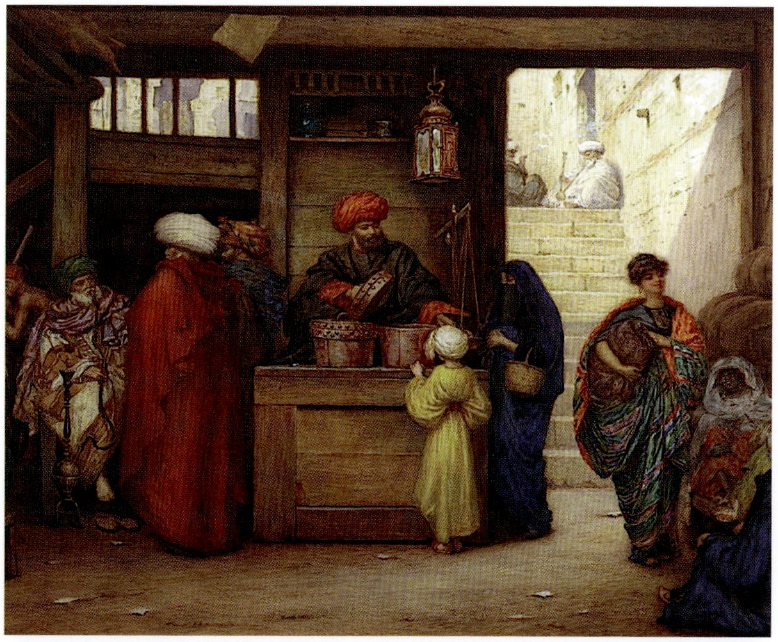

Henry Wallis, *The Pharmacy* [Cat. 262], *c.*1885-1905
PRIVATE COLLECTION. IMAGE COURTESY OF MATHAF GALLERY, LONDON

More important motives for the continued destruction were fanaticism and plunder, which had started with the edict of Theodosius establishing Christianity (AD 391) and worsened with the Arab conquest (AD 641). How great the devastation had been can be judged at Thebes, where only a few stones remained, and at Assiout, where walls had simply disappeared. A third cause to take into account is, or was, the zeal of the Egyptologists, who have too often left tombs and temples to the mercy of the elements. And "acts such as Mariette's employment of gunpowder in his excavations at the Pyramids, were inexcusable."[9] Last, but not least, preventive measures had never been undertaken by the Egyptian authorities: "The large majority of the monuments are unfenced; works of reparation are almost entirely neglected; there is neither inspector nor architect, but the inspection is supposed to be performed by the director of the national museum, an Egyptologist, who is expected to make an annual journey up the Nile, starting from his residence at Cairo. This arrangement has, during the past few years, been entirely ineffectual in preserving the monuments."[10]

This last point was particularly essential to Wallis, as he expressed in a typical Victorian Imperialist fashion in many letters. To Harold, in 1893, after a visit to Luxor, he complained that: "The native Egyptians, not one of whom, from the highest to the lowest, would stir a finger or spend a piaster to save any monument of their ancestors ancient or Mediaeval."[11] "The state of the monuments is, I am sorry to say, much worse than when I was here 3 years since."[12]

A memorandum was handed over to the Foreign Office, who asked the Antiquities Service to levy a charge of 100 piastres on each tourist, and to put the money aside in order to restore the tombs at Thebes. This was a good start but when the Society complained about the museum being moved from Bulaq to Gizeh, Sir Colin Scott-Moncrieff[13] blocked the memorandum and told them that the new museum was perfectly suited.

The second objective of the Society was to appoint a British inspector who would control the monuments and propose the necessary repairs. Confronted with the reluctance of the French, who had been in charge of the Antiquities Department since the time of Mariette, Flinders Petrie proposed to appoint one at their own expense. However, as they failed to come to a unanimous decision, it was proposed to devote the money they had raised to the restoration of the temple at Karnak. Flinders Petrie was so disgusted that he resigned and tried independently to appoint a private inspector.[14]

Another thorny point on the agenda was the use to be made of newly discovered items. Grébaut, the Antiquities Director, declared: "Il y aura partage des antiquités après prélèvement des pieces uniques au profit du Musée [de Boulaq]." [The antiques will be split once the unique items have been set aside in favour of the Bulaq Museum.][15] The problem, of course, was that it was not clear what was to be considered as "pièces uniques", because in Egyptology everything was unique. For the sake of good relations with France, a compromise was reached: the Museum would take possession of "unique" pieces; the discoverers would offer half of the remaining items to their own museums and publish the outcome of their research within the two following years.

Chapter Ten
WALLIS – THE MAN

Although Wallis was quite opiniated about art and politics, he was very much a man of his time and, following social convention, rarely spoke about his emotions; when he wrote to say he was sorry about a friend's death, it often sounded somewhat impersonal and dry. Only at his mother's death in February 1873 did he show some emotion in a letter to his friend Frederic Gard Fleay: "I have had trouble lately. I have lost my poor mother who died of bronchitis last month. She had been ailing all the winter & some severe weather we had more than a month since brought on an attack from wch she had not strength to rally. This is one of the trials which we feel the most – certainly I feel it so. Altogether we have been depressed lately. So many people one knows have been ill."[1]

A close study of Wallis's letters reveals him to have been a lonely man. Indeed, it is striking to note that, after his affair with Mary Ellen ended and after her death in 1861, he never mentions a new relationship, either to his son or to his friends.

As stated before (see Chapter Five), Joukovsky hypothesises that Wallis might have been homosexual.[2] Some details of his life might support that conclusion, such as his tender words about his friend Hotchkiss,[3] whom he remembered years after his death in Sicily. Alfred Tennyson, however, never completely got over the death of his beloved friend Arthur Hallam in 1833, for whom he wrote his poem "In Memoriam", published in 1850, and yet no one would suggest that Tennyson might be homosexual on this basis. Some of the works Wallis painted in the 1870s, largely inspired by the standard of masculine beauty in Carpaccio, and especially the more erotic masculine protagonists in Luca Signorelli's works, could possibly lend weight to the argument. Wallis was certainly not the only Victorian artist who remained unmarried to have his sexuality questioned: some scholars have suggested the same about Frederic Leighton, although recent evidence has thrown cold water on this theory.[4] It is equally possible, however, that Wallis remained a bachelor simply because he never fully recovered from the failure of his relationship with Mary Ellen Meredith.

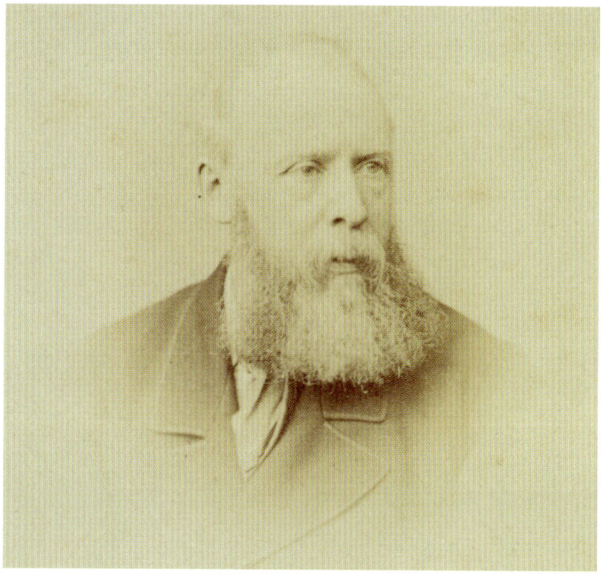

Henry Wallis
Cabinet photo
Image by permission of the Bodleian Libraries, University of Oxford

The Friend

Despite the lack of close personal relationships, Wallis maintained several friendships throughout his life (see Chapter Four). William Michael Rossetti wrote that Wallis was "a very agreeable companion, of solid character and open mind."[5]

His friendship with Fred and Clare Stephens was an intense and lasting one.[6] Stephens, who became an art critic and art historian, entered the Royal Academy Schools on 13 January 1844 at the early age of sixteen; he had probably left by the time Wallis entered. Wallis probably first made his acquaintance at about the same time that he met the Rossettis.

Stephens became the art critic for *The Athenaeum* and in the 1870s they exchanged letters on art matters and travelled together to review exhibitions. Wallis greatly benefitted from this friendship as Stephens seldom failed to review Wallis's contributions to exhibitions. His comments on Wallis's works were for the most part favourable, though he did not hesitate to criticize his friend if he thought the work required it (see Cats. 181, 188 and 189, for example). In December 1874, Wallis and Stephens travelled to Paris to review the Salon.[7] In April and May 1878, Wallis replaced Stephens, who was ill, to review the Paris Exposition Universelle.

At a time when Stephens felt uncomfortable at *The Athenaeum*, and was trying to find an alternative or additional income, Wallis, who had set up a network of correspondents and potential patrons, did his utmost to be supportive to his friend. In letters dated 17 June 1884, Wallis wrote: "Of course if you want to make more money & are sure you can

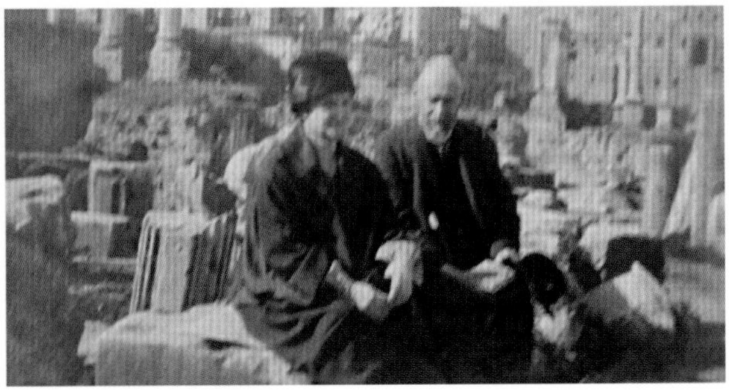

Above:
Wallis with an unknown lady (possibly the wife of a travelling companion or his daughter-in-law) at the *Foro Romano*, Rome, March(?) 1901; the date is mentioned in one of Wallis's sketchbooks (University of Oxford, Bodleian Library, MS Eng.e.3422). Wallis also visited Rome in 1903 and 1908.
Image by permission of the Bodleian Libraries, University of Oxford, MS Photogr.150, fol.30

by giving it up, why do so. But think carefully. I sh^{ld} say stick to the certainty. Let them have their way – wch will give you more time for other things – don't try to force even reviews on them. My belief is that they will like you better the less space you take even for Art matters. … – avoid slips – verify facts, & thus you will secure your position.

I don't at all agree that an article in a weekly is more valuable than a quarterly – or even monthly – even if read by 100 against 10, because the weekly is quickly thrown aside while the other remains on the table & is referred to. Then the quarterly, seen from a certain position, is not bad pay either.

As to getting that work I sh^{ld} fancy you w^{ld} not have much difficulty if you went the right way to work.

If you see any way in wch I can say a word to Maccoll point it out & I will find the opportunity.[8]

There is another alternative in the literary way if you don't care for review articles, write a book on some good subject. We might, just as well produce our own Art literature as have it translated – though you folk who have been so hard at work to thrust foreign Art on the British Public have the satisfaction of knowing that along wth the pictures have come the books."[9]

A few months later, Wallis insisted on introducing Stephens to the editor of a Berlin art journal: "The editor of a Berlin Journal has applied to me to write for him on modern English art. It is not in my line to do this except to help a friend or an emergency, or on some casual occasion. But it comes in the course of your regular business. Shall I give him your address & recommend him to apply to you? There is a very intelligent public in Berlin that it w^{ld} be a pleasure to write for. If you send me a reply by return to the Burlington F. A. Club, Savile Row, I expect to be there in the afternoon & w^{ld} write to Berlin at once."[10]

Stephens was conservative in art matters and detested Impressionism, which marked him as a man who was out of touch with his times – just like Wallis. In 1901, after forty years, Stephens's association with *The Athenaeum* came to an end and he was replaced by Roger Fry. It has been suggested that he was "dismissed because he wrote so badly."[11] Dianne S. Macleod also reports that Stephens's rival on *The Saturday Review*, Harry Quilter accused Stephens of inventing "a series of phrases to apply to pictures, painters and art subjects in general, which are absolutely excruciating in their combination of uselessness, affectation, and incomprehensibility."[12] Whatever the reason, Wallis remained the loyal friend and sought to comfort him: "I was sorry to hear though y^{r} account of the Ath: business. It is a matter in wch you can naturally do nothing, except take it philosophically – wch you will. One hears constantly the same thing happening to people writing for the press. Perhaps you may be considered fortunate in holding on so long to one Journal. I suppose you have already got similar work on another journal – perhaps better remuneration on one of [the] dailies. If you have not yet I sh^{ld} say y^{r} ability & experience will soon get you the place if you go the right way to work."[13]

The Victorian Man

In matters of emancipation, Wallis held the same opinions as most Victorian conservative gentlemen, which by modern standards, appears strikingly misogynistic. In December 1890, while he was in Cairo, something had happened at his home, and he wrote to his son: "My dear Felix. I am very concerned at the news in y^{r} letter of the 5th & very grieved that you sh^{ld} have had all this trouble in such bad weather. ... I suppose this sort of thing is only what is to be expected of women. To attempt to account for such conduct is waste of time. As to characters, all given by women are lies."[14]

Correspondence from later in his life, reveals Wallis to have been imperialist and anti-democratic, who showed little sympathy towards the ordinary population, the "vile crew"[15] as he called them, and even extolling the advantage of a strong leader.

Being a wealthy man, Wallis was not ready to accept socialism, and he made that clear in a letter to Harold, sent from Bologna and dated 1 December 1903: "I sh^{ld} have stayed 2 or 3 days but the Socialist Municipality has sealed up the Museum. My old friend Frati[16] (to whom I inscribed the Title Vol:) was the head Librarian. He died about a couple of years ago & this place is supplied by a distributore, a messenger! … The Socialists here show themselves in their true colours. What w^{ld} the idiots in England who play at Socialism say?"[17] These views would most certainly have put him at odds with his friend William Morris. Wallis was typical of the Victorian bourgeoisie and many of his letters to his son Harold show him more anxious about the stock exchange than the awful conditions in which the poor lived. No changes should be made to the world order established by a God in whom he did not appear to believe.

That is not to say, however, that Wallis was without sympathy towards the misfortune of others. When confronted with catastrophic events, such as the Messina earthquake of 28 December, 1908 that claimed over 100,000 lives, Wallis was

Opposite top:
Wallis at home, probably at no. 9 Beauchamp Road, Upper Norwood, *c.*1900
Image by permission of the Bodleian Libraries, University of Oxford, MS Photogr.150, fol.31

deeply touched. The day after the earthquake, he wrote to his son: "You will have got my letter posted yesterday stating that I was on the point of embarking for Messina. We arrived this morning & found the city destroyed by earthquake & the ruins burning.[18] It appears that the shock came at about 6 o'c. yesterday morning & communication was at once cut off, so that at Naples it was not known what had happened, although the news reached Naples, just as we were starting, of the destruction of cities in Calabria. In fact a man thrust a newspaper into my hand in the street, but I did not look at it till the evening. The destruction here is terrible, scarcely any house has escaped. In many places there are nothing but heaps of ruins, in others the walls are partly standing. The loss of life must have been very great but of course, the numbers stated are much lesser. This boat was going to Constantinople but it was at once seen that the Sicilian passengers c^ld^ not be landed, as there was no place to stay there. The railway is supposed to be damaged so the boat returns to Naples at 5 this afternoon. The captain sent provisions on shore & is taking as many people as can be stowed away between decks, taking them gratis to Naples. A few passengers have come on board, the German Consul & others, & the [...] terrible. One poor lady, the wife of the German Clergyman has just been brought on board, her 3 weeks baby was sleeping at her side. The floor fell whereby the baby was killed, the mother had a leg broken & a bad wound in the body. I shall post this tomorrow morning, & will also wire. As to my future plans I must wait till I get to Naples."[19]

In a letter from Naples to Charles Hercules Read, 30 December 1908, Wallis writes: "My course has been rather erratic lately, but today I reached here from Messina, having gone there on Monday even^g^; not knowing that the earthquake had destroyed the city on Monday morning at 5.30. I found the city, wch I knew so well, a heap of ruins, on fire from one end to the other. In places the buildings had fallen into the streets, blocking them up. Everywhere were mounds, from some of wch they had already begun to dig out the dead. It was said that the soldiers had been buried in their barracks, so an English man of war landed the marines & blue jackets to act as police...The spectacle was truly horrible and it will be long before I can get it out of my sight..."[20]

The Imperialist

For a traveller like Wallis, the concept of Empire was a reality and, he was in no doubt that the "barbarians" needed to be educated.[21] While he admired the pottery of ancient Egypt, he despised modern Egypt and her inhabitants, who were doing nothing to save their heritage. Wallis's opinions echoed well Edward Said's statement: "The relationship between Occident and Orient is a relationship of power, domination, of varying degrees of a complex hegemony."[22]

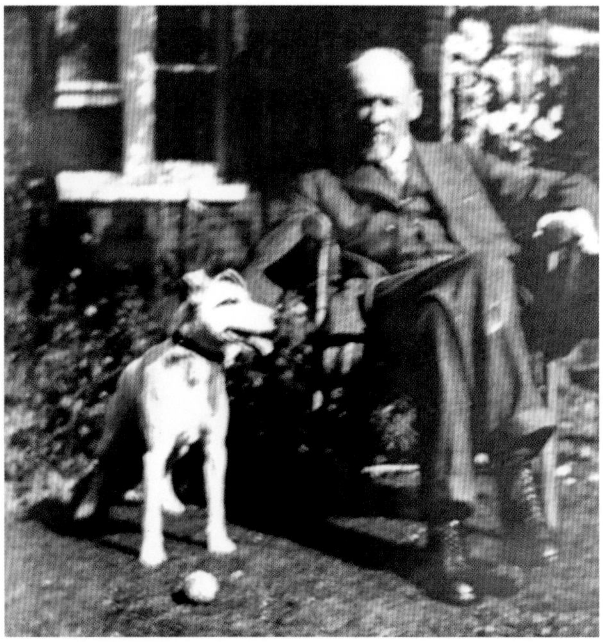

Indeed, rather than broadening Wallis's outlook and lending him an air of the cosmopolitan traveller, his journeys through the British Empire seem only to have affirmed his opinion that the British way was not only the *best*, but also the *only* acceptable way of life.

He often castigated French interference and he despised Gladstone, whom he had come to view as his personal enemy. An example of his imperialist views may be found in a letter to Frederic George Stephens, dated December 1895: "If the Italians w^ld^ only clear themselves of foreign influence, I think they w^ld^ take the first place in Europe. They have a natural artistic faculty such as is not found elsewhere, but after the centuries of repression time must be given them to recover lost ground. In all directions the revival of Italy is marvellous. The change since I first remember the country as a youth seems far greater than elsewhere. As to their future, the eastern part of the Mediterranean sh^ld^ be theirs & perhaps more. Theirs is the alliance we ought to cultivate & happily the intelligence of both countries clearly discerns where the true interest of each lie. If in the partition of Turkey we c^ld^ only help Italy to regain her old position at Constantinople we sh^ld^ be doing a wise thing. The Greeks as a governing race are hopeless, so also the people of the Balkan states."[23]

Wallis lived long enough to witness the beginning of the Great War. On Christmas Day 1914, he wrote to his son: "Thanks for your good wishes, & the same to Alice & Violet. But with all this savagery going on it seems rather a mockery to talk of the Christmas tide as it was understood in the days of Charles Dickens."[24]

On 20 December 1916, with The War still waging, Wallis, by now almost blind, died at home from cerebral thrombosis. He was buried at Highgate Cemetery.[25]

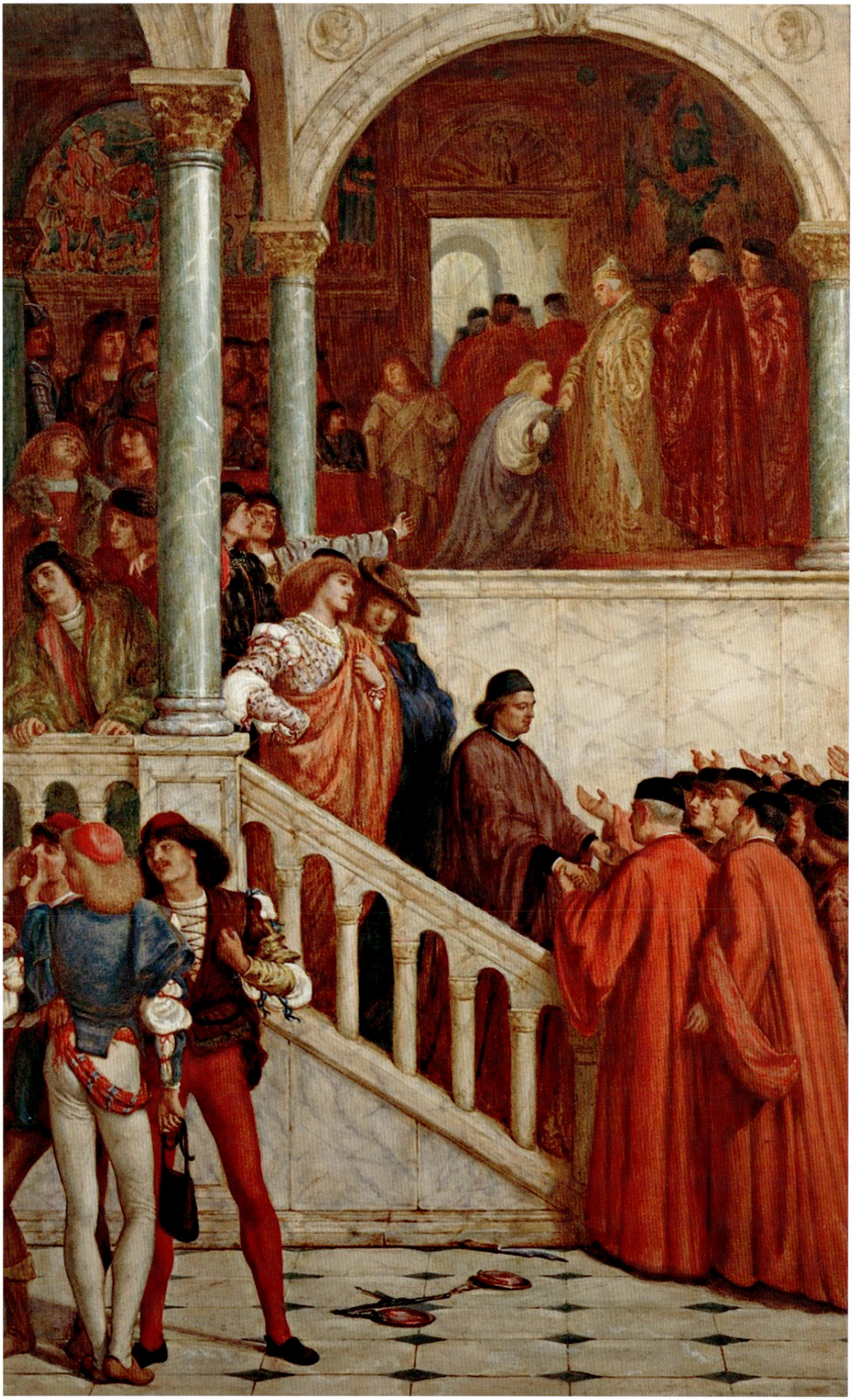

Henry Wallis, *After the Trial: Antonio receiving the Congratulations of his Friends (Antonio is released from Shylock's bond)* [Cat.125], *c.*1879
IMAGE COURTESY OF BONHAMS, LONDON

Chapter Eleven
WALLIS – THE ARTIST

As an artist Wallis was active during "The Restless Century",[1] of which Jeremy Maas gave the following overview: "During Queen Victoria's reign, the history of painting in England becomes an infinitely complex skein of extraordinary richness and variety. There were contradictions, movements and counter-movements; endless and labyrinthine courses were explored, false gods pursued; and a quantity of abysmal work was produced. It was nevertheless a great age for English painting. If the period produced few artists of world stature, this was balanced by the cumulative effect of the rich diversity of high talent, occasionally bordering on greatness. If the parts are sometimes leaden, the whole is a bright golden glow. This is nowhere more obvious than in the case of the Pre-Raphaelites: seen in isolation, the work of individual artists often appears maladroit, but grouped together their brilliance is manifest, and their very failings are forgiven in the way that one condones the eccentricities of genius."[2]

The Pre-Raphaelite

Wallis knew and was friends with most of the Pre-Raphaelites. He followed the path of the first phase of Pre-Raphaelitism during the 1850s and 1860s and adopted their painting techniques, although his chosen subjects tended to be taken from historical and literary figures. "The Pre-Raphaelites painted in bright strident colours, building up each form in thin layers with small brushes. This created a discordant equality of focus that represented an audacious departure from the hallowed practice of blending colours within a hierarchically organised composition where incidental features were subordinate to the main point of pictorial interest."[3] Paintings such as *Chatterton* [Cat. 22], *Dr Johnson at Cave's, the Publisher* [Cat. 10] and *A Sculptor's Workshop, Stratford-upon-Avon, A.D. 1617* [Cat. 25] are good examples of this. In his early works in oil, such as *Chatterton* or *Montaigne* [Cat. 26], Fleming has noted that "Wallis's forte was clearly the representation of light and

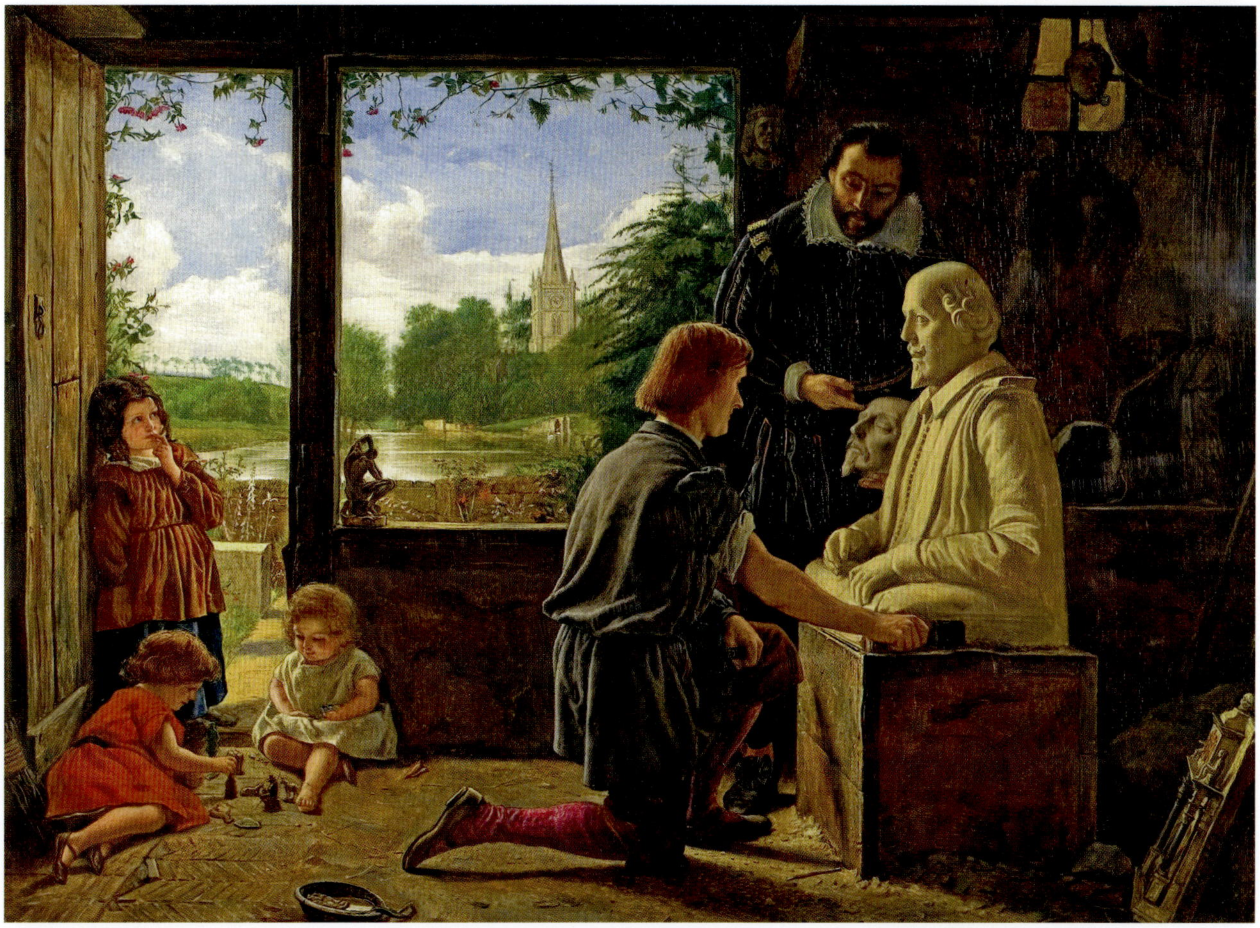

Henry Wallis, *A Sculptor's Workshop, Stratford-upon-Avon,* AD *1617* [Cat. 25a], 1857
Image by permission of Royal Shakespeare Company Collection, Stratford-upon-Avon/Bridgeman Images

shade."[4] This may have been fostered by Wallis's fondness for Dutch "Golden Age" painting. Wallis was also somewhat avant-garde as a colourist. For instance, he used blue shadows, presumably influenced by his Pre-Raphaelite colleagues. In his early works, Wallis has a penchant for interiors with views through windows. This might indicate the influence of Flemish art but also certainly that of the Pre-Raphaelites. Many early Pre-Raphaelite pictures have figures contained within a flat foreground space, occupying most of the picture plane; and distant landscapes visible in the background, were a standard compositional device. Their compositions were frequently flattened, producing pictures with little sense of depth. The device of a window allowed them to create a distant background without having to make the traditional middle-ground transition between it and the foreground plane.

Wallis was obviously aware of the changes taking place during the second phase of Pre-Raphaelitism and he adopted their ideas in his one work on an Arthurian theme, *Elaine* [Cat. 44] of 1861, and possibly also in his *Childe Roland to the Dark Tower Came* [Cat. 63], *c.*1868. In the early 1870s Wallis exhibited works dealing with social realism, such as *A January Morning* [Cat. 69], and Academic classicism, such as *Marsya*s [Cat. 68]. In the 1870s, his work also fell under the influence of Italian Renaissance painting, as was the case with many of the Pre-Raphaelite artists. In Wallis's Venetian-inspired paintings, however, such as *A Despatch from Trebizond* [Cat. 95] of 1873 or *Found at Naxos* [Cat. 97] of 1874, there is still very much of a "story telling" component to his works, rather than the "subjectless" manner of Aesthetic Movement painters like Burne-Jones, Solomon, or Prinsep. The closest Wallis comes to this is in the oil sketch of *Nude and Draped Figures* [Cat. 73] in the collection of Birmingham Museums and Art Gallery and, in particular, his *Pastorale* [Cat. 170] of 1883. Unfortunately, because the whereabouts of much of Wallis's oeuvre remains unlocated, it is not possible to judge whether he might have shown Aesthetic tendencies in his handling of such works as *Xarifa* [Cat. 36], 1859, or his female head studies like *Teresa* [Cat. 81], 1870, or *Assunta* [Cat. 87], 1871.

Wallis was a regular exhibitor at the Royal Academy, although it was not unusual for him to exhibit at other societies or galleries, especially once opposition to the Academy grew among his friends and colleagues. However, as he travelled more and more – first to Italy, then to Egypt – it appeared that watercolour painting was far more convenient to his purpose. This transition was also a natural one, for watercolour was regarded from the late eighteenth century as a peculiarly British medium.

The Watercolourist

In watercolour, a transparent dark colour is placed over a light one ('glazing') and the paper will still act as an illuminant. It was also not uncommon to cover parts of the work with bodycolour, as was often the case in Wallis's works. Wallis was not adverse to this Pre-Raphaelite tendency to make watercolours mimic oil paintings. The critic for *The Times* noted how his pictures exhibited at the Old Water-Colour Society were "set apart from the other work in the room by the depth and glow of its colour. Mr. Wallis evidently has no intention of allowing watercolour to remain at a disadvantage as compared with oils in these qualities."[5]

While he produced only a limited quantity of oil paintings, Wallis's watercolours must have been numerous and many are now untraced. He became an associate member of the Old Water-Colour Society (Society of Painters in Water Colours) in 1878, and a full member two years later, where he generally exhibited twice a year. Unfortunately, only a small number of these watercolours have appeared at public auctions and it is probable that we will never have a clear overview of his complete oeuvre. There can be no doubt, however, that Wallis was considered one of the most important members of the Old Water-Colour Society. In 1886, the Council on Education appointed a committee under the chairmanship of Frederic Leighton to consider the action of light upon watercolour drawings; Wallis was one of two members selected from the Old Water-Colour Society.[6] Wallis found himself in distinguished company: other members of the committee included such prominent artists and educators as Edward Poynter, Lawrence Alma-Tadema, Thomas Armstrong, Sidney Colvin, and J.D. Linton.

Inspiration of the Renaissance

Wallis executed surprisingly few portraits, except for those of his close family, like his son Harold [Cat. 72] and his mistress Mary Ellen Meredith [Cats. 32, 33] and her father Thomas Love Peacock [Cat. 34]. This was probably because he became a wealthy man at a relatively young age and did not have to venture into the lucrative, but often artistically unfulfilling, field of portraiture in order to make a living. During the first decade of his career, Wallis – like so many others – sought his inspiration in historical and Shakespearian subjects, which were immensely popular at that time. "In terms of sheer quantity the high point for all this production was the middle of the century, from about 1830 to 1860."[7] These historical representations can be seen as part of anecdotal genre painting in opposition to the "grand style" promoted and favoured by the Royal Academy. However, some academic painters like Frederic Leighton regarded Shakespeare's plays as

Top:
Henry Wallis, *The Lacemaker*, after Vermeer [Cat. 321]
Image by permission of the National Art Library, Victoria and Albert Museum, MSL 1939/1836

Right:
Henry Wallis, *Found at Naxos (Presenting a Sculpture)* [Cat. 97], 1874
Private collection. Image courtesy of Bukowskis Auction House, Stockholm

exhaustively finished works of art and considered "that it was too 'intimidating' to represent the incomparable, already existing complete."[8] Unlike his friend William Holman Hunt, who "felt that all good painting should have a controlling narrative and bear a message,"[9] Wallis wanted to represent single historical moments.

By the end of the 1860s, he started to produce exterior scenes as well as Renaissance-inspired subjects, which can be explained by his increasing love for Italian art, as a result of his journeys to Italy. His letters often refer to Italian artists such as Mantegna, Signorelli, Melozzo da Forlì, Carpaccio or Matteo Civitali. During the 1870s he produced a series of interesting watercolours in which the Italian influence is clearly visible. This includes his series based on Shakespeare's *Merchant of Venice*, which drew the attention of art critics, such as *The Merchant of Venice* (from Act II, Scene V) [Cat. 152] and *After the Trial: Antonio receiving the Congratulations of his Friends* [Cat.125], in 1879.

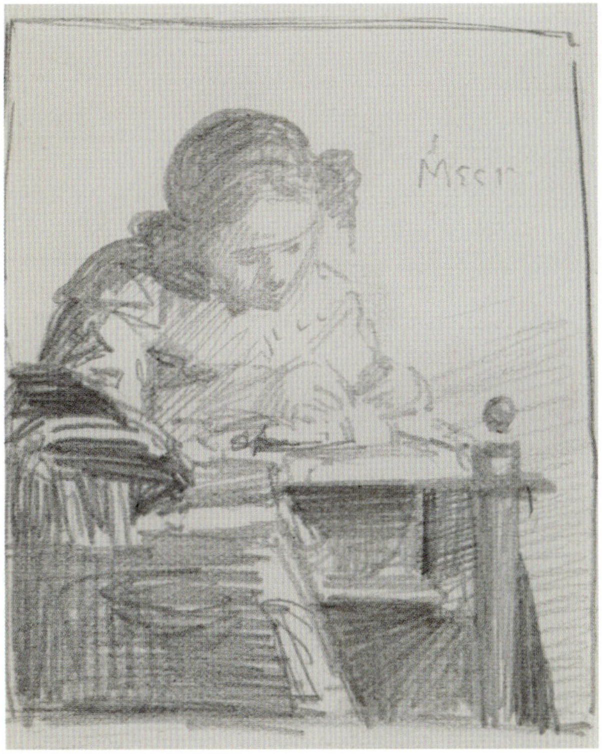

For Italian scenes, he not only found his inspiration in the landscapes and architectural features that he had noticed during his trips, but he also occasionally asked his friends to aid him to make certain he got specific details correct. For instance, in a letter dated 3 October 1874 from his friend and fellow Royal Academy exhibitor Henry Darvall, whom Wallis had asked to go to the Correr Museum: "I have been all the morning at the Correr Museum seeing what I could do for you about the Gondola. I started for that institution once before but found it was closed. There are lots of gondolas there, but I found they were all much later than your period, mostly about the time of Canaletto.... I made the two large sketches I now enclose, they are as nearly as possible the size of the originals. ... If you want further or more detailed information I think the best way will be for you to send me a rough drawing of a gondola or gondolas in position you want, marking the points about which you are uncertain, and I will do my best to complete them."[10]

During the 1870s, influence from Dutch 17th-century painters, especially Pieter De Hooghe, is

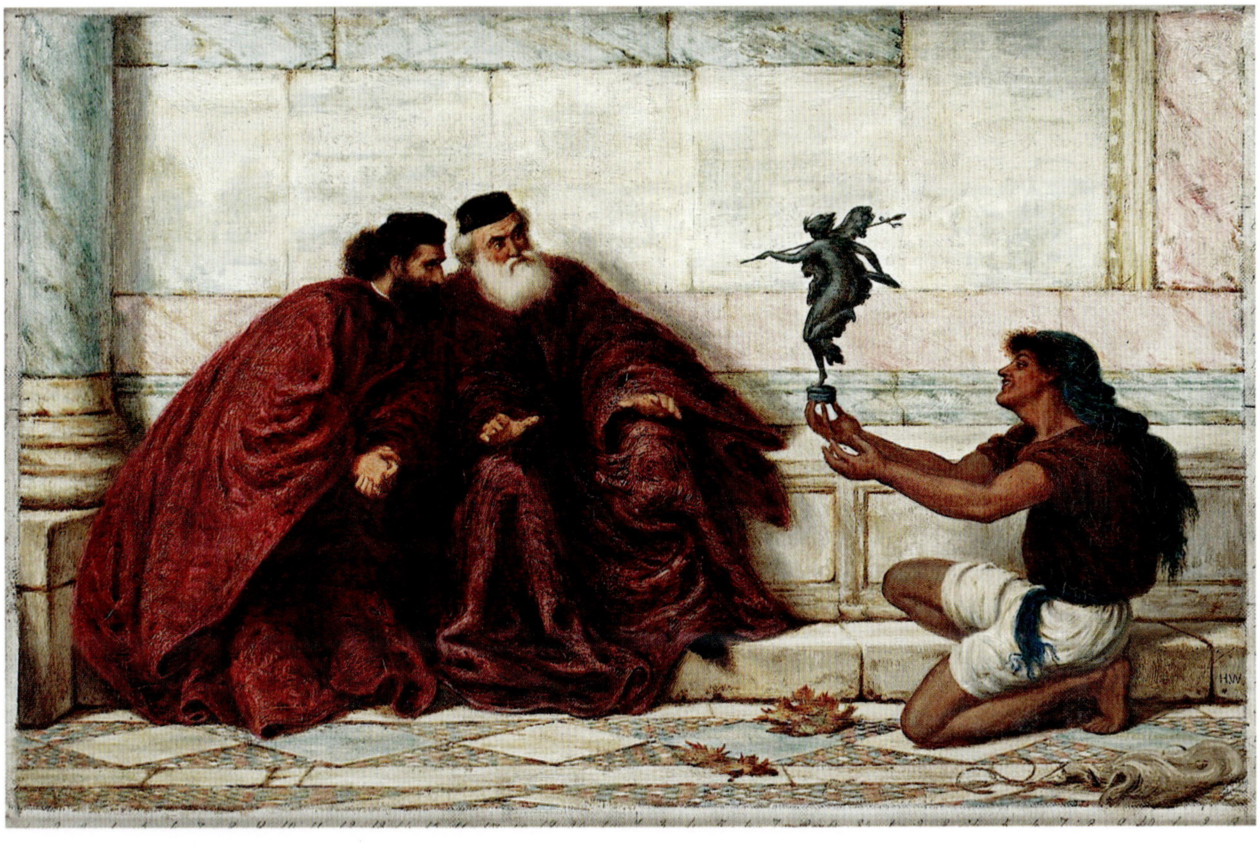

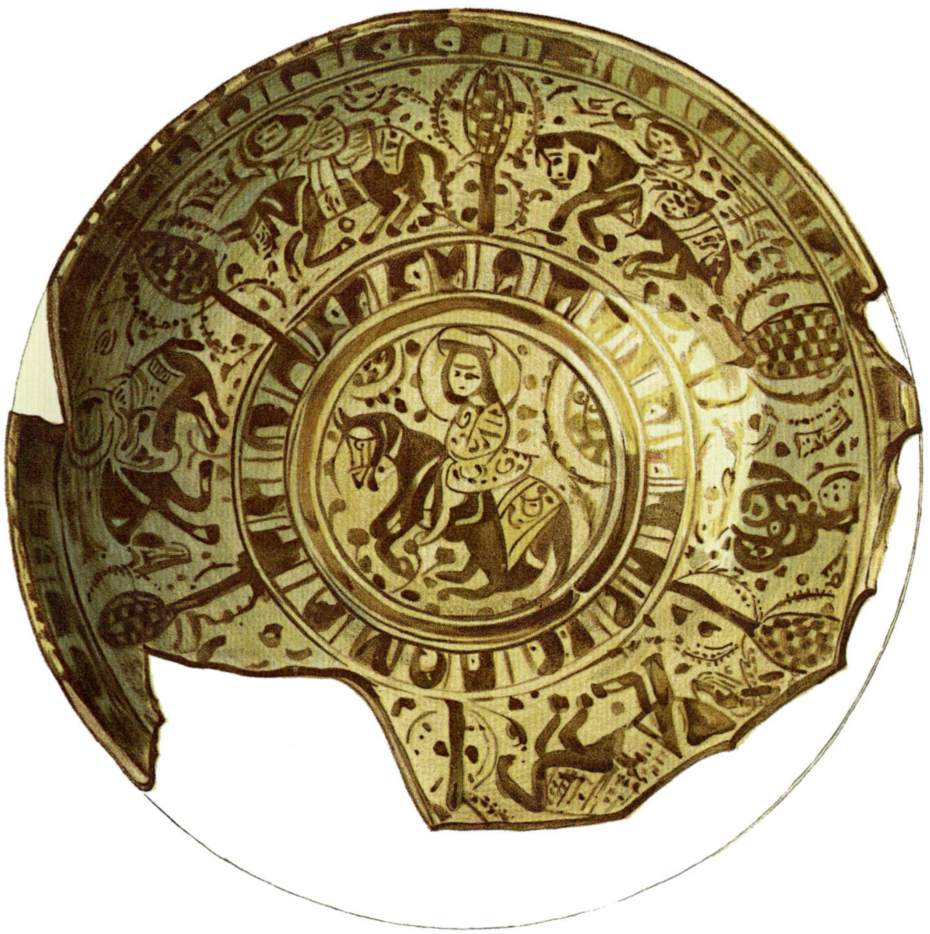

clearly visible in Wallis's works such as *Barnard's Inn Holborn* [Cat. 89], *A Flemish Interior* [Cat. 119], *A Dutch Hofje* [Cat. 130], and *A Musical Gathering* [Cat. 137]. Wallis's sketchbooks, although they generally show him copying Italian Renaissance works that interested him, also have examples after Dutch masters like Johannes Vermeer [Cat. 321] and Bartholomeus van der Helst [Cat. 323].

The Orientalist

Wallis's first journey to Egypt in 1885 opened a new world to him and, in addition to his archaeological work on pottery, it inspired a series of Orientalist paintings, which he would exhibit at the O.W.S. Wallis did not try to "Westernise" his street scenes, but on the contrary, he only described what he saw. This may possibly be seen by some as a lack of imagination because, according to Gerald Ackerman, "his Cairo street scenes are truthful, but they are not as lively as Lewis's and not as colourful as David Roberts's."[11]

Unfortunately, we know little about Wallis's working methods as an artist because he did not write about these in his letters and no contemporary assessment of his methods was written up in any of the magazines of the day. From his surviving sketchbooks Wallis appears to have jotted down artistic notes that he must have used occasionally to work up finished watercolours later in his studio. Unlike his academic colleagues, he does not seem to have consistently made nude and draped studies for the major figures within his paintings, although he did nude studies for figures in his oil sketch of nude and draped figures [Cat. 73]. We do know from some of P.A. Daniel's letters that Wallis worked on some of his early oil paintings of historical subjects on site and did not simply work them up in his studio. We do not know how many of his watercolours were painted *en plein air*. From the sepia drawings relating to his *Merchant of Venice* series of watercolours that he exhibited at the Old Water-Colour Society [Cats. 152a, 158a], it is obvious that he must occasionally have made very finished studies for some of his compositions.

The Illustrator

As time passed, likely because of his interest in ceramics, Wallis became convinced that artists were not superior to craftsmen. The dichotomy did not exist in ancient time, but was a recent concept, intended to maintain the artist's vanity. Wallis's thinking was in concordance with that of his friend William Morris and many artists later associated with the Arts and Crafts Movement. One aspect of Wallis's art for which he has received insufficient recognition, is his ability as an illustrator, particularly for the books he wrote on ceramics. His books not only included illustrations in black and white, but also wonderful chromolithographs produced by printmakers, like Samuel D. Hodson or William Griggs, based on the watercolours that Wallis painted especially for his publications. Some of these watercolours he even felt worthy of being exhibited at the Old Water Colour Society. *The Athenaeaum*

Persian Lustred Bowl, S.D. Hodson after Henry Wallis, 1891, chromolithograph on paper. Plate 13 *from Persian Ceramic Art in the Collection of Mr F. DuCane Godman, F.R.S. The Thirteenth Century Lustred Vases*, 1891. IMAGE COURTESY OF DENNIS LANIGAN COLLECTION

commented on these illustrations: "The drawings surpass anything produced in this country or abroad in felicitous recognition of the style, colours, lustring, and other characteristics of the beautiful ceramic wear of Persia. If the chromolithographs are not quite equal in purity of tint and crispness of touch to their originals, that is simply because no reproduction, however skilful and costly, can be absolutely perfect."[12] Albert Van De Put, in his obituary of Wallis, mentioned " A wonderful talent for seizing in paint, in black-and-white, or with the pencil, ceramic form and ornament, are resources of which few other investigators have disposed in anything like the same degree.[13]

Even Wallis himself acknowledged his love of illustrating ceramics: "If I had followed my own inclinations, I would have been content to draw vases."[14] Wallis's contributions as a book illustrator would have been sufficient to establish his reputation as an artist even had he not made a significant impact on the Victorian art world with his paintings. Unfortunately, we only know the present location of a few of Wallis's original drawings of ceramics. His black and white drawings for the book *XVII plates by Nicola Fontana da Urbino at the Correr Museum, Venice; a study in early sixteenth century maiolica with illustration by Henry Wallis*, and published by Taylor and Francis in 1905, are in the Victoria and Albert Museum.[15] Wallis's designs for *Egyptian Ceramic Art: The MacGregor Collection*, published by Taylor & Francis in 1898, are also in the V&A.[16] Should anyone doubt Wallis's ability to reproduce ceramics they need only consult these brilliant examples!

The Traditionalist

For someone who had been so curious and had taken such a fresh approach in his younger years, Wallis became rather stuck in his ways towards the end. Perhaps being a specialist in antiquities and a lover of Renaissance art, he may have lost his ability to look at modern art with a fresh and inquisitive eye. Not only did he dismiss the contemporary art of the day, but he was most forthright in his opinions. He was horrified to read that Art Nouveau had found its way into the South Kensington Museum and wrote to Read, on 20 July 1901: "I suppose you have seen the court of the 'new art' at S.K.M. The protest wch appeared in the *Times* the other day was not a bit too strong. It is like throwing up the sponge. After all the money the nation has spent, & all the hard work put into the cause, we are now to have this abominable and impertinent trash put before the students as models for imitation!"[17]

Certainly Pre-Raphaelite painters were unable to appreciate the beauty of French Impressionist art as it was contrary to everything they believed in. In a letter from Holman Hunt to Wallis of August 25, 1886 Hunt wrote: "The impressionists whose works I saw in King St. two years ago seemed to me to be the kind of artists who make you declare that both Art and Nature are hideous and intolerable still of course they ought to have no reasonable grievance. A fool the name of Chesneau[18] wrote to ask me to go and see the works when I wanted, and I could really scarcely believe that he was serious in speaking of them as deserving attention."[19]

It is also extremely unlikely that Wallis paid attention to the Post-Impressionist exhibition set up by Roger Fry, although in a letter to Wallis dated 23 December 1910, A.A.C. Boyce had drawn attention to it: "Avez-vous été voir les post-imperssionnistes à 'the Grafton'? Non, probablement, ni moi, j'en ai eu assez de ce que je vis en les journaux illustrés. Tout le monde en parle, ce qui plaît à ces artistes."[20] If Wallis had seen the Post-Impressionist exhibition, he almost certainly would not have liked it and his views undoubtedly would have coincided with those of his friends within the Pre-Raphaelite circle such as William Blake Richmond. In a letter to the *Morning Post* of 16 November 1910 Richmond stated: "The marvel is that these hysterical daubs should have been perpetrated at all, but various forms of disordered mentality are common to these times. That they should not have been exhibited is obvious. It was unkind to expose them. It is futile to attack the authors of these morbid excrescences... These incompetents neither could, nor can draw, paint or design. Blind to the beauty of line, colour or motive."[21]

***

Although Wallis as an artist may not have been in the first rank of Pre-Raphaelite painters, such as D.G. Rossetti, J.E. Millais, W. Holman Hunt or F. Madox Brown, he is certainly the equal to his friends Arthur Hughes and W. Bell Scott. Wallis painted two works considered amongst the masterpieces of the first phase of Pre-Raphaelitism, a not insignificant accomplishment. Wallis was an exceptionally skillful draughtsman and a fine watercolourist, whom contemporary reviewers considered to be amongst the leading members of the Old Water-Colour Society. He was also one of the most important British Orientalist painters of the second half of the 19th century. It is therefore quite clear, despite what some 20th century art historians believed, that Wallis did not disappear from the artistic scene after he had "eloped" with George Meredith's wife! His work continued to evolve through various phases, from his early historical and Pre-Raphaelite works in oil, to his later watercolours inspired by his travels, especially those influenced by Venetian Renaissance art and his Orientalist subjects. The quality of his work remained consistently high throughout his career as the catalogue section will show.

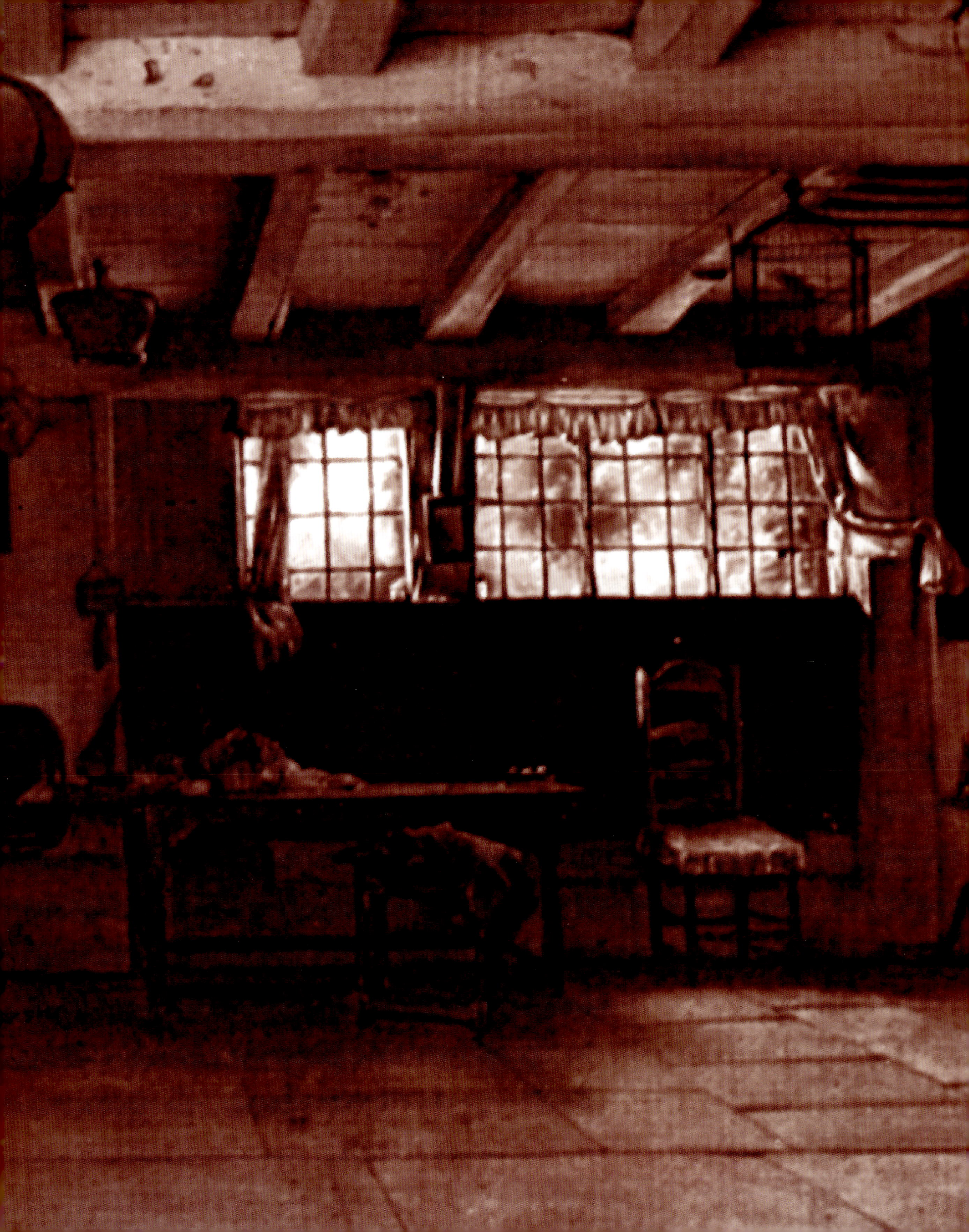

Part Two
An Illustrated Catalogue of Works

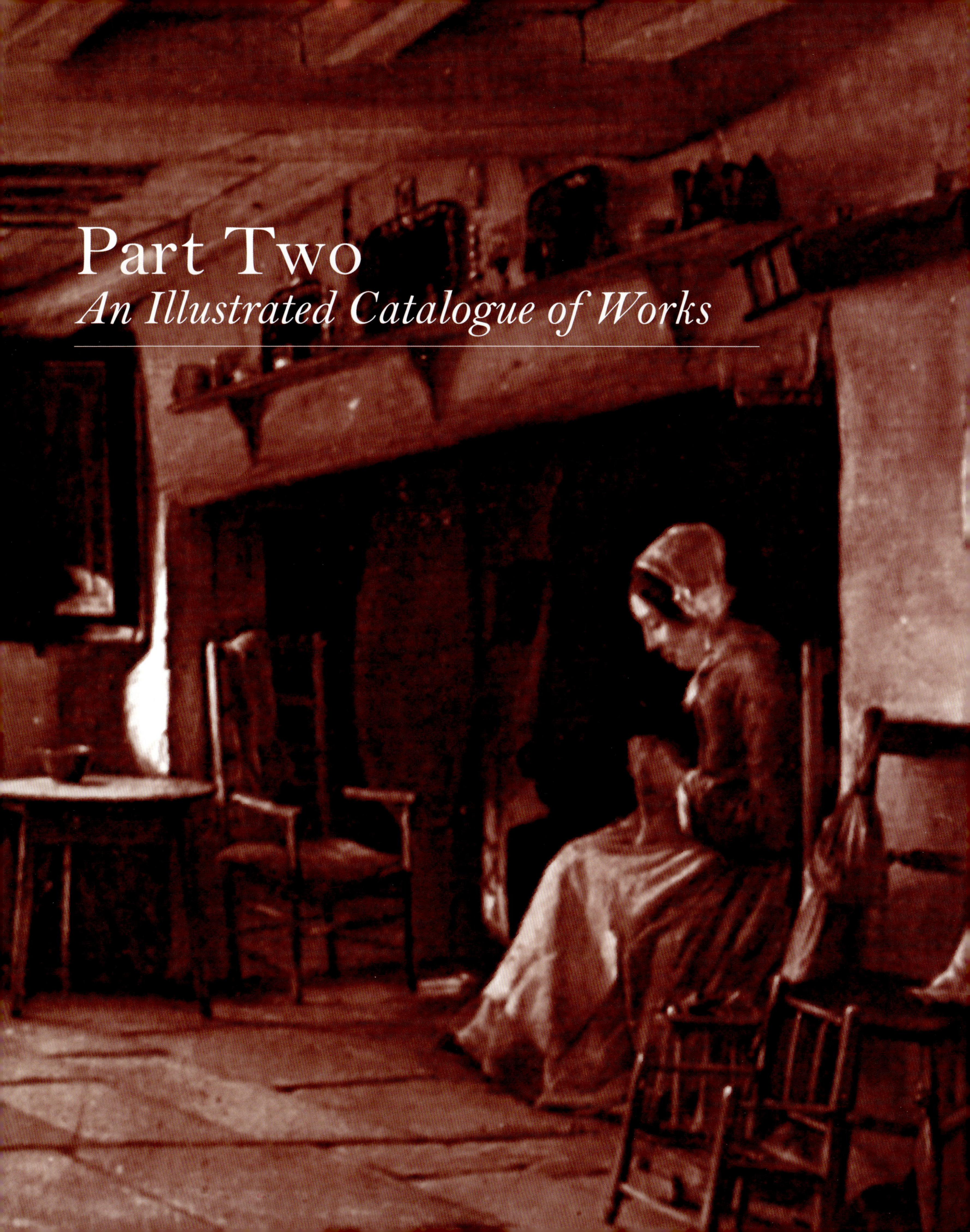

Catalogue Notes

Although the authors have tried to be as comprehensive as possible, works that have not yet been discovered will no doubt appear on the market from time to time. Works sold after 1970 are assumed to still survive. Most are in private collections unless otherwise specified.

The entries have been organised chronologically whenever possible. Works exhibited at the Royal Academy, the Old Water-Colour Society, and other institutions are, of course, easier to date. As Wallis seldom dated his works, these have normally been assigned according to when they were first exhibited, unless better documentary evidence exists; Wallis occasionally did not exhibit works until many years after he painted them so this system is not infallible. Watercolours and drawings that were not exhibited are harder to pin down and their style has been taken into account. When there is only a title, which may not even be the original title given to the work by Wallis, and no image of the work to look at, then dating becomes even more difficult and is often just a best guess. These works are, therefore, grouped sometimes by genre, as in the Orientalist watercolours, and sometimes by subject, as in *The Merchant of Venice* series. Dating the works made during his journeys has in many cases been possible, thanks to his abundant correspondence. There is always the possibility, however, that finished watercolours may have been worked up later in his studio from sketches made on much earlier trips.

There is very little information on Wallis's working methods. It is obvious that, particularly early in his career, he often did preliminary sketches in oil or watercolour of the overall composition, as well as drawings of individual figures for important compositions. Contemporary reviews are quoted whenever possible, particularly for those works where images are not currently available. This will facilitate later identification of a work should it subsequently appear on the art market. Contemporary reviews have also allowed us to determine the original titles for a number of works included in this catalogue.

Reproductive prints after Wallis are included under the same catalogue no. as the work itself. In many cases these provide the only clues to what the finished work looked like. The large number of missing works has, unfortunately, made it impossible to judge comprehensively Wallis's merits as an artist and to assess the evolution of his oeuvre.

Mention must also be made of the huge quantity of original drawings Wallis did for illustrations, particularly those done in watercolour, for the books that he wrote and illustrated on ceramics. Despite their merits, these drawings are not included in the catalogue section unless they were exhibited at the Old Water-Colour Society. In most cases, it is not known which specific illustrations Wallis exhibited there, so representative examples have been included here. To get as complete an overview of Wallis's work as possible, his books should also be considered. Some of Wallis's original drawings for ceramics are in the Prints and Drawings Department of the Victoria and Albert Museum. These works must also be consulted to get a full idea of Wallis's brilliance as an illustrator of ceramics.

In many cases, the artist signed his works 'H.W.' or 'H. Wallis'. The latter signature has led to some auction houses misattributing works to Henry Wallis that are actually by Hugh Wallis (1871-1943), a painter who also exhibited at the Royal Academy. A landscape painter named H. Wallis has also caused some confusion as to whether works at exhibition or sold at auction are by him or by Henry. It is possible that, on occasion, the authors have omitted works that were actually by Henry because on balance it was decided that the other artist was the more likely of the two. Sometimes a work has been attributed to Henry, but on no clear stylistic ground, and other times works have been attributed to him that are simply not executed skillfully enough to be by him. These doubtful works were not included until more definitive evidence becomes available. At times works attributed to Henry Wallis or H. Wallis have sold at auction, but no images are available to look at to make an informed judgment, so this catalogue should not be considered as definitive. Graves's and Redford's lists[1] of art sales are extremely useful, but are sometimes inaccurate.[2] Unfortunately, the authors have not had the opportunity to examine the majority of these works in person, and therefore have had to rely upon auction house records for inscriptions or annotations, which may not always have been accurate.

- Dimensions are given as height x width.
- Dimensions based on auction house measurements must be considered approximate.
- Dimensions followed by "sight" mean these were not examined out of the frame and are approximate.
- Watercolours are on paper unless otherwise stated.
- Inscriptions are in a hand known to be the artist's. Annotations are in an unknown hand.
- The Old Water-Colour Society (O.W.S.) is synonymous with the Society of Painters in Water Colours, which in 1881 became the Royal Society of Painters in Watercolours (R.W.S.).
- Sale prices are quoted in the currency of the country of sale.
- All auction sales are in London unless otherwise specified.
- Some reviews predate the completion of a painting as critics might be allowed to view a work in progress.

Cat. 1. ***Academic study of a Plaster Cast of the Laocoön***
*c.*1848; graphite on paper; 70.8 x 54.5 cm. (27⅞ x 17⅞ in.) - sight; Diane Johnson collection, Paris.
INSCRIPTION: signed *H. Wallis* and dated *Febr. 3rd; Gep. Jones*
PROVENANCE: Wallis's studio and then by descent from the artist to his daughter-in-law Alice Julyan Wallis (*née* Roberts), and thence to her great-niece Mrs. Vera G. Whiting, Purley, Surrey; given to Diane Johnson *c.*1973.

This is one of Wallis's earliest surviving drawings and dates from when he was a student at the Royal Academy Schools in London. George Jones R.A. (1786-1869) was obviously the "Visitor"[1] instructor in the Antique School at the particular time this study was done. Jones was Keeper of the Royal Academy from 1840-1850. This drawing would have been laid before the Council, accompanied with outline drawings of an anatomical figure and skeleton, together with the drawing originally presented for his admission as a probationer in order to gain acceptance as a full student of the Royal Academy Schools.

The Royal Academy had been presented with a plaster cast of the Roman marble version of the lost Greek bronze original by The Prince Regent in 1816. The marble statue was excavated in Rome in 1506 and has been on display in the Vatican since that time. This work is one of the most famous of ancient sculptures and most prominent 19th century drawing academies would have had a plaster cast of it.

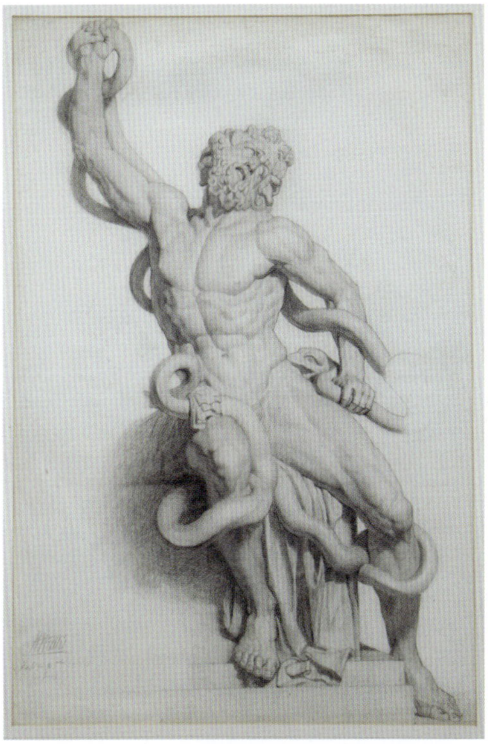

Cat. 1. Image courtesy of Diane Johnson collection, Paris; photograph by Alison Harris

Cat. 2. ***Academic study of a Plaster Cast of Cincinnatus***
*c.*1848; graphite on grey paper; 67 x 38 cm. (26⅜ x 15 in.) - sight; Diane Johnson collection, Paris.
PROVENANCE: Wallis's studio and then by descent from the artist to his daughter-in-law Alice Julyan Wallis (*née* Roberts), and thence to her great-niece Mrs. Vera G. Whiting, Purley, Surrey; given to Diane Johnson *c.*1973.

This is another of Wallis's earliest surviving drawings and likely dates from when he was studying at the Royal Academy Schools in London. In March 1848, Wallis graduated to the Antique School, where he would have made such studies from plaster casts. The cast from which this drawing was taken entered the Royal Academy collection in 1774. The subject is uncertain and it has been variously referred to as: *Cincinnatus*; *Hermes fastening his sandal*; *Jason*; or the *Lansdowne Sandal Binder*.[1] It was cast after a Roman marble copy of a Greek bronze original of the 3rd century BC that has been attributed to a pupil of Lysippos. The marble version, which had been discovered in Hadrian's Villa at Tivoli in 1769, was sold in 1772 to the Marquess of Shelburne, who later became the Earl of Lansdowne. The sculpture stayed in that family's collection until 1930, when it was sold and became part of the Glyptotek Collection in Copenhagen.

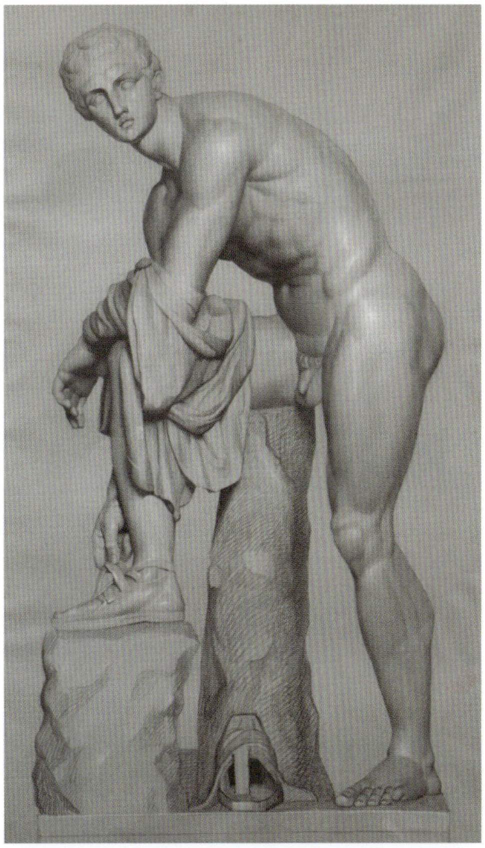

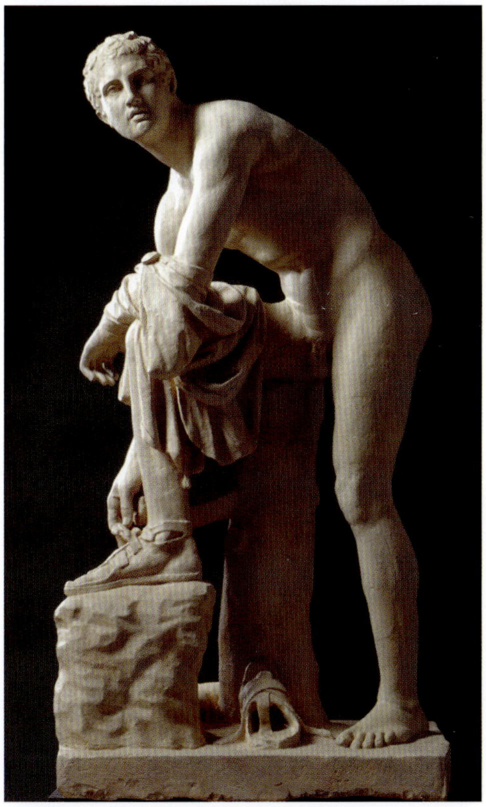

Cat. 2. (Above left) Image courtesy of Diane Johnson collection, Paris; photograph by Alison Harris (Above right) Plaster cast of Cincinnatus. Image by permission of the Royal Academy of Arts, London

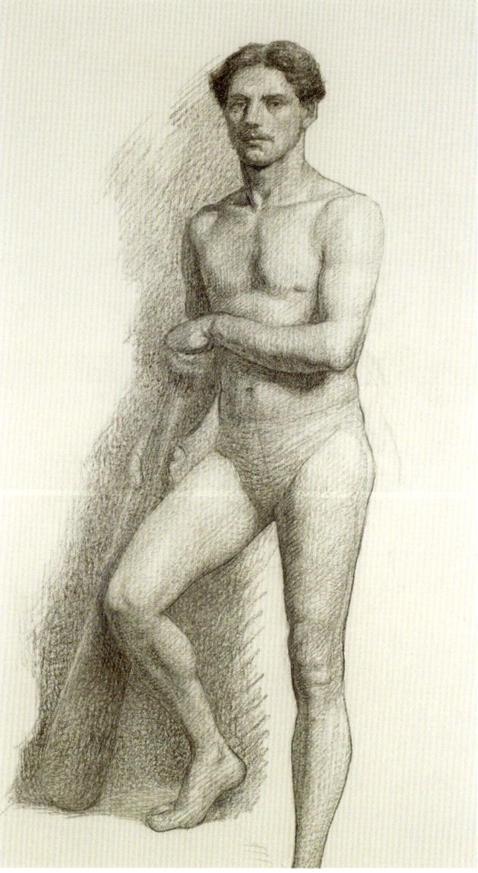

Cat. 3. Image by permission of Birmingham Museums Trust

Cat. 3. *Study of a Nude Man with Club*
*c.*1851; black chalk on paper; 62.9 x 35.5 cm. (24¾ x 14 in.); Birmingham Museum and Art Gallery.
Provenance: Presented by Harold Wallis to Birmingham Museum and Art Gallery in 1918, accession no. 1918P12.
Literature: Birmingham Museum and Art Gallery, *Catalogue of the Permanent Collection of Drawings*, 1939, p.415, no. 12'18.

The drawing likely dates either from the time Wallis attended the Royal Academy schools, or Gleyre's studio (*c.*1851-2), most probably the latter. If so, it is the only such academic drawing known to survive from this period. The model appears to be wearing short drawers and it is known that Gleyre, when girls were attending the lessons, did not want the students to draw completely nude men.[1] Moreover, when compared to Wallis's later surviving figure drawings, this drawing is far less elaborate and the modelling is flatter. Also, he has not quite captured the anatomy and proportions of the lower legs correctly.

Cat. 4. *Study of the Interior of a Blacksmith's Shop*
Date unknown; black and white chalk drawing on grey paper; 38.2 x 57.9 cm. (15 x 22⅞ in.); whereabouts unknown.
Inscriptions: signed with initials *H.W.*
Provenance: Given by Harold Wallis in 1918 to Birmingham Museums and Art Gallery (accession no.1918P14); de-accessioned and sold at Christie's, London, on 21 Feb 1958, lot 36, bought by Abbott, likely Robert Abbott of Abbott and Holder, London, for £3.
Literature: Birmingham Museum and Art Gallery, *Catalogue of the Permanent Collection of Drawings*, 1939, p.415, no. 14'18.

The drawing includes the figure of a man in the background heating a kettle.

Cat. 5. *Sketch of a Man Smoking a Pipe*
*c.*1852; pencil on white paper; dimensions unknown; private collection.
Provenance: The family by descent; Dominic Winter Auctions, 20 July 2011, part of lot 367, bought by Richard Macauley; sold to private collector, New York.

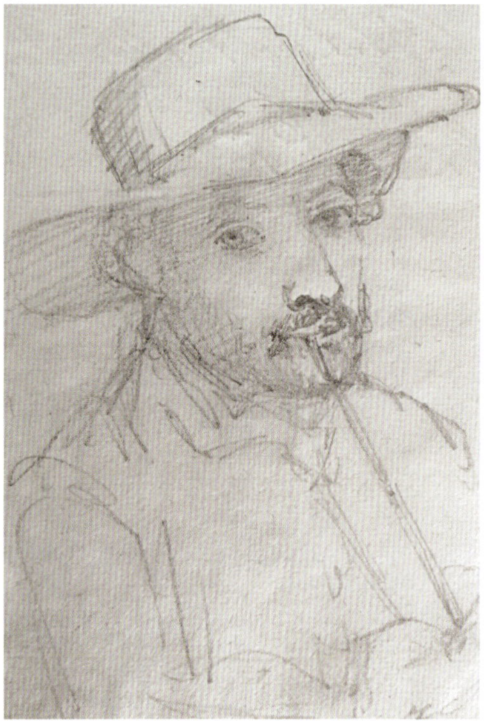

Cat. 5. Image courtesy of private collector

This drawing was found inside a passport stamped in 1852 used by Wallis when he visited Italy and crossed Switzerland, a journey obviously made while studying in Paris under Gleyre. This may be an early self-portrait, which would make sense considering it was drawn inside his passport. The facial features of this man are consistent with those of Wallis as a student in the drawing by Carl Haag [see: Chapter 1], although this is obviously not proof that the model is, in fact, Wallis. Certainly, pipe smoking was a common pastime for Wallis and his circle of friends. Peter Austin Daniel makes frequent references to this habit in his letters to his mother and in his journal.[1]

Cat. 6. *An Artist at his Easel*
*c.*1852; pencil on white paper; dimensions unknown; private collection.
Provenance: The family by descent; Dominic Winter Auctions, 20 July 2011, part of lot 367, bought by Richard Macauley; sold to private collector, New York.

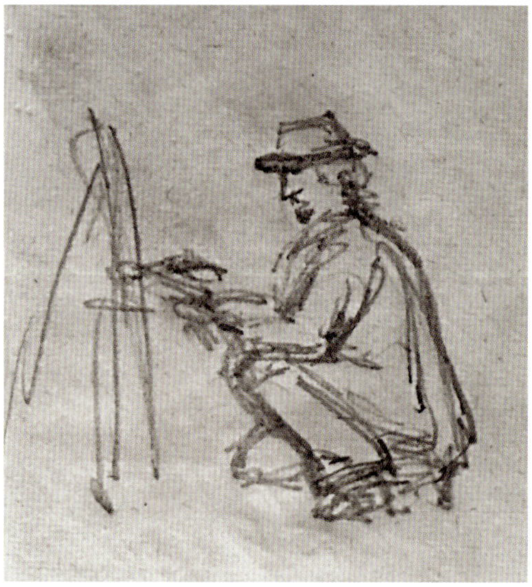

Cat. 6. Image courtesy of private collector

Another drawing found inside the 1852 passport [see previous item]. The fact that the subject is an artist supports the idea that these two drawings could be self-portraits.

Cat. 7. *Portrait of William Ashfield*
*c.*1853; oil on canvas; 21.5 x 16 cm (8½ x 6½ in.); private collection.
Inscriptions: Signed with initials *HW* and dated *1853*, lower left.
Provenance: Sotheby's Belgravia, 21 March 1972, lot 126; sold for £55 to Mrs. K. Morris of S. & K. Morris, art dealers, Stratford-upon-Avon.

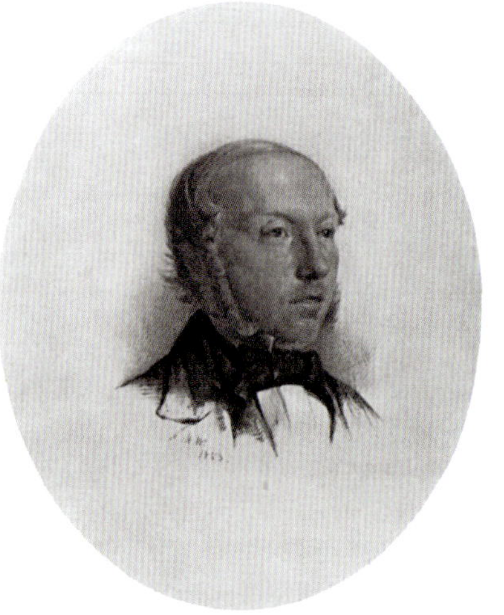

Cat. 7. Image courtesy of Sotheby's, London

A note on the reverse says that Wallis painted the portrait at the Falcon Hotel, Stratford-upon-Avon. William Ashfield (1827-1882) and his wife Marian (1840-1902) were probably the owners of the Falcon Hotel or Falcon Inn, a sixteenth-century Tudor

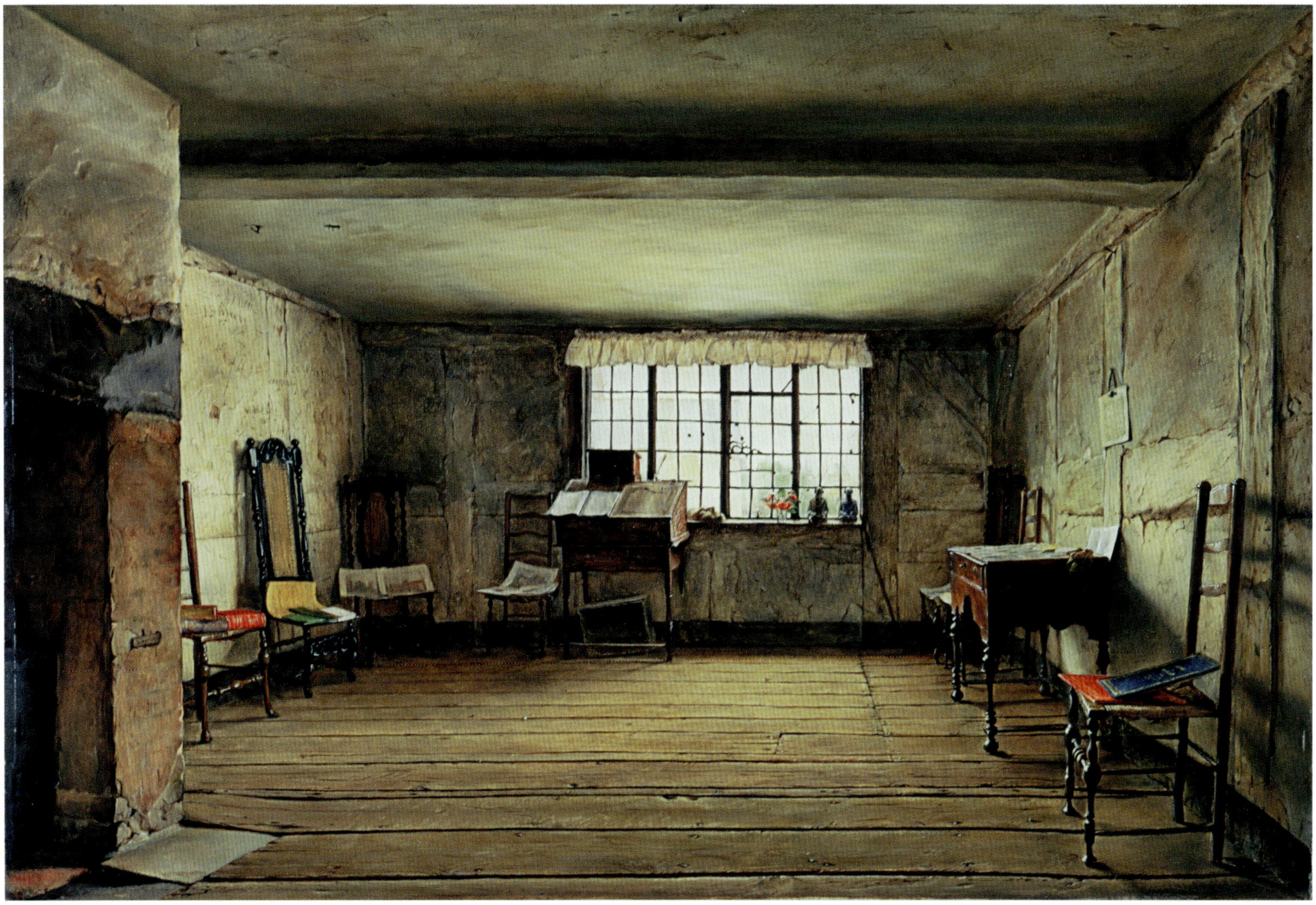

Cat. 8. Image by permission of Tate, London, 2016

residence that still stands, currently known as The Legacy Falcon Hotel. Wallis had, presumably, returned from studying in France and was staying at Stratford to prepare the paintings he would exhibit the following year (1854) at the Royal Academy. It is known that Wallis was back in England by May 1854 because of a letter P.A. Daniel wrote to his mother of 3 June 1854 in which he states: "I have been out of town for a fortnight on a sketching tour with a friend of mine (of course an artist) named Wallis."[1]

Cat. 8. *The Room in which Shakespeare was Born*
1853; oil on board; 29.2 x 41.9 cm. (11½ x 16½ in.); Tate Britain, London.
Provenance: Sir Charles Eastlake; possibly on his death in 1865 to his wife Elizabeth, Lady Eastlake (1809-1893); bequeathed the Tate Gallery in 1955 by Mrs. E. J. Thwaites, museum no. T00042.
Exhibitions: Royal Academy, 1854, no. 1303; Art Gallery of Western Australia and other venues, *The Pre-Raphaelite Dream*, 2003-2004, no. 25.
Literature: *The Academy and Literature*, Vol. 5, 6 June 1874, p.645; Hilton, Timothy: *The Pre-Raphaelites*, 1970, p.123; Altick, Richard D: *Paintings from Books*, Ohio State University Press, 1985, Part One, Chapter 7, pp.147-148, fig. 117, p.148; Upstone, Robert: *The Pre-Raphaelite Dream*, 2003, p.62.

Henry Wallis began his career by exhibiting a sequence of paintings of interior scenes connected with the life of William Shakespeare. Robert Upstone has noted about this work: "Wallis may have had in mind the commercial potential of such widespread enthusiasm for Shakespeare when he started this picture of the room in which he was born. Indeed, it was one of three such pictures he made at the same time… Accompanying *The Room in Shakespeare was Born* was a long descriptive quote from Charles Knight's 1842 biography of Shakespeare which described 'that mean room, with its massive joists and plastered walls, firm with ribs of oak, where we are told the poet of the human race was born' (p.30). On the same page is a woodcut illustration which takes the same viewpoint as Wallis's canvas, and it is possible that together with the text these two sources formed the basis for the composition. Nevertheless, in its simplicity and emptiness, and his concentration on rendering the textures of wood and plaster, Wallis produced a highly effective and atmospheric picture."[1]

Particularly Pre-Raphaelite in style, Wallis has included a remarkable level of detail in this painting; every nail securing the floorboards is visible. Wallis has even taken note of Knight's passage describing how "hundreds amongst the hundreds of thousands by whom that name is honoured have inscribed their names on the walls of the room".

When Wallis spent some time at Stratford in 1853 he visited its most iconic buildings. Among them was Shakespeare's birthplace, which the Shakespeare Birthplace Trust had purchased in 1847 by public subscription for preservation as a national memorial. A restoration of the fabric of the building was undertaken between 1857 and 1864.[2] The house had remained in the hands of the descendents of Shakespeare's sister Joan until the early nineteenth century, although it was in a state of semi-disrepair. The house was visited, amongst others, by such notables as John Keats, Sir Walter Scott and by Thomas Carlyle.[3]

The painting was purchased from Wallis by Sir Charles Eastlake, the President of the Royal Academy, which would have been quite a compliment for a young painter at the start of his career.

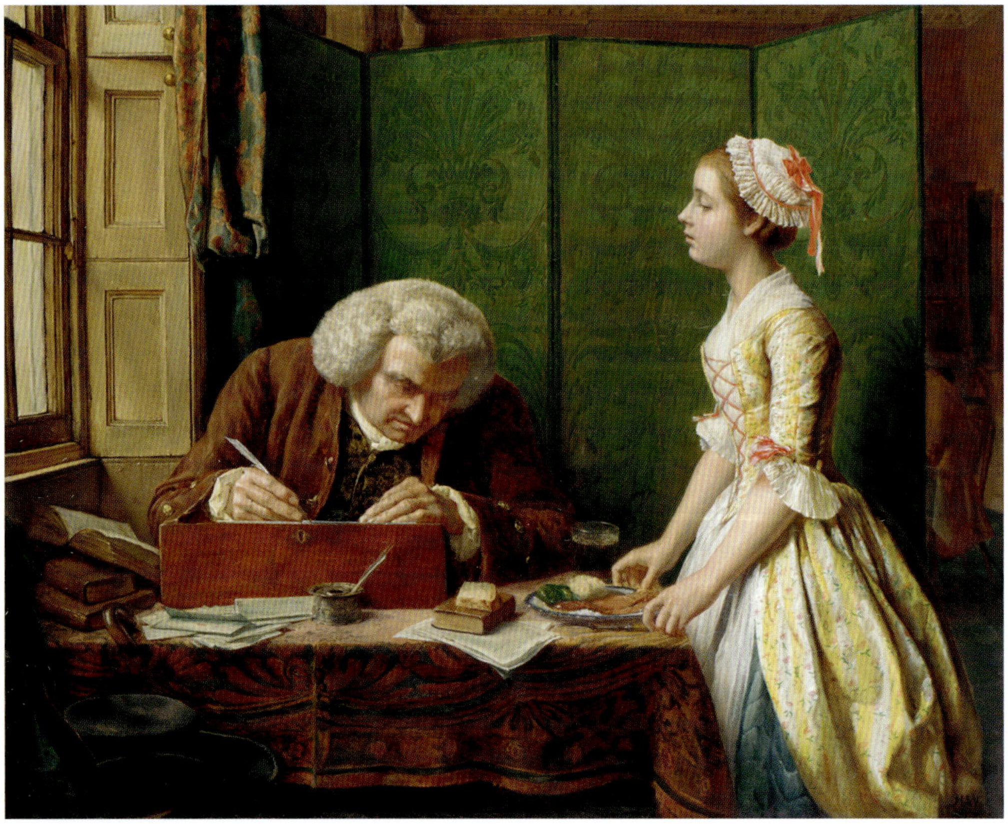

Cat. 10. Image courtesy of Sotheby's, London

Cat. 9. *Check*
1853; ?oil on canvas; dimensions unknown; whereabouts unknown.
Exhibitions: Royal Manchester Institution, *Exhibition of the Works of Modern Artists*, the thirty-fifth, 1853, no. 389, asking price £31 10s.

Unfortunately, no contemporary reviews of this work has been found to shed any light as to its subject matter.

Cat. 10. *Dr Johnson at Cave's, the Publisher*
1854; oil on canvas; 50.5 x 60.5 cm (19⅞ x 23¹³⁄₁₆ in.); private collection.
Inscriptions: Signed with initials *H.W.* and dated *1854*, lower right.
Provenance: Purchased for £42 from the Royal Academy exhibition by a prizeholder from the Art Union of London; Mr. Mann; his sale Christie's, London, May 19, 1866, lot 44, bought in; A.S. Dixon by 1883; his sale Christie's London, April 26, 1918, lot 116, purchased by William Walker Sampson (1865-1929) of W.W. Sampson & Sons, London for £22 1s; Lifford Antiques, their sale Sotheby's Belgravia, 27 March 1973, lot 47, purchased either by N. Drummond or J.S. Maas on behalf of Sir David Scott for £800; Lady Scott's estate sale, Sotheby's, 19 Nov 2008, lot 102, sold for £39,650.
Exhibitions: Royal Academy, 1854, no. 176; Huddersfield, *Fine Art and Industrial Exhibtion*, 1883, no. 66; National Gallery of Scotland, Edinburgh, *Sunshine & Shadow – The David Scott Collection of Victorian Paintings*, 1991, no. 7.
Literature: *Art Journal*, Vol. VI, 1854, p.161, p.188; *The Works of Eminent Masters in Painting, Sculpture, Architecture and Decorative Art*, Vol. I, 1854, p.411; *The Athenaeum*, No. 1384, 6 May 1854, p.560; *The Illustrated London News*, vol. 25, 12 August 1854, p.138; *Art Journal*, Vol. 13, 1866, p.220; *The Times*, 21 May 1866, p.12; *The Morning Post*, 22 May 1866, p.2; *The Burlington Magazine*: 'Mr. Henry Wallis', Vol. 30, No. 168, March 1917, p.123; Sotheby's, *Pictures from the Collection of Sir David and Lady Scott*, 2008, pp.92-93; Shrimpton, Nicholas (Ed.), *Trollope, Anthony, An Autobiography and Other Writings*, 2014, p.327.

This was the first painting Wallis exhibited at the Royal Academy and shows the obvious influence of the first phase of Pre-Raphaelitism. The reviewer for *The Art Journal* described the subject as: "Dr. Johnson at Cave's, the publisher; Johnson, too ragged to appear at Cave's, has a plate of victuals sent to him behind the screen.' Johnson is here labouring with his pen; he casts his eye from his paper to the plate, which a perking maid servant sets at the edge of the table. Beyond the screen appears one of the party who are seated at table. The picture is carefully wrought, but the life of Johnson is full of incident of a much more agreeable and not less telling character. The subject is unsuited to Art and ought not to have been painted. Its selection is not creditable to the artist."[1] The critic for *The Athenaeum* mentioned: "Mr. H. Wallis sends a cleverly conceived picture, which he calls *Dr. Johnson at Cave's the Publisher's* (176). The indomitable Johnson is seated writing at a desk, placed near a window, behind a screen, that separates him from Urban's more fashionable company. A pretty, smart servant, evidently recently culled from the upper classes of a parish school, is bringing him a plate of meat, with a contemptuous air and up-turned nose. He is eyeing it in an abstracted purblind way, as if he wondered what it could possibly be. The servant's impertinence would have been better given, we think, by representing her turning away, and not lingering as if she either pitied or wished to insult the learned but shabby stranger. Dr. Johnson is made rather too old, for the incident illustrated happened at a very early stage of Johnson's London life. Although carefully and firmly painted, the shadows of the Doctor's face are rather too hot."

When the painting sold at Sotheby's in 2008 Christopher Newall noted: "Henry Wallis' subject, showing the impoverished Dr Johnson being given an impromptu meal when visiting his publisher Edward Cave, was inspired by a note by Edward Malone in the third edition of *Boswell's Life of Johnson*, published in 1799. This describes how Johnson was living a hand-to-mouth existence in the period before he gained a professional reputation. Wallis shows him as prematurely aged (he was only in his mid-thirties at this time), and with worn and badly repaired clothes. He peers myopically (he had poor eyesight as a result of contracting scrofula as a child) at the writing slope at which he works, and appears not to be happy to be interrupted by the arrival of the young servant who brings food to him.

The visit to Edward Cave in fact represented a turning-point in Johnson's career, because it was from Cave that he received the commission to write a series of pieces for the *Gentleman's Magazine*, of which Cave was the founder and proprietor. The esteem in which these articles were held eventually led to Johnson becoming one of the most eminent literary figures of the day.

The colour and texture of the present work, and the careful observation of detail (when showing the painting to friends, Sir David used to point out the red marks on the arms of the servant, which he believed were burns from a hot oven), identify Wallis as one who was influenced by contemporary Pre-Raphaelitism."[2]

Wallis, as well as the present painting, is mentioned for the first time as being a member within the Pre-Raphaelite circle in a letter dated 14 May 1854, from Dante Gabriel Rossetti to the Belfast collector Francis MacCracken:[3] "Hughes could tell

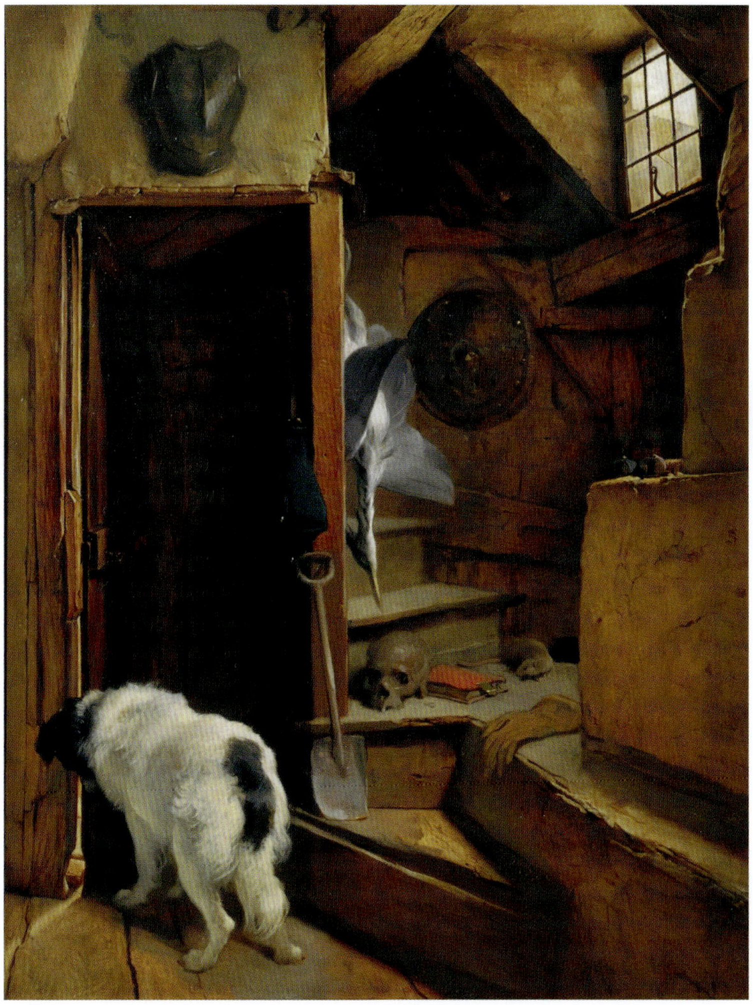

Cat. 11. Image by permission of Victoria and Albert Museum, London

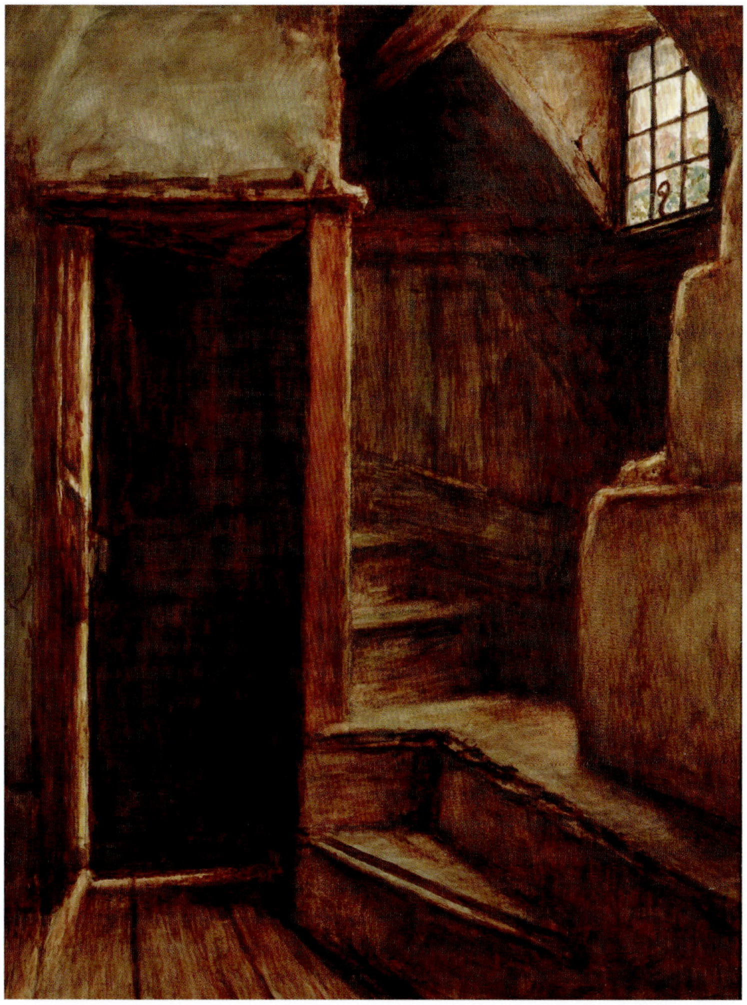

Cat. 12. Image courtesy of Bonhams, London.

you more than I could about Wallis and his works, as he knows him well I believe. I see by notices of the R.A. that he has a picture there from the life of Dr. Johnson, which seems to attract some attention."[4]

Cat. 11. *In Shakespeare's House, Stratford-upon-Avon*
1854; oil on canvas; 65.5 x 49.5 cm (25¾ x 19½ in.); Victoria & Albert Museum, London.
ANNOTATION: (on the frame) "Staircase leading to the room in which Shakespeare was born at Stratford-on-Avon. b.1830 Henry Wallis R.W.S. d. 1916."
PROVENANCE: John Forster, London, likely purchased from the R.A. exhibition;[1] bequeathed to the South Kensington Museum (V&A) in 1876, museum acquisition no. F.38, neg 53591.
EXHIBITIONS: Royal Academy, 1854, no. 267; Royal Scottish Academy, Edinburgh, 1867, no. 513;[2] *Shakespeare in Western Art*, no. 4, 1992-1993 at various museums in Japan including Isetan Museum of Art, Tokyo; The Museum of Modern Art, Ibaraki; Kintetsu Nara Hall; and Takamatsu City Museum of Art.
LITERATURE: *The Examiner*, 24 June 1854, p.392; *The Art Journal*, New Series Vol. VI, 1867, p.121; *The Times*, 21 February 1876, p.6; *The Bury and Norwich Post, and Suffolk Herald*, 22 February 1876, p.3; *Newcastle Courant*, 25 February 1876, p.6; *The Times*, 21 May 1877, p.6; *The British Architect and Northern Engineer*, Vol. 7, 1 June 1877, p.341; *The Art Journal*, Vol. 40, 1888, p.132; *Lloyd's Weekly Newspaper*, 28 July 1895, p.11; *Lloyd's Weekly Newspaper*, 3 September 1899, p.2; Altick, Richard D., *Paintings from Books*, Ohio State University Press, 1985, Part One, Chapter 7, p.147; Parkinson, Ronald, *Catalogue of British Oil Paintings 1820-1860*, London 1990, pp.292-94; Christian, John, *Shakespeare in Western Art*, 1992, pp.162-163; Upstone, Robert, *The Pre-Raphaelite Dream*, 2003, p.62.

The Examiner had these comments when the painting was shown at the Royal Academy in 1854: "A most poetical bit of homely literalness is an interior – a bit of old staircase, with a narrow landing and a window, *In Shakespeare's House*, by Mr. H. Wallis. Such a picture sets the mind at work, and is not to be forgotten."

The dog and the objects reminiscent of Shakespeare and of passages in his plays, were added later by Sir Edwin Landseer, R.A. Information from the Victoria and Albert Museum notes: "Painted by Wallis as a straightforward view of the staircase leading up to the room where Shakespeare is supposed to have been born, it was exhibited at the R.A. in 1854 and presumably bought there by Forster (although he may have commissioned it). Later, in 1866, Forster accepted Sir Edwin Landseer's offer to make additions of 'memorials of the marvelous man himself'." Forster first visited Stratford-upon-Avon and Shakespeare's birthplace with Daniel Maclise and Charles Dickens in 1840, and in the early 1850s, as chairman of the London committee of the Royal Shakespearian Club, was instrumental in securing the birthplace property for the nation. He corrected and edited the third of Alexander Dyce's editions of Shakespeare's Works.

Landseer's role is described in a letter of 2 February 1867. Forster wrote to him when the picture was exhibited in 1867 at the Royal Scottish Academy: "The picture in its first state – then an ancient stone staircase wonderfully painted by Mr Henry Wallis, the painter subsequently of the *Death of Chatterton*, - was purchased by me fourteen or fifteen years ago. You had often said, as you saw it in my dining-room, that you'd like some day to put something from your own hand into it; and last summer, generously indulging my earnest wish to possess some memorial of our thirty years of uninterrupted friendship, you desired me to send this particular picture to you. That the staircase as represented had been copied from Shakespeare's House at Stratford-upon-Avon, you did not then know, or had forgotten. After no longer interval I saw in your painting-room, not what had been familiar to me for so many years, but what the Edinburgh Academy will now see."[3]

Wallis, not surprisingly, was unhappy with Landseer's additions, which included the dog dominating the foreground [see: Letter 40]. This may be why Wallis made a smaller watercolour version [see next listing].

Dr Levi Fox, the former Director of the Shakespeare Birthplace Trust, confirms that Wallis's depiction is remarkably accurate and remains unchanged today. The view is of the original staircase leading from the first floor back room, originally one of the bedrooms, to the attic floor above the front part of the house; the doorway on the left leads to the front bedroom, which since the 18th century has traditionally been identified as where Shakespeare was born on 23 April 1564.[4]

Cat. 11a. ***In Shakespeare's House, Stratford-upon-Avon***
*c.*1854; ?oil on canvas; dimensions unknown; whereabouts unknown.
PROVENANCE: James Fallows, Sunny Bank, Longsight, Manchester;[1] his estate sale Christie's, 23 May 1868, lot 77 bought by Ag (?Agnew's) for £26 5s.

This can not be the same work as the painting owned by Forster and must either be the oil sketch for this picture or another version.

Cat. 12. ***A Staircase at the House at Stratford-upon-Avon, in which Shakespeare was Born***
*c.*1854; watercolour; 45.7 x 33.7 cm (18 x 13¼ in.); The Shakespeare Birthplace Trust Collection, Stratford-upon-Avon.
INSCRIPTION: Signed and inscribed on label on the verso.
PROVENANCE: Wallis's studio and then by descent from the artist to his son Harold Wallis, then to his daughter-in-law Mary Wallis (née Mary Elizabeth Aymes), then her great-niece Vera G. Cooper (née Langley) (1910-1989) and thence by direct descent to her son John Harold Cooper and family until sold at Bonhams, London, 05 March 2002, lot 76, sold for £800; the Shakespeare Birthplace Trust Collection, Stratford-upon-Avon.
EXHIBITIONS: Old Water-Colour Society, Winter exhibition 1910, no. 81.

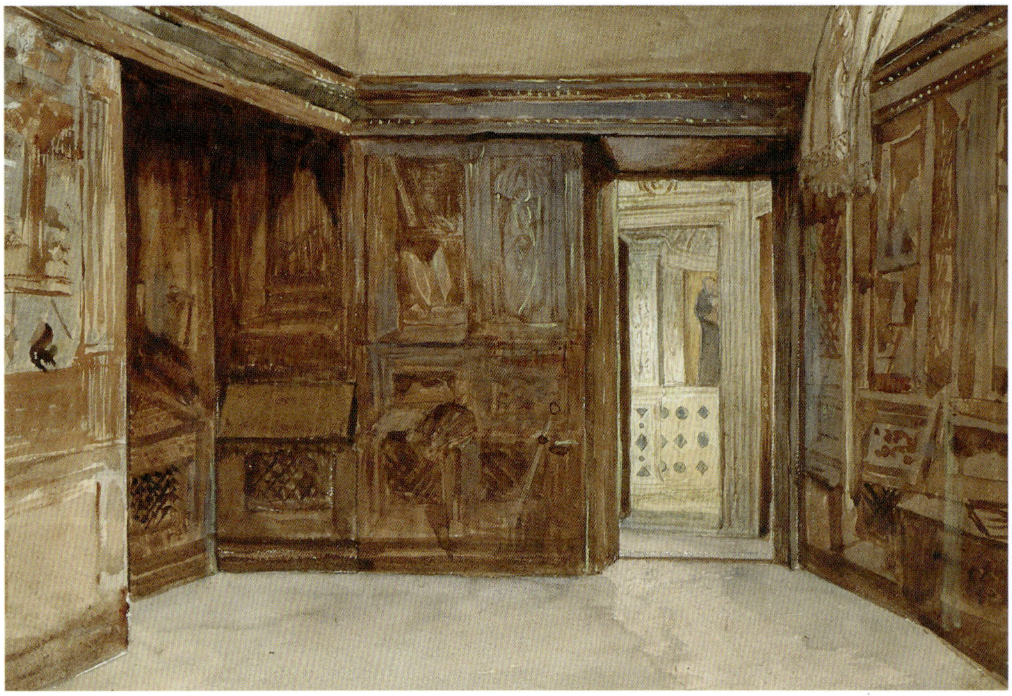

Cat. 13. Image courtesy of Bonhams, London

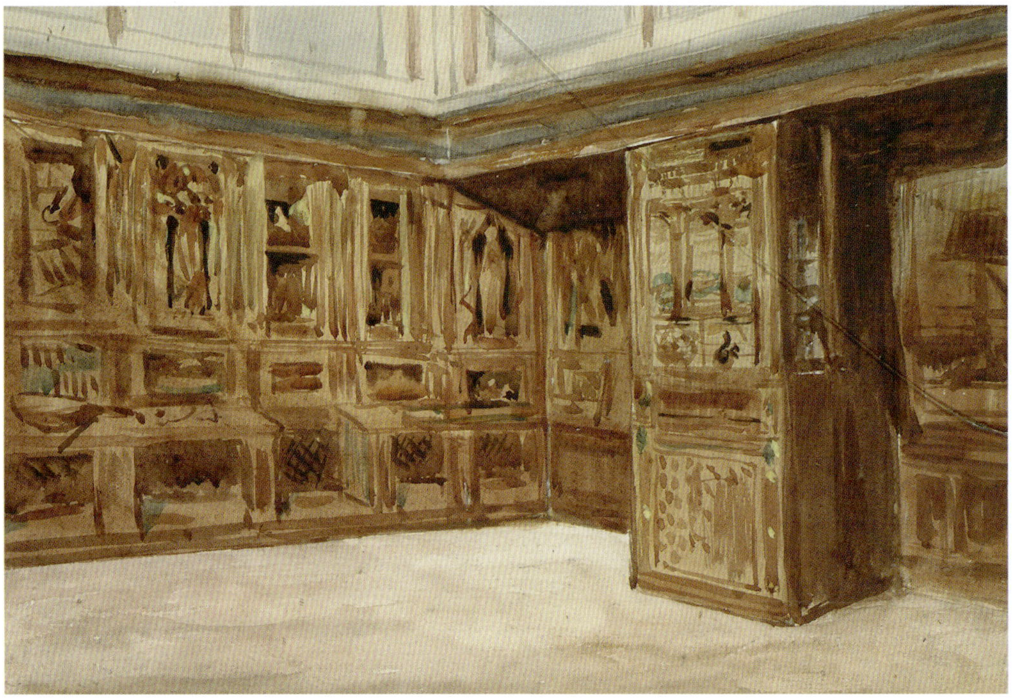

Cat. 13. Image courtesy of Bonhams, London

This is a smaller watercolour version of the oil painting, without Landseer's additions. Wallis probably made this copy after the original was bought by John Forster, but the exact date is uncertain. It may not even have been made until Wallis became aware of Landseer's additions to the oil painting. This version must have remained in Wallis's possession, however, for he exhibited it in 1910 at the Old Water-Colour Society's summer show, and it descended in his family.

Cat. 13. ***Interior Scenes of Shakespeare's Birthplace, Stratford-upon-Avon* – A pair**
*c.*1854; watercolour; 21.5 x 30.5 cm (8½ x 12 in.); private collection.
INSCRIPTION: Inscribed verso.
PROVENANCE: Anonymous sale, Bonhams, London, 8 March 2005, lot 104, bought in; Bonhams, London, 10 May 2005, lot 26, sold for £190; the watercolour illustrated superiorly was offered for sale on eBay in early July 2005.
EXHIBITIONS: ?Society of British Artists, 1854, no. 69

These two works continue Wallis's obvious fascination with Shakespeare's birthplace and were likely executed at about the same time as Cat. 8. In 1854 Wallis showed a work called *A Room in Shakespeare's House* at the Society of British Artists. This might possibly have been one of these two works.

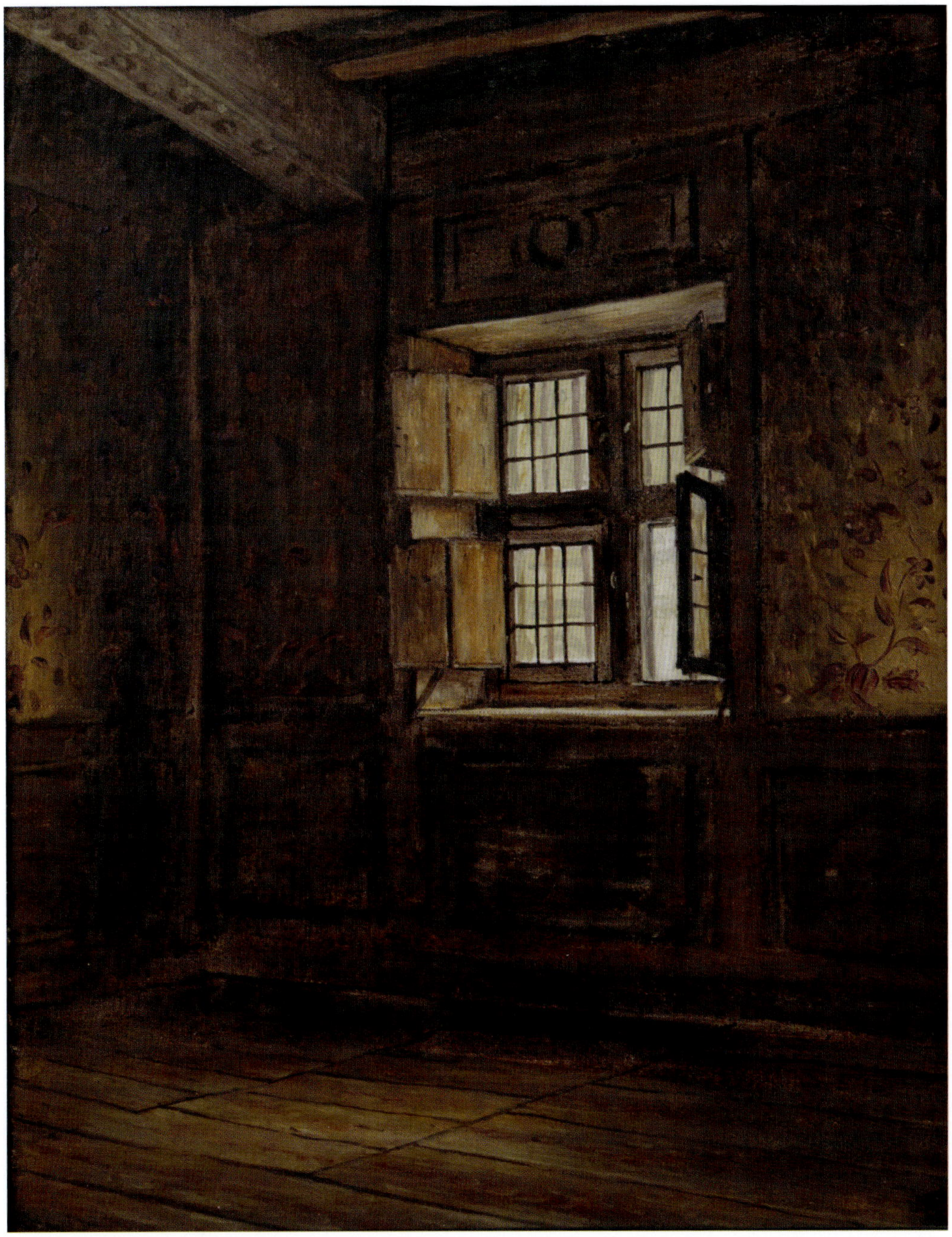

Cat. 14. Image courtesy of Diane Johnson, Paris; photograph by Alison Harris

Cat. 14. ***Interior of a Tudor House***
*c.*1854; oil on board; 32.6 x 25.2 cm (12⅞ x 9⅞ in.) - sight; private collection, Diane Johnson, Paris.
PROVENANCE: By descent from the artist to his daughter-in-law Alice Julyan Wallis (née Roberts), and thence to her great-niece Mrs. Vera G. Whiting, Purley, Surrey; given to Diane Johnson, in 1973.

When this work descended in the family it was referred to as *A Room in Shakespeare's House.* In 1854 Wallis had shown a work of this title at the Society of British Artists. This interior, however, looks far too grand to have been in Shakespeare's house. The wall covering appears to be Spanish stamped leather (*cuir de Cordoue*), which would have been very expensive in Tudor times and only the wealthy would have employed it. Jessie Petheram, the Museum Collections Officer for The Shakespeare's Birthplace Trust, agrees and points out that the interior has higher ceilings and deeper windows than Shakespeare's house.[1]

Cat. 15. ***The Font in which Shakespeare was Christened***
*c.*1853/54; oil on canvas; 20.3 x 30.5 cm (8 x 12 in.); whereabouts unknown.
PROVENANCE: This was still with Wallis in 1885 when he lent it to Frederic Fleay [see: Letter 40].
EXHIBITIONS: Royal Academy, 1854, no. 1269.
LITERATURE: *Notes and Queries,* 1904, p.159; Altick, Richard D., *Paintings from Books,* Ohio State University Press, 1985, Part One, Chapter 7, p.147; Upstone, Robert, *The Pre-Raphaelite Dream,* 2003, p.62.

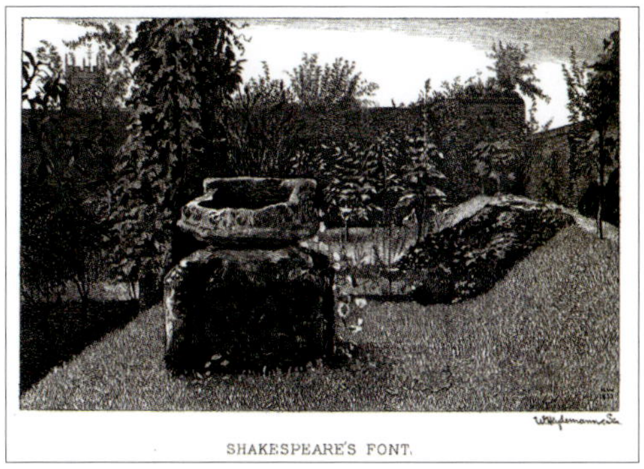

Cat. 15. Etching by William Heydemann after Henry Wallis

This work is known today only from an etching of 1886 by the British printmaker William Heydemann (1866-1917) which is reproduced before the introduction in Frederick Gard Fleay's *A chronicle history of the life and work of William Shakespeare* published in 1886. A note on p.364 states: "The *Font in which Shakespeare was baptized* has been obtained from a hitherto unreproduced original: an oil sketch made on the spot in 1853 by the world-known painter, Mr. Henry Wallis, and now [1886] in the artist's possession. It is with no little satisfaction that I find my work allowed to be associated with that of a painter so eminent." The flattering description no doubt reflects Fleay's long-standing friendship with Wallis.

The information is corroborated by a letter Wallis sent to his son from Cairo on 30 November 1885: "Fleay wants me to lend him an oil study of 'Shakespeare's Font'. It is carefully wrapped in brown paper, is about 12in by 8 & is, I think, in the back room, maybe on the drawers, if not it is resting on another picture. You will see it without removing anything. If you don't find it readily, I am afraid it is locked up. Look about it the first thing & communicate wth F. at once."[1]

Following an enquiry, Paul Taylor, from the Shakespeare Birthplace Trust Collection wrote: "Our Head of Research, Paul Edmondson did tell me something about what the image shows which relates to the history of the Norman font in which Shakespeare was baptised. It was removed from the church during the Reformation and turned up in the 19th century when it was being used as a cattle trough (so the story goes)."[2]

Cat. 16. ***The Parlour in Anne Hathaway's Cottage***
1854; oil on canvas; 25.4 x 50 cm (10 x 19¾ in.); private collection.
INSCRIPTIONS: Signed with title on an old label at the back.
PROVENANCE: T. Edwards; his sale Christie's, London, 14 July 1972, lot 136 as 'The Parlour in Anne Hathaway's Cottage, Stratford-on-Avon', bought Hancock for £900.

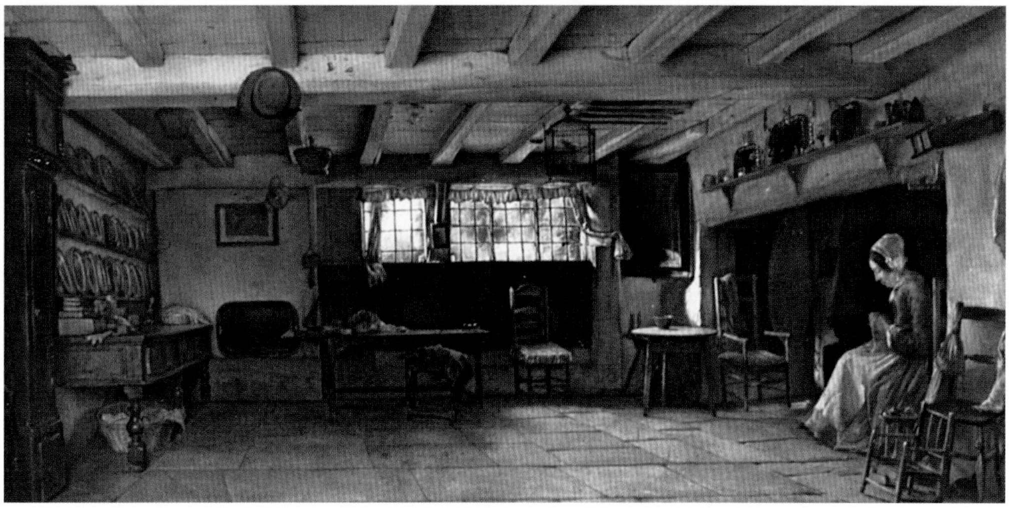

Cat. 16. Image courtesy of Christie's, London

Exhibitions: British Institution, 1854, no. 512, asking price £25 5s.[1]
Literature: *Morning Chronicle*, 16 February 1854, p.6; Altick, Richard D., *Paintings from Books*, Ohio State University Press, 1985, Part One, Chapter 7, p.148.

Altick has suggested the possibility that this work was shown at the British Institution because it had been rejected for the Royal Academy exhibition where Wallis showed three other related paintings that year. However, as the British Institution exhibition predates that of the Royal Academy, it obviously could not have been submitted to the Royal Academy first. The critic for the *Morning Chronicle* described this work as: "No. 512 is a representation by Mr. H. Wallis of 'The Parlour in Anne Hathaway's Cottage.' There is no attempt to reproduce any historic association. The room is delineated as it exists – a large low apartment, with a long range of old fashioned windows, an ample chimney on one side, and a well stocked dresser on the other. An eight-day clock is significant that the hat that is hanging on the rafter is not Shakespeare's hat, nor the girl who is at work in the corner of the chimney, Anne Hathaway."

Cat. 17. *A Night Study*
1854; ?oil on canvas; dimensions unknown; whereabouts unknown.
Exhibitions: Society of British Artists (Suffolk Street), 1854, no. 531; Royal Manchester Institution, *Exhibition of the works of Modern Artists*, 1854, no. 174, N.F.S.
Literature: *Manchester Courier and Lancashire General Advertiser*, 18 November 1854, p.9.

The reviewer for the *Manchester Courier* remarked: " 'A Night Study' is an ambitious project by H. Wallis, not successfully carried out; the production of such effects as that sought requires greater knowledge of peculiar aspects of light and shade than the artist has acquired." Unfortunately, there are no other details as to what exactly the subject was portrayed in this picture.

Cat. 18. *Fireside Reverie*
1855; oil on ?canvas; dimensions unknown; whereabouts unknown.
Provenance: John Miller,[1] Liverpool, likely purchased from the Liverpool Academy exhibition in 1855; his sale Christie's, 22 May 1858, lot 193, bought by the dealer Ernest Gambart for £26 5s.
Exhibitions: Royal Academy, 1855, no. 1150; Liverpool Academy, 1855, no. 743, priced at £40.[2]
Literature: *The Spectator*, Vol. 28, 2 June 1855, p.575; *The Literary Gazette*, 5 June 1858, p.546; *The Burlington Magazine*: 'Mr. Henry Wallis', Vol. 30, No. 168, March 1917, p.124; *The Connoisseur*, Vol. 94, part 2, 1934, pp.274-275; Darcy, Cornelius P., *The Encouragement of the Fine Arts in Lancashire 1760-1860*, 1976, p.148; Cooper, Robert M., *The Literary Guide and Companion to Southern England*, 1998, p.126; Haydock, James, *On a Darkling Plain: Victorian Poetry and Thought*, 2008, p.228; Joukovsky, Nicholas, 'The Merediths and their circle in 1856; a letter from Peter Augustin Daniel to Henry Wallis', *Notes and Queries*, Vol. 58, 2011, pp.557-561; Nicholas A. Joukovsky: 'The Early Meredithian Milieu: New Evidence from Letters of Peter Augustin Daniel', *Studies in Philology*, Vol. XV, Summer 2018, p.615.

When the painting was exhibited at the Royal Academy in 1855 it was accompanied by a quotation from George Meredith's poem of the same title: "Is she the star of one that is away? / She, that by the fire so gravely dreams, / In Evening's lulling stillness, while the ray / Tints her soft cheek, like Sunset on fair streams." The critic of *The Spectator* commented on the work: "A fourth Pre-raphaelite is Mr. Wallis; but his 'Fireside Reverie' though telling out very strongly in colour, is hardly up to his calibre. He has merely shown us he can paint; and that we knew before." Mary Ellen Meredith was the model for this picture.

The picture was purchased by the noted Liverpool collector John Miller, who interestingly also owned Ford Madox Brown's *Waiting: An English Fireside* of 1854-55, that is now in the collection of the Walker Art Gallery, Liverpool.

Cat. 19. *Study of a Girl Sitting in a Chair*
*c.*1855-58; pencil on paper; 40 x 29.5 cm. (16⅛ X 11⅝ in.); Tate Britain, London.
Provenance: By descent from the artist to his daughter-in-law Alice Julyan Wallis (née Roberts), and thence to her great-niece Mrs. Vera G. Whiting, Purley, Surrey; purchased from her by the Tate Gallery in 1973; museum acquisition no. T01723.

The sitter could possibly be Edith Nicolls, Mary Ellen Meredith's daughter by her first marriage. The drawing was supposedly made around 1855,[1] when Edith would have been aged 11, but the model appears slightly older, which makes the identification seem unlikely. Joukovsky, however, suggests a date for the drawing of *c.*1858.[2] Comparing the photo with the drawing, if she were the sitter, then it appears that Wallis has idealised her face, softening her features, particularly the nose. There is a physical resemblance between the model and Mary Ellen Meredith (below, right), then aged 34, so if a strong family resemblance existed between mother and teenaged daughter this would strengthen the potential identification.
The following points from the Tate Britain *Catalogue and acquisition files* appear to be relevant:

1. In a letter of 15 February 1974 from the former owner Mrs Whiting to Leslie Parris (former Tate curator), she writes: "I have no ideas about the identity of the model".

2. Both curators the authors spoke with at the Tate Britain think the model must have been aged 13 or 14, which means, assuming that Edith Nicolls was the model, that 1858 is a more likely date.

3. A letter from Robin Hamlyn, a former Tate curator, to Mrs. J.R. Haven, 1 May 1985 states: "I never discovered the present whereabouts of *Fireside Reverie* nor did I find a reproduction of it. However, I do feel that a drawing we have here (T01723) – a study of a girl sitting in a chair – may well be related to this painting. A note I made at the time I was researching indicates that I

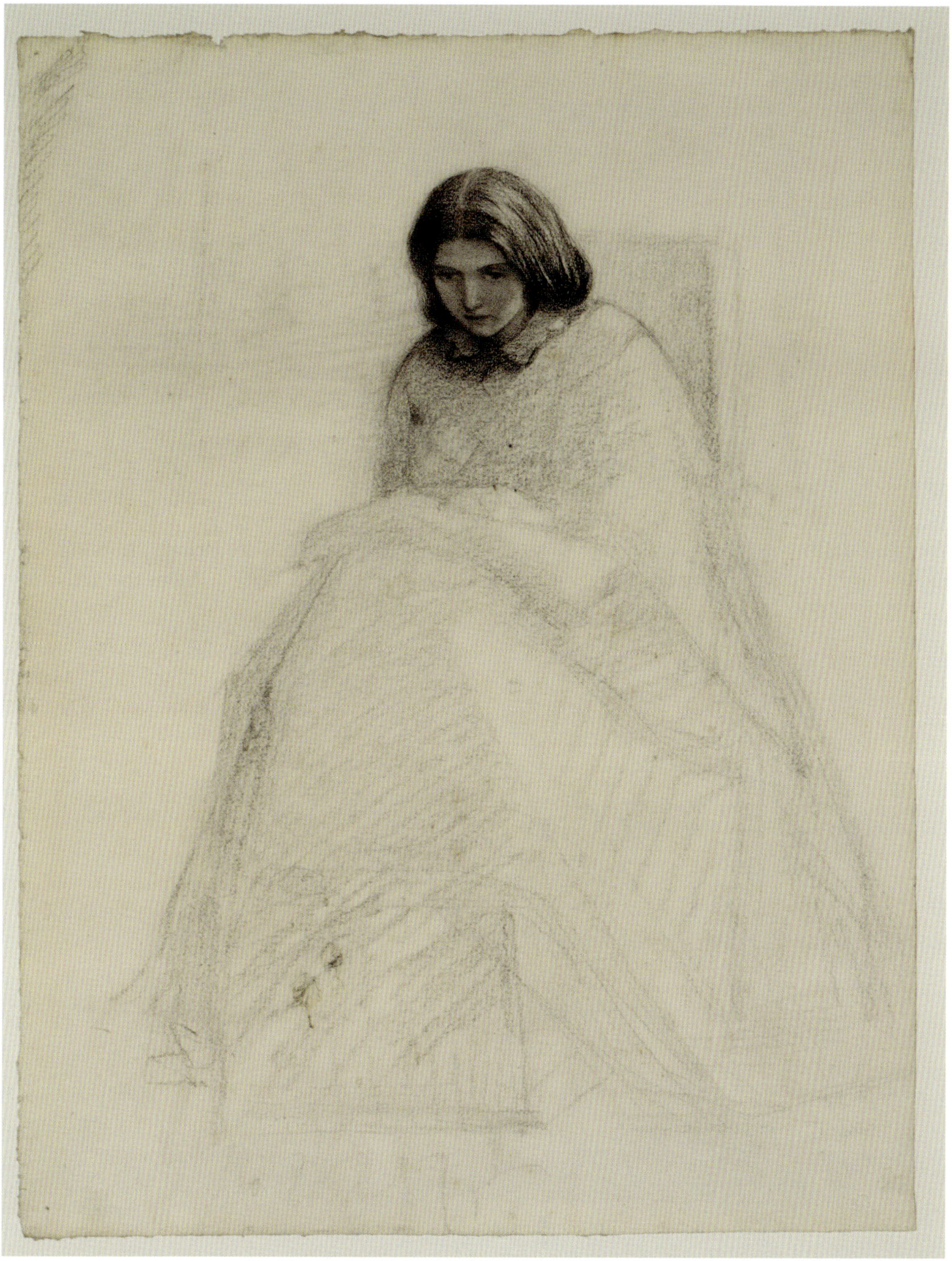

Cat. 19. Image by permission of Tate, London, 2016

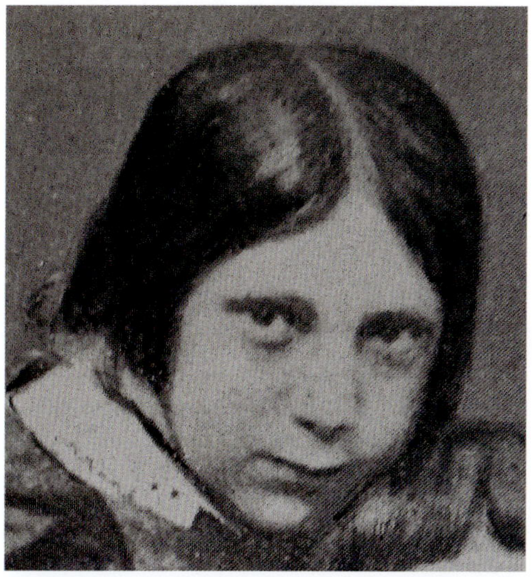

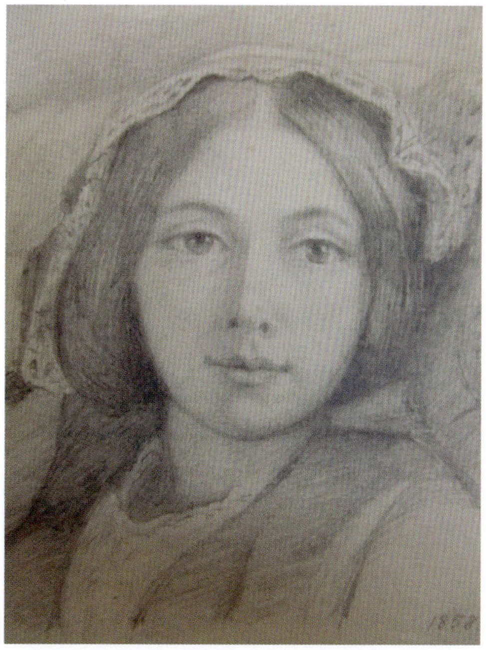

cf. Cat. 19. (Above) Photograph of Edith Nicholls, 1856 published in S.M. Ellis's biography of George Meredith, facing p.86. (Right) *Portrait of Mary Ellen Meredith* [Cat.32], 1858 Oxford, Ashmolean Museum. Image courtesy of Bonhams, London

thought our drawing was a portrait of Mrs Meredith. The pose and the mood seem to match the little we know about the picture's subject."

Cat. 20. ***A Study at Fontainebleau***
1855; ?oil on canvas; dimensions unknown; whereabouts unknown.
Exhibitions: Society of British Artists, 1855, no. 16, asking price £10 10s.

Fontainebleau was a village south-southeast of Paris and a suburb of Avon in the 19th century. The forest of Fontainbleau was a popular destination for the Barbizon school of painters. Wallis would have been familiar with their work from his earlier studies in Paris. Whether the Barbizon school influenced this work is unknown. It is known that Wallis was in Barbizon in the autumn of 1854. On 25 September, 1854, his friends P.A. Daniel and Arthur Hughes left London on a trip to France. Daniel tried unsuccessfully to find Wallis, first in Paris and then in Barbizon, before returning to England.[1]

Cat. 21. ***The Present***
1855; ?oil on canvas; dimensions unknown; whereabouts unknown.
Provenance: Thomas Miller,[1] No. 5, Wincley Square, Preston by 1855; after his death in 1865 possibly by descent to his son Thomas Horrocks Miller (1846-1916) but it was not in the sale of his son Thomas Pitt Miller at Christie's on 26 April 1946.
Exhibitions: Society of British Artists, 1855, no. 18, asking price: £31 10s; Royal Manchester Institution, *Exhibition of the Works of Modern Artists*, the thirty-seventh, 1855, no. 83, asking price £20 0s.

The exact subject of this work is unknown because no contemporary reviews have been found.

Cat. 22. ***The Death of Chatterton* (*Chatterton*)**
1855-56; oil on canvas; 62.2 x 93.3 cm. (24½ x 36 in.); Tate Britain, London.
Inscriptions: Signed *H. Wallis* and dated *1856*.
Annotation: (on the frame) "Cut is the branch that might have grown full straight, and burned is Apollo's laurel bough." [1]
Provenance: Purchased from Wallis by Augustus Egg R.A. in 1857; his sale Christie's, 18 May 1863, lot 146, purchased by Thos. Agnew & Sons for £813 15s; sold to Samuel Withers,[2] Liverpool, by 1867; his sale Foster's, 25 February 1868, bought J. Colls for Mr. Potts (?Major John

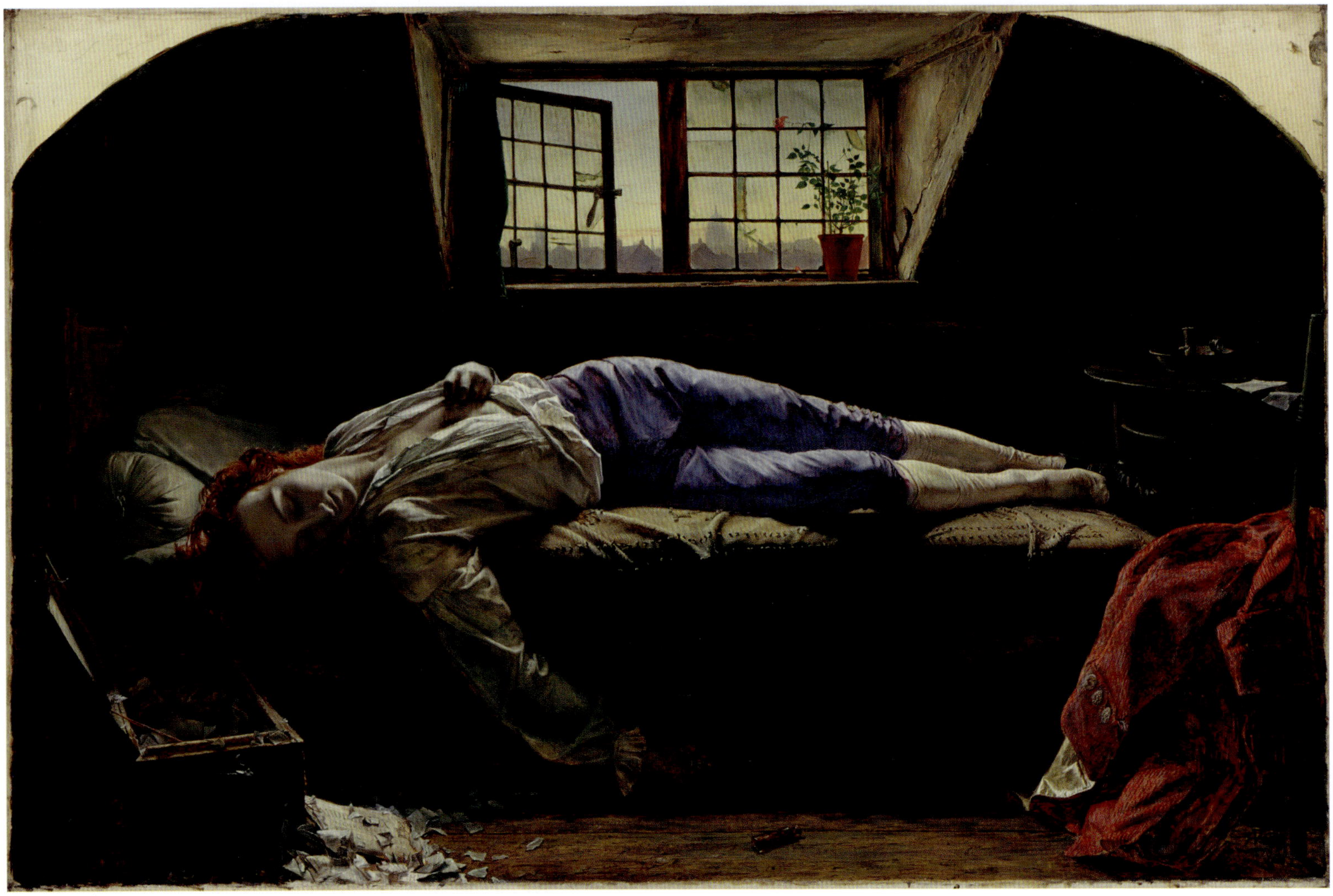

Cat. 22. Image by permission of Tate, London, 2016

Potts[3]) for 520 g; A.W. McDougall, Battle Fields, Lansdowne, Bath, by 1868; his sale Christie's, 13 March 1869, lot 91, bought in at £410; Charles Gent Clement[4] (1825-1899) by 1886; bequeathed to the Tate Gallery in 1899, museum acquisition no. N01685.

Exhibitions: Royal Academy, 1856, no. 352; Manchester, *Art Treasures Exhibition*, 1857, no. 371; Mr. Cranfield's Gallery, Grafton-street, Dublin, 1859; Birmingham, 1860, venue?; Mr. Haseé's Gallery, Leeds, 1860; Messrs. McClure & Son Gallery, Glasgow, 1862; Paris, *Exposition Universelle*, 1867, no. 150; Leeds, *National Exhibition of Works of Art*, 1868, no. 1391; Whitechapel Art Gallery, London, *Fine Art Exhibition*, 1886, no. 150; Birmingham Museum and Art Gallery, *The Pre-Raphaelites. Special Loan Collection of Modern Pictures in Oil and Water Colours*, 1891, no. 200; Liverpool Corporation, Walker Art Gallery, *Twenty-first Annual Autumn Exhibition of Modern Works of Art*, 1892, no. ?; Guildhall Gallery, *Loan Exhibition of Modern English Art*, 1895, no. 86; Tate Gallery, London, *Centenary Exhibition The Pre-Raphaelite* Brotherhood, 1948, no. 22; Bibliothèque Nationale, Paris, *Le Livre Anglais*, 1951, no. 497; Manchester, *Art Treasures Centenary*, 1957, no. 212; Royal Academy Bicentenary, 1968-69, no. 393; Arts Council, various venues, *Great Victorian Pictures*, 1978, no. 59; Tate Gallery, London, 1984, *The Pre-Raphaelites*, no. 75; National Gallery of Art, Washington, *The Victorians*, 1997, no. 20; Tate Britain, *Romantics*, 2000; Manchester Art Gallery, *Art Treasures in Manchester: 150 Years On*, 2007; Tate Britain, London, and other venues, *Pre-Raphaelites Victorian Avant-Garde*, 2012-2013, no. 45; Tate Britain, London, *Painting with Light*, 2016, p.60, fig.50.

Literature: *The Art Journal*, New Series, Vol. II, 1856, p.169, p.277; *The Morning Chronicle*, 5 May 1856, p.7; *The Athenaeum*, No. 1489, 10 May 1856, pp.590-1; *The Examiner*, 10 May 1856, p.293; *The Illustrated London News*, 10 May 1856, p.509, pp.512-14; *TheTimes*, 12 May 1856, p.12; *Literary Gazette*, 17 May 1856, p.284; *The Saturday Review*, 17 May 1856, p.58; *Lloyd's Weekly Newspaper*, 18 May 1856, p.8; *The London Daily News*, London, 21 May 1856, p.2; *The Spectator Supplement*, Vol. 29, 24 May 1856, p.570; *The Examiner*, 31 May 1856, p.341; *The Morning Chronicle*, 8 August 1856, p.5; Rossetti, William Michael: 'Art News from England. Letter XX', *The Crayon, vol.* 3, Dec. 1856, pp.372-373; *The Daily News*, London, 2 June 1857, p.2; *The Advocate* (Irish Industrial Journal), 30 March 1859, p.4; *The Lady's Newspaper*, 11 February 1860, p.101; *Birmingham Daily Post*, 16 April 1860, p.2; *Leeds Mercury*, No. 7158, 8 September 1860; *The Glasgow Daily Herald*, 22 May 1862, p.2; *The London Daily News*, 19 May 1863, p.6; *Freeman's Journal*, 21 December 1864, p.3; *The Art Journal*, New Series, Vol. 6, 1867,

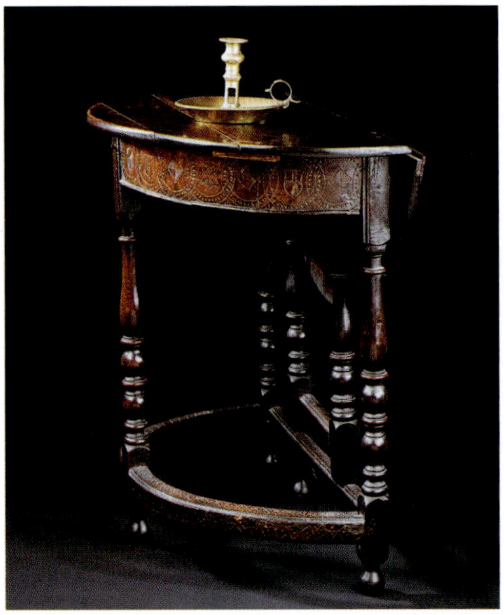

Wallis's oak credence-table and brass chamberstick, used as models for *Chatterton*; sold in 2002. Image courtesy of Bonhams, London

p.131, p.245; *The Times*, 6 June 1867, p.13; *The Leeds Mercury*, 7 June 1867, p.4; *The Art Journal*, New Series, Vol. 7, 1868, p.156; *The Leeds Mercury*, 19 May 1868, p.8; *The Leeds Mercury*, 4 July 1868, p.8; *Pall Mall Gazette*, 20 November 1868, p.10; *The Saturday Review*, Vol. 35, 10 May 1873, p.618; *The Era*, 21 June 1884, p.5; *Birmingham Daily Post*, 2 October 1891, p.4; *The Athenaeum*, No. 3337, 10 October 1891, p.491; *The British Architect*, Vol. 36, 1892, p.262; *The Magazine of Art*, Vol. 15, 1892, p.ii; *The Magazine of Art*, Vol. 18, 1895, p.317; *The Times*, 22 April 1895, p.4; *Daily Telegraph & Courier*, 22 April 1895, p.4; *The Athenaeum*, No. 3763, 9 December 1899, p.808; *The British Architect*, Vol. 52, 1900, p.419; Rowlands, Walter, *Among the Great Masters of Literature*, 1900, pp.145-151; *The Nation's Pictures*, 1901, Vol. IV, pl.17; Cook, E.T. & Wedderburn, A. [Eds.], *The Works of John Ruskin, Royal Academy Notes 1856*, Vol. XIV, London, 1904, p.60; Holman Hunt, William, *Pre-Raphaelitism and the Pre-Raphaelite Brotherhood*, 1905, Vol. II, p.88; Phythian, J. E., *Fifty Years of Modern Painting*, 1908, p.162; Bate, Percy, *The English Pre-Raphaelite Painters*, 1910, p.86; *The Burlington Magazine*, March 1917, p.124; Aitken, Charles, 'English 19th Century Art at the National Gallery', *The Burlington Magazine*, Vol. 31, No. 172, July 1917, p.9, p.124; Welby, T. Earle, *The Victorian Romantics 1850-70*, 1929, p.85; Gaunt, William, *The Pre-Raphaelite Tragedy*, 1942, p.64; Ironside, Robin & Gere, John, *Pre-Raphaelite Painters*, 1943, p.44, pl.71; Gaunt, William, *A Concise History of English Painting*, 1964, p.182, fig.140; Schiff, Gert, 'The Death of Chatterton', *Neue Zürcher Zeitung*, 5 February 1966; Graham Reynolds, *Victorian Painting*, 1966, pp.68-69; Parris, Leslie, *The Pre-Raphaelites*, 1966, fig.24; Bell, Quentin, *Victorian Artists*, 1967, p.44, pl.34; Maas, Jeremy, *Victorian Painters*, 1969, p.133 (illus.); Hilton, Timothy, *The Pre-Raphaelites*, 1970, pp.122-123, fig.87; Watkinson, Raymond, *Pre-Raphaelite Art and Design*, 1970, p.164; Nicoll. John, *The Pre-Raphaelites*, 1970, pl.90; Kelly, Linda, *The Marvellous Boy: The Life and Myth of Thomas Chatterton*, 1971, pp.116-119; Wood, Christopher, *Dictionary of Victorian Painters*, 1971, p.398; Lutyens, Mary, 'Letters from Sir John Everett Millais, Bart, P.R.A. (1829-1896) and William Holman Hunt, O.M. (1827-1910) in the Henry E. Huntington Library, San Marino, California', *The Volume of the Walpole Society*, Vol. 44, 1972-1974, p.45; Staley, Allen, *The Pre-Raphaelite Landscape*, 1973, p.88; Sambrook, James [Ed.], *Pre-Raphaelitism*, 1974, p.123; Larkin, David, *The English Dreamers*, 1975, pl.18; Williamson, Audrey, *Artists and Writers in Revolt The Pre-Raphaelites*, 1976, p.42; Harding, James, *The Pre-Raphaelites*, 1977, p.84; Wood, Christopher, *Dictionary of Victorian Painters*, 1978, p.748; Landow, G.P., *William Holman Hunt and Typological Symbolism*, 1979, p.80 (illus.); Landow, G. P., *Victorian Types, Victorian Shadows*, 1980, p.141; Wood, Christopher, *The Pre-Raphaelites*, 1981, p.61 and p.68(illus.); Bell, Quentin, *A New and Noble School The Pre-Raphaelties*, 1982, pp.90-91; Beninger, Kenneth, *An Introduction to Victorian Painting*, 1985, p.36; Altick, Richard D., *Paintings from Books*, Ohio State University Press, 1985, Part One, Chapter 7, pp.161-2, fig.127, p.16; Marchwinski, Alena, 'The Romantic Suicide and the Artists', *Gazette Des Beaux-Arts*, Vol. 6, February 1987, pp.70-72, fig. 4, p.70; Adams, Steven, *The Art of the Pre-Raphaelites*, 1988, p.8, p.74; Pointon, Marcia, *Pre-Raphaelites Re-viewed*, 1989, p.97, n. 3; Treuherz, Julian, *Victorian Painting*, 1993, p.94; Macleod, Dianne Sachko, *Art and the Victorian middle class*, Cambridge University Press, 1996, p.129; Hawksley, Lucinda, *Essential Pre-Raphaelites*, 1999, pp.182-183; Prettejohn, Elizabeth, *The Art of the Pre-Raphaelites*, 2000, pp.174, 192-193, 195, 205, 218, fig. 153; *Apollo*, CLV, June 2001, fig. 7, p.484; Crespon-Halotier, Brigitte, *Les peintres britanniques dans les Salons parisiens, des origines à 1939*, Répertoire, Dijon, 2002; Brown, Ron, 'Suicidal Tendencies', *Tate: The Art Magazine*, Spring 2002, p.54; Pergam, Elizabeth A., 'Creating a Furore, Annibale Carracci's 'The Three Maries', Thomas Gainsborough's 'Blue Boy' and Henry Wallis's 'Death of Chatterton' at the Manchester Art Treasures Exhibition', *Apollo*, vol 155, June 2002, pp.48-53, fig. 7; Upstone, Robert, *The Pre-Raphaelite Dream*, 2003, p.87; Hardy, Pat, *Art Treasures in Manchester: 150 Years On*, Manchester Art Gallery, 6 October 2007 - 27 January 2008, *The British Art Journal*, Vol. VIII, No. 3, pp.74-75, p.74 (ill.); Savu, Laura E., *Postmortem Postmodernists: the Afterlife of the Author in Recent Narrative*, 2009, pp.12-128; Robinson, Michael, *The Pre-Raphaelites*, 2012, p.97; Sanders, Andrew, *In the Olden Time. Victorians and the British Past*, 2013, cover illustration; Lessens, Ronald, 'Henry Wallis (1830-1916), a neglected Pre-Raphaelite', *The British Art Journal*, vol. XV, No. 1, 2014, p.47, p.48, p.51; Burchall, Heather, *Praraffaeliten*, 2016, p.94; Prettejohn, Elizabeth, *Modern Painters, Old Masters*, 2017, p.114; Petiot, Aurélie, *Le Préraphaélisme*, 2019, pp.103, 367-368.

The story of Thomas Chatterton (1752-1770), a young poet who committed suicide, has always been a favourite with poets and novelists, from Vigny to Ackroyd.[5] Born in Bristol, Chatterton started at an early age as a poet and a critic. At St. Mary Redcliffe, his father Thomas Chatterton, who was a schoolmaster, discovered some late medieval parchments, which he used to cover schoolbooks and his wife Sarah to fix the pins for her lacework. After his father's death, Chatterton, dazzled by their beauty, decided to make a different use of the parchments and wrote upon them some of his own poems that he made public, claiming they belonged to Thomas Rowley, a minor fifteenth-century poet. His forgery was exposed by Horace Walpole[6] and the embittered author left Bristol for London on 24 April 1770.

Chatterton led a miserable and dissolute life, contributing to several publications just for survival, including the *Middlesex Journal*, as may be seen in Wallis's painting.[7] Being aware of his poverty, some people around him proposed to help, but the proud poet declined their offer, claiming he was not hungry. His last days can be reconstructed on the basis of the judicial enquiry and has been described by Louise Kaplan in the following terms: "Based on the probably not entirely reliable report given to the coroner by Frederick Angel, husband of Mrs Angel (landlady). According to Angel, on the afternoon of August 22, Chatterton returned to his lodgings in a passion about the baker's wife, who had refused him a loaf of bread until he paid the three shillings he already owed to her. When on August 23, Chatterton still seemed extremely agitated, Mrs. Angel had inquired, 'What ails you?' The young poet had replied, 'Nothing. Nothing. Why do you ask?' Around 10 on the morning of August 24, he left with a bundle of papers under his arms saying that he was putting them in a place of safety lest they meet with an accident. Mr. Cross, the apothecary, saw him at 11:30 when he stopped in to ask for some arsenic, supposedly for an experiment he was conducting. Chatterton did not return to the Angels' until 7 P.M., and nobody seemed to know how Chatterton spent this last afternoon of his life or what happened to that bundle of papers. That evening he was pale and dejected. He sat with Mr. and Mrs. Angel moping about and muttering rhymes in some unintelligible language until retiring to his room a few hours later. The assumption was that when the baker's wife had denied Chatterton a loaf of bread, the dignity of suicide was the proud boy's only option."[8] Chatterton is said to have been buried in a workhouse graveyard, but Walter Thornbury, in his *Old & New London*,[9] claimed that his body had been buried at Bristol. So far, this point has not been confirmed.

Speculations have been made that Chatterton may have had gonorrhea and died of an accidental overdose of some combination of drugs, including arsenic, used to treat the condition. Nick Groom, in his DNB biographical entry on Chatterton suggests accidental death: "Everyone assumed his death was suicide, but from Chatterton's ongoing successes (he had by the time he died published fifty-three pieces and secured a book contract), his finances (Hamilton, for instance, was adamant that '*he did not die for want*') and his irrepressibly lusty spirits (in the last letters to Cary and Catcott), the devastating conclusion is that he died simply from unwisely mixing his venereal medicine with his recreational drugs".[10] Louise J. Kaplan is more cautious, however, and mentions this simply as a possibility.

In terms of the painting itself one must start with the simple question as to what the actual title of the painting is? It is often referred to as *The Death of Chatterton*, and frequently simply as *Chatterton*. When the work was exhibited at the Royal Academy in 1856 (no. 352), the catalogue lists the title as *Chatterton*. The reviewer of the *Athenaeum*, as well as Ruskin in his *Academy Notes* did the same. When the painting was exhibited at the Art Treasures Exhibition in Manchester in 1857, however, it was entitled *The Death of Chatterton* and when Wallis painted a copy of the original, now at the Birmingham Museums and Art Gallery, he entitled it *The Death of Chatterton* on the back. This was certainly the title prevailing in the Literature published during the second half of the nineteenth century and into the twentieth century. One may, therefore, conclude that the painting was originally entitled *Chatterton*, but soon became better known as *The Death of Chatterton*. Both names will therefore be used interchangeably, depending on the context.

In the first half of his career, Wallis was close to the Pre-Raphaelites and adopted their painting techniques of "truth to nature" for his pictures. At the same time, the painting is also an idealistic rendering, since "contemporaries described Chatterton's body as convulsed in agony, his features contorted and the bottle of poison clutched in his hand. Wallis's figure, by contrast, is stretched out across the bed in an attitude more reminiscent of erotic abandon, or a drugged sleep, than death. His expression is peaceful and his limbs are relaxed. One arm languidly pulls his shirt open to reveal his unblemished chest, while the other hangs limply over the edge of the bed, leading the spectator's gaze to the bottle of poison on the floor. These artistic liberties, like the flawless perfection of Chatterton's skin, create an image of the poet as an exquisite young martyr".[11] Andrew Sanders states that "Chatterton does attempt to endow an ordinary man with an iconic dignity which had formerly been reserved for religious or courtly figures. This is a *pietà* without supporting saints and a ceremonial lying-in-state without the ceremony and the state."[12]

This mix between realism and idealism is particular to the Pre-Raphaelite productions of the time. Wallis finished the painting in 1855 and exhibited it at the Royal Academy the following year. No portraits of Chatterton were known, so Wallis was free to invent his appearance.[13] "Like many artists associated with Pre-Raphaelitism, he preferred to use friends rather than professional models. He apparently chose George Meredith who, like Chatterton at the time of his death, was a young and unappreciated poet. Meredith's fine features and long hair were well-suited to the role."[14] However, no direct evidence has ever been found to prove beyond doubt that Meredith was indeed the model.

Wallis emphasised Chatterton's effeminate and narcissistic side, not only by the pose, but also with the elegant clothes. He allegedly painted it in the room where Chatterton had died (Brooke Street), and this "has been cited as one of the most notable instances of the Pre-Raphaelite concern for truth".[15] Thornbury published an engraving of no. 39 Brooke Street, in which it can be seen that the attic storey is identical to the one reproduced in Wallis's painting. However, it has been established that, seen from there, the view of St. Paul's could not have been identical. At the time the painting was finished, Wallis was sharing rooms at 8 Gray's Inn Square with his friend P.A. Daniel, a few minutes walk away from Brooke Street, and it is now known that *Chatterton* was painted there. P.A. Daniel's journal for 5 May 1856 reads: "Then to the opening of the Royal Academy – where of course was a great crowd. Met every body I knew there. The Exhibition is not a startling one but it contains many excellent works...Wallis too has made a great hit and established his name by his 'Death of Chatterton' an excellent picture but without the interest of novelty to me who have watched its progress from the first slight sketch to its completion – indeed it was painted in the very room I now write in."[16] The point about where it was painted may have some importance for art historians, but has no influence on our aesthetic appreciation of the work. An artist always uses disparate elements and pieces them together in his own particular way to create a new reality. Realistic elements portrayed in the painting, such as the brass chamberstick candle holder, and the oak Credence-table, remained in the Wallis family and were offered for sale in 2002.[17] The table was essentially 17th century with extensive restorations and later carved decoration; the brass chamberstick was 1st quarter of the 19th century.

Exhibited in 1856 at the Royal Academy and in 1857 at the Art Treasures Exhibition in Manchester, the painting was a tremendous success. When the picture was shown in Manchester it is said that two policemen were needed to protect it from the crowd.[18] The reviewer of *The Athenaeum* was enthusiastic about this picture: "One of the most thoughtful pictures exhibited this year is Mr. Wallis's *Chatterton* (352), a sad scene, full of pathos; though, perhaps, too sad for those whose path of life is softly carpeted, and who shut their doors on all unpleasant realities.... Mr. Wallis represents the dead poet, the poison-phial just slipped from his relaxed hand, stretched cold and stiff on a miserable pallet below a garret window, through whose horny, smoked panes, we see the careless city, crowned by the mountain dome that is for everlasting. This is the whole picture, the rest of the story being told by a candle just gone out, the blue stifling smoke of which curdles about the ceiling. By the bed-side is a chest full of torn poems, for the proud lad, who would rather starve than share his landlady's dinner, spent his last moments in carefully destroying all he had written. In how many garrets have such scenes been enacted with the same great city hushed below, careless of the forms whose shadows fall upon its stones and pass away. Mr. Wallis has flattered Chatterton as to face, without doing him justice, his great laughing eyes, rich flood of hair, and proud sullen mouth were worthy of the Apollo. The body is well drawn, and the satin coat and violet breeches for a pleasant unison of colour."[19]

John Ruskin had not yet declared war on some of the Pre-Raphaelites and his enthusiasm for this picture pervades his *Academy Notes*: "Faultless and wonderful: a most noble example of the great school. Examine it well inch by inch: it is one of the pictures which intend and accomplish the entire placing before your eyes of an actual fact – and that a solemn one. Give it much time."[20]

Like every fashionable Victorian, Charles Dickens visited the 1856 Royal Academy exhibition and *Chatterton* drew his attention. He wrote to his sister-in-law Georgina Hogarth: "There is a painful picture of a great deal of merit (Egg has bought it) in the exhibition, painted by the man who did those little interiors of Forster's.[21] It is called 'The Death of Chatterton'. The dead figure is good deal like Arthur Stone,[22] and I was touched on Saturday to see that tender old file standing before it, crying under his spectacles at the idea of seeing his son dead. It was a very tender manifestation of his gentle heart."[23]

Despite the general enthusiasm for the work, some journalists were bound to find fault: "the poison bottle is upon the floor; but in truth it was found on the window-sill"; for example, and "the tone throughout

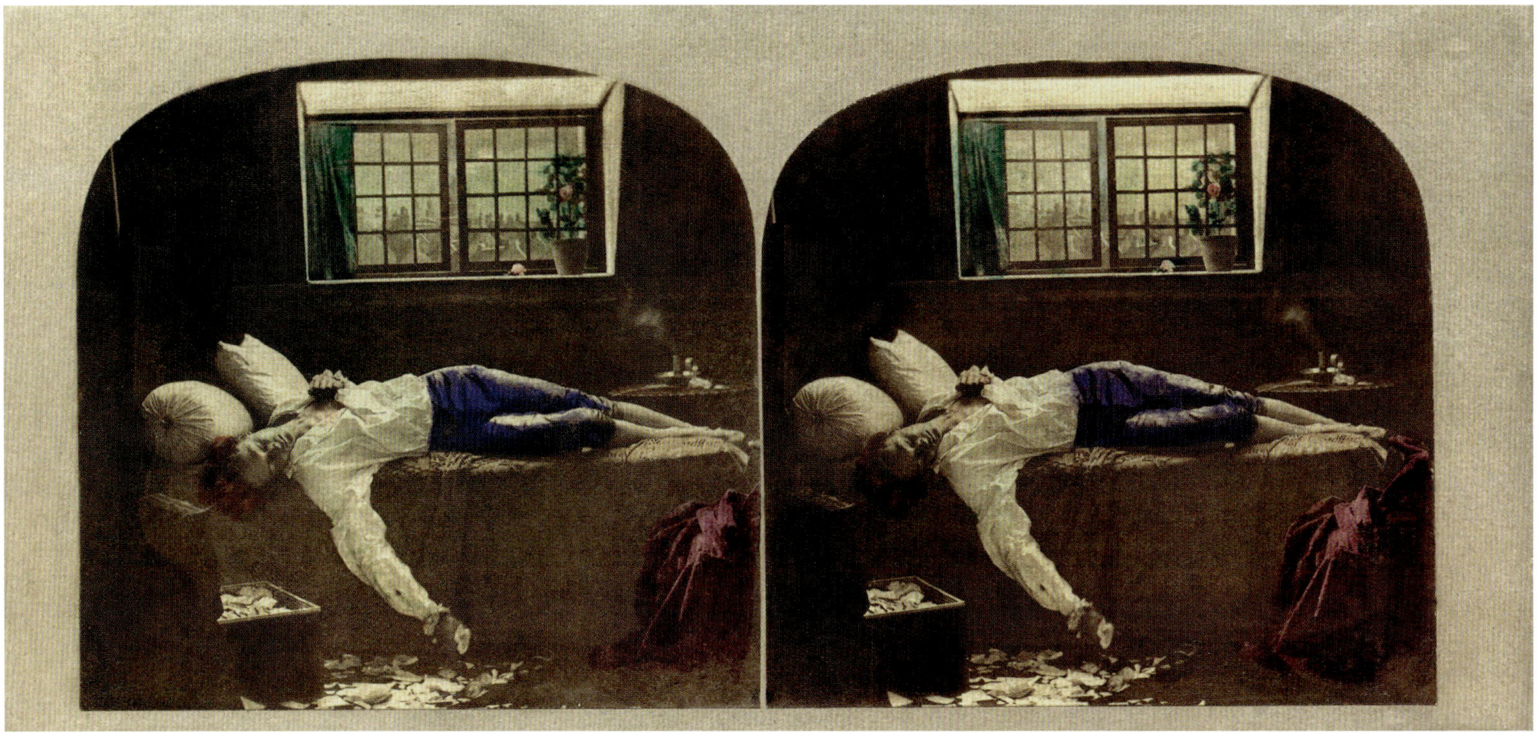

James Robinson, stereoscopic photograph, *The Death of Chatterton*, 1859. Image from Pellerin and May, *The Poor Man's Picture Gallery* (London Stereoscopic Company, 2014). Image © Dr. Brian May

[which] is too luxurious a description, too sensuous almost in its treatment, too unlike the poor boy who aspired to fame and was compelled to write for his living lampoons and laudatory poems on Lord Mayors."[24]

The privilege of fame was that Wallis himself, as well as other artists, made multiple copies and engravings of the picture.[25] Wallis's *Chatterton* was photographed by Charles Wright and the photograph was displayed in February 1857 at the Photographic Society. Counterfeits appeared and the makers of these *cartes de visite* and photographs were taken to court. The only person actually sued for breach of copyright was James Robinson over stereoscopic photographs he took based on Wallis's *Chatterton*. The original owner of the painting, Augustus Egg had sold the exclusive rights of publishing engravings of it to Robert Turner and had also given him the privilege of publically exhibiting the original painting for the purpose of securing subscribers for the anticipated print. It was exhibited widely, including in Dublin, where members of the public were charged the exorbitant entrance fee of six shillings; it was here that Robinson viewed *Chatterton*. The exhibition was attended with a restrictive notice to the spectators not to copy it in any way, or otherwise invade the owner's rights. Despite this, by 1856 Robinson had published his own meticulously recreated version of the painting with his young studio assistant posing as the dead poet. Robinson was sued, not by Wallis or Egg, but by Turner, for an alleged piracy of the painting and threatening the income of the printmaker who had the lucrative exclusive right to publish engravings of the painting. The case was decided in the Irish Chancery Court in Dublin in 1860. Turner won the case and Robinson was forced to destroy his stock of photographs.[26]

At that time, there was no Copyright Act in place to protect artists,[27] and they were furious at being constantly pirated by unscrupulous art dealers. On 19 June 1857, Holman Hunt wrote to Wallis (the 'picture' is, of course, *Chatterton*): "I hope that you will determinedly resist the publishing of the photograph of your picture. I find that Colnaghi has not given up the notion and it can only be stopped by a vigorous stand – which should be made by more than one. And to me it seems of the utmost importance that so bad a precedent should be crushed ere enactment."[28]

Cat. 22a. *The Death of Chatterton*
*c.*1855-56; oil on mahogany panel; 17.4 x 25.4 cm (6⅞ x 10 in.); Birmingham Museums and Art Gallery.
Inscriptions: Signed with initials *HW* in brown paint, lower left.
Annotation: (old label on the verso) "The Death of Chatterton / the original painting / Study by H. Wallis /-'The Marvellous Boy/The sleepless soul, that perished in its pride' / Wordsworth."
Provenance: Samuel Mendel, Manley Hall, Manchester;[1] his sale, Christie's 24 Apr 1875, lot 384, purchased by Agnew for 260 guineas; Baron Albert Grant;[2] his sale, Christie's 28 Apr 1877, lot 129, purchased by art dealer William Vokins for £157 10s;[3] sold in 1877 to the Rt. Hon. William Kenrick;[4] presented by him to Birmingham Museum and Art Gallery, 1918, accession no. 1918P43.
Exhibitions: Birmingham Museum and Art Gallery, *The Pre-Raphaelite Brotherhood*, 1947, no. 76; Birmingham Museum and Art Gallery, *Pictures from the City Art Gallery*, 1957, no. 46; Agnews, London, *Loan Exhibition of Pictures from Birmingham Art Gallery*, 1957, no. 46; Nottingham University Art Gallery, *Victorian Painting*, 1959, no. 73; Folkestone Art Gallery, *19th Century English Art*, 1965, no. 46; Mappin Art Gallery, Sheffield, *Victorian Paintings: 1837-1890*, 1968, no. 50; Royal Academy, *Bicentenary Exhibition 1768-1968*, 1968, no. 393; Brighton Museum and Art Gallery, *Death, Heaven and the Victorians*, 1970, no. 32; Manchester Art Gallery, Oct-Nov. 1986; Seattle Art Museum and other venues, *Visions of Love and Life*, 1995, no. 39; Alte Nationalgalerie, Berlin, *Fontane und die Bildende Kunst*, 1998, no. 70. *Victorian Radicals: From the Pre-Raphaelites to the Arts & Crafts Movement*, on loan from the Birmingham Museum and Art Gallery to eight American venues from October 2018 to May 2021, no. 44.
Literature: *The Art Journal*, New Series, Vol. IX, 1870, p.210; *The Architect*, Vol. 13, 20 February 1875, p.107: *Manchester Courier and Lancashire General Advertiser*, 26 March 1877, p.8; *The Sheffield and Rotherham Independent*, 29 March 1877, p.5; *The Manchester Times*, 7 April 1877, p.112; *London Daily News*, 30 April 1877, p.3; *The Morning Post*, 30 April 1877, p.2; *The Times*, 30 April 1877, p.6; *The British Architect*, Vol. 7, 1877, p.272; *The Architect*, Vol. 17, 5 May 1877, p.294; *The Academy*, 5 May 1877,

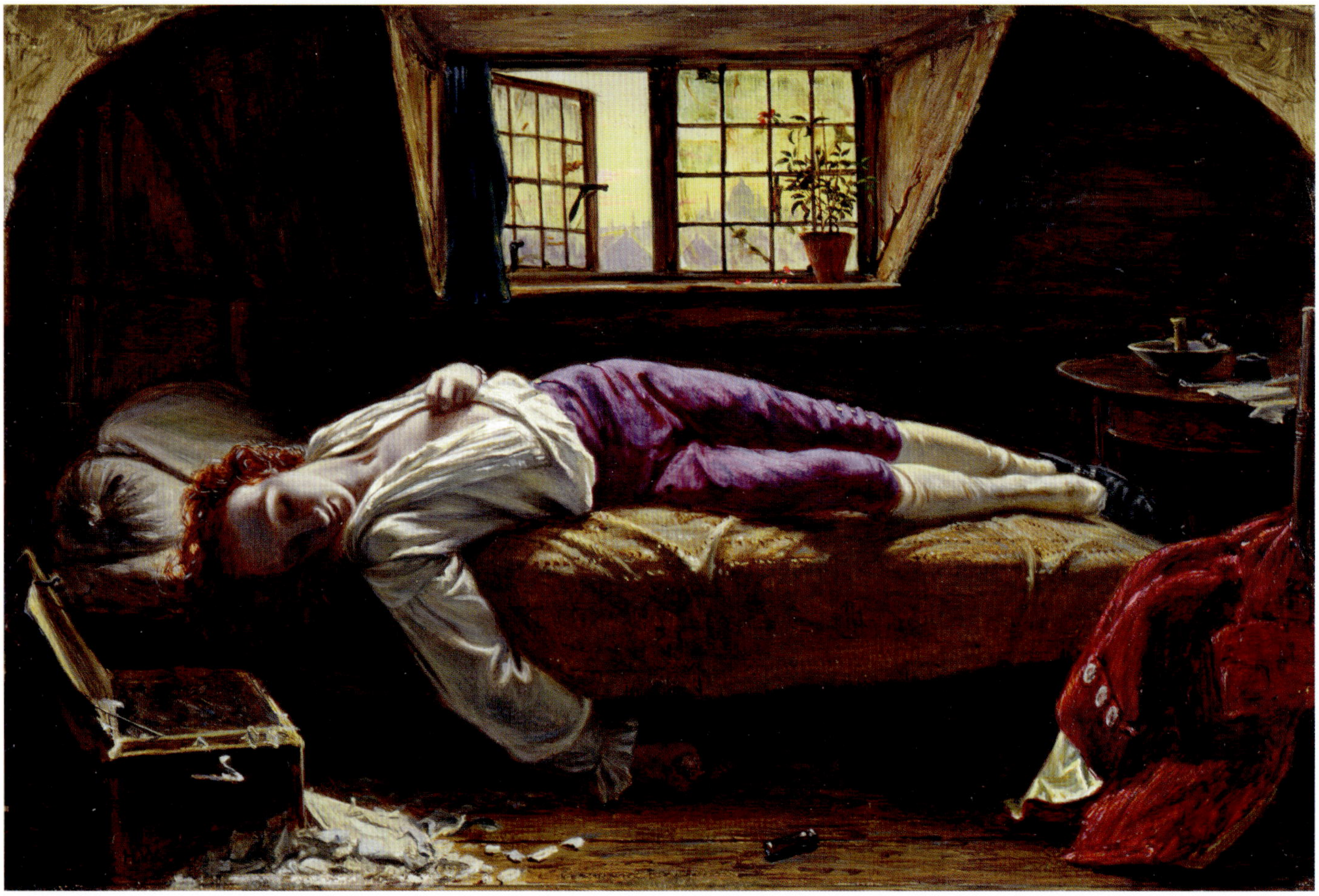

Cat. 22a. Image by permission of Birmingham Museums Trust

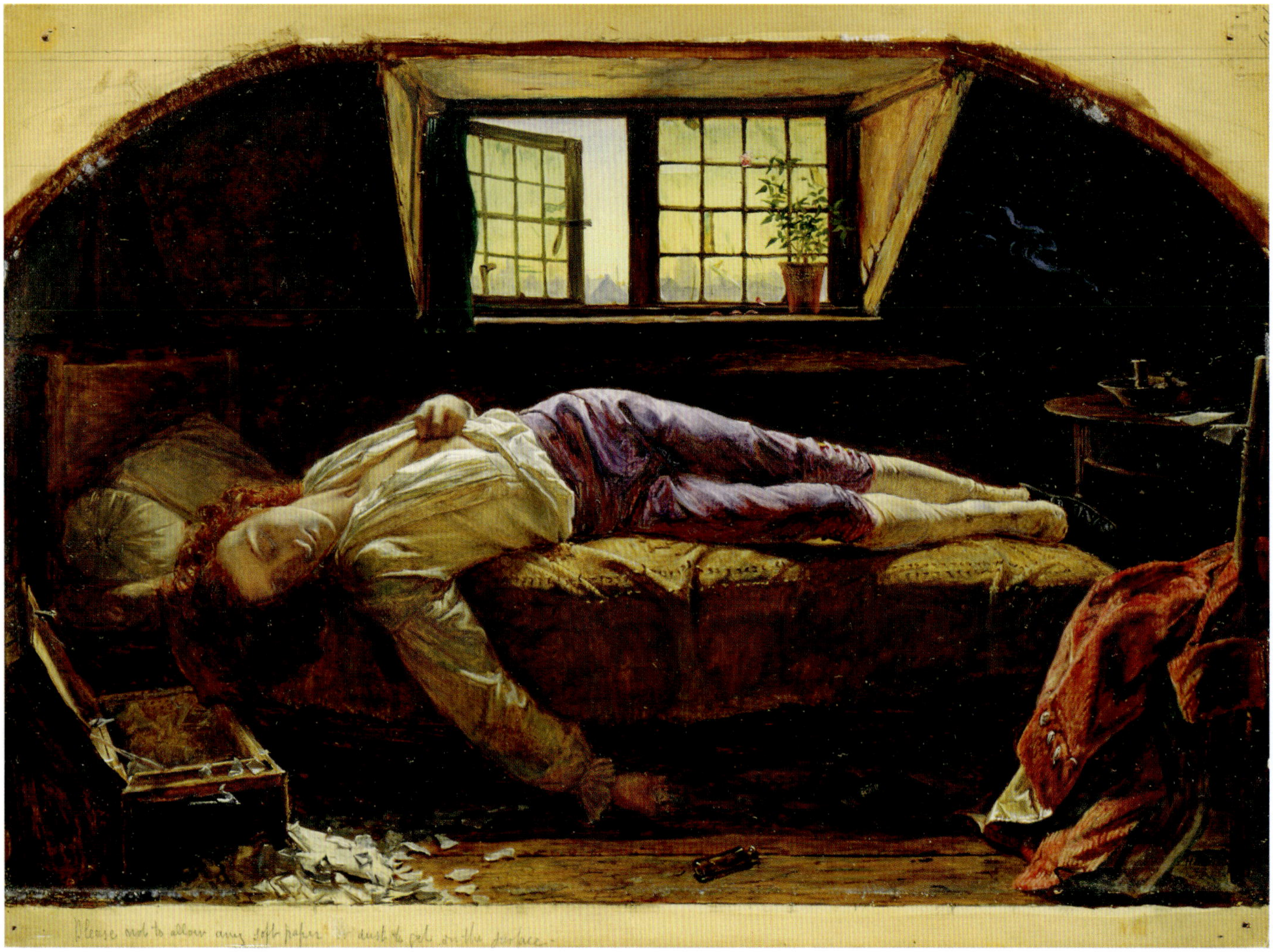

Cat. 22b. Image courtesy of Yale Center for British Art

p.399; Cook, E.T. & Wedderburn, A. [Eds.], *The Works of John Ruskin, Royal Academy Notes 1856*, Vol. XIV, London, 1904, p.60; Hunt, W.H., *Pre-Raphaelitism and the Pre-Raphaelite Brotherhood*, 1905, vol. 2, p.417; *Birmingham Mail*, 10 December 1918, p.3; City of Birmingham Art Gallery, *Catalogue of Paintings*, 1930, p.204, no. 43'18; Birmingham Museum, *Catalogue of Paintings*, 1960, p.149; Fredeman, William E., *Pre-Raphaelitism A Bibliocritical Study*, 1965, 2.1, p.44; Wildman, Stephen (Ed.), *Visions of Love and Life*, 1995, p.156; Schuster, Peter-Klaus, Wullen, Moritz et al (Eds.), *Fontane und die Bildende Kunst*, 1998, p.118 (repr. p.70); Hawksley, Lucinda: *Essential Pre-Raphaelites*, 1999, pp.184-185; Ellis, Andrew and Roe, Sonia, *Oil Paintings in Public Ownership in Birmingham*, Public Catalogue Foundation, 2008, p.195.

When this work was auctioned at Christie's in 1875 and 1877 it was sold as a "sketch" not as a copy. Stephen Wildman notes: "Whether, as the old inscription on the reverse suggests, this is a 'study' for the large oil on canvas now in the Tate Gallery, London, or a later replica, it is very difficult to tell. It would have accorded with Pre-Raphaelite practice for Wallis to have begun a small picture first, in preparation for painting on a larger scale, allowing the artist to work out details of perspective, lighting and costume. The question is complicated by the existence of a second small version (slightly larger than the Birmingham one), now in the Yale Center for British Art, New Haven. Some very minor differences of detail – most noticeable in the angle of the head, the rooftop view, the disposition of the leaves of the potted plant and the torn fragments of paper – are found when comparing the Birmingham version with the two others, leading to the conclusion that this is indeed the first design, and that the Yale oil is a replica."[5]

Cat. 22b. *The Death of Chatterton*
Date unknown; oil on panel; 22.7 x 30.2 cm. (8¹⁵⁄₁₆ x 11⅞ in.); Yale Center for British Art, New Haven, Connecticut.
INSCRIPTIONS: Signed *H. Wallis*, lower right.
PROVENANCE: Henry McConnel,[1] The Mansion, Cressbrook, Derbyshire; after his death in 1871 likely the trustees of the McConnel's estate (1871–85); Mary McConnel Worthington, his daughter, by descent (1885–86); Henry McConnel estate sale, Christie's, London, 27 March 1886, lot 21, bought by Joseph Dixon[2] of St John's Gardens, Ladbroke Grove, London for £21 5s; his estate sale Christie's, 18 March 1911, lot 42, withdrawn; K. Dorian; his sale Sotheby's Belgravia on 28 Nov.1972, lot 50, bought by art dealer John Baskett of Basket & Day for £18,000; Paul Mellon; donated to the *Yale Center for British Art* in 1981, acquisition no. B1981.25.648.
EXHIBITIONS: Whitechapel, *Spring Exhibition*, 1908, no. 34.
LITERATURE: *The Art Journal*, New Series, Vol. IX, 1870, p.286; *The Times*, 29 March 1886, p.10; *The Burlington Magazine*, Vol. 114, No. 836, November 1972, p.lxxxii; Yale Center for British Art, *Selected paintings, drawings & books*, Yale University Press, New Haven, CT, 1977, p.50; Robinson, Michael: *The Pre-Raphaelites*, 2012, p.136

This is an autograph copy by Wallis of the painting exhibited at the Royal Academy in 1856. The exact date it was painted is uncertain. It differs little from the original except in size. Wallis is alleged to have made even more copies of this, his most famous work, though the two paintings currently housed in the Birmingham Art Gallery and at the Yale Center are the only known autograph copies. Other artists also made copies of this painting of variable quality. Copies by other artists are in the Bristol City Art Gallery, Dove Cottage and Wordsworth Museum in Grasmere, Cumbria, and in private collections.

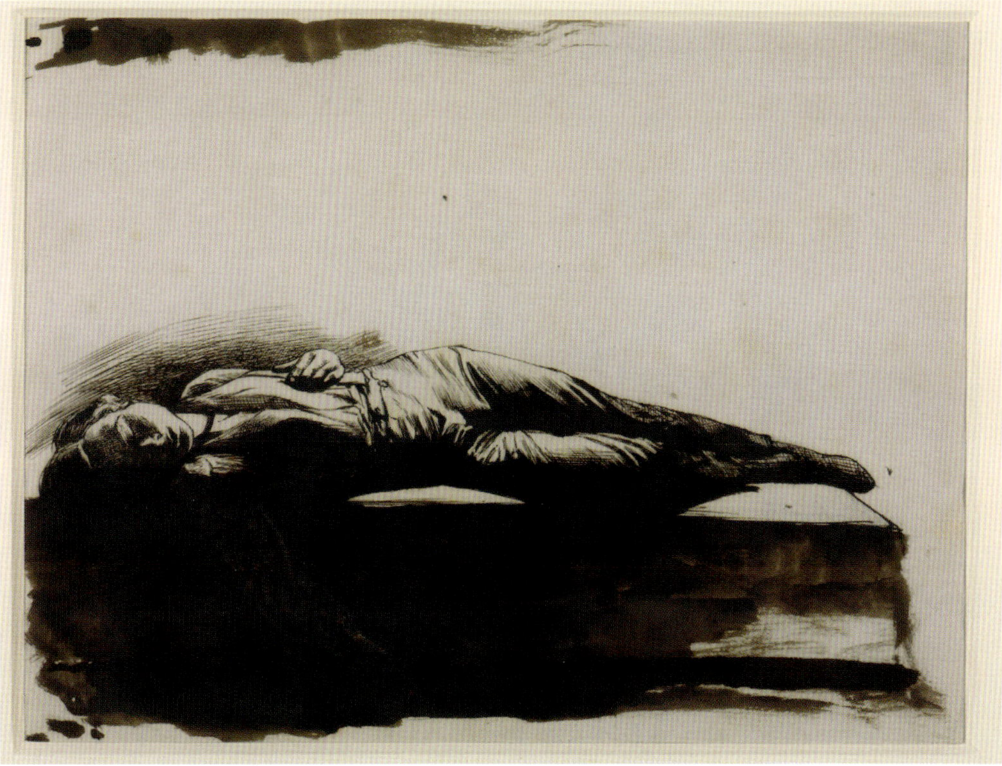

Cat. 22c. Image by permission of Tate, London, 2016

Cat. 22c. Study for *Chatterton*
*c.*1856; pen and ink on paper; 19.4 x 25.4 cm. (7⅝ x 10 in.); Tate Britain, London.
PROVENANCE: By descent from the artist to his daughter-in-law Alice Julyan Wallis (née Roberts), and thence to her great-niece Mrs Vera G. Whiting, Purley, Surrey; purchased by the Tate Gallery in 1973 for £550, acquisition no. T01721.
EXHIBITIONS: Art Gallery of Western Australia and other venues, *The Pre-Raphaelite Dream*, 2003-2004, no. 25.
LITERATURE: Billingsley, David: 'The drawings behind Pre-Raphaelite love and death', *PRS Review*, Vol. XXVI, No. 1, Spring 2018, pp.20-21.

According to the *Catalogue and acquisition files* at the Tate Britain, the pose of the figure in this drawing corresponds more or less with that in the painting while Cat. 22.d is less close. In the painting, Chatterton's face is considerably more idealized than in either drawing.

Cat. 22d. Study for *Chatterton*
*c.*1856; pencil on paper; 27.3 x 44.5 cm (10¾ X 17½ in.); Tate Britain, London.
PROVENANCE: By descent from the artist to his daughter-in-law Alice Julyan Wallis (née Roberts), and thence to her great-niece Mrs Vera G. Whiting, Purley, Surrey; purchased by the Tate Gallery in 1973 for £350, acquisition no. T01722.
LITERATURE: Billingsley, David: 'The drawings behind Pre-Raphaelite love and death', *PRS Review*, Vol. XXVI, No. 1, Spring 2018, pp.20-21.

The pose of Chatterton in this drawing differs slightly from the finished paintings, especially with Chatterton's head being more upright. It is, therefore, likely the

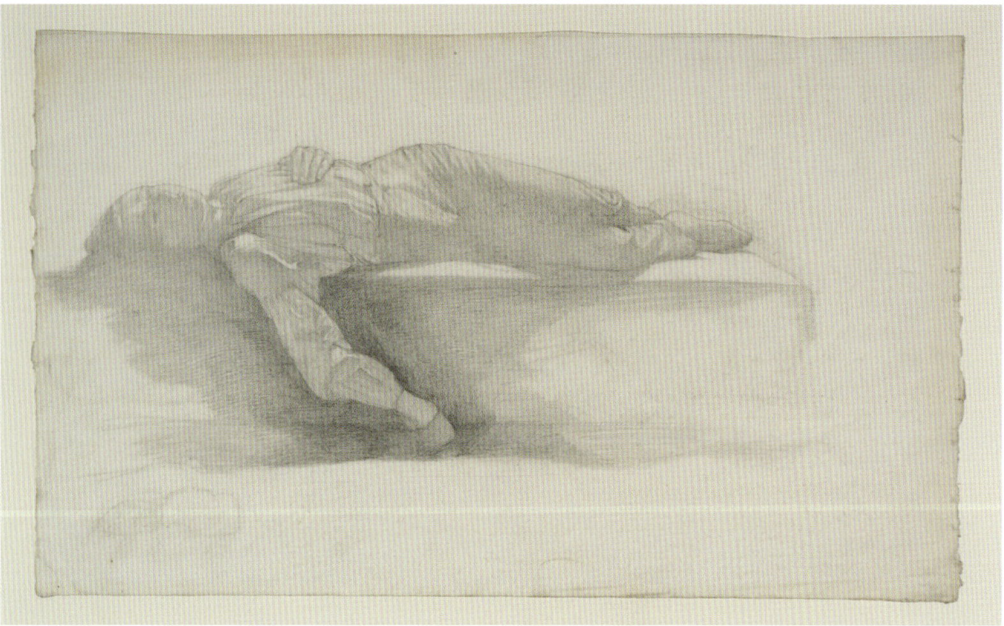

Cat. 22d. Image by permission of Tate, London, 2016

earlier of the two surviving drawings for this project.

Cat. 22e. Print after *The Death of Chatterton*
*c.*1856; wood engraving on chine collé; 21.1 x 278 cm. ($8\frac{5}{16}$ x $10\frac{15}{16}$ in.); The British Museum, London.

Annotations: (lettering below image, left) "Specimens from Recent Exhibitions: No II"; (lettering below image, right) "Painted by Henry Wallis"; (lettering below image, bottom) "CHATTERTON" and "Cut is the branch that might have grown full straight, And burned is Apollo's laurel-bough".[1]
Provenance: Purchased from the art dealer Edward Daniel (1807-92) in 1875 by The British Museum, Dept Prints & Drawings, registration no. 1875,0710.3739.
Literature: *Leeds Intelligencer*, 1 November 1856, p.12; *Leicester Journal*, 14 November 1856, p.6; Rossetti, William M.: *The Crayon*, Vol. 3, No. 12, December 1856, p.373; *The Lady's Newspaper*, 11 February 1860, p.101.

This wood-engraving was made with the permission of Henry Wallis and appeared in the *National Magazine*, Vol. I, 1857, p.33. Confirmation of the date comes from a discovery in the Wallis papers, of a letter dated 3 April 1858 from A.L. Egg (the first owner of *Chatterton*) to Wallis: "Since you ask me my feelings with respect to having the Chatterton engraved in *The Illustrated News*, I should recommend you most strongly not to have it done, and for two reasons. Firstly, it has been done very successfully once in a similar form for the National Magazine [the present work], and I feel certain it would not tell well done larger, that is to say on wood. Secondly, as I still think it not unlikely it may be perfectly engraved some day, a large wood cut having once appeared would alone prevent many publishers from undertaking it. I say by all means do not have it done."[2]

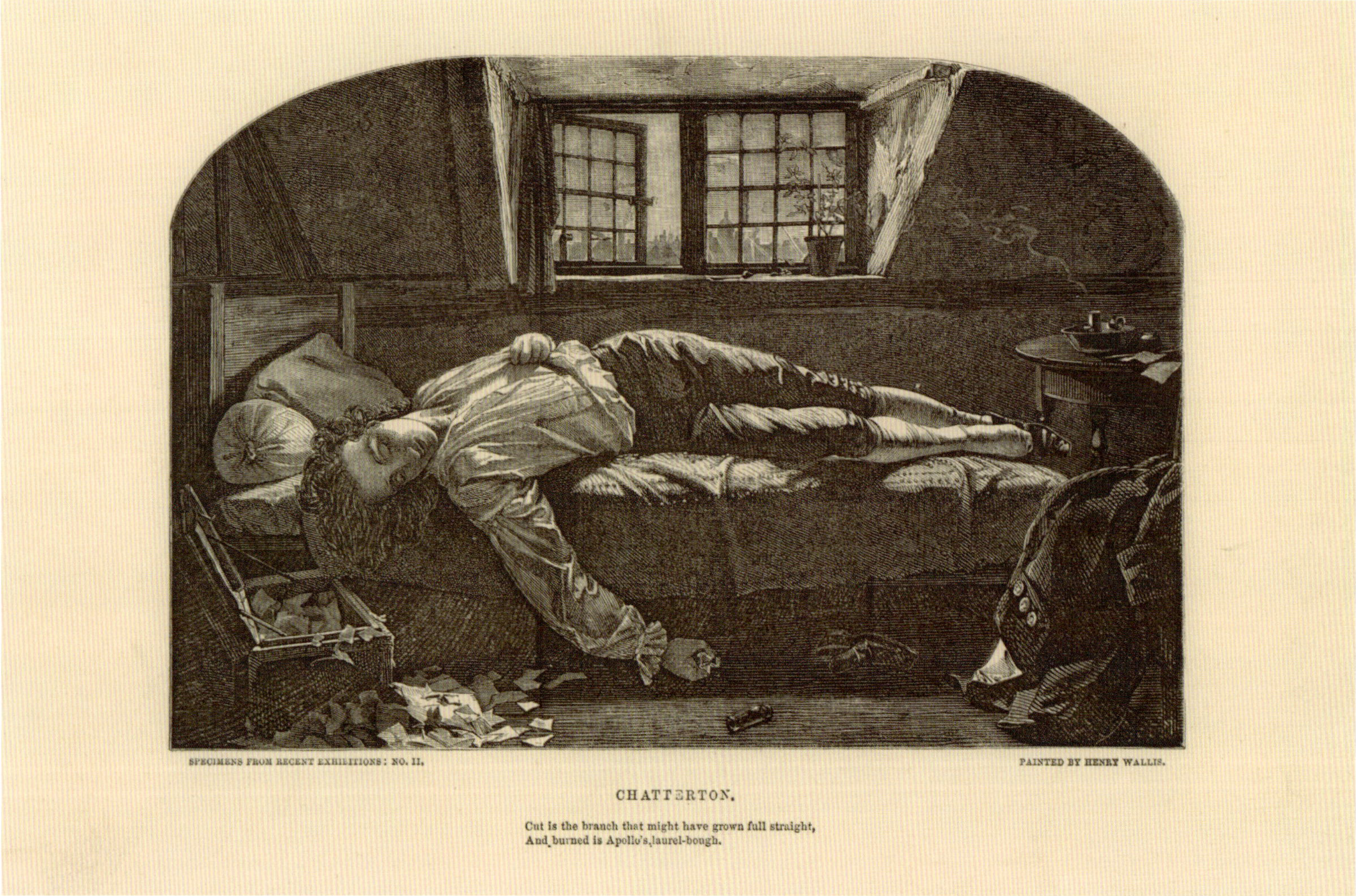

Cat. 22e. Image by permission of British Museum, London

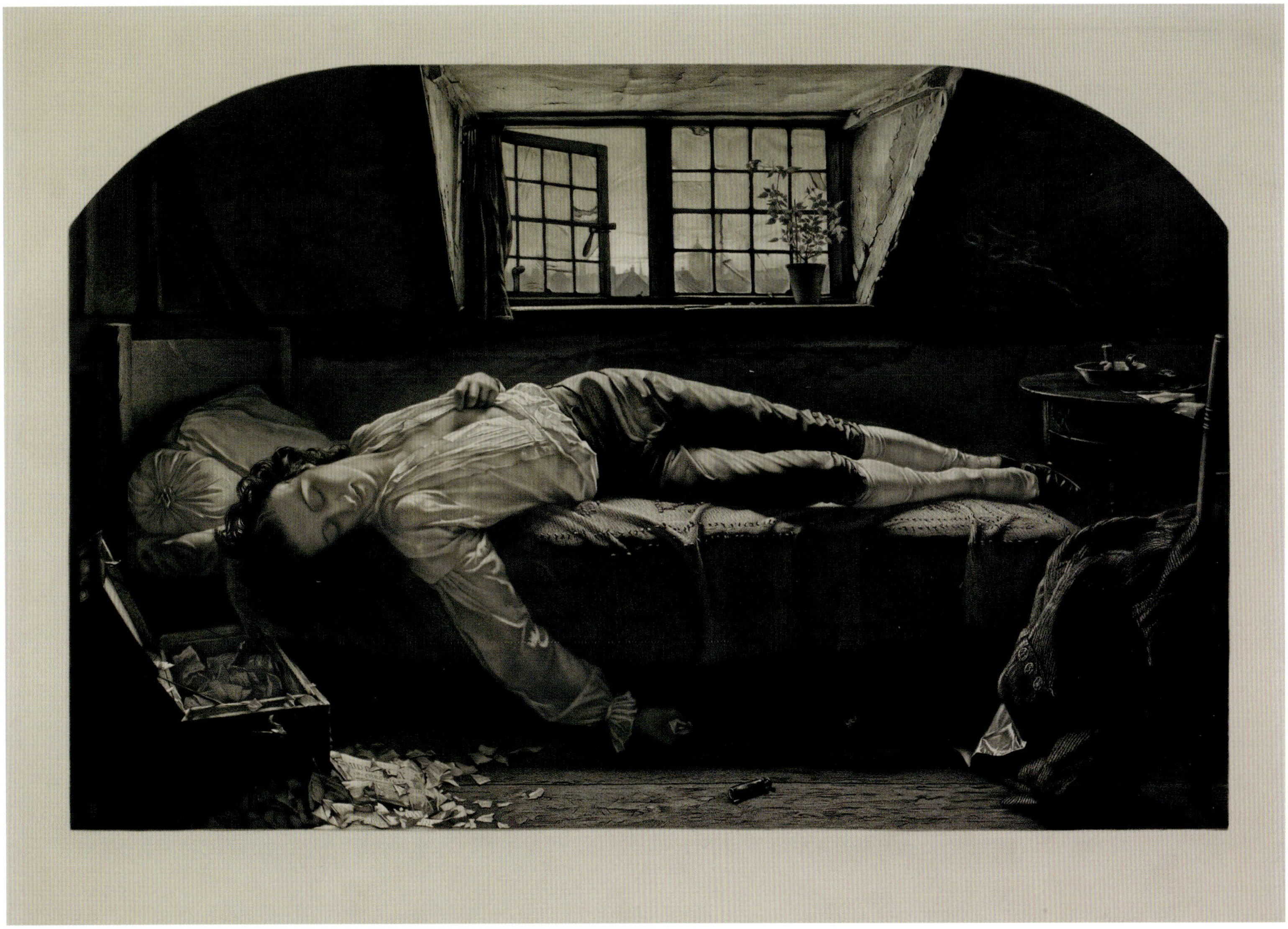

Cat. 22f. Image by permission of British Museum, London

Cat. 22f. Print after *The Death of Chatterton*
*c.*1860; mezzotint and stipple engraving on chine collé; 50.5 x 68.5 cm. (19⅞ x 27 in.); The British Museum, London.
ANNOTATIONS: Painter's name, dated 1856, and engraver's monogram, dated 1860, in the plate; signed with pencil at the bottom by the engraver.
PROVENANCE: Bequeathed in 1899 by T.O. Barlow to the British Museum, Dept of Prints & Drawings, registration no. 1889.0409.357.
LITERATURE: *Manchester Times*, 27 July 1861, p.4; *The Illustrated London News*, vol. 41, 16 August 1862, p.178; *The Illustrated London News*, 15 February 1873, p.158; Clement, Clara Erskine and Hutton, Lawrence, *Artists of the Nineteenth Century and Their Works*, Vol. I, 1889, p.34; *The British Architect*, Vol. 33, 3 January 1890, p.15; Tedeschi, Martha: 'Where the Picture Cannot Go, the Engavings Penetrate': Prints and the Victorian Art Market, *Art Institute of Chicago Museum Studies*, Vol. 31, no.1, Objects of Desire: Victorian Art at the Art Institute of Chicago, 2005, p.13; Rosenfeld, Jason M.: *The Post-Pre-Raphaelite Print*, Miriam & Ira D. Wallach Art Gallery, Columbia University, 1995, no.12.

The first copyright owner, Robert Turner, wanted the original painting to be engraved by T.O. Barlow. The text of the agreement between Mr. Turner and Augustus Leopold Egg (the first owner of the painting), was cited in the Chancery Reports, vol.10, Dublin, 1859-60, p.121-24: "And it has been further agreed between them, that the said Robert Turner shall cause the said picture to be engraved by Thomas Oldham Barlow, of Auburn-lodge, Victoria-road, Kensington, engraver, in his best style of engraving."[1] The work does not seem to have been completed before 1860 and was never commercialised. A pamphlet, printed either by Egg[2] or by Turner, announced that: "*The Death of Chatterton* painted by H. Wallis, Esq., now the property of Augustus Leopold Egg, Esq., A.R.A. [was] to be engraved in the highest style of the art, by T.O. Barlow Esq. (artists proofs 8/8/0; proofs before letters 6/6/0; proofs 4/4/0 and prints 2/2/0) with etchings and coloured copies, five guineas each." Besides the engraving in the British Museum, other known prints are in the collections of the Art Institute of Chicago[3] and the Metropolitan Museum of Art, New York. Although dated 1860, the engraving was not actually published until 20 March, 1862.

Johnson quotes an unknown source: "Many will be rejoiced to know that the talented Mr Barlow is engaged to reproduce an important plate from this picture, which is precisely one of that class of subjects better suited to the engraver than to receive the charm of colour from the painter. Others, no doubt, will suppose that a picture portraying 'The Death of Chatterton' will be painful: nothing of the kind; - here the most refined and sensitive cannot be offended. The Artist has invested his subject with a charm, a fascination that binds you to it, and is beyond description. It is the essence of poetry and teaches a moral beyond the power and capabilities of language."[4]

Thomas Oldham Barlow (1824-1889) was a mezzotint engraver whose prints helped to popularize many of the leading

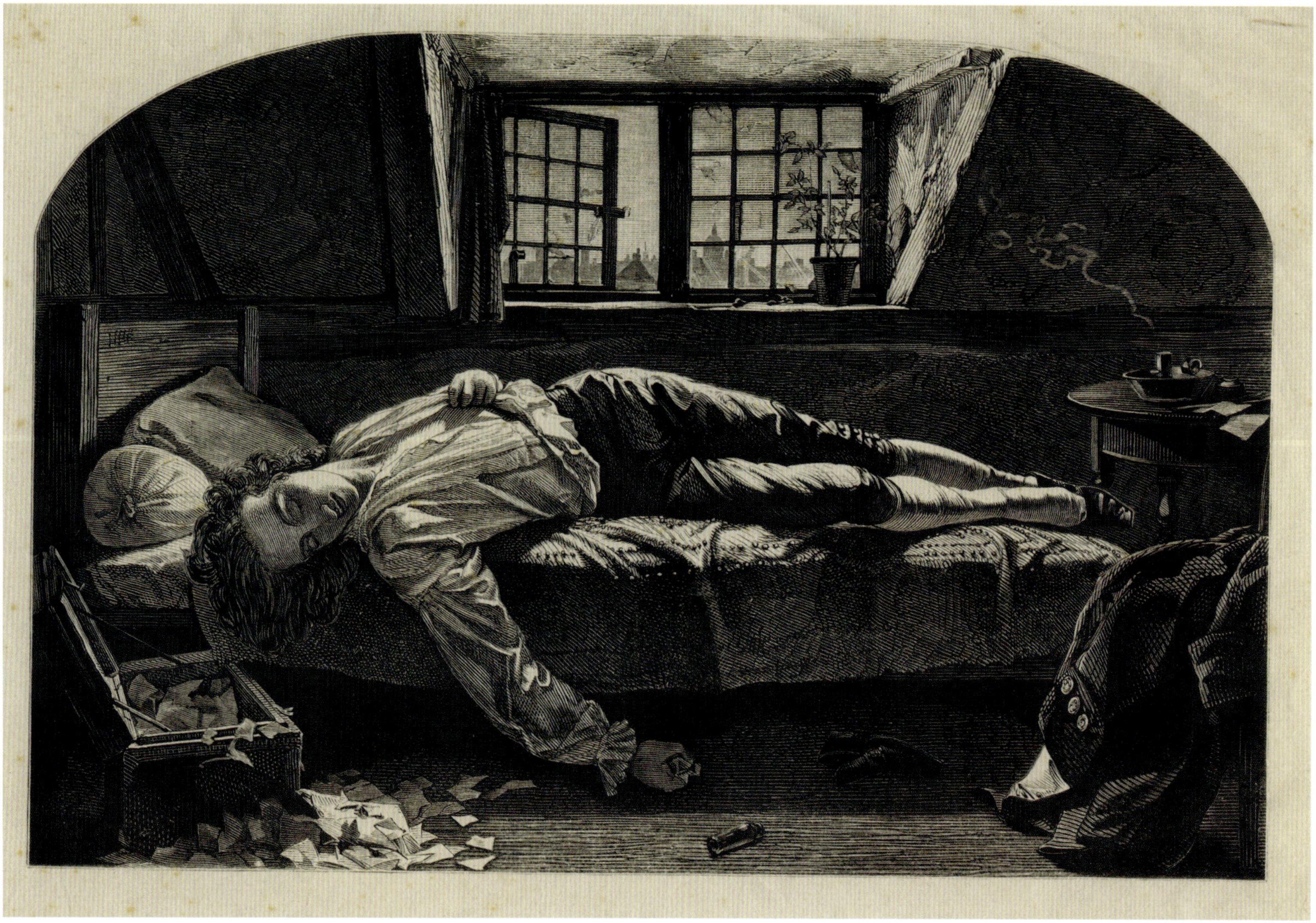

Cat. 22g. Image courtesy of the Dennis Lanigan collection

artists of his day, including especially Millais. Barlow was elected an A.R.A. in 1876, and a full academician of the Royal Academy in 1881. He was a member and, for many years, the secretary of The Etching Club

Cat. 22g. Print after *The Death of Chatterton*
*c.*1856; proof steel engraving on chine collé; 17.2 x 21.9 cm (6¾ x 8⅝ in.); Dennis T. Lanigan collection.
Annotations: (written in pencil in an unknown hand on the verso) "Death of Chatterton From painting in Bristol Art Gallery".
Provenance: Purchased from Richard M. Ford Ltd., Dealer in Manuscripts, Printed Ephemera and Antiquarian Books, London, Ford stock no. SKU:13273, on 29 June 2015.

The existence of this print was unknown to us until it appeared in the sales catalogue of an antiquarian book dealer in London. It had no earlier provenance and there were no publication details relating to place or date on the print itself to suggest its origin. It is obviously an early proof before lettering. Interestingly, a detail written on the verso, in an unknown hand and from an unknown date, says it was taken from the painting in the Bristol Art Gallery; Bristol only has a copy of the painting after Wallis. An engraving of *Chatterton* appeared in *The National Magazine*, Vol. I, 1857, p.33 so this is the most likely source for this print. The name of the engraver is not given. A print by Kurtz[1] of Wallis's picture was included in *Illustration of Great Men and Famous Women*, Vol. 7, p.110, edited by Charles Horne, and published by Selmar Hess, New York in 1894. However, this was a typogravure and, therefore, not the source of the steel engraving.[2] The likely source of this engraving remains unknown

Cat. 23. *Marten's Tower, Chepstow Castle*
1856; oil on canvas; dimensions unknown; whereabouts unknown.
Exhibitions: Royal Academy, 1856, no. 56.

This is the first of two paintings Wallis executed of Chepstow Castle in Wales. This picture likely showed the tower from the outside, while a later painting, *Henry Marten at Chepstow Castle* [Cat. 31], showed Marten as a prisoner.

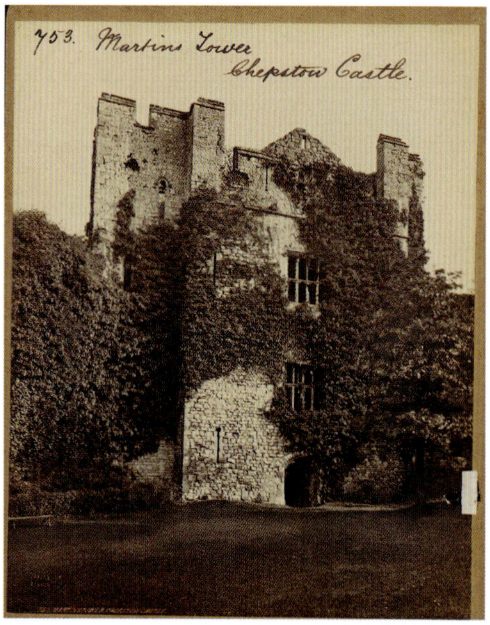

Cat. 23. Francis Frith, *Marten's Tower, Chepstow Castle*, albumen print, c.1850s-1870s. Image courtesy of Victoria and Albert Museum, museum no. E.208:981-1994

Cat. 24. *Andrew Marvell returning the Bribe*
1856; oil on canvas; dimensions unknown; whereabouts unknown.
Exhibitions: Royal Academy, 1856, no. 516.

Literature: *The Art Journal*, New Series, Vol. II, 1856, p.172, p.277; *The Athenaeum*, No. 1489, 10 May 1856, p.591; *The Times*, 12 May 1856, p.12; *Saturday Review*, 17 May 1856, p.58; *Lloyd's Weekly Newspaper*, 18 May 1856, p.8; *London Daily News*, 21 May 1856, p.2; *Lloyd's Weekly Newspaper*, 24 May 1856, p.7; Cook, E.T. & Wedderburn, A. [Eds.], *The Works of John Ruskin, Royal Academy Notes 1856*, Vol. XIV, London, 1904, p.60; Huish, Marcus B.: *British Watercolour Painting*, 1904, p.184; Ironside, Robin and Gere, John: *Pre-Raphaelite Painters*, 1948, p.44.

Wallis was obviously busily working on this picture by early 1856. An entry in P.A. Daniel's journal for 9 February 1856 states: "Called on Wallis in the afternoon and after smoking the pipe of peace and looking over the picture he is at work on (a scene from the life of Andrew Marvell) we walked together to the studio of a friend of his, an Artist named Wingfield who takes photographic portraits on an artistic principle."[1]

Although Andrew Marvell (1621-1678) was involved with politics, he is also known as one of the best of the 17th-century English metaphysical poets, of whom John Donne and George Herbert are the most famous. Marvell was for a time employed as a tutor, including to Oliver Cromwell's ward, before becoming an assistant to John Milton in the foreign office in 1657. After the monarchy was restored in 1660, Marvell wrote satirical verses against the corruption of the court, which Wallis illustrated in this picture. These verses circulated in manuscript form and were published under his name after his death. He avoided punishment for his own cooperation with republicanism and worked for the new Stuart regime of Charles II. From 1659 until his death, he was a member of Parliament and went on two diplomatic missions to the continent, including to Holland, Russia, Sweden and Denmark. He nevertheless continued to criticize the monarchy and to denounce censorship.[2]

The subject of this picture is explained by the following quotation: "Persuaded that Marvell would be theirs (the Administration's) for properly asking, they sent his old schoolfellow, the Lord Treasurer Danby, to renew acquaintance with him in his garret. At parting, the Lord Treasurer, out of pure affection, slipped into his hand an order upon the treasury for £1,000, and then went to his chariot. Marvell, looking at the paper, calls after the Treasurer, 'My lord, I request another moment'. They went up again to the garret, and Jack, the servant boy, was called. 'Jack, child, what had I for dinner yesterday?' 'Don't you remember, sir, you had the little shoulder of mutton that you ordered me to bring home from a woman in the market?' 'Very right, child. What have I for dinner to-day?' 'Don't you know, sir, that you bid me lay by the *blade bone to broil*?' 'T'is so; very right, child, go away.' 'My lord, do you hear that? Andrew Marvell's dinner is provided; there's your piece of paper. I want it not. I know the sort of kindness you intended. I live here to serve my constituents; the ministry may seek men for their purpose – *I am not one*'."[3]

The painting was not enthusiastically reviewed at the Royal Academy exhibition of 1856 by John Ruskin, who wrote: "Mr. Wallis has another very wonderful effort, [no.] 516, but it is harder and less successful [than *Chatterton*]. I suppose the face of Marvell is a portrait, but he does not look to me like a person who would return the bribe."[4] The art critic of *The Saturday Review*, however, expressed the opinion that: "Wallis's other work [the first one being *Chatterton*], though far inferior in sentiment and less complete as a picture, gives equal proof of power. The *chiaroscuro* is quite as skilful and there are some fine pieces of painting in it, such as the bit of Turkey carpet. The Lord Treasurer's head and whole figure are very fine – the great failure being the head of Andrew Marvell, which is neither honest nor intelligent." *The Athenaeum* stated: "Mr. Wallis's other picture, *Andrew Marvell returning the Bribe* (516), we cannot say much. It is nicely painted and well arranged, but it is a story impossible to tell in paint. There is a gentleman sitting down and one standing up, returning him a letter. In the background in an adjoining room is a boy preparing a dinner. This tells nothing, and is a mere conversational piece. It is the old mistake of a bad selection of subject, and is an instance – of talent thrown away. It can only be taken as an illustration of a passage in a book which should be kept at hand for the use of spectators. Mr. Wallis is one of the rising painters of the day – rising, not by overstrained mysticisms and untranslateable allegories, but by honest, hard thought, and dramatic representations of real passion and feeling; not varnished over with wearisome smooth prettiness."

Cat. 25. *A Sculptor's Workshop, Stratford-upon-Avon, AD 1617*
1857; oil on canvas; dimensions unknown; whereabouts unknown.
Provenance: Robert Platt,[1] Deanswater, Cheshire, by 1859.
Exhibitions: Royal Academy, 1857, no. 458; Summer Exhibition of Pictures at Peel Park, Salford, Manchester, 1859, no. 41; The Royal Manchester Institution, *Exhibition of the Works of Modern Artists*, 1865, no. 712, lent by R. Platt.
Literature: *The Art Journal*, New Series, Vol. III, 1857, p.173; *The Athenaeum*, No. 1541, 9 May 1857, p.602; *John Bull and Britannia*, 9 May 1857, p.298; *London Daily News*, 11 May 1857, p.2; *The Literary Gazette*, 16 May 1857, p.476; *The Saturday Review*, 23 May, 1857, pp.475-476; *The Illustrated London News*, Vol. 23, 23 May 1857, p.508; *Lloyd's Weekly Newspaper*, 24 May 1857, p.7; *The Examiner*, 4 July 1857, p.421; *The Crayon*, vol. 4, September 1857, p. 280; *Manchester Times*, 26 May 1860; Hilton, Timothy: *The Pre-Raphaelites*, 1970, pp.123-124, fig. 86.

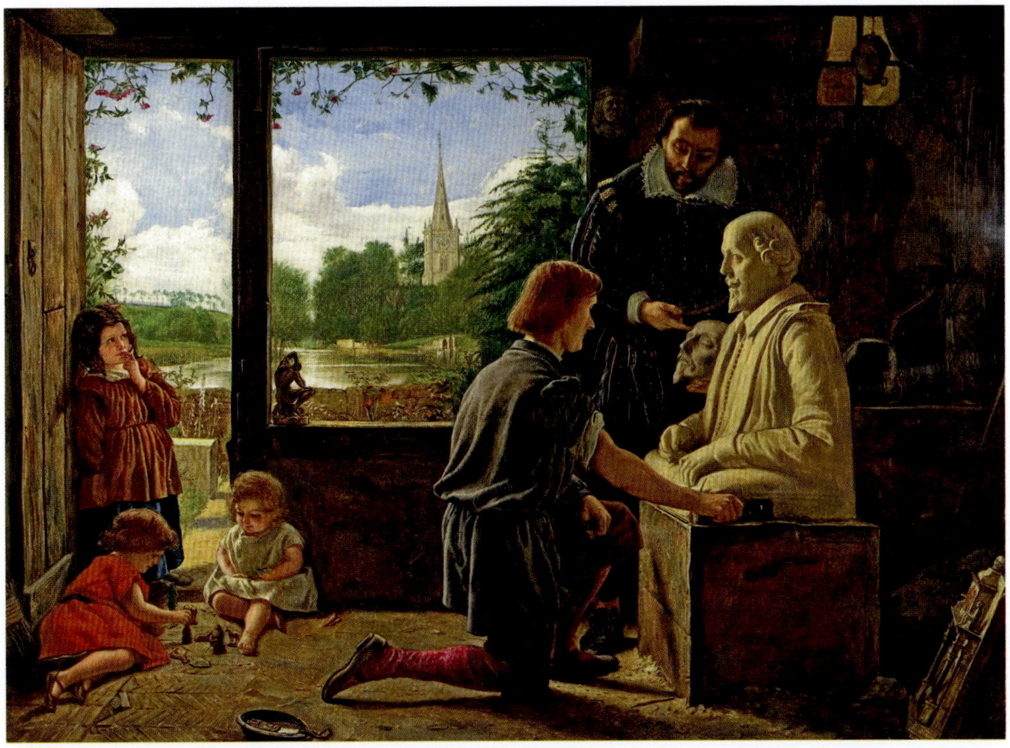

Cat. 25. Image by permission of Royal Shakespeare Company Collection, Stratford-upon-Avon/Bridgeman Images

The painting is sometimes also entitled *Gerard Johnson carving Shakespeare's funerary monument.*[2] The monument features a half-length sculpture of the poet, who holds a quill pen in one hand and a piece of paper in another. His arms are resting on a cushion. Above him is the Shakespeare's family's coat of arms. The monument must have been erected before 1627. In that year the first folio of Shakespeare's works was published, prefaced by a poem by Leonard Digges, that mentions 'thy Stratford monument'.

The reviewer of *The Art Journal* declared: "In this picture we find a sculptor at work, at the bust of Shakespeare, which is in Stratford Church. The bust is before him, and a gentleman stands near holding a plaster mask and suggesting some improvement. The subject is at once clear, but the picture is not so forcible as the Chatterton picture of last year." The reviewer for *The Athenaeum* stated: "Mr. Wallis makes no advance this year, but, nevertheless, holds his place. We must not expect a double crop every season. He has two pictures, one of which is only a sentiment, and another, which is only a historical portrait with real background. *A Sculptor's Workshop, Stratford-on-Avon, AD 1619* (458), shows us a red-haired eccentric sort of sculptor giving the finishing touch to the Stratford bust of Shakespeare, Ben Jonson looking on and comparing the post-mortem cast with the statuary's result. Some children play at the open door, and through the window we see the silver Avon, the church where the great man's ashes lie, and some harshly green turf and trees. An unpleasant foxiness besets and bars(?) the picture, red hair abounds, and one of the playing children is dressed in orange. The bust of Shakespeare, however, is painted with a most loving and well-spent care. It seems to live, and affects the mind with the feeling that it is about to speak. The gloom and dusk, too, of the shed throw a solemn feeling about the august face and the earnest, devotional look of the friend in his slashed dress, with its lines of scarlet. We see no reason, however, that the children should be in the dress of the nineteenth century."

The critic of *The Saturday Review* reported: "The 'Sculptor finishing Shakespeare's Stratford Bust,' appeals to the ordinary educated English sympathies, and is good, but not so good as the 'Montaigne.' It has a large scope of meaning; and in bringing together, as accessories, of this simple *atelier*, the Gothic corbels and a religious statue, together with an Italian model of the human muscles, Mr. Wallis, we presume, intended to indicate that meeting of the Old Art and the New which Shakespeare himself symbolized. There is much truthfulness in representing the sculptor of this famous bust as comparatively commonplace in character. He looks intelligent, but hardly equal to the great work which he has produced, instigated and encouraged by one of the poet's friends – Burbage is it or Southampton? – but scarcely conscious of his own success. There is a touch of German humour in the sculptor's children and their art-school of toys. By the way, the creeper, with its scarlet flowers, was not in England *regnante Jacobo* – or we have mistaken the botany; and the dull Stratford landscape is below the mark."

The reviewer for *The Satuday Review* commented: " 'A Sculptor's Workshop, Stratford-on-Avon, A.D.1617' (458), represents a long-faced, red-haired sculptor just completing the Stratford bust of Shakespeare; and Ben Jonson, with his wart, and in his best dress, pointing out – partly from the posthumous casts he holds in his hand, and partly from affectionate recollection – some little discrepancy in the sculptor's work. Three or four children are playing about, and a model of the monument which surrounds the bust is on the floor. The church is seen through the window; and the Avon, with of course some swans, flows gently between. In this picture the light and shade is again seen to be Mr. Wallis's *forte*. In respect to the authority for the posthumous cast Chantrey[3] was of the opinion that in the Stratford bust there was sufficient intenal evidence alone, as for instance in the dissimilarity of the two sides of the face, to prove that such a cast was taken."

Why Ben Jonson is holding Shakespeare's death mask is explained in Wallis's letter to William S. Brassington: "As a very intimate friend of the poet [he] would naturally have taken great interest in the monument and may have given suggestions on points of detail."[4] In the 1850s, it was argued by the scientist Richard Owen that Johnson probably used a death mask, discovered in Germany by Ludwig Becker in 1849, known as the Kesselstadt Death-Mask, to make the bust. The mask had been claimed to be of Shakespeare because of a similarity to an alleged Shakespeare portrait Becker had bought two years earlier. However, measurements of the mask and the monument bust did not correspond, most notably the bony structure of the forehead, and the idea was therefore discredited.

Wallis was also convinced that he had shown the true site of the sculptor's workshop: "It is interesting to know that my supposed site of the workshop coincides with the spot on which the memorial has been built." In fact, however, it had been carved in Southwark (near the Globe Theatre) and transported to Stratford to be painted in situ. It has also been pointed out that "in 1857, whitewash still obscured the original colour of the effigy in Holy Trinity. It was repainted only in 1861, but Wallis knew it had once been coloured, since the small maquette of the whole monument shown in the foreground is polychromed."[5]

Though Wallis had attempted to achieve a historically accurate setting, he did not achieve his aim, as has been pointed out by Sanders: "The painting is a complete theatrical fiction. As far as we know, Shakespeare's monument was made in Southwark and not in Stratford, and the death mask, shown being held by Ben Jonson in the painting, was a pious fraud discovered in Germany in 1849. Moreover, the stone spire of Holy Trinity, Stratford, which appears through the open frontage of the workshop, was only added to the church in 1763 (it replaced an earlier wooden spire)."[6]

W.M. Rossetti reported that Wallis was to lend this work or another to the *American Exhibition of British Art* being organized by himself, F. M. Brown, and others that was to tour New York, Philadelphia, and Boston in 1857-58.[7] There is no mention of any works by Wallis in the catalogues from these venues, however.

Cat. 25a. *A Sculptor's Workshop, Stratford-upon-Avon, AD 1617* (replica by Henry Wallis)

1857; oil on canvas; 39 x 53 cm (15⅜ x 21⅝ in.); The Royal Shakespeare Company Collection, Stratford-upon-Avon.
Inscriptions: Signed and dated on small maquette, *H Wallis 1857*, lower right.
Provenance: R.S. Richmond, Thornton, Crosby, near Liverpool; his sale Christie's, 2 April 1910, lot 137, bought by Shepherd, likely the art dealers Shepherd Brothers, London, for £15 15s; purchased in 1910 from the Leggatt brothers, art dealers, London, for £60 by The Royal Shakespeare Company, Stratford-upon-Avon, Warwickshire, accession no. STRPG-A: 1993-113.
Exhibitions: Royal Academy, Winter Exhibition, 1951-52, no. 343.
Literature: RSC Catalogue, no. 113, 1970, p.22 (illus.); Hilton, Timothy, *The Pre-Raphaelites*, 1970, pp.123-124, fig. 86; Altick, Richard D., *Paintings from Books*, Ohio State University Press, 1985, Part One, Chapter 7, pp.150-1, fig. 119, p.151; RSC List, 2003, no. 113.[1]

This small-scale replica of the larger painting [see: Cat. 25] was exhibited at the Royal Academy in 1857. It allows us to see what the major painting would have looked like.

Cat. 26. *Montaigne, the Library*
1856; oil on canvas; 101.6 x 71.1 cm. (40 x 28 in.); whereabouts unknown.
PROVENANCE: Robert Platt,[1] Deanswater, Cheshire by 1860; M.H. Copeland; his sale Sotheby's, 27 July 1938, lot 125, bought by Sawyer for £6.
EXHIBITIONS: Royal Academy, 1857, no. 501; Summer Exhibition of Pictures at Peel Park, Salford, Manchester, 1860, no. 96, lent by R. Platt; The Royal Manchester Institution, *Exhibition of the Works of Modern Artists*, 1864, no. 708, lent by R. Platt.
LITERATURE: *The Art Journal*, New Series, 1857, Vol. 3, p.173; *The Examiner*, 2 May 1857, p.278; *The Athenaeum*, No. 1541, 9 May 1857, p.602; *John Bull and Britannia*, 9 May 1857, p.298; *London Daily News*, 11 May 1857, p.2; *The Literary Gazette*, 16 May 1857, p.476; *The Saturday Review*, 23 May, 1857, pp.475-476; *The Illustrated London News*, Vol. 23, 23 May 1857, p.508; *The Spectator*, 23 May 1857, p.18; *Lloyd's Weekly Newspaper*, 24 May 1857, p.7; *The Examiner*, 4 July 1857, p.421; *Manchester Times*, 26 May 1860, p.4; Cook, E.T. & Wedderburn, A. [Eds.], *The Works of John Ruskin, Royal Academy Notes 1856*, Vol. XIV, London, 1904, p.113.

On 17 July, 1856 Wallis and his friend P.A. Daniel set off for France. After a day in Paris they then travelled to Orleans, Tours, Libourne, Saint-Émilion, and Castillion.[2] The principal reason for this trip was so that Wallis could visit the estate of Michel de Montaigne in Gascony. The famous writer and philosopher, was born into the minor French nobility in 1533, and died in 1592, both in his ancestral home the Château Montaigne in Saint-Michel-de-Montaigne. Wallis's painting *Montaigne: the library, from studies made at Montaigne's château in Gascony* was based on studies executed during his visit to France. A letter Mary Ellen Meredith wrote to Wallis on 4 August 1856 mentions the problems Wallis had from the owner, M. le Baron Curial, to gain access to the chateau's interior on 21 July: "What a misfortune that Montaigne's Tower should have fallen into the hands of such a brute, I am very glad you insisted on having admittance, I have no doubt your moral force controlled the wretched slave into yielding the miserable two hours he dared not withhold."[3] After much unpleasant argument, the owner had eventually allowed them to return for two hours the next day. The two artists then went on to Bordeaux.

Having heard of Wallis's journey to France, T.L. Peacock (Mary Ellen's father)

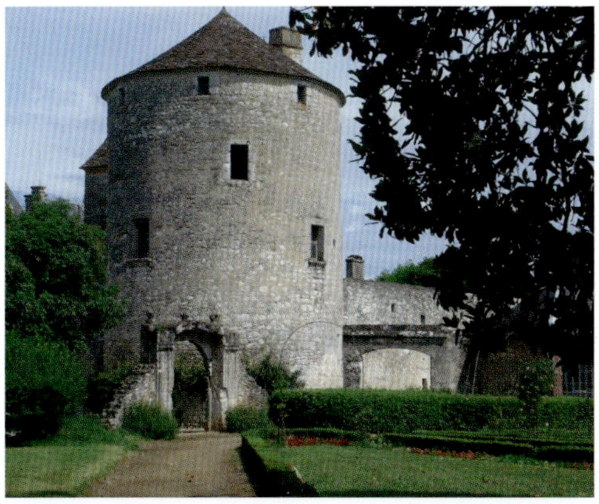

Montaigne's Château in France – exterior view and (below) interior view of the roof. Exterior photograph courtesy of Inge von der Ley. Interior photograph courtesy of R. Lessens.

made two suggestions to Wallis: either painting the writer in his library or painting the exterior of the building. This information is based on a letter to his daughter dated 4 November 1856: "Montaigne is best described by himself. There is an admirable portraiture of himself in his library: L.III.C.III.: the passage beginning: 'Chez moi, je me détourne un peu plus souvent à ma librarie.'...There is another passage, which would make a good picture in connection with the exterior of his house: himself and his family leaving their home in the plague."[4] Wallis did not follow Peacock's advice about an exterior

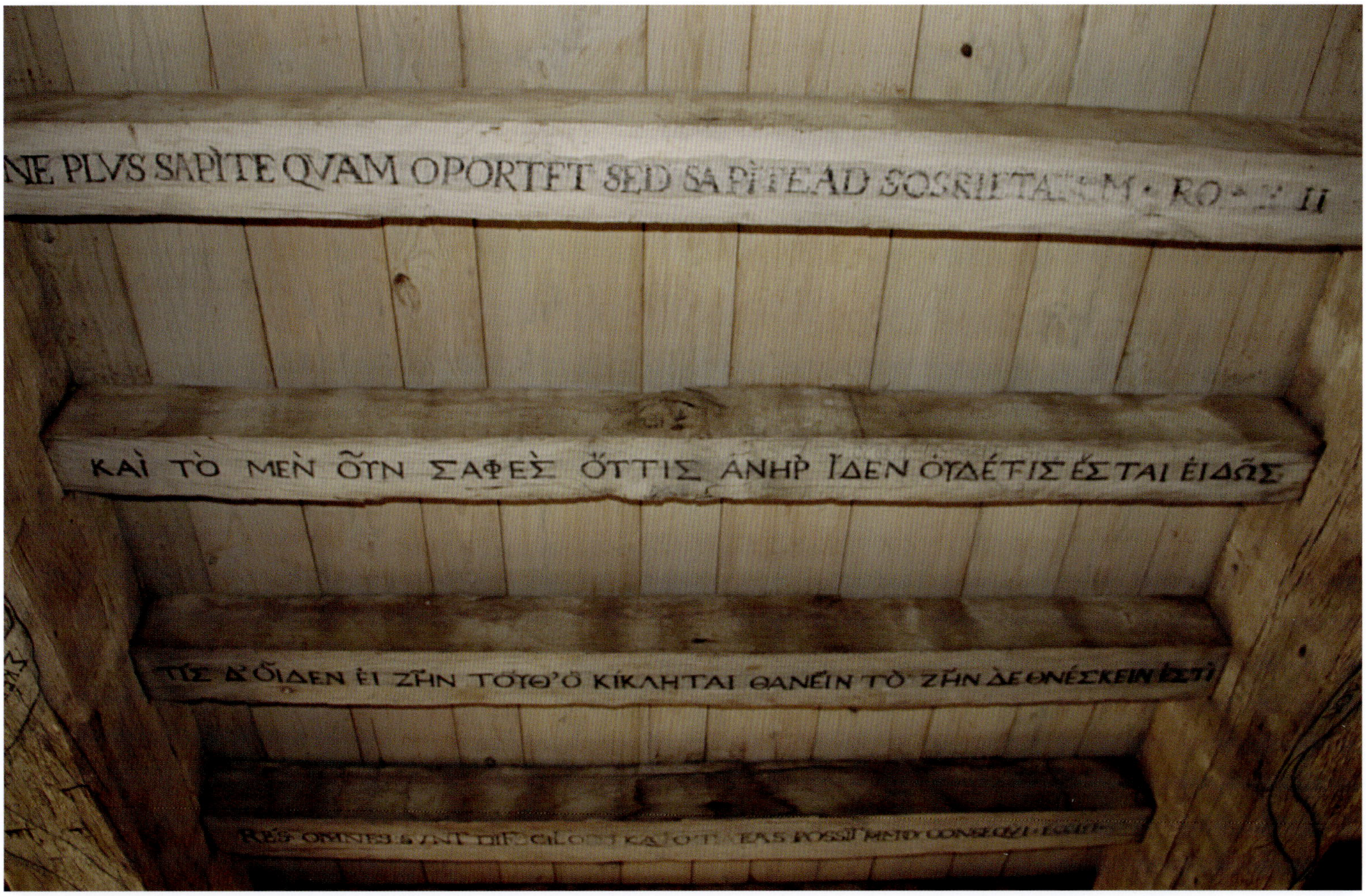

scene but did execute an interior scene of Montaigne in his library. In Ruskin's review of the Royal Academy exhibition of 1857 his comments were generally favourable: "Not, I think, quite so successful as the *Chatterton* of last year; but it contends with greater difficulties, and is full of marvellous painting. It is terribly hurt by its frame and by the surrounding colours and lights; seen through the hand, the effect is almost like reality. That is a beautifully characteristic fragment of homely French architecture seen through the window. I should think this picture required long looking at and that is seen to greater disadvantage by careless passers-by than almost any of its neighbours."[5] Montaigne's library was on the third floor of the tower, where he could look over the garden and the inner court. On the ground floor was his chapel, and on the first floor was a comfortable room in which he often slept alone. In 1885, the tower escaped destruction when a fire damaged large parts of the castle, parts which were later reconstructed.

The critic of *The Art Journal* voiced the opinion that: "The head of Montaigne, in this picture, is as successful with respect to the manner in which it is lighted as any similar study can be; the shaded passages are somewhat too warm, but the head is a speaking reality. Montaigne is introduced in his library, into which a young lady has penetrated, and on her knee supplicates that he will adopt her as his daughter. In every passage it merits the highest eulogy."

The reviewer of *The Spectator* noted: "Two works uncommonly complete in their differing excellence distinguish the West Room in Trafalgar Square – the 'Montaigne' of Mr. Wallis, and the 'Sick Child' of Mr. J. Clark. It would be difficult to cite a more thorough example of strong solid entire work, or of absolute realization, than the Montaigne: the artist has thought out and painted out his subject with a care that cannot be surpassed. The library in which the philosophic essayist is seated is done from the old château in Gascony itself, with the characteristic mottoes inscribed on its cornices, and its delightful glimpse out of window. He dictates, with a bunch of grapes in his hand, to his 'fille adoptive' Mademoiselle de Gournay, who writes seated low at his feet. The luswls [?], the lighting, the detail of the room – everything is so admirably and equally painted, with such an unqualified purpose of truth, and so much disciplined power, that the result is one of perfect satisfaction; there are no points to pick out here and there, but a whole to respect and to study. Mr. Wallis has adopted as his peculiar province subjects illustrating the career or character of men great in the literary past, and works upon them like a master."

The critic of *The Saturday Review*, however, was more favourably impressed with this work: "Wallis, the painter of the 'Death of Chatterton' of last year, has sent two pictures. We consider him and Philip to have achieved the great successes of the present Exhibition. Of Wallis's two pictures, (501) 'Montaigne in his Library' is by far the finest. It is very badly hung, discreditably so to the authorities; and we scarcely remember another fault of this kind. It recalls, and is evidently suggested by, the Van Eyck in the National Gallery – the mirror reproducing two out of the three windows, and the distant landscape seen through them, are copied from this source. The painter has scarcely caught the lady's character. She is not young, and though she may be...Molière's *Précieuses*, but here she only looks stupid. There should have been an element of the coquette in her, else were she no Frenchwoman. There is, perhaps, a little – diffidence, shall we call it, or pedantry? – in telling so much of Montaigne's character by the mottoes, and even by the frame, though these mottoes are what Montaigne himself inscribed in his library. But Mr. Wallis evidently aims at something of the illuminator's method. He will sacrifice no aid to being understood. In his accessories, his satin and velvet and furniture, he emulates the rich German profusion and luxury of invention; and his summer sun lights up the sumptuous pile of Montaigne's dress and its glossy, purpling depth with intense splendour. But the painted glass is not transparent, and we think we detect a coarseness in the lady's right hand. All, however, is redeemed by the power of Montaigne's face – the *seigneur* elevating the *littérateur*, and this, again, redeemed by satiric, mocking self-compression. Montaigne is rendered in every part of his character – cynic and sceptic, the precursor of Voltaire, yet earnest and true. If he doubts everything, he is also suspicious of himself. In the attitude of a lecturer, there is a proud humility, and yet a condescending stateliness, and all clouded over by a certain self-distrust. But great as is this picture we cannot think it of sufficient and large interest. It addresses itself to a small class; and there is probably not one person in ten thousand who can understand it or appreciate it."[6]

The critic of *The Illustrated London News* stated: "Mr. Wallis contributes nothing of such enchanting interest, or so exquisite in execution, as his 'Death of Chatterton' exhibited last year; but his present works show more various powers."

The Examiner critic, in his third notice of the Royal Academy Exhibition stated: "Mr. Wallis's *Montaigne* is only inferior to the same artist's *Chatterton* because its meaning is not to be read at a glance by every observer; otherwise, both as a piece of colouring and as a piece of thought, good as the *Chatterton* was, *Montaigne* is better."

It appears this was not the only historic French subject Wallis considered painting because around the same time he was also contemplating a picture featuring Voltaire, the famous philosopher, historian, and writer. T.L. Peacock again sent his daughter advice about this subject to pass on to Wallis in a letter of 25 May 1857, and in an undated memorandum that likely dates from this same time period.[7] As far as we know, this picture was never completed.

Cat. 26a. ***Montaigne, the Library***
*c.*1856; ?oil on canvas; 49.5 x 33 cm. (19½ x 13 in.); whereabouts unknown.
Provenance: Robert Kirkman Hodgson,[1] Ashgrove, Sevenoaks; his sale consigned through the dealer T. Agnew & Son, Christie's, 23 February 1907, lot 60; bought Bond for £9 9s.

When this painting sold from the Hodgson collection in 1907 it was referred to as *Montaigne and his Niece* but it is more likely to be either the oil sketch for, or a smaller version of, *Montaigne the Library*. The painting is dated 1867 in the Christie's catalogue. This is difficult to explain, unless the cataloguer mistakingly read 1867 instead of 1857, or Wallis made a copy much later than the original version.

Cat. 27. ***A Scene from Kenilworth***
1856; ?oil on canvas; dimensions unknown; whereabouts unknown.
Provenance: W. Thornton, 12 Alfred Terrace, Hanwell West London; his sale Christie's, 13 April 1881, lot 54, bought in at £12 12s.

Little is known about the actual subject of this work because Wallis did not exhibit it at any of the principal London venues. It can be dated fairly accurately, however, thanks to a letter from P.A. Daniel to Wallis of 24-26 June 1856 that was sent to him at Kenilworth in Warwickshire.[1] In the letter, Daniel discussed joining Wallis who had gone there on one of his sketching tours. It is highly likely that Wallis was there to begin, or at least make studies for, this painting.

This work was executed at a time when Wallis was interested in the great heroes of British history, in national monuments, and in subjects from literature. The source of the subject for the picture could possibly be Sir Walter Scott's famous novel *Kenilworth*. The book is set in the year 1575 and deals with the tragic secret marriage of Robert Dudley, the first Earl of Leicester, to Amy Robsart, the daughter of Sir Hugh Robsart.

Amy Robsart was a popular subject with Victorian painters, including W.F. Yeames's well-known picture of her tragic death painted in 1877, now in the Tate Britain. Kenilworth Castle, one of the largest and finest ruined castles in Britain, dates from the 12th to 16th centuries. In addition to Robert Dudley, the castle has been affiliated with other important figures in English history, including Henry II, King John, Simon de Montfort, Edward II, John of Gaunt, and Henry V.

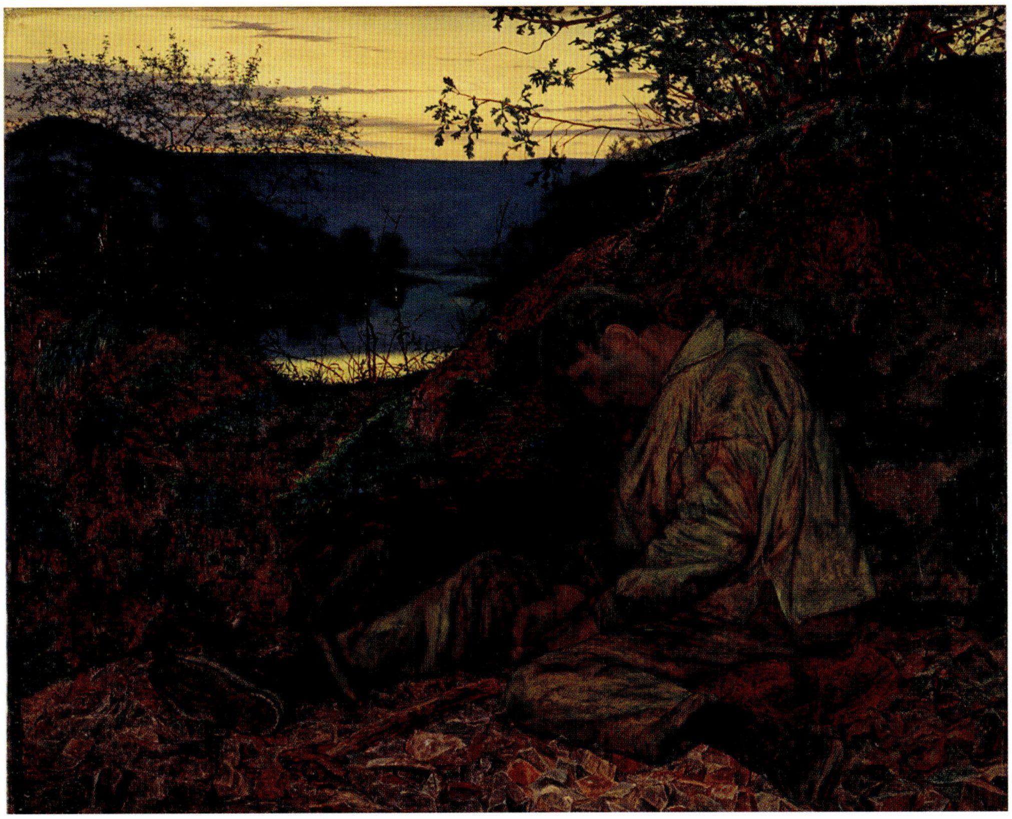

Cat. 28. Image by permission of the Birmingham Museums Trust

Cat. 28. ***The Stonebreaker***
1857; oil on canvas; 65.4 x 78.7 cm (25¾ x 31 in.); Birmingham Museums and Art Gallery.
Inscriptions: Signed and dated *H.WALLIS/1857*, lower right.
Annotations: (a note attached to the back of the painting by the artist, dated 18 May 1884) "The Stonebreaker was, I think, exhibited at the R.A. in 1858, also at Nat[l] Exb[n] at Dublin [1865] and again at Philadelphia [1868]."
Provenance: Exhibited at Liverpool Academy, 1860, and sold for 250 guineas; offered for sale at the *Dublin International Exhibition of Arts and Manufactures*, 1865, for £315, bought by Mervyn Wingfield, 7th Viscount Powerscourt (1836-1904); Temple Soanes,[1] (b.1822) Ethelburga House, Bishopgate Street, London, by 1876 and into the 1880s; Joseph Dixon of St John's Gardens, Ladbroke Grove, London, by 1887; his estate sale, Christie's, 18 March 1911, lot 44, withdrawn; Walter F. Morice, 8 De Vere Gardens, Kensington, London; his estate sale, Christie's, May 12, 1922, lot 101, bought Loveless for £89 5s; Charles Aitken;[2] presented to Birmingham Museum and Art Gallery in 1936.[3] Accession number 1936P506.
Exhibitions: Royal Academy, 1858, no. 562; Royal Manchester Institution, *Exhibition of Modern Pictures*, 1858, no. 188; Hogarth Club, summer exhibition, 1859; Liverpool Academy 36th Exhibition, 1860, no. 54; Birmingham Society of Artists, *Exhibition of Modern Works of Art*, 1861, no. 176; *Dublin International Exhibition of Arts and Manufactures*, 1865, no. 129; *International "Centennial" Exhibition of 1876*, Philadelphia, no. 170; Whitechapel Art Gallery, London, *Annual Exhibition*, 1887, no. 197; Birmingham Museum and Art Gallery, *The Pre-Raphaelites. Special Loan Collection of Modern Pictures in Oil and Water Colours*, 1891, no. 233; Leicester Galleries, London, *The Victorian Romantics*, 1941, no. 91; Birmingham Art Gallery and Museum, *The Pre-Raphaelite* Brotherhood, 1947, no. 77; Tate Gallery, London, *Centenary Exhibition The Pre-Raphaelite Brotherhood*, 1948, no. 23; Whitechapel Art Gallery, London, *the Pre-Raphaelites*, 1948, no. 118; Leicester Galleries, London, *The Victorian Romantics*, 1949, no. 91; National Library of Wales, Aberstwyth, *Some Pre-Raphaelite Paintings and Drawings*, 1955, no. 71 and Glynn Vivian Art Gallery, Swansea, 1955, no. 71; Aldeburgh [and elsewhere], Arts Council exhibition, *Victorian Paintings*, 1962, no. 64; Detroit Institute of Arts, *Romantic Art in Britain*, 1968, no. 232; Philadelphia Museum of Art, 1968, no. 232; Manchester City Art Gallery, 1968, no. 66; London, Royal Academy, 1968, no. 388; Welsh Arts Council, 1970, no. 56; London, Tate Gallery, *The Pre*-Raphaelites, 1984, no. 92; Manchester Art Gallery, *Hard Times. Social Realism in Victorian Art*, 1987-88, no. 23; Munich, Neue Pinakothek, 1993, no. 49; Madrid, Museo del Prado, 1993, no. 49; Seattle Art Museum and other venues, *Visions of Love and Life: Pre-Raphaelite Art from the Birmingham Collection*, 1995, no. 40; Tate Britain, London, *Ruskin, Turner and the Pre*-Raphaelites, 2000, no. 204; National Gallery of Victoria, Melbourne, 2005; Tate Britain, London, and other venues, *Pre-Raphaelites. Victorian Avant*-Garde, 2012, no. 103. *Victorian Radicals: From the Pre-Raphaelites to the Arts & Crafts Movement*, on loan from the Birmingham Museum and Art Gallery to eight American venues from October 2018 to May 2021, no. 47.
Literature: *The Art Journal*, New Series, Vol. IV, 1858, p.170; *The Royal Academy Review*, 1858, p.30; *The National Magazine*, Vol. 4, 1858, p.102; *The Spectator*, 1 May 1858, pp.470-1; *The Athenaeum*, No. 1592, 1 May 1858, p.567; *The Examiner*, 8 May 1858, p.293; *The London Daily News*, 10 May 1858, p.2; *The London Daily News*, 13 May 1858, p.2; *Illustrated London News*, 15 May 1858, p.498; *The Saturday Review*, 15 May 1858, p.500; *The Englishwoman's Review and Home Newspaper*, 15 May 1858, p.614; *The Times*, 22 May 1858, p.9; *The Literary Gazette*, 29 May 1858, p.522; *The Spectator*, 29 May 1858, p.579; *The Spectator*, 5 June 1858, p.603; *The Standard*, 11 September 1858, p.8; *The Spectator*, Vol. 31, 4 December 1858, p.1276; *The Dublin University Magazine*, Vol. 53, 1859, pp.150-151; *The Examiner*, 21 May 1859, p.326; *The Building News and Engineering Journal*, Vol. 7, 14 June 1861, p.507; *Birmingham Daily Post*, 26 August 1861, p.2; *The Times*, 26 August 1861, p.22; *The Times*, 13 May 1865, p.12; *The Illustrated London News*, 19 August 1865, p.166; *The Illustrated London News*, vol. 47, 4 November 1865, p.438; Parkinson, Henry and Simmonds, P. L. (Eds.), *The Illustrated Record and Descriptive Catalogue of the Dublin International Exhibition of 1865*, London, 1866, p.494; *The Art Journal*, New Series, Vol. X, 1871, p.202; *Official Catalogue of the International Exhibition of 1876*, Dept. IV - Art, p.65; *The Art Journal*, New Series, Vol. 2, 1876, pp.218-219; *The Times*, 18 February 1876, p.4; *The Architect*, 14 October 1876, p.233; *The Architect*, Vol. 24, 9 June 1883, p.378; Rowlands, Walter, *Among the Great Masters of Literature*, 1900, p.152; Cook, E.T. and Wedderburn, A. [Eds.], *The*

Works of John Ruskin, Vol. XIV, 1904, p.153, p.170; Birmingham City Museum and Art Gallery, *Catalogue of Paintings*, 1960, p.149; Reynolds, Graham, *Victorian* Painting, 1966, pp.68-69, pp.91-92, pl. 50; Royal Academy of Arts, London, *Bicentenary Exhibition 1768-1968*, 1968, p.388; Maas, Jeremy, *Victorian Painters*, 1969, p.133; Hilton, Timothy, *The Pre-Raphaelites*, 1970, p.122, fig. 85; Wood, Christopher, Nicoll, John, *The Pre-Raphaelites*, 1970, fig.32; Gaunt, William, *The Restless Century: Painting in Britain 1800-1900*, 1972, fig.106; Staley, Allen, *The Pre-Raphaelite Landscape*, 1973, pp.87-88 and 127, figs.5 and 43a; *Victorian Panorama: Paintings of Victorian Life*, 1976, pp.118-120, fig. 119; Harding, James, *The Pre-Raphaelites*, 1977, pp.84-85; *Studies in Romanticism*, Vol. 17, No. 3, 'Victorian Romanticism', Summer 1978, front cover; Cherry, Deborah, 'The Hogarth Club 1858-61', *Burlington Magazine*, 1980, pp.241-244, fig. 20; Rose, Andrea, *Pre-Raphaelite Portraits*, 1981, p.10, fig. 28; Wood, Christopher, *The Pre-Raphaelites*, 1981, p.61, p.64 (illus.); Rosenthal, Michael, *British Landscape Painting*, 1982, fig.143; Cordingly, David, 'The Stonebreaker', *Burlington Magazine*, 1982, p.141; Parris, Leslie [Ed.], *The Pre-Raphaelites*, 1984, p.92; Reynolds, Graham, *Victorian Painting*, 1987, fig.50; Treuherz, Julian, *Hard Times: Social Realism in Victorian Art*, 1987, p.23; Adams, Steven, *The Art of the Pre-Raphaelites*, 1988, p.74; Bennett, Mary, *Artists of the Pre-Raphaelite Circle*, 1988, p.16; Beutler, Christian, *Kunst um 1800 und die Folgen*, 1988, p.298; Wood, Christopher, *Paradise Lost: Paintings of English Country Life and Landscape, 1850-1914*, 1989, fig.11; Bayerische Staatsgemäldesammlungen, Munich, *Victorianische Malerei, von Turner bis Whistler*, 1993, p.49; Wildman, Stephen [Ed.], *Visions of Love and Life: Pre-Raphaelite Art from the Birmingham Collection*, Seattle, 1995, pp.157-9; Payne, Christiana and Hickox, Michael, 'Sermons in Stones: John Brett's "The Stonebreaker" reconsidered', in Harding, Ellen (Ed.), *Reframing the Pre-Raphaelites*, 1996, pp.106-107; Helmreich, Anne, in National Gallery of Art, Washington, *The Victorians*, 1997, p.101; Barringer, Tim, *the Pre-Raphaelites*, 1998, pp.106-107, fig. 74; Cowling, Mary, *Victorian Figurative Painting*, 2000, p.6, p.163; Hewison, R., Warrell, I. and Wildman, S. [Eds.], *Ruskin, Turner and the Pre-Raphaelites*, 2000, cat. 204; Prettejohn, Elizabeth, *The Art of the Pre-Raphaelties*, 2000, pp.239-240, fig. 188; Upstone, Robert, *The Pre-Raphaelite Dream*, 2003, p.189; Public Catalogue Foundation, London, *Oil Paintings in Public Ownership in Birmingham*, 2008, p.195; Payne, Christiana, *John Brett Pre-Raphaelite Landscape painter*, 2010, p.41, fig. 31; Robinson, Michael, *The Pre-Raphaelites*, 2012, p.97; Lessens, Ronald, 'Henry Wallis (1830-1916), a neglected Pre-Raphaelite', *British Art Journal*, Vol. 15, Issue 1, Autumn 2014, p.47, p.54; Petiot Aurélie, *Le Préraphaélisme*, 2019, p.234.
[See: Letter 3]

This work is considered Wallis's second masterpiece. Allen Staley points out that: "the *Death of Chatterton* is an interior scene, with only a view over the London skyline through a garret window, but [this] picture is an outdoor painting and a remarkable one. The stonebreaker lies dead upon his litter of rocks at sunset. Behind him are a fern-covered bank, a river in a valley below, and hills beyond. In a sense, the picture follows the Pre-Raphaelite pattern of the single figure in an elaborate and brightly coloured environment, but the extensive background and sunset effect reflect the later development of Pre-Raphaelitism in Millais's *Autumn Leaves*. Some details, such as the leaves above the horizon, are minutely and separately painted, but in the larger mass of the bank behind the dead man, the minutely drawn foliate detail of Hunt, Millais, or Hughes is absent. Throughout the foreground, Wallis's colours have an extremely high key. They are thinly painted over a white ground, and the effect is dazzling. As there is relatively little detail – simply areas of green and red, suggesting patches of grass and earth – the foreground comes to the surface primarily as abstract colour. Individual details such as the rodent at the dead worker's foot, and even the stonebreaker himself, do not stand out, but are absorbed as part of the pattern. The figure is painted in earthier colours than his setting. Nature glows vibrantly, but the dead man recedes into the landscape and becomes the quieter in death." Mike Hickox suggests the picture was painted during Wallis's trip to North Wales with Mary Ellen in summer 1857 and that the scenery depicted (e.g. the low hills) is consistent with the area. Hickox thinks that the location was near Maentwrog, where Mary Ellen's mother was born, and that the river in the mid-ground is the Dwyryd. During the 19th century, there was a slate quarry nearby.[4]

When the painting was exhibited at the RA in 1858, instead of a title, it was accompanied by a catalogue entry quoting Thomas Carlyle's (1795-1881) *Sartor Resartus*: "Venerable to me is the hard Hand, crooked, coarse; indefeasibly royal, as of the Sceptre of this Planet. Venerable, too is the rugged face, all weather tanned, besoiled, with its rude intelligence, for it is the face of a man living manlike. Oh, but the more venerable for thy rudeness, and even because we must pity as well as love thee. Hardly-entreated Brother! For us thy back was so bent, for us were thy straight limbs and fingers so deformed: thou wart our Conscript, on whom the lot fell, and fighting our battles wert so marred. For in thee too lay a god-created Form, but it was not to be unfolded; encrusted must it stand with the thick adhesions and defacements of labour; and thy body, like thy soul, was not to know freedom."

The original frame was inscribed with a line from Tennyson's poem 'A Dirge': "Now is done thy long day's work." The painting was exhibited under this title in Birmingham in 1861. In his *Academy Notes* of 1858, Ruskin was enthusiastic: "On the whole, to my mind, the picture of the year; and but narrowly missing being a first-rate of any year. It is entirely pathetic and beautiful in purpose and colour; its only fault being a somewhat too heavy laying of the body of paint, more especially in the distant sky, which has no joy nor clearness when it is looked close into, and in the blue of the hills that rise against it, which is, also, too uniform and dead. All perfect painting is light painting – light at some point of the touch at all events; no half inch of a good picture but tells, when it is looked at, 'None but my master could have laid me so.'"[5] "While Ruskin wrote that Wallis's foreground seemed somewhat hastily painted, he forgave it as the colours were beautiful and it would have been in false taste to elaborate the subject further. In treatment of both foreground and background, Wallis seems to have adopted Pre-Raphaelite effects of colour without basing them on the scrupulously detailed observation of Pre-Raphaelitism. But, although Ruskin partially disapproved, Wallis was remarkably successful in retaining the vibrancy of early Pre-Raphaelite colour and handling while incorporating them into a broader effect."[6]

Wallis had complained to Mary Ellen Meredith that his picture was badly hung. She replied: "It is too bad Beloved that your pictures are badly hung but they are too grand to be much injured by any such stupidity & will shine like the sun through clouds. Send me Ruskin's pamphlet when you have read it. You see even the *Spectator* speaks of the *Stonebreaker* as the best of the best."[7] The critic of *The Spectator* had written: "In the few words we have to say on the present occasion, we of course propose to accomplish nothing beyond the bare mention of the most prominent works… and the greatest work…is from one of the distinctly Praeraffaelite painters. We mean Mr. Wallis's dead Stonebreaker: a picture very wonderful dreadful, yet with a great peace in it too."

Not everyone recognized the greatness

of this painting initially. The painter Edward Lear noted in his diary: "I do not like it at all." [8] The reviewer for *The Athenaeum* was also less than enthusiastic about this picture: "Mr. Wallis is not very successful this year... His *Dead Stonebreaker* (562) may be a protest against the Poor-law, but still it is somewhat repulsive and unaccounted for. In a purple, mouldy, rather opaque twilight, on a heap of angular granite stones, in the vicinity of trees and brambles, dim and dark, against a thickened sky, lies a dead pauper stonebreaker – smock, cords, highlows, complete. His face, wan and sunken, is drooped against the bank, – they will wait long at home for him. His switchy hammer has dropped from his hand; a long, thin, wiry stoat has already, so quiet is he, so harmless and so uncomplaining, mounted on his foot, scenting death, and curious about who and what he is, whether dangerous or food. This may be a protest against the Poor-law – against a social system that makes the workhouse or stonebreaking the end of the model peasant; but it may also be a mere attempt to excite and to startle by the poetically horrible. If one dead man pleases, paint another, may be the argument, – the logic should be, if I make one triumph by a dead man, paint no more. There is the Morgue, there are dead-houses in Bedlam, there is the thief just down from the gallows, there is the suicide-painter, – but who but an undertaker would pelt us with skulls?"

The reviewer for *The Royal Academy Review* was also less than enthusiastic about the work: "Mr. Wallis in the charnel-house again! The dead body of a workhouse pauper on a stone-heap. He has died at his task. Night is falling, and a weazel stands fearlessly on the corpse. The whole painting is exaggerated in colour, and too low in tone, especially the dead pauper. The purple curtain at the back of the picture may be intended for a hill or a cloud: and it is only upon examination, and the discovery of certain trees on the summit, standing out from a bright lemon-coloured sky, that we arrive at any certain conclusion upon the matter. We are willing to admit that nature frequently exhibits extraordinarily twilight effects, and renders it extremely difficult to distinguish distant hills from clouds. Mr. Wallis, however, by his strong predilection for bright purples and lemon colours, and his hard outlines and want of gradation of light – dresses Nature in such fantastic attire, that renders confusion worse compounded. The corpse and the foreground are somewhat flimsily executed. The broke flints are not equal to those so photographically portrayed in Mr. Brett's 'Stone-breaker' (No.1089), and Mr. Wallis' reptilian delineation is inferior to Mr. Paton's in the 'Bluidy Tryste'."[9]

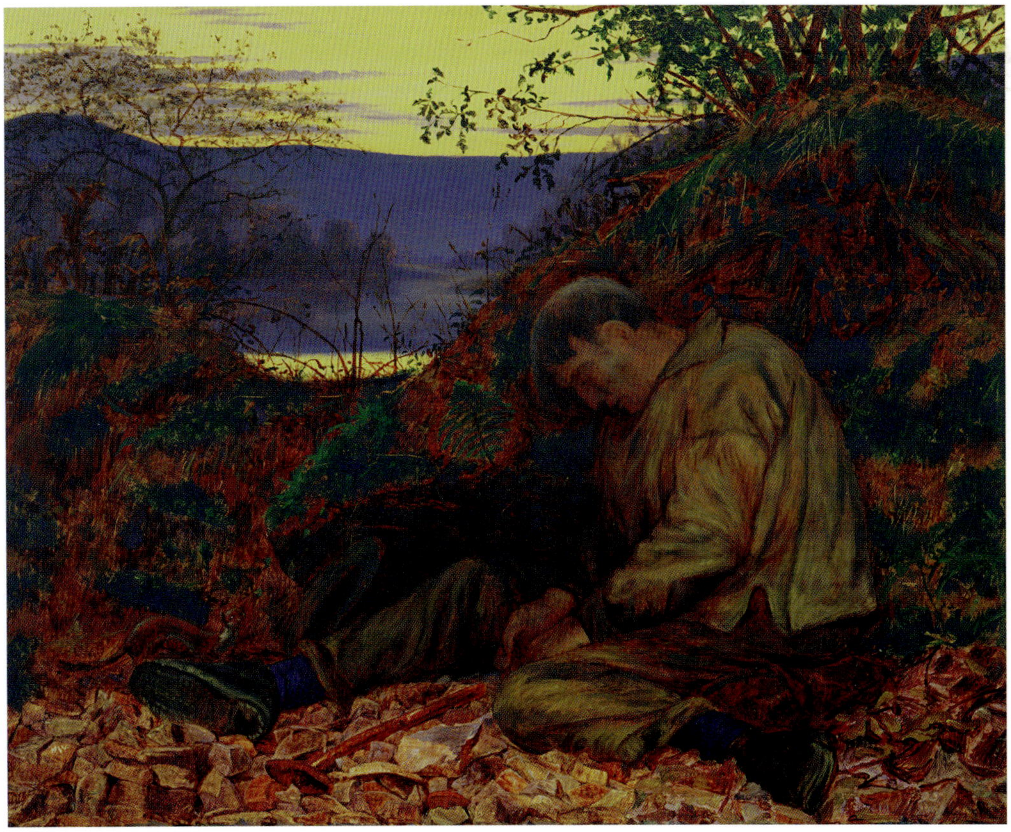

Cat. 28a. Image by permission of The Makins collection/Bridgeman Images

Unlike most other reviewers W.M. Rossetti writing in *The Saturday Review* had great praise for this work: "We do not hesitate to single out the Dead Stonebreaker of Mr. Wallis as the master-work of the gallery. It is at the head both of its thought and of its art, and presents a notable combination of the great qualities in the new movement. It takes the hard fact of our own day as its inspiration, finds that this too has elements of eternal pathos and significance, associates and calms its bitter human literality with the glory of external nature, and realizes all–the mournfulness, the strangeness, the beauty, the actual truth–to the uttermost. Mr. Wallis tells his meaning so well in the mottoes which he has selected, that we shall let them speak for him. The full-fraught line from Tennyson, inscribed on the frame, is almost enough of itself– Now is done thy long day's work; to which the catalogue adds that other from Carlyle– 'Hardly entreated brother! for us was thy back so bent, for us were thy straight limbs and fingers so deformed: thou wert our conscript on whom the lot fell, and, fighting our battles, wert so marred. For in thee too lay a God-created form, but it was not to be unfolded; encrusted must it stand with the thick adhesions and defacements of labour; and thy body, like thy soul, was not to know freedom.' The painter has probed low for his subject, but only to show us that we are wrong in calling it low. An old pauper set to break stones by the road-side, who has died over his work–that is all. No horror, no grimace no anti-poor-law stump oratory. It is mournful and terrible; yet there is more of peace at the heart of it than of terror. The old man is not a scarecrow, but a strong-knit stalwart labourer, not long past the vigour of his manhood. His task has been steadily worked at–the hammer has slipped quietly from his hand– grey under the twilight shadow, his face, which the inquisitive stoat stands to look at, has settled into calm. The yellow sunset broods over the blue bills, and, reflected in the still river, the sky comes nearer to the dead man than the hollow gloom of earth– Now is done thy long day's work: the great deliverer and changer has come. There is certainly no painter of the time who deserves better of the public than Mr. Wallis. He always gives them of his best. Whatever it is in him to think and do, he thinks gravely and does thoroughly."

Wallis was not the first artist to have painted stonebreakers. In 1830, early in his career, Sir Edwin Landseer (1802-1873) painted *The Stonebreaker and his Daughter*, now in the Victoria and Albert Museum. As Lionel Lambourne points out: "The theme was a topical one, for since the late 18th century the road system of Great Britain has been transformed by the work of Telford and Macadam, improvements accomplished not with sophisticated modern earth-moving techniques, but by the back breaking labour of stonebreakers and navvies."[10] Landseer's painting was engraved by John Burnet in 1844, so Wallis may have seen this print.

Wallis might have been influenced by Gustave Courbet's *The Stonebreakers*, painted in 1849 and exhibited at the 1851 Salon, at a time when Wallis was studying at Gleyre's studio in Paris, though there is no mention of this painting in his correspondence from this time. William Michael Rossetti, who did visit the exhibition, published a review in *The Spectator* and stated that: "Courbet seems to think that whatever he sees is what he ought to paint; he never invents a subject, but copies a fact."[11] Whether Rossetti's review might have encouraged Wallis and/or Brett[12] to take up the subject is unknown

Cat. 28a. *The Stonebreaker*
*c.*1857; oil on canvas; 38.1 x 45.7 cm (14½ x 18 in.); The Makins collection.
Inscriptions: Signed with initials *HW.*
Provenance: Joseph Dixon, 1 St. John's Gardens, Ladbroke Grove, London by 1887; his estate sale Christie's, 18 March 1911, lot 44, withdrawn; Sotheby's, Belgravia, 1 July 1975, lot 40 ('The Property of a Lady'), withdrawn from the sale; anonymous sale Sotheby's, Belgravia, 19 March 1979, lot 18, sold for £6,600 to the Makins collection, accession no. MAK 79790.
Exhibitions: Whitechapel (St Jude's), 1887, no. 197; on loan to the Delaware Art Gallery, Wilmington, 20 August 2012 to 17 June 2013.
Literature: *The Burlington Magazine* Vol. 117, No. 868, July 1975, p.xxi; *Art and Antiques Weekly*, 17 March 1979, p.52; Wildman, Stephan, *Visions of Love and Life: Pre-Raphaelite Art from the Birmingham Collection*, 1995, no. 40, p.158-159.

It is uncertain whether this is a preliminary oil sketch for the painting exhibited at the Royal Academy, or a later copy made because of the success of the major work, but the authors suspect it is the former because of minor differences between the two works.

Cat. 28b. Study for *The Stonebreaker*
1868; chalk or charcoal drawing; dimensions unknown; whereabouts unknown.
Provenance: Wallis's studio and then the family by descent.
Exhibitions: *London International Exhibition*, 1871, no. 1963.

That Wallis must have made a drawing after one of the paintings, rather than as a preliminary study, can be deduced because this drawing was dated to 1868 in the *London International Exhibition* catalogue of 1871. Further evidence of its existence is known from a letter dated 29 January 1968, sent to Diane Johnson by Marshall, Liddle & Downey, solicitors at Croydon and executors of Harold Wallis's will: "With regard to the pictures you mention, we see that in the Inventory of effects made on Mr. Harold Wallis' death, there was a charcoal drawing shown as 'the Dead Stone Breaker'. This may be the picture 'The Stone Breaker' which you mention."[1]

Cat. 29. *Sir Walter Raleigh in the Town*
1857; oil on panel; 61 x 75 cm (24 x 29½ in.); whereabouts unknown.
Provenance: Robert Kirkman Hodgson,[1] Ashgrove, Sevenoaks; his sale consigned through the dealer T. Agnew & Son, Christie's, 23 February, 1907, lot 59, bought by the art dealer Leggatt Brothers for £17 17s.

In R.K. Hodson's sale at Christie's in 1907 a picture by Wallis entitled *Raleigh in the Town* was included. Although this seems a strange title to choose if it is referring to a larger version of, *Sir Walter Raleigh in the Tower*, we suspect that Christie's has, in fact, made a mistake in identifying the subject.The painting is dated to 1857 in the Christie's catalogue. If we are correct in our supposition, this may therefore be the principal version of *Sir Walter Raleigh in the Tower* that was exhibited at the Royal Academy in 1858.

Cat. 30. *Sir Walter Raleigh in the Tower, circa AD 1600*
1858; oil on panel; 39.5 x 49 cm. (15½ X 19¼ in.); private collection.
Inscriptions: Signed recto, letter verso.
Provenance: E. J. Wythes,[1] Copped Hall, Epping Essex; his sale Christies, 20 January 1900, lot 61, bought for £14 14s by Wallis & Son, art dealers, London; their sale Christie's, 2 July 1904, lot 106, purchased by Wallis, possibly rebought by the art dealer Thomas Wallis of Wallis & Son, for £9 19s 6d; Messrs Mawson, Swan & Morgan Ltd., art dealers, 5 Grainger Street West, Newcastle-on-Tyne; their sale, Christie's, 15 July 1905, lot 26, bought by the art dealers Gooden & Fox, London; James Gresham[2] by 1906; his estate sale Christie's, London, July 12, 1917, lot 131, bought Mitchell, possibly the collector John Mitchell, for £27 7s; anonymous sale Rupert Toovey Auctions, Washington, West Sussex, U.K., 2 December 2009, lot 101, sold for £2,200.
Exhibitions: Royal Academy, 1858, no. 369; Whitechapel (Pageant), 1909, no. 66.
Literature: *The London University Magazine*, Vol. III, 1858, p.327; *The Royal Academy Review*, 1858, p.20; *The Art Journal*, New Series, Vol. IV, 1858, p.167; *The National Magazine*, Vol. 4, 1858, p.102; *The Athenaeum*, No. 1592, 1 May 1858, p.567; *The Times*, 1 May 1858, p.5; *The Birmingham Daily Post*, 7 May 1858, p.1; *The Examiner*, 8 May 1858, p.293; *The London Daily News*, London, 10 May 1858, p.2; *The Illustrated London News*, 15 May 1858, p. 498; *The Saturday Review*, 15 May 1858, p.502; *The Times*, 22 May 1858, p.9; *The Literary Gazette*, 29 May 1858, p.522; *The Sacristy*, Vol. II, 1872, p.86.

Sir Walter Raleigh (1552-1618) was an adventurer and a favourite of Elizabeth I, whose portrait is shown at the top left of the painting. Raleigh is perhaps best remembered for gallantly laying his cloak over a mud puddle for the Queen to walk upon. In 1578, he joined a privateering expedition against the Spanish, and in 1580 fought against the Irish rebels in Munster. He also led an unsuccessful expedition up the Orinoco River of South America in search of the gold of El Dorado in 1594.

When Queen Elizabeth died in 1603, he was accused of plotting to depose James I and was sentenced to death and imprisoned in the Tower of London. The sentence was reduced to life imprisonment. Raleigh was well treated, however, and his family was allowed to join him in a large apartment.[3] Upon being freed in 1616, he again sought the fabled gold of El Dorado in Guyana, but violated James's strict instructions to avoid attacking the Spanish colonists in the area. After his return, he was rearrested and, at the request of the Spanish ambassador, Raleigh's death sentence was re-instated. He was beheaded on October 29, 1618. [See: Cat. 43, *Gondomar Witnessing the Execution of Raleigh*].

An anonymous reviewer in the *Royal Academy Review* reported that the work was "the least objectionable picture exhibited this year by Mr. Wallis. The subject is a poor one, but portions of the painting are very good. A frowzy old man is sitting at a table, contemplating a little boy opposite him, who is coiled up in an arm chair, and blowing an impossible bubble. To people who are not well up in dates, it would be rather difficult to ascertain whether the old man or the little boy was intended for Sir Walter. Mr. Wallis has possibly foreseen the fact of this uncertainty arising, and he has, therefore, introduced near the old man, a Milo pipe to assist the public in arriving at a conclusion upon the matter."

The reviewer for the *London University Magazine* stated: "Mr. Wallis has two other paintings here: 'Sir Walter Raleigh in the Tower' (369) is a beautifully finished picture. The hero comes before us as we do not often think of him – as historian, with his reference books before him." *The Athenaeum* remarked: "Sir W. Raleigh in the Tower (369), though only a historical anecdote, is more interesting, though we hardly knew him again in fur and gown, looking so old and seedy and musty, seated at a table with stock books and other philosophic

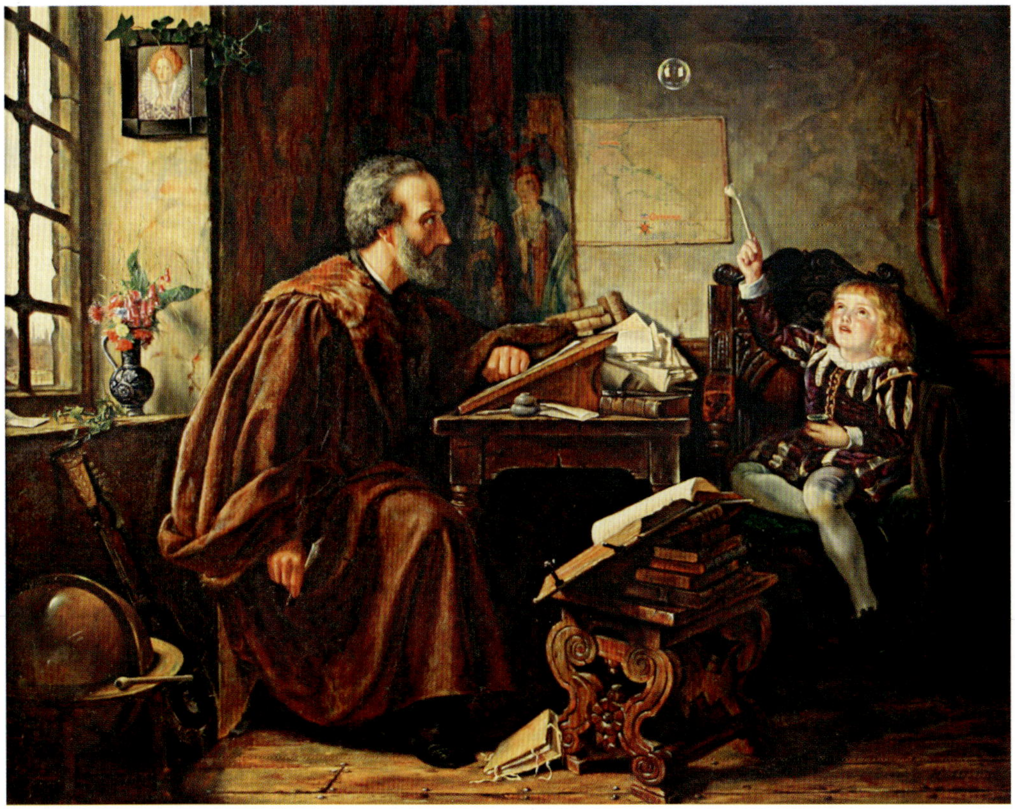

Cat. 30. Image courtesy of Toovey's, Fine Art Auctioneers and Valuers

implements. We rejoice in the thoughtless boy in slashed purple satin (fine contrast to his father's tawny bilious yellow) lounging on a chair and blowing bubbles, – glittering many-coloured evanescences, types of life. There is a sober thoughtfulness about this as there is about all Mr. Wallis does, an unaffected vigorous intensity: but this year he is unlucky in subjects."

The critic of *The Saturday Review* declared: "Mr. Wallis, whose greatest work we have already spoken of, [*The Stonebreaker*] appears again among the historical painters with 'Sir Walter Raleigh in the Tower' and 'Henry Martin in Chepstow Castle.' Both pictures have an abstract and individual dignity as well. The incident in the 'Raleigh' – his dim musing gaze at his boy who is blowing bubbles, which entail less disastrous consequences in their bursting than 'the bubble reputation' pursued through a life of service to the State, or a search after Eldorado – is well thought of, though not new as a general idea. We like, too, the portrait of his great mistress, the 'divine Eliza,' hung up, ivy-wreathed, to preside over the noble captive's fortunes."

The reviewer for the *Art Journal* commented: "'Sir Walter Raleigh in the Tower, *circa* AD 1600,' H. Wallis. This was about the commencement of his long imprisonment. We find him busied with his 'History of the World,' confined in a room presumed to be over the Water Gate. He is represented by a dignified and sadly thoughtful figure, seated with his back to the light, and opposite to him is a little boy, amusing himself by blowing bubbles. The impersonation is round and palpable, and the head is endowed with expression and argument. The room is furnished with a taste which discriminates between that which should be conceded and that which should be withheld; and what is made available here is most appropriate, and just sufficient. But Raleigh's best companion in his incarceration would have been the wife whom he so dearly cherished. The child blowing bubbles means something or nothing: if he means nothing, he ought not to be there; if it be intended to point a derisive allusion to Raleigh's works, on the authority of Ben Jonson and the author of 'Curiosities of Literature,' the unbecoming satire has visited an occasion worthy of an elevated sentiment." [4]

Cat. 30a. *Sir Walter Raleigh in the Tower, circa AD 1600*

*c.*1858; watercolour; 17.8 x 22.9 cm. (7 x 9 in.); whereabouts unknown.
Provenance: Ernest Gambart, London; his sale Christie's, 31 May 1871, lot 33, bought by Lewis Pocock for £5 10s.
Literature: *The Athenaeum*, No. 2267, 8 April 1871, p.440; *The Illustrated Review*, Vol. II. No. 18, 1 July 1871, p.32.

Like many prominent Victorian artists, Millais being a prime example, Wallis likely made a copy in watercolour of one of his successful Royal Academy exhibits. It could also possibly have been the initial sketch for the composition. It was purchased for resale by Ernest Gambart, the famous Victorian art dealer.

Cat. 31. *Henry Marten at Chepstow Castle (Henry Marten in Chepstow Gaol)*

1857-1858; oil on canvas; 95.3 x 57.2 cm. (37½ x 22½ in.); whereabouts unknown.
Inscriptions: Dated *1858*.
Provenance: John Mitchell,[1] Parkfield House, Bradford, Yorkshire; his sale Christie's, 28 May 1860, lot 209, bought Bentinck for 210 g; Thomas E. Plint;[2] his estate sale Christie's, 8 May 1862, no. 305, purchased by Anthony for £232 1s; Mervyn Wingfield, 7th Viscount Powerscourt (1836-1904), Powerscourt House, Enniskerry, Ireland by 1865;[3] his sale Christie's, 23 June 1894, lot 97, bought in.
Exhibitions: Royal Academy, 1858, no. 462; Canterbury Hall and Fine Arts Gallery, Waterloo Road, Lambeth, 1859; Dublin International Exhibition of Art and Manufacture, 1865, no. 141.
Literature: *The London University Magazine*, Vol. III, 1858, p.327; *The Art Journal*, Vol. 4, 1858, p.169; *The Royal Academy Review*, 1858, p.26; *The National Magazine*, Vol. 4, 1858, p.102; *The Athenaeum*, No. 1592, 1 May 1858, p.567; *The Times*, 1 May 1858, p.5; *The Birmingham Daily Post*, 4 May 1858, p.1; *The Birmingham Daily Post*, 7 May 1858, p.1; *The Examiner*, 8 May 1858, p.293; *The Daily News*, London, 10 May 1858, p.2; *The Illustrated London News*, 15 May 1858, p.498; *The Saturday Review*, 15 May 1858, p.502; *The Times*, 22 May 1858, p.9; *The Literary Gazette*, 29 May 1858, p.522; *The Spectator*, Vol. 32, 8 January 1859, p.53; *The Art Journal*, Vol. 6, 1860, p.215; *The Times*, 8 May 1860, p.32; *The Illustrated London News*, 2 June 1860, (supplement); *The Art Journal*, Vol. 1, 1862, p.105; *The Times*, 3 March 1862; *The Leeds Mercury*, 5 March 1862, p.4; *The Athenaeum*, No. 1794, 15 March 1862, p. 367-368; Bate, Percy: *The English Pre-Raphaelite Painters*, 1910, p.86; Stewart, Ann, *Irish Loan Exhibitions*, 1765-1927, Vol. 2, 1990, p.748.
[See: Letter 2]

Henry Marten (1602-1680) was a politician and ardent republican. In 1643, he was expelled from the Houses of Parliament and briefly imprisoned in the Tower of London for expressing the view that the monarchy should be brought to an end. As Governor of Aylesbury he took a direct part in the Civil War. He acted with Cromwell in bringing Charles I to trial and in signing his death warrant in 1649. He was chosen as a member of the Council of State that same year. After restoration of the monarchy, Charles II sent him into internal exile, first to Windsor Castle and then in 1668 to Chepstow Castle in Wales, where he remained for twelve years. His imprisonment does not seem to have been arduous; he had a suite of rooms in what is now known as Marten's Tower, as depicted in Wallis's painting, and was able to travel outside at times. Marten died at Chepstow Castle in 1680, having choked while eating his supper.[4]

Several letters from John Forster (1812-1876), the biographer and essayist, show that Wallis prior to starting the painting, asked whether Forster had a portrait of Marten upon which he could base the image of the politician. Forster answered: "It will give me very great pleasure if I am able to comply with your request for a portrait of Henry Marten. I think I possess one."[5] It is known from letters from P.A. Daniel to his mother that Wallis had visited Chepstow as early as late May of 1854. In another letter, dated 9 October 1857, Daniel said he went to Chepstow on October 1 where he stayed with Wallis at Tintern. Wallis had been staying there for some time and this must be when he did most of the work on the painting. This is, therefore, one of the clearest indications one has into Wallis's working methods where he obviously liked to do at least some of his painting onsite and not merely in his studio.

While the portrait of Marten appears to have been effective, the work as a whole does not appear to have been a success. An anonymous reviewer for *The Royal Academy Review* reported: "Mr. Wallis in another dungeon! [He refers to Wallis's *Sir Walter Raleigh in the Tower, c. AD 1600*, also on show that year]. Nothing but the head of Henry Martin [*sic*], in this picture, is at all worthy of Mr. Wallis. We object to the absence of all gradation of colour from the slab of lemon-coloured sky, to the dark lilac cloud, seen through the prison window; and in the painting of stone walls, we would refer Mr. Wallis to the study of Pickersgill's picture of 'The Bribe'."[6] The reviewer for *The Athenaeum* was also not favourably disposed towards this picture: "As for Henry Martin in Chepstow Castle (462), we see nothing but a portrait. Martin was an unestimable man as Cromwell denounced; he lived, local tradition says, in not uncomfortable retirement, and died, we believe, of apoplexy. He was a Republican in theory and a Cavalier in action."

The critic of *The Saturday Review* was more favourably inclined: "Mr. Wallis, whose greatest work we have already spoken of, [*The Stonebreaker*] appears again among the historical painters with 'Sir Walter Raleigh in the Tower' and 'Henry Martin in Chepstow Castle'. Both pictures have an abstract and individual dignity as well… Martin, the regicide, stands in the shadow of his prison-cell looking out, with a golden and purple sunset in the sky; but he looks to the twilight east, not the resplendent west, perhaps to gaze on that through the iron bars were rather bitterness than comfort. Mr. Wallis started a fine line of subject in these secluded but significant arts or moments of 'representative men'; and he is pursuing it with thought, and consistent but not monotonous purpose." The reviewer for the *Art Journal* commented: "'Henry Martin in Chepstow Castle,' H. Wallis. The figure is erect, standing by a window, the light of which falls on the face, which thus becomes in its sad expression the key to the narrative."

The reviewer for the *Birmingham Daily Post* was the critic most impressed with Wallis's contributions to the Royal Academy exhibition of 1858: "Mr. Wallis's 'Henry Martin the Regicide in Chepstow Tower' and 'Sir Walter Raleigh in the Tower,' deserve the highest praise they have received, and our local committee should make early application for some of these pictures for our local exhibition in autumn."

It is somewhat surprising that Wallis opted to exhibit two similar pictures at the Royal Academy exhibition in 1858, this work and *Sir Walter Raleigh in the Tower. Henry Marten in Chepstow Goal* is actually closer in compositon, however, to his *Sir Walter Raleigh in Durham House*, shown at the Royal Academy exhibiton of 1862. Wallis shared his Pre-Raphaelite colleagues' concerns to get the historical details correct, such as trying to obtain a portrait of Henry Marten so as to accurately portray his features.

Cat. 31a. *Henry Marten at Chepstow Castle (Henry Marten in Chepstow Gaol)*
*c.*1864; mezzotint engraving on off-white paper; image size: 63.5 x 41.8 cm. (25 x 16½ in.), sheet size: 71.3 x 48.7 cm (28 x 19¼ in.); Chepstow Museum, Chepstow, Wales.
INSCRIPTIONS: PAINTED BY HENRY WALLIS, lower left; London, Published Septr 22nd 1862, by Henry Graves & Co the Proprietors, Publishers to the Queen 6 Pall Mall, centre ; engraved by G.H. EVERY JUN^{R}, lower right; Embossed stamp: PRINTSELLERS KEZ ASSOCIATION; facsimile signature "Henry Marten", lower righty.
PROVENANCE: Donated by the private collector Anthony Marten to the Chepstow Museum, Chepstow, in 2012.[1]
EXHIBITIONS: Royal Academy, 1864, no. 830.

An engraving by G.H. Every after Wallis's *Henry Marten in Chepstow Goal* was exhibited at the Royal Academy in 1864, no. 830.[2] At the Viscount Powerscourt sale at Christie's held in 1894, lot 97 included an artist's proof of this engraving in addition to the picture. Another copy of this engraving sold at Mr. R. H. Grundy's sale at Christie's

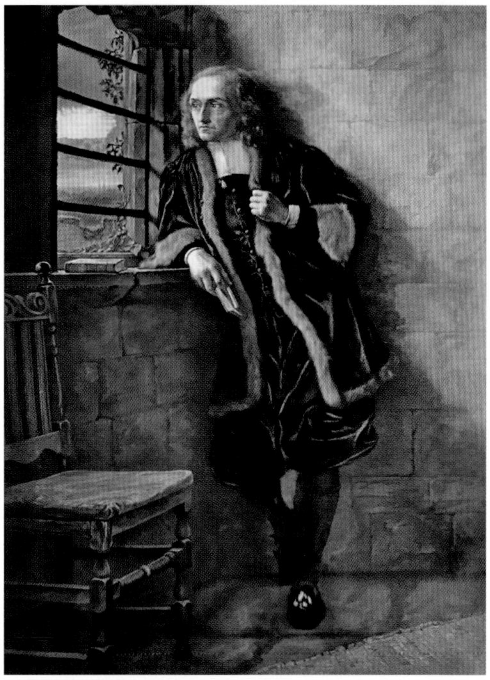

Cat. 31a. Image by permission of Chepstow Museum, Chepstow, Wales

on 21 December 1865, lot 918.

This reproductive print has similarities to Rembrandt's famous etching from 1647 of *Jan Six*, the famous writer and mayor of Amsterdam. Wallis was clearly influenced by Dutch 17th century art, so perhaps the finished painting was also influenced by Rembrandt.

Cat. 32. *Portrait of Mary Ellen Meredith*
1858; pencil on paper; 10.2 x 8.3 cm (4 x 3¼ in.); Ashmolean Museum, Oxford.
INSCRIPTION: Dated *1858*, lower right.
PROVENANCE: Wallis's studio and then by descent from the artist to his son Harold Wallis, then to his daughter-in-law Mary Wallis (née Aymes), then her great-niece Vera G. Cooper (née Langley) (1910-1989), and thence by direct descent to John Harold Cooper and family until sold at Bonhams, London, 5 March 2002, lot 62; bought by Neil Wilson of the Campbell Wilson Gallery, Hove, Sussex, for £8,000; subsequently sold to the Ashmolean Museum, accession no. WA2003.97.
LITERATURE: Johnson, D., *Lesser Lives*, 1972, facing p.112.

The present work depicts Mary Ellen Meredith (1821-1861), the daughter of the poet and novelist Thomas Love Peacock and the lover of Henry Wallis for several years [see: Chapter 5]. This drawing dates from 1858.

Mary Ellen had a weak constitution and during the winter of 1858 Wallis took her to Capri in the hope that she would regain her failing health. On her return from Capri, she lived in recluse with their son Felix near

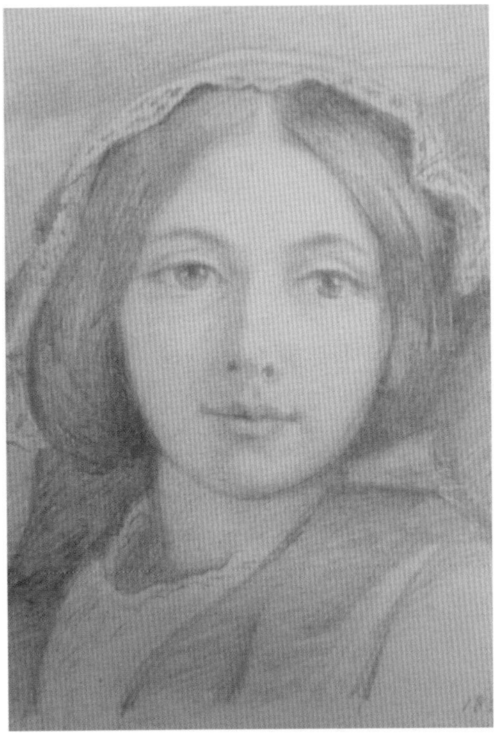

Cat. 32. Ashmolean Museum, Oxford. Image courtesy of Bonhams, London

to her father at Oatlands Park, Weybridge. After her death, Wallis kept certain of her possessions for the rest of his life, such as her green gown, matching parasol, and some of her writings and drawings.

This is an exquisite piece of draughts—manship and must rank amongst the most beautiful drawings Wallis ever executed. The love of Wallis for his subject is quite evident in this work which was executed at the height of their affair. It can be compared with D.G. Rossetti's drawings of Lizzie Siddal of a similar date. In comparison Wallis's portrait is far more direct and sensual.[1]

Cat. 33. *Portrait of Mary Ellen Meredith*(?)

Late 1850s-late 1860s; pencil on off-white paper; 19 x 15.2 cm (7½ x 6$\frac{9}{16}$ in.); Dr. Dennis T. Lanigan, Saskatoon, Canada.
Annotation: (on the backboard) "By Henry Wallis, Mrs Meredith, Nee Love, Thomas Peacock's Daughter"
Provenance: ? R.L. Cook, Sychamore, Norwich, Norfolk; private collection; Bonhams, New Bond Street, London, 8 March 2005, lot 103, sold for £3,200, purchased through Rachel Moss of Moss Galleries, London by Dr. Dennis T. Lanigan, Saskatoon; promised gift to the National Gallery of Canada.
Exhibitions: Mendel Art Gallery, *Drawing Inspiration from the Pre-Raphaelites*, 2007, no. 39; National Gallery of Canada, Ottawa, *Beauty's Awakening: Drawings by the Pre-Raphaelites and their Contemporaries*, 2015, no. 72; Leighton House, London, *Pre-Raphaelites on Paper*, 2016, no.72.

The identity of the sitter is controversial. The annotation on the old backboard is in an unknown hand. The drawing is neither signed nor inscribed so it is difficult to confirm whether or not Mary Ellen is the model. Colin Harrison, the Senior Curator of European Art at the Ashmolean Museum, Oxford states: "My feeling was that the technique was much less firm than in our drawing, and that the identification of the sitter is not very convincing when compared with our drawing. Also, given that Mrs Meredith died in 1861, I wonder if the chronology can really fit. The Bonhams drawing seems to me to be much later and of a different sitter, but that is just my instinct."[1] Nicholas Joukovsky, English professor at Pennsylvania State University comments: "If the eyes appear different, it may be because the Bonhams drawing is in profile. I do, however, think that the woman in the Bonhams drawing has the long, straight Peacock nose that is also evident in the Ashmolean drawing. It also seems to me that she looks younger than the Mary Ellen of the Ashmolean drawing, which is dated 1858. Wallis knew the Merediths well by 1855, and perhaps several years earlier."[2]

A more thorough appraisal has been given by Dennis Lanigan, the owner of the portrait: "As a maxillofacial surgeon, I have spent my professional career dealing with the correction of dentofacial deformities. I am therefore very used to analyzing patient's facial features from both a frontal and profile examination, much more than the usual art historian would be. I am very familiar with the drawing at the Ashmolean, having tried very hard to buy it myself when it came for auction at Bonhams in 2002. Comparing the drawings: both are suggestive of an individual with slightly decreased lower facial height and a deep labiomental fold, denoting a slight underdevelopment of the lower jaw. This fact strengthens the traditonal identification of the profile drawing as being of Mary Ellen."

In the Ashmolean drawing, the hair style is quite different and is not tied back into a bun and she is portrayed wearing an informal bonnet. Compounding the problem, is the existence of a drawing by Wallis, in the Birmingham City Museum and Art Gallery [Cat. 70]. The standing figure is of an elegant young woman in profile, whose facial features greatly resemble those of the model in this drawing. It is therefore possible this could be another study of Mary Ellen.

I think it is more convincing looking at the facial features that the subject of my drawing is the same model as in the drawing from Birmingham. Whether this model is Mary Ellen, however, remains the question. Certainly, the features of the lower jaw and relationship between the lower lip and

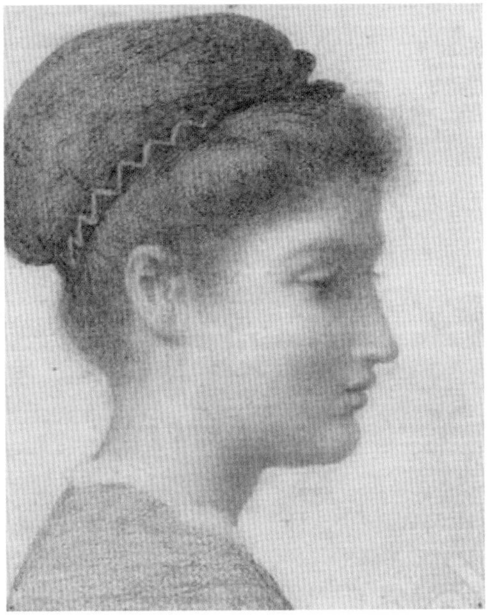

Cat. 33. Image courtesy of the National Gallery of Canada, Ottawa

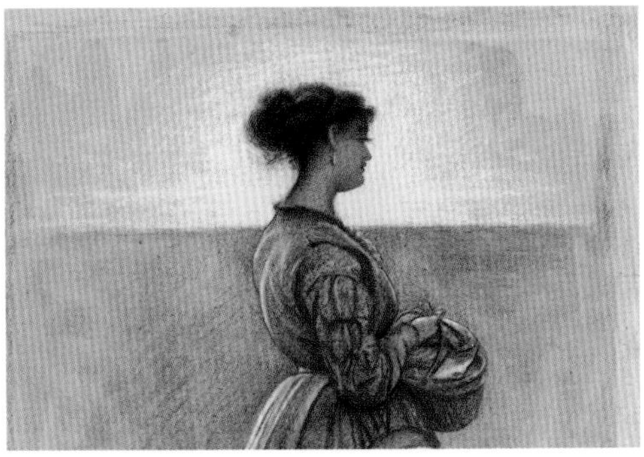

cf. Cat. 33. Detail of *Study of a Young Woman Standing* [*see:* Cat. 70]. Image by permission of Birmingham Museums Trust

chin are similar in both my drawing and the Ashmolean's. Class II malocclusions secondary to a retrusive lower jaw are a very common jaw deformity in the British population, however, so it is quite possible that two models could share a similar lower jaw pattern without necessarily being the same person. The noses are similar in that there are no obvious nasal dorsal humps but look quite straight. The length of the upper lip of the model in my drawing looks slightly shorter than the lip of Mary Ellen in the Ashmolean drawing, however. Comparing eyes is very difficult between a frontal and profile examination as is the area of the cheeks, unless one or both are obviously deficient in this area (midfacial retrusion) of which neither model is. Both models exhibit normal midfacial prominence. In summary, I think the resemblance is certainly possible but it would not be strong enough to be considered highly probable. Further drawings or photographs known to be of Mary Ellen would be needed for comparison to reach a more definite conclusion.

If the model in my drawing and the one in Birmingham are, in fact, one and the same, and the costume of the standing figure dates from later than 1861, this would obviously decrease the chance of my drawing being of Mary Ellen. I consulted two experts on nineteenth century dress for their opinions. Dr. Alexandra Palmer from the Royal Ontario Museum felt the dress was *c.*1861-1868. Dr. Kimberly Wahl from Ryerson University felt that while the bodice resembled earlier versions of 'Pre-Raphaelite' dress from the 1850s to the early 1860s, the length and volume of the back of the skirt suggested a later date of the late 1860s/early 1870s. She also felt the hairstyle was more consistent with this date. If her opinion is accurate this obviously decreases the chance of my drawing being Mary Ellen Meredith."

Cat. 34. *Thomas Love Peacock*
1858; mixed media on millboard; 16 x 14 cm. (6½ x 5½ in.); National Portrait Gallery, London.
INSCRIPTIONS: Dated *24.1.1858*, lower right.
PROVENANCE: Purchased from Henry Wallis in 1906 for the National Portrait Gallery for 20 guineas, accession no. NPG 1432.
EXHIBITIONS: *National Portrait Exhibition*, South Kensington, 1868, no. 623;[1] *Shelley: An Effectual Angel*, Dove Cottage, Grasmere, 1992.
LITERATURE: NPG Catalogue, 2004, illust.

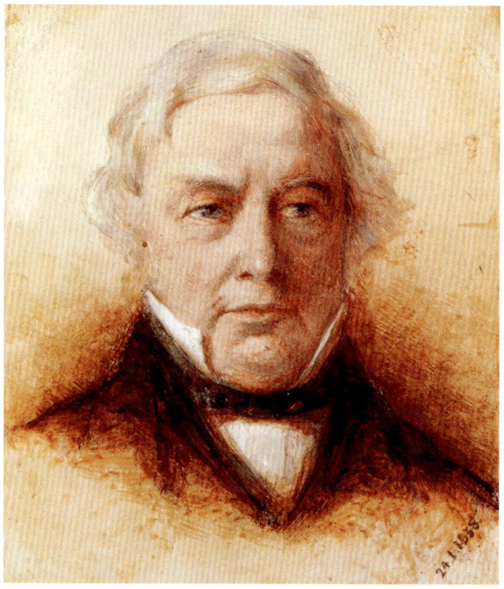

Cat. 34. Image by permission of the National Portrait Gallery/ Bridgeman Images

This portrait was painted when Wallis was staying with Mary Ellen at her father's house on the Thames at Lower Halliford. The fact that Mary Ellen was pregnant at the time must have meant that Peacock was comfortable, not only with the affair, but that Mary Ellen had left her husband. Wallis and Peacock were to remain on friendly terms even after Mary Ellen's death in 1861.

This portrait appears to have been executed in mixed media. Underdrawing in pencil can be visualized, and then the form appears to have been blocked in watercolour. This is most visible in the background and in the lower regions of the coat. The main portion of the face, hair and coat collar have then been built-up in rather thinned oil paint, which is matt and has a dry appearance. Wallis thought that the portrait he had done was the only one of Peacock in existence.[2] The National Portrait Gallery, however, also has a miniature portrait by Roger Jean in watercolour on ivory from *c.*1805, when Peacock was a young man.

Cat. 34a. *Thomas Love Peacock*
1910; etching on tan colour wove paper; image size: 11.4 x 9.2 cm. (4½ x 3⅝ in.), sheet size: 21.2 x 15.9 (8⅜ x 6¼ in.); Dennis T. Lanigan Collection.
INSCRIPTIONS: signed *W H W Bicknell* in pencil, lower right; inscribed in plate *W H W Bicknell del et sc 1910.*

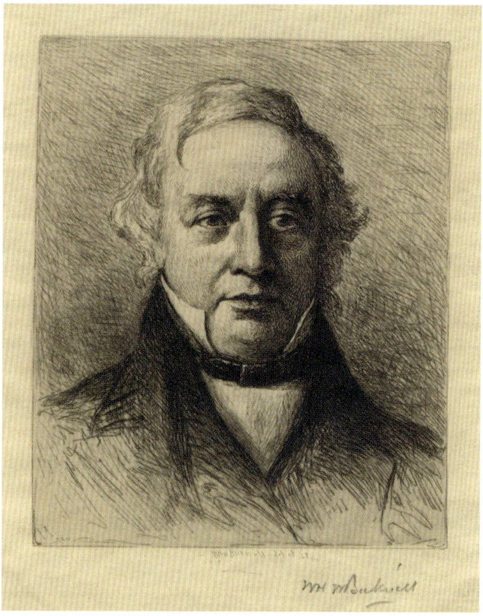

Cat. 34a. Image courtesy of the Dennis Lanigan collection

This etching after Wallis is by the American artist and etcher William Harry Warren Bicknell (1860-1947) who had trained at the Boston Museum School of Fine Arts. The Bibliophile Society of Boston asked him to do portraits of many well-known authors, including such English authors as Shakespeare and Robert Burns. This etching was used as the frontispiece for Garnett, Richard (Ed.), *Thomas Love Peacock. Letters to Edward Hookham and Percy B. Shelley with Fragments of Unpublished Mss*, published by The Bibliophile Society, Boston, in 1910.

Cat. 35. *The Bridge of Sighs*
1858; medium and dimensions unknown; whereabouts unknown.
EXHIBITIONS: Liverpool Academy, 1858, no. 143.

When the painting was shown in Liverpool in 1858 it was accompanied by the following lines from Thomas Hood's famous poem of 1844 'The Bridge of Sighs':

"Where the lamps quiver
So far in the river
With many a light
From window and casement,
From garret and basement.
She stood, with amazement,
Houseless by night,

…….with the daring
Last look of despairing
Fix'd on Futurity."[1]

Despite the exhibition at the Liverpool Academy being extensively reviewed in the *Liverpool Mercury*, there is no mention of Wallis's picture, suggesting that it failed to catch the attention of the critics. The so-called 'Bridge of Sighs' was Waterloo Bridge in London, infamous because of the number of young women in despair who had committed suicide by throwing themselves into the Thames to their deaths. It was a popular tragic subject for Victorian artists, perhaps now best known from one of J.E. Millais's most dramatic and beautiful etchings, *The Bridge of Sighs*, from *Passages from the Poems of Thomas Hood Illustrated by the Junior Etching Club* and published by E. Gambart & Co. in 1858, the same year as Wallis's picture. Other artists painting similar scenes included *Found Drowned*, ca. 1848-50, by George Frederic Watts, *Past and Present* of 1858 by Augustus Egg, and *Drowned! Drowned!* of 1860 by Abraham Solomon. Egg's work *Past and Present* was exhibited in Liverpool the same year as Wallis's painting.

The watercolour *A View of a City Bridge by Night* that sold at Sotheby's Belgravia in 1973 [Cat. 260] might be a study for this painting.

Cat. 36. *Xarifa*
1859; ?oil on canvas; dimensions unknown; whereabouts unknown.
EXHIBITIONS: French Gallery, *The Seventh Annual Winter Exhibition*, 1859, no. 154.
LITERATURE: *The London Daily News*, London, 14 November 1859, p.2; *The Athenaeum*, No. 1673, 19 November 1859, p.673; *Illustrated Times: Weekly Newspaper*, No. 242, Vol. 9, 19 November 1859, p.342; *The Illustrated London News*, Vol. 35, 19 November 1859, p.488; *The Era*, 20 November 1859, p.15; *The Illustrated London News*, Vol. 35, 26 November 1859, p.518; *The British Quarterly Review*, Vol. 31, 1860, p.268; *The Dublin University Magazine*, Vol. 55, April 1860, p.482.

This painting dates from 1859, the same year that D.G. Rossetti's *Bocca Baciata* introduced the influence of Venetian Renaissance painting into the second phase of Pre-Raphaelitism. It is unfortunate that Wallis's *Xarifa* is lost making it is impossible to know whether the Venetian colouring Wallis included in this painting was influenced by Rossetti's example. If so, this would certainly have placed Wallis amongst the avant-garde to have absorbed this influence so early. In terms of subject matter, the woman traumatized by a faithless lover harks back to early Pre-Raphaelite works such as Holman Hunt's *One step to the deathbed.*

The critic for *The Dublin University Magazine* commented: "Mr. Wallis's 'Xarifa' (154), indicates a revival of that power of colour he seemed to have lost with 'the return from Naseby' R.A. (1859), and although he deals to sad excess in purple flesh-tints there are harmonies in the present work pleasant to recognise. Xarifa is the Spanish heroine of the Ballad 'The Bridal of Andalla,' which Lockhardt translates thus: 'Rise up, rise up, Xarifa! Lay the golden cushion down;/ Rise up, come to the window, and gaze upon the town!/ From gay guitar and violin the silver notes are flowing,/ and lovely lute doth speak between the trumpet's lordly blowing;/ And the banners bright, from lattice light, are waving everywhere,/ And the tall, tall plume, of our cousin's bridegroom, floats proudly in the air./ Rise up, rise up, Xarifa! Lay the golden cushion down;/ Rise up, come to the window, and gaze with all the town.' But the Lady Xarifa would not rise, for it was the bridal of her false lover, and she sits here in the shadow of the room, gloomy, gaunt-eyed, and pale, her hands upon the golden cushion, and her features in a set despair."

The *Illustrated London News* said: "H. Wallis's 'Xarifa,' after Lockhart's heroine in 'The Spanish Ballad,' is a remarkable specimen of chiaroscuro and minute textural finish – vide more particularly the embroidered cushion on the lap, the tigerskin footstool, and the bright silk tapestry work on the floor." *The Athenaeum* stated: "Mr. Wallis's Xarifa (154) is a great advance, a gorgeous and most Venetian bit of colour – perhaps, rather of a decorative character: a room paneled with such figures would, indeed, be kaiserly, - not but what the expression of the hopeless, haggard, dark, red-eyed Moorish face, is beautiful and sad: but, still, what pleases most is the heavy richness of the violet velvet, the splendour of the gold-cloth cushion, the glowing crimson of the carpet, the pleasant round surface of the blue jar, the tiger-skin footstool, and the vivid green of the shrub that fills the right of the picture."

Cat. 37. *Paris Back Streets* (attributed)
1859; oil on panel; 27.9 x 22.8 cm (11 x 9 in.); private collection.
Inscriptions: Signed with the artist's *HW* monogram and dated *1859*.
Provenance: Belle Parker Gordon, New Rochelle, New York; her estate sale Sotheby's, Arcade, New York, 22 July 1993, lot 599, sold for $748.

It is difficult to say whether or not Wallis went to Paris that year. What is known, is that he spent the winter of 1858/59 at Capri with Mary Ellen Meredith. He came back from Capri on 14 February 1859, perhaps by way of Paris, which could corroborate the date on the painting, supposing the attribution is correct. The authors have not seen an image of this work to help determine whether or not it is by Wallis.

Cat. 38. *On the South-Coast, Seaford* (*A Coast Scene, Sunset, Seaford*)
1859; oil on board; 22.5 x 35.5 cm (8⅞ x 14 in.); Walker Art Gallery, Liverpool.
Annotations: (in ink, in an unknown hand,

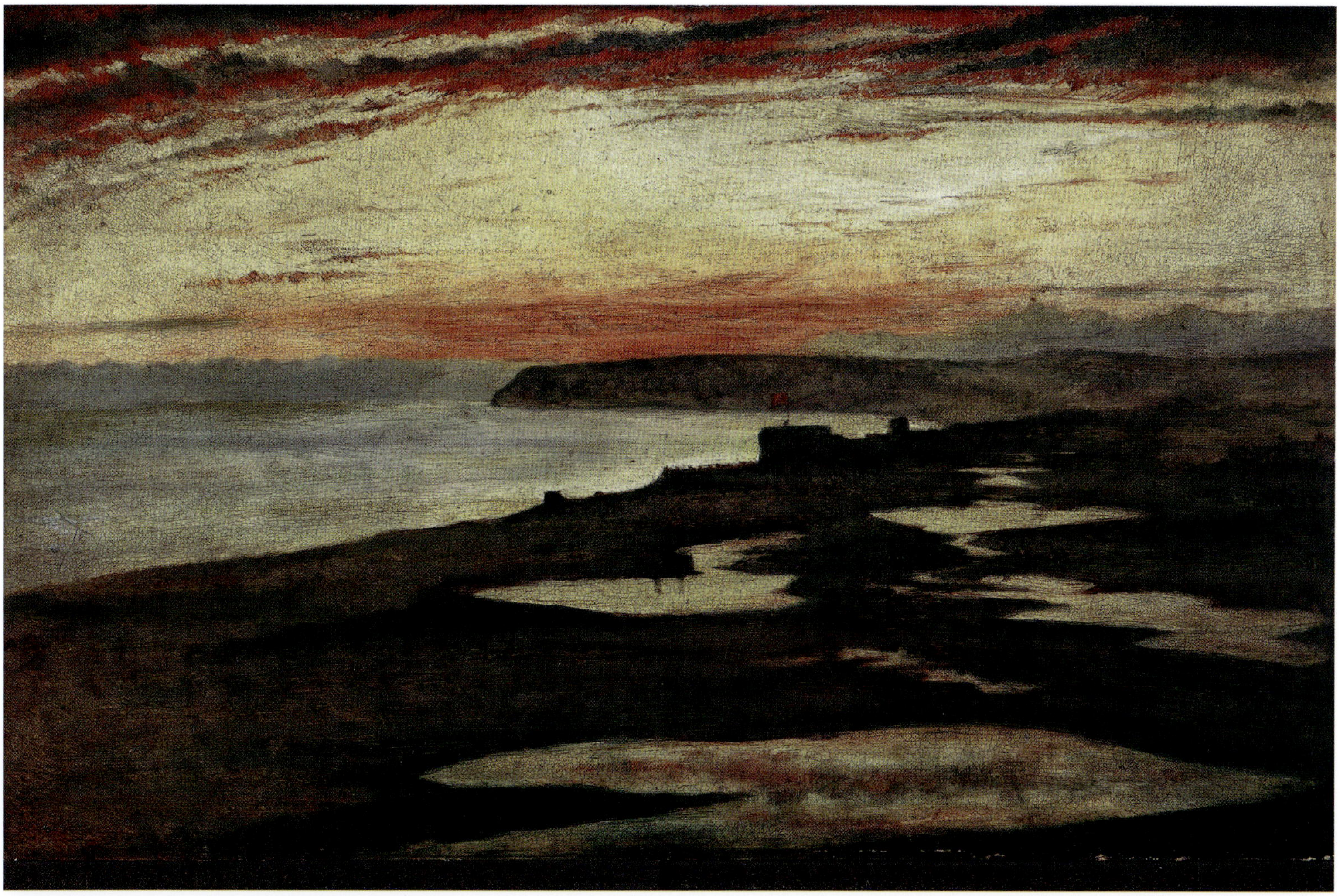

Cat. 38. Image by permission of the National Museums, Liverpool

verso) "By / Henry Wallis / 62 Great Russell Street / W.C."
PROVENANCE: Presented by the artist to G.P. Boyce; his executors' sale Christie's 1-3 July 1897, lot 218, bought by Charles Fairfax Murray; Augustine "Caroline" Boyce, widow of the artist; thence apparently to Dr P.R. Dodwell, London;[1] Miss Sylvia Browne, 39 Hawarden Avenue, Liverpool, from whom purchased for £10 by the Walker Art Gallery, 1954, acquisition no. WAG 1640.
EXHIBITIONS: The Picture Gallery, 14 Berners Street, 1862, no. 85; Arts Council, 1983-84, *Landscape in Britain, 1850-1950*, cat. 34; (venues included the Hayward Gallery, London; Bristol City Museum and Art Gallery; Stoke-on-Trent City Museum and Art Gallery; and Mappin Art Gallery, Sheffield).
LITERATURE: *The Athenaeum*, No. 1809, 28 June 1862, p.859; Staley, Allen: *The Pre-Raphaelite Landscape*, 1973, p.88; Bennett, Mary: *Artists of the Pre-Raphaelite Circle. The First Generation*, 1995, pp.190-91 (illus.); MacCulloch, Laura: *Pre-Raphaelite Treasures at National Museums Liverpool*, 2013, p.32.

A twentieth-century label on the back gives this work the title *A Coast Scene, Sunset, Seaford*, and the date 1859, but this is not the original title it was exhibited under in 1862.[2] The critic for *The Athenaeum* noted: "A new exhibition of pictures has opened in Berners Street...Mr. Wallis's *On the South-coast, Seaford* (85), twilight on the shore, with gleaming pools of water, and a fort darkening at evening, are excellent studies."

Mary Bennett has noted that "the view is of the coast line at Seaford, near Newhaven, Sussex, probably from a point by the Roman fort on the high ground above Seaford Head to the south-east of the town, over the saltings towards the Martello tower, with Selsey Bill in the far distance beyond. Seaford was the location of summer lodgings for George Meredith and his wife Mary Ellen during the mid-1850s...Mary Ellen appears to have stayed again at Seaford in the summer of 1857, in 1858 before she and Wallis went abroad, and once more in 1859. Wallis only took his lodgings in Great Russell Street in 1859, by which time they appear to have separated." MacCullough speculates: "This picture, which was painted the year they parted, may have been inspired by the bittersweet emotions of their love affair."

Bennett has pointed out that "twilight studies had already formed a part of the artist's interests, as they had for others of the Pre-Raphaelite circle. He exhibited a *Night Study* [Cat. 17] at the Society of British Artists in 1855 [1854]; the dying day and sunset sky are significant parts of his *Stonebreaker* [Cat. 28] of 1857-58; while a picture called *Nightfall* [Cat. 41] was exhibited at the Liverpool Academy 1860, for which the present painting might well be a candidate. The same meticulous and thoughtful vision apparent in his *Stonebreaker* also pervades this study of sunset clouds sharpened with red light, sweeping across the still and shadowy landscape and reflected in the saltings."

Cat. 39. *Back from Marston Moor*
1859; oil on canvas; 113 x 87.6 cm. (44½ x 34½ in.); whereabouts unknown.
PROVENANCE: Thomas E. Plint; his sale Christie's 8 March 1862, lot 327, bought in; Plint sale, Christie's, 17 June 1865, lot 121, bought by Ernest Gambart for £63;[1] his sale, Christie's, 31 May 1871, lot 229, bought Virtue, likely James Sprent Virtue (1829-1892) of Oaklands Park, Surrey, for £79 16s;[2] his sale Christie's, 1 March 1879, lot 158, purchased by W. Smith for £52 10s; Shepherd Brothers gallery, London, by 1881-1882; John Bibby III,[3] Liverpool by 1891; his estate sale Christie's 3 June 1899, lot 103 ["The Soldier's Return"], bought by T. Maclean, likely the art dealer Thomas McLean; Henry Wallis & Son of the French Gallery; their sale Christie's, London, March 23 & 24, 1916, lot 143, bought by the dealer W. W. Sampson for £37 16 s.
EXHIBITIONS: Royal Academy, 1859, no. 930; Birmingham Society of Artists, *Exhibition of Modern Works of Art*, 1860, no. 30, asking price £200; Yorkshire Art Exhibition, Leeds, 1880, no. 804; Shepherd Brothers, London, *Winter Exhibition*, 1881 and *Spring Exhibition*, 1882; *Liverpool International Exhibition*, 1886; Birmingham Museum and Art Gallery, *The Pre-Raphaelites. Special Loan Collection of Modern Pictures in Oil and Water Colours*, 1891, no. 201; Guildhall, 1900, no. 41.
LITERATURE: *The Royal Academy Review*, 1859, p.39; *The National Magazine*, Vol. VI, 1859, p.164; *The Dublin University Magazine*, Vol. 54, 1859, p.247; *The Athenaeum*, No. 1644, 30 April 1859, p.587; *The London Daily News*, London, 5 May 1859, p.2; *Gazette des Beaux-Arts*, 15 May 1859, p.243; *Lloyd's Weekly Newspaper*, 15 May 1859, p.8; *The Examiner*, 21 May 1859, p.326; *The Era*, 22 May 1859, p.5; *The Illustrated London News*, vol. 35, 13 July 1859, p.92; *The Illustrated London News*, 23 July 1859, p.90; *Blackwood's Edinburgh Magazine*, vol. 86, August 1859, p.127, p.132; *Aris's Birmingham Gazette*, 25 August 1860, p.5; *The Daily News*, 6 September 1860; *The Birmingham Daily Post*, 6 September 1860, p.2; *The Art Journal*, Vol. 1, 1862, p.105; *The Times*, 3 March 1862; *The Spectator*, Vol. 35, 8 March 1862, p.271; *The Building News and Engineering Journal*, Vol. 8, 14 March 1862, p.175; *The Athenaeum*, No. 1794, 15 March 1862, pp.367-368; *The Leeds Mercury*, 22 June 1880, p.8; *The Academy*, 22 September 1882, p.232; *The Artist*, Vol. III, 1 October 1882, p.328; *The Athenaeum*, No. 2970, 27 September 1884, p.409; *The Times*, 5 June 1889, p.4; *Birmingham Daily Post*, 2 October 1891, p.4; Rowlands, Walter, *Among the Great Masters of Literature*, 1900, p.151; Bate, Percy: *The English Pre-Raphaelite Painters*, 1910, p.86.

The Battle of Marston Moor on 2 July, 1644 was a critical battle during the English Civil Wars (1642-51). The Royalist forces (Cavaliers) under Prince Rupert were defeated by the Parliamentarian (Roundheads) and Scots Covenanter armies under Sir Thomas Fairfax and Oliver Cromwell. When Wallis's painting was exhibited at the Royal Academy in 1859 it was described as "A cavalier soldier entering his father's farmyard, wounded from the fight" but the soldier was obviously fighting for the Parliamentarians. Although this painting is now lost, its composition can be largely surmised from the later engraving. The painting, also referred to as *The Return from Marston Moor*, was exhibited at the Royal Academy in 1859, along with Augustus Egg's civil war picture *The Night before Naseby*. Contemporary reviews suggest this work was very avant-garde in terms of its colouring, such as the use of blue for shadows.

A critic for the *Royal Academy Review* expressed the unfavourable opinion that it was: "A sad retrogression of the painter of 'Chatterton's Death'. Everything is ugly and exaggerated; and the whole is a perpetual conflict of every extravagance that could have been introduced. The lights in the flesh tones are so hot, that the figures appear roasted, whilst the shadows remind us of blue cholera. The wounded trooper is on a horse of purple, to match his own face, which is set between a smeary gamboge and emerald green sky; the boy running to meet the trooper seems walking on red hot plough shares, as if going through the ordeal by fire, and the hay ricks are in a state of conflagration. It is a most unveracious work, and the acceptance and suspension in a good position of such a monstrosity can only be for the purpose of enticing the shillings by an eccentricity."

The critic for *Blackwoods Edinburgh Magazine* was also very obviously not an admirer of the Pre-Raphaelites. In his initial review, he denounced three works now generally regarded as minor masterpieces of the first phase of Pre-Raphaelitism: "We believe such works as 'Return from Marston

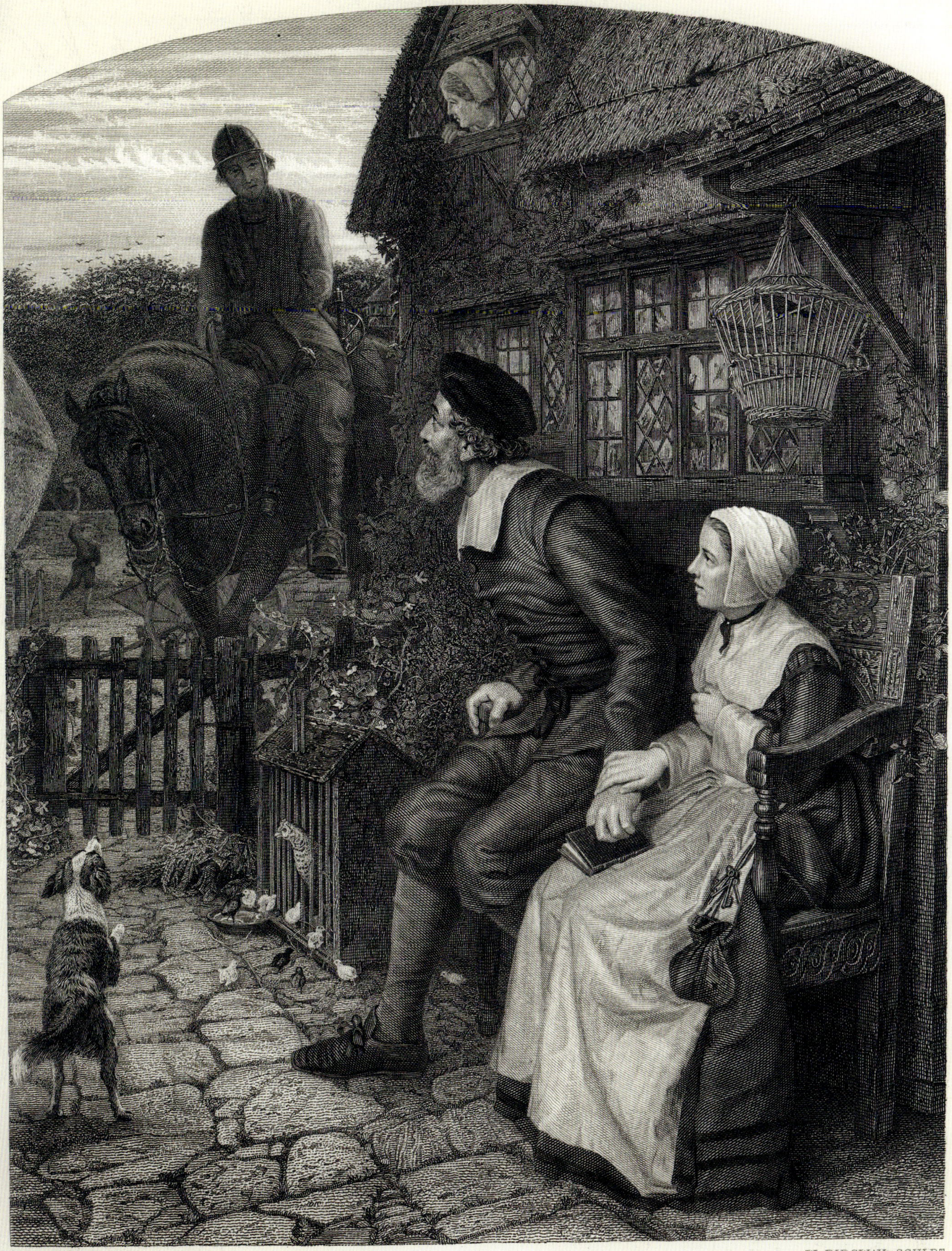

H. WALLIS. PINXT W. RIDGWAY. SCULPT

BACK FROM MARSTON MOOR.

Cat. 39b. Image courtesy of the Dennis Lanigan collection

Moor, by Mr. Wallis – 'Too Late,' by Mr. Windus – and 'The King's Orchard,' by Mr. Hughes – have for three long months attracted curiosity only to incite disgust or to provoke ridicule." In a later unfavourable review he maintained: "It is with deep regret that we have to record still another reputation wrecked in devotion to a cause which has this year betrayed its votaries into even more than accustomed extravagance. Mr Wallis, honoured as the painter of the 'Chatterton,' has now dishonoured both himself and his cause by the 'Return from Marston Moor'. This artist, with others of his school, would seem to hold that genius is best shown in the transgression of the limits and the laws which all previous genius had hitherto observed. The story and intention of the picture are undoubtedly simple and heartfelt. The return of a worn and wounded knight to home and anxious parents; the eager attitude of the father rising to meet the son's approach; the homeish housewife mother, the model of domestic solicitude, are sufficient to show what power of expression is within this artist's reach, did he but soberly follow the simplicity of nature. The imitation of nature which was once the watchword of the school, is here seen in colour the most outrageous, and detail absolutely impossible. The blaze of a sunset sky, red, green, and saffron yellow, the knight's features gory with blood, or glowing from the heat of battle; roses and flowers of brazen face and staring eye, verily blind the sober vision, and darken and dazzle by excess of light. In infinity of detail the work is not less distracting. The father's beard is counted hair for hair; the swallow swooping down with swift flight is yet painted with all the detail of beak, eye, and plumage; pigeons are cooing on the distant dovecot; a barn-door fowl is crowing between the stirrup of the rider and the horse's leg, and thus from centre to furthest corner is every inch crowded with incident, till the picture, like a drop of Thames water seen in the oxyhydrogen microscope, is amazingly wonderful, but monstrously disagreeable."[4]

The critic for *Lloyd's Weekly London Newspaper* gave the picture a more favourable review, however: "Mr. H. Wallis is strong this year, though not with the strength of 'Chatterton.' He has not given us a book-illustration or a horror. His story this time is complete in itself, 'Back from Marston Moor' (930), and requires no previous knowledge; but then the subject is not much – it is as simple as it can be, and it is rather a sun-set feeling than a story. The colouring is a little violent, not from any exaggeration of intensity, but from a slight want of fusing breadth and harmonious pervading atmosphere. In brief, the picture represents a young Puritan trooper slightly wounded, riding into his father's farm-yard at sunset, after the disbanding of Cromwell's army. There is nothing specially good about the young man's expression, – but he looks quietly, gravely happy, – as Puritan youth should do, – and is intent on observing his old father's and mother's first start of recognition. The old couple – true John Anderson and his wife[5] – are seated on the bench outside the cottage window, enjoying the serene grandeur of sunset, which turns them to the most alarming crimsons, yellows and purples. There is a fine rustic poetry and a true sense of the enjoyment and quietude of the country in this powerful picture. The old father, in his grave brown suit and plain hose, has caught sight of the brave lad, and is starting up to greet him, in spite of the old matron's checking and more cautious hand. Already the horse's knee is bumping against the wicket-gate, and the young brothers who have caught sight of him, are bounding over the farm-yard paling with a whoop and halloo. It is full of a fine muscular poetry is this picture, and a robust strength that is pure and healthy as can be. The moment is well chosen, because it is full of hope and surprise, and leaves so much to the imagination."

Cat. 39a. *Back from Marston Moor*
1859; oil on canvas; 54.6 x 41.9 cm. (21½ x 16½ in.); whereabouts unknown.
Provenance: James Knowles;[1] his sale Christie's, 31 May 1862, lot 103, bought Scott, possibly the dealer John Scott of Colnaghi's, for £15 15s; Thomas Blackburn, Liverpool, his sale Christie's, 13 March 1865, lot 75, bought in; Blackburn sale Christie's, October 23, 1865, lot 121, bought by the dealer Ernest Gambart for £63.

This would appear to be either a reduced version, or more likely the initial oil sketch, for the finished painting.

Cat. 39b. *Back from Marston Moor*
1875; steel engraving; image size: 23.8 x 18 cm (9⅜ x 7⅛ in.), sheet size: 31.9 x 24.3 cm (12⅝ x 9⁹⁄₁₆ in.); Dr Dennis T. Lanigan, Saskatoon, Canada.
Annotations: (lettered below image with title, production details, and publication line) "H. WALLIS, PINX^{T} / W. RIDGWAY, SCULP^{T}. / BACK FROM MARSTON MOOR. / D. APPLETON & Co. NEW YORK"
Literature: *The Times*, 2 December 1875, p.3; *The Art Journal*, New Series, Vol. XIV, 1875, p.360; *The Art Journal*, New Series, Vol XXIII, 1886, p.368.

An advertisment in *The Times* from 2 December 1875 stated: "*The Art Journal* for December contains the following engravings: 1. Back from Marston Moor. After H. Wallis." The engraving appeared in *The Art Journal*, Vol. XIV, opposite page 360. This print engraved by William Ridgway was later published by Virtue & Co. in London and appeared as an illustration in *Contemporary Art* of 1886. It was also published in New York by D. Appleton & Co. The print was described by *The Art Journal* as: "This picture represents an assumed passage from the history of the Civil War. The battle of Marston Moor, Yorkshire, fought on July 2nd, 1644, helped to decide the fate of Charles I, which culminated in that fought at Naseby in the year following. As we read the composition it shows one of Cromwell's troopers, probably one of his famous Ironsides, returning wounded to his native village, after the former engagement, so disastrous to the cause of the Royalist party. Seated in front of a picturesque cottage is the soldier's father, and probably a sister, for she appears too young to be his mother; both are of the true Puritan type, as regards costume. The sound of the horseman's feet stopping at the gate has withdrawn the elderly man's attention from the book he is reading, and he looks eagerly at the rider to ascertain who he may be. The female at his side does the same, but lays her hand gently on that of her companion, as if she half recognised the new comer and his condition, and would allay the excitement the old man might feel. The dog, however, true to the instinct of the animal, has no share in the doubt, but rushes forward to give the warrior a warm welcome, while the face of the girl peeping out of the casement-window has an expression of pleasure which shows but little uncertainty on her part. In the background are some of the villagers rushing across the farmyard, either to greet an old companion, or to hear news of the victory; perhaps both. As an illustration of the story of the period this picture merits attention, the subject itself being most pleasing; but the manner in which it is placed on the canvas would in itself find admirers altogether independent of the theme. The expression given to the two principal figures is forcibly suggestive of the feelings by which they are suddenly absorbed; and this is unmistakably manifested also in the attitude of the man and the action of his companion. The faces of the two are well-studied, and beautifully painted, while the trooper's horse looks over the gate, and seems as if it were neighing a recognition of some old friends. That pretty rustic cottage, with its surroundings of every kind, and its grave inmates, indicates a condition of social and mental quietude contrasting strongly with the appearance of the soldier fresh from the scenes of warfare and death. The picture was exhibited at the Royal Academy in 1859, but was unfavourably hung among the water-colour paintings and the miniatures."

The girl peeking out the window is reminiscent of similar women at windows in the work of Wallis's friend George Price Boyce of this same time period.[1]

Cat. 40. *Portrait of Henry Darvall in Military Dress*[1]
1859; oil on canvas; dimensions unknown; whereabouts unknown, likely destroyed.
LITERATURE: Nicholas A. Joukovsky: "The Early Meredithian Milieu: New Evidence from Letters of Peter Augustin Daniel," *Studies in Philology*, Vol. XV, Summer 2018, p.637.

In an undated letter from late 1859, P.A. Daniel describes the collective efforts of his artist friends, including Henry Wallis and Eyre Crowe, to help him fill the canvas covering a large screen that he was using to decrease the draftinesss of his rooms. Wallis apparently painted the six-foot-two-inch Henry Darvall in a military uniform, full-size, and scowling fiercely. While it would be interesting to think that Wallis was painting his friend in the uniform of the Artist Rifles this would be incorrect. The official formation of the corp did not happen until 10 August 1860. It was formed as part of a general volunteer movement to combat the possibility of French aggression under Napoleon III (Louis-Napoléon Bonaparte). As far as can be ascertained, neither Darvall nor Wallis ever joined the corp, although many artists in the Pre-Raphaelite circle did, including D.G. Rossetti, W. Holman Hunt, J.E. Millais, W. Morris, F. Leighton, W.B. Richmond and G.F. Watts. The military uniform may have, therefore, merely been a studio prop in Daniel's studio.

Cat. 41. *Nightfall*
*c.*1860, ?oil on canvas; dimensions unknown; whereabouts unknown.
EXHIBITIONS: Liverpool Academy, 1860, no. 766, sold for 35 guineas.[1]
LITERATURE: Bennett, Mary: *Artists of the Pre-Raphaelite Circle. The First Generation*, 1995, p.191

This was not Wallis's first nocturnal scene as he had previously exhibited a *Night Study* at the Society of British Artists in 1854. He later exhibited *On the South-coast, Seaford* (Cat. 38) at The Picture Gallery, London, in 1862. A contemporary description of *Nightfall* would be required to know exactly what Wallis portrayed in this painting. Mary Bennett speculates this could possibly even be the same work as *On the South-coast, Seaford.*

Cat. 42. *A Lady*
*c.*1860; medium and dimensions unknown; whereabouts unknown.
PROVENANCE: T.E. Plint; his sale Christie's, 8 May 1862, lot 286, purchased by Moore for £25 5s.

This work does not appear to have been exhibited by Wallis and was likely a direct commission from Plint. The fact that it sold for only £25 5s [25 guineas] at Plint's sale would suggest that it was either a drawing or an oil sketch and not a major finished painting, although works sold at the auction for far less than he had paid for them initially.

Cat. 43. *Gondomar Witnessing the Execution of Raleigh*
*c.*1859-1861; ?oil on canvas; dimensions unknown; whereabouts unknown.
PROVENANCE: Thomas E. Plint, his sale Christie's, 8 May 1862, lot 321, bought Smart, possibly Richard Thomas Smart (1825-1912) of the London picture dealers and conservators Seguier & Smart, for £199 10s; James Dorington, Hanover Square, London; his estate sale Christie's, 1 May 1880, lot 80, bought by Smart for £81 18s;
EXHIBITIONS: Royal Academy, 1861, no. 101.
LITERATURE: *The Spectator*, Vol. 34, 13 April 1861, p.389; *The Times*, 4 May 1861, p.12; *The Athenaeum*, No. 1750, 11 May 1861, p.635; *The Spectator*, 25 May 1861, p.556; *The Spectator*, 29 May, 1861; *The Art Journal*, Vol. 1, 1862, p.105; *The Times*, 3 March 1862; *The Spectator*, Vol. 35, 8 March 1862, p.271 *The Building News and Engineering Journal*, Vol. 8, 14 March 1862, p.175; *The Spectator*, 10 May 1862, p. 522; *The Athenaeum*, No. 1803, 17 May 1862, p.668; *The Artist and Journal of Home Culture*, Vol. I, June 1880, p.171; Lessens, Ronald, 'Henry Wallis (1830-1916), a neglected Pre-Raphaelite', *The British Art Journal*, vol. XV, No. 1, Autumn 2014, p.54.

Diego Sarmiento de Acuña, Count of Gondomar (1567-1626), was a Spanish diplomat and ambassador to England from 1613 to 1622. His task was to keep James I from aiding the Protestant states against Spain and Habsburg Austria, and to avert attacks on Spanish possessions in the Americas. The active part he took in promoting the execution of Sir Walter Raleigh aroused particular animosity towards him in England.[1]

When this painting sold at Christie's the auction house stated the work was painted in 1859, even though it was not exhibited until 1861.[2] William Michael Rossetti's review of this painting in *The Spectator* in 1862 stated: "In 'Gondomar' (101), the Spanish ambassador watching from a window the execution of Sir Walter Raleigh on Tower-hill, Mr. Wallis is more himself. The figure, though turning its back to the gazer, is full of meaning, and the colouring rich without the garishness displayed in the 'Elaine'." Rossetti's approval of Gondomar is significant because it reflects the praise he had given to two previous historical subjects by Wallis – *Sir Walter Raleigh in the Tower* and *Henry Marten in Chepstow Castle.*

The Athenaeum, in its review of the Royal Academy exhibition, stated: "Mr. H. Wallis has a telling little picture styled *Gondomar* (101), the famous Spanish ambassador, drawing back a window-curtain to look at an execution taking place on Tower Hill. There is a cruel triumph about this figure that is excellently given, and his character is aided by the sullen fervid colour of the picture, and the lute that lies on the couch by the window." The critic of *The Times* also admired this painting: "(101) 'Gondomar' – H. Wallis – that wily Spanish Ambassador, watching an execution (whose?) from behind a curtain window. His face is not seen, but the attitude is full of expression, and the colours – especially of the drapery of the window and furniture stuffs – excellent."

Cat. 44. *Elaine*
1861, oil on canvas; 62.2 x 127 cm (24½ x 50 in.); private collection.
INSCRIPTIONS: Signed with initials *HW*, dated *1861*, and inscribed on verso.
PROVENANCE: Thomas E. Plint; his sale Christie's, 8 May 1862, lot 317, purchased by Agnews, London, for £498 15s; Sir John Pender,[1] Crampsall House, near Manchester by 1865; his sale Christie's, 31 January 1873, lot 605, purchased by Agnew for £945; Holbrook Gaskell,[2] Woolton, Allerton, Liverpool, by 1884; his estate sale Christie's, 24 June 1909, lot 100, purchased by Agnew for £294; Sir Alexander Henderson,[3] by 1912; his sale Sotheby's, 13 June 1934, lot 129, bought by B. Samuel for £135; anonymous sale Hartleys Auctioneers & Valuers, Little-Lane, Ilkley, 23 April 1997, lot 486, bought for £940.
EXHIBITIONS: Royal Academy, 1861, no. 492; Royal Manchester Institution, *Exhibition of the Works of Modern Artists*, 1865, no. 728; *Royal Jubilee Exhibition*, Manchester, 1887, no. 939; *International Exhibition of Science, Art and Industry*, Glasgow, 1888, no. 369; Burlington Fine Arts Club, 1912, no. 22.
LITERATURE: 'Fine-Art Gossip', *The Athenaeum*, No. 1715, 8 September 1860, p.329; *The Art Journal*, New Series, Vol. VII, 1861, p.196; *The Spectator*, 13 April

1861, p.389; *The Examiner*, 4 May 1861, p.280; *The London Daily News*, London, 4 May 1861, p.5; *The Athenaeum*, No. 1750, 11 May 1861, p.635; *The Times*, 13 May 1861, p.6; *The London Daily News*, London, 21 May 1861, p.2; *The Spectator*, 25 May 1861, p.556; *The Illustrated London News*, 22 June 1861, p.594; *The Art Journal*, Vol. 1, 1862, p.105; *The Times*, 3 March 1862; *The Spectator*, Vol. 35, 8 March 1862, p.271; *The Building News and Engineering Journal*, Vol. 8, 14 March 1862, p.175; *Manchester Courier and Lancashire General Advertiser*, 6 September 1865, p.3; *Manchester Courier and Lancashire General Advertiser*, 9 September 1865, p.2; *The Athenaeum*, No. 2359, 11 January 1873, p.35; *The Athenaeum*, No. 2363, 8 February 1873, p.187; *The Athenaeum*, No. 2971, 4 October 1884, p.438; Armstrong, Walter, *Fine Art at the Royal Jubilee Exhibition, Manchester*, 1887, p.50; Arnold, William T.: *The Art Journal*, Vol. 49, 1887, p.252; *The Times*, 3 May 1887, p.10; *The Artist and Journal of Home Culture*, Vol. 8, 1 June 1887, p.190; White, William, *Notes and Queries*, Vol. III, 21 January 1893, p.45; White, William, *Notes and Queries*, Vol. III, 11 February 1893, p.117; *The Athenaeum*, No. 4262, 3 July 1909, p.21; *The Burlington Magazine*: 'Mr. Henry Wallis', Vol. 30, No. 168, March 1917, p.124; Carter, A. C.R., Forthcoming Sales-Lord Faringdon's Collection, *The Burlington Magazine*, Vol. 64, No. 375, June, 1934, p.xvii.

King Pelles's daughter Elaine had fallen in love with Sir Lancelot, yet her love was unrequited, for Lancelot loved only Queen Guinevere. At Case Castle, Lancelot found Elaine disguised by enchantment as Queen Guinevere. They slept together and she conceived a child, Galahad. Sir Lancelot felt that he had betrayed the King and left the castle. Lady Elaine fell into a deep sorrow at her loss of Lancelot. She died and was placed in a great barge, which was later found floating the river down to Camelot.[4] Wallis's picture shows the dead Elaine being placed in the barge. Wallis's painting was based on the following text from Tennyson's *Idylls of the King*:

> "In her right hand the lily, in her left
> The letter; all her bright hair streaming down;
> And all the coverlid was cloth of gold
> Drawn to her waist and she herself in white
> All but her face, and that clear featured face
> Was lovely, for she did not seem as dead,
> But fast asleep, and lay as though she smiled."[5]

The choice of subject, as well as the warm colour palette, is unusual for Wallis, and he may have been influenced by his friend D.G. Rossetti's "Froissartian" watercolours of the late 1850s, such as *Sir Galahad* or *The Blue Closet*. Certainly, Arthurian subjects were popular with members of the Rossetti circle at this time, but this is one of the few times one sees Wallis being influenced by the second phase of Pre-Raphaelitism. The subject of Elaine may also be the only known example of Wallis being inspired by Tennyson's poetry, with the possible exception of a short passage from Tennyson's 'A Dirge' being quoted in the catalogue when *The Stonebreaker* was exhibited at the Royal Academy. Mike Hickox comments on his website, The Victorian Web: "He returned to the Royal Academy with two major exhibits in 1861 *Elaine* and *Gondomar*. An oil sketch for the former survives. Elaine was included in the sale of Thomas Plint's pictures in 1862 and, since he died on July 11 the previous year, it is almost certain that he was the original purchaser. *Elaine* marks a change from Wallis's previously exhibited pictures both in its Arthurian subject matter and in its technique. Elaine of Astrolat, having died of unrequited love for Sir Lancelot, is shown floating down the river to Camelot accompanied by her mourning father and brother. The popularity of Arthurian subjects in Pre-Raphaelite and Victorian art makes it hard to identify Wallis's specific influences, though Arthur Hughes, who was friendly with Wallis, is one possibility. For example, Hughes's *Knight of the Sun* was completed in 1860…The technique also differs significantly from Wallis's other works. Not only does he employ a richer colour but the surface of the picture is flattened and there is little recession as compared to his earlier works. Furthermore, the figures are arranged in a frieze like pattern with no single figure dominating. The general effect is reminiscent of Dante Gabriel Rossetti's work, and it is possible that this may have influenced Wallis."

William Michael Rossetti's review in *The Spectator* was very hostile to *Elaine*, attacking both its use of colour and what Rossetti perceived as its false sentiment: "Mr. Wallis has a gorgeous assemblage of colours, but little good colour in 'Elaine' (492). The faces are emotionless and commonly painted. The best figure is the 'dumb old servitor', a Charon-like boatman. There is wondrous imitation of brocade and black satin, but the utter want of heart is painfully apparent." This criticism contrasts with the long ecstatic review he had given *The Stonebreaker* previously. Rossetti clearly believed Wallis had taken a wrong turn after the social realism of his previous picture.

In 1860, F.G. Stephens wrote in 'Fine-Art Gossip' in *The Athenaeum*: "Mr. Wallis is engaged upon a picture representing the deposition of Elaine in the barge before she 'floated down to Camelot.' We hope this work will be completed for next year." However, the reviewer for *The Athenaeum* did not care for the painting when it was exhibited in 1861: "This artist's, Elaine (492), – the placing of Mr. Tennyson's heroine in the barge, is neither worthy of himself nor the theme; it is over-tinted in colour, and should have been more thought out." The critic for *The Art Journal* also did not like the colouring in this work: " 'Elaine', No. 492, H. Wallis, is worth attention, from its excess of colour, and, to use a popular vulgarism, from its excessive 'loudness.' But it is not a picture so much as a crude imitation of the more recent style of stained glass, looking as if the artist had no higher aim than to imitate the brightest colours which the sun's rays pouring through the stained medium could produce. That some black velvet and some silk stuffs are tolerably well imitated, is, no doubt, something in the eyes of devotees of Pre-Raphaelitism, and that a flowing profusion of yellow hair is made to appear as hard spun silk, is evidently considered a feat of some importance by the artist; but what all this blaze of inharmonious colour has to do with the smooth, flowing, and quiet descriptions of the poet, or with the elements of a good picture, it would be very hard indeed to determine. Still, the multitude of the ignorant are attracted, just as children are charmed, by the brightness of colours; but such vulgar brilliancies bear the same relationship to legitimate colour that the reds, blues, yellows, and greens, on a country girl's dress, bear to the refined dressing of a

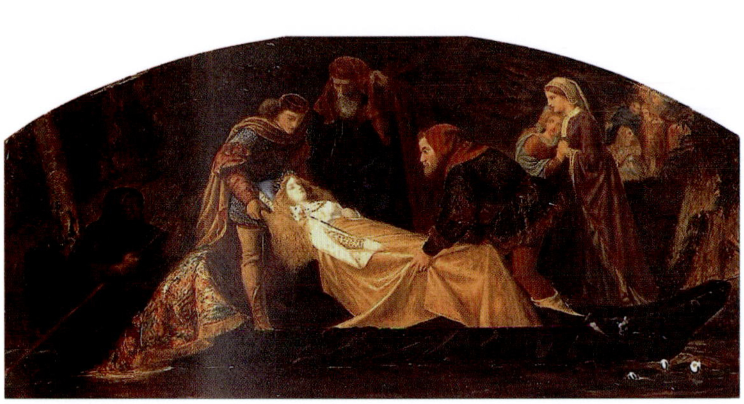

Cat. 44a. Image courtesy of Sotheby's

well-bred lady. The one is all vulgarity and show, the other simplicity and elegance; and painting to the top of the palette is no more good colour than screaming at the top of the voice is good singing. Unfortunately, Mr. Wallis has increasingly become one of the 'screaming' colourists, and he is rewarded with a place on the line for his loudness. Whether this be teaching the people wisely requires no answer; but that so many of this class of pictures have secured positions on or near the line this season cannot be ascribed to accident; and it deeply concerns the public to know whether the hanging committee were agreed upon the merits of such works."

The reviewer for *The Examiner* noted: "For how many bad pictures of *Elaine* exhibited this year is Mr. Tennyson answerable? There are three or four at the Academy, including, we fear we must say, Mr. H. Wallis's, which is incomparably the best we have yet seen. The boat is a simple canoe, wrapped in black satin, in which when she is laid, there will be room for none but the corpse and the dumb boatman. The canoe is moored by the river bank, and the dead Elaine is being carried down to it. But there is too much gay colouring in all the dresses, Elaine's hair is too obvious a match to the rich saffron-coloured quilt that is thrown over her, and, except that her eyes are closed, there is no sign of death in drop of jaw or in the sinking of a muscle. Mr Wallis's work is in many respects poetical, we can bear even with its gaiety of colour as part of the brightness of romance, but the legend of Elaine is not felt there as Mr Tennyson has made us feel it."

The critic of *The Times* felt this work a failure: " 'Elaine' (492), by T. Wallis, [*sic*] though a picture of the upmost elaboration, and showing a fine feeling for colour in the abstract with great delicacy of execution, does not escape the general verdict of 'not successful' passed on the many pictures of the same subject which this year has given birth to. This is one among the many examples of the all but insurmountable difficulties in the way of the painter when he takes to embodying a poet's conception."

Cat. 44a. *Elaine*
*c.*1861; oil on panel; 17.7 x 36.5 cm (7 x 14½ in.); private collection.
INSCRIPTIONS: Signed with initials *HW.*
PROVENANCE: Thomas E. Plint; his sale Christie's 8 March 1862, lot 218 purchased by James Watson Knight,[1] 33 Hyde Park Square W., London for £115 10s; his estate sale Christie's, 27 February 1904, lot 181, bought by the dealers Gooden & Fox for £31 10s; James Gresham;[2] his estate sale Christie's, 16 July, 1917, lot 419, bought Leggatt of the art dealers Leggatt Brothers, London, for £30 9s; property of a lady, her sale, Sotheby's Belgravia, 25 March 1975, lot 51, sold for £1000; Fine Art Society, London by 1977; private collection.
EXHIBITIONS: Mitsukoshi Department Store, Ginza, Tokyo, Japan, 1976, *Love and Poem. The 19th Century England. The Pre-Raphaelites – Painting and Graphics*, cat. no. 4917; The Fine Art Society, London, *Victorian Painting*, 1977, no. 22.
LITERATURE: *The Art Journal*, Vol. 1, 1862, p.105; *The Athenaeum*, No. 1794, 15 March 1862, pp.367-68; *The Times*, 16 February 1904, p.14.

This is either the preliminary sketch for, or a smaller version of, the painting exhibited in 1861 at the Royal Academy. It was initially in the collection of Thomas E. Plint, who also owned the major version. Wallis's painting appears to have been influenced by the Pre-Raphaelite illustrations for the *Moxon Tennyson* of 1857. The intense gaze of the bearded man lifting Elaine into the boat is very similar to that of Sir Lancelot looking at the dead maiden in D.G. Rossetti's tailpiece to 'The Lady of Shalott'.

Cat. 45. *Cleopatra's First Interview With Caesar*
1862; ?oil on canvas; dimensions unknown; whereabouts unknown.
LITERATURE: *The Spectator*, Vol. 35, 12 April 1862, p.410.

The critic of *The Spectator* discussed works to be submitted to the forthcoming Royal Academy summer exhibition and mentioned: "Mr. Wallis trys his hand successfully on a classical subject – 'Cleopatra's first interview with Ceasar'." If Wallis submitted this work to the hanging committee of the Royal Academy, either it was not selected for inclusion, or was selected but not hung because of a lack of space. If Wallis did complete such a work in 1862 this would make him one of the first English artists of his generation to adopt classical themes in his art.

Cat. 46. *Tobias Restoring the Eyesight of Tobit*
1862; medium and dimensions unknown; whereabouts unknown.
EXHIBITIONS: Liverpool Society of Fine Arts, 1862, no. 335.

When the painting was exhibited in Liverpool in 1862 it was accompanied with the quotation: "And he strake off the gall on his father's eyes, saying 'Be of a good hope, my father'." - Tobit, xi,2. The Book of Tobit is part of the canon of both the Roman Catholic and the Eastern Orthodox Churches. It is listed as a book of the *Apocrypha* in Article VI of the Thirty-Nine Articles of the Church of England. This book tells the story of a righteous Israelite named Tobit living in Nineveh. One night as he slept in the open he was blinded by bird droppings that fell in his eyes. Tobit's son Tobias catches a monstrous fish in the River Tigris with the help of the archangel Raphael who instructs Tobias to restore his father's eyesight using the gall of the fish.

The story of Tobit was a popular one for artists during the Renaissance. Drawings or engravings after Quentin Metsys (1466-1530) and Van Heemskerck were often used as models to decorate majolica plates and tiles. A well-known example is the tiles of the Ducal Palace at Vila Viçosa (Portugal) dated 1558.[1] It is possible that Wallis might have found his inspiration in Rembrandt's *Tobit and his Wife* of 1659 (collection, Museum Boijmans Van Beuningen, Rotterdam). On the other hand, in the first part of his career, Wallis was interested in contemporary French painting and would likely have known the painting *The Return of Tobias* that the French academic painter William-Adolphe Bouguereau exhibited at the Salon in 1857. Wallis could also have seen Bougereau's *Tobias Saying Good-Bye to his Father* of 1860, when he was in Paris with his son in December that year. Unfortunately, Wallis's picture is not discussed by the *Liverpool Mercury* in its reviews of the Liverpool Society of Arts exhibition so there are no clues as to what the picture looked like.

Artists within the Pre-Raphaelite circle who executed subjects from the story of Tobit included Frederic Leighton, William De Morgan, Evelyn De Morgan and James Smetham. Jane Benham Hay had exhibited a work of this same title at the Royal Academy the year previously in 1861, no. 308, and at the Winter Exhibition at the French Gallery in London in 1862.

Cat. 47. *The Death of Christopher Marlowe*
1862; ?oil on canvas; unknown dimensions.; whereabouts unknown.
PROVENANCE: Painting was still in Wallis's possession in 1873.
EXHIBITIONS: Royal Academy, 1862, no. 80; *Loan Museum of Art Treasures*, Industrial Exhibition Palace, Dublin, 1873, no. 69, lent by Wallis and priced at £36 15s.
LITERATURE: *London Society*, Vol. II, 1862, p.22; *The Examiner*, 3 May 1862, p.279; *The Times*, 8 May 1862, p.8; *The Spectator*, 10 May 1862, p.522; *The Athenaeum*, No. 1803, 17 May 1862, p.668; *The London Daily News*, London, 22 May 1862, p.3; *The Spectator*, 24 May 1862, p.578; Altick, Richard D., *Paintings from Books*, Ohio State University Press, 1985, Part One, Chapter 7, p.154.

Marlowe (1564-1593) was an English dramatist, poet, and translator during the Elizabethan era and is best known for his *Tragical History of Doctor Faustus.* A warrant was issued for Marlowe's arrest on 18 May 1593, possibly in connection with allegations of blasphemy. On 30 May, he was stabbed to death by Ingram Frizer.[1] The true events are shrouded in mystery and subject to many theories.

The critic of *The Times* in reviewing Wallis's painting voiced the opinion: "The same question might be proposed to Mr. Wallis, who in his devotion to great men should not forget what is worthiest, as well as what is saddest, in their careers…But why recall Marlowe's miserable end in a bagnio brawl? The corpse lies scarce seen amid the wreck of shattered chairs, upset candlesticks, flagons, and torn table-cover, by the light in the hands of the terror-stricken inmates of the foul place, who have gathered at the top of the stairs leading down to the room in which the brawl has taken place. Through the open window is seen the moonlit street with the assassins running away."

The critic of *The Athenaeum* noted: "Mr. H. Wallis's *Death of Christopher Marlowe* (80) shows a figure lying prostate in a dark tavern-room, with a broken sword beside it, while some people enter with lights. An open window displays figures running away." The critic of *The Spectator* preferred this painting to Wallis's other submission of this year to the R.A.: "A better picture by the same painter I find I have omitted to mention. It is hung under the line in the East Room, and represents in an effective way the death of 'Christopher Marlowe' (80)." The critic of *The Examiner* commented: "Mr. H. Wallis contributes two pictures, one of *Raleigh* looking out upon the port of London, the other of *Marlowe* lying slain in the dark after the night-brawl in the night-house where a dagger's thrust let out the young life-blood of a poet grand above most others with the untamed energies of genius. The chairs and stools are over-thrown, the light of the overturned candle flickers out in a red gleam. Through the window we see the retreating forms of the assassins; from a room on one side, summoned by the silence after the accustomed riot, come with lights some of the loose women of the house."

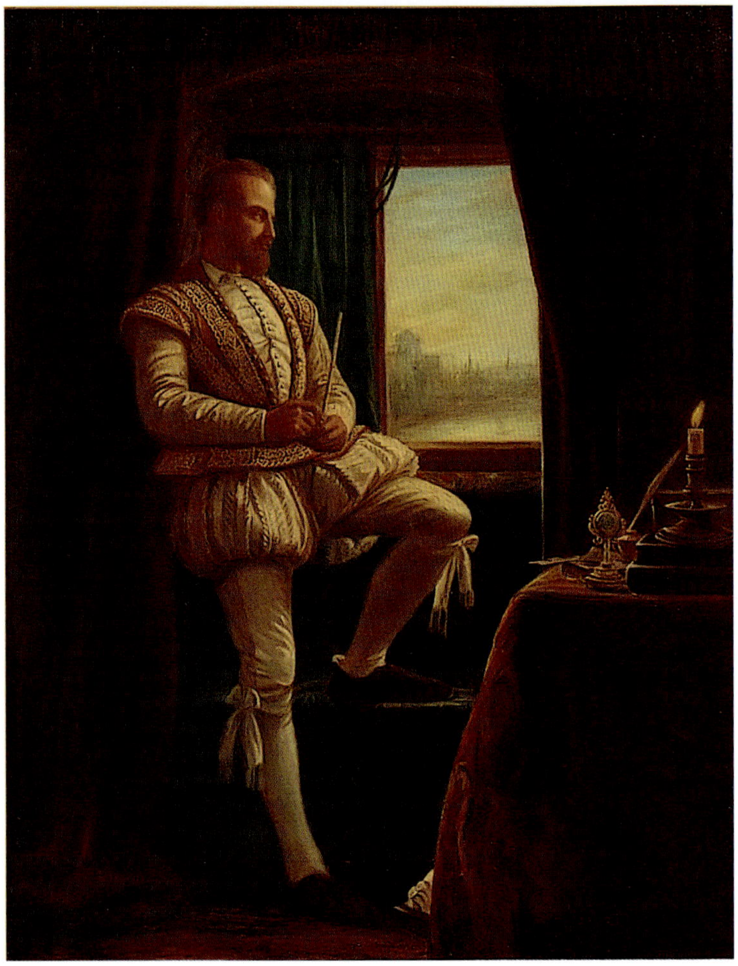

Cat. 48. Image courtesy of Keys Fine Art Auctioneers, Aylsham, Norwich

Cat. 48. ***Sir Walter Raleigh in Durham House***
1862; oil on canvas; 35 x 28 cm. (13¾ x 11 in.) – sight; private collection.
Provenance: Robert Martin, 94 Upper Brook St., Manchester; his sale Christie's, 9 June 1865, lot 28, bought in; Thomas McLean, art dealer, London; anonymous sale, Keys Fine Art Auctioneers, Aylsham, Norwich, 29 November, 2018, lot 1257, as English School (19th Century), "Raleigh at Durham House", sold for £1,350 hammer, private collection.
Exhibitions: Royal Academy, 1862, no. 268.
Literature: *London Society*, Vol. II, 1862, p.22; *The Examiner*, 3 May 1862, p.279; *The Times*, 8 May, 1862, p.8; *The Spectator*, 10 May 1862, p.522; *The Athenaeum*, No. 1803, 17 May 1862, p.668; *The Daily News*, London, 22 May 1862, p.3; *The Spectator*, 24 May 1862, p.578; *The Times*, 25 May, 1865, p.20.

Built by Bishop Thomas Hatfield, *c.*1345, Durham House was the historic London residence of the Bishop of Durham in the Strand, with its gardens descending to the Thames.

In 1583, Queen Elizabeth I granted the house to Sir Walter Raleigh, who spent £2,000 on repairs and lived there until Elizabeth's death. John Aubrey said that he well remembered the room that Raleigh used as his study; it was in a little turret that looked over the Thames and had a view of Westminster, Whitehall Palace, and the Surrey hills. It was in Durham House that Raleigh hosted Manteo and Wanchese, the first Native American Algonquin Indians to travel to England from the New World.

When the painting was exhibited at the Royal Academy in 1862 it was accompanied with the quotation: "Sir Walter's study at Durham House was a small chamber facing the river, and with a marvelously pleasant prospect from the window." The critic of *The Athenaeum* mentions in his review of the Royal Academy exhibition: "By the same is Sir Walter Raleigh (268), looking as 'Gondomar' did last year, out of a window; he fills his pipe with the new herb; has characteristic action and features." *The Spectator* critic said: " 'Sir Walter Raleigh' (268) is preferable to most of the works lately exhibited by Mr. Wallis, being less hard in execution, and quieter in colour." The reviewer for *The Daily News* declared: "We turn with pleasure from this purposeless and ignoble horror [Marlowe] to the little picture (268) of Raleigh filling his pipe at the window of his quiet study at Durham-house with the pleasant outlook over the then silvery Thames."

Cat. 48a. ***Sir Walter Raleigh in Durham House***
1871; heliotype print; 35.5 x 25 cm. (13¾ x 9⅞ in.); Sterling and Francine Clark Institute.
Literature: *The Illustrated Review*, Vol. II. No. 18, 1 July 1871, p.32; *The Spectator*, Vol. 43, 23 December 1871, p.1586, *The Saturday Review*, 23 December 1871, p.829.

A heliotype print of this work was reproduced in *Art: Pictorial and Industrial, an illustrated magazine*, published by Sampson Low, Marston, Lowe & Searle, London.[1] Twenty-four photomechanical prints were produced, of which this was number 3, for this publication by the Heliotype Company

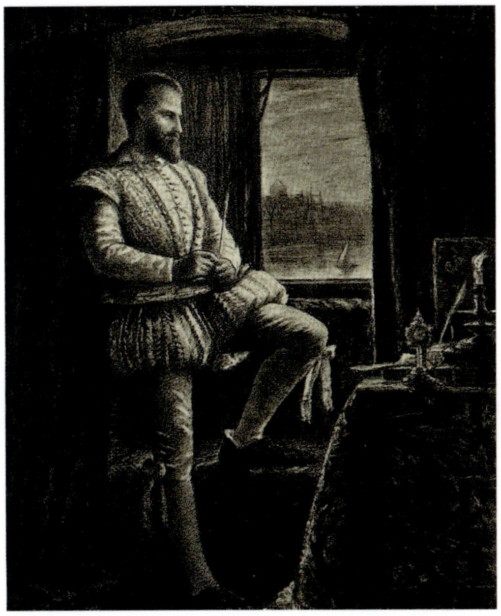

Cat. 48a. Image courtesy of Rare Book Collection, Sterling and Francine Clark Art Institute Library, Williamstown, MA

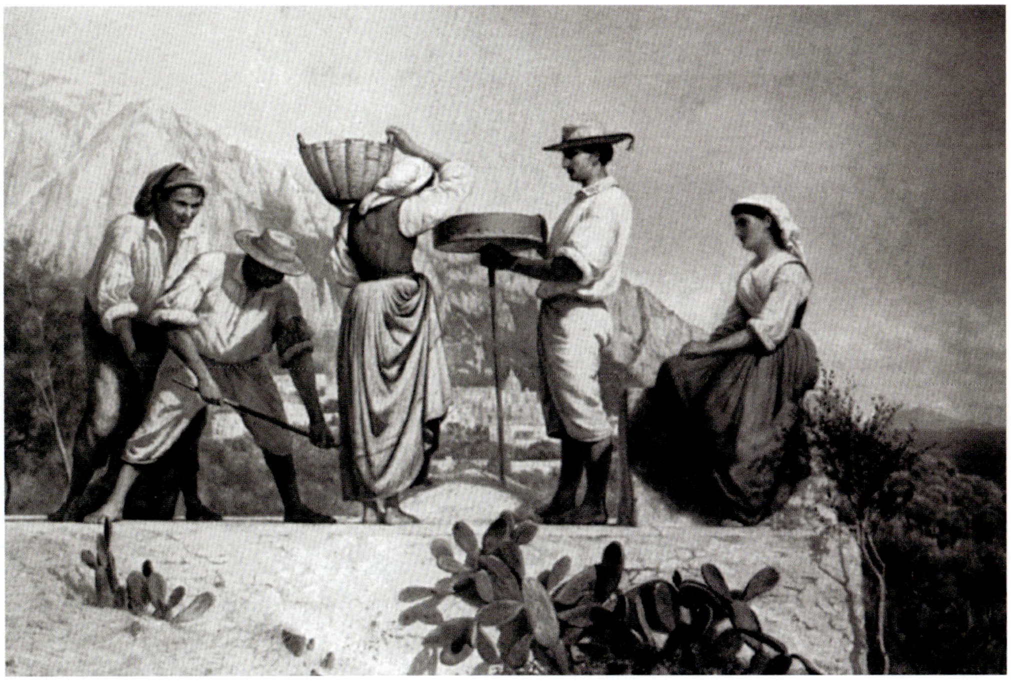

Cat. 49. Image courtesy of Sotheby's, London

Limited, 219 Regent Street, London between 1870-73. The Wallis print was published in Vol. II, No. 13, p.18, July 1871, and was apparently reproduced from a drawing by Wallis. Although the caption on the print calls it *Sir Walter Raleigh in the Tower* it clearly reproduces this later work.

Cat. 49. *Winnowing Corn, Capri*
1862; oil on canvas; 44.5 x 66 cm (17½ x 26 in.); private collection.
Inscriptions: Signed with initials *HW* and dated *1862* on recto; signed and inscribed on verso.
Provenance: Wallis's studio and then by descent from the artist to his daughter-in-law Alice Julyan Wallis (née Roberts), and thence to her great-niece Mrs. Vera G. Whiting, Purley, Surrey; her sale Sotheby's Belgravia, 10 April 1973, lot 196, purchased by J. Dell for £220.
Exhibitions: Royal Academy, 1864, no. 225.
Literature: *Fraser's Magazine*, vol. 70, 1864, p.73; *The Times*, 11 May 1864, p.5; *The Illustrated London News*, vol. 44, 14 May 1864, p.479; *The Athenaeum*, no. 1907, 14 May 1864, p.684; *The Saturday Review*, 21 May 1864, p.625.

Wallis presumably travelled to Capri in the autumn of 1858 accompanied by his lover Mary Ellen Meredith. They spent the entire winter on the island, the climate of which was supposed to be beneficial for Mary Ellen's failing health. After they had separated and following her death, Wallis came back with their son to spend the winters of 1861 and 1862. This painting must have been made during the visit of 1862 or was later worked up from earlier studies.

The reviewer for *The Athenaeum*, in his review of the Royal Academy exhibition of 1862, said: "Mr. *Wallis's Winnowing Corn, Capri* (225) has a greenness of tint about it which, amidst the glare of its companion pictures, is striking, and not wholly pleasant. There is some beautiful colour and great softness of effect in this painting. The landscape seems faithful." The critic for *The Saturday Review* stated: "One small and thinly, but gracefully, painted work, 'Winnowing Corn at Capri' (225), has been sent by that unequal though always interesting, artist, Mr. Wallis. Four or five peasants are here engaged on their picturesque employment, ranged in a line along the threshing floor almost with the severity of a bas-relief. The varieties in attitude are rendered with skill and grace, and the sculptureesque quality in the design which we have indicated is well balanced by the dispositon of the accessories and the landscape, which runs down obliquely behind the line of figures."

The Illustrated London News declared: "His 'Winnowing Corn, Capri' (225) is rather crude, though full of sunlight and remarkable for its couleur locale. How different is this conscientious study from nature from the Italian peasant and brigand of your conventional painters!" The critic of *The Times* praised this work: " Mr. A. [*sic*] Wallis's 'Winnowing Corn' at Capri – a group of sunburnt peasants on their walled thrashing-floor, plying their shovels among the heaps of golden maize, to which the women are adding the contents of their baskets – is an example of the interest that is imparted to the commonest incidents of Southern life in Italy by the beautiful nature among which it passes, and the impress of classical beauty still apparent in South Italian form and usage, though only to be detected and expressed by an eye, mind, and hand of requisite power and cultivation. Mr. Wallis's group, while perfectly true in form, colour, costume, and action reminds us of an antique bas-relief. The cliffs and town, standing out white against the blue sea of Naples, form a noble backgound, painted with the delicacy and truth it deserves."

Cat. 50. *Shakespeare and Spenser*
1864; oil on canvas; 51 x 66 cm (20 x 26 in.); private collection.
Inscriptions: Signed and dated *1864*.
Provenance: Wallis's studio and then by descent from the artist to his daughter-in-law Alice Julyan Wallis (née Roberts), and thence to her great-niece Mrs. Vera G. Whiting, Purley, Surrey; her sale Sotheby's Belgravia, 10 April 1973, lot 192, bought by B. Cohen for £130.
Exhibitions: Royal Academy, 1865, no. 7.
Literature: *Fraser's Magazine*, Vol. 71, 1865, p.751; *The Art Journal*, New Series, Vol. IV, 1865, p.166; *The Athenaeum*, No. 1953, 1 April 1865, p.462; *The Illustrated London News*, 22 April 1865, p.386; *Pall Mall Gazette*, 6 May 1865, p.10; *The Athenaeum*, No. 1959, 13 May 1865, p.657; *The Illustrated London News*, Vol. 46, 13 May 1865, p.451; *The Examiner*, 10 June 1865, p.362; Lessens, Ronald, "Henry Wallis (1830-1916), a neglected Pre-Raphaelite", *The British Art Journal*, vol. XV, No. 1, Autumn 2014, p.54.

Edmund Spenser (1552-1599) was an English poet, and the author of *The Faerie Queene*, composed as a glorification of England and Elizabeth I. He was part of a literary circle led by Sir Philip Sidney. In the Irish uprising of 1598, his domain was burned and Spenser died shortly after, probably in despair.[1]

Spenser and Shakespeare are considered

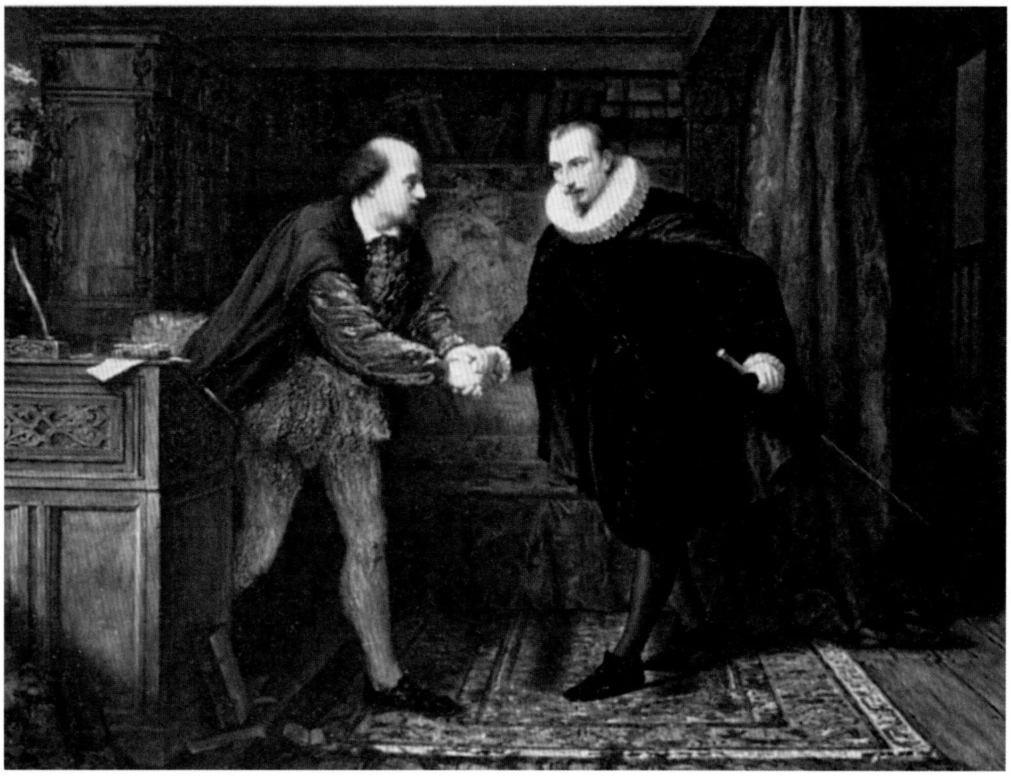

Cat. 50. Image courtesy of Sotheby's, London

two of the greatest of the English Renaissance poets and each influenced the other.

The critic for *The Athenaeum*, reviewing this painting, stated: "Mr. Wallis gives us a pleasant glimpse at Shakespeare's home life and the troubles of Spenser during the few months that preceded the death of the latter. *Shakespeare and Spenser* (7) shows how the latter might have visited the former in London, and just after his return from Kilcolman, or what remained of its ruins; he is pallid and worn with grief; his sensitive nature and delicate look are admirably expressed by the figure which that of the healthier Shakespeare so warmly, yet unaffectedly, shakes by the hand. Of several subjects of this class which Mr. Wallis has painted none have approached this one as a story or in execution."

The reviewer for *The Examiner* did not like this painting, however: "Mr. Wallis's other picture, *Shakespeare and Spenser* – each in his best clothes – is even less to our tastes. Spenser calls upon Shakespeare, who rises from his writing to receive him with a cordial grasp. But the artist has committed what in treatment of such a subject is the unpardonable sin, he has made both the heads unspiritual. One is fat, the other lean; and there is little more to see. Apart from indication of the study, Shakespeare might not be Shakespeare, but a butcher in his Sunday clothes, hurrying to grasp the hand of an old friend who has come to taste his mutton. The face seems to have been studied from the Stratford portrait, which we believe also to be the best authority, and do not doubt to be the picture that was copied from in modeling the monumental bust. But, if so, Mr. Wallis, who is one of the most promising of our painters – to say nothing of much good performance already achieved – has hardly used the insight of his genius in adding soul to form. Mr. Wallis always chooses subjects of the worthiest, and has a sound humour for marrying so far as he can, through his own work, English art to English literature. When we believe that a work of his fails, we know that it has been worthily attempted, and leave readers to take for granted full continuance of the mechanical skill through which he has heretofore made mind speak, and will make it speak again, we trust, in many a year for many years to come."

Cat. 51. *Paul Veronese painting the Portrait of Sir Philip Sidney*

1864; ?oil on canvas; dimensions unknown; whereabouts unknown.

Exhibitions: Royal Academy, 1865, no. 385.

Literature: *Fraser's Magazine*, Vol. 71, 1865, p.751; *The Art Journal*, New Series, Vol. IV, 1865, p.166; *The Athenaeum*, No. 1953, 1 April 1865, p.462; *The Illustrated London News*, 22 April 1865, p.386; *Pall Mall Gazette*, 6 May 1865, p.10; *The Athenaeum*, No. 1959, 13 May 1865, p.657; *The Illustrated London News*, Vol. 46, 13 May 1865, p.451; *The London Daily News*, London, 25 May 1865, p.3; *The Examiner*, 10 June 1865, p.362.

Sir Philip Sidney (1554-1586), a soldier and a poet, was born into an aristocratic family and educated to be a statesman and soldier. He served in minor official posts and also turned his hand to literature. His circle included his close childhood friend Fulke Greville[1] and the poet Edmund Spenser. Sidney had been a leader of the Puritan faction promoting English involvement in the wars of the Protestant Dutch against their Spanish rulers. In 1585, Elizabeth I finally acceded to this faction's demands and sent an army to the Netherlands. On 22 September in 1586 at the battle of Zutphen, Sidney was fatally wounded.[2]

Wallis's painting appears to have been painted during one of his trips to Italy. In a letter of 22 January 1864 to his mother from Rome he writes: "I have nearly finished my principal picture & shall send it to London."[3] Wallis's painting was shown at the Royal Academy in 1865 with this quotation in the catalogue: "Hodie effigiem meam inchoavit Paulus quidam Veronensis."[4]

The critic of *The Athenaeum* had this opinion on the work: "There is much that is brilliant in Veronese painting Sydney's Portrait (385); the latter, a rather stiff figure, sits in a chair that is raised on a dais; the painter is at his easel; between them, a little removed, is Titian, in a red robe, conversing with the Englishman; a page, who is seated on the platform, plays with a lap-dog; there are other figures, of which the best is that of a girl bringing fruit. There is much power of painting shown in this work; its materials are effectively put together; the colour and the chiaroscuro assist each other; and, except for the figure of Sydney – for the rigidity of which much, however, might be urged – there is great freedom and elegance in the composition; the design tells the story perfectly. The painting, however, – see Titian's robe and Veronese's face, – is not complete; the former of these important parts is thin, and looks like stained glass."

The reviewer for *The Art Journal* obviously liked this work: "The second picture of Mr. Wallis has a good subject, 'Paul Veronese painting the Portrait of Sir Philip Sidney' (385). Sir Philip is seated in due solemnity, and Veronese has just rubbed in the head upon canvas. The apartment is hung with rich curtains, and carpeted in bright colours. The grandees of Venice are in waiting on the artist and his sitter, and through an open window may be seen the well-known façade of the church of San Giorgio. The situation is altogether sumptuous, the colour resplendent; the picture, in fact, must be regarded expressly as a concatenation of colours. Assuredly there is widest interval between the 'Dead Stone Breaker' of former years and this luxurious show: the one is a work of decorative pomp, the other of vigorous naturalism."

The reviews were not all favourable, however. The critic for *The Examiner* was not impressed by this work: "Mr H. Wallis in his two pictures recals [*sic*] also the best days of Elizabeth, but they are not two of his own best. One shows *Paul Veronese painting the Portrait of Sir Philip Sidney*, a rich piece of composition but, as a transcript from real life and still more as an idealized memorial of a sitting that is actually upon record, all too fine. Sidney may have got himself up for the sitting, but the painter in silk and satin and the satin page, and the grand senator who holds a finger for the the sitter to fix his eye upon, and the general magnificence, are not very suggestive of a simple relation of art between two men of genius."

Wallis may have found his inspiration for this painting by seeing Veronese's portrait of Sidney at Leicester House or at an exhibition. Elizabeth Goldring writes: "The poet-courtier Sir Philip Sidney (1554-86) is unusual among members of the Elizabethan elite in having sat for his portrait on numerous occasions, including, most famously, to Paolo Veronese in 1574. Executed in Venice in the midst of a three-year period of continental travel and study which took Sidney as far north as Florence and as far east as Cracow, the resulting portrait was presented on completion to the Huguenot diplomat Hubert Languet (1528-81), who oversaw many of the day-to-day aspects of Sidney's 'Grand Tour'."

Cat. 52. ***A Scene in "Edward VI"***
Date unknown; watercolour; 35.5 x 24.1 cm (14 x 9½ in.); whereabouts unknown.
Provenance: Miss L. Caswall Smith,[1] 13 Rutland Park Mansions, Willesden Green, N.W.2, London; her sale Christie's, 26 March 1920, lot 57, bought for 19 19s by Bowden, likely one of the London dealers Bowden Bros. or G.W. Bowden.
Exhibitions: ? Nottingham, date unknown.

Unfortunately, little is known about this work beyond what was mentioned in the Christie's catalogue. The catalogue entry states it was "Exhibited at Nottingham", though the authors have not been able to match a work fitting this description to any of Wallis's works that are known to have been shown there. It is not even known if this is the correct title for the work. It is difficult to date this painting because Wallis's works dealing with the Tudor period, usually of the Elizabethan time, tend to be early from the mid-1850s to mid-1860s and are oil paintings and not watercolours. Wallis did not use watercolour with any regularity until the late 1870s but could have used it occasionally even prior to this time because he was already very fluent in this medium by the time he began exhibiting at the O.W.S. There is a possibility, however, that Christie's transcribed the title incorrectly. The authors have been unable to find a play based on Edward VI but there is a play by the Elizabethan dramatist Thomas Heywood entitled *Edward IV*. In view of Wallis's interest in subjects related to the Elizabethan period, a subject relating to Edward VI seems much more likely.

Cat. 53. ***Pippa***
1864; ?oil on canvas; dimensions unknown; whereabouts unknown.
Exhibitions: Birmingham Society of Artists, *Exhibition of Modern Works of Art*, 1864, no. 356, priced at £42.
Literature: *Aris's Birmingham Gazette*, issue 6405, 27 August 1864, p.7.

This painting might be related to Robert Browning's verse drama *Pippa Passes* first published in 1841. Wallis did base one painting on Browning for certain, his slightly later *Childe Roland to the Dark Tower came.*

Cat. 54. ***A Neapolitan Girl***
*c.*1857-1865; ?oil on canvas; dimensions unknown; whereabouts unknown.
Exhibitions: Birmingham Society of Artists, *Exhibition of Modern Works of Art*, 1865, no. 199, priced at £42

This was likely painted during the period from the late 1850s to the mid-1860s when Wallis made several trips to Capri and Naples. It was possibly one of the so-called "pot-boilers", painted by artists purely for commercial reasons to support their livelihood, but which the artist did not normally intend to exhibit. Frederic Leighton, for example, painted some very beautiful such portraits of Italian models over the course of his career. It could even have been a portrait of the girl Wallis mentions in a letter of 24 March 1857 to his friend Frederick Fleay when discussing the people of Sorrento [see: Letter 1].

Cat. 55. ***A Girl of Capri***
*c.*1860s; ?oil on canvas; dimensions unknown; whereabouts unknown.
Provenance: Messrs. Fores,[1] publishers, 41 Piccadilly, London; their sale Christie's, 22 May 1875, lot 711, bought in at £11 11s.

This could possibly be the same work as *A Neapolitan Girl* or perhaps another in a series of works that Wallis painted from local models during his trips to Italy. As this painting belonged to the firm of Messrs. Fores, who published prints, it is possible that they produced a print of this work for sale, as well as of *An English Girl*. If this were the case, no examples of any such prints have been located.

Cat. 56. ***An English* Girl**
*c.*1860s; ?oil on canvas; dimensions unknown; whereabouts unknown.
Provenance: Messrs. Fores, publishers, 41 Piccadilly, London; their sale Christie's, 22 May 1875, lot 710, bought in at £15 4s.

Nothing is really known about this work other than its title. It may have been a portrait or a "fancy picture" and could have been painted any time between the mid-1850s to the mid-1870s, when it first appeared at auction. No record of it having been exhibited has been found.

Cat. 57. ***The Last Days of the Cappuccini Monastery, at Sorrento***
(Also: ***The Cappuccini Monastery at Sorrento – Monks playing at Boccia*****)**
1865; oil on canvas; 56.5 x 91 cm (22¾ x 36 in.); private collection.
Inscriptions: Signed on the reverse.
Provenance: Wallis's studio and then by descent from the artist to his daughter-in-law Alice Julyan Wallis (née Roberts), and thence to her great-niece Mrs. Vera G. Whiting, Purley, Surrey; her sale Sotheby's Belgravia, 10 April 1973, lot 191, bought

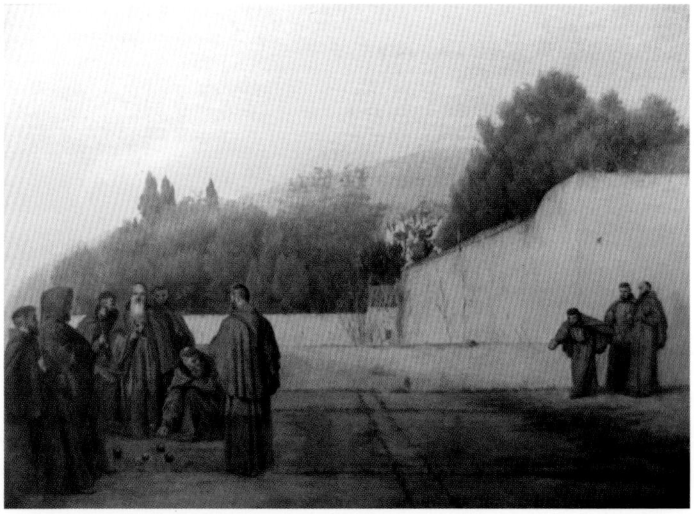

Cat. 57. Image courtesy of Sotheby's, London

by Caelt Gallery, London for £30; private collection.
Exhibitions: *London International Exhibition*, 1871, no. 275; *Dublin Exhibition of Arts, Industries, Manufactures and Loans*, 1872, no. 290, priced at £157 10s (lent by H. Wallis); Liverpool Corporation, Autumn Exhibition of Pictures, 1873, no. 440, priced at £150 0s.
Literature: Stewart, Ann, *Irish Loan Exhibitions, 1765-1927*, Vol. 2, 1990, p.748.

When this work was shown at the *London International Exhibition* in 1871 it was dated to 1865. It was entitled *The Cappuccini Monastery at Sorrento – Monks playing at Boccia* when it was exhibited at Liverpool in 1873. The subject of this painting seems to have been surprisingly popular in Victorian times. There was another painting entitled *Monks Playing at Bowls*, by the Belgian painter, Charles Hermans, exhibited at the *London International Exhibition* in 1871. At the Royal Manchester Institution, *Exhibition of Modern Pictures*, in 1867 a Mr. Graham had exhibited a painting of *Monks Playing at Bowls*, no. 26.[1]

Cat. 58. *The Golden Scarf*
1865; ?oil on canvas; dimensions unknown; whereabouts unknown.
Exhibitions: French Gallery, Thirteenth annual Winter Exhibition of Pictures, 1865, no. 103.
Literature: *The Illustrated London News*, vol. 47, 4 November 1865, p.438; *The Athenaeum*, No. 1984, 4 November 1865, p.618.

F.G. Stephens in *The Athenaeum* writes: "Mr. Wallis's *The Golden Scarf* (103) is a figure of a girl of Capri seated, with a scarf in her hand, very solidly and richly painted, life-size."

Cat. 59. *After Supper at Capri*
1865; ?oil on canvas; dimensions unknown; whereabouts unknown.
Exhibitions: French Gallery, Thirteenth annual Winter Exhibition of Pictures, 1865, no. 104.
Literature: *The Illustrated London News*, vol. 47, 4 November 1865, p.438; *The Athenaeum*, No. 1984, 4 November 1865, p.619; *The Saturday Review*, Vol. 21, 24 February 1866, p.233.

The critic of *The Saturday Review* had these comments on the work when it was shown at Ernest Gambart's The French Gallery: "Mr. Henry Wallis deserves praise for his very true moonlight in 'After Supper in Capri'; it is one of the most successful attempts at the colour of moonlight we remember to have met with." *The Athenaeum* noted: "Other pictures which merit attention are... and, especially, Mr. Wallis's *After Supper at Capri* (104)."

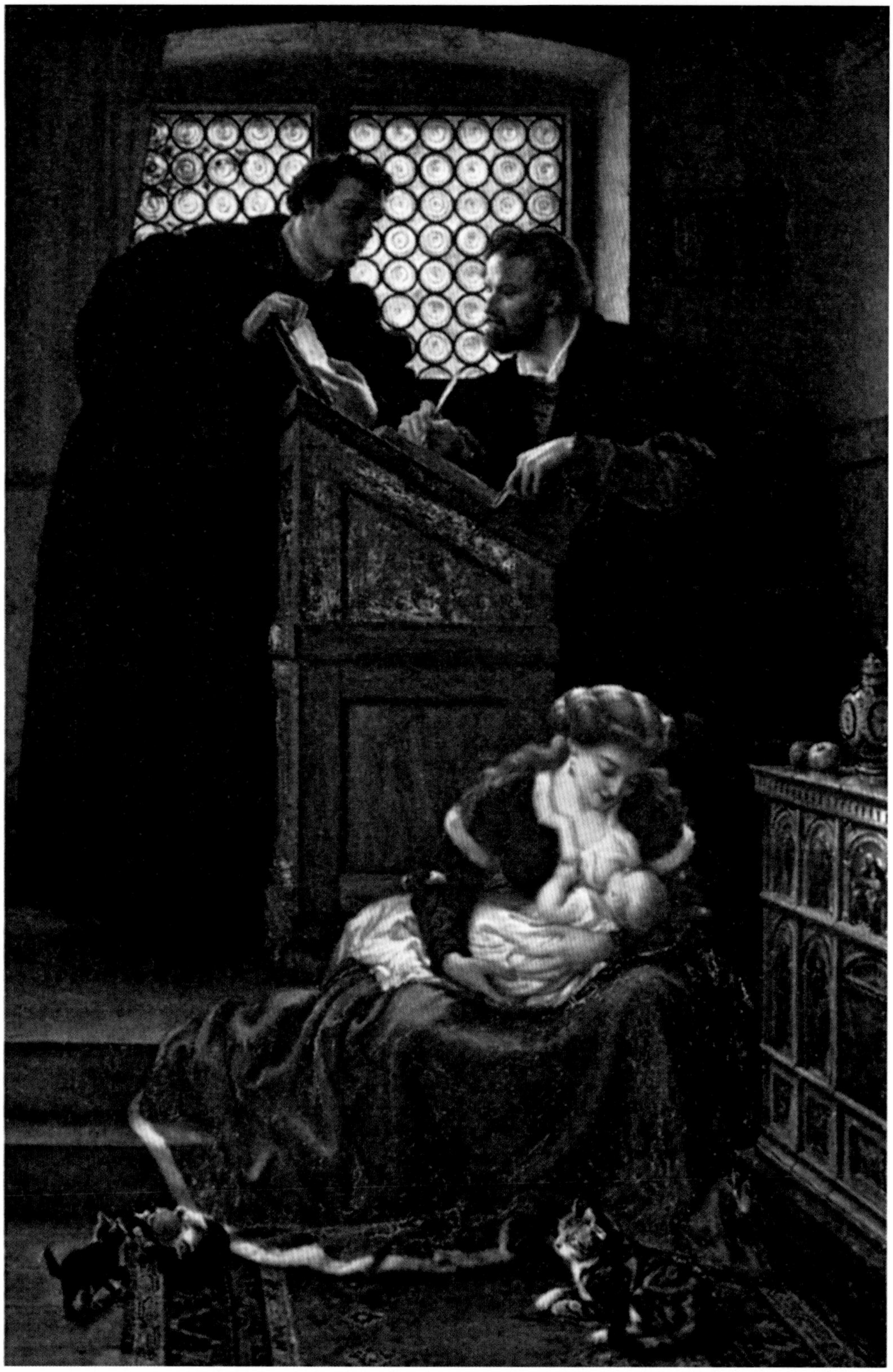
Cat. 60. Image courtesy of Sotheby's, London

Cat. 60. *Luther and Melancthon*
1867; oil on canvas; 99 x 66 cm (39 x 26 in.); private collection.
Inscription: Signed with *HW* initials.
Provenance: Wallis's studio and then by descent from the artist to his daughter-in-law Alice Julyan Wallis (née Roberts) and thence to her great-niece Mrs. Vera G. Whiting, Purley, Surrey; her sale Sotheby's Belgravia, London, 10 April 1973, lot 194, bought by M. Katz for £480.
Exhibitions: Royal Academy, 1867, no. 570; Royal Manchester Institution, *Exhibition of Modern Pictures*, 1867, no.3, priced at £157 10s; ?*Dublin International Exhibition*, 1907.[1]
Literature: *The Art Journal*, New Series, Vol. VI, 1867, p.140, p.234; *The Athenaeum*, No. 2065, 25 May 1867, p.697; *The Illustrated London News*, 25 May 1867, p.519; *The Preston Chronicle and Lancashire Advertiser*, 16 November 1867, p.6; Lessens, Ronald, 'Henry Wallis (1830-1916), a

neglected Pre-Raphaelite', *The British Art Journal*, vol. XV, No. 1, 2014, p.54.

Philipp Melanchthon (originally Philipp Schwartzerd; 1497-1560) was a German theologian, professor and religious reformer who worked closely with Martin Luther in establishing the tenets of Lutheranism. It was Luther who initially persuaded his colleague to join the Reformation movement. In 1560 Melanchthon married Katherine Krapp and they had four children – Anna, Philipp, Georg, and Magdalen. Wallis has portrayed Katherine and one of the children in the foreground of this painting. Wallis's inspiration for the present work may have come from his friend Eyre Crowe, who in November 1862, had started to work on a painting of Luther.[2] Wallis may have used Albrecht Durer's c.1526 engraving of Philip Melanchthon as his source for the image of the scholar.

This painting in general was not well received by the critics. *The Art Journal* had these comments on this work: "H. Wallis exhibits another carefully-elaborated work, which is indeed at the farthest possible remove from the naturalism of 'The Dead Stone-Breaker,'...We think it might be well for the painter to revert in some degree to his first manner. Certainly his present picture, 'Luther and Melancthon' [*sic*] (570), would be better for more vigour. Yet may the execution be commended for nice delicacy; the colour, too, shows refined harmonies."

The reviewer for *The Athenaeum* stated: "*Luther and Melancthon* [*sic*] (570), by Mr. H. Wallis, - the reformer showing a text to his friend, his wife and child seated near, - has finely designed figures of the woman and baby, much good colour throughout, delicate and tender expression, and well-rendered detail; Luther's face is full of animation." The critic of the *Preston Chronicle* voiced the opinion: "No. 3, Mr. Wallis's picture of 'Luther and Melancthon' [*sic*]. There is much careful work and conscientious study in it, still we must confess that it is not what we expect from Mr. Wallis. The general tone of the picture is not good, and there is a want of refinement which jars upon one." *The Illustrated London News* suggested: "Mr. Wallis, the painter of 'The Death of Chatterton,' does not well sustain his reputation with "Luther and Melancthon' [*sic*] (570)."

Cat. 61. *Laura*
1867; ?oil on canvas; dimensions unknown; whereabouts unknown.
Exhibitions: Royal Manchester Institution, *Exhibition of Modern Pictures*, 1867, no.?; Jarrow Mechanics' Institute, *Fine Art and Industrial Exhibition*, 1878, no. ?
Literature: *The Art Journal*, New Series, Vol. VI, 1867, p.234; *The Newcastle Courant*, Newcastle-upon-Tyne, 12 July 1878, p.8.

In terms of content, only this work's title is known as no contemporary review can be found. In view of Wallis's penchant for historical themes at this time, Laura may well be the great idealised love of the Italian poet and scholar Franceso Petrarch. Petrarch fell in love with Laura (possibly Laura de Noves of Avignon) at first sight on 6 April, 1327, but his love was unrequited because she was already married; she died in 1348.

Cat. 62. *Across the Common*
1867; oil on canvas; dimensions unknown; whereabouts unknown.
Provenance: Charles Gent Clement[1] by 1876.
Exhibitions: Dudley Gallery, *Cabinet Pictures in Oils*, 1867, no. 62; *Centennial International Exhibition of 1876*, Philadelphia, no. 169; *Whitechapel Fine Art Loan Exhibition*, St Jude's School House, 1887, no. 15.
Literature: *The Art Journal*, New Series, Vol. VI, 1867, p.269; *The Building News and Engineering Journal*, Vol. 14, 8 November 1867, p.769; *The Athenaeum*, No. 2089, 9 November 1867, p.617; *The Illustrated London News*, 16 November 1867, (supplement); *The Chromolithograph*, Vol. I, No. 1, 23 November 1867, p.15; *The Mask*, Vol. I, 1868, p.26; *Official Catalogue of the International Exhibition of 1876, Philadelphia*, Dept. IV – Art, p.65; Rowlands, Walter, *Among the Great Masters of Literature*, 1900, p.152.

It is an indication of the high reputation of this work that it was chosen for exhibition at Philadelphia in 1876. The reviewer for *The Art Journal* was quite obviously impressed by this work as professed in his review of the Dudley Gallery exhibition of 1867: "Not for many as year has Henry Wallis, of 'Chatterton,' and 'Dead Stone Breaker' repute, made so palpable a hit as that truly imaginative picture, 'Across the Common'. The canvas is brimful of nature and poetic feeling. What tone, colour, repose, settle on the face of nature! and how completely do the figures respond to the sentiment of the scene! The whole picture breathes the life of poetry." The critic for *The Building News and Engineering Journal* was equally impressed: "For the Exhibition, which was opened last Saturday, must be unquestionably cheering so long as it contains such pictures as 'Love in Oblivion' (No. 37) by Mr. Simeon Solomon; and 'Over the Common' [*sic*] (62), by Mr. H. Wallis. If there were nothing else in the Gallery but these two pictures, so opposite and yet so admirable of their kind, we should have no hesitation in bidding all who are interested in the painter's art (and that ought to mean all who are interested in architecture) to visit the Egyptian Hall, not so much as a pleasure but as a matter of duty...Mr. H. Wallis's very lovely work, like Mr. Leslie's, will be none the worse for keeping. If such a subject – a common in the twilight of a summer's day – is to be painted at all, Mr. Wallis has done it; but the very nature of the subject makes the truthfulness of the picture its own death warrant. 'Across the Common' is unfortunately placed between the bright lights and colour of Mr. Poynter's work on one side, and the snow in Mr. Mark's subject on the other. Under the circumstances, it takes a bright day and some patience to discover all the subtle changes in the mosaic of deep tones which give to this common not only all the reality of a common, but raises, so to speak, the whole spirit of the place. The sky line of the trees, the brooding mist, the charming standing figure, are all apparent even to the passerby; but the hollows and the hillocks, the still pools, the combined sense of openness and of loneliness – which is the very essence of a common – and the marvellous modeling of the ground, are things which require looking for, and which will be found if sought."

The reviewer for *The Athenaeum* noted: "Mr. H. Wallis is eminently fortunate in his beautiful and pathetic figure landscape, *Across the Common* (62) – a study of twilight on a marshy waste, where gleaming pools among rank herbage reflect the last light of day from a sky that is full of warm-tinted autumn clouds and glows softly in purples or blushes with rich rosy tints set in a plain of greyish hues. A line of trees on the far side of the common – we will not say what common it is, lest the builder should ravage its beauty for 'eligible sites' – makes a long mass of deep and finely-varied colour and texture; their summits are orange with the lustre of the hidden sun. Two ladies have crossed so much of the common as the picture shows; one sits to talk, the other, bonnet-less, whose figure is too tall, although capitally designed, stands to listen."

The critic of *The Mask*, in a satirical account, commented: "I have no hesitation in asking Mr. Henry Wallis to stand up for the First prize. Your picture *Across the Common*, which natural modesty prevented you calling *out of the common*, is one of the finest bits of English painting it has ever been our lot to criticize. The sun, already set behind those trees, which must be somewhere near Barnes or Wimbledon; there is still warmth in the atmosphere, and if you listen you can hear the gnats buzzing, and the rooks making their beds; while the carrier's cart adds a trotting accompaniment in the middle distance. It is a daring thing to introduce large figures into your foreground, when those figures are not intended to form the chief interest of your picture; but they stand."

Cat. 63. *Childe Roland to the Dark Tower Came*
1868-1877; ?oil on canvas; dimensions unknown; whereabouts unknown.
Exhibitions: Royal Society of Artists, Birmingham, 1877, *Autumn Exhibition*, no. 496, asking price £126.
Literature: Surtees, Virginia [Ed.], *The Diaries of George Price Boyce*, 1980, p.48.

The first mention of this work and the next item comes from George Price Boyce's diary entry for 28 May 1868: "Adjourned to Henry Wallis. He had on his easel an impressive picture (painted from studies made at Dartmoor) which he calls 'Childe Roland to the Dark Tower came'. He showed us also an interesting sketch of London from his studio window."[1] Seven years earlier, Burne-Jones had treated the same subject in one of his early pen-and-ink drawings. *Childe Roland to the Dark Tower Came* is based on a poem by Robert Browning, written in 1855, and published that year in the collection entitled *Men and Women.* Somewhat surprisingly Wallis's finished painting was not exhibited until much later, in 1877, and then in Birmingham rather than London. It would be interesting to know how much this work was influenced by the second phase of Pre-Raphaelitism or whether it was primarily a landscape.

Cat. 64. *London* (sketch)
1868; medium and dimensions unknown; whereabouts unknown.
Literature: Surtees, Virginia [Ed.], *The Diaries of George Price Boyce*, 1980, p.48.

See previous item. It is unknown if this was worked up further. It does not appear to have been exhibited.

Cat. 65. *Spring Flowers*
?*c.*1868; oil on canvas; dimensions unknown; whereabouts unknown.
Provenance: Henry Wallis; consigned to Christie's, 16 May 1868, lot 26, bought by Tooth, likely the art dealers Arthur Tooth & Sons, for £14 3s 6d.

Cat. 66. *Moorland*
1868; ?oil on canvas; 59.7 x 88.9 cm (23½ x 35 in.); whereabouts unknown.
Provenance: ?Walter F. Morice, 8 De Vere Gardens, Kensington W., London; his estate sale Christie's, London, 12 May 1922, lot 100, bought Loveless for £31 10s.
Exhibitions: Dudley Gallery, *Cabinet Pictures in Oil*, 1868, no. 3.
Literature: *The Art Journal*, New Series, Vol. VII, 1868, p.280; *The Athenaeum*, No. 2142, 14 November 1868, p.649; *Pall Mall Gazette*, 20 November 1868, p.10; *The Illustrated London News*, 21 November 1868, p.503.

After Wallis's recent success at the previous Dudley exhibition, this work was generally considered a failure by reviewers. For instance, the critic for *The Art Journal* was less than complimentary about this picture: "A word of caution might also be kindly given to Mr. Henry Wallis by his friends; never could we have thought it possible that the painter of 'The Dead Stonebreaker' would have perpetrated this 'Moorland'."

The reviewer for the *Pall Mall Gazette* also did not like this work: "The painter of 'Chatterton' has never yet fulfilled in his later work the expectations which were raised by that fortunate performance. In regard to his picture in this exhibition, called 'Moorland', nothing can be said, except that it derives its only interest from the name of the painter. Has Mr. Wallis ever tried his hand again in precisely the same department of work in which his early success was achieved? It was not the tragedy, but the *mise en scene* and accessories, which were really admirable in the 'Chatterton'. Except in the hands of the greatest men, Pre-Raphaelitism turned every kind of subject into genre, and it is quite possible that a painter might mistake the nature of his success, supposing that the praise which was intended for his dexterity and neatness of hand had been accorded to his attempts at greater things."

The Illustrated London News commented: "Mr. H. Wallis's representation of a monotonously-level tract of 'Moorland' (3) massed in dusky green and purple by the earth-shadow after sundown, and scarce broken by the figures of a belated girl and child, could scarcely fail to evince power, yet certainly misses the impressiveness intended. The sky is deficient in that force of orange light which would account for the intensity of the complementary purple of the farther plane of the moor."

F.G. Stephens, the critic of *The Athenaeum*, stated: "The ten pictures of our second class are Mr. H. Wallis's *Moorland* (3) – a girl crossing a brook and beckoning a child to follow; behind, the long, blue, sweeping lines of rolling land in twilight. A beautiful picture, the sky of which is peculiarly poetical, although it needs clearness and transparency to be perfect." This review shows that Stephens was not always the most impartial of reviewers.

It is possible that *Moorland* is the same painting called *Across the Moor*, from W.F. Morice's collection, that sold at his estate sale at Christie's in 1922.

Cat. 67. *Landscape Study of Moorland*
*c.*1868; black and white chalk drawing on grey paper; 41 x 55.6 cm. (16⅛ x 21⅞ in.); whereabouts unknown.
Inscription: Signed with initials *H.W.*
Provenance: Given in 1918 by Harold Wallis to Birmingham Museums and Art Gallery (accession no. 1918P13); de-accessioned and sold at Bonhams, London, 30 Jan 1958, lot 70.
Literature: Birmingham Museum and Art Gallery, *Catalogue of the Permanent Collection of Drawings*, 1939, p.415, no. 13'18.

This study is undated but it could possibly have been executed at the same time as the painting *Moorland* [Cat. 66]. The drawing is a landscape study of a moorland with heather in the foreground and a cottage in the right middle distance.

Cat. 68. *Marsyas*
1869; ?oil on canvas; dimensions unknown; whereabouts unknown.
Exhibitions: Royal Academy, 1869, no. 442.
Literature: *The Art Journal*, New Series, Vol. VIII, 1869, p.199; *The Athenaeum*, No. 2169, 22 May 1869, p.707; *The Illustrated London News*, vol. 54, 22 May 1869, p.526; *The Saturday Review*, Vol. 26, 5 June 1869, p.744; *The Times*, 11 June 1869, p.12; *The Tablet*, 19 June 1869, p.10.

This is one of Wallis's few forays into classicism, a movement that became important amongst English avant-garde painters like Leighton, Poynter, Moore, and Alma-Tadema in the late 1860s. Wallis's painting depicted the Greek myth of the Satyr who was punished by being flayed alive for his affront of challenging the god Apollo to a music contest and losing. The critic for *The Athenaeum* commented on this work: "Mr. H. Wallis's *Marsyas* (442), the preparations for flaying the presumptuous player, while Apollo reclines near the front of the scene, and a vista is formed by trees, is very rich and beautiful picture, full of light, solid in painting, and expressive. It suffers from its neighbours here." The critic of *The Art Journal* didn't like the work, however: "Mr. H. Wallis, known favourably in former years by 'The Death of Chatterton' and 'The Dead Stonebreaker,' has now, strange to say, forsaken nature. His aim in 'Marsyas' (442) is to represent a romantic classic phase of Art, which, if not spurious, is far from healthy or true. The colour may be considered by some the redeeming element in the picture." *The Illustrated London News* reported: "Mr. H. Wallis has an uncomfortable theme, in 'Marsyas' (442), and one scarcely redeemable by an extremely conventional golden tone, intended, we presume, to be Titianesque; however, there are some fine passages of colour in the work."

The Saturday Review had these comments on the work: "Thus, by the law of reactions, or of contraries, whereby Pre-Raffaelitism has flown to the opposite pole of classicism, Mr. H. Wallis, who of yore found sufficing grandeur in a 'Dead Stonebreaker,' now courts romantic beauty, even in the classic story of 'Marsyas.' Strange to say, the artist in this last consummation is lost to nature, and he would seem to seek compensation in colour." The reviewer for *The Times* declared: "The other is a bit of Academic classicality, a reclining Apollo in a shady glade, his warm flesh tolling from the green ground by help of a brilliant crimson-lake drapery, and further on in the shadow Nymphs lamenting over the fate of the presumptuous Satyr, who is seen in the distance strung up for flaying. Mr. Wallis evinces great cleverness in meeting two kinds of demand, which one can hardly imagine the same painter setting himself to supply."

Not having seen an image of this work it is uncleear as to whether Wallis was influenced by one of the many Old Master paintings of this subject. Wallis later did a pen-and-ink drawing of this subject based on a Maiolica plate by Nicola da Urbino.[1]

Cat. 69. *A January Morning*

1869; ?oil on canvas; dimensions unknown;whereabouts unknown.
PROVENANCE: Lewis Pocock,[1] London; his sale Christie's, May 13, 1871, lot 101, bought in.
EXHIBITIONS: Royal Academy, 1869, no. 745.
LITERATURE: *The Art Journal*, New Series, Vol. VIII, 1869, p.202; *The Morning Post*, 7 May 1869, p.6; *The Athenaeum*, No. 2273, 20 May 1871, p.630; *The Illustrated London News*, vol. 54, 22 May 1869, p.526; *The Athenaeum*, No. 2170, 29 May 1869, p.739; *The Times*, 11 June 1869, p.12; *The Tablet*, 19 June 1869, p.10; *The Annual Register of World Events. A Review of the Year*, Vol. 111, 1869, p.359; *The Art Journal*, New Series, Vol. X, 1871, p.189; *The Times*, 11 May, 1871, p.16; *The Athenaeum*, No. 2273, 20 May 1871, p.630.

The reviewer for *The Morning Post* praised this work: "The mistiness and raw cold of a winter's day are imitated with great felicity in a picture by Mr. H. Wallis entitled 'A January Morning' (745). The sky is densely draped with snow-fraught clouds; the snow lies thick upon the ground, and the air is keen and biting. The scene is a town view rather than a landscape in the rural sense of the word, and the most prominent figures are those of a number of girls, one of whom has parted from her companions, and retraced her steps for the charitable purpose of tying a kerchief round the neck of a little child, who, with her mother, sits shivering in the wintry blast at the gate of a workhouse. An expressive and well-finished picture, in all respects worthy of the artist's reputation." *The Athenaeum*, was also favourably impressed and mentioned that: "Mr. H. Wallis's *January Morning* (745) should not be overlooked." *The Illustrated London News* noted: "Curiously different in subject is the painful pathos of 'A January Morning' (745) – one of three young ladies stopping, compassionately, in a snowstorm to tie a woolen garment taken from her own person round the neck of an infant lying in the lap of a pale, wretched mother, seated on the step of a workhouse-door, waiting for relief." The critic for *The Annual Register of World Events* held the opinion: "'A January Morning' by Mr. H. Wallis is a good subject treated most tenderly." The critic for *The Times* commented: "Mr. H. Wallis seems to have set himself to show what a range his art can grasp, between his 'January Morning' (745), and his 'Marsyas' (442). The first is a painful bit of 'realism' from the London streets, a wretched widow with her starving child on the step of a closed workhouse door, with a compassionate girl of the period stopping to put a warm knitted handkerchief from her own neck round that of the shivering baby, while her companions, shop girls, apparently, wait for her, in the fog, a little further on."

This work of social realism can be compared to such contemporary works as Frederick Walker's *The Vagrants*[2] and *The Lost Path*,[3] or Luke Fildes's *Applicants for Admission to a Casual Ward*.[4]

Cat. 70. *Study of a Young Woman Standing*

*c.*late 1860s; black and white chalk with brown wash on blue-grey laid paper; 51.5 x 33.5 cm. (20$\frac{5}{16}$ x 13$\frac{3}{16}$ in.); Birmingham Museums and Art Gallery.
INSCRIPTIONS: signed by initials *H.W.*, lower right
PROVENANCE: Presented by Harold Wallis in 1918 to Birmingham Museums and Art Gallery, accession no.1918P2.
LITERATURE: Birmingham Museum and Art Gallery, *Catalogue of the Permanent Collection of Drawings*, 1939, p.414, no. 2'18.

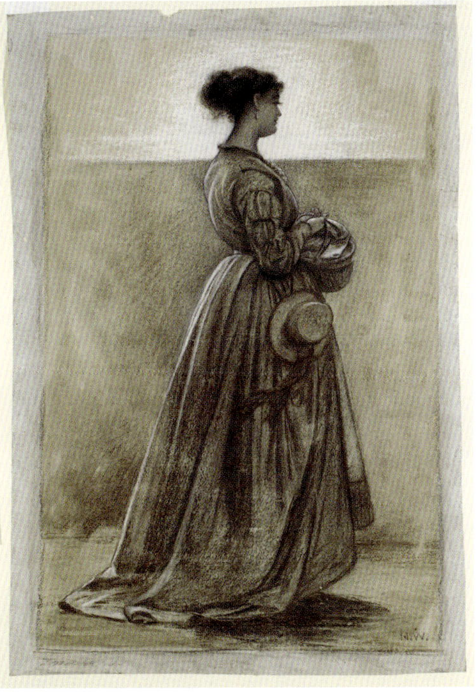

Cat. 70. Image by permission of Birmingham Museums Trust

The young woman stands in profile to the right, holding a basket, while a straw hat hangs from the area of her waist. Curators at Birmingham feel that the cut of the dress, with the skirt falling straight at the front and slightly flared at the back, suggests a date of the late 1860s. Similar dating is suggested by two dress historians. Alexandra Palmer of the Royal Ontario Museum in Toronto estimates the date of the costume to *c.*1861–68, while Kimberly Wahl of Ryerson University in Toronto associates the bodice to earlier versions of "Pre-Raphaelite" dress from the 1850s/early 1860s and the skirt to the late 1860s/early 1870s because of its length and volume at the back. She suggests the hairstyle is more consistent with this later date.[1] There is a possibility that this model may be the same young woman as that in the alleged portrait of Mary Ellen Meredith in the Lanigan collection.[2] [See: Cat. 33]

Cat. 71. *After the Storm*

1870; crayon drawing; dimensions unknown; whereabouts unknown.
EXHIBITIONS: Royal Academy, 1870, no. 837: ?Dudley Gallery, *Exhibition of Works of Art in Black and White*, 1874, no. 188.
LITERATURE: *The Athenaeum*, No. 2220, 14 May 1870, p.648; *The Athenaeum*, No. 2223, 4 June 1870, p.748; *The Athenaeum*, No. 2245, 5 November 1870, p.598; *The Athenaeum*, No. 2435, 27 June 1874, p.867.

F.G. Stephens, the critic of *The Athenaeum*, liked this drawing by Wallis: "We next come to the crayon drawings, a class of works with high claims to attention, - claims, however, that are not often regarded...We have already noticed Mr. Wallis's *After the Storm* (837), a noble study which deserves a better place than it has obtained." In an earlier review, Stephens had praised it by saying: "*After the Storm* (837), is a subject taken from Wooton Woods when a tornado had broken its way through them, prostrating the beeches which Evelyn planted; rent from the earth they lie in ranks, with boughs crushed and entangled; the artist has rendered the pathos of his subject with perfect skill in draughtsmanship and modelling." John Evelyn had begun the ornamental planting on his brother's grounds surrounding Wooton House in the mid-17th century.

This may be the same drawing, or perhaps a closely related one, that Wallis later showed at the Black and White exhibition at the Dudley Gallery in 1874. A review in *The Athenaeum* in 1874 remarks: "Mr. H. Wallis's *After a Storm in the Woods* (188), a glade, with trees lying prostrate in all their length, is grand in sentiment and style, two qualities rare in landscape. It is a fine design in every sense beautifully drawn."

Cat. 72. *Portrait of Harold (Felix) Wallis*
*c.*1870; oil on board; 15.5 x 14.5 cm. (6⅛ x 5¾ in.) - sight; private collection.
Annotation: (in red on the backboard) "Henry Wallis".
Provenance: Henry Wallis by descent to his son Harold Wallis, then to his wife Mary Wallis (née Mary Elizabeth Aymes), then her great-niece Vera G. Cooper (née Langley) (1910-1989), and thence by direct descent to John Harold Cooper and then to his family; private collection.

Harold 'Felix' Wallis was born on 18 April 1858. He appears to be about twelve or thirteen, making the date of its production *c.*1870. This is the only known portrait that Wallis made of his son. A photograph of Harold aged four or five is reproduced in Diane Johnson's book.[1]

Cat. 73. *Oil Sketch of Nude and Draped Figures (? Venus and Adonis)*
? 1870s. Monochrome brown oil paint, possibly burnt umber, on canvas; 18.1 x 36.6 cm. (7⅛ x 14⅜ in.); Birmingham Museum and Art Gallery.
Provenance: Presented by Harold Wallis in 1918 to Birmingham Museum and Art Gallery, accession no. 1918P8.
Literature: City of Birmingham Art Gallery, *Catalogue of Paintings*, 1930, p.204, no. 8'18; Birmingham Catalogue, 1960, p.148.

The subject of this work is obscure but is most likely based on a classical myth. Contemporary influences might include works by Albert Moore with women on benches, such as his *The Marble Seat* (private collection) exhibited at the Royal Academy in 1865. Moore's paintings, however, tend to be purely decorative and lack this overt eroticism. Contemporary French painting is another possible source. Considering Wallis's interest in Italian Renaissance painting at this time, however, it is far more likely he found his inspiration in works by High Renaissance masters like Titian, such as his *Venus and Adonis* (1554, Prado, Madrid) or *Diana and Actaeon* (finished 1556-9, National Gallery + National Gallery of Scotland). The possible influence of Titian on Wallis's work is supported by an almost illegible note by Wallis on *Venus and Adonis* in the Diane Johnson papers.[1]

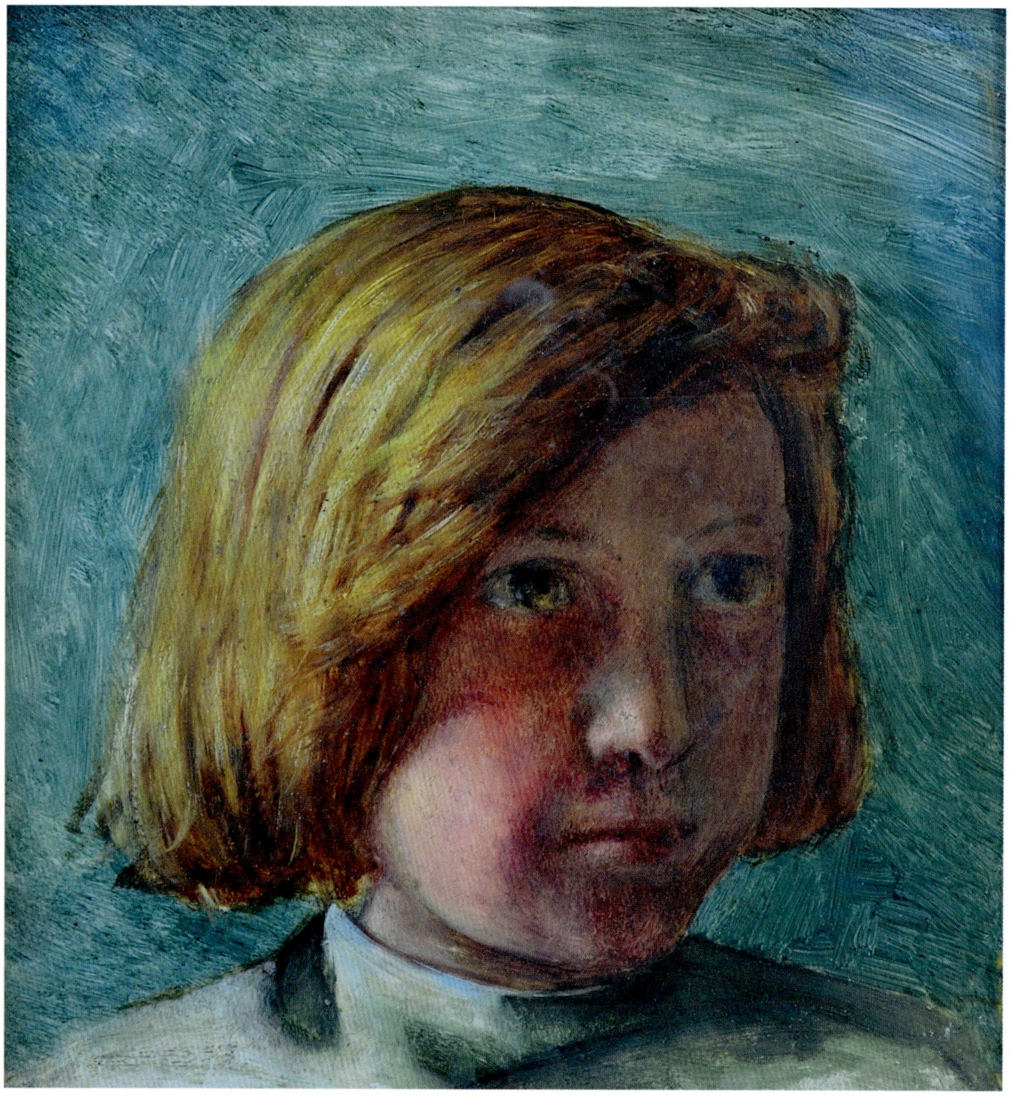
Cat. 72. Image courtesy of private collection

Cat. 73a. *A Study of a Reclining Woman and Two Nude Figures*
1870s; black chalk on grey paper; 33.1 x 30.7 cm. (13 x 12⅛ in.); Birmingham Museum and Art Gallery.
Inscriptions: Signed with initials *H.W.*, lower right.
Provenance: Presented by Harold Wallis in 1918 to Birmingham Museums and Art Gallery, accession no. 1918P10.
Literature: Birmingham Museum and Art Gallery, Catalogue of the Permanent Collection of Drawings, 1939, p.415, no. 10'18.
These studies are preparatory to the oil sketch [Cat. 73], although the pose of the woman in the top drawing is more upright and differs slightly from the sketch. These rare examples of working drawings make us wonder how many other prepatory drawings Wallis may have made for his paintings that do not survive.

Cat. 73b. *Study of a Nude Man, Seated on a Bench*
*c.*1870s; black chalk on grey paper; 29.6 x 31.5 cm. (11⁹⁄₁₆ x 12⅜ in.); Birmingham Museum and Art Gallery.
Provenance: Presented by Harold Wallis in 1918 to Birmingham Museum and Art Gallery, accession no. 1918P9.
Literature: Birmingham Museum and Art Gallery, *Catalogue of the Permanent Collection of Drawings*, 1939, p.414, no. 9'18.

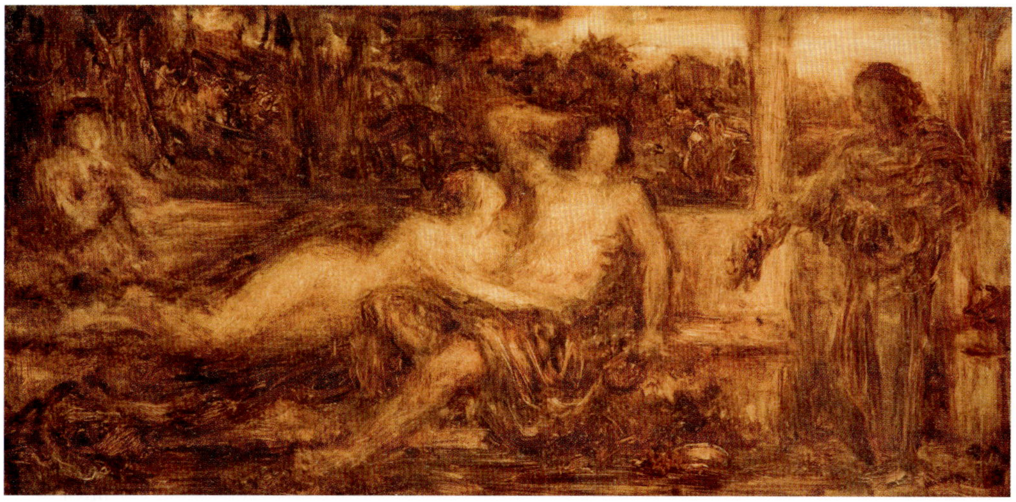

Cat. 73. Image by permission of Birmingham Museums Trust

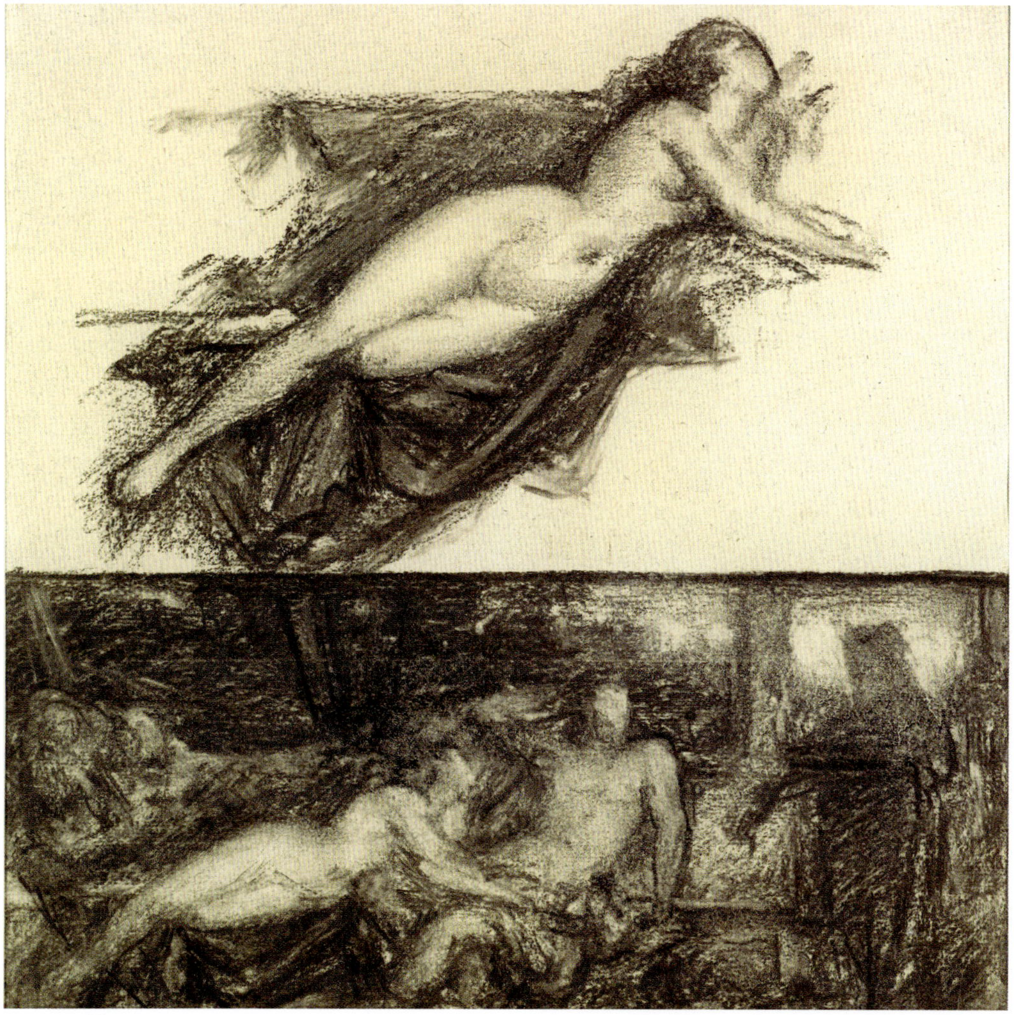

Cat. 73a. Image by permission of Birmingham Museums Trust

This drawing shows what an accomplished draughtsman Wallis had become; it relates to the previous drawing [Cat. 73a] and the oil sketch [Cat. 73], also in the Birmingham Collection. It is a study for the figure of the man sprawled on the bench to the right. These academic studies are not easy to date, but on stylistic grounds they likely date from the 1870s.

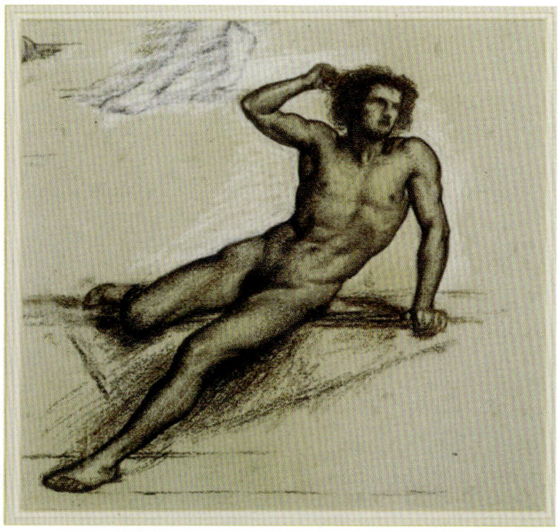

Cat. 73b. Image by permission of Birmingham Museums Trust

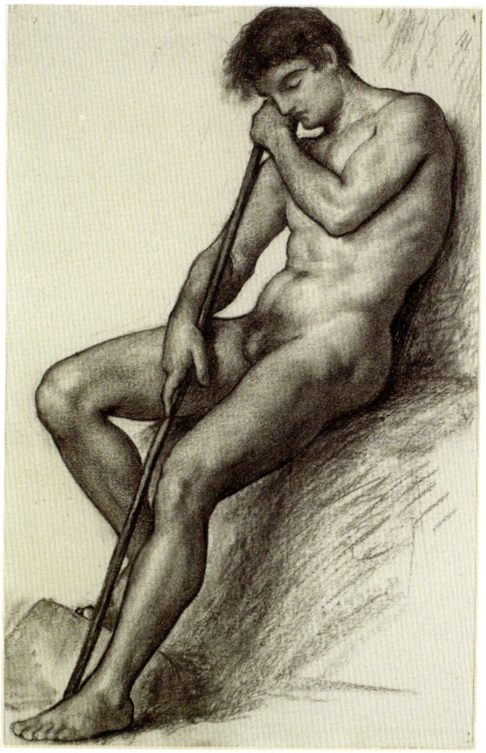

Cat. 74. Image by permission of Birmingham Museums Trust

Cat. 74. *Academic Study of a Seated Nude Man*
? 1870s; black chalk on greenish-grey paper; 46.2 x 29.1 cm. (18³⁄₁₆ x 11½ in.); Birmingham Museum and Art Gallery.
PROVENANCE: Presented by Harold Wallis in 1918 to Birmingham Museum and Art Gallery, accession no. 1918P11.
LITERATURE: Birmingham Museum and Art Gallery, *Catalogue of the Permanent Collection of Drawings*, 1939, p.415, no. 11'18.

The model holds a pole to help him maintain the pose. Although this drawing might have been made when he studied at the Royal Academy Schools (1848-49) or at Gleyre's studio (*c.*1851), it seems too accomplished for a twenty-year old young student. This becomes obvious if compared to his one known surviving early academic life study [Cat. 3] It therefore makes sense to give it a later date. The assured handling likely dates it to the 1870s, when he admired Renaissance Italian art in general, and the works of Carpaccio and of Melozzo da Forlì in particular.

Cat. 75. Blue Bells
1870; ?oil on canvas; dimensions unknown; whereabouts unknown.
PROVENANCE: Selected from the New British Institution exhibition in 1870 by J. Dickson, a prize-holder from the Art Union of London.
EXHIBITIONS: New British Institution, 1870, *First Spring Exhibition of Pictures*, no. 92, priced at £70.
LITERATURE: *The Art Journal*, Vol. 9, 1870,

p.219; *Report of the Committee of Management of the Art Union of London*, 1870, p 82; *The Architect*, Vol. 3, 12 March 1870, p.129; *The Morning Post*, 14 March 1870, p.6; *Pall Mall Gazette*, 30 March 1870, p.6; *The Saturday Review*, Vol. 29, 16 April, 1870, p.513; *The Morning Post*, 8 August 1870, p.6; *The Standard*, 8 August 1870, p.3; *The Illustrated London News*, 13 August 1870, p.180; *The Illustrated London News*, 7 January 1871, p.18; *Fun*, 19 March 1879, p.21.

When this work was exhibited in 1870 it was highly regarded. The critic of *The Architect*, in his review of the New British Institution exhibition, wrote: "There is more than one picture which not only evinces original genius in the artist, but at which the critic will look again and again with that feeling which is one of the greatest triumphs of the artist to produce – that which it is difficult to decide exactly what to say. Two or three of this sort may be referred to in illustration of our meaning. Thus 'Blue-bells' (No. 92), by H. Wallis, is a picture which it would be easy to criticize. A young mother, with her child, stands on a bank covered with blue-bells, and her sister stoops to pick one of the flowers. The ladies are delicately dressed in white; the hat of the period is worn by the married one, so as to be both picturesque in her attire and a valuable bit of shade in the picture. The distant hill is somewhat poor and bare. The whole painting must be looked at only from one especial standpoint; but, so viewed, it is a bit of nature, and very charming nature too." *The Saturday Review* held a high opinion: " Blue Bells are set like jewels in a field of emerald; the flowers throw off dazzling light and colour, and yet the picture is well kept together." The critic for *The Art Journal* also liked this work: "Lastly, we rejoice to see Mr. H. Wallis once more himself again, though he has long bid adieu to the realists: 'Blue Bells' (92) is a bright vision of early spring; these bells, more brilliant than turquoise or sapphire, are set in a field of emerald. We have seldom seen such flooding light or delicious colour brought within an exhibition-room."

The critic of *The Illustrated London News* was lavish in his praise: "Mr. Henry Wallis has not, since his 'Death of Chatterton,' painted anything so remarkable as his 'Blue Bells' (92). Quite a new quality of refinement, both in feeling and execution, seems to us to be developed in this beautiful work. The picture comes upon one as a surprise, but not more so than would such a scene in nature. It represents a woodland slope, dotted with the tufted roots of lately-felled trees, in spring time, when the whole hillside is carpeted with the purplish-blue of countless wild hyacinths. On the declivity are two females, dressed in white; one a young mother carrying her babe, the other stooping to gather some of the blue bells – human types of the season and its beauty. The figures are as lovely as the landscape setting, and the picture altogether seems redolent of the fresh and fragrant air of the sweet spring time."

This works sounds reminiscent of J.W. Inchbold's *Mid-Spring*, which was exhibited at the Royal Academy in 1856 and which Wallis likely saw.

Cat. 76. *Corner of an Eastern Courtyard*
*c.*1870; oil on canvas, 61 x 47 cm (24 x 18½ in.); Birmingham Museum and Art Gallery.
PROVENANCE: Presented by Harold Wallis in 1918 to Birmingham Museum and Art Gallery, accession no. 1918P17.
EXHIBITIONS: Hong Kong Museum of Art, *Pre-Raphaelite Art from the Birmingham Museum and Art Gallery*, 1984, cat. no. 64.
LITERATURE: City of Birmingham Art Gallery, *Catalogue of Paintings*, 1930, p.204, no. 17'18; Birmingham Catalogue, 1960, p.148; Lockett, Richard: *Pre-Raphaelite Art from the Birmingham Museum and Art Gallery*, 1984, pp.150-151; Wright, Christopher, et al., 1995, p.796, no. 92 (illus).[1]

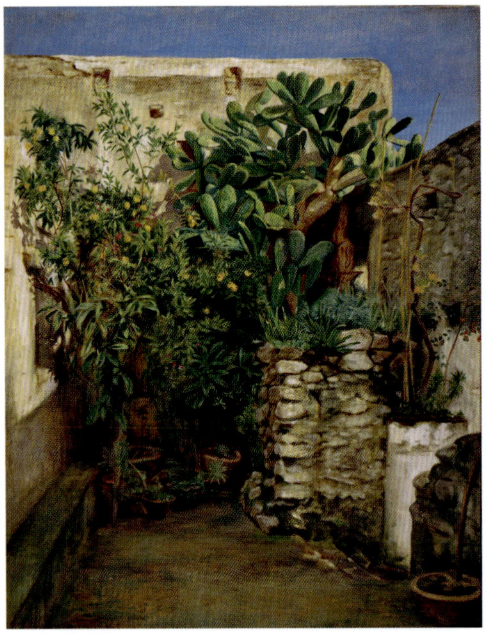

Cat. 76. Image by permission of Birmingham Museums Trust.

The Birmingham Museum curators date this work *c.*1870 and suggest the work may have been made at Capri. If this were true, the work could even date from earlier, perhaps even as early as the winter of 1858, when Henry and Mary Ellen stayed on the island, or 1861-1862, when Henry spent the winters with his son. No later journey to Capri has been recorded, but Wallis exhibited drawings of Capri at Colnaghi's in July 1869 making this a distinct possibility.[2] It is possible that the location is not Capri, however, and Wallis may have visited elsewhere in the Mediterranean area in *c.*1870.

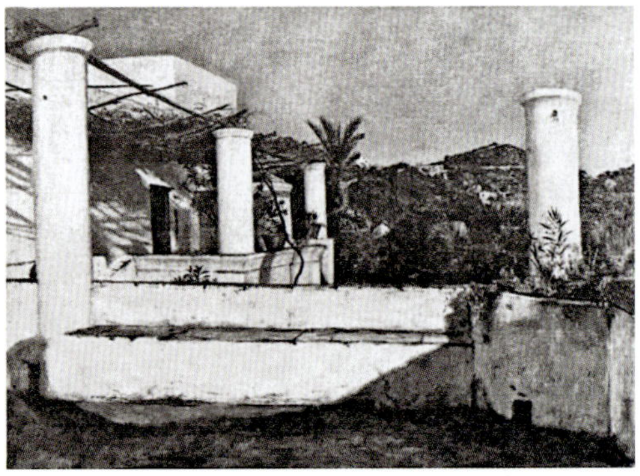

Cat. 77. Image courtesy of William Waters

Cat. 77. *Mediterranean Landscape seen from the Terrace of a Villa*
*c.*1870s, possibly as early as 1861/62; oil on canvas; 29.5 cm x 38.7 cm (11¾ x 16 in.); private collection.
PROVENANCE: Wallis's studio and then by descent from the artist to his daughter-in-law Alice Julyan Wallis (née Roberts), and thence to her great-niece Mrs. Vera G. Whiting, Purley, Surrey; her sale Sotheby's Belgravia, 10 April 1973, lot 193, bought by William Waters, Norham House, Cockermouth, Cumbria for £55; sold to John C. Constable, Southgate Gallery, Wolverhampton; Sotheby's Belgravia, 30 March 1982, lot 22.
EXHIBITIONS: Norham House: *The Pre-Raphaelite Fringe*, November 1973, no. 14.

The location is almost certainly in Capri. The picture could possibly have been made during the winter of 1858-59, supposing Mary Ellen and Henry were on the island then, but it could also date from the winters of 1861 or 1862, which Wallis spent in Capri with his son Harold, or even later [see: Cat. 76]. In the spring of 1859, Frederic Leighton had spent five weeks on the island and stayed at Pagano's Hotel, the oldest inn on the island, where he painted its gardens.[1] This is the same hotel where Wallis also stayed. Wallis's picture appears to represent the same gardens, but from a different angle.

Nearly 200 years have gone by since the notary Giuseppe Pagano decided to open his home as a lodging-house in 1820. In 1845, 'Casa Pagano' was extended and adapted to be better able to welcome the many foreign visitors coming to Capri, becoming the favourite haunt of scores of artists, poets, and writers who visited the island; today the hotel is known as La Palma.

Cat. 78. *A Mediterranean Courtyard*
*c.*1870s; oil on canvas; 35.6 x 45.8 cm (14 x 18 in.); private collection.
PROVENANCE: Wallis's studio and then by descent from the artist to his son Harold Wallis, then to his daughter-in-law Mary

Wallis (née Mary Elizabeth Aymes), then her great-niece Vera G. Cooper (née Langley) (1910-1989), and thence by direct descent to John Harold Cooper and family until sold at Bonhams, London, 05 March 2002, lot 68, for £380.

Cat. 79. *His Highness and His Excellency the Ambassador of the Florentine Republic (Cesare Borgia and Machiavelli)* (Also: *The Conversation*)
1870; oil on canvas; 66.4 x 92.1 cm (26⅛ x 36¼ in.); private collection.
Annnotations: Signed and inscribed on an old label on the verso *No 1/Henry Wallis/9 Red Lion Square/W.C.*
Provenance: Still in the possession of the artist in 1873; ?purchased at the exhibition in Dublin in 1873; T. O'Mahony, Castlecorner, Kilkenny, Ireland by 1973; anonymous sale Christie's, London, 8 November 1996, lot 62, sold for £9,200; Christie's, London, 12 June 2001, lot 51, bought in; purchased after the sale by a private collector, London; on consignment with Martin Beisly Fine Art, London, from 2016-2019; Bonhams, London, 26 September, 2019, lot 26.
Exhibitions: Dudley Gallery, *Cabinet Pictures in Oil*, 1870, no. 93, asking price £200; *London International Exhibition*, 1871, no. 473; *Loan Museum of Art Treasures*, Industrial Exhibition Palace, Dublin, 1873, no. 12, asking price £200.
Literature: *The Art Journal*, Vol. IX, 1870, p.372; *The Illustrated London News*, 5 November 1870, p.478; *The Athenaeum*, No. 2245, 5 November 1870, p.598; *Art, Pictorial and Industrial: An Illustrated Magazine*, Vol. I, 1870-71, p.124; *The Illustrated London News*, 7 January 1871, p.16; Lessens, Ronald, 'Henry Wallis (1830-1916), a neglected Pre-Raphaelite', *The British Art Journal*, vol. XV, No. 1, Autumn 2014, p.54.

This is the first of a series of Italian Renaissance-inspired works that would influence Wallis's work in the 1870s. The painting has sold twice recently under the title *The Conversation* but this was not its original title. The painting received mixed reviews at the Dudley Gallery exhibition. Not surprisingly, the most extensive review was by Wallis's friend F. G. Stephens in *The Athenaeum*: "Mr. Wallis has struck out into more than one fresh pathway, always with more or less success…the picture before us, shows the wealth of his mind, and the facility with which he turns its powers to account in divergent courses…We are heartily thankful for *His Highness and His Excellence the Ambassador of the Florentine Republic* (93) – C. Borgia and Machiavelli, resting on a marble bench by a garden wall in Rome, conversing, and not only dressed each suitably to his

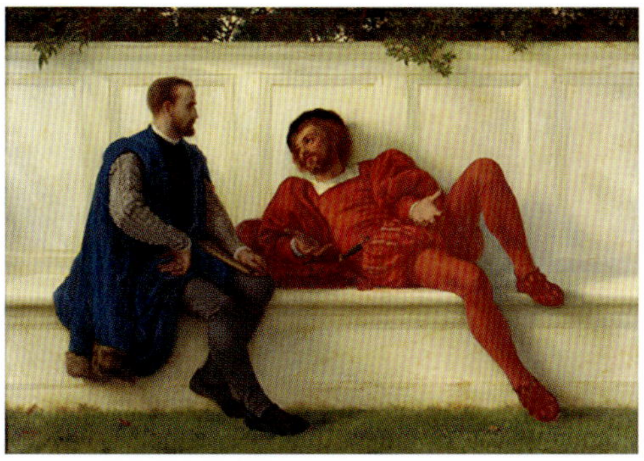

Cat. 79. Image courtesy of private collection c/o Martin Beisly Fine Art

nature, but posed and looking each after the mode of his kind. One sits nervously, almost on the edge of the bench, and listens to all appearance acquiescently, if not deferentially, to the other, who, clad in flame-colour from head to foot, lolls back, poses his foot on the marble, and demonstratively urges some apparently favoured scheme, looking, with his flushed and jovial face, his eager eyes and action, his restless limbs and mobile fingers, the very type of impulse and geniality, which by no means disclaimed the character of craft, yet seemed more open for being more profound. A big, robust, and luxurious, if not coarse, man, is this Caesar [*sic*]; whereas his companion is the type of Italian refinement and intellectual power. Dark while the other is red, slight of form, with strength of character marked on his brow and nose, astute, reticent, patient, Machiavelli is soberly, yet richly, clad in blue and grey. The design is admirable; the composition seems to us in need of enrichment by added elements, for the two figures are the sum of the picture, and each is alone, whereas we would not bring them closer together – this would mar the conception of the subject, than which it would be hard to invent a fairer – yet it may be that nothing of the expressiveness of the work would be lost if the figures were not isolated."

The critic for *The Art Journal* raised some concerns about this picture, however: "Mr. H. Wallis, we fear, has laid himself open to the charge of plagiarism in an otherwise commendable picture – 'His Highness and His Excellence the Ambassador of the Florentine Republic' (93). Certainly these figures on a bench are singularly like to Cabanel's well-known composition 'The Florentine Poet'. Mr. Wallis, however, whether or not he has stolen an idea, succeeds in making an agreeable picture: once more he pushes colour to a romantic pitch; his work, if not strong, is subtle and sensitive to beauty."

Cat. 80. *Ser Pandolfo*
1870; watercolour; dimensions unknown; whereabouts unknown.
Exhibitions: New British Institution, *First Winter Exhibition of Water-Colour Drawings*, 1870, no. 77; *London International Exhibition*, 1871, no. 1747; *Exhibition of Arts, Industries and Manufactures*, Dublin, 1872, no. 411, price 100 guineas.
Literature: *The Building News and Engineering Journal*, Vol. 19, 25 November 1870, p.383; *The Illustrated London News*, Vol. 57, 26 November 1870, p.543; *The Examiner*, 26 November 1870, p.761; *The Architect*, Vol. 4, 26 November 1870, p.306; *John Bull*, 3 December 1870, p.835; *The Morning Post*, 6 December 1870, p.6; *The Illustrated London News*, Vol. 58, 7 January 1871, pp.16-18.

The critic of *The Illustrated London News*, in its initial review, was very favourably impressed by this work: "There are several cases in this exhibition which may be adduced to show that oil-painters of ability have only to change their materials to successfully compete with or even surpass the old favourites whom the public may suppose enjoy a sort of monopoly in water colours. Among those artists known as oil-painters who lend novel interest to the display none has distinguished himself so highly as Mr. Henry Wallis in his 'Ser Pandolfo' (77). Since his 'Death of Chatterton' he has done nothing better calculated to enhance his reputation; but, unlike that celebrated early picture, the present is a work of the maturest art; indeed, we have seen few such drawings in our recent English school. Its colouring and force of effect; its texture, or what artists call 'quality' are of rare excellence. Nor is the conception inferior in originality and suggestiveness to the execution. 'Ser Pandolfo' is the type of a rich, self-indulging civic grandee of old Florence. His portly person buried in the ample folds of his scarlet robes, he sits, his plump hands folded over his stomach, on a marble bench, leaning, fast asleep, against the marble wall of (we may suppose) his palazzo. From the right, relieved against the mellowed hues of the sun-lighted marble with a vividness little short of that of nature, approaches one of the flower-girls who to this day present their tiny bouquets to every 'swell' they encounter in the hope of an occasional bajocco or Paulo [*sic*].[1] But with a charmingly-indicated expression, half timid, half roguish, the little gipsy pauses. Shall she dare wake so imposing a personage? Or shall she throw her flowers, with those which already lie unnoticed at the great man's feet?"

The reviewer for *The Examiner* also thought highly of this work: "We like Mr. Wallis's 'Ser Pandolfo' (77) better than any picture we have seen of his for some time. The two figures are well conceived and painted." *The Building News and Engineering Journal* reviewer also praised this picture: "No. 77, 'Sir Pandolfo,' by H. Wallis, is an excellent bit of colour; the warm lights in the marble seat are

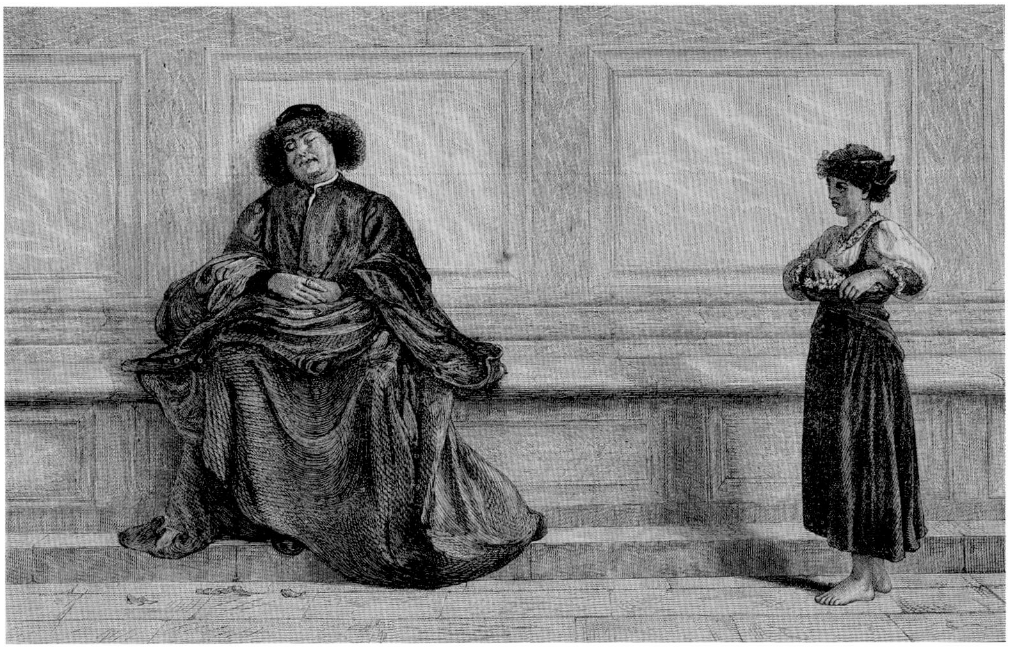

Cat. 80a. Image courtesy of Dennis Lanigan collection

truthfully rendered, as is also the rich shade of Sir Pandolfo's dress; on the right-hand side a pretty little Italian flower-girl timidly approaches." The popularity of the painting is also obvious from a letter of 13 November 1872 from P. W. Kennedy, secretary of the Society of Fine Arts Committee (Dublin), to Wallis. The Committee wanted to buy this painting that had been exhibited at the Exhibition of Arts, Industries and Manufactures in Dublin in 1872:

> Sir,
> Will you take seventy-five guineas for your Water Colour picture 'Sir Pandalfo' [*sic*].
> Your reply at your convenience will oblige
> Your obt servt.
> P.W. Kennedy, Sec. Fine Arts Committee.[2]

Cat. 80a. *Ser Pandolfo*
1871; wood engraving; image size: 19 x 29.2 cm (7½ x 11¾ in.); sheet size: 27 x 39.3 cm (10⅝ x 15½ in.); Dr Dennis T. Lanigan, Saskatoon, Canada.
Inscriptions: Signed in the plate *W. HOLLIDGE. Sc*, lower left.
Annotation: "SER PANDOLFO," BY H. WALLIS.
Literature: *The Illustrated London News*, 7 January 1871, pp.16-18.

The wood engraver William Hollidge who executed this print was a British printmaker active 1869-1895. *The Illustrated London News* was high in its praise of this work: "At first sight we imagined this drawing (which we have engraved from the current Exhibition of Water-Colour Paintings at the New British Institution) to be an illustration of some character of poetry or romance, or a representation of some specific historical personage. Higher praise is, however, due to the painter, for it is his own original conception. The artist who, in a recent oil painting gave us capital realizations of Machiavelli and Caesar Borgia, typical Florentine characters of the early part of the sixteenth century, here introduces an equally typical, although fictitious, Venetian personage of about the same date: and – with a power of imaginative sympathy which is not the less real because it is not vulgarly super-obvious – he gives us at the same time a glimpse as it were, of everyday Venetian life…This is one of those civic grandees of the palmy days of Venice, as we learn by the ample crimson silk robes which envelop his portly person. Magistrate and member of the Consiglio, he may be; but municipal duties sit light upon him, patriotic anxiety does not disturb his digestion or equanimity. 'Ser', the familiar contraction of his title, suggests that he is not held in high esteem among the populace, even by the poor flower-girl who chances to recognise him. He is, in short, the very personification in features, expression, and figure of a Venetian aldermanic Dives, luxuriously pampered, self-indulgent, and indolent. He has strolled out to air himself; but the warm, soft, moist breath of the Adriatic has a relaxing, somniferous influence. So he sits down on a marble bench, against a richly-inlaid outside wall of his own palazzo, as we suppose…Then his head loll's back, his plump hands fold themselves over his round, 'well-lined' stomach, and there he takes, al fresco, his siesta. And thus, in this undignified attitude of ease, he is found by a little flower girl, whose charming figure presents the strongest contrast, in her slender litheness, her arch vivacity of expression, her picturesque rags, and in every other respect…Technically, this picture is of very unusual interest. It is widely dissimilar in subject and treatment to the 'Blue Bells,' by the same artist, which was so much admired when exhibited at the same gallery last spring: and it is, we believe, the first painting in water colours that Mr. Wallis has exhibited. Yet it is remarkable for perfect command of the material, and it has a power and beauty of colour and richness of texture rarely found in water colours; indeed, it is long since we have seen a drawing, on the whole, so masterly. It is a considerable advance, in the higher artistic qualities, upon 'The Death of Chatterton,' the picture by which Mr. Wallis won his early fame. The celebrity of that picture was not undeserved; but it, perhaps, owed something of its renown to the rage for pre-Raphaelitism which prevailed about the time of its production. Since then, however, the artist has changed his style more than once, and his subjects have been extremely various. It is, probably, owing to these circumstances that some works of superior merit have not received due recognition from the public."

Cat. 81. *Teresa*
1870; medium and dimensions unknown, likely oil on canvas or board; whereabouts unknown.
Exhibitions: New British Institution, *Exhibition for Relief of Widows and Orphans of German Soldiers*, 1870, no. 9.
Literature: *The Daily News*, London, 26 September 1870, p.2; *The Illustrated London News*, vol. 57, 1 October 1870, p.359; *The Graphic*, 1 October 1870, p.322.

This exhibition, to which Wallis contributed a work, was established to help the dependants of German soldiers killed in the Franco-Prussian war. Queen Victoria's daughter, Princess Victoria, the Crown Princess of Prussia, was the patroness for the undertaking. *The Illustrated London News* describes this work as "an artistic study of an Italian girl". The critic for *The Graphic* indicated: "Teresa is a highly finished, richly coloured Italian head study seen in profile by Mr. H. Wallis."

A parallel *Exhibition of Paintings for the Distressed Peasantry of France* was organised by the picture dealer Henry Wallis and held at the premises of the Society of British Artists in Suffolk Street.[1] Wallis appears not to have contributed to this exhibition, which is somewhat surprising. Considering his artistic training in Paris one might have expected he would have been more sympathetic to the French than the German cause.

Cat. 82. *Study of a Standing Young Woman in Italian Peasant's Costume*
*c.*1870; black and white chalk on purple-grey paper; 61.8 x 40.6 cm. (24¼ x 16 in.); Birmingham Museum and Art Gallery.
Inscriptions: Signed with initials *H.W.*, lower right.
Provenance: Harold Wallis; given to Birmingham Museum and Art Gallery in 1918, accession no. 1918P3.
Literature: Birmingham Museum and Art Gallery, *Catalogue of the Permanent Collection of Drawings*, 1939, p.414, no. 3'18.

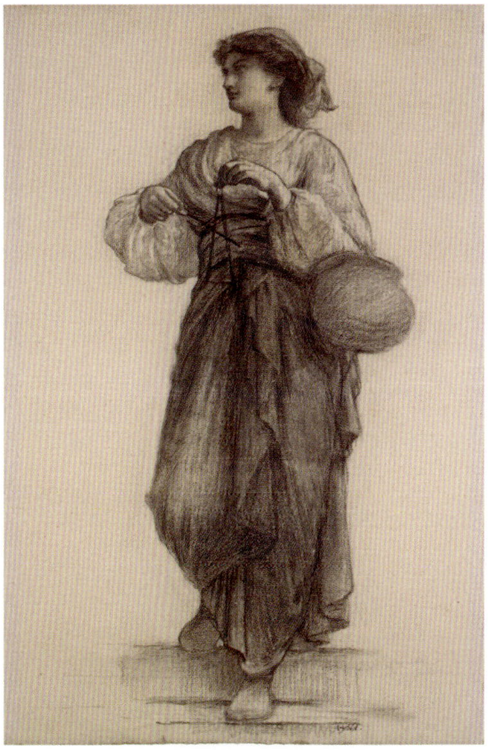

Cat. 82. Image by permission of the Birmingham Museums Trust

The young woman is standing on a step and playing a triangle. She is holding a basket in her left arm. This drawing certainly could have been made in the 1870s, during Wallis's Italian period, but this is difficult to determine without knowing exactly for which picture it is a study, or whether it was conceived as an independent work of art.

Cat. 83. *Burnham Beeches*
*c.*1871; black and white chalks on pale grey paper; 58.5 x 43 cm. (23⅒ x 17 in.) - sight; private collection.
Provenance: Wallis's studio and then by descent from the artist to his son Harold Wallis, then to his daughter-in-law Mary Wallis (née Mary Elizabeth Aymes), then her great-niece Vera G. Cooper (née Langley) (1910-1989), and thence by direct descent to John Harold Cooper and family; private collection.

This work again highlights Wallis's abilities as a draughtsman. Burnham seems to have been a favourite place with the Pre-Raphaelites, and it is not unlikely that Wallis showed the location to his friend Arthur Hughes or vice versa. Hughes writing to William Allingham in 1872 described familiar old trees at Burnham as "very solemn ...but cheering up wonderfully when a glimpse of the sun lights upon the green moss and brown heather". In a later letter of 1908 to the poet's widow, the watercolourist Helen Allingham (1848-1926), Hughes was moved to remember how "I showed and introduced Burnham Beeches to William Allingham".[1] Hughes and his nephew E.R. Hughes both loved to paint at this location.

A loose sketch entitled *Burnham Beeches* from a Wallis sketchbook is dated 11.4.71 and may have been executed at the same time as the more finished drawing.[2] [See: Cat. 308]

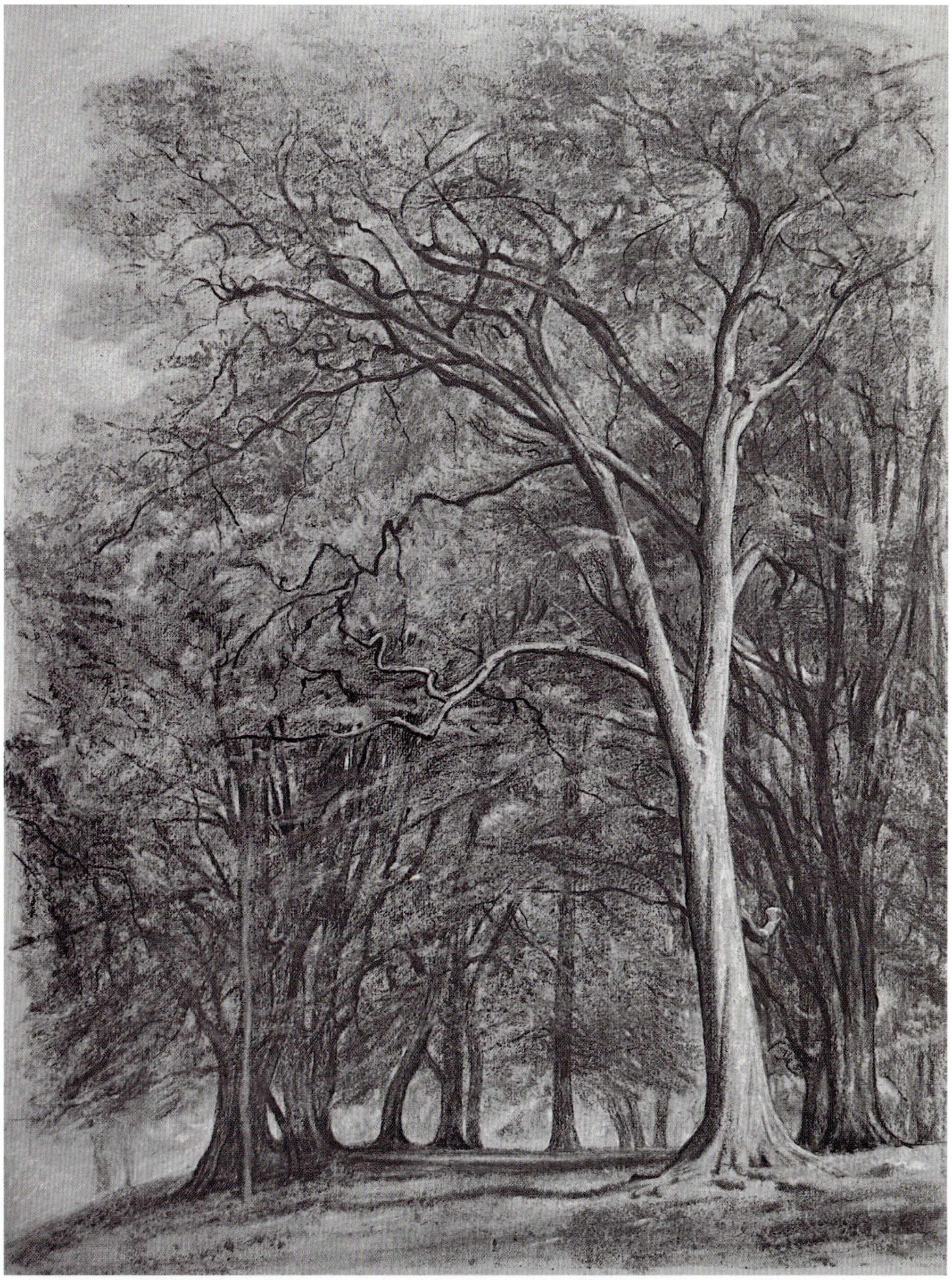

Cat. 83. Image courtesy of private collection

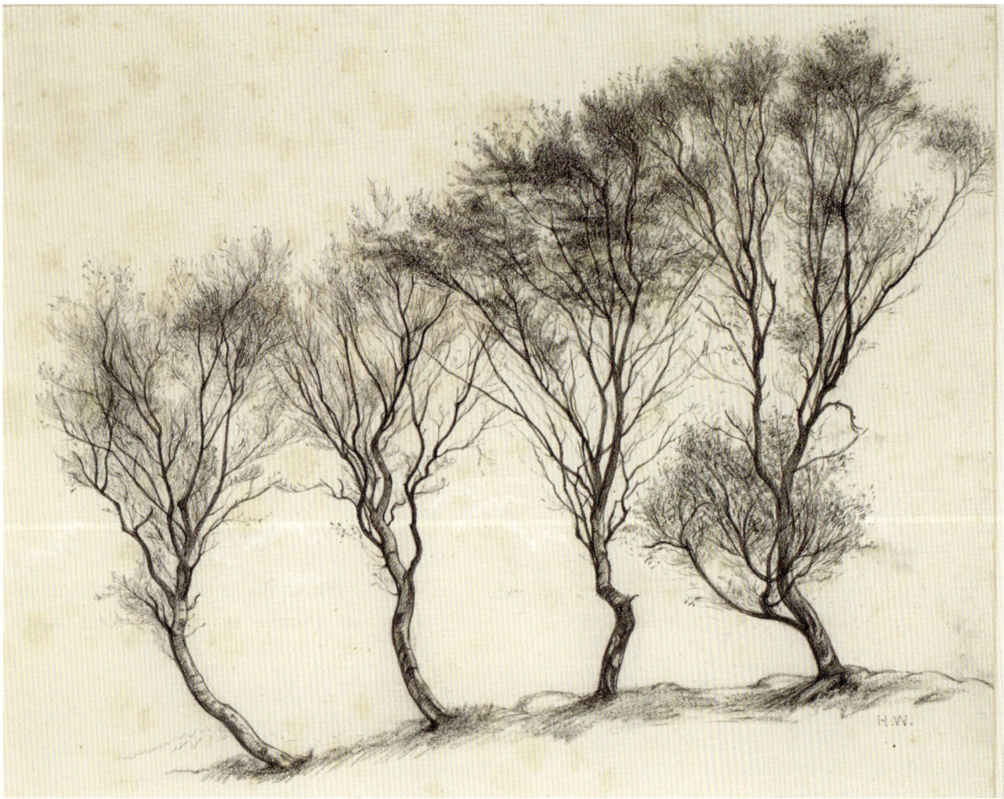

Cat. 84. Image by permission of the Birmingham Museums Trust

This drawing has always been known by Wallis's descendents as *The House in which Shakespeare Lived.* Although it bears some resemblance to the house in which Shakespeare was born, it is hard to reconcile the fact that the house in this drawing appears to abut directly on a river or stream. Jessie Petheram from the Shakespeare Birthplace Trust does not believe the house in this drawing can be Shakespeare's birthplace.[1] She felt it might, at a stretch, be a fanciful representation of New Place, the house Shakespeare owned until he died, but the site of this house did not abut the Avon river in Stratford either. Neither does this depiction resemble Hall's Croft, the home of Shakespeare's daughter Susanna Hall in Stratford-upon-Avon. Wallis visited Stratford as late as 1913 when he stayed in a house known as 'The Old Vicarage'. No house of this name from that time period appears to survive, so it is unknown as to whether this could be a possibility for the building depicted.

Cat. 84. *Study of Four Trees, on a Ridge*
*c.*1871; black chalk, heightened with white, on pale buff paper; 36.7 x 45.5 cm. (14 5/16 x 17 7/8 in.); Birmingham Museum and Art Gallery.
INSCRIPTION: Signed with initials *H.W.*, lower right.
PROVENANCE: Presented by Harold Wallis to Birmingham Museum and Art Gallery in 1918, acquisition no. 1918P16.
LITERATURE: Birmingham Museum and Art Gallery, *Catalogue of the Permanent Collection of Drawings*, 1939, p.415, no. 16'18.

This may well be another sketch that Wallis made at Burnham.

Cat. 85. *Landscape study with Trees*
*c.*1870s; charcoal on off-white paper; 41 x 56.8 cm (16 1/8 x 22 1/4 in.) - sight
Private collection, Diane Johnson, San Francisco. PROVENANCE: Wallis's studio and then by descent from the artist to his son Harold Wallis, then to his daughter-in-law Mary Wallis (née Mary Elizabeth Aymes), then her great-niece Vera Whiting; given to Diane Johnson, *c.*1973.

This is another of the many landscapes studies Wallis made. The authors are unable to ascertain whether it is one of the drawings he exhibited at venues such as Colnaghi's.

The location is probably in Italy, the home of upright Cypress trees, which are likely the tall trees in the background. This variety of tree is not native to England, and although they were planted in many arboreta, this scene appears to be a natural setting.

Cat. 86. *Study of a Tudor House*
*c.*1870s; grisaille watercolour and black and white chalks on pale grey paper; 57 x 42.5 cm. (22 7/16 x 16 3/4) - sight; private collection.
PROVENANCE: Wallis's studio and then by descent from the artist to his son Harold Wallis, then to his daughter-in-law Mary Wallis (née Mary Elizabeth Aymes), then her great-niece Vera G. Cooper (née Langley; 1910-1989), and thence by direct descent to John Harold Cooper and family; private collection.

Cat. 87. *Assunta*
1871; ?oil on canvas; dimensions unknown; whereabouts unknown.
EXHIBITIONS: New British Institution, Second Spring Exhibition of Cabinet Pictures, 1871, no. 64.
LITERATURE: *Art Pictorial and Industrial: An Illustrated Magazine*, Vol. 1, 1870-71, p.228; *The Art Journal*, New Series, Vol. X, 1871, p.120; *The Morning Post*, 27 February 1871, p.6; *The Illustrated London News*, vol. 58, 4 March 1871, p.199; *The Daily News*, London, 16 March 1871, p.2; *John Bull*, 18 March 1871, p.186.

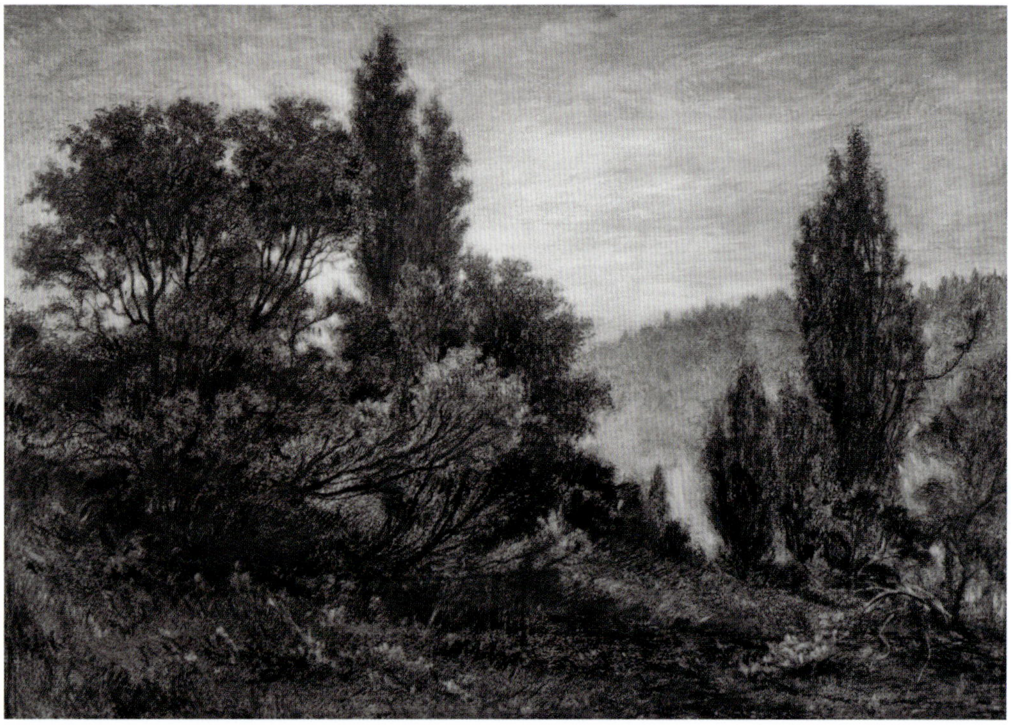

Cat. 85. Image courtesy of Diane Johnson, San Francisco

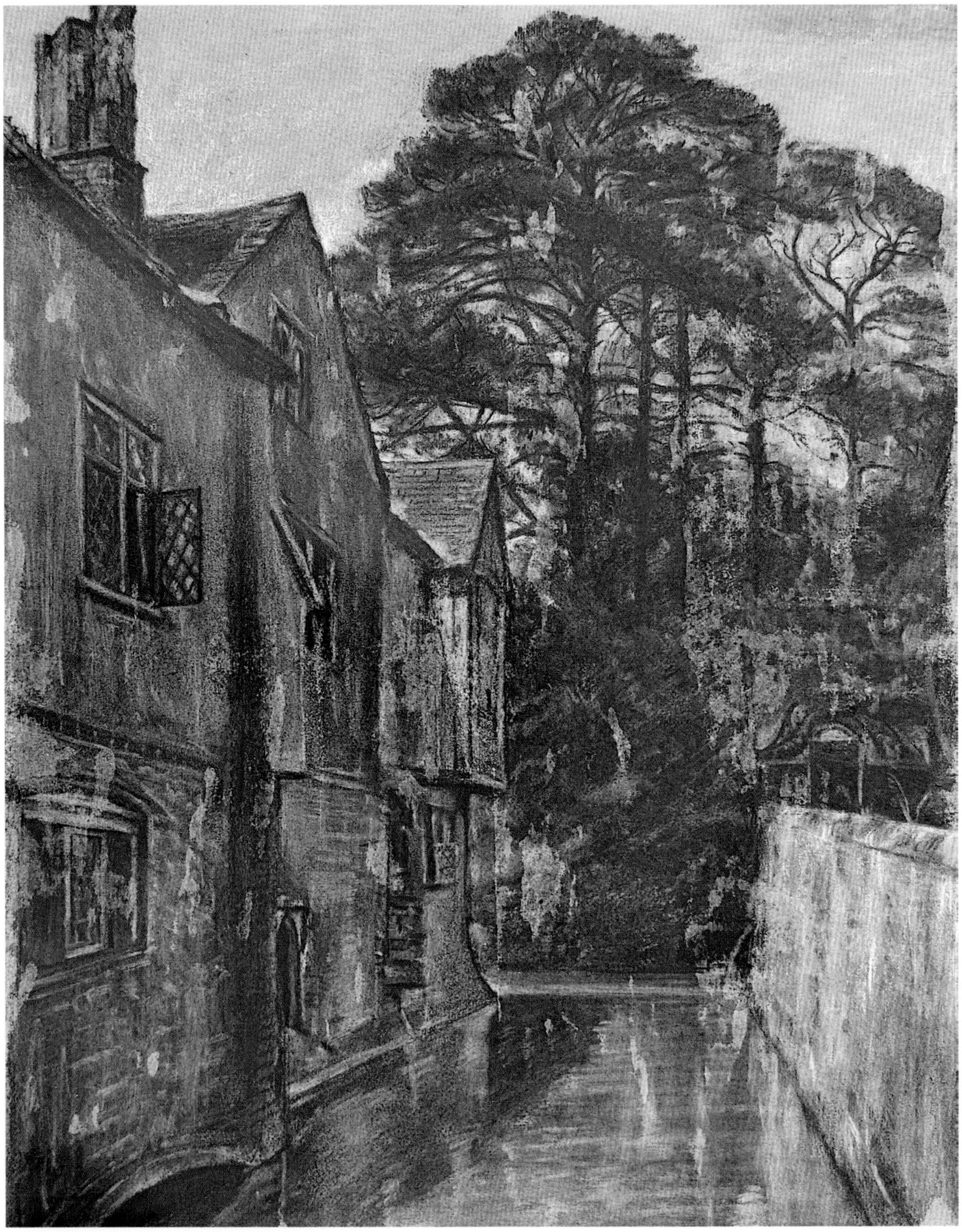

Cat. 86. Image courtesy private collection

The reviewer for *Art Pictorial and Industrial* commented: "H. Wallis sends the profile of a beautiful Italian lady in blue and white, which he calls 'Assunta' (64)." The critic of *The Art Journal* noted: " 'Assunta' (64), H. Wallis, a profile, it may be supposed, of an Italian model, rich enough in mellow brown tints to have been painted from a genuine *contadina*, certainly not imitated from any of those thin and blanched features of those presumed natives of the Campagna of recent importation among us." *The Illustrated London News* stated: "Mr. H. Wallis's small female study 'Assunta' (64) is quite Venetian in colour." *The Daily News* said: "and 64, 'Assunta,' by H. Wallis, has some nice points of colour which are worth notice". The reviewer for *John Bull* called this work "a small but very clever head by Mr. Wallis (64) 'Assunta'." *The Morning Post* called it "a splendid portrait".

Victorian artists such as Frederic Leighton and Val Prinsep made many such studies of the heads of beautiful Italian models. It would be interesting to know if Wallis treated this work in an Aesthetic manner influenced by Venetian Renaissance painting and his Victorian contemporaries.

Cat. 88. ***An Episode from the Life of Shelley***
1871; ?oil on canvas; dimensions unknown; whereabouts unknown.

As a young man Wallis was inclined to rank Shelley as a writer second to only Shakespeare. As early as 1857 Wallis had considered doing a portrait of Shelley, with Pompeii and Vesuvius for a background, but this was never executed. Later, as evidenced from D.G. Rossetti's surviving correspondence with Robert Browning and Henry Wallis, it is clear that Wallis had intended to paint a work with Shelley as the subject. On 8 April 1871, Rossetti wrote to Browning: "I think you have Mrs. Leigh Hunt's original bust of Shelley,[1] have you not? A friend of mine – Henry Wallis, painter of the 'Death of Chatterton' & many other good things – would like much to see it, as he is about to paint a picture from Shelley's life. Might I trouble you for one line saying when it would be convenient for him to call, as I feel sure you would allow him to do so." Browning replied on the 9 April that "Any day, or hour, that may suit Mr. Wallis to call here, will find the Bust ready for his inspection."[2] Rossetti then wrote to Wallis on 10 April telling him this and mentioning that he too had considered painting an episode from Shelley's life: "I don't know if I explained properly where the Shelley incident is to be met with. I found it in Leigh Hunt's 'Byron & his Contemporaries',[3] a book I think never reprinted, but I have no doubt that what relates to Shelley must have been transferred to some other work of Hunt's – probably his Autobiography. I remember I made some rough sketches myself for a picture of it, which I projected calling – 'Percy Bysshe Shelly, Cor. Cordium', followed by the quoted incident." Whether Rossetti's comments discouraged Wallis from carrying his own painting further is uncertain, but the only work known to survive is Wallis's drawing of Ant. Leisman, strongly resembling Shelley, which was found on the fly-leaf of a book of Shelley's poems that descended in the Wallis family.[4] Shelly was an obvious subject for Wallis because Shelley had been a great friend of Thomas Love Peacock and Shelley's work was greatly admired by the Pre-Raphaelites.[5]

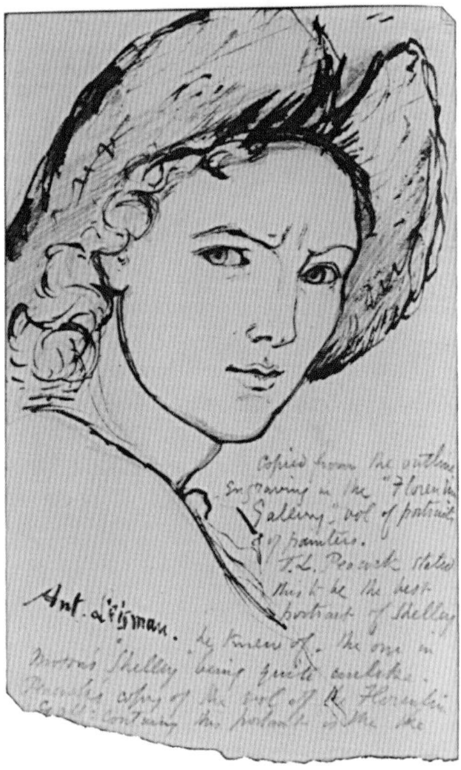

Wallis's sketch of a portrait of Ant. Leisman, said by T.L. Peacock to be a remarkable likeness of Shelley, superior to any portrait of Shelley himself. Image from D. Johnson, *Lesser Lives*, illus. no. 10. Image courtesy of Diane Johnson, San Francisco

Cat. 89. *Barnard's Inn, Holborn, in the 17th Century*
1872; oil on panel; 69.9 x 54.6 cm. (27½ x 21½ in.); whereabouts unknown.
PROVENANCE: Joseph Dixon,[1] of St John's Gardens, Ladbroke Grove, London; his estate sale Christie's, 18 March 1911, lot 43, bought by the dealer William Walker Sampson of W.W. Sampson & Sons, London for £17 17s.
EXHIBITIONS: Dudley Gallery, *Cabinet Pictures in Oil*, 1872, no. 269, asking price £100.
LITERATURE: *The Examiner*, 2 November 1872, p.1079; *The Graphic*, 2 November 1872, p.419; *The Athenaeum*, No. 2349, 2 November 1872, p.569; *The Illustrated London News*, 2 November 1872, p.419; *The Times*, 11 November 1872, p.4.

The reviewer of *The Times* remarked: "Mr. H. Wallis, in his 'Barnard's Inn' (269), rather challenges than sustains comparison with De Hooghe. The colouring and lines of the quaint old quadrangle may well have suggested a treatment in the manner of the great Pieter; but the comparison is a terrible one to provoke. Nor is it better borne by the buildings than by the figures of the tavern maiden in black, bearing the ale-glass and tray, and the two cloaked cavaliers in the background." The critic of *The Examiner* commented: "Mr. H. Wallis's 'Barnard's Inn, Holborn, in the Seventeenth Century' (269) is delightfully cool in its light and shade." *The Graphic* declared: " 'Barnard's Inn, Holborn, in the 17th century', by Mr. H. Wallis, is an interesting picture, richly and heedfully painted, with very happy management of light and atmosphere."

F.G. Stephens in *The Athenaeum* professed his admiration for this work: "Mr. H. Wallis's *Barnard's Inn, Holborn, in the Seventeenth Century* (269) is a picture which by its brilliancy, depth of colour, and fidelity worthily recalls De Hooghe's Dutch buildings. The little quadrangle of the old inn, and its ancient chapel, with a high-pitched, red-tiled roof, and on the ridge the louvre retaining Gothic forms, are admirably dealt with. The effect is at once powerful and broad, with the aerial prespective is most fortunately rendered. A buxom lass, clad in black, advances toward us bearing a tall glass, filled with ale, and standing on a tray."

90. Heather
1872; charcoal drawing; dimensions unknown; whereabouts unknown.
EXHIBITIONS: Dudley Gallery, *Exhibition of Works of Art in Black and White*, 1872, no. 130, asking price £20.
LITERATURE: *The Athenaeum*, no. 2333, 13 July 1872, p.56; *The Athenaeum*, No. 2577, 17 March 1877, p.357.

The Athenaeum twice discussed this drawing in the Dudley exhibition of 1872: "In this country Mr. Wallis's noble drawings are well known, and several examples of this mode of art have been seen at the Black and White Exhibition. This process is a highly artistic one, and possesses precious advantages for the skilled draughtsman. It combines some of the characteristics of painting with all those proper to drawing with chalk, great felicity, richness of colour, and unusual freedom. Besides these merits, *'paysage au fusain'*[1] has something which may, for want of a better name, be called pathetic in the sobriety, breadth, and severity of its peculiar subject. Sentiment is not, of course, to be had ready-made by this process, but every one familiar with its results will admit that it lends itself to pathetic touches, and assists in their expression." Later F.G. Stephens noted: "*Heather* (130), a drawing by Mr. H. Wallis, supplies a perfect contrast to the works to which we have just referred. Being essentially a painter's production, its renders effect and colour in a masculine mode, showing fine and broad understanding of nature."

Cat. 91. *Moorland Oaks*
*c.*1872; charcoal drawing; dimensions unknown; whereabouts unknown.
EXHIBITIONS: Dudley Gallery, *Exhibition of Works of Art in Black and White*, 1872, no. 143, asking price £20.
LITERATURE: *The Illustrated London News*, 29 June 1872, p.631; *The Athenaeum*, no. 2333, 13 July 1872, p.56.

F.G. Stephens noted: "See likewise Mr. Wallis's grand *Moorland Oaks* (143)." *The Illustrated London News* commented on: "charcoal studies of trees, &c, by H. Wallis". One suspects that this drawing could have been handled in a similar fashion to Wallis's Burnham Beeches [Cat. 83] although this drawing could possibly be the drawing now at the Tate Britain [Cat. 102]

Cat. 92. *A Moorland Stream*
*c.*1872; ?charcoal drawing; dimensions unknown; whereabouts unknown.
EXHIBITIONS: Dudley Gallery, *Exhibition of Works of Art in Black and White*, 1872, no. 335, asking price £20.

This drawing likely was executed in charcoal on the same visit as *Moorland Oaks*.

Cat. 93. *England and Italy* –a pair (attributed)
Early to mid-1870s; oil on panel; 27.9 x 22.8 cm (11 x 9 in.) each; whereabouts unknown.
PROVENANCE: Messrs. Fores, publishers, 41 Piccadilly, London; their sale Christie's, 27 June 1904, lot 108, bought in at £2 12s 6d.

There is no information about this pair of works beyond what is given in the Christie's catalogue. The artist is listed as "H. Wallis" so it cannot be certain that these are by *Henry* Wallis. The fact that the subjects are England and Italy suggest they could be by him, however. It is also known that the Messrs. Fores print publishing firm owned other works by Wallis, which strengthens the attribution to him. Whether the firm used these works to make reproductive prints is unknown, but it is likely. As the works are oil paintings and not watercolours, and because Henry was frequently visiting Italy in the early to mid-1870s, the authors of this book have tentatively dated them to this period, although he visited Italy both prior to and after this time. It is unknown whether these were landscape paintings or whether they could have been allegorical works. It is also possible that these could be Cat. nos. 55 and 56 being sold under different titles.

Cat. 94. *Maestro Sebastiano Guccato, Mosaic Worker, Titian's First Master*
1873; oil on ?canvas; dimensions unknown; whereabouts unknown.
EXHIBITIONS: Dudley Gallery, *Cabinet Pictures in Oil*, 1873, no. 355, asking price £105; Royal Hibernian Academy, Dublin, 1875, no. 181, asking price £100.
LITERATURE: *The Leeds Mercury*, 28 October 1873, p.7; *The Illustrated London News*, Vol. 63, 1 November 1873, p.418; *The Graphic*, 1 November 1873, p.418; *The Athenaeum*, No. 2401, 1 November 1873, p.567; *The Times*, 17 November 1873, p.4; *Bell's Life in London and Sporting Chronicle*, 29 November 1873, p.2.

The Illustrated London News noted: "Mr. H. Wallis is less happy in colour than usual (although the subject seems especially to demand that quality) in 'Maestro Sebastiano Guccato, Mosaic Worker, Titian's First Master' (355)." The critic for *The Graphic* observed: "Mr. Wallis is represented by an animated study of 'Titian's First Master - Maestro Sebastiano Guccato, Mosaic Worker,' an imposing processional figure robed in dull crimson, preceded by a page in striped hose bearing sunflowers." The reviewer for *Bell's Life in London* commented: "Mr. Wallis's representation of 'Maestro Sebastiano Guccato, Mosaic Worker, Titian's First Master' (355) is a solid quaint impersonation. A good contrast is afforded between the dignity of the maestro and the

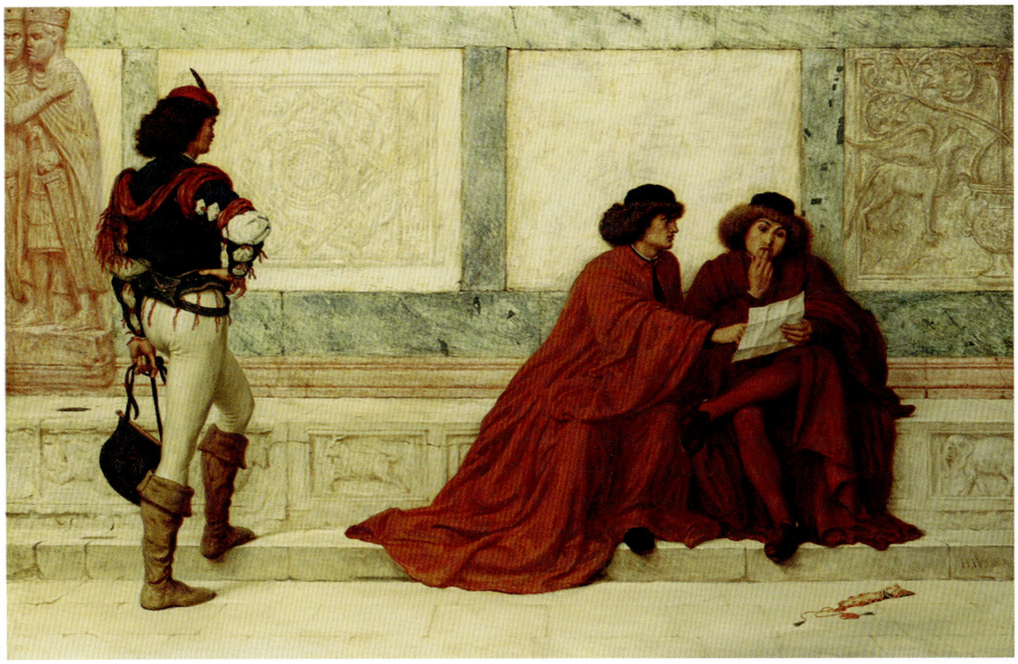

Cat. 95. Image by permission of Christie's Images/Bridgeman Images

boy who precedes him, bearing a bunch of sunflowers." *The Times* reviewer certainly liked this work: "Near this picture hangs one of the substantially good pictures of the Exhibition (355) by Henry Wallis – Maestro Sebastiano Zuccato, the mosaic painter, on the authority of Dolco [?Lodovico Dolce], the first master from whose hands Titian passed to the instructions of Gian Bellini. Mr. Wallis has painted the portly painter in his red gown of office, preceded by his page, carrying a big spray of sunflower, presumably for the purpose of some design in hand."

Cat. 95. ***A Despatch from Trebizond*** **(also: *The Announcement of War*)**
1873; oil on canvas; 91.5 x 137.8 cm (36 x 54¼ in.); private collection.
INSCRIPTIONS: Signed with initials *HW* and inscribed *Henry Wallis/9 Red Lion square/W.C.* on a label at the back.
PROVENANCE: J. S. Virtue of Virtue & Co. Ltd.; Virtue & Co. sale, Christie's, 14 March 1881, lot 245, bought by Graves, likely the art dealer Henry Graves of Henry Graves & Co.; Robert Kirkman Hodgson J.P., D.L. (1850-1924), 13 Eaton Terrace, S.W.1, London; his estate sale Christie's, London, 21 November 1924, lot 32, (entitled *The Announcement of War*), purchased by the dealer William Walker Sampson of W.W. Sampson & Sons, London, for £5 5s; anonymous sale Christie's, London, 1 November 1990, lot 296, sold for £17,600; private collection.
EXHIBITIONS: Royal Academy, 1873, no. 977.
LITERATURE: *The Athenaeum*, no. 2370, 29 March 1873, p.414; *The Athenaeum*, no. 2375, 3 May 1873, p.569; *Illustrated London News*, 17 May 1873, p.470; *The Times*, 19 May 1873, p.6; *The Graphic*, 23 May 1874, p.502; *The Athenaeum*, no. 2378, 24 May 1873, p.667; *The Tablet*, 14 June 1873, p.7; *The Art Journal*, vol. XIX, 1880, p.140, illus.; Hawksley, Lucinda: *Essential Pre-Raphaelites*, 1999, pp.186-187; Lessens, Ronald, 'Henry Wallis (1830-1916), a neglected Pre-Raphaelite', *The British Art Journal*, vol. XV, No. 1, 2014, pp.52 & 54.

When the picture was exhibited at the Royal Academy in 1873 the R.A. catalogue contained the following quotation: "Some news is come that turns their countenances – Shakespeare" (*Coriolanus*, Act IV, Scene VI). The painting was highly praised by F.G. Stephens in his reviews for *The Athenaeum*. In the review of 29 March 1873, he stated: "Mr. Henry Wallis has just finished a picture, entitled 'A Despatch from Trebizond', representing the lower part of the façade of St. Mark's, with its coating of rich marbles and quaint carvings, and the bench of white marble, which forms part of the building on the south side of the western front. On this bench sit two Venetian merchants of high degree, both clad in the red and flowing garments of their class and nation. One of them holds a letter, and reads it with an expression of extreme dismay, while his partner, equally interested, leans over him, and traces with a finger the lines announcing ill-luck to the firm, thus calling attention to the weight of the misfortune which has befallen them. Hardly out of earshot stands the tall, dark, lithe, reckless-looking courier, who has been the messenger of evil tidings, attired in white breeches, fitting him like a second skin, a dark blue jerkin, slashed and laced so as to show his white shirt; his bushy black hair is crowned by a dark red mortier cap. With one foot place down the step of the marble bench, one hand clenched against his hip, and his eyes cast down, the man awaits the answer he must carry over sea and land, from Venice to Trebizond." On 24 May 1873, Stephens wrote: "Mr. Wallis's *Despatch from Trebizond* (977), we have already mentioned, and now commend it to general attention. It is one of the most brilliant, original, and artistic pictures in the Exhibition. Two merchants of Venice are seated on a bench at St. Mark's, reading a letter which has been delivered to them by a courier, who stands before us, waiting to take the answer from Venice to Trebizond, or whatever they may require. The merchants wear red robes and black caps, and their hair is 'frizzed' in the mode of the 16th century in Italy. The 'colour' produced by these costumes, and the lucid surfaces of the wall – to which the figures are opposed, – the marble being of diverse tints, are enriched with sculptures, – is superb."

The critic for *The Times* also expressed his admiration: "In the same room hangs one of the most complete pictures of the year, Mr. H. Wallis's 'Despatch from Trebizond' (977), two Venetian merchant princes in costumes of the 14th century, of that red colour which has been christened from the city, on a seat with a dado of richly coloured marbles inlaid with old Lombard carvings, anxiously reading a letter of moment touching some venture of craft or cargo which has been brought to them by a sinewy and sun-burnt courier. The execution of the details, both of figures and architecture, in this design is among the completest in this year's Exhibition."

John Christian in his entry in the Christie's catalogue for 2 November 1990 noted: "What the picture does reflect is Wallis's interest in St Mark's Venice, an interest which would lead him to serve as Honorary Secretary to the committee for the Preservation of St Mark's from 1879 to 1882. The sweeping restoration of the Cathedral proposed and to some extent carried out at this time aroused great opposition in England. The Society for the Protection of Ancient Buildings, launched by William Morris in 1877, protested vigorously, and Burne-Jones was inspired to make the only public speech of his life (at Oxford in 1879). The figure of the courier is clearly inspired by Carpaccio, an artist who was receiving increasing attention in England at this time. G.F. Watts was struck by his work in 1853, Burne-Jones copied it extensively in 1859, and Ruskin 'discovered' Carpaccio in 1869. The picture's background is taken from the south façade of St. Mark's, where the wall is encrusted with Byzantine carvings looted from Constantinople in the 13th century, including the well-known porphyry group of Diocletian and his colleagues. Wallis's rendering of all this is remarkably accurate."

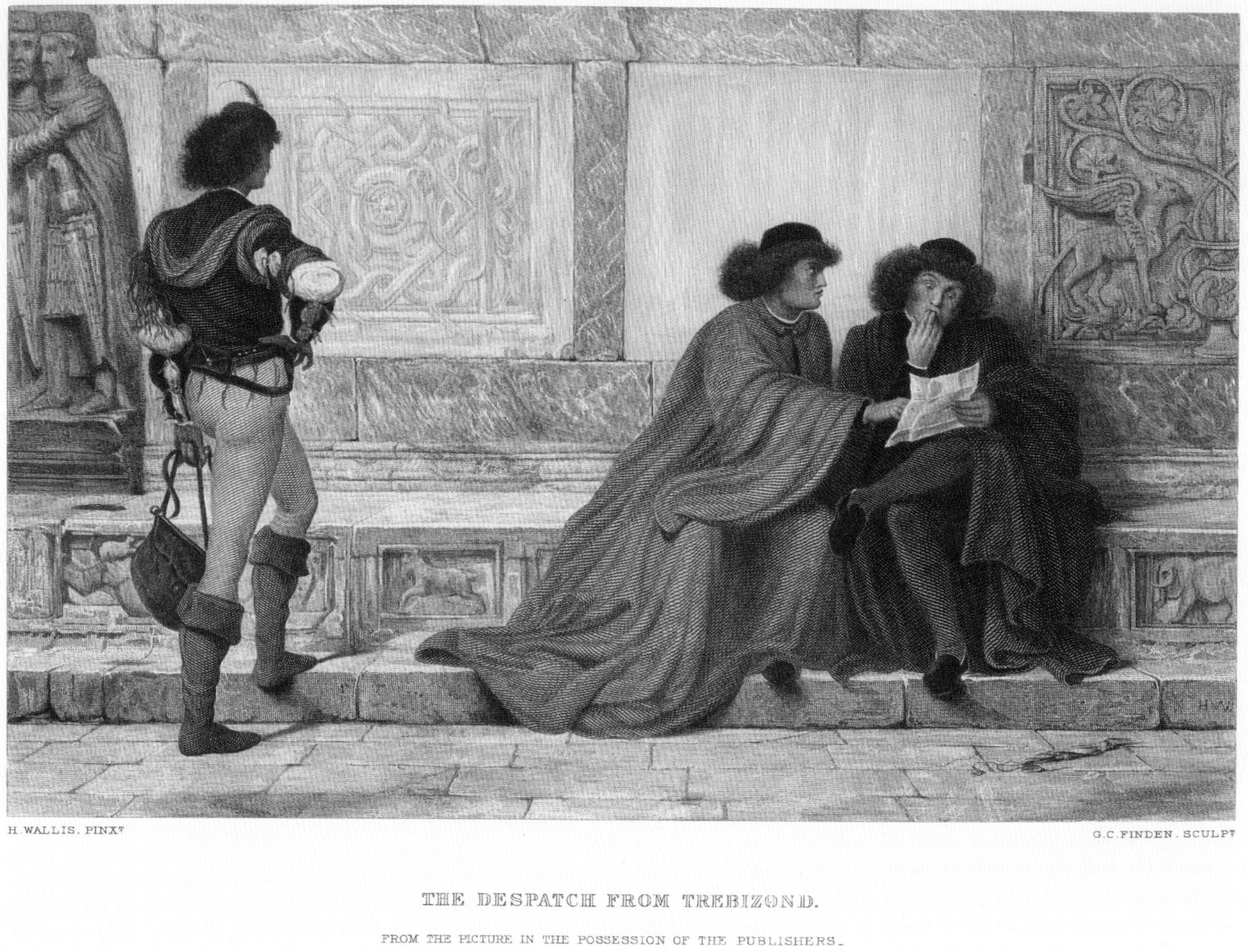

Cat. 95a. Image courtesy of Dennis Lanigan collection

Cat. 95a. ***A Despatch from Trebizond***
1880; steel engraving; image size: 16.9 x 25.2 cm (6⅝ x 9⅞ in.); sheet size: 22.8 x 29.1 cm (9 x 11$\frac{7}{16}$ in.); Dr Dennis T. Lanigan, Saskatoon, Canada.
Annotations: (lettering below image) "HENRY WALLIS, PINX.^{T} / THE DESPATCH FROM TREBIZOND. FROM THE PICTURE IN THE POSSESSION OF THE PUBLISHERS. / G. C. FINDEN. SCULPT^{T} "
Literature: *The Art Journal*, vol. VI, New Series, 1880, p.153; *The Athenaeum*, No. 2729, 14 February 1880, p.222; Rowlands, Walter, *Among the Great Masters of Literature*, 1900, p.151.

This print was engraved by George C. Finden and published by Virtue & Co. in the *Art Journal* in 1880. The *Art Journal* commented: "During the fifteenth century Trebizond was one of the most important cities of Asia Minor, and though greatly distracted both by internal warfare and the attacks of surrounding enemies, the city was regarded as the centre of the extensive commerce carried on between merchants of the Venetian and Genoese Republics, and the nations bordering the Euxine, or Black Sea. Greatly harassed they frequently were by the precarious condition of the government of the country which, about the year 1461, was surrendered by the brave monarch who fought long and gallantly for its freedom against his powerful adversary, the Sultan of Constantinople. In Mr. Wallis's very striking picture – exhibited at the London Royal Academy in 1873 – he has painted an historical episode of no uncommon occurrence: a messenger from Trebizond is the bearer of intelligence much affecting two Venetian merchants, filling them with surprise and apprehension. One is evidently in great perplexity, but the other points out with eagerness something in the document that he appears to consider may yet give a favourable turn to the tide of affairs. The men of business, who may also be senators in the famous city of Venice, are seated against the wall of the Bapistry of St. Mark's, an edifice wherein matters both of state and commerce were frequently discussed when the great Italian republics were in the height of their glory. The rich mosaics on the walls, the sculptures on the stone seats, and the well-known porphyry group of armed figures – generally accepted as Crusaders – greatly enrich a composition remarkably original both in conception and treatment."

The Athenaeum had these comments on the print: "Mr. George C. Finden has engraved a plate in the line manner after Mr. Wallis's 'A Messenger from Trebizonde [*sic*],' the capital picture which was at the Royal Academy a few years ago… Our business is now with the print, which is a noteworthy instance of successful use of 'the line manner,' although works of that kind are rare. There is a slight want of clearness in some of the darker parts of the reader's costume, but the tone, colour rendering, and reproduction of light are very good indeed – in fact, could hardly be better than they are. The design has been treated with commendable spirit and great success. Every one will admire the disposition of the chiaroscuro, the expressions of the faces and attitudes, and the 'colour' of the many-tinted and sculptured marbles of the background, here semi-transparent white, there grey, rose, red, and rich blue."

Cat. 96. ***Announcement of Peace***
*c.*1874; oil on canvas; 74.9 x 124.5 cm (29½ x 49 in.); whereabouts unknown.
PROVENANCE: Robert Kirkman Hodgson J.P., D.L, 13 Eaton Terrace, S.W.1, London; his estate sale Christie's, 21 November 1924, lot 33, bought by Amar for £9 9s.

This was obviously intended as the companion piece to *Announcement of War* (*A Despatch from Trebizond*) [Cat. 95], and both were at one time in the collection of R.K. Hodgson. This work does not appear to have been exhibited, as no contemporary description of it can be found; unless it was exhibited under another name. *A Despatch from Trebizond* was sold under an incorrect title, so it is certainly possible that this work was as well.

Cat. 97. ***Found at Naxos (Presenting a Sculpture)***
1874; oil on canvas; 31 x 47 cm (12 x 19 in.); private collection.
INSCRIPTIONS: Signed with initials *HW*, lower right.
PROVENANCE: James Sprent Virtue of Oatlands Park, Surrey;[1] his sale Christie's, March 1, 1879, lot 156, purchased by Thomas W. Waller, 10 Westbourne St., Hyde Park, London W., for £78; his estate sale, Christie's, 10 June 1910, lot 140, bought by C. Davis, likely Charles Davis of Frederick Davis & Son, art dealers, for £31 10s; anonymous sale Bukowskis, Stockholm, 30 November 2004, lot 267, sold for €995.
EXHIBITIONS: Royal Academy, 1874, no. 572; Bradford, *Fine Art and Industrial Exhibition*, 1882, no. 52, lent by T. W. Waller.
LITERATURE: Monkhouse, William Cosmo: *At the Royal Academy. A companion to the oil pictures in the exhibition of 1874*, London, 1874, p.29; *The Art Journal*, New Series, Vol. XIII, 1874, p.226; *Manchester Times*, 3 January 1874, p.8; *The Athenaeum*, No. 2428, 9 May 1874, p.638; *The Illustrated London News*, vol. 64, 16 May 1874, p.470; *The Graphic*, 23 May 1874, p.502; *The Times*, 26 May 1874, *The Athenaeum*, No. 2431, 30 May 1874, p.740; *The Spectator*, 30 May 1874, p.693; p.6; *Pall Mall Gazette*, 2 June 1874, p.11; Rowlands, Walter, *Among the Great Masters of Literature*, 1900, p.151.

In his Royal Academy review for 1874, Wallis's friend W. Cosmo Monkhouse described the work as follows: "Two rich old Venetians, gorgeous in crimson robes, are seated on a marble bench, scanning, with critical eyes, an antique bronze which has come from Naxos, and is being held up for their inspection, by a dark-haired, black-skinned youth, who is expatiating on its exquisite qualities. If that youth were a true critic, and had this picture to sell, his face might properly wear some expression not much less ecstatic, as he pointed out its many claims on our admiration as a pure work of art."

F.G. Stephens also praised this work in his review in *The Athenaeum*: "One of the by no means numerous designs which are marked by spontaneity of conception, and by their fine execution justify their existence, is Mr. Wallis's *From Naxos* (572), showing the marble wall of St. Mark's, at Venice, with the bench at its foot, and the two elderly merchants, in red robes and black caps, whom we saw last year seated in the same place, and in the receipt of 'News from Trebizond'; but in the interval between the two pictures more than a year has passed over the head of the worthies. Their hair has whitened, and, although still hale, their forms are less erect than before. They still wear red robes, but of a crimson tint, which does not become them quite so well as the red proper. Nevertheless, they remain fine old fellows, and a new phase of life has come on them. A man does not stand cap in hand, but kneels before them this time; for there is no need to return with a message to the old merchants' correspondents at Trebizond; all that is now over: the great carrack has, it may be, gone to pieces, or made their fortunes by its happy return. It seems more likely that the latter is the case, for what this kneeling man offers is a rarity of considerable price, and, apparently, not before known to the signors, being nothing less than Cupid, an antique relic, dug up, as it seems, in the Isle of Naxos, where our friends had dealings of yore, but for raisins and such like goods. They look at the relic with great interest and some hesitation. Here is Cupid at last, fresh as ever, though made in lustrous, dark, gold-hued bronze, and just rescued from the basket of that jovial Levantine sailor, himself a model of his kind, and one of the best designed figures Mr. Wallis has produced. We enjoy heartily the brilliant lighting, the rich colour, the rare spirit of this picture; but it suffers from tints, both of the gowns and the marble wall being a little forced, as if the artist had used gas-light too freely while he painted them, or, in an obedience to an afterthought, changed the gowns from red proper to crimson." Stephens was later forced to retract part of his comments on this work in his second *Athenaeum* review of the Royal Academy exhibition: "We come next to Mr. Wallis's picture. We have already described it but we owe him an apology for our error in our account of it. The figure in the hands of the Levantine is not a Cupid, now presented to the merchants, but a nymph, whirling with a thyrsus."[2]

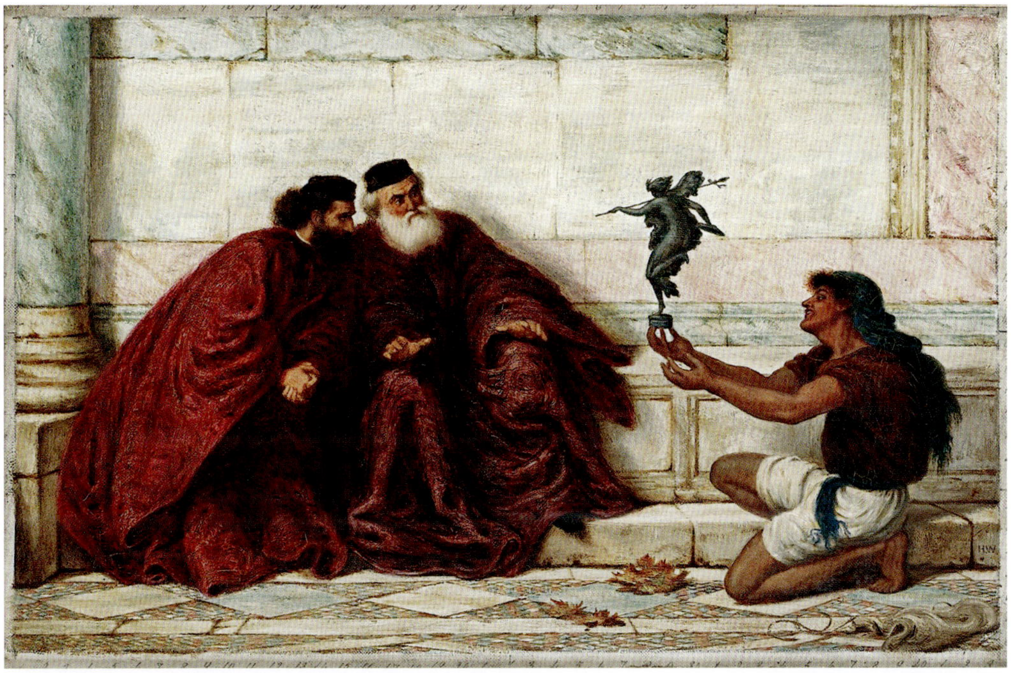

Cat. 97. Image courtesy of Bukowskis Auction House, Stockholm

Cat. 97a. ***Study of Two Venetian Senators seated on a Stone Bench***
*c.*1873; black and white chalk on grey paper; 47.1 x 60.5 cm. (18½ x 23¹³⁄₁₆ in.); Birmingham Museum and Art Gallery.
INSCRIPTIONS: Signed with initials *HW*, lower right.
PROVENANCE: Presented by Harold Wallis to Birmingham Museum and Art Gallery in 1918, accession no. 1918P1.
EXHIBITIONS: The Arts Council, *Pre-Raphaelite Drawings and Watercolours*, 1953, no. 76.
LITERATURE: Birmingham Museum and Art Gallery, *Catalogue of the Permanent Collection of Drawings*, 1939, p.414, no. 1'18; Lessens, Ronald, 'Henry Wallis (1830-1916), a neglected Pre-Raphaelite', *The British Art Journal*, vol. XV, No. 1, Autumn 2014, p.54.

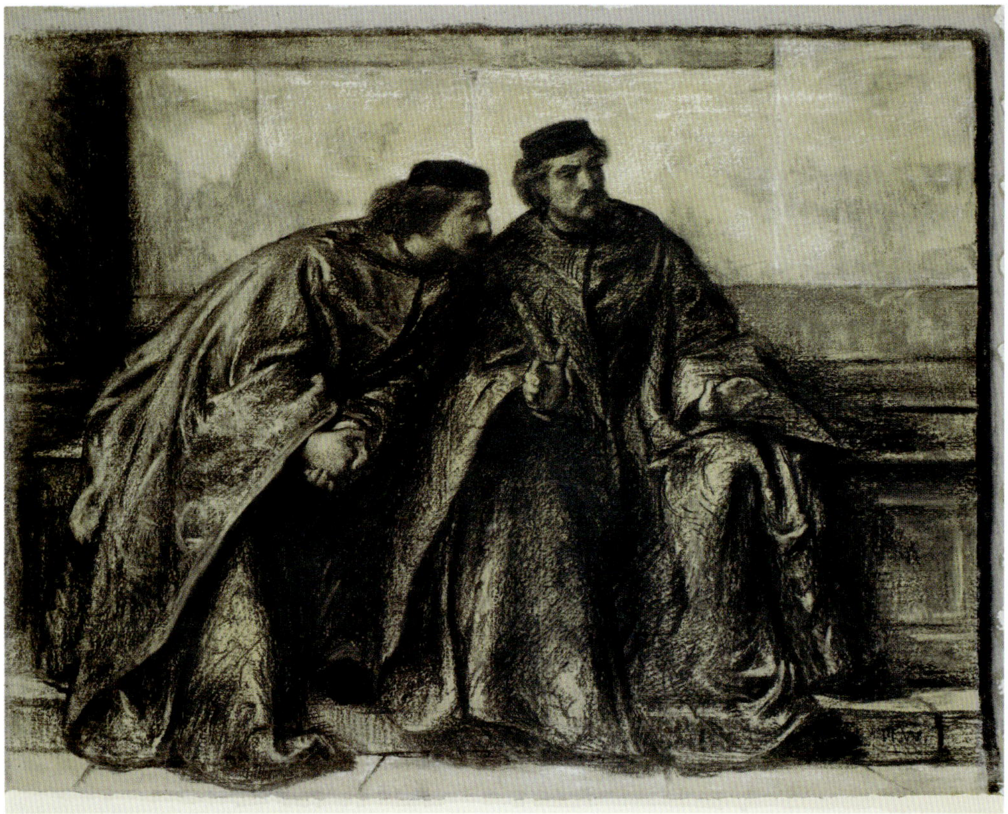

Cat. 97a. Image by permission of Birmingham Museums Trust

While these two figures are in a similar attitude as the figures in a previous painting, *A Despatch from Trebizond*, which shows two men seated on a marble bench in the Piazzetta near St Mark's, the positioning of these two figures is much closer to *Found at Naxos*. It is therefore more likely to be a preparatory drawing for this second painting.

Cat. 97b. *Found at Naxos (after Henry Wallis)*
1875; steel engraving by P. Lightfoot;
image size: 16.3 x 25.5 cm (6⅜ x 10 in.);
sheet size: 21.9 x 29.1 cm (8⅝ x 11⁷⁄₁₆ in.);
Dr Dennis T. Lanigan, Saskatoon, Canada.
ANNOTATION: (lettering below image) "HENRY WALLIS, PINX.T / "FOUND AT NAXOS" / P. LIGHTFOOT, SCULPT.T"
LITERATURE: *The Art Journal*, Vol. 4, "Our Steel Engravings: 'Found at Naxos'," 1878, p.282; *The Athenaeum*, No. 2622, 26 January 1878, p.111; *Leeds Mercury*, 4 September 1878, p.6.

The Art Journal commentary on this engraving by P. Lightfoot states: "This picture was exhibited at the London Royal Academy in 1874. Why Mr. Wallis intimated that the little bronze figure which gives the work its title was 'found at Naxos' we do not quite see. There were three places of this name known to the ancients, but neither of them appears to have been celebrated for artistic productions. The most famous of the three was an island, one of the large Cyclades in the Ægean Sea, about half-way between the coast of Greece and Asia Minor. It was taken by the Athenians in the time of Pisistratus,[1] about five hundred years before the Christian era, and subsequently fell under the dominion of the Venetians, who built the castle of Naxia, the chief town of the island, and made it the residence of their dukes. The principal deity of Naxos was Bacchus, in whose honour a temple was erected there, it being, as stated by some ancient writers, the place where he was educated, and held in much honour. The artist has associated his picture with Venetian history. A sailor of that country presents a small bronze, which is assumed to have been 'found at Naxos'— the title Mr. Wallis gave to the composition—to the Venetian noblemen, who are examining the 'antique' with wonder and admiration. Whomever the figure may represent, it is clearly not Bacchus, nor can we definitely identify it with any one of the numerous personages in the long catalogue of classic deities. As was said of the picture when it hung on the walls of the Academy, 'Mr. Wallis has not striven to present a picture of deeply significant meaning: he has only embodied certain types of national character in a graceful composition. There is just enough in the idea to create a certain fascination, imitative in some sort of that exercised over the two men attracted by the beauty of the small bronze. The composition is true and unforced. In the attitudes of the two figures there is no exaggeration, and the scheme of colour is a delicate harmony of warm tints carefully distributed over the space of the picture.' It is a picture of simple yet inviting composition."

Cat. 98. *After a Storm in the Woods*
1874; charcoal drawing; dimensions unknown, whereabouts unknown.
EXHIBITIONS: Dudley Gallery, *Exhibition of Works in Black and White*, 1874, no. 188.
LITERATURE: *The Tablet*, 13 June 1874, p.24; *The Times*, 23 June 1874, p.4; *The Athenaeum*, No. 2435, 27 June 1874, p.867.

This sketch appears closely related to another drawing, *After the Storm*, [Cat. 71] that Wallis exhibited at the Royal Academy in 1870. It is even possible it is the same work, either renamed, or perhaps reworked

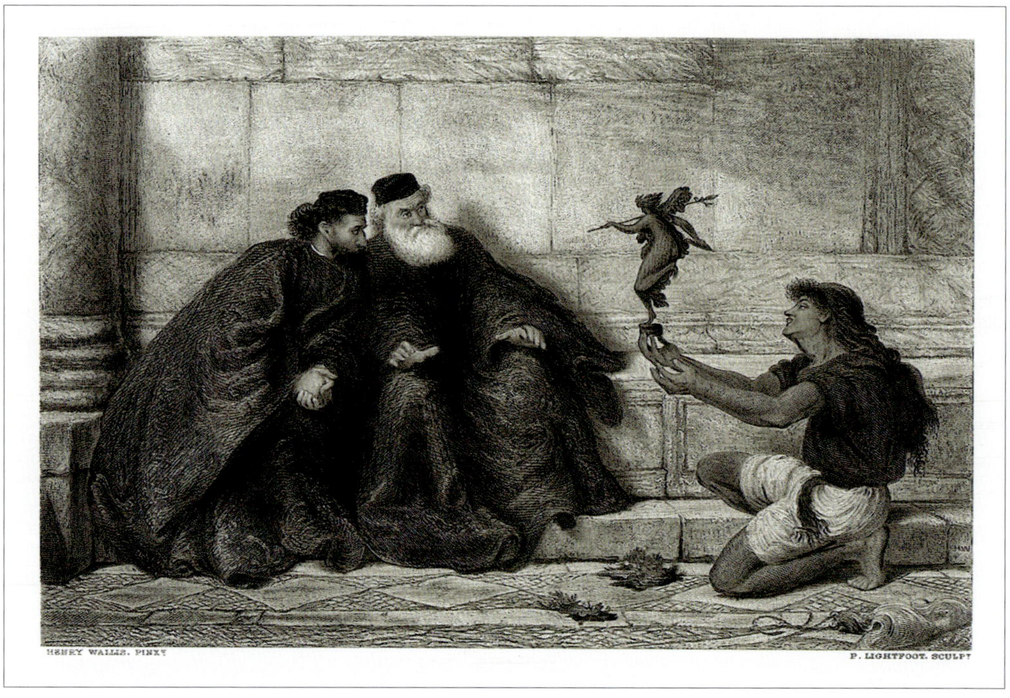

Cat. 97b. Image courtesy of Dennis Lanigan collection

slightly after its first exhibition. Cat. 145, *A Study*, may be another related work.

F.G. Stephens in *The Athenaeum* in 1874 remarks: "Mr. H. Wallis's *After a Storm in the Woods* (188), a glade, with trees lying prostrate in all their length, is grand in sentiment and style, two qualities rare in landscape. It is a fine design in every sense beautifully drawn." The critic for *The Times* said: "Among the charcoal studies in landscape or sepia there is none more comprehensive than Mr. H. Wallis's grand study for a picture 'After a Storm in the Wood' (188)."

Cat. 99. *Fugitives from Constantinople, 1453*
1875; ?oil on canvas; dimensions unknown; whereabouts unknown.
Exhibitions: Royal Academy, 1875, no. 386.
Literature: *The Athenaeum*, No. 2479, 1 May 1875, p.590; *The Bradford Observer*, 1 May 1875, p.7; *The Examiner*, 1 May 1875, p.501; *John Bull*, 8 May 1875, p.314; *The Illustrated London News*, 15 May 1875, p.470; *The Academy*, Vol. 7, 15 May 1875, p.513; *The Architect*, Vol. 13, 22 May 1875, p.300; *The Architect*, Vol. 13, 29 May 1875, p.314; *The Athenaeum*, No. 2484, 5 June 1875, p.756; *Harper's Weekly*, 18 September 1875, p.734, p.757; Blackburn, Henry: *Academy Notes*, 1875, p.29; *The British Almanac*, 1876, p.187; Lessens, Ronald, 'Henry Wallis (1830-1916), a neglected Pre-Raphaelite', *The British Art Journal*, vol. XV, No. 1, Autumn 2014, p.52.

The fall of Constantinople and the Byzantine Empire to the invading Turkish army of the Ottoman Empire led by Sultan Mehmed II occurred on 29 May, 1453. Many Greeks left the city, either prior to or during the siege, and fled to Italy, particularly Venice. The arrival of these intellectuals from Constantinople helped initiate the Renaissance in Italy.

The Academy critic remarked favourably upon this picture: "Mr. Wallis may always be counted upon for something realised thoughtfully so far as his purpose is concerned, and vigorously as regards execution. His richly-coloured *Fugitives from Constantinople, 1453*, responds to both these demands. It has a meaning, intense look: the eye is satiated with opulence of hue, and the mind led onward and inward. Seated on one of the marble benches of the patriarchal church of St. Mark in Venice, we see a splendidly handsome man, some thirty years of age, with a crutch under one armpit, and a youth of sixteen dozing fitfully beside him. Beyond the arcade of the piazza, a great crowd of Venetians has assembled to witness some sight of public or national moment. The sun blazes; the marbles glow and shine with their magical variety of tint; the immemorial pigeons flutter and settle for a moment; the air rings with cries of acclaim. These two, the Byzantine aliens and refugees, linger apart, in the scene and not of it. Sad memories and poignant thoughts ring them round with a personal solitude."

F.G. Stephens in *The Athenaeum* professed acclaim for the work: "We encounter an original and fine work in Mr. Wallis's *Fugitives from Constantinople* (386), a man with an eager Greek face, wearing black and dark red robes, and seated. He leans his armpit on the head of a stick, and watches a Venetian festival; a boy, his son, reclines on the man's knee. Behind this group are the coloured marbles of the wall of St. Mark's, on the bench of which, the pair are placed. This is a brilliant, rich, strongly-painted, and solid picture, the work of an accomplished painter, who does not care to reproduce the technical ideas of others, nor to repeat himself too often; accordingly this is one of the paintings of the year."

Cat. 99a. *Fugitives from Constantinople, 1453*
1875; wood engraving; image size: 20.3 x 33.9 cm (8 x 13⅜ in.); sheet size: 28.2 x 40.6 cm (11⅛ x 16 in.); Dr Dennis T. Lanigan, Saskatoon, Canada.
Annotations: "FUGITIVES FROM

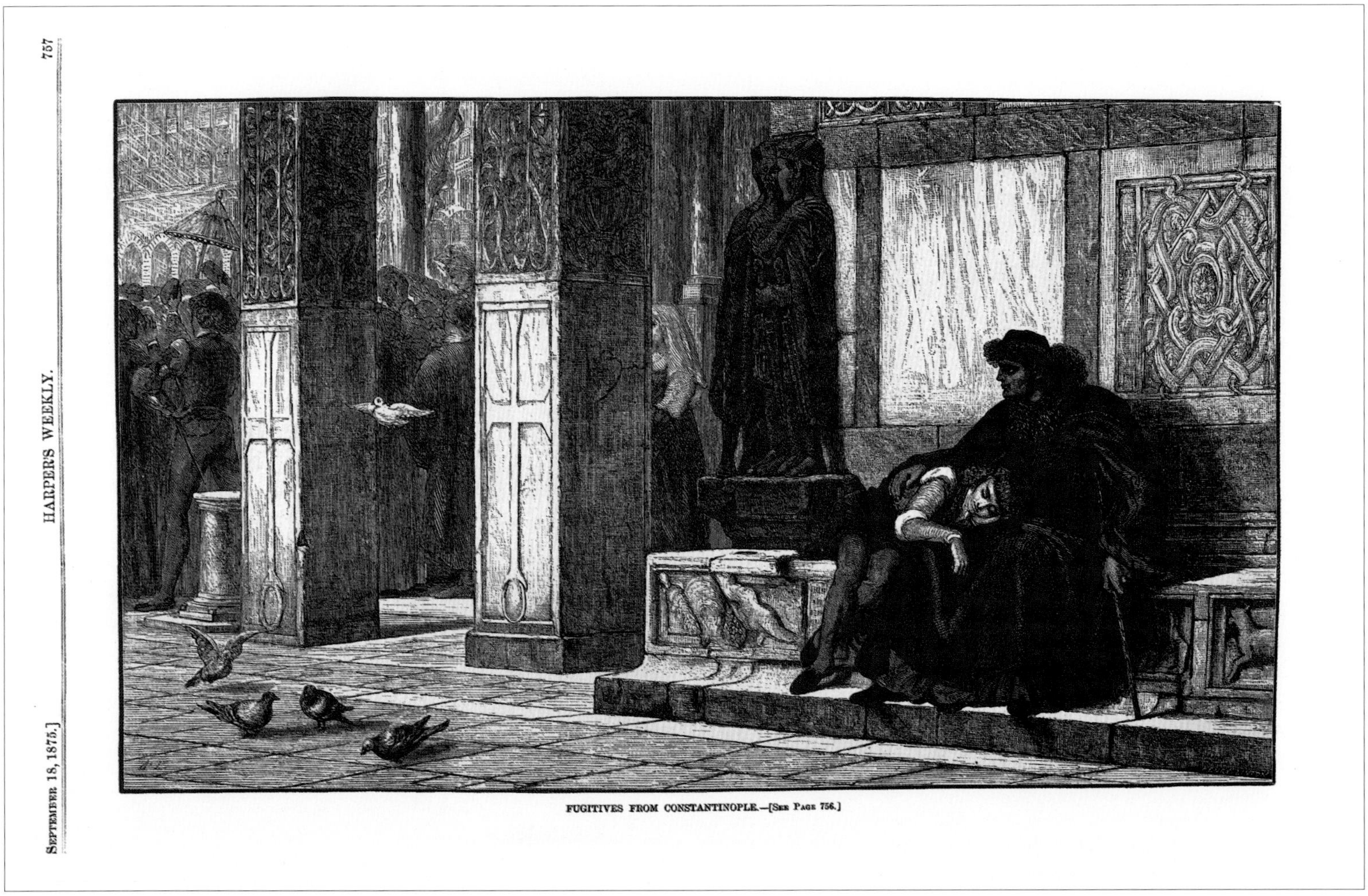

Cat. 99a. Image courtesy of Dennis Lanigan collection

CONSTANTINOPLE. – [SEE PAGE 756]"; signed in the plate *HENRY LINTON*, lower right; initialed A.L., lower left.
LITERATURE: *Harper's Weekly*, 18 September 1875, p.756.

This wood engraving was published in *Harper's Weekly* in 1875 on page 757. The engraver Henry Duff Linton (1815-1899) was an English wood engraver who contributed prints to many English, French and American publications [see: Cat. 100a and Cat. 107a]. Another wood engraving of this work, by A. Gilbert, was reproduced in the French publication *L'Art* in 1875.[1]

Cat. 100. *On the Ponte della Paglia, Going to the Council*
1875; ?oil on canvas; dimensions unknown; whereabouts unknown.
EXHIBITIONS: Royal Academy, 1875, no. 405.
LITERATURE: 'Fine-Art Gossip', *The Athenaeum*, No. 2457, 28 November 1874, p.721; *The Leeds Mercury*, 2 December 1874, p.3; *The Athenaeum*, No. 2479, 1 May 1875, p.590; *The Bradford Observer*, 1 May 1875, p.7; *John Bull*, 8 May 1875, p. 314; *The Academy*, Vol. 7, 15 May 1875, p.513; *The Illustrated London News*, 15 May 1875, p.470; *The Athenaeum*, No. 2484, 5 June 1875, p.756; *The British Almanac*, 1876, p.187; Cook, E.T. & Wedderburn, A. [Eds.], *The Works of John Ruskin, Royal Academy Notes 1856*, Vol. XIV, London, 1904, p.278.

The *Ponte della Paglia* (Bridge of Straw) is a Venetian bridge on the *Rio del Palazzo* from which the Bridge of Sighs can be seen, and opposite to it is the island of San Giorgio Maggiore.

In his *Academy Notes*, Ruskin wrote without enthusiasm of this work: "May be useful to travellers in at least clearly, if not quite accurately, showing the decorative use of the angle sculpture of the drunkenness of Noah on the Ducal Palace; and the Bridge of Sighs is better painted than usual." *The Academy* was somewhat more complimentary: "Mr. Wallis's second contribution is also a Venetian subject – *On the Ponte della Paglia, going to the Council*; slighter in import, but also worthy of his hand. A senator and a procurator of St. Mark are crossing the bridge, close to that angle of the Ducal Palace which is sculpted with the Drunkenness of Noah. The younger man whispers to the elder, with a subtle uninterpretable smile: pleasant and companionable, the two magnates are yet enfolded in statecraft and secrecy closer than in their crimson robes."

The Athenaeum had mentioned this work earlier in 1874 in Fine Art Gossip: "Mr. Wallis has just completed a picture of unusual interest, to be styled, 'A Fellow-Feeling makes us wondrous Kind,' and representing two crimson-robed Venetians, of noble race, walking side by side on a footway near the Bridge of Sighs. At the angle of a house approached by the gentlemen is a sculpture of the legend of Noah and the Vine. The Venetians are in the condition suggested by the carving, and cheerfully, but with unequal steps, keep on their way. We have a view of the canal, spanned by the Ponte dei Suspiri, and the eye ranges beyond the arch between grey walls, balconies of rich forms, parapets, windows, and roofs. The painting is a study in colour, generally representing the 'Despatch from Trebizond' of the artist, and its fellow of last year, but otherwise the motive is a totally different one, and the mode of treatment is distinct from that adopted in those works. Its effect on the spectator is due to the expressions of the faces, which, of course, we cannot describe, and the colour." F.G. Stephens subsequently reviewed the painting when it was shown at the Royal Academy: "By the same artist is *On the Ponte della Paglia - Going to the Council* (405). Two red-robed senators of Venice chatting as

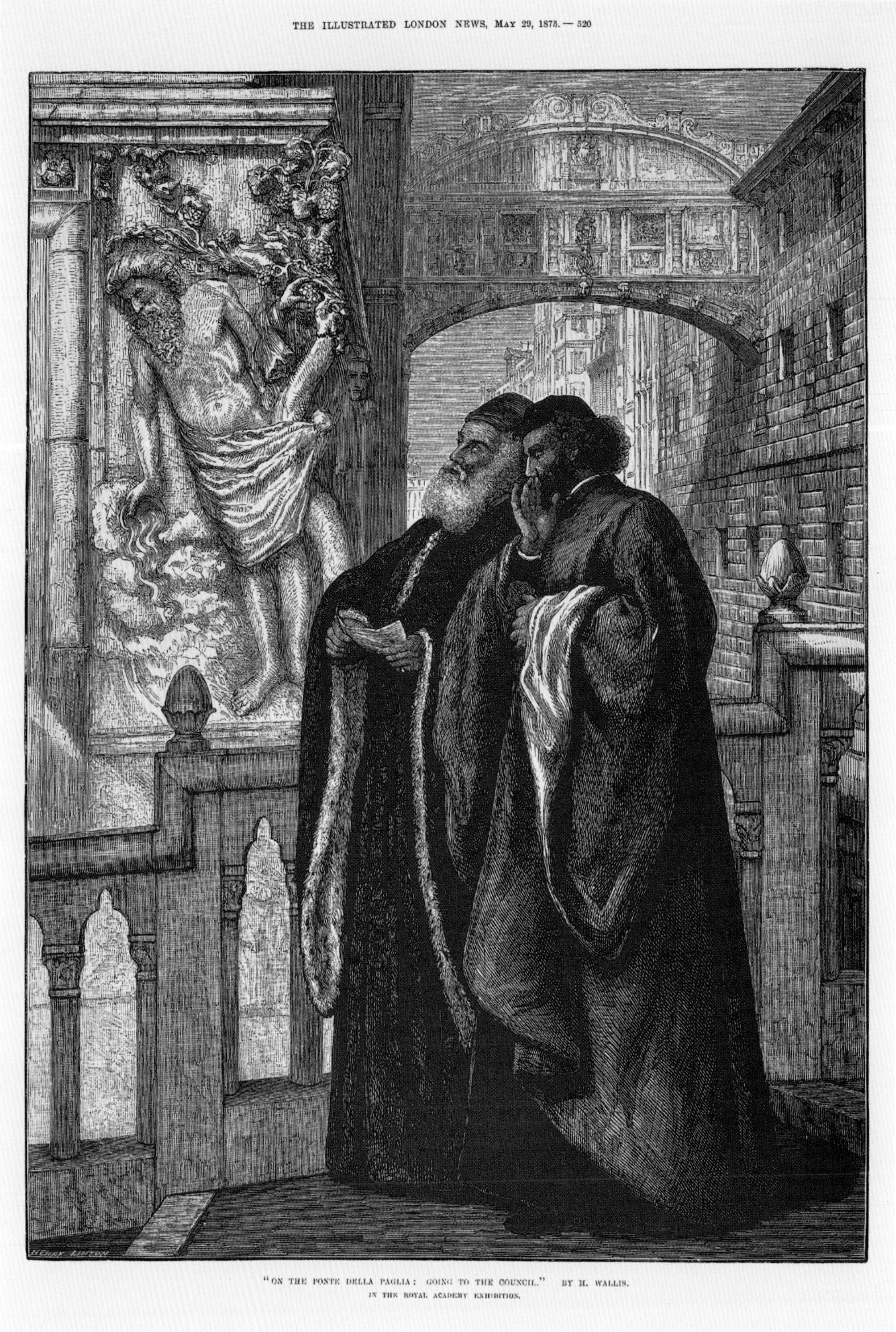

Cat. 100a. Image courtesy of Dennis Lanigan collection

they cross a bridge over the canal, which is likewise spanned by the Bridge of Sighs; there on high, connecting the tall opposed stone walls, is the famous bridge, and it is painted with fine feeling for light, as, indeed, the vista itself appears to be. The figures are capital as to colour, and both relieve on the light-toned walls behind them with unusual force. One senator whispers behind his hand to the other, and smiles craftily and gaily as he does so. The famous sculpture of Noah is at an angle of the building which the men are about to pass."

Cat. 100a. ***On the Ponte della Paglia, Going to the Council***
1875; wood engraving; image size: 34.2 x 24 cm (13½ x 9⅜ in.); sheet size: 39.8 x 26.9 cm (15⅝ x 10½ in.); Dr Dennis T. Lanigan, Saskatoon, Canada.
Annotations: "ON THE PONTE DELLA PAGLIA: GOING TO THE COUNCIL." BY H. WALLIS. IN THE ROYAL ACADEMY EXHIBITION; signed in the plate *HENRY LINTON*, lower left.

This wood engraved print by Linton was published in the *Illustrated London News* on 29 May 1875, p.520.

Cat. 101. ***Timon and Flavius***
1876; oil on panel; 60.6 x 49.2 cm (23⅞ x 19¼ in.); The Delaware Art Museum, Wilmington.
Inscriptions: Signed with initials *H.W.*, lower right.
Provenance: Painted for James Sprent Virtue, Oatlands Park, Surrey, the publisher of *The Art Journal*, 1876; his sale Christie's, 1 March 1879, lot 157, bought by Vokins, likely the art dealer William Vokins, for £36 15s; Mrs. Mackinlay (Madame Antoinette Sterling),[1] 40 Abbey Road, London; her sale Christie's, 3 February 1894, lot 117, bought by B. Smith for £2 5s; Hartnoll & Eyre, London, in 1971, from whom purchased by Joe Setton on behalf of The Pre-Raphaelite Trust; their sale Sotheby's Parke Bernet, New York, 11 February 1981, lot 120 for $1300; anonymous sale Christie's S. K., 20 March 1984, lot 78, where purchased by the Forbes Collection for £600; their sale Christie's, London, 20 February 2003, lot 69, bought in; their sale Lyon & Turnbull, Edinburgh, 1 November 2011, lot 153, bought in; given by the Forbes Collection to the Delaware Art Museum in 2013. Object number: 2013-46.
Exhibitions: Hartnoll & Eyre Ltd.: Catalogue 17, *Summer 1971*, no. 17; Japan, *The Pre-Raphaelites and their Times*, 1985 (venues included the Isetan Museum of Art, Tokyo, no. 19; Hamamatsu City Museum, Hamamatsu; The Aichi Prefectural Art Gallery, Aichi; Daimaru Museum of Art, Daimaru; and Yamanashi Prefectural Museum of Art, Yamanashi, no. 13).
Literature: *The Art Journal*, 1876, pp.172-3, illus.; Rowlands, Walter, *Among the Great Masters of Literature*, 1900, p.151.

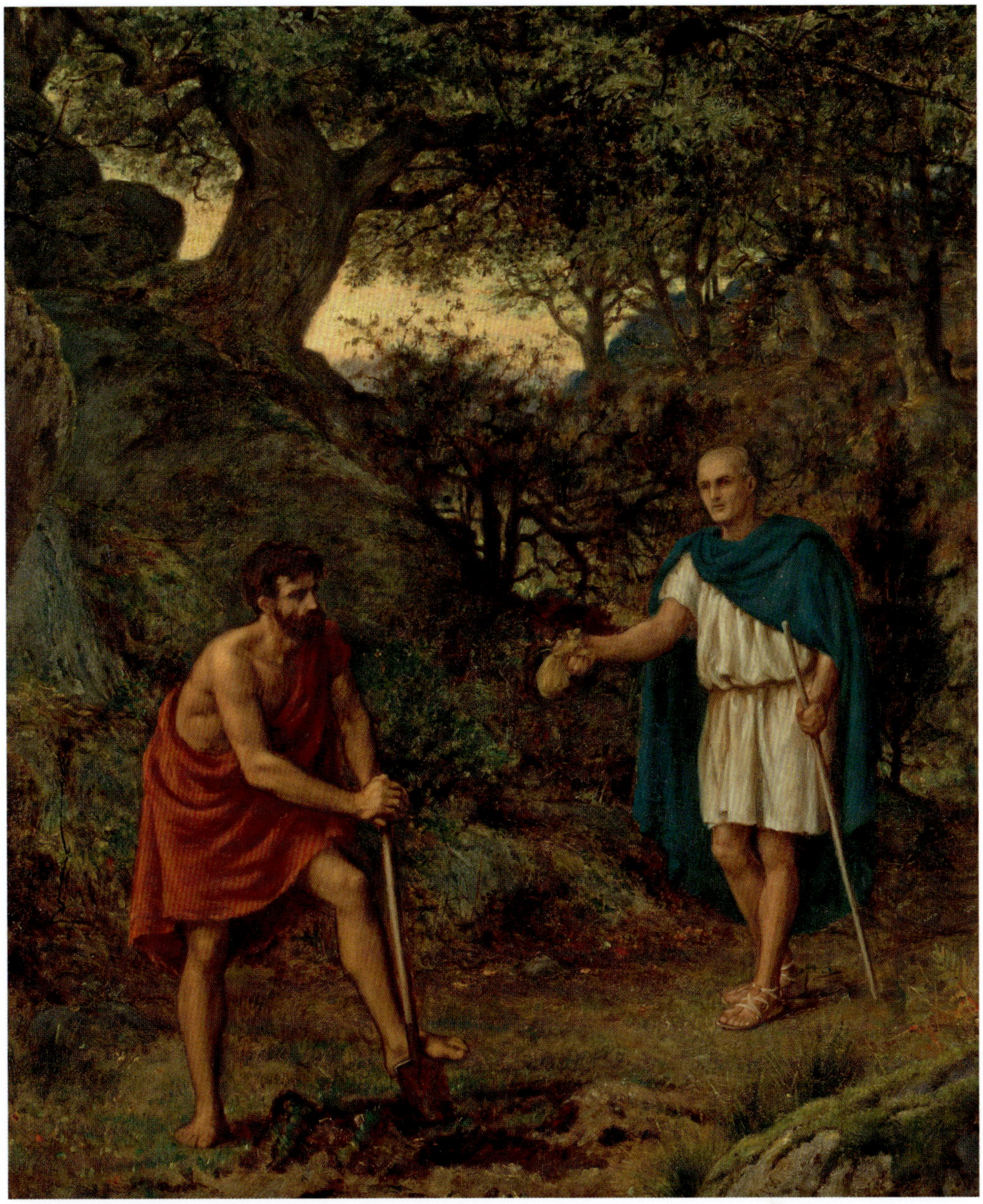
Cat. 101. Image courtesy of Delaware Art Museum, Wilmington

This work was not exhibited at the time it was executed because it had been painted expressly for the proprietors of the *Art Journal*. John Christian in his catalogue note for the Forbes sale at Christie's in 2003 states: "This picture illustrates Shakespeare's *Timon of Athens* (Act IV, Scene 3) and was painted about 1878 [*sic*], when it was engraved for the *Art Journal*. It therefore dates from many years after Wallis had painted such Pre-Raphaelite masterpieces as *The Death of Chatterton* and *The Stonebreaker*, and shows him reverting to a more conventional style. However, his choice of theme looks back to his Pre-Raphaelite origins. The Pre-Raphaelites had often mined Shakespeare in their search for meaningful subjects, and were invariably attracted, as Wallis is here, to ones rich in moral significance."

The *Art Journal* discusses the painting: "Our steel-plate frontispiece this month is from a painting by an English artist, H. Wallis, and depicts a scene from Shakespeare's 'Timon of Athens'. Timon in the intensity of his misanthropy, occasioned by loss of fortune and the consequent faithlessness of his friends, betook himself to the woods, it will be remembered, forsaking civilization, and refusing to consort further with mankind. But here Flavius, his faithful steward, followed him, and besought him to share his savings."

The Art Journal further states: "This is the point of Mr. Wallis's picture: the old steward, ignorant of the gold Timon himself has found, offers his former master 'the poor wealth' he has saved up, which the latter affects to regard as a bribe…The painter,

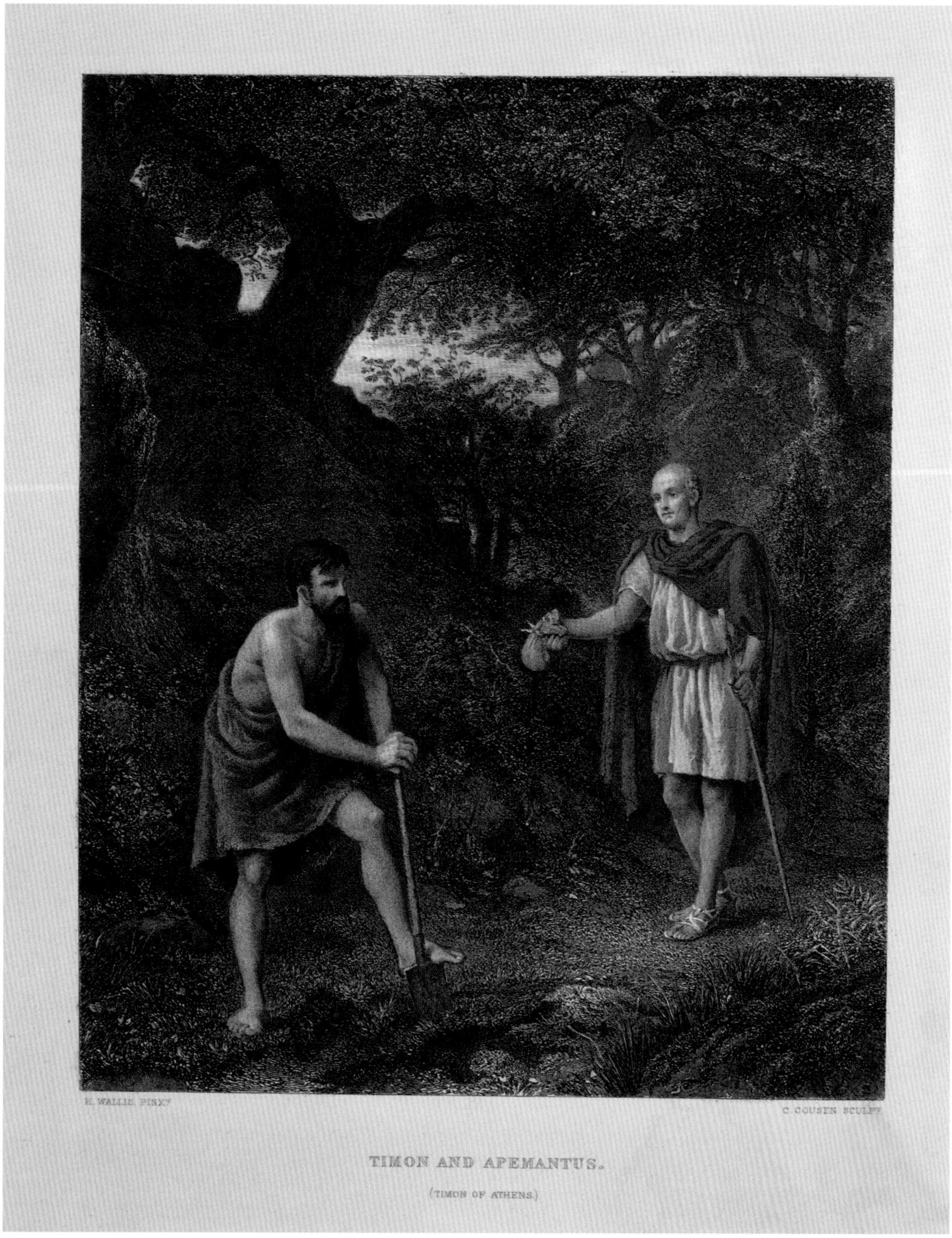

Cat. 101a. Image courtesy of Dennis Lanigan collection

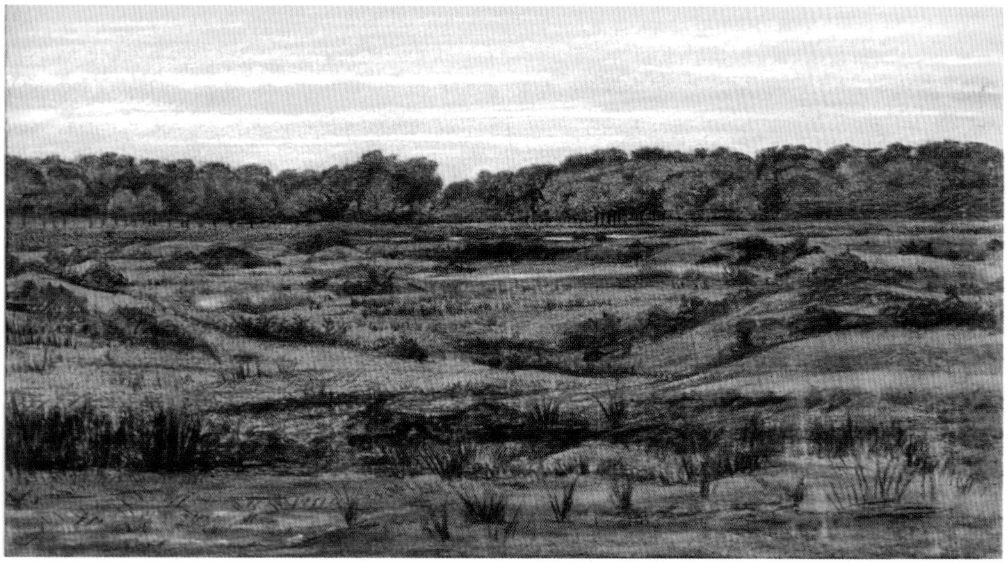

Cat. 102. Image by permission of Tate, London, 2016

in order to give effect to the locality and circumstances in which Timon has placed himself, has departed a little from the text of the play by representing him with a spade in his hands and digging: in an earlier part of the same scene he is thus employed, when he is visited by Apemantus…Mr. Wallis had not in this subject one that demanded much in the way of design, but the picture shows care and study, and some very pleasing composition in the landscape portion. It was painted expressly for the proprietors of this journal."[2]

Cat. 101a. *Timon and Apemantus*
1876; steel engraving; image size: 25.1 x 19.9 cm (9⅞ x 7¾ in.); sheet size: 36.8 x 27 cm. (14½ x 10⅝ in.); Dr Dennis T. Lanigan, Saskatoon, Canada.
ANNOTATIONS: "H. Wallis. pinx.[T] / TIMON AND APEMANTUS (TIMON OF ATHENS) / C. COUSEN SCULP[T]"
LITERATURE: *Art Journal*, June 1876, pp.172-3, p.177; *The Publishers' Weekly*, no. 229, 3 June 1876, p.751; *The Athenaeum*, No. 2536, 3 June 1876, p.751; *The Bristol Mercury*, 3 June 1876, p.6; *The Glasgow Herald*, 3 June 1876, p.3; *The Derby Mercury*, 14 June 1876, p.6.

This print, also called Timon of Athens, was engraved by the Yorkshire born line engraver Charles Cousen (1819-1889) for the *Art Journal* and taken from the *Imperial Edition of The Works of Shakespeare*, edited by Charles Knight, and published by Virtue and Company, London, 1873-76, in 2 volumes. The engraving undoubtedly copies *Timon and Flavius*. The second character can not be Apemantus, but rather Flavius [Cat. 101].

Cat. 102. *Landscape study (Study of Oaks, Dartmoor)*
1870s; black and white crayons on blue paper; 47.6 x 61 cm. (18¾ x 24 in.); Tate Britain, London.
PROVENANCE: Wallis's studio and then by descent from the artist to his daughter-in-law Alice Julyan Wallis (née Roberts), and thence to her great-niece Mrs. Vera G. Whiting, Purley, Surrey; sold to the Tate Gallery, 1973, acquisition no. T01724.
LITERATURE: *The Tate Gallery Report 1972–1974*, London 1975.

This drawing could possibly be *Moorland Oaks* [Cat. 91], which Wallis exhibited at the Dudley Gallery, *Exhibition of Works of Art in Black and White*, 1872, no. 143. *The Illustrated London News* commented on this work: "charcoal studies of trees, &c.".[1]

Cat. 103. *Dartmoor Oaks*
*c.*1875; watercolour and gouache; 35 x

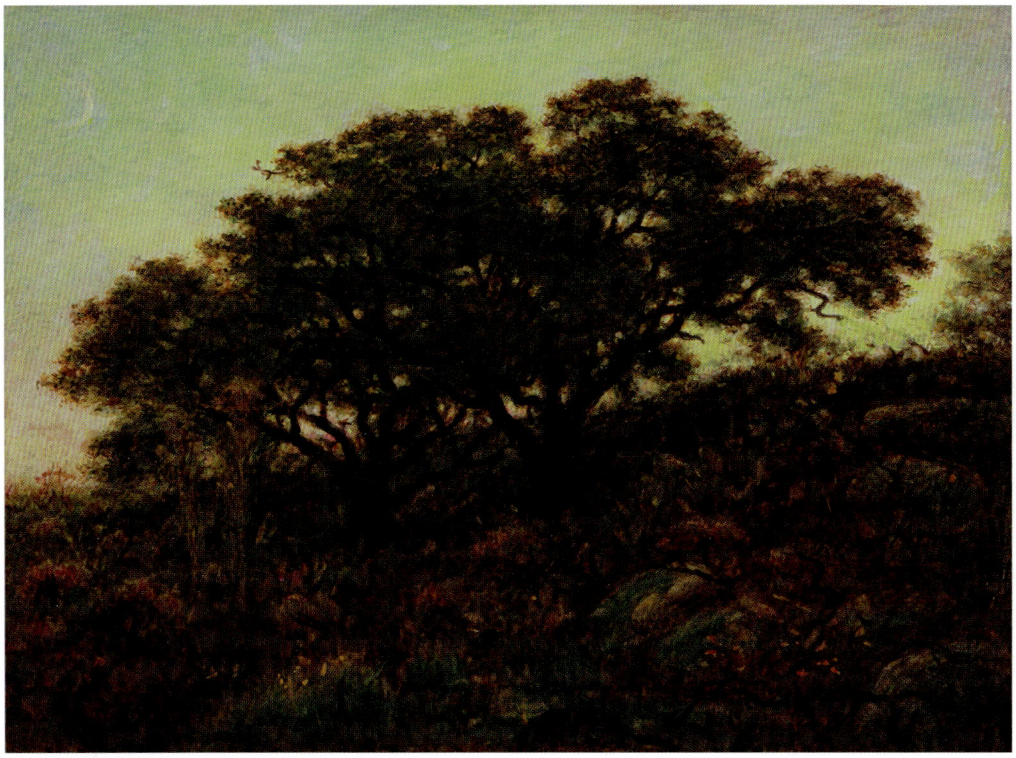

Cat. 103. Image courtesy of Diane Johnson, San Francisco, California

46 cm (13¾ x 18⅛ in.) - sight; private collection, Diane Johnson, San Francisco, California.
INSCRIPTIONS: On an old label on the backboard "Dartmoor Oaks Henry Wallis 9 Beauchamp Road, Upper Norwood S.E."
PROVENANCE: Wallis's studio and then by descent from the artist to his daughter-in-law Alice Julyan Wallis (née Roberts), and thence to her great-niece Mrs. Vera G. Whiting, Purley, Surrey; given to Diane Johnson, *c.*1973
EXHIBITIONS: The Society of French Artists (Mr. Deschamps's Gallery), 1875; Old Water-Colour Society, Winter exhibition, 1906-07, no. 106.
LITERATURE: *The Graphic*, 22 May 1875, p.495; *The Academy*, 29 May 1875, p.564.

The Academy discussing the exhibition of the Society of French artists in 1875 mentions: "Landscapes by Dupre, Corot, Courbet, C. F. Daubigny, Michel, and our very own Wallis (*Study of Oaks, Dartmoor*, very forcible in its juicy handling), appear on the walls to more or less advantage; however, not one of these is a work of exceptional importance." *The Graphic* describes this work as "the fine firm transcript of 'Oaks at Dartmoor' by Wallis". It seems possible, although surprising, that Wallis chose to exhibit this same drawing at the Old-Watercolour Society over thirty years later! There is no doubt, however that the present work is the one he showed at the O.W.S. in 1906 because Wallis lived from 1895 to 1908 at 9 Beauchamp Road, Upper Norwood S.E.

From a letter from Wallis to Charles Hercules Read (British Museum), dated 8 Oct 1908, it is evident that Wallis had visited the area around Dartmoor around 1875: "I was very glad to see your letter in the paper today. If the officials saw that your illustrious Society was in earnest, what remains of the Dartmoor monuments would be preserved. I hear that there are still many interesting ancient stone dwellings to be found. When I was painting there 30 years ago the farmers used to take the stone for the gateposts of their enclosures."[1] Wallis must have visited Dartmoor prior to this time, however, because he had exhibited drawings of three views of Dartmoor at Colnaghi's in July of 1869.[2]

The authors of this book first learned of the existence of a painting related to the drawing entitled *Study of Oaks, Dartmoor* through a letter from Leslie Parris, a former curator at the Tate Gallery, to Mrs V. G. Whiting (who sold 4 drawings to the Tate) on 26 February 1974: "I was interested to learn that Wallis painted a work called 'Dartmoor Oaks' and that our landscape drawing [Cat. 102] resembles it in some way." Mrs. Whiting had given a painting entitled *Dartmoor Oaks* to her friend Diane Johnson *c.*1973, which must be the work referred to. These two works appear to have little in common, however, apart from their titles.

Cat. 104. *Amidst the Moors*
1876. ?oil on canvas; dimensions unknown; whereabouts unknown.
EXHIBITIONS: Society of French Artists (Mr. Deschamps's Gallery), Winter Exhibition, 1876, no. 71.
LITERATURE: *The Glasgow Herald*, 7 November 1876, p.2; *Pall Mall Gazette*, 8 November 1876, p.10; *The Athenaeum*, No. 2559, 11 November 1876, p.632; *The Architect*, 11 November 1876, p.276; *The London Daily News*, 17 November 1876, p.2; *The Examiner*, 18 November 1876, p.1306; *The Academy*, Vol. 10, 25 November 1876, p.528.

F.G. Stephens, the critic of *The Athenaeum*, reported: "Finally, we recommend to all artists and amateurs Mr. Wallis's magnificent landscape, *Amidst the Moors* (71), that which is nearly twilight over a flat, marshy valley, closed on either hand by lofty hills of the deepest tone and richest colour, in the distance dark blue mountain sides. Over these huge bulks of slaty cumuli are slowly moving, their dazzling upper edges, full of light, shining against the profound blueness of the sky." The critic for *The Architect* echoed these comments about the sky: "Mr. H. Wallis paints a wonderfully blue sky *Amidst the Moors*." *The Examiner* noted: "Mr. Wallis's study of brown and purple moorland and heavy blue sky is very bold and effective in strong classical colour." The reviewer for *The Academy* also expressed praise for this work: "In the landscape branch of the collection nothing is more striking than Mr. Wallis's picture, *Amidst the Moors*; at once dark, rich, and luminous, in colour, to a singular degree – a lonely solemn scene, with a message of awe to the thoughtful or impressible, and of a certain physical disquietude even to the frivolous – the vast cumulous-clouds lemon-tinted in sunset as they surge and change over the obscure and limiting hills. Mr. Wallis has not unfrequently proved his uncommon depth of resource as a landscape-painter, but never perhaps, so superbly as in this picture." The critic of the *Pall Mall Gazette* remarked enthusiastically: "Mr. Henry Wallis in his striking picture entitled 'Amidst the Moors' (71), has striven for a more precise and forcible rendering of the enduring realities of the scene. He has chosen an effect of light which is consistent with precise design and he has produced a work of rich and harmonious colour which suggests by its method the example of the great Venetian painters."

Cat. 105. *Outside a Prison in Southern Italy (At the Prison Window)*
1876; ?oil on canvas; 73.7 x 81.3 cm (29 x 32 in.); whereabouts unknown.
PROVENANCE: Purchased at the Royal Hibernian Academy exhibition in 1877 by J. Wardell, likely John Wardell[1] of Thorncliffe, Rathgar, Co. Dublin.
EXHIBITIONS: Royal Academy, 1876, no. 322; The Royal Hibernian Academy, Dublin, 1877, no. 415; *Paris Exposition Universelle*,

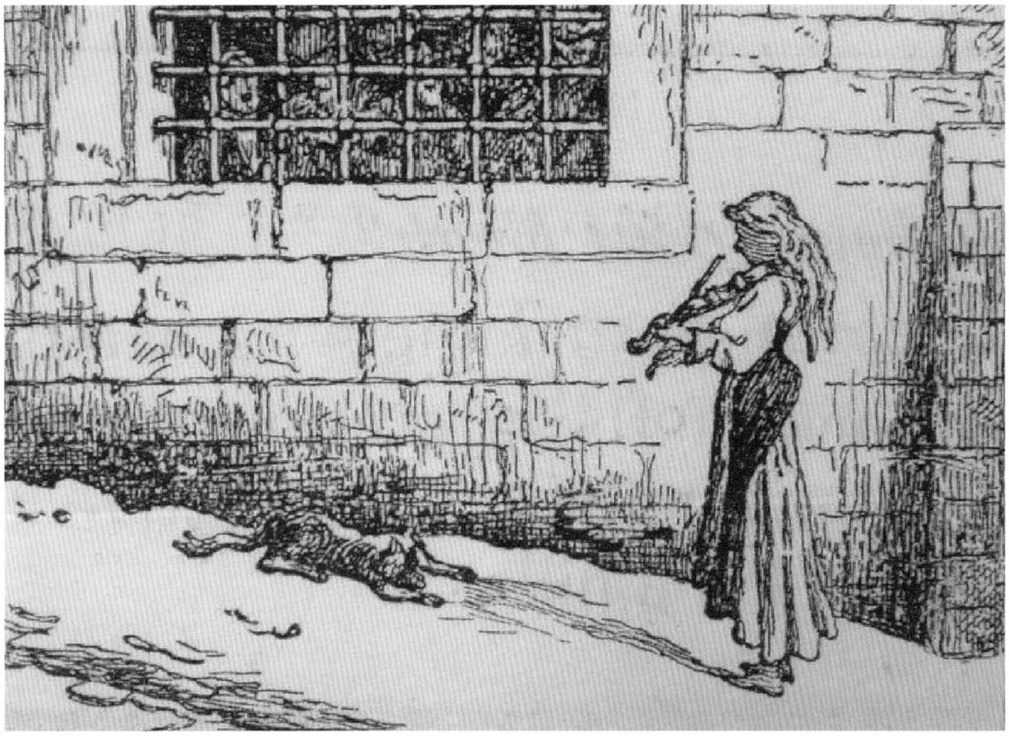

Image from Henry Blackburn, *Academy Notes* for 1876, p.34. See Cat. 105.

1878, no. 253; *National Exhibition of Arts and Manufactures*, Dublin, 1882.
Literature: Blackburn, Henry: *Academy Notes*, 1876, p.34; *The Academy*, Vol. 9, 1876, p.465; *The Athenaeum*, No. 2531, 29 April 1876, p.602; *John Bull*, 6 May 1876, p.305; *Illustrated London News*, 13 May 1876, p.475; *The Graphic*, 20 May 1876, p.491; *The Spectator*, 27 May 1876, p.13; *The Saturday Review*, Vol. 41, 27 May 1876, p.682; *The Tablet*, 3 June 1876, p.9; *The Art Journal*, Vol. 39, 1877, p.135; Enault, Louis: *Les Beaux-Arts à l'Exposition Universelle de 1878*, Paris, 1878, p.32; Exposition Universelle Paris, 1878, *Catalogue illustré de la section des Beaux-Arts. Ecole anglaise, avec notes par Henry Blackburn*, p.48; *The Athenaeum*, No. 2619, 5 January 1878, p.28; *The Architect*, Vol. 19, 4 May 1878, p.272; *The Saturday Review*, Vol. 45, 15 June 1878, p.755; *Reports of the United States Commissioners to the Paris Universal Exposition, 1878*, Vol. 2, 1880, p.61; Shepherd, George H.: *A Short History of the British School of Painting*, 1881, p.155; *The Artist and Journal of Home Culture*, Vol. 3, 1 October 1882, p.305.

When the painting was shown at the Royal Academy in 1876 the critic of *The Academy* observed: "*Outside a Prison in Southern Italy* shows the inmates collected close to the bars which face towards the pavement, killing time as best they may, and pretty nearly as if they were home: two of them smoke pipes, two others are preparing for the solace of a cigarette, and the fifth, a romantic-looking handsome young scion of the land of sun and song, who may perhaps have committed the trifling irregularity of stabbing a rival in love under the fifth rib, leans his cheek dejectedly upon his hand. In the street a sweet slim girl, pale and auburn-haired, pauses, playing her fiddle; a wiry dog, of the vulpi-lupine type so commonly seen in Italy, does his best with an already well-gnawed bone. Highly natural throughout, this picture condenses its sentiment into the figure of the girl, which is charming in its child-like abstracted tenderness."

F.G. Stephens in *The Athenaeum* also gave a favourable report: "A third picture will appeal to painters with more force than either of the above. It is styled *Outside a Prison in Southern Italy* (322), and represents technical experiments with colours and lights even more fortunately than it deals with the subject, a very pathetic one, of the visit of a pretty and innocent girl violin-player to the grating of a prison where, after the wonderful Italian wont, the scoundrels and murderers of the district are allowed to gather, smoke, swear, plot with their friends, and beg of the passersby. Here, behind the big bars of the grating, and in the darkness, is a group of rascals as ugly and villainous as one might desire to see hanged, the hideous visages glare so savagely or grin foolishly between the bars at the girl who, with her violin at her shoulder, charitably plays for them a tune, which may probably touch what hearts they have. There is beautiful and rich local colour in the girl's dress, but costume is one we are bored to death in seeing. Her pose is very graceful and simple; the picture is full of light, and very strong in all respects."

The critic for *The Graphic* held the opinion that: "Nothing in the exhibition is more exquisite in sentiment than the pathetic figure and face of the little girl, who plays a violin outside a prison-grate, through which a group of prisoners listen with sympathy for the little performer and relish for her music even among the goal-birds in Italy." Henry Blackburn in his *Academy Notes* for 1875 reported that this work was considered important enough that it was hung "on the line".

The painting was exhibited at the 1878 Paris Exposition Universelle, lent by J. Wardell[2] under the title *At the Prison Window.*

Cat. 106. *The Devotion of Sydney Carton: From the 'Tale of Two Cities'*
1876; ?oil on canvas; 137.6 x 101.6 cm (54 x 40 in.); whereabouts unknown.
Provenance: Lieutenant Colonel John Allen Bindley[1] by 1897; his sale Christie's, 12 July 1902, lot 80, bought in; Captain H.B. Norton,[2] Bournemouth, by 1926.
Exhibitions: Royal Academy, 1876, no. 902; The Royal Society of Artists, Birmingham, *Autumn Exhibition*, 1876, no. 73; *Victorian Era Exhibition*, Earl's Court, 1897, no. 563; Nottingham Castle Museum and Art Gallery, *Loan Collection of Modern Pictures*, 1898, no. 119; Russell-Cotes Art Gallery and Museum, *First Loan Exhibition of Pictures*, 1926, no. 72.
Literature: *The Academy*, Vol. 9, 1876, p.465; Blackburn, Henry: *Academy Notes*, Second Edition, 1876, p.58; *The Illustrated London News*, 1 April 1876, p.334; *The Athenaeum*, No. 2531, 29 April 1876, p.602; *John Bull*, 6 May 1876, p.305; *Illustrated London News*, 13 May 1876, p.475; *The Belfast News-Letter*, 1 June 1876; *Birmingham Daily Post*, 21 August 1876, p.5; *Illustrated London News*, 2 September 1876, p.218; *The Architect and Building News*, Vol. 16, 2 September 1876, p.134; Shepherd, George H.: *A Short History of the British School of Painting*, 1881, p.155; Kiralfy, Imre: *Victorian Era Exhibition, 1897, Earl's Court, London*, Riddle and Couchman, 1897, p.40; Kitton, Frederic: *Dickens and His Illustrators*, 1899, p.190; *Bulletin of the Russell-Cotes Art Gallery and Museum*, Vol. V, No. 4, December 1926, p.42.

Considered one of Charles Dickens's greatest novels, *A Tale of Two Cities* (1859), is set in London and Paris prior to and during the French Revolution. The painting depicts two of the main characters, Carton is a dissipated British barrister who goes to the guillotine in aristocrat Darnay's stead in an attempt to redeem his ill-spent life because of his unrequited love for Darnay's wife.

The critic of *The Academy* complimented this picture: "Mr. Wallis is, as usual, one of

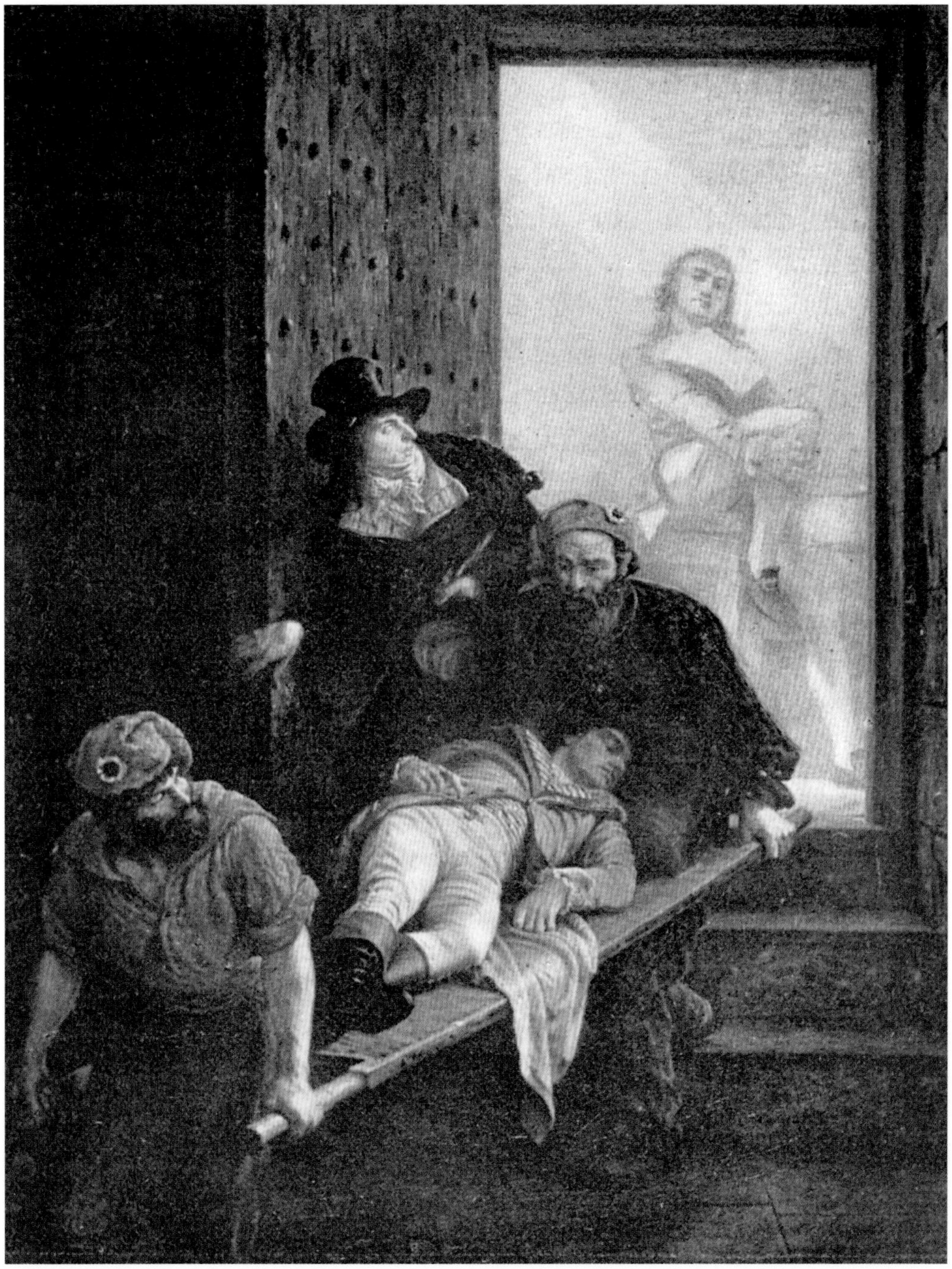

Cat. 106. Image by permission of Russell-Coates Museum, Bournemouth

the best exhibitors in this section. His two figure-pictures are of very diverse kind. *The Devotion of Sydney Carton (from the 'Tale of Two Cities')* is a genuinely dramatic presentment of a moving scene; the incident being that where Carton voluntarily devotes himself to take the place in prison of his rival, Darnay, who is borne away sleeping on a stretcher; a story, indeed, which cannot be absolutely told by painting, but which is nevertheless powerfully indicated in its visible form and inward significance. Carton remains in the cell with an air of triumphant satisfaction, illuminated by a vivid sun-gleam; the spy, who plays a principal part in the transaction, looks back at him with a meaning and clandestine glance. The figure of Darnay is a remarkably successful piece of foreshortening, and all is carried out with the painter's accustomed completeness."

Cat. 107. *An Oasis in the Desert: Fountain Court, the Temple*
1876; ?oil on canvas; dimensions unknown; whereabouts unknown.
Exhibitions: Royal Academy, 1876, no. 975.
Literature: *Illustrated London News*, 1 April 1876, p.334; *The Athenaeum*, No. 2531, 29 April 1876, p.602; *John Bull*, 6 May 1876, p.305; *Illustrated London News*, 13 May 1876, p.475; *Fun*, 7 June 1876, p.249; *The Graphic*, 17 June 1876, p.594; *Illustrated London News*, 9 September 1876, p.254; *The Athenaeum*, No. 2706, 6 September 1879, p.313; *The Hull Packet*, 12 September 1879, p.3.

The critic of *The Athenaeum* favoured this work above the other pictures that Wallis showed at the Royal Academy in 1876: "Mr. Wallis has three pictures, the most important of which we have already mentioned. It represents the charming court in the Temple, truly *An Oasis in the Desert* (975), as the picture is called, with the fountain in the background, which is now happily restored to its old simplicity, and the trumpery decorative sculpture in stucco banished. The fine and pretty jet springs in the air as a century ago it sprang to gladden Johnson's eyes. Here are the trees in their pale London verdure, the richly tinted, bulky houses with their ponderous cornices and steeply sloping tiled roofs, the houses which William Hunt painted so finely in that masterpiece in water colour, now at South Kensington,[1] here are the old steps, but newly arranged, and the old rails, before the new 'Gothic' building. The vista is formed by the flagged pathway leading to the steps and below the trees, its worn pavement is chequered in spaces of sunlight and shadow, and graceful figures of girls, ladies and children pass on their way. It is a beautiful picture, charming in sentiment, free from pretence, simple and pathetic, for its sweetness is not without sadness, and it brings before us the fact that this is truly an oasis in a horrid wilderness of bricks and stones, and even here the very trees are pale, the children slight and pallid, the graceful girls all too slender."

The *Illustrated London News* also wrote favourably: "Mr. Henry Wallis, the painter of this picture, which was in the Academy exhibition this year, could hardly have chosen a more fitting title than he has done. To pass from the crowded Strand or Fleet-street – from the arid desert of brick and mortar which constitutes the feverish heart of this great city – into Fountain-court, Middle Temple, with its pleasant patter of water and tall limes and beeches, is indeed suggestive of the eastern traveller – parched, worn, and faint – suddenly coming in mid-desert, upon an oasis of green pasturage and graceful palms, testifying to the presence of a cool, refreshing spring, needful sometimes to restore life itself to exhausted man and beast."

The *Graphic* commented: "(975) – 'An Oasis in the Desert' (H. Wallis). The Fountain Court in the Temple, with the elms in spring leaf and the bright thread of water leaping among the dry bricks and dusty pavement, and the dryer law-books and dustier chambers. Has been bought by a literary labourer in Serjeant's Inn, who is to be congratulated."[2]

Cat. 107a. *An Oasis in the Desert: Fountain Court, the Temple*
1876; wood engraving; image size: 33.9 x 49.1 cm. (13⅜ x 19⅞ in.); sheet size: 40 x 56.4 cm. (15¾ x 22¼ in.); Dr Dennis T. Lanigan, Saskatoon, Canada.
Annotation: (lettering below image) "AN OASIS IN THE DESERT: FOUNTAIN-

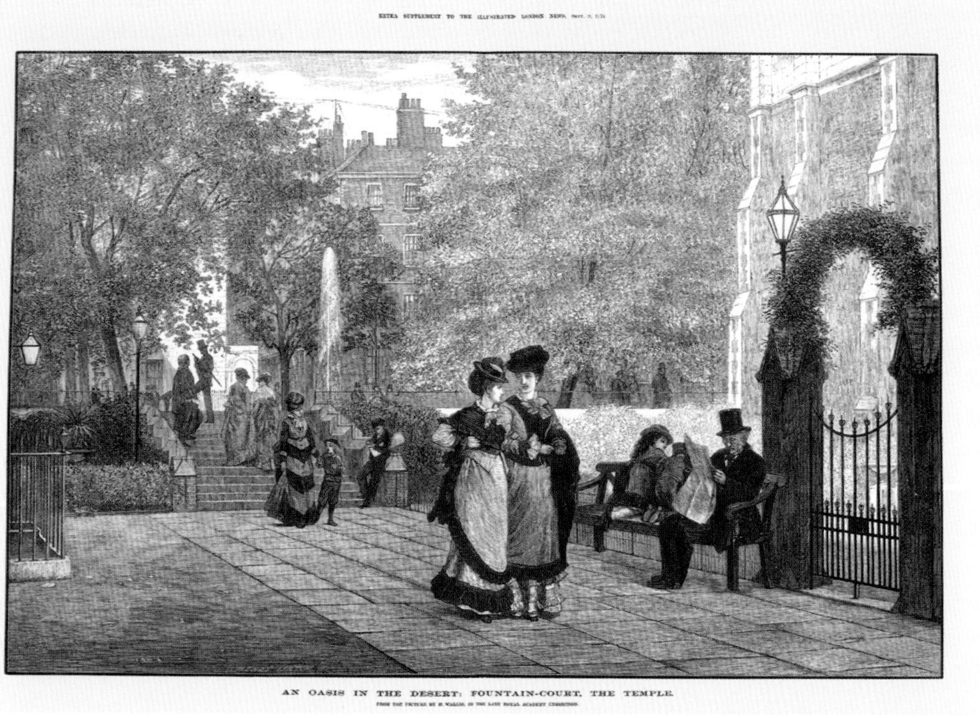

Cat. 107a. Fountain Court is part of the Temple complex, between the Middle Temple Hall and New Court (on the left) and Essex Court (on the right). Image courtesy of the Dennis Lanigan collection

COURT, THE TEMPLE / FROM THE PICTURE BY H. WALLIS, IN THE LATE ROYAL ACADEMY EXHIBITION"; signed in the plate *Henry Linton*, lower left.
Literature: *The Illustrated London News*, Vol. LXVIII, Extra Supplement, no. 1937, 9 September 1876, p.254; *The Times*, 28 December 1876, p.9.

This wood engraving by Henry Linton after the original painting was published in the *Illustrated London News* on 9 September 1876.

The Illustrated London News commented when discussing the print: "The celebrities associated with this spot and hereabout could scarcely be enumerated in a reasonable space… Some painters likewise are associated with the place – Reynolds, for instance, who visited Goldsmith in Brick-court; William Hunt, who painted the red-brick houses in the back of Mr. Wallis's picture; John Pettie, who lays the scene of a Shakespearean illustration in the Temple Gardens, and others not needful to name. But of all the celebrities associated with the Temple, he who endears himself most to memory is Charles Lamb." The buildings adjacent to the court forming our view are the Library, to the left, and the far more interesting Elizabethan Hall, on the right, which, besides many interesting relics, is remarkable as the only edifice now standing in which a play of Shakespeare was acted in the poet's lifetime. The gardens themselves are repeatedly referred to by Shakespeare.

A photoprint of this work was also produced in 1876 and included in *The Royal Academy Album*, a folio issued by L. Reeve and Co. and Fine Art Publishing Co.

Cat. 108. *Scene from the Merchant of Venice – How now, Tubal*
*c.*1876; watercolour; dimensions unknown; whereabouts unknown.
Exhibitions: Society Birmingham Society of Artists, Autumn Exhibition, 1876

Wallis may have painted this watercolour after attending the 1875 production of *The Merchant of Venice.*[1] He refers to the present work in a letter to Ford Madox Brown, dated 7 March 1876: "I am sending my water colour picture from the Merchant of Venice to the Birmingham Exb^{n}, rather wth a notion the town museum may purchase it. If you know anyone of the Com^{tee} who purchase will you kindly call his attention to it."[2] This watercolour that Wallis submitted in 1876 to the Birmingham Society of Artists was the start of a trend.

From 1879-1884 Wallis submitted many watercolours based on subjects from the *The Merchant of Venice* to the Old Water-Colour Society's exhibitions. The exact subject of this particular work is unknown because it does not appear to have been reviewed. It likely comes from Act III, scene I:

> *Shylock.* How now, Tubal! what news
> from Genoa? hast thou
> found my daughter?
> *Tubal.* I often came where I did hear of
> her, but cannot find her.

It is possible, therefore, that this is the same work as Cat. 158, *Tubal brings Shylock News of Jessica*, which Wallis later exhibited at the O.W.S. in 1882.

Cat. 109. *Arranging for the Marriage – An Idyll of the Sacristy*
1876; ?oil on canvas; 48.3 x 80 cm (19 x 31½ in.); whereabouts unknown.
Provenance: Frank K. Hurst, 18 Cadogan Pl. S.W. London; his estate sale Christie's, London, 15 July 1910, lot 108, bought by Morris,[1] for £19 19s.
Exhibitions: Society of British Artists (Suffolk Street), 1876-77, no. 191.
Literature: *The Academy*, Vol. 10, 18 November 1876, p.507; *The London Daily News*, 25 November 1876, p.2; *The Art Journal*, New Series, Vol. 3, 1877, pp.28-29.

The reviewer for *The Academy* stated: "Mr. Wallis sends *Arranging for the Marriage, an Idyll of the Sacristy*, in southern Italy. There are two priests, one of them in colloquy with the bride-elect, a barefoot peasant-girl in her early teens, the other conferring with the bridegroom. The former priest wipes his hand on a towel, and eyes with good-humoured complacency the dish of red mullets which the damsel and her little sister have brought round for acceptance: the other is seated on a marble bench projecting from the richly-decorated wall. This work is something between a sketch and a picture: the faces of the young people are extremely handsome, or one might say pretty, and would bear more of naturalistic development with great advantage to the whole."

The Art Journal said: "H. Wallis's 'Arranging for the Marriage' is certainly one of the most pleasing in this direction, excellent in rendering, brilliant in colour, careful in outline, and abounding in subtleties of quiet humour. A well-looking, well-bred priest, to judge from the rich purple and gold vestment which he wears over his broad shoulders, fresh from the service of the altar, stands wiping his comely hands with a fair linen towel hanging beside a marble piscina. His face is half turned around, to convey, by the language of the eyes, more telling strength to some utterance of kindly wit directed at a young Sicilian fishergirl, who stands immediately behind him. This maiden, a bronze-faced, bare-legged beauty in dainty-dress of white muslin and blue, bears to the father a rich tribute of freshly-caught red mullet, piled in an appetising heap on a dish overspread with emerald-green reeds. In the far-off corner of the sacristy stands the bridegroom, a handsome, well-shapen young fellow, evidently of the bride's own calling, engaged in conversation with a second priest, likewise clad in rich vestments of cloth of gold. This second priest, with pretension of listening to the speech of the lovesick boy, is in reality attentively scanning the eyes and countenance of his colleague, which would seem to betoken more knowledge and appreciation of worldly than of spiritual things. The story is admirably told, and the artist has bestowed upon the treatment of the faces much skill in the expression of thought and feeling. The marble is painted with painstaking attention to architectural detail, and discovers considerable ability in the blending of the various tints of green and white marble. Mr. Wallis's contribution, which seems, by-the-way, almost to have escaped notice in the brief criticisms of the exhibition given in the London press, is certainly one of the most noteworthy pictures among those sent in by non-members of the Society, not so much for its subject as for the capable way in which it has been handled."

Cat. 110. *In the Spring Time*
1877; watercolour; dimensions unknown; whereabouts unknown.
Exhibitions: Royal Academy, 1877, no. 762; Royal Hibernian Academy, Dublin, 1878, no. 534, asking price £63.
Literature: Richardson, H.C. [Ed.]: *Academy criticisms*, 1877, p.11.

When this picture was shown at the Royal Academy it was accompanied by a quotation from Shakespeare's *As You Like It*, Act V, Scene 3: "In the spring time, the only pretty ring time / When birds do sing, hey ding a ding, ding; / Sweet lovers love the spring."[1] The reviewer for *Academy criticisms* stated: "A charming drawing, the scene of which is an old church-yard (at Rye?) surrounded by houses; here two lovers sit, making love, on a tomb. It is a subtle study of effect and rich, fine, sober colour, with refined tones of the highest quality."

Cat. 111. *Louis XI and Cardinal Balue*
1877; ?oil on canvas; dimensions unknown; whereabouts unknown.
Exhibitions: Royal Academy, 1877, no. 987; Royal Manchester Institution, 1877, no. 654, priced at £105 0s.
Literature: *The Architect*, Vol. 17, 7 April 1877, p.225; *The Athenaeum*, No. 2584, 5 May 1877, p.583; *The Times*, 22 May 1877, p.11; *The Athenaeum*, No. 2587, 26 May 1877, p.677; *The Academy*, Vol. XI, 2 June 1877, p.496; *Fun*, 6 June 1877, p.222; *The Illustrated London News*, Vol. 70, 23 June 1877, p.587; Shepherd, George H.: *A Short History of the British School of Painting*, 1881, pp.155-56.

Jean Balue was a French cardinal (1421-1491), and a minister of Louis XI. The King imprisoned Balue from 1469 to 1480 for treason in favour of Charles the Rash, the Duke of Burgundy.[1]

None of the critics were particularly impressed with this work. *The Architect* described the painting thus: "Mr. Wallis's second contribution is 'Louis XI and Cardinal Balue', showing the wretched Cardinal imprisoned in the iron cage he designed for others, and in which he languished so many years. The King, with his back to the spectator, stands curiously regarding his fallen minister." W.M. Rossetti in his review in *The Academy* notes: "*Louis XI. and Cardinal Balue*, though it cannot be called one of Mr. Wallis's best pictures, is strongly expressive. The king, with the leaden saints in his hat, a light stick, and long, full, lanky grey hair, and companioned by a small terrier, contemplates with a serious unmoved countenance the kneeling cardinal as he pours forth an impassioned appeal: his iron cage, with an elaborate Gothic lock, and the cardinal's hat atop, would not, indeed, allow him to rise upright from his knees. Some straw and a pitcher of water are all his Eminence's present appurtenances. The contrast between the lean, cold-blooded, but triumphant King, and the grossly fleshy but dejected Cardinal, whose rotund proportions have not yet been brought down by incarceration, is no doubt intended on the artist's part, but the ecclesiastic's comparative size seems somewhat excessive."

The Illustrated London News stated: "Mr. H. Wallis does not manifest all his wonted power in 'Louis XI and Cardinal Balue' (987), albeit the scene is one abounding in materials for such a facile and such a dramatic pencil as as Mr. Wallis's. There is plenty of good drawing, colouring and finish in the work; but the two principal personages, the King and the Cardinal, cannot certainly be regarded as successful specimens of the artist's power of representing inexorable, sardonic, cynical cruelty on the one hand, and hopeless misery and despair on the other." *The Times* critic noted: "Mr. H. Wallis has a turn for odd subjects, but what on earth possessed him to (987) paint the hideous incident of Cardinal Balue shut like a wild beast in his iron cage, with Louis XI gloating over his degradation and misery?"

Cat. 112. *The Physician – A Visit of Charity*
1877; ?oil on canvas; dimensions unknown; whereabouts unknown.
Exhibitions: Royal Academy, 1877, no. 1359; Royal Society of Artists, Birmingham, 1877, no. 211.
Literature: *The Architect*, Vol. 17, 7 April 1877, p.225; *The Athenaeum*, No. 2584, 5 May 1877, p.583; *Illustrated London News*, Vol. LXX, no. 1975, 19 May 1877, p.467; *The Times*, 22 May 1877, p.11; *The Athenaeum*, No. 2587, 26 May 1877, p.677; *The Architect*, Vol. 18, 1 September 1877, p.113; *The Birmingham Daily Post*, 18 September 1877, p.5.

The Athenaeum, in its second of two reviews of the Royal Academy, stated: "A far superior work is *The Physician* (1359), the scene of which is outside an Italian building, at the window of which, accompanied by curious onlookers, is a doctor administering medicines to the sick inmates of the place. The effect is sunlight, given with richness and power; there is ample spirit, variety, and character in the numerous figures, and the damsel on our left of the doctor is a perfect type of southern grace; the colour and solidity here are first-rate." *The Architect* was also favourable in its review: "Mr. Henry Wallis has completed two pictures which will probably elicit considerable comment. 'The Physician – a Visit of Charity' represents a physician dispensing medicine to an ailing man, surrounded by a group of people who have brought their sick and afflicted ones. The scene is in Southern Italy, so that picturesque costume is added to the other attractions of a singularly fine work."

The critic for *The Birmingham Daily Post* stated: "Mr. Wallis's 'Physician' (211) is an Italian scene, perhaps leaning the least bit towards trickiness in its treatment, where the patients are coming or are being brought to the Healer; mothers with their babes, the strong man bearing his little one, the sister her brother – all with a wondrous patience, and a beautiful faith that interests us much, and makes us extremely curious about the mixture which the benevolent gentleman in the long black robes is compounding."

Cat. 112a. *The Physician – A Visit of Charity*
1877; wood engraving; image size: 33.1 x 49.1 (13 x 19⁵⁄₁₆ in.); sheet size: 40 x 55.2 cm. (15¾ x 21¾ in.); Dr Dennis T. Lanigan, Saskatoon, Canada.
Annotation: (lettering below image) "THE PHYSICIAN BY H. WALLIS. / IN THE EXHIBITION OF THE ROYAL ACADEMY"; signed in the plate *M. KLINKICHT*, lower right; unknown monogram, lower left.
Literature: *Illustrated London News*, vol. 70, no. 1975, Extra Supplement, 19 May 1877, p.467.

The *Illustrated London News* describes this wood engraving by Moritz Klinkicht,[1] thus: "The visitation of healing mercy and beneficent skill, in a village of those countries in south-eastern Europe, where pestilence and famine are too likely to follow in the train of war, is a subject worthy of the artist's serious conception. Mr. Wallis has treated a similar theme, in the picture

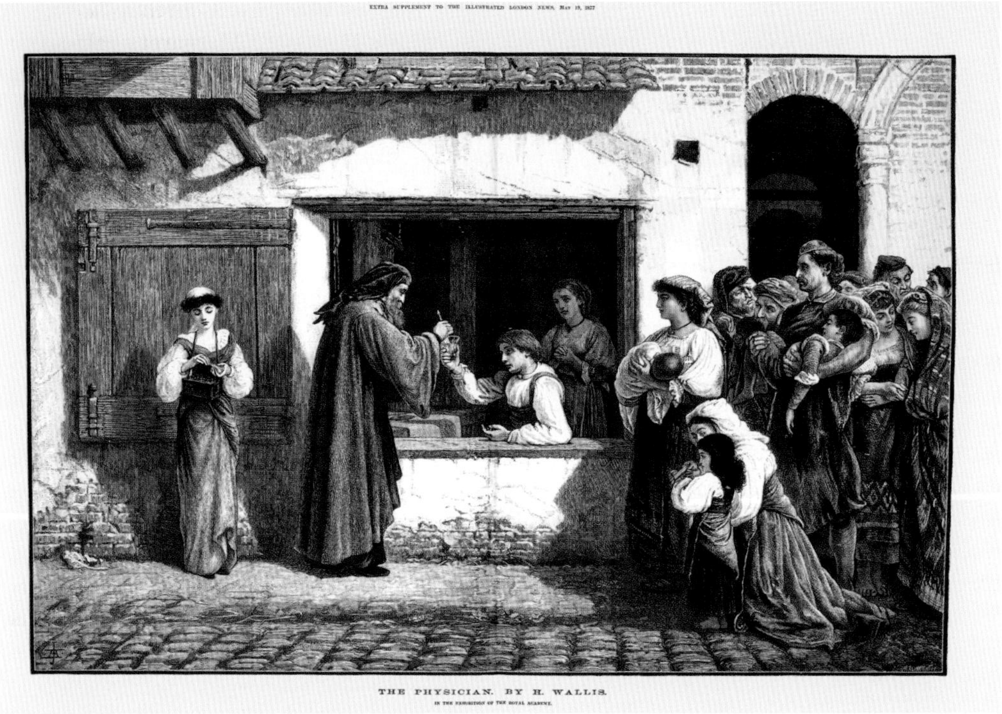

Cat. 112a. Image courtesy of the Dennis Lanigan collection

we have selected from the Royal Academy Exhibition for one of our Engravings, so forcibly, and with so much truth of feeling, as to convey a high moral lesson of the beauty of charity, in the gracious and winning performance of its holy behests. The attentive docility and expectancy of the waiting crowd, amongst whom are several patients, or fathers and mothers of younger patients, about to seek the aid of the foreign physician, is well expressed by their various attitudes, and by the countenances with which they regard him.

As he stands by the open window, ministering some potion of medicinal virtue to a sick woman of the household within, his noble figure is set off to much advantage by the flowing robe and head-dress of an Oriental costume. The maiden who attends his steps, bearing a little store of the drugs he is recustomed to use, may be supposed to be the physician's daughter; and her employment in this sacred service does not fail to enhance the particular interest of the scene."

Another print of this work by the British wood engraver John Watkins was reproduced in the French publication *L'Art* in 1877.[2] It was not of the same quality as the engraving from the *Illustrated London News*.

Cat. 113. *A Welsh Mountain Lake (Lyn Cae, North Wales)*
1878; watercolour heightened with white; 43 x 66 cm (17 x 26 in.); private collection.
Inscriptions: Signed with initials *HW* on recto and annotated on the back *Henry Wallis No. 3*.
Provenance: Wallis's studio and then by descent from the artist to his daughter-in-law Alice Julyan Wallis (née Roberts), and thence to her great-niece Mrs. Vera G. Whiting, Purley, Surrey; her sale Sotheby's Belgravia, 10 April 1973, lot 212, bought by Bill Waters of Norham House, Cockermouth, Cumbria for £55; sold to Hartnoll & Eyre, London by 1973; Sotheby's Belgravia, 29 July 1975, lot 249, sold for £40.
Exhibitions: Old Water-Colour Society, Winter Exhibition 1878-79, no. 66; Royal Birmingham Society of Artists, *Spring Exhibition of Water-colour Paintings*, 1879, no. 562, asking price £21; Hartnoll & Eyre Ltd., London: Catalogue Thirty-Three, September 25 – October 12, 1973, no. 42; Galerie des Luxembourg, *Le Paysage Anglais des Preraphaelites aux Symbolistes*, April 1974, no. 62.
Literature: *The Athenaeum*, No. 2667, 7 December 1878, p.730.

The critic for *The Athenaeum* noted: "There is abundant grandeur of subject, force of treatment, and epic simplicity in 'A Welsh Mountain Lake' (66)." This is likely the same work that Wallis exhibited in 1879 in Birmingham as *Lyn Cae, North Wales*, as 'lyn' means 'lake' in Welsh. This painting is traditionally picturesque, as if the mountain were posing for the camera, whereas the *Stonebreaker* is much more Pre-Raphaelite in that no attempt was made to arrange or prettify the landscape.

Cat. 114. *Between Hampstead and Highgate – A favourite haunt of Keats, Shelley and Coleridge*
1878; watercolour; dimensions unknown; whereabouts unknown.
Exhibitions: Old Water-Colour Society, Winter exhibition 1878-79, no. 68.
Literature: *Pall Mall Gazette*, 5 December 1878, p.11; *The Times*, 6 December 1878, p.3; *The Athenaeum*, No. 2667, 7 December 1878, p.730; *The Illustrated London News*, Vol. 73, 7 December 1878, p.542; *The Graphic*, 7 December 1878, p.583.

The critic for *The Athenaeum* said about this work: "Another, but less important, picture is full of artistic charm – a landscape of the environs of London during a solemn, glowing twilight, with the fierce luster of sundown on dense foliage, lush herbage, sward and shrubs, an old red-roofed cottage and its darker walls."

The reviewer for *The Illustrated London*

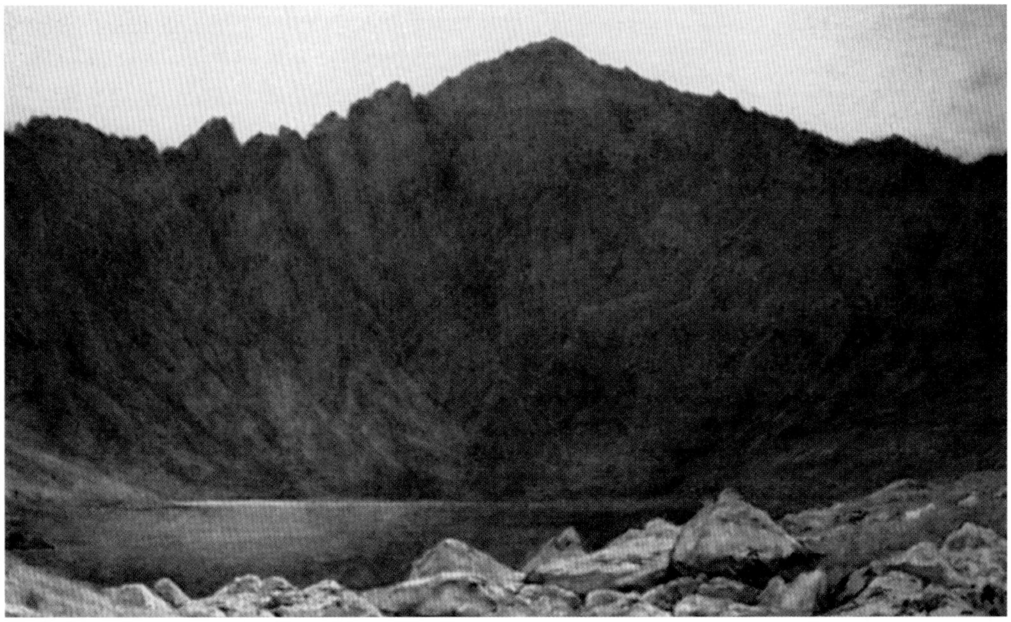

Cat. 113. Image courtesy of Sotheby's, London

News reported favourably: "Mr. Henry Wallis has often proved himself a colourist approaching the Venetian standard, and there is evidence of the fact here in his view of a favourite haunt of several of our poets, 'Between Hampstead and Highgate' (68), bathed in golden summer after-glow." *The Times* stated: "The same associate's study of a favourite haunt of Keats, Shelly, Leigh Hunt, and Coleridge, between Hampstead and Highgate, with its hedge-row timber, and its long, low pile of red-roofed farm buildings, is set apart from the other work in the room by the depth and glow of its colour. Mr. Wallis evidently has no intention of allowing watercolour to remain at a disadvantage as compared with oils in these qualities."

Cat. 115. *A Sextett during the Terror*
1878; black and coloured chalks; dimensions unknown; whereabouts unknown.
Exhibitions: Old Water-Colour Society, Winter exhibition 1878-79, no. 90.
Literature: *Pall Mall Gazette*, 5 December 1878, p.11; *The Athenaeum*, No. 2667, 7 December 1878, p.730; *The Illustrated London News*, Vol. 73, 7 December 1878, p.542; *The Examiner*, 7 December 1878, p.1550; *The Graphic*, 7 December 1878, p.583; *Judy, or The London Serio-Comic Journal*, 11 December 1878, p.234; *The Australasian*, 8 February 1879, p.168.

This picture depicts musicians playing while Paris is in the grip of the most violent period of the French Revolution; it may be based on a literary source though the authors have been unable to identify it.

The critic for *The Athenaeum*, undoubtedly Wallis's old friend F.G. Stephens, in his review of the Winter exhibition of the Old-Water Colour Society, noted: "The place of honour is filled with *A Sextett during the Terror* (No. 90), by Mr. Wallis, a party of French amateurs and their friends enjoying music in an upper chamber, the window of which reveals the houses and towers of Paris, while a purple evening twilight succeeds to the garish orange of declining day, and the luster still fills the room where the lovers of brass and string instruments are in the full swing of their performance, their figures strongly relieved against the light. Their attitudes and faces are full of animation, varied and dramatically rich in expression, rapt in the music, and not without a certain quaintness which is charming. The figure of the performer with the violin, who waits the march of the music so heedfully, and keeps his place so well, is particularly admirable. The harmony, local colour, greys, and illumination of this picture are most artistic."

The Illustrated London News indicated: "But his principal drawing, 'A Sextett during the Terror' (90), which occupies a post of honour, is a study of effect, merely in coloured, but mainly black, chalks. To paint a picture of the subject an additional study for the colour would be desirable. Otherwise there is great merit in this composition of amateur instrumentalists (as were some of the most blood-thirsty terrorists), playing so heedlessly, while the frequent clank and thud of the guillotine might be heard not far off – fiddling away, like Nero while Rome was burning. The important gestures of the first and second violin as they sway to the time are cleverly suggested; very good, also, is the management of lighting from the large casement, through which we see the towers of Notre-Dame and the picturesque spires and house-tops of old Paris in the *Cité*."

The reviewer for the *Pall Mall Gazette* had these comments: "Mr. Henry Wallis contributes by far the most striking picture of the exhibition to which the place of honour has accordingly been assigned. It is named 'A Sextett during the Terror' (90) and represents six gentlemen in the costume of the eighteenth century playing on various stringed and wind instruments; while another group of gentlemen, in similar attire, play the part of attentive listeners. Whether any particular incident of the history of the Revolution is illustrated does not appear from the picture. The faces can not be said to betray any anxiety beyond that to be accounted for by unmanageable semiquavers. Through the window some Paris architecture is dimly discovered, the colour of this background being surprisingly crude and unreal for so good an artists as Mr. Wallis. The attitudes of the performers on the other hand, are masterly, and the design as a whole is decidedly clever."

Cat. 116. *The Farmhouse by the Sea*
1877; medium, dimensions and whereabouts unknown.
Exhibitions: Birmingham Royal Society of Artists, Autumn Exhibition, 1877, no. 95, priced at £31 10s.

Nothing is known about the subject of this work other than what its title suggests.

Cat. 117. *A Portrait of Alice Boyd*
1878; oil on board; 35.6 x 30.5 cm (14 x 12 in.); private collection.
Inscriptions: Signed with initials *HW* and dated 1878.
Provenance: Alice Boyd, Penkill Castle, Ayrshire; thence by descent in 1897 to her niece Eleanor Margaret Courtney-Boyd, and thence in 1946 to Margaret's half-sister Evelyn May Courtney-Boyd; likely acquired by Elton A. Eckstrand when he became 18th Laird of Penkill; his sale Christie's, Girvan, Ayrshire, 15 December 1992, lot 175; private collection.

This full-length portrait is of a woman in a dark dress and black mantilla, standing by a chest or stand. The subject is, undoubtedly, Alice Boyd, the 14th Laird of Penkill Castle,[1] Ayrshire, herself a Pre-Raphaelite painter and William Bell Scott's mistress. Henry Wallis was befriended by them and he stayed at Penkill on several occasions. During the summer of 1873, for example, he spent several weeks with them and Scott painted his portrait (present whereabouts unknown). A comparison between this portrait and images known to be of Alice Boyd can leave little doubt that she was the model. Wallis's letter to Alice on the death of Scott at Penkill in November 1890 is among the Penkill Papers in the Library of the University of British Columbia.

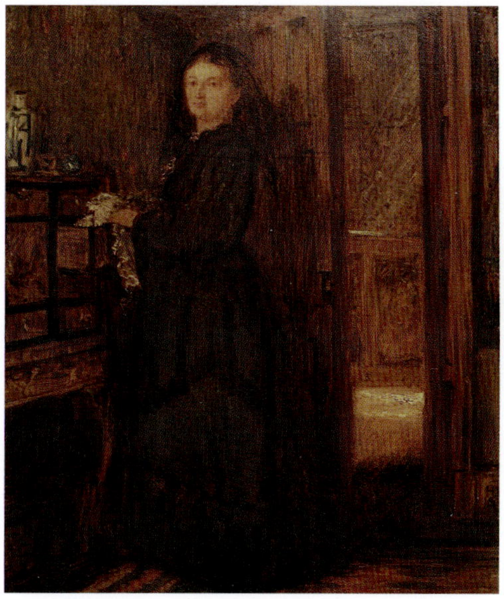

Cat. 117. Image courtesy of Christie's

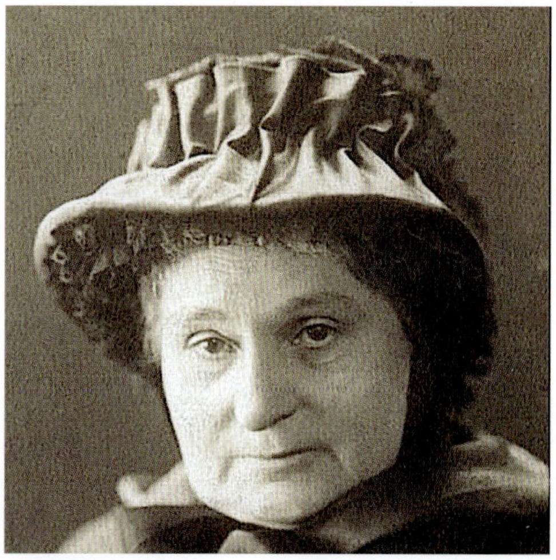

Alice Boyd in old age

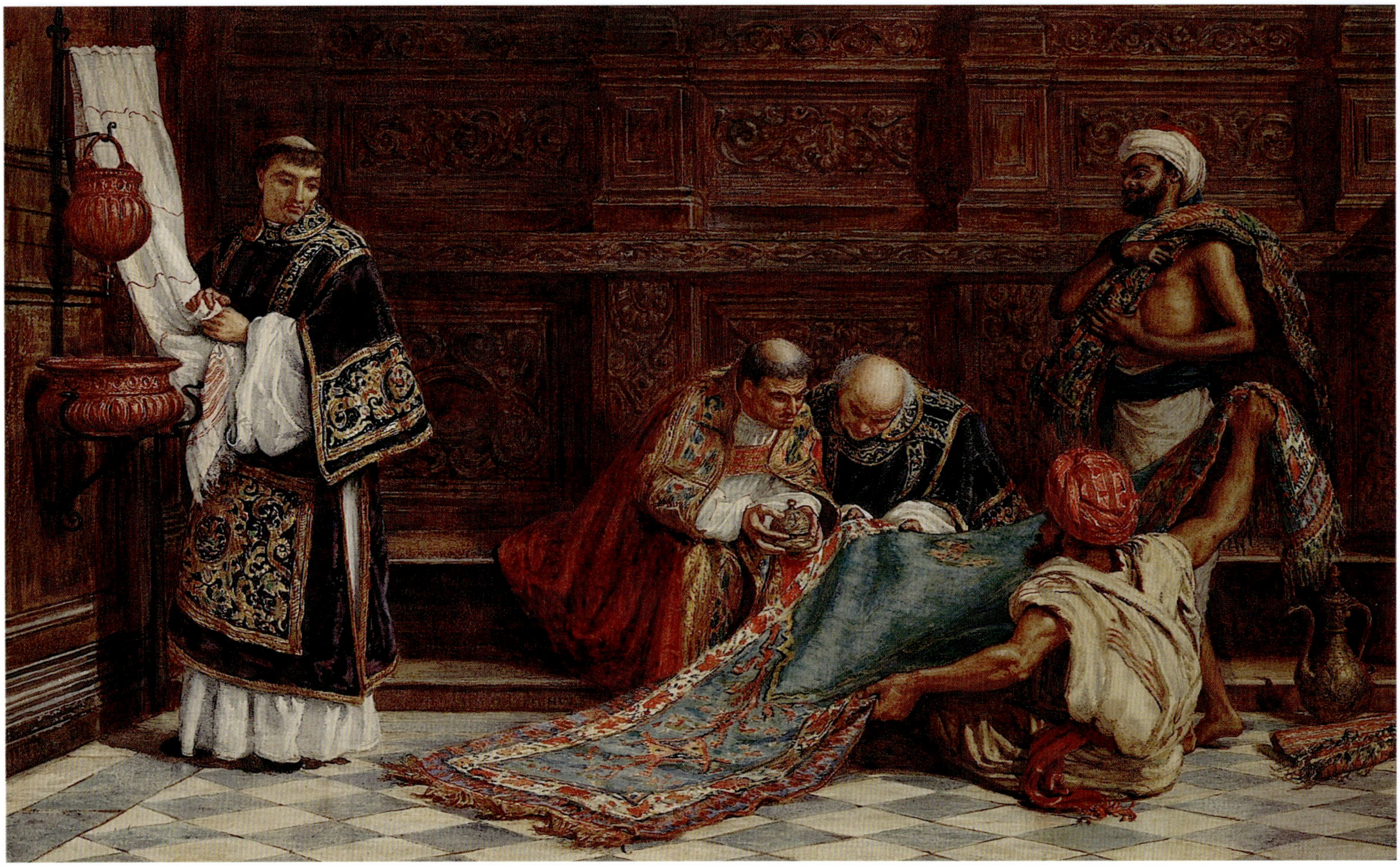

Cat. 120. Image courtesy of Bonhams, London

Cat. 118. *Autumn*
1878; ?oil on canvas; dimensions unknown; whereabouts unknown.
Exhibitions: Paris, *Exposition Universelle*, 1878, no. 254.[1]
Literature: 'Fine-Art Gossip', *The Athenaeum*, No. 2608, 20 October 1877, p.507; *The Architect*, Vol. 19, 4 May 1878, p.272.

Could this possibly be the picture F.G. Stephens discussed in Fine-Art Gossip in *The Athenaeum* in October 1877: "Mr. Wallis has just finished a fine landscape, consisting of a group of dense and richly foliaged oaks standing in a glowing evening light, with glimpses of golden and silver sky beneath, between and above the boughs. The verdure rises high, if that can be called verdure which is deepened with brown and purple, grey and marone, ash-like and amber hues suffusing the seemingly impenetrable wilderness of leaves that tower aloft and spread themselves to right and left in weird and gigantic bulks. It is a fine study of colour, and very rich and fine in tone; a poetic dignity and Poussin-like massiveness mark the design."

Cat. 119. *A Flemish Interior*
1878; watercolour; dimensions unknown; whereabouts unknown.
Exhibitions: Old Water-Colour Society, 1878, no. 55.
Literature: *The Athenaeum*, No. 2636, 4 May 1878, p.578; *The Illustrated London News*, vol. 72, 4 May 1878, p.418; *The Graphic*, 4 May 1878, p.446; *Fun*, 8 May 1878, p.191.

F.G. Stephens, in his review in *The Athenaeum* of the Old Water-Colour Society's exhibition of 1878, noted: "Mr. Wallis's third, *A Flemish Interior*, reminds us, both in composition and in sentiment of De Hoogh. This, perhaps, results from the yellows of the girl's hair, and the painting of the two windows, between which she stands dressing before the mirror, while an old lady sits at one side with an expression of motherly criticism. Whether from the horizon being too high, or from the lines of the floor radiating from the centre of the picture, we will not undertake to say, but the floor makes, to our eyes, a false impression of sloping, which could be easily obviated."

The critic of *The Illustrated London News* also noted the influence of 17th-century Dutch painting on this work: "The fourth Associate is Henry Wallis, to whom the compliment ought to have been paid years ago. His 'Flemish Interior' (55) is Van Hoogish in design, but it lacks the purity and charm of the Dutchman." The critic of *The Graphic* stated: "Two of Mr. Wallis's drawings, 'A Flemish Interior' and 'The Carpet Merchant', are rather reminiscent of Flemish *genre*-painters and Venetian colourists than really original works."

Cat. 120. *In a Sacristy, the Carpet Merchant*
1878; watercolour; 35.5 x 55.8 cm (14 x 22 in.); private collection.
Inscriptions: Signed with initials *HW*.
Provenance: Wallis's studio and then by descent from the artist to his son Harold Wallis, then to his daughter-in-law Mary Wallis (née Mary Elizabeth Aymes), then her great-niece Vera G. Cooper (née Langley) (1910-1989), and thence by direct descent to John Harold Cooper and family until sold at Bonhams, London, 05 March 2002, lot 65, sold for £2,200; private collection of Patrick Holden.
Exhibitions: Old Water-Colour Society, 1878, no. 107; Royal Birmingham Society of Artists, *Spring Exhibition of Water-colour Paintings*, 1879, no. 86, asking price £84.
Literature: *The Athenaeum*, No. 2636, 4 May 1878, p.578; *The Illustrated London News*, Vol. 72, 4 May 1878, p.418; *The Graphic*, 4 May 1878, p.446; *Fun*, 8 May 1878, p.191; *Birmingham Daily Post*, 28 March 1879, p.5.

Wallis introduces Oriental elements into his work for the first time. For a long time, he had shown an interest in ceramics and his fascination with the Middle East would certainly dominate his later years. As Wallis's first journey to Egypt was not until 1885, the Oriental elements in this work are clearly from his imagination rather than observation of real life. This type of subject was popularised by the well-known French academic painter Gérôme, another pupil of Gleyre.

F.G. Stephens, in *The Athenaeum*, wrote about this work: "*In a Sacristy – The Carpet Merchant* (107) is a gorgeous piece of colour; the Oriental seller of carpets and his slave bargain with two priests just come in from high mass in the neighbouring chapel, while a third washes his hands at a brazen lavatory, attached, as usual, to the wall. Every one of these figures is a rich study of powerful colour, and the group is posed against a carved wood panelling, madder-brown predominating, admirably painted. The propriety of expression on the faces and the lively concern shown in the transaction are notably represented."

The Illustrated London News stated: "The Arab carpet merchant (107) showing his wares to two priests who are clad in gorgeous vestments...are all charming pictures, and prove how wisely the council acted in electing their author." The year 1878, of course, was when Wallis was elected an associate of the Old Water-Colour Society.

Cat. 121. *The Sentinel*
1878; watercolour; dimensions unknown; whereabouts unknown.
EXHIBITIONS: Old Water-Colour Society, 1878, no. 187.
LITERATURE: *The Athenaeum*, No. 2636, 4 May 1878, p.578; *The Illustrated London News*, Vol. 72, 4 May 1878, p.418; *Fun*, 8 May 1878, p.191.

F.G. Stephens had these comments in his review of the Old Water-Colour Society exhibition of 1878: "The fourth and best contribution of this new member, or rather, we may say, most important is *The Sentinel* (187). An Arab, wrapped in one of the most admirable masses of striped silk drapery ever painted, perhaps, waits at the door, it may be, of a council-chamber, while a gazelle, the pet of the household, has come to see who the strange intruder is. Such are the simple materials, but the power and solidity of effect without loss of transparency show the immense value of an education in oil painting over undivided practice with water, which is so apt to make the painter work by thin washes, in the fear of losing his ground. Here not a line of the pattern of the striped silk is lost, while every fold is emphatically drawn with a firm hand. The background, again, is dispersed all over with a pattern that must have tried the artist's patience, like some elaborate portions of Lewis's pictures that used to excite our wonder.[1] Yet this background is kept down in a broad and sound manner, showing no desire to attract undue attention to the detail."

The Illustrated London News commented: " 'The Sentinel' (187), a lithe Arab in ample drapery, armed with a long rifle, regarding with pleased interest a lovely gazelle which has trotted up to the steps of the Sanctum which he guards."

[See also: Cat. 285]

Cat. 122. *The Prison Window*
1878; watercolour; 36.9 x 46.4 cm (14½ x 18¼ in.); whereabouts unknown.
PROVENANCE: Mrs. Fitzroy Johnstone, 23 Pelham Place S.W., London; her sale Christie's, 5 March 1917, lot 11, bought by the art dealer W.W. Sampson & Sons for £14 14s.
EXHIBITIONS: Old Water-Colour Society, 1878, no. 282.
LITERATURE: 'Fine-Art Gossip', *The Athenaeum*, No. 2619, 5 January 1878, p.28; *The Athenaeum*, No. 2636, 4 May 1878, p.578; *The Illustrated London News*, vol. 72, 4 May 1878, p.418; *The Graphic*, 4 May 1878, p.446; *Fun*, 8 May 1878, p.191.

F.G. Stephens, in *The Athenaeum* (May), stated: "...the fourth a reproduction in small of *The Prison Window* (No. 282) every one remembers with so much pleasure at the Academy. This replica, so different in size, possesses all the effect of the original, and the interest is rather enhanced by the increased expression of rough delight among the prisoners, to whom the amusement of the little performer is a godsend." *The Athenaeum* had previously announced: "Everybody will be glad to hear that Mr. Wallis's picture, 'The Prison Window', which was recognised as one of the unusually small number of works of art at the last Royal Academy, is to be etched by Prof. Unger."[1] No impression of this print has been found, if it was executed.

The Illustrated London News, in commenting on Wallis's election to the O.W.S., said: "...and the little strolling musician playing her violin before the window of an Italian prison (282) to the immense delight of the inmates, are all charming pictures, and prove how wisely the council acted in electing their author."

Cat. 123. *Awaiting the Distribution*
1878; watercolour; dimensions unknown; whereabouts unknown.
EXHIBITIONS: Old Water-Colour Society, Winter exhibition 1878, no. 50.
LITERATURE: *Pall Mall Gazette*, 5 December 1878, p.11; *The Times*, 6 December 1878, p.3; *The Graphic*, 7 December 1878, p.583; *The Athenaeum*, No. 2667, 7 December 1878, p.730; *The Australasian*, 8 February 1879, p.168.

Wallis made this watercolour either during or following his trip to Bruges and Brussels, 25 May–7 June 1877. He may have made sketches and notes for the picture during his Belgium tour and later worked up his finished watercolour in the studio. It was exhibited accompanied by this quotation: "It is a frequent custom at Bruges for persons to bequeath money to be expended in the distribution of bread to the poor."

In his review for *The Athenaeum* of the Old Water-Colour Society exhibition, F.G. Stephens reserved his greatest praise for Wallis's painting *A Sextet during the Terror*, but had these comments to make: "Hardly less attractive is this painter's *Awaiting the Distribution* (50), Belgian women gathered thick before the jube [rood screen] of a large church at Bruges, while behind them is a heap of brown loaves, the dole of some pious founder; the Suisse[1] and an attendant await the moment to distribute the bread, and the close line of black-robed women of all ages, buxom and luxurious, sedate and sad, withered and wan, with here and there a child or two, gossip eagerly after their kind. This is an admirable study of colour, the black and orange going finely with the grey, and interspersed with higher notes of the chromatic scale – the whole displayed with consummate skill in a perfect harmony of tints, and, while sober almost to a sadness, as rich in colour as it can be. Nor are the tones less fine, nor the chiaroscuro less complete."

The reviewer for *The Times* stated: "No figure drawing in the room is likely to make more impression than Mr. H. Wallis's 'Distribution of a Dole of Bread at Bruges', thanks to its simple elements of effect, the crowd of black-cloaked, white-coifed women and the great pile of golden loaves, against the dark background of carved oak."

The critic for *The Pall Mall Gazette* declared: "...but very graceful, also, is the same artist's 'Awaiting the Distribution' (50) – a number of women dressed in the long black cloaks and white hats peculiar to Bruges, awaiting the distribution of the good things doled out to them by a magnificent official adorned with a cocked hat and other insignia."

Cat. 124. *At a Window at St. Germain*
*c.*1878; medium and dimensions unknown; whereabouts unknown.
PROVENANCE: C.C. Grimes, Stonehouse, Gloucestershire; his estate sale Christie's, 18 February 1888, lot 82, bought for £4 4s by Cartwright.

In 1878 Wallis travelled to Paris to cover the Exposition Universelle for F.G. Stephens who was ill; it is likely that this work was executed during this visit. Saint-Germain-des-Prés is one of the four administrative quarters of the 6th arrondissement of Paris. The École des Beaux Arts is located in this quarter and during the 19th century the area was favoured by many foreign artists and writers, Wallis evidently being no exception.

Cat. 125. *After the Trial: Antonio receiving the Congratulations of his Friends (Antonio is released from Shylock's Bond)*
(The Merchant of Venice, Act IV, Scene 1)
1879; watercolour; 81.3 x 50.8 cm (32 x 20 in.); private collection.
Inscriptions: Signed with initials *HW* on recto; signed on label on reverse.
Provenance: Wallis's studio and then by descent from the artist to his son Harold Wallis; then to his daughter-in-law Mary Wallis (née Mary Elizabeth Aymes); then to her great-niece Vera G. Cooper (née Langley) (1910-1989); then by direct descent to John Harold Cooper and family until sold at Bonhams, London, 5 March 2002, lot 67; bought by Neil Wilson of Campbell Wilson for £3,800; on consignment with Shepherd & Derom Gallery, New York, in 2003; returned to Neil Wilson and sold to a private collector.
Exhibitions: Old Water-Colour Society, 1879, no. 14; Birmingham Royal Society of Artists, *Spring Exhibition of Water-colour Paintings*, 1880, no. 191; Shepherd & Derom Galleries, New York, *English Romantic Art 1850-1920*, 2003, no. 82.
Literature: *The Portfolio*, Vol. 11, 1879, p.108; *Pall Mall Gazette*, 2 May 1879, p.12; *The British Architect*, Vol.11, 2 May 1879, p.181; *The Architect*, 3 May 1879, p.258; *The Spectator*, Vol. 52, 7 June 1879, p.726; *The Illustrated London News*, Vol. 75, 4 October 1879, p.314; *Birmingham Daily Post*, 30 March 1880, p.6; *The Artist and Journal of Home Culture*, Vol. I, 15 April 1880, p.108.

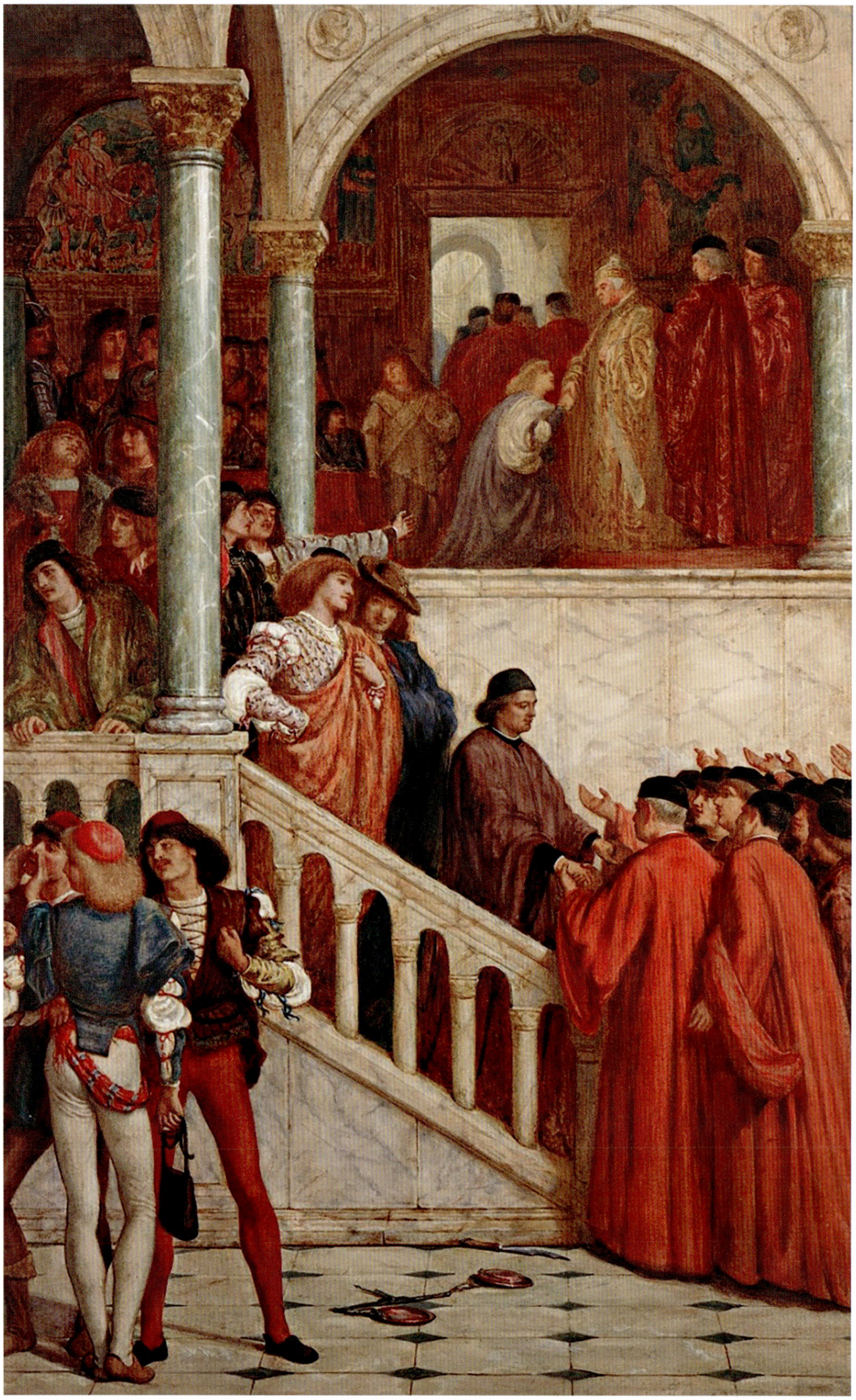

Cat. 125. Image courtesy of Bonhams, London

This particular play by Shakespeare obviously held a great attraction for Wallis as he chose to illustrate many scenes from it over the years.

This work was heavily influenced by Venetian early Renaissance painting, particularly by Carpaccio, who was a great favourite with the Pre-Raphaelites including Wallis. The back view of the standing male figure in pale tights in the foreground is also very reminiscent of a similar figure in Frederic Leighton's *Dante in Exile*, which Wallis undoubtedly would have seen in the Royal Academy exhibition of 1864. The reviewer for the *Pall Mall Budget* expressed this opinion on this watercolour: "By far the most important contributor to the Exhibition of the Society of Painters in Water Colours, as regards at least subject and size of pictures, is Mr. Henry Wallis. One of his pictures, No. 14, represents Antonio receiving the congratulations of his friends after the trial. There is not in Shakespeare's play a scene exactly answering to the situation, but the chief characters may without difficulty be recognised. In the centre of the picture we see the 'royal merchant' coming down a flight of steps, and receiving the congratulations of a crowd of friends, in a very dignified attitude. Among the latter are conspicuous some senators, or legal dignitaries, clad in the red robes which Mr. Wallis loves to paint. The other numerous figures in the picture, composing the crowd of lawyers, friends, and attendants which issues from the court, are grouped in an artistic way; but there is little of the

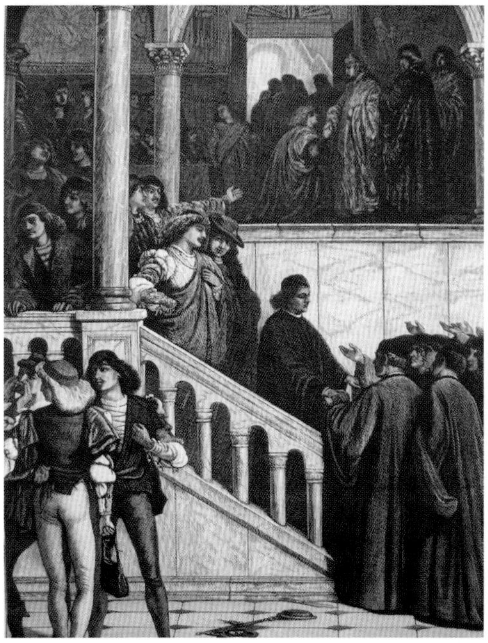

Cat. 125a. Image courtesy of Dennis Lanigan collection

dramatic life which such a scene might call forth – in other words, the design is too ornamental to be interesting."

The reviewer for *The Architect* commented: "Shakespeare used to be the especial topic of the President [John Gilbert], but the recent election of Mr. Henry Wallis has brought a competitor. This artist in every way brings novelty to the Gallery; his brilliant isolated colouring, his mode of composition, which delights in architectural accessories and dividing of masses after the example of the Venetians and the missal painters, are individualities quite refreshing. *After the Trial* (14), from the 'Merchant of Venice,' is a new reading from the ordinary stage version; Mr. Wallis's *Antonio*, who descends the staircase welcomed by outflung hands of congratulation, is not saturnine and sad of apparel, but a grave and dignified gentleman, senatorial in manner and costume, noble of visage, who smiles quietly with a look of comfort at escape from horror that has yet left its mark in the just tremulous mouth. The stairs and court swarm with courtiers, gay as butterflies, chattering, laughing, and congratulating; above, in the council chamber, the golden-draped doge is seen dimly, giving a hand to the kneeling Portia. As a study of colour this is as bold a piece of work as we ever saw; the frank splendour of the figures is thrown into balance by the expedient of marble buildings and pillars of bright green."

The reviewer for *Birmingham Daily Post* would later point this out as one of the chief pieces in the Royal Society of Artists, Birmingham, exhibition of 1880 and commented: "The gem of the exhibition is, undoubtedly, Mr. Wallis's 'After the Trial' (191) – a scene realised with great dramatic power, from 'The Merchant of Venice,' and rendered with consummate skill and rare feeling for the harmonies of rich and glowing colour."

Cat. 125a. ***After the Trial: Antonio receiving the Congratulations of his Friends – Merchant of Venice (after Henry Wallis)***
1879. Wood engraving; image size: 44.3 x 28.7 cm. (17⅝ x 11¼ in.); sheet size: 54.6 x 40.5 cm. (21½ x 15¹⁵⁄₁₆ in.); Dr Dennis T. Lanigan, Saskatoon, Canada.
Annotations: (lettering below image) "AFTER THE TRIAL: ANTONIO RECEIVING THE CONGRATULATIOS OF HIS FRIENDS. – 'Merchant of Venice.' By HENRY WALLIS"; signed in the plate with unidentified monogram, lower right.
Literature: *The Illustrated London News*, Vol. 75, 4 October 1879, p.314; *The Illustrated London News*, 15 November 1879, p.455.

An engraving by the British printmaker Frederick Wentworth (fl. 1865-94), after the watercolour, was published in the *Illustrated London News*, double-page from the 'Extra Supplement', Vol. 75, no. 2103, 4 October 1879, p.314.

The reviewer for *The Illustrated London News* had these comments on Wallis's picture: "The full title of this richly-coloured and otherwise remarkable drawing by Mr. Henry Wallis, which was noticed in one of the exhibitions of the Old Society of Painters in Water-Colours, is 'After the Trial: Antonio receives the Congratulations of his Friends'. This addition to the title distinguishes the particular incident in the dénouement of the drama intended to be most prominently represented; but the story altogether is here told pictorially and with singular completeness. The artist has taken the architecture of a portion of the Ducal Palace at Venice, and by an ingenious adaptation has rendered it subservient to the purposes of his composition. This has admitted a disposition of all the various groups essential to the dramatic situation. Nor are the characteristic gestures and expressions of the individual figures less aptly discriminated. The only personage of importance absent is Shylock; but the knife and scales on the pavement are sufficient memorials of that cruel Jewish money-dealer; and it is evident that he is hardly yet out of sight and of ear-shot, for in the lower corner on the left hand three friends of Antonio are watching the baffled murderer slink away, and one of them is shouting after him some taunting gibe, perhaps relating to his promised christening. Antonio, descending the staircase, unlike his companions, is very properly habited in the plainest possible garb, as befits a man who had resigned himself to probable death. He holds forth both hands to receive the congratulations of the 'troops of friends' who, as his noble character well deserved, are warmly attached to him. Behind follow, with other intimates, Gratiano, Salanio, and Salarino, his faithful debtor, the hardly less noble-minded Bassanio, for whom Antonio had risked his life, and who through his friend's aid had won the rich and beautiful heiress Portia. Above is Portia herself, in her robes, disguised as the young doctor-of-laws of Rome – 'another Daniel come to judgment.' At the happy termination of the trial the Duke of Venice entreats the clever supposed young doctor to come home with him to dinner. But she 'humbly desires his Grace of pardon' to decline, and in doing so would probably kneel, as indicated in the picture – alleging the necessity of setting forth at once to Padua. About the duke, or Doge, are some of the 'magnificoes' of Venice; and to the left is the table of the 'Court of Justice,' where the trial has been held. The costumes in which the artist has chosen to attire his figures are not, as usual upon the stage, those of the English Elizabethan fashion, but are of the Venetian style, as shown in the pictures of Bellini and Carpaccio. This work of Mr. H. Wallis is an attempt to give a decorative treatment to the subject, in the manner of wall-pictures by those Italian masters."

Cat. 126. ***An Operetta***
1879; watercolour; dimensions unknown; whereabouts unknown.
Exhibitions: Old Water-Colour Society, 1879, no. 62.
Literature: *The Portfolio*, Vol. 11, 1879, p.108; *Pall Mall Gazette*, 2 May 1879, p.12; *The Architect*, 3 May 1879, pp.258-59; *The Morning Post*, 8 May 1879, p.3.

When this picture was shown at the Old Water-Colour Society it was accompanied by this quotation in the catalogue: "At the commencement of the Revolution the Royalist prisoners amused themselves with theatrical representations, concerts and other diversions, only interrupted by the daily announcement of the list of those who were called for trial, but even this soon became subject for pleasantry." The reviewer for the *Pall Mall Budget* had these comments on this picture: "We recently commented upon a picture by the same artist, in which a quartet-party of French gentlemen were the actors and a Paris prison during the First Revolution the scene. In 'An Operetta' a similar motive is treated…On an improvised stage we see a shepherdess placed apparently between a father, or it may be an ancient lover, and a youthful and handsome Corydon, and singing to the accompaniment of an orchestra consisting of a violin, a violin-cello, a double-bass, and a clarinet, all playing with the zeal of dilettanti, while the conductor beats the time in an equally vigorous manner. A crowd of spectators composed of sweet-faced girls and gentlemen are evidently enjoying the fun with French carelessness and *gaité de coeur*. The tragic reverse of the medal is seen in the right corner of the picture, where a commissary of the Revolutionary Tribunal is just entering with a list of names in his hand. To determine who amongst the gay crowd will be the victim is left to the spectator's imagination; and in this vagueness of the danger, as well as in the contrast already pointed out, the most impressive feature of the composition must be discovered. The dramatic situation, however, has not been turned to sufficient pictorial account; the colour is uninteresting, and the facial expression of the various *dramatis personae* should have been more individual."

The critic of *The Architect* declared: "... *An Operetta* (62) represents an episode in the Days of Terror, when the irrepressible gaiety and *politesse* of the courtly Parisians made them get up musical and theatrical entertainments among themselves within the walls of their prison, and while each day summoned some of their number to a ghastly death; the subject does not lose its point in the artist's hand, though it might perhaps have been treated with greater emphasis."

Cat. 127. *Luca Signorelli*
1879; watercolour; dimensions unknown; whereabouts unknown.
Exhibitions: Old Water-Colour Society, Winter exhibition 1879, no. 122.
Literature: *The Globe*, 1879; *The Academy*, Vol. 17, 10 January 1879, p.34; *The Athenaeum*, No. 2717, 22 November 1879, p.667; *The Standard*, 12 December 1879, p.3; *The Athenaeum*, No. 2720, 13 December 1879, p.768; *The Illustrated London News*, Vol. 75, 13 December 1879, pp.558-559; *The Architect*, 13 December 1879, p.344; *The Times*, 26 December 1879, p.10; *The Saturday Review*, Vol. 49, 3 January 1880, p.19; *The Spectator*, Vol. 53, 3 January 1880, p.17; *The Artist and Journal of Home Culture*, Vol. I, 15 January 1880, p.26.

F.G. Stephens, in *The Athenaeum*, noted: "Mr. Wallis sends five works, of which the most important is *Luca Signorelli* (122), the painter, a stalwart and astute-looking sedate figure ascending a narrow street of many steps, and preceded by his son, a gallant youth, who looks up to laugh with the pretty children who peer at him from the garden wall above. The father and son are on their way to the *atelier*, and the latter carries a book of studies. The dark and rich costume of the artist and the more brilliant dress of the boy contrast vividly with the white walls, dashed by spaces of sunny light. This is a powerful and artistic work."

The critic for *The Times* also liked this work: "The figure painters are hardly as prominent as usual. H. Wallis is the most prominent in this branch. His 'Luca Signorelli' represents the grave painter in sober black, on his way home from his work, in Sienna, or Cortona, or Orvieto, descending a narrow alley, from over the wall of which two merry little girls laugh down to the merry apprentice who carries the master's portfolio. The contrast of sober, thoughtful age and light, laughing youth is very prettily and naturally brought out, and there is force and dignity without exaggeration in the painter's face and figure, his look and gait. The architecture looks solid and strong enough for the figures."

The critic for *The Globe* said: "The figure of the painter is dignified and characteristic, but the vitality of the work depends on that of the youth. In English art we have rarely met with a figure drawn with so much knowledge and skill, and at the same time so spontaneous and natural in movement."

The critic for *The Architect* added these favourable comments: "...the artist shows a large picture of *Luca Signorelli* (122) leisurely wending his way to his studio, down a flight of steps between walls, paint-brushes in hand, a dignified, self-contained figure, wrapt in a long dark mantle, and preceded in vivid contrast by a lithe youth, his pupil, dressed in the tight-fitting motley suit of the period, who bends back his laughing head to greet a couple of children that are pelting him with blossoms from the garden wall above. The motive of the picture is delightful, and the execution excellent. There is an emphatic manner of telling his story, which belongs to the artist. In this case the figures are kept in clear-cut isolation, against the pale grey walls, and the incident of the girls scattering flowers, with the sprays of blossoming foliage that fringe the wall, serves to connect the otherwise too-much separated chief figures, and to prevent the perpendicular lines of the composition from being too obtrusive. The face of SIGNORELLI has been studied from authentic sources – a strong, square-built physiognomy with keen eyes... Mr. Wallis has well individualised the dignified artist of 'upright life, sincere in all things,' who 'lived in the manner of a noble and a gentleman'."

Cat. 128. *Announcement of Marriage-Town Hall at Bruges*
1879; black and coloured chalks; dimensions unknown; whereabouts unknown.
Exhibitions: Old Water-Colour Society, Winter exhibition 1879, no. 258.
Literature: *The Athenaeum*, No. 2720, 13 December 1879, p.768; *The Illustrated London News*, Vol. 75, 13 December 1879, p.558; *The Architect*, 13 December 1879, p.344; *The Times*, 26 December 1879, p.10.

Wallis had previously travelled to Bruges and Brussels in 1877. In July and August of 1879, he made a grand tour of the Netherlands and of Belgium, including Bruges, and it appears that this painting and the following three works [Cats. 129, 130 and 131] are a result of this journey.

The critic of *The Illustrated London News* stated: "Mr. Henry Wallis is another artist who affords us interesting glimpses into the incipient stages of his work in two expressive drawings in black and coloured chalks. In one we see the poor of a congregation that remains 'Nearest the Door in the Cathedral of Bruges' (264) only so many backs are visible, but they are all bowed low in prayer [see: Cat 129]. The other shows a peasant couple making their 'Announcement of Marriage in the Townhall of Bruges' (258). There is humour in the slight touch of curiosity or *badinage* that peers through the business-like air of the clerks whose heads are seen over the desk of the bureau, and the face of the future wife is very sweet." F.G. Stephens in *The Athenaeum* commented on this drawing: "... a little piece sumptuously toned and soberly tinted. A bow-legged Belgian artisan, in a blue blouse and with shock hair, and his pretty bride have come to the office of the registrar of their parish, and a rakish clerk leers at the damsel. The 'serious' air of the whole and the rapt expressions of the women worshippers testify to the powers of the painter, and make this study a good picture."

Cat. 129. *Nearest the Door - Cathedral at Bruges*
1879; black and coloured chalks; dimensions unknown; whereabouts unknown.
Exhibitions: Old Water-Colour Society, Winter exhibition 1879, no. 264.
Literature: *The Illustrated London News*, Vol. 75, 13 December 1879, p.558; *The Architect*, 13 December 1879, p.344; *The Times*, 26 December 1879, p.10; *The Spectator*, Vol. 53, 3 January 1880, p.17; *The Building News and Engineering Journal*, Vol. 38, 16 January 1880, p.62.

The reviewer for *The Spectator* professed appreciatively: "We must leave unnoticed the other interesting works, only mentioning in conclusion that the contributions of Mr. Henry Wallis are almost the only figure ones of interest, and that of these, his picture of the tenants of the free seats in Bruges Cathedral seems to us to reach most nearly its mark. The large picture by this artist of Luca Signorelli must, we fear, be considered a meritorious failure." The critic of *The Times* reported: "Mr. Wallis has two groups in coloured crayons, from Antwerp [*sic*], one a youthful bridal pair, the other a row of poor worshippers – the poorest near the door, pitiful and pathetic." The critic for *The Architect* expressed the opinion that: "In the singular paucity of figure-subjects the contributions of Mr. Henry Wallis tell with increased value. Besides some capital little Dutch studies, interiors pitched in a somber key, reminding one of L'Hermitte,[1] and also, let us say, of the greater name of Rembrandt, the artist shows a large picture of *Luca Signorelli*." [See also: *The Illustrated London News* review under Cat. 128.]

Cat. 130. *A Dutch Hofje*
1879; watercolour; dimensions unknown; whereabouts unknown.
Exhibitions: Old Water-Colour Society, Winter exhibition 1879, no. 308.
Literature: *The Academy*, Vol. 17, 10 January 1879, p.34; *The Athenaeum*, No. 2720, 13 December 1879, pp.768-769; *The Illustrated London News*, Vol. 75, 13 December 1879, p.559; *The Times*, 26 December 1879, p.10.

No doubt Wallis is referring to the Hofje van Beresteyn near Haarlem, which housed a number of works by Frans Hals. On 6 August 1879, Wallis wrote to Frederic George Stephens from Haarlem: "Visitors to Haarlem who remember the pictures by Frans Hals in the Hofje van Beresteyn[1] will be surprised to hear that these celebrated works are no longer shown to the public. The rumour is that a money dealer of semitic origin has offered a large sum for the collection, wch two of the governors of the foundation are willing to accept, while the third – there are three – very rightly objects to the sale. Meanwhile the pictures are rigorously shut up. Is not this an instance in wch the Dutch government might well interfere to prevent the national disgrace of such important specimens of Dutch art leaving the country? If the pictures may be removed from the Hofje surely they shld find a permanent resting place in either the Stadhuis at Haarlem or the Nat. Gal. at Amsterdam."[2] Instead three of the pictures were purchased by the Louvre in Paris in 1885.[3]

F.G. Stephens, in his review in *The Athenaeum*, noted: "We recommend likewise *A Dutch Hofje* (308), the sunlit court and corridor of a hospital, with demure figures and large, splendid flowers; homely utensils are strewn about. De Hooghe would have been pleased with the ruddiness of the brick walls and tiled roofs, as displayed yet softened in the diffused splendours of the golden sunlight."

Cat. 131. *A Bridge at Delft – Market Day*
1879; watercolour; dimensions unknown; whereabouts unknown.
Exhibitions: Old Water-Colour Society, Winter exhibition 1879, no. 371.
Literature: *The Academy*, Vol. 17, 10 January 1879, p.34; *The Illustrated London News*, Vol. 75, 13 December 1879, p.559; *The Times*, 26 December 1879, p.10.

The critic of *The Illustrated London News* did not favour this work: "The artist also sends a view in Delft and other Dutch subjects, which appear to miss the aspect of the country and to be a little florid in colour; nor does one often meet so many fat vrouws[1] even in Holland." *The Times* was also critical: "He has besides some smaller Dutch quay scenes, not to our eye pleasing in colour, and clumsier in figures than Dutch housewives need to be made." The reviewer for *The Academy* was more complimentary, however: "By the same hand is *A Dutch Hofte* (almhouse) and two others, of which *A Bridge in Delft – Market Day*, is delightful; the group of three plump peasant women, standing in a triangle and having a regular good gossip, is excellent."

A drawing in one of Wallis's sketchbooks could be a study for this finished watercolour [See: Cat 312].

Cat. 132. *The School of Pan (after Luca Signorelli)*
?1877 ?1893; oil on panel; 35 x 46 cm (13¾ x 18⅛ in.); Gemaldegallerie, Staatliche Museen zu Berlin.
Provenance: Sotheby's Belgravia 29 June 1976, sold for £220; acquired in 1976 by the Gemäldegalerie, Staatliche Museen zu Berlin, invoice no.76.3.

Signorelli's original version of *The School of Pan* (*Das Reich des Pan*) dated 1489-90, formerly in the Kaiser-Friedrich-Museum, Berlin, was destroyed during the Second World War. This painting, also known as *The Realm of Pan*, numbered among the first Florentine paintings of large format devoted to a profane subject, along with Botticelli's *Primavera* and the *Birth of Venus*. Initially it was thought that Wallis's interest in Luca Signorelli had probably been aroused by Edward Burne-Jones, who had discovered the painter during his third journey to Italy in 1871. Wallis had actually seen Signorelli's work at Cortona and Orvieto the year previously, however, in April 1870, so it is thus possible that it was actually Wallis who suggested to Burne-Jones to visit these cities to see the painter's work. In an undated letter to Wallis, probably written during the period 1875-1880, Burne-Jones explains how much he admires the Italian master:[1]

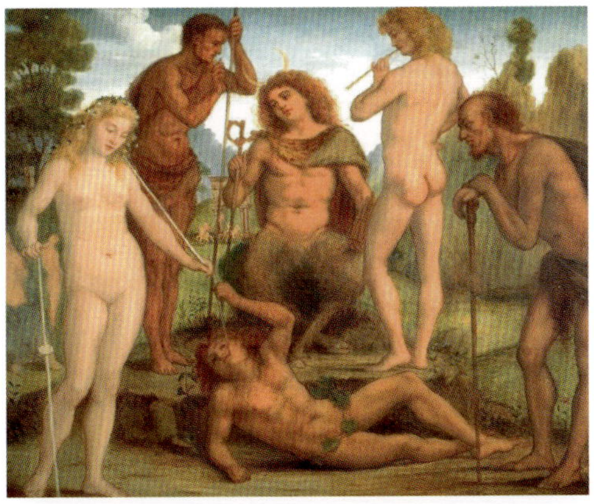

Cat. 132. Wallis's copy of *The School of Pan*. Image courtesy of Gemäldegalerie, Staatliche Museen zu Berlin

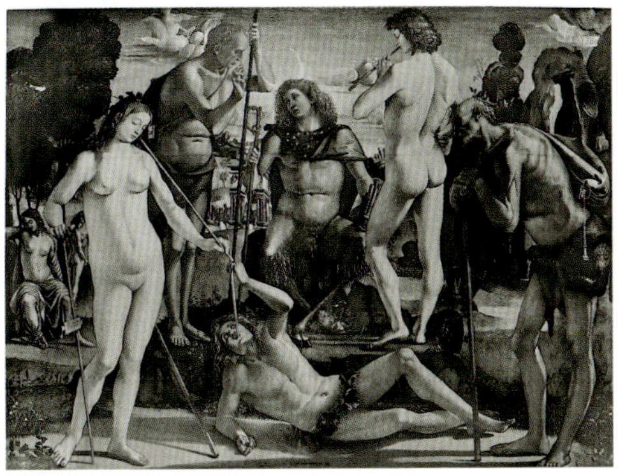

Original painting by Luca Signorelli, now destroyed. Image courtesy of Wikipedia Commons

> "Do you know how indistinct was your writing and that after four hours study I have come to certain conclusions about the substance of your letter that may after all have no warranty in fact. But on my assumption you have news of that sacred & divine volume of Signorelli woodcuts. Of course I want a copy more than I want any thing – but I can't, mustn't, daren't buy more, for I am much straightened this year – and no one would buy a copy that I know of but
> Morris1; Poynter1; Webb1; Colvin1; Howard1[2]
> I can think of no others, that's 6 with me. But I want the book terribly and pass sleepless nights, so to speak, because I haven't got it. O let me have it soon – please – my days in this soul sickening planet are shortening fast and nothing would restore me like that volume."[3]

Although it might be justified to date the present work to *c.*1877, there is no certainty. It is known, however, that Wallis visited the Prussian Royal Picture Gallery in Berlin in 1877 because he wrote about his visit and this particular painting in *The Athenaeum*.[4] Wallis remarked: "Chief among the recent acquisitions, perhaps foremost in the whole Gallery, is Luca Signorelli's 'Pan,' a picture which marks an epoch in the history of art…

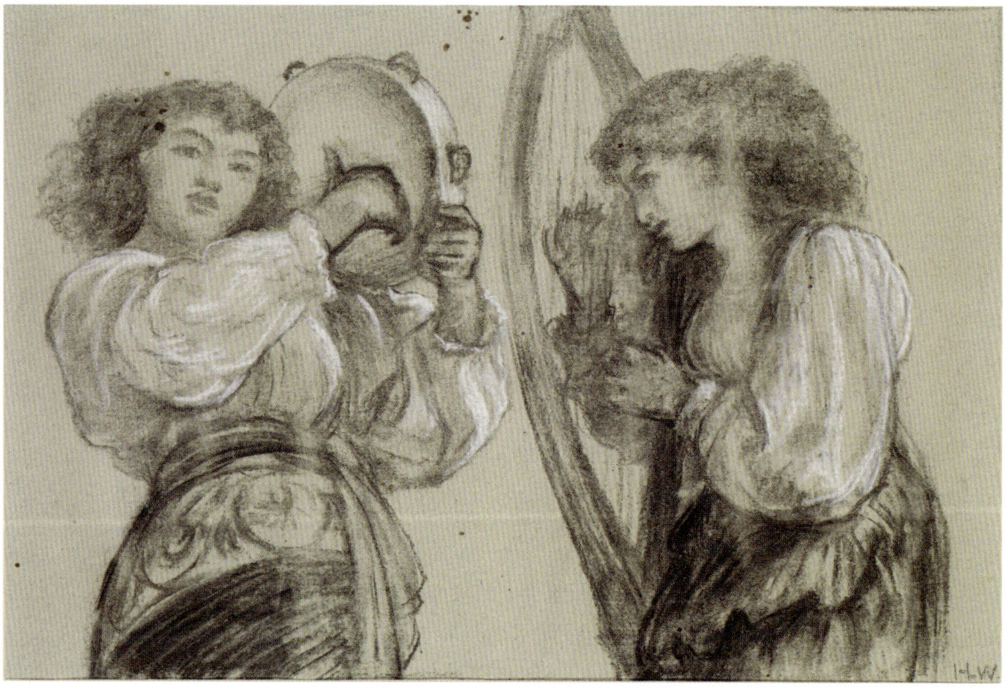

Cat. 133. Image by permission of Birmingham Museums Trust

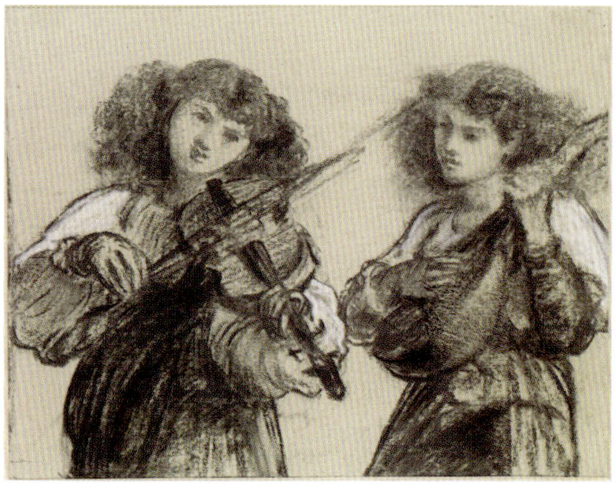

Cat. 134. Image by permission of Birmingham Museums Trust

Every Englishman must regret that we had the opportunity of acquiring such a priceless work and refused it, yet, seeing the rare and genuine enthusiasm evinced by the Berlin directors, one cannot help congratulating them on their treasure." Wallis was obviously very taken by this work and may very well have decided to copy it at that time. In 1893 the Burlington Fine Arts Club organised an 'Exhibition of the work of Luca Signorelli and his School'. This copy therefore could have been made soon thereafter, when Wallis travelled to Berlin, sometime between April 1893 and July 1894. Wallis, however, has stamped his own originality onto the work. The faces are more beautiful and reflect more closely the aesthetic sensibilities of the Victorian period. The background and foreground, and particularly the colouring and tone of the picture, have been considerably altered when one compares this to a coloured photograph of the original painting. Wallis's painting is, therefore, almost more of a pastiche of Signorelli's work, than it is a faithful copy.

Cat. 133. *Study of Two Italian girls Playing Tambourine and Harp*
*c.*1870s; black and white chalk on grey-green paper; 20.3 x 30 cm. (8 x 11¾ in.); Birmingham Museum and Art Gallery.
Inscriptions: Signed with initials *H.W.*, lower right.
Provenance: Harold Wallis; given to Birmingham Museum and Art Gallery in 1918, accession no. 1918P6.
Literature: Birmingham Museum and Art Gallery, *Catalogue of the Permanent Collection of Drawings*, 1939, p.414, no. 6'18.

This and the following three drawings appear strongly influenced by the 15th-century Renaissance painter Melozzo da Forlì's *Angels playing music.*[1]

Wallis definitely admired Italian art, in particular the art of the early Renaissance. Although in 1912, he had ordered a biography of Melozzo da Forlì,[2] it is highly improbable that the drawings were made then because the artist was by then aged 82 and afflicted with poor eyesight. It is more likely that these four drawings, now housed at the Birmingham Art Gallery, date from Wallis's Italian period during the 1870s when he painted such works as *His Highness and His Excellence the Ambassador of the Florentine Republic*, *A Despatch from Trebizond* and *Found at Naxos.* A letter from Wallis to Wilhelm Bode, dated 12 August [1880], confirms that by that time he was well acquainted with Melozzo's work: "Talking of saving, when I was at Forli I called attention in the 'Times' to Melozzo's frescoes in the roof of a chapel in the church of S.Francesco (?).[3] They are now full of cracks and pasted over with paper. The probability is that they will speedily fall down, or else that they will be restored so that none of Melozzo's work will remain."[4]

Cat. 134. *Study of Two Italian Girls Playing Violin and Lute*
*c.*1870s; black and white chalk on grey-green paper; 21.2 x 26.8 cm. (8⅜ x 10½ in.); Birmingham Museum and Art Gallery.
Provenance: Harold Wallis; given to Birmingham Museum and Art Gallery in 1918, accession no. 1918P4.
Literature: Birmingham Museum and Art Gallery, *Catalogue of the Permanent Collection of Drawings*, 1939, p.414, no. 4'18.

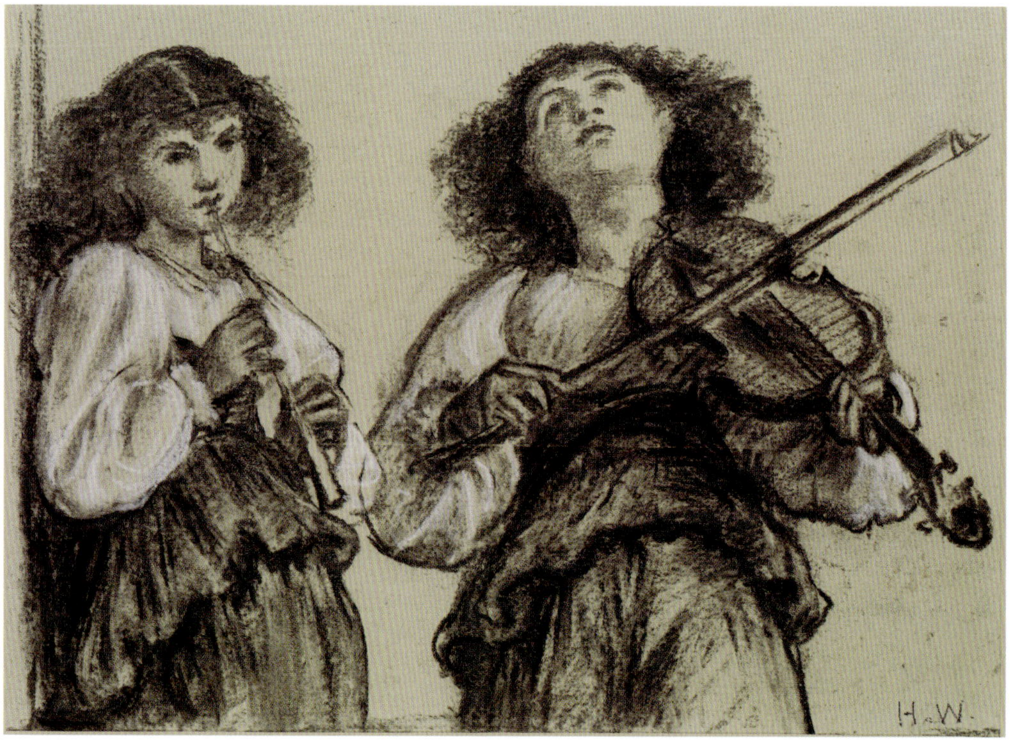

Cat. 135. Image by permission of Birmingham Museums Trust

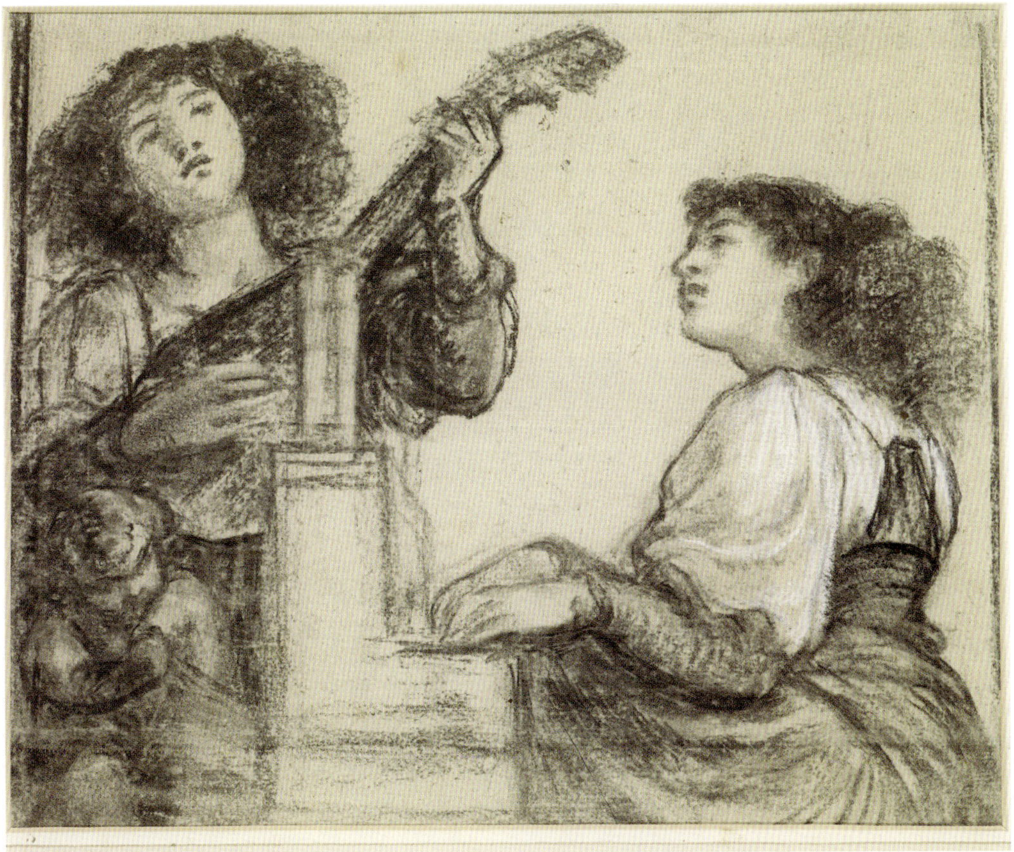

Cat. 136. Image by permission of Birmingham Museums Trust

The handling of the hair, the presence of the lute and, above all, the form of the bow indicate that Wallis admired and was influenced by Melozzo da Forlì (1438-1494), who is unfortunately largely forgotten now because so few of his works survive and he has been eclipsed by High Renaissance giants, such as Michelangelo, Leonardo da Vinci, and Raphael.

Cat. 135. *Study of Two Italian Girls Playing Violin and Pipe*
*c.*1870s; black and white chalk on pale grey-green paper; 21 x 26.7 cm. (8¼ x 10½ in.); Birmingham Museum and Art Gallery.
Inscriptions: Signed with initials *H.W.*, lower right.
Provenance: Harold Wallis; given to Birmingham Museum and Art Gallery in 1918, accession no. 1918P5.
Literature: Birmingham Museum and Art Gallery, *Catalogue of the Permanent Collection of Drawings*, 1939, p.414, no. 5'18; Harrison, Martin: *Pre-Raphaelite Paintings and Graphics*, 1970. Fig. 40.

Cat. 136. *Study of Two Italian Girls Playing Guitar and Organ*
*c.*1870s; black and white chalk on pale grey-green paper; 22.2 x 26.7 cm. (8¾ x 10½ in.); Birmingham Museum and Art Gallery
Provenance: Harold Wallis; given to Birmingham Museum and Art Gallery in 1918, accession no. 1918P7.
Literature: Birmingham Museum and Art Gallery, *Catalogue of the Permanent Collection of Drawings*, 1939, p.414, no. 7'18.

This work is somewhat reminiscent of Edward Burne-Jones's *Chant d'Amour.*[1] In Wallis's drawing, the organ is pumped by Cupid, the god of love, whereas in Burne-Jones's picture it is by Blind Love. These works by Wallis and by Burne-Jones were both, inturn, heavily influenced by Italian Renaissance painting, Wallis by Melozzo da Forlì, and Burne-Jones by Giorgione.

Cat. 137. *The Music Lesson (A Musical Gathering)*
*c.*1879; oil on canvas; 40.5 x 30 cm (16 x 11¾ in.); private collection.
Inscriptions: signed with initials *HW* on recto and signed on the back.
Provenance: Wallis's studio and then by descent from the artist to his daughter-in-law Alice Julyan Wallis (née Roberts), and thence to her great-niece Mrs. Vera G. Whiting, Purley, Surrey; her sale Sotheby's Belgravia, 10 April 1973, lot 195, bought B. Cohen for £280.

The influence of Flemish or Dutch 17th-century painting on this work seems obvious, especially De Hoogh,[1] whom Wallis particularly seemed to admire. Wallis made a journey through both Belgium and The Netherlands in July-August 1879, which makes 1879 a possible date for the painting. Note that the date on the watercolour sketch [Cat. 137a.] is barely legible and *could* read 1889, which would also then influence the date of this painting.

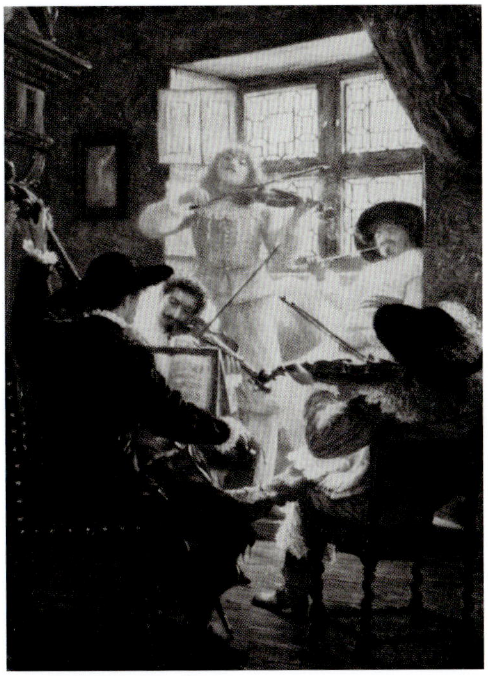

Cat. 137. Image courtesy of Sotheby's, London

Cat. 137a. *The Music Lesson*
*?c.*1879; watercolour heightened with bodycolour; 40.5 x 30 cm (16 x 11¾ in.); private collection.
Annnotations: "The Music Lesson/ Sketch for the original (which is in my possession) painted by my father Henry Wallis RWS/ signed Harold Wallis" (illegible date, possibly 22. ?. 89, and address)
Provenance: Harold Wallis; Holloway's Auctioneers, Banbury, Oxfordshire, 16 July 2013, lot 207; private collection.

This is an example of a Wallis opting to make a preliminary sketch in watercolour rather than oil for one of his major compositions.

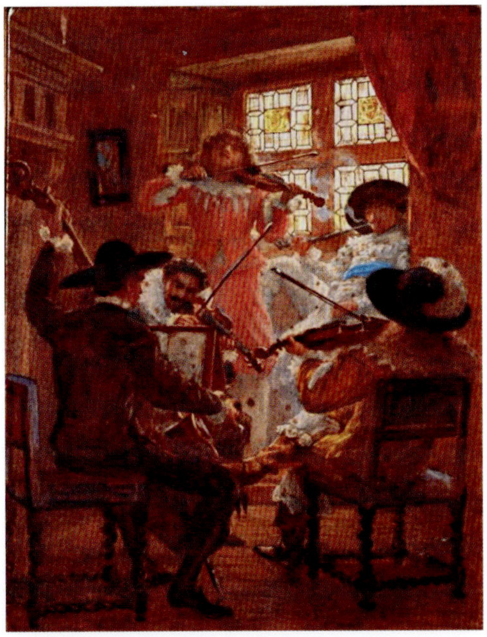

Cat. 137a. Image courtesy of Holloway's Auctioneers, Banbury

Cat. 138. *Vespers, Cathedral at Bruges*
1880; watercolour; dimensions unknown; whereabouts unknown.
Exhibitions: Old Water-Colour Society, 1880, no. 174.
Literature: *The Athenaeum*, No. 2733, 13 March 1880, p.352; *The Architect*, Vol. 23, 24 April 1880, p.276; *Pall Mall Gazette*, 29 April 1880, p.4; *The Building News and Engineering Journal*, 30 April 1880, p.508; *The Athenaeum*, No. 2740, 1 May 1880, p.574; *The Architect*, Vol. 23, 1 May 1880, p.296; *The Graphic*, 1 May 1880, p.446; *The Times*, 5 May 1880, p.8.

F.G. Stephens wrote in *The Athenaeum*: "Mr. Wallis has just finished some important water-colour drawings: 1. 'Vespers, Cathedral of Bruges', canons in black and white dresses, standing in their stalls of dark wood, holding their books of prayer, and facing the west, whence streams of orange light fall on their figures. At the side of one of the priests is an acolyte, in a rose-red and white dress, which supplies the high contrasting note to the scheme of colour of a powerful study in rich brown and black." Later Stephens commented: "Of Mr. Wallis's *Vespers, Cathedral at Bruges*, (174) we have already briefly written. It is, therefore, needless to add more than this picture represents a company of white-robed priests and their attendants at prayer, standing before their stalls, facing the sun, long lustrous rays from which penetrate the interior, and fall on the figures of the worshippers, the dark carvings of the stalls, and the high architectural masses before us. The light lacks a little of the golden tints of nature, the shadows need a more searching mode of representation."

The critic for *The Architect* was in general impressed by this work: "Mr. Henry Wallis, in the other gallery, runs Mr. Linton[1] hard in the matter of depth and nobility of colour…*Vespers – Cathedral at Bruges*, is a little wanting in motive. More might perhaps have been made out of the contrast between the perfunctory devotions of the priests in the stalls, and the worshipping upturned faces of the girls who kneel in the side chapel, where the light slants on their snowy caps; but as a study of tone the drawing is first rate."

Not every reviewer liked this work, however. *The Graphic* noted: "The large picture of Mr. H. Wallis 'Vespers – Cathedral at Bruges' (174) is somewhat disappointing. The heads of the ecclesiastics, each of whom stands in a separate stall, show considerable diversity of character; but the execution is wooly, and colour morbid and monotonous." The critic for *The Times* tended to agree with this assessment: "Mr. Wallis, though an old artist, is still comparatively a young member of the Society, and in that character demands notice for his elaborate picture of the canons at vespers in the Cathedral of Bruges, with the evening light warm on their surplices and bald heads, and the black-caped and white-robed figures standing each by his stall in somewhat rigid line. We should almost doubt it the labour spent on such a subject repays the painter, for we find little in these priestly heads and faces but various shades of dulness, stubbornness, and narrowness."

The reviewer for the *Pall Mall Gazette* agreed noting: "The painters of incident are not in great force. Mr. Herbert [*sic*] Wallis sends four drawings, of which the most important, 'Vespers – Bruges Cathedral', occupies the centre of one end of the room. It is a large and ambitious work but it cannot be considered a success. An attempt has beem made to imitate the glow of a Titian or Palma in an impossible medium. The want of richness and depth in the shadows has defeated the attempt, and there is no charm of composition, drawing, or general expression to make up for the failure."

Cat. 139. *The Fish Market at Bruges*
1880; watercolour; dimensions unknown; whereabouts unknown.
Exhibitions: Old Water-Colour Society, 1880, no. ?.
Literature: *The Athenaeum*, No. 2733, 13 March 1880, p.352.

Of this work *The Athenaeum* writes: " 'The Fish Market at Bruges', numerous figures gathered in an open space in the misty morning sunlight, and busily bargaining and talking." This work is not listed in the O.W.S. catalogue for 1880 and may have been added to the exhibition after the catalogue had been printed.

Cat. 140. *Literature in the Eighteenth Century*
1880; watercolour; dimensions unknown; whereabouts unknown.
Exhibitions: Old Water-Colour Society, 1880, no. 214.
Literature: *The Athenaeum*, No. 2733, 13 March 1880, p.352; *The Academy*, Vol. 17, 13 March 1880, p.204; *The Architect*, Vol. 23, 24 April 1880, p.276; *Pall Mall Gazette*, 29 April 1880, p.4; *The Building News and Engineering Journal*, 30 April 1880, p.508; *The Athenaeum*, No. 2740, 1 May 1880, p.574; *The Builder*, Vol. 38, 1 May 1880, p.532.

This watercolour looks back to Wallis's *Dr. Johnson at Cave's, the Publisher* of 1854 [Cat. 10] and we also see Wallis revisiting the theme of great English literary figures from the past. It is the first of several works [See also: Cats. 141, 146, 163 and 175] by Wallis set during the 18th century. Genre paintings set in this century were popularised by such prominent Victorian painters as Marcus Stone and G.D. Leslie. Like classical antiquity or the mediaeval period, for many Victorian painters this time represented a more idyllic world in comparison to the industrialised 19th century.

F.G. Stephens in *The Athenaeum* commented: "*Literature in the Eighteenth Century* (214) gives us a suggestion of Goldsmith during his first years in London, sitting in a 'peach-blossom' coat in one of those squalid chambers which were then affected by literary men. Being 'clean-shirt day', when the author could pay visits, a little girl has arrived with the all-important garment, and stands at the door demurely smiling on the tenant, who sits busily writing at his table. It is a richly tinted, strongly toned and effective picture, and the child's face and action are especially enjoyable."

The Building News and Engineering Journal observed: "On the screen Mr. Henry Wallis is represented by a humorous study depicting the Life of a Man of Letters in the eighteenth century, suggested by a passage from Boswell."

The reviewer for the *Pall Mall Gazette* remarked positively: "A much more satisfactory work by the same painter is 'Literature in the Eighteenth Century', which gives us a glimpse of a man of letters of the Goldsmith type in his dreary garret. He looks up from his writing as a little maid enters the room carrying the clean shirt which is to allow him to quit his den and go among friends. The compositon of this little work, its light and shade, tone and colour, are all alike good, and help enforce its meaning."

Cat. 141. *Old Friends*
1880; watercolour; dimensions unknown; whereabouts unknown.
Exhibitions: Old Water-Colour Society, 1880, no. 271.
Literature: *The Architect*, Vol. 23, 24 April 1880, p.276; *The Athenaeum*, No. 2740, 1 May 1880, p.574; *The Architect*, Vol. 23, 1 May 1880, p.296; *The Builder*, Vol. 38, 1 May 1880, p.532; *The Artist and Journal of Home Culture*, Vol. 1, 1 May 1880, p.133; *The Graphic*, 1 May 1880, p.446.

F.G. Stephens's laudatory remarks in *The Athenaeum* declared: "Old Friends (271), two gentlemen conversing and smoking by the window of an ancient room, reminds us of Metsu[1] in its brilliant lighting, fulness of colour, and richness of character. Very solid, it is thoroughly artistic. The actions and faces are first rate." In a later review, he added: " 'Old Friends', two gentlemen in costumes of the last century, seated near a window of an old room, which looks on a sunlit garden, deliberately enjoying their wine and tobacco, and gossiping about anything. It is a vivid piece of effect, and rich in colour of a vivid and strong order."

The reviewer for *The Artist* stated enthusiastically: "In 'Old Friends,' by Mr. Henry Wallis, the scene is an old room, hung with tapestry. The light of a summer evening streams through the low window, and we fancy we hear the singing of birds. Flowers and fruit are upon the table; a glass of red wine rests on the broad window sill. And there are the 'old friends', rich in the shining raiment of the good old times. He to whom the red wine belongs is a spare man. He is thoughtful, and puffs meditatively a long 'churchwarden.'[2] The other, the host we surmise, is more portly of form… The picture is as skilfully painted as poetically conceived, and is one of the very best in the exhibition."

The critic of *The Architect* voiced the opinion: "A little bit, entitled *Old Friends*, indicates pleasantly that cross between love of Venetian colour and delight of Dutch quaintness and precision which marks the art of Mr. Wallis."

Cat. 142. *A Study (of a Belgian Girl's Head)*
1880; watercolour; dimensions unknown; whereabouts unknown.
Exhibitions: Old Water-Colour Society, 1880, no. 257.
Literature: *The Architect and Building News*, Vol. 23, 1 May 1880, p.296.

The critic of *The Architect* commented on the Old Water-Colour exhibition of 1880: "In the three subjects which, with a study of a Belgian girl's head, form his contingent of contributions to the exhibition, he indulges in a warm yet subdued palette of rich liquorice browns, and reds, with mellow glow thrown into shadows. His use of green and yellow with grey tones is very noticeable."

Cat. 143. *A Morning Call, Ladies of Smyrna*
1880; oil on ?canvas; dimensions unknown; whereabouts unknown.
Exhibitions: Society of French Artists (Mr. Deschamps's Gallery), London, February 1880, no. 24; *International Exhibition*, Melbourne, 1880-1881, no. 229.
Literature: *Melbourne International Exhibition, The Official Catalogue of the Exhibits*, 1880, p.256; *The Athenaeum*, No. 2730, 21 February 1880, p.254; *Report of the Royal Commission for the Australian International Exhibitions*, 1882, p.435; *Melbourne International Exhibition, 1880-1881, Official Record and Catalogue of Exhibits*, 1882, p.303, p.518.

Wallis appears to have visited Smyrna[1] a number of times during the 1880s. In 1880, after this painting had been exhibited at the Society of French Artists, Wallis submitted it to the *Melbourne International Exhibition*, where it was awarded a diploma certificate under 'Second Order of Merit'.

Cat. 144. *In the Uffizi Gallery, Florence*
1880; watercolour; dimensions unknown; whereabouts unknown.
Exhibitions: Old Water-Colour Society, Winter exhibition 1880, no. 237.
Literature: *The Examiner*, 11 December 1880, p.1375; *The Athenaeum*, No. 2772, 11 December 1880, p.784; *The Saturday Review*, Vol. 50, 18 December 1880, p.769.

F.G. Stephens in *The Athenaeum* wrote: "Mr. Wallis has contributed an interesting study of colour and effect called *In the Uffizi Gallery* (237), where the warm and semi-lustrous white of an antique statue in full light contrasts with the almost dusky shadows and deep coolness of the wall. The contrast may be a little too positive for harmony in composition, but it is curious and fine, the local colouring is rich and broad, the picture luminous." The critic of *The Saturday Review* commented: "Mr. Wallis's 'In the Uffizi Gallery, Florence' (237), is a pleasing and attractive work, in which the representation of the stained and weather-beaten marble of the statue which is the principal object of the picture strikes us a being particularly happy. The figures of the spectators are less fortunate, but that perhaps is a matter of minor importance."

Cat. 145. *A Study*
1880; black and white chalks drawing on blue paper; dimensions unknown; whereabouts unknown.
Provenance:* Lord Sudeley,[1] 44 Grosvenor Gardens, London; his sale Christie's, 26 March 1887, lot 45 bought by ?Manville.[2]
Exhibitions:* Old Water-Colour Society, Winter exhibition 1880, no. 258.
Literature: *The Athenaeum*, No. 2772, 11 December 1880, p.784.

F.G. Stephens, in *The Athenaeum*, mentions: "By the same is *A Study* (258), a noble drawing in black and white chalks on blue paper, showing trees lying prostrate in a gloomy wood at evening after a storm, with glare between the distant trunks."

*A work entitled *A Study* sold at Christie's on 26 March 1887 but it is uncertain whether this is the same picture as that exhibited at the Old Water-Colour Society in 1880.

Cat. 146. *The Marriage Settlement*
1880; watercolour; dimensions unknown; whereabouts unknown.
Exhibitions: Old Water-Colour Society, Winter exhibition 1880, no. 381.
Literature: *The Daily Chronicle*, 7 December 1880; *The Athenaeum*, No. 2772, 11 December 1880, p.784; *The Spectator*, Vol. 53, 18 December 1880, p.1624; *Illustrated London News*, 18 December 1880, p.602.

The critic for *The Daily Chronicle* opined: "Of four contributions by Mr. Henry Wallis, two at least, 'The Marriage Settlement', four figures in a room, the young couple with the lady's father giving directions to 'a limb of the law' as to the settlement, and 'A Manuscript' [Cat. 147], in which an old gentleman perhaps the editor of a paper or a publisher, is seated, busily reading over an article brought to him by a young lady who anxiously awaits the verdict, will be examined with no little interest and profit. Whilst Mr. Wallis executes these subjects very beautifully, we can scarcely accept them as the true role of Art of the author of 'The Death of Chatterton', whose powers never appear properly displayed except in the historical scenes and characters with which he from time to time favours us."

The reviewer for *The Spectator* voiced his conviction that: "Mr. Henry Wallis's two small figure compositions, called, 'A Marriage Settlement' and 'A Manuscript' [Cat. 147], do not, in our opinion, show this earnest and conscientious painter at his best. They lack vitality and interest, and appear a trifle over-laboured. The colour, however, is pleasant throughout and the drawing as careful as usual."

F.G. Stephens, in *The Athenaeum*, noted: "*The Marriage Settlement* (381) comprises a somewhat uninteresting group of figures, clad in costumes of the eighteenth century, brilliantly and purely coloured, and exceptionally rich in tone. The deep blue of the lady's dress is as beautiful as the rosy hue of that of the bridegroom."

Cat. 147. *A Manuscript*
1880; watercolour; dimensions unknown; whereabouts unknown.
Exhibitions: Old Water-Colour Society,

Winter exhibition 1880, no. 404.
LITERATURE: *The Daily Chronicle*, 7 December 1880; *The Athenaeum*, No. 2772, 11 December 1880, p.784; *The Spectator*, Vol. 53, 18 December 1880, p.1624; *Illustrated London News*, 18 December 1880, p.602.

The Athenaeum noted: "No. 404, *A Manuscript*, a study of the interior of a room is very delicate in colour and firm in painting." [See also: *The Daily Chronicle* and *The Spectator* reviews under Cat. 146.]

Cat. 148. *Autumn in the Forest*
1880; ?oil on canvas; dimensions unknown; whereabouts unknown.
EXHIBITIONS: The Hanover Gallery, London, *Winter Exhibition of Oil Paintings by British Artists*, 1880, no. 87.
LITERATURE: *The Times*, 20 November 1880, p.11.

In the Hanover Gallery catalogue, the work is called *In the Forest – Autumn.* The reviewer for *The Times* stated: "Mr. Henry Wallis's 'Autumn in the Forest' is a painstaking, somewhat ambitious study of yellowing foliage which a little misses its mark." It is possible that this is the same work as Cat. 118 but under a different title.

Cat. 149. *A Genuine Cremona*
1881; watercolour; dimensions unknown; whereabouts unknown.
EXHIBITIONS: Old Water-Colour Society, 1881, no. 260.
LITERATURE: *The Daily News*, 12 April 1881; *The Illustrated London News*, Vol. 78, 16 April 1881, p.379.

The Daily News stated: "Mr. Henry Wallis sends a carefully executed, richly coloured study in No. 260 'A Genuine Cremona', wherein two old gentlemen are pointing out to a lady seated at a piano, the inestimable qualities of the violin one of them holds in his hands." *The Illustrated London News* mentioned: "Mr Henry Wallis sends but one small drawing, entitled 'A Genuine Cremona' (260) – two gentlemen examining a violin, with a lady listening to their comments."

Cat. 150. *Portia and Nerissa on the Morning of the Trial*
(The Merchant of Venice, Act III, Scene 4)
1881; watercolour; dimensions unknown; whereabouts unknown.
EXHIBITIONS: Old Water-Colour Society, Winter exhibition 1881, no. 11.
LITERATURE: *The Athenaeum*, No. 2822, 26 November 1881, pp.711-12; *Belfast News-Letter*, 26 November 1881, p.3; *The Times*, 5 December 1881, p.8; *The London Daily News*, London, 5 December 1881, p.3; *The Morning Post*, 6 December 1881, p.6; *The Graphic*, 10 December 1881, p.598; *The Athenaeum*, No. 2824, 10 December 1881, p.784; *The Architect*, Vol. 26, 10 December 1881, p.372; *The Illustrated London News*, 10 December 1881, p.567; *The Guardian*, 21 December 1881; *The Artist and Journal of Home Culture*, Vol. III, 1 January 1882, p.4.

This is the continuation of a large series of watercolours based on Shakespeare's Merchant of Venice that began when Wallis exhibited *After the Trial* at the O.W.S. in 1879. The critic of *The Graphic* professed the conviction: "Mr. Wallis contributes a series of seven drawings illustrating scenes in *The Merchant of Venice.* Besides being full of local colour, these are thoroughly original in conception and unconventional treatment. In his delineation of human character, he has not been very successful, both his Portia and his Jessica entirely fail to realise the idea of those characters conveyed by Shakespeare's words." The reviewer of *The Daily News* asserted: "Less pleasing and more ambitious is (11) one of Mr. Wallis's brilliant, almost garish, illustrations of *The Merchant of Venice.* The artist has as ususal rendered the Venetian colour with appropriate glow, but has sadly caricatured the beautiful heroines of Shakespeare." *The Illustrated London News* commented: "Mr. Henry Wallis has a series of illustrations of 'The Merchant of Venice,' some of the incidents being supposititious. All show acquaintance with Venetian architecture; all are rich in colour; but the figures and faces are not remarkable for dramatic character."

The Guardian, however, expressed this favourable opinion on the series shown at the O.W.S. exhibition: "The brilliant series of drawings, different scenes from *The Merchant of Venice*, by Mr. Wallis, form a prominent feature in the collection. Playful fancy, aptness of design, and unity of effect, pervade all these drawings. Four of them only are executed in colour; the remaining three are in sepia. The lighting and colour of the more finished works are exceptionally bright, and the drawings in the less advanced stage promise, when they are completed of being fully equal to their companions. It matters little that the course of the play is not consistently followed." Of this particular work, *The Guardian* said: "We see first *Portia and Nerissa on the Morning of the Trial* (11), before the sun has quite dispersed the early mists, going merrily in their gondolas over the smooth pale, gen. (?) green water. They are fair women rather than students learned in the law, but they are confident in themselves and full of spirit."

F.G. Stephens wrote in *The Athenaeum* in 'Fine Art Gossip': "The subject of the last work is not found in the play, but was derived from an incident which is referred to in Act III. Sc. iv. Portia and Nerissa, disguised as doctor and clerk, are going to the trial; the effect is that of bright, early morning; they sit in a gondola rowed by two men in blue jackets. The refined brilliancy and delicate, jewel-like 'colour' of the coloured drawings, the complete spontaneity of the designs, the animation of the movements and expressions of the figures, the prevailing brightness of the lighting, are charms common to all these works." In a later review, Stephens stated: "We have already mentioned Mr. Wallis's illustrations of the 'Merchant of Venice', the most important of which are signalized by delicious colour and brilliant yet harmonious illumination. These qualities are conspicuous in *Portia and Nerissa on the Morning of the Trial* (11), proceeding to court in a gondola, which the gaily clad boatmen urge swiftly over the calm, somewhat misty water. The blackness of the vessel sets off the glittering dresses and soft lustre of the sea."

The critic for the *Pall Mall Gazette* made an obvious objection to Wallis's treatment of this work: "He is seen at his best in the 'Shylock, Jessica, and Launcelot' (111), and at his worst in 'Portia and Nerissa' (11). It is difficult to understand how the artist who has painted the figure of Launcelot in the former work – a figure in which the vigour of young muscular form is seen in every line – could also paint the lank and ill-drawn gondoliers in the latter."

Cat. 150a. *Portia and Nerissa on the Morning of the Trial*
(The Merchant of Venice, Act III, Scene 4)
1882; wood engraving; image size: 20.1 x 30 cm. (7⅞ x 11¹³⁄₁₆ in.); sheet size: 29.9 x 40.3 cm. (11¾ x 15⅞ in.); Dr Dennis T. Lanigan, Saskatoon, Canada.
ANNOTATIONS: (lettering below image) "PORTIA AND NERISSA ON THE MORNING OF THE TRIAL' FROM THE PICTURE BY H. WALLIS, EXHIBITED IN THE GALLERY OF THE ROYAL SOCIETY OF PAINTERS IN WATER COLOURS"
LITERATURE: *The Graphic*, 27 May 1882, p.540.

Cat. 151. *Portia and Nerissa at Belmont*
(The Merchant of Venice, Act I, Scene 2)
1881; watercolour; dimensions unknown; whereabouts unknown.
EXHIBITIONS: Old Water-Colour Society, Winter exhibition 1881, no. 69.
LITERATURE: *The Guardian*, 21 December 1881; *The Athenaeum*, No. 2822, 26 November 1881, p.711; *Belfast News-Letter*, 26 November 1881, p.3; *The London Daily News*, London, 5 December 1881, p.3; *The Morning Post*, 6 December 1881, p.6; *The*

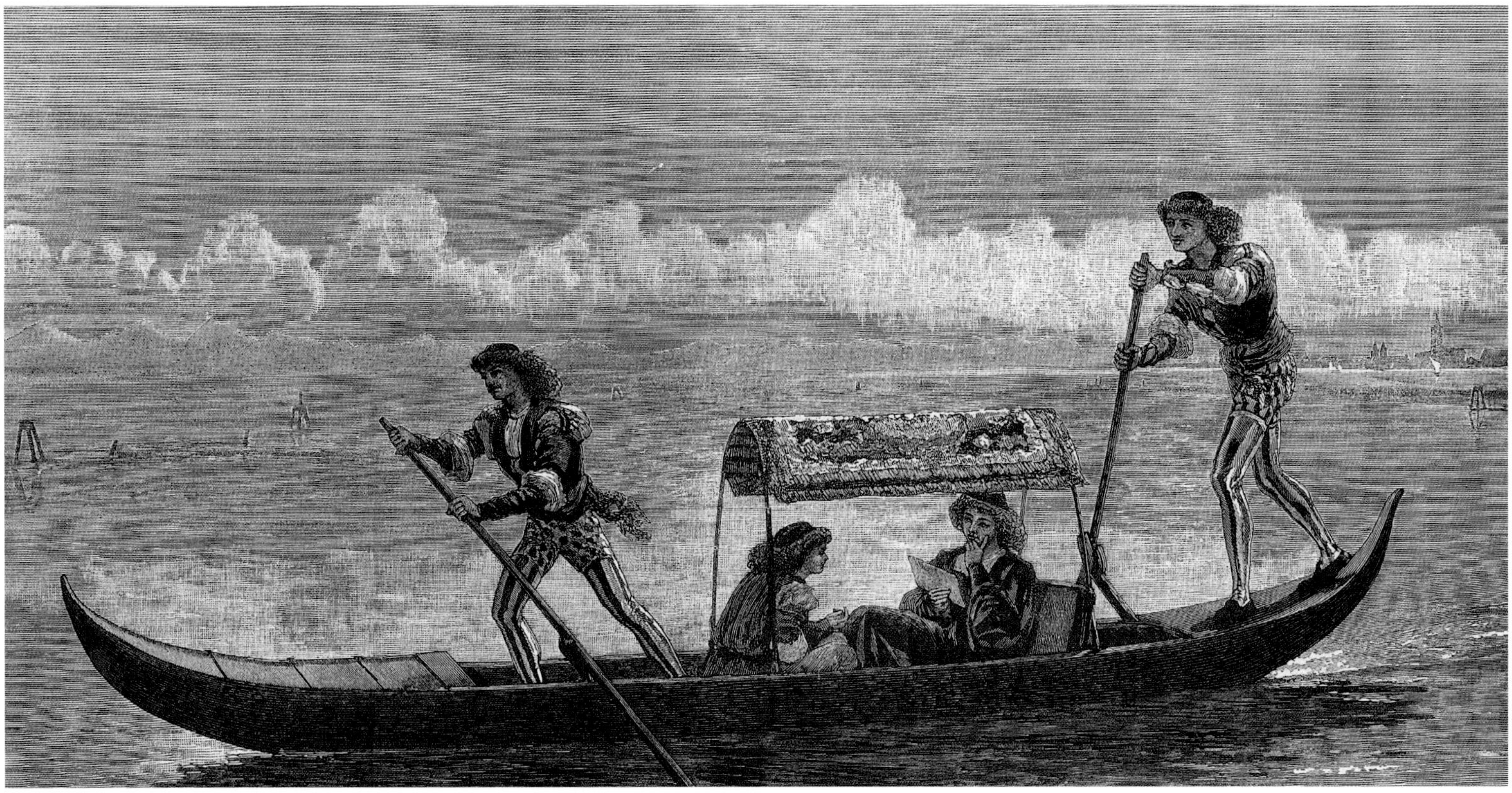

Cat. 150a. This print was reproduced in *The Graphic* on 27 May, 1882 (p.540). Image courtesy of the Dennis Lanigan collection

Athenaeum, No. 2824, 10 December 1881, p.784; *The Graphic*, 10 December 1881, p.598; *The Architect*, Vol. 26, 10 December 1881, p.372; *The Illustrated London News*, 10 December 1881, p.567; *The Artist and Journal of Home Culture*, Vol. III, 1 January 1882, p.4.

F.G. Stephens wrote enthusiastically in *The Athenaeum*'s 'Fine Art Gossip' section: "The fourth is the most brilliant picture of the series. It depicts Portia and Nerissa conversing at Belmont in a chamber which opens on apartments decorated with panels of mosaic. The gilding and paintings on the walls are sumptuous, and the shining and richly-tinted marbles of the floor reflect the warmer and cooler light. The whole is distinguished by luminosity and colour which is rich, brilliant, and soft. The draperies of the ladies and their gracious looks can hardly be admired too much." In his later formal review, Stephens maintained: "*Portia and Nerissa at Belmont* (69), however, is the best of this series, which ought, by the way, to have been hung all together and in the sequence of their subjects. No. 69 is precious on account of the intense luminosity and purity of its local colouring, its charming combinations of soft tints, as, for example, the exquisite keeping of Portia's dress with the surrounding tones and tints. The brilliancy of the richly decorated chamber is one of the most enjoyable things in the gallery. The illumination, too, deserves high praise, because it combines successfully the bright light which is admitted from the distance and the equally powerful light in front. The figures are placed where the lights meet and yet retain perfect solidity."

Cat. 152. *Shylock, Jessica and Launcelot (Shylock charging Jessica to see that Doors and Windows are secured).*
(The Merchant of Venice, Act II, Scene 5)
1881; watercolour; likely 41.2 x 57.1 cm (16$\frac{3}{16}$ x 22½ in.); whereabouts unknown.
Exhibitions: ?Old Water-Colour Society, Winter exhibition 1881, no. 111.
Literature: *Belfast News-Letter*, 26 November 1881, p.3; *The Athenaeum*, No. 2822, 26 November 1881, p.711; *The London Daily News*, London, 5 December 1881, p.3; *The Morning Post*, 6 December 1881, p.6; *Pall Mall Gazette*, 8 December 1881, p.11; *The Athenaeum*, No. 2824, 10 December 1881, p.784; *The Graphic*, 10 December 1881, p.598; *The Architect*, Vol. 26, 10 December 1881, p.372; *The Illustrated London News*, 10 December 1881, p.567; *The Guardian*, 21 December 1881; *The Artist and Journal of Home Culture*, Vol. III, 1 January 1882, p.4.

The *Pall Mall Gazette* critic had this interesting commentary to make on Wallis's series of watercolours: "We do not recollect to have ever seen such a profusion of gondolas and marble stairs. Mr. Henry Wallis's scenes from 'The Merchant of Venice', seven in number, are very ambitious in character, and form a leading feature of the exhibition. Their effect is not increased, however, by the fact that they are scattered promiscuously over the gallery; if a place could had been secured for them as a series on one of the screens it would have been better. Mr. Wallis is a painter who has never thoroughly mastered the technical part of his work; his colour is sometimes very full and beautiful, at other times painfully discordant. He is seen at his best in the 'Shylock, Jessica, and Launcelot' (111), and at his worst in 'Portia and Nerissa' (11)... Mr. Wallis has an eclectic style of his own, founded on selected types of early Italian art. He tries to be Venetian, but not always with success; a malicious critic might say that he aims at Gian Bellini and hits Pinturicchio.[1] But it is very intereresting to find a man with any serious aim at all, and Mr. Wallis seems a very great and original artist."

F.G. Stephens in *The Athenaeum* wrote in 'Fine Art Gossip': "The sixth picture depicts Shylock delivering the house key to Jessica with strident charges, which are illustrated by Launcelot's derisive pantomime behind his master's back. The yellow hood and black gabardine of the old man, his daughter's piquant Levantine dress of white, purple, gold, and orange, and the crisp surface of the serving man's new garments are effective elements in a sparkling little picture." *The Guardian* described the painting thus: "In the third drawing (111) Shylock, standing by the threshold of his house, gives charge to Jessica to see that doors and windows are secured, while Launcelot from behind him makes signs denoting how far he will be obeyed."

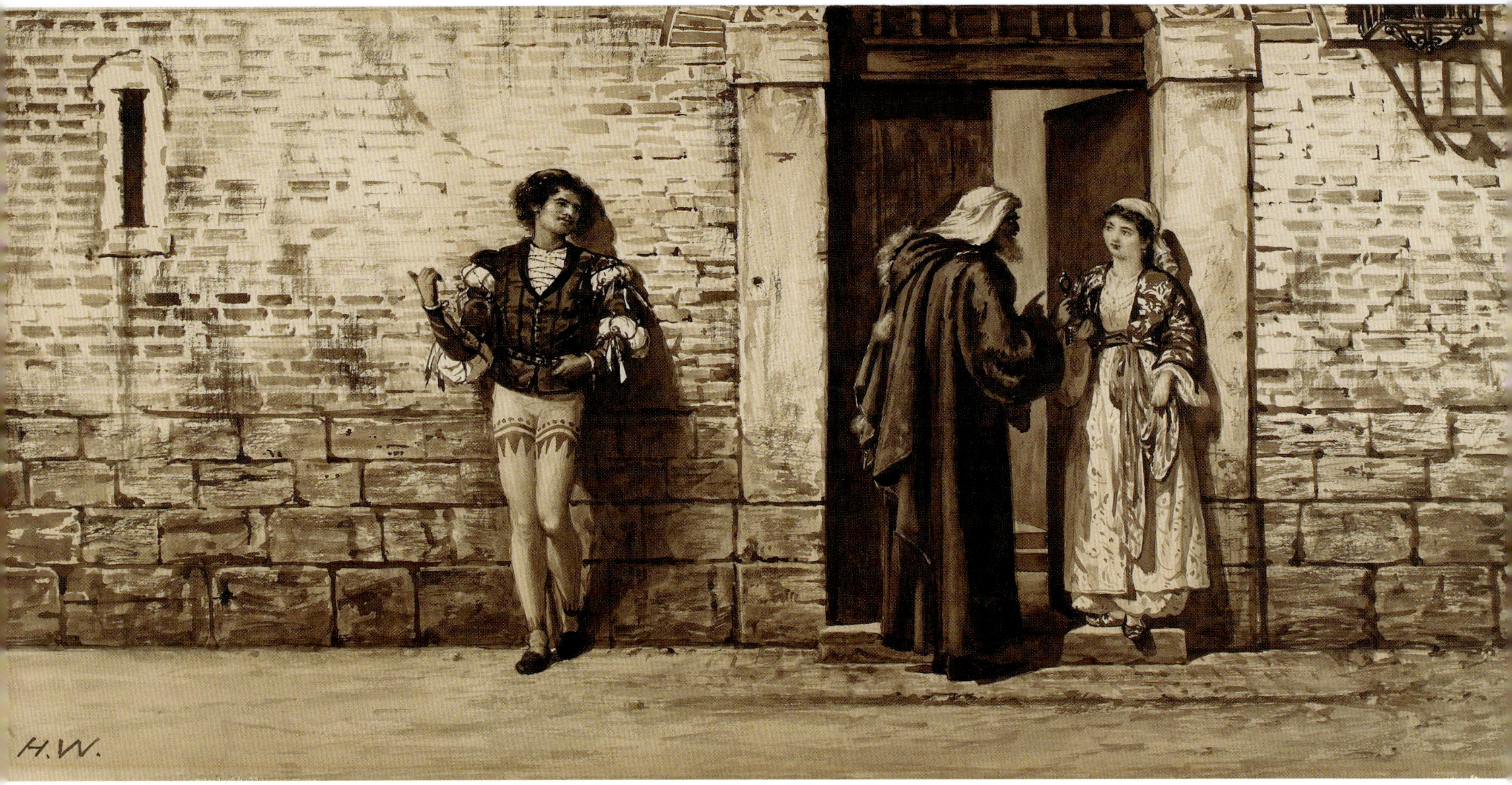

Cat. 152a. Image courtesy of the National Gallery of Canada, Ottawa

Cat. 152a. *Shylock, Jessica and Launcelot (Shylock charging Jessica to see that Doors and Windows are secured).*
(The Merchant of Venice, Act II, Scene 5)
1881; pen and ink and brown wash on off-white paper; 41.2 x 57.1 cm (16³⁄₁₆ x 22½ in.); National Gallery of Canada.
Inscriptions: Signed with initials *H.W.*
Provenance: Sotheby's Belgravia, 24 June 1980, part of lot 174,[1] bought in and purchased after sale by Abbott and Holder, London, and put away in a trunk for twenty-two years; purchased 15 November 2002 by Dr. Dennis T. Lanigan, Saskatoon, Canada; donated to the National Gallery of Canada, in 2008.
Exhibitions: ?Old Water-Colour Society, Winter exhibition 1881, no. 111; Abbott and Holder, London, November 2002, list 350, no. 90; National Gallery of Canada, Ottawa, *Beauty's Awakening. Drawings by the Pre-Raphaelites and their Contemporaries*, 2015, no. 116; Leighton House, London, *Pre-Raphaelites on Paper*, 2016, no. 116.
Literature: *The Athenaeum*, No. 2822, 26 November 1881, p.711-12; *Belfast News-Letter*, 26 November 1881, p.3; *The Graphic*, 10 December 1881; *The Athenaeum*, No. 2824, 10 December 1881, p.784; *The Architect*, Vol. 26, 10 December 1881, p.372; *The Guardian*, 21 December 1881.

It is unclear whether it was this monochrome study, or the finished watercolour, that was exhibited at the Old Water-Colour Society in 1881. In *The Athenaeum* in 'Fine Art Gossip' in November 1881 Stephens described this subject as a coloured watercolour and yet the reviewer for *The Guardian*, when discussing the Society of Painters in Water Colours exhibition, says that only four of the works in this series were executed in colour and the remaining three were in sepia. This raises the question whether Wallis decided not to exhibit this particular *Merchant of Venice* subject in colour and, rather, chose one of the monochrome sepia drawings to be shown?

The drawing is an illustration to *The Merchant of Venice*, Act II scene 5. Shylock is about to go to Antonio's feast and bids his daughter Jessica look to his house. The character to the left is Launcelot Gobbo, a clown, who used to work for Shylock, but who now works for Antonio. He will help Jessica elope that night with her Christian lover Lorenzo.

Cat. 153. *Antonio, Bassanio, Gratiano and Lorenzo; Exeunt Gratiano and Lorenzo*
(The Merchant of Venice, Act I, Scene 1)
1881; pen and ink and brown wash; dimensions unknown; whereabouts unknown.
Exhibitions: Old Water-Colour Society, Winter exhibition 1881, no. 125.
Literature: *Belfast News-Letter*, 26 November 1881, p.3; *The Athenaeum*, No. 2822, 26 November 1881, p.711; *The London Daily News*, London, 5 December 1881, p.3; *The Morning Post*, 6 December 1881, p.6; *The Athenaeum*, No. 2824, 10 December 1881, p.784; *The Graphic*, 10 December 1881, p.598; *The Architect*, Vol. 26, 10 December 1881, p.372; *The Illustrated London News*, 10 December 1881, p.567; *The Guardian*, 21 December 1881; *The Artist and Journal of Home Culture*, Vol. III, 1 January 1882, p.4.

F.G. Stephens in *The Athenaeum* wrote in 'Fine Art Gossip': "The second design represents the embarkation of Antonio and Bassanio, Gratiano and Lorenzo taking leave on the quay. The conception of the groups is spirited, and the figure of the gondolier about to row is admirably true and skilfully poised." The critic of *The Guardian* noted about Wallis's designs for his *The Merchant of Venice* series: "Four of them only are executed in colour; the remaining three are in sepia... In the designs in sepia, Antonio and Bassanio appear, and the figures are generally more numerous." This suggests this work must have been one of the sepia designs.

Cat. 154. *Jessica and Launcelot*
(The Merchant of Venice, Act II, Scene 3)
1881; watercolour; dimensions unknown; whereabouts unknown.
Exhibitions: Old Water-Colour Society, Winter exhibition 1881, no. 156.
Literature: Belfast News-Letter, 26 November 1881, p.3; *The Athenaeum*, No. 2822, 26 November 1881, p.711; *The Morning Post*, 6 December 1881, p.6; *The Athenaeum*, No. 2824, 10 December 1881, p.784; *The Graphic*, 10 December 1881, p.598; *The Architect*, Vol. 26, 10 December 1881, p.372; *The Illustrated London News*, 10 December 1881, p.567; *The Guardian*, 21 December 1881; *The Artist and Journal of Home Culture*, Vol. III, 1 Jan. 1882, p.4.

F.G. Stephens in *The Athenaeum* wrote in 'Fine Art Gossip': "The fifth picture shows Jessica at her father's door with Lancelot [*sic*], to whom she gives a ducat and a letter. She has a bright and sweet expression, and draws the letter from her bosom while standing with one hand on the lock. Her whimsical companion's loutish figure and attitude are full of humour. A touch of nature appears in the half-starved cat, who affectionately rubs her head against Lancelot's [*sic*] legs. As in the Belmont scene the architecture and its illumination are deliciously rich in tone and colour."

The Guardian stated: "... (156) Jessica and Launcelot are alone, the latter figure being most happily projected against the light." *The Graphic* declared: "and there is much truthful expression in *Jessica and Launcelot* (156). The half-starved cat rubbing his head against the legs of the serving-man in this drawing is well introduced, and the courtyard in the background suffused with sunlight is full of picturesque beauty."

Cat. 155. *Antonio and Bassanio – Bassanio unfolding his Plans for the Wooing of Portia*
(The Merchant of Venice, Act I, Scene 1)
1881; ?pen and ink and brown wash; dimensions unknown; whereabouts unknown.
Exhibitions: Old Water-Colour Society, Winter exhibition 1881, no. 235.
Literature: *Belfast News-Letter*, 26 November 1881, p.3; *The Athenaeum*, No. 2822, 26 November 1881, p.711; *The Morning Post*, 6 December 1881, p.6; *The London Daily News*, London, 5 December 1881, p.3; *The Athenaeum*, No. 2824, 10 December 1881, p.784; *The Graphic*, 10 December 1881, p.598; *The Architect*, Vol. 26, 10 December 1881, p.372; *The Illustrated London News*, 10 December 1881, p.567; *The Guardian*, 21 December 1881; *The Artist and Journal of Home Culture*, Vol. III, 1 January 1882, p.4.

F.G. Stephens in *The Athenaeum* wrote in 'Fine Art Gossip': "The third picture depicts Bassanio explaining his project to Antonio while they are seated under the canopy of the gondola; the rower stands behind and urges the boat over the smooth, semi-opaque sea. The design is so true that we seem to hear the ripples as the craft speeds over them. Strong tones give powerful daylight."

Cat. 156. *Antonio, Salarino and Solanio in Conversation*
(The Merchant of Venice, Act I, Scene 1)
1881; watercolour; dimensions unknown; whereabouts unknown.
Exhibitions: Old Water-Colour Society, Winter exhibition 1881, no. 271.
Literature: *Belfast News-Letter*, 26 November 1881, p.3; *The Athenaeum*, No. 2822, 26 November 1881, p.711; *The London Daily News*, London, 5 December 1881, p.3; *The Morning Post*, 6 December 1881, p.6; *The Athenaeum*, No. 2824, 10 December 1881, p.784; *The Graphic*, 10 December 1881, p.598; *The Architect*, Vol. 26, 10 December 1881, p.372; *The Illustrated London News*, 10 December 1881, p.567; *The Guardian*, 21 December 1881; *The Artist and Journal of Home Culture*, Vol. III, 1 January 1882, p.4.

F.G. Stephens in *The Athenaeum* wrote in Fine Art Gossip: "The first drawing shows the meeting of Antonio with Salarino and Solanio, who sit on a marble bench on the quay and gossip with their friend; a gondola is waiting, a water-seller fills a glass for one of the rowers. Behind, a glimpse of a canal displays buildings and masts of galleys on either side. The graceful Italian actions and expressions are animated and characteristic; the broad shadows and spaces of sunlight are charming."

Cat. 157. *The Trial, a Scene from the Merchant of Venice*
(The Merchant of Venice, Act IV, Scene 1)
*c.*1880; watercolour, sepia heightened with white; 47 x 33 cm (18½ x 13 in.); private collection.
Inscriptions: signed with *HW* initials.
Provenance: Sotheby's Belgravia, 24 June 1980, part of lot 174; bought in and purchased after sale by Abbott and Holder, London; sold to a private collector.

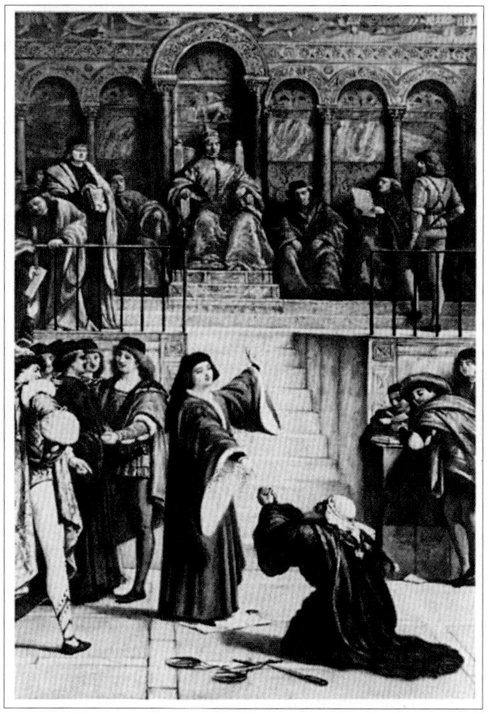

Cat. 157. Image courtesy of Sotheby's, London

This drawing shows Portia in her disguise as a doctor of civil law, arguing the case before the Duke with Shylock on his knees begging for mercy. Portia points out that the bargain between Antonio and Shylock called for no blood to be shed and exactly one pound of flesh to be taken. Shylock, realizing the impossibility of carrying out this agreement, recants and instead requests his 9,000 ducats back. Portia then argues that Shylock is himself guilty of the crime of conspiring to kill Antonio. As a punishment, the Duke and Antonio decide that Shylock must give half his belongings to the court. Although he can keep the other half for himself, he must promise to give all his remaining wealth to his daughter and son-in-law Lorenzo upon his death.

There were three preliminary drawings in this Sotheby's Belgravia sale in 1980. One drawing is now in the collection of the National Gallery of Canada [Cat. 152a], while another is the study for *Tubal brings Shylock news of Jessica* [Cat. 158a] at the Wichita Art Museum. These sepia drawings are of particular interest because of the insight they give us into Wallis's working methods. It is likely that he may have made similar studies, which do not survive, for others of his watercolours.

Cat. 158. *Tubal brings Shylock News of Jessica*
(The Merchant of Venice, Act III, Scene 1)
1882; watercolour; 42 x 55.9 cm (16½ x 22 in.); private collection.
Provenance: Wallis's studio and then by descent from the artist to his son Harold Wallis; then to his daughter-in-law Mary Wallis (née Mary Elizabeth Aymes); then her great-niece Vera G. Cooper (née Langley) (1910-1989); and thence by direct descent to John Harold Cooper and family; sold at Bonhams, London, 5 March 2002, lot 66, for £700; private collection.
Exhibitions: Old Water-Colour Society, 1882, no. 58.

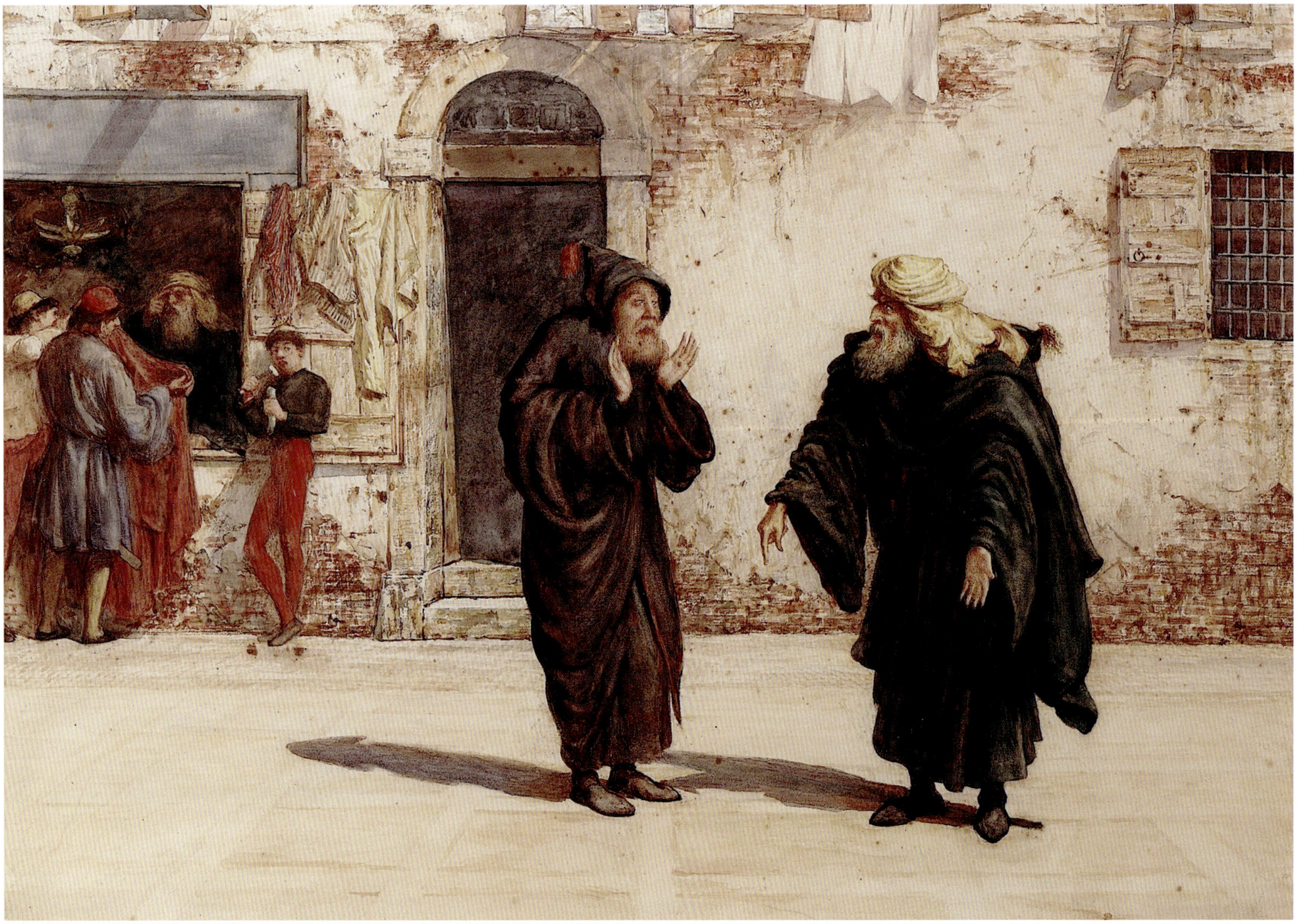

Cat. 158. Image courtesy of Bonham's, London

LITERATURE: *The Portfolio: An Artistic Periodical*, Vol. 13, 1882, p.22; *The Art Journal*, 1882, p.29, p.190; *The Times*, 25 April 1882, p.4; *Pall Mall Gazette*, 28 April 1882, p.4; *The Athenaeum*, No. 2844, 29 April 1882, p.546; *The Illustrated London News*, Vol. 80, 29 April 1882, p.414; *The Builder*, 29 April 1882, p.509; *The Graphic*, 29 April 1882, p.419; *The Academy and Literature*, Vol. 21, No. 521, 29 April 1882, pp.309-310. [See also: Cat. 108]

This work, in particular, suggests that Wallis was prone to the latent antisemetism common amongst middle-class Englishmen in Victorian England. This tendency was noticeable even amongst his Pre-Rapahelite colleagues, including Edward Burne-Jones who had several close friends who were Jewish. The portrayal of Shylock and Tubal in this work would generally be considered offensive today.

When this watercolour was exhibited at the O.W.S. in 1882 it was accompanied by the following quotation:

"*Tubal*: I often came where I did hear of her, but cannot find her.
Shylock: Why there, there, there, there! A diamond gone, cost me two thousand ducats in Frankfort! The curse never fell upon our nation till now; I never felt till now - two thousand ducats in that and other precious, precious jewels. I would my daughter were dead at my foot and the jewels in her ear! Would she were hears'd at my foot, and the ducats in her coffin!"

F.G. Stephens, in *The Athenaeum*, stated: "Eminent among the few figure pictures of this year's display are two of Mr. Wallis's illustrations of 'The Merchant of Venice', a series about we have spoken more than once. *Tubal brings Shylock News of Jessica* (58) is a charming study of sunlight on ancient walls covered in white plaster, a booth, the figures at its door, and the Venetian quay, on which stand the two Jews, clad in dark garments of the richest hues. In tone and local colouring this picture, although the figures in the distance are not quite complete, is of first-rate quality. The sunlight is vivid and brilliant, but the forms and extent of the shadows on the pavement are questionable. The figures are the best parts of the design, and they are marked by a humerous energy which is quite admirable."

The critic of *The Graphic* was of the position that: "The Merchant of Venice has supplied Mr. H. Wallis with the subjects of two excellent pictures. In the first in order, 'Tubal Brings Shylock News of Jessica' (58), we are inclined to think that the figure of Shylock is a little too grotesque and his gestures somewhat over-exuberant, but there can be no question as to the refined beauty of colour, or the admirable art displayed in the treatment of the subordinate group."

The reviewer for *The Academy* commented: "Of the treatment of the figure and its accessories in a spirit avowedly poetical, the work of Mr. Henry Wallis is generally a type. We have sometimes liked him better when he has worked upon a larger scale than he has adopted in the drawings just now exhibited; and his realization of Shakesperian heroines falls short of what is altogether satisfactory. But in his 'Meeting of Shylock and Tubal', where Tubal brings his comrade all the bad news of Jessica the spendthrift, Mr. Wallis shows himself able to deal adequately, even powerfully, with character and incident. His Shylock and Tubal are figures that remain in the memory."

Cat. 158a. *Study for Tubal brings Shylock News of Jessica*
(The Merchant of Venice, Act III, Scene 1)
*c.*1882; brown ink with white highlights over graphite on board; image size: 28.3 x 53.3 cm (11⅛ x 21 in.); sheet size: 41.4 x 57.1 cm. (16¼ x 22½ in.); Wichita Art Museum, Kansas.
Provenance: Sotheby's Belgravia, 24 June 1980, part of lot 174; bought after the sale by Abbott and Holder, London; bought from them by the Wichita Art Museum, Wichita, Kansas on 31 October 1987, with money from the *Virginia and George Ablah Fund*, museum acquisiton no. 1986.92.

This fascinating drawing appears unusual in Wallis's oeuvre, but is apparently common for his *Merchant of Venice* series. It is likely a preparatory study for the finished watercolour rather than a drawing after the watercolour worked up to be used as an illustration in some publication. The fact that it is the same size as the finished watercolour strongly suggests the former, as does the fact that it differs slightly in compositon. It is unknown how common it was for Wallis to make such studies for his other finished exhibition watercolours.

Cat. 159. *Gratiano having brought Portia Bassanio's Ring, is wheedled out of his Own by Nerissa, who is disguised as a Lawyer's Clerk*
(The Merchant of Venice, Act IV, Scene 2)
1882; watercolour; dimensions unknown; whereabouts unknown.
Exhibitions: Old Water-Colour Society, 1882, no. 64.
Literature: *The Art Journal*, 1882, p.9, p.190; *The Portfolio: An Artistic Periodical*, Vol. 13, 1882, p.22; *The Times*, 25 April 1882, p.4; *Pall Mall Gazette*, 28 April 1882, p.4; *The Athenaeum*, No. 2844, 29 April 1882, p.546; *The Illustrated London News*, vol. 80, 29 April 1882, p.414; *The Builder*, Vol. XLII, 29 April 1882, p.509; *The Graphic*, 29 April 1882, p.419.

F.G. Stephens commented in *The Athenaeum*: "The other picture, No. 64, represents the interview of Gratiano with Nerissa, disguised as a clerk, when the former was wheedled out of his ring. The daylight is less splendid than in the other example. The figures stand on the quay, while crowds cross a bridge behind; a gondola is at the quay-side, and is Raphaelesque in its riskiness. The best part is the stalwart form of Gratiano. The large style of his draperies is bold yet learned, and the figure is full of energy and admirably placed on its feet. Nerissa girl though she be, seems too small for her huge companion; her attitude and the arrangement of her costume are, we think, too boyish."

The critic of *The Builder* was more convinced of the merits of this work: "Among the best things in the exhibition are Mr. H. Wallis's two continuations of his 'Merchant of Venice' series; the one representing Tubal and Shylock (58), the other Nerissa obtaining the ring from Gratiano. The figure of Nerissa, in her man's costume, looks rather too small and boy-like; Gratiano is a good conception of the character, not too refined." The reviewer of *The Graphic* said: "The principal actors in the second picture, 'Gratiano Giving His Ring to Nerissa' (64), are dramatically expressive, but the background, in which Antonio surrounded by his friends is seen returning home in triumph after the trial, seems to us the best part of the work. Both pictures are conceived in an independent spirit, and they are remarkable besides for their striking truth of local colour, their admirable keeping, and finished workmanship."

The critic of the *Pall Mall Gazette* had this to say about Wallis's series from the *Merchant of Venice*, and this work in particular: "The figure painters who have chosen good subjects and painted them with intelligence are fewer than ever. Among water-colour painters whose work is marked by a stenuous effort after what is strong and serious, Mr. Wallis takes a high rank. We spoke last year of his series of pictures taken

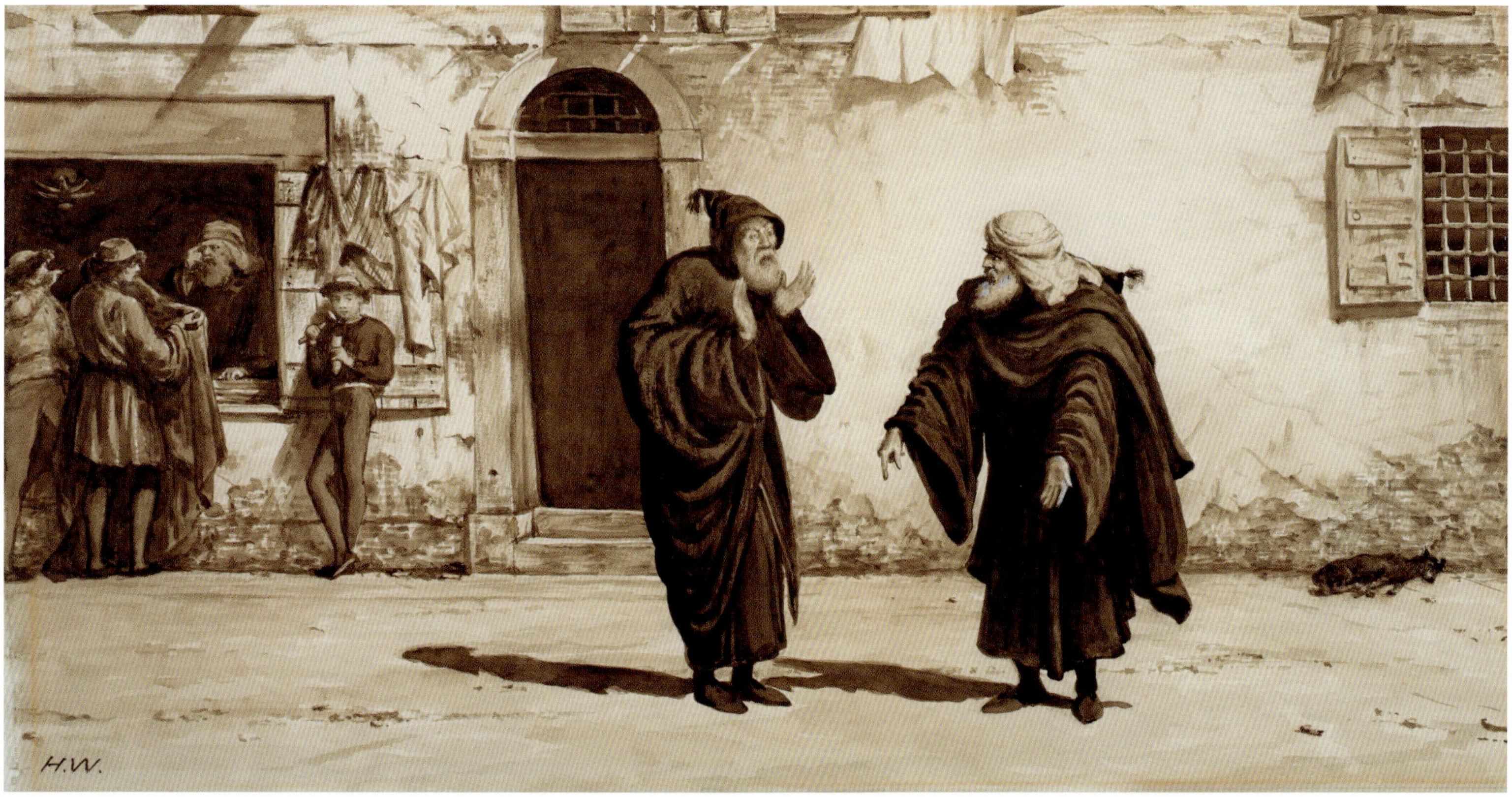

Cat. 158a. Image by permission of Wichita Art Museum, Witchita

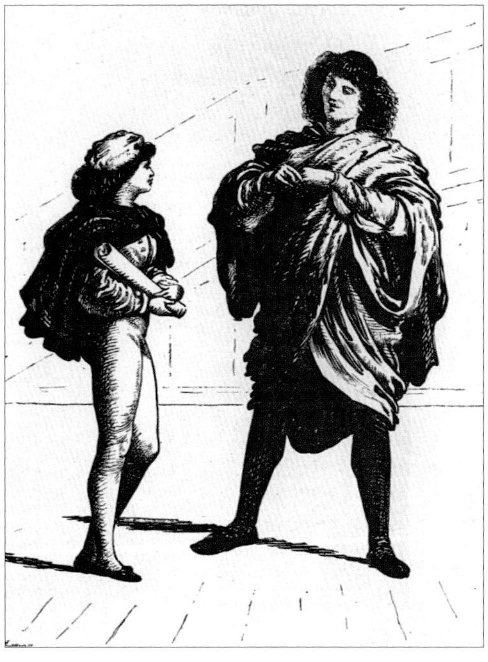

Drawing from the O.W.S.'s *Illustrated catalogue comprising 77 facsimiles of sketches by the artists*, giving a rough idea of how the central portion of the watercolour [Cat. 159] must have looked.

from 'The Merchant of Venice'; he continues that series this year. It is needless to say that his conception of the scenes and the dresses is as different as possible from that which regulated the late revival at the Lyceum. Mr. Wallis is a real antiquarian, and he gives us a Venice and a Venetian populace that might strictly have sat to Gentile Bellini for their portraits. Yet his pictures, this year as last year, are very unequal in execution. The best is (64) that in which Gratiano is wheedled out of his ring by Nerissa; the figure of the girl masquerading as 'a little scrubbed boy' could hardly be better. Gratiano too is painted with real skill and spirit. But Portia sitting in the boat seems very poorly put in."

Cat. 160. *A Scene from The Merchant of Venice*
(The Merchant of Venice, Act II, Scene 2)
1883; watercolour; 40.6 x 55.8 cm (16 x 22 in.); whereabouts unknown.
Provenance: Sir Henry James Veitch;[1] bequeathed in 1924 to the Royal Albert Memorial Museum, Exeter; Veitch Bequest Trust Fund sale, Christie's, 22 October 1954, lot 46; bought by Lang or Long for £14 14s.
Exhibitions: Old Water-Colour Society, 1883, no. 269; Liverpool Corporation, Fourteenth *Autumn Exhibition of Pictures*, Walker Art Gallery, 1884, no. 620, not for sale.
Literature: *The Times*, 3 May 1883, p.4. *The Athenaeum*, No. 2897, 5 May 1883, p.578.

This picture was accompanied by the following quotation from the play:

"*Launcelot, Gobbo and Old Gobbo.*
Launcelo: Father, I am glad you are come; give me your present to one Master Bassanio, who, indeed, gives rare new liveries; if I serve not him, I run as far as God has any ground. - O rare fortune! here comes the man; - to him, father; for I am a Jew, if I serve the Jew any longer.
Enter Bassanio with Leonardo and other Followers.
Bassanio: You may do so; - but let it be so hasted, that supper be ready at the farthest by five of the clock. See these letters deliver'd; put the liveries to making; and desire Gratiano to come anon to my lodging."

F.G. Stephens in his review in *The Athenaeum* stated: " 'A Scene from 'The Merchant of Venice' (269) continues the series of illustrations of this drama to which Mr. Wallis has devoted himself during several years. On the quay are Launcelot Gobbo and his father, Bassanio, and others – animated groups in picturesque costumes backed by sumptuous architecture. The whole is flooded with Venetian light, and distinguished by brilliant harmonies and purity of colour. The purple doves, each lighter in tone than its purple shadow on the pavement, sparkle as they move. The background gives beautifully the richly tinted marbles and many sculptures." The reviewer for *The Times* commented: "…a scene from the *Merchant of Venice*, treated by Mr. H. Wallis with his accustomed, perhaps excessive brightness."

Cat. 161. *A Scene from the Merchant of Venice (Antonio and Bassanio bargaining with Shylock)*
(The Merchant of Venice, Act I, Scene 3)
1884; watercolour; dimensions unknown; whereabouts unknown.
Provenance: Bought by Harry Weltsch, 34 Redcliffe Gardens, West Brompton, London, for £157 10s (a deposit of £31 10s was paid on 26 April 1884); ?anonymous sale, Robinson, Fisher and Harding auctions, London, 18 April 1918, lot 88.
Exhibitions: Old Water-Colour Society, 1884, no. 19.
Literature: *The Times*, 26 April 1884, p.10; *The Building News and Engineering Journal*, Vol. 46, 2 May 1884, p.661; *The Athenaeum*, No. 2950, 10 May 1884, p.604; *The Graphic*, 31 May 1884, p.535.
When the picture was shown at the Old Water-Colour Society in 1884 it was accompanied by this abridged quotation from the end of Act I, Scene 3:

"*Shylock*: O Father Abraham, what these Christians are
Whose own hard dealings teaches them suspect
The thoughts of others!
Antonio: Yes, Shylock, I will seal unto this bond.
Bassanio: I like not fair terms, and a villain's mind."

F.G. Stephens writing in *The Athenaeum* expressed his thoughts: "Mr. H. Wallis's figure pictures are welcome on account of their brilliancy, wealth of colour, and dramatic conception. He has been very happy in the *Scene from the 'Merchant of Venice'* (No. 19), where Shylock, with upraised hands, protests his innocent intentions, and Antonio and Bassanio regard him with disdain. The colouration and the lighting of this picture are clear as well as powerful and rich. The spontaneity of the design is greatly enhanced by the verisimilitude of the light and shade. The whole is, in the true sense of the phrase, admirably put upon the paper, the actions, colouring, and tones being forceful and harmonious."

The reviewer for *The Graphic* praised the work: "Mr. Henry Wallis's picture of Antonio and Bassanio bargaining with Shylock is one of the best of many illustrating *The Merchant of Venice* that he has produced. More distinct characterization in the figures and more intensity of expression would have rendered the work more dramatically effective, but the grouping is excellent and the disposition of the rich and brilliant local tints most artistic. The subordinate figures and the picturesque buildings in the background, glowing in the light of the mid-day sun, are admirably introduced, and their truth of local colour add greatly to the verisimilitude of the scene."

This may be the same watercolour that sold at Robinson, Fisher and Harding, London in 1918 described only as *Antonio* from the *Merchant of Venice.* Which one of Wallis's watercolours this was is difficult to ascertain for certain. The auction catalogue says it was "Exhibited at Manchester Exhibition" but it is not known which pieces from the *Merchant of Venice* series were exhibited there.

Cat. 162. *The Violin Player; the Fountain is attributed to Donatello*[1]
1882; watercolour; dimensions unknown; whereabouts unknown.
Exhibitions: Old Water-Colour Society, 1882, no. 196.
Literature: *Pall Mall Gazette*, 28 April 1882, p.4.

The critic of the *Pall Mall Gazette* stated: "Mr. Wallis also exhibits a female 'Violin Player' (196) who tucks her instrument under her arm, while she drinks at Donatello's marble fountain."

Cat. 163. *Springtide; Sitting in the Shade, in his Orchard*
1882; watercolour; dimensions unknown; whereabouts unknown.
Exhibitions: Old Water-Colour Society, 1882, no. 210.

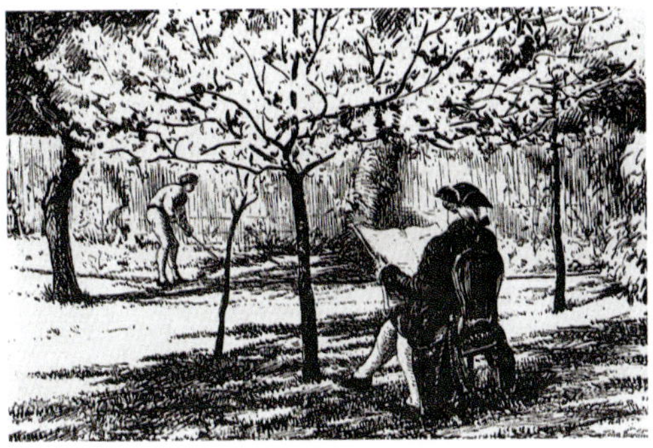

Drawing from the O.W.S.'s *Illustrated catalogue* including sketches by the artists.

This watercolour shows a gentleman in 18th-century dress, sitting in the shade in his orchard and reading a newspaper while a gardener labours in the background.

Cat. 164. *The Moorish Fountain and Patio de Lindaraja at the Alhambra*
1882; watercolour; 45.7 x 31.7 cm (18 x 12½ in.); private collection.
Inscriptions: Signed with *HW* initials, lower left.
Provenance: Wallis's studio and then by descent from the artist to his son Harold Wallis; then to his daughter-in-law Mary Wallis (née Mary Elizabeth Aymes); then her great-niece Vera G. Cooper (née Langley; 1910-1989); and thence by direct descent to John Harold Cooper and family; sold at Bonhams, London, 05 March 2002, lot 69 (*Figures in an Hispano-Moresque Courtyard*), sold for £1,900; private collection of Patrick Holden.
Exhibitions: Old Water-Colour Society, Winter exhibition 1882, no. 189.
Literature: *The Athenaeum*, No. 2876, 9 December 1882, p.780; *The Architect*, Vol. 28, 16 December 1882, p.375.

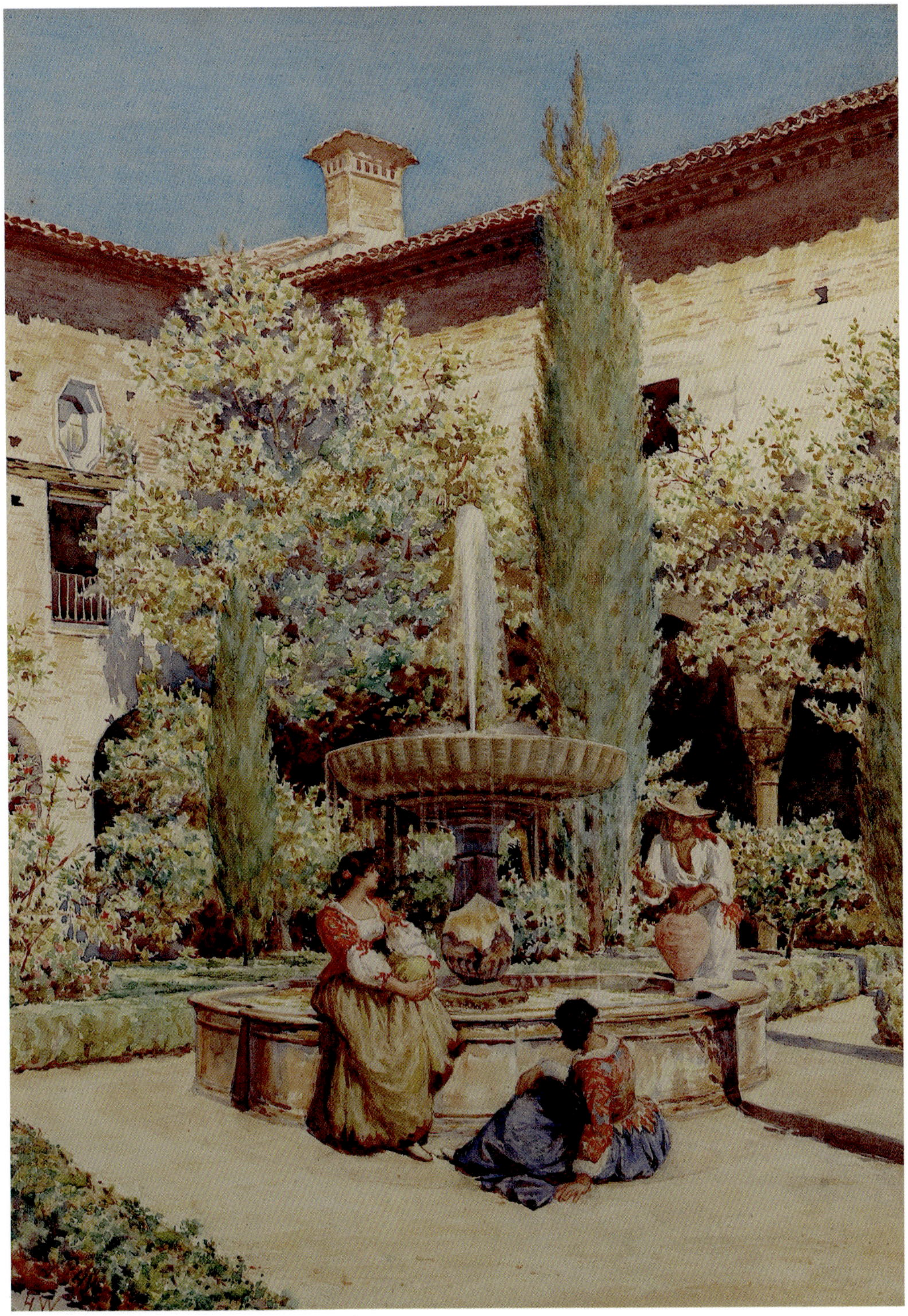

Cat. 164. Image courtesy of Bonhams, London

The critic of *The Architect* noted: "Mr. Henry Wallis has travelled to Spain in search of sunshine, and found it, to judge by The Moorish Fountain and Patio de Lindaraja at the Alhambra (189)." The watercolour shows two seated young Spanish women talking to a gardener. In view of the statuesque quality of the two female figures, one might also be tempted to equate this work with Wallis's picture *Gossip*, but F.G. Stephens describes that work as taking place in "a sunny street in an Italian town", which this obviously is not. This work is reminiscent of Luke Fildes's paintings of Venetian girls, such as his *The Venetians* of 1885 or *An al fresco toilette* of 1889.

Cat. 165. *A Spanish-Moorish Doorway at Toledo*
1883; watercolour; dimensions unknown; whereabouts unknown.
Provenance: Thomas Agnew & Sons Ltd., London, by 1884.
Exhibitions: Old Water-Colour Society, 1883, no. 233; Messrs. Agnew's Annual Exhibition of Water-Colour Art, 1884, no. 169.
Literature: *The Standard*, 4 May 1883, p.2; *The Builder*, Vol. XLIV, 5 May 1883, p.593; *The Athenaeum*, No. 2897, 5 May 1883, p.578; *The Guardian*, Supplement, 6 June 1883, p.17; *The Standard*, 25 February 1884, p.2.

F.G. Stephens in *The Athenaeum* discussed this picture enthusiastically: "Mr. Wallis sees everything with a painter's eye, and seeks for subjects in which light, colour, and picturesque costumes, and elegant architecture are happily blended. His tact was never used to more advantage than in *A Spanish-Moorish Doorway at Toledo* (233), where pure sunlight falls upon faded woodwork, which, originally a bright deep blue, has been blanched by twenty summers and winters till it has gained the fine and varied tints of an enamel. It is set in a white plaster wall made dazzling by the sun and splendidly contrasted by the yellow-orange garments of the figures posed in front of it. This is one of the most brilliant pictures of the year." The critic for *The Standard* commented: "Mr. Henry Wallis shows his

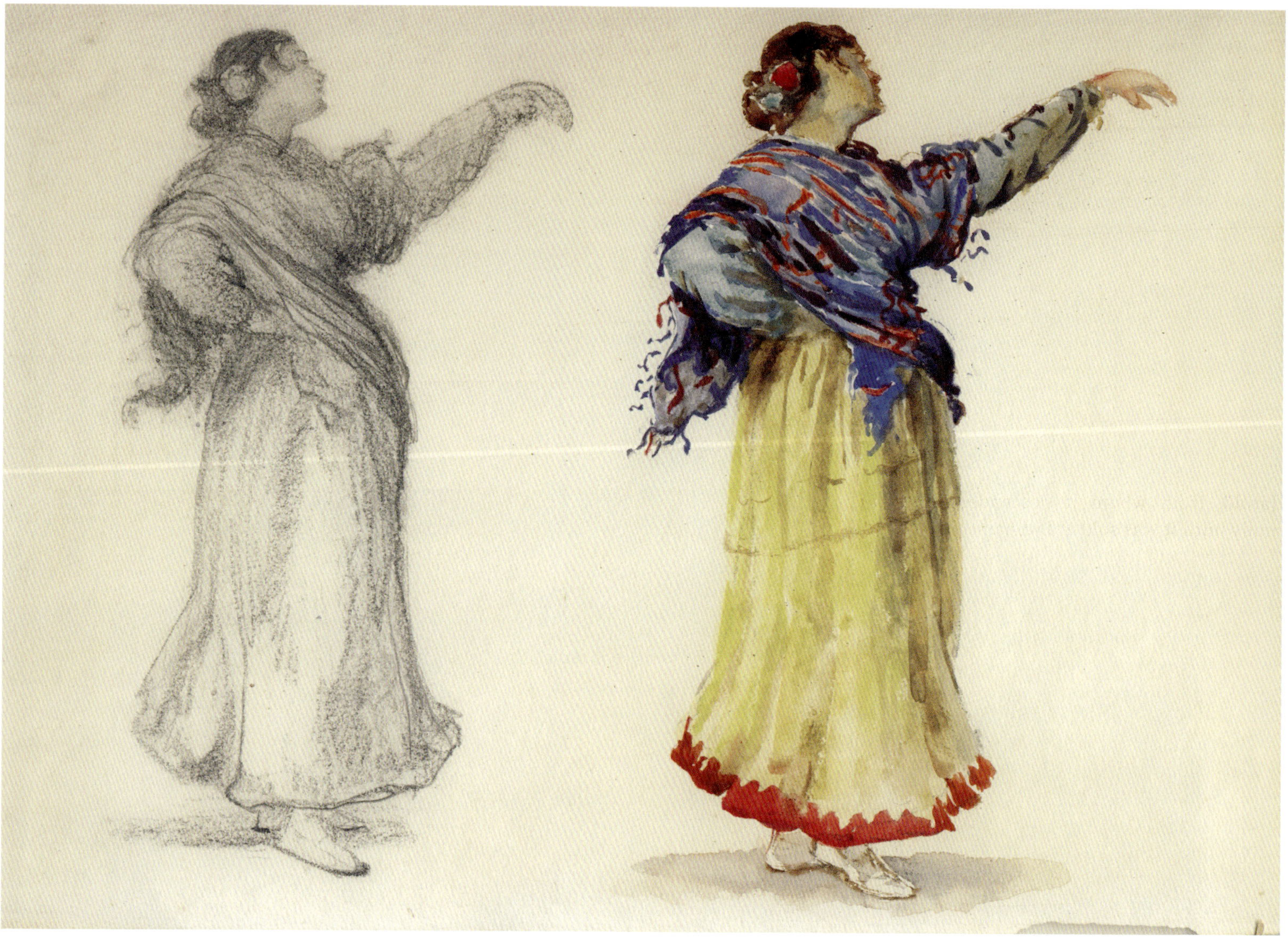

Cat. 167a. Image courtesy of Dennis Lanigan collection

most refined piece of execution, 'A Spanish Moorish Doorway at Toledo' (No. 233)."

Cat. 166. *Gossip*
1883; watercolour; dimensions unknown; whereabouts unknown.
Exhibitions: Old Water-Colour Society, Winter exhibition 1883, no. 145.
Literature: *The Times*, 3 December 1883, p.8; *The Athenaeum*, No. 2928, 8 December 1883, p.745.

This is the first of the pictures of the watercolour exhibition of 1883-84 described by F.G. Stephens in his review in *The Athenaeum*: "Mr. H. Wallis has sent a group of drawings of remarkable value on account of their tender colouration, brilliantly soft and pure local tints, and fine harmonies of tone. *Gossip* (145), the first we encounter is a vista of a sunny street in an Italian town, with two girls discussing local news; the statuesque elegance of the pose of one of them bespeaks the cultured taste of the artist, who recognised the antique in the types and contours of her draperies and the fine grace of her attitude." [See also: *The Times* review under Cat. 167.]

Cat. 167. *A Gipsy Dance, Granada*
1883; watercolour; dimensions unknown; whereabouts unknown.
Exhibitions: Old Water-Colour Society, Winter exhibition 1883, no. 158.
Literature: *The Standard*, 1 December 1883, p.2; *The Times*, 3 December 1883, p.8; *The Athenaeum*, No. 2928, 8 December 1883, p.745; *The Graphic*, 8 December 1883, p.575.

F.G. Stephens, in *The Athenaeum*, praised this painting: "A Gipsy Dance, Granada (158), depicts a girl dancing on the red-brick pavement of a Moorish atrium, while the aisles are occupied by lookers-on in costumes more gaudy, forced in contrasts of colour, and far less graceful than that of the elegant and animated performer. The sunlight effect here is very charming indeed. Nothing could be better than the general harmony of this capital work. The technical merits of this fine picture deserve the honours of a large canvas."

The critic of *The Graphic* stated: "Mr. H. Wallis has a characteristic scene of Southern Spanish life 'A Gipsy Dance, Granada'. The men, women, and children who are assembled in the *patio* of a stately house, besides being true types of Andalusian character, are naturally grouped and vivacious in expression." The reviewer for *The Times* commented: "Near them hang two drawings by Mr. Henry Wallis – 'Gossip' (145) [Cat. 166] and 'A Gipsy Dance, Granada' (158) – both of which are excellent specimens of this very accomplished figure painter. Mr. Wallis has probably never done anything better than the last-named drawing, with its gay, bright colour, its dancing, yellow-clad gipsy, and the happy Andalusian audience gathered together in the patio."

Cat. 167a. *Study of a Spanish Dancing Lady*
*c.*1883; watercolour and graphite on off-white Whatman paper watermarked 1881; 22.5 x 31.1 cm (8¹⁵⁄₁₆ x 12¼ in.); Dr Dennis T. Lanigan, Saskatoon, Canada.
Provenance: R.L. Cook, Norwich, Norfolk; private collection; his sale, Bonhams, Knightsbridge, London, 8 February 2005, lot 25, bought in; Bonhams, Knightsbridge, 9 August 2005, lot 138, bought by Dr Dennis T. Lanigan for £120.

This is an interesting sheet in that it includes, side-by-side, the same figure treated both in pencil and watercolour. It is reminiscent of the drawing exercises that John Ruskin devised for his students in which a figure or object would be drawn one way in pencil and then again in watercolour in order to demonstrate different techniques and approaches. Wallis would have been familiar with Ruskin and his writings, and may even have looked at, or owned, Ruskin's drawing manual, *Elements of Drawing; in Three Letters to Beginners* (1857). However, as this was drawn in the 1880s, Ruskin's influence is rather more pronounced than one might expect by this stage in Wallis's career. Upon his death, Wallis left his own copy of Ruskin's *Academy Notes* to his son Harold, from whom it descended in the family until it was sold at Bonhams in 2002.[1]

This drawing was undoubtedly executed on location in Spain. Based on a letter from Mary Ellen Meredith to Wallis on 4 August 1856, he is known to have visited Spain as early as July/August of 1856.[2] This was obviously not his only trip to Spain, however, because the paper on which this is drawn, is watermarked 1881. At the Old Water-Colour Society, Winter exhibition, in 1883-84, Wallis exhibited a watercolour entitled *A gypsy dance, Granada*; this study may well relate to that watercolour.

Cat. 168. ***At a Window, Seville***
1883; watercolour; dimensions unknown; whereabouts unknown.
Exhibitions: Old Water-Colour Society, Winter exhibition 1883, no. 243.
Literature: *The Athenaeum*, No. 2928, 8 December 1883, p.745; *London St James Gazette*, 10 December 1883, p.6.

F.G. Stephens discusses this work only briefly in *The Athenaeum*: "*At a Window, Seville* (243) is powerfully and freely drawn." Wallis obviously enjoyed his time in Spain and one of his sketchbooks is filled with drawings of the locations he saw and people he met in Seville and Granada. [See: Cats. 265-270 and 277-279].

Cat. 169. ***A Street Scene in Spain***
*c.*1882-1883; watercolour on paper; 18 x 8 cm (7⅛ x 3⅛ in.) – sight; private collection.
Provenance: Wallis's studio; by descent from the artist to his son Harold Wallis; then to his daughter-in-law Mary Wallis (née Mary Elizabeth Aymes); then her great-niece Vera G. Cooper (née Langley; 1910-1989); and thence by direct descent to John Harold Cooper and family; private collection.

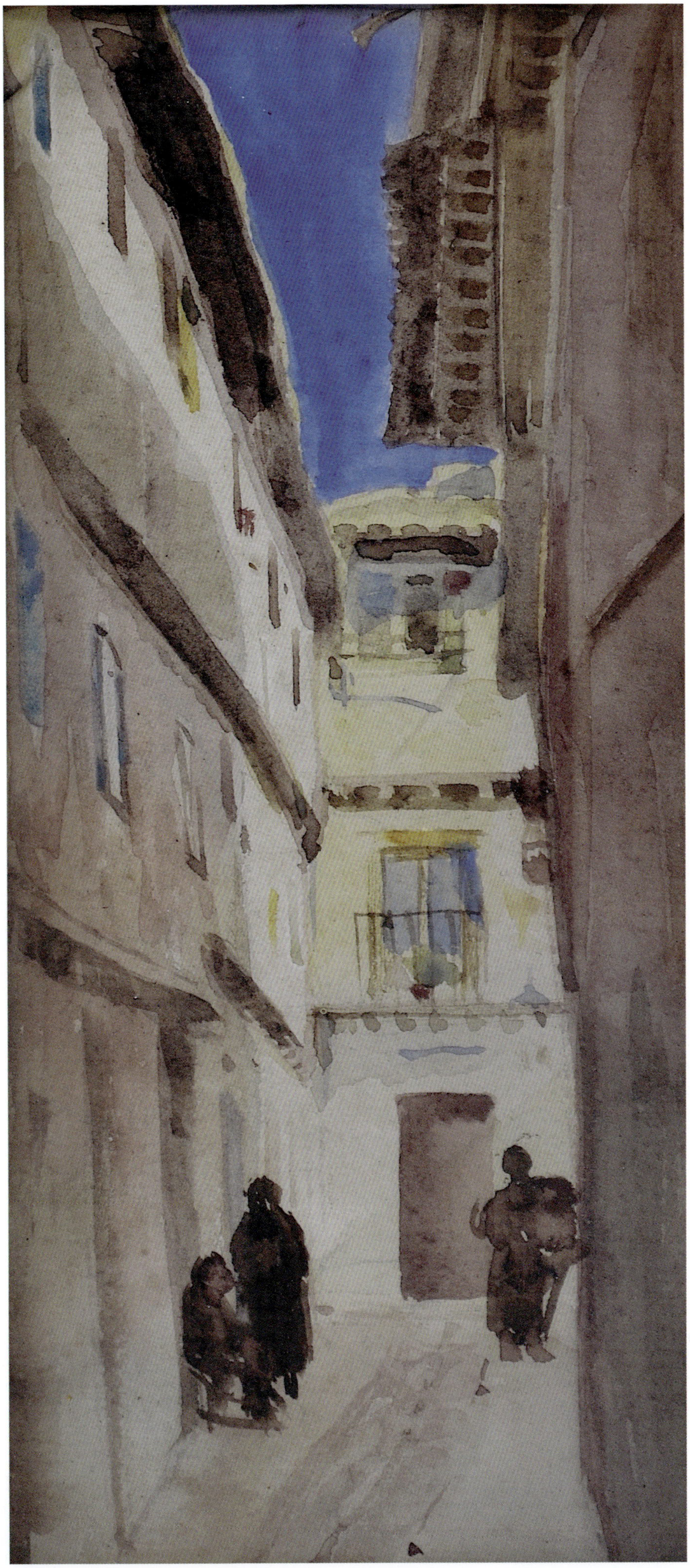

Cat. 169. Image courtesy of private collection

This scene is reminiscent of Wallis's drawings from his time spent travelling in Seville, Granada and Toledo. Wallis exhibited works with Spanish themes at the O.W.S. in 1882 and 1883 and this work might date from this same time period.

Cat. 170. *Pastorale*
1883; watercolour; dimensions unknown; whereabouts unknown.
Exhibitions: Old Water-Colour Society, Winter exhibition 1883, no. 402.
Literature: *The Portfolio*, Vol. 15, 1884, p.23; *The Standard*, 1 December 1883, p.2; *The Athenaeum*, No. 2928, 8 December 1883, p.745; *The Builder*, Vol. 45, No. 2109, 8 December 1883, p.747; *The Graphic*, 8 December 1883, p.575.

F.G. Stephens goes into more detail about this work, one of Wallis's few attempts at a work of Aesthetic Classicism and where he choses to paint the nude figure, another rarity in his art. "*Pastorale* (402) is an Italian romance in a very delicate art, suggestive of much that Samuel Palmer might have given us if he had drawn the nude figure with skill equal to Mr. Wallis's. It is the picture of a glade near a fountain, where some girls or nymphs loiter and turn to watch the coming of a piping youth. The light and shade, the disposition of the masses of foliage, verdure, sculpted stones, and the composing of the whole, are of rare value in design."

The critic for *The Builder* stated: "A fine piece of classicality in some respects is that by Mr. Henry Wallis…and is called 'Pastorale' (402). This is a small and lovely Titanesque study, representing three female figures in warm glowing evening light, the richness of the general colour being further heightened by the silken draperies introduced; the work is a little poem, a specimen of that abstract and truly imaginative painting, of which we see so little now-a-days."

The critic for *The Portfolio* liked this the best of Wallis's contributions to the exhibition: "In a very different manner Mr. Henry Wallis recalls the rich colour of Samuel Palmer, and hints at Titanesque memories, in a little picture of three nude female figures in a wooded landscape, which he calls a *Pastorale*: a beautiful drawing of the kind, very preferable to his motley notes from Spain." *The Graphic* noted: "His small picture, a 'Pastorale' glows with rich and well-harmonised colour." The reviewer for *The Standard* said approvingly: "…in 402, he gives us what is at once the most dignified and the most attractive rendering of the nude figure that the Exhibition contains – a great composition of serious grace and of glowing colour."

Cat. 171. *At the Well*
1884; watercolour; dimensions unknown; whereabouts unknown.
Exhibitions: Old Water-Colour Society, 1884, no. 218, asking price £63.
Literature: *The Athenaeum*, No. 2950, 10 May 1884, p.604.

The Athenaeum, comparing this painting to *The Nosegay*, stated briefly: "*At the Well* (218), a less important design, has nearly equal technical merits."

Cat. 172. The Nosegay
1884; watercolour; dimensions unknown; whereabouts unknown.
Exhibitions: Old Water-Colour Society, 1884, no. 275, asking price £105; Liverpool Corporation, Autumn Exhibition of Pictures, Walker Art Gallery, 1884, no. 460, N.F.S.
Literature: *The Building News and Engineering Journal*, Vol. 46, 2 May 1884, p.661; *The Athenaeum*, No. 2950, 10 May 1884, p.604.

F.G. Stephens, in *The Athenaeum*, complimented this watercolour: "The local and general colouring and tonality of *The Nosegay* (275) are extremely luminous. The velvety surface is not common in water colour painting, and due in this, as in other works by this artist, to his extensive practice in oil. In 'The Nosegay' a girl, wearing a blue petticoat and white upper garment, is seated on a bench before that famous wall in Venice, which Mr. Wallis has painted with sufficient frequency. The sculptures are charmingly delineated, and the marble of which they are formed has the true colour and semi-transparent surface. The girl amuses herself with a baby, who lies on the white marble pavement at her feet."

Cat. 173. The Bishop's Tomb
1884; watercolour; dimensions unknown; whereabouts unknown.
Exhibitions: Old Water-Colour Society, Winter exhibition 1884, no. 31, asking price £21.
Literature: *The Portfolio*, Vol. 16, 1885, p.22; *The Builder*, Vol. 47, 6 December 1884, p.754; *The Architect*, Vol. 32, 13 December 1884, p.383; *The Nation*, No. 1019, Vol. 40, 8 January 1885, p.32.

The critic for *The Nation* commented: "Henry Wallis sends two admirable drawings… 'The Bishop's Tomb', another Spanish study, the Bishop's reclining effigy surmounted by a beautiful figure bas-relief, with some ladies in black kneeling before the tomb." *The Builder* stated: "Mr. Wallis's 'the Bishop's Tomb' (31) is anther good architectural bit." The critic of *The Portfolio* was also well-disposed to this work: "Mr. Henry Wallis has an unusually impressive Spanish study of a Bishop's Tomb, with dark kneeling figures thrown out against subdued splendour of marble and bronze." The reviewer for *The Architect* declared: "It is disappointing to find no architectural or interior subjects by Mr. Hodson.[1] The best things in this line are by Mr. Henry Wallis a *Bishop's Tomb*, and *Doorway of Don Pedro's Palace, Toledo*, [Cat. 174] both impressive studies, splendid in colour and texture, though rather blurred in execution."

Cat. 174. *Gateway of the Palace of Don Pedro the Cruel, at Toledo*
1884; watercolour; 40.7 x 26 cm (16 x 10¼ in); whereabouts unknown.
Provenance: Bought on 29 November 1884 for £73 10s by John Graham, 18 Albert Gate, Hyde Park, London; his sale Christie's, 5 May 1894, lot 41, bought by Agnew's for £19 19s.
Exhibitions: Old Water-Colour Society, Winter exhibition 1884, no. 351.
Literature: *The Times*, 29 November 1884, p.8; *The Daily Chronicle*, 4 December 1884; *The Athenaeum*, No. 2980, 6 December 1884, p.739; *The Academy and Literature*, Vol. 26, No. 657, 6 December 1884, p.382; *The Architect*, Vol. 32, 13 December 1884, p.383; *The Portfolio*, Vol. 16, 1885, p.22; *The Nation*, No. 1019, Vol. 40, 8 January 1885, p.32.

F.G. Stephens reported favourably on this picture in *The Athenaeum*: "Another sincere piece of painting founded on knowledge, yet by no means innocent of the lamp, is the scholarly picture of a Spanish scene with domestic figures, entitled *Gateway of the Palace of Don Pedro* (351), by Mr. Wallis, a vigorous picture of sunlight and sharp, clear, dark shadow on a richly carved portal. The half-tints exceed in purple in the shades, in orange in the lights; such shortcomings and some lack of silvery hues we ascribe to the studio light rather than the sun."
[See also: *The Architect* review under Cat. 173.]

The reviewer of *The Daily Chronicle* professed his admiration: "The *Gateway of the Palace of Don Pedro the Cruel, Toledo* by Mr. Henry Wallis is a wonderfully fine study, broadly effective in treatment of the light and shade, delightful in elegant tracery and ornamentation of the gate itself, whilst the figures of the fish seller and others at the open door, give contrast and lend an interest to the subject." The critic for *The Nation* stated: "Henry Wallis sends two admirable drawings, 'The Gateway of the Palace of Don Pedro the Cruel, at Toledo', with an exquisite rendering of architectural detail and figures coming through the gateway,

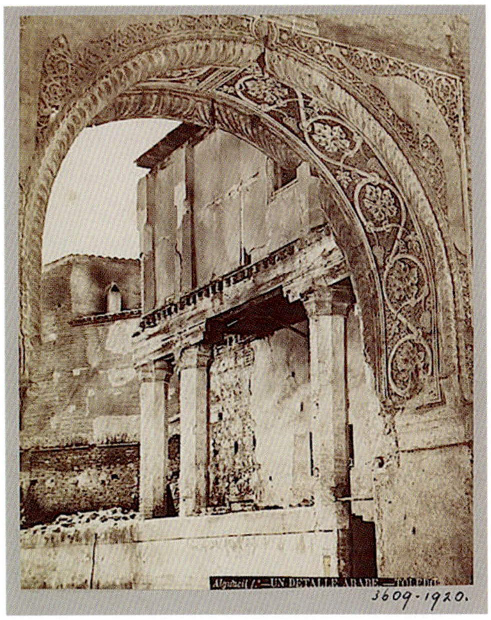

Gateway of the Palace of Don Pedro the Cruel by Spanish photographer Casiano Alguacil Blázquez (1832-1914), V&A collection, museum no. 3609-1920. Photograph courtesy of the Victoria and Albert Museum. See Cat. 174.

rich and harmonious in bright green and red attire." *The Times* referred to this as: "Mr. Henry Wallis again, is at his very best in No. 351, 'The Gateway of the Palace of Don Pedro the Cruel, at Toledo' a most dexterous and admirable piece of architectural drawing, relieved by the figures in the doorway."

Cat. 175. *Sedaine Reading to Diderot his Comedy 'Le philosophe sans le sçavoir'*[1]
1884-1899; watercolour; dimensions unknown; whereabouts unknown.
Exhibitions: Old Water-Colour Society, 1899, no. 65.
Literature: *The Athenaeum*, No. 2944, 29 March 1884, pp.417-18; *The Times*, 24 April 1899, p.6; *The Athenaeum*, No. 3734, 20 May 1899, p.630.

According to F. G. Stephens in Fine Art Gossip in *The Athenaeum* this work was virtually complete in 1884 but not exhibited until 1899: "Mr. Wallis has nearly finished a large watercolour drawing intended for the next exhibition of the society of which he is a member. It represents the interior of the study of Diderot while Sedaine is reading to him the play of 'Le Philosophe sans le Savoir'. The pair sit facing each other at a table which is covered with papers. The greater part of the walls of the room is lined with books in rich, quaint, and old bindings, so that the effect of tone and colour in the picture is made rich in variety and even in textures and light and shade." In a letter to Stephens written later in 1884, Wallis explained the reason for the delay in finishing the picture: " 'Le philosophe sans le savoir', I'm afraid I can't get it done. Can't get Houdon's bust of Diderot [?there]. Sh[ld] have to go to Paris for it. So am in a fix."[2]

In his review of the Old Water-Colour Society exhibition of 1899 Stephens remarked: "Mr. Wallis furnishes a highly artistic version of a subject Meissonier treated with signal success,[3] that is *Sedaine reading to Diderot his Comedy of 'Le Philosophe sans le Scavoir'*. Writer and critic face one another at a table laden with books, and the treatment of the incident is so appropriate and sincere, the design is so spontaneous and humorous, that the artist has imparted to it stronger and fresher attraction than really belongs to it. The picture, as a picture, is extremely strong and full of tone, and, withal, an admirable piece of colour; but the background and accessories are not so solid and highly finished as we expect from the artist." The critic of *The Times* commented: "...there is a good drawing by Mr. Henry Wallis, none the less interesting for it being somewhat of a 'new departure'."

Cat. 176. *Going to Market, Bruges*
1885; watercolour; dimensions unknown; whereabouts unknown.
Exhibitions: Old Water-Colour Society, 1885, no. 140, asking price £52 10s; Manchester Art Gallery, 1885, no. 499, not for sale.
Literature: *The Times*, 1 May 1885, p.3; *The Athenaeum*, No. 3001, 2 May 1885, p.573; *The Graphic*, 9 May 1885, p.463.

F.G. Stephens in *The Athenaeum* observed: "We turn from the chiaroscuro, atmospheric effects, and brilliancy of these landscapes to the comparatively conventional study of colour, tone, and character which Mr. Wallis has contributed under the name of *Going to the Market - Bruges* (140), representing a plump Flemish damsel whose Spanish descent is marked on her face as well as by her enormous black cloak worn over a scarlet petticoat, which is a legacy of the Spaniards' occupation of Flanders. Mr. Wallis produced a powerful piece of colouring in this figure, and observed the harmonies of the black and scarlet severally, when he imparted blue and warm tints to the one colour, orange and black to the other. It is rather a study of colour than a picture."

Cat. 177. *An Oriental Glass Merchant*
1885; watercolour; 30.5 x 42 cm (12 x 16½ in.); private collection.
Inscriptions: Signed and inscribed on a label on reverse.
Provenance: Wallis's studio and then by descent from the artist to his son Harold Wallis; then to his daughter-in-law Mary Wallis (née Mary Elizabeth Aymes); then her great-niece Vera G. Cooper (née Langley; 1910-1989); and thence by direct descent to John Harold Cooper and family; sold at Bonhams, London, 5 March 2002, lot 64, sold for £1800; private collection.
Exhibitions: Old Water-Colour Society, 1885, no. 265, asking price £105; Scottish Society of Painters in Water-Colours, Glasgow, 1885, no. 73.
Literature: *The Times*, 1 May 1885, p.3; *The Athenaeum*, No. 3001, 2 May 1885, p.573; *The Saturday Review*, Vol. 59, 2 May 1885, p.581; *The Graphic*, 9 May 1885, p.463; *The Artist and Journal of Home Culture*, Vol. 6, 1 June 1885, p.168; *The Illustrated London News*, 31 October 1885, p.443; *The Academy and Literature*, Vol. 28, No. 704, 31 October 1885, p.296; *The Daily Telegraph*, 1 December 1886.

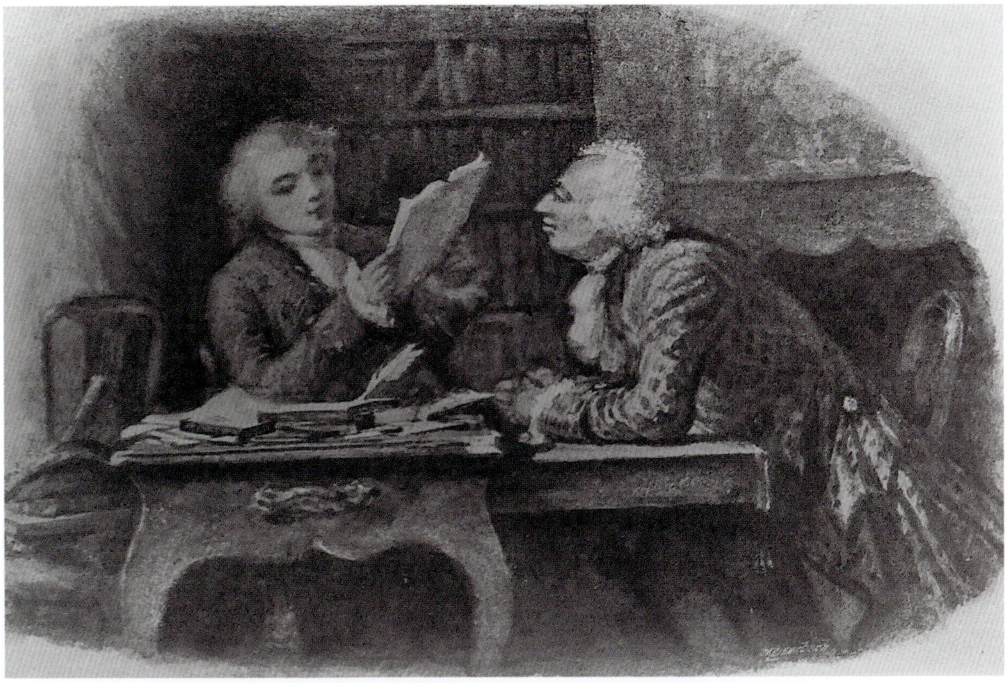

Illustration from the O.W.S.'s *Illustrated catalogue*. See Cat. 175.

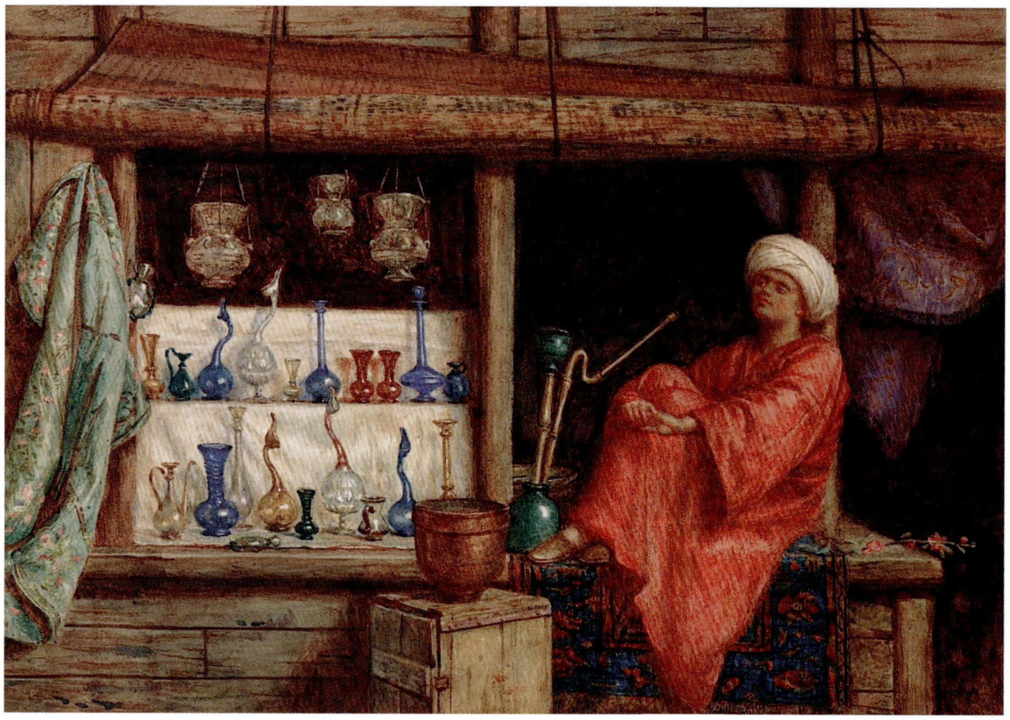

Cat. 177. Image courtesy of Bonhams, London

F.G. Stephens, in *The Athenaeum*, was laudatory in his remarks: "More like a picture is his *Oriental Glass Merchant* (265), in which an opportunity has been deftly seized for painting many fine specimens of glass on a white cloth, in company with the splendid red garment of the merchant lounging on one side, and the equally splendid green coat which hangs on the other side of the stall. Quite superb is the varied and contrasted colour and soft lustre which Mr. Wallis has made manifest in this picture. Tones of greater strength and tints of truer qualities have seldom been more delightfully combined. Each little bottle, beaker, vase, and cruet is craftily combined with its neighbours and the white, red, and green fabrics near it. But the man in the coat, his face, hands, and feet, to say nothing of the coat without the man his chromatic antagonist, should have been more carefully modelled and drawn."

Other reviewers were also lavish in their praise for this watercolour. The critic of *The Times* wrote: "...and an Eastern subject, which Mr. Henry Wallis has treated with a wealth of colour that will be a revelation even to his admirers. If it were a question of arranging the drawings in order of merit, we are not sure that we should not give the absolutely first place to this 'Oriental Glass Merchant' (265). In this small drawing, which hangs in the centre of the first screen, Mr. Wallis has painted a small shopkeeper of Damascus or Cairo, sitting and waiting for customers to buy his beautiful blue, green, and yellow glass jugs and long-necked phials. The subject is an admirable one for a colourist, and one wonders why the late John Lewis,[1] that illustrious searcher after all that was picturesque in Eastern life, never treated it; for of all the wares of the bazaar none are so brilliant or varied in hue as the delicate work of the glassmaker of old. Any one who wishes to see the reality should go to the Burlington Fine Art Club, and see the examples collected in the exhibition now being held there; or if he would prefer to see the same subject being treated in art, he cannot do better than come and study this minute and brilliant drawing of Mr. Wallis. We have classed it, however, among the figure subjects; and, indeed, the figure of the glass merchant, with his soft and dreamy countenance and his robe of brilliant red, is a notable feature of the drawing. But it is rather for the harmony of the whole that the work is remarkable, and in that respect it must rank extremely high."

Just as with *In the Sacristy, the Carpet Merchant*, Wallis did not paint this watercolour from life. In fact, Wallis would not make his first journey to Egypt until later that same winter. It is possible that he felt the need to be on site when designing his future visions of the Orient.

Cat. 178. *In the Bazaar, Smyrna*
1885; watercolour; dimensions unknown; whereabouts unknown.
Provenance: Bought on 2 December 1885 from the O.W.S. exhibition for £63 by John Godden,[1] West India House, 9 Leadenhall Street, London.
Exhibitions: Old Water-Colour Society, Winter exhibition 1885, no. 24.
Literature : *The British Almanac and Companion*, 1887, p.171 (of the *Companion*); *The Times*, 1 December 1885, p.17; *The Saturday Review*, Vol. 60, 5 December 1885, p.747; *The Athenaeum*, No. 3032, 5 December 1885, p.738; *The Graphic*, 12 December 1885, p.643; *The Portfolio*, Vol. 17, 1886, pp.21-22.

In 1885 Wallis returned to painting a subject from Smyrna that he had first explored in 1880 in his *A Morning Call, Ladies of Smyrna* [Cat. 143]. F.G. Stephens, in *The Athenaeum*, described this later work: "We turn with great pleasure to Mr. Wallis's superb exercise of subtle, rich, various, and powerful colouration called *In the Bazaar, Smyrna* (24), a lady bargaining with a merchant seated in a stall. A sumptuous garment of prophet green is brought in contact with a deep rose-coloured dress held by the dealer. The picture is so deep-toned and splendidly harmonious that it illuminates the place it hangs in, and might set a standard for tonality and colouration for the gallery. We cannot admire the drawing of the figures which is decidedly loose."

The critic of *The Times* had these comments: "It is not unfair to the society [Royal Society of Painters in Water Colours] thus to identify it with its landscape painters, for, in truth, figure painting has never been its strong point; and though there are artists in its ranks who can draw the figure, their work is, as a rule, hardly on a level with that of the best landscape painters. We ought, perhaps, to make an exception in the present case in favour of the drawings of Mr. Stacy Marks,[2] Mr. Henry Wallis, and one or two others;...and the great merit of Mr. Wallis's drawings lies in the rich and beautiful colour of the accessories...Mr. Wallis sends only one drawing, and that, as was the case last summer, of an Eastern subject. 'In the Bazaar, Smyrna' (24) is a brilliant and glowing performance, in which the carpets and the other wares of the stall-keeper are painted in a manner to recall the jewel-like work of the late John Lewis."

Cat. 179. *Portrait of a Girl Wearing an Embroidered Headdress*
1881 (?1886); watercolor heightened with gouache; 16 x 12 cm (6 1/4 x 4 3/4 in.); private collection.
Inscriptions: Signed with initials *HW* and dated *1881 (?1886)*
Provenance: Wallis's studio; then by descent from the artist to his daughter-in-law Alice Julyan Wallis (née Roberts); and thence to her great-niece Mrs. Vera G. Whiting, Purley, Surrey; her sale Sotheby's Belgravia, 10 April 1973, part of lot 211, bought by Abbott and Holder for £65; Sotheby's Belgravia, 5 July 1977, lot 12, sold for £170.

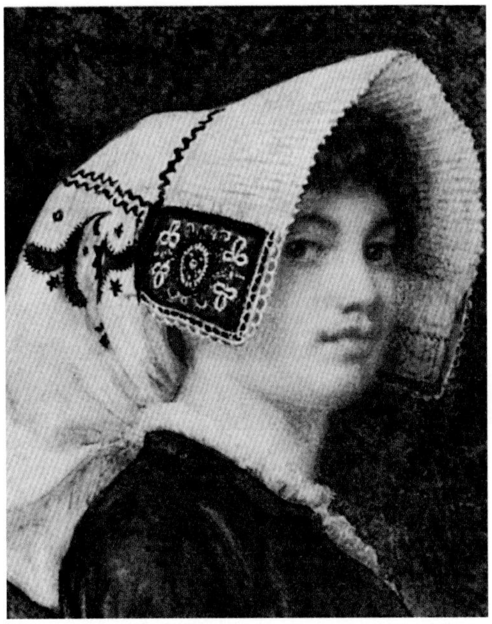

Cat. 179. Image courtesy of Sotheby's, London

The date of this drawing is difficult to verify as different dates were listed in the Sotheby's Belgravia catalogues. The model's head-dress is probably embroidered linen with lovely goffered pleating. According to a curator from the Fashion Museum, Antwerp, although the collar may be from Brittany, the head-dress is neither French nor German, nor indeed Flemish, Dutch or Belgian. The Belgian curator, Gwendoline d'Huart, in fact, has seen nothing similar and suggests that its design could be artistic licence on Wallis's part, which was not uncommon at the time.[1] It is possible, therefore, that this head-dress could be an "invention of tradition" of a typical 19th-century folk dress. However, Wallis was one of the Pre-Raphaelite painters, like Hunt and Brown, who strove for historical accuracy in his works, so it is more likely to be authentic and typical to a very specific regional site. The Belgian curator even suggested it could be Slavic in origin.

Cat. 180. *Outside the Door of the Mosque of Barkuk, Cairo*
1886; watercolour; 50.7 x 35.5 cm (20 x 14 in.); whereabouts unknown.
Provenance: Sold to John Postle Heseltine,[1] 196 Queen's Gate, London, on 15 May 1886 for £52; his sale Christie's, 24 May 1918, lot 52, bought for £27 6s by Bowden.[2]
Exhibitions: Old Water-Colour Society, 1886, no. 12.
Literature: *The Spectator*, Vol. 59, 1886, p.655; *The Times*, 5 May 1886, p.15; *The Athenaeum*, No. 3054, 8 May 1886, p.622.

F.G. Stephens, in *The Athenaeum*, commented: "A contrast to this delicately-toned picture of the ocean[3] is supplied by Mr. Wallis's rich and full-coloured Oriental example, *Outside the Door of the Mosque of Barkuk, Cairo* (12), a picture of broad and brilliant sun-light and sun-shadows, of figures in sumptuously tinted dresses, and of a door encrusted with plates of vivid green ancient bronze, patterned en repoussé. The walls are coloured with red, yellow, and white bands. The whole is a delightful and loyal study of light and colour, admirably harmonized and soft without lacking precision." The reviewer for *The Spectator* was less enthusiastic: "Mr. Henry Wallis has this year partially deserted his 'Merchant of Venice' and other Shakespearean subjects, and attacked Mr. Carl Haag's province of Eastern life.[4] But his work does not, we think, gain in consequence. For, in truth, Mr. Wallis's art is of a very peculiar character."

Cat. 181. *Twelfth Night – Act II, Scene 4*
1886; watercolour; dimensions unknown; whereabouts unknown.
Exhibitions: Old Water-Colour Society, 1886, no. 27, asking price £42; Midland Counties Art Museum Nottingham Castle, *Sixth Annual Autumn Exhibition of Modern Pictures*, 1886, no. 34A, priced at £42.
Literature: *The Times*, 5 May 1886, p.15; *The Athenaeum*, No. 3057, 29 May 1886, p.720; *The Academy and Literature*, Vol. 29, No. 735, 5 June 1886, p.404.

Wallis included this quotation from *Twelfth Night* in the Old Water-Colour Society catalogue:

> "Clown sings:
> *Come away, come away, death,*
> *And in sad cypress let me be laid;*
> *Fly away, Fly away, breath;*
> *I am slain by a fair cruel maid.*
> *My shroud of white, stuck all with yew,*
> *O, prepare it!*
> *My part of death, no one so true*
> *Did share it.*"

F.G. Stephens unusually was not particularly complimentary of this work in his 1886 review in *The Athenaeum*: "The best portion is the mouth with its pulpy lips – Mr. Wallis's *Twelfth Night, Act II. Scene 4* (27), represents that charming subject, the Clown singing Come away, come away Death. It is not one of the painter's best designs; indeed, in this respect it is a good deal below his standard, for it lacks spontaneity and character. On the other hand, it is an excellent piece of chiaroscuro, soft and broad. We have always felt that as a subject proper, i.e., apart from its technical advantages, this theme requires figures of some size. To be made interesting, in fact, it needs a scale sufficient for the full development of the expression of the fool, if not also those of his companions." However, the critic for *The Times* wrote: "Mr. Henry Wallis, divided between Egypt and Shakespeare, has sent two drawings full of brilliancy." The critic of *The Academy* also liked this work: "It is set besides Mr. Wallis's finest drawing – a scene from 'Twelfth Night', abundant in character and glowing of hue."

Cat. 182. *A Cairo Street Corner*
*c.*1886; watercolour; 44.5 x 30.5 cm (17½ x 12 in.); private collection.
Provenance: Wallis's studio and then by descent from the artist to his daughter-in-law Alice Julyan Wallis (née Roberts); and thence to her great-niece Mrs. Vera G. Whiting, Purley, Surrey; her sale Sotheby's Belgravia, 10 April 1973, lot 201, bought by Abbott & Holder for £26; private collection.

No work with this exact title was exhibited at the O.W.S., although the title is very vague and it might not even be the name Wallis originally gave it.

Cat. 183. *Cairo at Sunset, with Minarets in the Foreground, Pyramids in the Distance*
*c.*1886; watercolour; 25.5 x 35.5 cm (10 x 14 in.); private collection.
Provenance: Wallis's studio and then by descent from the artist to his daughter-in-law Alice Julyan Wallis (née Roberts); and thence to her great-niece Mrs. Vera G. Whiting, Purley, Surrey; her sale Sotheby's Belgravia, 10 April 1973, lot 201, bought by Hartnoll for Eyre for £36; private collection.
Exhibitions: Galerie des Luxembourg, *Le Paysage Anglais des Preraphaelites aux Symbolistes*, April 1974, no. 57.

Cat. 184. *Interior Courtyard of a Jew's House at Cairo – Preparing Coffee*
1886; watercolour; 40.7 x 30.5 cm (16 x 12 in.); private collection.
Inscription: Signed with initials *HW*, lower left; on the verso it states *No.1 Interior courtyard of a house at Cairo, preparing coffee* and signed underneath the inscription *Henry Wallis*.
Provenance: Wallis's studio and then by descent from the artist to his son Harold Wallis; then to his daughter-in-law Mary Wallis (née Mary Elizabeth Aymes); then her great-niece Vera G. Cooper (née Langley; 1910-1989); and thence by direct descent to John Harold Cooper and family; sold at Bonhams, London, 5 March 2002, lot 72, sold for £4000; private collection of Maurice Dixson.

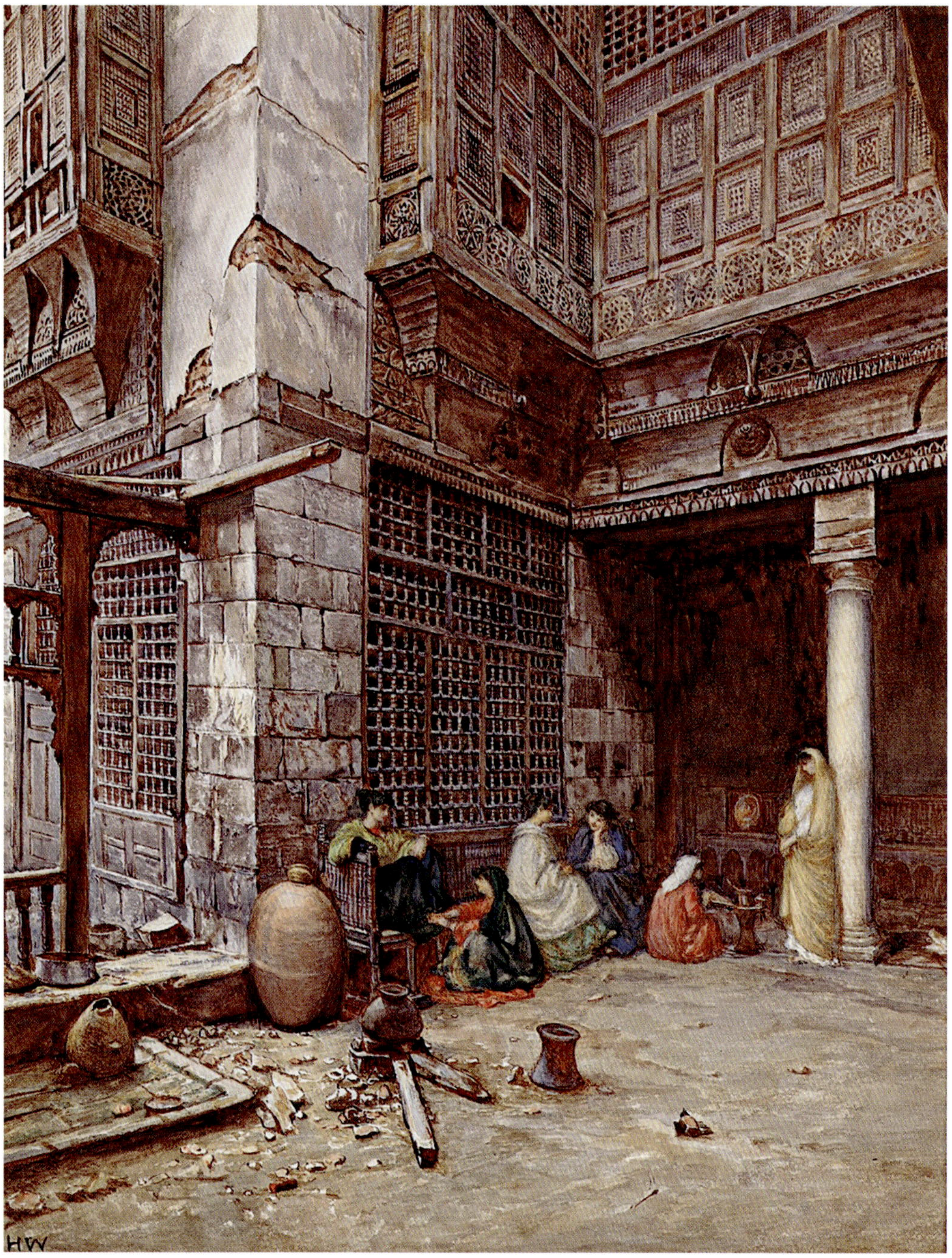

Cat. 184. Image courtesy of Bonhams, London

Exhibitions: Old Water-Colour Society, Winter exhibition 1886, no. 56, asking price £63.
Literature: *The Times*, 2 December 1886, p.8; *The Athenaeum*, No. 3084, 4 December 1886, p.750; *The Academy and Literature*, Vol. 30, No. 764, 25 December 1886, p.433.

F.G. Stephens, in his review in *The Athenaeum*, stated: "The *Interior Courtyard of a Jew's House at Cairo* (56) is the more important of Mr. Wallis's contributions. Its time-stained walls of white stone, here clad in stucco, there stripped bare, are surmounted by brown wood balconies of pierced work, characteristic of the city. It is made effective by light, shadow, and strong local colouring, solid, bright, rich in tints, and, if its shadows are rather hot and dark, highly artistic and skilful. The splendid luminosity of the costumes of the figures and the fine tonality of the whole show the power of the artist, which might be employed on nobler work." The reviewer for *The Times* said: "Two painters deal with the East, Mr. Wallis and Mr. Charles Robertson,[1] the latter sending a very ambitious performance which has a place of honour at one end of the room… In the higher qualities of a water-colour, Mr. Wallis's 'Interior of the Courtyard of a Jew's House – Cairo' (56) far surpasses Mr. Robertson's larger drawing."

Cat. 185. *The Second Cataract of the Nile from the Western Bank, above Wady Halfa*
1886; watercolour; dimensions unknow; whereabouts unknown.
Exhibitions: Old Water-Colour Society, Winter exhibition 1886, no. 120.
Literature: *The Times*, 2 December 1886, p.8; *The Athenaeum*, No. 3084, 4 December 1886, p.750; *The Tablet*, 8 January 1887, p.8.

Wallis spent the winter of 1885-86 in Egypt, and went as far as the second cataract, as we learn from a letter to his son Harold on 25 January 1886, and written aboard the SS *Water Lily*: "You will doubtless have got the post card I wrote yesterday at Assouan & the letter I posted at Luxor. On arriving at Assouan I went to the office of the Brigade Major to enquire if there was any possibility of going on to the 2nd Cataract. He very civilly gave me a pass wch allowed me to go up to Wady Halfa by the post boat & gratis, at the the same time he warned me there were no provisions to be got on board so I had to set to work at once to lay in rations."[1]

F.G. Stephens in *The Athenaeum* remarked on this picture: "He has sent a capital and vividly coloured study from nature of *The Second Cataract of the Nile* (120), which is interesting from its expanse of yellow sand, protruding black rocks, its river like blue steel, studded with huge angular boulders, and terraces of stone. The cloudless sky may owe something to the lamp."

Cat. 186. *Street Scene in Cairo (The Sheykh hears Mysterious Whispering)*
1887; watercolour; 48.2 x 34.4 cm (19 x 13½ in.); whereabouts unknown.
Provenance: Bought by Augustus Mordan,[1] Stone House, Reigate, on 10 May 1887 for £84; his estate sale, Christie's, 13 May 1901, lot 82A, bought Agnew's for £16 16 s.
Exhibitions: Old Water-Colour Society, 1887, no. 23.
Literature: Royal Society of Painters in Water Colours, *Illustrated Catalogue*, 1887, no. 23; *The Standard*, 18 April 1887; *The Times*, 18 April 1887, p.9; *The Athenaeum*, No. 3104, 23 April 1887, p.551; *The Illustrated London News*, Vol. 90, 23 April 1887, p.476; *The Graphic*, 23 April 1887, p.427; *The Academy and Literature*, Vol. 31, No. 782, 30 April 1887, p.314; *The Artist and Journal of Home Culture*, Vol. 8, 1 May 1887, p.150.

F.G. Stephens, in *The Athenaeum*, expressed the opinion: "Mr. Wallis's *Street Scene in Cairo* (23), Arabs conversing while a sheik holds a murmuring sea-shell to his ear, is hardly worthy of the brilliant powers of the painter or his early promise; yet the picture's force and general excellence make it conspicuous where these qualities are unusually scarce. It is a rich piece of colour, solid, and harmoniously disposed as to tone; the figures express the purpose of the artist, and their costumes could hardly be better painted."

The critic of *The Standard* claimed: "Mr. Henry Wallis's *Street Scene, Cairo* (N° 23) glows with Oriental colour; and this is some matter of importance and alarm, we take it, that is being discussed by the three men in presence of an unconcerned, but observant child." The reviewer for *The Graphic* described it thus: "... a characteristic picture of modern Oriental life, sunny in effect and strikingly true in local colour, by Mr. Henry Wallis. It is a 'Street Scene in Cairo,' with many figures, including three grave elders, one of whom is 'applying to his ear the convolutions of a thick-lipped shell' which he has purchased from a barefooted little girl." The critic of *The Artist*, somewhat surprisingly, commented: "but, on the other hand, Mr. Henry Wallis's 'Street Scene in Cairo' is better than we should have expected from him, and is decidedly agreeable in colour."

Cat. 187. *Herodotus at the Scribe's Bazaar, Memphis*
1887; watercolour; dimensions unknown; whereabouts unknown.
Exhibitions: Old Water-Colour Society, Winter exhibition 1887, no. 13, asking price £105.
Literature: *The Magazine of Art*, Vol. 11, 1888, p.114; *The Illustrated London News*, Vol. 91, p.110; *The Leeds Mercury*, 8 December 1887, p.8; *The Athenaeum*, No. 3137, 10 December 1887, p.789.

In a letter from Wallis to F.G. Stephens of the 18 December 1887 Wallis complains: "I see they made an absurd mistake in the Soc: catalogue [the Old Water-Colour Society] in my *Herodotus at the Scribe's*, leaving out *bazaar*."[1] This letter may have been prompted by Stephens's earlier review in *The Athenaeum*, in which he had commented: "Mr. Wallis's *Herodotus at the Scribes'* (no. 13), a picture proper with an awkward title, comes first to notice, while it provokes suspicions that the vista of an alley in an Oriental bazaar - where the Father of History, a stout Greek in a costume suspiciously like a comfortable toga (!), is studying a manuscript offered for sale – owes, to say the least, quite so much of the character, rich effect, and local colouring in which it abounds, to modern Cairo as to ancient Thebes. Yet very likely Herodotus did actually stand before a stall of this sort in a covered alley, the shadows of which were dashed with sunlight admitted by a dilapidated roof, while in front of him squatted on his shop-board the half-naked, eager-eyed Egyptian seller. On the other side of the alley a plump, voluptuous, and rather over-dressed lady tells her love tale to the impassive scribe seated there with the tablets before him, while an ardent-looking maiden, with her hair dressed in the extreme of Egyptian fashion and wearing embroidered garments of deep rose and green, waits her turn for a letter. Behind her is a dealer in what, if such they were or not, we call idols of quaint device, and his gods in brilliant green enamelled clay supply the complement to the coloration of the picture. Herodotus hardly suggests the Father of History to our mind, but the minor figures – about which Mr. Wallis, having seen them in Cairo, knows more – are charming. The tonality, breadth, homogeneity, and spirited chiaroscuro of his picture are creditable to the artist."

The critic for *The Magazine of Art* stated: "Mr. Henry Wallis in his 'Herodotus at the Scribes' shows technical skill in the realization of different qualities of light, but a total incapacity for grappling with the dramatic, or even the human, element in the subject attempted."

Cat. 188. *The Flute Player*
1887; watercolour; dimensions unknown; whereabouts unknown.
Exhibitions: Old Water-Colour Society, Winter exhibition 1887, no. 94, asking price £63.
Literature: *The Athenaeum*, No. 3137, 10 December 1887, p.789.

F.G. Stephens was less enthusiastic about Wallis's second contribution to the exhibition: "In neither of his two drawings does Mr. Wallis quite sustain his reputation; one of them is conspicuously below it... He can hardly expect us to say so much for No. 94, which is unhappily called the *Flute Player*, a group comprising a damsel, a young musician with double pipes, and a statue of bronze in an alcove, which seems dim because we look through its shadows to the outer day surcharged with light."

Cat. 189. *A Coffee Merchant, the Bazaar at Suez*
1888; watercolour on paper, mounted on wood panel; dimensions unknown; whereabouts unknown.
Provenance: Sold 25 April 1888 to Miss Annie Walters, The Oaklands, Reigate, Surrey, for £73 10s.
Exhibitions: Old Water-Colour Society, 1888, no. 63.
Literature: *The Portfolio*, Vol. 19, 1888, p.21-22; *The Times*, 23 April 1888, p.6; *The Athenaeum*, No. 3157, 28 April 1888, p.540; Gadoin, d'Isabelle et Palmier-Chatelain, Marie-Elise: *Rêver d'orient, connaître l'orient*, 2008, p.82.

When the painting was exhibited at the Old Water-Colour Society it did not receive a favourable review from F.G. Stephens in *The Athenaeum*: "Mr. Wallis's admirers can hardly be expected to be satisfied with his *Coffee Merchant, the Bazaar of Suez* (63), seated at his booth in a darkened alley accessible from a sunny street, despite the strong and deep colouration and tonality, and the other good technical qualities of the work, and the vivacious design of the buxom girl in parti-coloured draperies on our right. Her head is too small, and the merchant, who will never move from his seat, must have been there from time immemorial." The picture was subsequently mentioned in a letter from Wallis to F.G. Stephens of 4 May 1888: "The owner of my Coffee Merchant is a very fidgety lady, she has already sent me a long letter complaining of the warping (entirely imaginary) of the panel, & I was told that if she saw your contemptuous notice of the work, I should catch it hot. Curiously enough regarding this picture, I have had several complimenting letters from painters."[1]

The reviewer for *The Times* was more approving: "Mr. Henry Wallis is as striking and as true as ever in his Egyptian scenes, with their great brilliancy of colour that seems to be kept in order by a sober, controlling intelligence. 'A Coffee Merchant, the Bazaar, Suez (63) is a wonderful study of reds, yellows, blues and greens." *The Portfolio* critic encouragingly declared: "Here we meet Mr. Henry Wallis within Eastern bazaars blazing congenially in a kaleidoscopic, but harmonious effect."

Cat. 190. *Door of a Mosque, Cairo*
1888; watercolour; 31 x 21 mm (12¼ x 8¼ in.); private collection.
Provenance: Wallis's studio and then by descent from the artist to his daughter-in-law Alice Julyan Wallis (née Roberts); thence to her great-niece Mrs. Vera G. Whiting, Purley, Surrey; her sale Sotheby's Belgravia, 10 April 1973, lot 202, bought by Julian Hartnoll of Hartnoll & Eyre for £40; private collection.[1]
Exhibitions: Old Water-Colour Society, 1888, no. 258, asking price £73 10s; Liverpool Corporation, 18th *Autumn Exhibition of Pictures, Walker Art Gallery*, 1888, no. 545.
Literature: *The Times*, 23 April 1888, p.6; *The Athenaeum*, No. 3157, 28 April 1888, pp.540-541; *The Graphic*, 28 April 1888, p.458; *Liverpool Mercury*, 29 September 1888, p.5.
F.G. Stephens in *The Athenaeum* was more enthusiastic about this work, also exhibited in 1888: "Of much higher value is the same artist's carefully studied and solid *Door of a Mosque, Cairo* (258), in which the lamp is not apparent. Its draughtsmanship is in fine style, and contrasts with more than one unsuccessful delineation of similar subjects, where the stones have the colour and texture of old Cheddar cheese seen in the sunlight and well dried, and where the figures belong to British drawing-rooms and Books

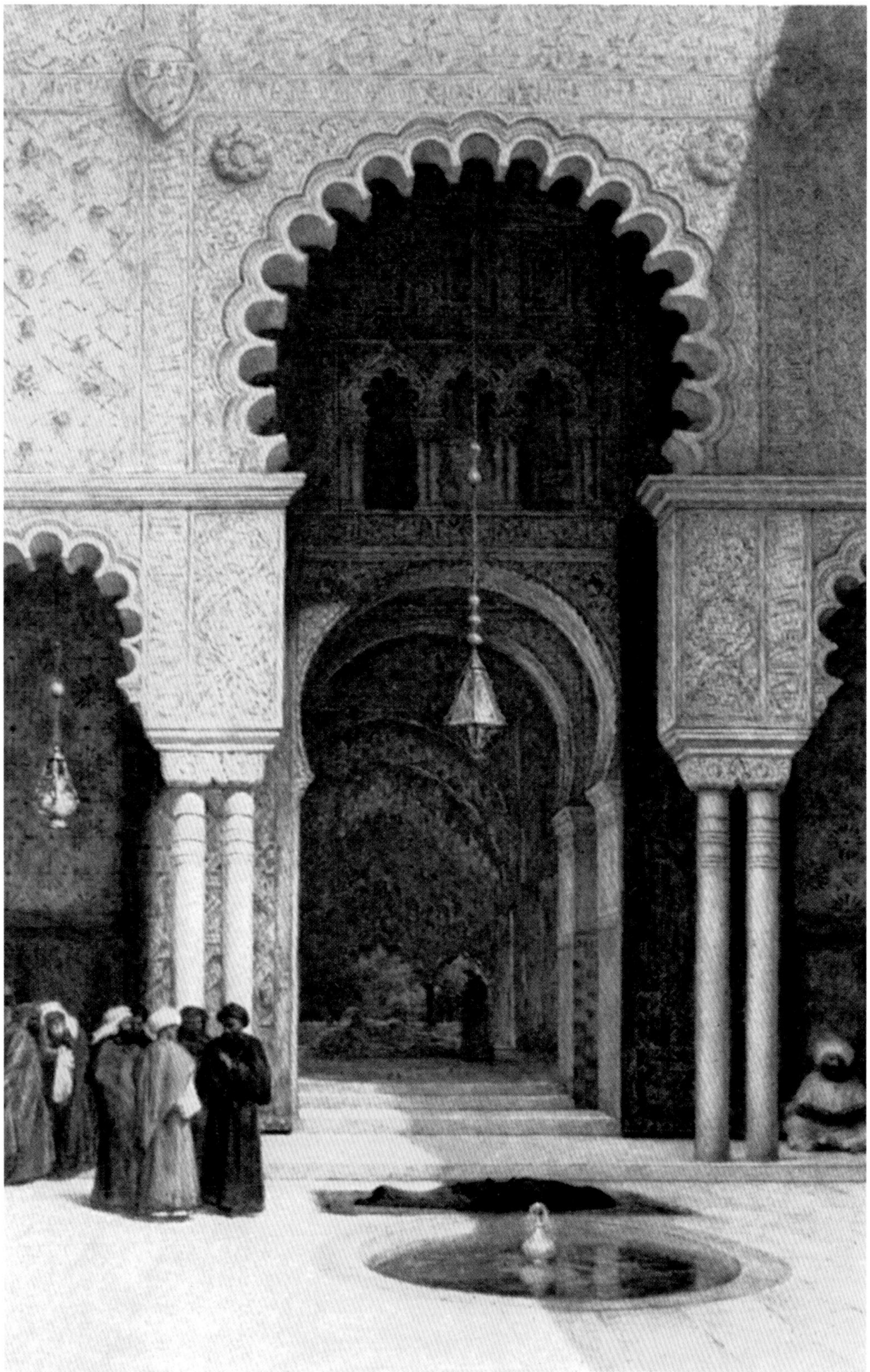

Cat. 192. Image courtesy of Sotheby's, London

of Beauty." *The Times* wrote: "The other drawing, 'The Door of a Mosque, Cairo' (258), is quieter, but is masterly as a study of tone." The critic of *The Graphic* stated: "…an elaborately-finished picture of 'The Door of a Mosque, Cairo,' in which the appearance of bright sunlight on crumbling stonework and picturesque figures is truthfully rendered."

Cat. 191. *Pot of Honey from Mount Hymettus*
1888; ?watercolour; dimensions unknown; whereabouts unknown.
EXHIBITIONS: New Gallery, 1888, no. 169.
LITERATURE: Blackburn, Henry: *New Gallery Notes*, Vol. I, 1888, p.55; *The Athenaeum*, No. 3162, 2 June 1888, p.701.

This is the only work that Wallis ever exhibited at the New Gallery, which replaced the Grosvenor Gallery as the principal venue for artists associated with the Aesthetic Movement. *The Athenaeum* mentions this work only superficially: "Mr. H. Wallis's *Pot of Honey from Mount Hymettus* (169), a pretty and sunny group of girls." Blackburn describes the picture simply as "Greek figures with child, and blue honey pot."

Cat. 192. *The Porch of the Mosque of Sultan Hassan, Cairo*
1888; watercolour, heightened with bodycolour; 84 x 53 cm (33 x 21 in.); private collection.
PROVENANCE: Wallis's studio and then by descent from the artist to his daughter-in-law Alice Julyan Wallis (née Roberts); thence to her great-niece Mrs. Vera G. Whiting, Purley, Surrey; her sale Sotheby's Belgravia, 10 April 1973, lot 204, bought by G. Sumner for £90; anonymous sale Sotheby's, London, 4 May 1977, lot 226, entitled *The Mosque Gates*, sold for £290; private collection.
EXHIBITIONS: Old Water-Colour Society, Winter exhibition 1888, no. 199, asking price £63.
LITERATURE: *The Globe*, 3 December 1888; *The Times*, 3 December 1888, p.4; *The Athenaeum*, No. 3190, 15 December 1888, p.819; *The Builder*, Vol. 55, 22 December 1888, p.448.

F.G. Stephens in *The Athenaeum* wrote: "Mr. Wallis is at his best when painting Cairo as it is (how long it will remain so is another matter). There is fine draughtsmanship in *The Porch of the Mosque of Sultan Hassan* (199), a beautiful and brilliant study of wall decoration in coloured and carved stones, in sharply contrasted sunlight and shadow. The figures deserved better drawing and more research; we are obliged to take Mr. Wallis's word for the brownness of the great shadow, although it suggests the lamp." Wallis in a letter of 4 May 1888 wrote to complain to Stephens about some of his comments: "To publish the slips or errors of a friend is not usually considered a friendly act. But what is to be said when the mistakes are pure in… [invention]? You state that I have not put in the lamp at the door of my Mosque. There it is, & has always been, precisely as it hangs in the original. Of course, I saw the article was written in grt haste & during an E. Wind, & if it only concerned me personally, I shld have thought no more about it, but that sort of thing does give one trouble & annoyance, wch you cld have hardly intended."[1]

The critic for *The Builder* called this work "a brilliant piece of painting of architectural detail". The reviewer for *The Globe* stated: "One of the best of many Oriental pictures in the collection is Mr. Wallis's 'In the Porch of the Mosque of Sultan Hassan, Cairo'. It is marked by excellent architectural draughtsmanship and broad simplicity of effect. The figures, though not in themselves interesting, are artistically introduced, and in perfect keeping with their surroundings." The reviewer for *The Times* appreciatively commented: "As

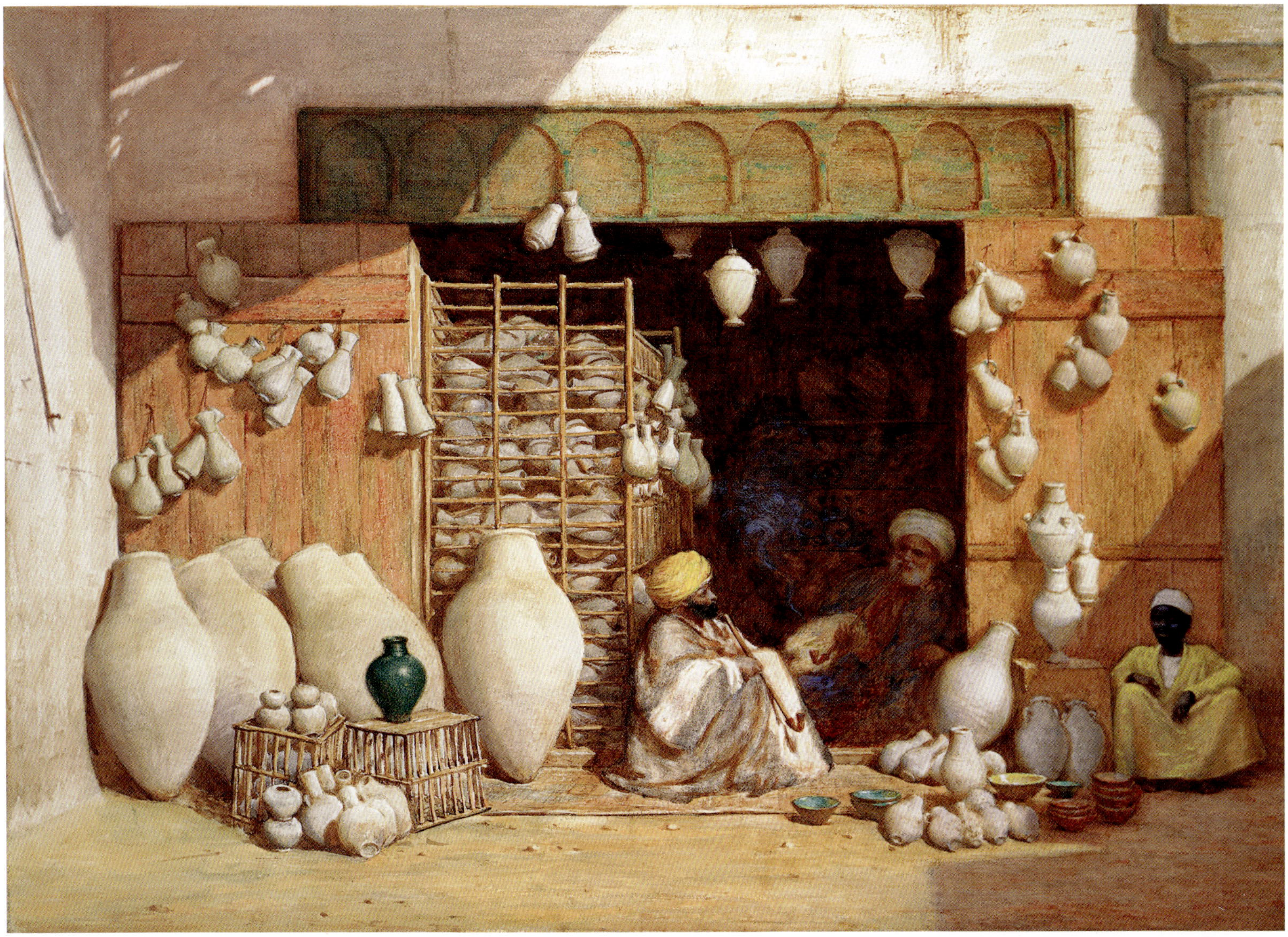

Cat. 194. Image courtesy of Professor Timothy Wilson, Oxford

to sheer executive skill nothing here surely passes Mr. H. Wallis's 'Porch of the Mosque of Sultan Hassan, Cairo.' That wall could only have been painted by a man who had been trained in the school of the pre-Raphaelites, and had emerged from it."

Thomas Seddon described this mosque in his memoirs: "The ornament in part of this and other earlier mosques is extremely like that of the early Gothic in Europe. The doors in most of the mosques are exquisitely worked in brass. In the great mosque of the Sultan Hassan, the door leading to his tomb is covered with bronze ornaments, inlaid with silver, as exquisitely as the finest jewellery; and the walls are covered to the height of twenty feet with mosaics and carved ornament, but so covered with dust that few people find it out." [2]

Cat. 193. *Street Scene in Smyrna: A Turkish Letter-Writer*
1888; watercolour; dimensions unknown; whereabouts unknown.
Exhibitions: Old Water-Colour Society, Winter exhibition 1888, no. 216; asking price £63.
Literature: *The Athenaeum*, No. 3190, 15 December 1888, p.819.

Wallis went to Smyrna and Constantinople in November 1887. F.G. Stephens in *The Athenaeum* commented on this work: "*Street Scene in Smyrna* (216) … demands similar criticism of the figures [see: Cat. 192], and still higher praise for the upper portion of the façade."

Cat. 194. *A Do'ruck and Chool'Leh Merchant, Cairo*[1]
1889; watercolour, heightened with white; 40 x 560 cm. (15¾ x 22 in.); private collection.
Provenance: Wallis's studio and then by descent from the artist to his daughter-in-law Alice Julyan Wallis (née Roberts); thence to her great-niece Mrs. Vera G. Whiting, Purley, Surrey; her sale Sotheby's Belgravia, 10 April 1973, lot 205, bought by J. Mallet for £200.
Exhibitions: Old Water-Colour Society, 1889, no. 101, asking price £63.
Literature: *The Times*, 30 April 1889, p. 8; *The Athenaeum*, No. 3210, 4 May 1889, p.574; *The Builder*, Vol. 56, 4 May 1889, p.331; *Fun*, 8 May 1889, p.202; *The Graphic*, 10 August 1889, p.170.

F.G. Stephens wote enthusiastically of this watercolour in his review in *The Athenaeum*: "Mr. Wallis contributes but one picture (an Eastern subject, such as he so often has chosen of late), and it is of very exceptional beauty indeed. It is called *A Do'ruck and Chool'leh Merchant* [seller of pots and pans], *Cairo* (101). The figure is very well drawn much better, indeed, than some of Mr. Wallis's. The distinguishing qualities of the work are its softened brilliance, the strength of colour, and the depth and clearness of the shadows. The visitor should notice the large space of deep shadow cast upon the wall by a projecting balcony near the top of the picture, as well as the lustre of the glowing space into which it falls, with edges sharply, but not harshly defined. This is a beautiful piece of painting, and it could not be purer in colour, softer, or more harmonious."

The critic for *The Times* mentioned: "Among the figure subjects one of the most brilliant is the Oriental scene of Mr. Henry Wallis (101), if, indeed, this can be properly classed with figure subjects, so elaborate are the surroundings, with such supreme care are they painted. Mr. Wallis has made a veritable collection of all forms of water-bottles that are to be found in modern Egypt, and a singularly picturesque setting do they make to his two merchants sitting in their shop under the brilliant Egyptian sun. A drawing like this is full of what painters call quality, which is quite different from pedantic imitation of details."

Cat. 195. *Eastern Scene*
1889; watercolour; dimensions unknown; whereabouts unknown.
Exhibitions: The Royal Glasgow Institute of Fine Arts, 1889, no. 870.
Literature: Billcliffe, Roger: *The Royal Glasgow Institute of Fine Arts 1861-1989*, Vol. 4, 1990, p.270.

This is most likely a work that Wallis would have shown previously at an Old Water-Colour Society exhibition but we have not been specifically able to identify which picture. *A Do'ruck and Chool'leh Merchant, Cairo* is an obvious candidate.

Cat. 196. *The Sick King in Bokhara*
1889; watercolour; dimensions unknown; whereabouts unknown.
Exhibitions: Old Water-Colour Society, Winter exhibition 1889, no. 33, asking price £105.
Literature: *The Magazine of Art*, Vol. 13, 1890, p.111; *London St. James Gazette*, 30 November, 1889, p.7; *The London Daily News*, London, 2 December 1889, p.3; *The Times*, 2 December 1889, p.4; *Pall Mall Gazette*, 5 December 1889, p.2; *The Athenaeum*, No. 3241, 7 December 1889, p.787; *The Graphic*, Vol. 40, 7 December 1889, p.702; *The Illustrated London News*, 7 December 1889, p.724; *The Spectator*, Vol. 63, 7 December 1889, p.807; *Glasgow Herald*, 13 December 1889, p.9; *The Academy*, Vol. 36, No. 920, 21 December 1889, p.411.

F.G. Stephens, in *The Athenaeum*, praised this work: "Another first-rate drawing is Mr. Wallis's large Oriental interior called, from the figures it contains, *The Sick King in Bokhara* (33), one of the most luminous and harmonious examples in the gallery. Mr. Wallis has painted the chamber under the dome of a royal palace. Its diapered walls and pillars are of white marble; its floor of coloured stones surrounds a slowly bubbling fountain, at the further side of which lies, under a black mantle, the corpse of the wretch whose fate Matthew Arnold has immortalized in fine verse.[1] Sunlight streams in from the lantern overhead. In the arcade facing us sits a moolah, chanting prayers from a book open upon his knees; his monotonous voice seems to fill the aisle behind and mix with the sound of water in the basin. A group of richly-clad men stand aloof from the dead man, and seem to whisper to each other about his fate. The brilliant and firm, yet soft and splendid chiaroscuro of the picture demands the highest praise."

Most of the critics agreed with Stephens and wrote with a laudatory pen. The reviewer for *The Daily News* stated: "Mr. Henry Wallis's brilliant picture of 'The Sick King in Bokhara', from the poem by Matthew Arnold is simply a triumph of technical completeness. The story is that of a certain Moolah, who having sinned against the law, demanded from his sovereign the punishment of death as the only just retribution. Upon the rejection of his petition he upbraided the king for cutting him off from the hope of salvation in the next world, so his prayer was granted and he was stoned to death. Then the King commanded that the corpse should be brought to the palace and buried in the Royal tomb. A pall covers the remains of the voluntary martyr, and the Royal spectator raises himself languidly on his couch of State, while a group of courtiers are assembled in quiet converse. The palace architecture is as realistic and solid as the details are artistically beautiful and lightly touched; and for depth and harmony of colour, vividness of light, transparency of shadows, and suggestions of space, this drawing would be difficult to rival."

The critic for *The Graphic* also commented favourably: "There are a few finished drawings of great excellence. One of the most important – Mr. Henry Wallis's 'The Sick King in Bokhara', suggested by a poem by Matthew Arnold – if not remarkable as realisation of dramatic incident, is an excellent picture, conveying a vivid impression of the clear atmosphere and glowing colour of the East. While the characteristic and well-grouped figures and all the details of the rich Oriental architecture are rendered with realistic truth, every individual fact bears its right relative value to the rest."

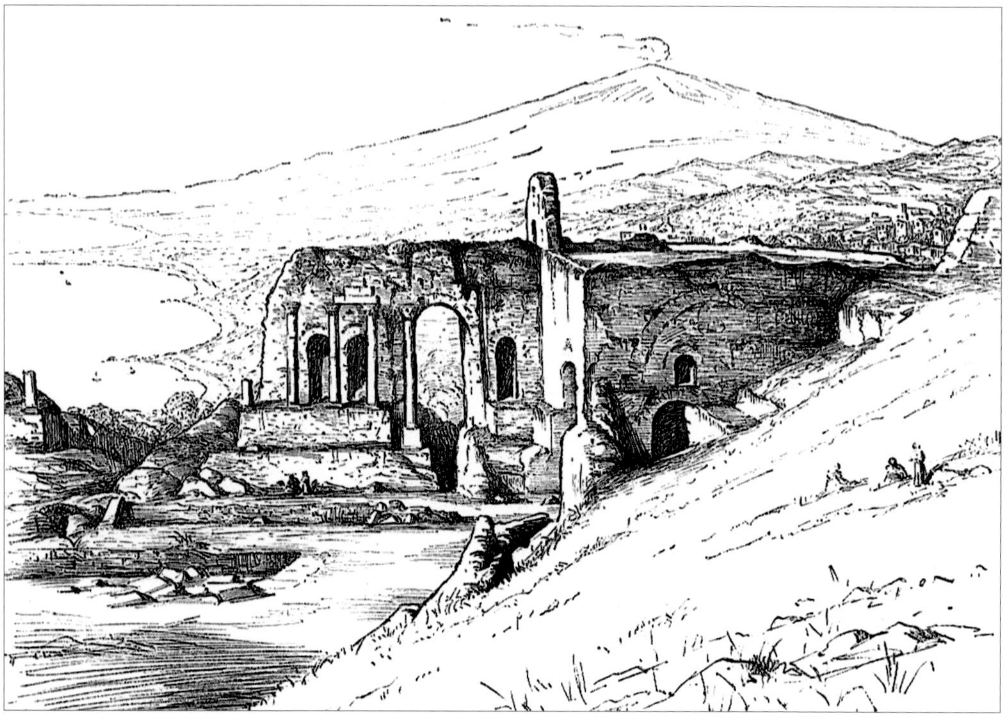
See Cat. 199. Drawing from the O.W.S.'s *Illustrated catalogue comprising 77 facsimiles of sketches by the artists.*

Cat. 197. *A Persian Mosque*
1889; medium, dimensions and whereabouts unknown.
Literature: *The Graphic*, Vol. 40, 6 July 1889, p.6.

The decorations of *A Persian Mosque* were designed by Wallis for the office of *The Graphic* and carried out by Art Students of *The Graphic* to honour the visit of Naser al-Din Shah Qajar, the Persian Monarch, to London in 1889. Exactly what the design portrayed and its fate are unknown.

Cat. 198. *A Thirteenth Century Spanish Moorish Vase*
1890; watercolour; dimensions unknown; whereabouts unknown.
Exhibitions: Old Water-Colour Society, Winter exhibition 1890, no. 105.
Literature: *The Times*, 1 December 1890, p.4; *The Athenaeum*, No. 3293, 6 December 1890, p.781.

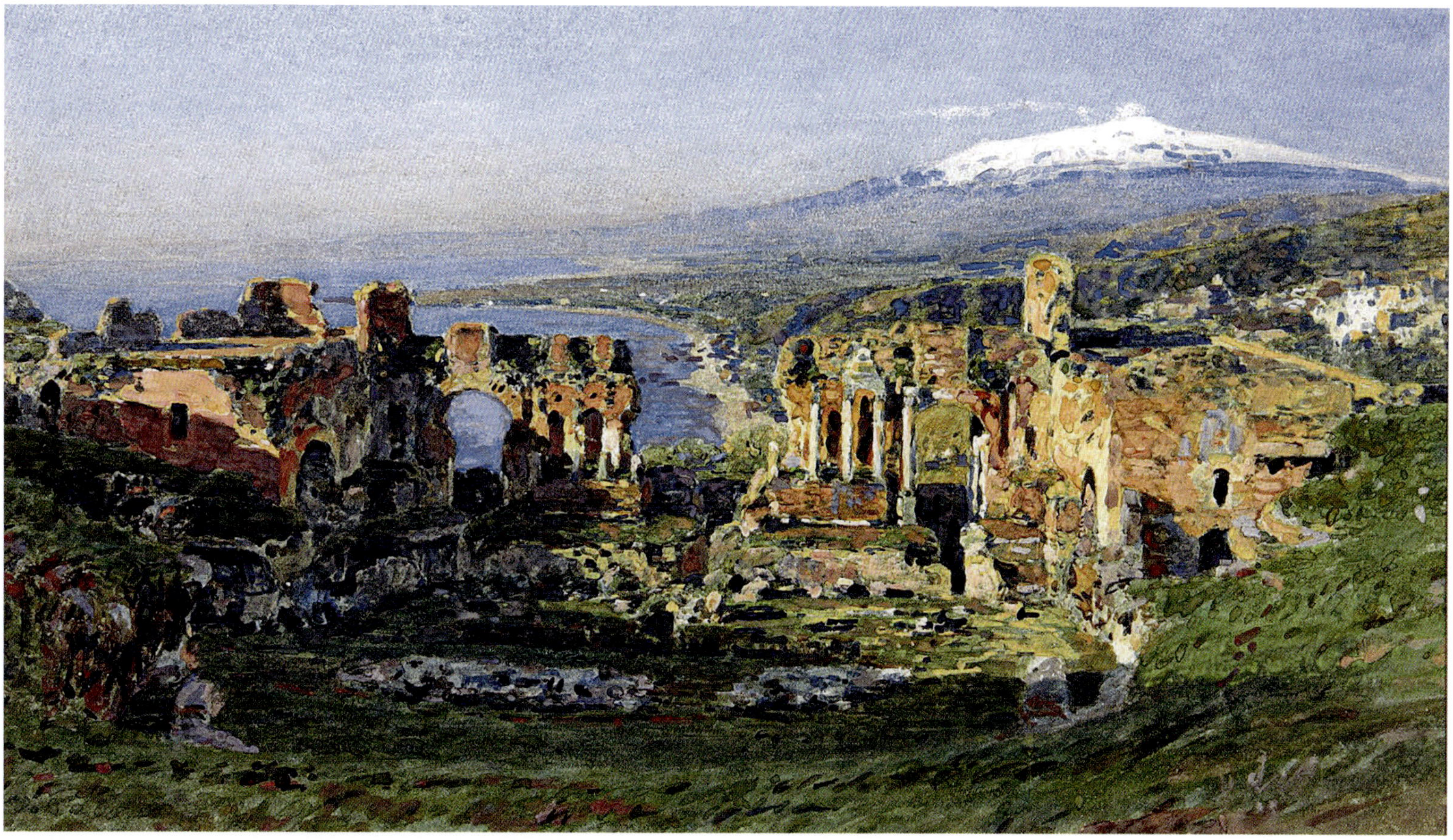

Cat. 200. Image courtesy of Bonhams, London

F.G. Stephens, in *The Athenaeum*, had these comments: "Fine as Mr. Wallis's single work is, we looked for something more ambitious than a picture of a still life. An accidental misunderstanding has delayed the exhibition of one of Mr. Henry Wallis's richest and strongest Oriental pictures, a Cairene scene, for which a distinguished place was reserved in the gallery. We have some compensation in the wealth of colours, masculine draughtsmanship, and extraordinary fidelity to nature displayed in his *A Thirteenth Century Spanish Moorish Vase* (105), one of the drawings prepared for his sumptuous book on ancient lustre ware.[1] It fails only to give the large size (four feet high) of the famous original. Few painters of our time could reproduce so finely the glow of the colours in the shadows as well as in the lights of the magnificent vase; it would be difficult for most of us to retain the splendour and the depth of the tints and tones of this noble piece." The reviewer for *The Times* stated: "A word should be said in praise of Mr. Henry Wallis's 'Spanish-Moorish Vase'."

Cat. 199. ***Etna, from the Theatre of Taormina***

*c.*1889-1891; watercolour; 45.7 x 58.4 cm (18 x 23 in.); private collection.
Inscriptions: Signed and inscribed on a label on the back.
Provenance: Sold to A.W. Cox,[1] 36 Conduit Street, London, on 21 Apr 1891 for £73 10s; anonymous sale, Christie's, South Kensington, 16 October 1985, lot 56, sold for £440; private collection.
Exhibitions: Old Water-Colour Society, 1891, no. 135.
Literature: *The Times*, 20 April 1891, p.7; *The Athenaeum*, No. 3313, 25 April 1891, p.543.

F.G. Stephens mentioned this work his *The Athenaeum* review of 1891: "Mr. H. Wallis's *Etna, from the Theatre at Taormino* (135), is a superb view of Sicily, with the volcano capped with snow and rising into the resplendent atmosphere, which is as broad as it is bright. The solid handling and fine draughtsmanship, however, suffer a little because the golden flush upon the ruin in the foreground, although it may be true to nature, is rather too yellow to be in harmony with the surrounding verdure." The reviewer for *The Times* said: "A word should be added in praise... the way in which Mr. Henry Wallis has striven to preserve the sunshine and colour of Taormina (135)."

It is not easy to date exactly when this work was executed because Wallis travelled to Italy frequently. According to his correspondence, he seems to have stayed at Taorminaon Sicily twice: from January to February 1889, and in March 1892. He also stayed at Palermo, in 1889 and 1891, from where Taormina could easily be reached. Since he exhibited this watercolour at the O.W.S. in 1891, the work was probably done either that year, or somewhat earlier in 1889. Of likely relevance to this work is a letter from Wallis to F.G. Stephens of 9 February 1889: "I am much struck with the ancient theatre here, which has more remaining than any other existing, and have set to work to make studies for a picture of it."[2]

Cat. 200. ***A View of Roman Ruins (Roman Theatre, Taormina), with Mt. Etna in the Distance***

*c.*1889-91; watercolour heightened with gouache; 21.8 x 36.7 cm (8 11/16 x 14 9/16 in.); private collection.
Provenance: Wallis's studio and then by descent from the artist to his daughter-in-law Alice Julyan Wallis (née Roberts); thence to her great-niece Mrs. Vera G. Whiting, Purley, Surrey; her sale Sotheby's Belgravia, 10 April 1973, lot 214, purchased by Bill Waters, Norham House, Cockermouth, Cumbria, for £100; sold to Rev. Clark for £150; anonymous sale Bonhams, Knightsbridge, 11 September 2012, lot 158, sold for £1,750; private collection.
Exhibitions: Norham House: *The Pre-Raphaelite Fringe*, November, 1973, no. 17.
This painting is another beautiful landscape view by Wallis of the famous ruins of the Roman theatre at Taormina with the snow-capped Mt. Etna in the distance. The theatre is built primarily of brick. Its arrangement corresponds to a Greek, rather than a

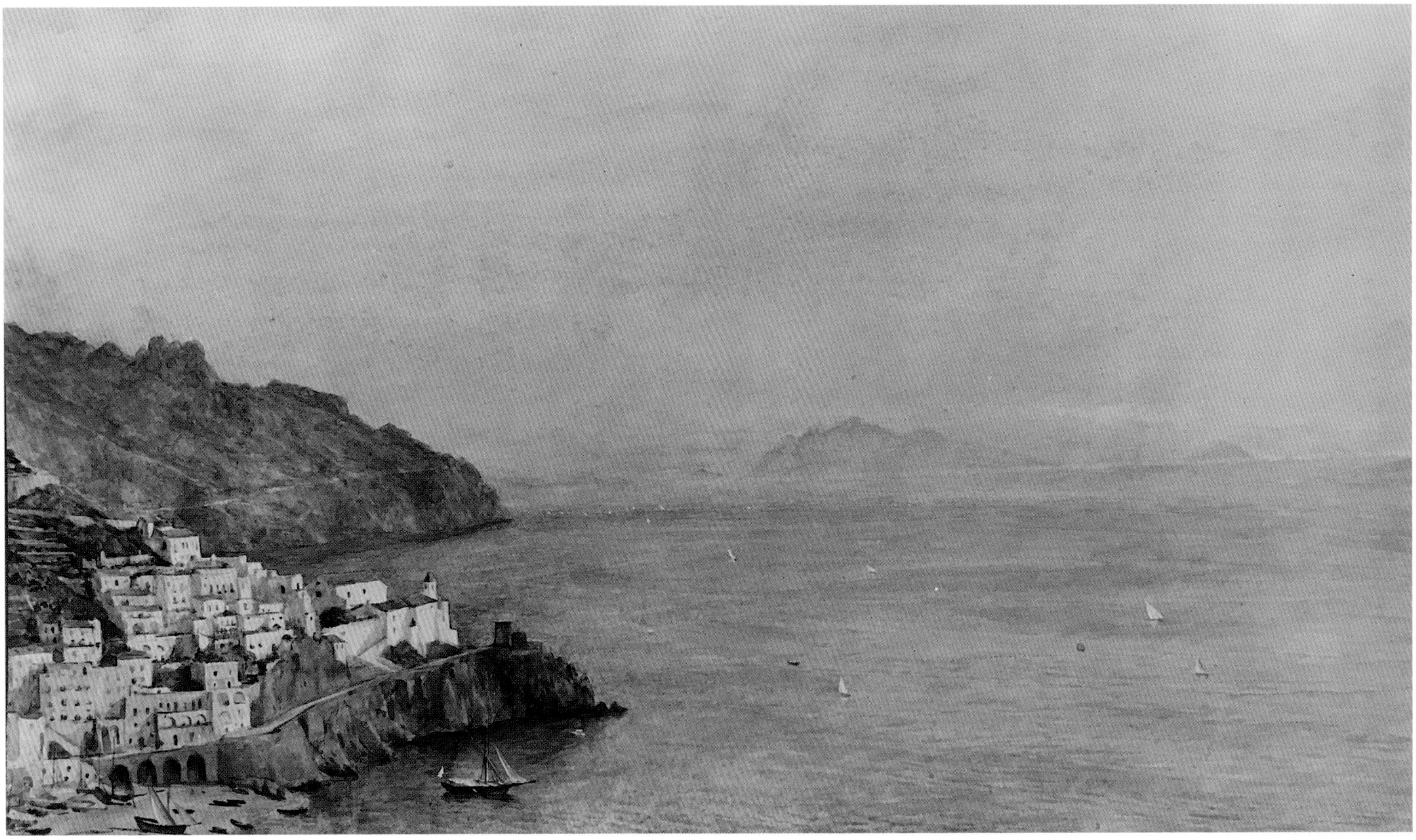

Cat. 201. Image courtesy of Julian Hartnoll, London

Roman theatre, so it was probably rebuilt on the foundation of an earlier structure dating from the Greek period. The theatre is the second largest in Sicily after Syracuse. The town was popular with tourists during the 19th century, including obviously Wallis.

Cat. 201. ***Amalfi***
*c.*1889-1892; watercolour heightened with white; 27.9 x 45.7 cm (10¾ x 17¾ in.); private collection.
Provenance: Wallis's studio and then by descent from the artist to his daughter-in-law Alice Julyan Wallis (née Roberts); thence to her great-niece Mrs. Vera G. Whiting, Purley, Surrey; her sale Sotheby's Belgravia, 10 April 1973, lot 210, bought Hartnoll & Eyre, London for £26; ?Sotheby's Belgravia, 22 April 1975, sold for £30; Christie's, London, 18 December 1984, lot 157, sold for £486, bought by Julian Hartnoll, London; private collection.
Exhibitions: Hartnoll & Eyre: Catalogue Thirty-Three, September 25 – October 12, 1973, no. 45; Galerie du Luxembourg, *Le Paysage Anglais des Préraphaelites aux Symbolistes*, April 1974, no. 53; Shepherd Gallery, New York, *English 19th Century Pre-Raphaelite and Academic*, Spring 1986, no. 101.

Amalfi lies at the mouth of a deep ravine, at the foot of Monte Cerreto, and is surrounded by dramatic cliffs and coastal scenery. Although it was a popular tourist destination in the latter parts of the 19th century, no known surviving letter from Wallis was sent from Amalfi. He was often in Naples, however, at least seven times between 1891 and 1908, from where Amalfi could easily be reached.

Cat. 202. ***Study of an Egyptian Village, with low Hills in the Background***
*c.*1880-1900; black and white chalk on purple-grey laid paper; 38 x 58.5 cm. (15 x 23⅛ in.); Birmingham Museum and Art Gallery.
Inscriptions: Signed with initials *H.W.*, lower right.
Provenance: Presented by Harold Wallis to Birmingham Museum and Art Gallery in 1918, accession no. 1918P15.
Literature: Birmingham Museum and Art Gallery, *Catalogue of the Permanent Collection of Drawings*, 1939, p.415, no. 15'18.

It is unclear which Egyptian village this is intended to represent.

Cat. 203. ***The Temple of Neptune, Paestum***
1891; watercolour and gouache; 32.9 x 47.4 cm (15½ x 19½ in.); private collection.
Provenance: Wallis's studio and then by descent from the artist to his daughter-in-law Alice Julyan Wallis (née Roberts); thence to her great-niece Mrs. Vera G. Whiting, Purley, Surrey; her sale Sotheby's Belgravia, 10 April 1973, part of lot 209, purchased by Bill Waters, Norham House, Cockermouth, Cumbria, for £240; private collection.
Exhibitions: Old Water-Colour Society, Winter exhibition 1891, no. 18; Norham House: *The Pre-Raphaelite Fringe*, November, 1973, no. 16.
Literature: *The Athenaeum*, No. 3345, 5 December 1891, p.767.

Paestum was a major city founded by the ancient Greek colonists on the Tyrrhenian coast in southern Italy. Three well-preserved ancient Greek temples survive at this site, including The Temple of Neptune. This work continues Wallis's interest in Mediterranean and Middle Eastern archeology.

F.G. Stephens in *The Athenaeum* commented: "Mr. Wallis's drawing of *The Temple of Neptune, Paestum* (18), standing, soft, yet distinct, in the silvery glow of a Sicilian summer noon, amid marshy ground full of flowers and weeds, against a background of purple mountains that are subdued in a tender haze, is very lovely in colour, and the effect is broad and soft. But the stupendous Doric temple loses in this fine version something of its sterness and that ponderous bulk for which it is remarkable."

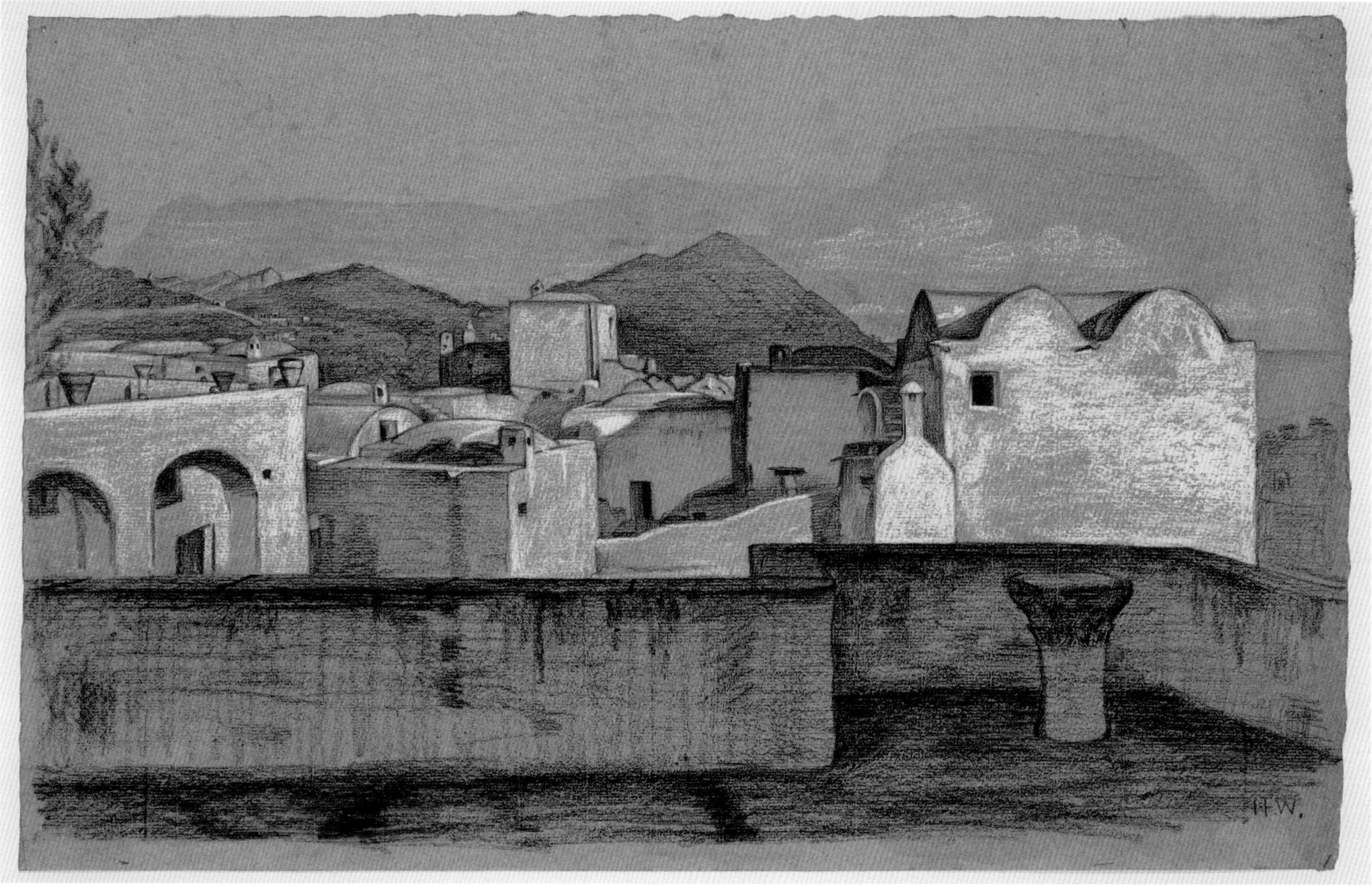

Cat. 202. Image by permission of Birmingham Museums Trust

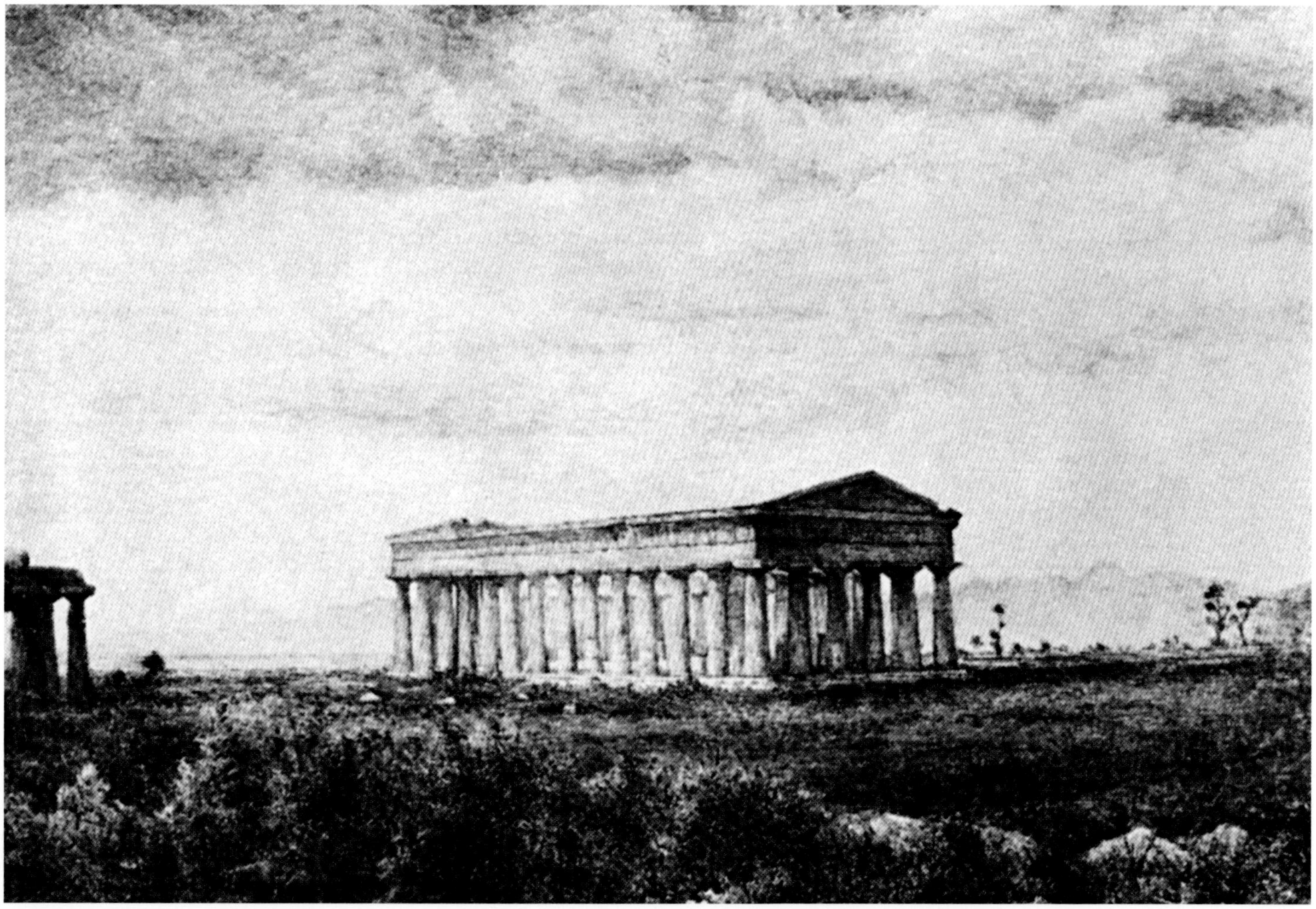

Cat. 203. Image courtesy of William Waters

Wallis's Illustrations to *Persian Ceramic Art*

Cat. 204. *Persian Tile, xiii* [1]
Exhibitions: Old Water-Colour Society, Winter exhibition 1891, no. 333.

Cat. 205. *Persian Lustre Vase, xiii*
Exhibitions: Old Water-Colour Society, Winter exhibition 1891, no. 334.

Cat. 206. *Persian Vase, xiii*
Exhibitions: Old Water-Colour Society, Winter exhibition 1891, no. 337.

Cat. 207. *Persian Lustre Vase, xiii*
Exhibitions: Old Water-Colour Society, Winter exhibition 1891, no. 340.

Cat. 208. *Persian Lustre Vase, xiii*
Exhibitions: Old Water-Colour Society, Winter exhibition 1891, no. 341.

Cat. 209. *Persian Tile, xiii*
Exhibitions: Old Water-Colour Society, Winter exhibition 1891, no. 343.

Cat. 210. *Persian Lustre Bowl, xiii*
Exhibitions: Old Water-Colour Society, Winter exhibition 1891, no. 347.

Cat. 211. *Persian Bowl, xiii*
Exhibitions: Old Water-Colour Society, Winter exhibition 1891, no. 348.

Literature: *The Athenaeum*, No. 3345, 5 December 1891, p.767.

F.G. Stephens in *The Athenaeum* commented: "The other group of studies was made by Mr. H. Wallis for the sumptuous volume he lately published, 'Persian Ceramic Art' as illustrated by thirteenth century vessels belonging to the collection of Mr. Godman.[2] Felicitous and powerful execution, absolute fidelity to originals of extraordinary difficulty, and most splendid colours, glowing in fiery golden or silvery *reflets* and amazing depths of tone, are the conspicuous qualities of these remarkable drawings. We select as especially pleasing to artistic eyes, *Persian Tile, xiii.* (333); *Persian Lustre Vase, xiii.* (334); *Persian Lustre Bowl, xiii.* (347); which excels in the perfect veracity of its foreshortening; and *Persian Bowl, xiii.* (348), the worthy companion of the last." Wallis's book on Godman's collection was published for private circulation and limited to 200 copies. The illustrations after drawings by Wallis comprised 24 full-page chromo-lithographs and about 225 illustrations in monochrome. The lithographic stones were destroyed after the book was printed.

A review of Wallis's book in *The Athenaeum* stated: "This handsome volume contains a number of superb plates, admirably copied in chromo-lithography by Mr. S. D. Hodson, after drawings by Mr. Henry Wallis contributed to the Winter Exhibition of the Old Water-Colour Society. The drawings surpass anything produced in this country or abroad in felicitous recognition of the style, colours, lustring, and other characteristics of the beautiful ceramic wear of Persia. If the chromolithographs are not quite equal in purity of tint and crispness of touch to their originals, that is simply because no reproduction, however skilful and costly, can be absolutely perfect."[3]

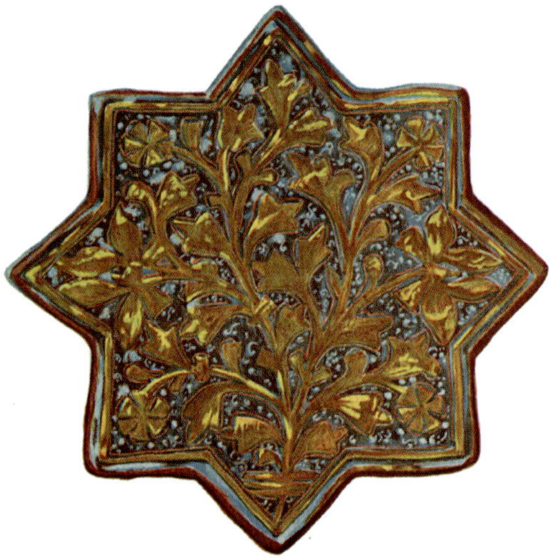

Cat. 204. Plate XV

The illustrations for Cats. 204-211 are all chromo-lithograph by S.D. Hodson after Henry Wallis's watercolours and were published in *The Godman collection. Persian Ceramic Art in the Collection of Mr. F. DuCane Godman, F.R.S. The Thirteenth Century Lustred Vases* (1891). The illustrations of the 13th-century Persian lustreware shown here are representative and it cannot be certain which specific plates in the book corresponded to Wallis's watercolours exhibited at the Old Water-Colour Society in 1891.

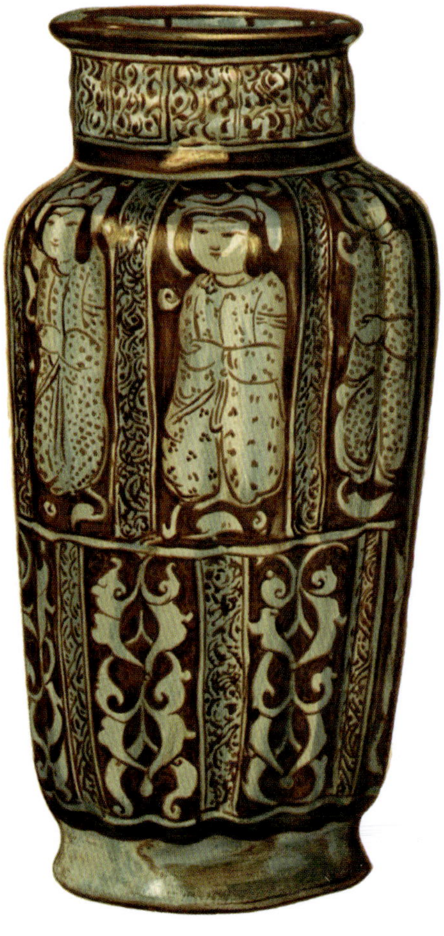

Cat. 205. Plate IV

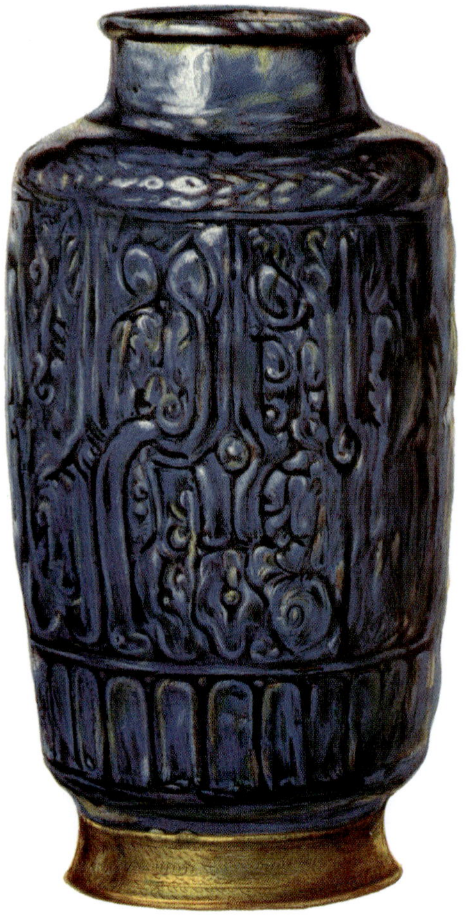

Cat. 206. Plate V

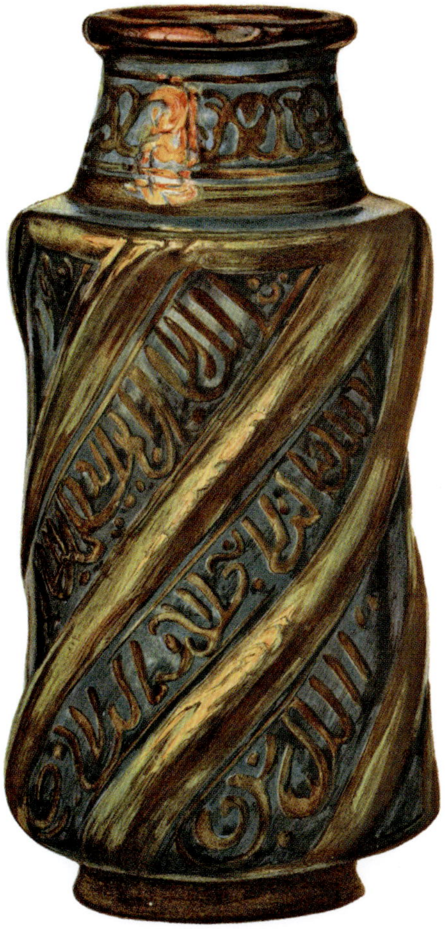

Cat. 207. Plate XI

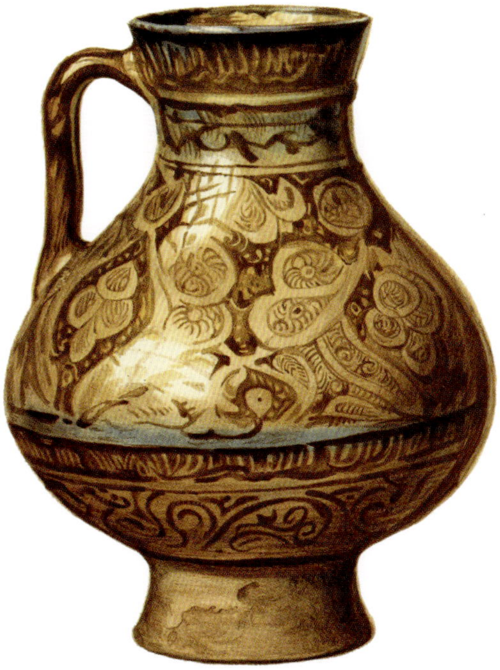

Cat. 208. Plate VII

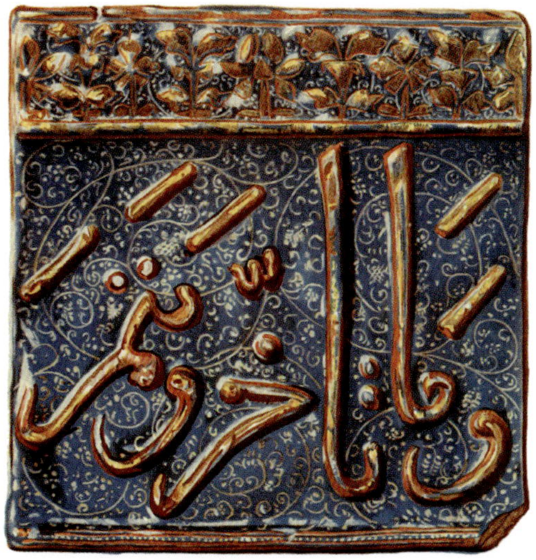

Cat. 209. Plate XVI

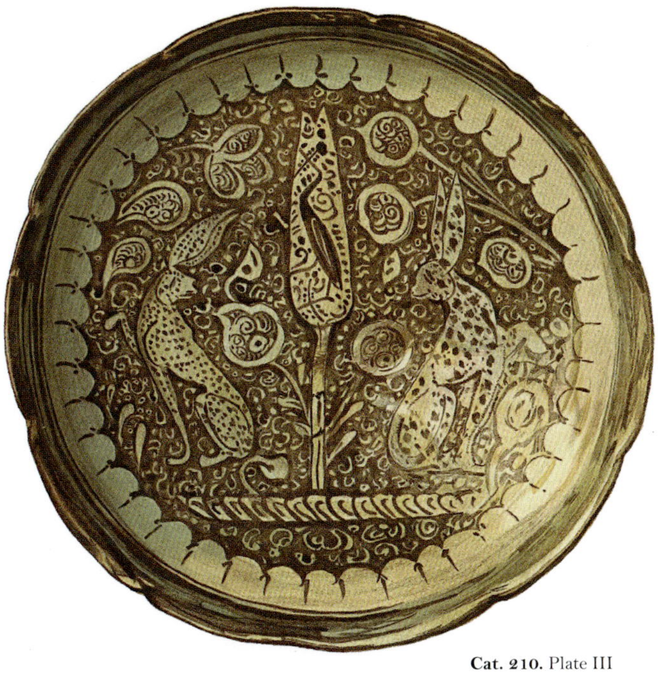

Cat. 210. Plate III

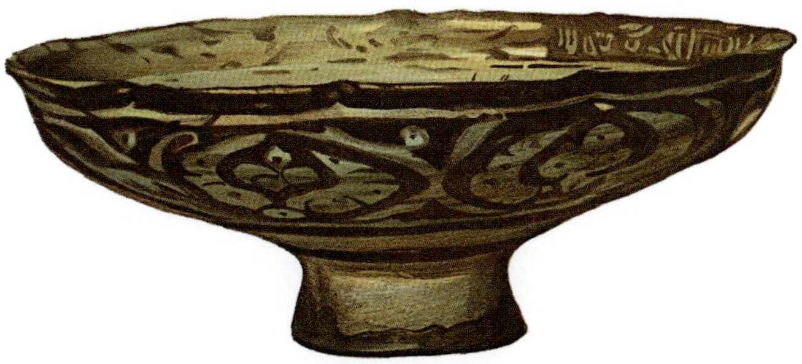

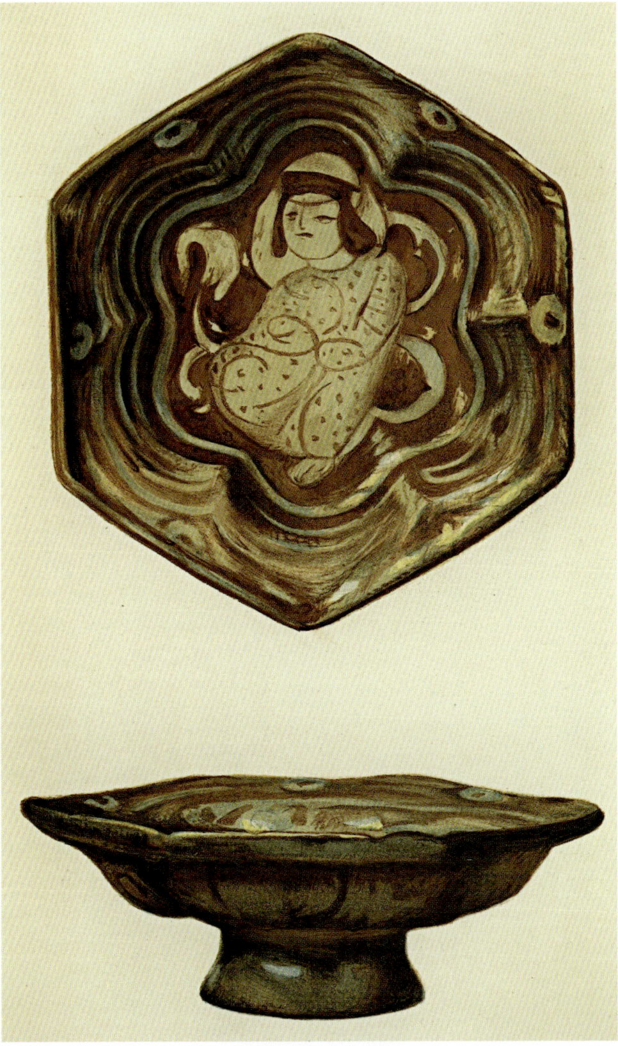

Cat. 211. Plate VI

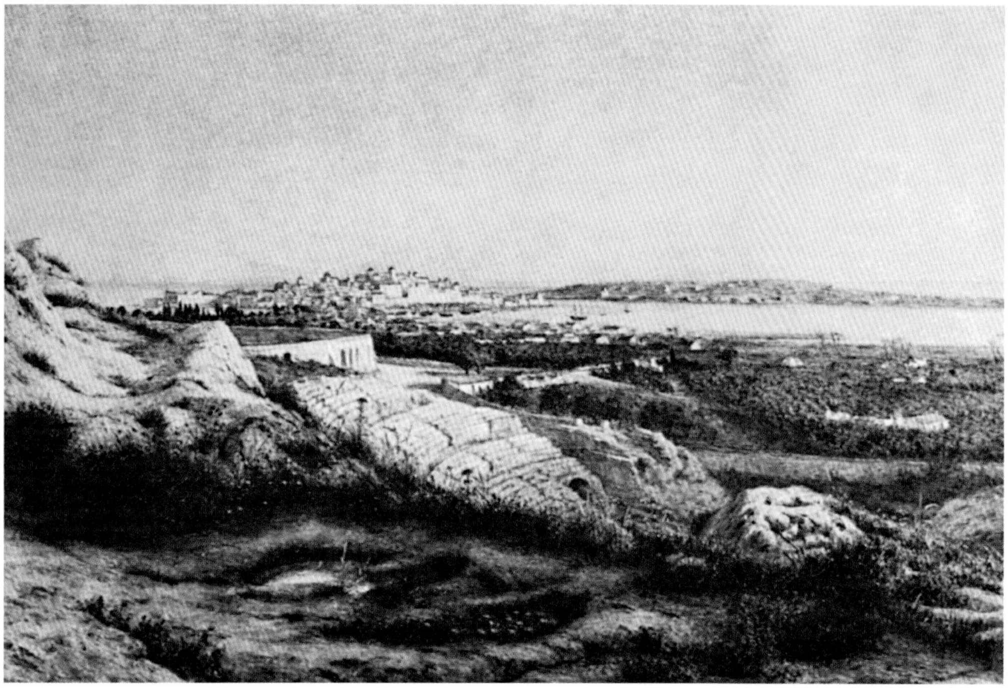

Cat. 212. Image courtesy of William Waters

Cat. 212. *A View of Syracuse with the Amphitheatre in the Foreground*
*c.*1892; watercolour heightened with gouache; 33 x 48.5 cm (13 x 19 in.); private collection.
Inscriptions: signed and inscribed on the reverse.
Provenance: Wallis's studio and then by descent from the artist to his daughter-in-law Alice Julyan Wallis (née Roberts); thence to her great-niece Mrs. Vera G. Whiting, Purley, Surrey; her sale Sotheby's Belgravia, 10 April 1973, lot 213, bought by Bill Waters, Norham House, Cockermouth, Cumbria for £110; sold in October 1973 to Julian Hartnoll of Hartnoll & Eyre, London; likely their sale Sotheby's Belgravia, 22 April 1975, lot 89, sold for £160; private collection.
Exhibitions: Norham House: *The Pre-Raphaelite Fringe*, November, 1973, no. 15; Galerie des Luxembourg, *Le Paysage Anglais des Preraphaelites aux Symbolistes*, April 1974, no. 58; Hartnoll & Eyre: Catalogue 40, September 23 – October 11, 1974, no. 21;

It is difficult to date this watercolour definitively because Wallis went to Sicily regularly. One surviving letter posted at Syracuse is dated January 1892.

Cat. 213. *The Fountain at Arethusa, at Ortygia, Syracuse*[1]
1892; watercolour; dimensions unknown; whereabouts unknown.
Exhibitions: Old Water-Colour Society, 1892, no. 231, asking price £52 10s.
Literature: *The Athenaeum*, No. 3367, 7 May 1892, p.606; *The Academy*, Vol. 41, No. 1045, 14 May 1892, p.475.

F.G. Stephens in his review in *The Athenaeum* tells us: "Mr. Wallis's *Arethusa* (231) charms us by its warmth and delicate tones, and especially by the beauty of the building on our right in the middle. The foliage seems too thin and of too light a colour." Cosmo Monkhouse, the critic for *The Academy* commented on: "… the Oriental feeling and richness of colour in Mr. Wallis's 'The Fountain of Arethusa at Ortygia, Syracuse' (231)."

Cat. 214. *In an Oriental Bazaar*
1892; watercolour; dimensions unknown; whereabouts unknown.
Exhibitions: Old Water-Colour Society, Winter exhibition 1892, no. 307, asking price £52 10s.
Literature: *The Times*, 28 November 1892, p.4; *The Athenaeum*, No. 3397, 3 December 1892, p.786; *The Academy*, Vol. 42, No. 1074, 3 December 1892, p.513.

F.G. Stephens remarked of this work: "Less interesting to us, although vigorous and finely coloured, is Mr. Wallis's picture of the outside of a Cairene shop, part of an *Oriental Bazaar* (307). Luminous, homogenous, and powerful in tone as this drawing is, it yet seems to us a little too much inspired by the lamp, and rather heavy in touch and tint." The critic of *The Times* remarked: "Mr. Henry Wallis sends two more of his marvelous studies of Persian glass or pottery, and another of his Oriental bazaar scenes; nobody is, in drawings of this kind, so splendid a colourist as he."

Cat. 215. A Persian Vase
1892; watercolour; dimensions unknown; whereabouts unknown.
Exhibitions: Old Water-Colour Society, Winter exhibition 1892, no. 327, asking price £12 12s.
Literature: *The Athenaeum*, No. 3380, 6 August 1892, p.200; *The Pottery Gazette*, 1 September 1892, p.90; *The Times*, 28 November 1892, p.4; *The Athenaeum*, No. 3397, 3 December 1892, p.786; *The Academy*, No. 1074, 3 December 1892, p.513.

F.G. Stephens, in *The Athenaeum*, commented: "Two more pieces, remarkable for colour, verisimilitude, and splendid illumination, may be noticed next, although their subjects and materials differ as widely as possible from Mr. Hunt's. These are Mr. Wallis's *A Persian Vase* (327) and *A Damascus Vase* (333), superb specimens of the precious lustre ware to which the artist has lately devoted much time and travel."
[See also: Cat. 216]

Cat. 216. *A Damascus Vase*
1892; watercolour; dimensions unknown; whereabouts unknown.
Exhibitions: Old Water-Colour Society, Winter exhibition 1892, no. 333, not for sale.
Literature: *The Athenaeum*, No. 3397, 3 December 1892, p.786; *The Times*, 28 November 1892, p.4.

The critic of *The Times* commented: "Mr. Henry Wallis sends two more of his marvelous studies of Persian glass or pottery… nobody is, in drawings of this kind, so splendid a colourist as he." *The Athenaeum* wrote of these plates for Wallis's book: "Finally, it is our duty to praise in the highest terms the beauty, fidelity, and extraordinary brilliance of the coloured illustrations, which reproduce the splendour of the lustre and the magnificent colouration of the relics to which the text is devoted. These plates were executed by Mr. Griggs after Mr. Wallis's own drawings."

Cat. 217. *The Interior of an Egyptian Temple, Assuan*
1893; watercolour; 21 x 13 cm (8½ x 5½ in.); private collection.
Inscriptions: dated *11-1-93.*
Provenance: Wallis's studio and then by descent from the artist to his son Harold Wallis; then to his daughter-in-law Mary Wallis (née Mary Elizabeth Aymes); then her great-niece Vera G. Cooper (née Langley; 1910-1989); and thence by direct descent to John Harold Cooper and family; sold at Bonhams, London, 5 March 2002, part of lot 71, bought by Neil Wilson of Campbell Wilson, Hove, East Sussex, for £3,400; private collection.

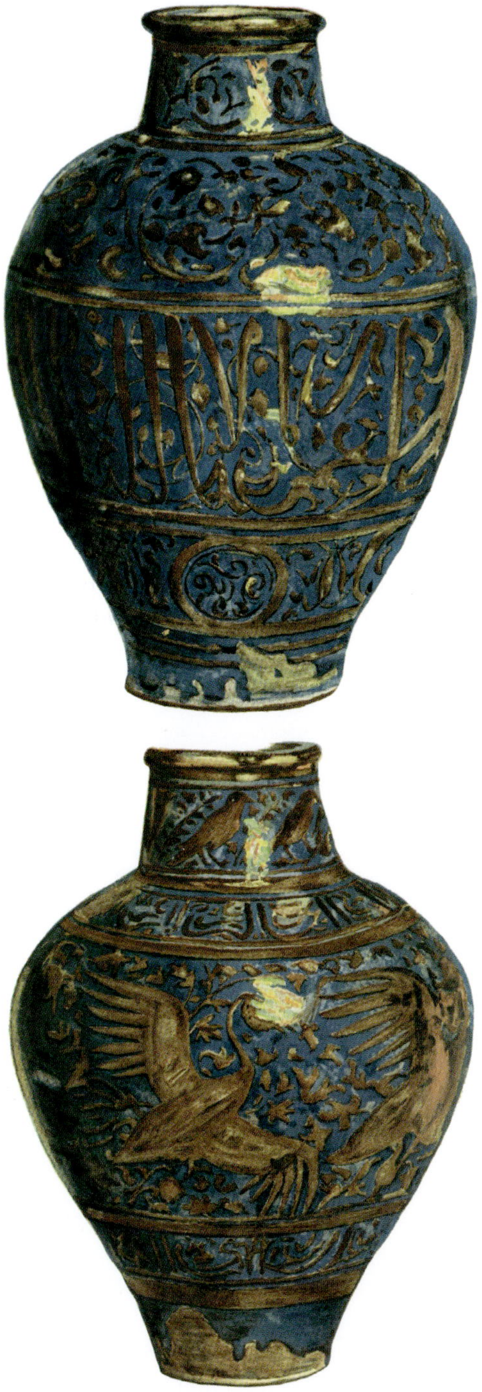

Cat. 216. Chromolithographs by W. Griggs after Wallis's original watercolours of lustre vases from *Notes on some Examples of Early Persian Lustre Ware*, published in 1889. The prints give an idea of the splendid quality of Wallis's illustrations for the books he wrote on Oriental pottery. Exactly which one of his illustrations matches *A Damascus Vase* shown at the O.W.S. is not known.

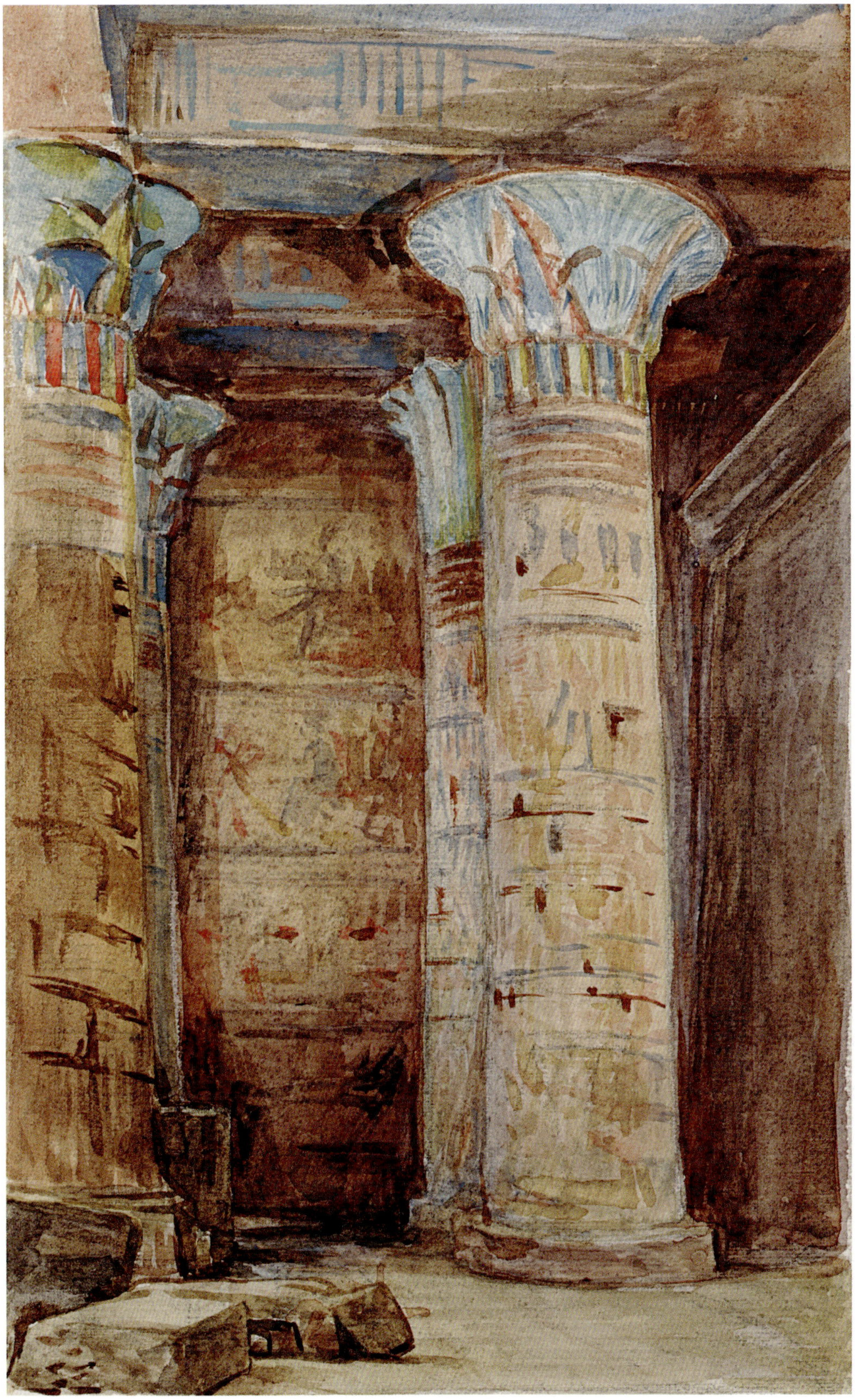

Cat. 217. Image courtesy of Bonhams, London

The Bonhams sale catalogue for 5 March 2002 mentions that this watercolor was included in one of 22 sketchbooks included in lot 71. This page was probably removed from a sketchbook so it could be sold as an individual work. A sketchbook in the Victoria & Albert Museum contains a related pencil drawing as well as a watercolour study of the detail of the top of a column.[1] Wallis was at, or near, Aswan (Assuan) between 30 December 1892 and 23 January 1893.

Cat. 218. *A Street Scene in Suez*
*c.*1890-1893; pencil and watercolour and bodycolour, heightened with gum arabic; 64.5 x 45.5 cm (25¾ x17¾ in.); Mathaf Gallery, London.
ANNOTATIONS: (by Felix Wallis on an old label attached to the backing) "A Street Scene in Suez/ by Henry Wallis."
PROVENANCE: Wallis's studio and then by descent from the artist to his daughter-in-law Alice Julyan Wallis (née Roberts); thence to her great-niece Mrs. Vera G. Whiting, Purley, Surrey; her sale Sotheby's Belgravia, 10 April 1973, part of lot 209, the lot bought by Bill Waters of Norham House, Cockermouth, Cumbria for £240; sold to Bolongare, Feb. 1977; sale Christie's, London, 29 September 1978, lot 199 for £350; Mathaf Gallery, London; sale Christie's, London, 2 April 1996, lot 104; Christie's, London, 8 April 1997, lot 103 (The Property of a Corporation), sold

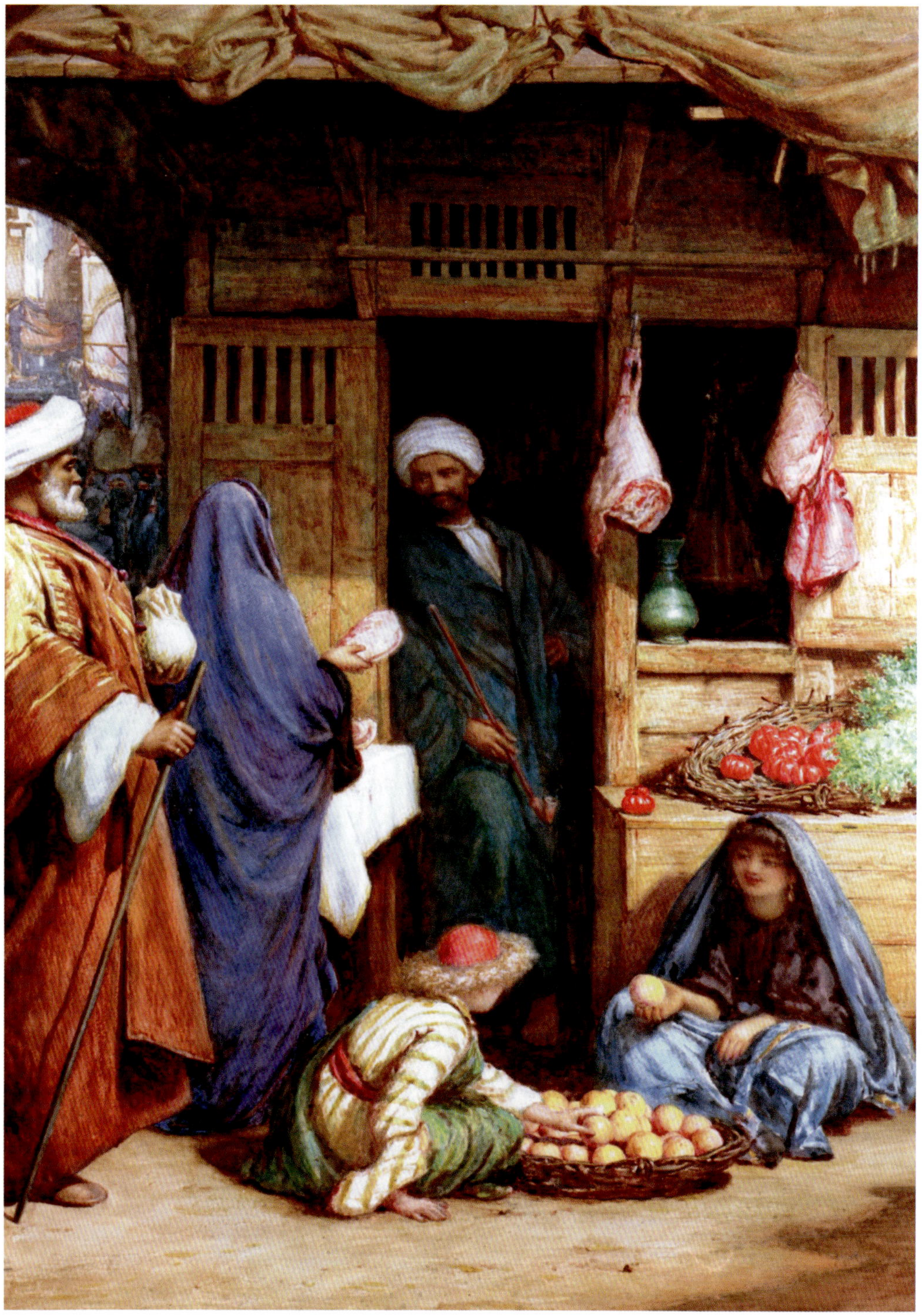

Cat. 218. Image courtesy of Mathaf Gallery, London

for £6,325; sale Christie's, London, 2 July 2008, lot 128, sold for £5,000; Mathaf Gallery, London.
Exhibitions: Old Water-Colour Society, London, 1893, no. 67; Norham House Gallery, Cockermouth: *The Pre-Raphaelite Fringe*, November 1973, no. 18.
Literature: *The Magazine of Art*, Vol. 16, 1893; *The Times*, 17 April 1893, p.12; *Paul Mall Gazette*, 20 April 1893, p.3; *The Athenaeum*, no. 3417, 22 April 1893, p.511; *The Illustrated London News*, 22 April 1893, p.492; *Bazaar Exchange and Mart, and Journal of the Household*, Vol. 48, 26 April 1893, p.737; *Fun*, 26 April 1893, p.174.

This painting received a very favourable review from F.G. Stephens in *The Athenaeum*: "…Mr. H. Wallis, the last of whom deserves the position of honour which is assigned on the walls to his picture called *A Street Scene in Suez* (No. 67). It represents, with extreme brilliancy and depth of tone and colour, the exterior of the shop, or booth, of a butcher, groups of figures assembled at it, and an intensely strong effect of sunlight and shadow in vigorously contrasted masses. In these respects it is a superb piece, its potency and harmony rivaling some of the strongest efforts of oil painting, and for much surpassing the richest and best of its neighbours on these walls. The drawing is excellent and the finish noteworthy. The painting of the draperies and that of the accessories – especially the meat hanging in front of the shop, and some of the faces – is most remarkable. While the composition is artistic in a high sense of the term, we cannot say that the design, strictly speaking, involves any subject; in fact, we are unable – it may be our fault – to see what is the business that occupies the figures, and every one who has studied the colouration and tone scheme of the work recommends Mr. Wallis to bring into harmony the too light and bright bunch of endive which lies on a board on our right, and troubles the eye of the visitor."

The Times critic approvingly declared: "Not for some years has Mr. Henry Wallis produced so important a drawing as that which he calls 'A Street Scene in Suez' (67) and which is deservedly hung in a place of honour at the end of the room…and nothing satisfies his love for glowing, almost dazzling, colours except the hues of Persian pottery or of Arab dresses seen under an Egyptian sky. He is, of course, not alone among the members of the society in his zeal for the East…Mr. Wallis spares no detail, and makes his brush compete with nature herself in adding colour to colour." In a letter to his son Felix, dated 14 March 1893, Wallis writes: "I find pictures here to be sent to the Gall. on Tuesday Ap. 4th. I proposed sending one that by mistake went in the winter 3 (?) years ago, & is in the studio covered wth a cloth. I think the outside one. It is an Oriental street scene – butcher's shop, etc. It has a card board mount (the part [?] next to picture.) This must be removed & a gold mount added. Will you put it out in the studio & ask Clayton (6 Red Lion Sqre) to fetch it, change the mount & deliver it at the Gally on the above date. You will have to write a label – my name & address + the title 'A Street scene at Suez' + paste it on the back."[1]

Cat. 219. *Erinna (Erinna - 'Ἠλακάτη - The Spindle')*
1893; watercolour; 21.3 x 29.4 cm (8½ x 10½ in.); private collection.
Provenance: Wallis's studio and then by descent from the artist to his daughter-in-law Alice Julyan Wallis (née Roberts); thence to her great-niece Mrs. Vera G. Whiting, Purley, Surrey; her sale Sotheby's Belgravia, 10 April 1973, part of lot 209, purchased by Bill Waters, Norham House, Cockermouth, Cumbria, for £240; sold to Keswick.
Exhibitions: Old Water-Colour Society, Winter Exhibition 1893, no. 92; Norham House: *The Pre-Raphaelite Fringe*, November, 1973, no. 19.
Literature: *The Athenaeum*, No. 3450, 9 December 1893, p.813; *The Era*, 6 January 1894, p.12.

The poet Erinna is portrayed as a muse who crowns a young woman who sits spinning. The style of this watercolour has

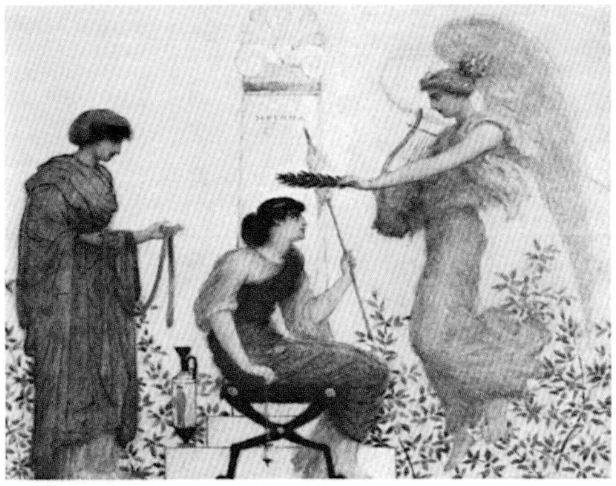

Cat. 219. Image courtesy of William Waters

obviously been influenced by Greek pottery decoration. In its two-dimensionality, it is also reminiscent of ancient Roman wall paintings. Erinna was very famous in her own time and had her likeness sculpted by at least two of the most famous sculptors living during that period.

F.G. Stephens in *The Athenaeum* commented: "Mr. Wallis, who is always alive to what is really fine art, has been attracted by the delicacy of certain painted Greek vases of the purest taste, which have been of late more studied than they used to be, and are justly admired for the elegant draughtsmanship of their figures, the charms of their expressions and attitudes, and especially for the beauty and brilliance of their colours, which are mainly rose, rich brown, and red, upon white grounds. In *Erinna* (92) he has added life and brightness, enhanced the tender colours, and made good the ravages of time in the models he has thus adopted; he has also eliminated as light stiffness and archaism the Greek decorator conceived himself bound to accept, and he has imparted that lucidity which is possible in modern water-colour art, though distemper could not attain to it."

Cat. 220. *The Music Master*
1893; watercolour; 22.4 x 34 cm (8¾ x 13½ in.); private collection.
PROVENANCE: Wallis's studio and then by descent from the artist to his daughter-in-law Alice Julyan Wallis (née Roberts); thence to her great-niece Mrs. Vera G. Whiting, Purley, Surrey; her sale Sotheby's Belgravia, 10 April 1973, part of lot 209, the lot bought by Bill Waters of Norham House, Cockermouth, Cumbria for £240; sold to Steigal Fine Art, Edinburgh; private collection.
EXHIBITIONS: Old Water-Colour Society, Winter Exhibition 1893, no. 313; Norham House, Cockermouth, *The Pre-Raphaelite Fringe*, November 1973, no. 21.
LITERATURE: *The Athenaeum*, No. 3450, 9 December 1893, p. 813.

The subject of this watercolour is unknown. Wallis may have found his inspiration for this work in his friend William Allingham's book of poetry, *The Music Master*, published in London by Routledge in 1854 and reissued 1863. The book contains illustrations by Arthur Hughes, J. E. Millais, and a particularly famous one by D.G. Rossetti. Arthur Hughes had met Allingham through Rossetti in 1854 and it was probably Hughes who later introduced Wallis to the Irish poet.

The Athenaeum commented that: "*The Music Master* (313), too, is attractive from its charming colour and graceful figures."

Cat. 221. *A Street in Cairo (A Mosque near the Goldsmiths' Market)*
1894; watercolour; 51 x 35.5 cm. (20⅛ x 14 in.; private collection.
INSCRIPTIONS: Signed with initials *HW*, signed on the verso.
PROVENANCE: Possibly sold in 1894 from the Old Water-Colour Society exhibition, buyer unknown; Wallis's studio at his death and then by descent from the artist to his daughter-in-law Alice Julyan Wallis (née Roberts); thence to her great-niece Mrs. Vera G. Whiting, Purley, Surrey; her sale Sotheby's Belgravia, 10 April 1973, lot 207 bought Hartnoll & Eyre, London for £95; sold to the dealer Joseph Soustiel,[1] Paris; purchased in 1975 by Alan Lesietre; ?Alder auctions, Paris, 19 November 1991, lot 299; private collection.
EXHIBITIONS: Old Water-Colour Society, 1894, no. 115; Hartnoll & Eyre Ltd., London: Catalogue Thirty-Three, September 25 – October 12, 1973, no. 43.
LITERATURE: *The Saturday Review*, Vol. 77, 1894, p.471; *The Athenaeum*, No. 3470, 28 April 1894, p.545; Jullian, Philippe: *Les Orientalistes*, Phaidon, 1977, pp.11 and 77; Ackerman, Gerald: *Les Orientalistes de l'école britannique*, Paris, 1992, p.299.
[Illustrated overleaf]

William Holman Hunt may be referring to this work when he wrote to Wallis, on the 22 August 1894: "Your drawing in the last Old Water colour was of a favourite façade of mine. But I don't know how you escaped the bad odour in the opposite Mosque."

F.G. Stephens in his review in *The Athenaeum* called this watercolour one of the most striking things in the gallery: "... Mr. Wallis's *Street in Cairo* (115) resplendent in light and colour, leaves nothing to the imagination. We have, in powerful sunlight, the clearest air, and vivid hues, buildings of sandstones in bands of red and yellow alternatively, and figures of Egyptians buying and selling, or loitering along the narrow way. The whole is carefully and brilliantly painted, with a firm crisp touch which ensures that there shall be no lack of breadth and solidity. Technically speaking, this is one of the finest works in the gallery; it wants nothing but a subject to attract popular admiration."

The critic for *The Saturday Review* commented: "Mr. Henry Wallis, whose work is always brilliant and individual, sends a 'Street in Cairo' (115), of very high technical interest."

Cat. 222. *Fetching Water, a Lane in Cairo*
1894; watercolour; dimensions unknown; whereabouts unknown.
PROVENANCE: Bought from the Old Water-Colour Society exhibition on 15 December 1894 by Mrs (?) Walter, Stoodhays, Wimbledon.
EXHIBITIONS: Old Water-Colour Society, Winter exhibition 1894, no. 92.
LITERATURE: *The Magazine of Art*, Vol. 18, 1895, p.127; *The Athenaeum*, No. 3502, 8 December 1894, p.797.

F.G. Stephens wrote in his review for *The Athenaeum*: "A shadowy, narrow street of lofty stone houses, with here and there carved balconies of wood, has afforded Mr. Wallis opportunities for utilizing his delicate perception of tone, aerial perspective, and opalescent colours exquisitely harmonized, in *Fetching Water, a Lane in Cairo* (92), his sole contribution of the season, and one of the few works of first-rate art now before us." The critic for *The Magazine of Art* indicated: "Mr. Henry Wallis is seen to much advantage in an Oriental scene, 'Fetching Water – a Lane in Cairo.' The deep, transparent shadow cast by walls of monumental massiveness and strength on the narrow street could hardly be better rendered."

Cat. 223. *The Principal Entrance to the Mosque of Sultan Kalaun, Cairo*
1895; watercolour, heightened with bodycolour; 42.8 x 33 cm (16⅞ x 13 in.) – sight; private collection, Diane Johnson, San Francisco.
ANNOTATION: (on the old backboard) "Henry Wallis Principal Entrance to the Mosque of Sultan Kalaun, Cairo".
PROVENANCE: Wallis's studio and then by descent from the artist to his daughter-in-law Alice Julyan Wallis (née Roberts); thence to her great-niece Mrs. Vera G. Whiting, Purley, Surrey; given to Diane Johnson *c.*1973.
EXHIBITIONS: Old Water-Colour Society, 1895, no. 6, asking price £52 10s; Liverpool Corporation, *Autumn Exhibition of Pictures*, Walker Art Gallery, 1895, no. 783, asking price £42 0s.
LITERATURE: *The Magazine of Art*, Vol. 18, 1895, pp.357-358; *The Times*, 20 April 1895, p.8; *The Athenaeum*, No. 3522, 27 April 1895, p.542.

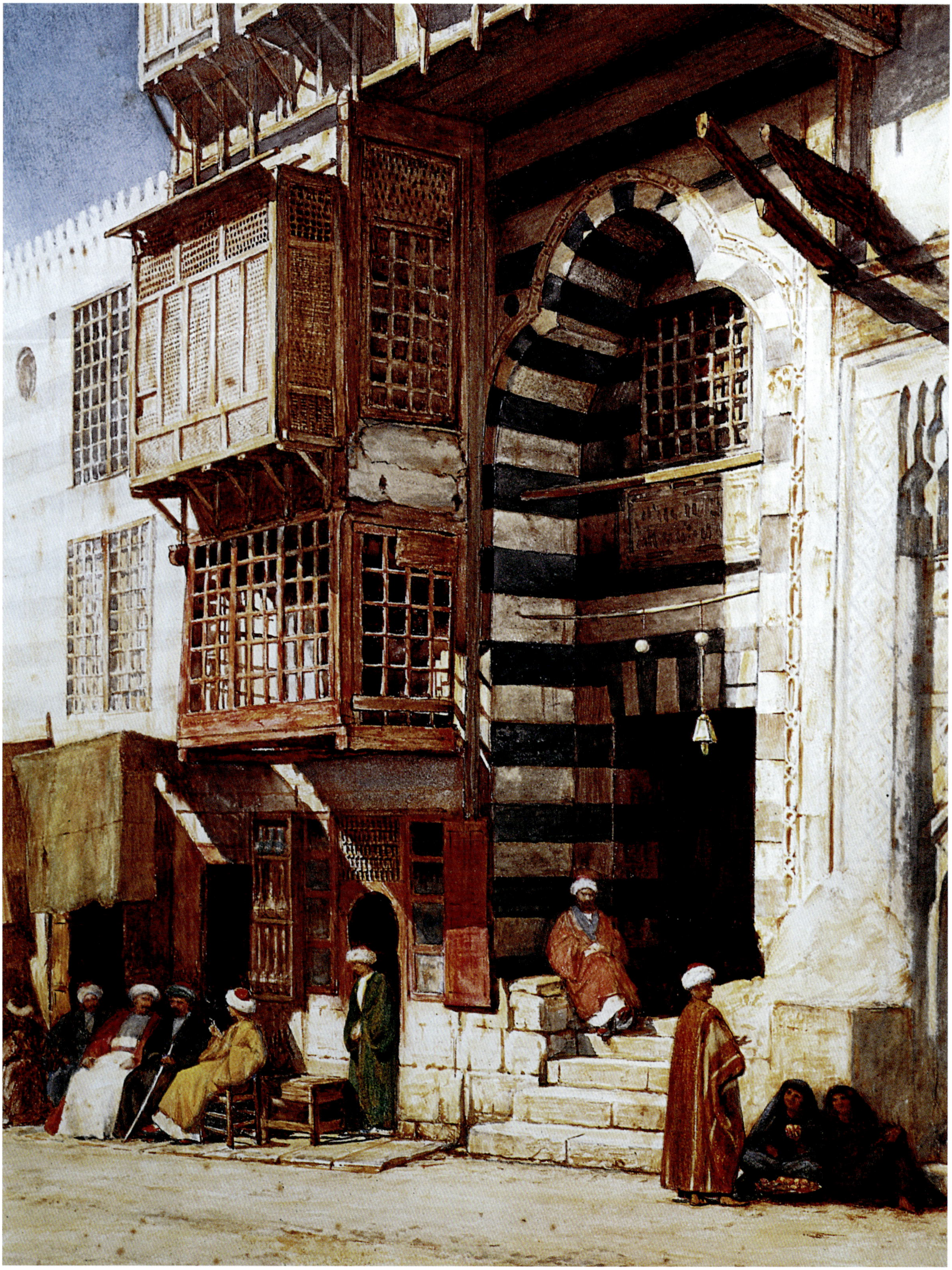

Cat. 221. Image from Ackerman, *Les Orientalistes de l'Ecole Britannique*, p.299.. Image courtesy of ACR Edition, Courbevoie.

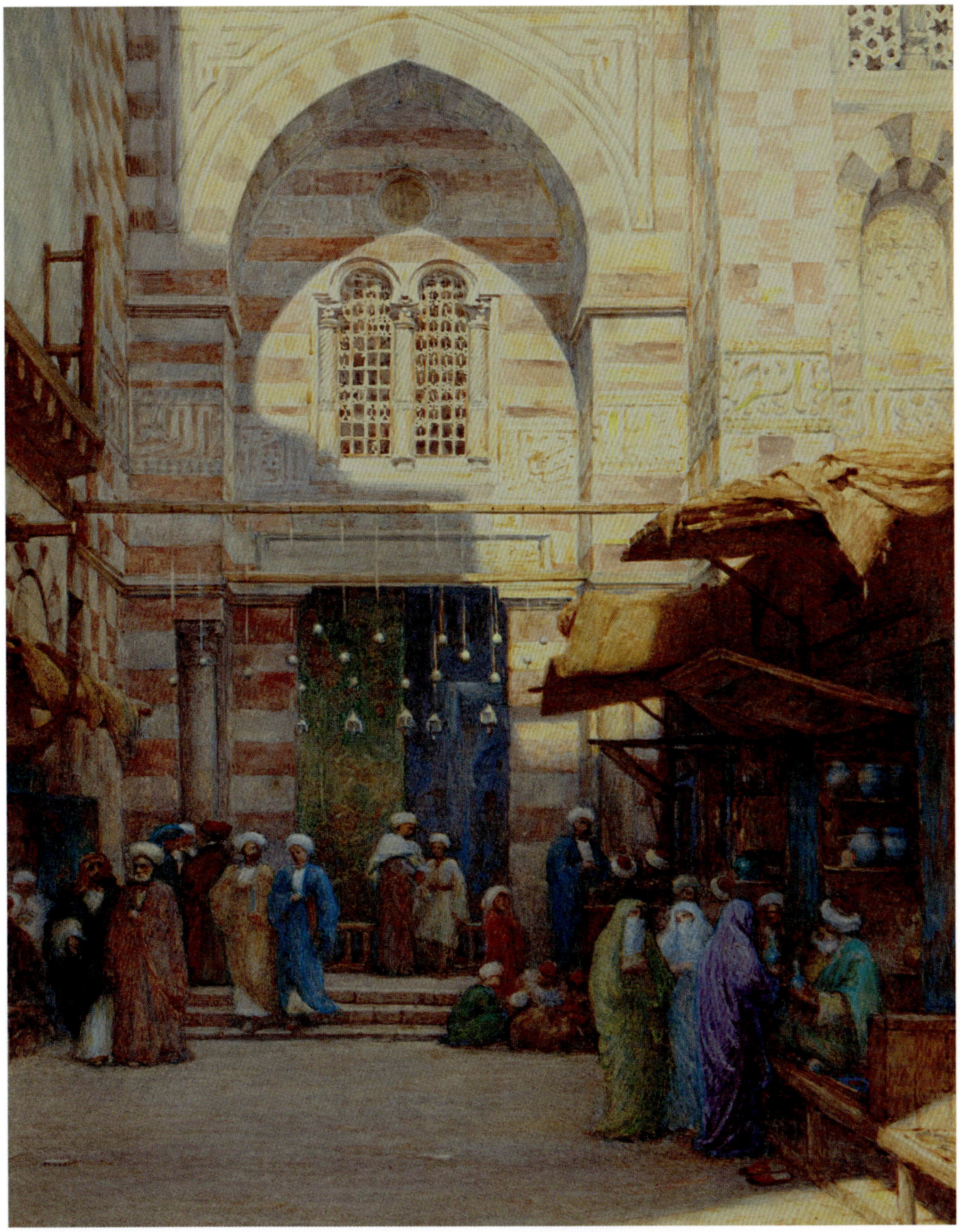

Cat. 223. Diane Johnson collection, San Francisco, California

F.G. Stephens in *The Athenaeum* stated: "Another fine piece of colour accompanied by powerful contrasts of light and shadow... is Mr. Wallis's *Principal Entrance to the Mosque of Sultan Kalaun, Cairo* (6), a true and complete picture, distinguished by deep and lucid tones, and comprising several excellent figures in Oriental costumes. Yet in painting but one such picture in a year Mr. Wallis is unjust to himself and unkind to the world." The critic for *The Magazine of Art* wrote: " 'The Principal Entrance to the Mosque of Sultan Kalaun, Cairo', by Mr. Henry Wallis is a wealth of orange, purple and gold."

Cat. 223a. *The Principal Entrance to the Mosque of Sultan Kalaun, Cairo*
1895; graphite; dimensions unknown; whereabouts unknown.
Literature: Old Water-Colour Society (R.W.S.), *Illustrated catalogue with sketches by the artists.*

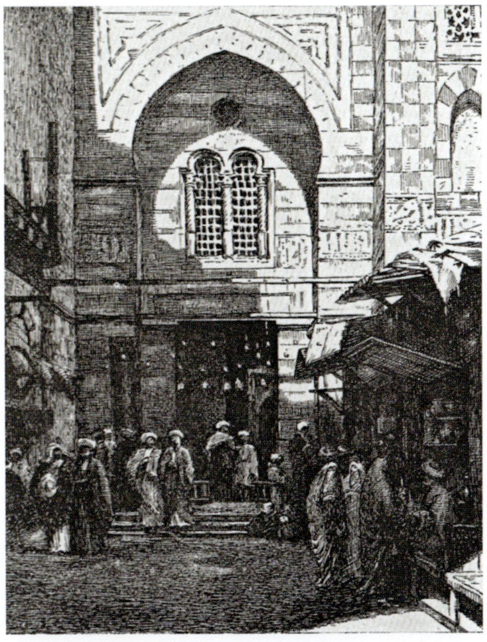

See Cat. 223a. Drawing by Wallis after the watercolour and reproduced in the O.W.C. Society's *Illustrated catalogue.*

Cat. 224. *Flinders Petrie Admiring a Find, the Ramesseum, Western Thebes*
1895; watercolour on paper, mounted on wood panel; 57.1 x 78.7 cm. (22½ x 31 in.); University College Art Museum, London
Provenance: Given to University College London Art Museum in 1964 by John H. L. Cooper and Harold Wallis, museum no. EDC2674.
Exhibitions: Old Water-Colour Society, 1898, no. 22.
Literature: *Lloyd's Weekly Newspaper*, 24 April 1898, p.4; *The Times*, 26 April 1898, p.3; The *Athenaeum*, No. 3681, 14 May 1898, p.636; Newberry, Percy E.: 'William Matthew Flinders Petrie, Kt., F.R.S., F.B.A.', *The Journal of Egyptian Archaeology*, Vol. 29, December 1943, p.70;Drower, Margaret S.: *Flinders Petrie: A Life in Archaelogy*, 1985, pl. 80; Harte N. and North J., *The World of UCL 1828-2004*, 2004, p.144, fig. 212.

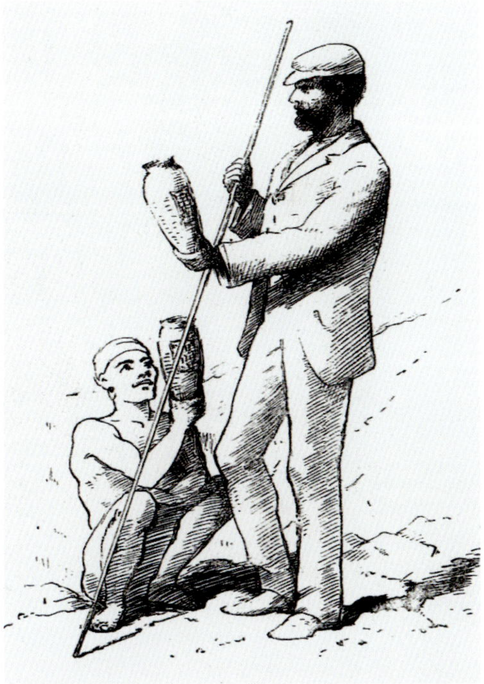

See Cat. 224 Drawing from the O.W.S.'s *Illustrated catalogue* showing a detail from the watercolour.

This is a larger version of the next painting whose compositions differ primarily in the figures found at the lower left. A quotation from the O.W.S. catalogue of 1898 states: "During the progress of his excavations Mr. Petrie makes the round of the trenches at stated intervals to measure the earth which has been removed, and to examine the objects which may have been found. The diggers are paid according to the quantity of earth excavated, but besides this fixed and determined wage Mr. Petrie, having appraised the objects discovered, credits the amount to the weekly accounts of the respective finders."

F.G. Stephens writing in *The Athenaeum* offered the opinion that: "No.22, Mr. Wallis's sole contribution, called *Excavating*

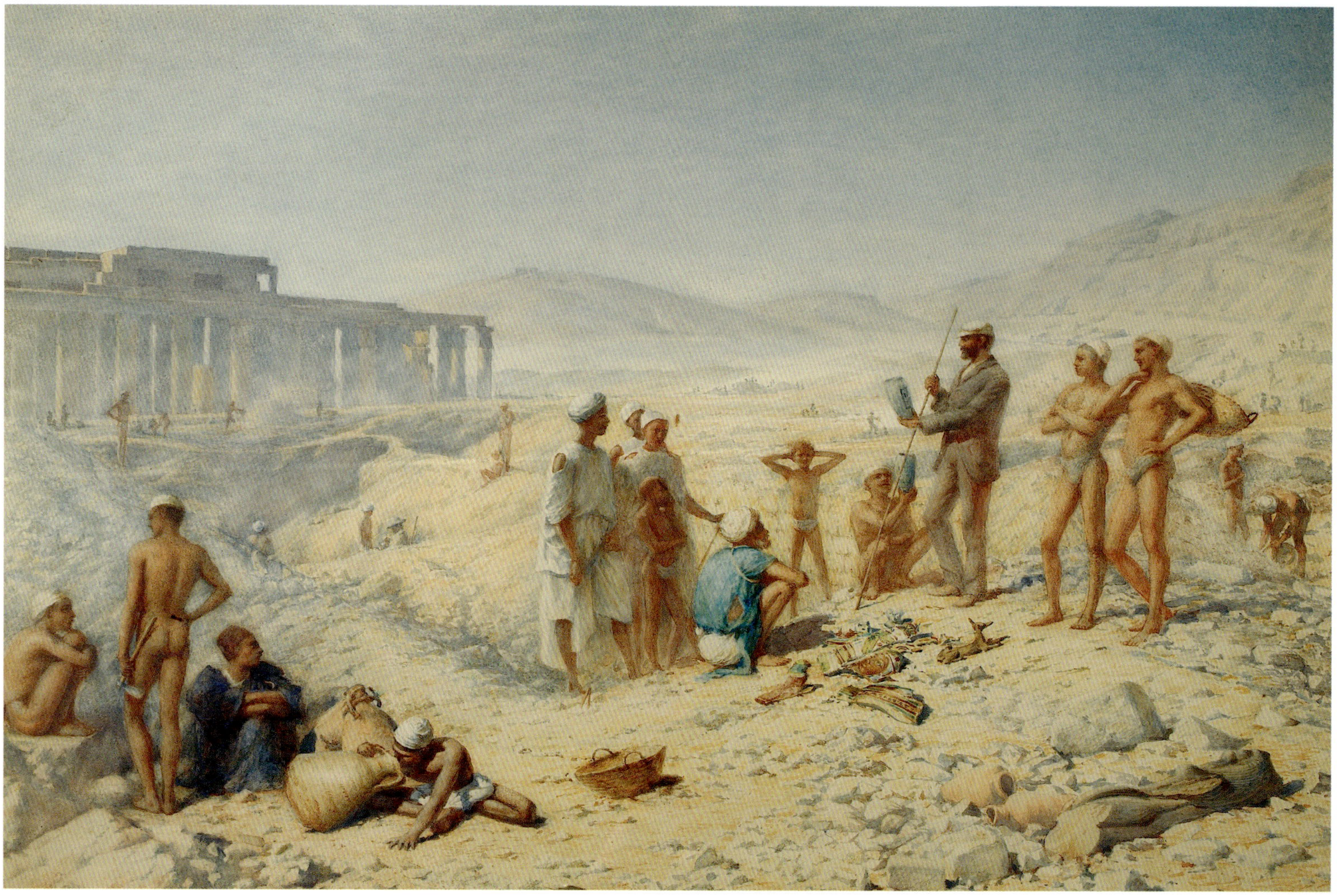

Cat. 224. Image by permission of UCL Art Museum, University College London

in Egypt: Prof. Petrie at Thebes, 1896, is no doubt beautifully coloured and thoroughly artistic; indeed, as a work of art it is equal to the best here; but we fear that the subject of excavation will interest comparatively few people. The enamel-like coloration that pervades the drawing serves like a setting to the higher tints which occur in the naked figures of Arab labourers and the dress of Prof. Petrie himself."

Wallis mentioned several times a painting that he finished at Deir-el-Bahari in January 1896. In a letter from Luxor to his son Harold, dated 30 December 1895: "I am still staying here as I have begun some painting at Dayr-el-Bahari – where the E. Exploration Fund is working.[1] They have a house – a little primitive but not uncomfortable. It is in the desert, where there is not a scrap of cultivation … I expect to stay here ten days or a fortnight longer then shall not go further but propose returning to Cairo."[2] In a letter to Frederic George Stephens, on 14 February 1896, Wallis wrote: "Returning to Cairo from upper Egypt, I painted a picture at Deir-el-Bahari in blazing sunshine & heat. I made studies for another subject – nude figures in sunshine."[3] The "nude figures in sunshine" may also refer to one of these two watercolours.

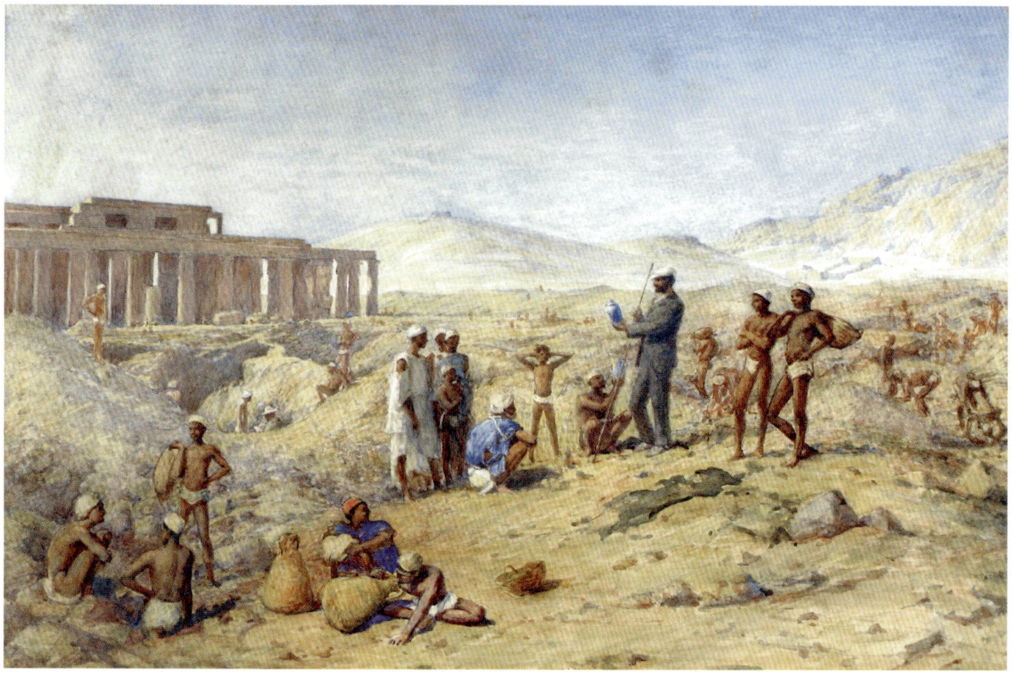

Cat. 224a. Image courtesy of Chris Beetles Gallery, London

Cat. 224a. ***Flinders Petrie admiring a find, the Ramesseum, Western Thebes***
1895; watercolour; 33 x 49.5 cm (12½ x 18¾ in); Chris Beetles Gallery, London.
PROVENANCE: Wallis's studio and then by descent from the artist to his son Harold Wallis; then to his daughter-in-law Mary Wallis (née Mary Elizabeth Aymes), then her great-niece Vera G. Cooper (née Langley; 1910-1989); thence by direct descent to John Harold Cooper and family; sold at Bonhams, London, 5 March 2002, lot 63, bought in; sale Bonhams, London, 25 June 2002, lot 94, sold for £1,300; Chris

Beetles, London, and still in his stock in 2018.
Exhibitions: Chris Beetles, *The Summer Show*, 2010, catalogued as *Excavating in Egypt: Professor Petrie at Thebes*, 1895; not sold.

Wallis and Petrie[1] knew each other quite well. During the 1895 excavations, Petrie stayed near Luxor and was cataloguing the Theban tombs. Petrie, Milne and others camped beside the Ramesseum. During that period, Wallis came over for a couple of days and made this and the previous watercolor,[2] which must have been executed between 18 December 1895 and 26 January 1896.

Cat. 225. *The Court of the Great Altar of the Temple of Queen Hatshepsu (Deir-el-Bahari), Thebes*
1896; watercolour; dimensions unknown; whereabouts unknown.
Exhibitions: Old Water-Colour Society, 1896, no. 137, asking price £50.
Literature: *The Morning Post*, 28 April 1896, p.5; *Globe*, 28 April 1896, p.3; *The Athenaeum*, No. 3576, 9 May 1896, p.625.

Wallis's watercolour of Queen Hatshepsut's magnificent temple[1] must have been made during his stay at Deir-el-Bahari from December 1895 – February 1896.

F.G. Stephens in the *The Athenaeum* discussed this work appreciatively: "The accomplished painter has represented with great force, breadth, and brilliance, a roofless compartment of white stone, strewn with huge blocks that have fallen from the upper walls, and full of light which glows intensely upon the time-stained walls, and casts from every projection, moulding, or piece of sculpture, a dark, purplish shadow sharply defined. The whole looks as if it had been painted with consummate art, but without reserve, from nature direct." The reviewer for *The Morning Post* stated: "The effect prevailing in this 'interior' [by Carl Haag] has its converse in the open-air scene limned by Mr. Henry Wallis in 'The Court of the Great Altar of the Queen Hatshepsu, Thebes.' Here the solid masonry of the walls is for the most part flooded with warm sunshine, but in such portions of the courtyard as are in shadow the tones are cold, with a blueish tendency." The critic of the *Globe* wrote: "Mr. Henry Wallis, who has not exhibited here of late, sends an admirable drawing of 'The Court of the Great Altar of the Temple of Queen Hatshepsu, Thebes,' with many devout Arabs in brilliant sunshine, full of Oriental colour, and painted in masterly style."

Cat. 226. *A Study of a Greek Vase*
1896; watercolour; dimensions unknown; whereabouts unknown.
Exhibitions: Old Water-Colour Society, Winter exhibition 1896, no. 261.
Literature: *The Builder*, Vol. 71, 1896, p.445; *London Evening Standard*, 28 November 1896, p.5; *The Times*, 30 November 1896, p.14; *The Athenaeum*, no. 3606, 5 December 1896, p.802.

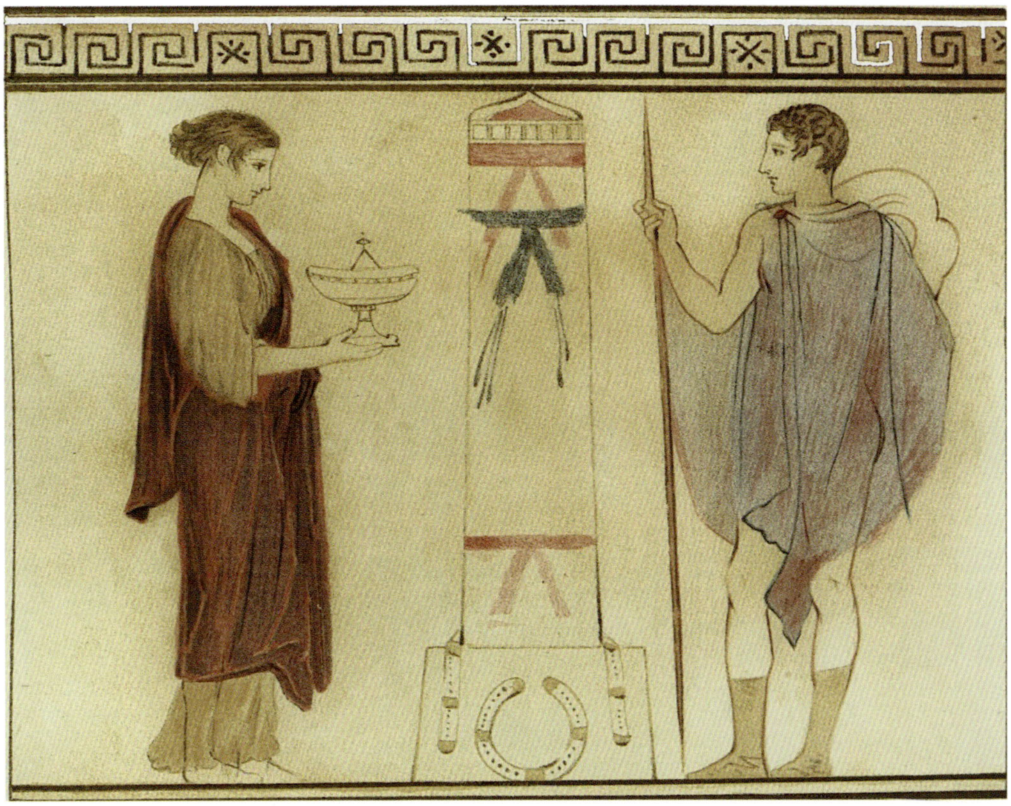

See Cat. 226. Lithographic reproduction after Wallis's drawing. Plate I in Wallis's book *Pictures from the Greek Vases: the White Athenina lekythi*, London, 1896. It is uncertain which of the original drawings for the plates in the book was exhibited as no. 261 in the O.W.S. exhibition.

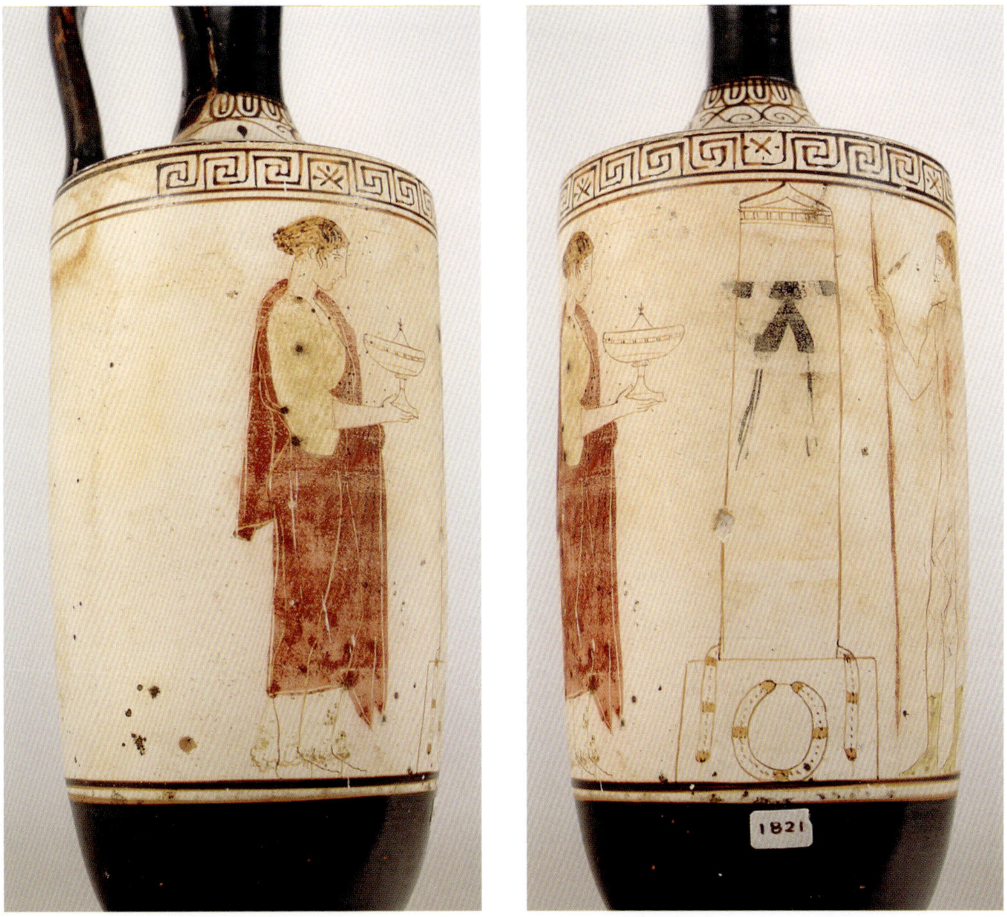

See Cat. 226. Lekythos vase, *c.*440 b.c. Attic white-ground, Eretia. Images by permission of National Archeological Museum, Athens

In a letter dated 9 October 1887 from Wallis in Athens to his son Harold, he mentions: "I am copying one or two of the glazed vases for the Magnus Opus." [Letter 29] F.G. Stephens, in *The Athenaeum*, stated:

"Mr. Wallis is, to our surprise, content to be represented by a most exquisitely drawn and painted *Study of a Greek (Athenian) Vase* (261) and charming *Study of the Ornamentation of an Athenian Lekythos* (265) [Cat. 227]. These are examples of the original drawings made by him for his recently published monograph. As before, the background is the luxurious warm white of a wall of Pentelican marble, not the cooler Carrara that Mr. Alma Tadema has so often painted...." The critic of *The Times* commented: "Mr. Henry Wallis, close by, hangs some of those charming copies of Greek vase paintings which he has just published in a book.[1] But Mr. Wallis is too refined and original an artist to give himself up to copies, though they be copies of Greek form or Persian colour."

Cat. 227. *A Study of the Ornamentation of a White Athenian Lekythos*
1896; watercolour; 17 x 20.8 cm (7 x 8¼ in); whereabouts unknown.
PROVENANCE: Wallis's studio and then by descent from the artist to his daughter-in-law Alice Julyan Wallis (née Roberts); thence to her great-niece Mrs. Vera G. Whiting, Purley, Surrey; her sale Sotheby's Belgravia, 10 April 1973, part of lot 209; lot purchased by Bill Waters, Norham House, Cockermouth, Cumbria, for £240.
EXHIBITIONS: Old Water-Colour Society, Winter Exhibition 1896, no. 265; Norham House: *The Pre-Raphaelite Fringe*, November, 1973, no. 20.
LITERATURE: *The Athenaeum*, no. 3606, 5 December 1896, p.802.
[See: Cat. 226 for review in *The Athenaeum*]

Cat 228. *A Study of the Ornamentation of a Greek Vase*
1896; watercolour; dimensions unknown; whereabouts unknown.
EXHIBITIONS: Old Water-Colour Society, Winter exhibition 1896, no. 271.

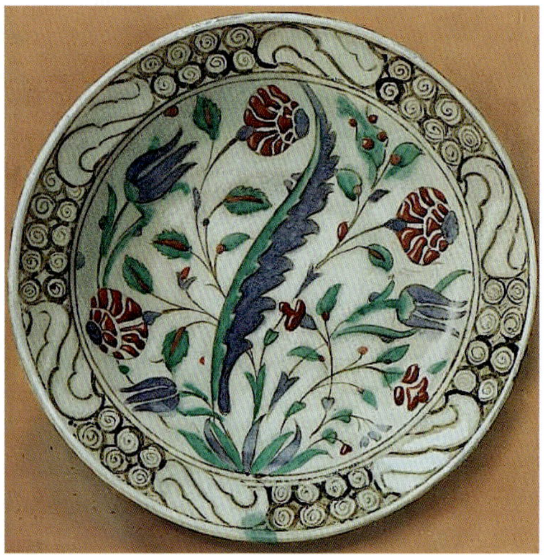

Cat. 229. Image courtesy of Bonhams, London

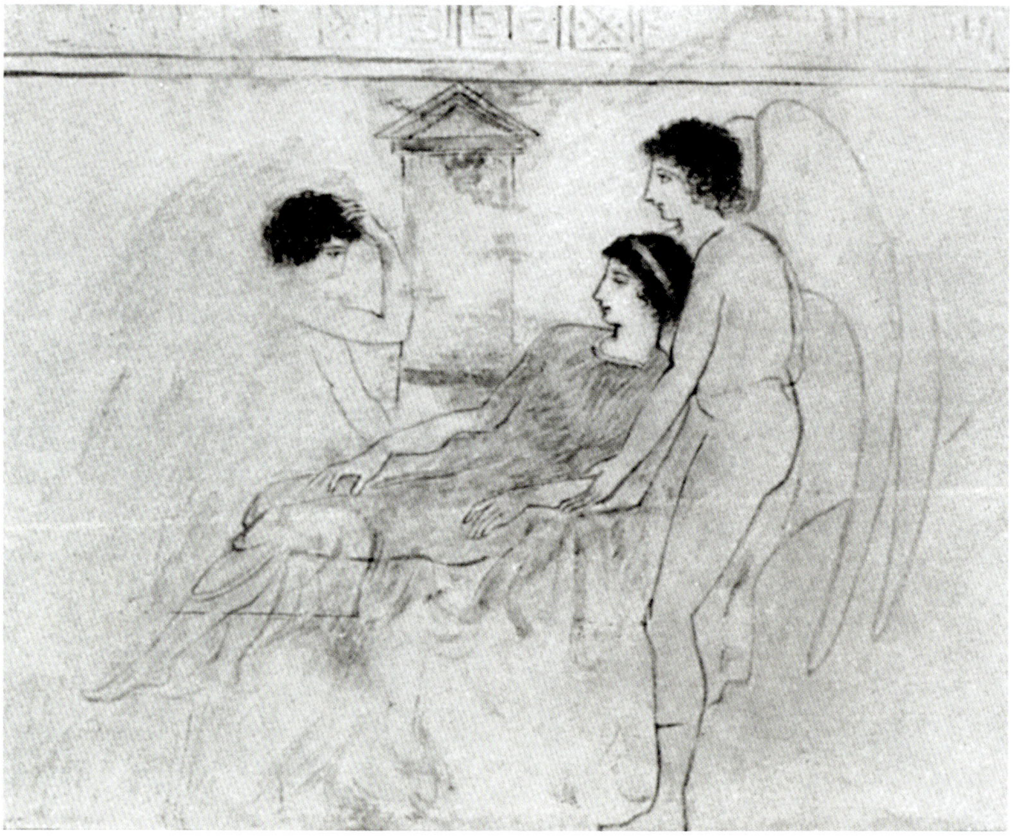

Cat. 227. Image courtesy of William Waters.

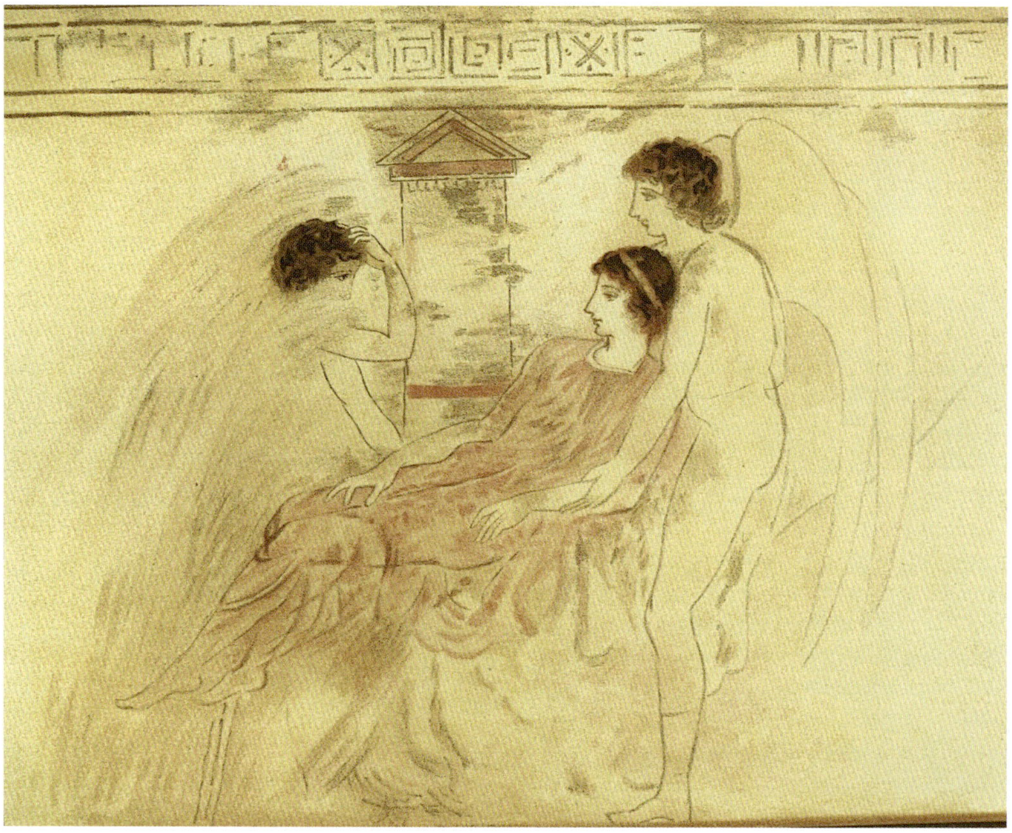

Cat. 227. Lekythos vases were made as grave offerings. This drawing, copied from a typical specimen of Greek vase painting, was reproduced as a lithograph by Hanhart[1] after Wallis's drawing in Wallis's book *Pictures from the Greek Vases: the White Athenina lekythi*, London, 1896.

Cat. 229. *Study of a late 16th Century Iznik Dish (and a Study of an Iznik drinking Vessel)*
c. mid-late 1890s; watercolour; 27.3 x 27.3 cm. (10¾ x 10¾ in.); private collection
PROVENANCE: Bonhams, London, 10 May 2005, lot 104, sold for £900.

Wallis was fascinated by the magnificent Iznik pottery[1] and shared this enthusiasm with others, including William De Morgan and Frederic Leighton, who particularly admired this style of pottery.

Some of Wallis's collection of Iznik pottery was sold to the British Musuem.

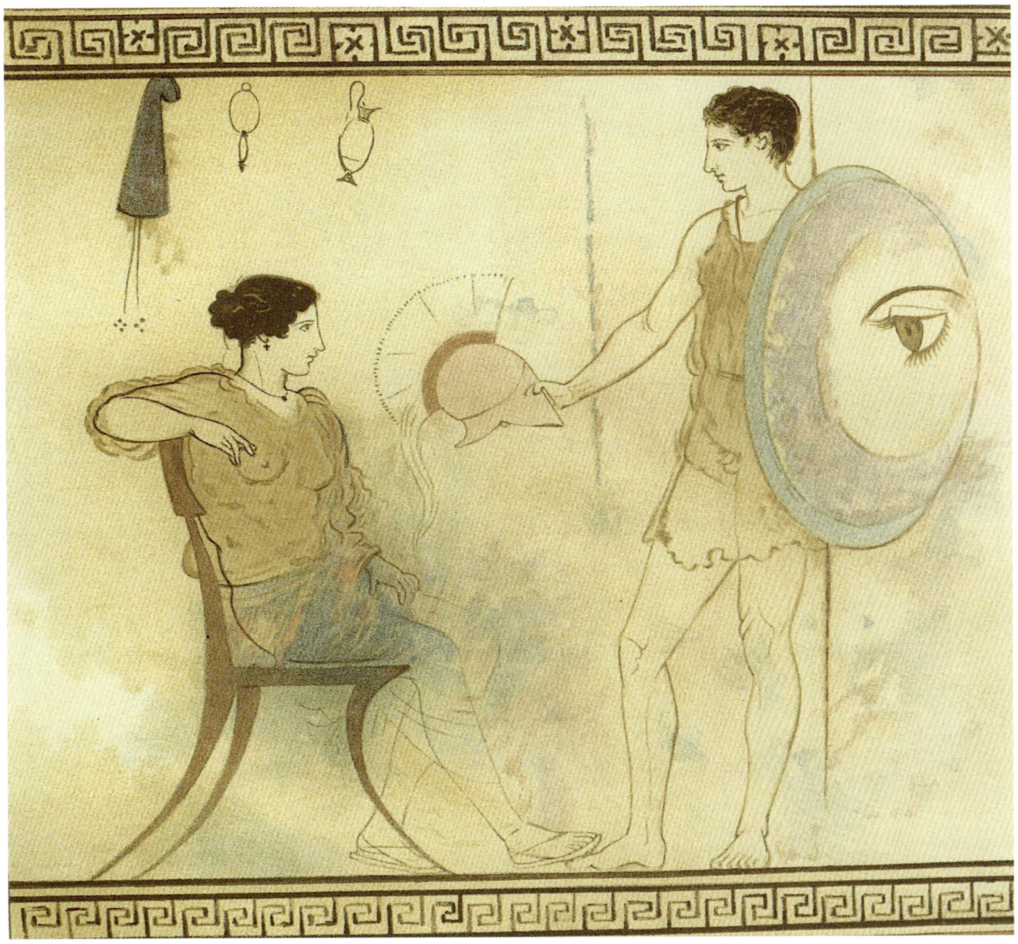

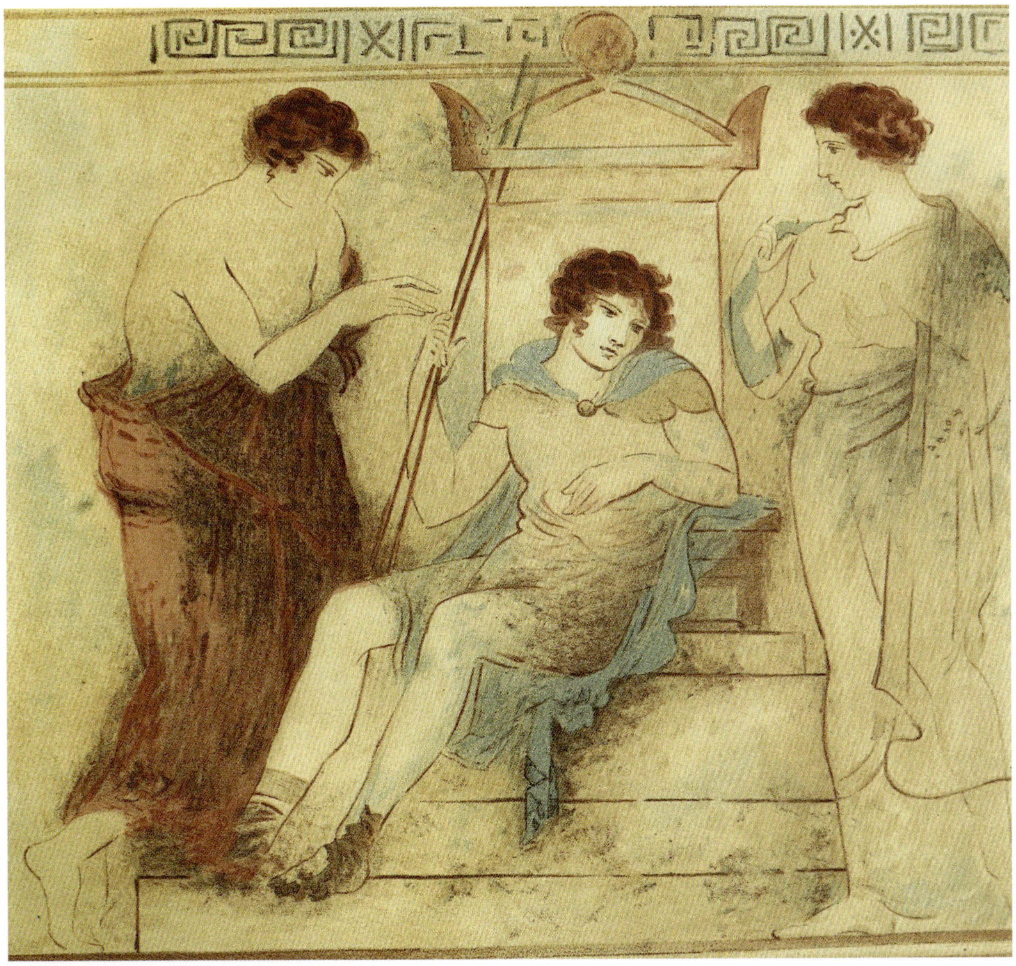

Lithographic reproductions after Wallis's drawings, which appeared in Wallis's book *Pictures from the Greek Vases: the White Athenina lekythi*, London, 1896 (Top: Plate III; below: Plate XI). It is uncertain which of the original drawings for the plates in the book was exhibited as no. 271 in the O.W.S. exhibition. See Cat. 228.

On 30 May 1897 Wallis wrote to Charles Hercules Read at the British Museum: "It has occurred to me that if I offer the [splendid Iznik or Kütahya] bowl at £300, & your people decline, it may be rather awkward for me, supposing that I sold it for double the price to someone else. There is a probability that some one who had seen it at the B.M. might come across it afterwards & might remark that it was offered at so much. I take it, however, that the Trustees wld accept your recommendation."[2]

Cat. 230. *Study of a 17th Century Kütahya Dish or Shallow Bowl* [1]
c. mid-late 1890s; watercolour and ink on paper; 12.5 x 12.5 cm. (4⅞ x 4⅞ in.) – sight; Diane Johnson collection, Paris.
Provenance: Wallis's studio and then by descent from the artist to his daughter-in-law Alice Julyan Wallis (née Roberts); and thence to her great-niece Mrs. Vera G. Whiting, Purley, Surrey; given to Diane Johnson *c.*1973.

Cat. 231. *Study of two Italian Renaissance Plates*
*c.*1900-1905; watercolour and ink on paper; 19.8 x 19.8 cm. (7⅞ x 7⅞ in.) – sight; Diane Johnson collection, Paris.
Provenance: Wallis's studio and then by descent from the artist to his daughter-in-law Alice Julyan Wallis (née Roberts); thence to her great-niece Mrs. Vera G. Whiting, Purley, Surrey; given to Diane Johnson *c.*1973.

The plate on the left is from Faenza of about 1480-1500, while that on the right is from Deruta of *c.*1510-50. Even prior to the turn of the 16th century, both Faenza and Deruta were well known as centres for making fine majolica. The letters in the centre of the plates are christograms IHS (or JHS).[1]

The plate on the right was from Henry Wallis's personal collection. He illustrated in sepia this plate with a raised centre, 36.6 cm in diameter, in his book *Italian Ceramic Art. Figure Design and Other Forms of Ornamentation in XVth Century Italian Maiolica*, Bernard Quaritch, London, 1905, fig. 78, p.78. Wallis noted in the book "similar ornamentation is found on lustred Diruta dishes." A circular plaque from the V&A's collection, similar to the plate on the left, is illustrated in the same book by Wallis, fig. 48, p.48. A mezzo-majolica shallow bowl from the V&A with similar ornamentation is illustrated in Wallis's book *The Art of the Precursors. A Study on the History of Early Italian Maiolica*, Bernard Quaritch, London, 1901, fig. 26, p.22.

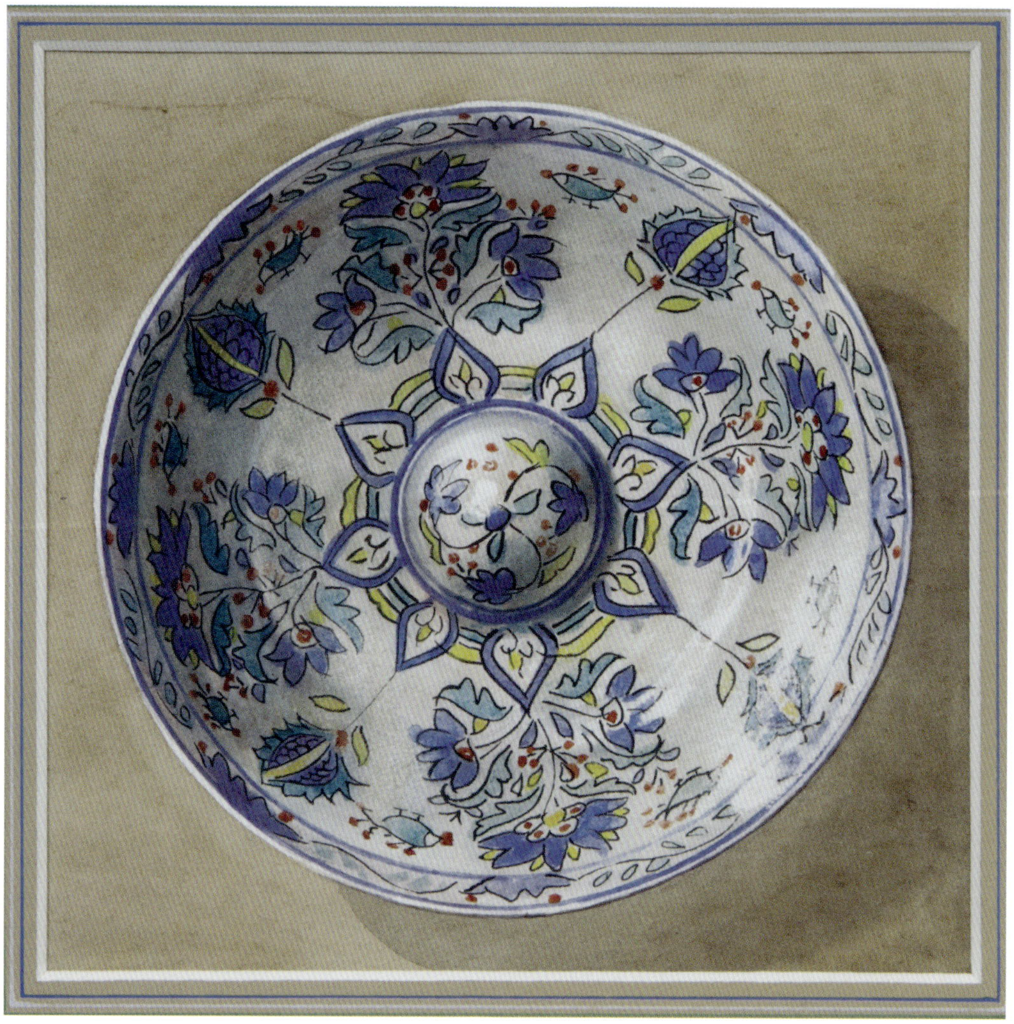

Cat. 230. Image courtesy Diane Johnson collection, Paris, photographer Alison Harris

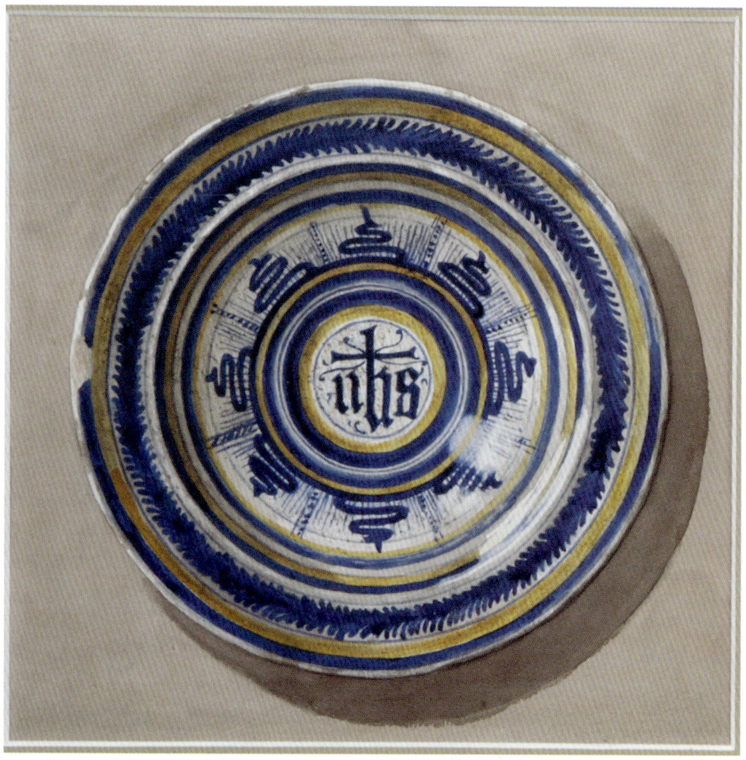

Cat. 231. Image courtesy Diane Johnson collection, Paris, photographer Alison Harris

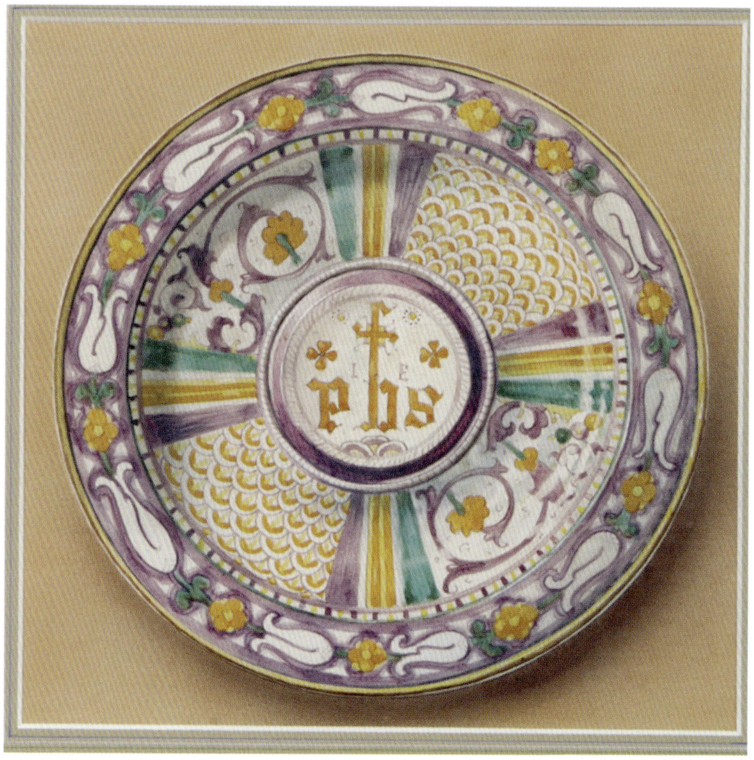

Cat. 231. Image courtesy Diane Johnson collection, Paris, photographer Alison Harris

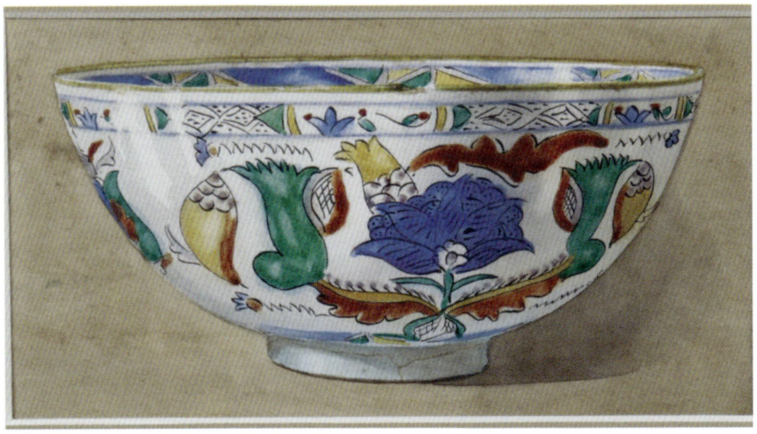

Cat. 232. Image courtesy Diane Johnson collection, Paris, photographer Alison Harris

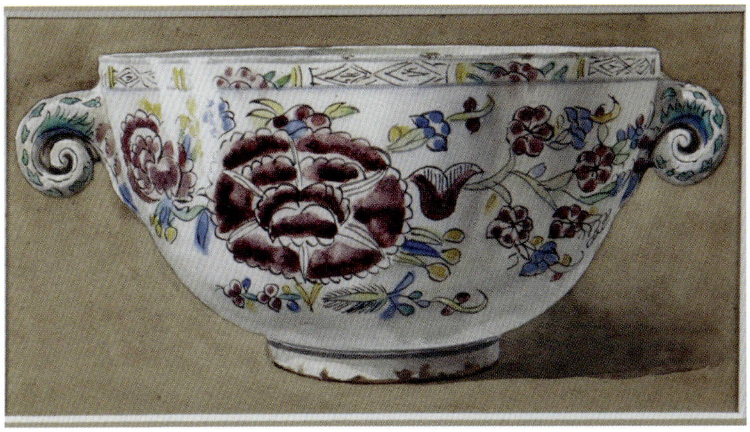

Cat. 232. Image courtesy Diane Johnson collection, Paris, photographer Alison Harris

Cat. 232. *Study of two Bowls*
c. mid-late 1890s; watercolour and ink on paper; 9 x 16 cm.each (3⅝ x 6⅜ in.); Diane Johnson collection, Paris.
Provenance: Wallis's studio and then by descent from the artist to his daughter-in-law Alice Julyan Wallis (née Roberts); thence to her great-niece Mrs. Vera G. Whiting, Purley, Surrey; given to Diane Johnson *c.*1973.

There is some difference of opinion amongst scholars whether both these bowls are French in origin. Dr Camille Leprince, an expert on French *faïence*, thinks the bowl on the left is Kütahya ware while the bowl to the right is from northern France, maybe Saint-Omer.[1] Italian majolica was imitated in early 16th-century France, where the term *faïence* was applied to this French tin-glazed earthenware."

233. *Study of a late 16th Century Iznik Dish or Plate*
c. mid-late 1890s; watercolour and ink on paper; 27 x 27 cm (10⅝ x 10⅝ in.) – sight; Diane Johnson collection, Paris.

Provenance: Wallis's studio and then by descent from the artist to his daughter-in-law Alice Julyan Wallis (née Roberts), and thence to her great-niece Mrs. Vera G. Whiting, Purley, Surrey; given to Diane Johnson *c.*1973.

The decoration of Iznik ceramics with a variety of real or fantastic animals began in the early decades of the 16th century. This plate probably dates from the end of the century, however, when its popularity began to increase. The animal iconography is primarily based on the metal art of the Balkan countries.

There is a ceramic bottle dating from the 17th century with a similar design in the collection of the British Museum (formerly in the collection of Frederick DuCane Godman).

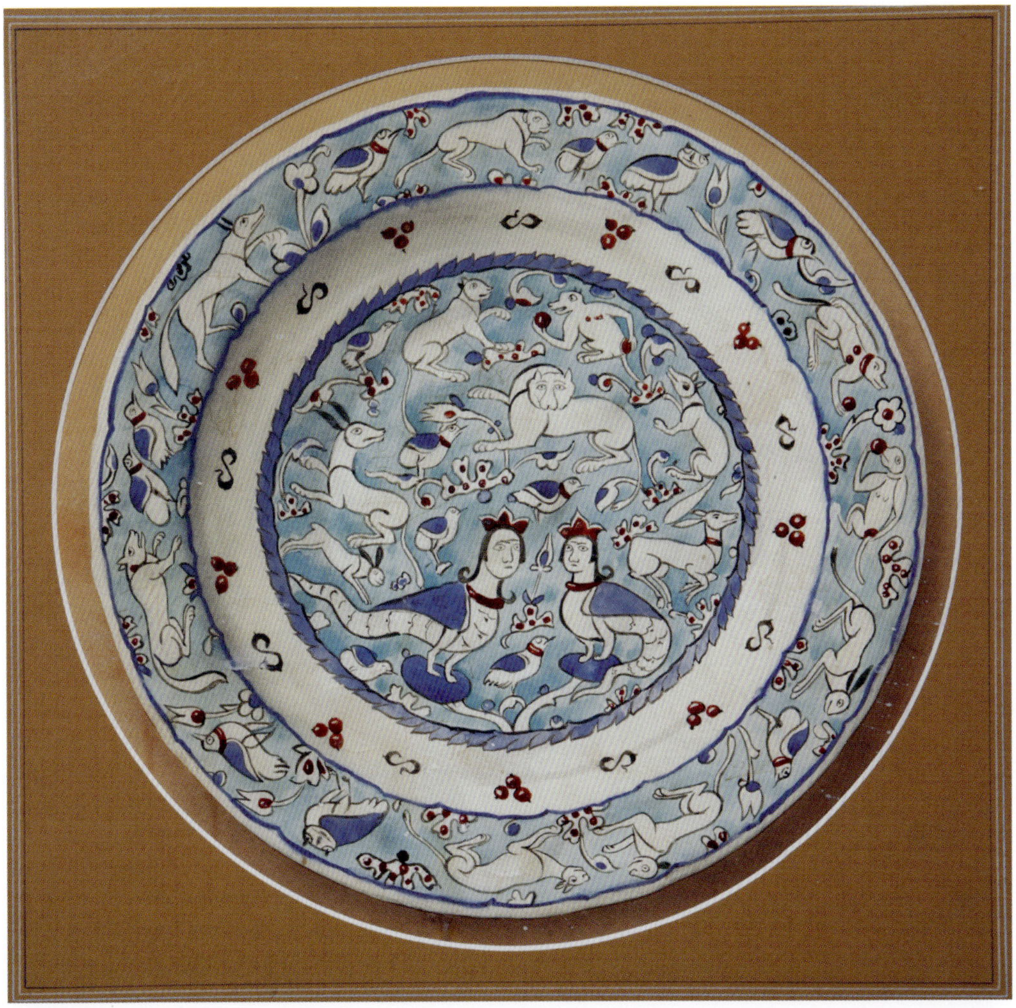

Cat. 233. Image courtesy Diane Johnson collection, Paris, photographer Alison Harris

Cat. 234. *The Door of a Mosque at Cairo*
1897; watercolour; 31 x 21 cm (12¼ x 8¼ in.); private collection.
Annotations: Inscribed with title and the artist's address on an old label on the recto.
Provenance: Wallis's studio and then by descent from the artist to his daughter-in-law Alice Julyan Wallis (née Roberts); thence to her great-niece Mrs. Vera G. Whiting, Purley, Surrey; her sale Sotheby's Belgravia, 10 April 1973, lot 202, bought by Hartnoll & Eyre, London; private collection.
Exhibitions: Old Water-Colour Society, Winter exhibition 1897, no. 25, asking price £42; Hartnoll & Eyre: Catalogue Thirty-Three, September 25 – October 12, 1973, no. 44.
Literature: *The Standard*, 26 November 1897, p.5; *The Morning Post*, 27 November 1897, p.4; *The Athenaeum*, No.3638, 4 December 1897, p.791.

F.G. Stephens, in *The Athenaeum*, wrote: "It is difficult to say whether Mr. Wallis's *Door of a Mosque, Cairo* (25) is more excellent

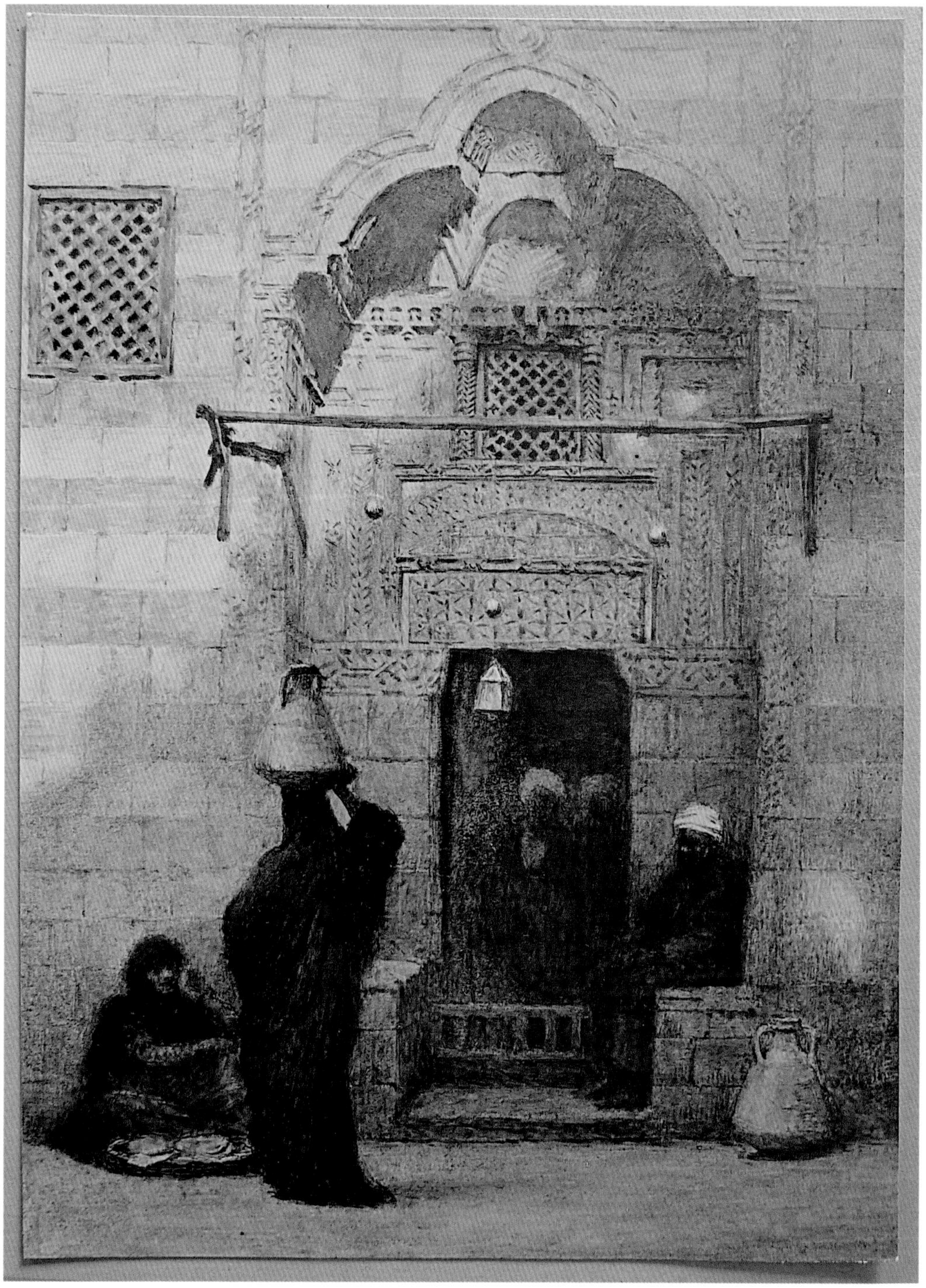

Cat. 234. Image courtesy of Julian Hartnoll, London

as a figure picture or as a powerful study of effect, colour, and light and shade. The group of sumptuously clad modern Egyptians is no doubt an important element of the background and, though in dignity or importance below the standard of the painter, it is a broad, homogeneous, and highly scientific work of art." The critic of *The Standard* suggested: "Mr. Henry Wallis is very tasteful in his 'Door of a Mosque, Cairo' where dark figures are seen against a background of salmon with points of turquoise." The reviewer for *The Morning Post* said: "A well-considered effect of light and shade, allied with richly varied colour, gives force to Mr. Henry Wallis's 'Door of a Mosque at Cairo'."

A watercolour heightened with bodycolour, entitled *A Mosque in Cairo*, sold at Sotheby's Belgravia on 6 May 1975, lot 7, 30 x 23.5 cm (11¾ x 9¼ in.), along with a pencil sketch for the same work. This might possibly be this watercolour but could be an entirely separate work.

Cat. 235. ***A Relic of the Native Quarter, Cairo***

1898; watercolour; dimensions unknown; whereabouts unknown.
Provenance: Bought by Alfred (?) Hay, 21 Fitz...[?Fitzjohn's] Avenue, London N.W. on 3 December 1898 for £26 5s.
Exhibitions: Old Water-Colour Society, Winter exhibition 1898, no. 76.
Literature: *The Times*, 3 December 1898, p.10; *Lloyd's Weekly Newspaper*, 4 December 1898, p.4; *Morning Post*, 9 December 1898, p.6; *The Athenaeum*, No. 3711, 10 December 1898, p.835.

F.G. Stephens in *The Athenaeum* remarked positively: "Mr. Wallis sends but one drawing, and only the last has kept up to his usual level of excellence. We turn to No. 76, *A Relic of the Native Quarter, Cairo*, the extremely brilliant and, so to say, thoroughly orientalized contribution of Mr. Wallis, which depicts with splendour, breadth, much force of tints, and intense contrasts of light and shade the vista of an Egyptian street in full sunlight. It is crowded with figures attired in strongly coloured robes." The reviewer for *Lloyd's Weekly Newspaper* stated: "...and Mr. Henry Wallis has one of his noble studies in 'A Relic of the Native Quarter, Cairo' the result being essentially Eastern, brilliant, and soft." *The Times* critic wrote: "There is one brilliant bit of Cairo from the ever-attractive brush of Mr. Henry Wallis, who revels as of old in Oriental colour (76)."

Cat. 236. ***A Street Corner in the Native Quarter, Cairo***

1899; watercolour; 40.6 x 30.5 cm. (16 x 12 in.); whereabouts unknown.
Exhibitions: Old Water-Colour Society, Winter exhibition 1899, no. 147.
Provenance: Bought at the O.W.S. exhibition by John Watson Knight,[1] 3 Hyde Park Square W., London, on 2 December 1899 for £26 5s; his estate sale Christie's, 27 February 1904, lot 66, bought by Leggatt,[2] for £27 6s.
Literature: *Morning Post*, 1 December 1899, p.2; *The Times*, 2 December 1899, p.13; *The Athenaeum*, No. 3763, 9 December 1899, p.807.

F.G. Stephens, in *The Athenaeum*, expressed the opinion: "In the forefront we may place Mr. H. Wallis's *Street Corner in the Native Quarter, Cairo* (147), a richly toned, luminous and harmoniously coloured view of white houses in sunlight." *The Times* critic noted: "In other regions than pure landscape we have an admirable little 'Street Corner in Cairo' (147), by Mr. Henry Wallis, jewel-like in colour."

Cat. 237. ***Outside the Bab-en-Nasir, Cairo***

1900; watercolour; dimensions unknown; whereabouts unknown.
Exhibitions: Old Water-Colour Society, 1900, no. 139.
Provenance: Bought by R. Corfield Bucknall,[1] 33 Prince's Gate S.W., London, on 27 April 1900 for £52 10s.
Literature: *The Times*, 27 April 1900 p.6; *Daily Telegraph & Courier*, 27 April 1900, p.5;

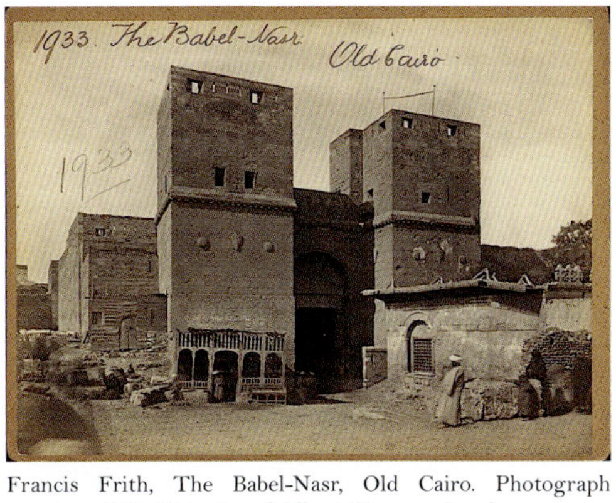

Francis Frith, The Babel-Nasr, Old Cairo. Photograph courtesy of the Victoria and Albert Museum, London, museum no. E.208:635-1994. See Cat. 237.

The Athenaeum, 5 May 1900, no 3874, p.569; *The Kentish Mercury*, 11 May 1900, p.3.

The Bab-en-Nasir must refer to the Bab al-Nasr (the Gate of Victory), one of the three remaining gates in the walls of the Old City of Cairo. This massive fortified gate has rectangular towers flanking the semicircular arch of the eastern portal.

F.G. Stephens, in *The Athenaeum*, wrote: "Mr. Henry Wallis's *Outside the Bab-en-Nasir, Cairo* (139) is one of the best of his powerfully painted Oriental street scenes, in which figures in dark and richly painted robes are placed against white walls, upon which the sunlight glows intensely. Practically, it contains no anecdote such as appeals to those who look on painting as a method of illustrating literature, but to lovers of art the vigour of Mr. Wallis's colouration, the force of his tones, and the wealth of high and harmonious keys of every kind must appeal strongly." The critic for *The Times* reported: "Standing quite by himself, and higher than ever, is Mr. Henry Wallis, whose 'Outside the Bab-en-Nasir, Cairo' (139) is a small drawing of great beauty and power. Some parts of it, especially the man in a brown dress against the white wall, reminds us of Decamps,[2] but Mr. Wallis has far greater fondness for positive colour than even Decamps had, and does not shrink from the reds, blues and greens which play such a large part in every Eastern street scene." The reviewer for the *Daily Telegraph & Courier* stated: " 'Outside the Bab-en-Nasir, Cairo,' by Mr. Henry Wallis, is a frank and brilliant exercise in the harmonizing of splendid Oriental hues, which is greatly wronged by being hung as it here is. If it were isolated, or more appropriately placed, the effect would be very different."

Cat. 238. *Bargaining, Cairo (An Arab Shoe Merchant Selling his Wares)*

1900; watercolour; 52 x 35.5 cm (20½ x 14 in); private collection.

Inscriptions: Signed and inscribed on a label on the verso.

Provenance: Wallis's studio and then by descent from the artist to his daughter-in-law Alice Julyan Wallis (née Roberts); thence to her great-niece Mrs. Vera G. Whiting, Purley, Surrey; her sale Sotheby's Belgravia, 10 April 1973, lot 206, bought by V. Friedman for £36; Christie's, 29 September 1978, lot 199, sold for £40;[1] private collection.

Exhibitions: Old Water-Colour Society, Winter exhibition 1900, no. 100; Manchester Art Gallery, *Exhibition of Water Colour Drawings*, Spring 1901, no. 34, N.F.S.

Literature: *London Evening Standard*, 29 November 1900, p.3; *The Times*, 30 November 1900, p.12; *The Athenaeum*, No. 3815, 8 December 1900, p.764; *The Lyle Official Arts Review*, 1979, p.451.

The critic in *The Athenaeum* wrote: "*Bargaining, Cairo* (100), and *The Door of a Mosque, Cairo* (118) by Mr. Wallis, both represent street scenes in intense sunlight, and are distinguished by technical power, yet we think the massive and powerful shadows are too hot, while the pictures lack some of Mr. Wallis's accustomed correctives, silveriness and breadth." The reviewer for *The Times* commented: "...while in figure subjects we have one or two brilliant bits of Oriental colour by Mr. Henry Wallis." The *London Evening Standard* critic wrote: "Mr. Henry Wallis is characteristic and certainly skilled in 'Bargaining Cairo'."

Cat. 239. *The Door of a Mosque, Cairo*

1900; watercolour; 50.8 x 35.5 cm (20 x 14 in.); whereabouts unknown.

Provenance: Bought on 30 November 1900 from the Old Water-Colour Society exhibition by R. Corfield Bucknall, 33 Prince's Gate S.W., London for £21; property of a gentleman; his sale Christie's, May 24, 1918, lot 52, bought by Bowden[1] for £27 6s.

Exhibitions: Old Water-Colour Society, Winter exhibition 1900, no. 118.

Literature: *The Times*, 30 November 1900, p.12; *The Kentish Mercury*, 7 December 1900, p.2; *The Athenaeum*, No. 3815, 8 December 1900, p.764.

[See: Cat. 238 for review in *The Athenaeum*]

Cat. 240. *The Gunsmith*

1901; watercolour; dimensions unknown; whereabouts unknown.

Exhibitions: Old Water-Colour Society, 1901, no. 31.

Literature: *The Times*, 1 May 1901, p.15.

There are no known contemporary descriptions of this watercolour.

Cat. 241. *The Courtyard of the House of Sheikh Abdullah: the Sheikh takes his Morning Coffee*

1901; watercolour; dimensions unknown; whereabouts unknown.

Provenance: Bought on 30 November 1900 by R. Corfield Bucknall, 33 Prince's Gate, London for £105 from the Old Water-Colour exhibition.

Exhibitions: Old Water-Colour Society, 1901, no. 90.

Literature: *The Pall Mall Gazette*, 27 April 1901, p.4; *Morning Post*, 29 April 1901, p.4; *The Times*, 1 May 1901, p.15.

The critic of *The Times* mentioned: "A painter who has of late years confined himself to Eastern scenes and subjects, Mr. Henry Wallis, sends two drawings, one of which, an Arab courtyard with figures, (90), literally glows with colour and light."

Cat. 242. *In the Bazaar, Suez*

1901; watercolour; dimensions unknown; whereabouts unknown.

Exhibitions: Old Water-Colour Society, Winter exhibition 1901, no. 14.

Literature: *The Times*, 5 December 1901, p.7.

The critic for *The Times* commented: "In other departments we notice a vivid bit of colour from Egypt, the work of Mr. Henry Wallis (14)."

Cat. 243. *Water Carriers, Old Cairo*

1902; watercolour; dimensions unknown; whereabouts unknown.

Exhibitions: Old Water-Colour Society, 1902, no. 147.

Some of the poorest Arab women were employed as water carriers to provide fresh water. Water vendors with goat skins filled with water and slung across their backs also provided water to thirsty travellers and patrons of the bazaars.

Cat. 244. *A Street in the Native Quarter, Cairo*

1902; watercolour; 37.5 x 26.7 mm (14¾ x 10½ in.); private collection.

Inscriptions: Signed and inscribed on a label on the verso with title and address 9 Beauchamp Road, Upper Norwood SE, where Wallis lived from 1895 to 1908.

Provenance: Wallis's studio and then by descent from the artist to his son Harold Wallis; then to his daughter-in-law Mary Wallis (née Mary Elizabeth Aymes); then her great-niece Vera G. Cooper (née Langley; 1910-1989); and thence by direct descent to John Harold Cooper and family;

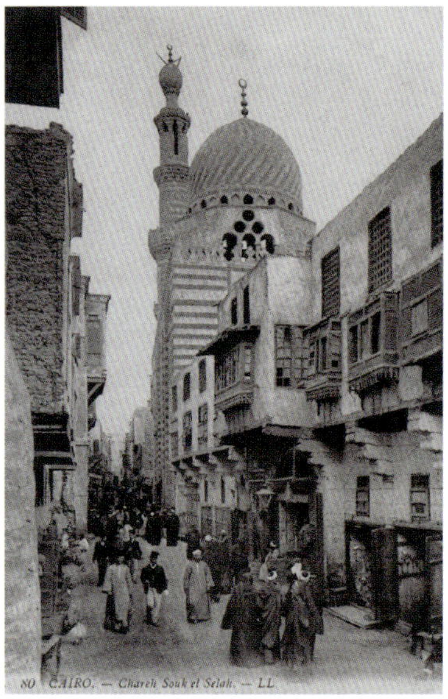

Photograph from Ben Mahmoud, *Le voyage en Orient 1850-1930*, 2008, p.103.

offered for sale at Bonhams, London, 5 March 2002, lot 75, bought in; Bonhams, London, 25 June, 2002, lot 96; Kent Auction Galleries Ltd., Folkestone, 30 June 2012, lot 100; private collection.
Exhibitions: Old Water-Colour Society, Winter exhibition 1902, no. 101.

A 19th-century photograph (left) identifies the location as Souk-el-Selah Street; the mosque in the background is clearly the same.[1]

There is a pencil study for the finished watercolour in a sketchbook held in the National Art Library at the Victoria and Albert Museum, MSL/1939/1948. The sketch, dated 5.11.93, contains all the architectural elements but omits the figures.

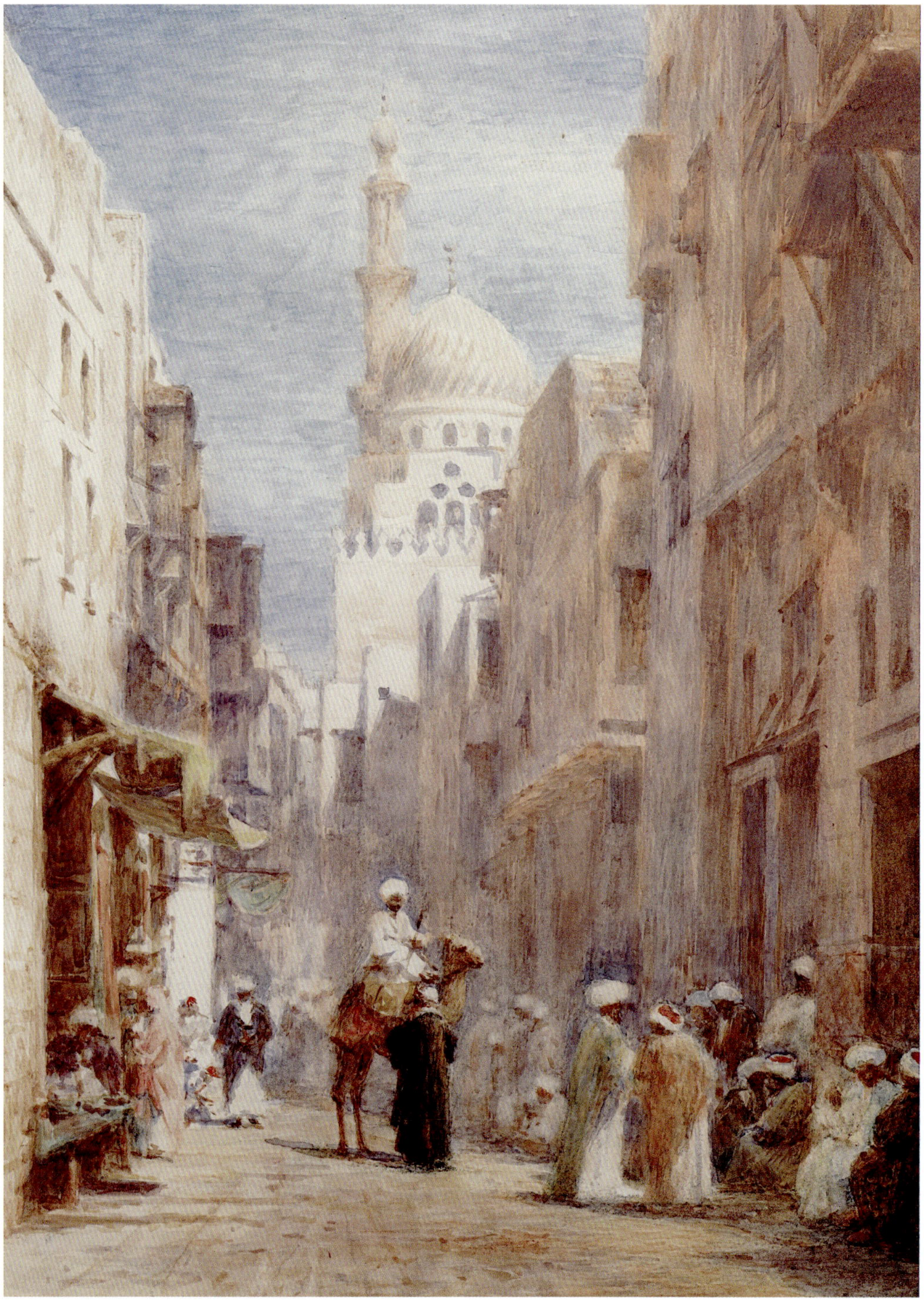

Cat. 244. Image courtesy of Bonhams, London

Cat. 245. ***An Ancient Highway at Syracuse***
1903; watercolour; dimensions unknown; whereabouts unknown.
Exhibitions: Old Water-Colour Society, 1903, no. 148.

A quotation from the O.W.S. exhibition catalogue stated: "In the time of antiquity the road led from Neapolis to the Great Theatre and the Temple of Apollo, it was then lined on either side with votive tablets let into the rock."

Cat. 246. ***Philae: the Hypaethral Temple ('Pharaoh's Bed')***[1]
1903; watercolour; 33 x 48.2 cm (13 3/4 x 19 3/4 in); private collection.
Inscriptions: Signed and inscribed on a label on the verso.
Provenance: Christie's, South Kensington, 3 October 1983, lot 48, sold for £420; private collection.
Exhibitions: Old Water-Colour Society, Winter exhibition 1903, no. 126.
Literature: Huish, Marcus B.: *British Water-Colour Art in the First Year of the Reign of King Edward the Seventh*, London 1904, p.184.

During the 1886-87 archeological excavation season, Wallis Budge, a curator at the British Museum, met Henry Wallis on several occasions. Budge reported: "Before I left Aswan for Wadi Halfah a company of Royal Engineers, under Captain Handcock, R.E., began to clear out some of the buildings on the Island of Philae, and they repaired many parts of the walls of the so-called 'Kiosk'. Several of the arches, by reason of the broken stones in them, were in imminent danger of collapsing, and many parts of the cornice had begun to crumble away, and large pieces of stone fell frequently. In the course of clearing the bases of the walls, Captain Handcock found many pieces of sculptured stone, which once formed parts of ancient buildings, and these he set aside for the British Museum."[2]

Wallis went several times to Philae, which he found to be a fascinating place; there are a number of drawings in his sketchbooks dated 1886 and 1893. In a letter to Frederic George Stephens, dated 9 January 1901, Wallis writes: "I came here mainly to see Philae before it is submerged, which there is every reason to expect it will be when the barrage is finished. And as the temples are built on sand – so I am informed – the result of constantly keeping them under water will probably be that they will collapse. I hope to get studies for a painting of the island: it has been done often but, perhaps, the fates being propitious, may yet

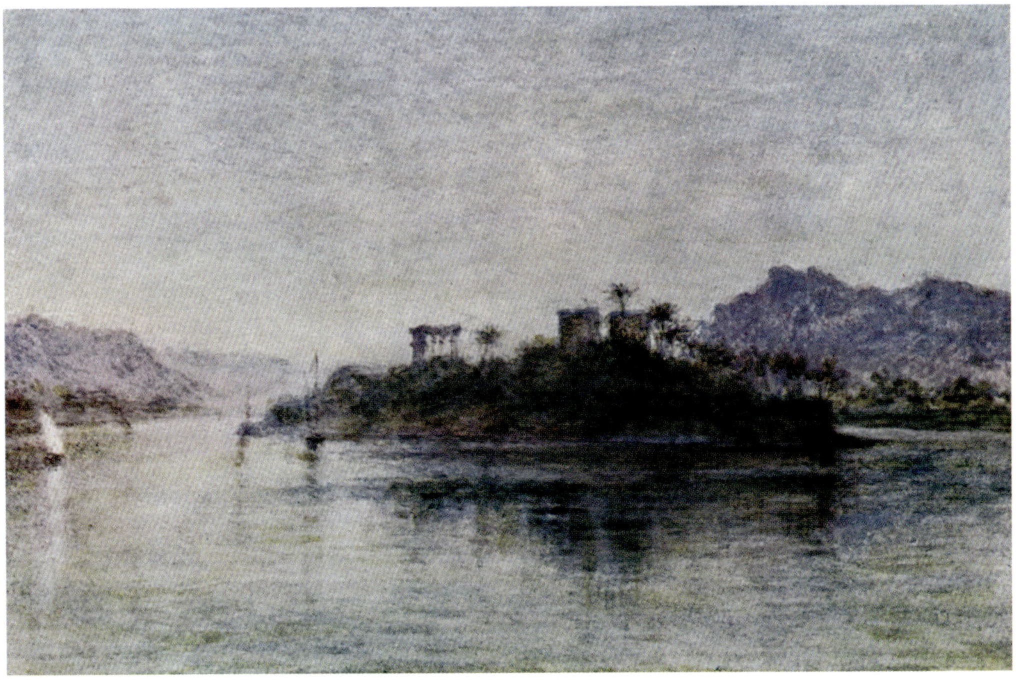

Cat. 246. Image from Marcus B. Huish, *British Water-Colour Art in the First Year of the Reign of King Edward the Seventh*, London, 1904, p.184

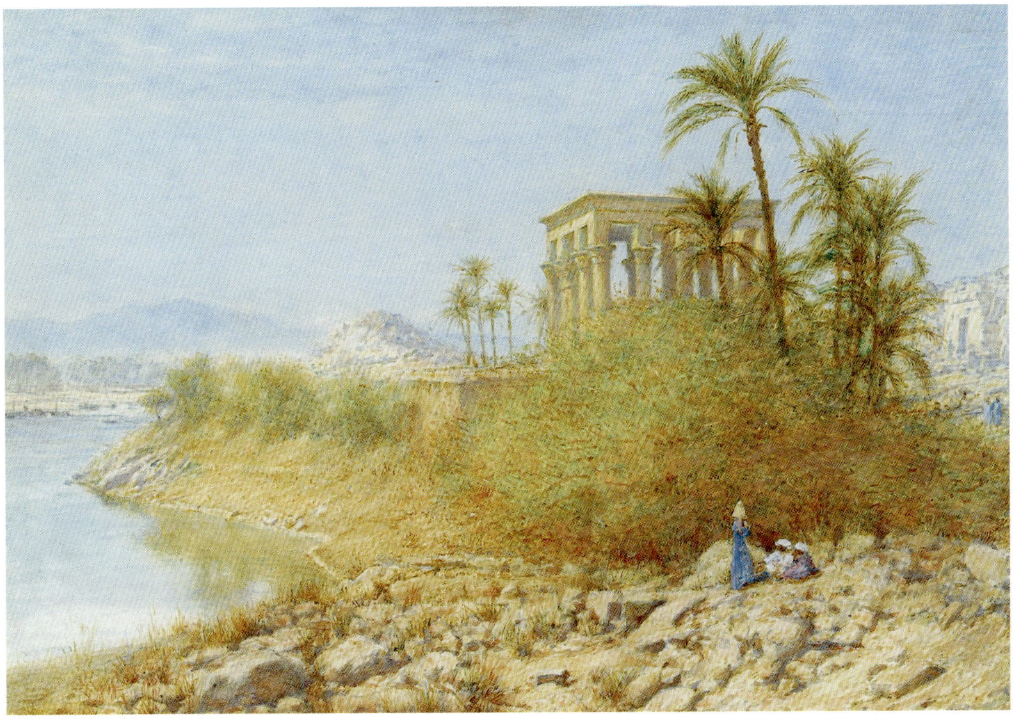

Cat. 247. Image courtesy of Dreweatts, Newbury.

be attempted again."[3] This watercolour and likely the next work seem to be the products of Wallis's intentions in this regard. During the 1960s, because of the building of the Aswan Dam, the temple was dismantled and moved to the island of Agilkia to prevent it being submerged by the rising levels of the Nile.

There is a pencil sketch dated 1.2.86 in one of Wallis's sketchbooks [See: Cat. 317].

Cat. 247. *Philae (attributed)*
*c.*1892; watercolour; 34 x 49 cm (13⅜ x 19¼ in); private collection.
Provenance: Dreweatts, Newbury, Berkshire, 8 December 2009, lot 29, sold for £400; private collection.

This work looks as if it could be an autograph watercolour by Wallis. In a letter to his son Harold, from Luxor aboard the S.S.*Memphis*, Wallis writes on 27 December 1892: "For beauty of scenery there is nothing more celebrated than the temple island of Philae just beyond the cataract at Aswan."[1]

Cat. 248. *A Street in Girgey,[1] Upper Egypt*
1904; watercolour; dimensions unknown; whereabouts unknown.
Exhibitions: Old Water-Colour Society, 1904, no. 101.
Literature: *The Architect and Contract Reporter*, 15 April 1904, p.250.

The reviewer for *The Architect and Contract Reporter* stated: "Mr. Wallis is one of the veterans of the Society. He contributes *A Street in Gorgey,* [*sic*] *Upper Egypt*, in which the white houses are occasionally varied by colour." In a letter to his son Harold, dated 21 March 1904, Wallis asks him to frame a drawing: "Please direct & post the enclosed to Messrs Harnell & Son. Frame makers. Lamb's Conduit St. W.C. & ask Mary to give them the drawing, wch is wrapped up in paper in the back drawing room. (It has a label on the back 'A street in Girgey, Upper Egypt')."[2]

Cat. 249. *In the Arab Quarter, Cairo*
1904; watercolour; 35.5 x 25.4 cm (14 x 10 in); private collection.
Inscriptions: Signed and inscribed on a label on the verso.
Provenance: Wallis's studio and then by descent from the artist to his son Harold Wallis; then to his daughter-in-law Mary Wallis (née Mary Elizabeth Aymes); then her great-niece Vera G. Cooper (née Langley; 1910-1989); and thence by direct descent to John Harold Cooper and family; sold at Bonhams, London, 5 March 2002, lot 73, sold for £1000; private collection.
Exhibitions: Old Water-Colour Society, Winter exhibition 1904, no. 288.
[Illustrated overleaf]

Wallis was clearly continuously fascinated by the streets of old Cairo and he wrote about them in the *Art Journal*: "At any point in those ancient streets in the old times, the painter could find materials for a picture, and materials intrinsically beautiful; masses of cool shade, brilliant passages of light, charming bits of decorative detail half hidden away, and often crowning the whole, and soaring in the sunshine, the shaft of some minaret, where elegant and fantastic forms meet in all sorts of unexpected combinations."[1]

Cat. 250. *Dahlias*
1905; watercolour; dimensions unknow; whereabouts unknown.
Exhibitions: Old Water-Colour Society, Winter exhibition 1905, no. 214.
Literature: *The Times*, 13 November 1905, p.4.

This work is a rare excursion by Wallis into the field of flower painting, which appears to have been successful. The critic of *The Times* noted: "For the rest, high praise is claimed by Mr. Henry Wallis's fine flower piece (214)."

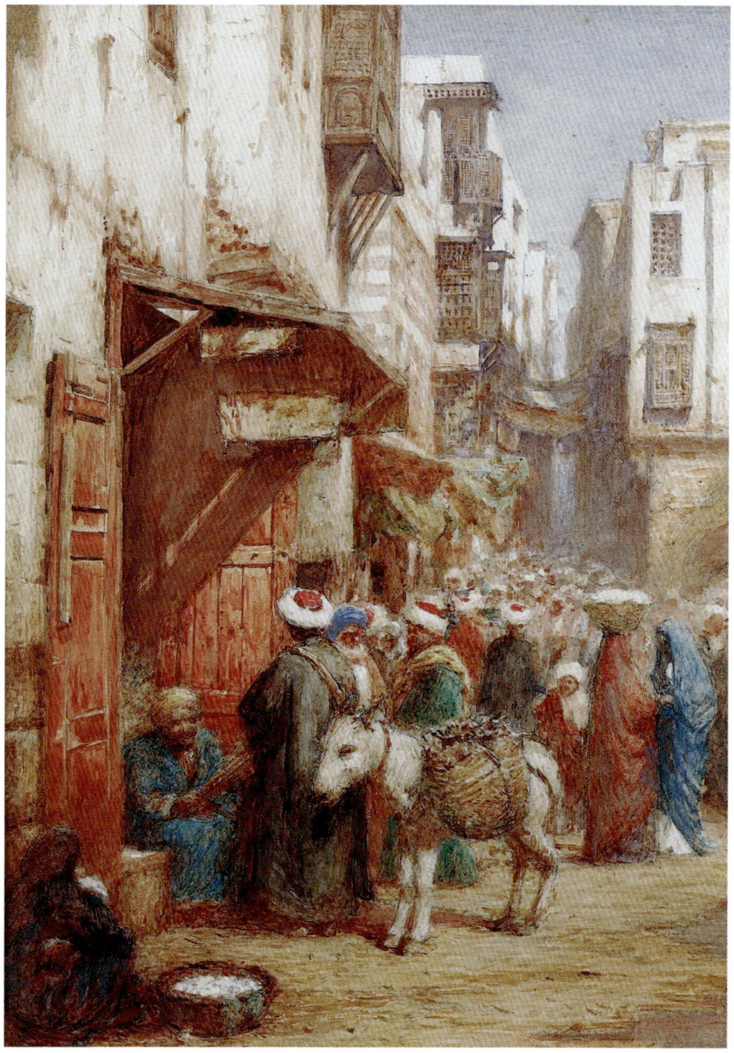

Cat. 249. Image courtesy of Bonhams, London

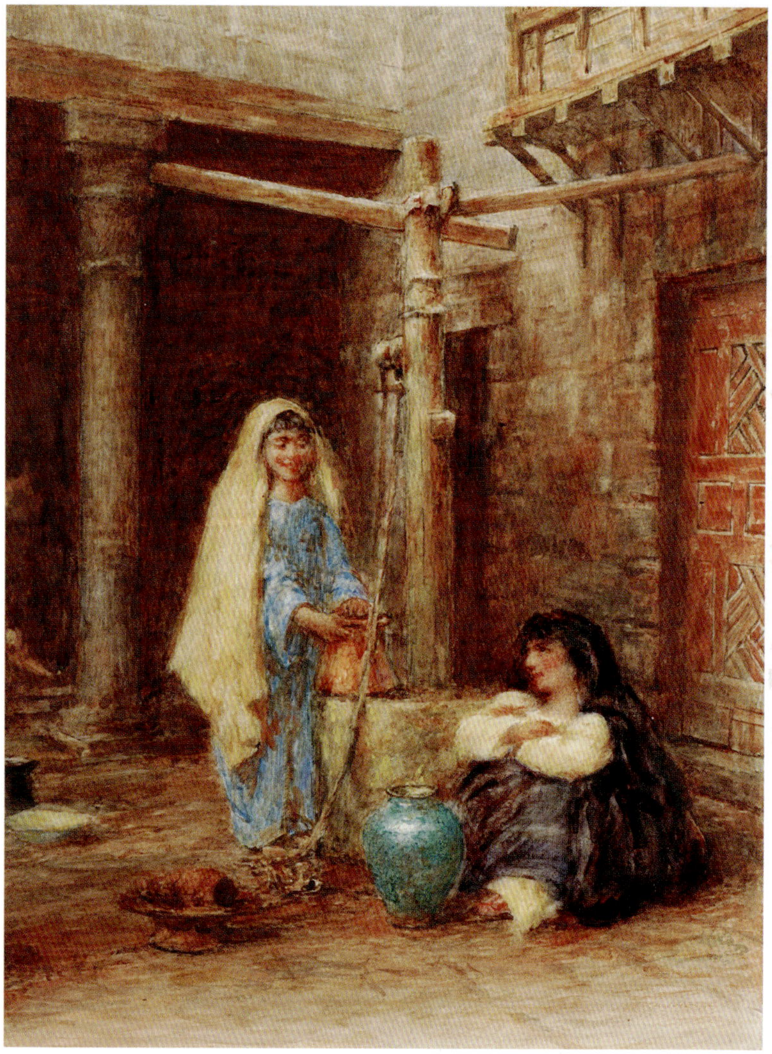

Cat. 252. Image courtesy of Bonhams, London

Cat. 251. ***A Vase of the Ming Dynasty (1368-1643)***
1907; watercolour; dimensions unknown; whereabouts unknown.
Exhibitions: Old Water-Colour Society, Winter exhibition 1907, no. 312.

It is uncertain whether the Ming dynasty vase depicted was ever part of Wallis's collection. Though Wallis himself never sold a Chinese vase to the V&A, his son Harold sold one from the collection showing Chinese influences in 1920.[1] This vase had been acquired in Sicily and was undoubtedly an item influenced by the large medieval export trade from the east. On 5 March 2002, 13 Chinese items from Wallis's collection that had been handed down through the family were sold at Bonhams, lot 70; it is also possible that the Ming vase was among these items.[2]

Cat. 252. ***Courtyard of a House in the Native Quarter, Cairo***
1908; watercolour; 33 x 24.1 cm (13 x 9½ in); private collection.
Inscriptions: Signed and inscribed on a label on the verso.
Provenance: Wallis's studio and then by descent from the artist to his son Harold Wallis; then to his daughter-in-law Mary Wallis (née Mary Elizabeth Aymes); then her great-niece Vera G. Cooper (née Langley; 1910-1989); and thence by direct descent to John Harold Cooper and family; offered for sale at Bonhams, London, 5 March 2002, lot 74, bought in; Bonhams, London, 25 June 2002, lot 95, sold for £500; private collection.
Exhibitions: Old Water-Colour Society, Winter exhibition 1908, no. 300.
Even as late as 1908 Wallis was was still painting Orientalist watercolours, which he exhibited at the O.W.S. This is a rather typical example showing two women working and resting in the architectural setting of a courtyard in Cairo.

Cat. 253. ***Amphora Shaped Glass Toilet Vase with Cameo Ornament – Roman period***
1911; watercolour; dimensions unknown; whereabouts unknown.
Exhibitions: Old Water-Colour Society, Winter exhibition 1911, no. 374.
Literature: *The Times*, 3 November 1911, p.10.

The reviewer for *The Times* commented: "Lastly Mr. Henry Wallis, one of the veterans of the Society, shows true artistic qualities, as well as extreme dexterity, in his beautiful little drawing of a small Roman vase (374)."

Cat. 254. Two studies *Blue Glass Vase – Roman period*
1912; watercolour; dimensions unknown; whereabouts unknown.
Exhibitions: Old Water-Colour Society, 1912, no. 180.

A quotation from the O.W.S. exhibition catalogue states: "The iridescent colour has come from the contact of the surface with damp soil. Found in excavations at Ancona." It should be noted that two studies of Roman blue glass vases, attributed to Wallis, sold at Keys auctions, Aylsham saleroom, 27 April 2007, lot 1, both 5½ x 3½ in.

Cat. 255. ***Arranging the Flowers***
Date unknown; oil on board; 35.5 x 29.2 cm (14 x 11½ in.); private collection.
Inscriptions: Inscribed on the reverse

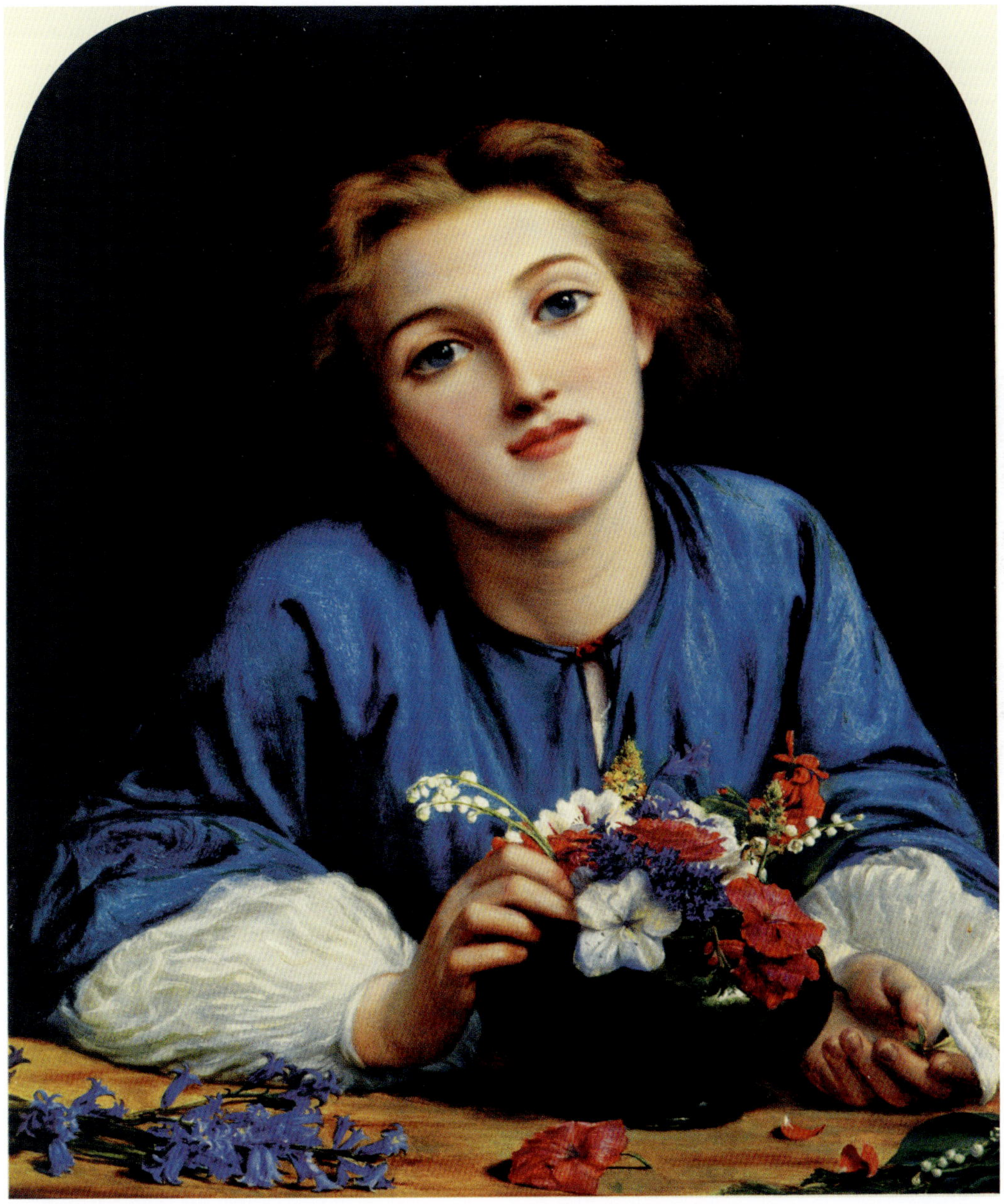

Cat. 255. Image courtesy Sotheby's, London

according to the 1988 Sotheby's catalogue.
PROVENANCE: Major F.G. Hill, O.B.E., Belfast; his sale Christie's, London, 17 November 1933, lot 125, bought by Field for £5 5s; anonymous sale, Sotheby's Belgravia, 15 December 1981, lot 239; anonymous sale, Sotheby's, London, 14 December 1988, lot 180, bought by Julian Hartnoll, London for £1,430; sold to John Schaeffer, Sydney, Australia; his sale Christie's, Sydney, 15 May 2004, lot 62, as *Young Girl with Flowers*, for 13,000 Australian dollars (£5,116); anonymous sale Sotheby's, New York, 20 April 2005, lot 78, bought in.

Although this painting has been accepted as an autograph work by Wallis by a major auction house and by a prominent dealer in Victorian art, this work appears rather unusual in Wallis's oeuvre. It is an oil painting, suggesting a date likely from the 1870s rather than later, and shows a young woman in rather Aesthetic dress arranging flowers. We would feel more confident in the attribution if we had images of other Wallis paintings of young women to compare it to such as *A Neapolitan Girl*, *A Girl of Capri*, *An English Girl* and *Teresa*.

Cat. 256. *Portrait of a Little Girl*
Date unknown; oil on panel; 23 x 17.5 cm (9 by 7 in); private collection.
PROVENANCE: Wallis's studio and then by descent from the artist to his daughter-in-law Alice Julyan Wallis (née Roberts); thence to her great-niece Mrs. Vera G. Whiting, Purley, Surrey; her sale Sotheby's Belgravia, 10 April 1973, lot 190, bought by Abbott & Holder for £26.

This work is described in the Sotheby's sales catalogue as a sketch. It was unusual for Wallis to do portraits of someone he did not know well, so perhaps it was a family member or the daughter of a close friend. It remained in the family until the 1970s. The Diane Johnson papers in the Harry Ransom Center refer to "a drawing of girl in Hat" in the collection of Vera Whiting, which may relate to this sketch.

Cat. 257. *Portrait of a Lady, said to be Mrs William Morris, in a Historical Costume*
*c.*1860-70s; oil on canvas; 58.5 x 49 cm (23 by 19¼ in.); private collection.
PROVENANCE: Wallis's studio and then by descent from the artist to his daughter-in-law Alice Julyan Wallis (née Roberts); thence to her great-niece Mrs. Vera G. Whiting, Purley, Surrey; her sale Sotheby's Belgravia, 10 April 1973, lot 188, bought by G. Sumner for £70.

It was suggested in the Sotheby's Belgravia sales catalogue from 1973 that Jane had modelled for Wallis for this painting, though some scholars question this. Although the model certainly does bear a resemblance to Jane Morris, she does not have the thick wavy hair with which Rossetti always portrayed Jane and that is so obvious in contemporary photographs of her. The second major concern is that this is a picture of a model in a historical costume. Other than Morris, Rossetti and, very early on, Burne-Jones, Jane is not known to have modelled for pictures by other painters.[1] Jane did sit for a number of artists later in life for portraits, including Evelyn De Morgan and Charles March Gere, which show her clad in her characteristic artistic dress, and with her easily recognisable hair. Wallis obviously knew Morris, but the majority of known letters from Morris to Wallis date from 1880 and relate to the S.P.A.B. There is a surviving letter from Morris to Wallis from as early 1867, however, [See: Cat. 266] and a letter from Morris to Charles Fairfax Murray from 1874 mentions Morris

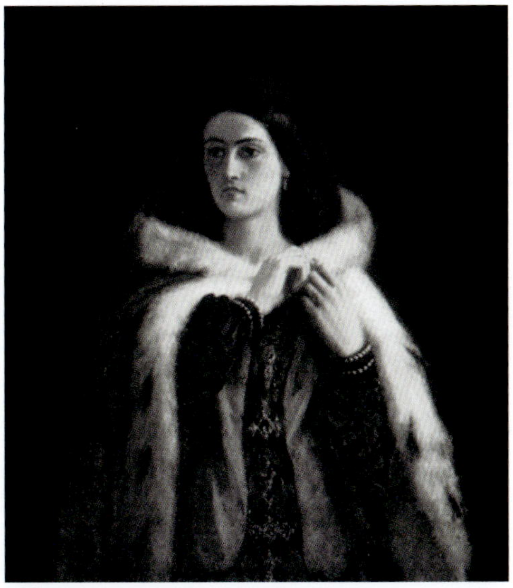

Cat. 257. Image courtesy of Sotheby's, London

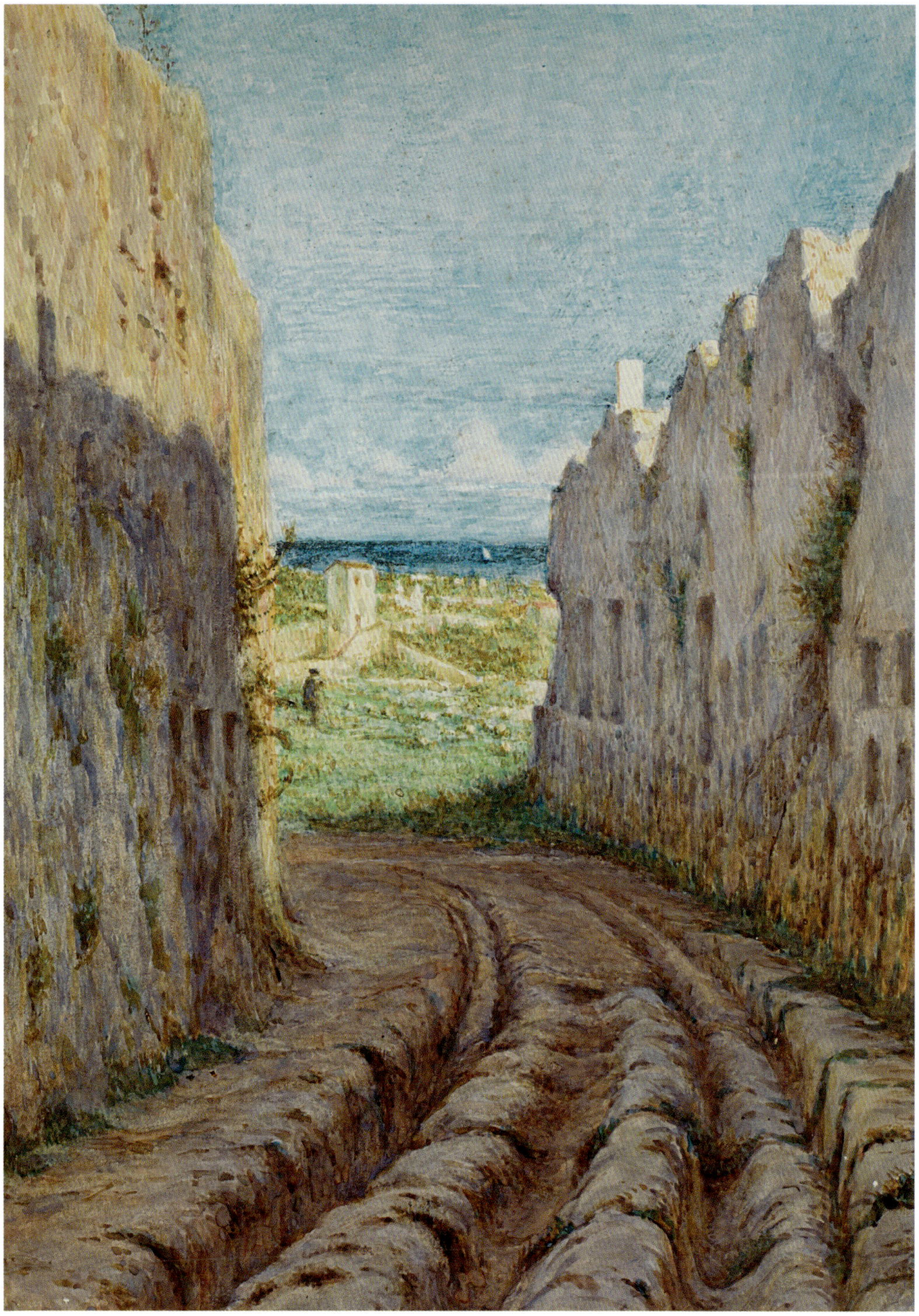

Cat. 261. Image courtesy Harry Moore-Gwyn auctions

dining at a tavern with Burne-Jones, Webb, Stanhope and Wallis.[2] The painting by Wallis is not a formal portrait of Jane Morris but is a "fancy" picture. Although Jane cannot entirely be ruled out as the model for this painting, it seems unlikely.

Cat. 258. ***A Sailing Ship Becalmed at Sunset***
Date unknown; oil on board; 25.5 x 46 cm (10 by 18 in.); private collection.
Provenance: Wallis's studio and then by descent from the artist to his daughter-in-law Alice Julyan Wallis (née Roberts); thence to her great-niece Mrs. Vera G. Whiting, Purley, Surrey; her sale Sotheby's Belgravia, 10 April 1973, lot 189, bought by Abbott & Holder for £26; private collection.

Cat 259. ***A View of a Lake at Dusk with Trees and a Village Beyond***
Date unknown; watercolour; 14 x 25 cm (5½ x 9¾ in.); private collection.
Provenance: Wallis's studio and then by descent from the artist to his daughter-in-law Alice Julyan Wallis (née Roberts); thence to her great-niece Mrs. Vera G. Whiting, Purley, Surrey; her sale Sotheby's Belgravia, 10 April 1973, part of lot 211, bought by Abbott & Holder for £65; private collection.

Cat 260. ***A View of a City Bridge by Night***
Date unknown; watercolour; 16 x 23 cm (6¼ x 9 in.); private collection.
Provenance: Wallis's studio and then by descent from the artist to his daughter-in-law Alice Julyan Wallis (née Roberts); thence to her great-niece Mrs. Vera G. Whiting, Purley, Surrey; her sale Sotheby's Belgravia, 10 April 1973, part of lot 211, bought by Abbott & Holder for £65; private collection.

This might be a study for *The Bridge of Sighs* shown at the Liverpool Academy in 1858 or it could be a totally unrelated work.

Cat. 261. ***A Street in Pompeii, with a Shepherd Beyond***
*c.*1891-1908; watercolour and crayon on paper; 51 x 35.5 cm (20 x 14 in.); private collection.
Provenance: Wallis's studio and then by descent from the artist to his daughter-in-law Alice Julyan Wallis (née Roberts); thence to her great-niece Mrs. Vera G. Whiting, Purley, Surrey; her sale Sotheby's Belgravia, 10 April 1973, lot 215, bought by N. Drummond for £42; anonymous sale Harry Moore-Gwyn auctions, London, October 25, 2017, lot 38, bought in; subsequently purchased by Jane Cohen, London for £550.
Exhibitions: Harry Moore-Gwyn, *British Pictures*, Catalogue Nine, Summer Exhibition 2005, Cat. 30, price £1900.

Although his work is difficult to date precisely, stylistically this watercolour was obviously executed later in Wallis's career. Wallis was frequently in nearby Naples, from as early as 1857, and is known to have visited Naples at least eight times between 1889 and 1908. Considering his interest in archaeological sites, Wallis undoubtedly visited Pompeii many times.

Cat. 262. ***The Pharmacy***
*c.*1885-1905; watercolour; 43.2 x 58.6 cm (17 by 23⅛ in.); private collection.
Inscriptions: Signed with initials *H.W.*
Provenance: Anonymous sale, Christie's, London, 19 June 1992, lot 81, sold for £6,050; Mathaf Gallery, London; private collection.
This is a highly accomplished watercolour, and one that Wallis might logically have been expected to show at the Old Water-Colour Society; however, it does not match any known exhibited work. Curiously, it is of higher quality than some of his works known to have been exhibited there. It is possible that *The Pharmacy* may not be its original title.

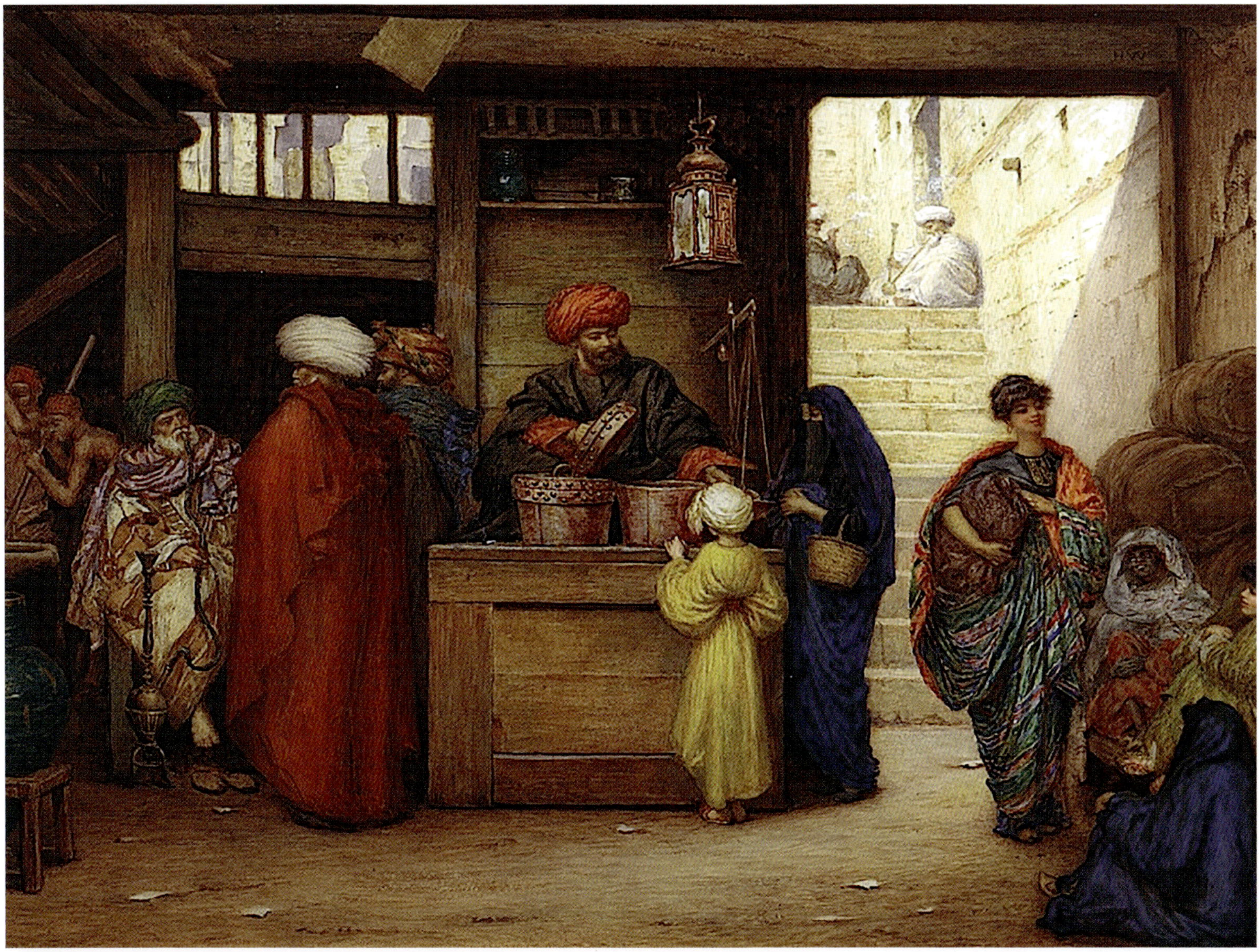

Cat. 262. Private collection. Image courtesy of Mathaf Gallery, London

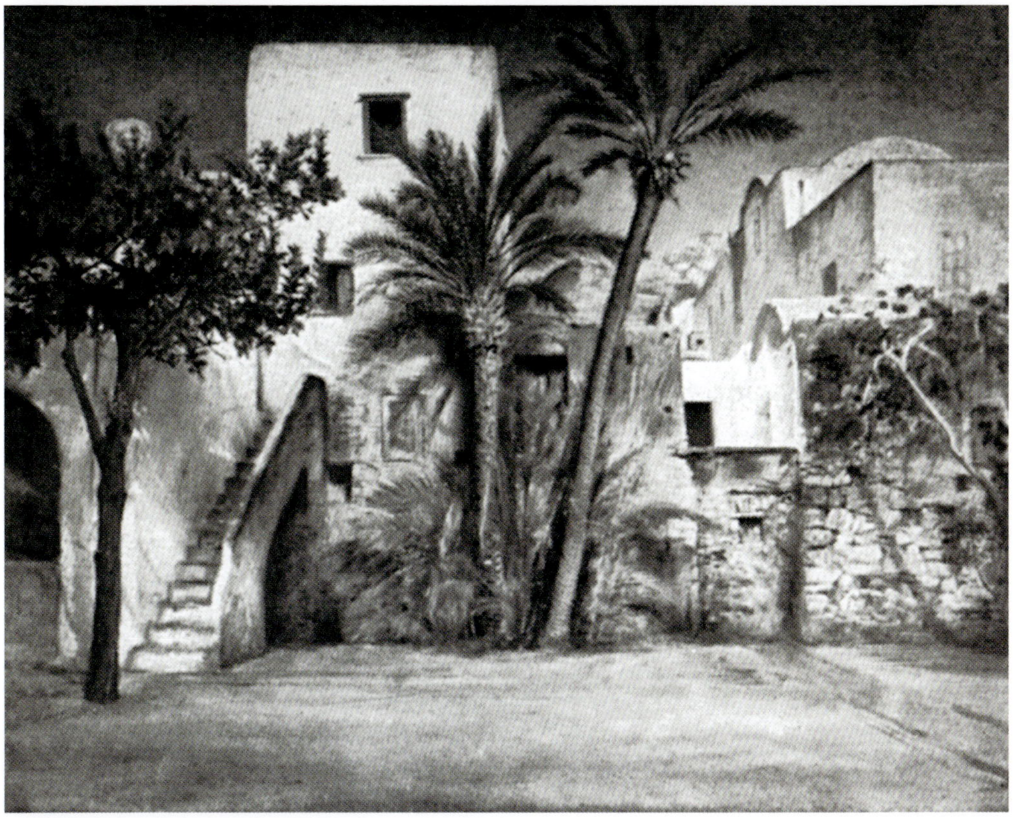

Cat. 263. Image courtesy of Sotheby's, London

Cat. 263. *A Village Square in North Africa, with Palm Trees and an Orange Tree*
*c.*1885–1905; oil on panel; 37.5 x 46 cm (14¾ x 18 in.); private collection.
PROVENANCE: Wallis's studio and then by descent from the artist to his daughter-in-law Alice Julyan Wallis (née Roberts); thence to her great-niece Mrs. Vera G. Whiting, Purley, Surrey; her sale Sotheby's Belgravia, 10 April 1973, lot 197, bought by Sorensen for £90.

Cat 264. *The Chrysanthemum Seller*
Date unknown; coloured chalks; 83.2 x 50.8 cm (33 x 20 in.); whereabouts unknown.
PROVENANCE: Christie's, London, July 3, 1922, lot 29, bought by Nicoll,[1] for £2 2s.

Cat. 265. *Fresh Herring*
Date unknown; drawing; 31.8 x 26.7 cm (12½ x 10½ in.); whereabouts unknown.
PROVENANCE: W.S. Hastings, 'Parham', No. 2, The Grange, Wimbledon; his estate sale Christie's, London, July 20, 1923, lot 29, bought by William Walker Sampson of W.W. Sampson & Sons, London for £12 12s.

Sheets from Sketchbooks

Cat. 266. *Studies of Armour*
*c.*1870s; pencil and white chalk on brown wove paper; 9.4 x 13.1 cm. (3¾ x 5⅛ in.); British Museum, London.
Inscriptions: upper right in graphite: *Helmut time Henry 8* -- ; lower left corner: *Jousting Helmut*; beside basket hilt: *Qui[l] lons*; in elbow of arm: *Car*(indecipherable).
Provenance: Wallis's studio and then by descent from the artist to his son Harold Wallis; then to his daughter-in-law Mary Wallis (née Mary Elizabeth Aymes); then to her great-niece Vera G. Cooper (née Langley; 1910-1989); thence by direct descent to John Harold Cooper and family; their sale Bonhams, London, 5 March 2002, part of lot 71, bought by Neil Wilson of Campbell Wilson, Hove, East Sussex; purchased by Douglas E. Schoenherr, Ottawa, Canada on 31 October 2003; given to the British Museum, London, in 2017, museum no. 2017,7020.9.

This study of armour, two helmets, the pommel of a sword, a sabaton, and a gauntlet and vambrace comes from a dismembered sketchbook, the sheets of which were sold separately by the dealer Campbell Wilson in 2003; *Studies of an [écorché] anatomical figure* [Cat. 267] comes from the same sketchbook. Though there was no date on any page of the broken-up sketchbook, the owner, retired art historian Douglas Schoenherr, is convinced that the drawings are not the work of a student. The study of armour in Cat. 288 might relate to this drawing as well.

It would be tempting to think that these studies of armour might be dated as far back as 1867. At that time Wallis wanted to borrow William Morris's suit of armour, as we learn in a letter from Morris dated 27 April 1867: "You are very welcome to borrow my armour with the rather startling proviso that I don't know where it is – however this is for your warrant to Hughes or others, - only fisticuffs to be avoided, it is not respectable; and you can't expect that any body who has had my armour for say 8 years can think it belongs to any body except himself."[1] Morris's armour, which he designed himself and had fabricated by a local blacksmith in Oxford in 1857,[2] would have been medieval in nature; the armour portrayed in this drawing is later, from the time of Henry VIII according to the inscription. Wallis probably studied it from one of the great London collections of arms and armour such as the Wallace Collection or the Royal Armouries in the Tower of London.

Cat. 267. *Studies of an Écorché Anatomical Drawing*
*c.*1870s; pen and brown ink over traces of graphite, heightened with white chalk, on light brown wove paper; two adjoining sketchbook pages height; 9.7 x 27.3 cm. (3⅞ x 10¾ in.); private collection.
Provenance: Wallis's studio and then by descent from the artist to his son Harold Wallis; then to his daughter-in-law Mary Wallis (née Mary Elizabeth Aymes); then her great-niece Vera G. Cooper (née Langley; 1910-1989); and thence by direct descent to John Harold Cooper and family; their sale Bonhams, London, 5 March 2002, part of lot 71, bought by Neil Wilson of Campbell Wilson, Hove, East Sussex;

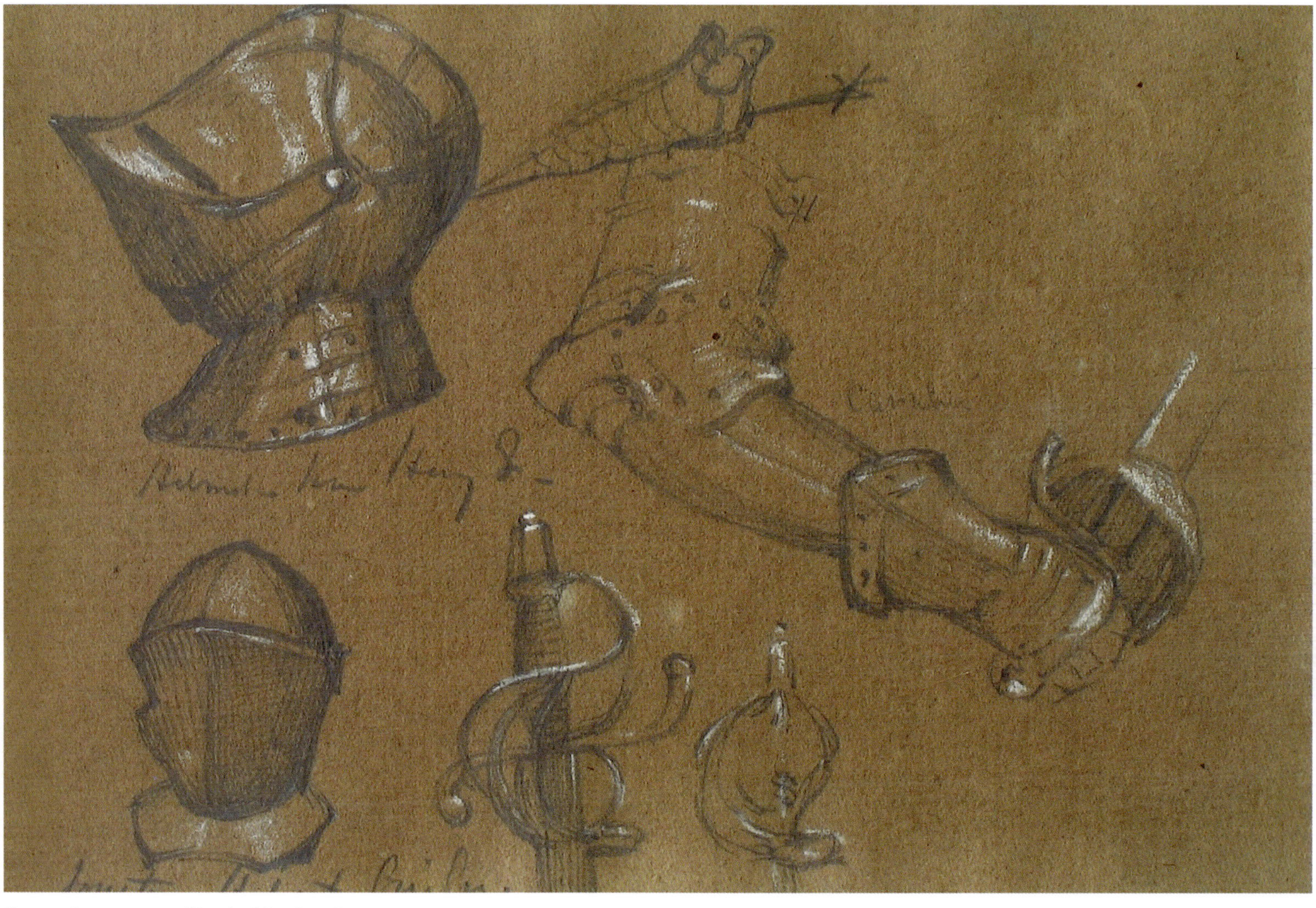

Cat. 266. Image courtesy of Douglas Schoenherr, Ottawa

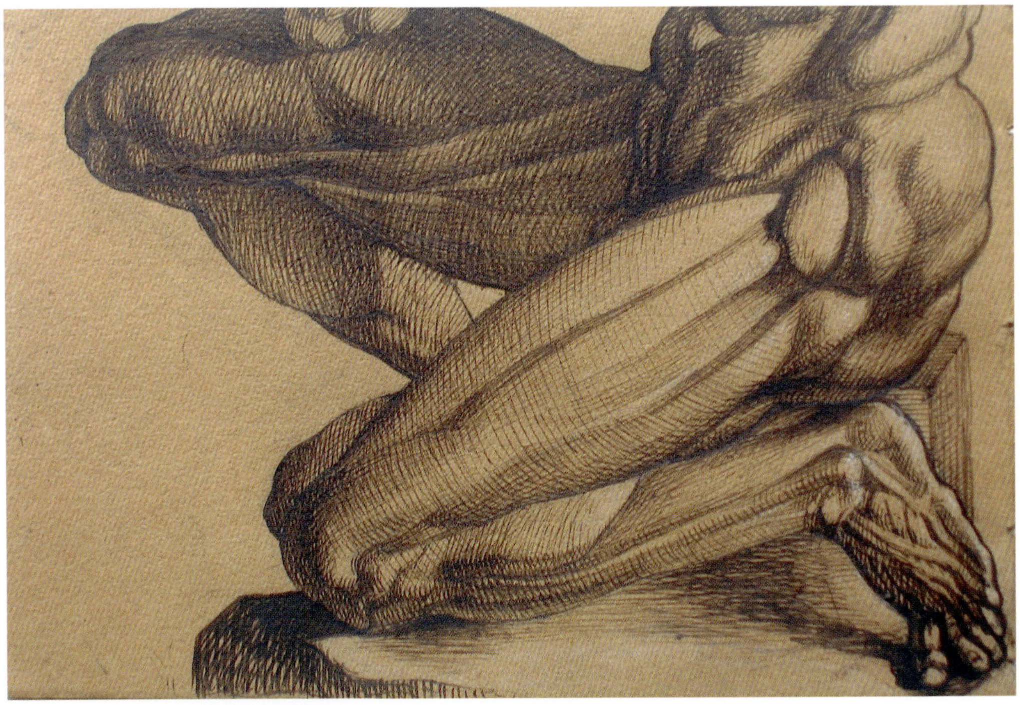

Cat. 267. Recto. Image courtesy of Douglas Schoenherr, Ottowa

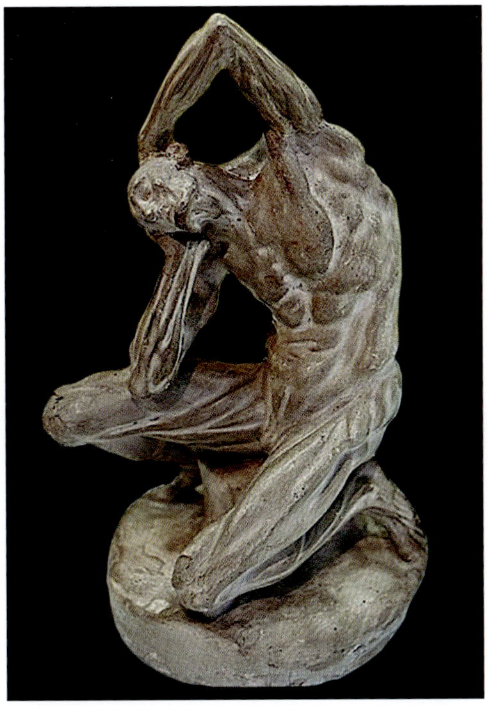

See Cat. 267. Plaster cast of the kneeling écorché figure. Image courtesy of Van Gogh Museum, Amsterdam

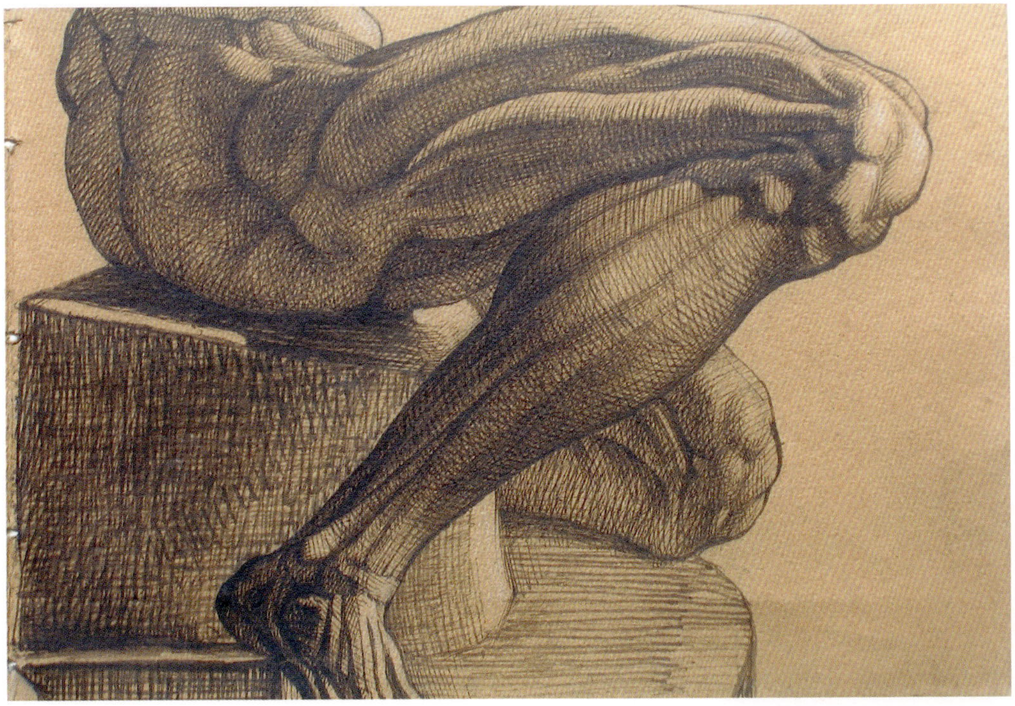

Cat. 267. Recto. Image courtesy of Douglas Schoenherr, Ottowa

purchased by Douglas E. Schoenherr, Ottawa, Canada on 4 October 2003.

This double page [recto and verso] comes from the same dismembered sketchbook as the previous drawing, *Studies of an Armour* [Cat 266]. These studies also appear too accomplished to be those of a student – especially on the recto pages, which suggest knowledge of Leonardo's anatomical drawings. It is not known when and where the drawings were made, but Dr. Schoenherr suggests that the studies on the left page of the verso seem to be from paintings or frescoes, possibly in Italy. Certainly other sheets from the same sketchbook can be identified as having been drawn in Italy. The study on the far left possibly represents a River God and that of a flying figure

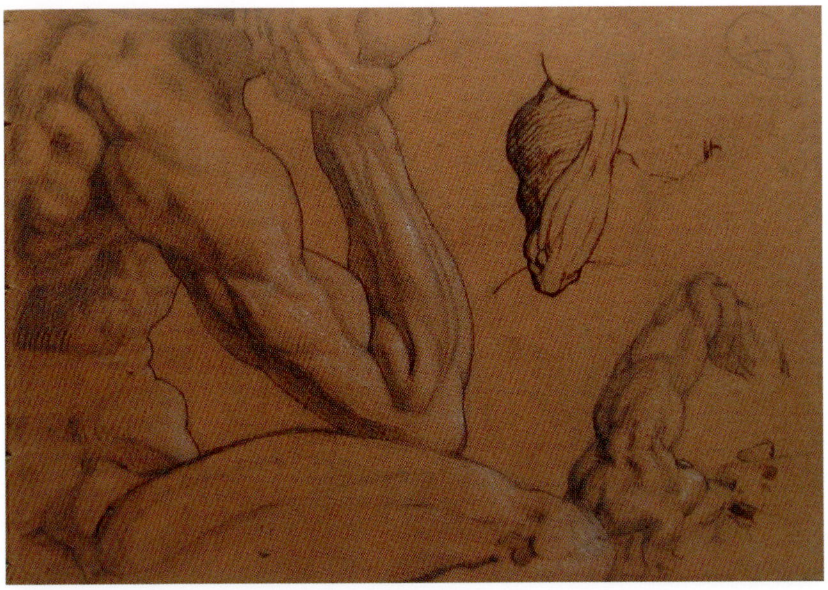

Cat. 267. Verso. Image courtesy of Douglas Schoenherr, Ottowa

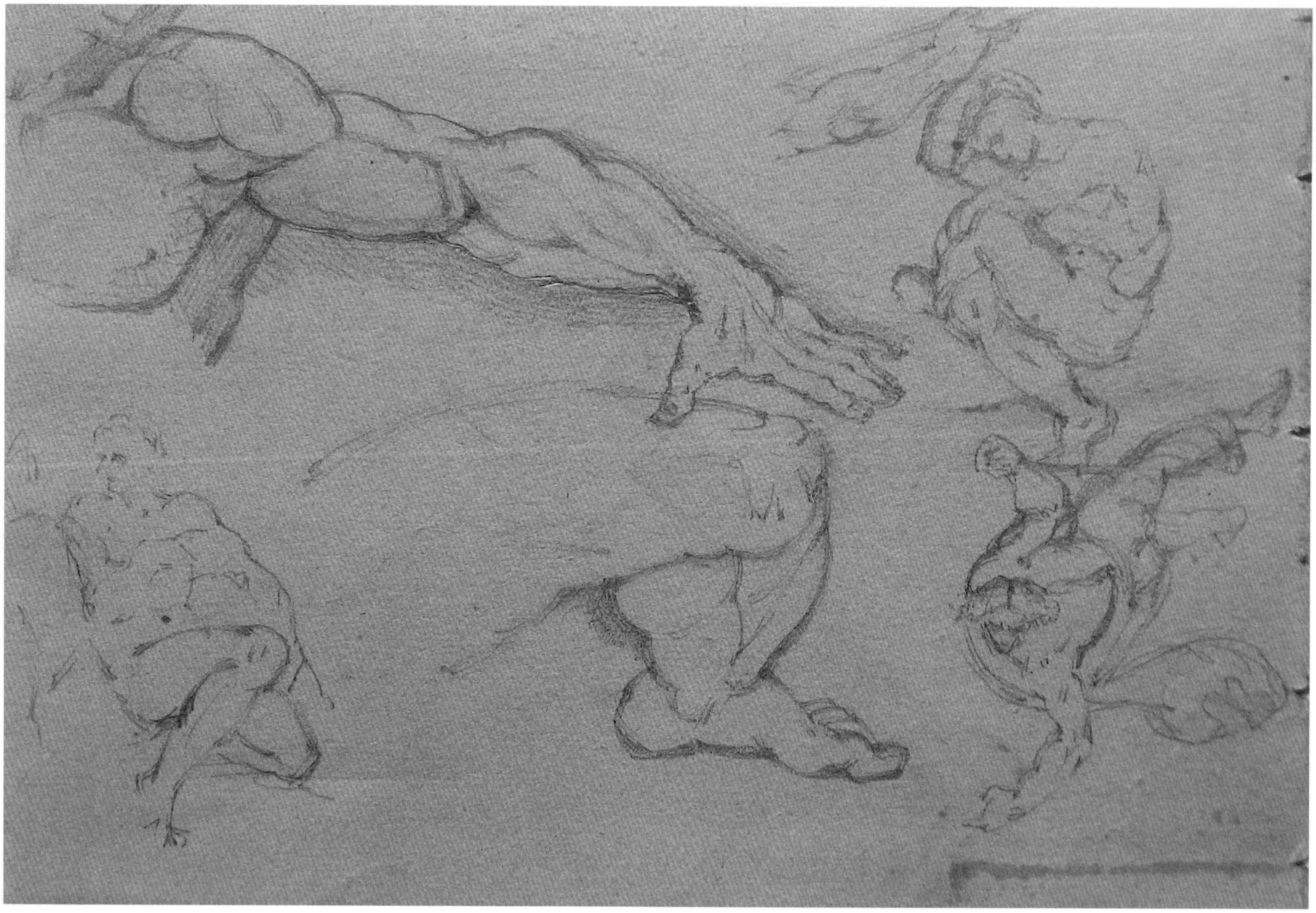

Cat. 267. Verso. Image courtesy of Douglas Schoenherr, Ottowa

descending on the right. A date from the first half of the 1870s might make sense as this was a period during which Wallis was fascinated by Italian art. It seems odd, however, that the drawings suggest Leonardo, for there is no evidence to suggest that Leonardo was one of Wallis's favourite Renaissance artists, who instead appears to have favoured Carpaccio, Luca Signorelli and Melozzo da Forlì.

No *écorché* specimens were available for study at the Royal Academy Schools during the time Wallis was a student there.[1] Such prepared specimens would, however, have been available for study in the 1870s at the medical school associated with St. George's Hospital. Wallis's drawings, however, were most likely drawn from a plaster cast of an écorché specimen that were used as early as the 17th and 18th centuries and were available in many arts schools during the 19th century. Wallis likely encountered such a cast during his training in Paris. Van Gogh, for instance, is known to have made a drawing of such a plaster cast in Paris in 1887.[2] Wallis illustrates an example of such an écorché sculpture in the middle left of his painting from 1857 entitled *A Sculptor's Workshop, Stratford-upon-Avon,* AD *1617*. This drawing, therefore, might have been executed much earlier in Wallis's career.

In Wallis's sketch, he is drawing while moving around the figure, and also on the verso. On the recto he is concentrating on the legs, one knee raised, one lowered, sitting on a square block with rounded base with an elbow on one knee. On the verso he shows more of the upper body, but omits the dramatically contorted raised elbow.[3]

Cat. 268. *Drawing of the Mona Lisa del Giocondo*

*c.*1870s; graphite on paper; 13.6 x 9.7 cm. (5⅜ x 3⅞ in.); verso – faint study of a draped standing female figure; private collection.

Provenance: Wallis's studio and then by descent from the artist to his son Harold Wallis; then to his daughter-in-law Mary Wallis (née Mary Elizabeth Aymes); then her great-niece Vera G. Cooper (née Langley; 1910-1989); thence by direct descent to John Harold Cooper and family; their sale Bonhams, London, 5 March 2002, part of lot 71, bought by Neil Wilson of Campbell Wilson, Hove, East Sussex; purchased by Scott Thomas Buckle, London, from the Olympia Fair on 12 November 2002.

Exhibitions: Olympia Art & Antiques Fair, Winter, 2012, exhibited by Campbell Wilson.

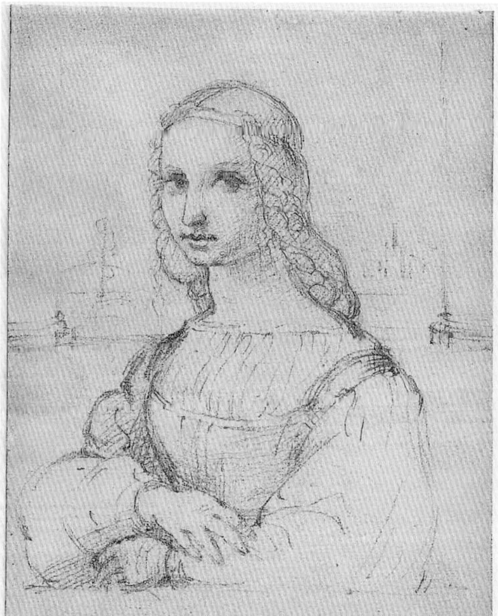

Cat. 268. Henry Wallis, drawing of the Mona Lisa. Image courtesy of Scott T. Buckle, London

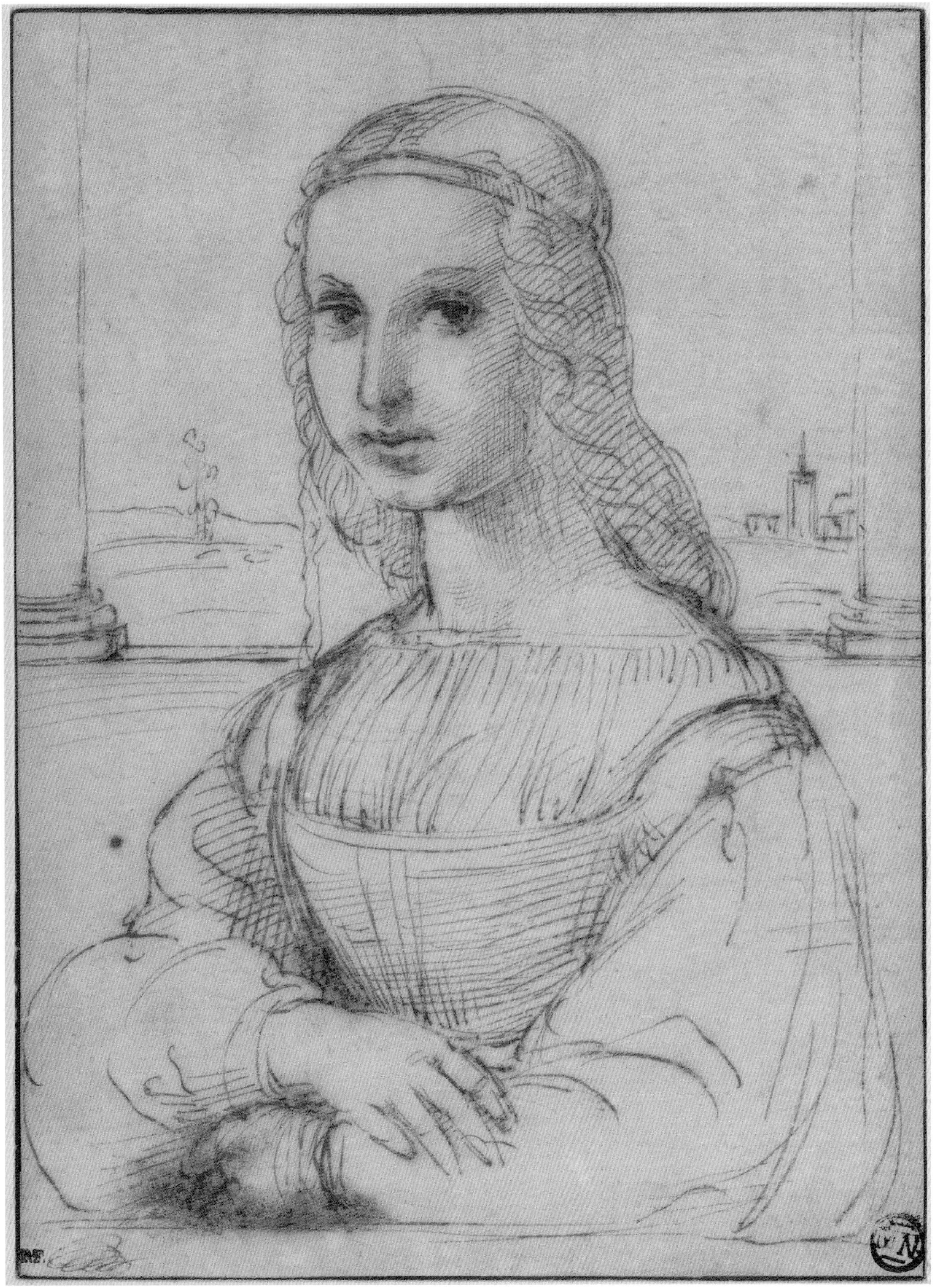

See Cat. 268. Raphael, drawing of the Mona Lisa, *c.*1504–1505, Louvre, Paris. Image by permission of the Louvre.

This is a copy by Wallis of a drawing by Raphael of *c.*1504–1505,[1] which some scholars think represents an earlier version by Leonardo of a more youthful Mona Lisa than the famous portrait of her now in the Louvre in Paris.[2] The whereabouts of this earlier painting is unknown. Raphael's drawing, executed while he was an apprentice to Leonardo in Florence in the early 1500s, is now in the Louvre, where Wallis must have seen and copied it.

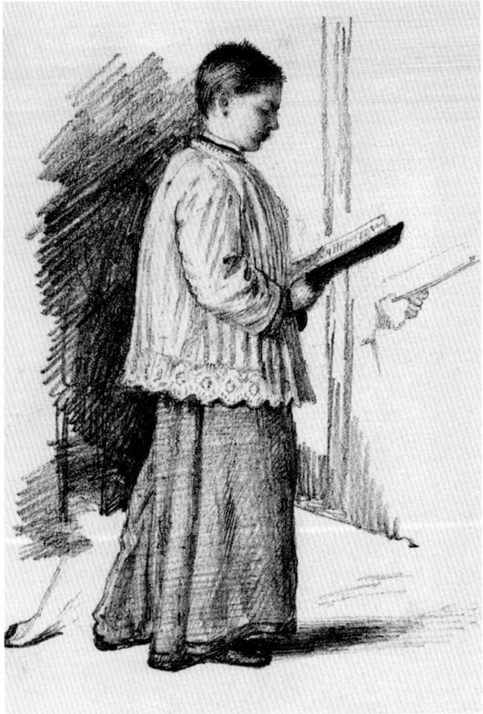

Cat. 269.

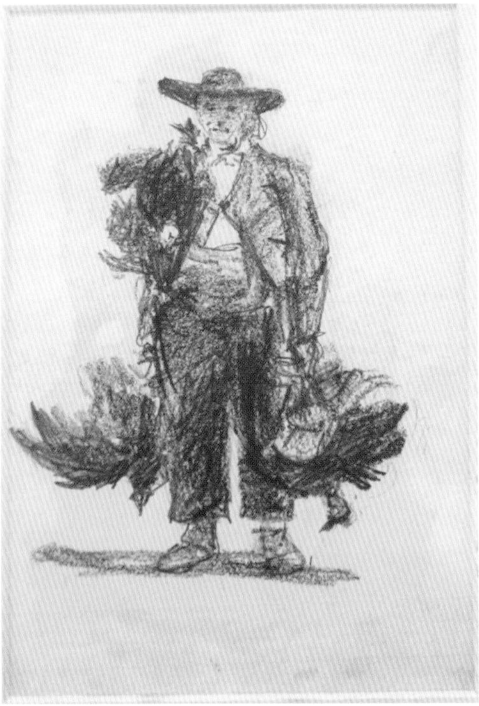

Cat. 271.

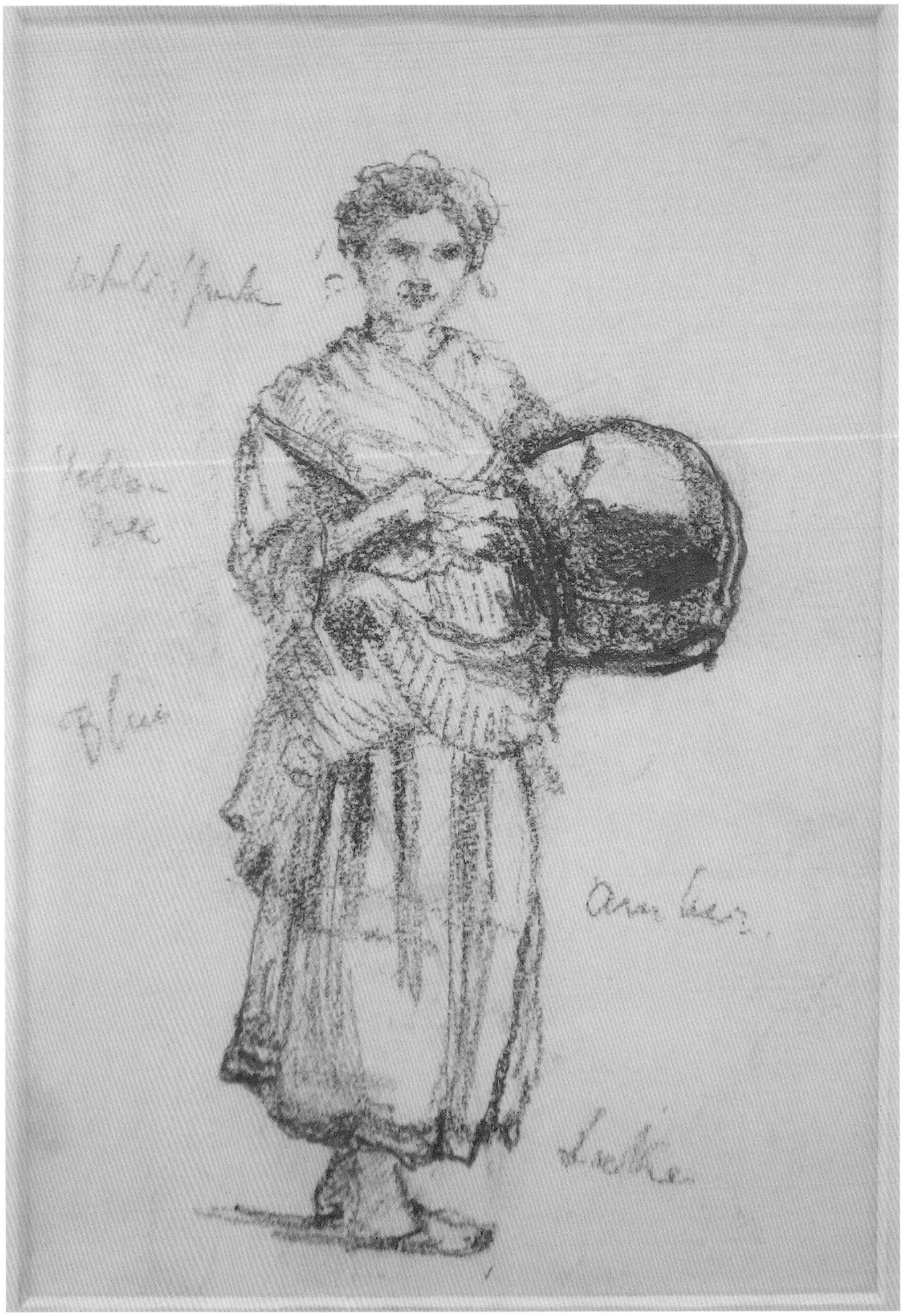

Cat. 270.

Cats. 269-280: images courtesy of Christie's South Kensington, London

Cats. 269-280. ***Study of a Choir Boy; and Eleven other Studies***
?1870s; sheets are various sizes; *Choir Boy* - pencil on paper; 22.3 x 13.3 cm (8¾ x 5¼ in.); private collections.
Provenance: Wallis's studio and then by descent from the artist to his son Harold Wallis; then to his daughter-in-law Mary Wallis (née Mary Elizabeth Aymes); then her great-niece Vera G. Cooper (née Langley; 1910-1989); thence by direct descent to John Harold Cooper and family; their sale Bonhams, London, 5 March 2002, part of lot 71, bought by Neil Wilson of Campbell Wilson, Hove, East Sussex; his estate sale Christie's South Kensington, 4 September 2014, lot 131, sold for £313, bought by a private collector in Spain.
Exhibitions: Shepherd & Derom Galleries, New York, 'English Romantic Art 1850-1920', 2003, no. 83 (*Choir Boy*); Campbell Wilson, Hassocks, West Sussex, 'Pre-Raphaelite Neo-Pre-Raphaelite, Post-Pre-Raphaelite', 2005, no. 45 (Choir Boy).

Sold as a single lot, these twelve drawings in graphite or watercolour by Wallis encompass landscape and architectural studies, including views of Seville and Granada, as well as figurative studies. Some of the figurative studies appear to have been copied from paintings in churches. A number of these studies were subsequently offered for sale at the Isbilya auction house in Seville. Cat. 269, the drawing of the choir boy, sold to a private collector for €250 in April 2015 prior to being auctioned.[1] On 21 January 2016 the following lots were offered for sale: Cat. 270, *Young Woman with a Basket*, lot 587, 22.5 x 14.9 cm; Cat. 271, *Spanish Farmer with Chickens*, lot 588, 22.5 x 14.9 cm, sold for 200 euros; Cat. 273, *A Street of Seville*, lot 585, 23.3 x 15.4 cm; and Cat. 274, *A Street of Seville*, lot 586, 23.3 x 15.4 cm.

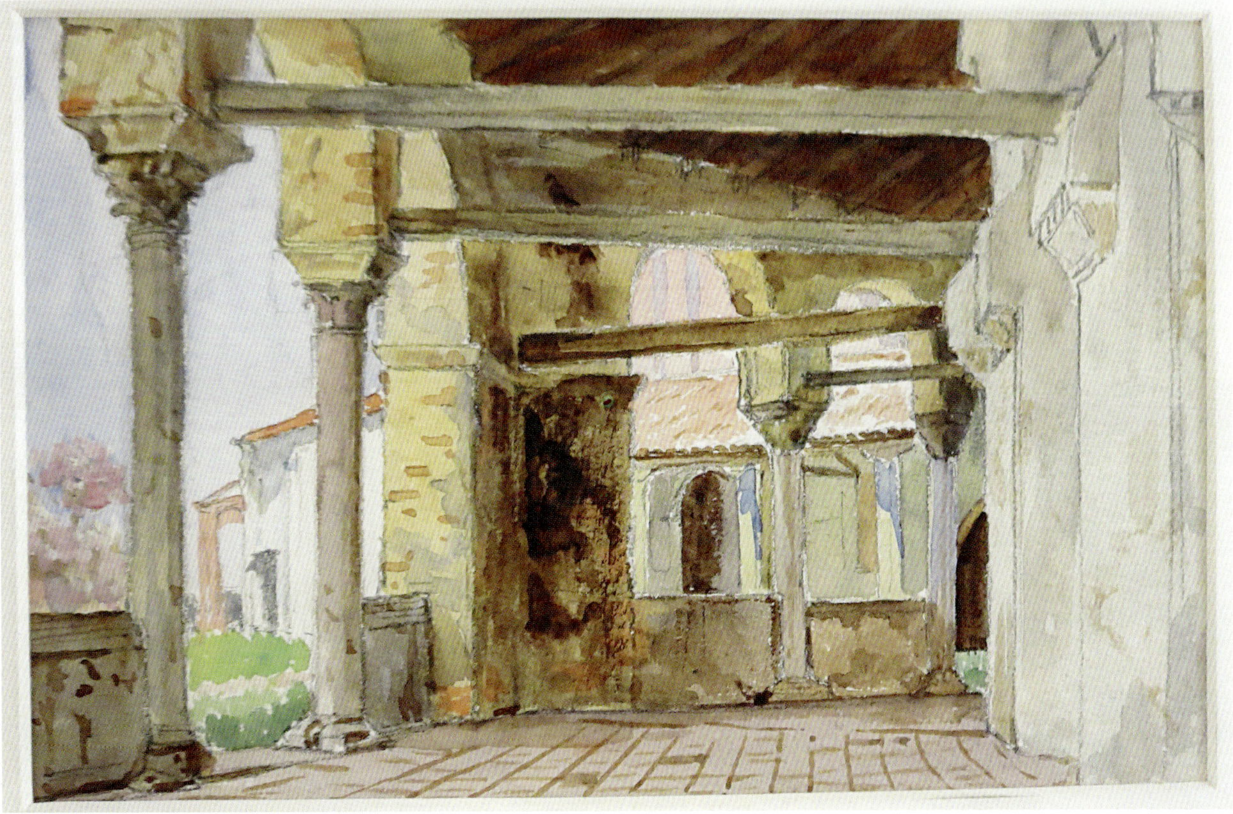

Cat. 272.

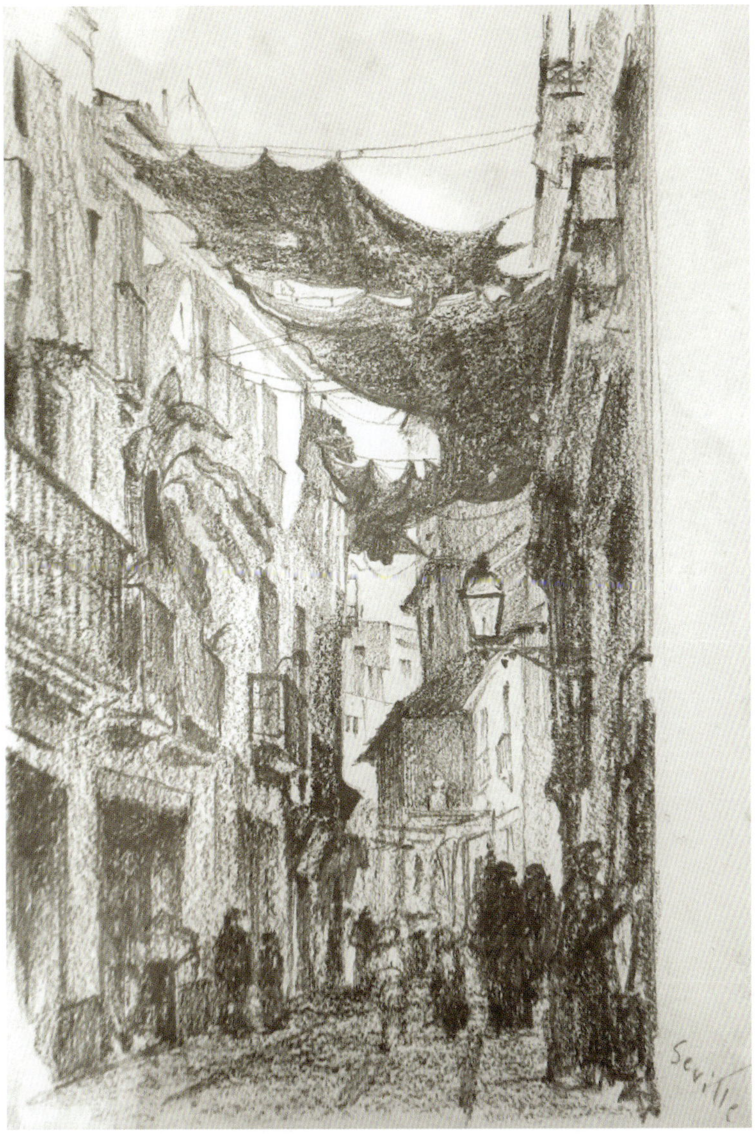

Cat. 273.

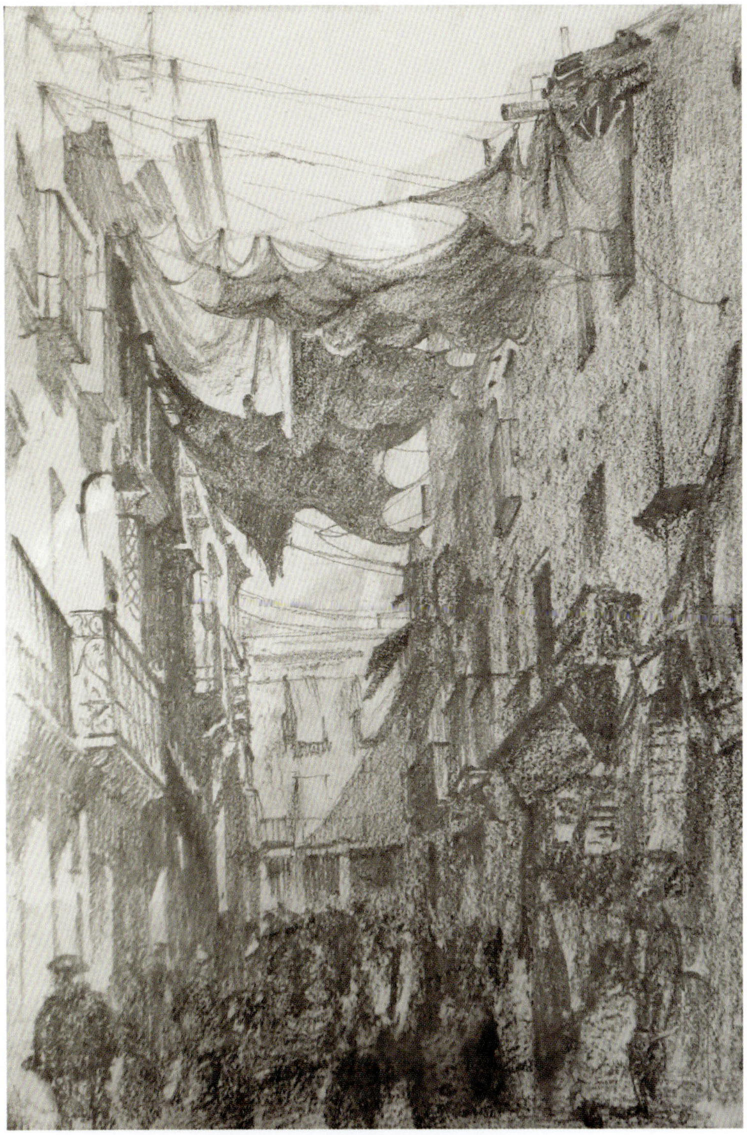

Cat. 274.

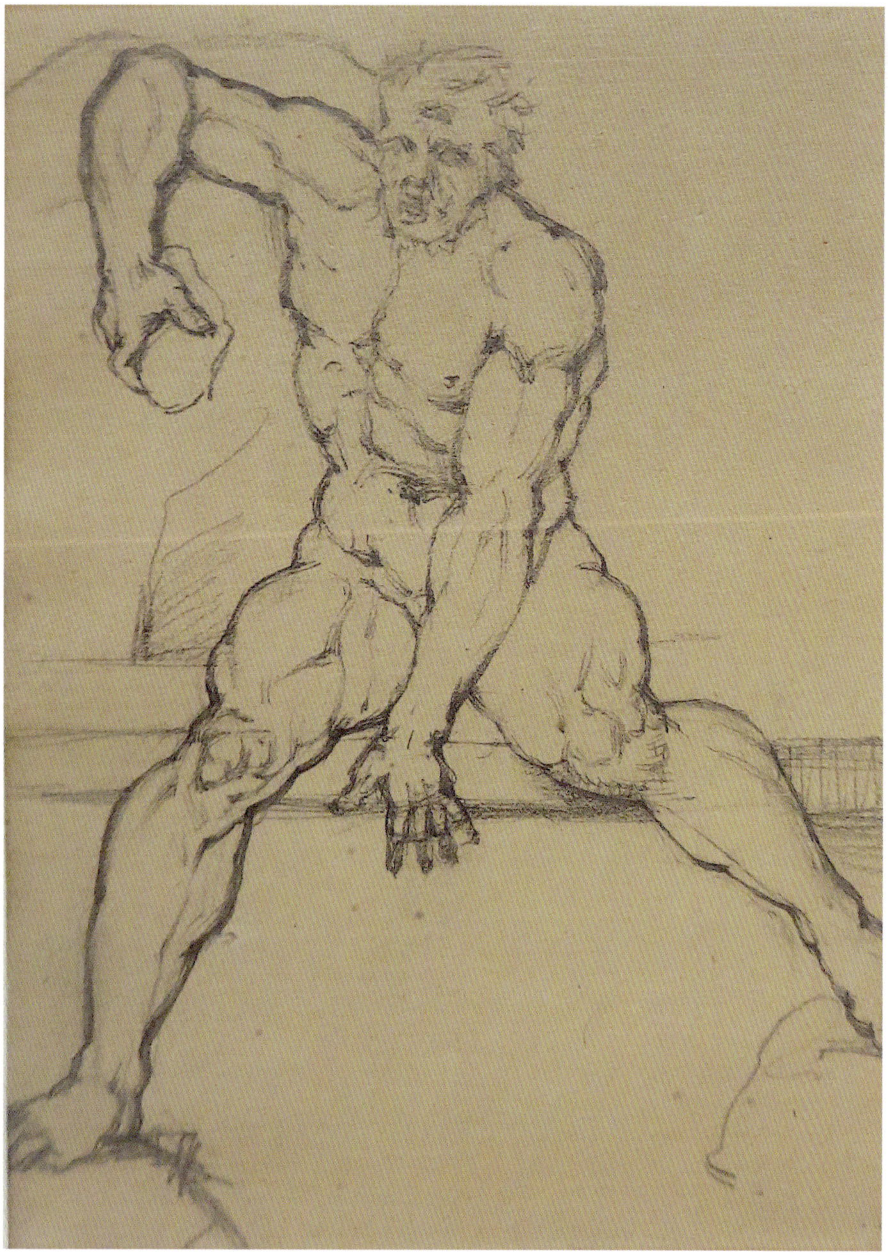

Cat. 275.

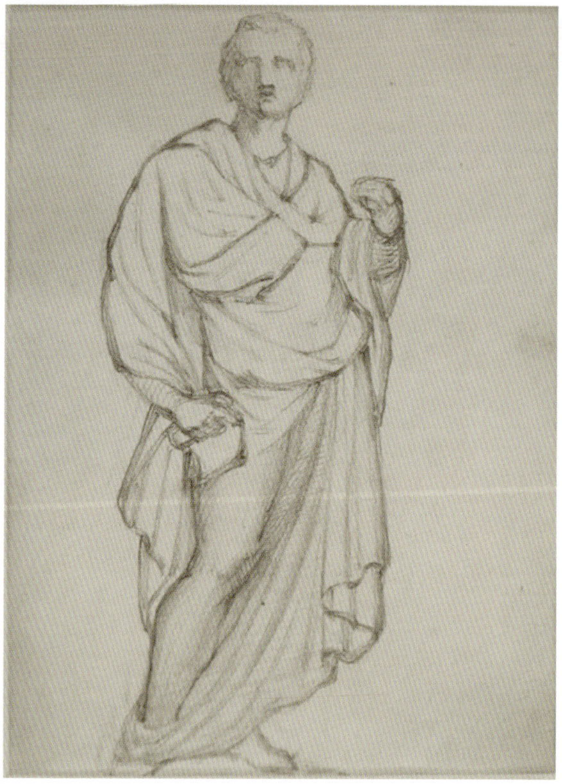

Cat. 278.

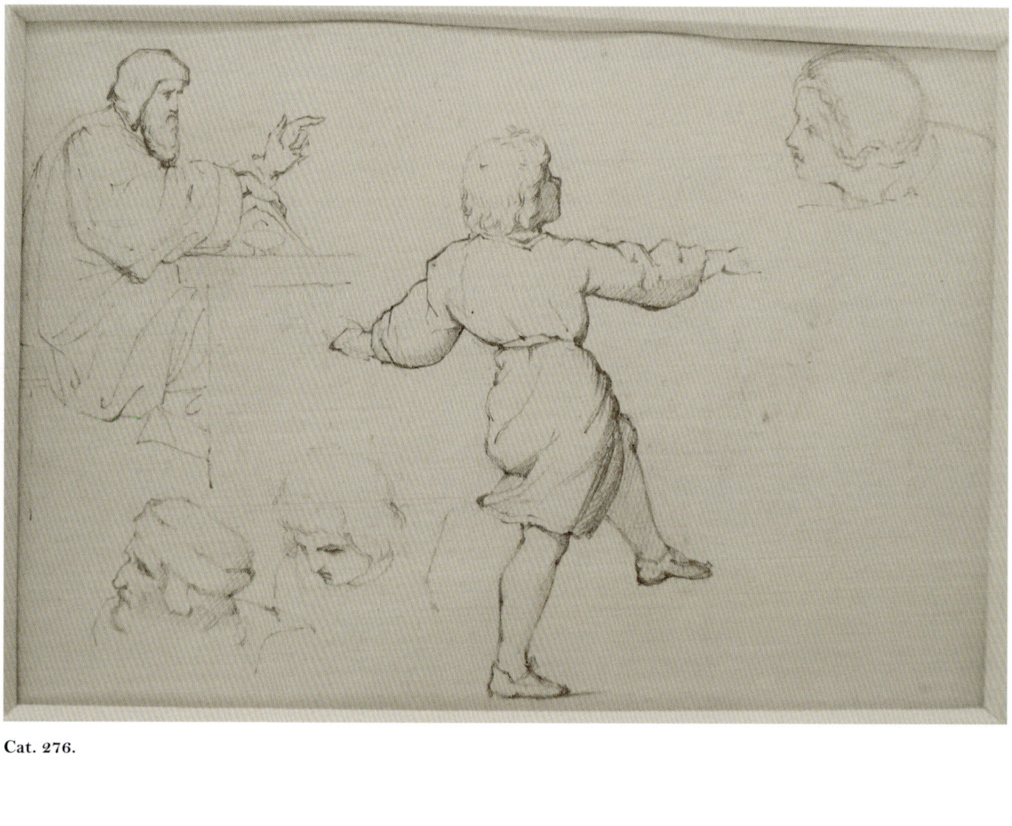

Cat. 276.

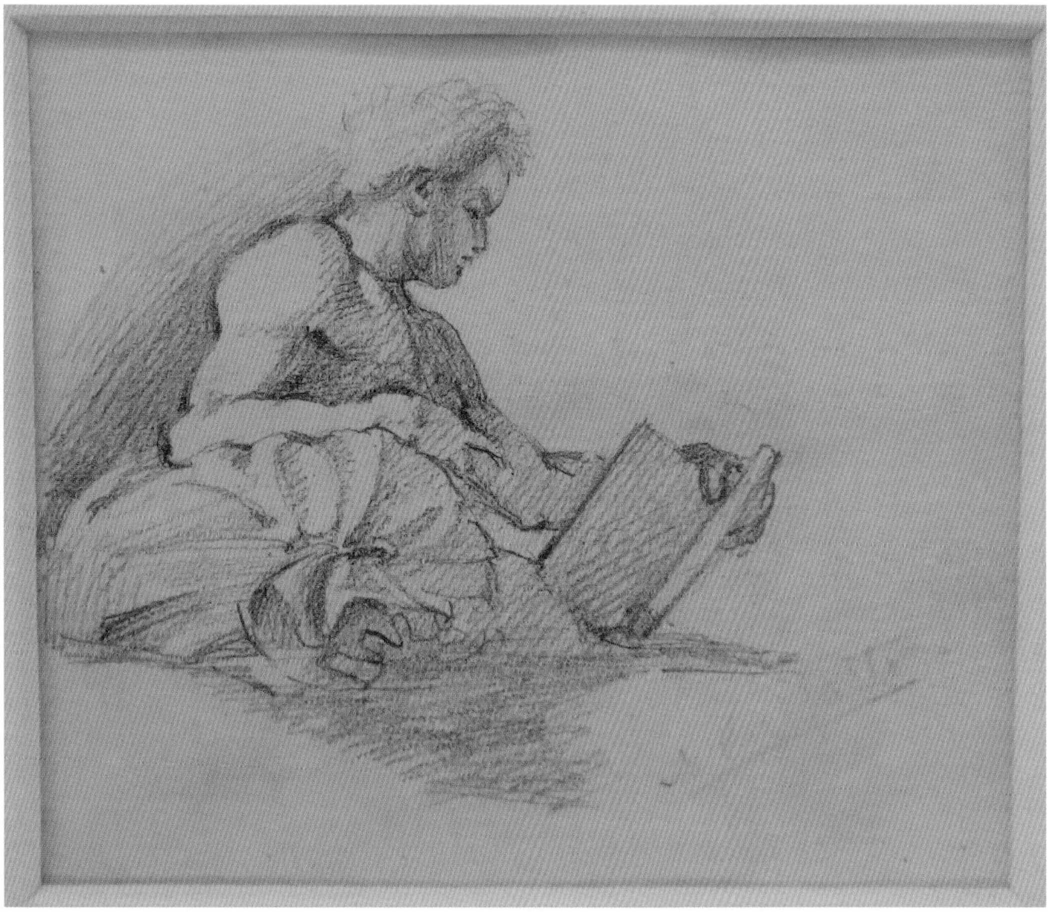

Cat. 277.

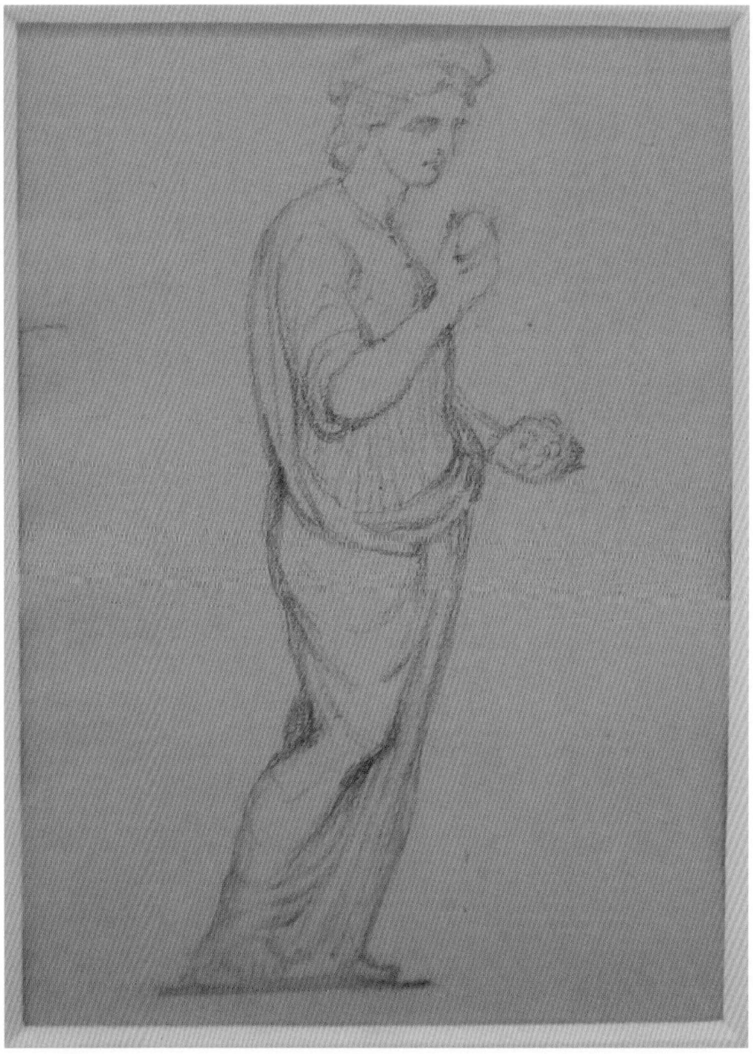

Cat. 279.

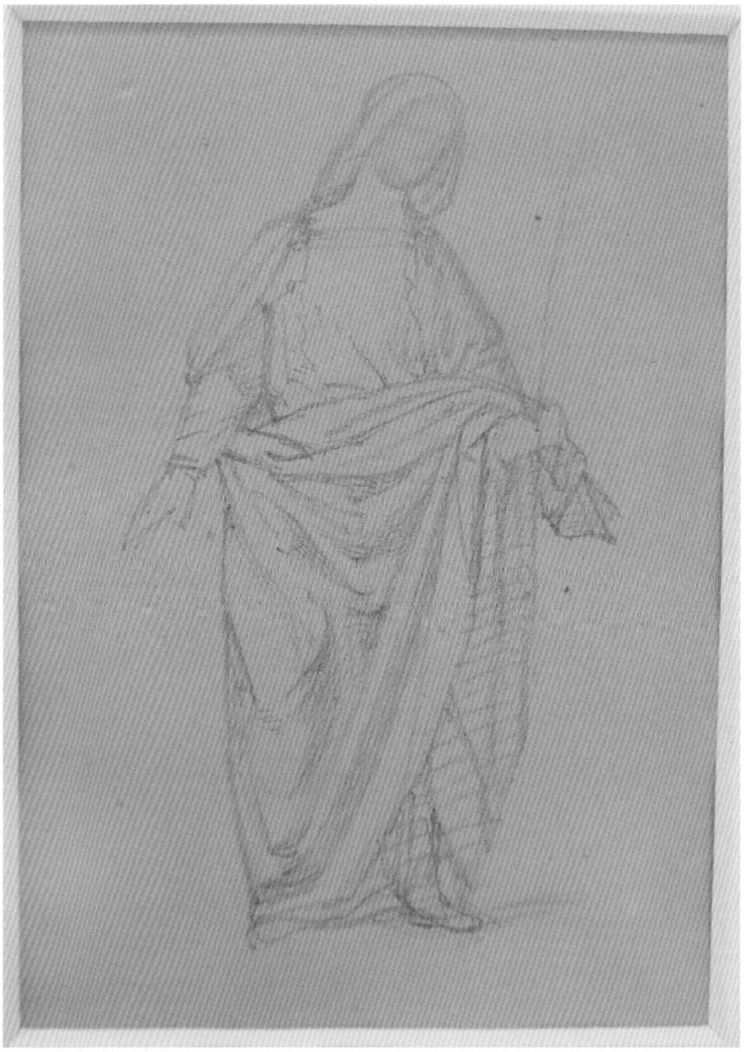

Cat. 280.

Cats. 281-284. *Sketchbook Studies*
Cat. 281 *Portrait sketch,* 7 x 13 cm (2¾ x 5⅛ in.); and *Balcony in Seville,* 22.5 x 14.9 cm (8⅞ x 5⅞ in.)
Cat. 282. *Portico and Basament,* 22.5 x 14.9 cm (8⅞ x 5⅞ in.)
Cat. 283. *Granada Fair,* 14.9 x 22.5 cm (5⅞ x 8⅞ in.); and *View of Granada,* 22.5 x 14.9 cm (8⅞ x 5⅞ in.)
Cat. 284. *Peasant woman with a shawl,* 22.5 x 14.9 cm (8⅞ x 5⅞ in.)
PROVENANCE: Wallis's studio and then by descent from the artist to his son Harold Wallis; then to his daughter-in-law Mary Wallis (née Mary Elizabeth Aymes); then her great-niece Vera G. Cooper (née Langley; 1910-1989), thence by direct descent to John Harold Cooper and family; their sale Bonhams, London, 5 March 2002, part of lot 71, bought by the art dealer Neil Wilson of Campbell Wilson; his estate sale Christie's South Kensington, 4 September 2014, part of lot 131; purchased by a private collector in Spain; his sale Isbilya auction house, Seville, on 21 January, 2016, lot 581 [Cat. 281], lot 582 [Cat. 282], lot 583 [Cat. 283], lot 584 [Cat. 284].

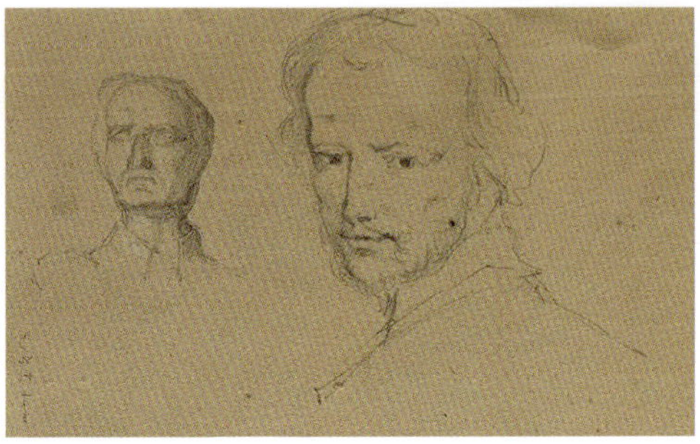
Cat. 281. Cats. 281-284 Images courtesy of Christie's South Kensington, London

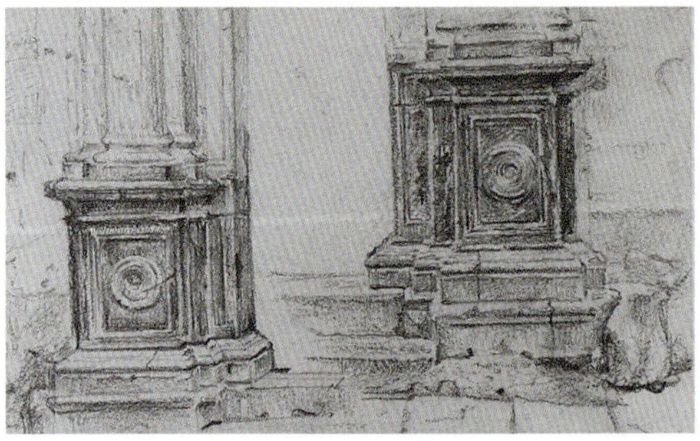
Cat. 282.

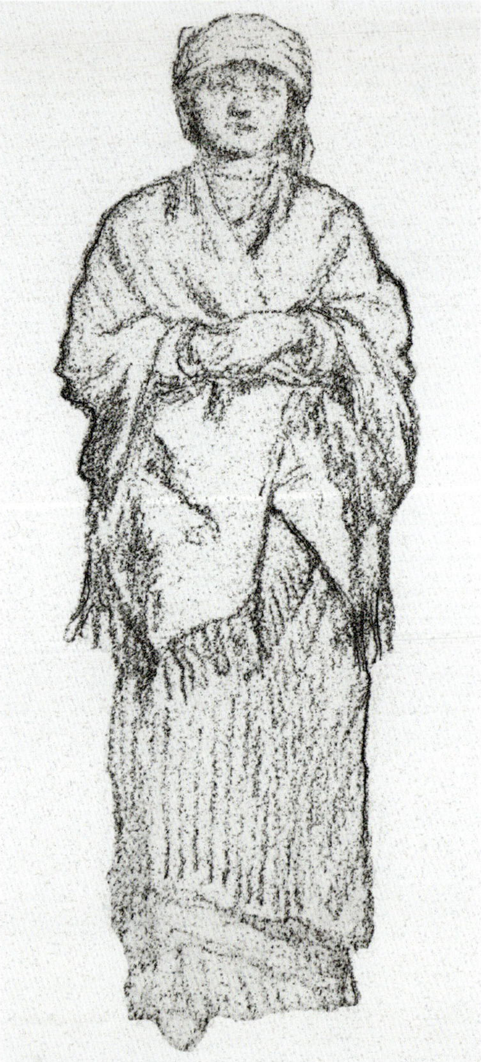
Cat. 284.

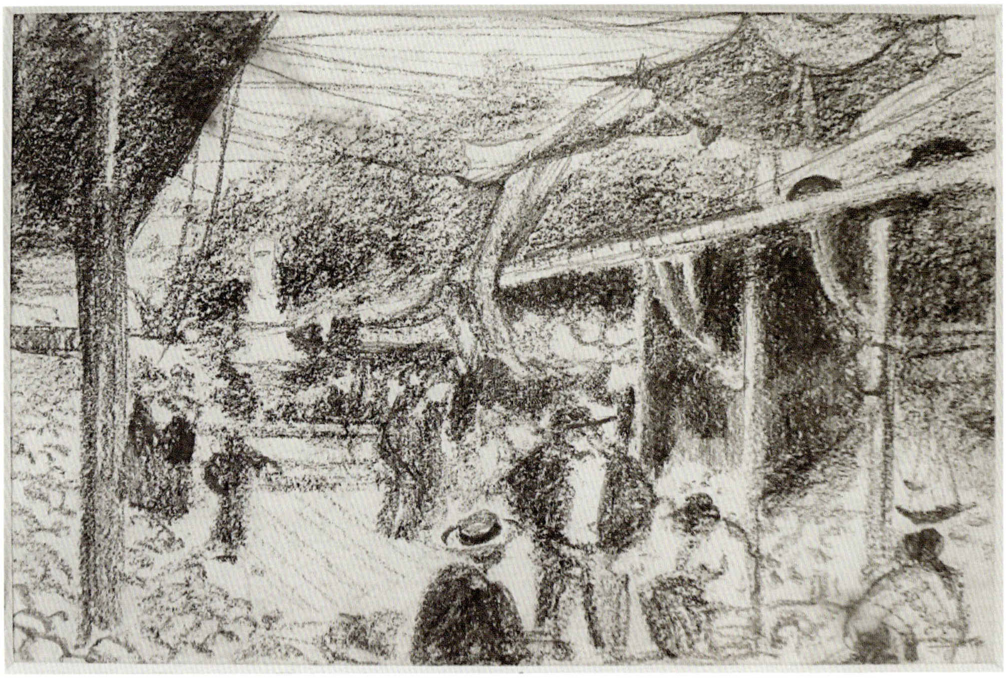
Cat. 283.

These studies may date from 1882-1883, when Wallis was known to have visited Spain, including Seville, Granada, and Toledo.

Cats. 285-286. *Study of a gazelle; A study of female heads,* 1870s
Cat. 285. *Gazelle,* pencil and watercolour, heightened with white on paper; 22.2 x 13.4 cm (8¾ x 5¼ in.)
Cat 286. *Female heads,* pencil on paper, dimensions unknown (smaller than *Gazelle*)
PROVENANCE: Wallis's studio and then by descent from the artist to his son Harold Wallis; then to his daughter-in-law Mary Wallis (née Mary Elizabeth Aymes); then her great-niece Vera G. Cooper (née Langley; 1910-1989); thence by direct

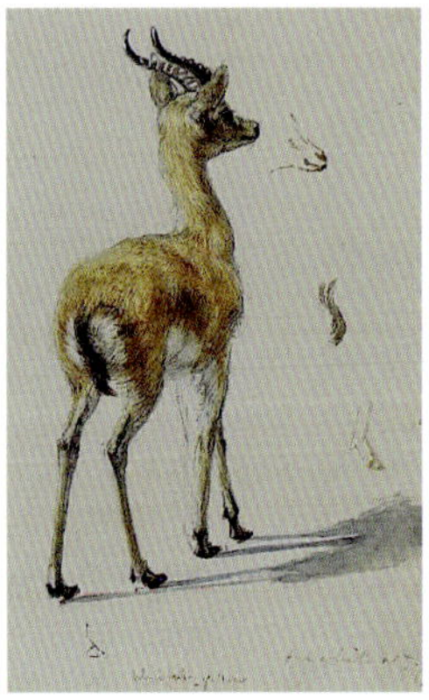
Left. Cat. 285.
Image courtesy of Christie's South Kensington, London

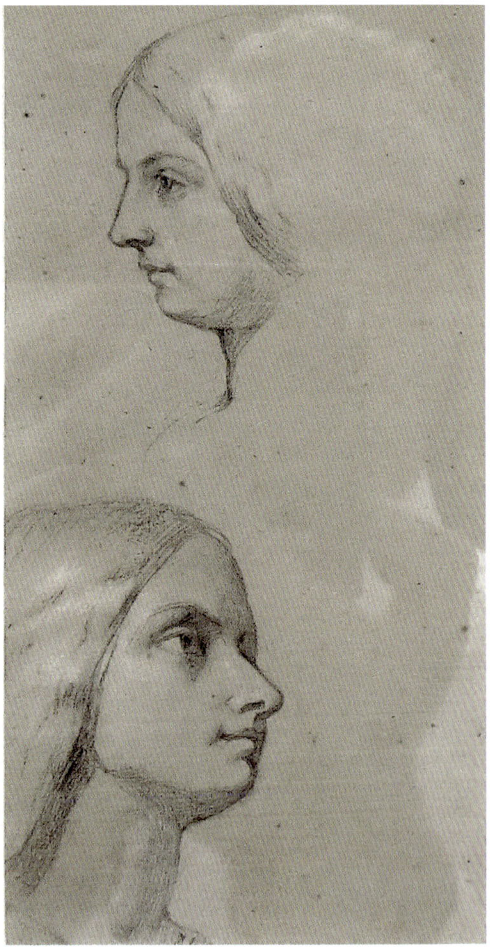
Right. Cat. 286.
Image courtesy of Christie's South Kensington, London

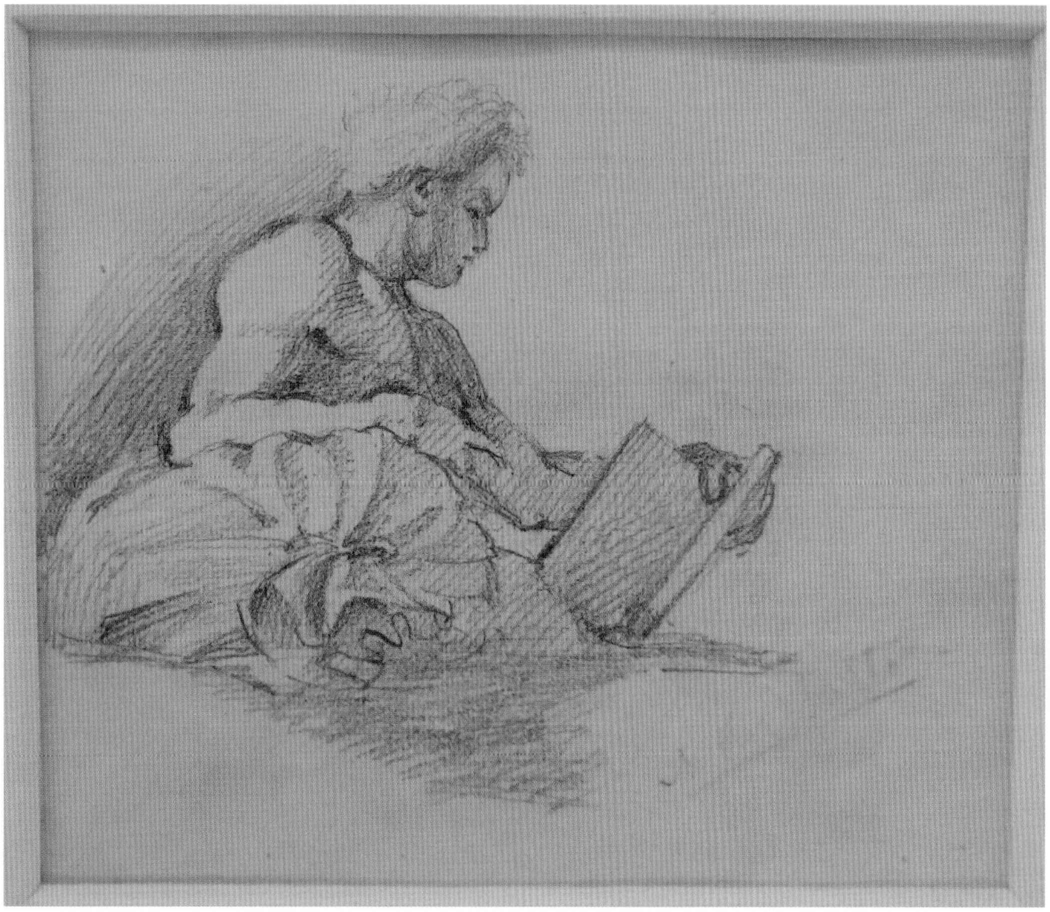

Cat. 277.

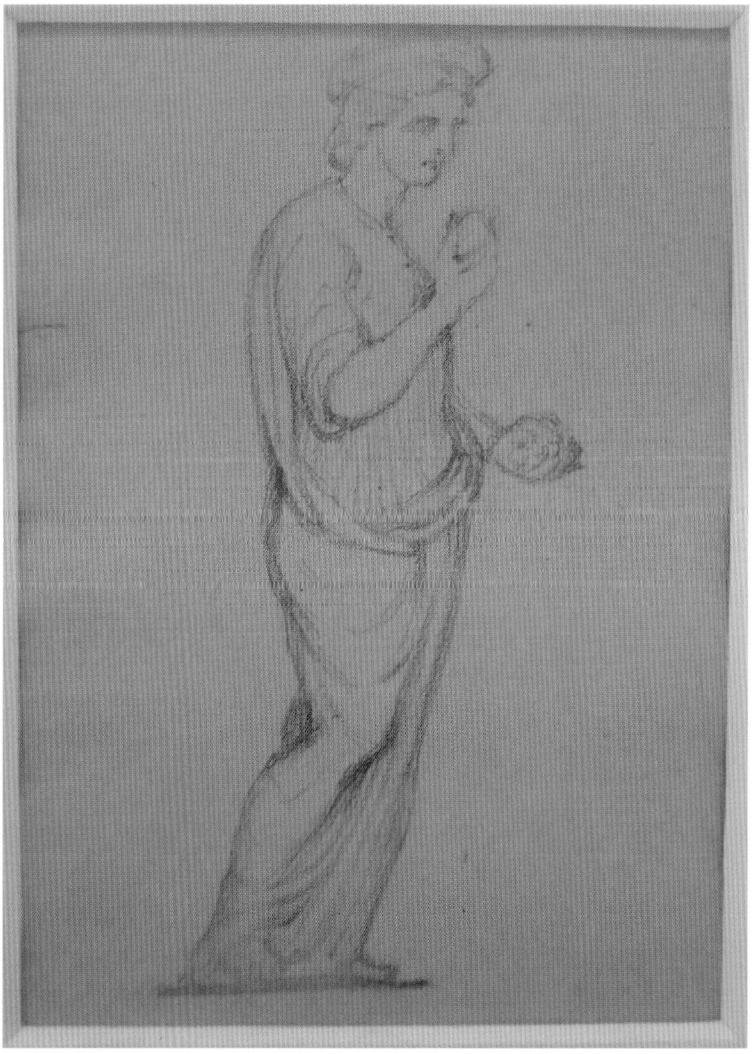

Cat. 279.

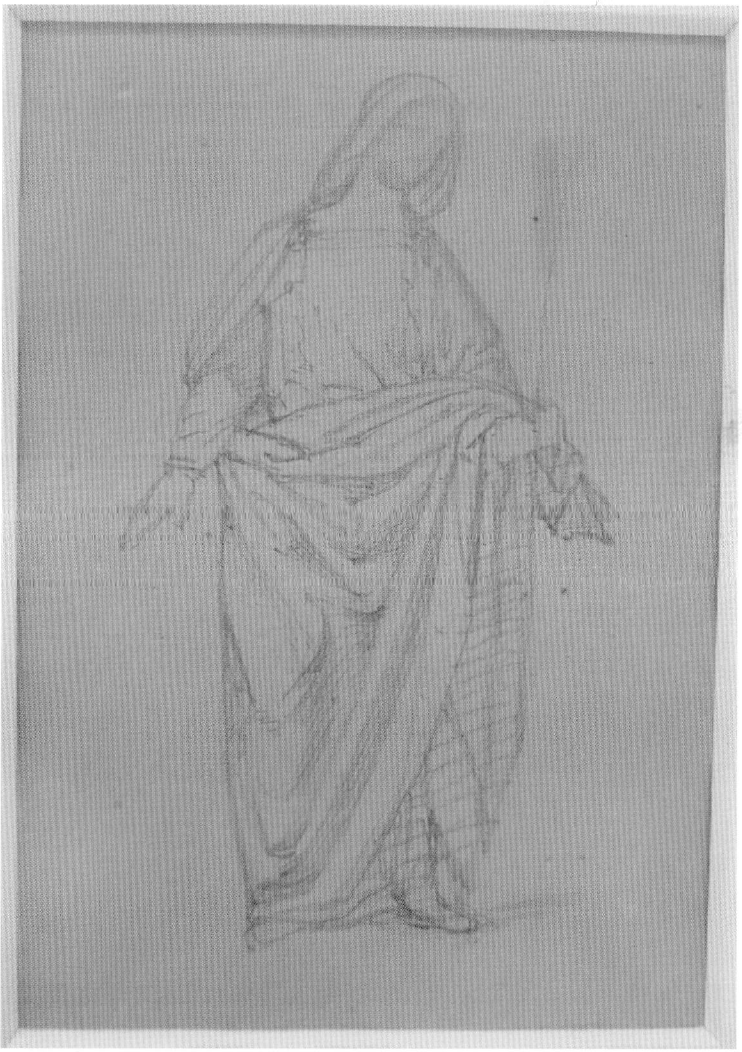

Cat. 280.

Cats. 281-284. *Sketchbook Studies*

Cat. 281 *Portrait sketch*, 7 x 13 cm (2¾ x 5⅛ in.); and *Balcony in Seville*, 22.5 x 14.9 cm (8⅞ x 5⅞ in.)

Cat. 282. *Portico and Basament*, 22.5 x 14.9 cm (8⅞ x 5⅞ in.)

Cat. 283. *Granada Fair*, 14.9 x 22.5 cm (5⅞ x 8⅞ in.); and *View of Granada*, 22.5 x 14.9 cm (8⅞ x 5⅞ in.)

Cat. 284. *Peasant woman with a shawl*, 22.5 x 14.9 cm (8⅞ x 5⅞ in.)

Provenance: Wallis's studio and then by descent from the artist to his son Harold Wallis; then to his daughter-in-law Mary Wallis (née Mary Elizabeth Aymes); then her great-niece Vera G. Cooper (née Langley; 1910-1989), thence by direct descent to John Harold Cooper and family; their sale Bonhams, London, 5 March 2002, part of lot 71, bought by the art dealer Neil Wilson of Campbell Wilson; his estate sale Christie's South Kensington, 4 September 2014, part of lot 131; purchased by a private collector in Spain; his sale Isbilya auction house, Seville, on 21 January, 2016, lot 581 [Cat. 281], lot 582 [Cat. 282], lot 583 [Cat. 283], lot 584 [Cat. 284].

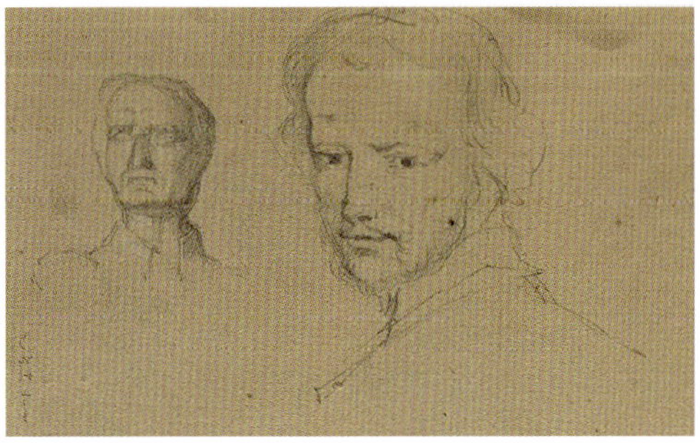

Cat. 281. Cats. 281-284 Images courtesy of Christie's South Kensington, London

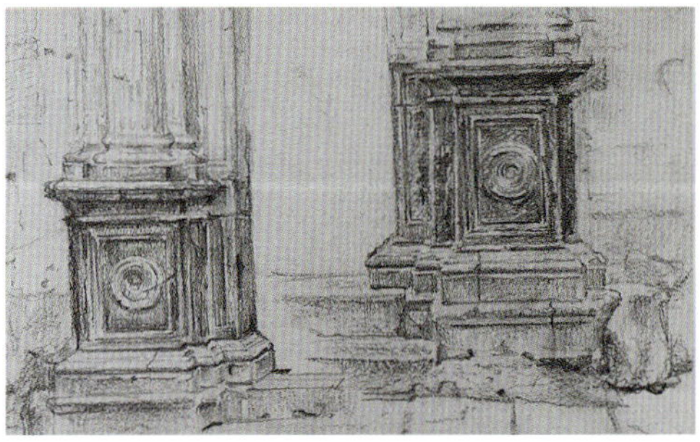

Cat. 282.

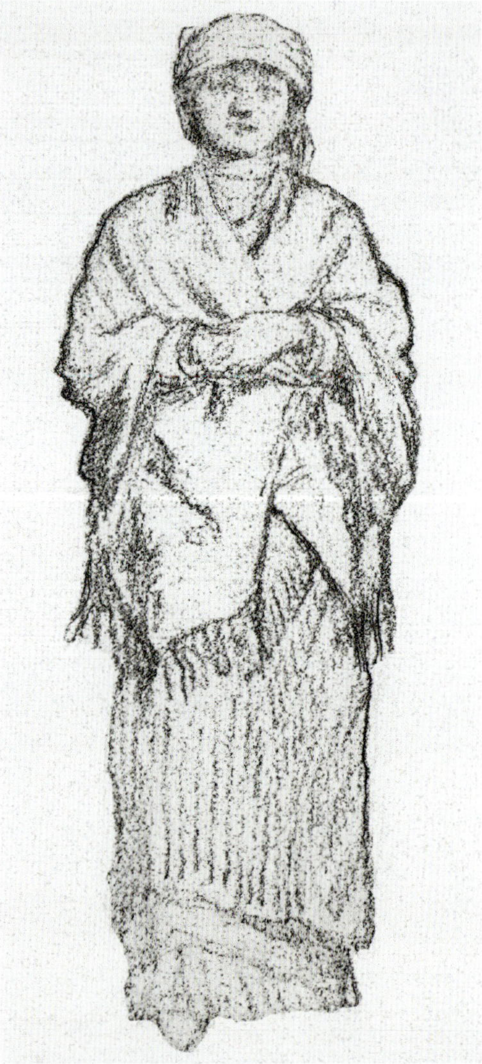

Cat. 284.

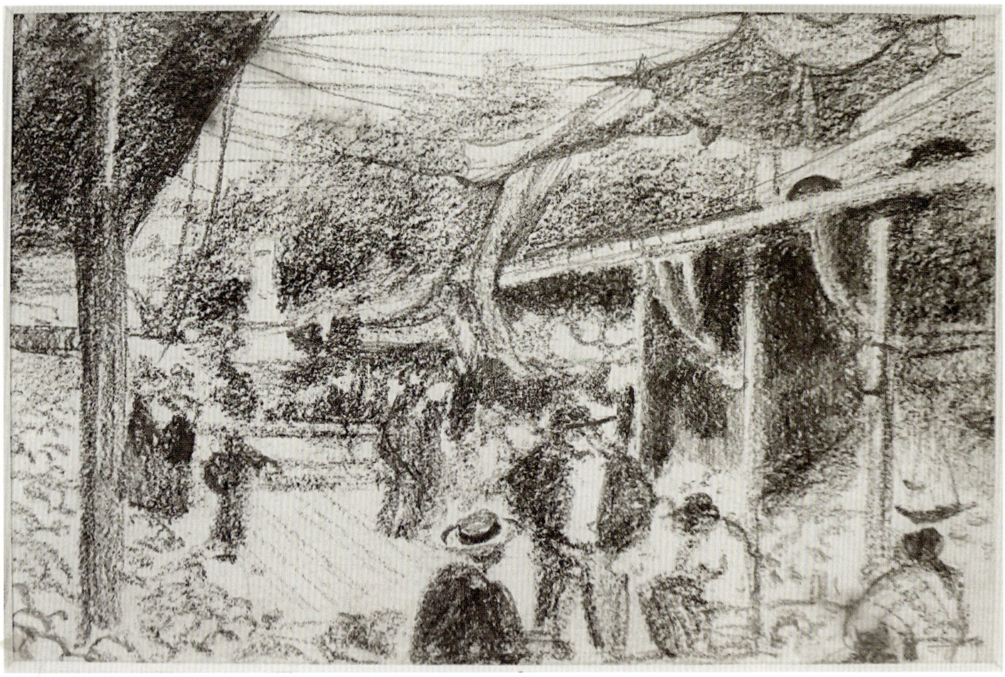

Cat. 283.

These studies may date from 1882-1883, when Wallis was known to have visited Spain, including Seville, Granada, and Toledo.

Cats. 285-286. *Study of a gazelle; A study of female heads*, 1870s

Cat. 285. *Gazelle*, pencil and watercolour, heightened with white on paper; 22.2 x 13.4 cm (8¾ x 5¼ in.)

Cat 286. *Female heads*, pencil on paper, dimensions unknown (smaller than *Gazelle*)

Provenance: Wallis's studio and then by descent from the artist to his son Harold Wallis; then to his daughter-in-law Mary Wallis (née Mary Elizabeth Aymes); then her great-niece Vera G. Cooper (née Langley; 1910-1989); thence by direct

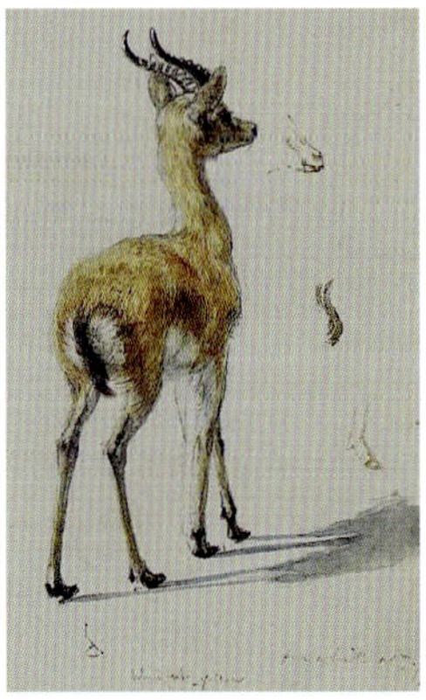

Left. Cat. 285. Image courtesy of Christie's South Kensington, London

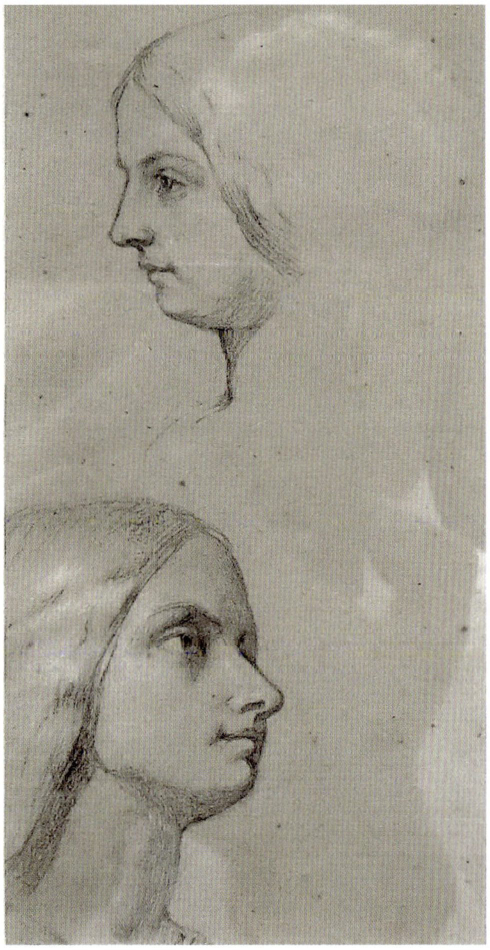

Right. Cat. 286. Image courtesy of Christie's South Kensington, London

descent to John Harold Cooper and family; their sale Bonhams, London, 5 March 2002, part of lot 71, bought by Neil Wilson of Campbell Wilson, Hove, East Sussex; his estate sale Christie's South Kensington, 4 September 2014, lot 132, sold for £1,063.

The study of the gazelle may relate to the painting *The Sentinel* [Cat. 121], which Wallis exhibited at the O.W.S. in 1878. In that work, the sentinel observes a lovely gazelle that has walked up to the steps of the Sanctum that he guards.

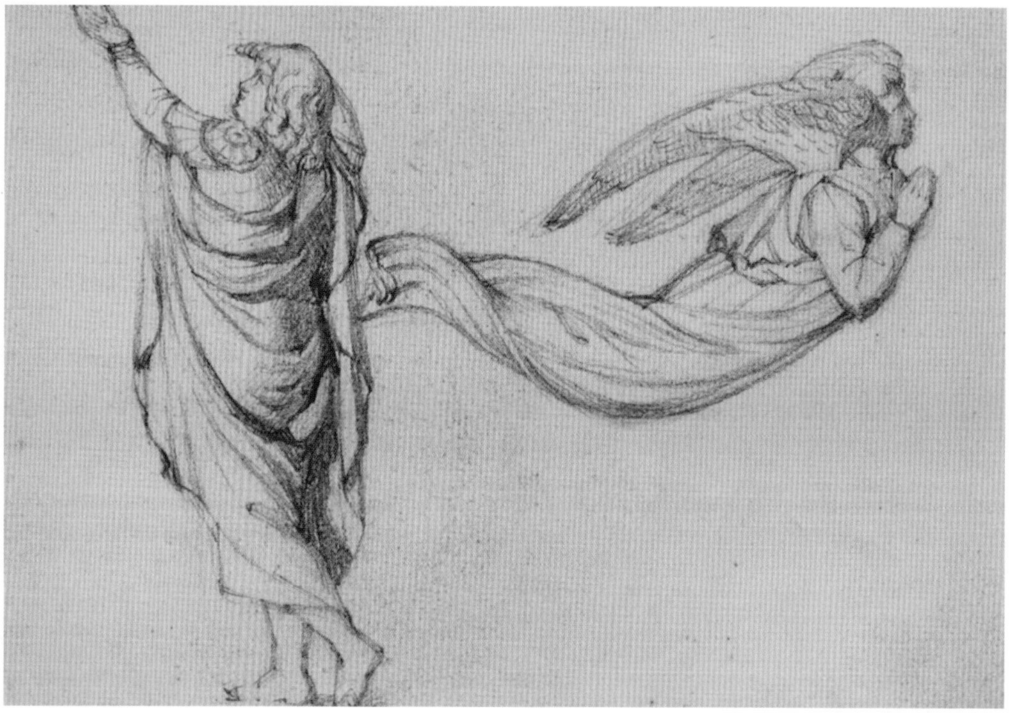

Cat. 287. Angel study

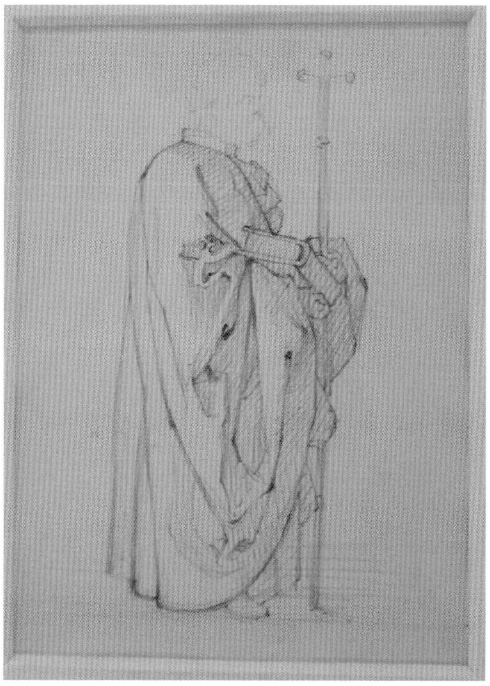

Cat. 289. Biblical figure, perhaps a martyred saint

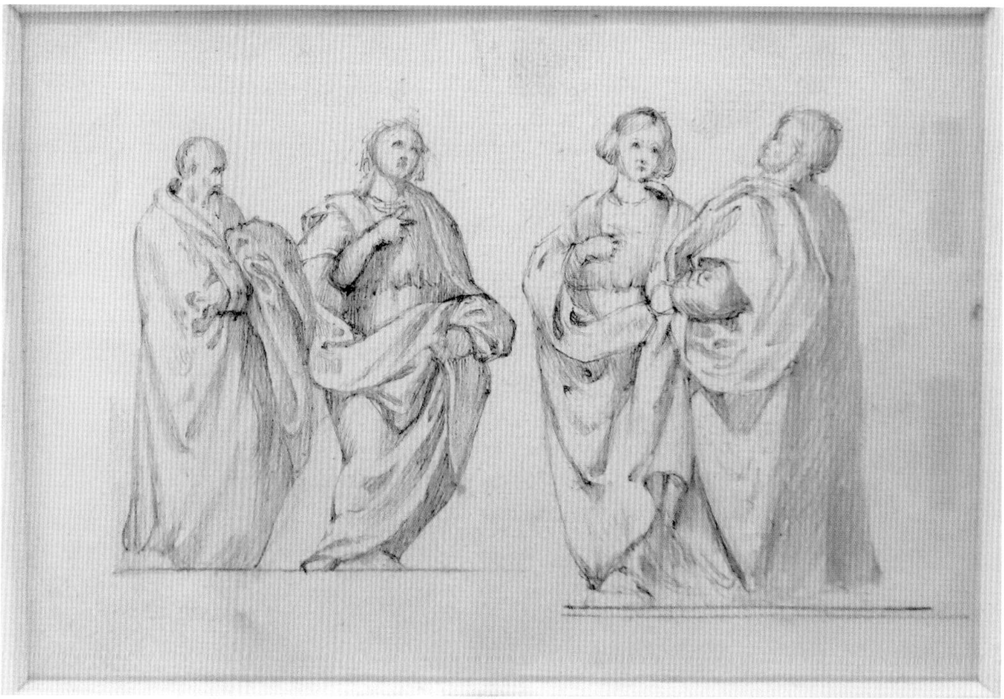

Cat. 288. Biblical figures, possibly saints

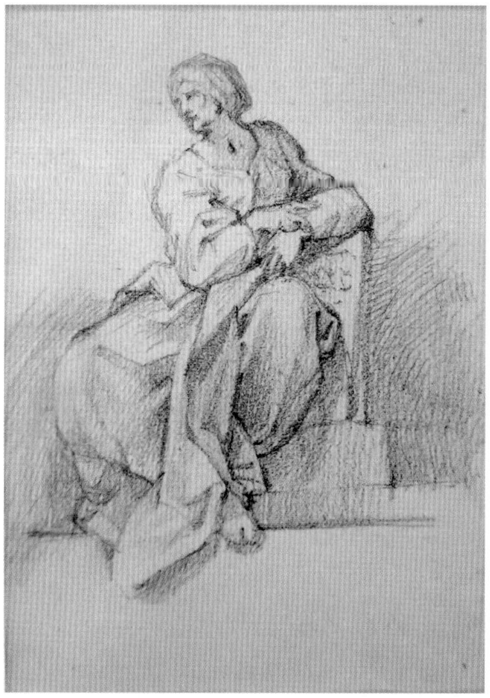

Cat. 290. Seated Biblical figure

Cats. 287-307. *A Figure Study with an Angel; Mother and Child; and Twenty other Drawings*

Cat. 287. *Angel study* (recto) and *Mother and Child* (verso), pencil on paper; 9.5 x 13.3 cm (3¾ x 5¼ in.). ?1870s/1880s; various sizes; private collection

Provenance: Wallis's studio and then by descent from the artist to his son Harold Wallis; then to his daughter-in-law Mary Wallis (née Mary Elizabeth Aymes); then her great-niece Vera G. Cooper (née Langley; 1910-1989); thence by direct descent to John Harold Cooper and family; their sale Bonhams, London, 5 March 2002, part of lot 71, bought by Neil Wilson of Campbell Wilson, Hove, East Sussex; his estate sale Christie's South Kensington, 4 September 2014, lot 133, sold for £188.

The majority of these drawings were Biblical, Renaissance or Classical figurative studies, some with drawings on both the recto and verso. Most of the figures appear to have been copied from paintings in churches, probably in Italy.

Cats. 287-307: Images courtesy of Christie's South Kensington, London.

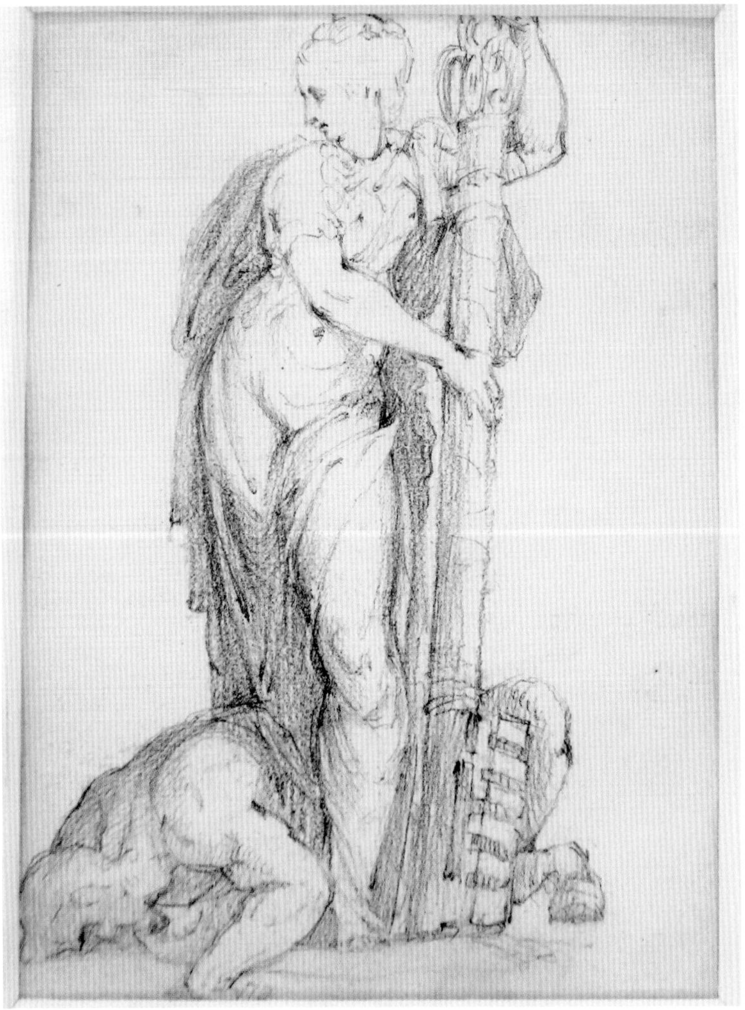

Cat. 291. Biblical figure, perhaps St. Peter, and an angel

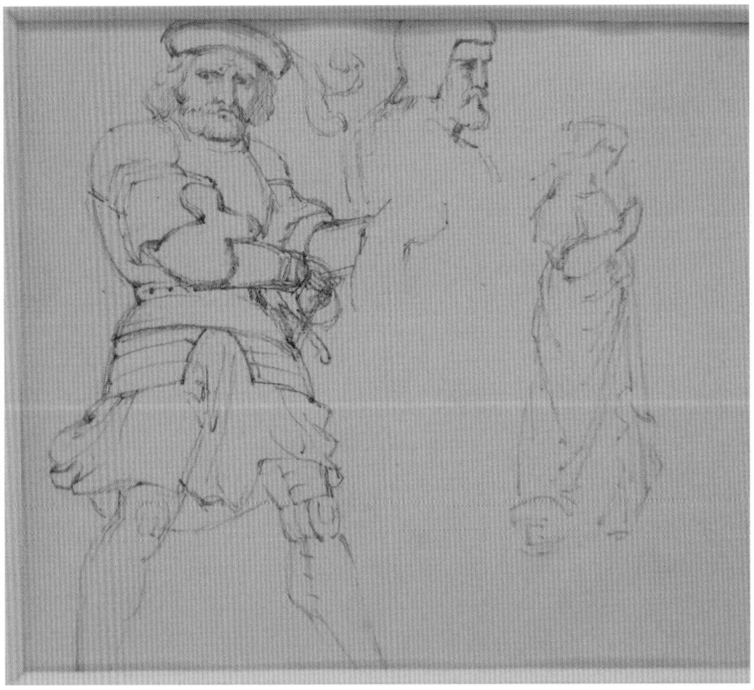

Cat. 292. Renaissance figures

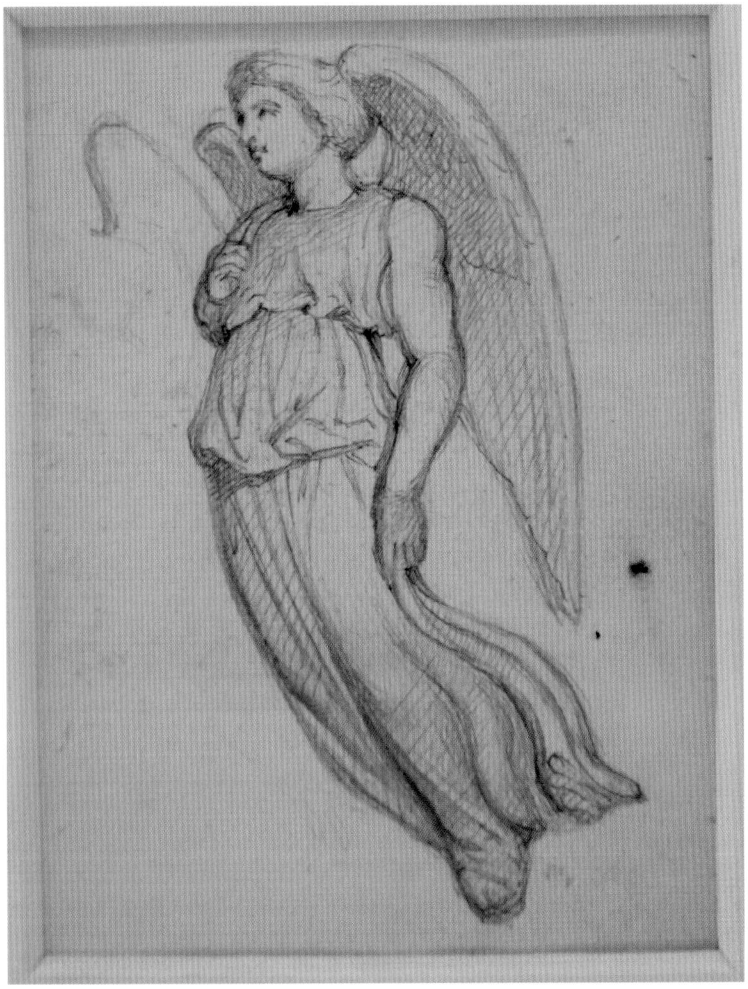

Cat. 293. Angel figure

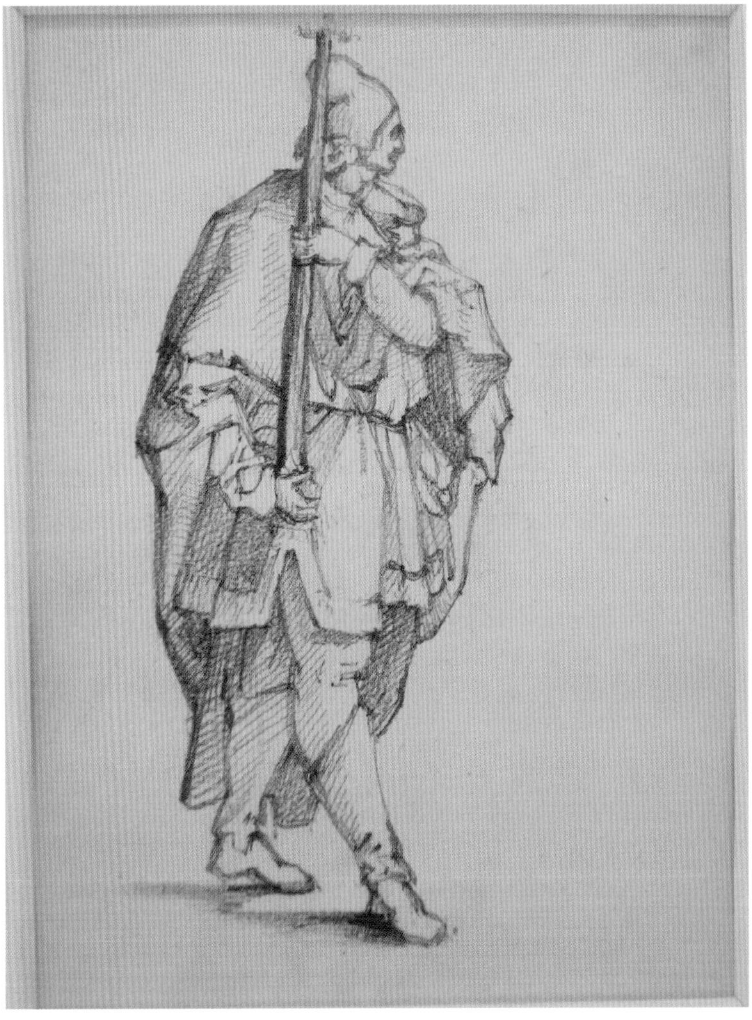

Cat. 294. Standing male Renaissance figure

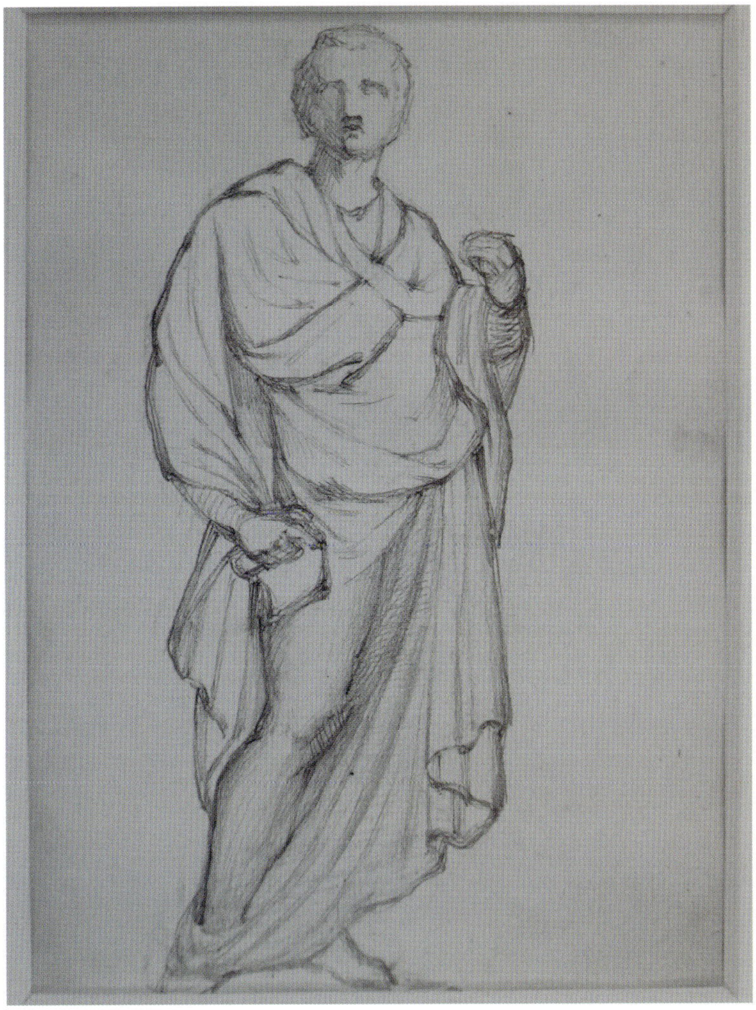

Cat. 295. Standing male Classical figure

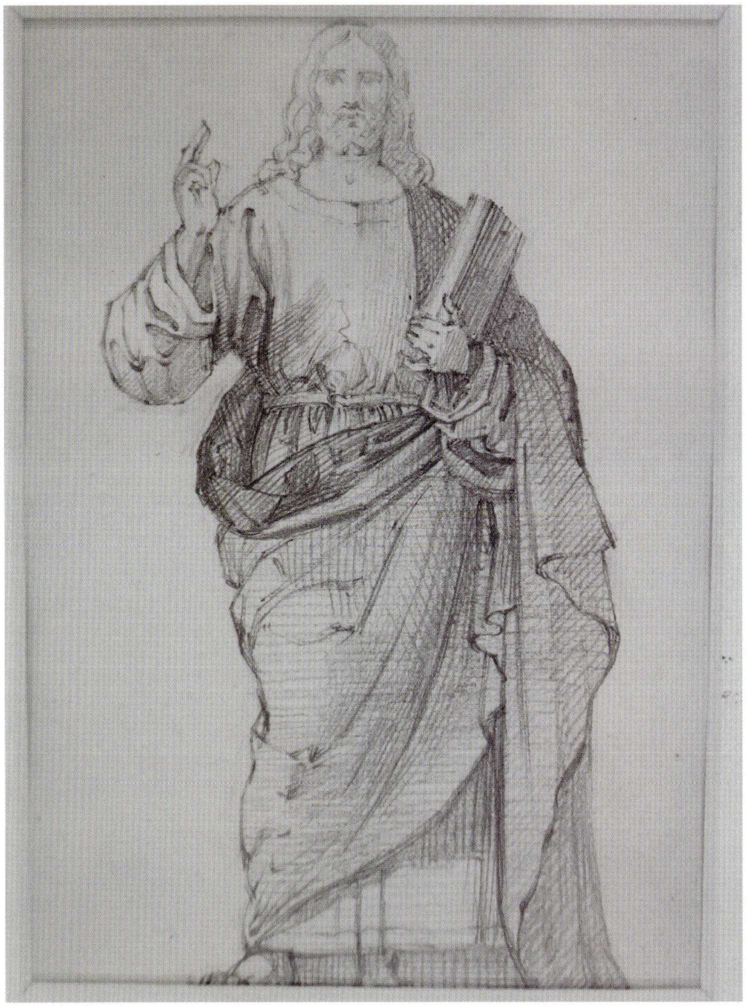

Cat. 296. Christ with his right hand raised in blessing (Christ Pantocrater)

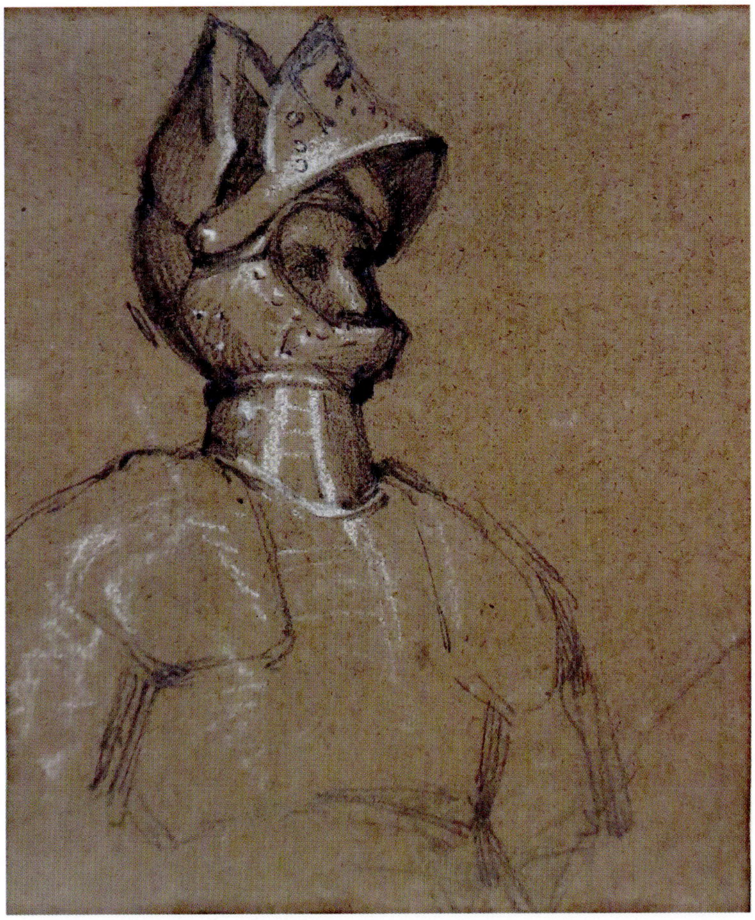

Cat. 297. Knight in armour

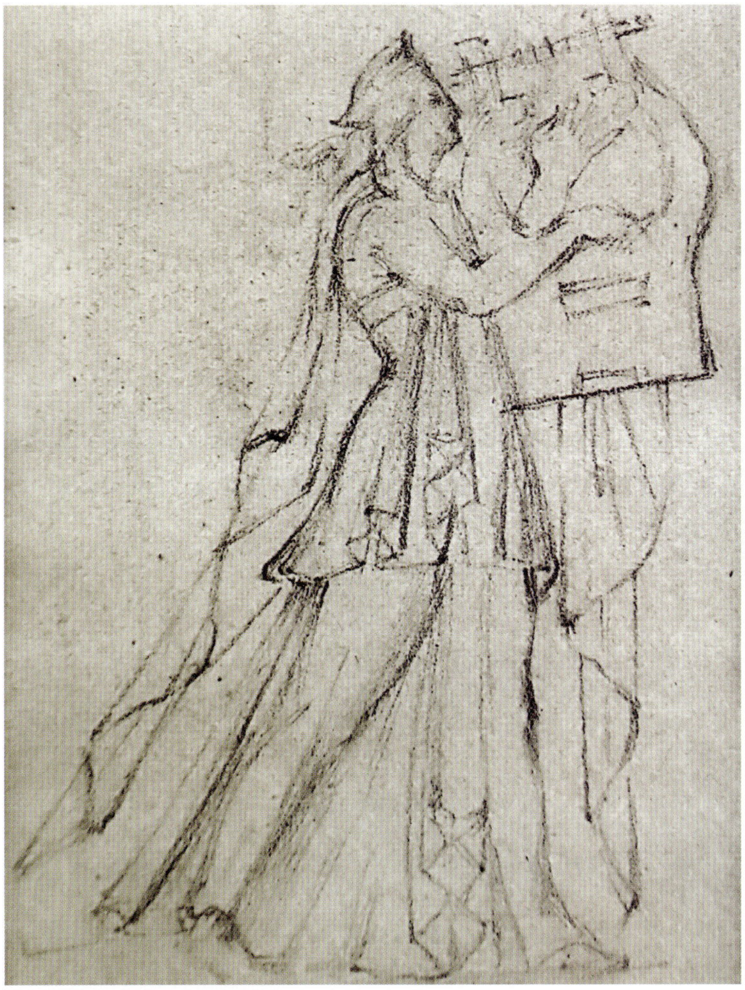

Cat. 298. Classical figure playing a lyre or kithara

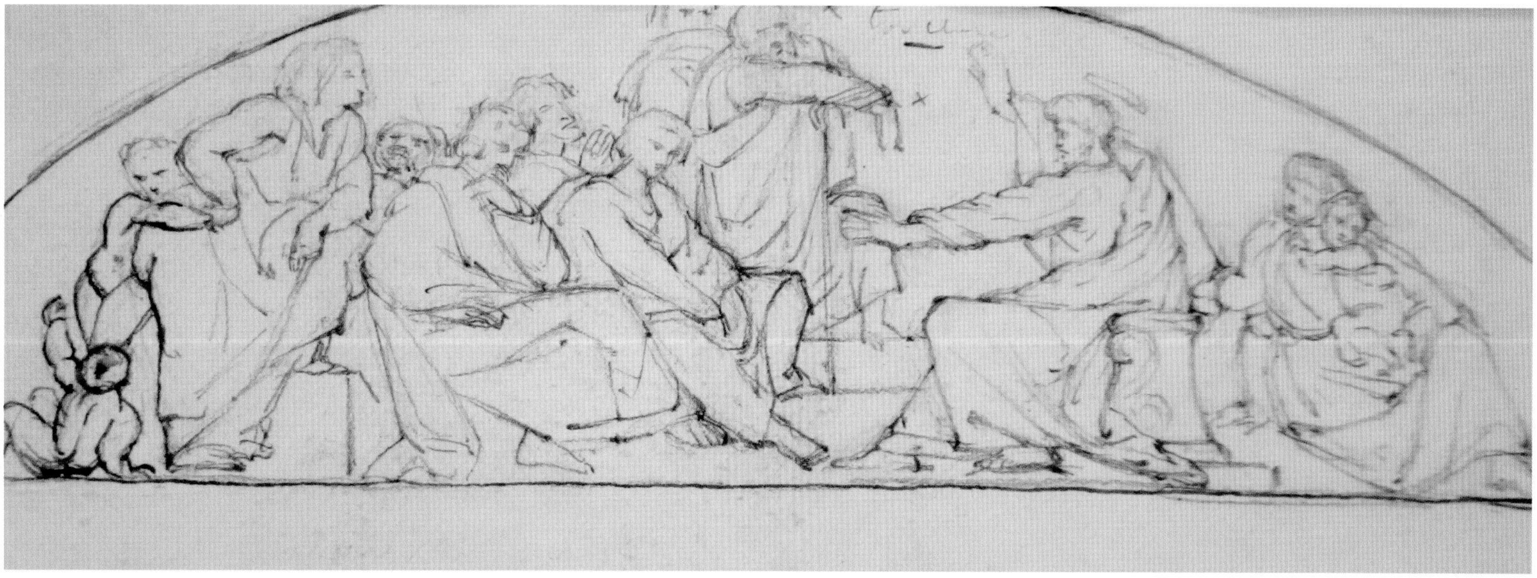

Cat. 299. Biblical scene

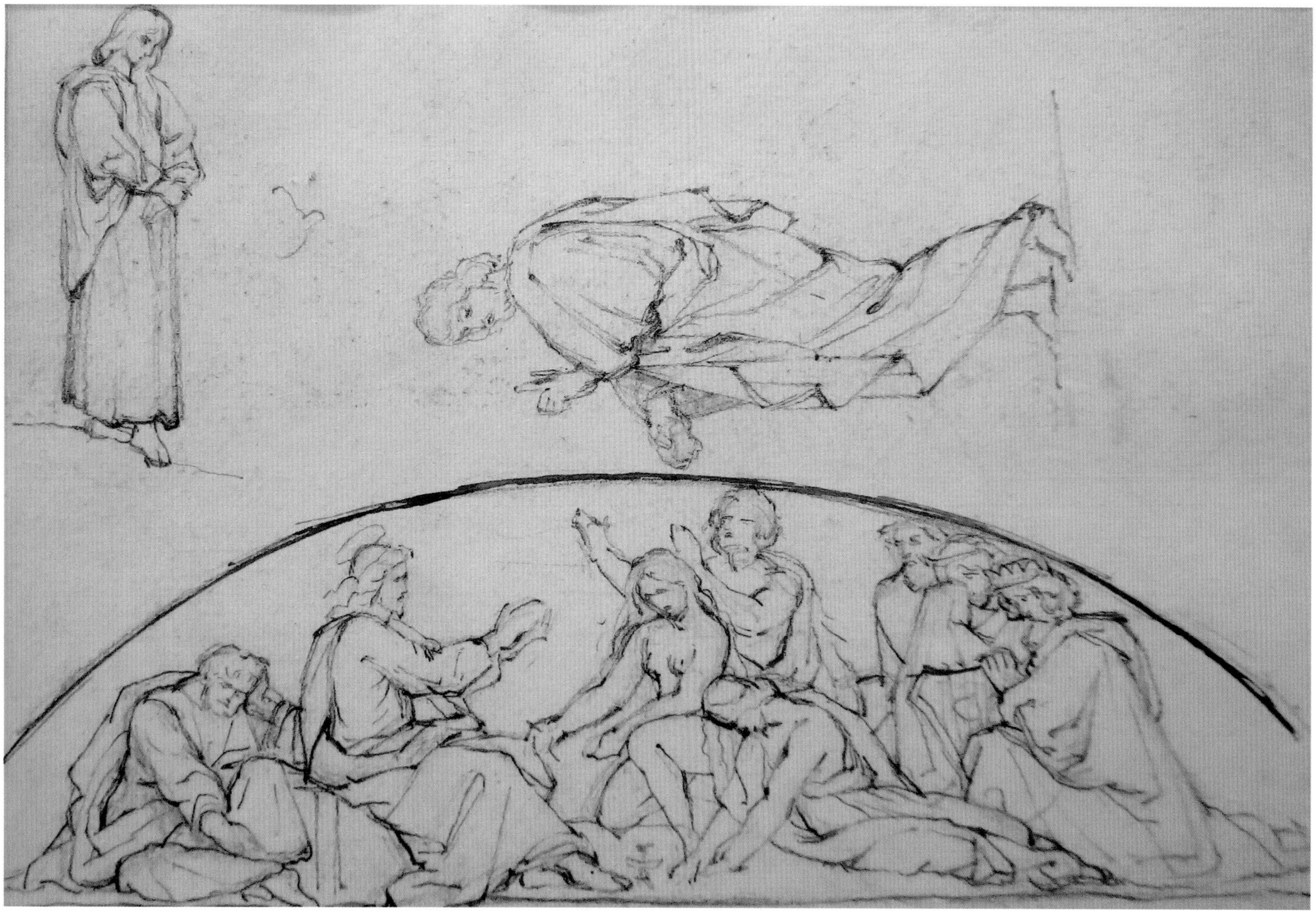

Cat. 300. Biblical scene

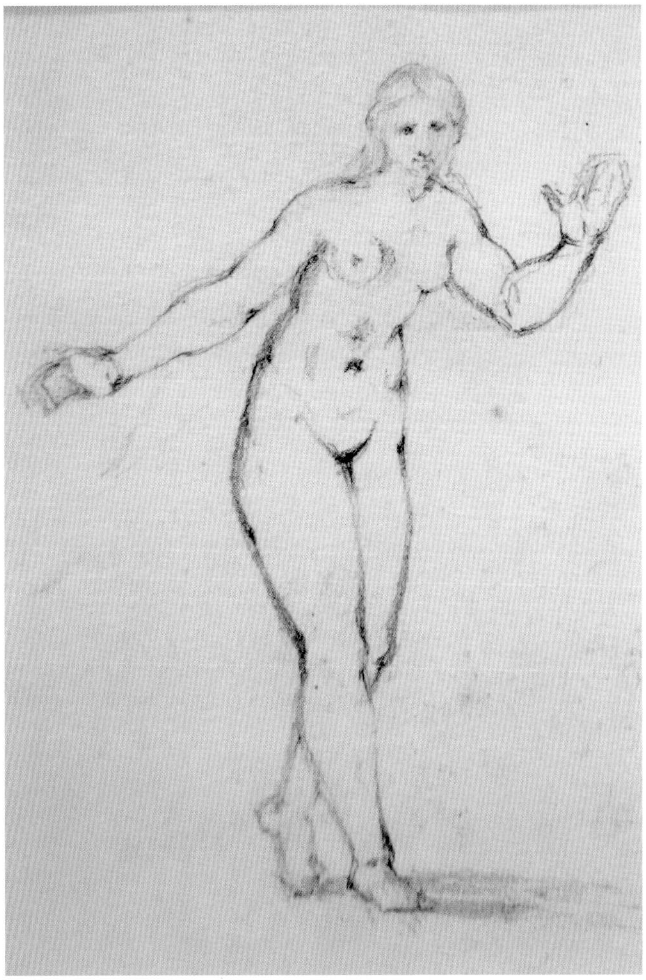

Cat. 301. Standing female nude

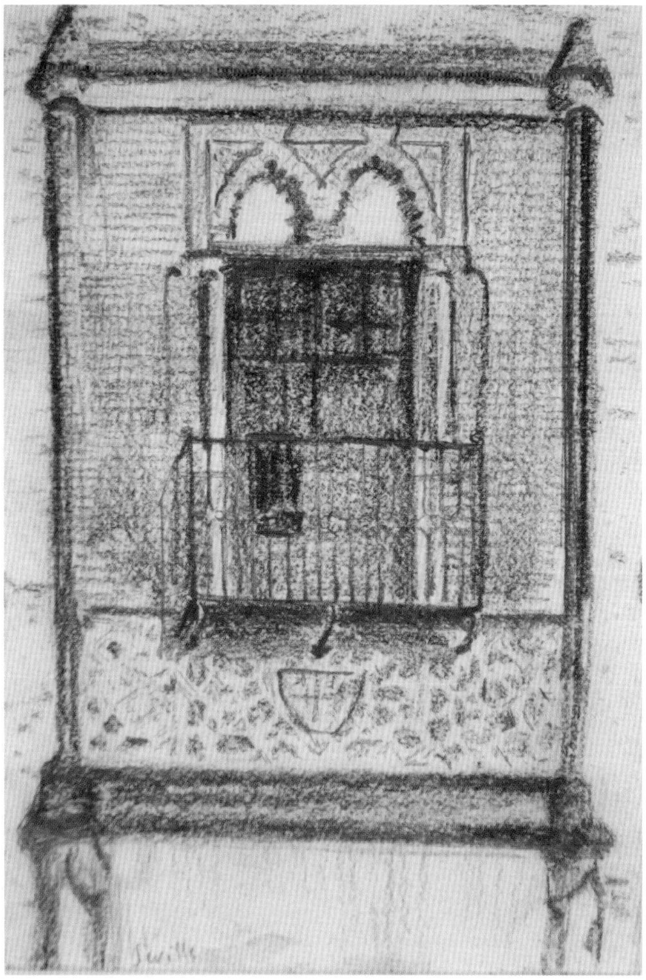

Cat. 306. Architectural study

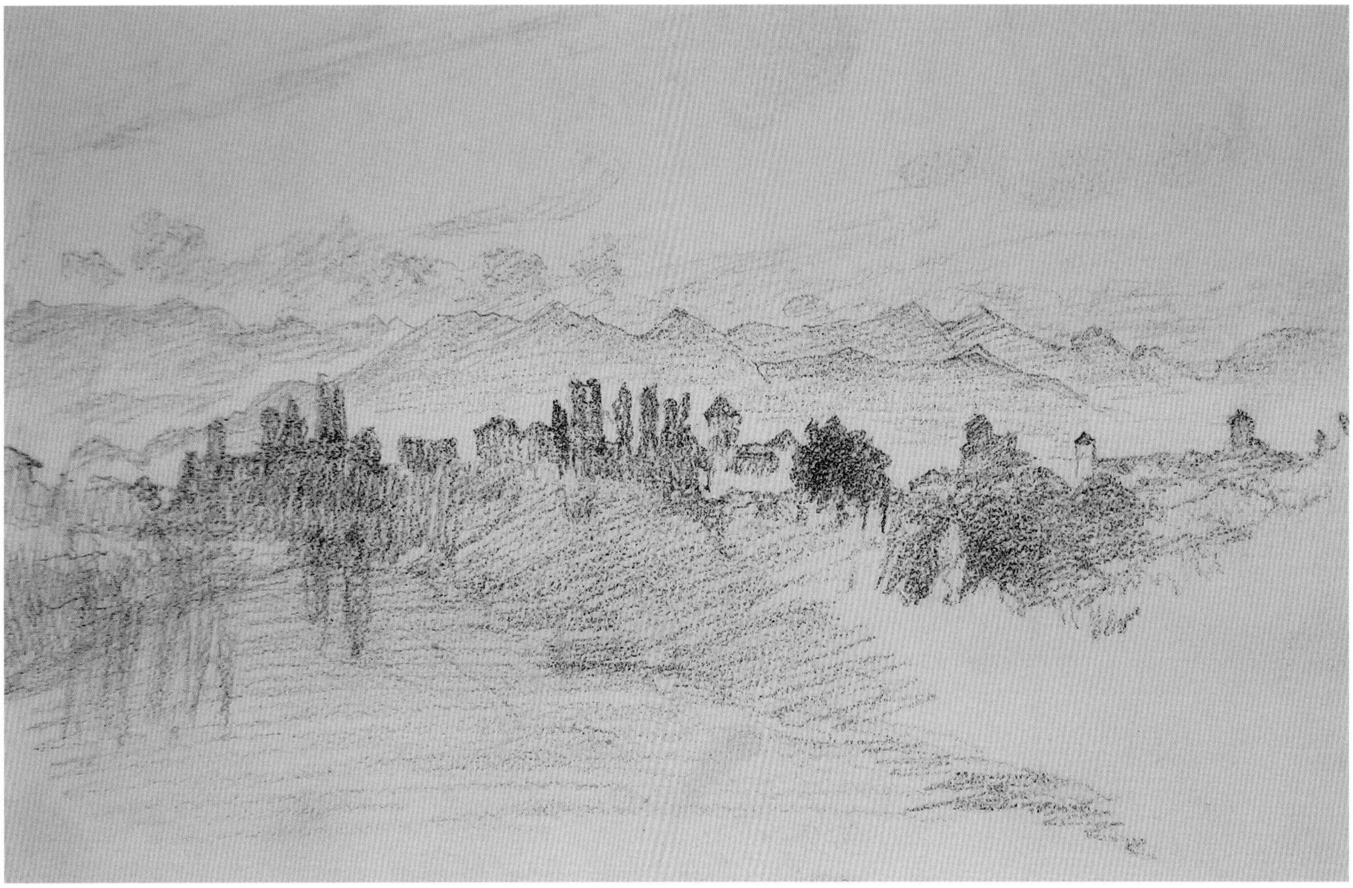

Cat. 307. Landscape study

Sheets from Sketchbooks in Public Collections

University of Oxford, Bodleian Library
Cats. 308-317.
1869-1910.
Provenance: Wallis's studio and then by descent from the artist to his son Harold Wallis; then to his daughter-in-law Mary Wallis (née Mary Elizabeth Aymes); then her great-niece Vera G. Cooper (née Langley; 1910-1989); thence by direct descent to John Harold Cooper and family; their sale Bonhams, London, 5 March 2002, part of lot 71, bought by the art dealer Neil Wilson of Campbell Wilson; sold to the Bodleian Library on 24 March 2003.

The Bodleian owns 21 of Wallis's sketchbooks, dating from 1869-1910 (Shelfmarks: MSS. Eng. d. 3552-8, e. 3414-27). According to staff at the Bodleian: "The sketchbooks mostly contain sketches in pencil, with some sketches in black crayon, charcoal, chalk, pen-and-ink and watercolours. The sketches depict Italian paintings, Egyptian and Italian artefacts, architectural details from buildings, towns, landscapes, figures and animals. Many of the landscapes and street scenes are Egyptian and Italian."

Cats. 308-317. Images by permission of the Bodleian Libraries, University of Oxford

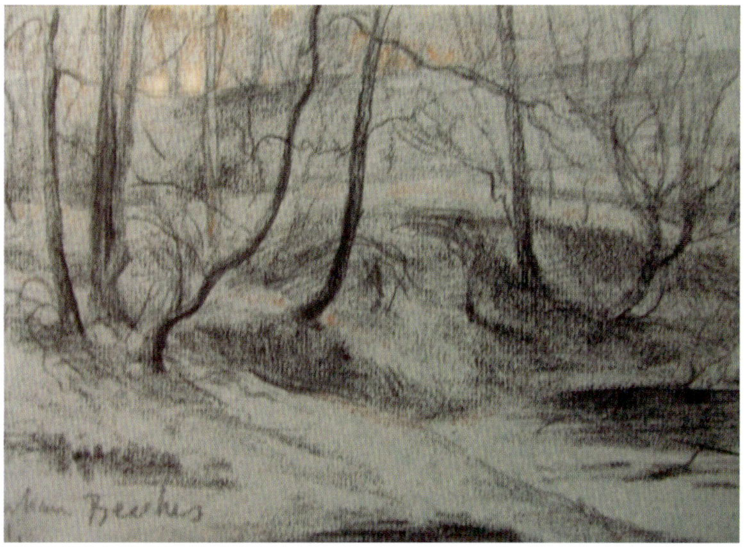

Cat. 308. *Burnham Beeches* [see: Cat. 83]. (MS. Eng. d. 3552, fol. 4r)

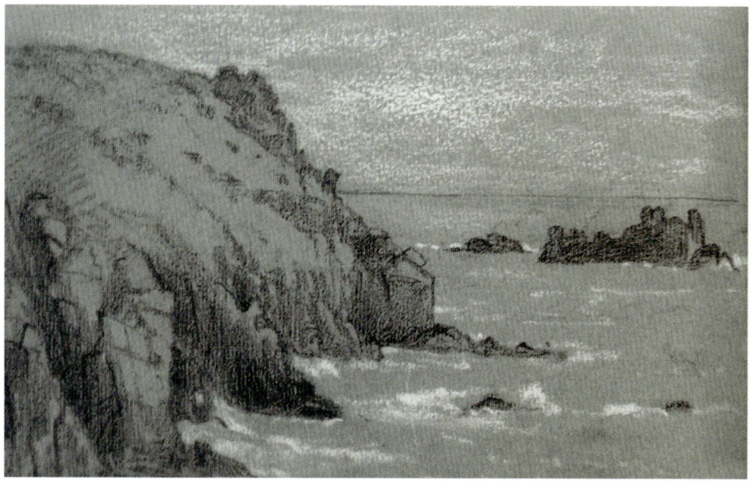

Cat. 309. *Passage.* (MS. Eng. d. 3552, fol. 2r rev)

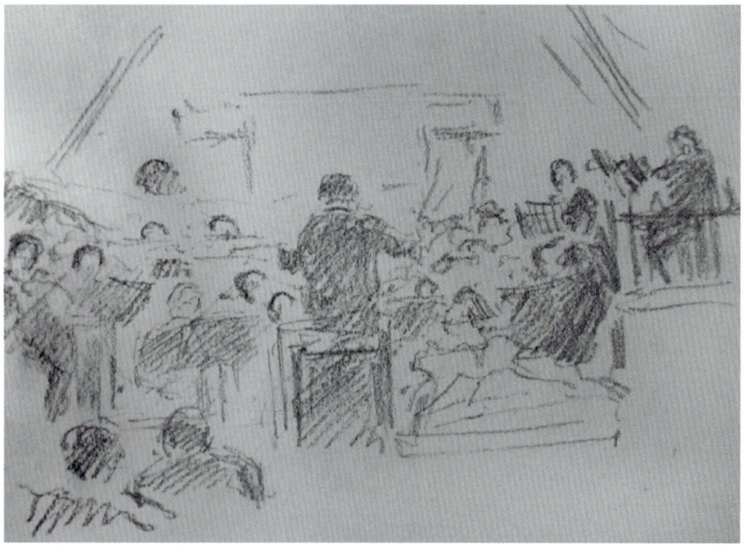

Cat 310. *At a Concert* (A). (MS. Eng. d. 3553, fol. 5r).

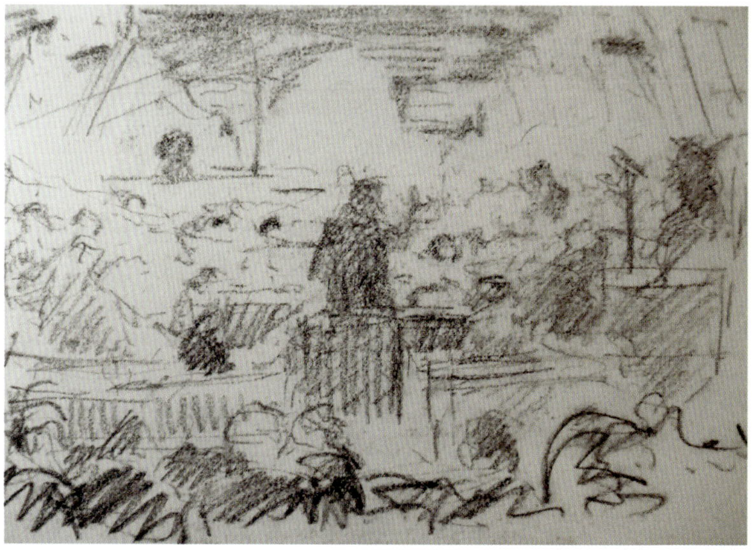

Cat. 311. *At a Concert* (B). (MS. Eng. d. 3553, fol. 4r).

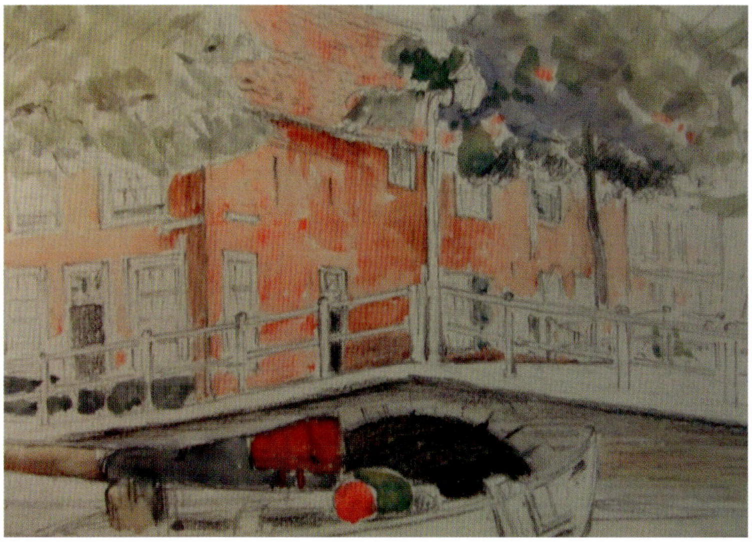

Cat. 312. *Delft (the Netherlands)* [see: Cat. 131]. (MS. Eng. d. 3553, fol. 11r).

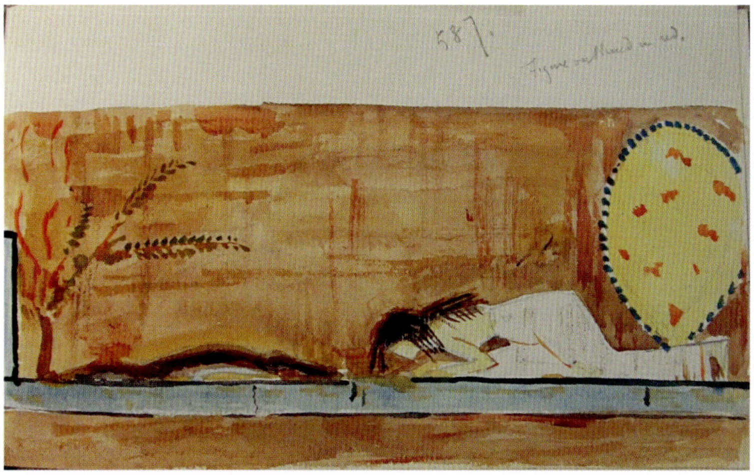

Cat. 313. *Egyptian Figure.* (MS. Eng. d. 3555, fol. 19r).

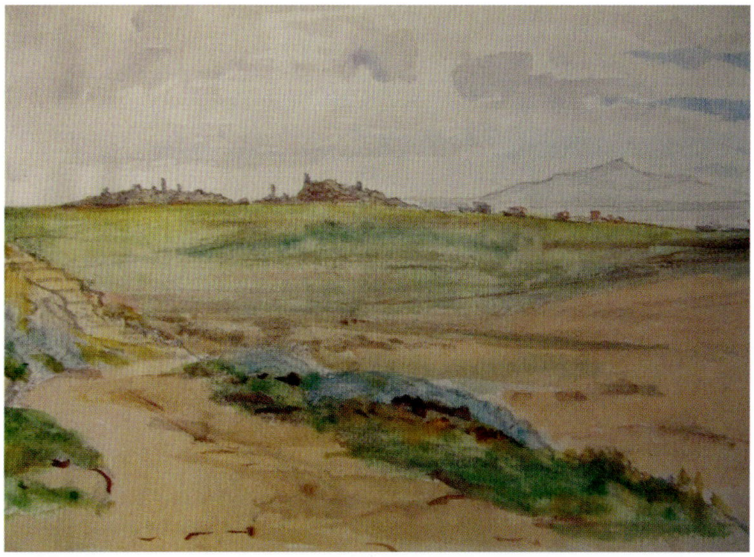

Cat. 314. *Selinus, Sicily* (A). (MS. Eng. d. 3555, fol. 6r).

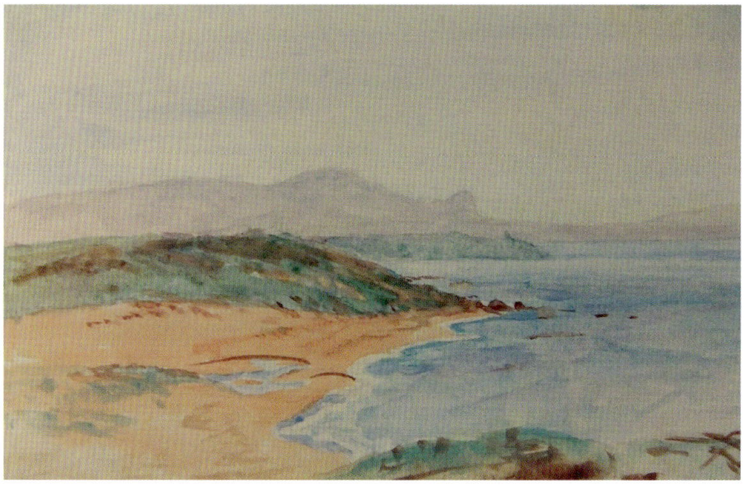

Cat. 315. *Selinus, Sicily* (B). (MS. Eng. d. 3555, fol. 7r).

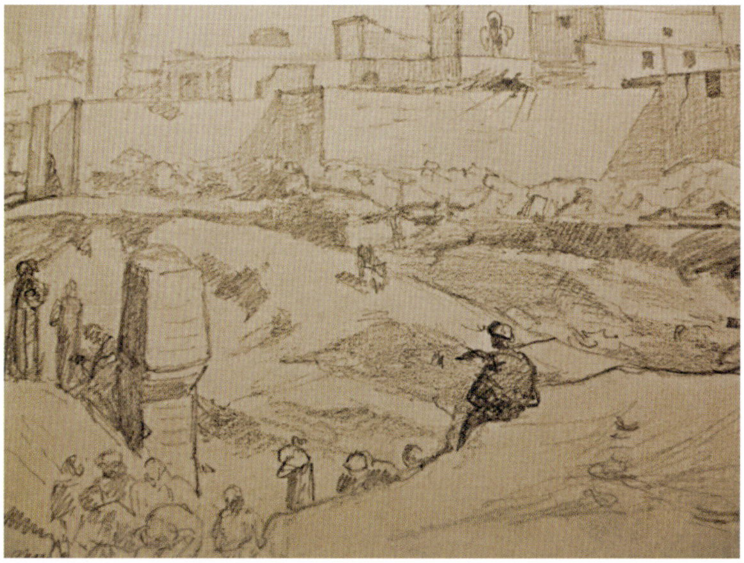

Cat. 316. *Excavating in Egypt.* (MS. Eng. e. 3418, fol. 14r).

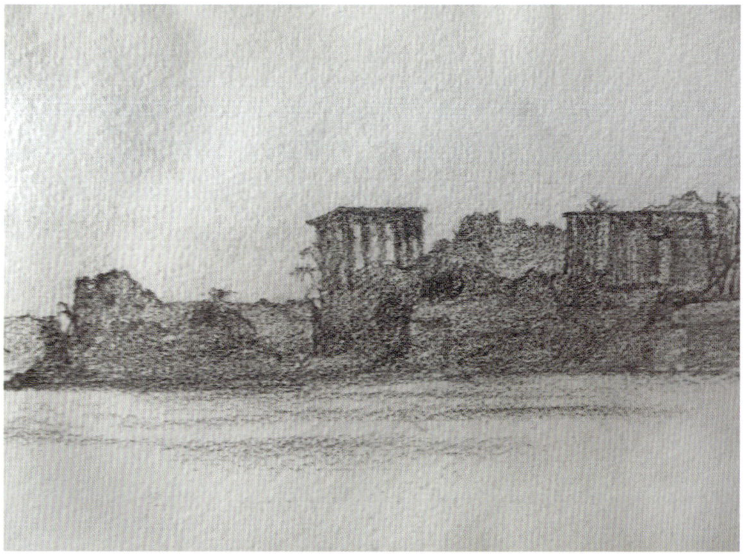

Cat. 317. *Philae* [see: Cat. 246]. (MS. Eng. e. 3418, fol. 4r).

Museo Internazionale delle Ceramiche, Faenza
Cats. 318-320.
*c.*1870s.

The drawings in this sketchbook appear to be have been copied from Italian Renaissance works. They include studies of Leda and the swan, an Italian landscape and a study either after a Renaissance tondo or a majolica plate.

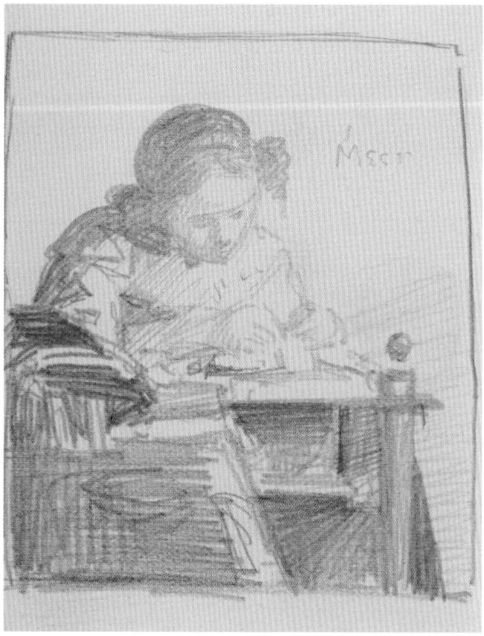

Cat. 321. After Johannes Vermeer's *The Lacemaker.* (MSL 1939/1836). Image by permission of the National Art Library, London (MSL/1939/1836)

National Art Library, London
Cats. 321-369.
c.1890-1910.
Provenance: Gift of Bernard Rackham CB, F.S.A. (through Mr. W.B. Honey, Keeper of Ceramics) on 24 July 1939.[1]

Cat. 321 After Johannes Vermeer's *The Lacemaker* (MSL 1939/1836)
Cat. 322 sketch of an Egyptian pottery merchant (MSL 1939/1946.)
Cat. 323 After Bartholomeus van der Helst (MSL/1939/1836)
Cat. 324 an Egyptian shop (MSL1939/1944)
Cat. 325 orientalist Figures (MSL 1939/1944)
Cat. 326 Cairo scene (MSL/1939/1944)
Cat. 327 Cairo scene (MSL/1939/1944)
Cat. 328 profile study of Dante Alighieri (MSL /1939/1946)
Cat. 329 sketch of Buckfastleigh, Devon, dated 7.4.09 (MSL/1939/1945)
Cat. 330 church interior, Totnes, Devon (MSL/1939/1949)
Cat. 331 various religious figures (MSL/1939/1946)
Cat. 332 male nude figure (MSL/1939/1946)
Cat. 333 Chiusi, Sienna, Italy 26.3.07 (MSL/1939/1946)
Cat. 334 Reggio [di Calabria], Southern Italy (MSL/1939/1946)
Cat. 335 landscape (MSL/1939/1946)
Cat. 336 rock formation (MSL/1939/1946)
Cat. 337 Egyptian male figures, including kneeling and bending figures (MSL 1939/1948)
Cat. 338 Egyptian male figures, sitting, standing and bending (MSL 1939/1948)
Cat. 339 the Souk-el-Selah Street, Cairo (MSL 1939/1948)
Cat. 340 Egyptian decorations in colour, including ceramic designs, 16.12.92. The date suggests he was in Cairo and probably drew these decorations at the Bulaq Museum (MSL/1939/1949)
Cat. 341 inside an Egyptian temple (MSL/1939/1949)
Cat. 342 inside an Egyptian temple (MSL/1939/1949)
Cat. 343 Egyptian decoration including hieroglyphs (MSL/1939/1949)
Cat. 344 inside an Egyptian temple, including a column with hieroglyphs

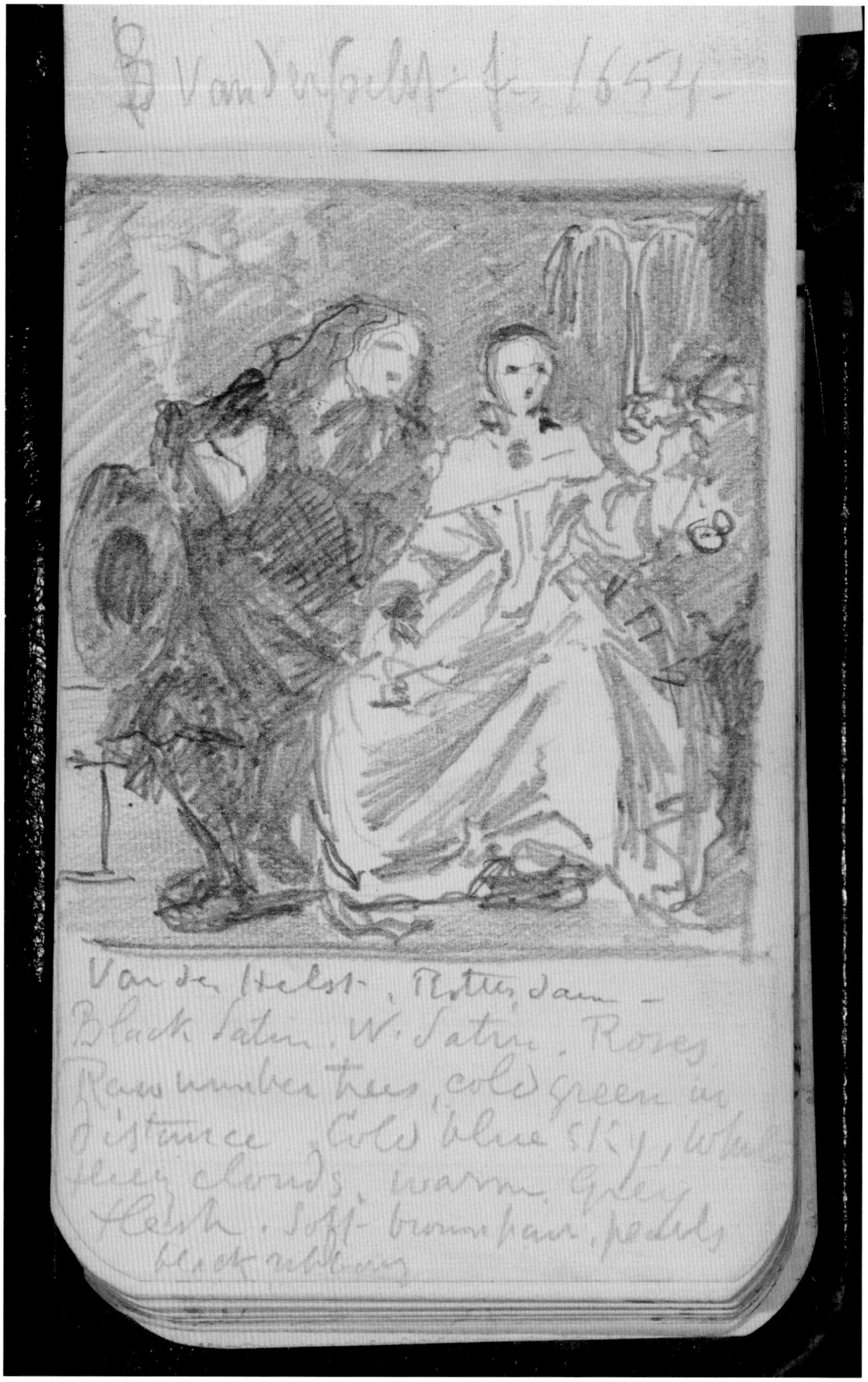

Cat. 323. After Bartholomeus van der Helst. Image by permission of the National Art Library, London (MSL/1939/1836).

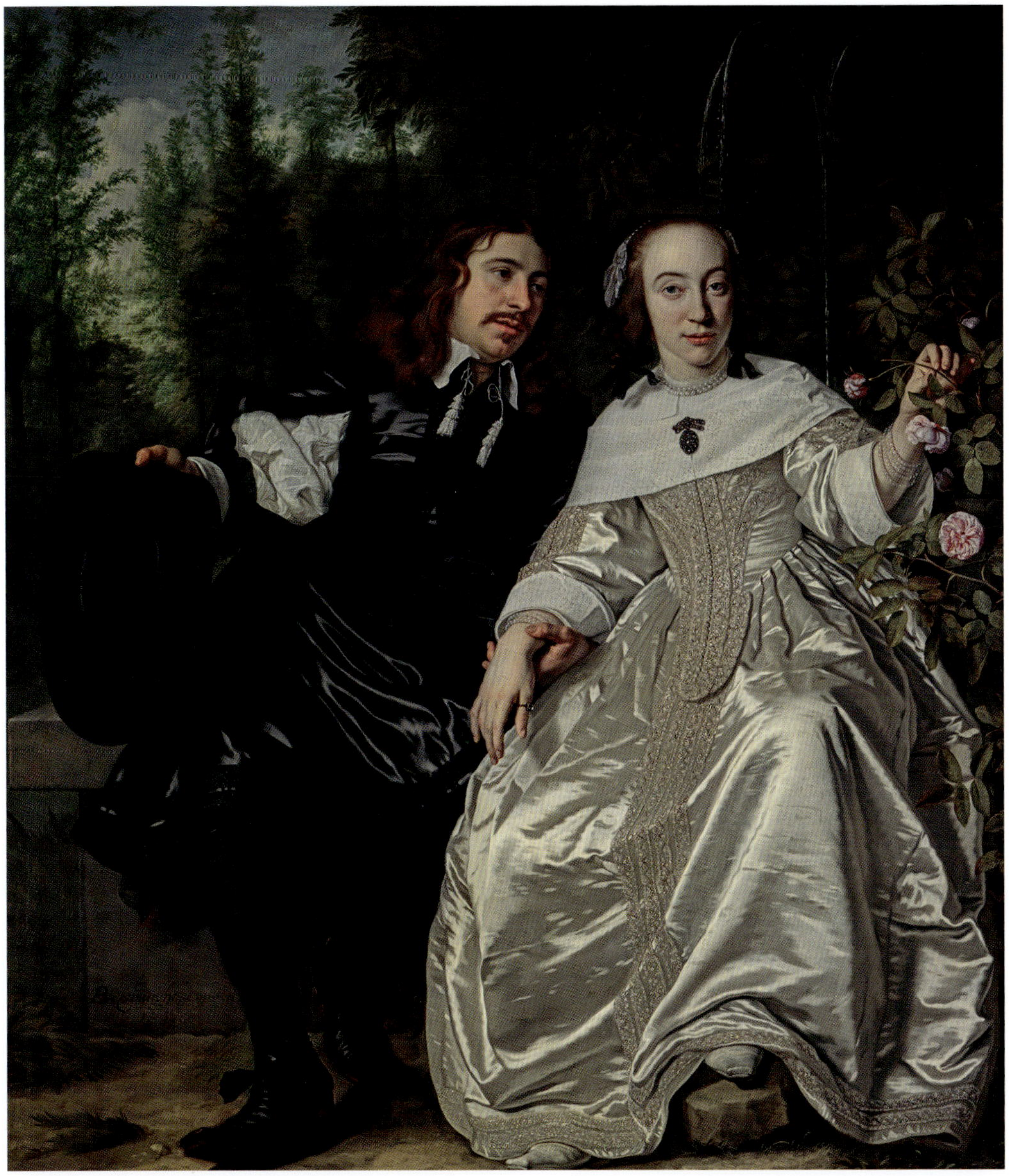

See Cat. 323. Bartholomeus van der Helst, *Abraham del Court and his wife*. Image by permission of Museum Boijmans Van Beuningen, Rotterdam

(MSL/1939/1949)
Cat. 345 inside a chamber, Philae, 14.1.93 (MSL/1939/1949)
Cat. 346 scenes from the Assouan tombs, 14-24.1.93 (MSL/1939/1949)
Cat. 347 Assouan, 30.12.92 (MSL/1939/1949)
Cat. 348 Shellal [south of Assouan], 14.1.93 (MSL/1939/1949)
Cat. 349. Philae, 14.1.93 (MSL/1939/1949)
Cats. 350-353 scenes from the Assouan tombs (MSL/1939/1949)
Cats. 354-355 Egyptian decorations, Karnak and surrounding area, 26-28.1.93 (MSL/1939/1949)
Cats. 356-357 interior of a temple at Assuan showing decorated columns (MSL 1939/1949). These studies relate to Cat. 217
Cat. 358 copy of a design of two standing wrestling figures from the Ghizeh museum, c.20.2.93 (MSL/1939/1949)
Cat. 359 designs, including for ceramics, copied from the Alexandria museum, c.8.3.93 (MSL/1939/1949)
Cat. 360 pencil sketch of a tomb sculpture, Girgeh museum, side view. (MSL 1939/1949)
Cat. 361 study of the same tomb sculpture in the Girgeh museum as Cat. 360, but from a frontal view, (MSL/1939/1949)
Cat. 362 seated Egyptian male figures (MSL/1939/1948)
Cat. 363 Egyptian male figure descending steps (MSL/1939/1948)
Cat. 364 Egyptian male figures, one bending (MSL/1939/1948)
Cat. 365 Coptos, Egypt (MSL/1939/1948)
Cat. 366 Egyptian city architecture (MSL/1939/1948)
Cat. 367 Egyptian architecture – arch (MSL/1939/1948)
Cat. 368 Mosque architecture in Cairo (MSL/1939/1948)
Cat. 369 Egyptian landscape with town (MSL/1939/1948)

The National Art Library at the Victoria and Albert Museum owns 9 notebooks by Wallis containing notes and sketches, some in colour. (Reference 86.BB.5; formerly nos. MSL/1939/1836 and MSL/1939/1942-1949). While some of these drawings show Wallis still making sketches based on his European travels and the Old Master paintings he saw, many are obviously from later, dealing with the sights Wallis had seen during his Egyptian travels. Two of the more interesting sketches relate to Dutch Golden Age paintings of the 17th century, which Wallis obviously admired.

Most of the drawings are in graphite but some are in graphite and watercolour, and many are inscribed with notes in Wallis's hand and dated.

Unfortunately, the high cost of photographing each sketch individually prohibits them all being illustrated here.

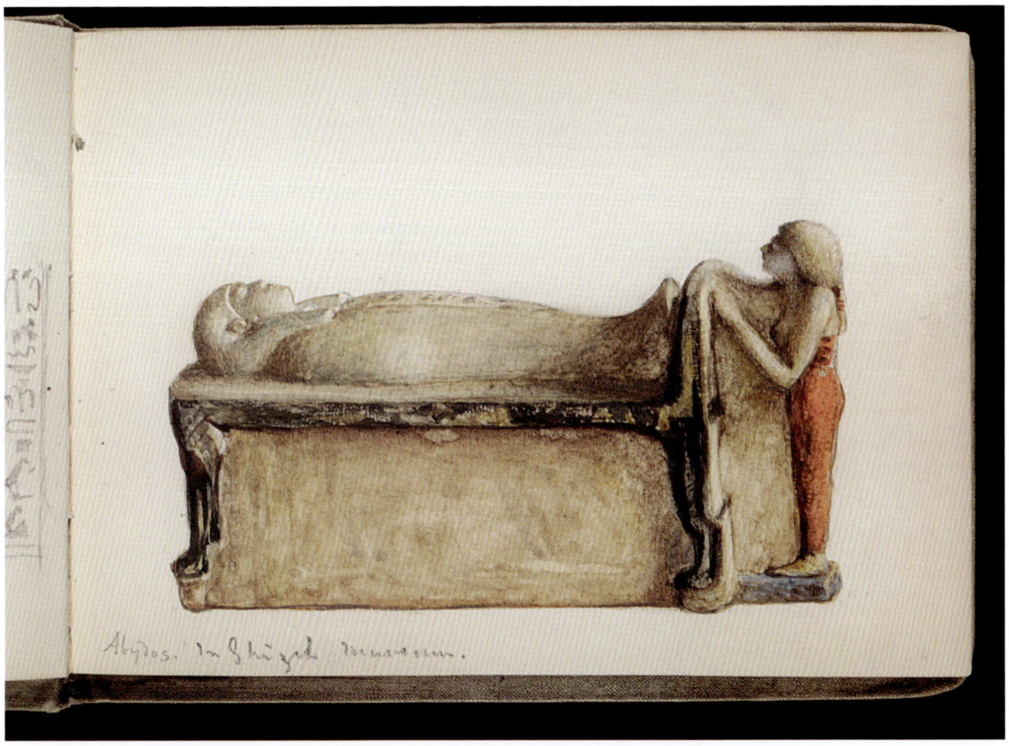

Cat. 360. Pencil sketch of a Tomb sculpture, Girgeh museum, side view. (MSL 1939/1949).

Addendum

Cat. 370. *Study of an Oak Tree*
Date unknown, possibly 1870s; pencil on off-white paper; 12.2 x 16.8 cm (4⅞ x 5⅝ in.) – sight; collection Timothy Wilson, Oxford.
PROVENANCE: Wallis's studio and then by descent from the artist to his son Harold Wallis; then to his daughter-in-law Mary Wallis (née Mary Elizabeth Aymes); then her great-niece Vera G. Cooper (née Langley; 1910-1989); thence by direct descent to John Harold Cooper and family; their sale Bonhams, London, 5 March 2002, part of lot 71; bought by Neil Wilson of Cambell Wilson, Hove, East Sussex; bought in 2002 by Professor Timothy Wilson, Oxford.

This drawing from one of Wallis's sketchbooks shows a grand old oak tree, probably either from Burnham Beeches or Dartmoor, where Wallis liked to sketch.

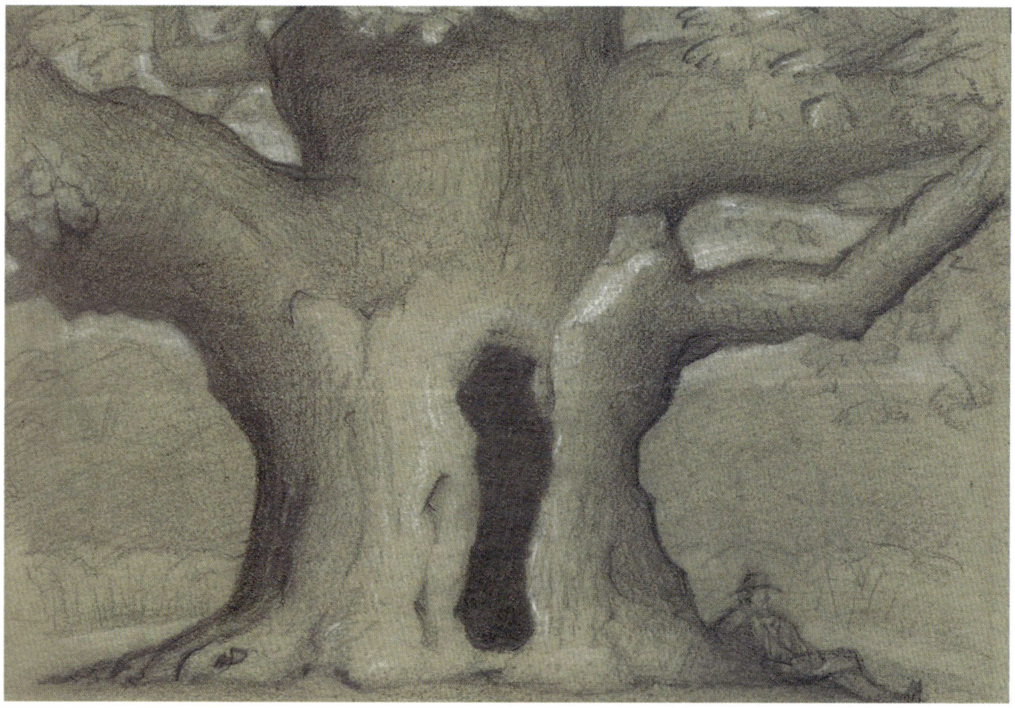

Cat. 370. Image courtesy of Timothy Wilson, Oxford

Cat. 371. *Study of two lions*
Date unknown; sepia watercolour over traces of pencil; 22 x 31 cm (8⅝ x 12¼ in.) – sight; private collection.
PROVENANCE: Wallis's studio and then by descent from the artist to his son Harold Wallis; then to his daughter-in-law Mary Wallis (née Mary Elizabeth Aymes); then her great-niece Vera G. Cooper (née Langley; 1910-1989); thence by direct descent to John Harold Cooper and family; private collection.

This drawing, although skillfully handled, is very unusual in the context of Wallis's oeuvre. If it were not for its good provenance, there would certainly be doubt about its authorship. There is no evidence that this study of a lion and a lioness was used as a study for a painting.

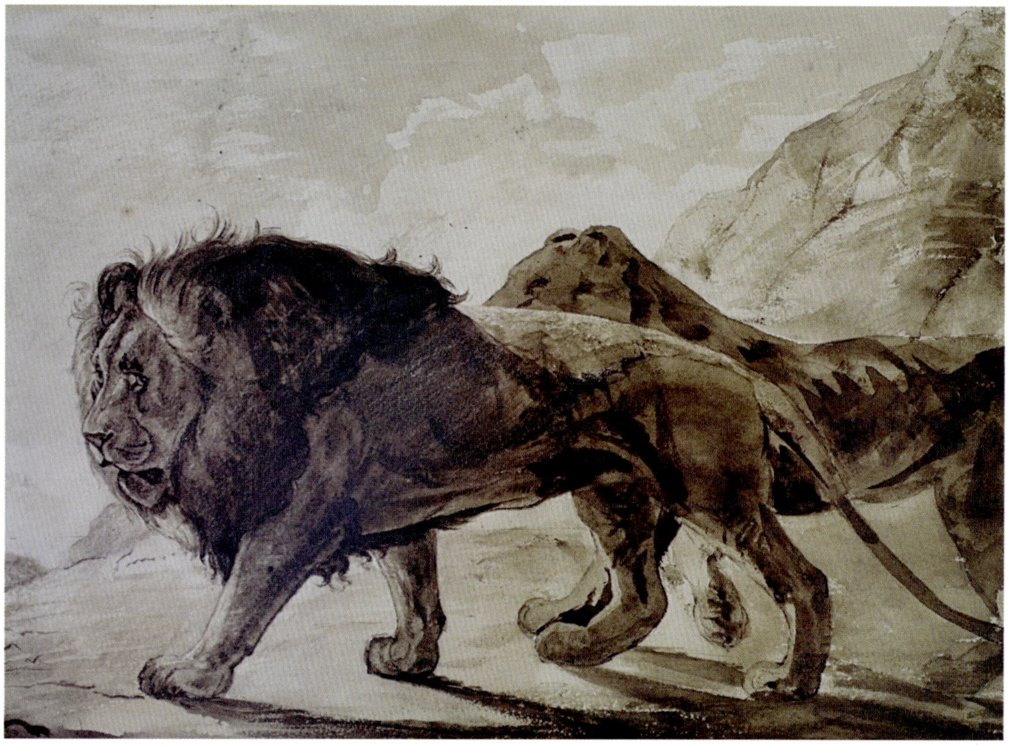

Cat. 371. Image courtesy of Private Collection

Cats. 372-374. *Sketches in Capri*
*c.*1860; graphite on off-white paper; private collection, Diane Johnson, San Francisco, California.

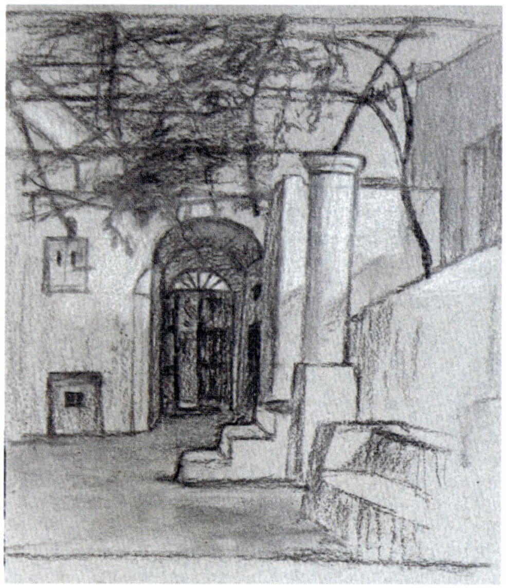

Cat. 372.

Cat. 372. *Architectural study*; image size: 23.5 x 22.5 cm (9¼ x 8⅞ in.).
Cat. 373. *Landscape study with trees in foreground and churches in background*; image size: 23.5 x 27.5 cm (9¼ x 10¾ in.)
Cat. 374. *Shoreline of Capri with mainland in the background*; image size: 30.5 x 24.5 cm (12 x 9⅝ in.).
PROVENANCE: Wallis's studio and then by descent from the artist to his daughter-in-law Alice Julyan Wallis (née Roberts); thence to her great-niece Mrs. Vera G. Whiting, Purley, Surrey; given to Diane Johnson, *c.*1973.
Images courtesy collection Diane Johnson, Paris

These sketches would all appear to have been executed during one of Wallis's trips to

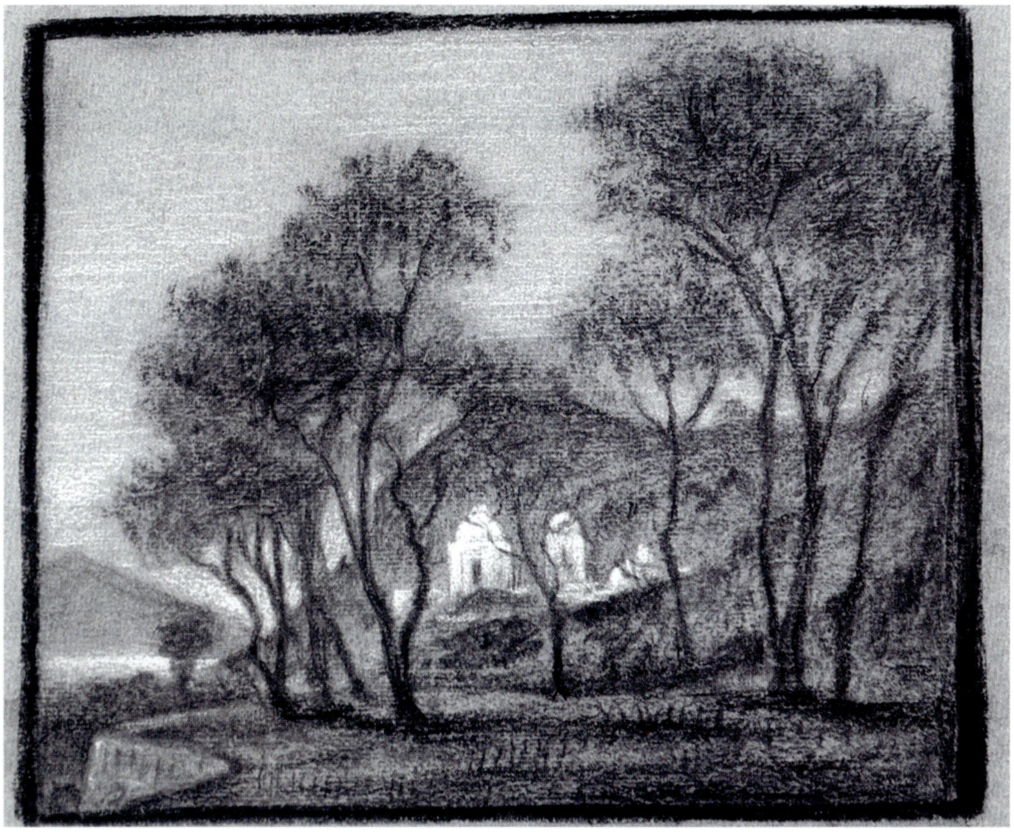

Cat. 373.

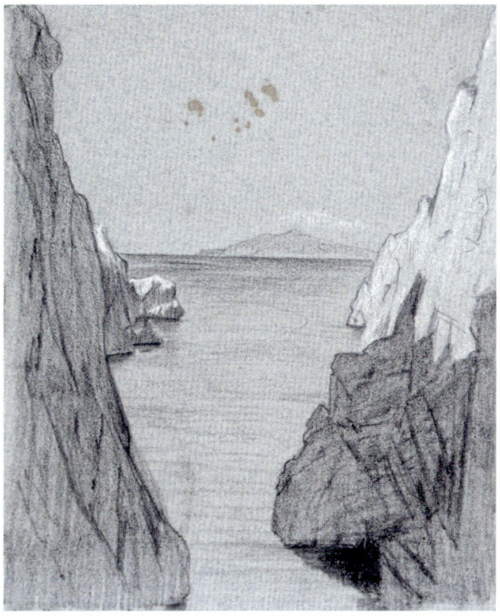

Cat. 374.

Capri, which he visited many times, especially in the late 1850s and early 1860s. The first drawing [Cat. 372] is probably of the Hotel Pagano where Wallis preferred to stay when in Capri. This drawing may be compared to Wallis's *Mediterranean Landscape seen from the Terrace of a Villa* [Cat. 77] and to Frederic Leighton's *The Staircase of a House at Capri* of 1859 in the Loyd Collection.

The second drawing [Cat. 373] is a landscape drawing with one of Capri's many churches seen in the background.

The third drawing [Cat. 374] shows the sheer rocky cliffs of the isle of Capri shoreline with Mount Vesuvius seen in the background on the mainland.

Cat. 375. *Sketch of an unknown Old Master Painting*
*c.*1860; black chalk heightened with white on off-white paper; image size: 6.3 x 9.2 cm (2½ x 3⅝ in.); private collection, Diane Johnson, San Francisco, California.
Provenance: Wallis's studio and then by descent from the artist to his daughter-in-law Alice Julyan Wallis (née Roberts); thence to her great-niece Mrs. Vera G. Whiting, Purley, Surrey; given to Diane Johnson, *c.*1973.

Although this could be a thumbnail sketch for a projected painting by Wallis for one of his *Merchant of Venice* series of watercolours, it is much more likely to be a study of an Old Master painting seen during one of his many travels. The contour/framing of this drawing[1] would be quite unusual for a preparatory drawing. It is, however, rather unusual in technique in comparison to other studies Wallis made of Old Master paintings, which were more normally executed in graphite. The prime focus of this sketch is the meeting of a couple, with the woman appearing to be bowing slightly, and perhaps being introduced by the man to a figure on a throne looking down. The couple are surrounded by a group of onlookers. Their costumes suggest that this could perhaps be a study of a Venetian Renaissance painting by an artist such as Veronese.

Cat. 376. *Study of an Old Lady*
Date unknown; pencil and black chalk, heightened with white, on light brown paper; 13 x 9 cm (5⅛ x 3½ in.) – sight; private collection.
Provenance: Wallis's studio and then by descent from the artist to his son Harold Wallis; then to his daughter-in-law Mary Wallis (née Mary Elizabeth Aymes); then her great-niece Vera G. Cooper (née Langley; 1910-1989); thence by direct descent to John Harold Cooper and family; their sale Bonhams, London, 5 March 2002, part of lot 71, purchased by Neil Wilson of Campbell Wilson, Hove, East Sussex; private collection; anonymous sale, Dawson's Auctioneers, Maidenhead, Berkshire, 24 November 2018, lot 105, bought in; Dawson's Auctioneers, 19 January 2019, lot 268.

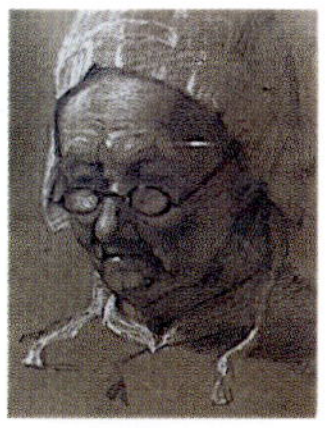

Cat. 376. Image courtesy of Dawson's Auctioneers, Maidenhead, Berkshire

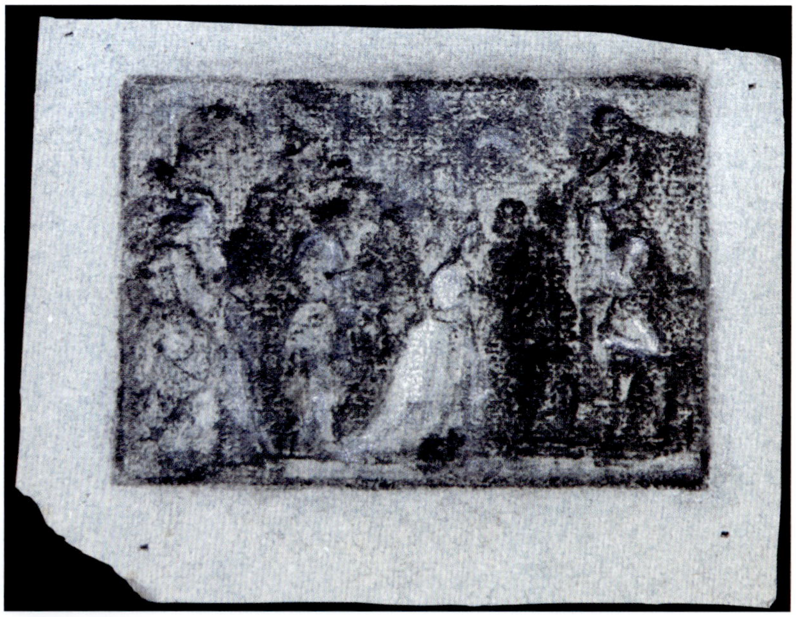

Cat. 375. Image courtesy of Diane Johnson Collection, San Francisco

Appendices

Appendix I
Exhibitions of Wallis's Works During his Lifetime

The list of exhibitions at London's major public galleries may be considered exhaustive but not necessarily for the private galleries. Unfortunately archives for regional galleries are less complete and access often limited. Although what is presented here is by no means a complete list, it is the result of considerable research. The authors would be grateful for any further information.

w = winter exhibition

BIRMINGHAM

Birmingham Museum and Art Gallery
'The Pre-Raphaelites. Special Loan Collection of Modern Pictures in Oil and Water Colours'

1891	No. 200	*The Death of Chatterton (Chatterton)* [Cat. 22]
	No. 201	*Back from Marston Moor* [Cat. 39]
	No. 233	*The Stonebreaker* [Cat. 28]

Birmingham Society of Artists/ Birmingham Royal Society of Artists

1877	No. 211	*The Physician – A Visit of Charity* [Cat. 112]

'Autumn exhibition'

1876	No. 73	*The Devotion of Sydney Carton* [Cat. 106]
	No. ?	*How now, Tubal* [Cat. 108]
1877	No. 95	*The Farmhouse by the Sea* [Cat. 116]
	No. 496	*Childe Roland to the Dark Tower Came* [Cat. 63]

'Exhibition of Modern Works of Art'

1860	No. 30	*Back from Marston Moor* [Cat. 39]
1861	No. 176	*The Stonebreaker* [Cat. 28]
1864	No. 356	*Pippa* [Cat. 53]
1865	No. 199	*A Neapolitan Girl* [Cat. 54]

'Spring Exhibition of Water-colour Paintings'

1876	No. 73	*The Devotion of Sydney Carton* [Cat. 106]
1879	No. 86	*In a Sacristy, the Carpet Merchant* [Cat. 120]
	No. 562	*A Welsh Mountain Lake* [Cat. 113]
1800	No. 191	*After the Trial: Antonio receiving the Congratulations…* [Cat. 125]

Private Gallery

1860		*The Death of Chatterton (Chatterton)* [Cat. 22]

BRADFORD

Bradford Fine Art and Industrial Exhibition

1882	No. 52	*Found at Naxos* [Cat. 97]

HUDDERSFIELD

Huddersfield Fine Art and Industrial Exhibition

1883	No. 66	*Dr. Johnson at Cave's, the Publisher* [Cat. 10]

LEEDS

Mr. Hasée's Gallery

1860		*The Death of Chatterton (Chatterton)* [Cat. 22]

National Exhibition of Works of Art

1868	No. 1391	*The Death of Chatterton (Chatterton)* [Cat. 22]

Yorkshire Art Exhibition

1880	No. 804	*Back from Marston Moor* [Cat. 39]

LIVERPOOL

International Exhibition

1886		*Back from Marston Moor* [Cat. 39]

Liverpool Academy

1855	No. 743	*Fireside Reverie* [Cat. 18]
1858	No. 143	*The Bridge of Sighs* [Cat. 35]
1860	No. 54	*The Stonebreaker* [Cat. 28]
	No. 766	*Nightfall* [Cat. 41]

Liverpool Corporation, Walker Art Gallery

Autumn Exhibition

1873	No. 440	*The Last Days of the Cappuccini Monastery, at Sorrento* [Cat. 57]
1884	No. 620	*A Scene from The Merchant of Venice* [Cat. 160]
	No. 460	*The Nosegay* [Cat. 172]
1888	No. 545	*Door of a Mosque* [Cat. 190]
1892	No. ?	*The Death of Chatterton (Chatterton)* [Cat. 22]
1895	No. 783	*The Principal Entrance to the Mosque of Sultan Kalaun, Cairo* [Cat. 223]

Liverpool Society of Fine Arts

1862	No. 335	Tobias Restoring the Eyesight of Tobit [Cat. 46]

LONDON

Agnew's

'Annual Exhibition of Water-Colour Art'

1884	No. 169	*A Spanish-Moorish Doorway at Toldeo* [Cat. 165]

British Institution

1854	No. 512	*The Parlour in Anne Hathaway's Cottage* [Cat. 16]

Burlington Fine Arts Club

1912	No. 22	*Elaine* [Cat. 44]

Canterbury Hall and Fine Arts Gallery, Waterloo Road, Lambeth

1859		*Henry Marten at Chepstow Castle* [Cat. 31]

Dudley Gallery

'Cabinet Pictures in Oil'

1867	No. 62	*Across the Common* [Cat. 62]
1868	No. 3	*Moorland* [Cat. 66]
1870	No. 93	*His Highness and His Excellency the Ambassador of the Florentine Republic* [Cat. 79]
1872	No. 269	*Barnard's Inn, Holborn, in the 17th Century* [Cat. 89]
1873	No. 355	*Maestro Sebastiano Guccato, Mosaic Worker, Titian's First Master* [Cat. 94]

'Exhibition of Works of Art in Black and White'

1872	No. 130	*Heather* [Cat. 90]
	No. 143	*Moorland Oaks* [Cat. 91; *see also*: Cat. 102]
	No. 335	*A Moorland Stream* [Cat. 92]
1874	No. 188	*After the Storm* [Cat. 71] / *After a Storm in the Woods* [Cat. 98]

Earl's Court

'Victorian Era Exhibition'

1897	No. 563	*The Devotion of Sydney Carton* [Cat. 106]

French Gallery

'Annual Winter Exhibition'

1859	No. 154	*Xarifa* [Cat. 36]
1865w	No. 103	*The Golden Scarf* [Cat. 58]
	No. 104	*After Supper at Capri* [Cat. 59]

Guildhall Gallery

'Loan Exhibition of Modern English Art'

1895	No. 86	*The Death of Chatterton (Chatterton)* [Cat. 22]

'Exhibition of Works of Art Presented by the Artists'

1900	No. 41	Back from Marston Moor [Cat. 39]

Hanover Gallery (47 New Bond Street)

'Winter Exhibition of Oil Paintings by British Artists'

1880	No. 87	*In the Forest – Autumn (Autumn in the Forest)* [Cat. 148]

Hogarth Club

1859 (summer)		*The Stonebreaker* [Cat. 28]
1860		?*Back from Marston Moor*[1] [Cat 39]

London International Exhibition

1871	No. 275	*The Last Days of the Cappuccini Monastery, at Sorrento* [Cat. 57]
	No. 473	*His Highness and His Excellency the Ambassador of the Florentine Republic* [Cat 79]
	No. 1747	*Ser Pandolfo* [Cat. 80]
	No. 1963	Chalk drawing of *The Stonebreaker* [28b]

New British Institution

'Exhibition for Relief of Widows and Orphans of German Soldiers'

1870	No. 9	*Teresa* [Cat. 81]

'First Spring Exhibition of Pictures'

1870	No. 92	*Blue Bells* [Cat. 75]

'First Winter Exhibition of Water-Colour Drawings'

1870	No. 77	*Ser Pandolfo* [Cat. 80]

'Second Spring Exhibition of Cabinet Pictures'

1871	No. 64.	*Assunta* [Cat. 87]

New Gallery

1888	No. 169	*Pot of Honey from Mount Hymettus* [Cat. 191]

Old Water-Colour Society

(also: Society of Painters in Water Colour; Royal Society of Painters in Water Colours)

1878	No. 55	*A Flemish Interior* [Cat. 119]
	No. 107	*In a Sacristy, the Carpet Merchant* [Cat. 120]
	No. 187	*The Sentinel* [Cat. 121]
	No. 282	*The Prison Window* [Cat. 122]

1878w	No. 50	*Awaiting the Distribution* [Cat.123]
	No. 66	*A Welsh Mountain Lake* [Cat. 113]
	No. 68	*Between Hampstead and Highgate…* [Cat. 114]
	No. 90	*A Sextett during the Terror* [Cat. 115]
1879	No. 14	*After the Trial. Antonio receiving the Congratulations of his Friends* [Cat. 125]
	No. 62	*An Operetta* [Cat. 126]
1879w	No. 122	*Luca Signorelli* [Cat. 127]
	No. 258	*Announcement of Marriage - Townhall at Bruges* [Cat. 128]
	No. 264	*Nearest the Door - Cathedral at Bruges* [Cat. 129]
	No. 308	*A Dutch Hofje* [Cat. 130]
	No. 371	*A Bridge at Delft - Market Day* [Cat. 131]
1880	No. 174	*Vespers, Cathedral at Bruges* [Cat. 138]
	No. ?	*The Fish Market at Bruges* [Cat. 139]
	No. 214	*Literature in the Eighteenth Century* [Cat. 140]
	No. 257	*A Study (of a Belgian Girl's Head)* [Cat. 142]
	No. 271	*Old Friends* [Cat. 141]
1880w	No. 237	*In the Uffizi Gallery, Florence* [Cat. 144]
	No. 258	*A Study* [Cat. 145]
	No. 381	*The Marriage Settlement* [Cat. 146]
	No. 404	*A Manuscript* [Cat. 147]
1881	No. 260	*A Genuine Cremona* [Cat. 149]
1881w	No. 11	*Portia and Nerissa on the Morning of the Trial* [Cat. 150]
	No. 69	*Portia and Nerissa at Belmont* [Cat. 151]
	No. 111	*Shylock, Jessica and Launcelot* [Cat. 152]
	No. 125	*Antonio, Bassanio, Gratiano and Lorenzo…* [Cat. 153]
	No. 156	*Jessica and Launcelot* [Cat. 154]
	No. 235	*Antonio and Bassanio…* [Cat. 155]
	No. 271	*Antonio, Salarino and Solanio in Conversation* [Cat. 156]
1882	No. 58	*Tubal bring Shylock News of Jessica* [Cat. 158]
	No. 64	*Gratiano having brought Portia Bassanio's Ring…* [Cat. 159]
	No. 196	*The Violin Player; the Fountain is attributed to Donatello* [Cat. 162]
	No. 210	*Springtide; Sitting in the Shade, in his Orchard* [Cat. 163]
1882w	No. 189	*The Moorish Fountain and Patio de Lindaraja at the Alhambra* [Cat. 164]
1883	No. 233	*A Spanish-Moorish Doorway at Toledo* [Cat. 165]
	No. 269	*A Scene from the Merchant of Venice* [Cat. 160]
1883w	No. 145	*Gossip* [Cat. 166]
	No. 158	*A Gipsy Dance, Granada* [Cat. 167]
	No. 243	*At a Window, Seville* [Cat. 168]
	No. 402	*Pastorale* [Cat. 170]
1884	No. 19	*A Scene from the Merchant of Venice* [Cat. 161]
	No. 218	*At the Well* [Cat. 171]
	No. 275	*The Nosegay* [Cat. 172]
1884w	No. 31	*The Bishop's Tomb* [Cat. 173]
	No. 351	*Gateway of the Palace of Don Pedro the Cruel, at Toledo* [Cat. 174]
1885	No. 140	*Going to Market, Bruges* [Cat. 176]
	No. 265	*An Oriental Glass Merchant* [Cat. 177]
1885w	No. 24	*In the Bazaar, Smyrna* [Cat. 178]
1886	No. 12	*Outside the Door of the Mosque of Barkuk, Cairo* [Cat. 180]
	No. 27	*Twelfth Night - Act II, Scene 4* [Cat. 181]
1886w	No. 56	*Interior Courtyard of a Jew's House at Cairo – Preparing Coffee* [Cat. 184]
	No. 120	*The Second Cataract of the Nile, from the Western Bank…* [Cat. 185]
1887	No. 23	*Street Scene in Cairo (The Sheykh hears Mysterious Whispering)* [Cat. 186]
1887w	No. 13	*Herodotus at the Scribes' Bazaar, Memphis* [Cat. 187]
	No. 94	*The Flute Player* [Cat. 188]
1888	No. 63	*A Coffee Merchant, the Bazaar at Suez* [Cat. 189]
	No. 258	*Door of a Mosque, Cairo* [Cat. 190]
1888w	No. 199	*The Porch of the Mosque of Sultan Hassan, Cairo* [Cat. 192]
	No. 216	*Street Scene in Smyrna; A Turkish Letter-Writer* [Cat. 193]
1889	No. 101	*A Do'ruck and Chool'leh Merchant, Cairo* [Cat. 194]

1889w	No. 33	*The Sick King in Bokhara* [Cat. 196]
1890w	No. 105	*A Thirteenth Century Spanish Moorish Vase* [Cat. 198]
1891	No. 135	*Etna, from the Theatre of Taormina* [Cat. 199]
1891w	No. 18	*The Temple of Neptune, Paestum* [Cat. 203] Illustrations to Persian Ceramic Art:
	No. 333	*Persian Tile, xiii* [Cat. 204]
	No. 334	*Persian Lustre Vase, xiii* [Cat. 205]
	No. 337	*Persian Vase, xiii* [Cat. 206]
	No. 340	*Persian Lustre Vase, xiii* [Cat. 207]
	No. 341	*Persian Lustre Vase, xiii* [Cat. 208]
	No. 343	*Persian Tile, xiii* [Cat. 209]
	No. 347	*Persian Lustre Bowl, xiii* [Cat. 210]
	No. 348	*Persian Bowl, xiii* [Cat. 211]
1892	No. 231	*The Fountain at Arethusa, at Ortygia, Syracuse* [Cat. 213]
1892w	No. 307	*In an Oriental Bazaar* [Cat. 214]
	No. 327	*A Persian Vase* [Cat. 215]
	No. 333	*A Damascus Vase* [Cat. 216]
1893	No. 67	*A Street Scene in Suez* [Cat. 218]
1893w	No. 92	*Erinna* [Cat. 219]
	No. 313	*The Music Master* [Cat. 220]
1894	No. 115	*A Street in Cairo* [Cat. 221]
1894w	No. 92	*Fetching Water, a Lane in Cairo* [Cat. 222]
1895	No. 6	*The Principal Entrance of the Mosque of Sultan Kalaun, Cairo* [Cat. 223]
1896	No. 137	*The Court of the Great Altar of the Temple of Queen Hatshepsu* [Cat. 225]
1896w	No. 261	*A Study of a Greek Vase* [Cat. 226]
	No. 265	*A Study of the Ornamentation of a White Athenian Lekythos* [Cat. 227]
	No. 271	*A Study of the Ornamentation of a Greek Vase* [Cat. 228]
1897w	No. 25	*The Door of a Mosque at Cairo* [Cat. 234]
1898	No. 22	*Excavating in Egypt; Professor Petrie admiring a Find, the Ramesseum (Flinders Petrie admiring a Find, the Ramesseum, Western Thebes)* [Cat. 224]
1898w	No. 76	*A Relic of the Native Quarter, Cairo* [Cat. 235]
1899	No. 65	*Sedaine Reading to Diderot his Comedy 'Le philosophe sans le s*çavoir*'* [Cat. 175]
1899w	No. 147	*A Street Corner in the Native Quarter, Cairo* [Cat. 236]
1900	No. 139	*Outside the Bab-en-Nasir, Cairo* [Cat. 237]
1900w	No. 100	*Bargaining, Cairo* [Cat. 238]
	No. 118	*The Door of a Mosque, Cairo* [Cat. 239]
1901	No. 31	*The Gunsmith* [Cat. 240]
	No. 90	*The Courtyard of the House of Sheikh Abdullah: the Sheikh takes his Morning Coffee* [Cat. 241]
1901w	No. 14	*In the Bazaar, Suez* [Cat. 242]
1902	No. 147	*Water Carriers, Old Cairo* [Cat. 243]
1902w	No. 101	*A Street in the Native Quarter, Cairo* [Cat. 244]
1903	No. 148	*An Ancient Highway at Syracuse* [Cat. 245]
1903w	No. 126	*Philae: the Hypaethral Temple ('Pharaoh's Bed')* [Cat. 246]
1904	No. 101	*A Street in Girgey, Upper Egypt* [Cat. 248]
1904w	No. 288	*In the Arab Quarter, Cairo* [Cat. 249]
1905w	No. 214	*Dahlias* [Cat. 250]
1906w	No. 106	*Dartmoor Oaks* [Cat. 103]
1907w	No. 312	*A Vase of the Ming Dynasty (1368-1643)* [Cat. 251]
1908w	No. 300	*Courtyard of a House in the Native Quarter, Cairo* [Cat. 252]
1910w	No. 81	*A Staircase in the House at Stratford-upon-Avon in which Shakespeare was born* [Cat. 12]
1911w	No. 374	*Amphora Shaped Glass Toilet Vase with Cameo Ornament* – Roman period [Cat. 253]
1912	No. 180	Two studies *Blue Glass Vase - Roman Period* [Cat. 254]

The Picture Gallery, 14 Berners Street

1862	No. 85	*On the South-Coast, Seaford* [Cat. 38]

Royal Academy

1854	No. 176	*Dr Johnson at Cave's, the Publisher* [Cat. 10]
	No. 267	*In Shakespeare's House, Stratford-upon-Avon* [Cat. 11]

	No. 1269	*The Font in which Shakespeare was Christened* [Cat. 15]
	No. 1303	*The Room in which Shakespeare was Born* [Cat. 8]
1855	No. 1150	*Fireside Reverie* [Cat. 18]
1856	No. 56	*Marten's Tower, Chepstow Castle* [Cat. 23]
	No. 352	*The Death of Chatterton (Chatterton)* [Cat. 22]
	No. 516	*Andrew Marvell returning the Bribe* [Cat. 24]
1857	No. 458	*A Sculptor's Workshop, Stratford-upon-Avon, AD 1617* [Cat.25]
	No. 501	*Montaigne, the Library* [Cat. 26]
1858	No. 369	*Sir Walter Raleigh in the Tower, circa AD 1600* [Cat. 30]
	No. 462	*Henry Marten, at Chepstow Castle* [Cat. 31]
	No. 562	*The Stonebreaker* [Cat. 28]
1859	No. 930	*Back from Marston Moor* [Cat. 39]
1861	No. 101	*Gondomar Witnessing the Execution of Raleigh* [Cat. 43]
	No. 492	*Elaine* [Cat. 44]
1862	No. 80	*The Death of Christopher Marlowe* [Cat. 47]
	No. 268	*Sir Walter Raleigh in Durham House* [Cat. 48]
1864	No. 225	*Winnowing Corn, Capri* [Cat. 49]
	No. 830	*Henry Marten, at Chepstow Castle* [Cat. 31a]
1865	No. 7	*Shakespeare and Spenser* [Cat. 50]
	No. 385	*Paul Veronese painting the Portrait of Sir Philip Sidney* [Cat. 51]
1867	No. 570	*Luther and Melancthon* [Cat. 60]
1869	No. 442	*Marsyas* [Cat. 68]
	No. 745	*A January Morning* [Cat. 69]
1870	No. 837	*After the Storm* [Cat. 71]
1873	No. 977	*A Despatch from Trebizond* [Cat. 95]
1874	No. 572	*From Naxos (Found at Naxos)* [Cat. 97]
1875	No. 386	*Fugitives from Constantinople, 1453* [Cat. 99]
	No. 405	*On the Ponte Della Paglia; Going to the Council* [Cat. 100]
1876	No. 322	*Outside a Prison in Southern Italy* [Cat. 105]
	No. 902	*The Devotion of Sydney Carton* [Cat. 106]
	No. 975	*An Oasis in the Desert: Fountain-Court, the Temple* [Cat. 107]
1877	No. 762	*In the Spring Time* [Cat. 110]
	No. 987	*Louis XI and Cardinal Balue* [Cat. 111]
	No. 1359	*The Physician – A Visit of Charity* [Cat. 112]

Shepherd Brothers (27, King's Street, St James's)

1881w		*Back from Marston Moor* [Cat. 39]
1882		*Back from Marston Moor* [Cat. 39]

Society of British Artists (Suffolk Street)

1854	No. 69	*A Room in Shakespeare's House, Stratford-on-Avon* [?Cat. 13]
	No. 531	*A Night Study* [Cat.17]
1855	No. 16	*A Study at Fontainebleau* [Cat. 20]
	No. 18	*The Present* [Cat. 21]
1876w	No. 191	*Arranging for the Marriage – An Idyll of the Sacristy* [Cat. 109]

Society of French Artists (Mr. Deschamps's Gallery)

1875	No. ?	*Study of, Dartmoor Oaks (Dartmoor Oaks)* [Cat. 103]
1876w	No. 71	*Amidst the Moors* [Cat. 104]
1880	No. 24	*Morning Call, Smyrna (A Morning Call, Ladies of Smyrna)* [Cat. 143]

South Kensington Museum

'National Portrait Exhibition - Portraits From 1800 onwards'

1868	No. 623	*Thomas Love Peacock* [Cat. 34]

Whitechapel Art Gallery

'Fine Art Exhibition'

1886	No. 150	*The Death of Chatterton (Chatterton)* [Cat. 22]

'Fine Art Loan exhibition' (St Jude's)
1887 No. 15 *Across the Common* [Cat. 62]

'Annual Art Exhibition'
1887 No. 197 *The Stonebreaker* [Cats. 28 or 28a]

'Spring Exhibition'
1908 No. 34 *The Death of Chatterton (autograph copy)* [Cat. 22b]

'Pageant'
1909 No. 66 *Sir Walter Raleigh in the Tower, circa* AD *1600* [Cat. 30]

MANCHESTER

Art Treasures Exhibition
1857 No. 371 *The Death of Chatterton (Chatterton)* [Cat. 22]

Manchester Art Gallery
1885 No. 499 *Going to Market, Bruges* [Cat. 176]

'Exhibition of Water Colour Drawings'
1901 No. 34 *Bargaining, Cairo* [Cat 238]

Royal Jubilee Exhibition
1887 No. 939 *Elaine* [Cat. 44]

Royal Manchester Institution
Exhibition of the Works of Modern Artists
1853 No. 389 *Check* [Cat. 9]
1854 No. 174 *A Night Study* [Cat. 17]
1855 No. 83 *The Present* [Cat. 21]
1858 No. 188 *The Stonebreaker* [Cat. 28]
1864 No. 708 *Montaigne, the Library* [Cat. 26]
1865 No. 712 *A Sculptor's Workshop, Stratford-upon-Avon,* AD *1617* [Cat. 25]
No. 728 *Elaine* [Cat. 44]

Exhibition of Modern Pictures
1867 No. 3 *Luther and Melancthon* [Cat. 60]
No. ? *Laura* [Cat. 61]
1877 No. 654 *Louis XI and Cardinal Balue* [Cat. 111]

Summer Exhibition of Pictures at Peel Park, Salford
1859 No. 41 *A Sculptor's Workshop, Stratford-upon-Avon,* AD *1617* [Cat. 25]
1860 No. 96 *Montaigne, the Library* [Cat. 26]

NOTTINGHAM

(Venue and date unknown) *A Scene in "Edward VI'* [Cat. 52]

Midland Counties Art Museum Nottingham Castle
'Annual Autumn Exhibition of Modern Pictures'
1886 No. 34A *Twelfth Night – Act II, Scene 4* [Cat. 181]

Nottingham Castle Museum and Art Gallery
'Loan Collection of Modern Pictures'
1898 No. 119 *The Devotion of Sydney Carton* [Cat. 106]

REPUBLIC OF IRELAND

DUBLIN

Dublin International Exhibition of Arts and Manufactures

1865 No. 129 *The Stonebreaker* [Cat. 28]
No. 141 *Henry Marten at Chepstow Castle* [Cat. 31]

Exhibition of Arts, Industries and Manufactures and Loans

1872 No. 290 *The Last Days of the Cappuccini Monastery, at Sorrento* [Cat. 57]
No. 411 *Ser Pandolfo* [Cat. 80]

Loan Museum of Art Treasures, Industrial Exhibition Palace

1873 No. 12 *His Highness and His Excellency the Ambassador…* [Cat. 79]
No. 69 *The Death of Christopher Marlowe* [Cat. 47]

Mr. Cranfield's Gallery (Grafton-Street)

1859 *The Death of Chatterton (Chatterton)* [Cat. 22]

National Exhibition of Arts and Manufactures

1882 *Outside a Prison in Southern Italy* [Cat. 105]

The Royal Hibernian Academy

1875 No. 181 *Maestro Sebastiano Guccato, Mosaic Worker, Titian's First Master* [Cat. 94]
1877 No. 415 *Outside a Prison in Southern Italy* [Cat. 105]
1878 No. 534 *In the Spring Time* [Cat. 110]

SCOTLAND

GLASGOW

Messrs. McClure & Son Gallery

1862 *The Death of Chatterton (Chatterton)* [Cat. 22]

Scottish Society of Painters in Water-Colours

1885 No. 73 *An Oriental Glass Merchant* [Cat. 177]

Glasgow International Exhibition of Science, Art and Industry

1888 No. 369 *Elaine* [Cat. 44]

Royal Glasgow Institute of Fine Arts

1889 No. 870 Eastern Scene [Cat. 195]

EDINBURGH

Royal Scottish Academy

1867 No. 513 *In Shakespeare's House, Stratford-upon-Avon* [Cat. 11]

FRANCE

PARIS

Expositions Universelles

1867 No. 150 *The Death of Chatterton (Chatterton)* [Cat. 22]
1878 No. 253 *The Gaol's window (Outside a Prison in Southern Italy)* [Cat. 105]
No. 254 *Autumn* [Cat 118]

USA

PHILADELPHIA

International "Centennial" Exhibition

1876	No. 169	*Across the Common* [Cat. 62]
	No. 170	*The Stonebreaker* [Cat. 28]

AUSTRALIA

Melbourne

International Exhibition

1880-81	No. 229	*A Morning Call, Ladies of Smyrna* [Cat 143]

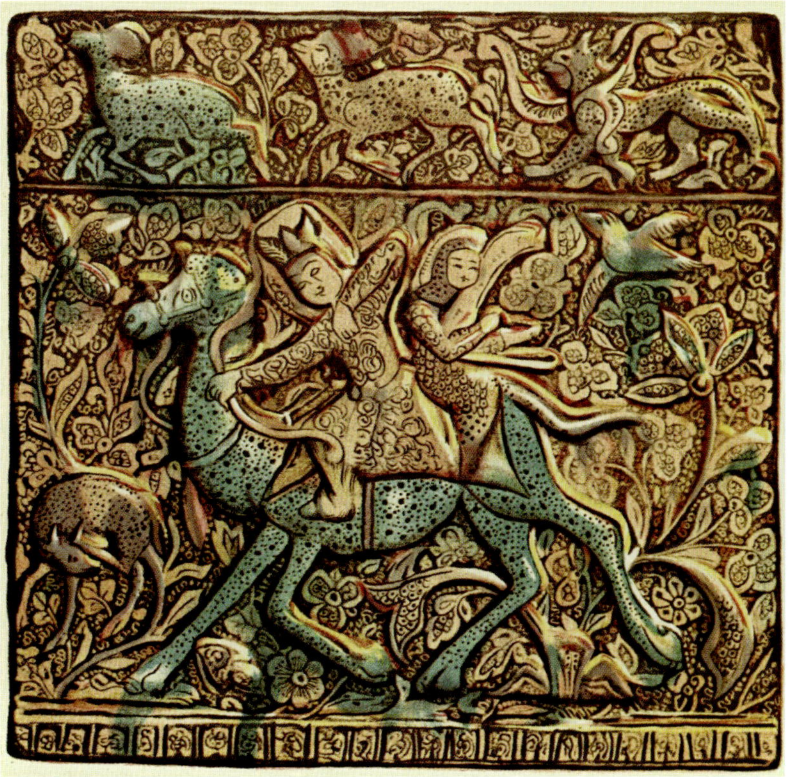

Chromolithograph after a watercolour by H. Wallis of a Persian Lustred Wall-Tile. From *Persian ceramic art belonging to Mr. F. DuCane Godman, F.R.S., with examples from other collections. The thirteenth century lustred wall-tiles*, 1894, Plate XXVI.

Appendix II

A Selection of Unpublished Letters

Henry Wallis is one of those lesser known artists whose personal documents have not been systematically analysed. Diane Johnson, who had access to the family papers, quoted from them in her biography of Mary Ellen Meredith, though without precise references.[1] Johnson was invited by the "heirs of Henry Wallis"[2] to a little house in Surrey, and examined "a dusty box room full of lost paintings and odd treasures. There was a lock of the poet Shelley's hair,[3] a book that had belonged to him, statues and jewelry from Egyptian tombs, Chinese fabrics, dozens of paintings, not only by Wallis but by Rossetti, Burne-Jones and Beardsley.[4] A fragment of a Titian canvas, Mary Ellen Meredith's clothes. Everything, in short, but anything that would reveal the True History. [But] inside a paintbox [I found] a small packet of letters from Mrs. Meredith to her lover Henry Wallis."[5]

The Bodleian Library, Oxford, purchased twenty-one sketchbooks from the art dealer Campbell-Wilson on 24 March 2003. Neil Wilson had obtained these, as well as the family papers – mainly letters, but also some photographs – at a Bonhams auction on 13 March 2002, lot 975. The lot consisted of letters from various correspondents and letters to his son Harold 'Felix' Wallis. These letters are an invaluable source of information on the living conditions in the second half of the nineteenth century, in England and abroad. They also allow us to peep into Wallis's personality and they show him as a cultivated though somewhat intolerant man, a typical Victorian male of his class. Fortunately, Wallis knew everyone in the Victorian art world and everyone knew him. The whole package of letters, therefore, provides a magnificent overview of the Victorian era, and are much more informative than the average summing up of dry facts.

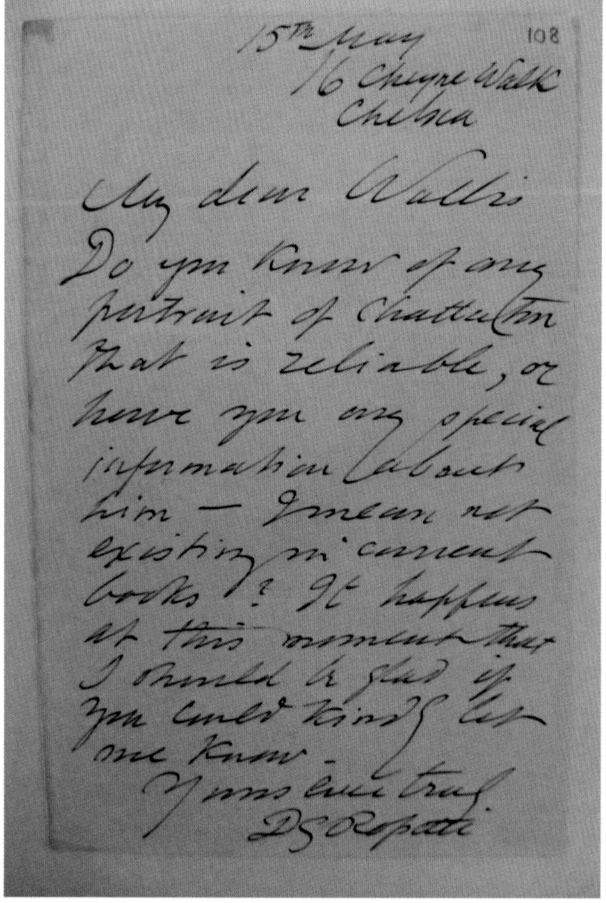

108

15th May
16 Cheyne Walk
Chelsea

My dear Wallis
Do you know of any portrait of Chatterton that is reliable, or have you any special information about him — I mean not existing in current books? It happens at this moment that I should be glad if you could kindly let me know.
Yours ever truly
D G Rossetti

A letter from D.G. Rossetti to Henry Wallis. [See: L13]
By permission of the Bodleian Libraries, University of Oxford, MSS Don.e.79, fol.39

Editorial principles

In editing and transcribing the following letters, accuracy has been a priority; Wallis's hand is not always very clear. Where a word is unreadable or a date missing, square brackets have been inserted. This is only a small selection of letters. Letters were chosen based largely on two principal criteria: firstly, information they provided on Wallis the person, his family, or his friends within the Pre-Raphaelite circle; secondly, on insights they gave about Wallis's art as well as his personal and political views. Where possible typographical arrangements of the original letters have been preserved. Though abbreviations are usual in scholarly editions, they are not used here, in order to facilitate reading.

L1. *To* Frederic Gard Fleay Sorrento 24 March, ?1857 or ?1863[1]

MS: Washington D.C., Folger Shakespeare Library, Y.c.1459 (1)

[See: Cat. 54]

This letter was probably written after Wallis's first visit to Capri with friends, and before he started a relationship with Mary Ellen Meredith, with whom he would travel around Wales in the later summer of the same year.

Villa Nardi

Sorrento

Tuesday 24th March

My dear Fleay,

Your letter was forwarded to me here and gladdened me to find you still displayed the same many sided activity. How different to us here,[2] who at best can only keep from stagnation. Tourists are of course only one remove from idiocy. Their main talk of what they have done and are going to do is perhaps the most painful reflection I know- of those who have settled here, not all have one subject of interest & their spurious [?] on that have long been stereotyped.

I who am here as a stranger, enjoy immensely the gorgeous nature I have seen for the first time and have a strong desire to stay here and work - only I fear the results.

I suppose it is the summer heat that brings on physical and mental las(s)itude.

Certainly these people are the lowest intellectuals I know. Have they ever produced any one but Tasso[3] & he I am inclined to think is more interesting in his life than works – for form and physique they are splendid. Many of the men and boys are very handsome & some of the girls ... There is one I have been painting today with a superb outline of face – a clearly cut, slightly aquiline nose: the hair just enough covering the forehead, a lovely mouth and chin with a short upper lip – blue eyes and light wavy hair, an English complexion only more creamy – a figure tall and finely rounded – however this is only a catalogue description; the charm of her presence I won't attempt to describe. That it is impossible to prevent oneself falling head over ears you may imagine – only her friends are decent and keep strict guard. The only pity is she is Italian and not English – and yet, for the life of me, I cannot help thinking, of the time when I shall see her tomorrow.

By the way she has a sister who is very jolly & so there are [...?] more so I would advise you to bring some new pens and spend your next vacation here – then you can give us a vol. of "Lemon blossoms".[4] The lemon trees are the great feature here. Fancy the combination of fruit, leaf (and?) blossom against the vivid blue sea or purple mountains, with the brilliant sky and white gleaming houses, opalescent in the shade – the ground covered with violets and bright coloured flowers, then there are richly mossed walls wth bright green lizards [waiting ?] about – rocks cropping up and streamlets making little waterfalls – here, as with my fair [...?] I am cataloguing again.

I came here to do a background for a Tasso coming home to his sister – it is true the wind has blown a little cold when you sit expo[sed ?] to it, as my John is – still I must confess to be rather glad of an excuse to roam about & simply enjoy the colour and sunshine.

I left Dan[5] at Capri – he seems determ[ined ?] to cut as soon as he gets his tin from the India Board. It is very odd he will shut his eyes to the beauty before him. He says I am only wasting my time here – but in that I hope and think he is mistaken. I have a considerable amount of work done, some of wch I fancy to [?be] able to turn to account – at any rate seeing a quite different kind of life as a gain – the difficulty is to assimilate and reproduce it. I want to do a subject wch may interest you – a portrait of Shelley, with Pompei [*sic*] and Vesuvius for background. You know the "Ode to Naples".[6] Since I have been here my admiration for Shelley has increased immensely. I am in a fair way to rank him as you do, 2nd to Shakespeare.

Let us hear from you before leaving. Are you going to publish the Horace? Can't you make a boy [...?] a bit?

Goodbye

Ever yrs

Henry Wallis

L2. *From* John Forster[1] London 1 May 1857
MS: Oxford, Bodleian Library, MS Eng.c. 7039, ff. 3-4.
[See: Cat. 31]
Wallis asked Forster to find a portrait of Henry Marten for a picture he had in mind.[2] On 1 May, Forster answered as follows:

46 Montagu Square W.
May 1st. 1857

Dear Sir
[...]
I wished to say to you that I have ascertained the fact of the existence of a portrait of Henry Marten in the family of the descendant of this Mr Lewis, whose house he occasionally visited during his Chepstow imprisonment. The house remains still, and the portrait.

Tell me if you still desire to obtain access to it, or whether you have laid aside your intention of pursuing the subject.

I much desired to possess a picture exhibited by you last year, and was not successful in my attempt to do so.[3]

I hear I have no better chance this year – though I'd very gladly be the owner (if possible yet) of either the Shakespeare or the Montaigne.[4]

Should this not be possible perhaps you will give me the privilege some day of visiting your studio & taking my chance there.
With best wishes, my dear Sir.
Always [?] believe me truly yrs.

John Forster
H. Wallis Esq.

L3. *From* William Holman Hunt London 16 June 1858
MS: University of Oxford, Bodleian Library, MS Eng. c.7039, ff 16-17
[See: Cat. 28]
Wanting his Stonebreaker *to be exhibited in Manchester or in Liverpool, Wallis asked Hunt for advice.*

16th June 1858
1 Tor Villa
Campden Hill
My dear Wallis
When you put the question to me the other night as to sending the Stone breaker to Liverpool or Manchester – it was in so independent a view from that I had taken that at first it seemed as if it was opposite and could not but reverse the decision. I am not quite certain yet that it may not seem so, but there are considerations which would have great weight with me that may not have occurred to you wherefore I write to present them to you.

Manchester people great patrons of / speculators in art ? granted but of perculiarly sensitive / extremely calculating taste[1] which as a body makes them declare against any picture of a sad character not only as unsuitable to them, but as wrong, false to the purposes of Art. They admired Chatterton prodigiously – yes! but that was bought, had earned glory which they were afraid not to endorse. Moreover it did not say "Woe unto you!" as the Stone breaker does to them in particular. On this account it won't get the prize or sell there. They will be consistent and again endorse the London opinion both in praise and neglect. The Liverpool Academy is very pig-headed – has shewn a strong disposition to prove itself before the Age in flying in the face of a disputing world. I think therefore you might get the prize by which the unsuccessful character in a monetary point of view would be removed and so the old woman would get home that night.

In all this I may be miscalculating. I leave you to consider it however. I have not a hint of authority from Liverpool for the expectation I express about the Academy decision.[2]
Yours ever truly.
W. Holman Hunt

L4. *To* his mother, Mary Ann Wallis Rome 27 December 1863

Copy: Harry Ransom Center, Austin, Texas. Diane Johnson papers, box 13.2

After Mary Ellen's death in 1861, Henry spent two winters at Capri with his son, but from 1863 to 1865 he spent them at Rome, which is where this letter was written to his widowed mother.

Note: the parentheses are Diane Johnson's; the square brackets are this author's

Messrs Pakenham Hooker & Co.
Prazzi di Sp (?)[1]
Roma

Sunday Dec 27 Dec. '63 [written in pencil]

My dear Mother,

We have just finished our Xmas here which has certainly not been like the same season in England, in one respect it has been to our advantage for the weather has been clear and warm like spring, that is in the sun. Yet in the shade and the wind is decidedly m--ing [?]. I suppose you know there are grand ceremonies at St Peters and other churches, at least they are called grand but in reality are rather tiresome affairs. On Xmas eve I went to the Sistine Chapel in the evening. Men are obliged to go in evening dress and the ladies in black with veils of the same colour. There was a grand mass at which a lot of cardinals attended, who looked very picturesque in their red silk dresses. They evidently found the ceremony wearisome as they yawned a good deal. It was curious that the whole congregation were Protestants, being nearly all English. On Xmas day there was high mass in St Peters the only part of it worth seeing was the procession at the end in which the Pope is carried in a dias on mens shoulders down the c[h]urch attended by numerous cardinals, Bishops, etc. in very gorgeous costumes. It struck me that there were not as many people attended as when I was there before. I had a quiet dinner at home with a friend. I was invited out to dine but did not go till the evening, as I did not like to leave Harold alone. Afterwards I went to a party of Americans, very nice people. The lady was very proud at having made a genuine English plum pudding - though it was not the size I recollect you used to make. I hope you had a pleasant day and that the pudding turned out a success – did the Yorstons come & how were they? The other day an old Friend[2] of mine turned up he is in a public office & has come here for a couple of months holiday. Living close by he clubs in with me for dinner which makes it pleasant. I don't have dinner cooked at home but brought from a cook in a wonderful apparatus with a charcoal fire [l]it which keeps everything as hot as if it was dressed in the house. Meat is good here and game plentiful and very cheap, living is dearer than when I was here before but still cheaper than London. I bought a few days ago some old lace that you would enjoy immensely. It has been part of altar cloths. I think the pattern is wonderfully rich. It was at an old shop in the jews quarter. I saw at the same time some net would do for collars but was not sure that it was genuine. I will ask some lady about it and if good will buy you some. I picked up some bits of old silk brocade with silver worked in it, and a large piece of tapestry enough to cover the side of a room for 12/. You would be amused to see the Ghetto or Jews Quarter, it is the most dirty, ramshackle place in the world though very picturesque. We often go and have a regular rummage in it. Harold is pretty well, looks better than in England though not quite equal to last winter at Capri. He is very fond of acquiring languages. I think I shall let him begin German. He has been trying his hand on Greek lately – the joke against him is that he begins a fresh language every day.

Did Henry say he had paid the money with (into?) the bank? Remember me to him. I hope you have recovered from your attack of lumbago. I am certain you would derive benefit a warm bath daily. It would bring about a healthy action of the skin – H was pleased with his picture. (Mrs?) Daniel sent him Punch's Almanac that amused him much. He sends his love and a kiss.

A happy New year
And with kind love
I remain
Ever affectionately
Henry Wallis

L5. *To* his mother, Mary Ann Wallis Rome 22 January 1864
Copy: Harry Ransom Center, Austin, Texas. Diane Johnson papers, box 13.2
Note : the parentheses are Diane Johnson's.
This and the previous letter indicate that as early as the 1860s Wallis was already becoming a collector.

Rome
22nd Jany 1864

My dear Mother,

I take advantage of a friend returning to England to send you a line & so evade the swindle of the Papal postage. Since I last wrote we have had some exceedingly cold weather, colder than it has been here for thirty years. I did not find it so very bad myself but I heard others say that it was sharper than they experienced in England. Our rooms are very sunny and warm, so much so that a fire has been necessary only morning and evening. Some of the fountains with figures of Tritons and Neptunes etc. presented rather a curious appearance being quite draped in ice with icicles hanging from their arms and legs, which amused Harold immensely. I put in extra flannels & he seems to have got on very well. The last few days it has been decidedly warmer and we hope the spring will commence. The Carnival begins in a few days – such as it is – for now the more respectable of the Romans never join in the festivities; the only people who go to the Corso[1] are the ragamuffins and some foreigners.

I send you by my friend some lace collars which I have asked him to direct to you by the Parcels Delivery Comp. There are five, you can give one to Emma (Mrs. Yorston)[2] & one to Henry's wife if you like. I will tie a bit of worsted on the ones I think best and that you had better keep – tell me what you think of them. I have besides got some more lace that will do well for trimming to a table cover. I received a letter from Henry, please thank him for sending me this account and give him my kind remembrances. I am glad to say I have nearly finished my principal picture & shall send it to London I think the end of next month.[3]

I propose returning about April 10. Harold sends his love and a kiss. Hoping to hear you have been quite well & with kind love.

I remain
Ever affectionately
Henry Wallis

Please send me half a dozen postage stamps.

L6. *To his mother* Mary Ann Wallis Rome 26 February 1864
MS: Private collector, New York.
Copy: Harry Ransom Center, Austin, Texas. Diane Johnson papers, box 13.2
Note: the parentheses are Diane Johnson's; the square brackets are the authors'.
Every letter from Wallis's early period is important and sheds light on the way he lived at the time. Even as early as 1864 he seemed to have been unsettled and this would continue until the end of the century.

Rome
Friday 26 Feb.

My dear mother,

I have an opportunity of sending letters tomorrow so shall scribble away this evening (?). I received yrs the other day & was glad to find you were coming on so well and had got Spring to come so soon. We have not had pleasant weather & very little likelihood of its improving, worse luck for a background or two I wanted to make. I have finished my picture and think of sending it to England next week. I shall at the same time send the things I have bought. You are quite full I know so I shall have them warehoused at the agents. The Carnival this year was a very poor affair – The Romans not joining in the festivities & this weather this year helping it dull. Visitors are making themselves scarce, going down to Naples, where if work did not prevent I should like to go for a week or so before returning. I may leave here in about a month or six weeks, & shall certainly not stay longer if I can help it. It seems advisable to give notice for [?Mi... ?Nu...]. I have not yet decided where I shall look after a place, though it is very doubtful if I can get one where I want it.[1] I was sorry to hear such a poor account of Mrs. Shirley. I am afraid this winter has been trying to her. Harold has been much better lately, getting considerably stouter and I suppose about ready to begin to go to school – he sends his best love in which I unite.

& believe me
Ever affectionately yrs
Henry Wallis

L7. *From* Edward Burne-Jones – January 1867

MS: Oxford, Bodleian Library, MS Eng.c. 7039, fols. 79-80.

This letter confirms the longstanding friendship between Edward Burne-Jones and Wallis.

My dear Wallis.

I was aggravated to find your card the other night & to think that the only night you had come to see me for a year, I should be dissipating at *Rouge et Noir* – it was at the Lyceum[1] & very harmless, & I must say you had your revenge for any annoyance the journey out here cost you. I should be very glad to be of any help, but Swinburne has surely much overestimated my knowledge, though not my interest in the subject – I greatly question if I can be of any good to you, but if you will tell me when you shall be in, I will come & talk it over and see more exactly what you mean.

If one had a perfect memory of what struck ones imagination most as a child, doubtless that would [be] a good direction to work in, but unfortunately for my self in this way I had the stupidest of infancies & childhoods, & don't think I was taught or told anything but Hymns – how the word makes one creep.

Write & fix a time & I will be your

Affec[t]

E.B. Jones

L8. *From* Edith Nicolls Blackheath 13 June 1874

MS: University of Oxford, Bodleian Library, MS Eng. c.7041, f.115

PUBL.: Excerpt in D. Johnson, op cit, p.158

Edith Nicolls was Mary Ellen's daughter by her first marriage. After her mother's death, Edith stayed at Lower Halliford at her grandfather's. Following his death, she contributed to an edition of Thomas Love Peacock's collected works for which she wrote a biographical introduction. In 1875, Edith became Lady Superintendent of the National Training School of Cookery *and married Charles Clarke, who was employed at the India Office. Although the couple had three daughters, she continued working to the age of seventy-five. Edith and Henry kept in touch intermittently and a daughter remembers Wallis calling on her mother as late as 1911. The outcome of her request is unknown.*

12, New Vanburgh Terrace
Blackheath S.E.
June 13th 1874

Dear Mr Wallis,

You will be surprised at receiving after so many years of silence, another note from me. I write to ask you a favour, which is this. Have you any Photo or likeness of my Mother which you will give to me? I have no likeness of any kind of her and I much desire to get one. I understand that the miniature of her taken as a girl with long curls, was given either to you or Harold, by Mary Ann(e) Rosewell,[1] this should surely have come to me, as it was painted for my Father, at the same time that one was painted of him for Mamma, this latter I have. If you or Harold object to give me that miniature, then will you please lend it to me, that I may have a copy made of it ? when I will faithfully return it to you again.

Arthur is coming here today, this is his birthday he is 21: he has been for some months with Tom Taylor, as tutor to his son,[2] but he goes next month into a merchants house in Havré,[3] he is a queer lad, very small, quiet & very studious. He found it quite impossible to live with the Merediths.[4] I am sorry for the lad, he has been kept so long abroad that he seems to have no idea of home-life, & his affections seem to me never to have been awakened, & there is, I grieve to say, little sympathy between our natures some how or other. I do not know why I should trouble you with all this, it has run from my pen without the least premeditation. I have been for a long while very busy preparing a complete edition of Grandpapa's works for publication. I hope it will be out in Sep[t]. I hope you will grant me the favor [*sic*] I ask of you?

And believe me yours sincerely,

Edith Nicolls

Please tell me of Harold. Have you a Photo of him to give me?

L9. *To* Frederic George Stephens London April 1878

MS: University of Oxford, Bodleian Library, MSS Don.e. 79, ff. 6-9

Stephens was one of Wallis's best friends, sharing with him his interest and concerns about art. Stephens, who was ill, could not attend the Exposition Universelle in Paris in 1878; he asked Wallis to go and write the review for The Athenaeum in his stead.

Brecknock Cres: N.W.
Thursday

My dear Stephens.

I found y^{r} note the other day at my return, & was touched by y^{r} affectionate words. I accept y^{r} thanks – but on one condition – (for I reckon I still have you in charge) & that is that when you recover there shall be no more night work, finish y^{r} business by nine o'clock, wife & family! Do you think y^{r} wife & family want you to work y^{r}self into an early grave, or a lunatic asylum?

Y^{r} note today shows a noble ardour & so far is a good sign, but I think I w^{ld} just quietly recruit & so ensure a complete cure. Maccoll[1] and I agreed the other day that this year the Salon w^{ld} only require one article (all the best work will of course go into the International) & I don't think it is worth while troubling y^{r}self for that.

Of course you w^{ld} like to see the Exb^{n}, take y^{r} wife for a week in September when the weather is cool & simply have a holiday, but if you want to do any Exb^{n} work (wch I decidedly don't advise) I know Jackson will be only too glad only to have one article on the R.A. By the way, we must arrange the Exb^{n}. I say (R.A. & watercolour on the 4 May) Grosvenor, R.A. & Paris on the 11th? Then who will do the Grosvenor? There again I advise you to let some one else have the labour. In wch case we might rely on Scott.[2]

You clearly understand I have not the slightest desire to do the Salon, only being there I sh^{ld} look on the 4 or 5 columns as so many hours work after I had seen it. How long I shall stay at Paris I have a very vague idea, probably 3 weeks, for you may rest assured I am not going to spend my days in the Exb^{n} & my nights in writing: I shall do all my work by daylight.

I am detained in town tomorrow & Saturday on business, so Felix has gone to S^{t} [Margarets ?] without me, if I have an opportunity I shall drop in to the Editors Friday or Saturday.

(haste) Always sincerely.
Henry Wallis

L10. *To* Frederic George Stephens London 18 January 1879

MS: University of Oxford, Bodleian Library, MSS Don.e. 79, ff.13-14

After he had reviewed the Exposition Universelle and the Salon on behalf of Stephens, Wallis seems to have had some problems in recovering his expenses. This letter is an attempt to explain things to his friend.

24 Brec Cres[1] NW
Saturday
Private

Dear Stephens.

Wth regard to the Athenaeum payment I had not previously made any calculation. Now I find I went to Paris 2 or 3 days before 1st May: left 9 June say 40 days. Living, cabs, tips, etc. cost me £1 a day. R^{lwy} fare £4.15. I took a monthly ticket thinking that w^{ld} be long enough, but staying longer had to pay another £3. In short altogether I reckon I paid £50 wch agrees wth what I took over, considering other expenses on my own account.

Then there is the payment for work, the quantity I have not calculated; but it must be remembered that it was condensed; Salon/notice, wch is harder work than doing it in 2 & so throughout. I sh^{ld} put the work at a moderate calculation at £1 a day, remembering that journalistic work is not paid nearly as well as artistic. Still I know that besides corrections there are very few who have the knowledge to have done the notices so as to be of value. This of the modern, besides them was the ancient.

I sh^{ld} have much preferred only staying 3 weeks instead of 6, but I left the day after the Historic Gall^{y} opened to public & gave my time to the whole business as long as I was there.

This for the Paris business for wch I only consider I have claim. The editorship, till I left, I said I w^{ld} do for you without payment, & abide by my statement of course you know the reason I offered to take y^{r} duties. When I heard you were likely to have a long bout of it, I thought the work friendly office I c^{ld} do your way to do my best to secure y^{r} place for you, very aware that the temporary occupant might make efforts to the permanent one. For in the press gratitude is the rarest thing. I have known men who have given their best years to it, flung aside like a suckled orange. Of course there are exceptions & Dilke[2] may be one. I simply know nothing of him, except that he is a sound Radical member, but Roebuck[3] is an example that a man may begin as a sound radical & yet be a knave & double dyed villain at heart. However, when you happened to fall ill the duties were very light. I did them after my regular work. Maccoll is a very pleasant fellow to work wth & the business was a pleasure rather than otherwise, so I stick to my proposal.

You can tell them my notion of the Paris work if you like. I am not going to discuss the matter wth them, as I had no agreement. It w^{ld} make no difference to me if they send me £70 of £170 or £7, fortunately for me. Still it is just as well they sh^{ld} know that sound work sh^{ld} be fairly paid for.

Do you see one of y^{r} craft is dead? Dallas, predecessor of T.T.[4] By the way I went last night to ask you for the Delacroix letter you promised me & the Museum pamphlet.
In haste. Ever y^{rs}.

Henry Wallis

L11. *To* Frederic George Stephens   Brussels   17 August 1879

MS: University of Oxford, Bodleian Library, MSS Don.e. 79, ff.19-20

During the summer of 1879, Wallis travelled through The Netherlands and Belgium and studied the local art in detail. In this letter, he expresses his feeling that fine oil paintings cannot be properly seen and studied in churches.

Hotel de Suede. Brussels
Sunday 17 Aug.
My dear Stephens.
[...]

The Belgian government have acquired for the sum of 200.000 frs the triptych by Quentin Massys,[1] his masterpiece, in the church of St Peter at Louvain. It is not yet removed but will be at an early opportunity. The Belgian art authorities must be heartily congratulated on having secured this picture for the Brussels Gall^{y} where it will be placed opposite the Adam & Eve of Van Eyck, & when there it can be properly seen wch was certainly not the case at the ridiculous height & between the cross lights of the church windows. It is to be hoped that the removal of this work to Brussels will be followed by Van Eycks masterpiece from St Bavon's at Ghent.[2]

We are perfectly aware there are some who desire to see pictures kept in the churches for wch they are placed. No one w^{ld} wish frescoes removed but there is not a single instance in wch a really fine oil picture can be properly seen & studied in a church, their usual altitude, distance from the eyes, obscurity, reflecting light & the colour of the wall entirely destroys their effect & makes of a masterpiece merely a mess of dark colours wth grey lights on its surface. How much better w^{ld} Rubens' Descent & Elevation of the Cross at Antwerp be in the gallery rather than in their present position.[3]
Always understood that fair copies be given to churches, wch will be the case wth the 2 Massys at Louvain. Among recent addition to the Brussels Gall^{y} is a large tryptich by Heemskirk,[4] a deposition in the centre, wings donator & donatrice, life size figures, dead body of X^{t} vigorous drawing & modelling, reverse of wings standing saints, fine colour & good preservation – while the centre (dep^{n}) is much rubbed. / A landscape by Moucheron / A dead cock hanging against a wall by Hondecouter, rich in colour & strong in l. & shade / A half length portrait of man by N. Maes.[5] A large landscape & figures (small) by J. Jordaens[6] & J. Wildens.[7] Subject, Eleazer & Rebecca. ... decorative – mountains – the most interesting part a town in middistance wth citadel, bridge & above all a superb portrait by Rubens[8] of an English peer, fit to rank wth Vandycke's Gervatius.[9] This was bought from Burlington House Exb. What were trustees of Nat. Gall. doing not to secure for the Eng^{h} public & artists this one of the finest & most artistic of R's portraits?

L12. *From* William Morris London 8 November 1879

MS: University of Oxford, Bodleian Library, MS Eng.c.7039, ff. 93-94

William Morris created an International Committee for the Preservation of the Basilica of St Mark, *of which Wallis was the Honorary Secretary from 1879 to 1882. The documents related to this committee can be consulted at the British Library, ref.* Add. 38831. *An excellent summary of the St Mark's affair can be found in Edward Tyas Cook's* The Life of John Ruskin, *vol .2, ch XVII (London, 1911), as well as in John Dominic Standish's* Venice in Environmental Peril: Myth and Reality, *University Press of America, 2011.*

26, Queen Square
Bloomsbury, London.
Nov: 8th 1879

My dear Wallis

Thanks for your note, which I was very glad to get. As you will see the S.P.A.B.[1] is flitting a memorial to the Minister of Works which I will send you, & ask you to get good signatures to. Meantime you have done the best thing possible by writing the letter to the Times which I have just read, & which is first rate. There is to be a meeting at Oxford on Saturday 13th Nov: Dean of Ch: Ch:[2] in the Chair. Though this latter is rather like the Devil saying fie for shame to sin. Yet we must work by instruments, even if necessary by the Devil (when we can catch him) & I hope it may do good. I think there is a good deal of stir in the matter, & we may do some good, if everything is not settled already, as I much fear it is. I think we want most is direct undeniable information as to what is intended. I mean to say coming from officials but not in an official manner, which would be sure to gloss over facts, & cool people.

Of course our information is undoubted, but it does not come direct from an official. I have written again to Venice to get at the very day the Commission is to be called for. Any suggestion you can make will be thankfully received by me. Meantime many thanks for the good service you have done already.

Yrs very truly.

William Morris

P.S. I hope a general election won't tumble on the midst of this; but I think not: the jingoes must be dispirited by the municipal elections.

L13. *From* Dante Gabriel Rossetti London 15 May ?1880[1]

MS: University of Oxford, Bodleian Library, MS Eng.c.7039, f.108

Long after Wallis's successful Death of Chatterton, *D.G. Rossetti, too, became interested in the fate of the unfortunate genius. His poem* Chatterton *was finished by April 1880 and a few weeks later he wrote the following two letters to Wallis to enquire whether he knew of some likeness of the poet.*

15th May
16 Cheyne Walk
Chelsea

My dear Wallis

Do you know of any portrait of Chatterton that is reliable, or have you any special information about him[2] – I mean not existing in current books? It happens at this moment that I should be glad if you could kindly let me know.

Yours ever truly.
D.G. Rossetti

L14. *From* Dante Gabriel Rossetti London ?May ?1880[1]

MS: University of Oxford, Bodleian Library, MS Eng.c.7039, ff.109-110

Monday

My dear Wallis

Thanks for your note. I should be but a fool indeed to poach on your well-won preserves! My enquiry was on behalf of Theod: Watts[2] who is writing something about Chatterton, & did not think he knew you well enough for personal enquiry.

The question of the portraits is certainly a puzzle & I as well as he wanted to know what you thought of it. I have seen 3 different versions (2 prints & an Arundel[3] photo: all doubtless familiar to you) which certainly seem to represent the same individual at somewhat varying ages, yet common sense seems quite against the idea that Chatterton was ever painted till you painted him. He certainly seems to have numbered among his intimates at Bristol one Alcock a miniature painter.[4] Had A. painted C. in his lifetime it w[d] surely be known, but it seems conceivable that A. may after his death & growing fame have made some reminiscent sketch of him which was the foundation for these portraits.

One (called a Hogarth!) is in the Salford Museum[5] – another (seeming boyish but not as in the Colston's School[6] tonsure – the hair being very luxuriant) is in possession of Sir Henry Taylor.[7] All this again you doubtless know, & had probably come to your conclusion as to the portraits very early, as I can still remember that I sent you a young man who answered your purpose as a model for the picture.[8]

Yours sincerely
D G Rossetti.

L15. *From* William Morris London 4 August 1880
MS: B.M. add. MS 38,831. See Kelvin, Norman, *Collected Letters of William Morris*, Vol. I, 1848-1880, letter 638, p.576.

9 Buckingham St.
August 4, 1880
St. Marks Committee

My dear Wallis

I understood when I saw you last that we were to meet here at ½ past 4 today: so I came; but after waiting till ¼ past 5 concluded there must be some mistake; so I write. Ruskin written to by Jones has telegraphed to say that he joins: Burne-Jones joins also Walter Crane (asked by me) the latter is to ask W. Spottis Woode (P.R.S.).[1]

Civil note from the American Legation on Lowells part, accepting. Also from Mark Pattison[2] Rector of Lincoln Coll: Oxford accepting. Also from Talbot[3] Warden of Keble Coll: accepting. So please put these names down, which will give us a tolerable list pro: tem:.

I suppose you had better notify their being on the Committee officially. Talbots letter being humble as well as civil I answered at once. I have also a letter from Max Müller[4] declining, but speaking sympathetically of the movement.

I sent my letter to Lowell[5] to the American Legation.

Ruskins address is Brantwood Coniston Lancashire

On Tuesday next I go out of town for a week. I have no letter yet from the Dean of Ch[rist Church].

Yours very truly
William Morris

L16. *From* William Holman Hunt London 31 October 1880
MS: University of Oxford, Bodleian Library, MS Eng.c.7039, ff.23-24
The following letter deals with Hunt's hatred of the academical world and with his finances.

2 Warwick Gardens
Kensington W.
Oct 31. 1880

My dear Wallis

I trust that your cold is better and that you are better prepared to meet the coming winter which threatens to be a severe one. For my own individual part I am prepared to regard this country as one with very little more life in it, and I am inclined to care for little that does not have reference to some future nation of a non diplomaed type. Your beloved bishops and royal academicians and royal academicians toadies, you may hope to see scotched but I have no such faith. You will go on to the end with Lord Elchos[1] and Lord Overstones[2] and Deans and Canon forming themselves into committees of conscience and taste to frame laws and decide who shall make statues to heroes great edifices built with public money and pictures for the nation – who shall find the plausiblest of humbugs to patronize. And when the result is found out to be a disgrace, you – not you individually, but you the proud English XIXth century gentleman – shall decide that it would be ungentlemanly to enquire too closely about the last concern. But in all senses highly salutary and proper to trust to a new committee framed on the same principle for the defilement of the metropolis and the country at large. Hold your tongue about all jobs but to be a good fellow is every thing. And the first condition for getting a good share of the plunder and public laudation in your town. For my part, as I say, the end seems not far distant and I don't therefore regard Syria[3] as so far away from home as I otherwise should. This is the explanation of my aberration of common sense in living so far away from the blessed land with its perfect constitutional government which is about as ideal as any thing else.

I did not mean to promise a subscription to the offshoot from the "Ancient Buildings" – only that I had promised to the last and I knew that the money must be found somehow – but indeed just now I have no little difficulty in finding means for all the calls on me and 10/- is 10/-.

The Guild taxes my ready money very heavily. And this must be borne patiently for the sake of the prospects which I think are important for future Art.

I hope to see you on Wednesday at 8.

Yours ever.

W. Holman Hunt

L17. *From* William Morris London 24 December 1880

MS: University of Oxford, Bodleian Library, MS Eng.c.7039, f.95

Morris expresses his sorrow for the death of their mutual friend George Edmund Street.[1] Wallis would have known the famous architect initially through the Hogarth Club. Wallis once claimed that he had once been an architect himself,[2] although no evidence to support this statement has ever been found. Wallis attended Street's funeral as the representative for the St. Mark's (Venice) Committee, of which he was Honorary Secretary. Street had been the Vice-Chairman of the Committee.

Kelmscott House,
Upper Mall, Hammersmith.
Dec : 24th 1881

My dear Wallis

I have every wish to show that I am sorry for Street's death as I really am, and I think he behaved very well in the St Mark's affair, also I always had much respect for his hard-working & genuine qualities, which however did not include any real artistic faculty. But it is a matter of principle with me to have nothing to do with funeral pomp in general, and I am bound in particular to set my face against any Westminster Abbey funeral, which includes the double nuisance of a disgraceful intramural burial, and a disgraceful stone insult to the most beautiful building in England.

I can't help thinking that poor Street would by no means have agreed to such an idiocy himself.

Yours very truly.

William Morris

L18. *From* William Morris London 11 March 1882

MS: University of Oxford, Bodleian Library, MS Eng.c.7039, ff. 96-100

PUBL.: Excerpt in T. Wilson, op cit, p.154

In this important and telling letter from Morris to Wallis, the former describes the disarray at the South Kensington Museum (later the Victoria and Albert Museum).

Kelmscott House,
Upper Mall, Hammersmith.

March 11th 1882

My dear Wallis

Thanks for your note and enclosure. I suppose you have seen our notice in this morning's Daily News. No, Ravenna is impossible, or any other travel for me for years to come, I fear, however glad I should be to go.

As to the question of the Museums, I don't think I quite agree, all the more as I have just this moment come from S.K.M. which I have found in its usual state of muddle. That museum is overburdened with articles & don't know where to put them. It is true that about one third of the articles are useless & ought to be destroyed, but even if that were done there still would not be room for a proper arrangement of what is left. That arrangement should be nearly a permanent one, or the museum is of no use to students. Take an example: the S.K.M. possesses in the Bock Collection a treasure of textile examples which is invaluable;[1] it is now several years (15 I should think) since the public has been able to see any thing but a small part of this stowed away in a dark corner. In the mean time the SKM has exhibited all sorts of sickening rubbish: fans, rococo embroideries, the sweepings of the Venice dealers' shops and other twaddle: now it really would be better that these things should be visible at Manchester or Nottingham **or** Birmingham than invisible in London. Besides (I am speaking of industrial art as the slang goes, not of pictures all this while), it seems to me that if museums are of use to the art of today (which may be questioned) they are wanted in manufacturing towns more than in London. At the same time I don't agree with the extension of the lending system, which I think a bad one in any case.

Not to bore you with my opinion of what I should call a difficult question here it is.

1. The S.K.M. wants thorough reform.

2. That reform should consist A. of weeding out the useless articles, a committee of artists to sit upon them as works of art not curiosities, no dealer's opinion to be asked on them. & B. of arrangement: a Committee of artists should settle where the things could be put to best advantage, and that arrangement should be permanent. One court might be kept for articles on loan (as now) but the permanent arrangement should never be disturbed.

3rd this collection should consist of things typical of their kinds, and all duplicates, and all things so much alike as to approach the nature of duplicates should be set aside and handed over to the provincial museums as a nucleus in each case for their collections.

4th I don't see why, in buying new things those provincial museums should not have some share of things acquired. All the more as the S.K.M. would not if properly arranged want many more articles, would only have to supply certain difficiencies [deficiencies] which would become obvious when a systematic and permanent arrangement was set about there.

You see I would not on any account do anything which would injure the Museum as a collection of typical works of art; but at present its condition is chaotic; I believe chiefly because it has more things than it knows what to do with. As to the lending business, once more I think that a mistake from beginning to end. Things are no use in a museum if a student can't come to them whenever he wants to study them & bring his master or scholar to look at them – also the risk makes one shudder. If I had a fine picture I would see everybody Italians[2] before I would lend it to go jig-jog on a railway.

Well pray excuse my scrawl: only I am as much interested in the matter as you are, & am glad of a chance of airing my views in a crude & irresponsible manner.

Yours very truly.

William Morris

P.S. I think whatever is bought in future every museum should have a good copy of it in some form or other.

L19. *From* William Holman Hunt Fulham 30 April 1882

MS: University of Oxford, Bodleian Library, MS Eng.c.7039, ff. 27-28

On the 10th of April 1882, Dante Gabriel Rossetti died at Birchington-on-Sea, Kent. After his death, several exhibitions were organised, one of them at the Royal Academy. Hunt was displeased, as he considered that the Academy had never recognised Rossetti's genius.

April 30. 1882
Draycott Lodge, Fulham. S.W.

My dear Wallis

I have seen W[illiam] Rossetti this eveng and he tells me that he objects to the Academy being the exhibitor of his brother's pictures, but that Leyland[1] has entered into communications with the august body to place his set of pictures in their hands, and that Graham[2] and one or two others have done so (the first I hear independently says his pictures will sell better by this course). Agnew[3] aids the Academy and thus regards the decision which he has made as inevitable.[4]

The fact however is more cruelly disgusting with all the facts known than it appears on the surface.

Gabriel, in addition to the money which in early days William had given, had borrowed very large sums of money from him – literally I believe thousands. William thus, and by reason of other life long charities of his, is a very poor man. He has a family of five or so, and his widow has[5] no pension from Government, so he ought to get all that is possible out of his brother's estate but he has relinquished his claim to the lent money to reduce the debts, which are very considerable. The Academy will now put all the profits from the exhibition into their own pockets, and this blessed Institution in its "generosity" not only did every thing to make Rossetti's career a failure and did succeed in making it much harder, and probably also aided thus in cramping his powers but generously abstained from sending him a ticket for the "Private View" during the whole course of his life!

But the body are rich, have a thousand men paying court to them who are ready to do all their dirty work. Do you think it of any use to protest in the name of honesty? I confess I have given up all hope of doing good by such means. I believe the country is so far gone in snobbism and sneaking in the worship of humbug, that the only cure that can come will be by an explosion, spontaneous and conclusive. Brown is, I hear, not yet asking for election, so there is one prophet.

Still yours.

W.H.H.

L20. *To* Harold Wallis Cairo 8 November 1885

MS: private collector, New York.

Wallis started his first journey to Egypt in October 1885, travelling via Venice, Brindisi and Port Said to arrive at Cairo. The freshness of the first impressions makes his weekly letters particularly interesting.

Hotel du Nil. Cairo

Sunday 8 Nov.

My dear Felix.

Behold me, at last, arrived. And thankful I am to rest a bit after a journey wch was certainly fatiguing. You got the letter I wrote from the steamer at Brindisi last Sunday I suppose. On Sunday night the mail train arrived bringing the bulk of the passengers & they pretty well filled the ship! Nearly all the cabins were full. I happened to be in about the only one that was not, having 2 instead of 4 occupants. We started before daybreak on Monday in bad & ominous looking weather, that increased to a gale the next night, & as the wind was in our teeth we made little way. However, the weather gradually mended from Tuesday but we were not able to make up, lost time I arrived at Port Said just before midnight on Thursday instead of daybreak of the same day. You may imagine the gladness wth wch we heard the reply to the first question put to the pilot before he got on board, "Is there quarantine?" "No." All the Indian, Australian & Chinese passengers went on board the 3 steamers waiting for them. I & a man belonging to the Italian Consulate had arranged to take the steamer – a launch for Ismailia, but the only other Cairo passenger told me it w^{ld} be a wretched journey, start at midnight, dirty, wait at Ismailia for train & recommended returning in the *Tanjore* to Alexandria (160 miles). We sh^{ld} have gone there instead of Port Said if there had been no quarantine. So again I found myself at sea, this time in more comfort, for I left my previous hot quarters & appropriated the cabin for two up for L.D. Carring who went out to his governorship. The luxury was not palatial but the breathing space was grateful.

It looked dubious when we started, but the threatened storm passed off & we arrived all right at Alexandria yesterday morning. The voyage was interesting. The different groups of Indian civilians, officers, Australians etc. presented types offering plenty of variety & many were very intelligent & all tried to make themselves pleasant under the somewhat trying circumstances. To me the noise of the engines was very wearying, I wasn't sick but felt an almost continual headache, wch has not gone away yet.

I started by the first train from Alexandria. Yes, today 10 a.m. & found at the station my fellow passenger of the *Tanjore*, he turned out to be the Inspector of Egyptian railways, or some such title. He gave me a seat in his reserved compartment wch insured considerably more comfort than I sh^{ld} otherwise have got. I sh^{ld} think he received as much respect from the officials as the Khedive himself. It struck me they were glad to see him back. He seemed a good specimen of the best sort of English official, a man who saw everything, was not to be trifled wth yet spoke kindly to the officials. He had been in some such post in India & seemed to think the work easier there than here, however he p... to improve the railway system here, if only the wretched Home Gov^{t} w^{ld} behave decently.

There is no doubt about it the policy or no policy of the Gladstone Gov^{t} wth relation to Egypt was infamous. Probably the other side w^{ld} not have done better, but I think if I had a seat in the next Parliament I sh^{ld} be half inclined to do what [Rochefort?][1] proposes – impeach the minister who was responsible for the Egyptian muddle.

From half an hour's stroll I had ... ... Cairo seems to be the most picturesque place I was ever in. I have of course made no plans but may stay in this hotel for a week or so.

Send me letters (wth enclosures) to the Poste Restante. Find out the right way of addressing. Tell me how you are & how all goes on. Give date of previous letter.
Your loving father,

Henry Wallis

L21. *To* Harold Wallis Cairo 16 November 1885
MS: private collector, New York.
Wallis's first impressions of Cairo, a city that would fascinate him for the rest of his life, and which he employed as a setting for numerous watercolours.

Cairo. 16 Nov.

My dear Felix.

I wrote you a week ago & now send by this mail. I have not yet heard from you here, the post coming in I think, on Thursday. You had better find out the day the Brindisi mail leaves & write every week by that way. There are letters come by on French & Italian boats but they are not so rapid or punctual as the P. & O.

We still have what w^{ld} be called warm summer weather in England. I went to the English Church yesterday & the ladies wore July dresses. It was curious, by the way, to see the large majority of the congregation in uniform. I've been doing a good deal of exploring the bazaars, mosques & old parts of the city this past week & find that the destruction & demolition that has been accomplished & is taking place is frightful. Cairo will be a new city in a few years wth scarcely anything of the old, except a few mosques. The rage is for wide streets & houses built after the fashion of 4th rate French towns.

Just now the pilgrims are returning from Mecca & the occasion is invariably taken to get up a "fantasia" for the pious man. His friends meet him at the station, a band is hired & also cre..., who carry blazing baskets of fire on the tops of poles. A procession is made of these materials who precede, then the man arrives on a horse or donkey & his friends mounted on donkeys. The pilgrim is in gorgeous attire. The procession is closed by 2 or 3 carriages containing the women of the family. The whole [business?] looks very picturesque coming down the streets but the noise & din is deafening. That is the normal state of the streets of Cairo, every one seems to think it to be his duty to bawl & shout continually. The Pilgrims seem to entertain their friends for a day or 10 after their return.

A day ago I was going along wth an officer & we looked into a courtyard where there were sounds of music. We were invited to take seats near the sheykh & were served wth hot cinnamon water, cigarettes, etc., the pilgrim in a huge state of glorification & in most brilliant coloured clothes doing the honours in person. The holy carpet & camels are expected to arrive in a few days, where there will be still [?] junks (see Lane's [?] Egyptians).[1]

I can't say the climate has agreed with me altogether, having had a diarrhea, the streets are horribly dirty in some places & I expect there must be a frightful deal of cesspool about, for bad smells [?]. If I'm well enough I'm going tomorrow to Sakkarah[2] on an invitation from the great cook who is out here.

There appear to be no visitors. There is an English Colonel for his health at the Hotel & a son of Horsley the painter[3] came to make sketches, but I don't expect there will be any tourists. They say the Arabs are massing in the Soudan & are coming down to Wady Halfa, or where ever the troops are, and soldiers are being sent up the Nile now.

I suppose you sent off my picture all right.[4] How about the add^t in the catalogue? Have you seen any notices of the notes in my papers?[5] How do you come on about a servant? Got a respectable party? Tell me all the news & how you are. I hope you have not got as many fleas about y^r legs as I have just now, nor as many mosquito bites as I am decorated with. The number of [critters?] that graze upon a human here is legion.

Good bye, all good wishes from y^r affectionate father

Henry Wallis

L22. *To* Harold Wallis   Cairo   30 November 1885

MS: University of Oxford, Bodleian Library, MS Eng.c.7049, ff. 3-4

During his first journey to Egypt, Wallis went as far as Assouan and Philae and was back in England by March. In one of his weekly letters to his son, he describes a trip outside Cairo to see the Coptic churches, as well as the return of the camel from Mecca bringing the sacred carpet.

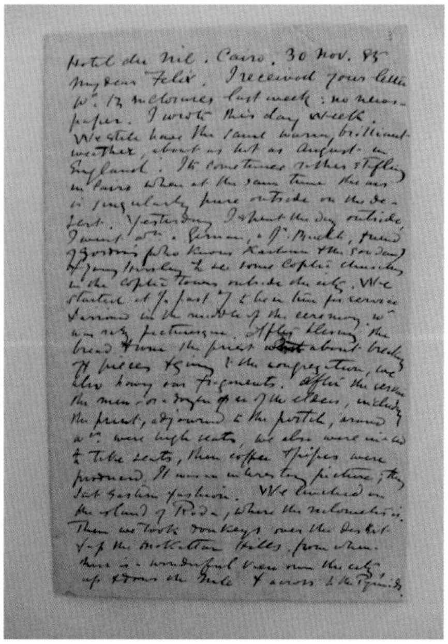

A letter from Henry Wallis in Cairo to his son Harold 'Felix' Wallis. [See: L22]
By permission of the Bodleian Libraries, University of Oxford, MSS Don.e.79, fol.39

Hotel du Nil. Cairo. 30 Nov. 85.

My dear Felix.

I received your letter wth 13 enclosures last week: no newspaper. I wrote this day week. We still have the same warm, brilliant weather, about as hot as August in England. It's sometimes rather stifling in Cairo when at the same time the air is singularly pure outside in the desert. Yesterday, I spent the day outside. I went wth a German, a Mr Brecht, friend of Gordon's[1] (who knows Khartoum & the Sudan) & young Horsley[2] to see some Coptic churches, in the Coptic town outside the city. We started at ½ past 7 to be in time for service & arrived in the middle of the ceremony, wch was very picturesque. After blessing the bread & wine the priest went about breaking off pieces & giving to the congregation, we also having our fragments. After the service the men – or a dozen or so of the elders, including the priest, adjourned to the por[t]ch, around wch were high seats. We also were invited to take seats, then coffee & pipes were produced. It was an interesting picture; they sat eastern fashion.[3] We lunched on the island of Roda, where the nilometer[4] is. Then we took donkeys over the desert & up the Mokattan Hills from where there is a wonderful view over the city, up & down the Nile & across to the Pyramids. We had a practical experience of the persistence wth wch the Egyptians will use the railway line when they can & wch was such a grief to my Rlwy [Railway] manager friend. Numbers of natives & animals of all kinds from camels to sheep get killed annually. Coming to a line the donkey boys insisted we c^{ld} make a short cut by going along it, but possibly we got into a very deep cutting. Only one line, scarcely any sideway, a serpentine road wth rapid curves. Suddenly they thought they heard a train & took fright, proposing we sh^{ld} return, wch if this had been done w^{ld} have got us all killed. However we dismounted & I went on ahead to give [?] another rearguard. Fortunately no train appeared, if one had we might have escaped but the donkeys c^{ld} not have been saved. And it turned out after all that taking the rail we went along way further than if we had stuck to the desert.

Last week one of the g^{rt} annual festivals came off. The return of the sacred camel from Mecca bringing the carpet.[5] The spectacle was not remarkable for the splendour of the apparition or their decoration, but interesting from the motley groups of dervishes & pilgrims, in picturesque costume. There were native troups wth their execrable bands; there were pashas & officials who looked bored; there was one English officer who rode by himself, but the principal personage was the sheykh of the carpet, fat naked to the waist & who rolled about on his camel. Some of the banner [hewns?] staggered along, supported by their friends & the flag poles going anywhere. It struck me the [?] were under the influence of liquor or hasheesh.

[...]

L23. ***To* Frederic George Stephens Cairo 12 December 1885**
MS: University of Oxford, Bodleian Library, MSS Don.e.79, ff.77-78
Wallis gives Stephens his impression of Cairo and the surrounding area.

Hotel du Nil. Cairo. 12 Dec – 85

My dear Stephens.

I am afraid the climate of Cairo is not of the most bracing, it induces habits of procrastination. I have been going to write you any time the last five weeks, to learn how you come on, & wth the hope of extracting a whole budget of home news from you, & yet post after post have gone by. The fact is I had expected bright weather but I was not prepared for 35 successive days of sunshine in Nov: & Dec: & for all I can see there is every prospect of the same state of affairs going on to the end of time. You get an occasional blood red sunrise, well, that ought to bring rain in any well conducted atmosphere, devil a bit, here. Mare's tails appear & vanish, but nothing comes of them, & so wth all the infallible prognostics of rain & change in Europe.

Things generally have a topsy turvy air here. It is all [?]; wch accounts for the general state of dilapidation & muddle, & dirt & filth. What is really exhilarating is the air of the desert – of the country – Get outside the city & the air is of wonderful purity & freshness, the colour also is of corresponding purity & delicacy.

The lines of the landscape are of extreme simplicity, but there is sufficient incident to remove any appearance of monotony. I am too late to see Cairo under its aspect as an Arab town. The old houses are being pulled down in all directions & they must have been very fine in structure & ornamentation & where the walls are standing, they are as solid & the [?] often as sharp as if they had been set up yesterday.

Many of the mosques have been destroyed, some of the old ones will I suppose escape – after restoration. The new streets that are replacing the old ones, & the new quarter, are dull & absolutely w^th^out interest - when not positively offensive. Cairo will soon be an ugly Frenchified third rate capital, where probably much of the swindledom & rascality of Europe will congregate, though any imported corruption will never match the native article.

[...]

L24. ***To* Harold Wallis Cairo 21 December 1885**
MS: University of Oxford, Bodleian Library, MS Eng.c.7049, ff.5-6
Like any artist, Wallis was keen to learn and his descriptions of people and sites are often interesting, but he lacked an open mind and was perplexed by "idiotic" ceremony of the dervishes he described so accurately. His attitude was imperialistic and patronising, typical of an English gentleman of his time.

Hotel du Nil. Cairo. 21 Decr 1885.

My dear Felix.

[...]

Last week was the annual fête of Mohammed, the Mooled el Nebby, it is a compound of religious festival & Bartholomew fair lasting a couple of weeks. The religious portion is held in a series of tents inside an enclosure. The tents are large & grandily decorated & at night when the devotional exercises take place are brilliantly illuminated. I went the last night & found the various companies of dervishes in full swing, each in their separate tents. The services are conducted on various principles, partaking of the nature of systematic exercises, more or less violent. For instance, 80 or 110 men will stand in two rows facing each other, every man touching his neighbours. In the centre will stand 2 or 3 single men who gabble a litany or something of that nature. The rank & file will sway their bodies, from side to side & after the two lateral motions incline their bodies forward, keeping up a monotonous chant, while the motion is slow. But as it quickens the chant becomes a wheeze, a [?] or a low howl. Some roll their heads about as if they wanted to dislocate their necks. This goes on for hours, until they drop from their exhaustion. Some are seized wth phrensy [*sic*] & will fling up their arms & fall in convulsions. Then their friends rush in forcing the wretched men away, kicking & moaning & yelling. In some of the tents they sit in rows several deep putting their shoes in the centre, & read the Koran, taken at the double. It appears as if it was a race to see who c^ld^ get through it first. A little swinging is going on all the while to give a cheerful & convivial air to the proceedings. The tents are crowded wth people, consequently the air is stifling. Crowds pass on outside & carriages containing the ladies of the harems also pass slowly along. Otherwise there are no women to be seen in tents or crowd. There are official tents where solemn swells sit & smoke & there is a display of fireworks wch opens the evenings' entertainment. In the pleasure part of the fair there are swings & roundabouts & [?] of various kinds [?] & a noise & uproar absolutely deafening. It's a curious sight to see once, but a little of it goes a long way. Formerly the Sheykh of the Dervishes used to ride over the prostrate forms of his disciples (sudane - ?Sudan) but that has been abolished 5 or 6 years.[1] Also I believe they don't eat snakes or swallow glass & other disgusting exb^{n} now, and I suppose the idiotic spectacle I witnessed will not last long. At any rate if we c^{ld} only govern the country for a certain time, establish a decent system of education & give the people justice, many degrading customs w^{ld} be certain to disappear. [...]

L25. *From* William Holman Hunt Fulham 30 September 1886
MS: Oxford, Bodleian Library, MS Eng.c. 7039, fols. 47-48.
Hunt is referring to Henry Tamworth Wells, R.A. (1828-1903)

Draycott Lodge Fulham
Sept 30th 1886

My dear Wallis.

I shall not perhaps take any further notice of Wells' letters unless there should be something quite unexpected. Nothing for the moment can be counted upon from the discussion but as you say, I believe the revelations have stirred up much interest and when the question comes up the public will insist upon a serious readjustment of the Academy. I was talking to an M.P. on Sunday who is not one professing to understand Art. But he referred to my letters which he assured me he had followed most attentively. And he declared they had been quite a revelation to him, and to many others and would not fail to bear fruit.

What you say about the young men I should like to talk over with you. For the last two or three years my malady has so hampered me that I have but rarely been able to count upon a full hour's freedom from discomfort and pain. And so I have not been to exhibitions of young men, and I have not looked for their works in the old [?], so I don't know any young men's works. Now and then I hear of a highly successful picture of a dirty dog having his fleas washed out of him – or two dogs represented inimitably – dragging at a dead duck – one at his head, the other at his tail. Of course there are other sorts of work but little I think of the poetic or imaginative kind.

On Tuesday evening one of the Nat. Art Exh. Soc. named Thomas,[1] a sculptor, has a gathering at his studio in Manresa Rd. Last time I set out to go but I was unwell on the way and had to come back. Thus far therefore I know nothing of them. Were there any one strong as half a dozen men that I could name about the year 1856 I would not fear competition. But then what can you do – if some do prove themselves equal – against the temptations of the Academy ? Only Rossetti, you, Brown and I were staunch. Crane thinks all of these new men will be, but what security is there they will not be like the ordinary men of modern Britishers, who seem to have forgotten the firmness of their fathers.

Yours ever truly.
W. Holman Hunt

L26. *From* William Holman Hunt Fulham 17 November 1886
MS: University of Oxford, Bodleian Library, MS Eng.c.7039, f.53
The following two extracts show how much Hunt liked to gossip, here about George Frederic Watts, who spent his honeymoon in Egypt. The second letter [L27] also reinforces Hunt's concerns regarding finances and his ongoing concerns about the running of the Royal Academy.

Draycott Lodge Fulham
Nov 17. 1886

My dear Wallis

[...]

If you go I hope you will have a pleasant time. All the artists go to Egypt this year. You will meet the bridegroom and his bride – G.F. Watts and the lady who has adored him for twenty five years.[1] The world gets funnier as it gets more tragic.

L27. *From* William Holman Hunt Fulham 30 January 1887

MS: University of Oxford, Bodleian Library, MS Eng.c.7039, ff.55-56

Draycott Lodge Fulham
Jan[y] 30th 1887

My dear Wallis.

I am in difficulty to keep a business promise just now, or I would not have left so long a time go by without sending a return to your welcome letter, which came with a breath of the sunny south which I can only enjoy in such distant manner. I had indeed made forecasts for a journey to Egypt this winter and the gods forbid it. And as far as I see I must die where I am, as people seem to deserve to do when they are poor.

I do believe that a few months of the delightful climate of Egypt in the winter would sit me right now, for I think it is quite proved that organically I am still all sound. But the long tension I suffered with that Jerusalem canvas[1] and all the lamentable consequences – sleeplessness and incessant vomittings – have so racked my breathing tubes that nothing but balmy and soothing air and life could afford me the rest necessary to allow me to recuperate. The constant drain on my purse nearby maddened me – Even now great bills come in, and I have to pay them, when under ordinary circumstance I might expect payments that would more than free me from the losses I have suffered. Don't say any thing of this but I am teased out of my life by people saying "Oh I thought you were going to Egypt", as if I was doing them great wrong by not having kept my promise. And I don't want you to think that I act waywardly without the guidance of reason.

You will be amused to learn that Wells has presented a great scheme of reform for the Academy to adopt.[2] It was announced in last night's *Pall Mall Gazette*, and the writer speaks of it as the great project which he inaugurated. And he adds that he cannot repine at the great pains he unceasingly took to bring about this grand end. (I quote from memory but it is at least as strong as this). I am too lazy at this moment to get the paper, but as far as I remember the plan is to have 150 or more outside members of the R.A. who shall have special claims upon space for exhibition. And they will have the first chance of election as A.R.A.s. It is amusing and it goes some way to confirm me in a suspicion that there is not much hope for England until it has met with tremendous trial and humiliation to shake the Almighty humbug out of it. The National men it seems to me are inactive, but my illness has prevented me from going to see them. Walter Crane wrote to me expressing surprise that I had refused to be on the provisional Committee, but I told him this was impossible in my state unless I left the work to others, while I took the responsibility, which was out of the question. But I offered to appear in name as a patron, or an honorary member, and so it stands.

My picture has come back from Manchester[3] with the frame disgracefully damaged. Three screw holes in the gold surface from behind and the gilt and gesso too torn off for about 5 feet. There is to be a great exhibition at Adelaide this year[4] but it is to be all in the hands of the R.A. and I don't see how one can send.

You will have heard of Watts' marriage and of his honeymoon in Egypt.[5] The deceiver had been making love to several ladies, and he never let them meet. One now is in the greatest distress confined to her bed. She had courted him for years and she did not know of the existence of this rival.[6]

Yours affectionately.
W. Holman Hunt

L28. *To* William Holman Hunt Benisouéf 14 February 1887

MS: The Huntington Library, San Marino, California, MS. HH 579.

From Dah[1] Lotus, above Benisouéf [2]
14 February 1887

My dear Hunt

I was grieved to hear that you had not got rid of your bronchial ailment & sorry to find that you are not coming to Egypt, because I think to have escaped a London winter & to have had 3 or 4 months of this genial temperature would have put you right again. I rather fancy if you had passed the last ten weeks on the upper deck of this boat, simply doing nothing but looking at the passing landscape, turning over the leaves of a book, wth an occasional cigarette, you w[ld] have got quit of y[r] ailments. I don't think I sh[ld] have let you make any of the expeditions I have gone through, for the atmosphere of tombs approaches the stifling, & a long walk of 8 miles over the desert in the broiling sun is not the regime for an invalid. When it is a quiet ride on a donkey through the green cornfields, the barley, that is now in the ear, or through the long stretches of the perfume of the bean fields the gentle exercise w^{ld} not be fatiguing, but donkeys are not always available & monuments not always within the belt of civilization. However, it is too late to come to Egypt this spring but cannot you go to some genial climate for a couple of months, so avoiding the English spring, wch is often more trying than the winter? If you don't mind the sea it is an easy voyage to Gibraltar & then to Malaga, from thence to Granada is not a long way & you have an air of extraordinary purity & the most lovely scenery in Europe & a comfortable Hotel at the Washington Irving. The journey through Spain by France is very trying, but you might see the Madrid Gall^{y} coming home. Arcachon, beyond Bordeaux has a fine genial climate. I believe. If you won't leave England, Mount's Bay, in Cornwall is delightfully sunny when there is snow and sleet in London. There are nooks there equal to the Bay of Naples for temperature. Now, pray go to one of these places, or some other such like, stop for a couple of months and don't do any work, or think at all about business of any kind. And you will come back refreshed & invigorated & ready for anything. It is depressing not to sell the result of ones work at once. But in times of depression, like the present, there are few can buy high priced pictures. In all human probability another season of prosperity will arrive & then your larger works will find purchasers. Or you might organize a scheme to find your payment from exhibiting them. C^{ld} not the 'Triumph of the Innocents' go to the colonies and America? Portraits pay, & wth a certain amount of tact and diplomacy you might, I sh^{ld} think, secure your share of these. Your account of Wells' proposal amused me.[3] Bad times are coming for that institution. We can afford to contemplate the evolution of the decomposition wth perfect serenity. I do not think the painters are yet educated up to the point of a rational system, & it is a mistake to give people better institutions than they desire, or can appreciate. Let the leaven work. After the effort you made last autumn you can wth a quiet conscience retire to your own tent – in no sullen spirit but in assured confidence as to the final result. The Anglo Saxon is a slow & unready animal, & morally, I fear, the painters are not the most favourable specimens of the race. Still, I believe in the race, in its capacity to work out its salvation in its own plodding way, often going astray, groping its way back into the true path & reaching the goal at last.

I am glad to say my voyage from an artistic point of view has been tolerably successful. I have got a subject or two I hope to be able to work out;[4] not that I count much on it from that side, for Egyptian subjects will never greatly interest the English public, but from the insight one has been able to acquire in the mysteries of Egyptian Art I cannot consider the time wasted. I don't pretend to have solved the riddle of those mysteries, only I have more distinct impressions than before I had carefully examined the monuments. On the direction of so-called Arab Art & the early Xtian I think I have found something – but of these matters when we meet.

Pray try & take a season of entire rest in some pure & genial climate & where the air is lighter and the skies brighter than our damp & smoky metropolis. Pray give my kind regards to Mrs Hunt & believe me ever sincerely yrs

Henry Wallis

L29. *To* Harold Wallis Athens 9 October 1887

MS: Private collection, New York.

In 1887, instead of reaching Egypt via Brindisi, Wallis decided to go by way of Trieste, Corfu, Athens, Smyrna and Constantinople, before reaching Alexandria.

Hôtel des Etrangers. Athens.

Friday; 9th Oct.

My dear Felix.

I wrote you last just before leaving Corfu…

I arrived on Wednesday, went of course first up to the Acropolis, but have not yet attempted to see anything, it being much too hot for the slightest unnecessary exertion. Finding a good Egyptian coll^{n} at the Museum. I am copying one or two of the glazed vases for the Magnum Opus. I suppose this heat will not continue much longer. I shall go to the post to see if y^{r} letter [of?] Triest has arrived.

With respect to the "letter" for the Exb^{n} – water colour – you can fill it in. No. 1. Herodotus at the Scribe's Bazaar at Memphis. Price 100 Gns. No. 2. The Flute Player. Price 60 Gns.[1] You will see how to do it, enclose in envelope & direct to the Sec: Clayton will take the letter wth the pictures. Write the titles & my name (not price) on slips of paper & paste them on the backs of the pictures. The prices are deadfully low, but I am afraid things will sell wth increased difficulty this winter.

I think you had better write here to the hotel. Find the best day for the post. I've made no plans yet. Shall I address to Bank?

Ever y^r loving father.

Henry Wallis

Did you hear of the earthquake at Corinth 3 or 4 days ago? It was a sharp shock here I am told & the people are very alarmed.

L30. *To* Harold Wallis Constantinople 25 October 1887
MS: private collector, New York.

Constantinople. Oct 25th. Tuesday

My dear Felix.

I wrote you last on Saturday. There are 2 mails a week for London via Vienna.

The 4 days I have been here have not been of the most genial, in fact such continuous heavy rain I scarcely ever remember. And when you have to walk through miles of them Devonshire lane streets in it nothing more c^ld be desired.

Last Sunday I went wth the consul to call on Hamdy Bey, the Director of the Museum. He lives a long way down the Bosphorus, a short distance from his villa, on returning, the carriage broke down, so there was nothing for it but to tramp!

I have left the hotel & taken a room, having my meals at the Club, a very comfortable place, & where visitors are allowed to have the advantages if for a limited time. Below my windows I have a view of the Golden Horn & this morning, at 7, it being fine, the view is fine, perhaps too much mist[?] from the water.

There is another painter here, Tristam Ellis,[1] but I hear the visits of artists are of extreme variety. It is a deprivation not hearing from you or getting letters. Keep on writing to Cairo - Cook & Son.

I propose leaving here on Thursday on a Messagerie boat for Smyrna & from thence after a couple of days to Alexandria. A pleasant time & good weather for y^r holidays. Have you seen Mr Clement.[2] Did he pay Roberson?[3] Have you taken the things to B. M. & S. K. M.?

Ever y^r loving father.

Henry Wallis

L31. *To* Frederic George Stephens Smyrna 2 November 1887
MS: Oxford, Bodleian Library, MSS Don e. 79, fols.87-88.

Smyrna. 2 Nov 87

My dear Stephens.

[...]

I have for a long while been leading a kind of Ulysses life, [?or ?on river] since I left Trieste. The voyage among the Ionian islands is enchanting & Corfu has wonderful landscape when one goes ashore. I only stopped a couple of days there. Then the gulf of Corinth keeps up the same scenery. From Corinth I went to Athens by rail & stopped there a fortnight, & sh^ld have remained longer but the heat & dust were intolerable. From thence I took steamer for Constantinople & after having seen St Sophia & other antiquities, was glad to leave it after a week. The filth in the streets is overpowering. Arid through the beauty of the site is unquestionable, seen from the water. Yet the cupolas & minarets are poor in form & the mass of the secular buildings mean. The voyage here through the Peloponnese, past the plains of Troy, between Lesbos & the coast of Asia Minor is a thing to remember. So also the Gulf of Smyrna, but it sh^ld be done in a yacht. One continually wants to land & explore the vales into wch one gets such enchanting glimpses. Splendid as is the seduction of this "capital of Asia Minor", it is not cheerful. The rule of the Turk is cunningly continued to wreck commerce & make life dreary. The talk of the residents is all of murders & robberies (varied wth earthquakes). The latter I look on wth indifference, since my first experience in Greece. I sh^ld like to go to Ephesus & Hierapolis[1] but the risk is too great & I shall presently take steamer for Alexandria.

L32. *To* Harold Wallis Cairo 14 November 1887
MS: private collector, New York.

Care of Messrs Cook & Son:
Cairo.
Monday 14 Nov.

My dear Felix.

I wrote you yesterday week. And received a letter from you on my arrival here. On Thursday - the arrival post day - I got a weekly Times but no letter. I did not get one addressed to the H. des Etrangers, Athens. In fact I have only received three from you - the last dated 28 Oct: As I suppose you have sent more had you not better write to the P. Office.

Tano,[1] the dealer here, tells me he has sent me a wooden object, wth inscriptions & animals on it. His account is so vague I cannot make out even what it is, but I suspect it is a boomerang – used by the ancient Egyptians found in tombs[?]. He says the price of this is £30. If I don't buy it or the British Museum, he wishes it sent back. Its artistic value may be nil, or it may be important, its monetary value may be 5/- or £50 – but if the latter there is no reason why he sh^ld^ have £30, w^ch^ [is?] a ballon d'essai.[2] I think you had better take it to the British Museum & leave it wth Budge[3] who can bargain for it if they want it – or send it back. Or it may have an artistic value in wch case I think Poynter sh^ld^ see it.[4] Write to him 25 Albert Gate - tell him when you could bring it & ask him if he will see it - that is before you take it to Budge. W^ld^ it be in the way of S. K. M.? When you come back can you take the object to Poynter when you write to him you had better copy what I have said. On the other side, it will give him an idea how the matter stands. You can describe the thing to me.

It is still very hot here. Almost every body has had the fever. I don't mean to – if I can help it. If you went on your holiday on the 5th I suppose you will return on the 26th? & this sh^ld^ reach town on the 21st. Let me hear all about where you have been, hope you had nice weather.

Your loving father

Henry Wallis

How was it at Woodbury on your return?

L33. *To* Harold Wallis Cairo 27 November 1887
MS: private collector, New York.

c/o Messrs Cook & Son. Cairo.
27 Nov. Sunday

My dear Felix.

I received last Thursday yours of the 18th but no papers. I wrote to you last week.

I have sent George Wallis[1] 3 invoices

– hasp[?] £5 : 3 shoes 30/- : 3 pieces of textiles 32/- I have asked him to pay the money unto the B[ank] of E[ngland]. If he can't & sends them to you, you consign & send them to B. of E. W. Bi...Look at the last of things & see what price I put on the sculpture sent to S. K. M. & let me know. Did you tell them the price? I asked you to.

One of the letters you sent me was from Lambros, Athens.[2] He was to send 2 glass vases & one agate funnel & one glass vase, broken to A.W. Franks[3] F. R. S. Keeper of Antiquities, British Museum. I wrote to F. telling him he might like the broken vase, & if so to have it at the price I gave, £2. The others I keep. £22 in all. I told F. he need not write to me. Now, will you write to him, asking to let you know when the vases arrive (enumerate them) to tell you if he keeps the one I thought he w^ld^ like & whether you should fetch them or whether he will allow them to remain at the B. M. till my return? I am to send Lambros a cheque as soon as I hear of their arrival.

Have you heard from Budge? I have not had the letter you sent to the Hotel des Etrangers, A. Did it contain enclosures?

Write to young Poynter[4] telling him what Kenny says, ask him if he w^ld^ like any more copies of the Report. If so he sh^ld^ ask for them & then he sh^ld^ tell K. to distribute. Can you not call & see Mr Clement & see if he is equal to the "little outside pressure"?

You say...I am in cloudless skies. However dark you may have had it in London you have not nearly all been down wth Denghi [*sic*] Fever – like the people here. I am thankful to say I have not had it but almost every body I know has, doctors tell. They are so hard worked they can't attend all their patients. This evening I have been doctoring the man in the next room to me. Col: ..olled Smith.

The weather keeps up wonderfully fine, a little cooler than at first. The Mooled al Neblyi[5] has been going on (I think I told you of it 2 years ago), the religious part is the same, but the fair has lost some of its saturnalian character, thanks, I suppose, to the British hands of the police. The city has much improved in cleanliness & in the state of the roads since first I saw Cairo. What is absolutely necessary is a system of drainage, then much of the disease wld disappear. But while we continue our policy of shilly shally that, wth so many other things, will never be accomplished. And there is no chance of improvement or decent government here anywhere else in our dominions while that wretched old humbug cannot hold his tongue.[6]

I have not seen an account of the riots but have heard there were people killed. I hold that he is responsible for their deaths[?].[7]

I sent by parcels post this week some things to Armstrong[8] S. K. M. 3 pieces of Egyptian textiles, for the museum, & in the parcel <u>3 pieces of Rhodian embroideries + 2 silk & gold woman's robes</u>. I have asked A. either to send these to you or to keep them at the museum till my return.

Is the studio all right & dry? I supposed Mr Daniel has really started.

Ever your loving father.

Henry Wallis

L34. *To* Harold Wallis Girga 22 December 1887

MS: University of Oxford, Bodleian Library, MS Eng.c.7049, ff.19-20

This letter shows Wallis travelling with E.A. Wallis Budge, a curator from the British Museum, and how they tried to secure pieces for their own collections and for that of the British Museum.

c/o Mess. Cook & Son. Cairo. Thursday 22.12.87
S.S. Amosis above Girgey[1]

My dear Felix.

I have not received a letter from you this week. As I left Cairo on Tuesday & post does not arrive till Thursday, I write now in hopes this will get to Cairo by Sunday, in time for the Brindisi Mail.

I started early on Tuesday morning wth Budge[2] on the dirtiest bit of railway travelling in the world, the line to Asyout, & we had 10 hours of it arriving at 6.30. We came on board the steamer at once & started the next morning at a little after six, just as the day was dawning, a time that I never like to miss on the Nile. I don't know [if] there is any particular merit in early rising here, because the starting of the boat always wakes you up & you have only to open yr door to find yrself in the open & you need not put on anything more than an Ulster [overcoat] & a pair of slippers, over yr pyjamas. We have wonderfully fine weather, wth the sun perceptibly hotter than at Cairo – the air perceptibly sweeter. We are not a large party. Cook's eldest son,[3] Canon Isaac Taylor[4] & his wife & daughter & a mild & ?worked out M.P. & his wife. He is but a fledgling & it might perhaps be thought cruel to nip his young existence in the bud, but as he is a Separatist we feel that we shall be guilty of a culpable neglect of the best interests of the Commonweal[th] if we don't bind him to a wild ass & send him soon in the desert to be devoured by jackals & vultures.

It is not as satisfactory being steamed past so many interesting places, as when you are in yr own boat & can stop where you like. Girgey, for instance, is the place where one cld take a donkey for Abydos, & where last year I went & slept at the house of the Sheykh, & where temples & landscape are among the most interesting in Egypt, it lies 8 miles or so from the Nile.[5] One can see the gap in the mountains, whereby the souls went to the land of Osiris, but we must be content wth a distant view. Last night we tied up at Akhmeem, where the textiles come from, & where there are several dealers.[6] A good natured Frenchman, who manages a mill there, took us – B. & myself – to several of these worthies, who had all gone to bed, it being after 8 o'clock. At one place we had a mummy case opened & there was considerable excitement to know how it wld turn out; if successful B. was to give £5 for it, but it was a very indifferent one damaged. So he did not buy it. The groups in the dim light of a couple of lanterns was [...bly] picturesque. In spite of the lateness of the hour the usual amount of haggling over the price of every thing had to be gone through. Some times the seller insists on you making the price, or he may suggest a sum absolutely preposterous, then he is very coy in producing his best things. We did not get finished till 2 a.m. & then some men came & made bazaar at B's cabin, wch took half an hour more. He got some interesting things in the way of inscriptions & I got a couple of bits of blue wth some trifling things. A great haul of Coptic mss. had to be left undecided. We expect to be at Keneh[7] tonight where I know a man who has inscribed potsherds that B. will go for, so we may have another late night. K. is celebrated for its dates, sold now in boxes, if they w[ld] not get dried upon the passage, I sh[ld] like to send you a box.

We ought to arrive at Luxor tomorrow. There I may stay some time, depend[ing] on whether I can get any material for work. Wish you c[ld] drop in on Xmas day in the lightest of summer costume. The uncertainty in the characters of this letter is <u>not</u> from ague or inebriation, but because the *Amosis* is getting into decrepitude – in fact it is despisably shaky. Let me hear all you have seen.

Y[r] loving father.

Henry Wallis

L35. *From* William Bell Scott Penkill Castle 11 October 1889

MS : Bodleian Library, MS Eng.c. 7041, fols. 211-2.

This letter seems to be the last that Scott sent to Wallis; Scott would die the following year.

Penkill, Girvan, Ayrshire
11 October 1889

My Dear Wallis,

Perhaps you have heard that I have at last (after reaping it on all those years I have been invalided here at immense expense) sold the lease of my dear old Bellevue House at Chelsea, and am therefore clearing out all my old collections to deliver it up.

There is to be a sale in the house, but <u>when</u> I don't yet know, and if you want the little early Italian pots you once called to see or anything else, I advise you to go. There are a number of Hispano-Moros if you still collect such, and a remarkable Majolica platter with the subject of Jupiter & Juno in an interesting position (not improper) on it. The Hispano Moresque water vessel I have presented to the SK Museum. I expect things will go dirt cheap. All my Nankin ware will go with the rest and the wine in the cellar, among w[h] is 3 or 4 dozen very old Port, really regretted by me, but impossible to send down here.

How have you been this long time? I am rather better; my lungs seem quite safely well just at present, but general health bad, making me give up the hope of getting again to London, and I have got accustomed to the quiet life of the country and have a studio here where I am going to put all my pictures (my own and the few others I possess), but all my books must go at Sothebys. The time for that is not yet determined, but a Cat. will be got up by Mr Hodge of the firm.[1]

Give me a few words and believe me

Ever very sincerely yours

William Bell Scott

To my old friend Henry Wallis.

L36. *From* William Matthew Flinders Petrie Cairo 4 February 1890

MS: University of Oxford, Bodleian Library, MS Eng.c.7041, ff. 121-122

[See: L37]

Wallis and Petrie met often during the period 1890-1895 and shared their passion for Egyptian art. On one occasion, Wallis accompanied him to Naucratis where Petrie had made discoveries.

Cairo
4 Feb 90

My dear Sir,

Tano[1] says that he is selling off & wants to clear his stock, & take to travelling dealing in Europe. He now offers the fine Ramesses II green brick, with double cartouche on top, & inscription all round, together with the poor one with trace of cartouche & broken, for £20 together. He says he gave Farag £30. I told him I would write to you. If you want them send him the money, & tell him to deliver them to D[r] Grant's,[2] & I will include them in a box of mine, when I leave, so their cost of carriage would be only a few shillings. This would be your cheapest way to get them over.

He also has about 100 leaves of a fine old Koran, sheet 36 x 24 in., thick paper, 9 lines & 1 illuminated at bottom, also patch of illumination in margin: writing about 1 ½ in high, very beautiful, red numeration &c. The illumination is in gold & blue. I am no judge of the age, but it is certainly not late, nor is the writing cufic on the other hand. He wants £30, or £1 a leaf. Being imperfect, a few leaves would be as good as the whole for the style & art.

I have bought some stuff, but nothing in your way here.

Yours sincerely,

W.M. Flinders Petrie

L37. *To* Harold Wallis Cairo 17 November 1890

MS: University of Oxford, Bodleian Library, MS Eng.c.7049, ff.40-41

Wallis describes his trip to Naucratis with Flinders Petrie.

Cairo. Egypt. 17.11.90

My dear Felix.

Yours of the 7th recvd wth paper. You will have recvd my letter from Marseilles & I hope in your next I shall get the information about the 4th vol: of Sterling.

We had a very pleasant voyage to Alexandria, arriving there on Thursday morning, the wind was favourable & we had no bad weather though it was not exactly smooth. It was very cold on starting & fairly warm on arriving. We stayed the day at Alexandria & then on Friday left by an early train for the nearest station to Naucratis,[1] a five miles walk in a brilliant sun. Petrie was glad to visit the scene of his former labours. We passed most of the day in walking about the site of the ancient city & among the myriads of fragments of pottery found some interesting pieces. Then we took the evening train arriving at Cairo at night. We were welcomed by the proprietor of the hotel as ancient clients & now are settling down. Petrie trying for permission to excavate at Maydum,[2] wch, if he gets it will occupy him the winter.

One hears a good deal about the monuments, nothing definite, but the agitation has roused the officials here. Send me all you hear about it from the English papers.[3] There are very few visitors as yet. It is very hot, although today has been cloudy, wth the first rain.

I have several letters to write & post goes soon & I don't want to miss this mail.

Ever your loving father.

Henry Wallis

L38. *To* Harold Wallis Luxor 13 January 1891

MS: University of Oxford, Bodleian Library, MS Eng.c.7049, ff.52-53

Wallis was obviously concerned about the damage caused to the Egyptian monuments. It is also clear that his anti-French feelings intensified during the 1890s.

(Société Égyptienne Thewfikieh de Navigation-Remorquage et de Commerce)

<u>Address as usual</u>

No need to put Poste restante

Luxor, 13.1.91

My dear Felix.

Yrs of the 2nd recvd yesterday, wth Ath: [Athenaeum magazine] but no Times. I was very sorry to hear that the inclement weather still continued in London. Its duration is almost unprecedented. I hope you will escape serious indisposition. Here we have the usual brilliant sunshine, hot in the day, & rather sharply cold towards morning, but wch vanishes at sunrise.

As yet I am the sole resident at this hotel, but expect some others in a few days. Being new, the arrangements are on an improved system to the other two hotels, though in a climate like this, it does not much matter as to the accommodation, & then one is not [? in] all day. Excavations are being made at the Temple of Luxor, & at Medinet Habou,[1] on the other side – the Western – of the Nile. The state of the monuments is, I am sorry to say, much worse than when I was here three years since. The agitation of the last years has had the smallest effect, no repairs are done, no practical supervision is exercised. The

French display an incapacity w[ch] is simply incredible – unless it is intentional. Their paper, the Bosphore – the organ of the French Consul General is more rabid & abusive than ever. I suppose it is on a par wth the Irish home rule papers. I occasionally see Paris papers, & they are equally virulent in their anti-English feeling, now they are furious at the fiasco of the Irish, showing that their rooted feeling is a malignant hatred of England. It is true their hatred of Germany & Italy is equally intense. It seems that there will be nothing for it but to effectually draw their teeth, & I think it is a pity Germany did not do so 20 years ago.

I am not at all sure about getting to Abydos, & may stay here till the end of the month & then return to Cairo.

I thought the Argentine funds were for £100. How is it I only got £40? How do matters come on in those regions now? [2]

I did not find any dates worth sending this year – nothing as good as those boxes from the stores. The ripe dates were good but this year they don't seem to preserve well.
Ever y[r] affectionate father.

Henry Wallis

L39. *From* William Holman Hunt Cairo / Jerusalem 9 March 1892 / 4 April 1892
MS: Oxford, Bodleian Library, MS Eng.c. 7039, fols. 57-59.
This important letter is the longest Hunt ever wrote to Wallis, and is published here for the first time. In it he explains his religious and political beliefs. Hunt forecasts the horrors of the Great War and the possibility of a European Union.

Continental Hotel
Cairo. Egypt

March 9th 1892

My dear Wallis.

I received your letter from Naples just as it had been determined that instead of facing further the difficulties of the winter in England I should go abroad and as my house in Jerusalem has been neglected of necessity thro all of the difficulties occasioned by that terrible Jerusalem canvas[1] it seemed desirable to combine health and business and come on to the East before my return. To write at once was impossible. I could not tell whether you were to stay in Naples but I put your letter in my pocket with the idea that in that beautiful but bedevilled city I might hear of you and follow you up, but the letter quickly got put away into a more fitting packet, so that never since have I been able to find it. And here where there was some hope during the two months since my arrival I have not heard of you. Just now when we were on the point of our departure my wife has fallen ill and after three or four days battling with the malady here I have as she desired sent her to the German Hospice where she will be better nursed. She is already, I rejoice to say, better and soon I hope she will be quite well.

About the special matter of your letter I can scarcely hope to argue to much effect in a letter. What degree of folly there is mixed up with the Peace & Arbitration agitation[2] I see very clearly myself. To propose that an Empire like England should by way of bringing about the reign of Peace dismand [disband?] the army and put down the navy is only to retard the accomplishment. And to call soldiers murderers is what I should be the last to join in. I admire soldiers, and I have the greatest interest in the annals of our wars, and the hig[h]est admiration for the men who have proved so often superior to all others. Indeed I question whether you would go so far as I do in this respect, for I should not be surprised to find that you with many modern intellects go with Morris and disapprove of our conquest of India and our occupation of Egypt, while I think this and such domination part of the duty of the hig(h)est race. (I like Morris, and I admire Gladstone, but when they talk I am dispose[d] even at 65 to take up a sword and stand in the ranks again). But I can't disregard the evidence shewing itself around, as that war between civilized nations when it breaks out next will be outrageously horrible that after the first crash, each nation will stand appalled at the havoc that has been wrought, and they will, at least the best of them, will say. There is no longer room for heroism in such a struggle and if it is to continue all the best of mankind will be destroyed, and the world will go back in culture many thousands of years; and there can scarcely be calculation of the time needed to produce another set of great leaders. In prospect of such a moment of sobriety, I regard every word that can be uttered now in favor [*sic*] of making Europe into one great united States as inestimably precious. The froth will all evaporate and I should be sorry now not to dare the misunderstanding and contempt which supporting a movement in advance of the age ensures. That it is more than this I don't think you will maintain. Since one thousand years since quite as much could be said against the unification of England as is now said against the cashiering of all the useless or worse than useless kings and potentates who manage to perpetuate the prejudices and ill feelings of the different peoples of the Continent of Europe. But you may say why bring in Monk?[3] Well my dear fellow he was the first man I ever met in the world who had worked out the idea, and who was so sensible as to avoid the follies which so many indulge who take up this idea. I must say further that one difference between you and me is, I still think, that you don't believe in an overruling Providence, while I do. It may be very foolish, but I have really taken a good deal of pains to cure myself. I have read Voltaire, Volney, Gibbon, Bolingbroke, Hume, Payne, and a man you once recommend[ed] strongly to me as good medicine for the malady. I mean Renan, as well as Strauss, and they do me good in different degrees by making me laugh. The contemporary Parisian is the most amusing dog of all. And I feel that he must have been sent by the gods who love fun to spoil his case completely. I feel sure that you cannot have read him yourself, or that you had not done so when you spoke. It was many years ago that you spoke, when I had not read him. The others however in less degrees but not less surely, in my mind do spoil their case. And so I still believe that in some mysterious manner the ruler of the world has dimly made known his programme of events by the pens of men of old belonging to the Jewish race, and it can be doubted that the idea they expressed was that in the far future war should cease. All the people now working to encourage this idea are not believers in revelation. I know of some who would call themselves atheists, and many more who are professed agnostics. Their idea of the superiority of insight of these predecessors of theirs of three thousand years back is, and could not but be, extraordinary. They don't now act with any thought of fulfilling prophecy. They judge of the value of the proposal without allowing prejudice to turn them from the work of hastening its accomplishment. I believe my dear fellow that you too on further thought will agree that they are right. If I were of their philosophy I should still feel bound to keep the cause. As it is I must avow that I see in the growth of the movement additional reason for believing that the great Father of all is leavening men's minds, be they what they may, to see that the angels shall ascend to and descend from Heaven in the end.

I often wish that I could have a quiet talk with you about other matters. I know that we agree about some art questions, and I think we ought to concur in many others, but I can't tell: if we did we might be stronger for good influence. But to write to you on the questions would be unsatisfactory, because I might be assuming too much and I would not on any account be appearing to wish to separate you from people of your choice whose views and courses I may not like to leave unblamed. And now the wilderness of counsellors objectionable in my eyes is both fierce and unlimited. You may too not think the outlook of art in England so disastrous as I do. The splendid prospect it once had has been destroyed by charlatans and fools, and knaves of all kinds. And they are so strongly banded together that every one fears to attack them. Since my health was destroyed by that Jerusalem bother of fifteen years ago origin,[4] I have had more than enough to attend to keep my own head any how above water. I have spoken out clearly about one great power and principality – and this I doubt not will do good in the end – as all truth does, but I have sometimes wished to talk over the question whether I ought to leave the quarrel to rest, or whether doing so will lead the world to think that I have been converted to a better opinion of the Kingdom of Satan. Writing here without knowing when I shall come home, I can only leave the doubt for you to reflect upon. And I must trust to chance for the opportunity of conferring with you about it.

Jerusalem April 4th 92

Happily after having written the above, my wife got better and as it was evident that Cairo was pestilential we came away at once. And this letter was packed away in a box which of course got belated, and so done without that it has only recently been unpacked. Had not this box been kept back I should have had time to finish two drawings for the Old Water Color. As it was I had to give up the hope, and write my excuses to Fripp.[5] Going up the Nile was a novelty to me. I had before been down from Cairo to Damietta and that was delightful, but up to the first cataract was an experience of the newest as well as highest kind, because of the wonderful changes from day to day. I had expected to find some monotony, but of this there was none. The only difficulty was in want of time to secure some of the lovely effects – but even in this region the curse which comes elsewhere on the world has advanced, for every twenty miles are great sugar factories with chimneys ranged like organ pipes belching out black smoke which spreads over leagues of country like a great storm, blackening the atmosphere worse than one sees on the Thames. But I think I may secure from my venture one drawing. If you have not been I recommend you to go ere the country again gets altogether covered with Egyptian darkness. Here every thing is defaced. Some wretches have built on the mount of Olives a hideous tower which is something like the Eifel tower in height, and all over the sides are erections rivalling the pavilion at Brighton in elegance. On the western side the view of the city is obscured by horrible nightmares of habitations with more squalid specimens of the Hebrew race than could be imagined. My house built half a mile outside the walls is now surrounded by new buildings and my light is spoilt.

I cannot stay much longer here but I am busy and may accomplish something to bring home. We wish to see our children again and so are impatient. I wonder what your boy is doing.

Good bye. Yours ever.

W. Holman Hunt

L40. *To* Frederic Gard Fleay Cairo 30 November 1892

MS: Washington D.C., Folger Shakespeare Library, Y.c.1459 (18)

[See: Cats. 11, 15]

Frederic Gard Fleay's A Chronicle History of the Life and Work of William Shakespeare *was published in 1886. Fleay had previously written to Wallis asking permission to reproduce some of his paintings dealing with the life of Shakespeare. Fleay was one of the founders of the New Shakespeare Society in 1873.*

Hotel du Nil. Cairo. 30 Nov

My dear Fleay.

I will give my consent wth pleasure. One of the series is in S.K.M. Landseer borrowed it of Forster in the understanding he was to make a copy of it for the introduction of figures etc.[1] The vulgar & insolent ass daubed his drivelling notions on the actual panel. You will please ask the draughtsman to omit the dog, heron, handsaw[2] & all the rubbish that Landseer added to the simple representation of the place, wch will restore the impressiveness of the light & shade. You can ask Lady Eastlake, she lives in Fitzroy Sq^{re} about the one Sir C.E.[3] bought of me. It was the so-called "room in wch S. was born".[4] You had better call on Lady E. She asked me the other day to back a protégée of hers: wch I did. Another one (the "interior of Anne Hathaway's Cottage")[5] was bought by some one through either Eastlake or Forster. You might find it. The Font I have.[6] I have asked Felix to look it up & give it you. It is just possible that it is locked up, then he c^{ld} not get it. I only got your letter by last mail – post comes once a week.

We have had it & still is blazing hot. The only time when it is truly pleasant is early morning, so I rise before the sun. The air in the desert outside Cairo, however, is always delicious in spite of the heat.

You have had your heat I suppose in the form of elections.[7] W^{ch} side is going to win? What is the subject of your book & when does it come out.

Hope you are all quite well & [?]. Kind regards to mrs Fleay.

......

Always sincerely y^{rs}.

Henry Wallis

L41. *To* Harold Wallis Cairo 1 January 1893

MS: University of Oxford, Bodleian Library, MS Eng.c.7049, fols 96-97

Wallis expresses his views on architecture and powerfully describes the crossing of the first cataract, starting from Philae.

(Cairo. Egypte. For postal address)
The Assouan Hotel. Assouan, Upper Egypt. 1.1.93

My dear Felix. I arrived here last Thursday, just in time to miss the post boat, & the next only leaves tomorrow, so this letter will not reach you for a fortnight. Your letter wch I sh^{ld} have rec^{vd} at Cairo last Thursday has of course not yet come here. I take it you got my last from Luxor, posted a week ago. As I mentioned, I was not certain about staying here but as I find a hotel (only opened a week) I propose remaining for at least a week or so. Assouan presents a very different appearance to when I was last here (when there were a number of English troops), now there is only one native regiment wth four English officers. Building operations, however, are going on apace, as at all these Egyptian towns, and quite respectable, substantial towns are being constructed. This one contains upwards of fifty rooms, it belongs to a wealthy Khartoum merchant, & he indulged in the pastime of being his own architect. Consequently there are all sorts of novelties of construction wch are a constant source of interest to those living in it. The staircases alone give one all the amusement of a visit to Hampton Court maze. Some of the problems wch arose as to lighting were too much for the worthy merchant & you find good sized rooms without windows. A pleasing feature, common to all the rooms, great & small, is that no corner is a right angle. However, the house is very comfortable & the situation very pleasant. It is on the bank of the river wth the island of Elephantine opposite & looks down the long stretch of river wch forms the approach to Assouan. Up above is the cataract, wch may be said to terminate at Elephantine. The cataract, as I suppose you know, is about six miles of river bed having a descent and running amidst rocks. The passage for dahabeeyehs & large craft is a serious affair, they have in some places to be dragged up against a rush of water that comes down in great waves, & wch it seems that no amount of pulling & hauling c^{ld} overcome. The ascent takes two or three days, the work being performed by the inhabitants of a couple of Nubian villages. The men & boys are all expert swimmers, they also float about on logs of wood, sitting as surely as if they were on terra firma. I made the descent of the cataract yesterday wth a party of two men staying at this hotel & Sir G. Grant[1] & his wife & son & daughter, who have come in a dahabeeyeh. We had a boat wth eight rowers & started from Philoe, wch is at the top of the cataract. At the commencement the stream glides smoothly between the high granite cliffs, burnt black by the sun & wherever the water has reached them shining brilliantly, as if covered wth a vitreous glaze, possibly the result of some ingredient in the Nile deposit. Soon the boat goes among the granite rocks rising out of the river bed, & the stream becomes more disturbed. Then the boat stops at an island & you walk a few hundred yards to the top of a precipitous descent at the bottom of wch is the great fall. There a few men & boys enter the water from the upper end & swim down some wth logs – or rather they are whirled down, frequently dragged under water. It looks a dangerous game but I suppose is not to creatures so amphibious: the object is, of course, backshish.[2] Having seen this performance you reenter the boat & the serious part of the descent begins, by a passage that avoids the above mentioned fall. The agitation of the water, especially in two places, is considerable & in both of these, it appears as if the boat must dash against the rocks, when by a sudden turn of the rudder the boat in an instant changes its course & is swept past the apparently certain destruction. It is certainly the cleverest bit of steering imaginable; the rowers pull their hardest, to get way on the boat, so that, wth the current, the velocity is very high; therefore all depends on the exact moment being seized; missed, the boat w^{ld} be smashed to pieces, & though the crew might escape I am afraid the chances of the passengers getting to what the country counsellor called terra cotta w^{ld} be small. I noticed the Scottish knight looked very serious, & evidently for the moment regretted his foot was not on his native heather.

Just now the temperature is agreeable, although so hot in the sun that a parasol is desirable. I am not sure how long I shall remain at present. I shall probably not go higher up the Nile. Write, of course, as before. I shall hope to hear that you have been well & that all is right at Woodbury. Have you seen Mr Daniel?[3] Wth best wishes for the new year. Ever y^{r} affec^{t} father.
Henry Wallis

L42. *From* William Holman Hunt Liverpool 22 September 1894

MS: Oxford, Bodleian Library, MS Eng.c. 7039, fols. 62-63.

Hunt laments Wallis taking time away from his painting to write books. It also shows Hunt to be a thorough Imperialist and, much like Wallis, a typical Englishman of his time and class.

North Western Hotel. Liverpool.
Sept 22. 1894

My dear Wallis.

I was, and am grateful for your reply of 24.8 to mine, but at the time of its arrival a Greek friend of ours heard of my trouble and spoke of a scarf which she had and this she sent.[1] It differed in many points, but had many resemblances, sufficient to encourage the thought that with some ribands sewn on, it might serve as a model, if on trial my brush and colors [*sic*] would prove to have sufficient imagination. When models for my other work left me free, and the scarf was ready I had to come away to the north, and now I am only on my way back with yet Oxford as a halting place to detain me a day or two. I think I may be able to make shift with the loaned scarf, and in that case I have only to thank you for your offer to help me without taxing your good nature further.

Your book, judging from your previous volume, cannot but be extremely precious and beautiful, yet I do begrudge the time it will take from you, which otherwise would be spent in poetic work.

The silly people who are always blundering with sentimental theories about Egypt, and India, are men and women who have never lived among Asiatics and Africans, or who have done so with neither brains, limbs or poverty sufficient, to allow of actual contact with the natives. Half the rule of the world is in the hands of newspaper young graduates, who learn the views that will be thought smart and state these smoothly. Previously in England the trick was done in Parliament. Now the only hope is that people like Clive, Warren Hastings, Nelson and Wellington (not to go back to later time when England was often on the point of perishing from doctrinaires) and that the rebellious will justify their independence by success. I have great admiration of heroism in war. Yet I think the time has come for courage now to declare for its abolition by the Union of all European states.

My wife left me at Preston to go on straight to London.

Ever yours truly.

W. Holman Hunt

L43. ***To*** **Frederic George Stephens** **Upper Norwood** **5 August 1896**

MS: University of Oxford, Bodleian Library, MSS Don.e.79, ff.127-128

Some reminiscences of Robert Braithwaite Martineau's well-known painting The Last Day in the Old Home, *now in the collection of Tate Britain. Wallis knew Martineau quite well during his Pre-Raphaelite period; in 1860, Martineau had found him an apartment in Great Russell Street, facing the British Museum.*

9 Beauchamp Rd.
Up: Norwood: S.E.
5.8.96

Dear Stephens.

Somebody sent me – perhaps it was you? – a ticket to see Martineau's "Last day at the old home."[1] I went to see it today & thought it looked very fine. Poor Hotchkiss said that there was more old masterly quality in Martineau's work than in that of any other modern painter. I was struck wth the truth of the remark when standing befor[e] the work today. I sh^ld^ much like to see it in the Nat: Gall: Do you see any way of getting it there? A Dr Martineau bought his relative's picture from the Leathart coll: the other day. I wonder, whether he w^ld^ buy this & present it to the nation? [2]

Afterwards I went to the Leathart coll:[3] & I there thought how desirable it w^ld^ be if Hunt's "Hireling Shepherd" was also in the N.G.[4] Why does not Tate buy it? I see some idiot in trying to throw cold water on the proposal for the N.G. to buy the Colonna Raphael![5]

We are fast going on the downward road to the Devil in matters artistic.

Kind regards to Mrs Stephens.

Ever y^rs^.

Henry Wallis

L44. ***From*** **William Holman Hunt** **Fulham** **12 August 1896**

MS: Oxford, Bodleian Library, MS Eng.c. 7039, fols. 64-65.

Draycott Lodge Fulham
Aug 12. 1896

My dear Wallis

Tomorrow I hope to get to town and then I shall try and see Bob's[1] picture. It seems there is some cracking in it and I want to judge of this, and of what otherwise might have to be done to put the work in the best condition.

It does not belong to the widow, but to the original family, and they were scarcely daring to think of its being accepted by N[ational] G[allery]. But I told them to keep their hands still till this could be worked for. Of course it ought to be there. And I think the officials and council could make no difficulty about the matter seeing that the possessor asks no price but would give it.

Yours ever truly.

W. Holman Hunt

L45. ***To*** **Frederic George Stephens** **Florence** **3 March 1897**

MS: University of Oxford, Bodleian Library, MSS Don.e.79, ff.136-137

Wallis returned from Egypt at the end of January 1897, just in time, as it appears, to attend the funeral service of George Price Boyce, who had died on 9 February. Wallis then started on a grand tour of Italy.

Florence. 3.3.97

My dear Stephens.

Many thanks for y[r] good wishes, w[ch] reached me here.

I left on the Monday after poor Boyce's funeral[1] & went to Marseilles, where I had some matters to see after, & then came into Italy by the Riviera. The weather was so warm & delightful there that I sh[ld] liked to have stayed, only the places were full of visitors & idiotic carnival festivities (?) were going on. I therefore only stopped a couple of days at S[t] Remo, where it was like fine June weather. However, even for there it was exceptional there, though [f...] for time of year, it is still March.

I propose going on to Rome on Friday, am not sure where I shall put up, so my address will be <u>Poste Restante</u>.

I don't know that there is any one here wth whom you are acquainted except Stanhope,[2] who has been better this winter than usual. M[rs] de Morgan[3] works away at her studio. Otherwise there is nothing particular in the art world. We are all so delighted at the declaration of the Wallace bequest[4] that all other matters are as naught. I suppose it is the most magnificent art donation that was ever made in all time – & precisely the things we wanted. Now we must have a good building, not so much ornamental outside as the best thing in the way of arrangement w[ch] can be contrived. You have only to come to Italy to see how splendid things are thrown away by bad exhibition.

I hear there was no election at the [Old Water-Colour] Soc:? Privately I may say that I expect the more respectable members are disgusted at Herkomer & the clique who are destroying all the Traditions of the Soc: Have you heard anything lately about the business?[5]

Hope you did not get cold at the funeral.

Give my kind regards to M[rs] Stephens.

Ever y[rs].

Henry Wallis

L46. *To* Charles Hercules Read Rome 19 October 1897

MS: British Museum, Department Prehistory & Europe.

PUBL.: Excerpts in T. Wilson, 238b-239a.

Wallis describes a fine Byzantine bowl he bought and sent to the British Museum for conservation, while he was on his way to Egypt.

Rome. 19.10.1897

My dear Read.

Today I took to the Embassy a parcel for you w[ch] will go to the F[oreign] O[ffice] – should reach London on Saturday – addressed to Thompson.[1] I have written to him begging him to send for it if you have not returned: if you have, perhaps you will send for it, or drop a line to the F.O. to forward it. It contains a piece of Byzantine pottery of a kind – as far as I am aware – entirely unknown, & of great beauty. It is a bowl, 5[in] D, the outside in blue & white, cloisonné, crisply & delicately worked. When it was put into my hands the inside appeared to be in a fine enamel, warm toned white in colour, equal, but wth indication of three faint circles.

I was told before purchasing to take it away & put it in warmish water, not hot. Imagine my surprise when I saw appear a figure of Our Lord seated on a throne, one hand raised in benediction, & on either side on the ground two medallions containing heads. Below the edge (inside) was visible an inscription : - ... (a piece is broken out) ... A.VAL.COSTANTINVS. PIVS.FELIX. AVGVSTVS. CVM. FLAV.MAX. FAVSTA. Figure & inscription in toned white outline on pale fawn coloured ground. When found this ornamentation was imperceptible & was only discovered some days after when the piece was washed. In a day or so the fawn colour faded, as it did a day after I tried, though it was faintly perceptible when I packed the bowl this afternoon. I did not read the inscription myself (only seeing some of the letters when I immersed it. I was afraid to keep it more than 5 minutes in the water). It is especially interesting to me, who have been seeking Byzantine pottery for so many years. And I think you will agree it is a rare find. As I propose going to Naples, & leave there on the 7th Nov for Egypt, I did not like to take it wth me & was afraid to send it by the ordinary methods of transport. So I tried the Embassy & found them helpful. Will you kindly keep the bowl under lock & key till my return? I may say the technique is Egyptian, same as the Tel-el-Yahoudi (Ramses III), only there is no instance known there of the ornament appearing & disappearing.[2]

[...]

L47. *To* Harold Wallis Cairo 20 December 1897
MS: private collector, New York.
Another letter commenting on the unfavourable transformation of Cairo.

Cairo. 20 Dec. Monday

My dear Felix.

Arriving here I find y^{rs} of the 11th. I suppose you got my letter from Suez, we could not hear if the route was practicable at this season, & as in no case c^{ld} the chaplain get away for a week we abandoned the project, at least for the present. The residents here say that the cool weather has commenced, but for a newcomer it is decidedly hot – warmer than we had it last summer in London at any time.

Besides the mosquitoes are in extra numbers, on account of the high Nile this year, so that one is bitten night & day. There are very few visitors as yet, the hotel keepers are sanguine respecting the numbers they expect will come, but I sh^{ld} say it is probable there will be fewer than usual.

Building is still going on at a great rate, & the city is becoming more than ever Europeanized & will doubtless within a not very protracted period lose its Oriental character entirely.

I wish you w^{ld} send me by the next post a copy of the proof of the 'Tiles' (book post, registered).[1] You will find several copies on the table in the library, the first eight pages have the borders, the rest without them. You will find a stitched copy. They may possibly be in dining room, but I think not. Hope you will see that the studio is all right & that Mary keeps a fire there for 2 or 3 days every now & again - especially when the weather is damp.

Did drawings go all right to the Gallery?[2]

Sorry to hear that the fog has been so bad & hope it will finish with this month.

If you have an interesting paper put a stamp upon it.

Ever y^{r} affec^{t} father.

Henry Wallis

L48. *To* Charles Hercules Read on board the *Prinz Heinrich* 8 January 1900
MS: British Museum, Department Prehistory & Europe.
PUBL.: Excerpt in T. Wilson, op cit,242.
This letter deals with the famous MacGregor collection of Egyptian antiquities, which the owner intended to leave to a college or a museum.[1]

Dampfer[2] *Prinz Heinrich*
Thursday. 8.11.00

My dear Read

As usual I was occupied before leaving London or I sh^{ld} have come to see you at the B.M. to tell you of a matter in wch I think you will be interested. You may have heard that MacGregor has for some time announced his intention of leaving his Egyptian Coll^{n} to Rugby. The other day I happened to mention to him the circumstance of poor Myers having bequeathed his Coll^{n} to Eton,[3] & wth results that have been far from happy. M.G. then told me he had abandoned the idea of leaving his treasures to Rugby & now rather thought they w^{ld} go to the Birmingham Museum. I told him I thought the proposed bequest was most judicious, but suggested that the proper destination for the ceramic section was the B.M.; the reason being that the series was altogether about the most important wch has been brought together & united wth what is already at the Museum w^{ld} constitute a collection such as cannot be found in any other Natl: Museum, or that perhaps can be got together in the future. Probably you will agree wth me. And if so I think no one c^{ld} better carry the matter through than y^{r}self.

There is the difficulty of Budge, wth whom M.G. is not (I believe) on the most friendly terms. But I don't think he w^{ld} be a serious obstacle – certainly not if Thompson was to take the business in hand. B[udge] w^{ld} probably be glad if the pottery was altogether removed from his rooms & the space filled up wth papyri or mummies, or inscribed posthers [?potshards]. C^{ld} not all the glazed pottery of antiquity be put under y^{r} charge (not, of course, including the very small amount of glazed Greek ware)? Anyhow, I am sure you can arrange a scheme, if you can induce M.G. to give you his pottery (I say, give not leave), so I hope you will communicate wth him. Make it so that the proposal appears to come from him & only refer to my having incidentally told you that he had visibly given up the Rugby scheme.

We passed Crete last night & expect to get to Port Said tomorrow. From thence I proceed to Cairo.

My full address is – Henry Wallis. Cairo. Egypt.

Hope you are going to be spared the usual Nov: fogs. Just now the temperature in this particular part of the Mediterranean is perfect. I only wish you c^ld^ join me in my before breakfast constitutional from sunrise to 8.30, when one has the deck almost to oneself, saving for the silent Chinese who softly & quietly clean the saloon windows & metal work. It strikes me they w^ld^ make ideal Museum attendants. The P.H. is not a bad boat, & the Teutons very decent fellows. We have about 60 officers on their way to join the German fleet in China. They display a most commendable industry in teaching themselves & each other all sorts of exercises from small manuals.

Always sincerely.

Henry Wallis

L49. *To* Harold Wallis – 5 October 1901

MS: University of Oxford, Bodleian Library, MS Eng.c.7050, ff.48-49

This document, pencil written, seems to be a letter or memorandum accompanying a will. It stops abruptly, is not signed, and was probably never sent.

5-10-01

Dear Felix

I have made the stipulation respecting sale by auction, because I should like if possible, the objects of art to be offered to Museums, with the view of keeping them together. I should wish the ancient glass to be offered to the British Museum, the Spanish Moorish & Italian pottery to the Vic. & Albert Ms. (S.K.M.), also to the same the Italian furniture, tapestries, etc.

The Egyptian pottery & bronzes might be offered to the B.M. Supposing these two Museums did not wish to acquire, there are the provincial Museums. As to prices, it would be desirable not to put the figures too high, but to endeavour to come to any amicable agreement with the Directors.

I have alas other reason for objecting to sale by auction, there is a chance that the objects might not fetch their value for causes which the seller cannot reckon upon. Alas, the things often get much damaged altogether, unless managed by people understanding the business & themselves owning the property. Sale by auction is not the most desirable way of disposing of works of art.

L50. *To* Frederic George Stephens Syracuse 15 February 1903

MS: University of Oxford, Bodleian Library, MSS Don.e.79, ff.183-184

Wallis decided to spend the winter of 1902-3 in Italy rather than Egypt. Starting in December, he first stayed at Naples, then visited southern Italy and Sicily, coming back in March by way of Siena. He was especially fond of Syracuse, of which he made several beautiful watercolours.

Grand Hotel. Villa Acradania.
Siracusa
15.2.03

My dear Stephens,

I was sorry to hear from your letter received at Naples that Mrs Stephens had been so unwell, but it was satisfactory to know she was improving when you wrote & I hope before this she has quite recovered, & ready for a trip to Naples, wch ought to complete the cure. What do you say?

I have been waiting to write from an address where there was a chance of getting letters, having been on the move since last I heard from you.

I landed in Sicily at Messina & then went along the N. coast, where there are very interesting places out of the tourist route. One you w^ld^ have liked to have seen – Cefalu wth its magnificent Norman church decorated by Byzantine mosaic workers – wch you doubtless know from works on Norman architecture.[1] I also explored the extreme west of the island, wch is also a part out of the beaten tract of the tripper. There the interest is mainly in the Carthagian remains, but including the Greek Selinonte & Segeste.[2] Sicily still keeps to its old customs in the way of brigandage. When I was at Marsala, they seized a landowner at a Villa close by where I was staying, & I see from the papers they demand 200,000 lire as a ransom. The capture was made just outside the city & near the establishment of Mr Whitaker who makes the famous Marsala wine.[3] It seems that the brigandage exists entirely from the cowardice of the upper class, who are afraid to turn out & defend themselves against the robbers. As to the authorities, civil & military, one w^ld^ not say they are in league wth the brigands. They are probably merely incapable. The worst is that popular

& journalistic sympathy is on the side of criminals.

Now I have come to Syracusa [Syracuse], a locality of wch I am very fond. I am sorry to say that the new buildings springing up at the part of the island where the old fortress formerly stood, are deplorably out of character wth the place & constitute a suburb wch spoils the effect of the city when seen from the heights or the main land.

However, I hope to have some work done, hitherto the weather has been singularly inclement & sunless, so as to prevent any attempt at more than a hasty sketch in the open air.

Give my very kind remembrance to Mrs Stephens, & let me know all y^r news.
Ever sincerely y^rs

Henry Wallis

L51. *To* Harold Wallis Berlin 26 March 1905?[1]
MS: private collector, New York.

[Grand Hôtel de Rome u. du Nord]
Berlin, 26 Mar 190

Dear Felix,

I arrived here yesterday evening after a not unpleasant journey, barring fogs in Holland & on the W. frontier. Here it is bright & sunshiny but wth a cold wind.

Respecting the packet (wch will be about 1 foot by 9 in.) in brown paper, & bearing the label of Taylor & Francis. Please write to Mary on receipt of this – enclosing your address written on a label that she can paste on it – asking her to send it to you at once. It ought to contain two sets of text proof & two sets of proofs of 17 circular plates. If it does take the one marked duplicate & post it on to Messrs Matt Bell & co., Temple Works. Cursitor St. EC.[2] & ask them to be so good as to make of(?) them specimen binding at once & post it on to 9. B[eauchamp]. Rd. You can mention that I am not at home today but hope to receive it tomorrow. But if the packet does not include the 17 circular plates please do not send it. Then write to Taylor & Francis, Red Lion Court. Fleet St. asking them to send you at once the two sets, put one wth the text for Matt Bell & the other wth the text & post them to G. B. Rd.

I ought to have had the proofs a month ago, they were promised for yesterday or Friday night, but they may not have come. Matt Bell are also dilatory, promising a thing for tomorrow & sending it in a fortnight.

I think it will be less trouble to you thus, than if you went down to Norwood, & if the proof has really been sent it won't much matter them getting it a day later – the only thing I want is for Matt Bell to have a copy of text & plates to know the size & thinness for their specimen binding – for wch they have had full instructions from me.

I have a note from Mr Bode[3] asking me to come to him at Charlottenburg, this afternoon, wch I propose doing after having had a look at his new museum. He says he is not very well.

I cannot say yet how long I may stay – perhaps not more than 3 days, so please answer by return.

Hoping you are well, ever affec^t

Henry Wallis

L52. *To* Harold Wallis Exmouth 18 December 1906
MS: private collector, New York.
During the final decade of his life, Wallis liked to spend some time on the south coast of England, from Dover to Cornwall. He continued to carry out some research and to correct previous publications.

Dec 18
4 Alexandra Terrace.
Exmouth. Devon.

Dr Felix.

I find myself here in pleasanter quarters than at Exeter & as there is nothing to do on the way of house seeking. I remember there is the text of a 2nd edition of one of the Italian Pavements to be written up – that on the Tile pavement at S. Paolo, Parma. But in order to do so I sh^{ld} have the Vol. of XV Cent Italian Ceramic Art. The Pavement Tiles.[1] The series stands on the top shelf of the book case beside the fireplace in dining room. Can you kindly send it me. There are to be more illustrations - proofs (where?) of are on the large table in the large room up stairs. There were 10 illustrations to the original notice, & I have added another 10. If you can send me a set of all the proofs, the old ones & those unpublished wch are together in the same parcel, I sh^{ld} be much obliged.

It has been a brilliant day here after a storm in the early morning.

Ever affect^{y}.

H. W.

If you have been to Sutton already this week pray depose it till next week.
The proofs of the Illustrations are printed 8 or 10 on sheet of cream coloured paper.

L53. *To* James Milner Upper Norwood 17 March 1906

MS: London, National Portrait Gallery, NPG 1432 Acquisition file
[See: L54]

Wallis's portrait of Thomas Love Peacock, Mary Ellen's father, was purchased by the National Portrait Gallery in 1906. Richard Garnett, who posthumously published some of Peacock's letters, was instrumental in this, but he died one month after the acquisition.

[Red ink:] ack^{d} receipt of portrait 28 Mch 1906
9 Beauchamp Road
Upper Norwood S.E.
17.3.06

Sir,

Dr Richard Garnett has sent me your letter relating to the portrait of Thomas Love Peacock, wch he suggests I sh^{ld} submit to your Board for purchase.[1]

I propose sending it to you on Monday.

The portrait was painted by me on the 24th Jan^{y}: 1858, Mr Peacock being in his 73rd year. He told me that it was the first time he had sat for his portrait & he was never painted again.[2]

The price of the painting is 20 gns.

Will you kindly tell me if the above particular[s] are all that is necessary, & also send me a line acknowledging the receipt of picture when it arrives.

I am, Sir,
Sincerely y^{rs}
Henry Wallis

L54. *To* Charles Hercules Read Bologna 15 April 1906

MS: British Museum, Department Prehistory & Europe

Hôtel Pellegrino. Bologna.
15.4.06

My dear Read.

I was shocked last night to see a notice in the Corriere della Sera that Rick: Garnett[1] died on Friday. I had a letter from him a fortnight ago saying that he had an affection [*sic*] of the eye wch prevented him going out, but there was no mention of other indisposition. You will probably know if any members of his family lived wth him at Hampstead, if so, kindly tell me to whom I sh^{ld} write respecting a portrait of Thomas Love Peacock that he asked me to get reproduced. It is for a publication of some posthumous work by T.L.P. of wch Garnett had bought for the B.M. & was seeing through the press for a Boston bibliophile club.[2] Unfortunately the portrait was reproduced by a 3 tint process & is far from satisfactory – so much so that I have been advised not to pass it. The Nat: Portrait Gall^{y} has acquired the portrait, & I want to know if fresh negatives can be taken.

[...]

L55. *To* Harold Wallis   Teignmouth   21 December 1906

MS: University of Oxford, Bodleian Library, MS Eng.c.7050, ff.82-83

The S.K.M. asked Wallis to send them an albarello,[1] being part of a collection they acquired.

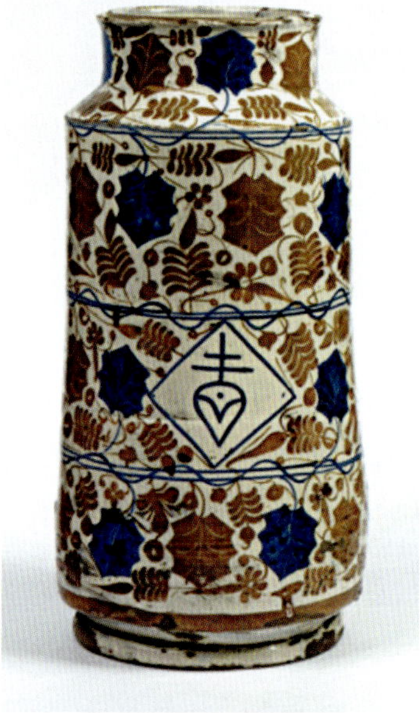

Hispano-Moresque albarello (drug jar), tin-glazed earthenware, painted in cobalt blue and lustre. Made in Valencia, 1435-1475. The diamond-shaped panel has an apothecary's mark in blue. Museum no. 52-1907. Image courtesy of Victoria and Albert Museum

Venice House
Teignmouth Devon
21.12.06

Dear Felix.

S. Kensington Museum ask me to send them a large Hispano Moresco Albarello which is at 9 Beauchamp Rd., or rather they ask when I can give it to a messenger that they will send for it.

I am afraid Mary[2] might make some mistake, so perhaps you will kindly run up & show her wch it is.

It is in the back drawing room, & I either left it lying down on the table or on the large Italian seat facing the window. It is about 15 inches high, wth an ornament of alternate gold lustre & blue vine leaves. There is an illustration in my Oriental Influence on Italian Maiolica of a similar albarello in the Louvre. The shape is this [sketch]. The Oriental Influence is the first of 6 small 4° vols.

I suppose they w^ld like to have it as soon as possible, but I don't think they c^ld send a man before the 27th, so any time that w^ld be convenient to you before then w^ld do. You might drop me a line to say the days.

The Museum has made the acquisition of the Coll^n & this is included in it, it is one of a pair, the other being in the Museum at present. You must tell Mary to hold it in two hands when giving it to messenger, as it is restored (broken & stuck together).

Ever affect^ly.

Henry Wallis

Friday night

P.S. You might send me a wire on Sunday morn^g saying the day you can go to Norwood. If you have a cold – wch I hope you have not – do not go – they can wait

L56. *From* Arthur Hughes   Kew Green   March 1907

MS: University of Oxford, Bodleian Library, MS Eng.c.7040, ff.262-263

Hunt published his history of the Pre-Raphaelite movement, Pre-Raphaelitism and the Pre-Raphaelite Brotherhood, *at the end of 1905 and asked Arthur Hughes to forward Wallis a copy. This request seems odd because Hunt and Wallis had always been on good terms and one might have expected Hunt to send Wallis a copy direct. The answer may be related to Hunt's poor eyesight in his old age and the lack of cooperation from his wife Edith. The book put Wallis in a difficult position between his two old friends, Hunt and Stephens. Wallis urged Stephens not to reply to Hunt's allegations in the book and that a letter to* The Times *was an "irrevocable step".*

Eastside House
Kew green

My dear Wallis

Holman Hunt has asked me to forward to you this copy of His Book (coming by Parcel post) and says "He will I know like it as a tribute of old friendship and admiration, and with his understanding of all the perplexities of life, not put a bad construction upon the request even to him not to write to me to acknowledge the gift, every word that comes to me now has to be read by another, and I want to escape enquiry about such personal inclinations."

This seems curious, but I believe the book is and always has been full of difficulties and worries at home, and I know he has great trouble sometimes to get his wishes carried out.[1]

So if you will write to me instead of to him saying you have got it. I will be seeing him shortly and make him happy in the knowle(d)ge of it.

I was so sorry not to see you at the funeral yesterday.[2] Tadema afterward told me that you were in the church. I had expected to see you and Wm Rossetti at the house but I do not think he turned up at all.

Hoping you are well and defying Influenza and without my Rheumatics.
I am ever yours.

Arthur Hughes

L57. *From* Lawrence Alma-Tadema London 13 January 1912
MS: University of Oxford, Bodleian Library, MS Eng.c.7039, f.118
Since there are only a handful of short letters from Alma-Tadema or his daughter to Wallis, it is not possible to know how well they were acquainted, though this letter suggests a fairly close intimacy with the most famous artist of the day.

Telegrams Tadema, London
34, Grove End Road
St John's Wood,
N.W.
13.1.12

My dear Wallis

It was truly nice to receive your wishes on my birthday. I felt much gratified. One loses so many friends who depart forever that those who remain are somehow doubly precious especially when life feeds principally on recollections.
Yours always sincerely.
L. Alma Tadema

L58. *From* David Croal Thomson London 28 January 1914
MS: University of Oxford, Bodleian Library, MS Eng.c.7041, ff.231-232
David Croal Thomson (1855-1930), an art critic, dealer and manager of the Goupil Gallery, intended to write on the French Barbizon painter Jean-Baptiste-Camille Corot (1796-1875), and asked Wallis for information about Corot's trip to London. In July 1862, Corot and his friend Badin took their one week journey to London, because of the International Exhibition, to which Corot had contributed a landscape. Henry Wallis, Eyre Crowe and Val Prinsep, all of whom had trained in France, were instrumental in welcoming the artist.

Corot was well known among British artists. As early as 1857, George Price Boyce had paid Corot a visit when he travelled to Paris. Giovanni Costa came to know Corot well in the early 1860s and he introduced Corot to Frederic Leighton a year or two later. Leighton owned important works by Corot and he influenced Leighton's landscape sketches.

Kenleith,
Broadlands Road,
Highgate, N.
28th January, 1914
Henry Wallis, Esq.

Dear Mr Wallis,

When I published my book on the Barbizon School in 1882,[1] you gave me some information about the visit of Corot to London about twenty years previous to that time.

I am now writing a kind of popular dissertation on Corot for "The Studio" Magazine, and as it specially appeals to English people I would like to say something more, if possible, about Corot's visit to this country.

He came to England only for one week, to see the 1862 Exhibition, and so far as is known, he only made three little sketches. The one I remember best being a *View from the Bridge on the Serpentine*, but it was only about a quarter of an hour's work and very slight.[2]

When you told me about Corot, you described a walk you had with him up the river at Marlow,[3] and in my book I mention this and speak of the astonishment with which Corot experienced the sunshine and heat of the English climate, which, like most other French people, he thought was always dull and foggy.

What I would specially like to know is: Can you tell me where Corot lived, or with whom? I know that he had special introductions to Val Prinsep and Eyre Crowe, but I cannot find out if he lived with them or how he fared generally in London.

If you do not know of your own knowledge, can you refer me to anybody still living who would be likely to remember.

It is many years since I have had the pleasure of seeing you, and I hope you enjoy good health.

I am,
Very faithfully yours,

D. Croal Thomson

Wallis's reply dated 1st February is not in the Wallis papers. Fortunately, Thomson quoted parts of it in The Landscapes of Corot (pp.24–25)*: Corot's coming to London was "so short and uneventful that when you have stated the fact, you have almost exhausted the subject. He evidently was attracted with the Marlow country and wished to make some studies there; indeed, I had arranged to find quarters for him in the neighbourhood. However, on seeing Eyre Crowe a day or two after, he told me that Corot had arranged to return to Paris with some friends; and I remember we both agreed it was the wiser course for him to take considering his age."*

L59. *To* Harold Wallis Sutton 5 August 1914

MS: University of Oxford, Bodleian Library, MS Eng.c.7050, ff.153-154

This letter, dated 5 August 1914, is the first one to have been sent to his son after war had broken out on 28 July. Like so many others, Wallis naively assumed that Belgium – which had been guaranteed neutrality by all Europe, including Germany – would not be invaded.

Claverton, Sutton, Surrey
Aug. 5. [1914]

Dear Felix.

Yours of yesterday received. The post I suppose is rather disorganized at present but I suppose will soon get into working order again.

It must have been a busy scene at Dover yesterday. But I suppose the Belgians have really nothing to fear. Their territory may be occupied on the frontier next to Germany but the armies of France & Germany are scarcely likely to meet there? The question is wch will be the attacking party at sea, England or Germany.

However, it is useless speculating on the point now. This state of affairs will send the holiday folks back to London?

Wth kind regards.
Ever affectly.
Henry Wallis

L60. *From* Peter Austin Daniel *to* Harold Wallis – 24 December 1916

MS: Diane Johnson papers, Harry Ransom Center, University of Texas at Austin.

After Wallis's death, his lifelong friend P.A. Daniel sent this moving letter to Harold in which he summarises their long friendship.

3, St Peter's Square
24 Decr 1916

My dear Harold,

The death of your dear Father on the 20th instant ends for me a long life of intimacy and friendship: I first made his acquaintance on the benches of the Antique school of the Royal Academy and on Saturday, 23rd of December, I reached my 89th year. He was a few years my junior, tho' as a distinguished man he was always my senior and I always looked on him as such. In fact I felt distinguished by his recognition of me.

I regret therefore that I cannot be present at the last sad scene to do honour to his memory. For years now bodily weakness will not permit me to venture into the streets or even into our little garden.

You did not mention where, in Highgate, the ceremony is to take place. I should like to know, at your leisure, and I hope I need not say that I would always be glad to see you whenever you would care to call.

Excuse my writing, and
Believe me,
Yours very truly
P.A. Daniel

Appendix III

The Wallis objects at the V&A and at the British Museum

Victoria and Albert Museum

Museum No.	*Description*	*Origin and date*	*Gallery location (R=room ; C=case ; S=shelf)*
8306-1863	Textile fragment	Italy (14th-15th C.)	
651-1886	Tapestry	Egypt (300-500)	R.8, C.2
666-1886	Panel	Akhmim, Egypt (300-699)	
218-1887	Woven linen	Egypt (700-899)	In storage
434-1888	Manuscript, Coptic	Akhmim, Egypt (8th-11th C.)	Print & Drawings room, level C, C.2, S.H., box 15
434.B-1888	Manuscript, Coptic	Akhmim, Egypt (8th-11th C.)	Print & Drawings room, level C, C.2, S.H., box 15
435-1888	Door of a cabinet	Egypt	
1683:1-1888	Casket	Egypt (400-500)	R.8, C.14
600-1890	Cross	Egypt (600-700)	R.8, C.13
601-1890	Cross	Egypt (600-700)	R.8, C.13
604-1890	Cross	Egypt (400-700)	R.8, C.13
605-1890	Cross	Egypt (400-700)	R.8, C.13
148-1896	Gravestone	Egypt (6th-8th C.)	
785A-H-1896	Panel	Egypt	
392-1898	Bowl	Cyprus (13th-14th C.)	
393-1898	Bowl	Cyprus (13th-14th C.)	In storage
394-1898	Cup	Cyprus (13th-14th C.)	
395-1898	Bowl	Cyprus (13th-14th C.)	
407:1-1898	Tile	Syria (Damascus) (1420-1450)	
443-1898	Coat	Turkish (1800s)	
689-1898	Jar fragment	Iran (9th-10th C.)	R.137, C.25, S.3
690-1898	Jug	Italy	R.137, C.36, S.2
753-1898	Textile fragment	China (1300-1399)	
61:1-8-1900	Fragments	Malkata, Egypt (1410-1375 BC)	R.131, C.86, S.1
855-1901	Pilaster	Egypt (7th-11^{th}C.)	
1384-1901	Bowl	Cyprus (13th-14th C.)	R.137, C.33, S.7
1385-1901	Bowl	Cyprus (13th-14th C.)	
1388-1901	Bowl	Cyprus (13th-14th C.)	
1389-1901	Bowl	Cyprus (13th-14th C.)	
1390-1901	Bowl	Cyprus (13th-14th C.)	
1392-1901	Bowl	Cyprus (13th-14th C.)	
1396-1901	Bowl	Cyprus (13th-14th C.)	
1401-1901	Bowl	Cyprus (13th-14th C.)	
1405-1901	Bowl	Cyprus (13th-14th C.)	
1406-1901	Bowl	Cyprus (13th-14th C.)	
1409-1901	Cup	Cyprus (13th-14th C.)	
1410-1901	Cup	Cyprus (13th-14th C.)	R.137, C.33, S.7
1411-1901	Bowl	Cyprus (14th-15th C.)	
906-1903	Lamp	Egypt (11th-12th C.)	R.137, C.25, S.6
1108-1903	Tile	Seville, Spain (1513-1521)	R.137, C. E1, S.3

Museum No.	*Description*	*Origin and date*	*Gallery location (R=room ; C=case ; S=shelf)*
1109-1903	Floor tile	Umbria, Italy (1450-1475)	R.137, C.37, S.8
1110-1903	Floor tile	Siena, Italy (1507)	R.137, C.37, S.8
1433-1903	Bottle		
1116-1904	Drug jar	Italy	R.137, C.37, S.6
1118-1904	Drug jar	Italy	R.137, C.36, S.1
1119-1904	Drug jar	Florence, Italy (1450-1470)	R.137, C.36, S.3
1120-1904	Drug jar	Deruta, Italy (1470-1480)	R.137, C.36, S.3
1121-1904	Drug jar	Deruta, Italy (1475-1500)	R.137, C.36, S.1
1122-1904	Jug	Italy (2nd half 15th C.)	R.137, C.36, S.2
1123-1904	Jug	Italy (2nd half 15th C.)	R.137, C.36, S.1
1126-1904	Drug jar	Pesaro; Italy (1480)	R.137, C.36, S.4
1127-1904	Drug bottle	Italy (1540)	R.137, C.36, S.5
1129-1904	Drug jar	Naples, Italy (1450)	R.137, C.36, S.4
1131-1904	Drug jar	Florence, Italy (1450-1470)	R.137, C.36, S.1
1132-1904	Drug jar	Florence, Italy (1450-1475)	R.137, C.11, S.3
1133-1904	Jug	Arezzo, Italy (early 15th C.)	R.137, C.36, S.2
1135-1904	Drug jar	Italy (1450-1475)	R.137, C.36, S.1
1136-1904	Drug jar	Florence, Italy (1450-1475)	R.137, C.11, S.3
1137-1904	Jug	Florence, Italy (1450-1475)	R.137, C.11, S.3
1138-1904	Drug jar	Umbria or Latium (late 15th C.)	R.137, C.36, S.1
1140-1904	Jug	Italy (2nd half 15th C.)	R.137, C.36, S.2
1141-1904	Jug	Italy (1st half 15th C.)	R.137, C.36, S.2
1142-1904	Drug jar	Deruta, Italy (1475)	R.137, C.11, S.4
1144-1904	Drug jar	Deruta, Italy (1475)	R.137, C.36, S.3
1146-1904	Drug jar	Italy	R.137, C.42, S.3
1148-1904	Jug	Tuscany, Italy (14th-15th C.)	R.137, C.11, S.2
1151-1904	Drug jar	Florence, Italy (2nd half 15th C.)	R.137, C.36, S.1
793-1905	Bowl		
377-1906	Fragment		
433-1906	Drug jar	Montelupo, Italy (1490)	R.137, C.11, S.3
1-1907	Tile panel	Seville, Spain (1538-1539)	R.137, C. WS
2-1907	Bowl	Manises, Spain (1700-1750)	R.137, C.34, S.7
3-1907	Plaque	Manises, Spain (1700-1750)	R.137, C.34, S.7
4-1907	Serving dish	Manises, Spain (1500-1525)	R.137, C. D1, S.3
5-1907	Jar	Spain (17th-18th C.)	
6-1907	Jar	Spain (18th C.)	
7-1907	Jar	Manises, Spain (1625-1700)	R.137, C.34, S.5
8-1907	Vase	Manises, Spain (1625-1700)	R.137, C.34, S.5

Museum No.	*Description*	*Origin and date*	*Gallery location (R=room ; C=case ; S=shelf)*
9-1907	Vase	Manises, Spain (1675-1700)	R.137, C. F1, S.1
10-1907	Drug jar	Valencia, Spain (1450-1475)	R.143, C.11, S.2
11-1907	Jar	Manises, Spain (1500-1700)	R.137, C.34, S.5
12-1907	Bowl	Muel, Spain (1550-1610)	R.137, C. E1, S.4
13-1907	Bowl cover	Paterna or Manises, Spain (1450-1475)	R.137, C. D1, S.2
14-1907	Dish	Manises, Spain (1435-1460)	R.137, C.1, S.1
15-1907	Dish	Valencia, Spain (1500)	
16-1907	Dish	Manises, Spain (1500)	R.137, C.33, S.4
17-1907	Plate	Spain (18th C.)	
18-1907	Bowl	Hispano-Moresque, last quarter 15th C.	
19-1907	Bowl	Manises, Spain (1475-1500)	R.137, C. D1, S.2
20-1907	Dish	Manises, Spain (1625-1700)	R.137, C.33, S.1
21-1907	Dish	Manises, Spain (1625-1700)	R.137, C.33, S.1
22-1907	Dish	Manises, Spain (mid-16th C.)	
23-1907	Dish	Manises, Spain (1435-1475)	R.137, C.1, S.1
24-1907	Dish	Manises, Spain (1625-1700)	R.137, C.33, S.3
25-1907	Dish	Valencia, Spain (1500)	
26-1907	Dish	Manises, Spain (1500)	R.137, C. D1, S4
24-1907	Dish	Valencia, Spain (1525-1550)	R.137, C.33, S.3
28-1907	Dish	Manises, Spain (1470-1500)	R.137, C.33, S.5
29-1907	Dish	Reus, Spain (1639)	
30-1907	Plate	Valencia, Spain (mid-16th C.)	
31-1907	Bowl	Muel, Spain (1550-1610)	R.137, C.34, S.5
32-1907	Drug jar	Manises, Spain (1435-1460)	R.137, C.34, S.5
33-1907	Drug jar	Manises, Spain (1435-1460)	R.137, C.34, S.5
34-1907	Jug	Manises, Spain (1500)	R.137, C. D1, S.3
35-1907	Dish	Seville, Spain (1470-1500)	R.137, C.34, S.4
36-1907	Dish	Seville, Spain (1470-1500)	R.143, C.13, S.2
37-1907	Plate	Manises, Spain (1400-1500)	R.137, C. C1, S.3
38-1907	Dish	Manises, Spain (1st half 18th C.)	
39-1907	Pedestal	Iran (13th C.)	
40-1907	Drug ajr	Manises, Spain (1435-1460)	R.137, C.34, S.5

Museum No.	*Description*	*Origin and date*	*Gallery location (R=room ; C=case ; S=shelf)*
41-1907	Drug jar	Manises, Spain (1435-1460)	R.137, C. C1, S.1
42-1907	Dish	Muel, Spain (1550-1600)	R.137, C. E1, S.2
43-1907	Dish	Manises, Spain (1450-1475)	R.137, C.33, S.6
44-1907	Drug jar	Manises, Spain (1450-1475)	R.137, C. D1, S.1
45-1907	Drug jar	Manises, Spain (1450-1475)	R.137, C.34, S.5
46-1907	Jar	Valencia, Spain (1400-1450)	R.64, C. SS3
47-1907	Drug jar	Paterna or Manises, Spain (1400)	R.137, C. C1, S.2
48-1907	Drug jar	Paterna or Manises, Spain (1450)	R.137, C. C1, S.2
49-1907	Drug jar	Paterna or Manises (1400-1500)	R.137, C.34, S.5
50-1907	Drug jar	Paterna or Manises (1400-1500)	
51-1907	Dish	Reus, Spain (1600-1625)	R.137, C.35, S.3
52-1907	Drug jar	Valencia, Spain (1435-1475)	R.145, C.4, S.1
53-1907	Drug jar	Valencia, Spain (mid-15th C.)	R.137, C. D1, S.1
54-1907	Dish	Seville or Valencia, Spain (1550-1600)	R.137, C.33, S.3
55-1907	Dish	Manises, Spain (1430-1470)	R.137, C.33, S.4
56-1907	Ewer	Manises, Spain (1500)	R.137, C. D1, S.4
458-1907	Bowl	Manises, Spain (1500)	R.137, C. D1, S.3
331-1908	Dish	Manises, Spain (1500-1700)	R.137, C.35, S.5
332-1908	Stand	Manises, Spain (1625-1700)	R.137, C.33, S.3
333-1908	Fragment (plate)		
C.566-1917	Dish fragment	Valencia, Spain (2nd half 14th C.)	In storage
C.574-1917	Dish fragment	Triana, Spain (1500-1525)	In storage
C.598-1917	Jug	Florence, Italy (1450-1475)	R.137, C.36, S.3
C.613-1917	Bowl fragment	Manises, Spain (1400-1450)	In storage
C.614-1917	Jug	Italy (1st half 15th C.)	R.137, C.36, S.2
C.630-1917	Fragment	Deruta, Italy	
C.632-1917	Fragment	Deruta, Italy	R.143, C.10, S.3
C.634-1917	Fragment	Deruta, Italy	
C.635-1917	Fragment	Deruta, Italy	
C.649-1917	Dish (fragment)	Tuscany (1520-1530)	
C.653-1917	Bowl (part)	Italy (1450-1499)	
C.661-1917	Tile	Manises or Murcia, Spain (1450)	In storage
M.76-1917	Signet ring	Roman (100-200)	R.91, C.4, S. A,Box 26
M.85-1917	Cross	Egypt (5th-7th C.)	

Museum No.	*Description*	*Origin and date*	*Gallery location (R=room ; C=case ; S=shelf)*
C.413-1918	Vase	Syria (1400-1500)	R.145, C.30, S.2
C.414-1918	Bowl	Iran (1260-1350)	R.137, C.26, S.1
C.415-1918	Dish	Syria (1200-1300)	R.137, C. V, S.3
E.494-1918	Drawing		Print & drawings room, case C, shelf 133
T.758-1919	Dalmatic	Spain (16th C.)	
T.766-1919	Dalmatic	Spain (16th C.)	
C.19-1920	Jar	Syria (Damascus), 1300-1400	
C.20-1920	Dish	Turkey, 1750-1850	
C.21-1920	Bowl	Iran (12th-13th C.)	
C.22-1920	Cup		
C.5-1920	Jug	Faenza, Italy (1480)	R.145, C.4, S.2
C.6-1922	Jug	Faenza, Italy (1400-1450)	R.137, C.36, S.2
A.53-1926	Jug (rock cristal)	Egypt (1080-1100)	R.111, C.2
C.332-1928	Vase		
C.333-1928	Cup		
C.334-1928	Unguent bottle	Syria or Palestina	
C.335-1928	Unguent bottle	Rhodes (550-400 BC)	
C.336-1928	Bowl		
C.337-1928	Lamp		
C.338-1928	Bottle	Iran (9th-10th C.)	
C.339-1928	Oil flask (Aryballos)	Egypt (200-299)	
C.340-1928	Bowl	Iran (13th C.)	R.137, C.26, S.1
C.137-1929	Vase	Syria (12th-13th C.)	R.137, C.27, S.7
W.31:1-1935	Writing case		In storage
C.901&A-1936	Box & lid	Egypt (900-1100)	
C.902-1936	Jug	Syria (300-399)	
C.903-1936	Mosque lamp	Prob. Syria (1100-1300)	
C.904-1936	Bowl	Japan, Edo period (prob. 18th C.)	
C.905-1936	Fragment		
C.906-1936	Fragment		
C.907-1936	Tile	Iran (13th C.)	
C.908-1936	Drug jar	Castelli, Italy (1520)	R.62, C.9
C.909-1936	Bowl	Italy (1450)	R.137, C.43, S.7
C.910-1936	Dish	Spain	
C.911-1936	Jug	Faenza, Italy (early 15th C.)	R.137, C.11, S.3

Museum No.	*Description*	*Origin*	*Gallery location*
On display			
1888, 215.1	Plate		Prehistory & Europe. G46/dc2
1891, 401.3	Pyxis	Greek	Greek & Roman. G69/balcony/3B
1891, 401.5	Jar	Roman	Greek & Roman. G69/balcony/4D
1894, 517.4	Ewer		Prehistory & Europe. G34/11
1894, 517.5	Lamp	Byzantine	Prehistory & Europe. G41/dc/N°43
1895, 105.2	Ink-well	Roman	Greek & Roman. G69/7
1895, 1023.5	Tile		Prehistory & Europe. G46/dc2
1895, 1023.6	Tile		Prehistory & Europe. G46/dc2
1896, 523.1	Tile		Prehistory & Europe. G46/dc2
1896, 523.2	Tile		Prehistory & Europe. G46/dc2
1896, 1116.6	Lamp-filter		Prehistory & Europe. G41/dc7/N°15
1897, 511.12	Tile		Prehistory & Europe. G46/dc2
1897, 511.13	Tile		Prehistory & Europe. G46/dc2
1898, 523.11	Apothecary jar		Prehistory & Europe. G1/WP177
1898, 523.12	Albarello		Prehistory & Europe. G1/WP177
1902, 529.2	Bowl	Islamic	G34/12
1902, 529.10	Flask	Islamic	G34/3
1902, 529.24	Ampulla	Byzantine	Prehistory & Europe. G41/dc3/N°26
1903, 515.1	Storage-jar		Prehistory & Europe. G46/dc2
1903, 714.6	Strigil		Greek & Roman. G69/18
1904, 706.9	Tile		Prehistory & Europe. G46/dc2
1904, 706.19	Beaker		Prehistory & Europe. G46/dc8
1905, 710.1	Figure ; stand. Etruscan fitting		Greek & Roman. G71/25
1905, 710.2	Figure ; stand. Etruscan fitting		Greek & Roman. G71/25
1905, 710.9	Askos	Attic	Greek & Roman. G20A/13
1905, 710.10	Lekythos	Attic	Greek & Roman. G20A/17
1905, 710.11	Lekythos	Attic	Greek & Roman. G20A/17
1906, 418.2	Jar		Prehistory & Europe. G46/dc1
1906, 418.3	Jar		Prehistory & Europe. G46/dc1
1913, 419.1	Askos	Apulian	Greek &Roman. G73/36
In storage			
1870, 510.1	Bowl	Roman	Greek & Roman
1880, 1211.56	Drawing		Prints & Drawings
1885, 711.1	Handle	Islamic	Middle East
1885, 1009.1	Bowl	Islamic	Middle East
1886, 416.1	Brazier		
1886, 504.1	Stamp		Ancient Egypt & Sudan
1886, 507.1	Ostracon	Coptic	Ancient Egypt & Sudan
1886, 507.2	Ostracon	Coptic	Ancient Egypt & Sudan
1886, 507.3	Ostracon	Coptic	Ancient Egypt & Sudan
1886, 507.4	Ostracon	Coptic	Ancient Egypt & Sudan
1886, 507.5	Ostracon	Coptic	Ancient Egypt & Sudan
1887, 713.1	Writing-board	Graeco-Roman	Ancient Egypt & Sudan
1887, 713.2	Writing-board	Roman period	Ancient Egypt & Sudan
1887, 713.3	Artefact	Roman period	Ancient Egypt & Sudan
1887, 713.4	Ostracon	Graeco-Roman	Ancient Egypt & Sudan
1887, 713.5	Writing-board	Graeco-Roman	Ancient Egypt & Sudan
1887, 713.6	Writing-board	Coptic	Ancient Egypt & Sudan
1888, 521.1	Necklace		Greek & Roman
1888, 806.9	Pilaster	Roman perod	Ancient Egypt & Sudan
1888, 806.10	Stela	Ptolemaic	Ancient Egypt & Sudan

Museum No.	*Description*	*Origin*	*Gallery location*
1888, 806.12	Coffin		Ancient Egypt & Sudan
1889, 620.1	Lamp	Roman	Greek & Roman
1890, 517.4	Jug	Fatimid dynasty	Middle East
1890, 1011.1	Mosaic	Islamic	Middle East
1890, 1011.3	Mosaic, tessera	Islamic	Middle East
1890, 1011.4	Window	Islamic	Middle East
1890, 1011.5	Window	Islamic	Middle East
1890, 1011.6	Window	Islamic	Middle East
1890, 1011.7	Window	Islamic	Middle East
1891, 401.4	Jar	Roman	Greek & Roman
1891, 401.6	Jar	Roman	Greek & Roman
1891, 401.7	Flask	Roman	Greek & Roman
1891, 401.8	Jug	Roman	Greek & Roman
1891, 401.9	Jug	Roman	Greek & Roman
1891, 401.10	Cup	Roman	Greek & Roman
1891, 401.11	Cup	Roman	Greek & Roman
1891, 401.12	Lamp	Roman	Greek & Roman
1891, 401.13	Candlestick		Prehistory & Europe
1891, 423.1	Painting	Roman	Greek & Roman
1891, 423.2	Painting	Roman	Greek & Roman
1891, 424.1	Strigil		Greek & Roman
1891, 424.2	Simpulum		Greek & Roman
1891, 424.3	Nail-file		Greek & Roman
1891, 424.4	Figure	Roman	Greek & Roman
1891, 516.2	Bowl	Mamluk dynasty	Middle East
1891, 701.37	Vessel	Mamluk dynasty	Middle East
1893, 101.1	Tile	Islamic	Middle East
1894, 313.1	Pectoral		Ancient Egypt & Sudan
1894, 516.2	Cross pendant		Prehistory & Europe
1894, 517.2	Crucifix		Prehistory & Europe
1894, 517.3	Statuette		Prehistory & Europe
1895, 105.1	Figure		Greek & Roman
1895, 105.4	Statuette		Greek & Roman
1895, 1023.3	Bowl		Prehistory & Europe
1895, 1023.4	Dish		Prehistory & Europe
1895, 1023.7	Jug		Prehistory & Europe
1895, 1023.8	Dish		Prehistory & Europe
1895, 1023.9	Dish		Prehistory & Europe
1895, 1023.10	Bowl		Prehistory & Europe
1895, 1025.2	Bowl		Prehistory & Europe
1895, 1025.3	Bowl		Prehistory & Europe
1896, 523.3	Bowl		Prehistory & Europe
1896, 615.1	Candlestick		Prehistory & Europe
1896, 615.2	Candlestick		Prehistory & Europe
1896, 1116.5	Bucket		Prehistory & Europe
1896, 1116.7	Figure		Prehistory & Europe
1896, 1116.8	Figure		Prehistory & Europe
1896, 1116.9	Cross pendant		Prehistory & Europe
1896, 1124.1	Inlay	Coptic	Prehistory & Europe
1896, 1124.2	Inlay	Coptic	Prehistory & Europe
1897, 511.1	Jug		Prehistory & Europe
1897, 511.2	Jug		Prehistory & Europe
1897, 511.3	Jug		Prehistory & Europe
1897, 511.4	Jug		Prehistory & Europe
1897, 511.5	Jug		Prehistory & Europe
1897, 511.6	Jug		Prehistory & Europe
1897, 511.7	Jug		Prehistory & Europe

Museum No.	*Description*	*Origin*	*Gallery location*
1897, 511.8	Jug		Prehistory & Europe
1897, 511.9	Jug	Medieval	Prehistory & Europe
1897, 511.10	Jug		Prehistory & Europe
1897, 511.11	Jug		Prehistory & Europe
1897, 511.14	Tile		Prehistory & Europe
1897, 511.15	Tile		Prehistory & Europe
1897, 511.16	Tile		Prehistory & Europe
1897, 511.17	Tile		Prehistory & Europe
1898, 523.1	Albarello		Prehistory & Europe
1898, 523.2	Albarello		Prehistory & Europe
1898, 523.3	Jug		Prehistory & Europe
1898, 523.4	Storage-jar		Prehistory & Europe
1898, 523.5	Albarello		Prehistory & Europe
1898, 523.6	Albarello		Prehistory & Europe
1898, 523.7	Storage-jar		Prehistory & Europe
1898, 523.8	Jug		Prehistory & Europe
1898, 523.9	Jug		Prehistory & Europe
1898, 523.10	Bottle		Prehistory & Europe
1898, 523.13	Dish		Prehistory & Europe
1898, 523.14	Dish		Prehistory & Europe
1898, 523.15	Plate		Prehistory & Europe
1898, 714.1	Vessel	18th Dynasty	Ancient Egypt & Sudan
1898, 714.2	Amphora	18th Dynasty	Ancient Egypt & Sudan
1898, 714.3	Vessel	18th Dynasty	Ancient Egypt & Sudan
1898, 714.4	Vessel	18th Dynasty	Ancient Egypt & Sudan
1898, 714.5	Amphora	18th Dynasty	Ancient Egypt & Sudan
1898, 714.6	Vessel	18th Dynasty	Ancient Egypt & Sudan
1898, 714.7	Vessel	18th Dynasty	Ancient Egypt & Sudan
1898, 1019.1	Bowl		Prehistory & Europe
1898, 1019.2	Bowl		Prehistory & Europe
1898, 1019.3	Bowl		Prehistory & Europe
1898, 1019.4	Bowl		Prehistory & Europe
1898, 1019.5	Bowl		Prehistory & Europe
1898, 1019.6	Bowl		Prehistory & Europe
1898, 1019.7	Bowl		Prehistory & Europe
1898, 1019.8	Bowl		Prehistory & Europe
1898, 1019.9	Bowl		Prehistory & Europe
1898, 1019.10	Dish		Prehistory & Europe
1898, 1019.11	Dish		Prehistory & Europe
1898, 1019.12	Bowl		Prehistory & Europe
1898, 1019.13	Bowl		Prehistory & Europe
1898, 1019.14	Dish		Prehistory & Europe
1898, 1019.15	Bowl		Prehistory & Europe
1898, 1019.16	Bowl		Prehistory & Europe
1898, 1019.17	Bowl		Prehistory & Europe
1898, 1019.18	Kiln-furniture		Prehistory & Europe
1898, 1019.19	Jug		Prehistory & Europe
1898, 1019.20	Baluster jug		Prehistory & Europe
1898, 1019.22	Jug		Prehistory & Europe
1898, 1019.23	Jug		Prehistory & Europe
1898, 1019.24	Jug		Prehistory & Europe
1898, 1019.25	Jug		Prehistory & Europe
1898, 1019.26	Jug		Prehistory & Europe
1898, 1019.27	Jug		Prehistory & Europe
1898, 1019.28	Jug		Prehistory & Europe
1898, 1019.29	Jug		Prehistory & Europe
1898, 1019.30	Jug		Prehistory & Europe

Museum No.	*Description*	*Origin*	*Gallery location*
1898, 1019.31	Jug		Prehistory & Europe
1898, 1019.32	Bowl		Prehistory & Europe
1898, 1019.33	Bowl		Prehistory & Europe
1898, 1019.34	Dish		Prehistory & Europe
1898, 1019.35	Tile		Prehistory & Europe
1898, 1019.36	Bowl		Prehistory & Europe
1898, 1019.37	Bowl, waster		Prehistory & Europe
1898, 1019.38	Bowl		Prehistory & Europe
1898, 1019.39	Bowl		Prehistory & Europe
1898, 1019.40	Plate		Prehistory & Europe
1900, 1006.1	Tile		Prehistory & Europe
1900, 1006.2	Tile		Prehistory & Europe
1902, 529.4	Lamp		Prehistory & Europe
1902, 529.5	Lamp		Prehistory & Europe
1902, 529.11	Bottle	Islamic	Middle East
1902, 529.12	Unguentarium	Islamic	Middle East
1902, 529.18	Mirror-case		Prehistory & Europe
1902, 529.25	Finger-ring		Prehistory & Europe
1902, 529.29	Kohl-stick	Coptic	Africa, Oceania & the Americas (AOA)
1902, 529.37	Cosmetic-box	Coptic	AOA
1902, 529.39	Kohl-pot	Coptic	AOA
1902, 628.1	Tile		Prehistory & Europe
1903, 714.1	Relief		Greek & Roman
1903, 714.2	Relief		Greek & Roman
1903, 714.3	Figure	Ptolemaic	Greek & Roman
1903, 714.4	Phial	Hellenistic	Greek & Roman
1903, 714.5	Simpulum		Greek & Roman
1903, 714.7	Strigil		Greek & Roman
1903, 1010.1	Vase		Prehistory & Europe
1903, 1010.2	Vase		Prehistory & Europe
1903, 1217.1	Vessel-cover	Roman	Greek & Roman
1904, 706.1	Albarello		Prehistory & Europe
1904, 706.3	Albarello	Islamic	Middle East
1904, 706.5	Cup		Prehistory & Europe
1904, 706.6	Tile		Prehistory & Europe
1904, 706.7	Tile		Prehistory & Europe
1904, 706.8	Tile		Prehistory & Europe
1904, 706.10	Tile		Prehistory & Europe
1904, 706.11	Tile		Prehistory & Europe
1904, 706.12	Tile		Prehistory & Europe
1904, 706.13	Tile		Prehistory & Europe
1904, 706.14	Tile		Prehistory & Europe
1904, 706.15	Tile		Prehistory & Europe
1904, 706.16	Tile		Prehistory & Europe
1904, 706.17	Tile		Prehistory & Europe
1904, 706.18	Tile		Prehistory & Europe
1904, 706.20	Vessel-case		Prehistory & Europe
1904, 706.25	Pot	Islamic	Middel East
1904, 706.26	Dish	Islamic	Middel East
1904, 706.27	CosmeticpPot	Islamic	Middel East
1904, 706.28	CosmeticpPot	Islamic	Middel East
1904, 706.30	Vessel	Fatimid dynasty	Middle East
1904, 706.31	Beaker	Early Islamic	Middle East
1904, 706.32	Vessel	Islamic	Middle East
1904, 706.33	Vessel	Islamic	Middle East
1904, 706.34	Bottle	Islamic	Middle East

Museum No.	*Description*	*Origin*	*Gallery location*
1904, 706.35	Vessel		Prehistory & Europe
1904, 706.36	Bottle	Islamic	Middle East
1904, 706.37	Vessel	Islamic	Middle East
1904, 706.38	Bowl	Islamic	Middle East
1904, 706.39	Vessel	Islamic	Middle East
1904, 706.40	Figure		Prehistory & Europe
1904, 706.41	Tunic		Prehistory & Europe
1905, 710.3	Figure	Roman	Greek & Roman
1905, 710.4	Figure	Roman	Greek & Roman
1905, 710.5	Mirror	Western Greece	Greek & Roman
1905, 710.6	Belt-fitting		Greek & Roman
1905, 710.7	Krater		Greek & Roman
1905, 710.8	Lamp		Greek & Roman
1905, 1016.1	Vase	Roman	Greek & Roman
1905, 1016.2	Jug	Roman	Greek & Roman
1906, 418.1	Albarello		Prehistory & Europe
1906, 1121.1	Vase	Roman	Greek & Roman
1907, 718.1	Dagger		Prehistory & Europe
1907, 1009.1	Bowl		Prehistory & Europe
1907, 1009.2	Bowl		Prehistory & Europe
1907, 1009.3	Bowl		Prehistory & Europe
1907, 1009.4	Bowl		Prehistory & Europe
1907, 1009.5	Bowl		Prehistory & Europe
1908, 729.1	Jug		Prehistory & Europe
1908, 729.2	Jug		Prehistory & Europe
1908, 729.3	Baluster jug		Prehistory & Europe
1908, 729.4	Baluster jug		Prehistory & Europe
1908, 729.5	Jug		Prehistory & Europe
1908, 729.6	Bowl		Prehistory & Europe
1908, 729.7	Bowl		Prehistory & Europe
1909, 503.1	Lekythos	Attic	Greek & Roman
1912, 1211.1	Vase; lid	Qing dynasty	Asia
1913, 419.2	Skyphos	Roman	Greek & Roman
1913, 419.3	Vessel	Roman	Greek & Roman
1913, 419.4	Krater	Roman	Greek & Roman
1913, 419.5	Figure	Western Greece	Greek & Roman
1915, 512.1	Cameo	Roman	Greek & Roman
1915, 512.2	Cameo	Roman	Greek & Roman
1920, 327.2	Bead	Phoenician	Ancien Egypt & Sudan
1963, 1113.1	Jar	Safavid dynasty	Middle East
1963, 1113.2	Bowl	Islamic	Middle East
1963, 1113.3	Bangle	Islamic	Middle East
1971, 603.1	Plaque	Roman	Greek & Roman
1979, 1017.8	Trial-piece	26th Dynasty	Ancient Egypt & Sudan
1979, 1017.43	Model	Ptolemaic	Ancient Egypt & Sudan
1979, 1017.167	Kohl-pot	New Kingdom	Ancient Egypt & Sudan
1979, 1017.169	Patera ; votive offering	Roman period	Ancient Egypt & Sudan
1917, 1017.170	Dish	Roman	Ancient Egypt & Sudan
1979, 1017.171	Mirror		Ancient Egypt & Sudan
1980, 1010.1	Lamp	Roman	Greek & Roman
1980, 1128.1	Figure		Greek & Roman
1980, 1128.2	Figure		Greek & Roman
1980, 1128.3	Figure		Greek & Roman
1980, 1128.4	Figure		Greek & Roman
1980, 1128.5	Fitting		Greek & Roman
1980, 1128.6	Fitting		Greek & Roman
1980, 1128.7	Fitting		Greek & Roman

Museum No.	*Description*	*Origin*	*Gallery location*
1980, 1128.8	Fitting		Greek & Roman
1982, 526.215	Tile	New Kingdom	Ancient Egypt & Sudan
1982, 526.216	Bowl	New Kingdom	Ancient Egypt & Sudan
1982, 526.217	Tile	New Kingdom	Ancient Egypt & Sudan
1982, 526.218	Bowl	New Kingdom	Ancient Egypt & Sudan
OA.4434	Tile		Prehistory & Europe
OA.9169	Vessel		Prehistory & Europe
OA.9170	Vessel		Prehistory & Europe
OA.9171	Vessel		Prehistory & Europe
OA+2696	Vessel	Islamic	Middle East
OA+2698	Vessel	Islamic	Middle East
OA+2711	Vessel	Islamic	Middle East
OA+2727	Vessel	Islamic	Middle East
OA+2728	Vessel	Islamic	Middle East
OA+6441	Vessel	Islamic	Middle East
OA+6442	Vessel	Islamic	Middle East
OA+6443	Vessel	Islamic	Middle East
OA+6444	Vessel	Islamic	Middle East

Appendix IV

Personal Information

Timeline

1830 Born in London on 21 February
1845 His mother Mary Ann Thomas marries Andrew Wallis
1848 Enters the Royal Academy Schools
1851 Enters Gleyre's studio (Paris)
1852 France (Paris, Bellegarde); Switzerland (Geneva); Italy (Bologna, Venice, Ferrara, Milan, Turin)
1853 Stratford-upon-Avon
1854 First exhibition at the R.A.
1856 Paints *The Death of Chatterton*; to Spain
1857 ?Capri, Sorrento; Wales with Mary Ellen Meredith
1858 (?late summer) Capri with Mary Ellen
1861 (?late summer) Capri with Harold
Death of Mary Ellen Meredith
1862 (Jul) welcomes Corot in England
(winter) Capri with Harold
1863-65 Winters in Rome with Harold
1866 (Jul) Weymouth, Lulworth
1870 (Mar-May) Milan, Venice, Murano, Florence, Chiusi, Orvieto, Arezzo, Cortona, Perugia, Turin
1872 (Aug) Scilly Isles?
1873 (summer) Penkill Castle (guest of William Bell Scott)
1874 (Apr-May) Turin, Milan, Verona, Padua, Venice, Florence, Sienna
1875 (Apr) Chapford
1877 (May-Jun) Bruges, Brussels
1878 (Apr-Jun) Paris, Auvers-sur-Oise
1879 (Jul-Aug) Delft, Haarlem, Amsterdam, The Hague, Brussels, Ghent, Bruges, Ypres
1882-1883 Spain, including Seville, Granada and Toledo
1884 (Mar-May) Pisa, Siena, Orvieto, Rome, Assisi, Perugia, Florence, Turin
1885-1886 (December-March) first journey to Egypt via Venice and Brindisi; then Cairo, Assouan, Philae, Ghizeh
1886-1887 (Sept-Feb?) Cairo
1887-1888 (Oct-Feb) Corfu, Athens, Smyrna, Constantinople, Cairo, Luxor, Helouan
1889 (Jan-Apr) Paris, Lyon, Naples, Taormina, Tarento, Reggio, Messina, Syracuse, Palermo, Rome
1890 (Mar-May) Munich, Vienna, Istanbul, Patras, Paris
1890-1891 (Nov-Feb) Cairo, Assiout, Luxor, Maidoom
1891-1892 (Sept-Apr) Paris, Rome, Naples, Palermo, Selinonte, Syracuse, Modica, Taormina, Mesina, Rome, Ravenna, Bologna, Turin
1892-1893 (Nov-Apr) Cairo, Luxor, Assouan, Philae, Medinet Habu, Karnak, Alexandria, Athens, Patras, Vienna, Berlin, Paris
1893-1894 (Oct-Jan) Milan, Trieste, Alexandria, Cairo, Luxor, Naples
1894 (Jul) Berlin, Frankfurt; (Dec) Hastings
1895-1896 (Oct-Mar) Paris, Rome, Naples, Cairo, Luxor, Deir-el-Bahri
1896 (summer) the Midlands; (Nov-Dec) Hastings
1897 (Feb-Mar) Florence, San Remo, Rome
1897-1898 (Oct-Feb) Bologna, Florence, Faenza, Rome, Naples, Cairo, Assiout, Luxor
1899 (Mar-Apr) Sienna, Lucca, Pisa, Florence, Rome, Gubbio, Arezzo, Ravenna, Faenza, Bologna, Paris
1900-1901 (Nov-Apr) Cairo, Luxor, Upper Egypt, Rome, Faenza
1901-1902 (Nov-Apr) Paris, Genoa, Cairo, Luxor, Florence
1902-1903 (Dec-Apr) Naples, Palermo, Castellamare, Syracuse, Reggio, Chiusi, Sienna, Foligno
1903-1904 (Oct-Apr) Rome, Venice, Florence, Naples, Ravello, Salerno, Amalfi, Rimini, Ancona
1904-1905 (Dec-Feb) Hastings, Exmouth
1905 (Aug) Berlin, Dresden, Vienna
1905-1906 (Oct-Apr) Venice, Pisa, Bologna, Padua, Milan
1906 (Nov-Dec) Exmouth, Teignmouth
1907 (Mar-Apr) Italy (Ravenna)
1908-1909 (Dec-Jan) Rome, Naples, Messina, Florence
1910-1911 (Dec-Jan) Worthing, Exmouth
1911 Germany
1911-1912 (Dec-Feb) St Leonards-on-Sea, Weymouth
1913 (Jul) Stratford-upon-Avon; (Aug) Antwerp; (Oct-Dec) Sidmoouth, Worthing
1915 (Jun-Jul) Bath
1916 Died 20 December from cerebral thrombosis

Wallis's addresses

1845 Clarence Place, Pentonville
1848 17 Devonshire Place, Maida Hill
1851 13 Mornington Road, London
1854 17 Talbot Road, Camden Road Villas, Sutton
1855 8 Gray's Inn Square
185? 198 Marylebone Road
1857 12 Queen Charlotte Row, New Road
1859 62 Great Russell Street
1861 Pembridge Villa, 5 Paragon Place, Streatham Hill
1862 6 Gray's Inn Square
186? 29 Soho Square
186? Holstein Cottage, Queens Road
1864 'The Studio', Campden House Mews, Kensington
1865 4 Grove End Road, St Johns Wood
1867 1 Westminster Chambers, Victoria Street
1869 10 Adelphi Terrace
1871 129 Lupus Street
1873 9 Red Lion Square
1874 24 Brecknock Crescent, Camden Road
1881 Woodbury Cottage, Biggin Hill, Norwood
1895 9 Beauchamp Road, Upper Norwood
1909 'Claverton', Cheam Road, Sutton, Surrey
1916 1 Walpole Road, Croydon

Family Tree

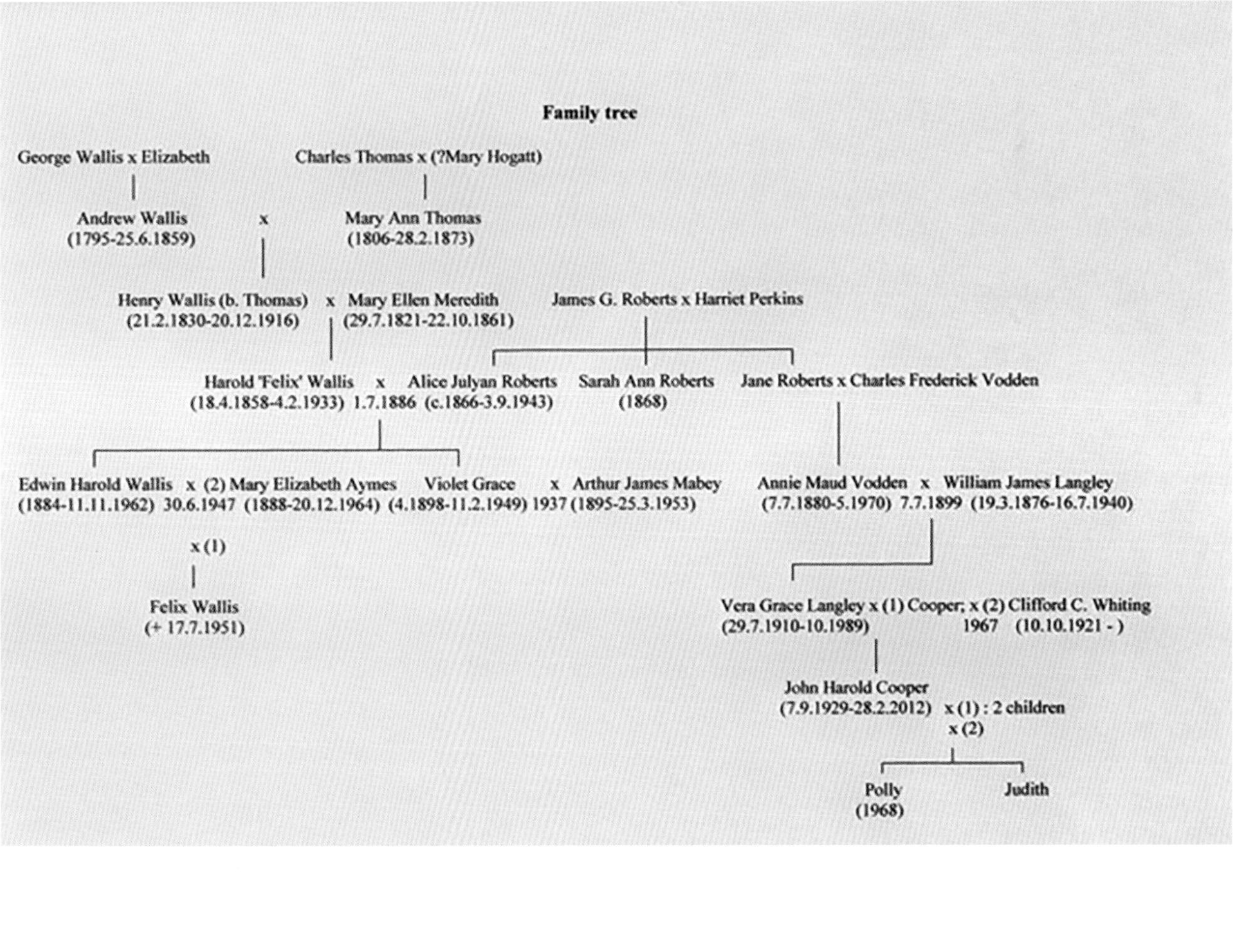

Henry Wallis's Last Will and Testament

I HENRY WALLIS of 9 Beauchamp Road, Upper Norwood, in the County of Surrey, revoke all Wills and testamentary dispositions heretofore made by me and declare this to be my last Will. I appoint Peter Austin Daniel of 6 Gray's Inn Square, London W.C. and Harold Wallis of the Bank of England and No. 104 Lordship Road, Stoke Newington, London N. to be the EXECUTORS of this my Will. I give to the said Peter Austin Daniel any two pieces of Chinese Porcelain belonging to me which he may select and the sum of Twenty pounds, the said bequests to be free of legacy duty. I give to every servant who may be in my service at the time of my death and have been in my service for six years or more previously the sum of Fifty two pounds ten shillings. I give to my son Harold Wallis all my pictures and objects of art upon condition of his not disposing of them by public auction, though he may dispose of them privately and if he shall attempt to dispose of them by public auction then I give the same to The Victoria and Albert Museum at South Kensington, London. I give to my said son Harold Wallis all my stocks and shares, my freehold land and houses at Finchley and at Whitfield Street, St Pancras, London, my cash in hand and on deposit at the Western Branch of the Bank of England in London and at the London and South Western Bank, Upper Norwood, also all my household goods and chattels and books (it being my wish that my son shall present volumes to any personal friends of mine who may wish to have them) and all other my property of every description not hereby otherwise disposed of. IN WITNESS whereof I have hereunto set my hand this twenty fifth day of September One thousand nine hundred and one. - HENRY WALLIS - Signed by the Testator as his last Will in the presence of us both present at such signing and who at his request and in his and each others presence hereto subscribe our names as witnesses - ROBERT MARSHALL, Solicitor, Croydon - E. C. DOHOO , Clerk to Messrs Marshall & Liddle, Solicitors, Croydon.

I the above named Testator declare this to be a Codicil to the above Will whereby I revoke the appointment of Peter Austin Daniel as one of my Executors and revoke the bequests to him and in lieu thereof I appoint the Public Trustee to be an EXECUTOR of my Will jointly with my son Harold. And I give to the said Peter Austin Daniel Ten pounds free of duty to purchase a ring. And in all other respects I confirm my said Will. IN WITNESS whereof I have hereto set my hand this twenty ninth day of October One thousand nine hundred and fourteen. - HENRY WALLIS - Signed by the Testator as a Codicil to his Will in our presence and by us in his presence. - ROBERT MARSHALL, Solicitor, Croydon - FREDERICK A. SAVAGE, Clerk to Messrs Marshall & Liddle, Solicitors, Croydon.

I HENRY WALLIS formerly of 9 Beauchamp Road, Upper Norwood and afterwards of "Claverton", Cheam Road, Sutton, and at present residing at No. 1 Walpose Road, Croydon, all in the County of Surrey, Esquire, declare this to be a Codicil to my Will dated the twenty fifth day of September One thousand nine hundred and one by which Codicil declare that all gifts contained in my said Will to and in favour of Harold Wallis therein named shall not lapse by reason of his death in my lifetime, but shall take effect and all the premises respectively devised and bequeathed to the said Harold Wallis shall devolve as if he had survived me and died immediately after my death subject as aforesaid I confirm my said Will except so far as it is revoked or varied by a Codicil thereto dated the twenty ninth day of October One thousand nine hundred and fourteen and I confirm that Codicil. IN WITNESS whereof I have hereunto set my hand this twenty fourth day of March One thousand nine hundred and sixteen. - HENRY WALLIS - Signed by the Testator as a Codicil to his Will in our presence and by us in his presence. - ROBERT MARSHALL, Solicitor, Croydon - W. C. CROUCH, Clerk to Messrs Marshall & Liddle, Solrs, Croydon.

On the 9th day of February 1917 Probate of this Will and two Codicils was granted to The Public Trustee the executor in Codicil.

Endnotes

INTRODUCTION

1. Boime, Albert, 'The instruction of Charles Gleyre and the Evolution of Painting in the Nineteenth Century', in Exh.cat., *Charles Gleyre ou Les Illusions perdues*, Winterthur, 1974, p.102a.
2. Johnson, Diane, *The True History of the First Mrs Meredith and Other Lesser Lives*, London, 1973, p.xiii.
3. Krzysztof Z. Cieszkowski, 'The Legend Makers: Chatterton, Wallis & Meredith', *History Today*, Vol. 32, Issue 11, November 1982. This gives some idea of the state of Wallis scholarship in the early 1980s.
4. Johnson, Diane, 'Lady in the Shadow of Great Lives', *San Francisco Sunday Examiner & Chronicle* [1973]. Harry Ransom Center, University of Texas at Austin, Diane Johnson papers, box 13.2, p.1.
5. Nicholas Joukovsky has annotated and published this letter in *Notes & Queries*, 3 November, 2011.

PART I - AN UNCOMMON LIFE

CHAPTER ONE

1. Diane Johnson suggests that Andrew was an architect, but no evidence to prove this conjecture could be found (Diane Johnson papers, box 13.1 - Harry Ransom Center, University of Texas at Austin).
2. We also learn that Andrew's father was named George and identified as a gentleman, which means he had independent means. Mary Ann's father, Charles, was a bookbinder.
3. Frith, William Powell, *My Autobiography and Reminiscences*, New York, 1888, p.23.
4. Mancoff, D.N., ' "The Play's the Thing": Victorian Literary Paintings as Theatre', *The Forbes Collection of Victorian Pictures and Works of Art*, 3 vols, Christie's London 2003, vol. 2, p.92.
5. W. P. Frith, op cit, pp.25-26.
6. Valentine, Helen, 'The Royal Academy Schools in the Victorian Period', *Art in the Age of Queen Victoria*, Helen Valentine, ed., New York & London, 1999, p.42.
7. The Royal Academy's 'Probationers book' authenticates Wallis's presence:

– 1848, Jan 7 – Henry Wallis – Painting – Recommended by F.S. Cary

The 'Admissions book' confirms his admission in the Antique School:

– 1848, Mar 31 – Henry Wallis – Painting – Age 18. Address: 17 Devonshire Place, Maida Hill.

8. In his entry for *Chatterton* in the Tate catalogue 2012 (p.70), Tim Barringer claims that Wallis had only been a student at the Royal Academy Schools briefly in 1848-9, but recognises that he only "relied on standard sources (*Dictionary of National Biography*; Grove; Benezit; C. Wood's *Dictionary of Victorian Artists*)" (personal communication to Ronald Lessens).
9. Letter to Frederic George Stephens, dated April 1881. University of Oxford, Bodleian Library, MSS Don.e. 79, ff. 41-42.

CHAPTER TWO

1. 'A travelling scholarship of £200 a year was now given with every gold medal, instead of with every other one as formerly.' (Leslie, G.D., op cit, p.54).
2. Lamont, Thomas Reynolds, *Thomas Armstrong. A Memoir (1832-1901)*, London, 1912, pp.5 & 7.
3. Morris, Edward & McKay, Amanda, 'British art students in Paris 1814-1890', *Apollo*, CXXXV, no. 360, (February 1992), p.84a. At a Dominic Winter auction in Cirencester in June 2011 a passport sold that had belonged to Wallis. It was stamped in 1852 and proves that he travelled to Switzerland and to Italy, which means that he must have crossed France, probably starting from Paris. (private collection, New York).
4. Charles Gleyre (1806-1874) was born at Chevilly, Switzerland. After the deaths of his parents, he spent his youth with his uncle at Lyon. Gleyre started his artistic training in Paris in 1825 and attended Louis Hersent's studio, before travelling to Rome, where he was in touch with Horace Vernet, then Headmaster of the École de Rome. The latter introduced him to John Lowell Jr. (1779-1836), a politician and philanthropist, who was seeking consolation in travel following the deaths of his wife and his two daughters. Lowell wanted to visit the Orient and to have an artist at his disposal to reproduce landscapes, monuments and people. With Lowell, Gleyre visited Sicily, Corfu, Turkey, Rhodes, Egypt and Nubia as witnessed by his numerous watercolours. Lowell would pay Gleyre's expenses and give him pocket money, in return for ownership of all works the artist created during their trip. Two years after they had started their travels, Gleyre left his patron. They did not really quarrel, but having reached Khartoum, Gleyre felt exhausted and wanted to rest. While in the Orient, an ophthalmic disorder left him almost completely blind and disabled for the rest of his life. He came back to France in 1837 in poor physical health. Upon his return, he started to paint seriously again.
5. "In the summer of 1843, the eminent painter Paul Delaroche abandoned his teaching studio, advising his students to seek instruction from other masters, including Charles Gleyre." (Hauptman, William, 'Delaroche's and Gleyre's Teaching Ateliers and Their Group Portraits', *Studies in the History of Art*, vol. 18, Washington, 1985, p.79).
6. Boime, Albert, *The Academy and French Painting in the Nineteenth Century*, New Haven and London, 1986, p.48. This study is essential for an understanding of the French academic world in the 19th century.
7. Hauptman, William, *Charles Gleyre. Life and Works*, Princeton, 1996, p.328.
8. Staiger-Gayler, Brigit, 'Gleyre und seine Schweizer Schüler', *Charles Gleyre ou Les Illusions Perdues*, Winterthur 1974, p.134a. Further memories are quoted in the same article.
9. In his novel, *Trilby*, George du Maurier evoked the memory of Gleyre as the great teacher: "Every Friday Monsieur Carrel, a great artist, and also a stately, well-dressed, and most courteous gentleman (duly decorated with the red rosette of the Legion of Honour), came for two or three hours and went the round, spending a few minutes at each drawing-board or easel – ten or even twelve when the pupil was an industrious and promising one. He did this for love, not money, and deserved all the reverence with which he inspired this somewhat irreverent and most unruly company, which was made up of all sorts." (Wordsworth Ed., Ware, 1995, p.41.) A similar description was made by the Swiss student Auguste Bachelin; see: W. Hauptman, *Gleyre...*, vol.I, p.331. Gleyre had become "Carrel"; Alecco Ionides, the son of a Greek patron living in London, was "the Greek"; Lamont was the "Laird of Cockpen"; Armstrong – or Val Prinsep – was "Taffy"; Poynter, a studious apprentice, was "Lorimer" and the opposite of the lazy "Joe Sibley" (whom everyone recognised as Whistler, and the latter was angry with du Maurier – but then Whistler seems to have been contentious with everyone at some point!).
10. The studio started in 1843 and was situated in the rue d'Erfurth, before moving after 1850 to no. 36 rue de l'Ouest, near Montparnasse railway station and cemetery. In 1859, it settled at no. 69 rue de Vaugirard. See: W. Hauptman, *Gleyre*, vol. I, p.330.
11. Renoir, Jean, *Renoir, my father*, London, 1988, p.95. Also: Hauptman, W., *Delaroche...*, p.84b: 'The master had a certain timidity in allowing male models to pose in the nude when female students were present.'
12. W. Hauptman, *Charles Gleyre...*, vol. I, p.329. Also: Prinsep, Val, 'A Student's Life in Paris in 1859', *Magazine of Art*, February 1904, pp.338-342.
13. Felix Moscheles, *Fragments of an Autobiography*, London, 1899, chapter 5, p.8.
14. D. Johnson, op cit, p.177.
15. Reymond, Nathalie, *Claude Monet*, Paris, 1992, p.40.
16. Boime, Albert, 'The Instruction of Charles Gleyre and the Evolution of Painting in the Nineteenth Century', *Charles Gleyre ou les illusions perdues*, exh. cat. Winterthur, 1974, p.106b.
17. Lechien, Isabelle Énaud, *James Whistler*, Paris. 1995, p.9.
18. Leonée Ormond points out that "the indifference of Du Maurier and his friends to avant-garde experiments in French painting is typical of the insularity of English art, and of the gulf which divided it from the continent." (Ormond, Leonée, *George du Maurier*, Pittsburgh, 1969, p.46.)
19. Monneret, Sophie, *L'Impressionnisme et son époque*, 2 vols, Paris, 1978-9, vol 1, p.300.
20. W. Hauptman, *Delaroche...*, p.88b.
21. Distel, Anne, *Renoir*, Paris, p.27a.
22. F.G. Stephens, *The Athenaeum*, no. 2577, 17 March 1877, p. 357.
23. *The Illustrated London News*, Vol. 73, 7 December 1878, p. 542.

CHAPTER THREE

1. The Government School of Design, of which William Dyce was the Director.
2. Dakers, Caroline, *The Holland Park Circle, Artists and Victorian Society*, New Haven and London, 1999, p.5; £5,000 a year is the equivalent today of over £500,000.
3. Fredeman, William E.: 'The Letters of Pictor Ignotus: William Bell Scott's Correspondence with Alice Boyd, 1859-1884', The John Rylands University Library of Manchester, 1976, pp. 67-68. Scott's article had appeared in *The Gentleman's Magazine*, Vol. CCXLI, August 1877, 'The Royal Academy and the Exhibition', pp.173-196.
4. Hutchison, Sidney C., *The History of the Royal Academy 1768-1968*, London, 1968, p.101.
5. *The Royal Academy Review. A Guide to the Exhibition of the Royal Academy of Arts, 1859*, London, 1859.
6. Id, pp.1 and 5.
7. Id, p.7.
8. Francis Richard Charteris (1818-1914) was styled Lord Elcho from 1853 to 1883. When his father died in 1883 he became the tenth Earl of Wemyss. He was educated at Eton and Oxford, a conservative MP from 1841 to 1883, a Lord of the Treasury, and a founder of the National Rifle Association. He was also a close friend of George Frederic Watts and a collector of Italian Renaissance art.
9. Avery-Quash, Susanna & Sheldon, Julie, *Art for the Nation. The Eastlakes and the Victorian Art World*, London, 2011, p.110.
10. Amor, Anne Clark, *William Holman Hunt*, London, 1989, p.216. This is from Hunt's letter of 27 March 1886 to Sir Charles Dilke, MS. British Museum Addit MS.43910 fol.116.
11. Spielman, Marion H., 'The Proposed Royal Academy Reform', *Contemporary Review*, August 1889, p.261. Spielman (1858-1948) was a prolific Victorian art critic, writer, and the editor of *Connoisseur* and *The Magazine of Art*.
12. M. H. Spielman, op cit, p.272.

13. The Academy reluctantly admitted watercolours to its exhibitions, but did not welcome watercolourists as members until 1943. Even engravers had been able to become members from 1853. See: Denney, Colleen, *At the Temple of Art. The Grosvenor Gallery, 1877-1890*, London, 2000.
14. In 1812, the Society reformed as the *Society of Painters in Oil and Watercolours*, reverting to its original name in 1820. After it obtained its Royal charter in 1881, it became the *Royal Society of Painters in Watercolours*. Finally, in 1988, it changed its name again to the *Royal Watercolour Society*.
15. "Gilbert was to be President of the Society for twenty-six years, the longest term in office of any of its Presidents in either the nineteenth or the twentieth centuries. However, this genial, confident and able man was to grow more and more conservative with the passing of time, more and more concerned with matters of status and increasingly out of touch with its members". (Fenwick, Simon, *The Enchanted River. Two Hundred Years of the Royal Watercolour Society*, Bristol, 2004, p.79.)
16. For more details about these negotiations, see: S. Fenwick, op cit, pp.84-86.
17. Graves, Algernon, *The British Institution 1806-1867*, London, 1908, p.vii.
18. Scott, William Bell, *Autobiographical Notes of the Life of William Bell Scott*, New York, 1892, vol 1, p.109.
19. *The Architect*, 12 March 1870, p. 129.
20. The Old Watercolour Society, for example, victimised both Boyce and Burne-Jones at the 1864 summer exhibition, and "even in the early 1890s, when [Edward Robert] Hughes was elected an Associate Member, the R.W.S. held a reputation as a traditionalist, even reactionary, institution". (Osborne, Victoria J., *A British Symbolist in Pre-Raphaelite Circles: Edward Robert Hughes RWS [1851-1914]*, Birmingham, 2009, pp.27-28.)
21. For more details, see: Lanigan, Dennis T., "The Dudley Gallery: Watercolour drawings exhibitions", *Journal of Pre-Raphaelite Studies*, vol 12, Spring 2003, pp.74-96.
22. C. Denney, op cit, p.43a.
23. Hauptman, William: "Hanging The Pre-Raphaelites and others. The Royal Academy Exhibition of 1851." *The British Art Journal*, Vol. XIX, No. 1, Spring 2018, pp. 4-28.
24. "The Grosvenor's financial footing had never been a sound one. The income of the gallery came almost entirely from the shilling entrance fee charged to the public. It seems that no commission was taken from the artist when a painting was sold and in any case many of the pictures on show at the Grosvenor were on loan from private collections. The restaurant did not pay and the gallery's finances were always under threat from Sir Coutts's endemic extravagance: for instance the 3,600 plates adorned with the Lindsay crest with which he had equipped the restaurant." (MacCarthy, Fiona, *The Last Pre-Raphaelite. Edward Burne-Jones and the Victorian Imagination*, London, 2011, p.372).
25. "It may have been Lady Lindsay's influence which led to the establishment of the general principle that a good proportion of women should be invited to send to the gallery." (Newall, Christopher, *The Grosvenor Gallery Exhibitions*, Cambridge, 1995, p.23a.)
26. More details about art business in nineteenth century London can be found in Fletcher, Pamela & Helmreich, Anne, eds, *The Rise of the Modern Art Market in London, 1850-1939*, Manchester, 2011, as well as on two internet projects: the *London Gallery Project* [http://learn.bowdoin.edu/fletcher/london-gallery/] at Bowdoin College, and the University of Glasgow's *Exhibition Culture in 19th Century London 1878-1908* [http://www.exhibitionculture.arts.gla.ac.uk/index.php].
27. Macleod, Dianne Sachko, *Art and the Victorian middle class*, Cambridge University Press, 1996.
28. In 1867, before retiring to his mansion "Les Palmiers" in Nice, France, Gambart sold the lease of his gallery to a London art dealer, by coincidence, also named Henry Wallis (1804-1890). He was the younger brother of the engraver Robert Wallis. "Henry Wallis started his career as a line-engraver but following two strokes became a picture dealer and dealt in good pictures by contemporary painters such as Turner, Clarkson Stanfield, Frith, Landseer and Roberts. ... He began to have serious financial worries in 1858 and in 1860 he rented his house in Bedford Square to Joseph Gillott. ... After his financial recovery in 1862, Wallis exhibited pictures again at the French Gallery, 120 Pall Mall; he later took over the lease from Ernest Gambart for £1,000 in 1867, having worked previously as his manager." (Chapel, Jeannie, 'The Papers of Joseph Gillott [1799-1872]', Oxford, *Journal of the History of Collections*, 2007, p.24a.)

CHAPTER FOUR

1. His friends among artists not part of the immediate Pre-Raphaelite circle included P.A. Daniel, Henry Darvall, and Eyre Crowe. Both Daniel and Crowe were members of the Hogarth Club.
2. R.A. Admissions book.
3. V. Surtees, op cit, p.22.
4. This is odd, since we know that Hughes's wealth at death was £6,037 19s 5d, quite a respectable amount for the time (DNB, online version 2013).
5. University of Oxford, Bodleian Library, MS Eng.c.7040, f. 257.
6. University of Oxford, Bodleian Library, MS Eng.c.7040, ff .258-9.
7. University of Oxford, Bodleian Library, MS Eng.c.7040, ff.260-1.
8. Roberts, Leonard & Wildman, Steven, *Arthur Hughes: his life and work*. Woodbridge, 1997, p.13.
9. V. Surtees, op cit, p.11.
10. Belfast businessman who had bought Hunt's *Two Gentlemen of Verona*. Many artists had reason to complain about McCracken: "In January 1854 [Arthur] Hughes had at last sold a painting, 'Ophelia', to the devious Belfast collector Francis MacCracken, who promised sixty guineas but gave only thirty. Within six months, MacCracken consigned the picture to Christie's, where it was bought for sixty guineas by Thomas Edward Plint, an act causing great indignation among Hughes's friends, and occasioning a rare outburst of animosity from the artist himself (who was still owed five guineas) against such a 'frightful scoundrel'." (L. Roberts & S. Wildman, op cit, p.14).
11. Fredeman, William E., *Correspondence of Dante Gabriel Rossetti*, 9 vols, Cambridge, 2002, vol. 1, p.350. The painting was *Dr. Johnson at Cave's the Publisher*. Brandard was likely the landscape painter Edward Paxman Brandard (1819-1898). John Bridges (fl. 1818-1854) was an Oxford portrait and genre painter. Redgrave was Richard Redgrave R.A. (1804-1888), a leading genre and landscape painter.
12. Ruskin, John, *Modern Painters*, Smith Elder & Co., London, Sixth Edition, 1857, Vol. I, Chap. III, p.417.
13. Leslie, George Dunlop, *The Inner Life of the Royal Academy*, London, 1914, p.86.
14. Hunt won the prize in 1851 with *Valentine Rescuing Sylvia from Proteus* and in 1853 with *Claudio and Isabella*; Millais in 1852 with *A Huguenot* and in 1857 with *The Blind Girl*; Madox Brown was the 1856 winner with *Christ Washing Peter's Feet* (see: Rudersdorf, Tina, *Die Ausstellungen der Präraffaeliten. Präsentationsformen viktorianischer Malerei und ihre Wirkung*, Bonn, 2009, p.44, n.164).
15. Ann Bukantas, 'John Miller of Liverpool' and 'Portrait of a collector', pp.74-79, in Newall, Christopher: *Pre-Raphaelites Beauty and Rebellion*, Walker Art Gallery, Liverpool, 2016.
16. Bennett, Mary, 'A Check-List of Pre-Raphaelite Pictures Exhibited at Liverpool 1846-67, and Some of Their Northern Collectors', *The Burlington Magazine*, vol. 105, no. 728, Nov. 1963, p.486a.
17. Surtees, Virginia [ed.], *The Diaries of George Price Boyce*, Norwich, 1980, p.24.
18. For more information about these 'patrons of the arts', see: MacLeod, Dianne Sachko, *Art and the Victorian middle class: Money and the Making of Cultural Identity*, Cambridge University Press, 1996.
19. Lewis, Brian, 'Thomas E. Plint. A Patron of Pre-Raphaelite Painters', *The Journal of Pre-Raphaelite Studies*, vol. 3, May 1980, p.83.
20. Redgrave, George, *Art Sales. A History of Sales of Pictures and Other Works of Art*, 2 vols, London, 1888, vol. 1, p.164; William Roberts, *Memorials of Christie's A Record of Art Sales from 1766 to 1896*, vol. I, digital edition, Edizione Savine, 2017.
21. V. Surtees, op cit, p.51. The Princeton University Library also has a letter (C0705, Box 1, folder 42) dated 20 October 1865 from Wallis to Boyce, with musical references: a composed line of music with the description "Spirit of Joachim" - likely Joseph Joachim (1831-1907), the famous violinist.
22. George Price Boyce mentions a "great gathering" on 23 April 1864 (Surtees, op cit, p.40). In a letter to William Hardman dated 1 March 1864, George Meredith writes he has dined with Arthur Lewis (Cline, C. L. [ed.], *The Letters of George Meredith*, 3 vols, Oxford, 1970, Vol. I, p.245). Since Wallis was a guest at the parties, it is possible he could have met Meredith on such an occasion. It seems unlikely and would have been awkward, especially after Henry's affair with Mary Ellen and her death in 1861.
23. W.H. Hunt, op cit, Vol. II, p.151: "He [Fred Walker] was constant as a guest at Lewis' parties, and was ever conspicuous in a knot composed of Calderon, Storey, Wallis, Du Maurier, and Stacey Marks; the two latter often delivered humorous recitals."
24. T.R. Lamont, op cit, p.19. Also: L. Ormond, op cit, pp.105-107.
25. V. Surtees, op cit, pp.41-42. J.R. Clayton: best known for his work with the stained-glass firm Clayton and Bell. Henry Wells: painter who married Boyce's sister Joanna. Frederick William Burton: the Irish watercolour painter, who would later become Director of the National Gallery.
26. Holman-Hunt, Diana: "The Holman Hunt Collection, A Personal Recollection", in Parris, Leslie: *Pre-Raphaelite Papers*, 1984, pp. 206-225.
27. Tromans, Nicholas, 'Palestine: Picture of Prophecy', exh. cat. *Holman Hunt and the Pre-Raphaelite Vision*, Toronto, 2008, p.138.
28. All well-known philosophers particularly engaged with the issues of organised religion.
29. University of Oxford, Bodleian Library, MS Eng.c.7039, ff. 57-59.
30. The work was published in 1906 and Wallis died in 1916.
31. Rossetti, William Michael, *Some Reminiscences*, 2 Vols, New York, 1906, Vol. I, p.158. We have been unable to ascertain with certainty for which Wallis picture Rossetti sat.
32. William Bell Scott had earlier been associated with the painters of The Clique (Augustus Egg, Richard Dadd, William Powell Frith, John Phillip, Alfred Elmore); he was the brother of the historical painter David Scott.
33. Dominic Winter Auctions, *Fine Art & Antiques*, 5 October 2017, lot 264, pencil on off-white paper, 48 x 51 cm. The auction house attributes the drawing to D.G. Rossetti and others. Wallis is mistakenly identified as "Captain Weatherly", but since the initials say "HW" and Weatherly was James Dent Weatherly, this is obviously erroneous.
34. As reported in Fredeman, William E., *The Letters of Pictor Ignotus*, p.49. So far, the whereabouts of this portrait is untraced.
35. Scott died on 22 November 1890. Up until his death, he had been occupied with writing his reminiscences, which were published posthumously in 1892 as *Autobiographical Notes*. Controversy arose about the book and "opinion was sharply divided on its total veracity." Fredeman also stated: "Indeed, many reviewers predicted – rightly as it has turned out – that Scott would be better and longer remembered

for the *Notes* than for his work as either a painter or a poet." (Fredeman, W.E., *Pictor Ignotus*, pp.34-42 gives more details.)
36. Scott had recurrent attacks of *angina pectoris*, the first spasms of which struck him in late April 1885.
37. Alice Boyd owned Penkill Castle and was William Bell Scott's companion from 1859 until his death in 1890. From Scott's *Autobiographical Notes* (vol. 2, p.57): "18/3/1859. I had a visit from a lady some few years over thirty, ill and weary from watching by the death-bed of her mother. I had not heard her name before. She wanted to find a new interest in life, and thought to find it in art. [...] This ancient house [Penkill Castle] has been my summer home and that of my wife, for many years, and all the friends, with few exceptions, mentioned in these pages have come to see us here; the winter half of the year Miss Boyd is our guest in London."
38. University of Oxford, Bodleian Library, MS Eng.c.7041, ff. 201-2.
39. At the beginning of December 1885, Wallis started his first journey via Venice and Brindisi, and then took the boat to Alexandria. He stayed at Cairo and travelled up the Nile as far as Assouan and Philae. He remained at Cairo until the end of February.
40. At the time of this letter, Harold 'Felix' was a clerk at the Bank of England and still lived at his father's house (Woodbury, Biggin Hill, Norwood).
41. University of Oxford, Bodleian Library, MS Eng.c.7041, ff. 203-4.
42. University of Oxford, Bodleian Library, MS Eng.c.7041, ff. 205-6.
43. 21 sketchbooks are at the Bodleian, 9 at the National Art Library, and 1 at the *Museo Internazionale delle Ceramiche*, Faenza, Italy.

CHAPTER FIVE

1. Sir Walter Peacock (1871-1956), a barrister, was Keeper of the Records of the Duchy of Cornwall from 1908-30.
2. Letter dated 30 May 1968. Diane Johnson papers box 12.6. Harry Ransom Center, Austin, Texas.
3. 'Mary Ellen's exact date of birth is not known, but Peacock said in a letter to Shelley of [?11-16] October [1821]: "We have a charming little girl (now eleven weeks old) who grows and flourishes delightfully in this fumose and cinereous atmosphere." (Joukovsky, Nicholas, 'New Correspondence of Mary Ellen Meredith', *Studies in Philology*, Vol. 106, Fall 2009, p.486).
4. D. Johnson, op cit, p.48.
5. Joukovsky, Nicholas, "According to Mrs. Bennett. A document sheds a new and kinder light on George Meredith's first wife", *Times Literary Supplement*, 8 October 2004, p.14a.
6. Peter Augustin Daniel (1827-1917) was one of the Merediths' oldest friends. Besides his contributions to *The Monthly Observer*, he exhibited works at the Royal Academy and at the British Institution and became a Shakespearean scholar, publishing introductions to facsimile editions or reprints of Shakespeare quartos or source texts. He was a non-artistic member of the Hogarth Club. For a living, he worked as a clerk in the Examiner's Office of the East India Company at India House, where he was acquainted with his colleague Edward Gryffydh Peacock, Mary Ellen's brother. It is highly probable that Daniel introduced Wallis to the Meredith circle.
7. Nick Joukovsky: "New Correspondence of Mary Ellen Meredith", *Studies in Philology*, Vol. 106 (Fall 2009), p.489.
8. D. Johnson, op cit, p.83.
9. Sencourt, Robert, *La vie de Meredith*, Paris, 1931. We cite Sencourt, although he is less reliable than Galland and Stevenson, because his viewpoint is opposed to Johnson's, a point which we like to emphasize.
10. Ellis, Stewart Marsh, *George Meredith. His Life and Friends in Relation to his Work*, London, 1920, p.15.
11. See: Joukovsky, Nicholas, 'Mary Ellen's First Affair. New Light on the Biographical Background to *Modern Love*', *Times Literary Supplement*, 15 June, 2007, p.13d: "On 13 June (1853), Mary Ellen had given birth to her son Arthur Gryffydh Meredith. However, the Meredith's marriage had been deteriorating for the past three years." Also: Shaheen, Mohammed [ed.], *Selected Letters of George Meredith*, London, 1997, pp.26 & 27.
12. Banerjee, Jacqueline: 'A Cut Above. George Meredith and the Landlady's Daughter', *The Times Literary Supplement*, 2 September 2015, pp.13-14.
13. Mary Ellen's *Commonplace Book of Extracts* is in the Beinecke Rare Books and Manuscript Library, Yale University, New Haven, Conn. Quoted in D. Johnson, *Lesser Lives*, p.108.
14. Anne Ramsden Bennett (1817-1906) was the eldest child of David Gladstone, a Liverpool merchant whose brother John was the father of William Ewart Gladstone. In 1836, she married Thomas France Bennett, a Liverpool merchant who died in 1866. The Bennetts lived at *Joy Farm* near Birkenhead. The fact of the Meredith's early quarrels was first established from Mrs. Bennett's accounts, as published by N. Joukovsky in 'According to Mrs Bennett', in *The Times Literary Supplement*, No. 5297, 2004, pp.13-16.
15. Joukovsky, N., *According...*, p.14c.
16. A letter from George Meredith to his friend and solicitor William Hardman, dated 3 June 1864, points out that a few years after her death, he still found her guilty: "You can say the truth that incompatibility of temper separated two people of whom the man was eight years the junior, the woman very clever: – her qualities we may leave where they lie. To say that she approached near madness without being quite mad is to express her mental and moral character. She dallied with responsibility, played with passions; rose suddenly to a height of exaltation, sank to a terrible level. And was very clever." (C.L. Cline, op cit, vol. 1, p.262).
17. Joukovsky, N., *According...*, p.13d. See also: Banerjee, J., op cit, pp.13-14.
18. Joukovsky, N., 'George and Mary Meredith, the East India Company, and the Society of Arts: New Light on the Author's Early Career', *Studies in Philology*, vol. 97, Fall 2000, pp.473-493.
19. Letter dated 4 August 1856. University of Oxford, Bodleian Library, MS Eng.c. 7039, f 86.
20. Jones, Frederic L. [ed.], *Mary Shelley's Journal* (Oklahoma, 1947, p.35): "Thursday, Jan 12 [1835]. Letter from Peacock to say that he is in prison; the foolish man lived up to Charlotte's expectancies [see: Mary Shelley's remark of 3 Jan 1815, p.34: "A rich heiress has fallen in love with Peacock, and lives with him."], who turns out to have nothing. Her behaviour is inexplicable. There is a terrible mystery in this affair. His debt is 40 l [£40 1s]." The word "prison" is used because that is what Mary Shelley termed it, but Joukovsky points out that it was a "sponging house" for debtors.
21. Joukovsky, N., *George and Mary Meredith* ...., p.476.
22. N. Joukovsky, *According...*, p.14.
23. Shaheen, Mohammed (ed.), *Selected Letters of George Meredith*, 1997, pp. 26-27. Richard Hengist Horne (1802-1884) was an English poet and critic and a mentor to Meredith. Catherine Horne had been abandoned by her husband, who left for Australia in 1852, and the separation became permanent after 1855.
24. See: N. Joukovsky, 'Mary Ellen's First Affair', p.13-15. Mansfield was acquainted with the Christian Socialists Charles Kingsley, John Malcolm Ludlow, Frederick Denison Maurice and Thomas Hughes. In 1853-54, with the help of Mansfield and his friends, Mary Ellen attempted to establish a school for female domestic servants, but insufficient funds were raised. Furthermore, it appeared that F.D. Maurice wanted the house in Red Lion Square for the projected Working Men's College.
25. Email from N. Joukovsky of 23 September 2015. See also: N. Joukovsky: 'Dearest Susie Pye': New Meredith Letters to Peacock's Natural Daughter, *Studies in Philology*, Vol. 111, No. 3, 2004, p. 617.
26. University of Oxford, Bodleian Library, MS Eng.c. 7040, ff..160-2. Joukovsky has published and annotated the letter in *Notes and Queries*, November 3, 2011, which we reproduce in part here with his kind permission.
27. Cf. William Makepeace Thackeray, *The Newcomes* (1853–5), Vol. II, chap. XXXVI, p.393: "What the deuce does Warrington want with the effigy of his grim old mug?"
28. University of Oxford, Bodleian Library, MS Eng.c.7039, ff..85-86.
29. Nicholas A. Joukovsky: 'The Early Meredithian Milieu: New Evidence from Letters of Peter Augustin Daniel', *Studies in Philology*, Vol. XV, Summer 2018, pp. 615-641.
30. S.M. Ellis, *George Meredith; his life and friends in relation to his work*, 1920, pp.85-86.
31. University of Oxford, Bodleian Library, MS Eng.c.7039, ff..87-88.
32. D. Johnson, op cit, pp.124-5.
33. These lines are from Lord Byron's well-known poem "Elegy on Thyrza" or "And Thou Art Dead, As Young and Fair", written in 1812.
34. M. Shaheen, op cit, pp.30-32. Manuscript is in the Beinecke Library at Yale.
35. Johnson thinks that he was called Felix only after his mother's death. D. Johnson, op cit, p.210, n.30. She also states (p.8) that the baby was christened Harold Meredith.
36. University of Oxford, Bodleian Library, MS Eng.c.7039, ff..89-90.
37. D. Johnson, op cit, p.132.
38. It was here where Leighton painted his first oil landscape sketches, which were influenced by his friend Giovanni Costa and the French artist Corot, whom he admired.
39. That is what D. Johnson claims, however, Joukovsky is suspicious of this statement, which may have been an invention of some early Meredith biographer.
40. R. Sencourt, op cit, p.60.
41. D. Johnson, op cit, p.133.
42. Ibid.
43. Jones, Mervyn, *The Amazing Victorian. A Life of George Meredith*, London, 1999, p.81.
44. Mike Hickox, email to Ronald Lessens, 9 August 2015.
45. Nicholas A. Joukovsky, 'The Early Meredithian Milieu: New Evidence from Letters of Peter Augustin Daniel', *Studies in Philology*, Vol. XV, Summer 2018, pp. 615-641.
46. Mike Hickox, email to Ronald Lessens, August 1, 2015.
47. Georgiana Burne-Jones remembered the place quite well: "Before the birth of our first child we removed from Russell Place into a larger set of rooms just left by Mr. Henry Wallis, at No.62, Great Russell Street. Here Edward's studio was again only the front room of the first floor, but as the house was opposite to the British Museum the large open space before it gave a better painting light than usual. Behind the studio and communicating with it by a door was our sitting-room, and beyond that a very small third one. The outlook of the sitting-room was upon a little back-yard entirely built over and covered with a skylight; beyond this was the high blank wall of the back of a house. This had once been coloured and was now blotched in a leprous way. Our own walls inside were beautified with some old tapestry left there by Mr. Wallis while he was travelling abroad." (G. Burne-Jones, op cit, vol. 1, p.228).
48. D. Johnson, op cit, p.103. Hunt's granddaughter Diana also reported: "Meredith had been the model for the corpse on the bed in *The death of Chatterton*. She [Edith Holman Hunt] had told me long ago that the painter Henry Wallis stole his wife, as if one could steal a person." (Holman-Hunt, Diana, *My Grandmothers and I*, London, 1987, p.110).

49. N. Joukovsky, *According to Mrs. Bennett…*, p. 622.
50. Some time ago, we discovered at the Bodleian Library (MS Eng.c. 7050, f.186), an answer from Highgate cemetery to Harold's request: "Grave 9688, Sqre 18, Dear Sir, Mr Andrew Wallis was interred in the above grave on July 1st 1859. Death would occur four or five days previously." Wallis would therefore surely been in a financial position to aid Mary Ellen prior to her death.
51. Madden, Mary & Lionel, 'Thomas Love Peacock, George and Mary Meredith, and John Parker Jr,' *Victorian Periodicals Review* 27/1, Spring 1994, p.32.
52. M. & L. Madden, op cit, p.38.
53. Joukovsky, Nicholas, *The Letters of Thomas Love Peacock*, 2 vols, Oxford, 2001, vol. 1, p.429.
54. D. Johnson, op cit, p.144.
55. C. L. Cline, op cit, vol. 1, p.119.
56. Why she allowed Wallis to take Felix with him to Europe is unknown. Did she not suspect she was ill enough to die during her young son's absence? Or, perhaps, she did not want him to witness her death.
57. A sketch for a tombstone was found amongst Peacock's papers, along with an epitaph.
58. S.M. Ellis, op cit, p.92. The poem is by Alfred Tennyson, first published in *The Keepsake* in 1851.
59. Joukovsky, N., 'New Correspondence…,' p.488, n.29.
60. Diane Johnson papers, box 13.2, p.92.
61. Diane Johnson papers, box 13.2, p.110.
62. C.L. Cline, op cit, Vol .1, p.262.
63. Edmond, Rod, *Affairs of the hearth: Victorian poetry and domestic narrative*, London and New York, 1988, p.211.
64. C.L. Cline, op cit, vol. 1, pp.269-271.
65. D. Johnson, op cit, p.209, n.25.
66. Bell, Alan Nigel, *The male novelist and the 'Woman question': George Meredith's presentation of his heroines in* The Egoist *(1879) and* Diana of the Crossways *(1885)*, Rhodes University. 2007, p.6.
67. Letter dated 21 March 1865, quoted in D. Johnson, op cit, pp.171-2.
68. D. Johnson, *op cit*, p.170.
69. University of Oxford, Bodleian Library, MS Eng.e.3395.
70. Burne-Jones, Georgiana, *Memorials of Edward Burne-Jones*, 2 vols. London, 1904, vol. 1, p.228.
71. *Vacation tourists. Notes of travel 1860*, accessible on *archive.org*
72. He does not seem to have met John Brett, who spent the winters of 1863 and 1864 on the island of Capri with his two mistresses: Mathilde Loeser (a professional singer) and Georgina Weldon (a talented amateur singer who also became Charles Gounod's mistress).
73. Diane Johnson papers, box 13.2.
74. In the papers purchased by a private collector in New York, was an account of Harold's school expenses:

Henry Wallis Esq. to Rev. Chas Wicksteed
Midsummer 1868
Half Year's Board & Education of son Harold (with)

Washing & extras (Music &c)	33	0	0
Money for Journey,			
1£ Pocket money 3/6	1	3	6
Medical Attendance		10	0
Mending boot-laces to ? 3° Music		4	0
	£34	17	6

75. Diane Johnson papers, box 13.2, p.57.
76. Harold's entrance into the bank was bonded by Henry Wallis's artist friend Eyre Crowe A.R.A., and his patron Charles G. Clement, for £500 apiece. The Bank's Election Memorandum book specifies that he was in good health, that he was Unitarian, that he was free from debt and living with his father at no. 24 Brecknock Crescent, Camden Town. (Bank of England, Candidates for Election Memorandum book, E45/1.) Harold started as an assistant on a yearly salary of £70, but was regularly advanced and ended his career as a 1st Class Clerk, on a salary of £280. On 10 October 1918 – at the age of 60 – he retired and was granted a pension of £245 6s 8d a year, quite a respectable amount at the time.
77. Biographers have always assumed it was "Julia", but in his will Harold mentions "my dear Wife Alice Julyan Wallis": this is not a transcription fault, for the 1911 census also lists her as *Alice Julyan*.
78. Although Edwin seems to have been born in 1884, the 1891 census shows that Harold was still living with his father. In his letters Henry often mentions Alice and Violet, but only them. The 1901 census, Harold's will, as well as his death certificate, never mention a son.

Census 1901 - household members:

Harold	42y	Bank clerk	b. Bristol
Alice	35		b. London, St James
Violet	2		b. Stoke Newington
Harriet Roberts (Alice's mother)	67	Living on own means	b. London, Holborn

Furthermore, in a letter addressed to Harold and dated 27 December 1919, Bernard Rackham, from the Victoria and Albert Museum, states he hoped "you & Mrs. & Miss Wallis have had an enjoyable Christmas." (University of Oxford, Bodleian Library, MS Eng.c. 7050, ff.189-190.) While this almost makes it appear that Edwin never existed, Johnson had access to original family documents to refute this. For example, she transcribed Violet Grace's will, dated 1943, where she left part of her £10,000 wealth to her "Brother Edwin Harold Wallis." (D. Johnson papers, box 13.1.) According to immigration reports an Edwin H. Wallis, aged twenty-eight, who was born in London, is known to have emigrated to the United States in February 1913. We know he married Mary Elizabeth Aymes because she donated antiquities in his memory to the Victoria and Albert and British Museums. If Edwin Harold Wallis did at some point live in the United Sates he must have returned to England because when he died in 1962 he and his wife were living at The Hedges, Hartley Down, Purley, Surrey. After Harold's death, Violet Grace married Arthur James Mabey (1895-1953), a Fellow of the Society of Antiquaries of Scotland, 1930-1953.
79. General Register Office, death certificate.
80. University of Oxford, Bodleian Library, MS Don.e.79, f.17."

CHAPTER SIX

1. Bennett, Mary: *Artists of the pre-Raphaelite Circle: The First Generation*, Lund Humphries, London, 1988, p. 190; Wood, Christopher: *The Pre-Raphaelites*, Crescent Books, New York, 1994, p. 64.
2. For example: "As to selling Argentines, it is as far as I have observed a mistake to sell in time of panic. The thing is to get information before the event. It is unfortunate one gets no information here till so long after the event." (Letter to Harold, from Cairo, 1.12.1890 – Bodleian Library, MS Eng.c.7049, fol.41); "Sorry to hear such a bad account S. American securities & must get back as soon as I can to go into the matter." (Letter to Harold Wallis, from Luxor, 27.1.1891 – Bodleian Library, MS Eng.c;7049, fol.57)
3. Gadoin, Isabelle, 'Henry Wallis: du peintre préraphaélite au spécialiste en céramique islamique', in: Gadoin, Isabelle & Palmier-Chatelain, Marie-Élise, *Rêver l'Orient, connaître l'Orient*, Paris, 2008, p.83.
4. C. Dakers, op cit, p.46.
5. In a letter from December 1858 to Madox Brown, D. G. Rossetti gives a list of "artistic members" for the year 1859: G.F. Bodley, G.P. Boyce, John Brett, F. Madox Brown, W.S. Burton, James Campbell, J.M. Carrick, John R. Clayton, Eyre Crowe Jun., William Davis, Alfred D. Fripp, Michael F. Halliday, Arthur Hughes, Alfred W. Hunt, W. Holman Hunt, J.W. Inchbold, E. Burne-Jones, Edward Lear, F. Leighton, Robert B. Martineau, William Morris, T. Morten, J.W. Oakes, J.H. Pollen, Val Prinsep, D.G. Rossetti, John Ruskin, W.B. Scott, J.R. Spencer Stanhope, F.G. Stephens, G.E. Street, John L. Tupper, Henry Wallis, G.F. Watts, Philip Webb, W.L. Windus, Benjamin Woodward, Thomas Woolner. Honorary members were: David Cox, F. Danby, Eugene Delacroix, W. Dyce, William Hunt, J.F. Lewis, and W. Mulready. (W.M. Rossetti, *Ruskin, Rossetti, Preraphaelitism Papers 1854 to 1862*, London, 1899, pp.216-7).
6. Newman, Teresa & Watkinson, Ray, *Ford Madox Brown and the Pre-Raphaelite Circle*, London, 1991, p.131.
7. For a more detailed report, see: William Michael Rossetti's letter to William Bell Scott, dated 28 April 1861, in R. Peattie (ed.), *The Selected Letters of William Michael Rossetti*, Pennsylvania State University Press, 1990, p.114.
8. Bornand, Odette [ed.], *The Diary of W.M. Rossetti*, Oxford, 1977, pp.236-7.
9. University of Oxford, Bodleian Library, MS Don.e.79, f.23.
10. University of Oxford, Bodleian Library, MS Eng.c.7049, f.83.
11. Private Clubs for gentlemen, although they had been set up initially in the late seventeenth century, assumed their full identity after Waterloo instituted by officers who wanted to share their modest earnings and have the advantages of a first-class mess. It was a huge success and other professions followed suit. Oxford and Cambridge had their clubs for clerics and professors, the Athenaeum was meant for judges, solicitors and doctors, the Reform Club for politicians, the Academy Club for Academicians and their Associates, etc. Artists had plenty of choices and could affiliate with the Arts Club, the Athenaeum, the Savile Club and the Burlington Fine Arts Club. The Arts Club, founded in 1863, and established in Tenterden Street, Hanover Square, was frequented by artists such as Thomas Armstrong, John Frederick Lewis and George Dunlop Leslie. The latter points out that, on election day, it was a meeting place for Academicians, and that champagne was offered by the newly elected Associates. (G. D. Leslie, op cit, pp.224-5.) Artist members of the Athenaeum included Lawrence Alma-Tadema, John Brett, Edward Burne-Jones, Frederick Burton, William Holman Hunt, Frederic Leighton, J.E. Millais, Edward Poynter, Val Prinsep, W.B. Richmond, G.F. Watts, and Thomas Woolner. The Savile Club, established in 1868, at first had its premises in Savile Row, but after eleven years it moved to no. 107 Piccadilly. The literary world was especially welcome, but also artists as it appears from a letter dated 3 August 1889 from Wallis to the critic Cosmo Monkhouse: "Thanks, I shall have much pleasure in dining wth you at the Savile on Wednesday next." (University of Texas at Austin, Harry Ransom Center.)
12. Letter to Wallis from George Price Boyce's widow Caroline, dated 1 July 1915: "Je vous remercie de la lettre d'introduction au Burlington Club que vous avez eu la bonne pensée de m'envoyer." ["I thank you for the introduction letter to the Burlington Club which was very thoughtful of you to have sent me."] (University of Oxford, Bodleian Library, MS Eng.c.7040, f.34.)

CHAPTER SEVEN

1. For example, Reynolds-Ball, E.A., *Cairo of To-Day: A Practical Guide to Cairo and the Nile*, 1904, accessible on *archive.org*.
2. Bar-Yosef, Eitan, *The Holy Land in English Culture 1799-1917*, 2005, pp.64-65.
3. British Museum, Department of Prehistory and Europe.
4. University of Oxford, Bodleian Library, MS Eng.c.7049, ff. 92-119.
5. University of Oxford, Bodleian Library, MS Eng.c.7039, f. 59.
6. University of Bodleian Library, MSS Don.e.79, f.115.
7. Napoleon occupied this palace during his Egypt campaign. It opened as a hotel in 1841 and housed

Cook's agency. Shepheard's was the leading hotel in Cairo and one of the most celebrated hotels in the world from the middle of the 19th century until it was destroyed by fire in 1952.
8. This would be Flinders Petrie's choice of hotel for eleven years.
9. Lemaire, Gérard-Georges, *L'univers des Orientalistes*, Paris, 2000, p.185b.
10. Titmarsh, M.A., *Notes of a Journey from Cornhill to Grand Cairo*. London, 1846, pp.278-279.
11. John Mason Cook, Thomas Cook's son.
12. Village close to Memphis, 20 miles from Cairo.
13. "Memphis had been the capital of Egypt since the dawn of history, and it retained its role as the headquarters of the national administration right through the Ramesside Period. Thebes may have taken on the mantle of the nation's religious capital, but it was at Memphis that royal decrees were issued, officials appointed and kings crowned." (Wilkinson, Toby, *The Rise and Fall of Ancient Egypt*, New York, 2010, pp.369-70.)
14. University of Oxford, Bodleian Library, MS Eng.c.7049, ff. 1-2.
15. After the conquest of Egypt in 1517, the Turks had divided the country into 24 provinces, each one being led by a Bey, or prince. The Beys formed the Government's Council (*Diwan*), chaired by a Pasha, or Khedive appointed by the Turks. In Wallis's time, British foreign policy was alternately conducted by Gladstone or by Disraeli and, since the opening of the Suez Canal, Egypt had become a vital passage to India. The bad financial management of the Khedive led to an agreement by Britain and France to jointly control the Egyptian debt. After riots had broken out, causing some Europeans to be killed at Alexandria, the European powers decided to intervene; however, in an attempt to avoid any escalation, France withdrew its fleet, with the result that the British army "temporarily" occupied Cairo as well as the rest of Egypt (1882). Gradually, the relations between the two countries became strained, especially after the Sudan expedition, during which General Gordon and his army perished. A Muslim fanatic had proclaimed himself the *Mahdi* ("Messiah") and, with the help of his followers the dervishes, had cut Lieutenant-General Hicks's army into pieces. (William Hicks, a retired colonel in the Indian army, had been hired by the Egyptian Governor Raouf Pasha to take command of the Egyptian army in the Sudan. Hicks' request for British troops to assist was refused. His army was massacred at the Battle of El Obeid on November 3-5, 1883.) Gordon, who had been sent to pacify the region, locked himself up in Khartoum, instead of evacuating the country. By the time Gladstone eventually decided to send reinforcements, it was too late and Gordon was killed. In the second half of the 1890s, Kitchener had been sent to avenge Gordon's death and to reassert British control of the upper waters of the Nile. At Omdurman, near Khartoum, he had defeated the Mahdi's successor and his army. The French had always regretted their decision not to take part in the occupation of Egypt and decided to take control of the Nile headwaters under the command of General Marchand. Kitchener reacted at once and raced up the Nile to Fachoda in Upper Sudan. The scene was set for a major confrontation, but after negotiations, the French government gave in and ordered their troops to withdraw. (*Looking back at Britain. 1890s. Victoria's final decade*. London, 2009, p.135.) Wallis's letters to his son often mention the political tension in southern Egypt and allow us to understand the vehemence of his anti-French feelings.
16. That year (1885), Wolseley's troops battled with the Mahdi's forces north of Khartoum, where Gordon's situation had become critical. After Gordon's death, the region remained troubled and Wallis was a key witness to these events.
17. University of Oxford, Bodleian Library, MS Don.e.79, ff. 77-78.
18. University of Oxford, Bodleian Library, MS Eng.c.7049, ff. 52-53. Wallis was referring to the German victory over the French in the Franco-Prussian war of 1870.
19. Sir Ernest Alfred Thompson Wallis Budge (1857-1934) was Keeper of Egyptian and Assyrian Antiquities, 1894-1924. His integrity has come into question, however: "In future years Petrie appears to have been scrupulous in submitting everything that he found to the [Cairo] Museum and obtain export permits; he was condemnatory of those, like Wallis Budge, who boasted that they smuggled out of the country what they would not have been permitted to take legally." (Drower, Margaret, *Flinders Petrie. A Life in Archaeology*, Wisconsin, 1995, p.64).
20. Budge, E.A. Wallis, *By Nile and Tigris. A narrative of journeys in Egypt and Mesopotamia on behalf of the British Museum between the years 1886 and 1913*, London, 1920, pp.108-9. Even the French archaeologist Gaston Maspero, who was a nice man, spoke of Schliemann as "quarrelsome and tactless". (T.G.H. James, *Excavating in Egypt: The Egypt Exploration Society 1882-1982*. University of Chicago Press, 1982, p.15). Schliemann, of course, was famous at this time as the "discoverer of Troy".
21. E.A.W. Budge, op cit, p.132.
22. University of Oxford, Bodleian Library, MS Eng.c.7049, ff. 19-20. Letter dated 22 December 1887.
23. Howard was a friend of Wallis and other Pre-Raphaelites, especially Burne-Jones and William Morris. Wanting to become a painter, he studied in Italy with Giovanni Costa before returning to London in 1865 to continue his training at the Kensington School of Art and Heatherley's. He wanted to work with Burne-Jones and learn from him but Burne-Jones recommended Alphonse Legros. Howard also became a considerable patron. (F. MacCarthy, op cit, p.192-3.)
24. Seti I, king of the XIXth dynasty, reigned from 1290 to 1279 BC. His richly decorated tomb (KV17), in the Valley of Kings, was discovered by Giovanni Belzoni in 1817.
25. Sir John Soane (1753-1837) was an architect who taught at the Royal Academy and was the architect and the surveyor of the Bank of England. His Museum remains much as it was in his day and houses the enormous sarcophagus of Seti I, which he purchased in 1824.
26. University of Oxford, Bodleian Library, MS Eng.c.7049, ff. 21-22.
27. M. Drower, op cit, p.219. The Wallis Papers at the Bodleian Library contain several letters mentioning Petrie, for example: MS Don.e.79, fol 106, letter to F.G. Stephens, dated 25 Jan 1894: "I did not go further up than Luxor & when there went for a few days to see Flinders Petrie."; MS Eng.c.7050, f.2, letter to his son Harold, from Cairo, dated 4 December 1895: "Petrie has come & will soon start for his winter's diggings."; British Museum, Dept Prehistory & Europe, to A.W. Franks, 18 December 1895: "Petrie is at work here (I write from Luxor)."
28. Naucratis was at the centre of the XXVIth Saïte dynasty (664-525 BC). A Greek colony had been founded during the reign of Psammetichus I (664-610 BC) and Naucratis was a key commercial site. It was one of the first places to be explored by Flinders Petrie (1885).
29. University of Oxford, Bodleian Library, MS Eng.c.7049, ff. 39

CHAPTER EIGHT

1. Gadoin, Isabelle, "Henry Wallis, du peintre préraphaélite au spécialiste en céramique islamique," pp. 77-97 in Gadoin, Isabelle et Palmier-Chatelain, Marie-Elise: *Rêver d'orient, connaître l'orient*, 2008.
2. The Diane Johnson papers discuss her finding residuals from Wallis's estate when she visited Vera Whiting in 1973. Johnson discovered works by Wallis's Pre-Raphaelite friends, a Beardsley drawing, as well as a fragment of a painting attributed to Titian. Some of these works, including works by Burne-Jones and Rossetti, were subsequently sold at auction at Christie's, London, on 13 March 1973. When Diane Johnson examined the Wallis archive she discovered four letters from the well-known collector J.R. Holliday to Wallis concerning Burne-Jones drawings. Wallis at some point, therefore, may have had many more drawings by Burne-Jones.
3. Wilson, Timothy, 'A Victorian artist as ceramic-collector: The letters of Henry Wallis', *Journal of the History of Collections*, vol. 14, no. 1, Oxford, 2002, p.140b.
4. Van de Put, Albert, 'Henry Wallis 1830-1916', *Faenza. Bolletino del Museo Internazionale delle Ceramiche*. Fasc. Vol. V, Issue 2, 1917.
5. A. Van de Put, op cit, pp. 3-4.
6. A. Van de Put, Albert, op cit.
7. Gadoin, Isabelle, 'Les collections victoriennes d'art persan: images exposées, sous-exposées, sur-exposées', *Images de l'*étranger: actes du colloque. *Université de Limoges, 28-29 mars 2003*, Limoges, 2003, p.95.
8. T. Wilson, op cit, p.141b. A waster is a vessel that has been damaged during manufacture, in particular during firing, but which is not necessarily rendered unusable.
9. Id, pp.142b-143a. Nicola da Urbino (*c.*1480-1540/47), the Italian ceramist from Castel Durante, was formerly confused with Nicola Pellipario. In 1985, Franco Negroni set out to demonstrate that "Nicola Pellipario" was a phantom of art-historical imagination and that the Urbino master with his own shop by 1520 was Nicola da Urbino.
10. Ibid.
11. Id., p.156, n.32; also: Giacomotti, Jeanne, *La majolique de la Renaissance*, Paris, 1961, p.34.
12. I. Gadoin, *Les collections victoriennes...*, p.94.
13. MS: PP/University of British Columbia.
14. T. Wilson, op cit, p.144a. There were three hundred textiles in the collection that Wallis sold.
15. London, National Art Library: MA/1/W330. Correspondence of Henry Wallis with the Victoria and Albert Museum.
16. A.B. Skinner (1861-1911) was Assistant Director to the S.K.M. from 1896; Art Director 1905; Keeper of the Department of Architecture and Sculpture from 1909.
17. "The V&A's own collection of Spanish pottery was less comprehensive than its collection of Italian maiolica, and Wallis's loan of Hispano-Moresque was visually more spectacular than the maiolica. In 1907 Wallis's collection of Spanish lustreware was, therefore, purchased at a price of £3,000. (T. Wilson, op cit, p.146a).
18. N.A.L., MA/1/W330.
19. Godman (1834-1919) was a collector of Iznik, Hispano-Moresque and early Iranian pottery. His collection was donated to the British Museum by his younger daughter Catherine.
20. Gadoin, op cit, p.93. The exhibition was entitled *Catalogue of Specimens Illustrative of Persian and Arab Art. Exhibited in 1885.*
21. He had been recommended in December 1884 by Virtue Hobbs and Frank Dillon, and elected a member in June 1885 (BFAC, Candidates Books, IV, n° 541 - National Art Library, ref. 86.KK.28).
22. Small funerary figures buried in a tomb with a person to act as a worker in the afterworld.
23. *Exhibition of the Art of Ancient Egypt*, 1895, p.vi.
24. The Saïte Period, the Twenty-Sixth Dynasty, lasted from 664 BC to 525 BC, during the Late Period of ancient Egypt.
25. Friedrich Overbeck (1789-1869) was one of the founders of the German *Nazarene* movement.
26. *Exhibition of the Art of Ancient Egypt*, p.xi.
27. *The Academy*, Vol. 36, no. 919, 14 December 1889, p.393.
28. Kirby, Thomas E. [Ed.], *Catalogue of the Art and Library Property Collected by the Late Henry G. Marquand*, New York, 1903, lot 1133.

29. *The Athenaeum*, no. 3494, 13 October 1894, p.498.
30. *The Times*, 6 April 1894, p.13.
31. Holman Hunt, Diana, 'The Holman Hunt Collection, A Personal Recollection', *Pre-Raphaelite Papers*, 1984, pp.206-225.
32. In a letter from Bell Scott to Wallis of 11 October 1889 he mentions the sale of ceramics from his collection at his upcoming house sale: "and if you want the little early Italian pots you once called to see or anything else, I advise you to go. There are a number of Hispano-Moros if you still collect such, and a remarkable Majolica platter with the subject of Jupiter & Juno in an interesting position (not improper) on it. The Hispano Moresque water vessel I have presented to the SK Museum. I expect things will go dirt cheap. All my Nankin ware will go with the rest." (University of Oxford, Bodleian Library, MS Eng.c. 7041, ff.211-2.)
33. T. Wilson, op cit, p.147. See also: MS: University of Oxford, Bodleian Library, MS Eng.c.7040, ff.61-62
34. T. Wilson, op cit, p.250.
35. T. Wilson, op cit, p.258.
36. I. Gadoin, *Les collections victoriennes...*, p.89.
37. University of Oxford, Bodleian Library, MS Eng.c.7039, ff. 96-100.
38. Gadoin, I., *Henry Wallis, du peintre préraphaélite au spécialiste en céramique islamique*, pp. 77-97. "Ce sont ces vastes perspectives ouvertes par les collectionneurs victoriens que la suite de l'histoire de l'art islamique a continué à sonder. Mais Wallis occupe dans ces découvertes une place de choix. C'est qu'il jouait sur plusieurs cordes : il possédait non seulement l'œil de l'expert mais aussi la main de l'artiste, et non content d'exceller au jeu des attributions, des classifications et des datations, en tant que « connoisseur » au sens le plus noble du terme, il possédait aussi de rares qualités de diffuseur des images, par sa virtuosité d'illustrateur ; enfin, par ses contacts étroits avec les marchands, joints à une diplomatie enjouée, évidente à la lecture de ses lettres, il fut un émissaire de choix des musées et des grands collectionneurs. Son parcours montre de manière irréfutable qu'entre le rêve et la connaissance, il n'y a pas d'antithèse. Mieux, que l'un ne saurait jouer, ni se constituer sans l'autre : on tente de connaître ce que l'on a d'abord aimé, fantasmé ; et dans cette connaissance progressivement acquise se glissent à parts égales l'investigation respectueuse et la prise de possession typiquement impérialiste. Mais l'amour de l'art, uni chez le collectionneur à la passion de l'acquisition, en viennent aussi à développer le savoir que l'Occident peut avoir de l'Orient – un savoir nécessairement subjectif (chargé de l'affect de l'amateur) en même temps qu'objectif (sondant les objets). "

CHAPTER NINE

1. Morris had first developed his ideas after having toured Northern France with Burne-Jones in 1855 when they were students at Oxford. Morris was convinced that "restoration falsified the architects' and craftmen's original intentions, smoothing out the original vigour of the workmanship. Better to let buildings decay than to restore them." (F. MacCarthy, *The Last Pre-Raphaelite*, p.49). Other prominent Victorians who were members of the Society for the Protection of Ancient Buildings included G. Aitchison, L. Alma-Tadema, G.P. Boyce, E. Burne-Jones, F.W. Burton, Edward Poynter, and Philip Webb.
2. See: in Appendix II, letter 12, p.236 and letter 15, p.237. Morris's letters to Wallis on the subject of the Basilica of St. Mark.
3. MacCarthy, Fiona, *William Morris. A Life for Our Time*, London, 1994, p. 378.
4. In his *Life of John Ruskin*, Edward Tyas Cook has given an excellent summary of the campaign against the restoration of St. Mark's. Letters related to the SPAB and sent by William Morris, Charles Yriarte and others can be found in the Wallis papers at the British Library (Add. 38831).
5. Wallis wrote a letter to *The Times*, published on 20 April 1880, on the condition of the Bapistry in Ravenna and his fears for the mosaics. Wallis's concerns about the proposed restoration of the chapel painted by Melozzo da Forlì can be found in *The Architect*, 24 April 1880, p. 293 and 22 May 1880, p. 360.
6. See: *The* Athenaeum, no. 3180, December 1888, p.779. The society ceased activities in 1910.
7. M. Drower, op cit, p.43.
8. *The Academy and Literature*, Vol. 37, No. 933, 22 March 1890, p.212. General Sir Henry Brackenbury (1837-1914) had served in the Gordon Relief Expedition to the Sudan in 1884-1885. Professor Archibald Sayce (1845-1933) was Professor of Assyriology at Oxford University from 1891-1919.
9. Henry Wallis, 'The Destruction of Egyptian Monuments', *The Nineteenth Century*, XXVIII, no. 165, Nov. 1890, p.725. The French archeologist Auguste Mariette (1821-1881) was appointed the first director of ancient monuments in Egypt and established the first National Museum of Antiquities in the Middle East at Bulaq, north-east of Cairo.
10. Id, p.726.
11. T. Wilson, op cit, p.145a.
12. University of Oxford, Bodleian Library, MS Eng.c.7049, f.55.
13. Sir Colin Scott-Moncrieff (1836-1916). Head of the Irrigation and Canal Department; Under-Secretary of State for Public Works in Cairo. He was the man under whom the general direction of the Bulaq Museum and the Department of Antiquities would come. (M. Drower, op cit, p.73).
14. Drower, Margaret: *Flinders Petrie. A Life in Archeology*, 1995, p.171.
15. M. Drower, op cit, p.176.

CHAPTER TEN

1. Folger Shakespeare Library, Washington D.C., Y.c. 1459 (14).
2. Personal communication to Ronald Lessens.
3. Little is known about this mysterious friend of Wallis's, the American painter Thomas H. Hotchkiss. He was born in 1833 in Coxsackie, N.Y., and died in 1869 in Sicily from tuberculosis, having spent much of his short career in poverty painting Rome and its surrounding countryside as well as other picturesque corners of Italy. Wallis had introduced him to Holman Hunt, as can be deduced from a note sent by Hunt to Wallis, dated 17 August 1865: "My dear Wallis. I was sorry to find that your friend Hotchkiss had called while I was out yesterday: his card has no address upon it, so I have no means of writing to him. I shall be at home on Monday as also on Saturday. If I knew where he lived I would call and see his sketches and pictures and then I should be better able to decide how I could help him." (University of Oxford, Bodleian Library, MS Eng.c.7039, f.18). In a letter dated 8 June 1868, an unidentified correspondent writes: "... see your friend the American painter." (University of Oxford, Bodleian Library, MS Eng.c.7041, f. 310). In a letter to his son, dated 28 January 1889, Wallis recalled: "the Campo Santo Inglese [Messina, Southern Italy], where poor Hotchkiss was buried." This seems to indicate that even years after the painter's death, Wallis was still emotional about it.
4. Martin, Philippa, "The Tragic Muse", *Apollo*, November 2014, pp.76-80. This article on the secret life of Frederic Leighton confirms that his favourite model, Dorothy Dene, was also his mistress.
5. W.M. Rossetti, *Some Reminiscences*, 2 vols, New York, 1906, Vol..I, p.158.
6. They both attended the meeting of the Hogarth Club on 4 May 1858. Wallis's first surviving letter to Stephens is dated 27 May 1862. (University of Oxford, Bodleian Library, MSS Don.e.79, f.1.)
7. University of Oxford, Bodleian Library, MSS Don.e.79, ff. 4-5.
8. Norman MacColl (1843-1904) was editor of *The Athenaeum* from 1871-1900.
9. Letter dated 17 June 1884. University of Oxford, Bodleian Library, MSS Don.e.79, ff. 61-62.
10. Letter dated 23 February 1885. University of Oxford, Bodleian Library, MSS Don.e.79, f.63.
11. Macleod, Dianne Sachko, 'F.G. Stephens, Pre-Raphaelite critic and art historian', *The Burlington Magazine*, vol. 128, no. 999, June 1986, p.402, n.45.
12. Id, p.402.
13. University of Oxford, Bodleian Library, MSS Don.e.79, ff.163-4.
14. University of Oxford, Bodleian Library, MS Eng.c.7049, ff. 46-47.
15. University of Oxford, Bodleian Library, MS Eng.c.7049, f. 77. Letter to Harold, 24 January 1892.
16. Dr. Luigi Frati was the head librarian of the Municipal Library of the Archiginnasio Palace, Bologna, and an expert on Italian majolica.
17. University of Oxford, Bodleian Library, MS Eng.c.7050, ff. 50-51.
18. The earthquake struck at about 5:20 am and lasted for more than 20 seconds, reaching a magnitude of 7.5 on the Richter Scale. It was closely followed by a tsunami, now thought to have been caused by an unrelated underwater landslide. More than 80,000 people were killed in the double disaster, which almost completely destroyed the towns of Messina, Reggio and Calabria and many local coastal towns and villages.
19. University of Oxford, Bodleian Library, MS Eng.c.7049, ff. 66-67.
20. T. Wilson, op cit, p.250.
21. Letter - University of Oxford, Bodleian Library, MS Eng.c.7049, ff. 5-6.
22. Said, Edward W., *Orientalism. Western conceptions of the Orient.* London, 1995, p.5.
23. University of Oxford, Bodleian Library, MSS Don.e.79, f.116b.
24. University of Oxford, Bodleian Library, MS Eng.c. 7050, f.110.
25. Tomb no. 19216.

CHAPTER ELEVEN

1. Gaunt, William, *The Restless Century. Painting in Britain 1800-1900*, Oxford, 1978.
2. Maas, Jeremy, *Victorian Painting*, London, 1975, p.10.
3. Smith, Alison, *in* Townsend, Joyce et al., *Pre-Raphaelite Painting Techniques*, London, 2004, p.1.
4. Fleming, G.H.: *That Ne'er Shall Meet Again*, 1971, p. 145.
5. *The Times*, 6 December 1878, p. 3.
6. *Liverpool Mercury*, 3 August 1886. The other member from the O.W.S. was Carl Haag.
7. Poole, Adrian, *Shakespeare and the Victorians*, London, 2004, p.41.
8. Newall, Christopher, *Frederic Leighton 1830-1896*, exh. cat. London, 1996, p.74.
9. Silver, Carol, in *Holman Hunt and the Pre-Raphaelite Vision*, exh. cat. Ontario, 2008, p.16.
10. 77University of Oxford, Bodleian Library, MS Eng.c.7040, ff.166-7. The only Wallis paintings we are aware of that feature gondolas come from his *Merchant of Venice* series in 1881, such as *Portia and Nerissa on the Morning of the Trial* [Cat. 150] or *Shylock, Jessica and Launcelot* [Cat. 152].
11. G. Ackerman, op cit, p.129.
12. *The Athenaeum*, No. 3380, 6 August 1892, p. 200.
13. Van De Put, A., *Bolletino del museo di interzionale debt Ceramiche Faenza*, Vol.V, Issue. 2, 1917, p.3.
14. Wallis, H., *Persian Ceramic Art Belonging to F. DuCane Godman*, quoted in Gadoin, Isabelle, 'Henry Wallis the Pre-Raphaelite painter specialist in Islamic ceramics', pp. 77-97 in Gadoin, Isabelle et Palmier-Chatelain, Marie-Elise: *Rêver d'orient, connaître l'orient*, 2008.
15. These drawings are in pen and ink, approx. 7 3/4 in. in diameter, and were given by Harold Wallis in 1918. They are museum nos. E.497-1918 to E.513 -1918 and are located in the Prints & Drawings Study Room, level D, case C, shelf 133.
16. These drawings were given by Harold Wallis in 1917 and 1918. Museum nos. E.484-1918 and

E.485-1918 are in pen, touched with white, on paper and are approx. 2 ½ in. in height and 8 ¾ in. in width. They are designs for the frontispiece. Museum nos. E.1832-1917 to E.1865-1917 are all watercolours on paper, approx, 19 in. in height by 14 ½ in. in width. These drawings are located in Prints & Drawings Study Room, level D, case C, shelf 127 and level C, case WM, shelf 3, box B.
17. T. Wilson, op cit, p.244.
18. Ernest Chesneau (1833-1890) was a well-known French art critic. His book *The English School of Painting* (London, 1885) was the first comprehensive study made by a Frenchman, in which the Pre-Raphaelite movement was described and analyzed. Comparing the French artists to the Pre-Raphaelites, he stated (pp.197-8) that: "It may be that they succeed in gathering together the elements of truth in their infinity of detail, but the appearance of reality is always wanting to complete the faithfulness of their productions; they never arrive at a life-like harmonious ensemble. We sacrifice detail to general effect, and they neglect general effect for detail... Is it truth to represent a landscape without any atmosphere, and a body without projection? What does it signify that every smallest detail of that body is present if, when finished, it fails to convey the general appearance of life?"
19. University of Oxford, Bodleian Library, MS Eng.c. 7039, ff.35-36.
20. "Have you seen the post-impressionists at the Grafton's? Probably not, me neither, for I am fed up with what I have seen in the illustrated periodicals. Everybody talks about them, that's what these artists like." (University of Oxford, Bodleian Library, MS Eng.c;7040, f.32.)
21. Quoted in Reynolds, Simon, *William Blake Richmond. An Artist's Life*, 1995, p.310.

Part II - The Catalogue

Introduction

1. Redford, George, *Art Sales. A History of Sales of Pictures and Other Works of Art (1628-1887)*, 2 Vols., London, Agnew & Co., 1888.

Graves, Algernon, *The Royal Academy: dictionary of contributors, 1769-1904*, 8 Vols. Accessible on *archive.org*.

Graves, A., *The British Institution, 1806-1867*, London, George Bell & Sons, 1884; Bath, Kingsmead Reprints, 1969.

Graves, A., *Art Sales from early in the eighteenth century to early in the twentieth century*, New York, Burt Franklin, 1970, Vol. IV.

Graves, A., *A Century of Loan Exhibitions, 1813-1912*, London, A. Graves, 1914.

2. Redford's *Art Sales*, for instance, lists two works attributed to Wallis that are actually by H.B. Willis – *L. Wales* and *A Surrey Pastoral*.

Cat. 1: 1. Royal Academicians were elected as "Visitors" and served in rotation for nine months of the year. Each Visitor would attend for one month. They set the poses of models in the life school and instructed and judged the performances of the art students. This teaching system continued until the 1920s when Visitors were replaced by permanent instructors.

Cat 2: 1 . The Royal Academy of Arts cast measures 162 x 80 x 42 cm in size. Another cast is at the Ashmolean Museum in Oxford.

Cat. 3: 1. J. Renoir, op cit, p.95.

Cat. 5: 1. Nicholas A. Joukovsky: 'The Early Meredithian Milieu: New Evidence from Letters of Peter Augustin Daniel', *Studies in Philology*, Vol. XV, Summer 2018, pp. 615-641. Daniel's journal from 4 January 1856, for example, states: "Wallis, Terry, Martineau and a mr Machonchie a clerk at the Home Office were there and we smoked pipes and as usual discussed art, literature, and politics."

Cat. 7: 1. Nicholas A. Joukovsky: 'The Early Meredithian Milieu: New Evidence from Letters of Peter Augustin Daniel', *Studies in Philology*, Vol. XV, Summer 2018, pp. 615-641. Daniel describes their sketching tour in more detail in a letter of 3 August 1854; in the first week he mentions that they visited Winchester, Southampton, Salisbury, Stonehenge, and Shaftesbury. Later, they visited Netley Abbey, Stalbridge, Yeovil and Bristol, before Wallis set off alone to Chepstow and the Wye Valley.

Cat. 8: 1. R. Upstone, 2003, op cit, p. 62. *William Shakespeare a biography* by Charles Knight was published by C. Knight and Co., London, in 1843.

2. Fox, Levi, *In Honour of Shakespeare. The History and Collections of the Shakespeare Birthplace Trust*, Norwich, 1972, p.7.

3. A. Sanders, op cit, p.61.

Cat. 10: 1. *The Art Journal*, 1854, p.161.

2. Sotheby's, *Pictures from the Collection of Sir David and Lady Scott*, 2008, pp. 92-93.

3. Belfast businessman who had bought Hunt's *Two Gentlemen of Verona* as well as other Pre-Raphaelite works.

4. W.E. Fredeman, *Correspondence of Dante Gabriel Rossetti*, Vol I, p.350.

Cat. 11: 1. John Forster (1812-1876) was a noted biographer, critic, essayist, historian and Shakespeare scholar, probably best remembered for his biography of his close friend Charles Dickens. Forster was literary editor of the weekly *Examiner* from 1833 to 1847, and then its editor from 1847 to 1855. He bequeathed his collection of books and art to the V&A.

2. The exhibition catalogue (Edinburgh 1867, pp. 26-27) attributes the work to: W. Wallis [*sic*] and Sir Edwin Landseer.

3. Folger Shakespeare Library, Washington D.C., Y.c. 1459 (18). Letter dated 30 November 1892.

4. Dr Levi Fox, OBE, was Director of the *Shakespeare Birthplace Trust* from 1945 to 1989.

Cat. 11a: 1. James Fallows was a partner in the firm of Fallows and Keymer, Manufacturers and Calico Printers and Dyers, Manchester.

Cat. 14: 1. Personal communication, email to D.T.L. of 20 March 2017.

Cat 15: 1. University of Oxford, Bodleian Library, MS Eng.c.7049, ff. 3-4.

2. Personal communication to R. L., 4 May 2013.

Cat. 16: 1. A. Graves, *The British Institution*, p. 559; British Institution, Catalogue 1854, no. 512, London, 1854.

Cat. 18: 1. John Miller (1796-1876) was an important Liverpool collector and a member of the Hogarth Club. He owned many important early Pre-Raphaelite paintings, including J.E. Millais's *Autumn Leaves* and William Windus's *Too Late*.

2. Bennett, Mary, 'A Check-List of Pre-Raphaelite Pictures Exhibited at Liverpool 1846-67, and Some of Their Northern Collectors', *The Burlington Magazine*, Vol.105, no. 728, November 1963, p.491a.

Cat. 19: 1. In the acquisition file (Tate Britain), a note from the Conservation Department mentions a "J. Whatman watermark d. 1854".

2. Nicholas A. Joukovsky, personal communication to R. L.

Cat. 20: 1. Nicholas A. Joukovsky: "The Early Meredithian Milieu: New Evidence from Letters of Peter Augustin Daniel," *Studies in Philology*, Vol. XV, Summer 2018, pp. 615-641.

Cat. 21: 1. Thomas Miller (1811-1865) ran the Horrocks, Miller & Co. cotton textile manufacturing business in Preston. He is known to have been a keen art collector, particularly of Pre-Raphaelite and early Victorian oils and watercolours.

Cat. 22: 1. This is a quotation from Christopher Marlowe's 1604 version of *The Tragical History of the Life and Death of Doctor Faustus*.

2. Probably Samuel Withers (1841-1922), a manufacturer of safes and iron doors in West Bromich, West Midlands.

3. John Potts (d.1896) was from a wealthy coalmine owner's family from Wallsend, Newcastle. He was an art collector and may well have been the father of W.W. Sampson, the well-known art dealer, who was his executor.

4. Clement was a business partner with Temple Hillyard Hick Soanes, who owned Wallis's *The Stonebreaker*. Clement became a personal friend of Wallis and one of his principal patrons.

5. Chatterton has also been a source of inspiration for composers such as Ruggero Leoncavallo (*Chatterton*), the German composer Matthias Pintscher (his opera *Thomas Chatterton* was performed in 1998 at the Semper Opera House, Dresden) or the Australian composer Matthew Dewey (chamber opera *The Death of Chatterton*, 2007).

6. Horatio (Horace) Walpole, 4th Earl of Oxford (1717-1797); author of the first Gothic novel, *The Castle of Otranto*, and the youngest son of Prime Minister Sir Robert Walpole.

7. "An open chest contains torn-up samples of the poet's writings, and extracts from his contributions to the Middlesex Journal and other journals are scattered on the floor." (Banham, Joanna, *Beautiful and damned*, *TES* (Times Educational Supplement) Magazine, 4 June 2004, p.1.

8. Kaplan, Louise J., *The Family Romance of the Impostor-Poet Thomas Chatterton*, Berkeley, 1989, pp.222-3.

9. Thornbury, Walter, *Old & New London: a narrative of its history, its people and its places*, 5 Vols, London, 1873-78, Vol. I, pp.134-5; Vol. II, pp.545-7.

10. Groom, Nick, *Chatterton*, DNB, 2011, pp.235-242.

11. J. Banham, op cit, p. 2. The spandrels in the top corners of the painting gives it a religious dimension as well, suggestive of martyrdom.

12. Sanders, Andrew, *In the Olden Time. Victorians and the British Past*, New Haven and London, 2013, p.4.

13. Thomas Dixon sent William Michael Rossetti an alleged likeness of Chatterton, as we learn from a letter Rossetti wrote to Dixon of early January 1859: "I am very much obliged for your kindness in sending me the enclosed. The portrait of Chatterton (indeed, *any* portrait of him) is new to me, and most interesting; showing a very remarkable head indeed, full of fire and strangeness: and, as it happens, we were all here wishing to see a head of him, having lately been reading Masson's narrative of his life." (Peattie, Roger, [ed.], *Selected Letters of William Michael Rossetti*, Pennsylvania 1990, p.103. Whether or not it was Chatterton's portrait and by whom, we can not say.)

14. J. Banham, op cit, p.2. Meredith is known to have had brown, not the reddish-brown chestnut coloured hair of the model in the painting.

15. Robin Hamlyn, in *The Pre-Raphaelites*, Tate Gallery Publications, 1984, cat.75, p. 142. Hamlyn notes, however, "the evidence is such that this assumption must be questioned".

16. Nicholas A. Joukovsky: "The Early Meredithian Milieu: New Evidence form Letters of Peter Augustin Daniel," *Studies in Philology*, Vol. XV, Summer 2018, pp. 615-641. Wallis and Daniel shared rooms at Gray's Inn Square from Christmas 1854 until September 1855.

17. Bonhams, London, 5 March 2002, lot 6; estimate: £2,000-3,000, purchased by Neil Wilson of Campbell Wilson.

18. That is what the reviewer of the *Art Journal* claimed but no contemporary testimony confirms this. On October 18, 1857, however, the critic of *The Era* reported: "In the interior the crowd has been so great that it has been impossible to see the notable pictures, such as Wallis's 'Death of Chatterton', 'The Awakening Conscience.' [Holman Hunt] or Caracci's 'Three Marys', without a hard struggle, and a policeman has been placed inside the rails to make something like a stream, so that all could catch a glimpse." (p.9). See also: Pergam, E. A., 'Creating a furore: Annibale Caracci's "The Three Marie", Thomas Gainsborough's "Blue Boy"

and Henry Wallis's "Death of Chatterton" at the Manchester Art Treasures Exhibition', *Apollo. The International Magazine of the Arts*, June 2002, pp. 48-53. At the Manchester Art Treasures Exhibition of 1857 *Chatterton* was a huge success: "This huge exhibition, the biggest of its kind in the north, not only brought art to the people, but set the seal on collecting as a respectable and worthwhile activity. Art in the north, and especially at Manchester, was linked to civic pride, and also to the idea of social responsibility. The chairman of the exhibition was Sir Thomas Fairbairn (1823-91), a successful engineer; he was a noted patron of the Pre-Raphaelites, and especially of Holman Hunt. His main adviser was Augustus Egg, Frith's close friend and neighbour. The most popular picture in the exhibition was Henry Wallis's *Death of Chatterton.*" (C. Wood, op cit, p. 94). This should perhaps be qualified to say that it was the greatest attraction of the modern works of art on view.

19. 'Fine Arts: Royal Academy', *Athenaeum*, 10 May 1856, pp.589-590.
20. Cook & Wedderburn [eds.], *The Works of John Ruskin*, vol. XIV, London, 1904, p.60.
21. Dickens, who was a friend of his biographer John Forster, is likely referring to Wallis's *In Shakespeare's House, Stratford-upon-Avon*, now at the V&A Museum, painted in 1854, and bought by Forster. Dickens could also be referring to a pair of small watercolours of *Interior Scenes of Shakespeare's Birthplace, Stratford-upon-Avon*, probably painted in the same year.
22. Arthur Stone was the son of Dickens's friend the illustrator Frank Stone. In 1859, after Frank Stone's death, Dickens became a second father to Stone's sons, Arthur and Marcus, and helped them to advance their respective careers. Marcus Stone R.A. (1840-1921) became a well-known painter.
23. Storey, Graham & Tillotson, Kathleen [eds.], *The Letters of Charles Dickens*, Oxford, 1995, vol. 8, pp.109-111.
24. *The Examiner*, 31 May, 1856, p.5; *Morning Chronicle*, 8 August, 1856, p.5, both quoted in Pellerin, Denis & May, Brian, *The Poor Man's Picture Gallery*, p.25.
25. Wallis is known to have made at least two copies – now at the Birmingham Museum and at the Yale Center for British Art.
26. *The American Law Review*, Vol. IX, 1874-1875, p.240.
27 The *Copyright Act* was not voted in until 1862.
28. University of Oxford, Bodleian Library, MS Eng.c.7039, ff.14-15. The photographs to which Hunt refers were published by Colnaghi's in 1858 in a very expensive folio edition, *Gems from the Art Treasures Exhibition, Modern Series.* Although far from piracies, Hunt was concerned that if he allowed a photograph of one of his pictures to be published he would lose the right to a crucial form of income, royalties on any graphic reproduction after the work.

Cat. 22a: 1. Samuel Mendel (1811-1884) was a wealthy Manchester textile merchant and art collector.
2. Albert Grant (1831-1899), born Abraham Gottheimer, was a wealthy but unscrupulous company promoter who was also elected as a Conservative M.P. He was created a hereditary baron in 1868 by King Victor Emmanuel II of Italy.
3. William Vokins (1815-1895) was a leading London dealer and a noted judge of English watercolours.
4. William Kenrick was a wealthy industrialist who sat as Liberal M.P. for Birmingham from 1885 to 1899. He was closely connected to members of the Arts and Crafts Movement.
5. S. Wildman, [ed.], 1995, p. 156. Wallis was not the only Victorian artist to paint replicas of his successful paintings. It was a fairly common practice.

Cat. 22b: 1. Henry McConnel was the owner of McConnel & Co. of Manchester, cotton spinners, which in the mid-1830s was the largest private company in Britain. McConnel owned a mill in Cressbrook, Derbyshire, and he built his grand house Cressbrook Hall there in 1843. He assembled an important art collection.
2. Joseph Dixon not only had important Pre-Raphaelite pictures in his collection but also Persian and Hispano-Mauro faience pottery. His ceramic collection sold at Christie's on 16-17 March 1911.

Cat. 22e: 1. This is a quotation from Marlowe's *Dr Faustus.*
2. University of Oxford, Bodleian Library, MS Eng.c.7040, ff.200-201.

Cat. 22f: 1. Greenhill, Gillian B.: 'The Death of Chatterton, or Photography and the Law', *History of Photography*, vol. 5, no. 3, 1981, p.205. See also: *Manchester Times*, 27 July 1861, p. 4.
2. D. Johnson: op cit, p.92.
3. Art Institute of Chicago, mixed method engraving on ivory chine mounted on off-white plate paper, by Thomas Barlow.
4. D. Johnson, op cit, p.92.

Cat. 22g: 1. Likely William Kurtz (1833-1904), who was born in Germany and trained as an artist and lithographer but primarily worked in the United States as an engraver and photographer.
2. A typogravure is a half-tone relief photoengraving.

Cat. 24: 1. This was likely David Wilkie Wynfield (1837-1887), an artist and photographer and a prominent member of the St. John's Wood Clique.
2. www.answers.com/topic/andrew-marvell
3. Coleridge, H., *Lives of Northern Worthies*, London, 1852, vol. 1, pp. 88-89.
4. Cook & Wedderburn, *The Works of John Ruskin*, Vol. XIV, p 60.

Cat. 25: 1. Robert Platt (1802-1882) was a wealthy cotton manufacturer, art patron, and philanthropist. He later lived at "Woodlands", Mottram Road, Stalybridge, Cheshire.
2. Catherine Simpson (Collections Officer at the R.S.C.) points out that "the Sculptor depicted in the pictures is believed to be Gheerart Janssen, whose workshop was near the Globe Theatre in London. It is therefore very probable that Janssen knew Shakespeare. The figure in the centre may be whoever commissioned the bust for Holy Trinity Church. He is holding Shakespeare's death mask". (Personal communication to R.L., 15 July 2013)
3. Sir Francis Chantrey (1781-1841) was the foremost English portrait sculptor of the Regency period in Britain.
4. Letter dated 4 October 1910, collection of The Royal Shakespeare Company, Stratford-upon-Avon. Quoted in Martineau, Jane et al.: *Shakespeare in Art*, London-New York, 2003, p.214.
5. Ibid.
6. A. Sanders, op cit, p.57.
7. Rossetti, W.M., 'Sketchings: Exhibition of the Works of British Artists', *The Crayon*, Vol. 4, September 1857, p.280.

Cat. 25a: 1. Wright, Christopher, et al., *British and Irish paintings in public collections.* New Haven & London, 2006, p.796.

Cat. 26: 1. Robert Platt also owned the major version of *A Sculptor's Workshop, Stratford-upon-Avon, AD 1619*.
2. Nicholas A. Joukovsky: 'The Early Meredithian Milieu: New Evidence from Letters of Peter Augustin Daniel', *Studies in Philology*, Vol. XV, Summer 2018, pp. 615-641.
3. University of Oxford, Bodleian Library, MS Eng.c.7039, ff. 85-86.
4. Joukovsky, N: *The Letters of Thomas Love Peacock*, Vol. II, pp. 357-358.
5. Cook & Wedderburn, *The Works of John Ruskin*, Vol. XIV, p. 113.
6. See: Prettejohn, Elizabeth, *Modern Painters, Old Masters*, Yale University Press, 2017, Chaper 2, 'Artist and Mirror: Pre-Raphaelites and Others', pp. 58-97 for the importance of the Arnolfini Portrait on the Pre-Raphaelites.
7. Nicholas A. Joukovsky: 2018, and Thomas Love Peacock Letters, Vol.2: 1828-1866, 2001, pp.357-58 and 367-68.

Cat. 26a: 1. R. Kirkman Hodgson was the son of Kirkman Daniel Hodson J.P., M.P., who had made a fortune as an East Indian merchant and a banker. R.K. Hodgson also owned several other works by Wallis including as *A Despatch from Trebizond.* His sale at Christie's also included pictures by many artists associated with the Pre-Raphaelites including J.W. Inchbold, F. Leighton, R.B. Martineau, J.E. Millais, V. Prinsep, and D.G. Rossetti.

Cat. 27: 1. Nicholas A. Joukovsky: 'The Merediths and their circle in 1856: A letter from Peter Augustin Daniel to Henry Wallis', *Notes and Queries*, Nov. 3, 2011, p.2

Cat. 28: 1. Temple Hillyard Hicks Soanes was a banker and a merchant in the Russia trade. His wife, Alice, was painted by Frederick Sandys. His former residence, Hill House in Upminster, featured stained-glass windows by Morris & Co. after designs by Burne-Jones and Morris. He was in partnership with C.G. Clement, who also owned works by Wallis.
2. Charles Aitken (1869-1936) was the third keeper of the Tate Gallery (1911-1917) and its first Director (1917-1930).
3. M. Bennett, op cit, p.495a; Morris, E., & Roberts, E., *The Liverpool Academy...*, p.621.
4. Mike Hickox, personal communication to R. L.
5 D. Johnson, op cit, .p129; Cook and Wedderburn, op cit, Vol. XIV, p.170.
6. Staley, Allen, *The Pre-Raphaelite Landscape.* Oxford, 1973, pp.116-117.
7. Joukovsky, N., *New Correspondence ...*, p.518 and n.175.
8. Edward Lear's diary entry, 10 September 1858. Quoted in Barringer T, Rosenfeld J, and Smith A, 2012, p.142.
9. *The Royal Academy Review. A guide to the exhibition of the Royal Academy of Arts, 1858*, London, 1858, p. 30. J.N. Paton's *Bluidy Tryste* is in the Kelvingrove Art Museum, Glasgow.
10. Kauffmann, Michael, *100 Great Paintings in The Victoria & Albert Museum*, London, 1985, p.124.
11. Harding, Ellen, [Ed.], *Re-framing the Pre-Raphaelites*, Aldershot, 1996, p.107.
12. Curiously, the 1858 R.A. exhibition showed another *Stonebreaker* painted by John Brett (1830-1902), now at the Walker Art Gallery, Liverpool. Brett was also a member of the Pre-Raphaelite circle and Ruskin's *Modern Painters* had a profound effect on his painting.

Cat. 28b: 1. Diane Johnson papers, box 13.2, p. 38.

Cat. 29: 1. Robert Kirkman Hodgson J.P., D.L. (1850-1924) was the only son of Kirkman Daniel Hodgson, Governor of the Bank of England (1863-65).

Cat. 30: 1. Ernest Wythes (1868-1949) was the grandson of the wealthy railway magnate George Wythes. A nine-page article on his country seat, Copped Hall, appeared in *Country Life*, Vol. XXVIII, No. 722, 5 Nov. 1910.
2. James Gresham (1836-1914) was an inventor of improvements to steam locomotives and a prominent art collector who owned works by many leading Victorian artists, including L Alma-Tadema, F. M. Brown, W. Crane, W.P. Frith, W.H. Hunt, F. Leighton, J.E. Millais, A. Moore, E. Poynter and D.G. Rossetti. The sale of his collection took place over three days at Christie's in July 1917.
3. Wood, Lesley, 'The Sir Walter Raleigh "Tower portrait" of 1613', *British Art Journal*, Vol. XVI, No. 3, 2015, p.61. "It is well documented that initially he was allowed servants living in, and also his wife Bess and young Wat."
4. Isaac D'israeli (1766-1848) was an English writer whose best-known work was a collection of essays entitled *Curiosities of Literature*, which contained anecdotes about historical persons and events. In his book, D'israeli impugned Raleigh's claim that his *History of the World* was a work of his own hand, as the Elizabethan playwright Ben Jonson (1572-1637) had done earlier. His eldest son, Benjamin Disraeli, went on to become Prime Minister.

Cat. 31: 1. John Mitchell was a prominent Bradford

merchant who served as an alderman from 1856 to 1868.
2. Thomas Edward Plint (1823-61) was a Leeds stockbroker who formed an important collection of paintings particularly by Turner and the Pre-Raphaelites.
3. Mervyn Wingfield, 7th Viscount Powerscourt, (1836-1904), was an Irish Representative Peer from 1865 to 1885.
4. www.answers.com/topic/Henry-marten
5. University of Oxford, Bodleian Library, MS Eng.c.7039, ff 1-2. Forster was able to locate a portrait of Marten in the collection of a descendant of a Mr. Lewis, whose house Marten visited occasionally during his imprisonment.
6. Frederick Richard Pickersgill R.A. (1820-1900), *The Bribe*, 1857, collection of the Royal Academy of Arts, London.

Cat. 31a.: 1. We are grateful to Dr. John Rees, Visiting Research Fellow, Goldsmiths, University of London, for bringing the location of this engraving to our attention in an email to D.T.L., 9 May, 2017.
2. George H. Every (1837-1910) exhibited nine mezzotint engravings after works by popular artists at the Royal Academy, from 1864 until 1905.

Cat. 32: 1. Surtees, Virginia, *Rossetti's Portraits of Lizzie Siddal*, Scholar Press, 1991. See particularly: figs. 26, 27, 69 & 60.

Cat. 33: 1. Personal communication to R. L.
2. Personal communication to R. L. Joukovsky has written extensively on the Merediths and their circle.

Cat. 34: 1. Graves, A., *A Century…*, Vol. IV, p.1599. Three exhibitions were held at the South Kensington Museum between 1866 and 1868. The first exhibition (April 1866) showed portraits up to the Glorious Revolution; the second exhibited portraits up to 1800; and the third, portraits from 1800 onwards.
2. While Wallis may have felt this at the time, he must later have made a copy of this portrait when he decided to sell the original to the National Portrait Gallery in 1906. The copy is also mixed media, though is slightly smaller at 16 x 14 cm (6½ x 5½ in.). It has been handed down in the family. That he should want to retain a likeness of Peacock almost 50 years after he painted the initial version, shows the esteem in which Wallis held his former lover's father.

Cat. 35: 1. M. Bennett, op cit, p. 492a; E. Morris & E. Roberts, op cit, p. 621.

Cat. 38: 1. Dodwell was a physician practising in the Battersea area of London. He was the Assistant Resident Medical Officer, Hospital for Consumption, Brompton, in the 1890s.
2. *Manchester Times*, 15 March 1862, p.192.

Cat. 39: 1. W.E. Fredeman, *Correspondence of DGR*, Vol. III, pp. 303-04. In a letter from D.G. Rossetti to F.M. Brown he relates that many works either did not sell or went for well below their estimated value. "Gambart was here just now, and it seems things were desperate indeed at the Plint Sale. Brett's £420 *Chepstow Castle* fetched £20, Wallis's *Marston Moor* came down from £250 to £60, and Hughes *Belle Dame* from the same to £30." Ernest Gambart was a leading Victorian art dealer.
2. J.S. Virtue was a British publisher and proprietor of *The Art Journal*. He took over from his father George Virtue who had purchased *The Art Union* in 1848 and renamed it *The Art Journal* in 1849.
3. John Bibby III (1839-1898) of Hart Hill Lodge, Allerton, was the grandson of John Bibby (1775-1840), the shipping magnate and the founder of the Bibby Line.
4. The critic for Blackwood's, a very conservative periodical, was likely J.B. Atkinson.
5. The reviewer is referring to Robert Burns's famous poem 'John Anderson my Jo' written in 1789.

Cat. 39a: 1. Possibly James Thomas Knowles (1806-1884), a prominent architect. His son Sir James Knowles (1831-1908) was an English architect and later editor of *The Contemporary Review* and *The Nineteenth Century*. He was a prominent art collector so he is the more likely candidate to have bought this work.

Cat. 39b: 1. I am indebted to Judith Bronkhurst for this suggestion. See: Newall, Christopher and Egerton, Judy, *George Price Boyce*, Tate Gallery, 1987, colour plates 4 & 5.

Cat. 40: 1. The artist Henry Darvall (1829-1891) and Wallis were great friends. Originally a figure painter, Darvall became a scenic painter following his move to Venice in 1875.

Cat. 41: 1. M. Bennett, op cit, p. 495a; E. Morris & E. Roberts, op cit, p. 621.

Cat. 43: 1. www.britannica.com
2. Graves, *Art sales*...Vol. III, p.312.

Cat. 44: 1. Sir John Pender M.P. (1816-1896) was a cotton textile merchant but best known as the British pioneer of submarine telegraph communication. He amassed a large art collection.
2. Holbrook Gaskell (1813-1909) made his money initially manufacturing engines and machine tools and then later with a chemical manufacturing plant.
3. Alexander Henderson, 1st Baron Faringdon (1850-1934) owned an important art collection, including many works by J.W. Waterhouse as well as Burne-Jones's large *Briar Rose* series.
4. Souter, Keith, *The Classic Guide to King Arthur*, Newhaven, 2012, pp.56-57.
5. *Poems of Tennyson*. Oxford Edition, 1918, p. 578.

Cat. 44a: 1. J.W. Knight was a London barrister or stockbroker and an art collector.
2. James Gresham (1836-1914), Woodheys Park in Ashton-on-Mersey, was the founder of Gresham & Graven, which manufactured brake equipment for railway vehicles. He was considered a connoisseur of contemporary art.

Cat. 46: 1. Dumortier, Claire, *Céramique de la Renaissance à Anvers*, Bruxelles, 2002, pp. 121-2 and figs 49-52.

Cat. 47: 1. www.britannica.com

Cat. 48a.: 1. A heliotype print is a photomechanically produced plate for pictures made by exposing a gelatin film under a negative, hardening it with chrome alum, and printing in ink directly from it.

Cat. 50: 1. www.britannica.com

Cat. 51: 1. Fulke Greville (1554-1628), 1st Baron Brooke, was an English statesman during the reigns of Elizabeth I and James I, and was also a poet and playwright.
2. www.britannica.com
3. This letter is in a private collection, Crosskeys, South Wales.
4. The Exhibition of the Royal Academy, The Ninety-Second, 1860, p. 21. This line translated from Latin reads "Today a certain Paulus Veronensis [Paolo Veronese] began my portrait."

Cat. 52: 1. Lizzie Caswall Smith was a well-known early 20th-century photographer whose specialities included studio portraits of celebrities and society people.

Cat. 55: 1. Messrs. Fores, the firm of publishers and printsellers, was first established by Samuel William Fores (1761-1838) in 1783. After his death, his sons George Thomas Fores (1806-1858) and Arthur Blucher Fores (1814-1883) continued the business.

Cat. 57: 1. Likely either Peter Graham R.A. (1836-1921) or Thomas Alexander Graham H.R.S.A. (1840-1906), two Scottish painters who regularly exhibited at the Royal Academy and elsewhere.

Cat. 60: 1. The *Catalogue of the International Exhibition – Dublin & Belfast*, 1907, printed by MacCaw, Stevenson & Orr, makes no mention of this work, however.
2. Eyre Crowe papers, 1555. Garthewin Additional Collection, University of Wales, Bangor. Crowe's *Martin Luther Nailing his Theses to the Doors of Wittenberg* is now in the Museum & Gallery at Bob Jones University, Greenvile, South Carolina, U.S.A.

Cat. 62: 1. Charles Gent Clement (1825-1899) was a wealthy merchant and art collector. He bequeathed *The Death of Chatterton* to the Tate Gallery. His business partner Temple Hillyard Hick Soanes owned Wallis's other masterpiece, *The Stonebreaker*.

Cat. 63: 1. V. Surtees, op cit, p. 48. Wallis had lodgings at no.1, Westminster Chambers at this time.

Cat. 68: 1. Wallis, Henry: XVII Plates by Nicola Fontana da Urbino at the Correr Museum Venice: A Study in Early XVIth century Maiolica, 1905, Fig. 16. The drawing is in the collection of the Victoria and Albert Museum, museum no. E502-1918.

Cat. 69: 1. Macleod, Dianne Sachko: *Art and the Victorian middle class*, 1996, pp. 162-163. Lewis Pocock (1801-1882) was a co-founder and the honorary secretary of the Art Union of London, treasurer of the Graphic Society, and secretary of the Old Water-Colour Society. He played an important role in promoting the reputation of the Pre-Raphaelites on the London art scene and owned works by them, including several by Wallis.
2. Exhibited at the Royal Academy in 1869.
3. Painted in 1863 and illustrated in *The Graphic* on 25 December 1869.
4. Exhibited at the Royal Academy in 1874.

Cat. 70: 1. Emails to D.T.L. from Alexandra Palmer on 5 September 2014 and Kimberly Wahl on 11 September 2014 .
2. Lanigan, Dennis: *Beauty's Awakening*, National Gallery of Canada, 2015, cat. no. 72.

Cat. 72: 1. Johnson, D, 1972, illus. 12, following p.110 (source: Wallis family)

Cat. 73: 1. Diane Johnson papers, box 13.2, p.83. Wallis could have seen Titian's *Venus and Adonis* during one of his trips to Madrid and certainly would have known the copy by the workshop of Titian at the National Gallery in London, purchased in 1824. According to Johnson, Wallis owned a fragment of a work attributed to Titian.

Cat. 76: 1. Wright, Christopher, et al., *British and Irish paintings in public collections*. New Haven & London, Yale University Press, 2006, p.796.
2. *The Athenaeum*, no. 2177, 17 July 1869, p.89. Views of Capri are mentioned amongst the drawings exhibited at Colnaghi's, as well as three views of Dartmoor, and a large picture of a wood in Surrey.

Cat. 77: 1. *Leighton, Garden of an Inn, Capri*, exh. cat. Royal Academy of Arts, 1996, p.116.

Cat. 80: 1. The baiocco and paolo were coins in the currency of the Papal States of Rome.
2. University of Oxford, Bodleian Library, MS Eng.c.7040, f.189. It is not known whether they were successful in buying the painting.

Cat. 81: 1. *London Daily News*, 19 December 1870, p.2.

Cat. 83: 1. L. Roberts & S. Wildman, op cit, 1997, p.15.
2. University of Oxford, Bodleian Library, MS Eng.d.3552.

Cat. 86: 1. Jessie Petheram, Museum Collections Officer, The Shakespeare Birthplace Trust, personal communication, email to D.T.L. dated 16 June, 2016.

Cat. 88: 1. Marianne Hunt's plaster bust of Shelley is now at Eton College. The bust, which was given to Browning by Thomas Carlyle, was originally intended for Shelley's grave but was rejected by the family as too unflattering. The bust is reproduced (Pl. 26) in Michael Meredith's *Meeting the Brownings*. [Fredeman, *Corr. of DGR*, 5:45] Rossetti's letter is published in W.E. Fredeman, *Correspondence of Dante Gabriel Rossetti*, 5: 45.
2. Letter of 9 April, 1871 from Browning to Rossetti (Add ms 38794, I).
3. James Henry Leigh Hunt's book, *Lord Byron and Some of his Contemporaries; with recollections of the author's life, and of his visit to Italy* (Henry Colburn, 1828), published first as a single volume and then as 2. It was also published in 3 volumes in Paris (A. & W. Galignani, 1828).
4. Shelley, P.B. *Poetical Works*, Routledges Excelsior Series. London. n.d. The book is inscribed by Wallis "Bought at Smyrna." Ant. Leisman was John Anthony Leisman a 17th-century German painter. Wallis wrote that he copied this portrait from the outline engraving in the Florentine Gallery volume of portraits of painters. Wallis inscribed on the

drawing that "T.L. Peacock stated this must be the best portrait of Shelley he knew of." The drawing is currently in the collection of Diane Johnson, Paris.

5. Shelley was amongst the "List of Immortals" drawn up by the Pre-Raphaelite Brotherhood of the men they particularly admired.

Cat. 89: 1. Joseph Dixon not only collected Pre-Raphaelite art but also pottery. After his death, the sale of his collection of Rhodian, Damascene, Persian and Hispano-Mauro faience was held at Christie's on 16-17 March 191. In view of his interests, it is likely he knew Wallis personally.

Cat. 90: 1. A landscape rendered in charcoal.

Cat. 97: 1. James Sprent Virtue ((1829-92) was the son and business successor of George Virtue (1793-1868), who had founded Virtue & Co., a publishing firm, and was also the publisher of *The Art Journal.*

2. A thyrsus was a staff or spear topped with an ornament like a pine cone carried by Dionysus and his revellers in ancient Greece or Rome.

Cat. 97b: 1. Pisistratus, or Peisistratus, was a 6th century BC ruler of ancient Athens, who did much to promote the arts.

Cat. 99a: 1. *L'Art*, Vol. II, 1875, p.214, in the article by Yriarte, Charles: 'Exhibition of the Royal Academy of Arts', pp.212-216. A. Gilbert was likely the French printmaker Achille-Isidore Gilbert (1828-1899).

Cat. 101: 1. Antoinette Sterling (1850-1904) was a famous Anglo-American vocalist who, in 1875, married the Scottish-American John Mackinlay.

2. *Art Journal*, quoted in Hartnoll & Eyre, catalogue 17, 1971.

Cat. 102: 1. *The Illustrated London News*, 29 June 1872, p.631.

Cat. 103: 1. British Museum, *Department Prehistory and Europe.*

2. *The Athenaeum*, No. 2177, 17 July 1869, p.89. The exhibition also included a drawing of a view of Capri ("a noteworthy specimen of the artist's ability") and a large picture of a wood in Surrey.

Cat. 105: 1. John Wardell (1824-1878) was best known for his collection of Old Masters, which were sold after his death at Christie's on 10 May 1879. He also collected contemporary art.

2. B. Crespon-Halotier, op.cit.

Cat. 106: 1. J.A. Bindley was the owner of Bindley & Co. Brewery, an inventor and a Fellow of the Royal Geographic Society. He was also an officer in the Rifle Volunteers of the Auxillary Forces of the British Army.

2. H.B. Norton was a former officer in the British Army who later became operations manager for the police department in Bournemouth as well as a magistrate and councillor.

Cat. 107: 1. William Henry Hunt (1790-1864), *New Court, the Temple, London*, watercolour, William Smith Bequest, V&A Museum no.:3022-1876.

2. The identity of the "literary labourer in Serjeant's Inn" is unknown. W.S. Gilbert, the well-known dramatist, librettist and poet, had a brief career as a barrister in the Inner Temple, so he is a possible candidate.

Cat. 108: 1. D.N. Mancoff, op cit, vol. 2, p.91. Mrs. Bancroft's production of Shakespeare's *The Merchant of Venice* was first performed at the Prince of Wales Theatre, London, on 17 April 1875, with Ellen Terry as 'Portia'.

2. London, National Art Library, MSL/1995/14/123/1.

Cat. 109: 1. Possibly either of the London art dealers Morris, Hy. & Co., or J. Morris.

Cat. 110: 1. A. Graves, *The Royal Academy...*, Vol. VIII, p.116.

Cat. 111: 1. Petit Larousse 1991, p.1130.

Cat. 112a: 1. Moritz Klinkicht was born in Germany in 1845. He settled in London from 1868-1883 and continued to work for London periodicals even after he moved back to Freiburg in 1883.

2. *L'Art*, vol. X, 1877, p. 44, in the article by J. Comyns Carr: 'La saison d'art à Londres', V. La Royal Academy, III, pp.38-44.

Cat. 117: 1. When Alice Boyd died in 1897, she bequeathed Penkill to the descendants of her half-brother Henry Courtney, the child of her mother's second marriage. For the next 75 years, the castle was the home of his spinster daughters, during which time Penkill Castle was left to deteriorate. In 1978, Dr Elton August Eckstrand, an American lawyer and passionate admirer of Pre-Raphaelite art and philosophy, bought the castle complete with contents. Although he initially worked to ensure Penkill's preservation, he later sold off the castle and its contents in 1992.

Cat. 118: 1. B. Crespon-Halotier, op.cit.

Cat. 121: 1. John Frederick Lewis (1804-1876) was the most important of the British Orientalist painters.

Cat. 122: 1. Professor William Unger (1837-1932) was important not merely as an etcher but also as an influential teacher and scholar; he was professor of Graphic Arts at the Vienna Academy.

Cat. 123: 1. The 'Suisse' was a church layperson who could usher, keep order, and assist in religious ceremonies.

Cat. 129: 1. Léon Augustin Lhermitte (1844-1925) was a French realist painter who worked in oils, pastel and charcoal and favoured rural scenes depicting peasant workers.

Cat. 130: 1. A 'Hofje' is a Dutch almshouse built around a courtyard. The Hofje van Codde en Beresteyn (Haarlem) originally provided housing for poor elderly Catholic women. During the 19th century, the families of van Codde and van Beresteyn sold paintings to fund rebuilding. One of the Frans Hals paintings was sold to Mathilde Rothschild in 1882.

2. Letter in University of Oxford, Bodleian Library, MSS Don.e.79, ff.17-18.

3. The portrait of the painter Claes van Berestyn is by Hals. The portrait of Beresteyn's third wife Catharina Both van der Eem has been variously attributed to Hals and the Haarlem painter Pieter Soutman. The group portrait of the couple and their children is now attributed to Soutman.

Cat. 131: 1. A Dutch married woman.

Cat. 132: 1. MS: University of Oxford, Bodleian Library, MS Eng.c.7039, ff.77-78. In 1871, during his third Italian journey, Burne-Jones was "lastingly impressed by Luca Signorelli's extraordinary frescoes in the Chapel of San Brizio in Orvieto Cathedral, carried out from 1499 to 1502. At the dramatic centre of the cycle are the scenes from the Apocalypse, Signorelli's brilliantly inventive, ribald, erotic and frightening account of the end of the world." (MacCarthy, F.: *The Last Pre-Raphaelite*, p. 229). Since Wallis's friendship with the second-phase Pre-Raphaelites was at its height in the second half of the 1870s and the beginning of the 1880s, it seems judicious to date the present letter between 1875 and 1880. It is not impossible, however, that the letter dates from 1893-4, when Wallis had been to Berlin and where he admired Signorelli's *Pan*, of which he made the present copy.

2. William Morris, Edward Poynter, Philip Webb, Sidney Colvin, and George Howard. The prominent art historian Sidney Colvin had entered the Pre-Raphaelite circle in 1868, introduced by Burne-Jones.

3. Herbert Horne, *The Century Guild Hobby Horse*, Vol. III, 1888, pp.36-38. Burne-Jones is almost certainly referring to the wood-cut illustrations in the Florentine edition of 1508 to the *Il Quadriregio*, a poem by Federico Frezzi, composed in the early part of the 15th century. Some of the wood-cuts bear the initials "LV". Charles Fairfax Murray initially attributed them to Luca Signorelli, although later both he and Sidney Colvin were inclined to "think the whole matter undecidable." The initials "LV" were thought to relate to Signorelli's real name Luca Egidio di Venturi but it appears that he never signed "LV" and his usual signature was "LC", for Luca di Cortona. Regardless, the illustrations would have greatly appealed to Burne-Jones.

4. *The Athenaeum*, No. 2615, 8 December, 1877, p.741.

Cat. 133: 1. Melozzo da Forli's fresco depicting the Ascension of Christ in the Santi Apostoli apse in Rome, painted *c.*1480. In 1711, during restoration work on the church, the fresco was removed and broken into 16 pieces, which are now housed variously at the Quirinal Palace (fragment with the figure of Christ), the sacristy of Peter's, the Prado and the Vatican Pinacoteca, which displays 14 fragments depicting the Apostles and Angels playing instruments such as a tambourine, a viola, and a lute. The *Santi Apostoli* apse can be seen as the forerunner of certain features of Michelangelo's Sistine Chapel ceiling, of Raphael's Chigi Chapel in Santa Maria del Popolo, of Corregio's cupola in Parma Cathedral, and of Pordenone's works in Treviso and Piacenza. (www.museivaticana.va; N. Clark, op cit, p.69.)

2. University of Oxford, Bodleian library, Eng.c.7051/1, f.15. The book was Ricci, C., *Melozzo da Forlì*, Rome, 1911.

3. The church in Forlì was San Girolamo. (*The Architect*, 24 April 1880, p.293 and 22 May 1880, p.360).

4. Quoted in T. Wilson, op cit, p.251a. The letter was written on St Mark's Venice Committee letterheaded paper.

Cat. 136: 1. The first version of Burne-Jones's *Chant d'Amour* was in watercolour and dates to 1865 and was shown at the Old Water-Colour Society exhibition of 1866. The later oil version dates to 1868-77 and was exhibited at the Grosvenor Gallery in 1878.

Cat. 137: 1. Pieter de Hoogh (1629-1684), also spelled de Hooch or de Hooghe, was one of the most important genre painters during the so-called "Dutch Golden Age" and a contemporary of Jan Vermeer.

Cat. 138: 1. Sir James Dromgole Linton (1840-1916) was a well-known English painter. He served as president of the Royal Institute of Painters in Water Colours from 1884-1899 and from 1909-1916.

Cat. 141: 1. Gabriël Metsu (1629-1667) was a Dutch 17th-century realist artist who produced some of the greatest genre paintings of the period.

2. A 'churchwarden' is a slender pipe with a particularly long stem.

Cat. 143: 1. Smyrna was a city located in present-day Turkey on the Aegean coast of Anatolia. Initially, it was controlled by the ancient Greeks and then later by the Romans.

Cat. 145: 1. Charles Douglas Richard Hanbury-Tracy (1840-1922), 4th Baron Sudeley, was a Liberal politician and a Fellow of the Royal Society.

2. Possibly the London art dealer C.T. Manvell.

Cat. 152: 1. Giovanni Bellini (1430-1516) and Bernardino di Betto, aka Pinturicchio (1454-1513), were both well-known Italian Renaissance painters.

Cat. 152a: 1. Three drawings in brown ink that depicted scenes from *The Merchant of Venice*, including this particular drawing, formed lot 174. Two were 11 x 21 in and one was 18 1/2 x 13 in. The dimensions given in the Sotheby's catalogue, however, do not appear to match with the size of the drawings at the National Gallery of Canada or the Wichita Art Museum.

Cat. 160: 1. Henry James Veitch (1840-1924) was a member of the Council of the Royal Horticultural Society, and one of the best-known horticulturalists in Britain, for which reason he was knighted by King Edward VII.

Cat. 162: 1. There are two fountains by, or at least attributed to, Donatello. The first fountain, the basin of which is now lost, was carved of granite and decorated with marble ornaments, and crowned by Donatello's bronze statue of Judith and Holofernes. It was originally in the Medici Palace in Florence before being seized by the state in 1495 and the statue transferred to the Palazzo Vecchio. The second one was in the Villa di Castello, the country residence of Cosimo I de' Medici near Florence.

Cat. 167a: 1. Munro-Faure, Alice, in 'Bonhams, New Bond Street', *Fine British & Continental Watercolours* *and Drawings*, 5 March, 2002, p.25.

2. N. Joukovsky, *New Correspondence...*, pp.512-513.

Cat. 173: 1. Samuel John Hodson (1836-1908) was a landscape and architectural painter. He was elected an associate of the Society of Painters in Water-Colours in 1882 and a full member in 1890.

Cat. 175: 1. *Savoir* [knowledge] was written *sçavoir* in the 18th century and Wallis has obviously taken the original title of the play, The Philosopher without Knowledge.

2. A terracotta bust of Denis Diderot by the French sculptor Jean-Antoine Houdon (1741-1828) was shown at the Salon of 1771. It is currently in the Louvre. A marble version, now at the Metropolitan Museum in New York, was exhibited at the Salon in 1773.

3. Jean Louis Ernest Meissonier's painting, *A Reading at Diderot's*, was exhibited at the Salon in Paris in 1857.

Cat. 177: 1. John Frederick Lewis R.A. (1804-1876) was the most famous of the British Orientalist painters. He served as President of the Society of Painters in Water-Colours from 1855 until 1858, when he resigned to concentrate on painting in oils.

Cat. 178: 1. John Godden & Co. owned extensive phosphate deposits on the Caribbean island of Klein Curaçao, West Indies, which were mined and shipped to Europe for use in fertiliser.

2. Henry Stacy Marks R.A. (1829-1898) was a well-known Victorian painter and illustrator and a founding member of the St. John's Wood Clique.

Cat. 179: 1. Personal communication to R. L. August 20, 2015.

Cat. 180: 1. J.P. Heseltine (1843-1929) was a stockbroker by profession, an art collector, and an accomplished amateur etcher. He was a trustee of the National Gallery, London, from 1893.

2. Likely one of the London dealers Bowden Bros. or G.W. Bowden.

3. This is being compared to F. Powell's watercolour *The World's Highway* (no. 8). Francis Powell R.W.S., P.R.S.W. (1833-1914) was a well-known and distinguished Victorian watercolour painter.

4. Carl Haag (1820-1915) was born in Bavaria but moved to England in 1847. He was a member of the R.W.S. and specialised in Middle Eastern subjects.

Cat. 184: 1. Charles Robertson A.R.W.S. (1844-1891) was a landscape and genre painter, frequently of Orientalist subjects.

Cat. 185: 1. University of Oxford, Bodleian Library, MS Eng.c.7049, f.11.

Cat. 186: 1. Augustus Mordan (1821-1901) was a partner in S. Mordan & Co., London, founded by his father, which manufactured writing and stationery related goods. He retired in 1884.

Cat. 187: 1. University of Oxford, Bodleian Library, Don.e.79, f.32.

Cat. 189: 1. University of Oxford, Bodleian Library, Don.e.79, f.91.

Cat. 190: 1. A watercolour heightened with bodycolour, entitled *A Mosque in Cairo*, sold at Sotheby's Belgravia on 6 May 1975, lot 7, 30 x 23.5 cm (11 3/4 x 9 1/4 in.), along with a pencil sketch for the same work. This might possibly be this watercolour, but is more likely to be a different composition.

Cat. 192: 1. University of Oxford, Bodleian Library, MSS Don.e.79, f. 91.

2. Seddon, John Paul (Ed.): *Memoirs and Letters of the Late Thomas Seddon, artist*, James Nisbet & Co., London, 1858, p.45.

Cat. 194: 'Doraks' and 'Kullehs' were types of earthenware water pots used in 19th-century Egypt.

Cat. 196: 1. The poem 'The Sick King in Bokhara' was composed in 1847-48 and was included in Arnold's first volume of poems *The Strayed Reveller and other Poems* that dates to 1849.

Cat. 198: 1. Wallis, Henry, *The Godman collection. Persian ceramic art in the collection of Mr. F. DuCane Godman, F.R.S. The thirteenth century lustred vases.* London, priv. circulation, 1891. We have been unable to ascertain exactly which vase this represents in Wallis's publication since none match this description.

Cat. 199: 1. A.W. Cox obviously had a longstanding interest in art. He won a £75 prize from the Art Union of London in 1876 but that time selected a landscape from the S.B.A. exhibition by an obscure artist H. Stokes as his prize.

2 . University of Oxford, Bodleian Library, Don.e.79, ff.92-93.

Cats. 204-211: 1. The Roman numerals 'xiii' are taken directly from F.G. Stephens' review (*The* Athenaeum) and refers to the 13th century.

2. Wallis, Henry, *Persian Ceramic Art in the Collection of Mr. F. Ducane Godman, F.R.S. - The Thirteenth Century Lustred Vases*, printed for private circulation, 1891.

3. *The Athenaeum*, No. 3380, 6 August 1892, p.200.

Cat. 213:

1. The Arthuse is a natural fountain on the island of Ortygia in Syracuse, Sicily. This freshwater spring, famous since ancient times, flows directly into the sea. In the Greek myth, the nymph Arethusa was transformed into a spring by the goddess Artemis in order to escape the unwanted sexual advances of the river god Alpheios. The appearance of the fountain has changed a number of times over the centuries. In 1540 the Spanish reduced the size of the lake created by the spring to the much smaller semicircular pool present today.

Cat. 217: 1. Victoria & Albert Museum, *Notebook MSL/1939/1949* – these two studies date to December 1892.

Cat. 218: 1. University of Oxford, Bodleian Library, MS Eng.c.7049, ff.111-2. The 'Gallery' refers to the Old Water-Colour Society.

Cat. 221: 1. Joseph Soustiel (1904-1990) was a Paris dealer and connoisseur of Islamic art. His collection of Archéologie - Art Islamique sold at Christie's, Paris, on May 6, 2015.

Cat. 224: 1. The Egypt Exploration Fund – later Society – began its activities in 1882. The Fund sent Professor Naville and the Count d'Hulst to the site of Deir-el-Bahari, where they remained active between 1893 and 1896. See: T.G.H. James, op cit, pp.51-70.

2. University of Oxford, Bodleian Library, MS Eng.c.7050, ff. 8-9.

3. University of Oxford, Bodleian Library, MS Don.e.79, f.119.

Cat. 224a: 1. The catalogue note from the Bonhams sale of 5 March, 2002 states: "Sir William Matthew Flinders Petrie (1853-1942) was an Egyptologist of great note and in the late nineteenth and early twentieth centuries, when the sciences of Egyptology and archaeology were still in their infancy, he contributed very important methodologies to these fields. While other archaeologists were only saving whole pots or whole mummies, Petrie was the first to dig systematically and to pay attention to even minute details. His close attention to pottery led him to develop the technique of sequence dating for Egyptian pottery. His main contribution to Egyptology was the information he gathered about the Predynastic period, which then was little-known. He later became Edwards Professor of Egyptology at University College, London."

2. M. Drower, op cit, p. 219. The Wallis Papers at the Bodleian Library contain several letters mentioning Petrie, for example: MS Don.e.79, fol. 106, letter to F.G. Stephens, dated 25 Jan 1894: "I did not go further up than Luxor & when there went for a few days to see Flinders Petrie." MS Eng.c.7050, fol.2, letter to his son Harold, from Cairo, dated 4 December 1895: "Petrie has come & will soon start for his winter's diggings."; British Museum, Dept Prehistory & Europe, to A. W. Franks, 18 December 1895: "Petrie is at work here (I write from Luxor)."

Cat. 225: 1. The temple of Queen Hatshepsut of the XVIII Dynasty was built in a valley beneath the bay of cliffs known as Deir el-Bahri, near the Valley of the Kings. The temple was known as Djeser-djeseru in ancient times, meaning the 'sacred of sacreds'. Hatshepsut's temple surpassed anything which had been built previously, both in its architectural style and in its beautifully carved coloured reliefs.

Cat. 226: 1. *Pictures from Greek vases, the white Athenian lekythi: a series of twelve polychrome plates representing the paintings on typical examples of the white Athenian lekythi*, London, J.M. Dent, 1896.

Cat. 227: 1. M. & N. Hanhart was a London lithographic publishing firm best known for its chromolithographs.

Cat. 229: 1. Iznik pottery originated in Turkey and is named after the town in western Anatolia, where it was produced from the last quarter of the 15th century until the end of the 17th century. It was during the 16th century that additional colours were added, including pastel shades of sage green and pale purple.

2. British Museum, Department Prehistory & Europe. Partly published in Wilson, op cit, p.237a.

Cat. 230: 1. Some of the later pottery from the 17th century that is sometimes labelled as 'Iznik' was actually manufactured in Kütahya, a town close to Iznik. Although ceramics were made there from the 15th century onwards, production in this centre peaked when Iznik declined.

Cat. 231: 1. The letters HIS are the first three letters of *Ihsus*, the name of Jesus in Greek, although these letters are sometime misinterpreted as being an abbreviation of the Latin phrase "Jesus Hominum Salvator", meaning Jesus Saviour of mankind. The letters in these plates appear to be just variations in orthography.

Cat. 232: 1. We are grateful to Professor Timothy Wilson for contacting Dr. Leprince on our behalf.

Cat. 236: 1. J.W. Knight (b.1823/24) was a London stockbroker and art collector.

2. Likely the art dealers, Leggatt Brothers, London.

Cat. 237: 1. Bucknall must have been a man of considerable wealth and social standing to own a home in this fashionable area of South Kensington. He lent a work by Ernest Waterlow to the *Franco-British Exhibition* of 1908 and owned several works by Wallis.

2. Alexandre-Gabriel Decamps (1803-1860) was a French artist who was one of the founders of Orientalism in painting. He was known for his striking contrasts of colour and light and shade in his work.

Cat. 238: 1. Although the *Lyle Official Arts Review* lists this work selling at Christie's in 1979 the auction actually took place on 29 September, 1978.

Cat. 239: 1. Likely the London dealers Bowden Brothers or G.W. Bowden.

Cat. 244: 1. Ben Mahmoud, op cit, p103.

Cat. 246: 1. Trajan's kiosk on the island of Philae, which the local Egyptian populace referred to as 'Pharaoh's Bed', was first called a 'hypaethral', or roofless temple, by the British artist David Roberts. In actuality, the temple was originally covered by a wooden roof. The temple was constructed by the Roman Emperor Trajan and had served as a place of worship for ceremonies honouring the goddess Isis.

2. E.A.W. Budge, op cit p. 102.

3. University of Oxford, Bodleian Library, Don.e.79, ff.159-160.

Cat. 247: 1. University of Oxford, Bodleian Library, MS Eng.c.7049, f.95.

Cat. 248: 1. The former capital of Upper Egypt, Girgeh (George) had derived its name from a Roman Catholic monastery dedicated to St. George, the patron saint of Egyptian Christians, and was the oldest of four such ancient establishments in the country. In Victorian times a large proportion of the population was Coptic Christian, who could be distinguished from their Muslim neighbours by their black turbans and kaftans. (Murray, John: *A Handbook for Travellers in Lower and Upper Egypt*, 1880, Part 1, p. 433.)

2. University of Oxford, Bodleian Library, MS

Eng.c.7050, f.56.

Cat. 249: 1. Wallis, Henry: 'Ancient Cairo houses', *Art Journal*, 1888, pp.144-49, quoted in Wilson: op cit, p.140a.

Cat. 251: 1. See: Victoria and Albert Museum, *Review of the Principal Acquisitions of the Year*, 1920, Plate 7, p.20. Wallis discussed this vase in *The Oriental influence on the ceramic art of the Italian Renaissance*, 1900, fig. 20. It was exhibited on loan at the V&A, 1908-11 (No. 226) and 1917 till date of purchase (No.10), also in the *Exhibition of the Faïence of Persia and the Nearer East* at the Burlington Fine Arts Club, London, 1908, see: Catalogue p.2 (A.No.3).

2. Bonhams, London, 5 March 2002, lot 70 included two Tslin, one decorated with trigrams from the Book of Changes, one robins-egg glazed vase; a powder blue water pot, Qianlong four-character mark and a pale-celadon water pot, Qianlong six-character mark in Zhuanshu script, and various others.

Cat. 257: 1. Simeon Solomon is known to have made caricatures of Jane Morris but these would not have been drawn from life.

2. Kelvin, Norman [ed.]: *The Collected Letters of William Morris*, Vol. I 1848-1880, pp. 216-217, letter dated 9 March, 1874.

Cat. 264: 1. Likely J.A.C. Nicoll. Dr. James Nicholl was a well-known collector of both art and porcelain in the 1920s. He was medical superintendent of the Fountain Hospital in Tooting and died in 1959.

Cat. 266: 1. MS: Oxford, Bodleian Library, MS Eng.c. 7039, f.91.

2. Mackail, J.W.: *The Life of William Morris*, 1907, p.120. "Therefore Morris set to work to make designs for an ancient kind of helmet called a basinet, and for a great surcoat of ringed mail with a hood of mail and the skirt coming below the knee."

Cat. 267: 1. Postle, Martin, 'Flayed for art. The écorché figure in the English art academy', *British Art Journal*, Vol. V, No. 1, 2004, pp.55-63.

2. Van Gogh's drawing and an example of the cast is now in the collection of the Van Gogh Museum in Amsterdam. The cast is invoice number v35V1978, artist unknown, dimensions 13 x 22 cm. This is similar to the size of the sculpture portrayed in Wallis's painting *A Sculptor's Workshop*.

3. Douglas Schoenherr, email to D.T.L., dated 23 July 2015.

Cat. 268: 1. Raphael later used this same sketch as the basis for his early masterpiece *Lady with a Unicorn*, which is supposedly a portrait of Maddalena Strozzi.

2. See: http://monalisa.org/2012/09/10/the-raphael-sketch/

Cats. 269-280: 1. Carmen Íñiguez of Isbilya Subastas auction house, email to D.T.L. of 11 July 2016.

Cats. 321-369: 1. Bernard Rackham (1876-1964) was an English writer and lecturer on ceramics and stained glass, who spent his career as a curator at the Victoria and Albert Museum, starting there in 1898. He was known for his pioneering research on Italian maiolica, so probably knew Wallis personally and admired him.

Cat. 375: 1. I am grateful to Dr. Sonia Delre, National Gallery of Canada, Ottawa, and Dr. Stacey Sell, National Gallery of Art, Washington, for their insights into this drawing in emails dated 29 September 2017.

Appendix I - London Exhibitions

1. Deborah Cherry, 'The Hogarth Club: 1858-1861', *The Burlington Magazine*, Vol. 122, 1980, p.242. Cherry mentions Wallis exhibited a work this year but gives no title. In an email from Cherry to D.T.L. of 30 June 2016 she states that she does not know which specific work Wallis showed. *Back from Marston Moor* is likely but not the only possibility.

Appendix II - Letters

1. Unfortunately, some of these documents have since disappeared.

2. Johnson does not give any names; it is assumed that she is referring to Mrs. Vera G. Whiting, of Purley, Surrey.

3. Wallis once gave William Michael Rossetti a lock of the poet's hair, but WMR unfortunately lost it. In the Wallis estate, only a lock of Mary Ellen's hair had been preserved; it was recently sold at an auction at Bonhams in London and purchased by private collector, New York.

4. Johnson was instrumental in helping the Wallis heirs to sell drawings and paintings through Christie's (13 March 1973) and Sotheby's (10 April 1973). In a letter dated April 1973 addressed to Martin Butlin (Tate), she explained: 'I thought you might be interested in the fate of the rest of the stuff – being sold at Christie's, mostly, and so far the Whitings have gotten about £20,000! And that's without the various old paintings you saw, or some good prints, which are in forthcoming sales. Not too bad. The ingenious Christie fellows, by the way, dug around and found that one of those frames of "Beardsleys" *was* by Beardsley. A pleasant £1,300 discovery. The Whitings kept a dozen watercolors and all the charcoals by Wallis.' (Tate Britain, Acquisition file - ref. TG 4/2/1075/1). For more details about the acquisitions by the Tate Britain, see the catalogue. Drawings by Burne-Jones owned by Wallis included a study for the mural *The Marriage of Sir Degravaunt* at William Morris's The Red House, *Buondelmonte's Wedding: The arrival of Buondelmonte*, and a study for *Sir Galahad*.

5. Diane Johnson papers, box 13.2, p.1.

L1: 1. It has been assumed that this was written in 1857 because the letter mentions it being Wallis's first visit to the area and since he refers to the poem 'Almond Blossoms', which Fleay published in 1857. Moreover, 24 March in 1857 was a Tuesday, making this date likely. Other scholars, including Nicholas Joukovsky and Mike Hickox, favour a later date of Tuesday 24 March 1863. However, it is certain that Wallis and his son travelled to Capri in 1862, possibly even as early as 1861, which means that Wallis's first visit to Sorrento and then Capri could not have occured in 1863. The letter does seem to refer to Daniel's pension from the India Board, which was granted around 1860 or 1861. Prior to August 1858, India was governed by the private East India Company, under the supervision of a government entity known as the India Board. In August 1858, the East India Company was abolished and its assets were transferred to a new government entity called the India Office. Before August 1858, Daniel's salary as a Company clerk would have been paid by the East India Company and not by the Board. His pension, however, would have been paid by the India Office. Joukovsky feels that prior to August 1858, the East India Company would almost certainly not have allowed their clerk sufficient time off to take a long vacation trip to southern Italy. (Email dated 16 August 2015).

2. The 'us' is repeated at the end of the letter. Does he refer to his friend Peter Austin Daniel or to someone else? It is not likely to have been Mary Ellen Meredith because she and Wallis left for Capri in the autumn of 1858 and came back in the beginning of the following year, but not as late as the end of March.

3. Torquato Tasso (1544-1595) is considered the greatest Italian poet of the late Renaissance.

4. Fleay published 'Almond Blossoms' in 1857.

5. His Academy fellow and lifelong friend Peter Augustin Daniel. In March 1847, Daniel had obtained a clerkship in the Examiner's Office of the East India Company, headed by Thomas Love Peacock. After the powers of the Company were transferred to the Crown in 1858, Daniel served in a similar capacity in the India Office until 1861, when he retired with an annual pension of £367, twothirds of his final salary of £550.

6. Shelley composed it at San Juliano di Pisa, 17-25 August, 1820.

L2: 1. John Forster (1812-1876) was a noted biographer, critic, essayist and historian; he was particularly interested in Wallis's works.

2. This would be *Henry Marten at Chepstow Castle*, exhibited at the Royal Academy in 1858.

3. Most likely *The Death of Chatterton*, which was bought by Augustus Leopold Egg.

4. *A Sculptor's Workshop, Stratford-upon-Avon, AD 1617* and *Montaigne, the Library*, which were both exhibited at the R.A. that year. Forster was eventually successful in acquiring a work by Wallis, his *In Shakespeare's House* of 1854.

L3: 1. Hunt obviously did not have a high opinion of Manchester collectors and struggled to find the right phase to express his reservations about them.

2. In 1858 *The Stonebreaker* was exhibited at the Royal Academy and then the Royal Manchester Institution. In 1859 it was shown at the Hogarth Club and in 1860 at the Liverpool Academy, where it finally sold for 250 guineas.

L4: 1. Piazza di Spagnia.

2. The friend was P.A. Daniel.

L5: 1. The via del Corso is a main street in the historic centre of Rome, which had, from the 15th century, served as the racetrack during the Roman Carnival.

2. The 1861 census lists an Emma Yorston (b.1813) married to Robert Yorston and living in Middlesex, a county in southeast England that is now mostly part of Greater London.

3. In 1864, he only exhibited one picture at the Royal Academy: *Winnowing Corn, Capri*, [Cat. 49] painted in 1862. It is highly likely, therefore, that Wallis is referring to *Paul Veronese painting the Portrait of Sir Philip Sidney* [Cat. 51], which was the major picture Wallis exhibited in 1865.

L6: 1. It is unknown where Wallis moved to in 1864 following his return from Italy, although at least by 1865 he was living at 4 Grove End Road, London. Both James Tissot and Lawrence Alma-Tadema would later live on this same street in St. John's Wood.

L7: 1. Henry Leslie's play *Rouge et Noir* was performed for the first time at the Lyceum Theatre in London in January 1867.

L8: 1. Mary Ann 'May' Rosewell (1823-83) was Mary Ellen Meredith's foster-sister, who came to stay with her for some three weeks after Harold's birth. Peacock wrote to Claire Clairmont on 12 May 1858: "May has been more than three weeks with Mary Ellen, at a place near Bristol. She comes home tomorrow." (N. Joukovsky, Peacock Letters, Vol. II, p.371).

2. Tom Taylor's son, John Wycliffe Taylor, was born 24 April 1859, making him fifteen at the time.

3. Le Havre, France.

4. George Meredith had married Marie Vulliamy on 20 September 1864.

L9: 1. Norman Maccoll (1843-1904) was editor of *The Athenaeum* from December 1869 to December 1900. Educated at Downing College, Cambridge, he applied himself to journalism and literary criticism. Sir Charles Dilke appointed him editor of that periodical, an office that he held for over 30 years. He resigned on 1 January, 1901.

2. Their mutual friend, the artist and educator, William Bell Scott.

L10: 1. Brecknock Crescent.

2. Sir Charles Dilke (1843-1911), a Liberal politician and the owner of *The Athenaeum*.

3. John Arthur Roebuck (1802-1879) was a British parliamentarian born in Madras, India. He became a Member of Parliament for Bath.

4. Eneas Sweetland Dallas (1828-1879) was a journalist who primarily wrote for *The Times* but also for periodicals like *The Saturday Review* and the *Pall Mall Gazette*. T.T. = Tom Taylor (1817-1880), an art critic of *The Times* and *The Graphic* and editor of *Punch* from 1873 until his death in 1880.

L11: 1. Quentin Metsys the Elder (Louvain, 1465-Antwerp, 1530) painted his tryptich of the

Brotherhood of St Anne at Louvain in 1504. It is now in the collection of the Musée Royaux des Beaux-Arts, Brussels.
2. The Ghent Altarpiece (*The Adoration of the Mystic Lamb*) by Jan and Hubert Van Eyck is in St. Bavo's Cathedral, Ghent.
3. Rubens's two great altarpieces *The Descent of the Cross* and *The Elevation of the Cross* are in the Cathedral of Our Lady in Antwerp. During Napoleon's rule, the paintings were taken to Paris to the Louvre but were returned in 1815.
4. The triptych of the *Entombment* was painted by the Dutch portrait and religious painter Maarten van Heemskerk (1498-1574).
5. The Brussels Museum has several portraits by Nicolaes Maes (Dordrecht, the Netherlands, 1634-1693).
6. Jacob Jordaens (Antwerp, 1593-1678).
7. *The Encounter of Eliezer and Rebecca*, painted by Jan Wildens (Antwerp, 1586-1693).
8. Peter Paul Rubens (Siegen, Germany, 1577-1640 Antwerp, Belgium). This portrait, supposedly of an English nobleman, has since been attributed to Van Dyck.
9. The Flemish painter Anthony Van Dyck (1599-1641), his *Portrait of Cornelis van der Geest* in the National Gallery, London.

L12: 1. *Society for the Protection of Ancient Buildings*, the pioneer conservation body that Morris founded in 1877 to protect buildings in Britain. Early members included E. Burne-Jones, G.P. Boyce, E.J. Poynter, P. Webb, J. Ruskin, and Wallis. The society soon campaigned against the restoration, or as the members saw it, the 'destruction' of the west front of St Mark's in Venice and mounted an international protest. This was the Society's first major public campaign, with meetings being called in London, Birmingham and Oxford. (F. MacCarthy, *The Last Pre-Raphaelite*, p.298).
2. Christ Church College, Oxford. The Dean was Henry George Liddell, the father of Alice Liddell of Louis Carroll's *Alice in Wonderland* fame.

L13: 1. Since Rossetti finished his poem in April 1880, it is likely that this letter was written that same year.
2. On 7 May, Rossetti had written to Theodore Watts-Dunton: "I know you'll try & come on Sunday if you can, & if so, I should be much obliged if you'd bring me Masson's *Chatterton* unless cumbrous." (See: W.E. Fredeman, *Correspondence of DGR*, Vol. IX, pp.170-1). Masson refers to Masson, David, *Essays biographical and critical: chiefly on English poets*, Macmillan, 1856.

L14: 1. Date based on Rossetti's previous letter dated 15 May ?1880.
2. Theodore Watts-Dunton (1832-1914) was Rossetti's friend as well as his solicitor. He was also a poet and critic and was commissioned to edit selections of Chatterton for T.H. Ward's *English Poets*.
3. The Arundel Society published chromolithographs of art works, especially fresco paintings in order to raise public awareness for the preservation of the works of the old Italian and Flemish masters.
4. Edward Alcock was a portrait and miniature painter who flourished from 1745-1778.
5. Peter N. Ogilvie, Collections Manager, Salford Museum & Art Gallery, Peel Park, Salford, personal communication, email to D.T.L. dated 9 November 2018: "The painting in question came into our museum in 1877. In 1909 it was described as a portrait of "Thomas Chatterton", however it goes on to say that it is unlikely to be by Hogarth because at the time of his death Chatterton was twelve years old. In 1926 Prof. Richardson declares it to be a self portrait by Hogarth. In 1952 Mr. Sewter supports the attribution to Hogarth. In 2011, Michael Doble, Chairman of "The Thomas Chatterton Society" thinks it is a self portrait of Hogarth." The Salford Museum & Art Gallery in Salford, Greater Manchester, was opened in 1850, and has a significant collection of Victorian art.
6. The school, founded in 1710, was created by the Bristol philanthropist Edward Colston.
7. Henry Taylor (1800-1886) spent his working life at the Colonial Office, though he was also a prolific author. His best-known works were four verse plays, including *Philip van Artevelde*, a drama based on the Elizabethan model, and *The Statesman*, his ironic view on the art of success. He was a favourite model of the pioneer photographer Julia Margaret Cameron.
8. Among biographers, it has always been assumed that George Meredith was the model for Chatterton, but Rossetti's claim in this letter to have sent someone to Wallis to model raises questions about this. Jerome McGann's *The Complete Writings and Pictures of Dante Gabriel Rossetti A Hypermedia Archive*, states that D.G. Rossetti did not meet George Meredith until 1861. If this is the case, Meredith obviously could not have been the young man Rossetti sent to Wallis as a possible model. Of course, it is entirely possible that Wallis decided against using Rossetti's suggested model.

L15: 1. William Spottiswoode (1825-1883) was a mathematician and physicist. He served as president of the Royal Society from 1878 to 1883.
2. Mark Pattison (1813-1884) was an Anglican cleryman and educator.
3. Edward Stuart Talbot (1844-1934) was the first warden of Keble College, Oxford from 1864 to 1888. He later became the Bishop of, successively, Rochester, Southwark, and Winchester.
4. Friedrich "Max" Muller (1823-1900) was an Orientalist and philologist. Although born in Germany, he studied and lived the majority of his life in Britain.
5. James Russell Lowell (1819-1891) was an American diplomat who was minister to Great Britain from 1880 to 1885.

L16: 1. Lord Elcho (1818-1914), Francis Richard Charteris, the tenth earl of Wemyss and March [see: ch3, note 8].
2. Lord Overstone (1796-1883). Samuel Jones-Loyd became a partner in his father's bank. A passionate art collector, he became a trustee of the National Gallery in 1850. He was created Baron Overstone the same year. Dickens is said to have used him as a model for the character of Paul Dombey in *Dombey and Son* (1848).
3. Hunt travelled to Palestine and to Syria in 1854-1856.

L17: 1. George Edmund Street (1824-1881) was a leading English Gothic Revivalist architect in whose offices William Morris had spent the year 1856 as an apprentice and met his life-long friend and collaborator Philip Webb (1831-1915).
2. "I was an architect once myself." (Letter to Bode, the Director of the Berlin Museums, winter of 1897. Quoted in T. Wilson, op cit., p.253a).

L18: 1. Dr. Franz Johann Bock (1823-1899) was a German ecclesiologist and collector who sold an important collection of textiles to the South Kensington Museum in 1862. During the 1860s and 1870s he also advised the Museum on its textile purchases. In 1882 he attempted to sell the S.K.M. his entire collection of textiles, but this did not occur when Morris suggested that they should just buy a selection of the outstanding items.
2. Unlike his friends Edward Burne-Jones, George Howard, Charles Fairfax Murray and Wallis, Morris was not fond of Italy but greatly preferred Iceland. Morris accompanied Burne-Jones once to Italy in 1873, stayed a fortnight, and then returned to England. As Morris's biographer J.W. Mackail said, Burne-Jones "found him a rather exacting companion, and a little determined to make the worst of things." [Mackail, J.W.: The Life of William Morris, Vol. I. 1907, p.293] Possibly this comment reflects Morris's unfavourable view of Italy and Italians.

L19: 1. Frederick Leyland (1832-92) was the director of a Liverpool shipping line and a patron to the Pre-Raphaelites and to Whistler.
2. William Graham (1817-85) was a Liberal MP for the city of Glasgow and also a patron of the arts who supported Burne-Jones, among many others. See: MacCarthy, F., *The Last Pre-Raphaelite*. pp.186-9.
3. The art dealer Thomas Agnew (1794-1871) founded the firm in 1817. In 1850, he called it Thomas Agnew & Sons Ltd upon his two sons becoming business partners: Sir William Agnew (1825-1910) and Thomas Agnew (1827-1883). Since 1876, the premises were for many years in Old Bond Street. The gallery closed in 2013 but has subsequently reopened under new management.
4. "At Leyland's suggestion, Leighton arranged for a retrospective exhibition of Rossetti's works at the Royal Academy. 'And do you think such an exhibition will do Rossetti's reputation any good?' A smirking Academician asked Holman Hunt. 'Not it. It will rather ruin it altogether.' But at the end of the year, a total of 84 works were duly displayed in a limited space at the RA Winter Exhibition alongside those of Blake's friend John Linnell, who also died in 1882, in his ninetieth year. Simultaneously, 153 works were exhibited at the Burlington Fine Arts Club, with a catalogue compiled by H.V. Tebbs. These two 'official' shows were complemented by a small one held in Bond Street premises hired by John Schott, where various works and photographs belonging to his wife Fanny were displayed." (Marsh, Jan, *Rossetti*, p.533). Fanny, of course, was Rossetti's former mistress and housekeeper, Fanny Cornforth.
5. William was still alive, so Hunt probably means "will have no pension".

L20: 1. Possibly the controversial French journalist and politician Victor Henri Rochefort (1830-1913) who sat in the Council of Deputies of the French parliament in Paris for a short time in 1885-86.

L21: 1. *An Account of the Manners and Customs of the Modern Egyptians* by Edward William Lane (1801-1876), published in 1836.
2. Sakkara or Saqqara is a huge, ancient burial ground in Egypt that served as the necropolis for the Ancient Egyptian capital of Memphis. Royal tombs located here date from the first dynasty (3200 BC) until the Graeco-Roman period. The oldest pyramid in Egypt, the Step Pyramid, is located here.
3. The son of John Callcott Horsley R.A. (1817-1903), Walter Charles Horsley (1855-1934) was an Orientalist painter. His *The French in Cairo*, in Museums Sheffield, is dated c.1884.
4. *In the Bazaar, Smyrna* [Cat. 178.] was the only work Wallis sent in that winter to be exhibited at the Old Water-Colour Society (Winter Exhibition 1885-86, No. 24).
5. Wallis refers to his *Notes on some early Persian lustre vases*, which Quaritch published that year.

L22: 1. Major General Charles George Gordon (1833-1885) had been Governor-General of the Sudan. He was killed in 1885 when the Mahdi's forces took Khartoum.
2. Walter Charles Horsley (1855-1934).
3. A similar description has been made by Georges Legrain, *Une famille copte de Haute-Égypte*, Bruxelles, 1945, p.23.
4. The nilometer, situated on the south end of Roda Island, is one of the oldest structures in Cairo built after the Arab conquest. Nilometers were used since antiquity to measure the flood levels of the Nile River.
5. *Boston Evening Transcript*, 9 March 1914, p.14. "Once a year pilgrims set out from Cairo to carry a wonderfully wrought carpet to Mecca, and as often they return, bringing with them the old one made holy by its twelve months in the tomb of the Prophet."

L24: 1. Meir Hatina, 'Religious Culture Contested: The Sufi Ritual of *Dawsa* in Nineteenth-Century Cairo', *International Journal for the Study of Modern Islam*, New Series, Vol. 47, Issue 1, 2007. p.33: "An illuminating example is the *dawsa* ritual – a ceremony involving the *shaykh* of the Sa'diyya order riding his horse over the backs of his prostrate disciples, which was widespread in the Cairene milieu. This practice, intended to prove that true believers are protected from all harm, was officially abolished in 1881 in the name of enlightenment and human dignity."

L25: 1. Possibly John Harvard Thomas R.W.A., 1854–1921. Thomas had returned to London from studying in Paris in 1884.

L26: 1. On 20 November 1886, George Frederic Watts had married Mary Fraser Tytler, who had revered him since she first met him in 1870, so not quite 25 years, though long enough! At first, the engagement was kept secret, perhaps because of the difference in their ages and the problems Watts had encountered in his first marriage to Ellen Terry. His second marriage proved to be a happy one, however.

L27: *The Triumph of the Innocents* (Walker Art Gallery, Liverpool), which he started in 1876 but did not finish until 1887 because of problems with the canvas.

2. Henry Tanworth Wells R.A. (1828-1903) was a member of the Council of the Royal Academy and a strong supporter of its constitutional rights and privileges, He had strongly defended the existing system against the agitation for reform lead by Hunt as outlined in Hunt's letters to *The Times* in August and September of 1886.
3. Hunt had a number of works included in the *Royal Jubilee Exhibition* held in Manchester in 1887 including *Claudio and Isabella*, *Our English Coasts*, *The Scapegoat*, *The Shadow of Death*, and a *Portrait of Professor Owen*. The extent of damage to the frame suggests a large work so it was probably the frame for *The Shadow of Death*.
4. The *Adelaide Jubilee International Exhibition* was held in 1887. Hunt sent *The Ship* where it was awarded the second order of merit.
5. See previous letter. After their marriage, the couple travelled to Cairo where they arrived on Christmas Eve. They hired a *dahabeeyah* and, on 4 January, they set sail for a seventy-day cruise up the Nile. Back in Alexandria, they then set sail for Constantinople, via Greece. Whether they met with Wallis is unknown, but nothing is mentioned in Wallis's letters to his son.
6. The Watts scholar Veronica Franklin Gould is unable to ascertain with certainty the lady to whom Hunt is referring: "The truth is that yes, Watts did compartmentalise his women friends. I have not heard of a lady being jilted for Mary Fraser Tytler and taking to her bed in distress. Letters would indicate the likeliest candidate to be the American Mary Gertrude Mead, who first wrote to him in 1883, and who instigated the Watts exhibition at the Metropolitan Museum of Art. Watts came to feel that her interest was more than artistic, but because she was not resident in England, she may not have been aware of Mary FT in the studio." (Personal communication to D.T.L., email dated 29 December, 2015)

From Mary's perspective, her chief rival was not an unmarried woman but Watts' close friend, neighbour, and later biographer, Mrs. Russell Barrington, to whom Mary once referred as "a poisonous snake".

L28: 1. Dahabeeyuh

2. Beni Suef is now the capital of the Beni Suef Governate and situated on the west bank of the Nile in northern Upper Egypt.
3. [See: L27].
4. Wallis was to exhibit three works at the O.W.S. in 1887 including *Street Scene in Cairo* (*The Sheykh hears Mysterious Whispering*) [Cat.186], *Herodotus at the Scribe's Bazaar, Memphis* [Cat. 187], and *The Flute Player* [Cat. 188].

L29: 1. *Herodotus at the Scribe's Bazaar. Memphis* [Cat. 187], and *The Flute Player* [Cat. 188] were both exhibited that winter at the Old Water-Colour Society, nos. 13 and 94 respectively.

L30: 1. Tristam Ellis (1844–1922) was an English artist who specialised in Middle Eastern and eastern Mediterranean subjects.

2. Charles Gent Clement, Wallis's friend and a principal patron.
3. Charles Roberson & Co., Artists' Colourmen, Manufacturers of Water and Oil Colours, Materials for Drawing and Painting, 51, Long Acre, London. Wallis had an account with them for many years.

L31: 1. Epheseus is the remains of the ancient Greek and Roman city in the central Aegean region of Turkey. During the 5th and 6th centuries A.D. it was the second most important city of the Byzantine Empire after Constantinople. Hierapolis is the modern city of Pamukkale in Southern Turkey.

L32: 1. Nicholas Tano (d.1924) was a prominent Greek Cypriot antiquities dealer in Cairo with premises at 51 Sharia Ibrahim Pasha, opposite the old Shepheards Hotel.

2. A *ballon d'essai* = a measure or policy put forward to test reactions to it.
3. E.A.T. Wallis Budge, (1857-1934). Keeper of Egyptian and Assyrian Antiquities, British Museum, 1894–1924. For his contacts with Wallis in Egypt, see: Budge, op cit, pp.82, 109 and 132.
4. Edward John Poynter P.R.A. (1836-1919), artist, educator and administrator. He was Director of the National Gallery from 1894–1904. He lived for many years at 28 Albert Gate S.W., London.

L33: 1. George Wallis, FSA (1811-1891) was appointed senior keeper of the Fine Art Collection at the South Kensington Museum in 1863 and remained in that post until just prior to his death.

2. Jean P. Lambros (1843-1909) was a prominent antique and art dealer in Athens.
3. Augustus Wollaston Franks KCB (1826-1897) joined the British Museum staff in 1851. From 1866-1896 he served as its first Keeper of British and Medieval Antiquities and Ethnography.
4. Probably Edward Poynter's son, Ambrose Macdonald Poynter (1867-1923), who went on to become an architect.
5. Mawlid al-Nabi al-Sharif is the festival celebrating the birthday of Muhammad held in the third month of the Islamic calendar on the 12th day of Rabi' al-awwal. This festival would have occurred in November in 1887.
6. Wallis is probably referring to the then British Prime Minister, Lord Salisbury.
7. The "Bloody Sunday" march to Trafalgar Square on 13 November 1887 culminated in violent confrontation with the authorities. There were some 400 arrests and many injuries. Although one purpose of the demonstration was to protest about the handling of the Irish situation by the Conservative government of the day, it had a much wider context of discontent among the poor and unemployed. William Morris and George Bernardf Shaw were among the protesters. Three days later another demonstration took place and again turned violent; a young man died later from wounds he sustained having been trampled by a police horse.
8. Thomas Armstrong (1832-1911) was an artist and director for art at the South Kensington Museum.

L34: 1. Girgeh, now Girga, halfway between Cairo and Aswan, is sometimes associated with Thinis, the ancient capital of Middle Egypt during the Thinite dynasty.

2. E.A.T. Wallis Budge, (1857-1934). Keeper of Egyptian and Assyrian Antiquities, British Museum, 1894–1924. For his contacts with Wallis in Egypt, see: Budge, op cit, pp.82, 109 and 132.
3. John Mason Cook (1834-1899). He took over the business when his father retired in 1879.
4. Isaac Taylor (1829-1901) was Anglican canon of York from 1885. He was also a philogist and pioneer toponymist. He was an advocate for Home Rule for Ireland.
5. Abydos is one of the oldest cities in Upper Egypt, 500 km south of Cairo. Founded before the 1st Dynasty, the town was incessantly reconstructed until the XXVIth dynasty. Mariette and Maspero discovered the temples of Seti I and Ramses II. Five royal tombs were discovered on the site, where Flinders Petrie worked between 1899 and 1904.
6. Petrie tried to start excavations there, but Grébaut, the Director of excavations, refused to allow it. (M. Drower, op cit, p.118).
7. Keneh is about 20 miles north of Luxor. For a description, see: Maspero, Gaston, *Ruines et paysages d'Égypte*, Paris, 2003, pp.98-103.

L35: 1. Scott's household furnishings from No. 92 Cheyne Walk, Chelsea, were auctioned by Williamson's on 5 December 1889. A portion of his library was sold by Sotheby's on 7 and 8 March 1890. A sale of engravings, etchings and drawings from his collection was held at Sotheby's 14 July 1892.

L36: 1. Nicholas Tano was a well-known antiquities dealer living in Cairo, who died in 1924.

2. Dr. James Grant, physician to the Khedive, lived in Cairo and was a friend of Petrie's. Grant also collected Egyptian antiquities, which he later donated, to the University of Aberdeen.

L37: 1. Naucratis, or Naukratis, was at the centre of the (XXVIth) Saïte dynasty (664–525B.C.). A Greek colony had formed during the reign of Psammetichus I [Psamtek] (664–610B.C.) and Naucratis was a key commercial centre. It was one of the first places explored by Flinders Petrie (1885). See: T. Wilkinson, op cit, p.418.

2. Grébaut, the Director of Antiquities, allowed Petrie to excavate at Meidum during the winter of 1890–91. "Flinders Petrie had decided the year before what he wanted to do. The great stone pyramid of Meydum stands like a sentinel on the desert edge looking over the wide green Fayum depression. The Arabs call it the 'False Pyramid', for its walls rise tower-like from a mound of stone chips at the base and the sloping outer case has quite gone. Its builder was unknown, but it was attributed by most Egyptologists to Snoferu, the father of Khufu, the builder of the Great Pyramid." (M. Drower, op cit, p.173).
3. A.L. Frothingham Jr.: *The American Journal of Archeology and the History of the Fine Arts*, Vol. VII, pp.81-82. "The following letter has been received by the Earl of Wharncliffe, in answer to the memorial concerning the ancient monuments of Egypt presented by him to the Marquis of Salisbury: 'Foreign Office, Dec. 25, 1890. My Lord, – I am directed by the Marquis of Salisbury to acknowledge the receipt of your letter of the 10 inst., and to inform you that the memorial enclosed there, praying for the appointment of an official inspector with a view to a better preservation of the ancient monuments in Egypt, will be forwarded to Her Majesty's Agent and Consul-General at Cairo for presentation to the Egyptian government. Sir E. Baring will be instructed to state that Her Majesty's Government consider the question of the nationality of the official to be appointed to such a post to be a matter that lies wholly within the competence of the Egyptian Government, and their only desire is that adequate steps should be taken to preserve the monuments from further destruction or mutilation. Sir E. Baring will also explain to the Egyptian Government how the memorial came to be signed in two different forms. [signed] P. W. Currie' " The Egyptian Government thereafter decided to appoint two European inspectors to insure the preservation of ancient monuments. The Earl of Wharncliffe and Henry Wallis were both prominent members of The Society for Preserving the Monuments of Ancient Egypt. See also: Wallis's letter on this subject, published in the *Academy* on 31 January, 1891.

L38: 1. The Mortuary Temple of Ramesses III at Medinet Habu, dating from the New Kingdom period, is a famous structure amongst a complex of temples on the West Bank of the Nile opposite Luxor.

2. For information on the financial problems in the

Argentine Republic in 1890-91, see: *The Statist: A Journal of Practical Finance and Trade*, Vol. 28, 26 December 1891, pp.708-709. This led to a financial crisis in London at Baring Brothers Bank. Wallis is known to have had investments in Argentina. In a letter to Harold from Cairo dated 1.12.1890, Wallis writes 'As to selling Argentines, it is as far as I have observed a mistake to sell in time of panic. The thing is to get information before the event. It is unfortunate one gets no information here till so long after the event.' (Bodleian Library, MS Eng.c.7049, fol.41).

L39: 1. Hunt had encountered major technical difficulties when painting his first version of *The Triumph of the Innocents* because he had used local Egyptian linen rather than canvas to paint on. His problems continued even after he had the linen backed with canvas.

2. The International Arbitration and Peace Association (IAPA) was created by Hodgson Pratt in London in 1880, but was most active between 1892 and 1913, with the stated aims of promoting peace in places of armed conflict.

3. Henry Wentworth Monk (1827-1896) was a Canadian Christian Zionist known as "The Prophet". He travelled widely throughout the Middle East and Europe advocating universal peace. Hunt was his friend and painted his portrait, which now hangs in the National Gallery of Canada.

4. It is uncertain exactly to which health problem in Jerusalem Hunt is referring. In mid-June 1877 Hunt was suffering from a fever while in early 1878 he was ill with dysentery. He came closest to death later in the year, however, when after a visit to Paris he contracted typhoid fever, which laid him up for ten weeks.

5. The watercolourist George Arthur Fripp (1813-1896) was a prominent member of the Old Water-Colour Society and its secretary from 1848-54. See: Wilcox, Scott and Newall, Christopher, *Victorian landscape watercolours.*

L40: 1. Wallis is referring here to his painting *In Shakespeare's House, Stratford-upon-Avon* [Cat. 11], now at the Victoria & Albert Museum.

2. Landseer was possibly making an allusion to Shakespeare's *Hamlet*, II, 2: "I know a hawk from a handsaw".

3. Sir Charles Eastlake (1793-1865) was President of the Royal Academy from1850-1865.

4. [See: Cat. 8].

5. *The Parlour in Anne Hathaway's Cottage* [Cat. 16].

6. *The Font in which Shakespeare was christened* [Cat. 15]. This was the only one of Wallis's works ultimately reproduced in the book.

7. The General Election in Great Britain held from 24 November to 18 December 1885. The Liberals, under William Gladstone, formed a minority government where the balance of power was held by the Irish Nationalists under Charles Stewart Parnell.

L41: 1. Sir George Macpherson-Grant, 3rd Baronet of Ballindalloch (1839-1907) was the M.P. (Liberal) for Elgin and Nairn between 1879 and 1886.

2. A small tip given for services rendered.

3. Peter Augustin Daniel, a Shakespeare scholar and Wallis's lifelong friend.

L42: 1. In a previous letter, dated 22 August 1894, Hunt had written of a silk scarf that that he had purchased in Cairo in 1854 that he was using in a portrait of Miss Gladys M. Holman Hunt (*The School of Nature*). It had been stolen from his studio and Hunt requested Wallis's help in finding a suitable replacement. Hunt told Wallis that the original scarf was made of substantial silk of a delicate pink tint with stripes of hyacinth colour at either end.

L43: 1. "A pupil of Hunt, Robert Braithwaite Martineau (1826-1869) had interest in social themes and in the Pre-Raphaelite taste for detail. He painted his *Last Day in the Old Home* in 1862; it shows how a family was forced to sell the ancestral home and its contents, thanks to the irresponsible behavior of a feckless spendthrift." (Upstone, Robert, *The Pre-Raphaelite Dream*, London, 2003, p.126.). See also: L44.

2. The painting was in fact presented to the Tate by the architect E.H. Martineau in 1896.

3. James Leathart (1820-1895) of Newcastle was one of the most important patrons of the Pre-Raphaelites. Most of his pictures were shown in the exhibition *A Pre-Raphaelite Collection* at the Goupil Gallery in 1896. A later executors' sale of his pictures was held at Christie's, London, on 19 June 1897.

4. It was purchased in 1896 for the collection of the Manchester City Art Gallery.

5. The *Colonna Altarpiece* was painted by Raphael early in his career, and hung originally in Perugia. The centrepart took its name from the Colonna family that bought it after the altarpiece had been broken up in 1663 and its panels scattered to buyers around Europe. In 1901, J. Pierpont Morgan paid two million French francs for the central part and lunette.

L44: 1. Robert Braithwaite Martineau's painting *Last Day in the Old Home*. See also: L43.

L45: 1. The closing years of Boyce's life were affected by dementia and he died from the result of a stroke on 9 February 1897 at the age of seventy. His wife survived him by many years. Notifying Stephens of his death, Mrs. Boyce enquired whether he would like to "follow your old friend George to his last resting place", the service taking place at St. Luke's, Sydney Street, followed by burial at Kensal Green." (V. Surtees, op cit, p.ix). Boyce had been a good enough friend of Wallis's that he had given him D.G. Rossetti's study for *My Lady Greensleeves* on 14 July, 1884. This work was subsequently sold by a descendant of Wallis at Christie's on 13 March 1973, lot 38.

2. John Roddam Spencer Stanhope (1829-1908) was the grandson of the Earl of Leicester and a pupil of George Frederic Watts. "He was one of the many late Victorian painters to be influenced by Burne-Jones. But his style is distinctly personal, and also highly Italianate. From 1880 onwards, he lived permanently in Florence and his pictures reflect his obvious admiration for Florentine Renaissance art, especially Botticelli. He was the uncle, and also the teacher, of Evelyn De Morgan." (Wood, Christopher, *The Pre-Raphaelites*, London, 1994, p.137.) Evelyn often stayed at the Villa Nuti, her uncle's home in Florence.

3. Evelyn Pickering married the potter William De Morgan in 1887. They spent many winters living in Florence for the sake of William's health.

4. Richard Wallace (1818-1890), the illegitimate son of the fourth Marquess of Hertford, died in 1890, and his widow Amélie-Julie Castelnau (1819-1897) did not show a great interest in the collections, which she left to the British nation. Hertford House now houses the famous Wallace Collection, which opened in 1900.

5. Hubert von Herkomer (1849-1914), born in Bavaria, became a famous and rich Victorian artist, even being appointed as Slade Professor of Art at Oxford University in 1884. Despite this Herkomer was never fully accepted by the British art establishment. The controversy Wallis refers to may relate to Herkomer's great ambition to become President of the Old Water-Colour Society. In the election of 1897 the candidates were Herkomer and Ernest Waterlow and the latter was elected. The results ended the friendship between J.W. North and Herkomer when he found that North had actively opposed his election despite all that Herkomer had done to further North's career, including getting him elected as an Associate of the Royal Academy. North, although believing Herkomer was by far the more talented artist, thought he did not possess the necessary tact for the office, and that an English society should have an English president.

L46: 1. Probably Richard Anthony Thompson (c.1819-1908), who joined the staff of the S.K.M. in 1857 and later became an Assistant Director until 1892. Another possibility is the eminent surgeon Sir Henry Thompson (1820-1904), who was a collector of Chinese porcelain and, like Wallis, a member of the Burlington Fine Arts Club.

2. The bowl was bought by Wallis from Count Tyskiewicz in Rome in 1897, and subsequently purchased by the British Museum in 1901. "Wallis believed what came to be known as 'the Constantine bowl' to be of the fourth century AD. Its authenticity was called into question by a German scholar soon afterwards and Wallis's letters to Read reveal the sensitivity of the issue. Wallis must have been enraged when Joseph Wilpert, who had never studied the bowl directly, published in 1907 a detailed argument that it was a fake and insultingly dismissed Wallis's views as not worth attention because he was 'a painter by profession, not an archaeologist!' This is unjust: Wallis constantly stressed the importance to ceramic studies of archaeological excavation, and was the first to give the British Museum fragments of post-medieval Italian pottery from kiln sites. The date of the bowl is still an unresolved problem, but new research suggests it may after all be Byzantine, if not as early as Wallis believed. A recent discussion concludes 'if it is genuine it is arguably the finest piece of late Byzantine pottery now known'." (T. Wilson, op cit, p.233).

L47: 1. Wallis refers to his *The Godman collection. Persian ceramic art belonging to Mr. F. DuCane Godman, F.R.S., with examples from other collections. The thirteenth century lustred wall-tiles.* London, Taylor & Francis, 1894.

2. Wallis is perhaps referring to *The Door of a Mosque at Cairo*, which he showed at the Winter exhibition of the O.W.S. (R.W.S.) in 1897.

L48: 1. The Rev. William MacGregor (1848-1937) was a collector of antiquities, vicar of Tamworth, and on the Committee of the Egypt Exploration Fund, 1888-1930. He formed one of the most remarkable collections of Egyptian antiquities ever made by a private individual, the ceramic portion of which was described by Wallis in his book, *Egyptian ceramic art: the MacGregor collection: a contribution towards the history of Egyptian pottery* (London, 1898). MacGregor's collection was auctioned off at Sotheby's in 1922 in a 7-day sale, making a total of £34,000.

2. Dampfer = Steamer. The *Prinz Heinrich* was part of the fleet of the Bremen shipping company, Norddeutscher Lloyd.

3. Major William Joseph Myers fought with the King's Royal Rifle Corps in the South African War and was killed in action on 30 October 1899 at the battle of Ladysmith. Myers, who had been educated at Eton, bequeathed his fine collection of Egyptian art to the school. However, on the 3 January 1900 the Victoria and Albert Museum was offered Myers's collection of Arab glass and wall tiles. The V&A purchased this part of the collection, which was subsequently divided and shared with the Dublin Science and Art Museum and the Edinburgh Museum of Science and Art. The remainder of Myers's collection remained at Eton where it forms the core of the Myers Museum of Antiquities. The collection is best known for its outstanding Egyptian faience from the 18th to 22nd dynasties.

L50: 1. Construction of the Roman Catholic Cathedral-Basilica of Cefalù, Sicily started in 1131 and the apse mosaics began in 1145.

2. Selinunte (Selinus) was one of the most important ancient Greek cities on the southwestern coast of Sicily. Its archeological site consisted of five temples centered on an Acropolis. Selinunte was destroyed by the Carthagians in 409 B.C. Segesta, situated north of Selinunte was one of the major cities of the Elymian people, one of the indigenous tribes of Sicily. In ancient times it was in constant conflict with Selinunte.

3. The Whitaker family were wealthy 19th-century

tycoons from West Yorkshire, who had developed the wine industry in Marsala, Sicily, starting in 1806. Many members of the family moved to Sicily permanently.

L51: 1. The date is uncertain as the letterhead gives a date of "190_". The only year we know for certain that Wallis travelled to Berlin is 1905. However, there is only evidence that he was there in August (he continued to Dresden and Vienna) of that year, not in March. The reference of text proofs from his publisher also lends weight to this date as Taylor & Francis published Wallis's *XVII plates by Nicola Fontana da Urbino at the Correr Museum, Venice; a study in early sixteenth century maiolica with illustrations* in 1905.

2. Matthew Bell, Colley & Co., Publishers' Bookbinders, were located at Temple Works, Cursitor St., Chancery Lane, London, E.C.

3. Probably Wilhelm Bode, the Director of the Berlin Museums and an expert in potteries of all kinds.

L52: 1. Wallis, Henry. *Italian ceramic art. The maiolica pavement tiles of the fifteenth century.* London, Quaritch, 1902.

L53: 1.The portrait of Peacock was used as the frontispiece for Garnett's posthumously published volume of Peacock letters and manuscripts. Garnett was a Trustee of the National Portrait Gallery.

2. This statement is not quite accurate as the National Portrait Gallery has a watercolour on ivory miniature of Peacock as a young man done in c.1805 by Roger Jean (NPG 1994).

L54: 1. Richard Garnett was the Keeper of Printed Books at the British Museum. He quarrelled publicly with Peacock over his "Memoirs" of Shelley in 1860 and 1862. He later gained the trust of Peacock's granddaughter Edith Nicolls and misappropriated many of Peacock's manuscripts. The whole sordid story is told in the last section of the introduction to Peacock's *Letters*, edited by N. Joukovsky. (Personal communication to R.L. from Nicholas Joukovsky).

2. An etched version by William Harry Warren Bicknell of Wallis's portrait was used as the frontispiece for Garnett's posthumously published volume of Peacock's letters and MSS by the Bibliophile Society, Boston, in 1910. [See: Cat. 34a.]

L55: 1. A type of maiolica medicinal jar. "The albarello is the clearest example of the development of a shared tradition. This cylindrical, lidded, slightly waisted drug jar, with a Latin inscription often richly embellished with decorative flourishes, probably originates from Persia or Syria. There it was used to store precious spices. In such a container these would travel the trade routes to the Christian lands. The name is Italian in origin, meaning little tree and is thought to refer to an earlier wooden version, made of a hollow piece of bamboo. The shape at least supports this theory. This type of pottery accompanied the Arab conquerors to the Iberian peninsula during the eighth century and retained its position among the export faiences. It was taken from Spain to France, Burgundy and Italy.. In the wake of the Reconquista, when the Balearic Islands, Sardinia, Corsica and Sicily also came under the rule of the Kings of Aragon during the fourteenth and fifteenth centuries, these trading connections were intensified." (Weinhold, Rudolf, *The Many Faces of Clay*, Leipzig, 1983, pp.151-2.)

2. Wallis's servant, the widow Mary A. Ely, who had been born in 1834 in Wye, Kent.

L56: 1. For the authors of this book, Hughes's letter seems to confirm the idea that Edith Holman Hunt was not an easy person and that, in her "adoration" of her husband, she wanted him to withdraw any bit of information that could fade his aura. While Edith never interfered in Holman Hunt's art, she definitely seemed to control the other aspects of their lives. For a fuller description of her personality, see: D. Holman-Hunt, *My Grandmothers and I*, London, 1987.

2. The funeral of their mutual close friend F.G. Stephens, who died 9 March, 1907.

L58: 1. Thomson, David Croal, *The Barbizon school of painters: Corot, Rousseau, Diaz, Millet, Daubigny*, New York, 1890. Thomson must have remembered incorrectly the date of the initial publication of this book.

2. Corot also painted *Richmond, near London* (oil on canvas), now in a private collection.

3. Marlow, Buckinghamshire is located on the River Thames, about 30 miles west of London.

Bibliography

Wallis's publications

'The Destruction of Egyptian Monuments', *The Nineteenth Century*, Vol. XXVIII, N° 165, Nov. 1890, pp.720-732.

'La céramique persane au XIIIe siècle', *Gazette des Beaux-Arts*, 1892/07-12, pp.69-80.

Catalogue of specimens illustrative of Persian and Arab art, exhibited in 1885. London, Burlington Fine Arts Club, 1885.

Notes on some early Persian lustre vases. London, Quaritch, 1885.

Notes on some examples of early Persian lustre ware. London, 1889.

The Godman collection. Persian ceramic art in the collection of Mr. F. DuCane Godman, F.R.S. The thirteenth century lustred vases. London, priv. circulation, 1891.

Typical examples of Persian and Oriental ceramic art. London, Lawrence & Bullen, 1893.

The Godman collection. Persian ceramic art belonging to Mr. F. DuCane Godman, F.R.S., with examples from other collections. The thirteenth century lustred wall-tiles. London, Taylor & Francis, 1894.

The art of ancient Egypt: a series of photographic plates representing objects from the exhibition of the art of ancient Egypt. London, Burlington Fine Arts Club, 1895.

Pictures from Greek vase, the white Athenian lekythi: a series of twelve polychrome plates representing the paintings on typical examples of the white Athenian lekythi. London, J.M. Dent, 1896.

Italian ceramic art: examples of maiolica and mezza-maiolica fabricated before 1500. Privately printed, 1897.

Egyptian ceramic art: the MacGregor collection: a contribution towards the history of Egyptian pottery. London, Taylor & Francis, 1898.

Persian lustre vases…with illustrations by the author. London, Taylor & Francis, 1899.

Thirteenth-century Persian lustre pottery. London, 1899.

Ancient Egyptian ceramic art. New York, 1900.

Egyptian ceramic art: typical examples of the art of the Egyptian pottery. London, Taylor & Francis, 1900.

The oriental influence on the ceramic art of the Italian renaissance. London, Quaritch, 1900.

The art of the precursors: a study in the history of early Italian Maiolica. London, Quaritch, 1901.

Italian ceramic art. The maiolica pavement tiles of the fifteenth century. London, Quaritch, 1902.

Italian ceramic art: XV-century pharmacy jars in Moresco Italian ware. 1902.

Oak-leaf jars: a 15th century Italian ware showing Moresco influence. London, Quaritch, 1903.

Exhibition of Ancient Greek Art. London, Burlington Fine Arts club, 1903.

Italian ceramic art. The albarello, a study in early renaissance maiolica, with illustrations. London, Quaritch, 1904.

Italian ceramic art. Figure design and other forms of ornamentation in fifteenth century Italian maiolica, with illustrations. London, Quaritch, 1905.

XVII plates by Nicola Fontana da Urbino at the Correr Museum, Venice; a study in early sixteenth century maiolica with illustrations. London, Taylor & Francis, 1905.

Byzantine ceramic art: Notes on examples of Byzantine pottery recently found at Constantinople with illustrations. London, Quaritch, 1907.

Primary sources

Austin, University of Texas (Harry Ransom Center)
1 letter to Dante Gabriel Rossetti
3 letters to William Bemrose. Enquiries as to whether Bemrose would like to publish his books.
1 letter to William Monkhouse
Diane Johnson Papers, *box 12, folders 4-6 and box 13, folders 1-2*

Berlin, Zentralarchiv der staatlichen museen Berlin, Preussischer Kulturbesitz
75 letters from Wallis to Bode

Bologna, Biblioteca dell'Archiginnasio
Carteggio Carlo Frati xxvii, n° 3. *Letter from Wallis to Carlo Frati, son of Luigi Frati.*

Faenza, Museo Internazionale delle Ceramiche, Archivio Storico

Ballardini II : *Letters between Wallis and Ballardini (7 folios)*
1 sketchbook (given by B.Rackham to G.Ballardini)
Inv. 8904, Collocazione : I E 4 20

HARVARD, HOUGHTON LIBRARY

MS Eng 1265.1, Series III : *13 letters and telegram, 1905-06,* concerning the reproduction of a portrait of Thomas Love Peacock for Garnett's editing of Peacock's letters.

LONDON, THE BRITISH LIBRARY

Add. 38831. *Correspondence of Henry Wallis, R.W.S., Secretary of the International Committee for the Preservation of the Basilica of St.Mark's, Venice, 1879-1882.*

LONDON, THE BRITISH MUSEUM

Dept of the Ancient Near East : *Letters to E.A. Wallis Budge.*
Dept of Medieval and Modern Europe : *150 letters to A.W. Franks and C.H. Read.*
Dept of Greek and Roman Antiquities : *Letters from Wallis to A.S. Murray.*

LONDON, NATIONAL ART LIBRARY (VICTORIA & ALBERT MUSEUM)

MSL/1995/14 F.M.Brown Box 23. *7 letters from Ford Madox Brown to Henry Wallis on various subjects*
MSL/1939/1836. *9 notebooks containing notes and sketches some in colour.*
MSL/1948/251. *38 letters to Albert Van de Put concerning Italian maiolica, pottery, etc.*
MSL/1976/5451 Box 1, fol. 42. *Correspondence of Thomas Armstrong.* Letter from Wallis (4 May 1894).
40.F Box IV. *The destruction of Egyptian monuments.*
MA/1/W330. *Correspondence of Henry Wallis with the Victoria & Albert Museum.*
Print room : *Drawings for Wallis's books.*

MANCHESTER, UNIVERSITY OF (JOHN RYLANDS LIBRARY)

English MS 1281/678-684. *Letters from Wallis dated between 1894 and 1906, dealing with a variety of matters.*

OXFORD, ASHMOLEAN MUSEUM, DEPARTMENT OF WESTERN ART

Fortnum Archive : F/9/x/22 ; F/2/x/37 ; F/9/x/16 ; other letters inserted into copies of Wallis's books.

OXFORD, BODLEIAN LIBRARY

MS. Photogr. 150, fol. 29-40. *Twelve photographs of unidentified people.*
MSS. Eng. c. 7039, 7040, 7041. *Letters to Henry Wallis, 1856-1915.*
MSS. Eng. c. 7051, e. 3394, 3395, 3396, e. 3401. *Miscellaneous papers of Henry Wallis, 1846-1952.*
MS. Eng. c. 7049, 7050. *Papers of Harold Wallis, 1885-1918.*
MSS. Eng. d. 3552-8, e. 3414-27. *Sketch-books of Henry Wallis, 1869-1910.*
MS. Don.e.79. *120 letters to F.G. Stephens, 1828-1907.*
MS. Don.d.116, fol. 123. *Letter to F.G. Stephens.*

OXFORD, ORIENTAL INSTITUTE LIBRARY, UNIVERSITY OF OXFORD

Letter to C.D.E. Fortnum inserted into Fortnum's copy of Wallis's *Notes on some Examples of Persian Lustreware,* No 3.

PARIS, ARCHIVES NATIONALES (ECOLE NATIONALE SUPÉRIEURE DES BEAUX-ARTS)

AJ/52*/235. *Registres matricules des élèves peintres et sculpteurs.*
AJ/52*/273. *Dossiers individuels des élèves peintres.*
AJ/52*/553. *Inscriptions dans les ateliers.*
AJ/52/916. *Inscriptions : dossiers de demandes des aspirants peintres, sculpteurs et architectes pour le concours des places et demandes d'autorisation de se présenter au concours émanant d'aspirants étrangers.*
AJ/52/926. *Inscriptions et contrôles de la présence des élèves.*

PRINCETON UNIVERSITY LIBRARY, DEPT OF RARE BOOKS AND SPECIAL COLLECTIONS

C0705. Pre-Raphaelite Correspondence of George Price Boyce, 1852-1917. Letter from Henry Wallis, 1865 October 20. Box 1, folder 42.

SAN MARINO, CALIFORNIA, HUNTINGTON LIBRARY

3 letters to William Holman Hunt, 1858-1896 (HH 578-580)
1 letter to Marion Edith Hunt, Feb 1875 (HH 577)
2 letters to Edward Robert Hughes, 1901-1908 (William Morris Papers, Box 13, MOR 568-569)

Stratford-upon-Avon, Royal Shakespeare Company
1 letter from Henry Wallis to William S.Brassington, 4 October 1910

Vancouver, University of British Columbia
Penkill Papers
6-2 Letter from Henry Wallis to Alice Boyd (on the death of William Bell Scott)
6-20 Letter from Henry Wallis to William Bell Scott (n.d.)
Angeli-Dennis Papers
4-7 Letters from H.Wallis to D.G.Rossetti. 4 items (ca.1874-ca.1880)
24-18 (17-19) From H.Wallis: 20 Mar 1870, 24 Jum 1887, 11 Apr 1882.

Washington D.C., The Folger Shakespeare Library
27 Letters to Frederick Gard Fleay (Y.c.1459, 1-27)

Yale University, Beinecke Library
1 letter from Mary Ellen Meredith to Wallis, 29 September 1857.
1 letter from A.W. Hunt to Wallis, 28 October 1885.
1 letter from D.G.Rossetti to Wallis, 'Wednesday'.
1 letter from Wallis to his son Harold 'Felix', 27 November 1893.

Private owners
Private Collector (New York), *24 autograph letters to his son Felix, 2 autograph letters to his mother, 2 letters to Violet, passport, a lock of 'father's hair'.* (Dominic Winter Auction, 19 July 2011)

Printed documents

Able (Augustus Henry), *George Meredith and Thomas Love Peacock. A Study in literary influence.* Thesis Univ. of Pennsylvania, 1930; Gorgian Press, 1970.
Ackerman (Gerald-M.), *Les Orientalistes de l'école britannique.* Paris, ACR, 1991, 2000.
———, *Jean-Léon Gérôme. Sa vie, son oeuvre.* Paris, ACR Édition/PocheCouleur, 1997.
Ackroyd (Peter), *Chatterton.* Paris, Gallimard, "Le Promeneur", 1988.
———, *Shakespeare. De biografie.* Amsterdam, J.M. Meulenhoff, 2006 .
(Alexandria 1995), *Visions of Love and Life* (S. Wildman, Ed.). Alexandria, Virginia, 1995.
Altick (Richard D.), *Paintings from Books. Art and Literature in Britain, 1760-1900.* Columbus, Ohio State University Press, 1985.
Amor (Anne Clark), *William Holman Hunt. The True Pre-Raphaelite.* London, Constable, 1989.
Andreu (Guillemette) et al., *L'Égypte ancienne au Louvre.* Paris, Hachette, 1997.
Angeli (Helen Rossetti), *Dante Gabriel Rossetti, His Friends and Enemies.* London, Hamish Hamilton, 1949.
(Anon.), *Dr.Johnson at Cave's, the publisher.* Art Journal, 1854, p.161.
(Anon.), *Notes and Queries*, 1893, pp.47, 117, 363; 1904, p.159; 1964, p.480. Oxford University Press.
(Anon.), *The Burlington Magazine*, xxix, 1916, p.510; xxx, 1917, pp.123-4.
(Anon.), *The Royal Academy Review. A Guide to the Exhibition of the Royal Academy of Arts, 1858-60, containing original, critical and descriptive notices.* By the Council of Four. London, F.A. Day, 1858; Kent & Co, 1859 & 1860.
Arberry (Arthur J.), *British Orientalists.* London, W. Collins, 1943.
(Arrest Court of Appeal), 'Turner v. Robinson', *The Irish Jurist*, vol. 12, Dublin, F. Ponsonby, 1860, pp.385-398.
Ashton (Geoffrey) et al., *Shakespeare and British Art.* New Haven & London, Yale University Press, 1981.
Assouline (Pierre), *Grâces lui soient rendues. Paul Durand-Ruel, le marchand des impressionnistes.* Paris, Gallimard, "Folio" n° 3999, 2002.
Avery-Quash (Susanna) & Sheldon (Julie), *Art for the Nation. The Eastlakes and the Victorian Art World.* London, The National Gallery Company, 2011

BARRINGTON (Mrs. Russell), *The Life, Letters and Work of Frederic Leighton.* 2 vol. New York, MacMillan, 1906.
BATE (Percy H.), *The English Pre-Raphaelite Painters: their Associates and Successors.* London, G.Bell & Sons, 1905. Accessible on *archive.org.*
BAYLY (C.A.), *La naissance du monde moderne (1780-1914).* Paris, Les Éditions de l'Atelier/Éditions Ouvrières, 2007.
BELL (Alan Nigel), *The male novelist and the 'Woman question': George Meredith's presentation of his heroines in* The Egoist *(1879) and* Diana of the Crossways *(1885).* Thesis, Rhodes University, 2007.
BENEDETTI (Maria Teresa), *I Preraffaelliti.* Firenze, Giunti, 1986.
BÉNÉZIT, (E.), *Dictionnaire critique et documentaire des peintres, sculpteurs, dessinateurs et graveurs.* Vol.14. Paris, Gründ, 1999.
BEN MAHMOUD (Feriel) & DANIEL (Nicolas), *Le voyage en Orient, 1850-1930.* Paris, Éditions Place des Victoires, 2008.
BENNETT (Mary), 'A Check-List of Pre-Raphaelite Pictures Exhibited at Liverpool 1846-67, and Some of Their Northern Collectors', *The Burlington Magazine,* Vol.105, N° 728, Nov.1963, pp.486-495.
———, *Ford Madox Brown. A Catalogue Raisonné.* 2 vol. New Haven & London, Yale University Press, 2010.
———, 'Artists of the Pre-Raphaelite Circle. The First Generation'. *Catalogue of Works in the Walker Art Gallery, Lady Lever Art Gallery and Sudley Art Gallery.* London, 1988.
———, 'The Pre-Raphaelites and the Liverpool Prize', *Apollo,* vol.76 (Dec 1962), pp.748-53.
BENOIST-MÉCHIN, *Bonaparte en Égypte ou Le rêve inassouvi.* Lausanne, Clairefontaine, 1966.
BILLCLIFFE (Roger), *The Royal Institute of Fine Arts 1861-1989,* 4 vols., Glasgow, 1992, IV, p270.
BIRCHALL (Heather), *Préraphaélites.* Paris, Taschen, 2010.
(BIRMINGHAM 2011), *Pre-Raphaelite Drawing* (C. Cruise, Ed.). Exh. cat. Birmingham Museum and Art Gallery, 2011.
BOIME (Albert), *The Academy of French Painting in the Nineteenth Century.* 2nd ed., New Haven, Yale University Press, 1986.
———, 'The Instruction of Charles Gleyre and the Evolution of Painting in the Nineteenth Century'; in Exh. cat., *Charles Gleyre ou Les Illusions perdues,* Winterthur, 1974.
BONAFOUX (Pascal), *Renoir.* Paris, Perrin, 2009.
BOYCE (George Price), *The Diaries of G.P. Boyce* (V. Surtees ed.). Norwich, Real World, 1980.
BRADSHAW (Maurice), *Royal Society of British Artists: members exhibiting 1824-1962.* Leigh-on-Sea, F. Lewis, 1973-77.
BRECCIA (E.), *Alexandrea ad Aegyptum. Guide de la ville ancienne et moderne et du musée Gréco-Romain.* Bergamo, Istituto Italiano d'Arti Grafiche, 1914.
(BRIGHTON 1983), *The Inspiration of Egypt. Its Influence on British Artists, Travellers and Designers, 1700-1900.* Exhibition held at Brighton Museum, 7 May-17 July 1983 and at Manchester City Art Gallery, 4 August-17 September 1983. Brighton Borough Council, 1983.
(BRISTOL 2006), *John Brett. A Pre-Raphaelite in Cornwall* (C. Brett, Ed.). Exh. cat. Bristol, Samson & Company Ltd., 2006.
BRITISH ALMANAC AND COMPANION (THE), 1887. London, The Stationers' Company, 1887.
BRONKHURST (Judith), *William Holman Hunt. A Catalogue Raisonné.* 2 vol. New Haven & London, Yale University Press, 2006.
BROWN (Ford Madox), *The Diary of Ford Madox Brown* (V. Surtees, Ed.). Newhaven, Yale University Press, 1981.
BRUCKMULLER-GENLOT (Danielle), *Les Préraphaélites, 1848-1884.* Paris, Armand Colin, 1994.
(BRUSSELS 2010), *L'Orientalisme. De Delacroix à Kandinsky.* Bruxelles, Musées Royaux des Beaux-Arts, 2010.
BUDGE (E.A. Wallis), *Cook's Handbook for Egypt and the Sudan.* London, Cook, 1906.
———, *By Nile and Tigris. A narrative of journeys in Egypt and Mesopotamia on behalf of the British Museum between the years 1886 and 1913.* London, John Murray, 1920.
BULL (Deborah) & LORIMER (Donald), *Up the Nile: A Photographic Excursion, Egypt 1839-1898.* New York, C.N. Potter, 1979.
(BURLINGTON), *The Burlington Fine Arts Club. Its early members and Mr. Holford,* in *The Holford Collection,* exh. cat. Burlington Fine Arts Club, London, 1924, pp.19-24.
(BURLINGTON), *The Burlington Fine Arts Club,* editorial in *Burlington Magazine* 94 (1952), pp.97-99.
(BURLINGTON), *The Burlington Fine Arts Club, 17, Savile Row, W. Rules, Regulations and Bye-Laws, with List of Members.* London, Metchim & Son, 1899.
BURNE-JONES (Georgiana), *Memorials of Edward Burne-Jones.* 2 vol. London, Macmillan, 1904.

Butler (Marilyn), *Peacock displayed. A Satirist in his Context.* London, Routledge & Kegan Paul, 1979.
Casanova (Giacomo), *Mémoires.* 3 vols. Paris, Robert Laffont, "Bouquins", 1992.
Castagna (André), *Panorama du siècle élisabéthain.* Paris, Seghers, 1970.
Casteras (Susan P.), *English Pre-Raphaelitism and its Reception in America in the Nineteenth Century.* London and Toronto, Associated University Presses, 1990.
Caubet (Annie) & Pierrat-Bonnefois (Geneviève), *Faïences. Faïences de l'Antiquité, de l'Égypte à l'Iran.* Paris, Musée du Louvre Éditions, 2005.
Cazar (Dominique-Marie), *Faïences et Porcelaines. La faïence et la porcelaine dans le monde.* Lausanne, Edita, 1996.
Champneys (Basil), *Memoirs and correspondence of Coventry Patmore.* 2 vols. London, G. Bell & Sons, 1900.
Chapel (Jeannie), 'The Papers of Joseph Gillott (1799-1872)'. Oxford, *Journal of the History of Collections,* 2007, 1-48.
Cherry (Deborah), 'The Hogarth Club, 1858-1861'. *The Burlington Magazine* 122, April 1980, pp.237-44.
Chesneau (Ernest), *La Peinture Anglaise.* Paris, A. Quantin, 1882; *The English School of Painting.* London, Cassell & Co., 1885.
Cieszkowski (Krzysztof Z.), 'Chatterton, Wallis & Meredith', *History Today,* Vol.32, Issue 11, November 1982.
Clark (Nicholas), *Melozzo da Forlí.* London, Sotheby's Publications, 1990.
Clayton (Peter), *The Rediscovery of Ancient Egypt: Artists and Travellers in the Nineteenth Century.* London, Thames & Hudson, 1982.
Clément (Charles), *Gleyre. Étude biographique et critique avec le catalogue raisonné de l'œuvre du Maître.* Paris, Perrin, 1886.
———, Études sur les Beaux-Arts en France. Paris, Michel Lévy, 1865.
Cobley (John), *The death of Chatterton. Suggestions from the celebrated painting by Wallis.* Manchester, William Bremner; London, F. Pitman, 1857.
Codell (Julie), *The Victorian Artist. Artists' Lifewritings in Britain, 1870-1910.* London, 2003.
Cook (E.T.), *The Life of John Ruskin.* London, George Allen & Co, 1911.
Coombs (James) et al., *A Pre-Raphaelite friendship: the correspondence of William Holman Hunt and John Lucas Tupper.* Ann Arbor, Michigan, UMI Research Press,1986.
Cottrell (Leonard, Ed.), *Dictionnaire encyclopédique d'Archéologie.* Paris, S.E.D.E., 1962.
Crespon-Halotier (Béatrice), *Les peintres britanniques dans les Salons parisiens, des origines à 1939. Répertoire.* Dijon, L'Échelle de Jacob, 2002.
Dakers (Caroline), *The Holland Park Circle, Artists and Victorian Society.* Newhaven, Yale University Press, 1999.
Damiano-Appia (Maurizio), *L'Égypte. Dictionnaire encyclopédique de l'ancienne Égypte et des civilisations nubiennes.*Paris, Gründ, 1999.
Davis (Frank), *Victorian Patrons of the Arts.* Country Life Limited London, 1963.
Denison (Cara D.), Phimister (Evelyn J.) & Wiles (Stephanie), *De Gainsborough à Ruskin. Le grand siècle du paysage. Aquarelles et dessins de la Morgan Library.* New York, The Pierpont Morgan Library, 1994.
Denney (Colleen), *At the temple of Art: the Grosvenor Gallery, 1877-1890.* Cranbury/London, Associated University Presses, 2000.
Denon (Vivant), *Voyage dans la Basse et la Haute Égypte.* Paris, Pygmalion, 1990.
Distel (Anne), *Renoir.* Paris, Citadelle & Mazenod, 2009.
Donovan (Andrea Elizabeth), *William Morris and the Protection of Ancient Buildings.* New York & London, Routledge, 2008.
Drower (Margaret S.), *Flinders Petrie. A life in archaeology.* The University of Wisconsin Press, 1995.
Dubernard-Laurent (Annie), *Le Pré-Raphaélisme en Angleterre. Les Arts et les Lettres en France: essai d'étude comparative.* Thesis, Sorbonne-Paris IV, 1996.
(Dublin 1873), *Loan Museum of Art Treasures.* Industrial Exhibition Palace, Dublin, 1873.
(Dublin 1988), *The East: imagined, experienced, remembered. Orientalist Nineteenth Century Painting.* Dublin, The National Gallery of Ireland, 1988.
Dunn (Henry Treffry), *Recollections of Dante Gabriel Rossetti.* London, Elkin Mathews, 1904; Dalrymple Press, 1984.
(Edinburgh 1991), *Sunshine and Shadow. The David Scott Collection of Victorian Paintings.* National Galleries of Scotland, Edinburgh, 1991.
Edmond (Rod), *Affairs of the hearth: Victorian poetry and domestic narrative.* London & New York, Routledge, 1988.
Edwards (Amelia B.), *A Thousand Miles up the Nile.* London, Century, 1982.
Elliott (David B.), *Charles Fairfax Murray. The Unknown Pre-Raphaelite.* Lewes, The Book Guild Ltd &

New Castle, DE, Oak Knoll Press, 2000.
———, *A Pre-Raphaelite Marriage. The Lives and Works of Marie Spartali Stillman & William James Stillman*. Woodbridge, Antique Collectors' Club, 2006.
Ellis (Stewart Marsh), *George Meredith. His life and friends in relation to his work*. London, Grant Richards Ltd., 1920.
Énaud Lechien (Isabelle), *James Whistler*. Paris, ACR Édition/PocheCouleur, 1995.
Énault (Louis), *Les Beaux-Arts à l'Exposition Universelle de 1878*. Paris, E.Gros, 1878.
Énault (Louis) & Doré (Gustave), *Londres et les Londoniens en 1875*. Paris, SACELP, 1984.
Engen (Rodney K.), *Dictionary of Victorian engravers, print publishers and their works*. Cambridge, Chadwyck-Healey, 1979.
Erman (Adolf), *Life in Ancient Egypt*. New York, Dover, 1971.
Eyre (R.H.S.), *Royal Academy Reform*. London, Hardwicke & Bogue, May 1876.
Fagan (Brian M.), *L'aventure archéologique en Égypte*. Paris, Pygmalion, 1981.
Fenwick (Simon) & Smith (Greg), *The business of watercolour: A guide to the archives of the Royal Watercolour Society*. Ashgate, 1997.
———, *The Enchanted River. Two Hundred Years of the Royal Watercolour Society*. Bristol, Samson & Company, 2004.
Fildes (L.V.), *Luke Fildes*. London, Michael Joseph, 1968.
Fleay (Frederic Gard), *A Chronicle History of the Life and Work of William Shakespeare, Player, Poet and Playmaker*. London, John C. Nimmo, 1886.
Fletcher (Pamela) & Helmreich (Anne), *The Rise of the Modern Art Market in London, 1850-1939*. Manchester University Press, 2011.
Forbes (Christopher), *The Royal Academy (1837-1901) Revisited: Victorian Paintings from the Forbes Magazine Collection*. New York, The Metropolitan Museum of Art, 1975.
Fouquet (Dr D.), *Contribution à l'*étude de la céramique orientale. Mémoires présentés à l'Institut Égyptien, Tome IV, Le Caire, 1901.
Fox (Levi), *In Honour of Shakespeare. The History and Collections of the Shakespeare Birthplace Trust*. (Norwich, Jarrold & Sons, 1972).
Frank (Katherine), *Lucie Duff Gordon. A Passage to Egypt*. London, Hamish Hamilton, 1994.
Fredeman (William E.), *Pre-Raphaelitism: a Bibliocritical Survey*. Harvard University Press, Cambridge, Mass., 1965.
———, *The Correspondence of Dante Gabriel Rossetti*. 9 vol. Cambridge, D.S. Brewer, 2002-2009. See: Rossetti
———, 'The Letters of Pictor Ignotus: William Bell Scott's correspondence with Alice Boyd, 1859-1884'. *Manchester, Bulletin of the John Rylands Library*, vol. 58, 1976, part I: pp.66-111; part II: pp.306-352.
———, 'A Pre-Raphaelite Gazette: the Penkill letters of Arthur Hughes to William Bell Scott and Alice Boyd, 1886-97'. *Manchester, Bulletin of the John Rylands Library*, 1967, pp.323-62; 1968, pp.34-82.
Frith (Francis), L'Égypte à la chambre noire. Paris, Découvertes Gallimard Albums, 1992.
Frith (William Powell), *My Autobiography and Reminiscences*. New York, Harper & Brothers, 1888.
Gadoin (Isabelle), 'Les collections victoriennes d'art persan : images exposées, sous-exposées, sur-exposées', *Images de l'*étranger : actes du colloque. *Université de Limoges, 28-29 mars 2003*. Limoges, Pulim, Collection Espaces Humains, 2003, pp.217-244.
Gadoin (Isabelle) & Palmier-Chatelain (Marie-Élise), *Rêver d'Orient, connaître l'Orient*. Paris, ENS Éditions, 2008.
Galland (René), *George Meredith: les cinquante premières années*. Paris, Les presses françaises, 1923.
Gallon (D.N.), 'Peacock's later years: the evidence of unpublished letters'. *Review of English Studies*, August 1969, XX, pp.315-319.
Garrigan (Kristine Ottesen), *Victorian Art Reproductions in Modern Sources. A Bibliography*, London, Garland Publishing Inc., 1991.
Gaunt (William), *The Pre-Raphaelite Tragedy*, London, Cardinal, 1988.
Gaunt (William), *Painting in Britain 1800-1900. The restless century*. Oxford, Phaidon, 1978.
———, *The Pre-Raphaelite Tragedy*, London, Cardinal, 1988.
(Ghent 2007), *British Vision. Observation and Imagination in British Art 1750-1950*, exh. cat., Museum voor Schone Kunsten Ghent, 2007 (R.Hoozee, Ed.).
(Glasgow 1888) See: Henley and Walker
Goldring (Elizabeth), 'A portrait of Sir Philip Sidney by Veronese at Leicester House, London'. *The Burlington Magazine*, vol.154, n°1313, August 2012, pp.548-54.
Golvin (Jean-Claude) & Traunecker (Claude), *Karnak. Résurrection d'un site*. Fribourg, Office du Livre,

1984.
Goncourt (Edmond et Jules de), *Manette Salomon.* Paris, Folio Classique.
Goodall (Frederick), *The Reminiscences of Frederick Goodall, R.A.* London & Newcastle-on-Tyne, The Walter Scott Publishing, 1902.
Graves (Algernon), *The Royal Academy: dictionary of contributors, 1769-1904.* 1905-1906, 8 vol. Accessible on *archive.org.*
———, *Dictionary of artists who have exhibited works in the principal London exhibitions of oil paintings from 1760-1880.* London, G. Bell & Sons, 1884 ; Bath, Kingsmead Reprints, 1969.
———, *The British Institution, 1806-1867.* London, George Bell & Sons, 1908; Bath, Kingsmead, 1875; reprint, Facsimile Edition, 1969.
———, *Art Sales from early in the eighteenth century to early in the twentieth century,*Vol. IV. New York, Burt Franklin, 1970.
———, *A Century of Loan Exhibitions, 1813-1912.* London, A. Graves, 1914.
Grearson (Edward), *Storm Bird: The Strange Life of Georgina* Weldon. London, Chatto & Windus, 1959.
Greenhill (Gillian B.), 'The Death of Chatterton, or Photography and the Law'. *History of Photography,* 1981, vol. 5, N° 3, pp.199-205.
Groom (Nick), *Chatterton.* Oxford, DNB, 2011.
Grylls (Rosalie G.), *Portrait of Rossetti.* London, Macdonald, 1964.
Hackney (Stephen) : see Townsend.
Hamlyn (Robin), *Henry Wallis + Chatterton, 1855-56.* Accessible on *www.friedrichshainerschule.de / WALLIS.htm*
Hardie (Martin), *Water-Colour Painting in Britain.* 3 vol. London, B.T. Batsford, 1968.
Harding (Ellen, Ed.), *Re-framing the Pre-Raphaelites.* Aldershot, Scolar Press, 1996.
Hauptman (William), 'Delaroche's and Gleyre's Teaching Ateliers and their Group Portraits'. *National Galleries Washington, Studies in the History of Art,* vol. 18, 1985, pp.79-119.
———, *Charles Gleyre.* Princeton University Press, 1996.
Henderson (Philip), *The Letters of William Morris to his Family and Friends.* London, Longmans, Green & Co., 1950.
Henisch (Heinz K.) & Bridget (Ann), *The photographic experience, 1839-1914 images and attitudes.* The Pennsylvania State University Press, 1994.
Henley (William Ernest) & Walker (Robert), *A Century of Artists. A Memorial of the Glasgow International Exhibition 1888.*Glasgow, James MacLehose & Sons, 1889.
Henry (Tom) & Kanter (Laurence B.), *Luca Signorelli. The Complete Paintings.* London, Thames & Hudson, 2001.
Hilton (Tim), *John Ruskin.* New Haven & London, Yale University Press, 2002 (paperback).
Hogg (Thomas Jefferson), *The Life of Percy Bysshe Shelley.* London, J.M. Dent, 1933
Holman-Hunt (Diana), *My Grandmothers and I.* London, A Hamish Hamilton Paperback, 1987.
———, *My Grandfather, His Wives and Loves.* London, Columbus Books, 1987.
Holme (Charles), *The Royal Institute of Painters in Water-Colours.* London, The Studio, Special Spring Number 1906.
———, *The Old Water-Colour Society, 1804-1904.* London, The Studio, Special Spring Number 1905.
Holmes (Richard), *Shelley. The pursuit.* London, Harper Perennial, 2005.
Hopkinson (Martin), 'Drawings in the Dudley Gallery's Black and White Exhibitions', *The British Art Journal,* vol. XV, No.1 (Autumn 2014), pp.21-26.
Houfe (Simon), *The dictionary of 19th century British book illustrators and caricaturists.* Woodbridge, Antique Collectors' Club, 1996.
Hubbard (Hesketh), *An Outline History of the Royal society of British Artists.* 3 vol. London, Royal Society of British Artists' Art Club, 1937.
Huish (Marcus B.), *British Water-Colour Art.* London, The Fine Art Society; A. & C. Black, 1904.
Humbert (Jean-Marcel), *L'Égyptomanie dans l'art occidental.* Paris, ACR, 1989.
Hunt (Violet), *The Wife of Rossetti, her Life and Death.* New York, E.P. Dutton, 1932.
Hunt (William Holman), *Pre-Raphaelitism and the Pre-Raphaelite Brotherhood.* London, MacMillan & Co, 1905.
Hutchinson (Sidney C.), *The History of the Royal Academy 1768-1968.* London, Chapman and Hall, 1968.
James (T.G.H.), *Excavating in Egypt: The Egypt Exploration Society 1882-1982.* University of Chicago Press, 1982.
Jarrah (Nagham), *Valentine Cameron Prinsep.* Dissertation, University of London, 1983. A copy at the Courtauld Institute, London.
Johnson (Diane), *Lesser lives. The true history of the first Mrs. Meredith and other lesser lives.* London,

Heinemann, 1973.
Johnson (Jane), *Works exhibited at the Royal Society of British Artists 1824-1893 and at The New English Art Club 1888-1917*. Woodbridge, Antique Collectors' Club, 1975.
Johnson (Jane) & Greutzner (A.), *The dictionary of British artists 1880-1940*. Woodbridge, Antique Collectors' Club, 1976.
Johnson (Wendell Stacy), *Living in sin: the Victorian sexual revolution*. London, Nelson-Hall, 1979.
Jones (Frederick L.), *Mary Shelley's Journal*. University of Oklahoma Press, 1947.
———, *The Letters of Bysshe Shelley*. Oxford, Clarendon Press, 1964.
Jones (Mervyn), *The amazing Victorian, a life of George Meredith*. London, Constable, 1999.
Joukovsky (Nicholas A.), 'George and Mary Meredith, the East India company, and the Society of Arts: New Light on the Author's Early Career'. *Studies in Philology*, Vol. 97, Fall 2000, pp.473-493.
———, 'According to Mrs. Bennett. A document sheds a new and kinder light on George Meredith's first wife'. *Times Literary Supplement*, October 8, 2004, pp.13-15.
———, 'Mary Ellen's first affair. New light on the biographical background to *Modern Love*'. *Times Literary Supplement*, June 15, 2007, pp.13-15.
———, 'New Correspondence of Mary Ellen Meredith'. *Studies in Philology*, Vol. 106, Fall 2009, pp.483-522.
———, 'The Hoggs and the Peacocks: Some Later Correspondence'. *Keats-Shelley Journal* 52 (2003), p.166-194.
———, *The Letters of Thomas Love Peacock*. Oxford, Clarendon Press, 2001.
——— & Powell (Jim), *A Peacock in the Attic. Insights and secrets from newly discovered letters by George Meredith*. Times Literary Supplement, 22 July 2011.
——— , 'The Early Meredithian Milieu: New Evidence from Letters of Peter Augustin Daniel', *Studies in Philology*, Vol. XV, Summer 2018, pp.615-641.
Jullian (Philippe), *Les Orientalistes*. Fribourg, Office du Livre, 1977.
Kanter (Laurence B.) : see Henry (Tom).
Kaplan (Louise J.), *The family romance of the imposter-poet Thomas Chatterton*. Berkeley, University of California Press, 1989.
Labat-Poussin (Brigitte), *Archives de l'École Nationale Supérieure des Beaux-Arts*. Paris, Centre Historique des Archives Nationales, 1998.
Laffon (Juliette), *Catalogue sommaire illustré des peintures*. Paris, Musée du Petit Palais, 1982.
Lagier (Camille), *L'Égypte Monumentale & Pittoresque*. Bruxelles, Vromant, 1914.
Lambourne (Lionel) & Hamilton (Jean), *British Watercolours in the Victoria and Albert Museum: an illustrated summary catalogue of the national collection*. London, Sotheby Parke Bernet, 1980.
Lamont (T.R.), *Thomas Armstrong. A Memoir (1832-1911)*. London, Martin Secker, 1912.
Lanigan (Dennis T.), 'The Dudley Gallery: Watercolour drawings exhibitions 1865-1882', *Journal of Pre-Raphaelite Studies*, 12, Spring 2003, 74-96.
Laurent (Jeanne), À propos de l'École des Beaux-Arts. Paris, École nationale supérieure des Beaux-Arts, 1980.
(Lausanne 2005), *Charles Gleyre. Le genie de l'invention*. Lausanne, Éditions 5 Continents, 2005.
Lauts (Jan), *Carpaccio. Paintings and drawings*. London, The Phaidon Press, 1962.
Laver (James), *Les idées et les mœurs au siècle de l'optimisme, 1848/1914*. Paris, Flammarion, 1969.
Lecoq de Boisbaudran (Horace), *Coups d'œil sur l'enseignement des Beaux-Arts*. Paris, Éd. Vve Morel & Cie, 1871.
———, *Lettres à un jeune professeur, sommaire d'une méthode pour l'enseignement du dessin et de la peinture*. Paris, Éd. Vve Morel & Cie, 1877.
Legrain (Georges), *Une famille Copte de Haute-Égypte*. Bruxelles, Édition de la Fondation égyptologique Reine Élisabeth, 1945.
Lemaire (Gérard-Georges), *L'univers des Orientalistes*. Paris, Place des Victoires, 2000.
———, *Les Préraphaélites entre l'enfer et le ciel. Une anthologie*. Paris, C.Bourgois, 1989.
Leslie (George D.), *The Inner Life of the Royal Academy*. London, John Murray, 1914.
Lessens (Ronald.), 'Henry Wallis (1830-1916), a neglected Pre-Raphaelite', *British Art Journal*, Vol. 15, Issue 1, Autumn 2014, pp.47-59.
Lessing (Erich, Ed.), *La Renaissance italienne*. Paris, Hatier, 1985.
Lethève (Jacques), 'Connaissance des peintres pré-raphaélites en France 1855-1900'. *Gazette des Beaux-Arts*, vol. 53, 1959, pp.315-328.
———, *La vie quotidienne des artistes français au XIXe siècle*. Paris, Hachette, 1968.
Lewis (Brian), 'Thomas E. Plint. A Patron of Pre-Raphaelite Painters', *The Journal of Pre-Raphaelite Studies*, Vol.3, May 1980, pp.77-101.

Lindsay (Jack), *Gustave Courbet. His life and art.* Bath, Adams & Dart, 1973.
(London 1977), *Victorian Painting.* London, The Fine Art Society, 15 Nov-9 Dec 1977.
(London 1978), *Eastern Encounters. Orientalist Painters of the Nineteenth Century.* London, The Fine Art Society, 1978.
(London 1984), *The Orientalists: Delacroix to Matisse.* London, Royal Academy of Arts, 1984.
(London 1985), *100 Great paintings in The Victoria & Albert Museum.* London, Victoria and Albert Museum, 1985.
(London 1987), *Ceramic Art of the Italian Renaissance* (T. Wilson, Ed.). London, British Museum, 1987.
(London 1990), *Catalogue of British Oil Paintings, 1820-1860.* London, Victoria and Albert Museum, HMSO, 1990.
(London 1996), *Frederic Leighton 1830-1896.* London, Royal Academy of Arts, 1996.
(London 2003), *The Forbes Collection of Victorian Pictures and Works of Art.* 3 vols. Christie's, London, 2003.
(London & Ferrara 2003), *Shakespeare in Art.* See: Martineau.
(London 2008), *The Lure of the East. British Orientalist Painting, 1830-1925.* London, Tate Britain & Yale Centre for British Art, 2008.
(London 2012), *Pre-Raphaelites. Victorian Avant-Garde* (T. Barringer, J. Rosenfeld & A. Smith, Eds). London, Tate Publishing, 2012.
(London 2014), *The Poor Man's Picture Gallery. Stereoscopy* versus *paintings in the Victorian era* (Eds. Brian May & Denis Pellerin). The London Stereoscopic Company, 2014.
(Los Angeles 2010), *Jean-Léon Gérôme (1824-1904).* Los Angeles, The J. Paul Getty Museum, 15 June-12 September 2010. Also: Paris 2010 and Madrid 2011.
Maas (Jeremy), *Victorian Painters.* London, Barrie & Jenkins, 1978.
———, *The Victorian Art World in Photographs.* London, Barrie & Jenkins, 1984.
———, *Gambart, Prince of the Victorian Art World.* London, Barrie & Jenkins, 1975.
MacCarthy (Fiona), *The Last Pre-Raphaelite. Edward Burne-Jones and the Victorian Imagination.* London, Faber and Faber, 2011.
———, *William Morris.* London, Faber and Faber, 1995.
Mackail (J.W.), *The Life of William Morris.* London, Longmans, Green & Co., 1901.
MacKenzie (Ian), *British prints: dictionary and price guide.* Woodbridge, Antique Collectors' Club, 1998.
MacKenzie (John M.), *Orientalism. History, Theory and the Arts.* Manchester University Press, 1995.
Macleod (Dianne Sachko), *Art and the Victorian Middle Class.* Cambridge University Press, 1996.
———, 'Frederic George Stephens as an art critic', *Burlington Magazine*, vol.128, June 1986, pp.398-406.
Madden (Mary & Lionel), 'Thomas Love Peacock, George and Mary Meredith, and John Parker Jr.' *Victorian Periodicals Review* 27/1, Spring 1994, pp.32-39.
(Madrid 2011), *Jean-Léon Gérôme (1824-1904).* Madrid, Museo Thyssen-Bornemisza, 1 March-22 May 2011.
Maguin (Jean-Marie & Angela), *Shakespeare.* Paris, Fayard, 1996.
Mallallieu (Huon L.), *The Dictionary of British Watercolour Artists up to 1920.* Woodbridge, Antique Collectors' Club, 2002.
Mantz (Paul), 'Charles Gleyre', *Gazette des Beaux-Arts,* 1 March 1875, pp.233-244 & 1 May 1875, pp.404-414.
Marks (J.G.), *The life and letters of Frederick Walker.* London, MacMillan, 1896
Marks (Henry Stacy), *Pen and Pencil Sketches.* London, Chatto & Windus, 1894, 2 vols.
Marsh (Jan), *Dante Gabriel Rossetti. Painter and Poet.* London, Phoenix, 2005.
———, *Pre-Raphaelite Women.* London, Weidenfeld & Nicolson, 1987.
Marshall (Mrs. Julian), *The Life and Letters of Mary Wollstonecraft Shelley.* 2 vols. London, Bentley and Son, 1889.
Martineau (Jane) et al., *Shakespeare in Art.* London-New York, Merrell, 2003.
Maspero (Gaston), *Ruines et paysages d'Égypte.* Paris, Payot "PBP/Voyageurs", 2003.
Maurier (George du), *Trilby.* Ware, Wordsworth Editions, 1995.
Maurier (Daphne du), *The Young George du Maurier.* New York, Doubleday & C^y^, 1952.
Maurois (André), *Ariel ou La vie de Shelley.* Paris, Calmann-Lévy, 1927.
———, *Histoire de l'Angleterre.* Paris, Hachette, 1963.
May (Brian), see : London 2014.
Mély (F. de), 'Les origines de la céramique italienne'. *Gazette des Beaux-Arts,* 1884, pp.111-133.
Meredith (George) (Cline, C.L., Ed.), *The Letters of George Meredith.* 3 vols. Oxford, Clarendon Press, 1970.
———, *Selected Letters of George Meredith* (M.Shaheen, Ed.). London, Macmillan Press Ltd., 1997.

Meyerstein (E.H.W.), *A Life of Thomas Chatterton.* 1930.
Millar (Oliver), *Victorian Pictures in the Collection of Her Majesty the Queen.* Cambridge University Press, 1992.
Millais (John G.), *The Life and Letters of Sir J.E. Millais.* London, Methuen & Co., 1899.
Monkhouse (William Cosmo), *British contemporary artists.* London, 1899.
———, *At the Royal Academy. A companion to the oil pictures in the exhibition of 1874.* London: Virtue, Spalding and Deldy, 1874.
Monneret (Sophie), *L'Impressionnisme et son époque.* Paris, Laffont, "Bouquins", 1978-79.
Montegut (Émile), 'Charles Gleyre', *Revue des Deux-Mondes,* 48, 1878, p.p395-425 (?).
Moore (A.), 'The Fountaine collection of maiolica', *Burlington Magazine* 130 (1988), pp.435-7.
Moorehead (Alan), *The White Nile.* London, Penguin Books, 1971.
Morgan (Hilary) & Nahum (Peter), *Burne-Jones, the Pre-Raphaelites and their Century.* London, Peter Nahum, 1989.
Morris (Edward) & Roberts (Emma), *The Liverpool Academy and other exhibitions of contemporary art in Liverpool 1774-1867.* Liverpool University Press, 1998.
Morris (Edward) & McKay (Amanda), 'British Art Students in Paris 1814-1890', *Apollo* CXXXV, n° 360, February 1992, pp.78-84.
Morris (James), *I. Heaven's Command. An Imperial Progress. II. Pax Britannica. The Climax of Empire. III. Farewell the Trumpets. An Imperial Retreat.* Penguin Books, 1979.
Morris (William) (Henderson, Philip, ed.), *The Letters of William Morris to his Family and Friends.* London, Longmans, Green & Co., 1950.
———, *The Collected Letters of William Morris.* 4 vol. Princeton University Press, 1984.
Moscheles (Felix), *In Bohemia with Du Maurier.* London, T. Fisher Unwin, 1896.
Mouliérac (Jeanne), *Céramiques du monde musulman.* Paris, Institut du Monde Arabe, 1999.
Mourey (Gabriel), *D.G.Rossetti et les Préraphélites Anglais.* Paris, Henri Laurens, "Les grands artistes", n.d.
Mowl (Timothy), *Horace Walpole. The Great Outsider.* London, John Murray, 1996.
Murray (Venetia), *Castle Howard. The Life and Times of a Stately Home.* London, Viking, 1994.
Newall (Christopher), *The Grosvenor Gallery Exhibitions.* Cambridge University Press, 1995.
(Newcastle 1990), *Pre-Raphaelites. Painters and Patrons in the North-East.* Newcastle-upon-Tyne, Laing Art Gallery, 1990.
Newman (Teresa) & Watkinson (Ray), *Ford Madox Brown and the Pre-Raphaelite Circle.* London, Chatto & Windus, 1991.
Norman (Geraldine), *Nineteenth Century Painters and Painting: a Dictionary.* London, Thames & Hudson, 1977.
O'Kane (Bernard), *Trésors de l'Islam. Les richesses de l'art musulman.* Potsdam, h. f.ullmann, 2011.
(Ontario 2008), *Holman Hunt and the Pre-Raphaelite Vision* (K. Lochnan & C. Jacobi, Ed.). Art Gallery of Ontario, 2008.
Osborne (Victoria J.), *A British Symbolist in Pre-Raphaelite Circles: Edward Robert Hughes RWS (1851-1914).* The University of Birmingham, Thesis, 2009.
(Paris 1993), *Album de voyage. Des artistes en expédition au pays du Levant.* Tel-Aviv, Musée d'Art; Bayonne, Musée Léon-Bonnat ; Paris, Musée Hébert. Paris, Réunion des Musées Nationaux, 1993.
(Paris 2010), *Jean-Léon Gérôme (1824-1904). L'Histoire en spectacle.* Paris, Musée d'Orsay, 19 October 2010-23 January 2011.
Parris (Leslie Ed.), *Pre-Raphaelite Papers.* London, The Tate Gallery, 1984.
Peacock (Thomas Love), (N. Joukovsky, ed.). *The Letters of Thomas Love Peacock.* 2 vol. Oxford, Clarendon Press, 2001.
Pellerin (Denis), see : London 2014.
Peltre (Christine), *L'atelier du voyage: les peintres en Orient au XIXe siècle.* Paris, Gallimard, 1995.
———, *Les Orientalistes.* Paris, Hazan, 2003.
———, *Orientalisme.* Paris, Terrail, 2004.
———, *Les Arts de l'Islam. Itinéraire d'une redécouverte.* Paris, Gallimard, 2006.
———, *Dictionnaire culturel de l'orientalisme.* Paris, Hazan, 2008.
Pennell (Elizabeth Robins & Joseph), *The life of James McNeill Whistler.* 2 vol. London, Heinemann, 1908.
Pergam (Elizabeth A.), 'Creating a furore: Annibale Caracci's 'The Three Marie', Thomas Gainsborough's 'Blue Boy' and Henry Wallis's 'Death of Chatterton' at the Manchester Art Treasures Exhibition', *Apollo. The International Magazine of the Arts,* June 2002, pp.48-53.
———, *The Manchester Art Treasures Exhibition of 1857.* Farnham, Ashgate, 2011.
Perkus (Gerald H.), 'Meredith's Unhappy Love Life : Worthy of the Muse', *Cithara,* Vol. IX, N° 2, May

1970, pp.32-46 (St Bonaventure University).
Perruchot (Henri), *La vie de Renoir.* Paris, Hachette, 1964.
Peters (Catherine), *The King of Inventors. A Life of Wilkie Collins.* A Minerva Paperback, 1992.
Phillips (Lawrence), *A mighty mass of brick and smoke. Victorian and Edwardian representations of London.* Amsterdam-New York, Editions Rodopi, 2007.
Picard (Liza), *Victorian London.* London, Phoenix, 2006.
Poole (Adrian), *Shakespeare and the Victorians.* London, Arden Critical Companions, 2004.
Poulson (Christine), 'A checklist of Pre-Raphaelite illustrations of Shakespeare's Plays', *The Burlington Magazine*, No 925, vol. CXXII, April 1980, pp.244-250.
———, *The Quest for the Grail.Arthurian Legend in British Art, 1840-1920.* Manchester University Press, 1999.
Powell (Jim), *The early life of Susan Mary Abbott.* Web document, 11 October 2013.
———, see: Joukovsky
Prettejohn (Elizabeth), *The Art of the Pre-Raphaelites.* Princeton University Press, 2000.
Prinsep (Val C.), 'A Student's Life in Paris in 1859', *Magazine of Art*, Feb., May 1904.
Pulford (J.S.L.), *George & Mary Meredith in Weybridge, Shepperton & Esher, 1849-61.* Walton & Weybridge Local History Society, 1989.
Rachet (Guy) & Simoën (Jean-Claude), *David Roberts. Voyage en Égypte.* Paris, Bibliothèque de l'image, 1995.
Ramm (John), 'The Forgotten Pre-Raphaelite', *Antique Dealer and Collector's Guide*, March-April 2003, pp.32-35.
Raphael (Frederic), *Byron.* London, Thames & Hudson, 1982.
Redford (George), *Art Sales. A History of Sales of Pictures and Other Works of Art (1628-1887).* 2 vols. London, Bradbury, Agnew & Co., 1888.
Redgrave (Samuel), *A dictionary of artists of the English School : painters, sculptors, architects, engravers and ornamentalists with notices of their lives and work.* Bath, Kingsmead Reprints, 1970.
Reeves (Nicholas) & Taylor (John H.), *Howard Carter before Tutankhamen.* London, The British Museum Press, 1992.
Régamey (Raymond), 'La Formation de Claude Monet', *Gazette des Beaux-Arts*, February 1927.
Renoir (Jean), *Renoir, my father.* London, Columbus Books, 1988.
Reveillac (Gérard) : see Tuccelli (Nicole)
Reymond (Nathalie), *Claude Monet.* Paris, Jean-Claude Lattès, 1992.
Reynolds-Ball (E.A.), *Cairo of To-Day: A Practical Guide to Cairo and the Nile.* 1904. Accessible on *archive.org.*
Rice (David Talbot), *L'Art de l'Islam.* London, Thames & Hudson, 1994.
Ridge (Jacqueline): see Townsend.
Roberts (Leonard) and Wildman (Steven), *Arthur Hughes: his life and work.* Woodbridge, Antique Collectors' Club, 1997.
Roe (Dinah), *The Rossettis in Wonderland.* London, Haus Publishing, 2011.
Roget (John Lewis), *The 'Old' Water-Colour Society.* London, Longmans, Green & Co, 1891.
Rooke (Thomas Matthews), *Burne-Jones Talking.* (M. Lago, Ed.). London, John Murray, 1982.
Rose (Phyllis), *Mariages victoriens.* Paris, Albin Michel, 1988.
Rossetti (V. Surtees, Ed.), *The Paintings and Drawings of Dante Gabriel Rossetti.* Oxford, At the Clarendon Press, 1971.
rossetti (Dante Gabriel) (Doughty, O. & Wahl, J.R., Ed.), *Letters of Dante Gabriel Rossetti.* Oxford, Clarendon Press, 1965-67.
———, *The Correspondence of Dante Gabriel Rossetti* (W.E. Fredeman, Ed.). Cambridge, D.S. Brewer, 2003-2010. *The formative years, 1835-1862. I. 1835-1854 (vol. 1). II. 1855-1862 (vol. 2). The Chelsea years, 1863-1872. I. 1863-1867 (vol. 3). II. 1868-1870 (vol. 4). III. 1871-1872 (vol. 5). The last decade, 1873-1882. I. 1873-1874 (vol. 6). II. 1875-1877 (vol. 7). III. 1878-1879 (vol. 8). IV. 1880-1882 (vol. 9).*
———, *Letters of Dante Gabriel Rossetti to William Allingham 1854-1870.* (Birkbeck Hill, G., Ed. New York, Frederick A. Stokes, 1898.
Rossetti (William Michael), *Dante Gabriel Rossetti: His Family letters.* London, Ellis and Elvey, 1895.
———, *Ruskin, Rossetti, Preraphaelitism. Papers 1854 to 1862.* London, George Allen, 1899.
———, *Rossetti papers 1862 to 1870.* New York, Charles Scribner's Sons, 1903.
———, *Some reminiscences.* New York, Charles Scribner's Sons, 1906.
———, *Preraphaelite Diaries & Letters.* London, Hurst & Blackett Ltd., 1900.
———, *Dante Gabriel Rossetti. His family-letters. With a memoir.* London, Ellis & Elvey, 1895.
———, *The Selected Letters of William Michael Rossetti* (Peattie, R., Ed.). The Pennsylvania State

University Press, 1990.
———, *The Diary of W.M. Rossetti* (Bornand, O., Ed.). Oxford, Clarendon Press, 1977.
Rudersdorf (Tina), *Die Ausstellungen der Präraffaeliten. Präsentationsformen viktorianischer Malerei und ihre Wirkung.* Ph.D. thesis, University of Bonn, 2009.
Ruskin (John), *Modern Painters* (D.Barrie, Ed.). London, Pilkington Press, 2000.
———, *The Works of John Ruskin* (Cook & Wedderburn, Ed.). Vol. XIV London, George Allen, 1904.
Said (Edward W.), *Orientalism. Western conceptions of the Orient.* London, Penguin Books, 1995.
Sandby (William), *The History of the Royal Academy of Arts, from its foundation in 1768 to the present time.* London, Longman, Roberts, & Green, 1862.
Sanders (Andrew), *In the Olden Time. Victorians and the British Past.* Hew Haven & London, Yale University Press, 2013.
Saville (Paul), *Valentine Cameron Prinsep in relation to the practice and theory of academic painting in late nineteenth century England.* Unpublished B. Litt. Thesis, University of Oxford, 1970.
Sayce (A.H.), *Reminiscences.* London, 1923.
Scott (William Bell), *Autobiographical notes of the life of William Bell Scott* (W. Minto, Ed.). 2 vol. New York, Harper & Brothers, 1892.
Searight (Sarah), *The British in the Middle East.* London, Weidenfeld and Nicolson, 1969.
Sencourt (Robert), *La vie de Meredith.* Paris, Gallimard, 1931.
Shaheen (M.Y.), see Meredith.
Shakespeare (William), *Le Marchand de Venise.* Paris, Les Belles Éditions, 1935.
———, *Oeuvres completes, 4.* Paris, Le club français du livre, 1963.
Shelley (Mary Wollstonecraft), *The Letters of Mary Wollstonecraft Shelley* (B.T. Bennett, Ed.). 3 vol. Baltimore, Johns Hopkins University Press, 1980-88.
———, *Mary Shelley's Journal.* See: Jones, F.L.
Shelley (Percy Bysshe), *The Letters of Percy Bysshe Shelley.* See: Jones F.L.
Sillars (Stuart), *Shakespeare, Time and the Victorians. A Pictorial Exploration.* Cambridge University Press, 2012.
———, *The Illustrated Shakespeare 1709-1875.* Cambridge University Press, 2008.
Simoën (Jean-Claude), *Le Voyage en Égypte.* Paris, J'ai lu en images, 2010.
Sizeranne (Robert de la), *Le Préraphaélisme.* New York, Parkstone Press International, 2008.
———, *La peinture anglaise contemporaine 1844-1894.* Paris, Hachette, 1922.
Skidelsky (Robert), *John Maynard Keynes.* London, Macmillan, 1983.
Solé (Robert) & Walter (Marc), *Voyage en Égypte.* Paris, Éditions du Chêne, 2003.
Souter (Keith), *The Classic Guide to King Arthur.* Newhaven, Golden Guides Press, 2012.
Spencer (Robin), *Whistler. A Retrospective.* New York, Wings Books, 1989
Spielmann (Marion H.), 'The Proposed Royal Academy Reform', *Contemporary Review,* August 1889, p259-271.
Staley (Allan), *The Pre-Raphaelite Landscape.* Oxford, Clarendon Press, 1973.
Starkey (Pat, ed.), *Riches into Art. Liverpool Collectors 1770-1880. Essays in honour of Margaret T.Gibson.* Liverpool University Press, 1993.
Stevens (Bethan), *The British Museum Pre-Raphaelites.* London, The British Museum Press, 2008.
Stewart (Brian) & Cutten (Mervyn), *The dictionary of portrait painters in Britain up to 1920.* Woodbridge, Antique Collectors' Club, 1997.
Stirling (A.M.W.), *A Painter of Dreams, the life of Rodham Spencer Stanhope.* London, John Lane, 1916; William Heinemann, 1926.
Sturgis (Alexander), *Rebels and Martyrs the image of the artist in the nineteenth century.* London, National Gallery, 2006.
Surtees (Virginia), *Coutts Lindsay, 1824-1913.* Norwich, Michael Russell, 1993.
Sweetman (John), *The Oriental Obsession. Islamic inspiration in British and American Art and Architecture 1500-1920.* Cambridge University Press, 1988.
Tabarant (Adolphe), *La vie artistique au temps de Baudelaire.* Paris, Mercure de France, 1942.
Tesson (Thierry), *Ferdinand de Lesseps.* Paris, Jean-Claude Lattès/Ushuaia, 1992.
Thompson (Brian), *A Monkey among Crocodiles. The Disastrous Life of Mrs Georgina Weldon.* London, HarperCollins, 2000.
Thomson (David Croal), *The Landscapes of Corot.* London, "The Studio", 1920.
Thornbury (Walter), *Old and new London: a narrative of its history, its people, and its places.* 6 vol. London, Cassell, Petter & Galpin, 1873-78.
Thornton (Lynne), *Les Orientalistes Peintres-Voyageurs.* Paris, ACR, 2001.
———, *Du Maroc aux Indes, voyages en Orient.* Paris, 1998.

———, *La femme dans la peinture orientaliste.* Paris, ACR Poche, 1993.
Tiradritti (Francesco, Ed.), *Egyptian treasures from the Egyptian Museum in Cairo.* Eni/leoc, 1998.
Tobin (Thomas), *Pre-Raphaelitism in the Nineteenth-Century Press. A Bibliography.* Victoria (Canada), 2002.
Todd (Pamela), *The Pre-Raphaelites at Home.* London, Pavilion, 2001.
Townsend (Joyce H.) et al., *Pre-Raphaelite Painting Techniques.* London, Tate Publishing, 2004.
Trevelyan (Raleigh), *A Pre-Raphaelite Circle.* London, Faber & Faber, 2011.
Trodd (Colin), 'The Authority of Art. Cultural Criticism and the Idea of the Royal Academy in Mid-Victorian Britain'. *Art History,* XX (1997), pp.3-22.
Tuccelli (Nicole) & Reveillac (Gérard), *Le Nil en dahabieh.* Paris, Éditions Paris-Méditerranée, 2001.
Tyldesley (Joyce), *Egypt. How a lost civilization was rediscovered.* London, BBC Books, 2008.
Upstone (Robert), *The Pre-Raphaelite Dream. Paintings & Drawings from the Tate Collection.* London, Tate Publishing, 2003.
Valentine (Helen), *Art in the Age of Queen Victoria. Treasures of the Royal Academy of Arts.* New York & London, Yale University Press, 1999.
Vernus (Pascal), *Dictionnaire amoureux de l'Égypte pharaonique.* Paris, Plon, 2009.
Vigny (Alfred de), *Chatterton.* Bruxelles, Louis Hauman, 1835.
Volait (M.), *Fous du Caire. Excentriques, architectes & amateurs d'art en Égypte, 1863-1914.* L'Archange Minotaure, s.l., 2009.
Walkley (Giles), *Artists' Houses in London 1764-1914.* Aldershot, Scolar Press, 1994.
Waters (Grant M.), *The dictionary of British artists working 1900-1950.* Eastbourne Fine Art, 1975.
Watts-Dunton (Theodore), *Old Familiar Faces.* New York, E.P. Dutton & Co., 1916.
Weinhold (Rudolf), *Argile aux cent visages / The many faces of Clay.* Edition Leipzig, 1983.
Whistler (James McNeill), *Whistler.* Exhibition catalogue. London, Tate Gallery; Paris, Musée d'Orsay, 1995-1996. (R. Dorment & M. MacDonald, Ed.)
White (Harrison & Cynthia), *La carrière des peintres au XIXe siècle.* Paris, Flammarion, 2009.
Whiteley (Jon), The Combe Bequest'. *Apollo,* 117 (1983), pp.302-307.
Wilcox (Scott) & Newall (Christopher), *Victorian landscape watercolors.* Yale Center for British Art, Cleveland Museum of Art, Birmingham Museums & Art Gallery, 1992.
Wilkinson (Toby), *The Rise and Fall of Ancient Egypt.* New York, Random House, 2010.
Williams (David), *George Meredith. His Life and Lost Love.* London, Hamish Hamilton, 1977.
Wilson (A.N.), *The Victorians.* London, Hutchinson, 2007.
Wilson (Timothy), 'A Victorian artist as ceramic-collector: The letters of Henry Wallis'. Oxford, *Journal of the History of Collections,* Vol. 14, N° 1, 2002, pp.139-159 ; Vol. 14, N° 2, 2002, pp.231-269.
———, 'The origins of the maiolica collections of the British Museum and the Victoria and Albert Museum 1851-55', *Faenza* 71 (1985), pp.68-81.
———, *Maiolica. Italian Renaissance ceramics in the Ashmolean Museum.* Oxford, Ashmolean Museum, 2003.
(Winterthur 1974), *Charles Gleyre ou les illusions perdues.* Winterthur, Kunstmuseum, 1974.
Wood (Christopher), *Victorian painters.* Woodbridge, Antique Collectors' Club, 1995.
———, *William Powell Frith. A Painter & his world.* Stroud, Sutton Publishing Limited, 2006.
———, *The Pre-Raphaelites.* London, Weidenfeld & Nicolson, 2nd ed., 1994.
———, *Victorian Panorama.* London, Faber and Faber, 2nd ed., 1990.
Wood (Jeremy), *Hidden talents: a dictionary of neglected artists working 1880-1950.* Billinghurst, Jeremy Wood Fine Art, 1994.
Woolner (Amy), *Thomas Woolner, R.A., Sculptor & Poet : His Life in Letters.* 1917.
Wright (Christopher, et al.), *British and Irish paintings in public collections.* New Haven & London, Yale University Press, 2006.

Acknowledgements

We should like to offer our thanks to the many people – strangers or colleagues – who have given their time to helping us writing the first biography of this neglected artist whose place in the Victorian art world was not negligible. Dr. Judith Bronkhurst read through a draft of our manuscript and we are grateful to her for her very helpful advice. A special thank you to Polly Lockwood, a Wallis descendant, for all her help and to Doina Zugravescu for her translations. Victorian scholar Scott Thomas Buckle was of great assistance to us by helping look through auction catalogues at the National Portrait Gallery in order to research Wallis works sold at auction. We are extremely grateful to the team at ACC, in particular: to Senior Editor, Susannah Hecht, who expertly brought this project to fruition; to the designer, Steve Farrow, who made the appearance of the book exceed our expectations; and, especially, to our Publisher, James Smith, who supported this project from the beginning.

We also particularly want to thank: Raed A. AL-RIFAI, Ambassador of the State of Kuwait in Athens □ Abigail ARMISTEAD, Yale Center for British Art □ Bruce BARKER-BENFIELD, Bodleian Libraries, Oxford □ Chris BEETLES, Chris Beetles Gallery, London □ Charlotte BERGSTRÖM, Bukowski Auktioner, Stockholm □ Brad David BLATHERWICK □ Annie BLOOD, The Burlington Magazine □ Molly BRAGG, Duke University Library □ F Amaryllis and Charles BRETT □ Judith BRONKHURST □ Ann BUKANTAS, Walker Art Gallery, Liverpool □ Julia CARVER, Bristol's City Museum & Art Gallery □ Areti CHAVALE, Bonhams London □ Deborah CLIFFE, Bonhams London □ Lisa COLE, Tate Library & Archive □ Sarah COLEGRAVE, Sarah Colegrave Fine Art □ Jeff COWLEY, The Wordsworth Trust, Grasmere, Cumbria □Anne DISTEL, Conservateur général du patrimoine – Ministère de la Culture et de la Communication, Paris □ Dr Maurice DIXSON □ Lauren DUDLEY, Birmingham Museums and Art Gallery □ Dr Donato ESPOSITO □ Andrea FAJRAJSL, National Gallery of Canada □ Andrea FREDERICKSEN, Art Museum, University College London □ Andrew GENT, Tate Library and Archive □ Charlotte GERE, London □ Andrew GORDON, New York □ Jacky HARDCASTLE, John Rylands Library, University of Manchester □ Colin HARRIS, Bodleian Library, Oxford □ Colin HARRISON, Ashmolean Museum, Oxford □ Andrew D. HARTLEY, Hartleys Auctioneers and Valuers □ Hannah HAWKSWORTH, Royal Watercolour Society □ Elspeth HEALEY, Harry Ransom Center, The University of Texas at Austin □ Mike HICKOX □ John HODGSON, John Rylands Library, University of Manchester □ Patrick HOLDEN □ Edward HOPEWELL-ASH, Toovey's Antique & Fine Art Auctioneers & Valuers □ Diane JOHNSON □ Nicholas JOUKOVSKY, Pennsylvania State University □ Andrew KING, Nottingham Art Gallery □ Bryony LEVENTHALL, British Museum □ Brandon LINDBERG, Christie's London □ Roddy LLOYD, Rowley Fine Art □ Gina MACDERMOT, Mathaf Gallery Ltd □ Wendy MAKINS, Makins collection □ Angela McDERMOTT, Lots Road Auctions □ Lynda McLEOD, Christie's Archives □ Brian MAY □ Louisa MEEKS, National Gallery, Washington □ Sarah MILLARD, Bank of England Archive □ Elizabeth MORCOM, Senate House Library □ Angela NACOL, The Forbes Collection □ Victoria OSBORNE, Birmingham Museums and Art Gallery □ Christiana PAYNE □ Denis PELLERIN □ Jessie PETHERAM, The Shakespeare Birthplace Trust □ Stephen QUIRKE, Art Museum, University College London □ John RAMM □ Lorella RANZI, Museo Internazionale delle Ceramiche, Faenza □ Leonard ROBERTS □ Nicola ROBERTS, Tate Library & Archive □ Emily ROEHL, Harry Ransom Center, The University of Texas at Austin □ Tom ROTH, Christie's South Kensington □ Dr Douglas SCHOENHERR, Retired Curator □ Andrew SHAPLAND, Greek Bronze Age Curator, British Museum □ Richard SHONE, The Burlington Magazine □ Catherine SIMPSON, Royal Shakespeare Company □ Elen Wyn SIMPSON, University of Wales, Bangor □ Maria SINGER, Yale Center for British Art □ Alison SMITH, National Portrait Gallery, London □ Michael StJOHN-McALISTER, British Library, London □ James SUTTON, Victoria and Albert Museum Archives □ Paul TAYLOR, Royal Shakespeare Company □ Abigail THOMAS, British Museum, London □ Simon TOLL, Sotheby's, London □ Duncan WALKER, Russell-Cotes Art Gallery and Museum, Bournemouth □ Betsy WALSH, The Folger Shakespeare Library, Washington D.C. □ Lottie WIHL, Christie's, London □ Hannah WILLIAMSON, Manchester Art Gallery □ Timothy WILSON, Ashmolean Museum, Oxford □ The staff of the MRBAB Library (Musées Royaux des Beaux-Arts de Belgique, Brussels) □ The staff of the BODLEIAN LIBRARY Oxford □ Cyndie CAMPBELL and the staff of the NATIONAL GALLERY OF CANADA LIBRARY – Ottawa □ The staff of the COURTAULD INSTITUTE OF ART LIBRARIES and THE NATIONAL PORTRAIT GALLERY LIBRARY – London □ The staff of the archives ROYAL BIRMINGHAM SOCIETY OF ARTISTS □ The staff of the archives MANCHESTER CENTRAL REFERENCE LIBRARY.

Index of Known Works

Page numbers in **bold** refer to illustrations

Provenance Index for Works by Henry Wallis

General Index

Page numbers in **bold** refer to illustrations

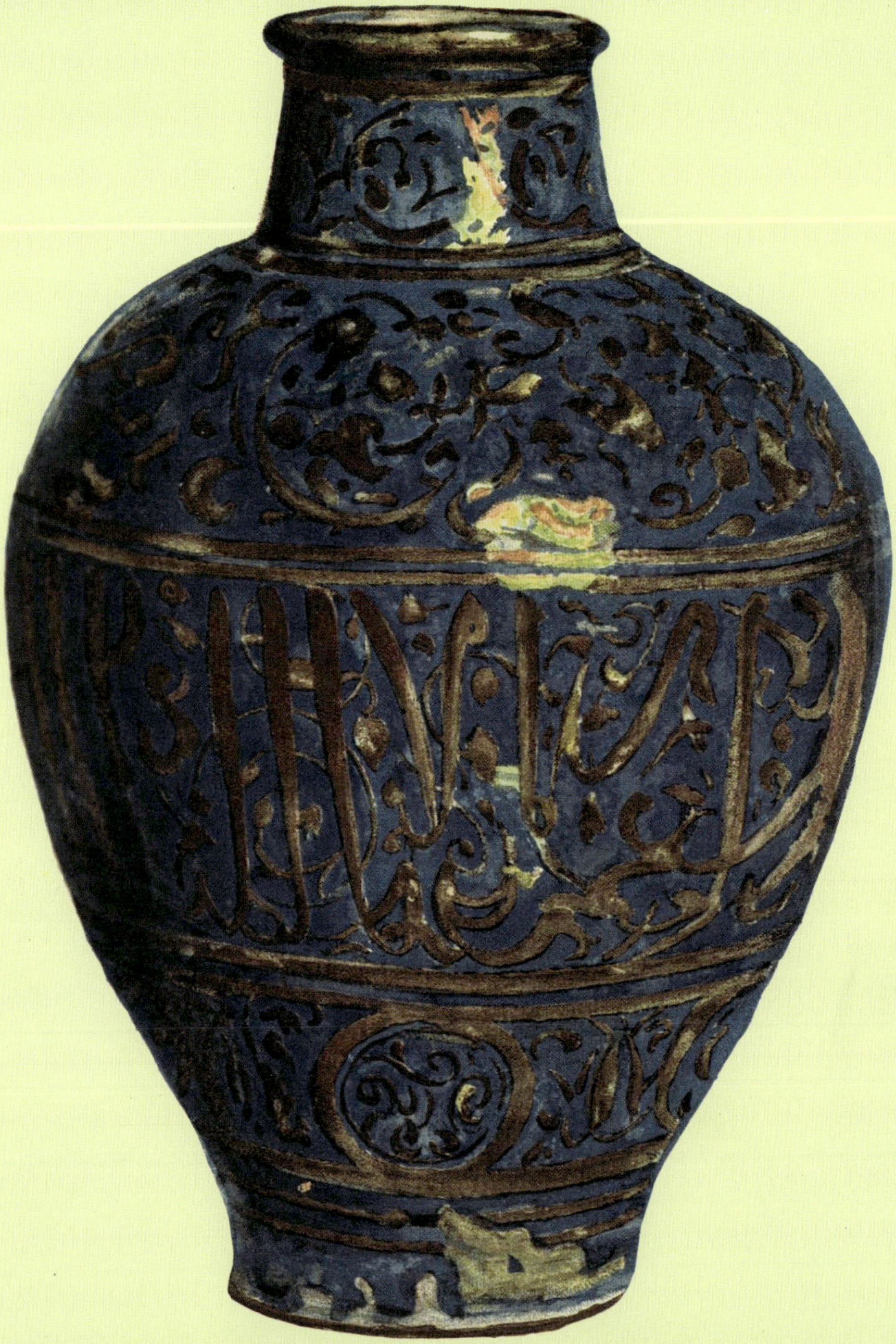